HOLT McDOUGAL

TEACHER'S EDITION

Bien dit!™

FRENCH 2

John DeMado

Séverine Champeny

Marie Ponterio

Robert Ponterio

HOLT McDOUGAL

 HOUGHTON MIFFLIN HARCOURT

Teacher to Teacher Contributors

Jon Baker
Westmoore High School
Oklahoma City, OK

Sandra Behensky
Rock Island High School
Rock Island, IL

Elaine Bind
McDonogh School
Ownings Mills, MD

Todd Bowen
Barrington High School
Barrington, IL

Geneviève Delfosse
Thomas Jefferson High School for Science and Technology
Alexandria, VA

Laura Grable
Riverhead Middle School
Riverhead, NY

Bill Heller
Perry High School
Perry, NY

Dena Hooley
Mt. Vernon City Schools
Mr. Vernon, OH

Todd Losié
Renaissance High School
Detroit, MI

Jodi Mahlmann
Seven Lakes High School
Katy, TX

Cindy McDaniel
Rushville Consolidated High School
Rushville, IN

Sue Mistric
Mount St. Mary Academy
Little Rock, AR

Rachel Norwood
Athens Academy
Athens, GA

Lynn Payne
Hidden Valley Middle School
Roanoke, VA

Karen Query
Lincoln High School
Vincennes, IN

Nancy Rodman
The Blake School
Minneapolis, MN

Pam Seccombe
Nathan Hale High School
West Allis, WI

Barbara Tentinger
Papillion-LaVista High School
Papillion, NE

Printed in the U.S.A.

ISBN 978-0-547-87172-1

4 5 6 7 8 9 10 2266 21 20 19 18 17 16 15 14

4500456911 A B C D E F G

Contributing Authors

John DeMado

John DeMado has been a vocal advocate for second-language acquisition in the United States for many years. He started his career as a middle/ high school French and Spanish teacher, before entering the educational publishing profession. Since 1993, Mr. DeMado has directed his own business, John DeMado Language Seminars, Inc., a company devoted exclusively to language acquisition issues. He has authored numerous books in French, Spanish, and ESL that span the K–12 curriculum. Mr. DeMado served as the lead consultant for program content at all levels. He created and recorded the **On rappe!** songs for Levels 1 and 2.

Séverine Champeny

Séverine Champeny, a native of Provence, has been involved in the development of French language educational programs for over 17 years. She has worked on print and media products ranging from introductory middle-school texts to advanced college-level texts. She created activities for the core sections of the chapters. She authored the **Télé-roman** scripts and wrote activities for the DVD Tutor.

Marie Ponterio

Marie Ponterio is a native of France and teaches French language and civilization at the State University of New York College at Cortland. She's the author of the web site **Civilisation française** and the recipient of several awards from Multimedia Educational Resource for Learning and Online Resources. She has co-authored video activities for several high-school textbooks for Harcourt. She has co-authored the culture notes in the program and reviewed all the **Géoculture** sections.

Robert Ponterio

Bob Ponterio is Professor of French at the State University of New York College at Cortland where he teaches all levels of French. He is a moderator of FLTEACH, the Foreign Language Teaching Forum e-mail list. He has published numerous articles and is a recipient of the Anthony Papalia Award for Outstanding Article on Foreign Language Education and the Dorothy S. Ludwig Award for Service to the FL profession. He has co-authored the culture notes in the program and reviewed all the **Géoculture** sections.

Student Edition

Contributing Writers

Dana Chicchelly
Missoula, MT

Serge Lainé
Austin, TX

Karine Letellier
Paris, France

Stuart Smith
Austin, TX

Alisa Trachtenberg
Ridgefield, CT

Samuel J. Trees
Christoval, TX

Mayanne Wright
Austin, TX

Reviewers

These educators reviewed one or more chapters of the Student Edition.

Todd Bowen
Barrington HS
Barrington, IL

Janet Bowman
Ithaca HS
Ithaca, NY

J. Blake Carpenter
Department of Modern Languages
The University of Texas at Arlington
Arlington, TX

Mari Kathryn Drefs
Butler Middle School
Waukesha, WI

Magda Khoury
West Covina HS
West Covina, CA

Todd Losie
Renaissance HS
Detroit, MI

Jean McDaniel
Garinger HS
Charlotte, NC

Jennifer Wells
Hamilton HS
Hamilton, IN

Thomasina I. White
School District of Philadelphia
Philadelphia, PA

Lori Wickert
Wilson HS
West Lawn, PA

Teacher's Edition

Contributing Writers

Joan Altobelli
Cedar Park, TX

Elizabeth Baird
Garfield Heights, OH

Dana Chicchelly
Missoula, MT

Ruthie Ford
Austin, TX

Chris Hiltenbrand
Austin, TX

Todd Losié
Detroit, MI

Julie McCracken
Austin, TX

Cherie Mitschke
Giddings, TX

Mary Moermond
Des Moines, IA

Rachel Norwood
Athens, GA

Annick Penant
Austin, TX

Marci Reed
Buda, TX

Pamela Taborsky
Austin, TX

Renate Wise
Austin, TX

Mayanne Wright
Austin, TX

Erika Zettl
Austin, TX

Reviewers

These individuals reviewed one or more chapters of the Teacher's Edition.

Robert Didsbury
Raleigh, NC

Richard Lindley
Dripping Springs, TX

Field Test Participants

Stéphane Allagnon
Sandy Creek High School
Tyrone, GA

Normand Brousseau
Westside High School
Macon, GA

Melanie Calhoun
Sullivan South High School
Kingsport, TN

Karen Crystal
Austin High School
Chicago, IL

Magalie Danier-O'Connor
William Allen High School
Allentown, PA

Svetoslava Dimova
Campbell High School
Smyrna, GA

Isha Gardner
Booker T. Washington High School
Atlanta, GA

Melinda Jones
Diamond Bar High School
Diamond Bar, CA

Cynthia Madsen
St. Joseph High School
Lakewood, CA

Johanna Norman
Hernando High School
Memphis, TN

Patricia Shanahan
Swampscott High School
Swampscott, MA

Nitya Viswanath
Roosevelt High School
Chicago, IL

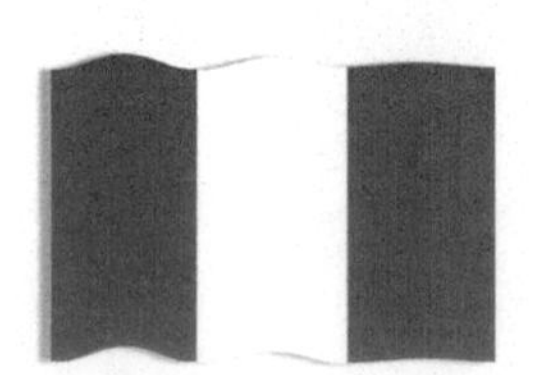

Teacher's Edition

Sommaire

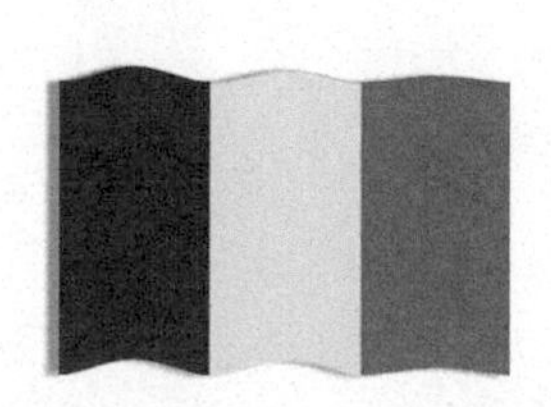

To The Teacher

Bien dit!—a new program with real-world photos, on-location video, animated grammar, and solid pedagogy—is an exciting, motivational, and effective French series that will appeal to all types of learners and keep them coming back for more. Based on the "five C's" of the national standards, this new program has an easy-to-use format that allows students to achieve success, and gives teachers a host of teaching tools to make sure all students can focus on each lesson's goals.

Communication

Bien dit! engages students right from the start of each lesson and carefully leads them from structured practice to open-ended communication. Unique image-based **Vocabulaire** presentations introduce a thematic context and provide a reason and motivation for using the language. Colorful **Grammaire** presentations, accompanied by **animated grammar** explanations, help students achieve accuracy in their communication.

Cultures

The **Géoculture** feature that precedes every other chapter, hands-on projects, realia-based readings and activities, and culture notes in each chapter offer high-interest cultural information and a chance to learn about the **products, practices,** and **perspectives** of the target cultures.

Connections

Links to other subject areas, such as social studies, math, language arts, music, and fine arts are found throughout each chapter of *Bien dit!* Additional opportunities for connections are found at point of use in the *Teacher's Edition.*

Comparisons

To enable students to acquire a broader and a deeper understanding of language and culture, *Bien dit!* offers them multiple opportunities to compare the new language and culture with their own.

Communities

The ultimate goal of learning to communicate in a new language should be the ability to function in an increasingly diverse community and an increasingly demanding world market. *Bien dit!* is built on the theory that the global community has its roots in the second language classroom. If learning language and culture is enjoyable and accessible, all students will become productive members of their community.

For any language program to be successful, the needs of teachers and students have to be the primary consideration. From suggestions for differentiated instruction to the latest in technology products, *Bien dit!* provides an abundance of teacher support and learning tools to help ensure success for all teachers and students.

Sommaire

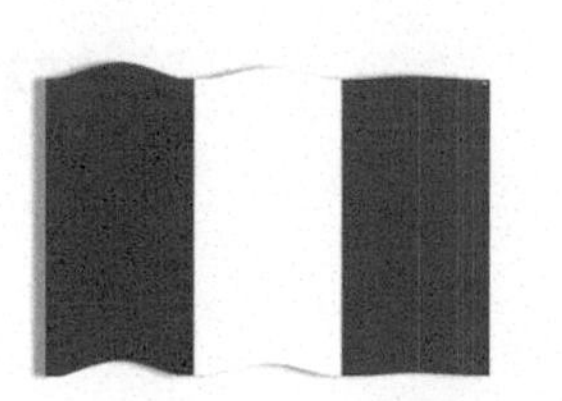

Chapitre 1 Ma famille et mes copains

Chapter Interleaf with Teaching Resources

Objectifs

In this chapter you will review how to
- describe yourself and ask about others
- talk about likes and dislikes
- inquire
- tell when you do something

Video

Géoculture	Géoculture
Vocabulaire 1 et 2	Télé-vocab
Grammaire 1 et 2	Grammavision
Télé-roman	Télé-roman

Online Practice
my.hrw.com
Online Edition

Géoculture

Chapitre 2 On fait la fête 40

Chapter Interleaf with Teaching Resources

Objectifs

In this chapter you will learn to
- wish someone a good time
- ask for and give advice
- ask for help
- check if things have been done

Video

Géoculture	Géoculture
Vocabulaire 1 et 2	Télé-vocab
Grammaire 1 et 2	Grammavision
Télé-roman	Télé-roman

Online Practice
my.hrw.com
Online Edition

Chapitre 3 Faisons les courses 80

Chapter Interleaf with Teaching Resources

Objectifs

In this chapter you will learn to
- ask about food preparation
- make requests
- shop for groceries
- ask where things are

Video

DVD

Géoculture	Géoculture
Vocabulaire 1 et 2	Télé-vocab
Grammaire 1 et 2	Grammavision
Télé-roman	Télé-roman

Online Practice
my.hrw.com
Online Edition

Géoculture

Chapitre 4 Au lycée 116

Chapter Interleaf with Teaching Resources

Objectifs

In this chapter you will learn to
- ask how something turned out
- wonder what happened
- ask for information
- express frustration

Video

Géoculture	**Géoculture**
Vocabulaire 1 et 2	**Télé-vocab**
Grammaire 1 et 2	**Grammavision**
Télé-roman	**Télé-roman**

Online Practice
my.hrw.com
Online Edition

Rennes
Chapitres 5 et 6

Chapitre 5 Une journée typique 156

Chapter Interleaf with Teaching Resources

Objectifs

In this chapter you will learn to
- talk about your routine
- express impatience
- say when you do things
- make recommendations

Video

Géoculture	**Géoculture**
Vocabulaire 1 et 2	**Télé-vocab**
Grammaire 1 et 2	**Grammavision**
Télé-roman	**Télé-roman**

my.hrw.com
Online Edition

Géoculture

Chapitre 6 Le bon vieux temps 182

Chapter Interleaf with Teaching Resources

Objectifs

In this chapter you will learn to
- talk about when you were a child
- tell about an event in the past
- compare life in the country and in the city
- describe life in the country

Video

Géoculture	Géoculture
Vocabulaire 1 et 2	Télé-vocab
Grammaire 1 et 2	Grammavision
Télé-roman	Télé-roman

Online Practice
my.hrw.com
Online Edition

Dakar

Chapitres 7 et 8

Chapitre 7 Un week-end en plein air 232

Chapter Interleaf with Teaching Resources

Objectifs

In this chapter you will learn to
- say what happened
- describe circumstances
- tell what you will do
- wonder what will happen

Video

Géoculture	Géoculture
Vocabulaire 1 et 2	Télé-vocab
Grammaire 1 et 2	Grammavision
Télé-roman	Télé-roman

my.hrw.com
Online Edition

Géoculture

Chapitre 8 Es-tu en forme? 268

Chapter Interleaf with Teaching Resources

Objectifs

In this chapter you will learn to
- ask and tell how you feel
- describe symptoms and give advice
- complain about health and give advice
- sympathize with someone

Video

Géoculture	Géoculture
Vocabulaire 1 et 2	Télé-vocab
Grammaire 1 et 2	Grammavision
Télé-roman	Télé-roman

Online Practice
my.hrw.com
Online Edition

Nice

Chapitres 9 et 10

Chapitre 9 On s'amuse!

Chapter Interleaf with Teaching Resources

Objectifs

In this chapter you will learn to
- describe a movie or a book
- ask for and give information
- ask about preferences
- recommend or advise against something

Video

Géoculture	Géoculture
Vocabulaire 1 et 2	Télé-vocab
Grammaire 1 et 2	Grammavision
Télé-roman	Télé-roman

Online Practice
my.hrw.com
Online Edition

Géoculture

Chapitre 10 Partons en vacances! 344

Chapter Interleaf with Teaching Resources

Objectifs

In this chapter you will learn to
- ask about a vacation
- say what you would do if you could
- express necessity
- ask about what has been done

Video

Géoculture	**Géoculture**
Vocabulaire 1 et 2	**Télé-vocab**
Grammaire 1 et 2	**Grammavision**
Télé-roman	**Télé-roman**

Online Practice
my.hrw.com
Online Edition

Scope and Sequence
Bien dit! Level 1

L'Île-de-France

La gastronomie
Les beaux-arts
L'histoire
Les loisirs

La tour Eiffel

Vocabulary	Functions	Grammar	Culture	Strategies
Chapitre 1 Salut, les copains! pp. 4–37				
• Greetings • Numbers 0–30	• Greet someone and say goodbye • Ask how someone is • Introduce someone • Ask how old someone is	• Subjects and verbs • Subject pronouns	• Kissing or shaking hands while greeting • Personal space and formal versus informal greetings • **Culture appliquée: Les gestes** • **Comparaisons:** Greetings • **Communauté:** Join a French club	• **Video Strategy:** Analyzing the opening • **Reading Strategy:** Recognizing cognates • **Writing Strategy:** Making a list
• Classroom objects and expressions • Accents and special characters	• Ask about things in a classroom • Give classroom commands and ask the teacher something • Ask how words are spelled • Ask for and give e-mail addresses	• Indefinite articles and plural of nouns • The verb **avoir** and negation	• Saying "hello" in the street FINE ART • ***Dans la classe,*** Théophile Duverger	
Review/Re-Entry	• **Révisions cumulatives,** pp. 36–37			

Notre Dame de Chartres

Vocabulary	Functions	Grammar	Culture	Strategies
Chapitre 2 Qu'est-ce qui te plaît? pp. 38–71				
• Likes and dislikes	• Ask about likes or dislikes • Agree and disagree	• Definite articles • **-er** verbs • Irregular plurals	• Music in France • French-language comic books • **Culture appliquée: Danses traditionnelles** • **Comparaisons: On joue au foot?** • **Communauté:** Folk dances	• **Video Strategy:** Gathering information • **Reading Strategy:** Using visual clues • **Writing Strategy:** Cluster diagrams
• Leisure activities	• Ask how often you do an activity • Ask how well you do an activity and talk about preferences	• Contractions with **à** • Conjunctions • **Est-ce que**	• Movie theaters in France FINE ART • ***Une baignade, Asnières,*** Georges Seurat	
Review/Re-Entry	• **Révisions cumulatives,** pp. 70–71		• Irregular plurals	

La province de Québec

La gastronomie
Les sports
Les fêtes et les festivals
L'histoire

La biosphère de Montréal

Vue panoramique de Québec

Vocabulary	Functions	Grammar	Culture	Strategies
Chapitre 3 Comment est ta famille? pp. 76–109				
• Physical descriptions and personality traits	• Ask about and describe people • Ask for and give opinions	• The verb **être** • Adjective agreement • More irregular adjectives 	• Last names • Motto of Quebec • **Culture appliquée: Le blason familial** • **Comparaisons: En famille** • **Communauté:** Your city's coat of arms	• **Video Strategy:** Separating essential information from non-essential information • **Reading Strategy:** Using genre to set expectations • **Writing Strategy:** Graphic organizers
• Family and pets	• Identify family members • Ask about someone's family	• Possessive adjectives • Contractions with **de** • **C'est** versus **Il/Elle est** 	• **Festival d'été et Fête de la famille** • **Carnaval de Québec**  FINE ART • ***Le traditionnel gâteau des Rois,*** Edmond-Joseph Massicotte	
Review/Re-Entry	• **Révisions cumulatives,** pp. 108–109			

Vocabulary	Functions	Grammar	Culture	Strategies
Chapitre 4 Mon année scolaire pp. 110–143				
• School subjects • Days of the week • Time	• Ask about classes • Ask for and give an opinion	• **-re** verbs • **-ger** and **-cer** verbs • **Le** with days of the week	• Bill 101 • 24-hour clock • **Culture appliquée: Les jours de la semaine** • **Comparaisons: Les délégués de classe** • **Communauté:** Vacations	• **Video Strategy:** Understanding a character's motives • **Reading Strategy:** Using background knowledge • **Writing Strategy:** Using chronology
• School supplies • Colors and numbers 31–201 	• Ask others what they need and tell what you need • Inquire about and buy something	• The verbs **préférer** and **acheter** • Adjectives as nouns • Agreement with numbers	• The school system • The **Cégep** FINE ART • ***L'Hôpital Saint-Paul à Saint-Rémy,*** Vincent van Gogh	
Review/Re-Entry	• **Révisions cumulatives,** pp. 142–143			

L'Ouest de la France

L'histoire
L'architecture
La gastronomie
Les sports

Le château de Chambord

Vocabulary	Functions	Grammar	Culture	Strategies
Chapitre 5 Le temps libre pp. 148–181				
• Sports and activities • Seasons and months of the year	• Ask about interests • Ask how often someone does an activity	• The verb **faire** • Question words • Adverbs	• School sports • **Sports de glisse** • French sports teams • **Culture appliquée: La pétanque** • **Comparaisons: Vive le sport!** • **Communauté: Un club de pétanque**	• **Video Strategy:** Looking for clues • **Reading Strategy:** Making predictions • **Writing Strategy:** An outline
• Places in town • Weather	• Extend, accept, and refuse an invitation • Make plans	• **Aller** and the **futur proche** • **Venir** and the **passé récent** • Idioms with **avoir**	• The Celsius scale FINE ART • ***Sur la plage à Trouville,*** Claude Monet	
Review/Re-Entry	• **Révisions cumulatives,** pp. 180–181	• Likes and dislikes		

Scope and Sequence

LIAISON

Les Champs-Elysées et l'Arc de Triomphe

Liaison Bien dit! Level 1B pp. xxii–L33

Vocabulary	Functions	Grammar
• Greetings • Physical descriptions and personality traits • Likes and dislikes • Sports and leisure activities • Weather • School supplies • Time • School subjects	• Ask for personal information • Ask for and give an opinion • Ask about one's interests • Make plans • Ask about school and classes • Ask and tell about family relationships	• The verbs **être** and **avoir** • Adjective agreement • **aller** and the **futur proche** • Contractions with **à** and **de** • Possessive adjectives • The present tense of **-er** and **-re** verbs

Maisons à poutres apparentes

Chapitre 6 Bon appétit! pp. 182–215

Vocabulary	Functions	Grammar	Culture	Strategies
• Breakfast foods and drinks • Place settings	• Offer, accept, and refuse food • Ask for and give an opinion	• The partitive • **-ir** verbs • The verb **vouloir** 	• A typical breakfast • Table manners in France • **Viennoiseries** • **Culture appliquée: La tarte** • **Comparaisons: À table!** • **Communauté: Des desserts**	• **Video Strategy:** Keeping track of the plot • **Reading Strategy:** Context clues and visual clues • **Writing Strategy:** Organizing via charts
• **Café** foods	• Inquire about food and place an order • Ask about prices and pay the check	• The verb **prendre** • The imperative • The verb **boire**	• Tipping in France • The euro • **Menu à prix fixe**  FINE ART • ***Le déjeuner des canotiers,*** Pierre Auguste Renoir	
Review/Re-Entry	• Contractions with **de** • **Révisions cumulatives,** pp. 214–215	• Sports and pastime activities		

Le Sénégal

L'artisanat
La musique
Les sports
La gastronomie

Marché en plein air

Chapitre 7 On fait les magasins? pp. 220–253

Vocabulary	Functions	Grammar	Culture	Strategies
• Clothing and accessories	• Offer and ask for help in a store • Ask for and give opinions	• Demonstrative adjectives • Interrogative adjectives • The verb **mettre** 	• Clothing sizes • **Batik** • Bargaining in Senegal • **Culture appliquée: Le boubou** • **Comparaisons: Les soldes** • **Communauté: Des costumes traditionnels**	• **Video Strategy:** Recognizing different points of view • **Reading Strategy:** Facts and opinions • **Writing Strategy:** Using charts to visualize and contrast
• Sports equipment, leather goods, and jewelry • Numbers 1,000–1,000,000	• Ask about and give prices • Make a decision	• The **passé composé** of **-er** verbs • The **passé composé** of irregular verbs • Adverbs with the **passé composé** 	• The Senegalese **franc CFA** FINE ART • ***Un souwère,*** M'Bida	
Review/Re-Entry	• Giving opinions • **Révisions cumulatives,** pp. 252–253	• Adjective agreement • **Avoir**		

Le lac Rose, Sénégal

Le Midi

L'artisanat
Les fêtes et les festivals
La gastronomie
Les arts

Marché en plein air à Nice

La gare de Nice

Vocabulary	Functions	Grammar	Culture	Strategies
Chapitre 8 À la maison pp. 254–287				
• Chores	• Ask for, give or refuse permission • Tell how often you do things	• The verbs **pouvoir** and **devoir** • The **passé composé** of **-ir** and **-re** verbs • Negative expressions 	• Tea ceremony in Senegal • **Culture appliquée: La cérémonie du thé** • **Comparaisons: Où sont les toilettes?** • **Communauté: C'est comment chez toi?**	• **Video Strategy:** Making deductions • **Reading Strategy:** Scanning for specific information • **Writing Strategy:** Using visuals
• House and furniture	• Describe a house • Tell where things are	• The verbs **dormir, sortir,** and **partir** • The **passé composé** with **être** • **-yer** verbs 	• Numbering floors in Senegal • Senegalese **cases** FINE ART • ***La chambre de Van Gogh à Arles,*** Vincent Van Gogh	
Review/Re-Entry	• Places and activities • **Révisions cumulatives,** pp. 286–287		• The **passé composé** of regular **-er** verbs • The past participles of **-er**, **-ir**, and **-re** verbs	
Chapitre 9 Allons en ville! pp. 292–325				
• Places in the city • Means of transportation	• Plan your day • Ask for and give directions	• The verb **voir** • The verbs **savoir** and **connaître** • The imperative	• **Code de la route** • Public transportation • The metric system • **Culture appliquée: La ville en chanson** • **Comparaisons: Les médicaments** • **Communauté: Plan de ta ville**	• **Video Strategy:** Making predictions • **Reading Strategy:** Reading aloud • **Writing Strategy:** Using a map to write directions
• At the pharmacy, bank, and post office	• Tell what you need • Make and respond to requests	• The present tense • Inversion • The partitive	• **La carte bleue** • **Pharmacie** versus **droguerie** • Banking at the post office  FINE ART • ***La Maison jaune,*** Vincent van Gogh	
Review/Re-Entry	• The imperative • The partitive	• The present tense • **Révisions cumulatives,** pp. 324–325	• Questions with intonation and **est-ce que**	
Chapitre 10 Enfin les vacances! pp. 326–359				
• Travel items • At the hotel	• Give advice • Get information	• The verb **appeler** • Prepositions with countries and cities • Idioms with **faire** 	• **Gîtes** • Hotel ratings • **Culture appliquée: Les santons** • **Comparaisons: L'électricité** • **Communauté: Souvenirs**	• **Video Strategy:** Summarizing • **Reading Strategy:** Improving comprehension • **Writing Strategy:** Create a timeline
• At the train station and airport	• Ask for information • Buy tickets and make a transaction	• The **passé composé** with **avoir** • The **passé composé** with **être** • Ordinal numbers	• **SNCF** and **TGV** • **Un composteur** FINE ART • ***La gare,*** Daniel Lordey	
Review/Re-Entry	• Contractions with **à** and **de** • Cardinal numbers • Places		• **Passé composé** with **avoir** • **Passé composé** with **être** • **Révisions cumulatives,** pp. 358–359	

Scope and Sequence
Bien dit! Level 2

Paris
Les sports
Les sciences
La gastronomie
La mode

Le Louvre

Les Invalides

Vocabulary	Functions	Grammar	Culture	Strategies
Chapitre 1 Ma famille et mes copains pp. 4–39				
• Describing friends and family	• Describe yourself and ask about others • Talk about your likes and dislikes	• The verbs **avoir** and **être** • Adjective agreement • The adjectives **beau, nouveau,** and **vieux**	• Sundays • Family nicknames • **La cursive** • **La famille au Maroc** • **Le français et l'enseignement**	• **Video Strategy:** Looking for clues • **Reading Strategy:** Genre of a text • **Writing Strategy:** Writing plan
• After-school activities	• Inquire • Tell when you do something	• **-er** verbs • **-ir** and **-re** verbs • Verbs like **dormir** 	• After-school activities • Cafés  FINE ART • ***Yvonne et Christine Lerolle au piano,*** Renoir	
Review/Re-Entry	• **tu** vs. **vous** • The verbs **avoir** and **être** • Adjective agreement • The adjectives **beau, nouveau,** and **vieux** • Days and months		• **-er** verbs • **-ir** and **-re** verbs • Verbs like **dormir** • **Révisions cumulatives,** pp. 38–39	
Chapitre 2 On fait la fête pp. 40–75				
• Celebrations	• Wish someone a good time • Ask for and give advice	• Direct object pronouns • Indirect object pronouns • The verb **offrir** 	• **L'Épiphanie, le jour des Rois** • **Le 14 juillet** • **Le carnaval** • **Invitation à manger** • **Spécialités pour les fêtes**	• **Video Strategy:** Gathering information • **Reading Strategy:** Using cognates • **Writing Strategy:** Good use of dialogue
• Party preparations	• Ask for help • Check if things have been done	• The **passé composé** with **avoir** • The **passé composé** with **être** • Negative expressions 	• **Noël** • Holidays FINE ART • ***La Rue Montorgueil, la Fête du 30 juin 1878,*** Claude Monet	
Review/Re-Entry	• The **passé composé** • The **passé composé** with **avoir**		• The **passé composé** with **être** • **Révisions cumulatives,** pp. 74–75	

Scope and Sequence

Québec
L' architecture
La gastronomie
Les fêtes et festivals
Les arts

Le château Frontenac

Bâtiment gouvernemental

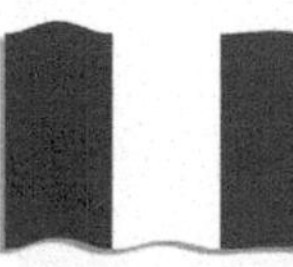

Rennes
L'architecture
Les fêtes et festivals
La musique
Les arts

L'Opéra de Rennes

Chapitre 3 Faisons les courses pp. 80–115

Vocabulary	Functions	Grammar	Culture	Strategies
• Fruits, vegetables, and cooking	• Ask about food preparation • Make requests 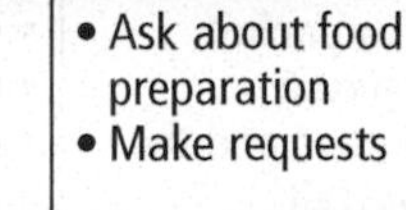	• The partitive • The pronoun **y** • Question formation 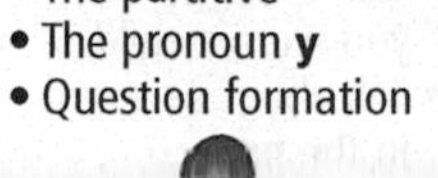	• The metric system • Typical foods of Quebec • **Le sirop d'érable** • **Le couscous** • **Le français dans les cuisines**	• **Video Strategy:** Comparing attitudes • **Reading Strategy:** Making inferences • **Writing Strategy:** Arranging your ideas chronologically
• Food shopping 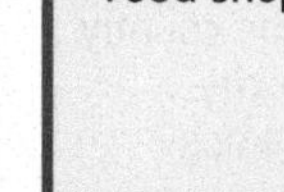	• Shop for groceries • Ask where things are in a store	• The pronoun **en** • Placement of object pronouns • Contractions with **à** and **de**	• Shopping FINE ART • ***La Rue des Abbesses,*** Maximilien Luce	
Review/Re-Entry	• Indefinite articles **un, une, des** • The partitive • Question formation • Prepositions		• In town • Contractions with **à** and **de** • **Révisions cumulatives,** pp. 114–115	

Chapitre 4 Au lycée pp. 116–151

Vocabulary	Functions	Grammar	Culture	Strategies
• School places and events	• Ask how something turned out • Wonder what happened	• Object pronouns with the **passé composé** • **Quelqu'un, quelque chose, ne...personne, ne... rien, ne...que** • The verb **recevoir**	• **Diplôme d'études collégiales (Québec)** • School books • **La ringuette** • **On mange où?** • **Être professeur de français**	• **Video Strategy:** Understanding subtext • **Reading Strategy:** The genre of a text • **Writing Strategy:** Answering the five "W" questions
• Computer terms	• Ask for information • Express frustration	• The verb **suivre** • **Depuis, il y a, ça fait...** • The verb **ouvrir** 	• Computer key-boards • Web sites FINE ART • ***Le Hockey,*** Henri Masson	
Review/Re-Entry 	• Direct and indirect object pronouns • **ne...personne; ne...rien**		• Party preparations • **Révisions cumulatives,** pp. 150–151	

Chapitre 5 Une journée typique pp. 156–191

Vocabulary	Functions	Grammar	Culture	Strategies
• Morning routine	• Talk about your routine • Express impatience	• Reflexive verbs • **tout, tous, toute, toutes** • The verbs **s'appeler** and **se lever**	• Typical French teen's day • The **métro** in Rennes • **La faïence de Quimper** • **À pied, à vélo ou en bus?** • **Le français et les produits de beauté**	• **Video Strategy:** Evaluating choices • **Reading Strategy:** Using the context • **Writing Strategy:** Identifying your audience
• Daily routine	• Say when you do things • Make recommendations	• Reflexive verbs in the **passé composé** • The imperative with reflexive verbs • Reflexive verbs with infinitives	• **Le goûter** • Shopping FINE ART • ***Nana,*** Edouard Manet	
Review/Re-Entry	• Verbs like **balayer** and **essayer** • **Tu, vous, nous** commands		• **Révisions cumulatives,** pp. 190–191	

Scope and Sequence

Place de la Mairie

Dakar
Les arts
La mode
Les fêtes et festivals
Le cinéma

Bateaux de pêche

La porte du Troisième Millénaire

Chapitre 6 Le bon vieux temps pp. 102–227

Vocabulary	Functions	Grammar	Culture	Strategies
• Childhood activities	• Talk about when you were a child • Tell about an event in the past	• The **imparfait** • The **passé composé** and the **imparfait** • Adverb placement	• Children's games • Comic books • **Les comptines** • **À la ferme** • **Au pair**	• **Video Strategy:** Making deductions • **Reading Strategy:** Using images and symbols • **Writing Strategy:** Symbols, imagery, metaphors, similes
• Country life	• Compare life in the country and in the city • Describe life in the country	• The comparative with adjectives and nouns • The superlative with adjectives • Irregular comparatives and superlatives	• Living in the country versus the city • Summer camps FINE ART • ***Paysage de Pont-Aven,*** Paul Gauguin	
Review/Re-Entry	• The **passé composé** • Adverbs • Adverb placement	• Contractions with **de** • **Révisions cumulatives,** pp. 226–227		

Chapitre 7 Un week-end en plein air pp. 232–267

Vocabulary	Functions	Grammar	Culture	Strategies
• Camping	• Say what happened • Describe circumstances	• The **passé composé** and the **imparfait** • **être en train de** • Verbs with **être** or **avoir** in the **passé composé**	• Camping • Nautical sports • **Le Parc national de la Langue de Barbarie** • **Le camping** • **Le français dans le monde du tourisme**	• **Video Strategy:** Getting confirmation • **Reading Strategy:** Focusing on ideas • **Writing Strategy:** Create the setting
• Nature, animals, and activities	• Tell what you will do • Wonder what will happen	• The future • The future of irregular verbs • The verb **courir**	• Fishing • The **pirogue** FINE ART • Jean Metzinger	
Review/Re-Entry	• The **passé composé** and the **imparfait** • Childhood activities • Verbs with **être** in the **passé composé** • **Révisions cumulatives,** pp. 266–267			

Chapitre 8 Es-tu en forme? pp. 268–303

Vocabulary	Functions	Grammar	Culture	Strategies
• Parts of the body; injuries and illnesses	• Ask and tell how you feel • Describe symptoms and give advice	• The subjunctive of regular verbs • The subjunctive of irregular verbs • More expressions with the subjunctive	• Health care • **L'awalé** • **Malade en France** • **Le français dans le monde médical**	• **Video Strategy:** Following the plot • **Reading Strategy:** Using background knowledge • **Writing Strategy:** Providing specific details
• Improving one's health	• Complain about health and give advice • Sympathize with someone	• The conditional • **Si** clauses • The conditional to make polite requests	• Gyms • Senegalese foods FINE ART • ***Un souwère du Sénégal***	
Review/Re-Entry	• Body parts • Family • Future stems of irregular verbs		• **Imparfait** endings • Fruits and vegetables • **Révisions cumulatives,** pp. 302–303	

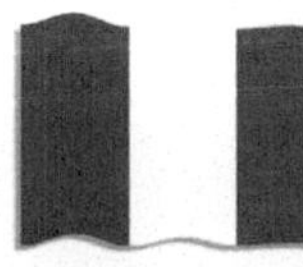

Nice

Les arts
Les fêtes et festivals
L'architecture
La gastronomie

La FNAC

Chapitre 9 On s'amuse! pp. 308–343

Vocabulary	Functions	Grammar	Culture	Strategies
• Movies and books	• Describe a movie or a book • Ask for and give information	• The relative pronouns **qui, que,** and **dont** • Present participles • **C'est** and **Il/Elle est** 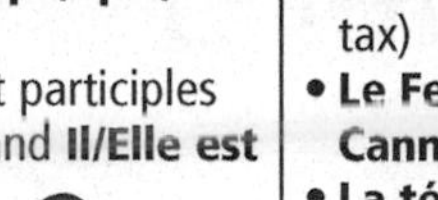  	• Movies • The **TVA** (French tax) • **Le Festival de Cannes** • **La télévision en France** • **Être traducteur ou interprète**	• **Video Strategy:** Predicting • **Reading Strategy:** Recognizing the main idea • **Writing Strategy:** Using conjunctions and relative pronouns
• Television shows and music	• Ask about preferences • Recommend and advise against something	• Interrogative pronouns • Demonstrative pronouns • Comparatives and superlatives	• The TVA • Television FINE ART • ***Pont de Langlois,*** Vincent Van Gogh	
Review/Re-Entry	• Expressions followed by **de** • **C'est** and **Il/Elle est** • **Quel**	• Comparatives and superlatives • **Révisions cumulatives,** pp. 342–343		

Musée d'Art moderne et d'art contemporain (MAMAC)

Chapitre 10 Partons en vacances! pp. 344–379

Vocabulary	Functions	Grammar	Culture	Strategies
• Vacation	• Ask about a vacation • Say what you would do if you could	• Object pronouns • The conditional • **Si** clauses	• Tourism • Vacations • **Le tourisme à Nice** • **En vacances!** • **Le français et le tourisme**	• **Video Strategy**: Putting the pieces together • **Reading Strategy:** Personification • **Writing Strategy:** Purpose for writing
• Making preparations for vacation	• Express necessity • Ask about what has been done	• The subjunctive • The **passé composé** and the **imparfait** • **être en train de**	• School holidays • Vacation schedules FINE ART • ***Scène du jardin en Bretagne,*** Pierre Auguste Renoir	
Review/Re-Entry	• To say in, to, from a country • Object pronouns • The conditional • Clothes and accessories • **Révisions cumulatives,** pp. 378–379	• The **passé composé** and the **imparfait** • **être en train de** • **Si** clauses • The subjunctive		

Scope and Sequence
Bien dit! Level 3

Chapitre 1 Retour de vacances pp. 4–41

	Vocabulary	Functions	Grammar	Culture	Strategies
La France **La géographie** **L'histoire**	• Back-to-school activities and classes • After-school activities	• Express likes, dislikes, and preferences • Ask about plans	• Regular verbs in the present • Irregular verbs in the present • Verbs followed by the infinitive	• The **baccalauréat** and professional studies • The **baccalauréat** • **Chevaux de polo** • **Les moniteurs** • **Le français et le développement des loisirs et du tourisme**	• **Reading Strategy:** Creating mental images • **Writing Strategy:** Sensory details
Marché aux fleurs	• What you did last summer: activities, things, and places	• Tell when and how often you did something • Describe a place in the past	• The **passé composé** • The **passé composé** and the **imparfait** • Reflexive verbs in the **passé composé**	• Summer vacation for French youth • Festivals in France FINE ART • ***Un dimanche après-midi à l'Île de la Grande Jatte*** de Georges Seurat	
	Review/Re-Entry	• Regular verbs in the present • Irregular verbs in the present • Verbs followed by the infinitive • The **passé composé**		• The **passé composé** and the **imparfait** • Reflexive verbs in the **passé composé** • **Révisions cumulatives,** pp. 40–41	

Chapitre 2 Le monde du travail pp. 42–79

	Vocabulary	Functions	Grammar	Culture	Strategies
Fontaine et fleurs	• Professions and services	• Ask about future plans • Make polite requests	• The future • Feminine forms of nouns • The verb **conduire**	• The three parts of the French economy • The French work year • **Designer olfactif** • **Curriculum vitae** • **Le français et la publicité**	• **Reading Strategy:** Summarizing ideas • **Writing Strategy:** Details and organization
	• Telephone and formal letter vocabulary	• Make a phone call • Write a formal letter	• The future perfect • The present participle • **Conditionnel de politesse**	• Finding a job in France, the ANPE • Unions and strikes in France FINE ART • ***Les Constructeurs*** de Fernand Léger	
	Review/Re-Entry	• The future • Present participles	• The **conditionnel de politesse** • **Révisions cumulatives,** pp. 78–79		

L'Afrique francophone
La géographie
L'histoire

Femmes en costume traditionnel

Chapitre 3 Il était une fois... pp. 94–131

Vocabulary	Functions	Grammar	Culture	Strategies
• Legends, fairy tales, and fables	• Set the scene for a story • Continue and end a story	• The **passé simple** • Relative pronouns with **ce** • Adjective placement and meaning	• Oral tradition • The **médina** • **La littérature maghrébine en français** • **Écrire en français** • **Doubleur: un métier en plein boum**	• **Reading Strategy:** Using chronology • **Writing Strategy:** Using realistic dialogue
• Historical accounts from Africa	• Relate a sequence of events • Tell what happened to someone else	• The past perfect • Sequence of tenses in indirect discourse • The past infinitive	• French colonists in Algeria FINE ART • Cave art painting from Aounrhet, Tassili, Algeria	

Review/Re-Entry	
• **Imparfait et passé composé** • The pronouns **qui, que,** and **dont**	• Reflexive verbs in the **passé composé** • **Révisions cumulatives,** pp. 130–131

Perles et colliers sur un marché à Dakar

Chapitre 4 Amours et amitiés pp. 132–169

Vocabulary	Functions	Grammar	Culture	Strategies
• Reciprocal actions and emotions	• Say what happened • Ask for and give advice	• Reciprocal verbs • The past conditional • The verbs **manquer** and **plaire**	• Hospitality in Africa • **Maroc: nouveau code de la famille** • **Sorties entre copains!** • **Les formateurs multiculturels**	• **Reading Strategy:** Using background knowledge • **Writing Strategy:** Using similes
• Life events and emotions	• Share good and bad news • Renew old acquaintances	• The subjunctive • The subjunctive with necessity, desire, and emotions • Disjunctive (stress) pronouns	• Weddings in North Africa • Family politics FINE ART • ***La Noce*** d'Henri-Julien Félix Rousseau dit Le Douanier	

Review/Re-Entry	
• Reflexive verbs in the **passé composé** • The conditional • **Révisions cumulatives,** pp. 168–169	• The subjunctive • Activities

L'Amérique francophone
La géographie
L'histoire

Bâtiment gouvernemental

Chapitre 5 En pleine nature pp. 184–221

Vocabulary	Functions	Grammar	Culture	Strategies
• Nature and animals	• Express astonishment and fear • Forbid and give warning	• The subjunctive with expressions of fear • The imperative • The verbs **voir** and **regarder**	• Parks in Louisiana • French and Cajun influence • **Les oies voyageuses** • **Les parcs publics en France** • **Moniteurs/Guides de sports extrêmes**	• **Reading Strategy:** Using inferences • **Writing Strategy:** Using multiple techniques
• Exploration (hiking, rafting, extreme outdoor sports)	• Give general directions • Complain and offer encouragement	• **Apporter, amener, emporter** and **emmener** • Verbs followed by **à/de** and the infinitive • Verbs with idioms	• Canadian sports FINE ART • ***Louisiana heron*** de Jean-Jacques Audubon	

Review/Re-Entry	
• The subjunctive • The imperative • **Révisions cumulatives,** pp. 220–221	• **Voir** and **regarder** • Idiomatic expressions

Scope and Sequence

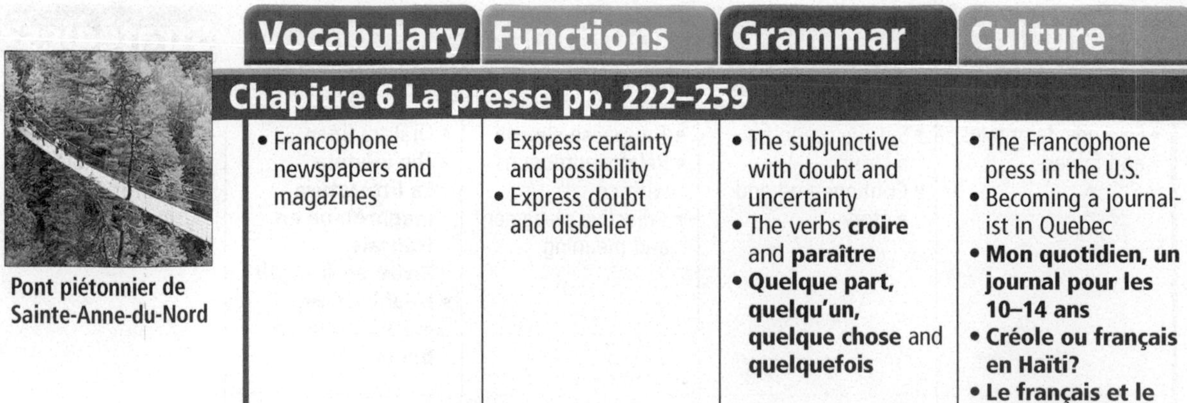

Pont piétonnier de Sainte-Anne-du-Nord

Chapitre 6 La presse pp. 222–259

Vocabulary	Functions	Grammar	Culture	Strategies
• Francophone newspapers and magazines	• Express certainty and possibility • Express doubt and disbelief	• The subjunctive with doubt and uncertainty • The verbs **croire** and **paraître** • **Quelque part, quelqu'un, quelque chose** and **quelquefois**	• The Francophone press in the U.S. • Becoming a journalist in Quebec • **Mon quotidien, un journal pour les 10–14 ans** • **Créole ou français en Haïti?** • **Le français et le journalisme**	• **Reading Strategy:** Background knowledge and context clues • **Writing Strategy:** Defining your style
• The news	• Break news • Ask about information	• Object pronouns • **Qui est-ce qui, qui est-ce que, qu'est-ce qui** and **qu'est-ce que** • More negative expressions	• Blogs FINE ART • ***Le Snobisme*** de Toulouse-Lautrec	
Review/Re-Entry	• Subjunctive forms, regular and irregular • **quelque** • Sequence of tenses		• Direct object agreement of the past participle • Object pronouns • **Révisions cumulatives,** pp. 258–259	

Chapitre 7 Notre planète pp. 274–311

L'Europe francophone
La géographie
L'histoire

Les Alpes françaises

Vocabulary	Functions	Grammar	Culture	Strategies
• Natural phenomena	• Caution • Tell why something happened	• The comparative and superlative • The passive voice • Prepositions	• The climate • **Dépollution par le lombric** • **La minuterie** • **Le français et le monde de la recherche**	• **Reading Strategy:** Identifying the main idea • **Writing Strategy:** Defining your audience
• Environmental issues and solutions	• Make predictions and express assumptions • Express and support an opinion	• **Quand, lorsque,** and **dès que** • Subjunctive after a conjunction • The verb **éteindre**	• Kyoto treaty for Environmental protection • Electric cars FINE ART • **La Jetée du Havre par mauvais temps** de Claude Monet	
Review/Re-Entry	• Irregular comparative and superlative of **bon** and **bien** • The future and future perfect • **Révisions cumulatives,** pp. 310–311		• The subjunctive • The verb **éteindre**	

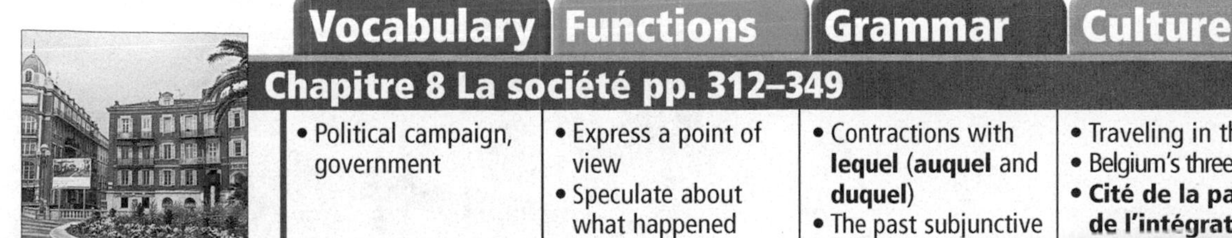

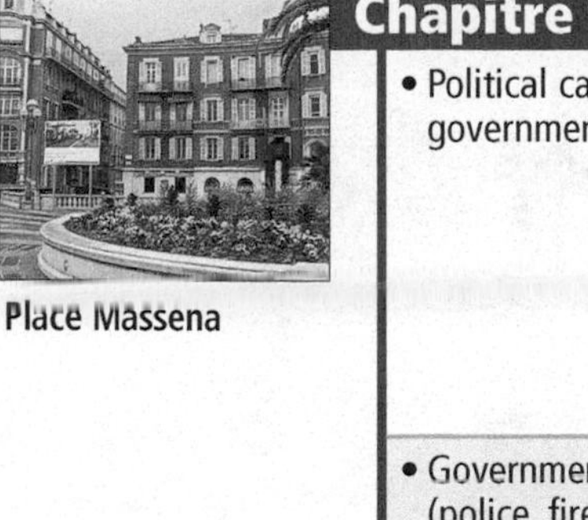
Place Massena

Chapitre 8 La société pp. 312–349

Vocabulary	Functions	Grammar	Culture	Strategies
• Political campaign, government	• Express a point of view • Speculate about what happened	• Contractions with **lequel** (**auquel** and **duquel**) • The past subjunctive • Adverbs	• Traveling in the EU • Belgium's three cultures • **Cité de la paix et de l'intégration** • **Les Juges en France** • **Le français et les organisations internationales**	• **Reading Strategy:** Taking notes • **Writing Strategy:** Good introductions and conclusions
• Government services (police, firefighter, administration)	• Ask for assistance • Get information and explain	• The conditional • The verb **vaincre** • **Chacun/chacune**	• Swiss government FINE ART • ***Les Représentants des puissances étrangères venant saluer la République en signe de paix*** d'Henri Rousseau	

Review/Re-Entry
- The interrogative pronoun **lequel**
- The subjunctive
- Adverbs
- The **imparfait**
- The conditional
- **Révisions cumulatives,** pp. 348–349

Chapitre 9 L'art en fête pp. 364–401

L'outre-mer
La géographie
L'histoire

Forteresse à la Martinique

Vocabulary	Functions	Grammar	Culture	Strategies
• Types of fine arts	• Ask for and give opinions • Introduce and change a topic of conversation	• The inversion • Present participles used as adjectives • **Si** and **oui**	• Tahitian crafts • **La sculpture, l'âme des Marquises** • **Les musées en France** • **Le français et la musique**	• **Reading Strategy:** Dialoguing with the text • **Writing Strategy:** Using note cards
• Music and other performing arts	• Make suggestions and recommendations • Give an impression	• The comparative and superlative • Demonstrative pronouns • **Savoir** and **connaître**	• Music of the Antilles • Tahitian song and dance 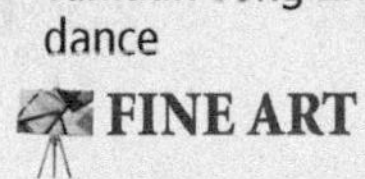 FINE ART • ***Danseuse au bouquet*** d'Edgar Degas	

Review/Re-Entry
- Intonation
- Inversion
- Present participles used as adjectives
- Adjective agreement
- The comparative and superlative
- Demonstrative pronouns
- **Savoir** and **connaître**
- **Révisions cumulatives,** pp. 400–401

Bateaux à la Martinique

Chapitre 10 Bon voyage! pp. 402–439

Vocabulary	Functions	Grammar	Culture	Strategies
• At the airport	• Ask for and give information and clarifications • Remind and reassure	• Prepositions with places • The subjunctive	• DROM • **A380 Naissance d'un géant** • **Les autoroutes en France** • **Le français et les métiers du tourisme**	• **Reading Strategy:** Combining strategies • **Writing Strategy:** Creating mood
• Travel by car	• Ask for and give help • Ask for directions	• The future • The past perfect • The causative **faire**	• French driver's license • French driver's license – the point system FINE ART • ***The Regattas at Nice*** d'Henri Matisse	

Review/Re-Entry
- Gender of countries
- Preposition with places
- The subjunctive
- Adverbs and adverb placement
- The future
- The **plus-que-parfait**
- The causative **faire**
- **Révisions cumulatives,** pp. 438–439

Language takes you there!

Remarkable Culture

Vivid, inspiring, and focused culture goes beyond the textbook with on-site videos, News Networking and more!

Relevant Instruction

Multi-tiered differentiation in presentation, practice, assessments, and in FRENCH InterActive Reader create a truly personalized learning environment.

Real Interaction

Students show what they know with performance space, a virtual one-to-one environment that allows students to record spoken and written responses.

Digital French

TEACHER ONE STOP
- Resources available on DVD and at my.hrw.com
- All Print Resources
- Interactive Teacher Edition
- Projectable Transparencies
- Lesson Plans
- Reading Strategy and Skills Handbook
- Media Guide
- Cahier de vocabulaire et grammaire, Teacher Edition
- Cahier d'activités, Teacher Edition
- ExamView® Assessment Suite

ONLINE STUDENT EDITION
- Fully interactive student edition
- Interactive activities with immediate feedback
- Performance Space

eTEXTBOOKS
- Available for delivery on a variety of devices

STUDENT ONE STOP
- Entire Student Edition with Audio and Video at point-of-use

INTERACTIVE WHITEBOARD LESSONS

ONLINE PRACTICE
- @Home Tutor
- On rappe!
- Grammavision Animated Grammar

HOLT MCDOUGAL FRENCH APPS

PERFORMANCE SPACE

Practice and Assess Performance In this Virtual Environment!
- Teacher Dashboard to Manage Student Responses
- Student Dashboard to Track Completion and Feedback

NEWS AND NETWORKING
- High-interest articles at appropriate levels of difficulty
- Current cultural and newsworthy videos
- Monitored blogs

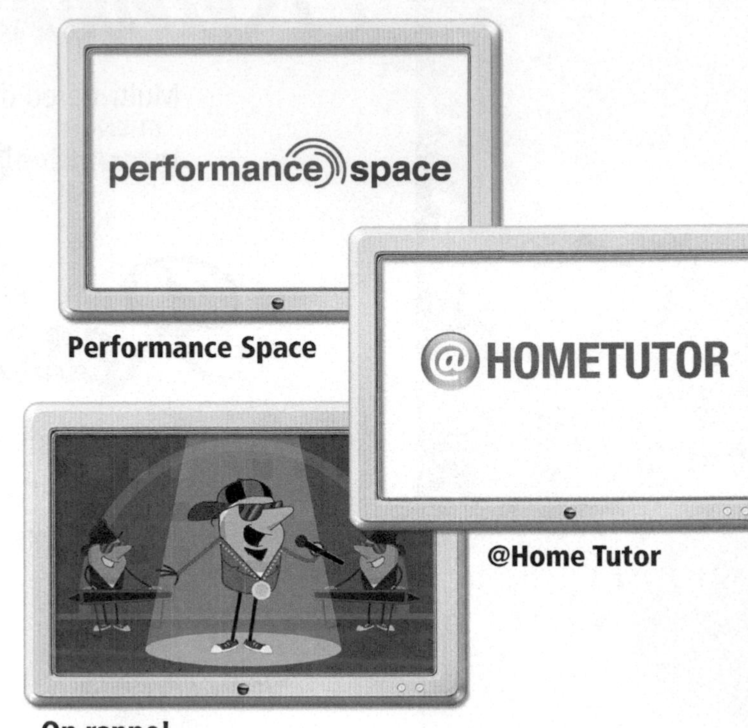

Performance Space

@Home Tutor

On rappe!

FRENCH INTERACTIVE READER
- Authentic texts
- Reading in the Content Areas
- Leveled for Difficulty

VIDEO AND AUDIO

Downloads available at my.hrw.com
- On rappe! Video (Animations of songs with Karaoke track, Teaching Suggestions, Activity Masters, Video Scripts and Answers)
- Bien dit! Video Program
- Audio Program

MP3

ONLINE ASSESSMENT
- ExamView on Teacher One Stop
- Holt McDougal Online Assessment
- Generate Success Rubric Generator

DIFFERENTIATED PRACTICE AND ASSESSMENT CD-ROM

Two versions of the Cahier de vocabulaire et grammaire and Assessment Program—one for advanced learners and one for slower paced learners

Print Resources

FOR THE STUDENT

Student Edition

Cahier de vocabulaire et grammaire
- Presentation of major grammar points
- Additional practice activities

Cahier d'activités
- Additional reading and Writing Activities

Beginning/Intermediate/Advanced Readers

FOR THE TEACHER

Teacher's Edition

Assessment Program

Grammar Tutor for Students of French
- Comparisons of Grammar concepts in English and French
- Additional grammar practice

Reading Strategies and Skills Handbook
(Available on the Teacher One Stop)

Articulation Across Levels

From Middle School through Level 3

Begin the learning experience with **Level 1**

...or

set a slower pace for middle school with **Level 1A** and **Level 1B**

Level 1A

+

Level 1B

Level 2 thoroughly reviews the basics and continues to build a solid foundation for communication.

Level 3 begins with a review of the major points covered in Level 2, then builds student skills to the Intermediate Proficiency level.

Culture from the start

provides high-interest articles, cultural videos and blog!

Chapitres 3 et 4

Géoculture
Québec

DVD
Géoculture

La Chute Montmorency est plus haute que les chutes du Niagara. En hiver, elle gèle *(freezes)* et on peut l'escalader *(climb)*. 3

Les fortifications Québec est la seule ville fortifiée d'Amérique du Nord. 4

Le Petit-Champlain Dans ce quartier sympathique, il y a beaucoup d'ateliers *(workshops)* d'artistes, de cafés et de boutiques. 5

La place Royale C'est ici que Samuel de Champlain a fondé la ville de Québec en 1608. 2

La terrasse Saint-Denis Cette large promenade offre une belle vue du Saint-Laurent. C'est un des lieux de rendez-vous préférés des jeunes Québécois. 1

Le château Frontenac Les châteaux de la Loire en France ont inspiré l'architecture de cet hôtel. 6

Almanach

Nom des habitants
Les Québécois

Population
Plus de 160.000 habitants

Personnages célèbres
Marie-Claire Blais, Yves Thériault, Félix Leclerc, Guy Laliberté

Économie
industrie alimentaire, textile, trafic portuaire, tourisme

Savais-tu que...?
La terrasse Saint-Denis était un des endroits favoris des poètes et écrivains.

Les plaines d'Abraham En 1759, les Anglais ont battu les Français à cet endroit. Aujourd'hui, c'est un grand parc. 7

Géo-quiz
Qu'est-ce qui différencie Québec des autres villes d'Amérique du Nord?

76 soixante-seize Chapitres 3–4 Géoculture soixante-dix-sept 77

The ***Géoculture*** video brings each location to life.

Géoculture

The ***Géoculture*** pages introduce students to a new country. Students make connections with geography, art, architecture, food, and celebrations.

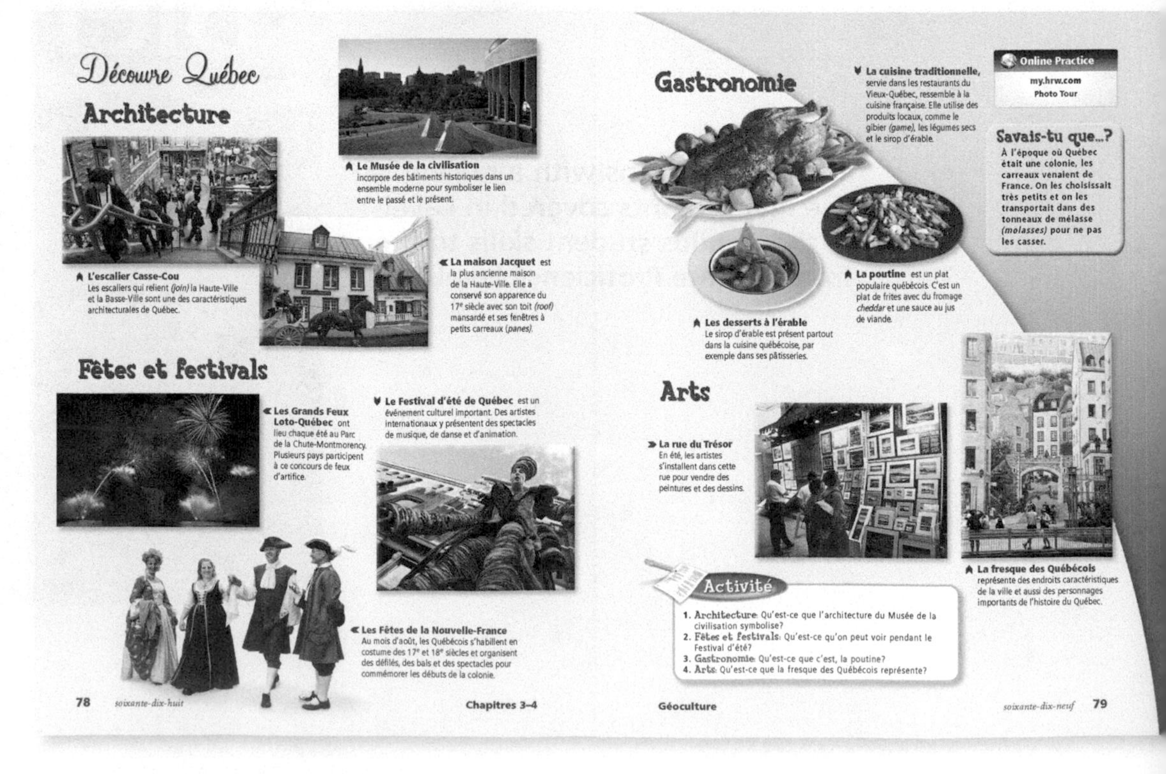

Découvre Québec

Architecture

Le Musée de la civilisation incorpore des bâtiments historiques dans un ensemble moderne pour symboliser le lien entre le passé et le présent.

L'escalier Casse-Cou Les escaliers qui relient *(join)* la Haute-Ville et la Basse-Ville sont une des caractéristiques architecturales de Québec.

La maison Jacquet est la plus ancienne maison de la Haute-Ville. Elle a conservé son apparence du 17e siècle avec son toit *(roof)* mansardé et ses fenêtres à petits carreaux *(panes)*.

Fêtes et festivals

Les Grands Feux Loto-Québec ont lieu chaque été au Parc de la Chute-Montmorency. Plusieurs pays participent à ce concours de feux d'artifice.

Le Festival d'été de Québec est un événement culturel important. Des artistes internationaux y présentent des spectacles de musique, de danse et d'animation.

Les Fêtes de la Nouvelle-France Au mois d'août, les Québécois s'habillent en costume des 17e et 18e siècles et organisent des défilés, des bals et des spectacles pour commémorer les débuts de la colonie.

Gastronomie

La cuisine traditionnelle, servie dans les restaurants du Vieux-Québec, ressemble à la cuisine française. Elle utilise des produits locaux, comme le gibier *(game)*, les légumes secs et le sirop d'érable.

Online Practice
my.hrw.com
Photo Tour

Savais-tu que...?
À l'époque où Québec était une colonie, les carreaux venaient de France. On les choisissait très petits et on les transportait dans des tonneaux de mélasse *(molasses)* pour ne pas les casser.

La poutine est un plat populaire québécois. C'est un plat de frites avec du fromage *cheddar* et une sauce au jus de viande.

Les desserts à l'érable Le sirop d'érable est présent partout dans la cuisine québécoise, par exemple dans ses pâtisseries.

Arts

La rue du Trésor En été, les artistes s'installent dans cette rue pour vendre des peintures et des dessins.

La fresque des Québécois représente des endroits caractéristiques de la ville et aussi des personnages importants de l'histoire du Québec.

Activité

1. Architecture Qu'est-ce que l'architecture du Musée de la civilisation symbolise?
2. Fêtes et festivals Qu'est-ce qu'on peut voir pendant le Festival d'été?
3. Gastronomie Qu'est-ce que c'est, la poutine?
4. Arts Qu'est-ce que la fresque des Québécois représente?

78 soixante-dix-huit Chapitres 3–4 Géoculture soixante-dix-neuf 79

Vocabulary

and functional phrases are the foundation of meaningful communication. Interactive Whiteboard activities provide a great way to get the whole class involved.

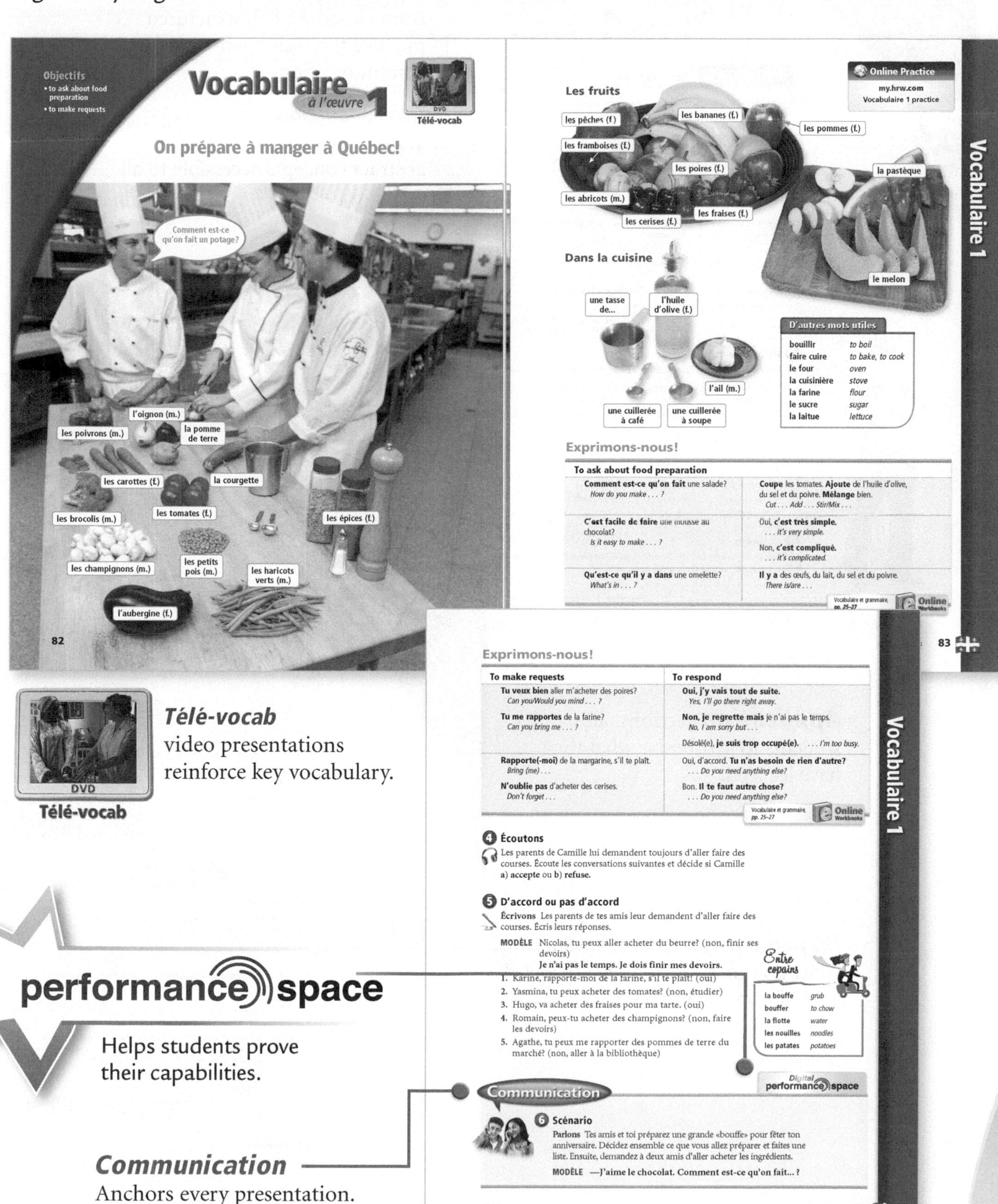

Objectifs
- to ask about food preparation
- to make requests

Vocabulaire à l'œuvre 1

DVD Télé-vocab

On prépare à manger à Québec!

82

Les fruits

Online Practice
my.hrw.com
Vocabulaire 1 practice

Dans la cuisine

D'autres mots utiles

bouillir	*to boil*
faire cuire	*to bake, to cook*
le four	*oven*
la cuisinière	*stove*
la farine	*flour*
le sucre	*sugar*
la laitue	*lettuce*

Exprimons-nous!

To ask about food preparation	
Comment est-ce qu'on fait une salade? *How do you make . . . ?*	**Coupe** les tomates. **Ajoute** de l'huile d'olive, du sel et du poivre. **Mélange** bien. *Cut . . . Add . . . Stir/Mix . . .*
C'est facile de faire une mousse au chocolat? *Is it easy to make . . . ?*	Oui, **c'est très simple.** *. . . it's very simple.* Non, **c'est compliqué.** *. . . it's complicated.*
Qu'est-ce qu'il y a dans une omelette? *What's in . . . ?*	**Il y a** des œufs, du lait, du sel et du poivre. *There is/are . . .*

Vocabulaire et grammaire, pp. 25–27 Online Workbooks

83

Vocabulaire 1

Exprimons-nous!

To make requests	To respond
Tu veux bien aller m'acheter des poires? *Can you/Would you mind . . . ?* **Tu me rapportes** de la farine? *Can you bring me . . . ?*	**Oui, j'y vais tout de suite.** *Yes, I'll go there right away.* **Non, je regrette mais** je n'ai pas le temps. *No, I am sorry but . . .* Désolé(e), **je suis trop occupé(e).** *. . . I'm too busy.*
Rapporte(-moi) de la margarine, s'il te plaît. *Bring (me) . . .* **N'oublie pas** d'acheter des cerises. *Don't forget . . .*	Oui, d'accord. **Tu n'as besoin de rien d'autre?** *. . . Do you need anything else?* Bon. **Il te faut autre chose?** *. . . Do you need anything else?*

Vocabulaire et grammaire, pp. 25–27 Online Workbooks

4 Écoutons

Les parents de Camille lui demandent toujours d'aller faire des courses. Écoute les conversations suivantes et décide si Camille a) **accepte** ou b) **refuse.**

5 D'accord ou pas d'accord

Écrivons Les parents de tes amis leur demandent d'aller faire des courses. Écris leurs réponses.

MODÈLE Nicolas, tu peux aller acheter du beurre? (non, finir ses devoirs)
Je n'ai pas le temps. Je dois finir mes devoirs.

1. Karine, rapporte-moi de la farine, s'il te plaît! (oui)
2. Yasmina, tu peux acheter des tomates? (non, étudier)
3. Hugo, va acheter des fraises pour ma tarte. (oui)
4. Romain, peux-tu acheter des champignons? (non, faire les devoirs)
5. Agathe, tu peux me rapporter des pommes de terre du marché? (non, aller à la bibliothèque)

Entre copains

la bouffe	*grub*
bouffer	*to chow*
la flotte	*water*
les nouilles	*noodles*
les patates	*potatoes*

Digital performance space

Communication

6 Scénario

Parlons Tes amis et toi préparez une grande «bouffe» pour fêter ton anniversaire. Décidez ensemble ce que vous allez préparer et faites une liste. Ensuite, demandez à deux amis d'aller acheter les ingrédients.

MODÈLE —**J'aime le chocolat. Comment est-ce qu'on fait... ?**

Québec *quatre-vingt-cinq* 85

DVD Télé-vocab

Télé-vocab video presentations reinforce key vocabulary.

performance space

Helps students prove their capabilities.

Communication Anchors every presentation.

Grammar and Application

Objectifs
- the partitive
- the pronoun *y*

Grammaire à l'œuvre 1

DVD Grammavision

Révisions The partitive

1 The partitive articles express the idea of *some* or *any*, or a *part/portion* of a whole item.

Masculine	Feminine	Sing word beginning with a vowel	Plural
du sucre	de la farine	de l'huile	des petits pois

—Tu veux du gâteau ou de la tarte?
—*Do you want (some) cake or (some) pie?*

2 The forms of the partitive change to de (d') in a negative sentence and after words of quantity like **beaucoup**.

Il y a de la farine, mais il n'y a pas d'ail.
Karine mange beaucoup de cerises!

3 To talk about a whole item, use the indefinite article un, une, or des.

Nous achetons une tarte aux pommes.

Vocabulaire et grammaire, *pp. 28–29*
Cahier d'activités, *pp. 21–23*
Online Workbooks

Déjà vu!
The indefinite articles are **un**, **une**, and **des**. They mean **a**, **an**, or **some**. The definite articles are le, la, and les. They mean **the**. To say that you like something, use a definite article.
Ariane achète **une** tarte.
J'aime les fraises.

7 Parlons de cuisine
Lisons Choisis l'article qui convient pour compléter chaque phrase.

1. Marianne et ses amis aiment bien _____ salade.
 a. de la b. la c. les
2. Je mange _____ légumes, mais pas de viande.
 a. des b. de c. un
3. Il y a beaucoup _____ épices dans ces légumes.
 a. des b. de c. d'
4. Je vais préparer une tarte et il me faut _____ sucre.
 a. des b. du c. de la
5. Il n'y a pas _____ tomates dans cette salade.
 a. de l' b. de c. une

8 Écoutons
Des amis parlent au café. Écoute chaque phrase et dis si **a) il y a un partitif** ou si **b) il n'y a pas de partitif**.

86 *quatre-vingt-six* **Chapitre 3** · Faisons les courses

Grammar sections lead students from closed-ended, structured practice through open-ended communication.

Grammavision animation makes even the most abstract concepts accessible to all students.

Application sections allow students to synthesize what they have learned.

Un peu plus presents or reviews a short grammar topic and is followed by additional activities.

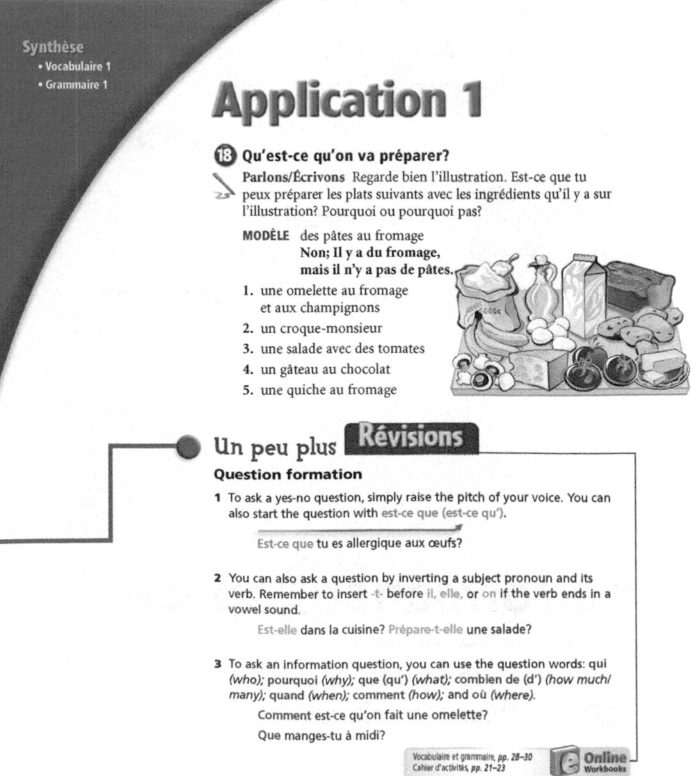

Synthèse
- Vocabulaire 1
- Grammaire 1

Application 1

18 Qu'est-ce qu'on va préparer?
Parlons/Écrivons Regarde bien l'illustration. Est-ce que tu peux préparer les plats suivants avec les ingrédients qu'il y a sur l'illustration? Pourquoi ou pourquoi pas?

MODÈLE des pâtes au fromage
Non; Il y a du fromage, mais il n'y a pas de pâtes.

1. une omelette au fromage et aux champignons
2. un croque-monsieur
3. une salade avec des tomates
4. un gâteau au chocolat
5. une quiche au fromage

Un peu plus Révisions
Question formation

1 To ask a yes-no question, simply raise the pitch of your voice. You can also start the question with est-ce que (est-ce qu').

Est-ce que tu es allergique aux œufs?

2 You can also ask a question by inverting a subject pronoun and its verb. Remember to insert -t- before il, elle, or on if the verb ends in a vowel sound.

Est-elle dans la cuisine? Prépare-t-elle une salade?

3 To ask an information question, you can use the question words: qui *(who)*; pourquoi *(why)*; que (qu') *(what)*; combien de (d') *(how much/many)*; quand *(when)*; comment *(how)*; and où *(where)*.

Comment est-ce qu'on fait une omelette?
Que manges-tu à midi?

Vocabulaire et grammaire, *pp. 28–30*
Cahier d'activités, *pp. 21–23*
Online Workbooks

19 Écoutons
Écoute chaque phrase et dis si c'est **a) une question** ou **b) une phrase affirmative**.

90 *quatre-vingt-dix* **Chapitre 3** · Faisons les courses

Culture and on-going story

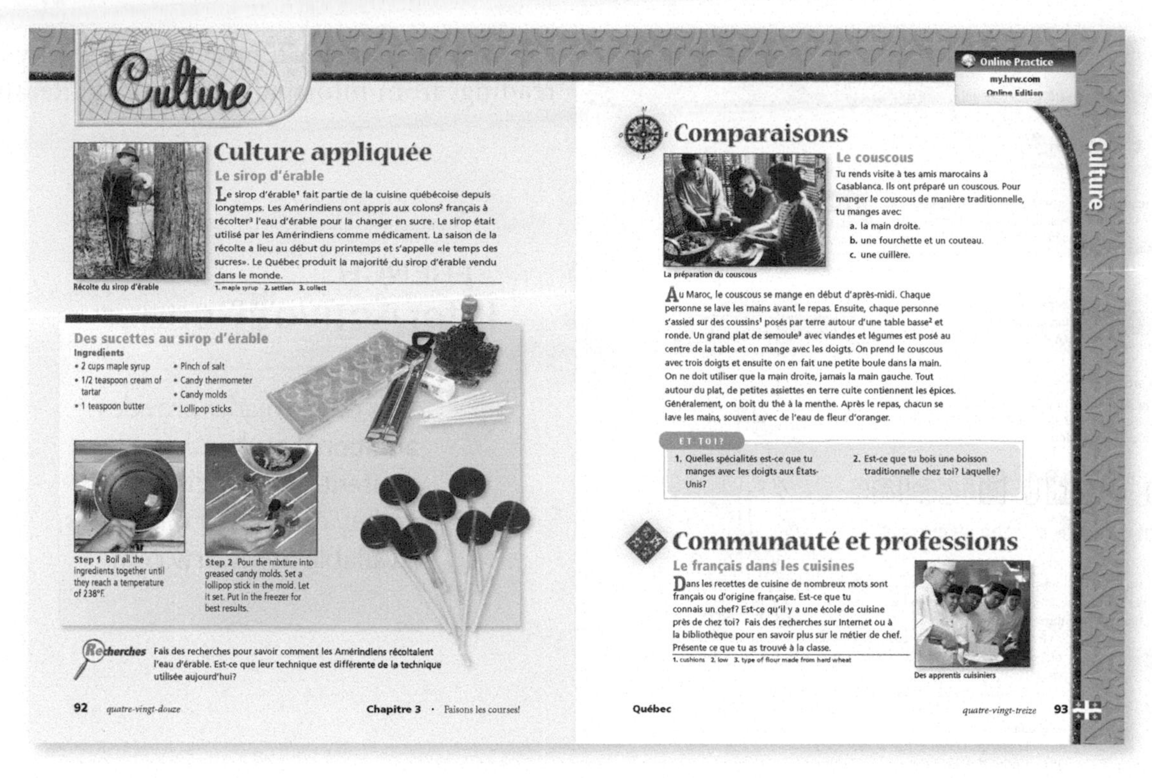

Culture

Culture appliquée

Le sirop d'érable

Le sirop d'érable[1] fait partie de la cuisine québécoise depuis longtemps. Les Amérindiens ont appris aux colons[2] français à récolter[3] l'eau d'érable pour la changer en sucre. Le sirop était utilisé par les Amérindiens comme médicament. La saison de la récolte a lieu au début du printemps et s'appelle «le temps des sucres». Le Québec produit la majorité du sirop d'érable vendu dans le monde.

Récolte du sirop d'érable

1. maple syrup 2. settlers 3. collect

Des sucettes au sirop d'érable

Ingredients
- 2 cups maple syrup
- 1/2 teaspoon cream of tartar
- 1 teaspoon butter
- Pinch of salt
- Candy thermometer
- Candy molds
- Lollipop sticks

Step 1 Boil all the ingredients together until they reach a temperature of 238°F.

Step 2 Pour the mixture into greased candy molds. Set a lollipop stick in the mold. Let it set. Put in the freezer for best results.

Recherches Fais des recherches pour savoir comment les Amérindiens récoltaient l'eau d'érable. Est-ce que leur technique est différente de la technique utilisée aujourd'hui?

92 quatre-vingt-douze Chapitre 3 · Faisons les courses!

Online Practice
my.hrw.com
Online Edition

Comparaisons

Le couscous

Tu rends visite à tes amis marocains à Casablanca. Ils ont préparé un couscous. Pour manger le couscous de manière traditionnelle, tu manges avec:

a. la main droite.
b. une fourchette et un couteau.
c. une cuillère.

La préparation du couscous

Au Maroc, le couscous se mange en début d'après-midi. Chaque personne se lave les mains avant le repas. Ensuite, chaque personne s'assied sur des coussins[1] posés par terre autour d'une table basse[2] et ronde. Un grand plat de semoule[3] avec viandes et légumes est posé au centre de la table et on mange avec les doigts. On prend le couscous avec trois doigts et ensuite on en fait une petite boule dans la main. On ne doit utiliser que la main droite, jamais la main gauche. Tout autour du plat, de petites assiettes en terre cuite contiennent les épices. Généralement, on boit du thé à la menthe. Après le repas, chacun se lave les mains, souvent avec de l'eau de fleur d'oranger.

ET TOI?

1. Quelles spécialités est-ce que tu manges avec les doigts aux États-Unis?
2. Est-ce que tu bois une boisson traditionnelle chez toi? Laquelle?

Communauté et professions

Le français dans les cuisines

Dans les recettes de cuisine de nombreux mots sont français ou d'origine française. Est-ce que tu connais un chef? Est-ce qu'il y a une école de cuisine près de chez toi? Fais des recherches sur Internet ou à la bibliothèque pour en savoir plus sur le métier de chef. Présente ce que tu as trouvé à la classe.

1. cushions 2. low 3. type of flour made from hard wheat

Des apprentis cuisiniers

Québec quatre-vingt-treize 93

Culture

Culture engages students while they learn more about cultural products and practices in the French-speaking world.

- ***Culture appliquée*** introduces students to a topic and then provides a hands-on activity.
- ***Recherches*** invites students to expand their knowledge through independent research.
- ***Comparaisons*** challenges students to compare the culture studied with their own.
- ***Communauté*** asks students to think critically about their own community.

An engaging storyline makes students want to follow along!

Télé-roman

Le Secret de la statuette *Épisode 3*

STRATÉGIE

Comparing attitudes Comparing the characters' attitudes toward an idea or an event can help you to understand their motives and their actions. In **Episode 3**, Seydou and Léa react differently to the mysterious disappearance of the statuette. Who detains the information at the beginning of the episode? Who decides to take action? Do the two characters react in the same way when they find out that Charles Rigaud is on the island? Based on what you learn in the episode, who do you think is the most adventurous? The most cautious?

Quelques jours plus tard, chez les Gadio...

1 **Seydou** Tu sais, l'inspecteur Sonko a dit à mon père qu'il n'y a pas de Charles Rigaud à Dakar.
Léa Ah oui? Et alors?
Seydou Eh bien, peut-être que l'homme qui a apporté la statuette à mon père ne s'appelle pas vraiment Charles Rigaud.

2 **Seydou** L'inspecteur Sonko a trouvé quelque chose. Il a fait analyser le sable qu'il a trouvé dans le bureau de mon père. C'est du sable de l'île de Gorée.

3 **Léa** Alors, on y va?
Seydou Où?
Léa Sur l'île de Gorée. C'est peut-être là que les voleurs se cachent.

4 *Seydou et Léa prennent le bateau pour l'île de Gorée.*

104 cent quatre Chapitre 3 · Faisons les courses

Visit Us Online
my.hrw.com
Online Edition

Sur l'île de Gorée...

5 **Seydou** Pardon, monsieur. Nous faisons une petite enquête sur un vol. Est-ce que vous avez remarqué quelque chose de bizarre ces jours-ci?
Le commerçant Attendez un peu! Il y a cet homme qui vient au magasin depuis une semaine ou deux.

6 **Le commerçant** Il a l'air d'un explorateur, avec le chapeau et tout! Il se tire toujours l'oreille, comme ça...

7 **Seydou** Charles Rigaud! Je suis sûr que c'est lui!
Léa Mais pourquoi? C'est pas logique du tout! C'est lui qui a apporté la statuette à ton père et maintenant, il la vole? Ça n'a aucun sens!

8 **Seydou** Bon, on téléphone à l'inspecteur Sonko?
Léa D'abord, je pense qu'on devrait attendre ici. Rigaud va peut-être passer au magasin.
Seydou Bon. D'accord.

9 *Seydou et Léa attendent Charles Rigaud devant le magasin de l'île de Gorée.*

AS-TU COMPRIS?

1. Qu'est-ce que l'inspecteur Sonko a dit à monsieur Gadio?
2. Pourquoi Seydou et Léa décident d'aller sur l'île de Gorée?
3. Le commerçant décrit un homme. Qui est cet homme?
4. Quand Seydou dit «Charles Rigaud! Je suis sûr que c'est lui!», qu'est-ce qu'il veut dire?
5. Qu'est-que Seydou et Léa décident de faire à la fin de l'épisode?

Prochain épisode: *Peux-tu deviner qui va venir au magasin dans l'épisode 4?*

Québec cent cinq 105

Télé-roman

Le Secret de la statuette an intriguing video story, will have students guessing all year long.

Télé-roman provides optional French captions.

Reading and Writing

Jean-Jacques Sempé (1932–) est un des dessinateurs français les plus connus. Il commence à publier des dessins humoristiques vers l'âge de 19 ans. À partir de 1960, *Le Petit Nicolas* prend la forme de romans écrits par **René Goscinny** (1926–1977) et illustrés par Sempé. Goscinny est aussi le scénariste[1] de la bande dessinée *Astérix*.

Jean-Jacques Sempé

René Goscinny

STRATÉGIE pour lire
Making inferences is drawing conclusions based on evidence that is hinted at, or implied. While you read, pause after each paragraph, or exchange to think about the details the author includes, why they are included, and what those details tell you.

A Avant la lecture
Lis le titre et regarde les illustrations. D'après toi, qui est le narrateur? Qu'est-ce qu'il fait? Avec qui? Essaie d'imaginer l'histoire à partir des illustrations.

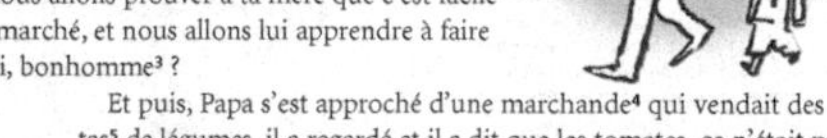

Le Petit Nicolas
On a fait le marché avec papa

[...]

— Bien, a dit Papa, nous allons prouver à ta mère que c'est facile comme tout de faire le marché, et nous allons lui apprendre à faire des économies[2]. Pas vrai, bonhomme[3] ?

Et puis, Papa s'est approché d'une marchande[4] qui vendait des tas[5] de légumes, il a regardé et il a dit que les tomates, ce n'était pas cher.

— Donnez-moi un kilo de tomates, il a demandé, Papa.

La marchande a mis cinq tomates dans le filet à provisions[6] et elle a dit :

— Et avec ça. Qu'est-ce que je vous mets ?

Papa a regardé dans le filet, et puis il a dit :

— Comment ? Il n'y a que cinq tomates dans un kilo ?

— Et qu'est-ce que vous croyez, a demandé la dame, que pour le prix vous aurez une plantation ? Les maris, quand ça vient faire le marché, c'est tous du pareil au même[7].

— Les maris, on se laisse moins rouler[8] que nos femmes, voilà tout ! a dit Papa.

1. writer 2. save money 3. young man 4. saleswoman 5. loads of 6. string bag 7. all the same 8. we are not easy to con

106 *cent six* **Chapitre 3** · Faisons les courses

The ***Lecture*** section provides students with readings from informational texts to literature.

FRENCH InterActive Reader

This online reader provides additional authentic and content-area readings at a variety of levels of difficulties. Available at my.hrw.com

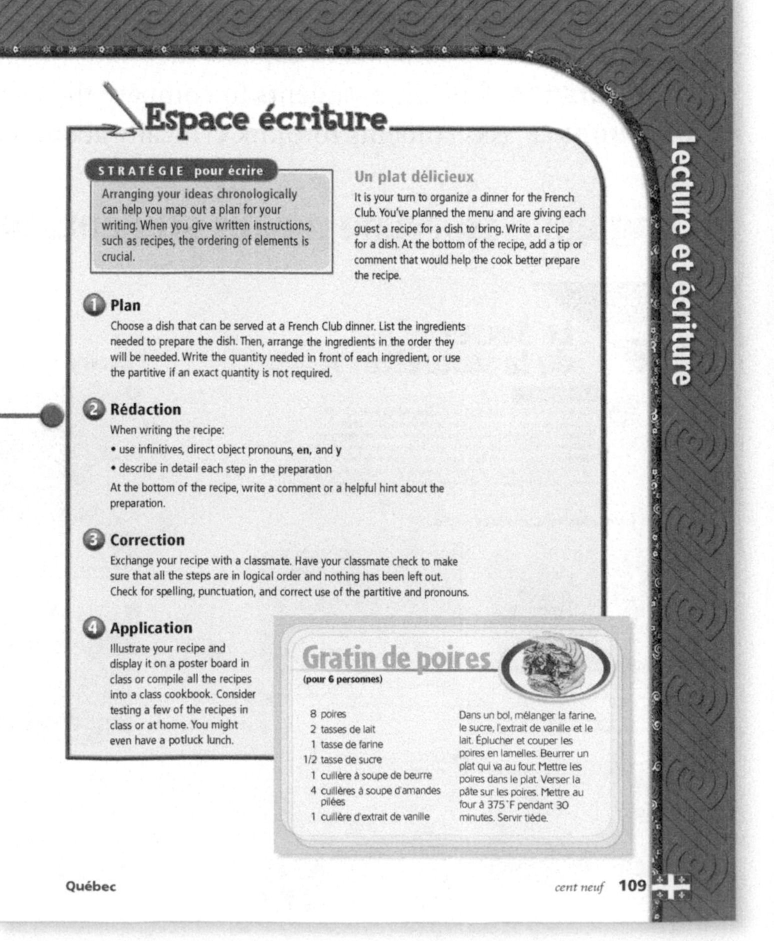
Espace écriture

STRATÉGIE pour écrire
Arranging your ideas chronologically can help you map out a plan for your writing. When you give written instructions, such as recipes, the ordering of elements is crucial.

Un plat délicieux
It is your turn to organize a dinner for the French Club. You've planned the menu and are giving each guest a recipe for a dish to bring. Write a recipe for a dish. At the bottom of the recipe, add a tip or comment that would help the cook better prepare the recipe.

1 Plan
Choose a dish that can be served at a French Club dinner. List the ingredients needed to prepare the dish. Then, arrange the ingredients in the order they will be needed. Write the quantity needed in front of each ingredient, or use the partitive if an exact quantity is not required.

2 Rédaction
When writing the recipe:
- use infinitives, direct object pronouns, **en**, and y
- describe in detail each step in the preparation

At the bottom of the recipe, write a comment or a helpful hint about the preparation.

3 Correction
Exchange your recipe with a classmate. Have your classmate check to make sure that all the steps are in logical order and nothing has been left out. Check for spelling, punctuation, and correct use of the partitive and pronouns.

4 Application
Illustrate your recipe and display it on a poster board in class or compile all the recipes into a class cookbook. Consider testing a few of the recipes in class or at home. You might even have a potluck lunch.

Gratin de poires
(pour 6 personnes)

8 poires
2 tasses de lait
1 tasse de farine
1/2 tasse de sucre
1 cuillère à soupe de beurre
4 cuillères à soupe d'amandes pilées
1 cuillère d'extrait de vanille

Dans un bol, mélanger la farine, le sucre, l'extrait de vanille et le lait. Éplucher et couper les poires en lamelles. Beurrer un plat qui va au four. Mettre les poires dans le plat. Verser la pâte sur les poires. Mettre au four à 375 °F pendant 30 minutes. Servir tiède.

Lecture et écriture

Québec *cent neuf* 109

Espace écriture follows each reading and steps students through the writing process, gradually building their writing skills in French. Teachers may use **Generate Success** to customize their rubrics.

Review

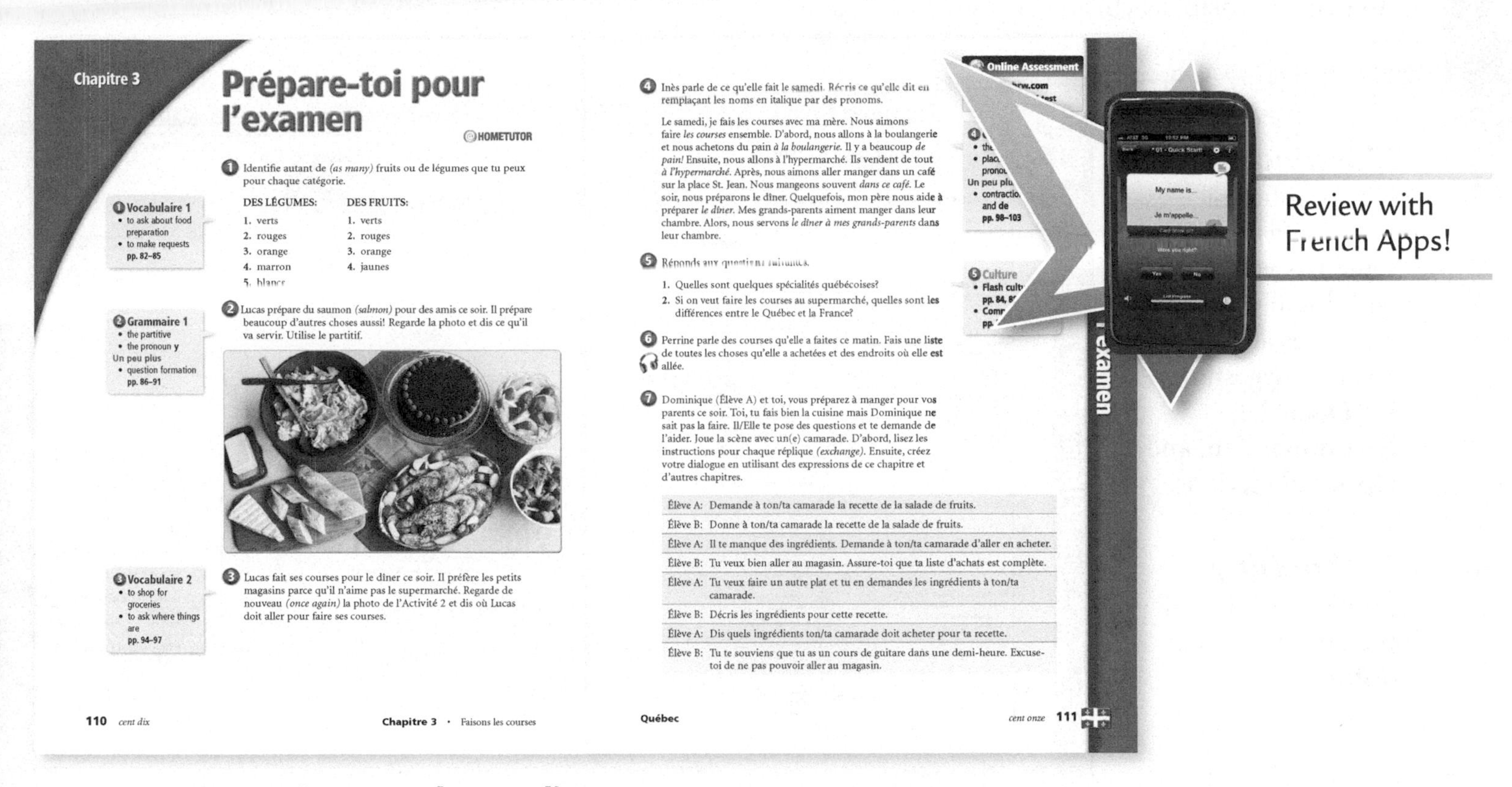

Chapitre 3

Prépare-toi pour l'examen

HOMETUTOR

1 Vocabulaire 1
- to ask about food preparation
- to make requests

pp. 82–85

1 Identifie autant de *(as many)* fruits ou de légumes que tu peux pour chaque catégorie.

DES LÉGUMES:	DES FRUITS:
1. verts	1. verts
2. rouges	2. rouges
3. orange	3. orange
4. marron	4. jaunes
5. blancs	

2 Grammaire 1
- the partitive
- the pronoun y

Un peu plus
- question formation

pp. 86–91

2 Lucas prépare du saumon *(salmon)* pour des amis ce soir. Il prépare beaucoup d'autres choses aussi! Regarde la photo et dis ce qu'il va servir. Utilise le partitif.

3 Vocabulaire 2
- to shop for groceries
- to ask where things are

pp. 94–97

3 Lucas fait ses courses pour le dîner ce soir. Il préfère les petits magasins parce qu'il n'aime pas le supermarché. Regarde de nouveau *(once again)* la photo de l'Activité 2 et dis où Lucas doit aller pour faire ses courses.

4 Inès parle de ce qu'elle fait le samedi. Récris ce qu'elle dit en remplaçant les noms en italique par des pronoms.

Le samedi, je fais les courses avec ma mère. Nous aimons faire *les courses* ensemble. D'abord, nous allons à la boulangerie et nous achetons du pain *à la boulangerie*. Il y a beaucoup *de pain*! Ensuite, nous allons à l'hypermarché. Ils vendent de tout *à l'hypermarché*. Après, nous aimons aller manger dans un café sur la place St. Jean. Nous mangeons souvent *dans ce café*. Le soir, nous préparons le dîner. Quelquefois, mon père nous aide à préparer *le dîner*. Mes grands-parents aiment manger dans leur chambre. Alors, nous servons *le dîner à mes grands-parents* dans leur chambre.

5 Réponds aux questions suivantes.

1. Quelles sont quelques spécialités québécoises?
2. Si on veut faire les courses au supermarché, quelles sont les différences entre le Québec et la France?

6 Perrine parle des courses qu'elle a faites ce matin. Fais une liste de toutes les choses qu'elle a achetées et des endroits où elle est allée.

7 Dominique (Élève A) et toi, vous préparez à manger pour vos parents ce soir. Toi, tu fais bien la cuisine mais Dominique ne sait pas la faire. Il/Elle te pose des questions et te demande de l'aider. Joue la scène avec un(e) camarade. D'abord, lisez les instructions pour chaque réplique *(exchange)*. Ensuite, créez votre dialogue en utilisant des expressions de ce chapitre et d'autres chapitres.

Élève A: Demande à ton/ta camarade la recette de la salade de fruits.
Élève B: Donne à ton/ta camarade la recette de la salade de fruits.
Élève A: Il te manque des ingrédients. Demande à ton/ta camarade d'aller en acheter.
Élève B: Tu veux bien aller au magasin. Assure-toi que ta liste d'achats est complète.
Élève A: Tu veux faire un autre plat et tu en demandes les ingrédients à ton/ta camarade.
Élève B: Décris les ingrédients pour cette recette.
Élève A: Dis quels ingrédients ton/ta camarade doit acheter pour ta recette.
Élève B: Tu te souviens que tu as un cours de guitare dans une demi-heure. Excuse-toi de ne pas pouvoir aller au magasin.

Online Assessment

5 Culture
- Flash culture

110 *cent dix* Chapitre 3 · Faisons les courses Québec *cent onze* 111

Review with French Apps!

The ***Prépare-toi pour l'examen*** review section offers discrete, chapter-specific practice with references back into the chapter if students need further review.

Chapitres 1–3

Révisions cumulatives

1 Tu écoutes des recettes à la radio à Québec. Écoute ces extraits et choisis la photo qui correspond à chacune des recettes.

a. b. c. d.

2 Les légumes et les fruits, sont-ils vraiment importants? Lis les publicités et décide si les phrases suivantes sont **a) vraies** ou **b) fausses**.

Mangez des légumes!
Faites votre plein en vitamines, en fer, en magnésium et en fibre !
Conseils :
• Chaque catégorie de légumes apporte son lot de nutriments. Diversifiez votre consommation de légumes.
• Mangez-les crus ou cuits.
(au moins 5 par jour combinés avec les fruits)
Mangez des fruits!
Faites votre plein de vitamines A et C sans oublier le potassium !
Conseils :
• Les jus de fruit 100 % fruit sont les meilleurs.
• Préférez les fruits nature : ils contiennent plus de fibres que les jus de fruits.
• Mangez des fruits riches en vitamine C.
(au moins 5 par jour combinés avec les légumes)

1. Les fruits nous apportent des vitamines A et C.
2. Les fruits contiennent une forte quantité de sodium.
3. Les jus de fruit contiennent plus de fibres que les fruits.
4. Les légumes nous apportent de nombreuses vitamines et des minéraux.
5. Chaque catégorie de légumes apporte les mêmes nutriments. Vous pouvez donc vous limiter à manger une seule catégorie de légumes.

3 Tu vas bientôt fêter ton anniversaire! Imagine que tu fais des achats dans une épicerie à Québec. Avec un(e) camarade, créez une conversation entre le/la commerçant(e) et le/la client(e).

4 Aujourd'hui, c'est le jour du marché. Imagine ce qui se passe dans l'image. Qu'est-ce que les marchands vendent? De quoi parlent les personnes? Est-ce qu'il y a des marchés comme ça aujourd'hui? Écris un paragraphe qui décrit le jour du marché.

La rue des abbesses de Maximilien Luce

5 Écris une lettre à une amie québécoise. Parle de ce que tu manges souvent le matin, à midi et le soir. Dis aussi quand, où et avec qui tu manges. Pose-lui des questions pour tout savoir sur ses habitudes alimentaires *(eating habits)*.

6 À ton tour

Émission de cuisine You will host a cooking show for your classmates. Working with a partner, think of or research a recipe you would like to make. List all the ingredients you will need and their quantities. Then compile the steps needed in order to complete the recipe. You and your partner will present your recipe and demonstrate how to cook your recipe for the class.

Online Assessment
my.hrw.com
Cumulative Self-test

114 *cent quatorze* Chapitres 1–3 Révisions cumulatives *cent quinze* 115

The ***Révisions cumulatives*** section provides students with cumulative practice after every chapter.

Chapter Interleaf

Each chapter of the ***Bien dit!*** Teacher's Edition includes interleaf pages to help you plan, teach, and expand your lessons.

Planning Guide is a snapshot of the material presented as well as the additional practice resources available. Pacing Suggestions list **Essential, Recommended,** and **Optional** sections.

Technology provides a list of all the options at your disposal!

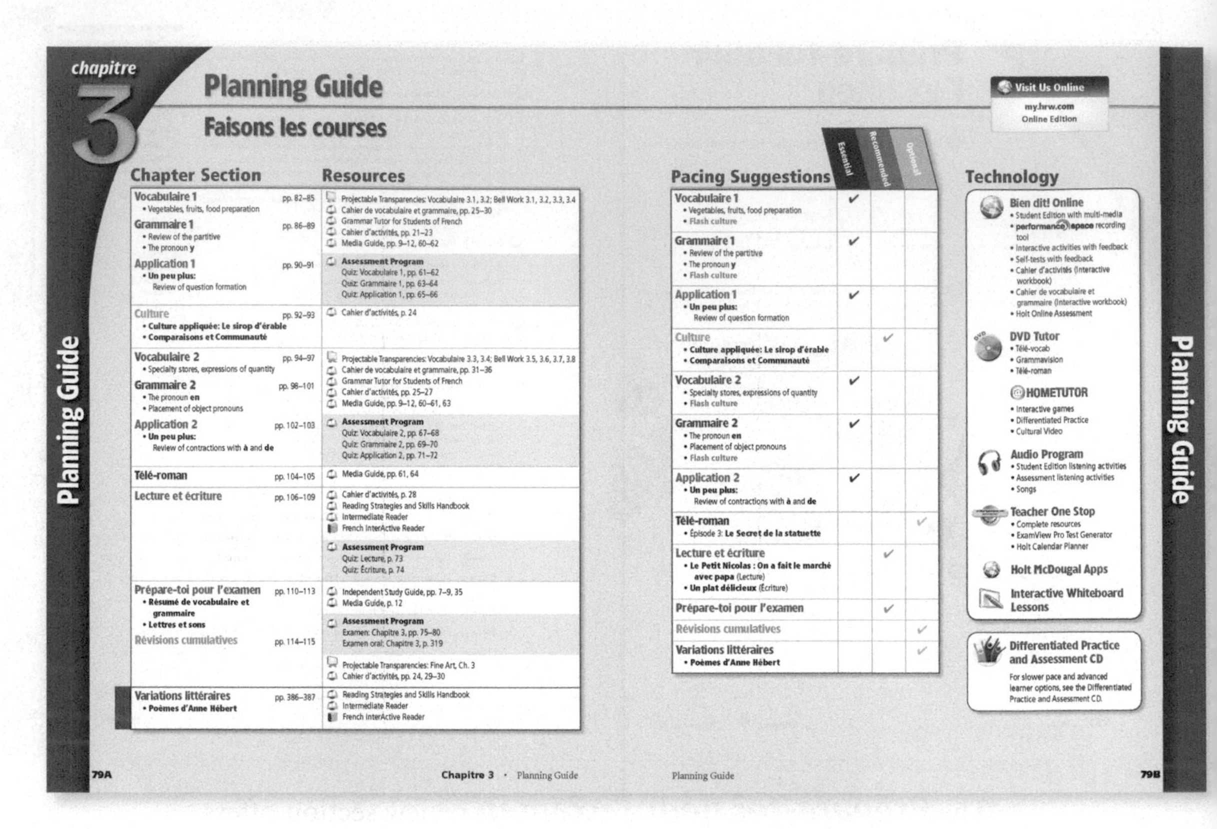

chapitre 3

Planning Guide

Faisons les courses

Chapter Section		Resources
Vocabulaire 1 • Vegetables, fruits, food preparation **Grammaire 1** • Review of the partitive • The pronoun **y** **Application 1** • **Un peu plus:** Review of question formation	pp. 82–85 pp. 86–89 pp. 90–91	Projectable Transparencies: Vocabulaire 3.1, 3.2; Bell Work 3.1, 3.2, 3.3, 3.4 Cahier de vocabulaire et grammaire, pp. 25–30 Grammar Tutor for Students of French Cahier d'activités, pp. 21–23 Media Guide, pp. 9–12, 60–62 **Assessment Program** Quiz: Vocabulaire 1, pp. 61–62 Quiz: Grammaire 1, pp. 63–64 Quiz: Application 1, pp. 65–66
Culture • **Culture appliquée: Le sirop d'érable** • **Comparaisons et Communauté**	pp. 92–93	Cahier d'activités, p. 24
Vocabulaire 2 • Specialty stores, expressions of quantity **Grammaire 2** • The pronoun **en** • Placement of object pronouns **Application 2** • **Un peu plus:** Review of contractions with **à** and **de**	pp. 94–97 pp. 98–101 pp. 102–103	Projectable Transparencies: Vocabulaire 3.3, 3.4; Bell Work 3.5, 3.6, 3.7, 3.8 Cahier de vocabulaire et grammaire, pp. 31–36 Grammar Tutor for Students of French Cahier d'activités, pp. 25–27 Media Guide, pp. 9–12, 60–61, 63 **Assessment Program** Quiz: Vocabulaire 2, pp. 67–68 Quiz: Grammaire 2, pp. 69–70 Quiz: Application 2, pp. 71–72
Télé-roman	pp. 104–105	Media Guide, pp. 61, 64
Lecture et écriture	pp. 106–109	Cahier d'activités, p. 28 Reading Strategies and Skills Handbook Intermediate Reader French InterActive Reader **Assessment Program** Quiz: Lecture, p. 73 Quiz: Écriture, p. 74
Prépare-toi pour l'examen • **Résumé de vocabulaire et grammaire** • **Lettres et sons** **Révisions cumulatives**	pp. 110–113 pp. 114–115	Independent Study Guide, pp. 7–9, 35 Media Guide, p. 12 **Assessment Program** Examen: Chapitre 3, pp. 75–80 Examen oral: Chapitre 3, p. 319 Projectable Transparencies: Fine Art, Ch. 3 Cahier d'activités, pp. 24, 29–30
Variations littéraires • **Poèmes d'Anne Hébert**	pp. 386–387	Reading Strategies and Skills Handbook Intermediate Reader French InterActive Reader

Visit Us Online
my.hrw.com
Online Edition

Pacing Suggestions	Essential	Recommended	Optional
Vocabulaire 1 • Vegetables, fruits, food preparation • Flash culture	✔		
Grammaire 1 • Review of the partitive • The pronoun **y** • Flash culture	✔		
Application 1 • **Un peu plus:** Review of question formation	✔		
Culture • **Culture appliquée: Le sirop d'érable** • **Comparaisons et Communauté**		✔	
Vocabulaire 2 • Specialty stores, expressions of quantity • Flash culture	✔		
Grammaire 2 • The pronoun **en** • Placement of object pronouns • Flash culture	✔		
Application 2 • **Un peu plus:** Review of contractions with **à** and **de**	✔		
Télé-roman • Épisode 3: **Le Secret de la statuette**			✔
Lecture et écriture • **Le Petit Nicolas : On a fait le marché avec papa** (Lecture) • **Un plat délicieux** (Écriture)		✔	
Prépare-toi pour l'examen		✔	
Révisions cumulatives			✔
Variations littéraires • **Poèmes d'Anne Hébert**			✔

Technology

Bien dit! Online
- Student Edition with multi-media
- performance space recording tool
- Interactive activities with feedback
- Self-tests with feedback
- Cahier d'activités (interactive workbook)
- Cahier de vocabulaire et grammaire (interactive workbook)
- Holt Online Assessment

DVD Tutor
- Télé-vocab
- Grammavision
- Télé-roman

HOMETUTOR
- Interactive games
- Differentiated Practice
- Cultural Video

Audio Program
- Student Edition listening activities
- Assessment listening activities
- Songs

Teacher One Stop
- Complete resources
- ExamView Pro Test Generator
- Holt Calendar Planner

Holt McDougal Apps

Interactive Whiteboard Lessons

Differentiated Practice and Assessment CD

For slower pace and advanced learner options, see the Differentiated Practice and Assessment CD.

79A Chapitre 3 · Planning Guide

Planning Guide 79B

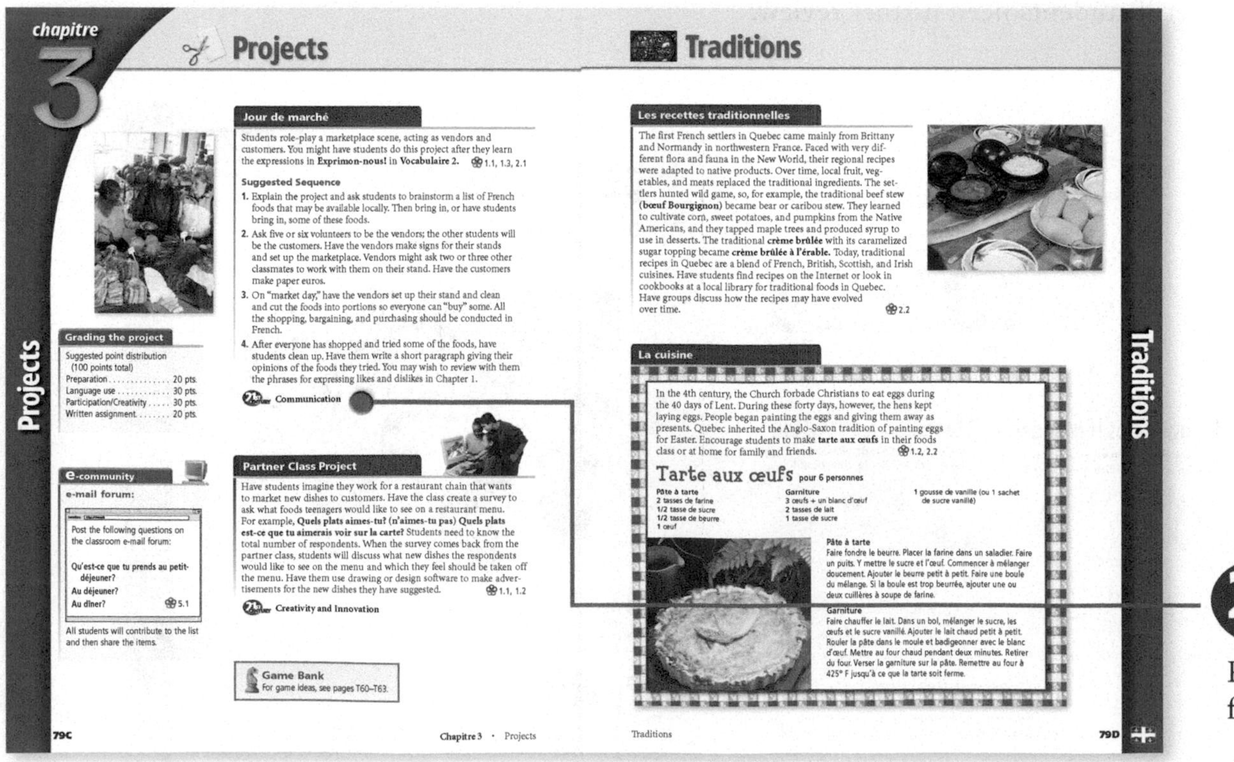

chapitre 3

Projects

Jour de marché

Students role-play a marketplace scene, acting as vendors and customers. You might have students do this project after they learn the expressions in **Exprimon-nous!** in **Vocabulaire 2.** 1.1, 1.3, 2.1

Suggested Sequence

1. Explain the project and ask students to brainstorm a list of French foods that may be available locally. Then bring in, or have students bring in, some of these foods.
2. Ask five or six volunteers to be the vendors; the other students will be the customers. Have the vendors make signs for their stands and set up the marketplace. Vendors might ask two or three other classmates to work with them on their stand. Have the customers make paper euros.
3. On "market day," have the vendors set up their stand and clean and cut the foods into portions so everyone can "buy" some. All the shopping, bargaining, and purchasing should be conducted in French.
4. After everyone has shopped and tried some of the foods, have students clean up. Have them write a short paragraph giving their opinions of the foods they tried. You may wish to review with them the phrases for expressing likes and dislikes in Chapter 1.

21st Century Communication

Grading the project

Suggested point distribution (100 points total)

Preparation	20 pts.
Language use	30 pts.
Participation/Creativity	30 pts.
Written assignment	20 pts.

e-community

e-mail forum:

Post the following questions on the classroom e-mail forum:

Qu'est-ce que tu prends au petit-déjeuner?
Au déjeuner?
Au dîner? 5.1

All students will contribute to the list and then share the items.

Partner Class Project

Have students imagine they work for a restaurant chain that wants to market new dishes to customers. Have the class create a survey to ask what foods teenagers would like to see on a restaurant menu. For example, **Quels plats aimes-tu? (n'aimes-tu pas) Quels plats est-ce que tu aimerais voir sur la carte?** Students need to know the total number of respondents. When the survey comes back from the partner class, students will discuss what new dishes the respondents would like to see on the menu and which they feel should be taken off the menu. Have them use drawing or design software to make advertisements for the new dishes they have suggested. 1.1, 1.2

21st Century Creativity and Innovation

Game Bank
For game ideas, see pages T60–T63.

79C Chapitre 3 · Projects

Traditions

Les recettes traditionnelles

The first French settlers in Quebec came mainly from Brittany and Normandy in northwestern France. Faced with very different flora and fauna in the New World, their regional recipes were adapted to native products. Over time, local fruit, vegetables, and meats replaced the traditional ingredients. The settlers hunted wild game, so, for example, the traditional beef stew (**bœuf Bourgignon**) became bear or caribou stew. They learned to cultivate corn, sweet potatoes, and pumpkins from the Native Americans, and they tapped maple trees and produced syrup to use in desserts. The traditional **crème brûlée** with its caramelized sugar topping became **crème brûlée à l'érable.** Today, traditional recipes in Quebec are a blend of French, British, Scottish, and Irish cuisines. Have students find recipes on the Internet or look in cookbooks at a local library for traditional foods in Quebec. Have groups discuss how the recipes may have evolved over time. 2.2

La cuisine

In the 4th century, the Church forbade Christians to eat eggs during the 40 days of Lent. During these forty days, however, the hens kept laying eggs. People began painting the eggs and giving them away as presents. Quebec inherited the Anglo-Saxon tradition of painting eggs for Easter. Encourage students to make **tarte aux œufs** in their foods class or at home for family and friends. 1.2, 2.2

Tarte aux œufs pour 6 personnes

Pâte à tarte
2 tasses de farine
1/2 tasse de sucre
1/2 tasse de beurre
1 œuf

Garniture
3 œufs + un blanc d'œuf
2 tasses de lait
1 tasse de sucre
1 gousse de vanille (ou 1 sachet de sucre vanillé)

Pâte à tarte
Faire fondre le beurre. Placer la farine dans un saladier. Faire un puits. Y mettre le sucre et l'œuf. Commencer à mélanger doucement. Ajouter le beurre petit à petit. Faire une boule du mélange. Si la boule est trop beurrée, ajouter une ou deux cuillères à soupe de farine.

Garniture
Faire chauffer le lait. Dans un bol, mélanger le sucre, les œufs et le sucre vanillé. Ajouter le lait chaud petit à petit. Rouler la pâte dans le moule et badigeonner avec le blanc d'œuf. Mettre au four chaud pendant deux minutes. Retirer du four. Verser la garniture sur la pâte. Remettre au four à 425° F jusqu'à ce que la tarte soit ferme.

Traditions 79D

21ST CENTURY SKILLS

Preparing for their future today.

Projects and Traditions allow students to work at different levels to expand on the information in the chapter—individually, in pairs or groups, or with a partner class.

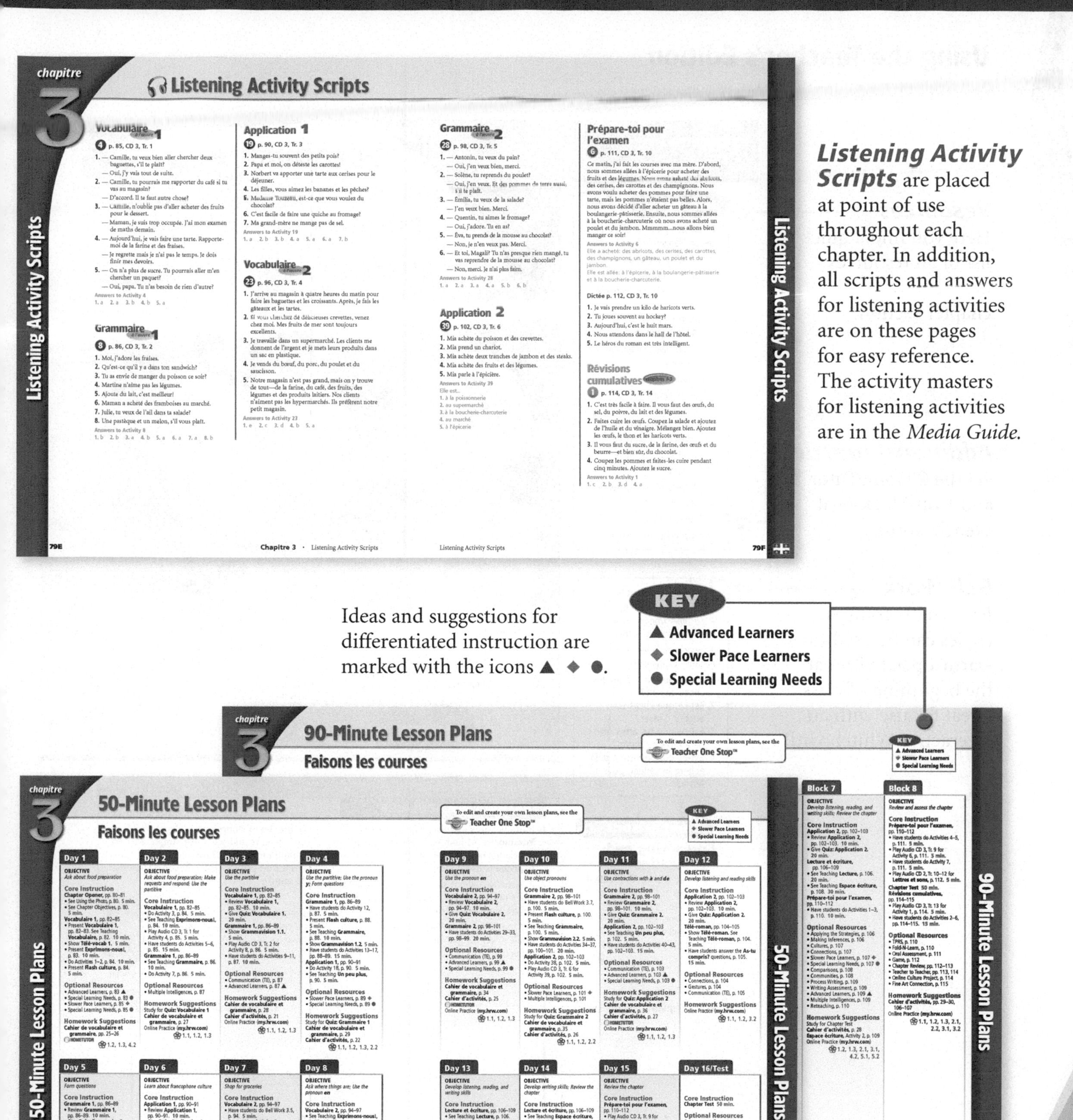

Listening Activity Scripts are placed at point of use throughout each chapter. In addition, all scripts and answers for listening activities are on these pages for easy reference. The activity masters for listening activities are in the *Media Guide.*

Ideas and suggestions for differentiated instruction are marked with the icons ▲ ◆ ●.

KEY

- ▲ Advanced Learners
- ◆ Slower Pace Learners
- ● Special Learning Needs

Suggested Lesson Plans provide a logical sequence of instruction along with suggestions for optional practice and homework. Both **50-minute** and **90-minute** block plans are provided.

Using the Teacher's Edition

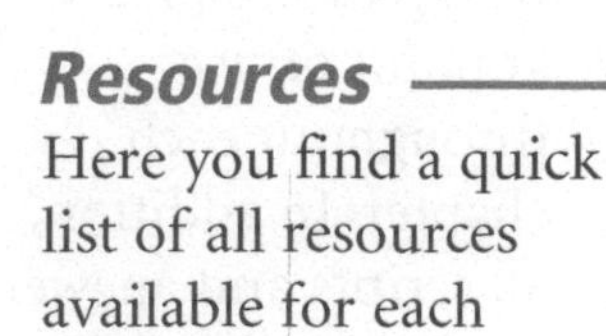

Resources
Here you find a quick list of all resources available for each chapter section.

Additional practice
via the @HomeTutor and Holt McDougal French Apps!

Bell Work
Projectable transparencies can be used for warm-up activities at the beginning of class. Great for use with an Interactive Whiteboard!

Chapitre 3
Vocabulaire 1

Resources

Planning:
Lesson Planner
Teacher One Stop

Presentation:
Projectable Transparencies **Vocabulaire 3.1, 3.2**
DVD Tutor, Disc 1 **Télé-vocab 1**
Interactive Whiteboard Lessons

Practice:
Cahier de vocabulaire et grammaire
Differentiated Practice and Assessment CD-ROM
Independent Study Guide
Media Guide
Projectable Transparencies Bell Work 3.1
@HOMETUTOR
Holt McDougal French Apps

Bell Work
Use Bell Work 3.1 in the *Projectable Transparencies* or write this activity on the board.

Answer each question with a negative expression.

1. **Est-ce que tu fais quelque chose ce soir?**
2. **Est-ce que Lucas veut encore danser?**
3. **Est-ce que tes amis sont déjà allés au Japon?**
4. **Est-ce que Juliette a déjà acheté le cadeau pour Astrid?** 1.2

Comparisons

Comparing and Contrasting
The photo features the **École de l'Hôtelier** in Quebec City. Have students research information on both a French and an American culinary school and prepare a presentation to contrast the two schools. 4.2

Objectifs
- to ask about food preparation
- to make requests

Vocabulaire à l'œuvre 1

DVD Télé-vocab

On prépare à manger à Québec!

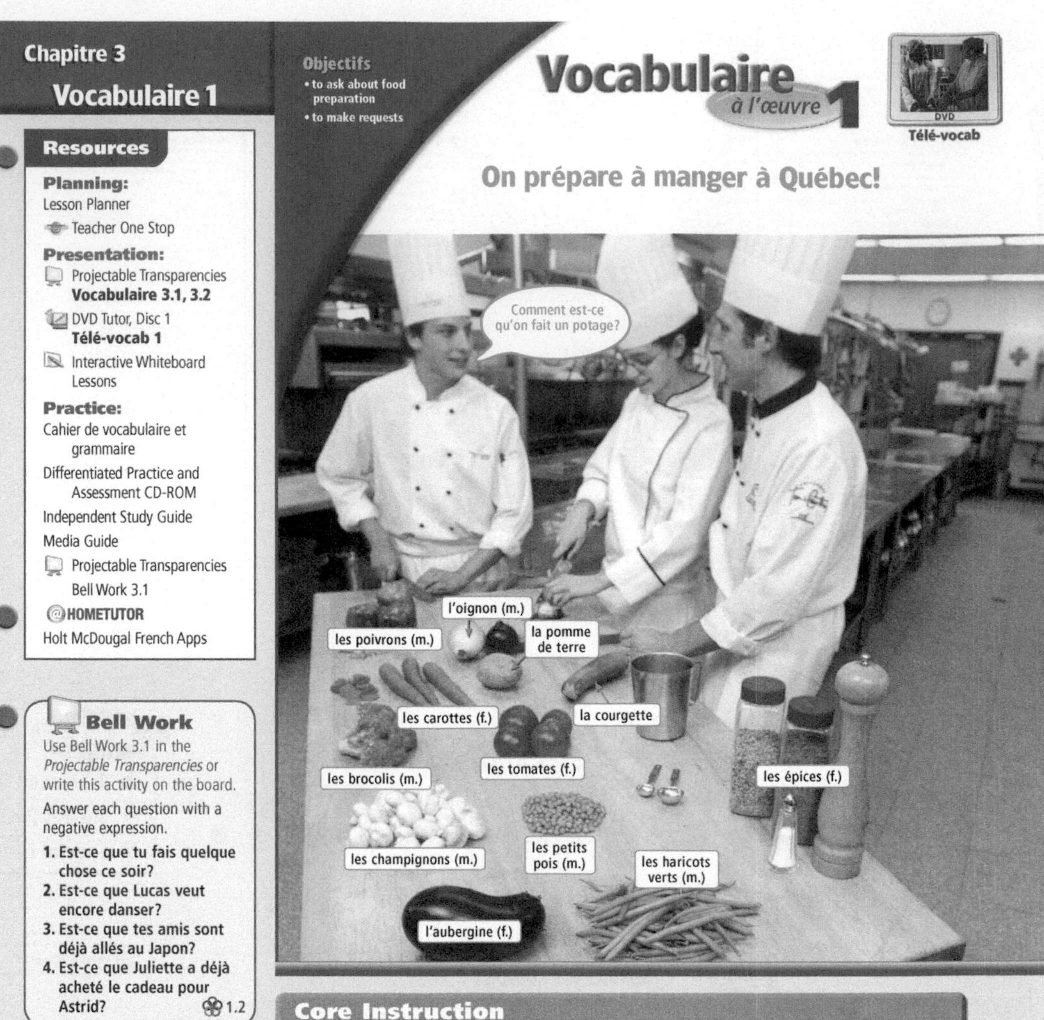

Core Instruction

TEACHING VOCABULAIRE

1. Introduce the vocabulary with transparencies **Vocabulaire 3.1** and **3.2** and model the pronunciation of each word using expressions in **Exprimons-nous! (2 min.)**
2. Ask students about the items. **Est-ce qu'il y a des tomates dans une salade? Le sel et le poivre, sont-ils des fruits? (3 min.)**
3. On the board, draw two columns with the heads **C'est simple** and **C'est compliqué.** Bring in magazine pictures of some common French foods (**mousse au chocolat, omelette, soupe, bœuf bourgignon, glace**). Hold up each picture and ask **C'est simple ou c'est compliqué à faire?** Have students take turns posting the pictures under the correct heading. **(2 min.)**

Télé-vocab 1
For a video presentation of this vocabulary, see the *DVD Tutor.*

DVD Télé-vocab

82 *quatre-vingt-deux* **Chapitre 3** · Faisons les courses

Teaching Vocabulaire
Timed suggestions for each presentation in the chapter provide guidance to newer teachers and a quick reference for more experienced teachers.

Video Support is provided for each presentation.

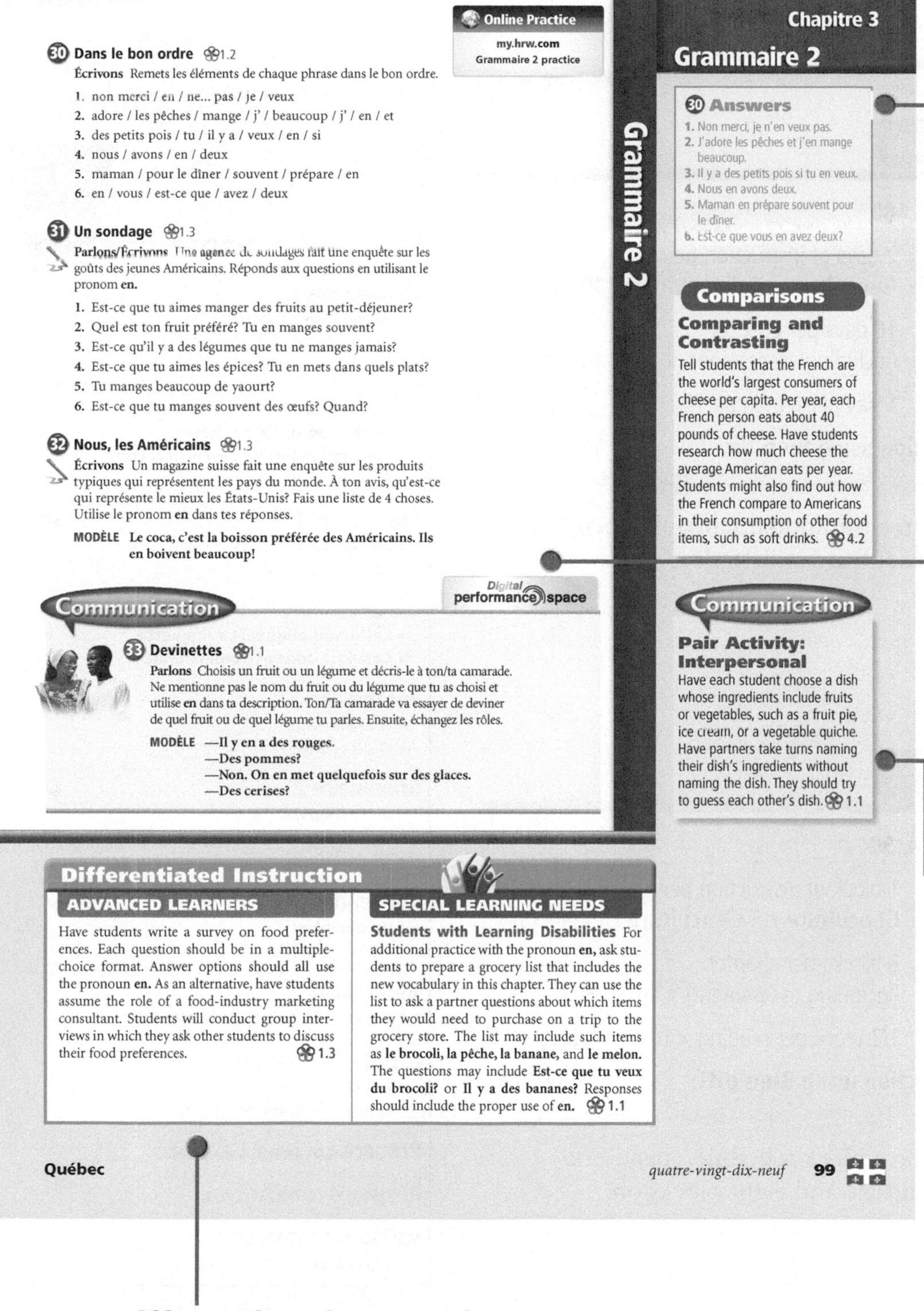

Online Practice
my.hrw.com
Grammaire 2 practice

Chapitre 3
Grammaire 2

30 Dans le bon ordre 1.2

Écrivons Remets les éléments de chaque phrase dans le bon ordre.

1. non merci / en / ne... pas / je / veux
2. adore / les pêches / mange / j' / beaucoup / j' / en / et
3. des petits pois / tu / il y a / veux / en / si
4. nous / avons / en / deux
5. maman / pour le dîner / souvent / prépare / en
6. en / vous / est-ce que / avez / deux

31 Un sondage 1.3

Parlons/Écrivons Une agence de sondages fait une enquête sur les goûts des jeunes Américains. Réponds aux questions en utilisant le pronom **en**.

1. Est-ce que tu aimes manger des fruits au petit-déjeuner?
2. Quel est ton fruit préféré? Tu en manges souvent?
3. Est-ce qu'il y a des légumes que tu ne manges jamais?
4. Est-ce que tu aimes les épices? Tu en mets dans quels plats?
5. Tu manges beaucoup de yaourt?
6. Est-ce que tu manges souvent des œufs? Quand?

32 Nous, les Américains 1.3

Écrivons Un magazine suisse fait une enquête sur les produits typiques qui représentent les pays du monde. À ton avis, qu'est-ce qui représente le mieux les États-Unis? Fais une liste de 4 choses. Utilise le pronom **en** dans tes réponses.

MODÈLE **Le coca, c'est la boisson préférée des Américains. Ils en boivent beaucoup!**

Digital performance space

Communication

33 Devinettes 1.1

Parlons Choisis un fruit ou un légume et décris-le à ton/ta camarade. Ne mentionne pas le nom du fruit ou du légume que tu as choisi et utilise **en** dans ta description. Ton/Ta camarade va essayer de deviner de quel fruit ou de quel légume tu parles. Ensuite, échangez les rôles.

MODÈLE **—Il y en a des rouges.**
—Des pommes?
—Non. On en met quelquefois sur des glaces.
—Des cerises?

30 Answers

1. Non merci, je n'en veux pas.
2. J'adore les pêches et j'en mange beaucoup.
3. Il y a des petits pois si tu en veux.
4. Nous en avons deux.
5. Maman en prépare souvent pour le dîner.
6. Est-ce que vous en avez deux?

Comparisons

Comparing and Contrasting

Tell students that the French are the world's largest consumers of cheese per capita. Per year, each French person eats about 40 pounds of cheese. Have students research how much cheese the average American eats per year. Students might also find out how the French compare to Americans in their consumption of other food items, such as soft drinks. 4.2

Communication

Pair Activity: Interpersonal

Have each student choose a dish whose ingredients include fruits or vegetables, such as a fruit pie, ice cream, or a vegetable quiche. Have partners take turns naming their dish's ingredients without naming the dish. They should try to guess each other's dish. 1.1

Differentiated Instruction

ADVANCED LEARNERS

Have students write a survey on food preferences. Each question should be in a multiple-choice format. Answer options should all use the pronoun **en.** As an alternative, have students assume the role of a food-industry marketing consultant. Students will conduct group interviews in which they ask other students to discuss their food preferences. 1.3

SPECIAL LEARNING NEEDS

Students with Learning Disabilities For additional practice with the pronoun **en,** ask students to prepare a grocery list that includes the new vocabulary in this chapter. They can use the list to ask a partner questions about which items they would need to purchase on a trip to the grocery store. The list may include such items as **le brocoli, la pêche, la banane,** and **le melon.** The questions may include **Est-ce que tu veux du brocoli?** or **Il y a des bananes?** Responses should include the proper use of **en.** 1.1

Québec *quatre-vingt-dix-neuf* 99

Answers at point of use are a quick reference for all *Student Edition* activities.

Performance Space Teacher Dashboard allows teachers to give students audio, video, or written feedback.

Communication The activities suggested here focus on one of the three kinds of communication: **interpersonal, interpretive,** or **presentational.**

Differentiated Instruction suggests ways to address the diversity of any classroom. The suggestions on the left provide support for teaching advanced or slower-pace learners. Those on the right help accomodate students with special learning needs or reach learners through multiple intelligences.

Pacing and Planning

Bien dit! Levels 1, 2 and 3

Base your pacing on your schedule...

Traditional Schedule

Days of Instruction: 180		
Géoculture	2 days of instruction per **Géoculture** x 5 **Géoculture**	10 days
Chapter	16 days per chapter (including assessment) x 10	160 days
Variations littéraires	1 day per reading x 10	10 days
Total days of instruction using Bien dit!:		**180 days**

If you are teaching on a traditional schedule, spend two days on each **Géoculture** and 16 days on each chapter.

Block Schedule

Blocks of instruction: 90		
Géoculture	1 block of instruction per **Géoculture** x 5 **Géoculture**	5 blocks
Chapter	8 blocks per chapter (including assessment) x 10	80 blocks
Variations littéraires	1/2 block per reading x 10	5 blocks
Total blocks of instruction using Bien dit!:		**90 blocks**

If you are teaching on a block schedule, spend one block on each **Géoculture** and eight blocks on each chapter.

Pacing Suggestions

	Essential	Recommended	Optional
Vocabulaire 1 • School places and events • Flash culture	✔		
Grammaire 1 • Object pronouns in the **passé composé** • **Quelqu'un, quelque chose, ne... personne, ne... rien, ne... que** • Flash culture	✔		
Application 1 • **Un peu plus:** The verb **recevoir**	✔		
Culture • **Culture appliquée: La ringuette** • **Comparaisons et Communauté**		✔	
Vocabulaire 2 • Computer terms • Flash culture	✔		
Grammaire 2 • The verb **suivre** • **Depuis, il y a, ça fait...** • Flash culture	✔		
Application 2 • **Un peu plus:** The verb **ouvrir**	✔		
Télé-roman • Épisode 4: **Le Secret de la statuette**			✔
Lecture et écriture • **Intermezzo** (Lecture) • **Tout va de travers!** (Écriture)		✔	
Prépare-toi pour l'examen		✔	
Révisions cumulatives			✔
Variations littéraires • **L'alouette**			✔

Pacing and Planning

Use the **Teacher One Stop** to make *Bien dit!* work for you...

- **PDF format lesson plans** with links to **all** teaching resources, including video and audio
- **Editable tests and lesson plans** are available for all chapters on the *Teacher One Stop.*
- **ExamView® Assessment Suite**
- **All audio and video resources**

...or customize lesson plans to suit your style or individual classes.

Lesson Plans are available for both 50-minute and 90-minute classes.

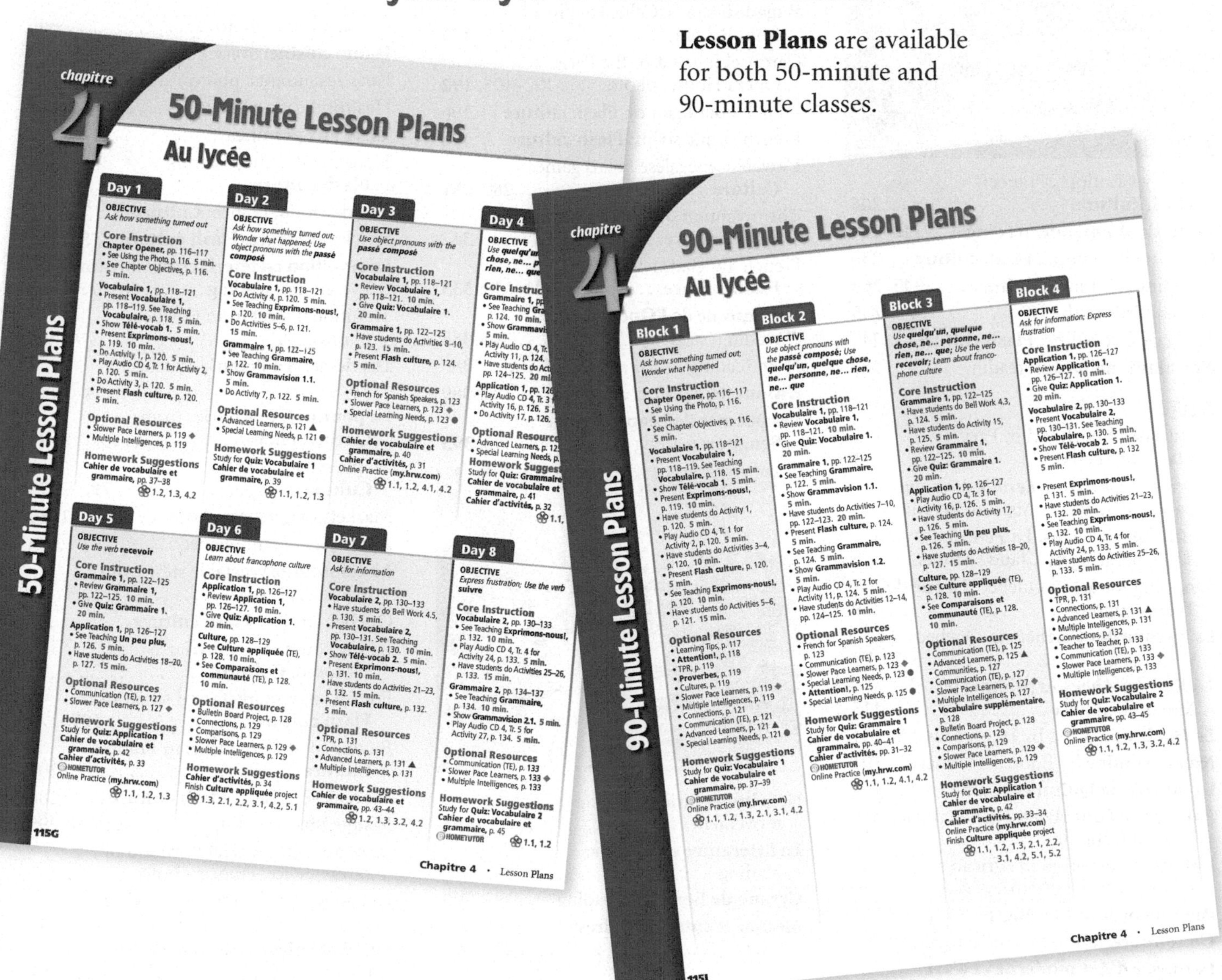

chapitre 4

50-Minute Lesson Plans

Au lycée

Day 1
OBJECTIVE
Ask how something turned out
Core Instruction
Chapter Opener, pp. 116–117
- See Using the Photo, p. 116. 5 min.
- See Chapter Objectives, p. 116. 5 min.

Vocabulaire 1, pp. 118–121
- Present **Vocabulaire 1,** pp. 118–119. See Teaching **Vocabulaire,** p. 118. 5 min.
- Show **Télé-vocab 1.** 5 min.
- Present **Exprimons-nous!,** p. 119. 10 min.
- Do Activity 1, p. 120. 5 min.
- Play Audio CD 4, Tr. 1 for Activity 2, p. 120. 5 min.
- Do Activity 3, p. 120. 5 min.
- Present **Flash culture,** p. 120. 5 min.

Optional Resources
- Slower Pace Learners, p. 119 ◆
- Multiple Intelligences, p. 119

Homework Suggestions
Cahier de vocabulaire et grammaire, pp. 37–38
1.2, 1.3, 4.2

Day 2
OBJECTIVE
Ask how something turned out; Wonder what happened; Use object pronouns with the ***passé composé***
Core Instruction
Vocabulaire 1, pp. 118–121
- Do Activity 4, p. 120. 5 min.
- See Teaching **Exprimons-nous!,** p. 120. 10 min.
- Do Activities 5–6, p. 121. 15 min.

Grammaire 1, pp. 122–125
- See Teaching **Grammaire,** p. 122. 10 min.
- Show **Grammavision 1.1.** 5 min.
- Do Activity 7, p. 122. 5 min.

Optional Resources
- Advanced Learners, p. 121 ▲
- Special Learning Needs, p. 121 ●

Homework Suggestions
Study for **Quiz: Vocabulaire 1**
Cahier de vocabulaire et grammaire, p. 39
1.1, 1.2, 1.3

Day 3
OBJECTIVE
Use object pronouns with the ***passé composé***
Core Instruction
Vocabulaire 1, pp. 118–121
- Review **Vocabulaire 1,** pp. 118–121. 10 min.
- Give **Quiz: Vocabulaire 1.** 20 min.

Grammaire 1, pp. 122–125
- Have students do Activities 8–10, p. 123. 15 min.
- Present **Flash culture,** p. 124. 5 min.

Optional Resources
- French for Spanish Speakers, p. 123
- Slower Pace Learners, p. 123 ◆
- Special Learning Needs, p. 123 ●

Homework Suggestions
Cahier de vocabulaire et grammaire, p. 40
Cahier d'activités, p. 31
Online Practice (**my.hrw.com**)
1.1, 1.2, 4.1, 4.2

Day 4
OBJECTIVE
Use ***quelqu'un...***
Core Instruction
Grammaire 1, pp...
- See Teaching **Gra...** p. 124. 10 min.
- Show **Grammavi...** 5 min.
- Play Audio CD 4, Tr... Activity 11, p. 124.
- Have students do Act... pp. 124–125. 20 mi...

Application 1, pp. 126...
- Play Audio CD 4, Tr. 3... Activity 16, p. 126. 5...
- Do Activity 17, p. 126...

Optional Resource...
- Advanced Learners, p. 12...
- Special Learning Needs, p...

Homework Sugges...
Study for **Quiz: Grammaire...**
Cahier de vocabulaire et grammaire, p. 41
Cahier d'activités, p. 32
1.1, ...

Day 5
OBJECTIVE
Use the verb ***recevoir***
Core Instruction
Grammaire 1, pp. 122–125
- Review **Grammaire 1,** pp. 122–125. 10 min.
- Give **Quiz: Grammaire 1.** 20 min.

Application 1, pp. 126–127
- See Teaching **Un peu plus,** p. 126. 5 min.
- Have students do Activities 18–20, p. 127. 15 min.

Optional Resources
- Communication (TE), p. 127
- Slower Pace Learners, p. 127 ◆

Homework Suggestions
Study for **Quiz: Application 1**
Cahier de vocabulaire et grammaire, p. 42
Cahier d'activités, p. 33
HOMETUTOR
Online Practice (**my.hrw.com**)
1.1, 1.2, 1.3

Day 6
OBJECTIVE
Learn about francophone culture
Core Instruction
Application 1, pp. 126–127
- Review **Application 1,** pp. 126–127. 10 min.
- Give **Quiz: Application 1.** 20 min.

Culture, pp. 128–129
- See **Culture appliquée** (TE), p. 128. 10 min.
- See **Comparaisons et communauté** (TE), p. 128. 10 min.

Optional Resources
- Bulletin Board Project, p. 128
- Connections, p. 129
- Comparisons, p. 129
- Slower Pace Learners, p. 129 ◆
- Multiple Intelligences, p. 129

Homework Suggestions
Cahier d'activités, p. 34
Finish **Culture appliquée** project
1.3, 2.1, 2.2, 3.1, 4.2, 5.1

Day 7
OBJECTIVE
Ask for information
Core Instruction
Vocabulaire 2, pp. 130–133
- Have students do Bell Work 4.5, p. 130. 5 min.
- Present **Vocabulaire 2,** pp. 130–131. See Teaching **Vocabulaire,** p. 130. 10 min.
- Show **Télé-vocab 2.** 5 min.
- Present **Exprimons-nous!,** p. 131. 10 min.
- Have students do Activities 21–23, p. 132. 15 min.
- Present **Flash culture,** p. 132. 5 min.

Optional Resources
- TPR, p. 131
- Connections, p. 131
- Advanced Learners, p. 131 ▲
- Multiple Intelligences, p. 131

Homework Suggestions
Cahier de vocabulaire et grammaire, pp. 43–44
1.2, 1.3, 3.2, 4.2

Day 8
OBJECTIVE
Express frustration; Use the verb ***suivre***
Core Instruction
Vocabulaire 2, pp. 130–133
- See Teaching **Exprimons-nous!,** p. 132. 10 min.
- Play Audio CD 4, Tr. 4 for Activity 24, p. 133. 5 min.
- Have students do Activities 25–26, p. 133. 15 min.

Grammaire 2, pp. 134–137
- See Teaching **Grammaire,** p. 134. 10 min.
- Show **Grammavision 2.1.** 5 min.
- Play Audio CD 4, Tr. 5 for Activity 27, p. 134. 5 min.

Optional Resources
- Communication (TE), p. 133
- Slower Pace Learners, p. 133 ◆
- Multiple Intelligences, p. 133

Homework Suggestions
Study for **Quiz: Vocabulaire 2**
Cahier de vocabulaire et grammaire, p. 45
HOMETUTOR
1.1, 1.2

115G

Chapitre 4 · Lesson Plans

chapitre 4

90-Minute Lesson Plans

Au lycée

Block 1
OBJECTIVE
Ask how something turned out; Wonder what happened
Core Instruction
Chapter Opener, pp. 116–117
- See Using the Photo, p. 116. 5 min.
- See Chapter Objectives, p. 116. 5 min.

Vocabulaire 1, pp. 118–121
- Present **Vocabulaire 1,** pp. 118–119. See Teaching **Vocabulaire,** p. 118. 15 min.
- Show **Télé-vocab 1.** 5 min.
- Present **Exprimons-nous!,** p. 119. 10 min.
- Have students do Activity 1, p. 120. 5 min.
- Play Audio CD 4, Tr. 1 for Activity 2, p. 120. 5 min.
- Have students do Activities 3–4, p. 120. 10 min.
- Present **Flash culture,** p. 120. 5 min.
- See Teaching **Exprimons-nous!,** p. 120. 10 min.
- Have students do Activities 5–6, p. 121. 15 min.

Optional Resources
- Learning Tips, p. 117
- **Attention!,** p. 118
- TPR, p. 119
- **Proverbes,** p. 119
- Cultures, p. 119
- Slower Pace Learners, p. 119 ◆
- Multiple Intelligences, p. 119
- Connections, p. 121
- Communication (TE), p. 121
- Advanced Learners, p. 121 ▲
- Special Learning Needs, p. 121 ●

Homework Suggestions
Study for **Quiz: Vocabulaire 1**
Cahier de vocabulaire et grammaire, pp. 37–39
HOMETUTOR
Online Practice (**my.hrw.com**)
1.1, 1.2, 1.3, 2.1, 3.1, 4.2

Block 2
OBJECTIVE
Use object pronouns with the ***passé composé****; Use* ***quelqu'un, quelque chose, ne... personne, ne... rien, ne... que***
Core Instruction
Vocabulaire 1, pp. 118–121
- Review **Vocabulaire 1,** pp. 118–121. 10 min.
- Give **Quiz: Vocabulaire 1.** 20 min.

Grammaire 1, pp. 122–125
- See Teaching **Grammaire,** p. 122. 5 min.
- Show **Grammavision 1.1.** 5 min.
- Have students do Activities 7–10, pp. 122–123. 20 min.
- Present **Flash culture,** p. 124. 5 min.
- See Teaching **Grammaire,** p. 124. 5 min.
- Show **Grammavision 1.2.** 5 min.
- Play Audio CD 4, Tr. 2 for Activity 11, p. 124. 5 min.
- Have students do Activities 12–14, pp. 124–125. 10 min.

Optional Resources
- French for Spanish Speakers, p. 123
- Communication (TE), p. 123
- Slower Pace Learners, p. 123 ◆
- Special Learning Needs, p. 123 ●
- **Attention!,** p. 125
- Special Learning Needs, p. 125 ●

Homework Suggestions
Study for **Quiz: Grammaire 1**
Cahier de vocabulaire et grammaire, pp. 40–41
Cahier d'activités, pp. 31–32
HOMETUTOR
Online Practice (**my.hrw.com**)
1.1, 1.2, 4.1, 4.2

Block 3
OBJECTIVE
Use ***quelqu'un, quelque chose, ne... personne, ne... rien, ne... que****; Use the verb* ***recevoir****; Learn about francophone culture*
Core Instruction
Grammaire 1, pp. 122–125
- Have students do Bell Work 4.3, p. 124. 5 min.
- Have students do Activity 15, p. 125. 5 min.
- Review **Grammaire 1,** pp. 122–125. 10 min.
- Give **Quiz: Grammaire 1.** 20 min.

Application 1, pp. 126–127
- Play Audio CD 4, Tr. 3 for Activity 16, p. 126. 5 min.
- Have students do Activity 17, p. 126. 5 min.
- See Teaching **Un peu plus,** p. 126. 5 min.
- Have students do Activities 18–20, p. 127. 15 min.

Culture, pp. 128–129
- See **Culture appliquée** (TE), p. 128. 10 min.
- See **Comparaisons et communauté** (TE), p. 128. 10 min.

Optional Resources
- Communication (TE), p. 125
- Advanced Learners, p. 125 ▲
- Communities, p. 127
- Communication (TE), p. 127
- Slower Pace Learners, p. 127 ◆
- Multiple Intelligences, p. 127
- **Vocabulaire supplémentaire,** p. 128
- Bulletin Board Project, p. 128
- Connections, p. 129
- Comparisons, p. 129
- Slower Pace Learners, p. 129 ◆
- Multiple Intelligences, p. 129

Homework Suggestions
Study for **Quiz: Application 1**
Cahier de vocabulaire et grammaire, p. 42
Cahier d'activités, pp. 33–34
Online Practice (**my.hrw.com**)
Finish **Culture appliquée** project
1.1, 1.2, 1.3, 2.1, 2.2, 3.1, 4.2, 5.1, 5.2

Block 4
OBJECTIVE
Ask for information; Express frustration
Core Instruction
Application 1, pp. 126–127
- Review **Application 1,** pp. 126–127. 10 min.
- Give **Quiz: Application 1.** 20 min.

Vocabulaire 2, pp. 130–133
- Present **Vocabulaire 2,** pp. 130–131. See Teaching **Vocabulaire,** p. 130. 5 min.
- Show **Télé-vocab 2.** 5 min.
- Present **Flash culture,** p. 132 5 min.
- Present **Exprimons-nous!,** p. 131. 5 min.
- Have students do Activities 21–23, p. 132. 20 min.
- See Teaching **Exprimons-nous!,** p. 132. 10 min.
- Play Audio CD 4, Tr. 4 for Activity 24, p. 133. 5 min.
- Have students do Activities 25–26, p. 133. 5 min.

Optional Resources
- TPR, p. 131
- Connections, p. 131
- Advanced Learners, p. 131 ▲
- Multiple Intelligences, p. 131
- Connections, p. 132
- Teacher to Teacher, p. 133
- Communication (TE), p. 133
- Slower Pace Learners, p. 133 ◆
- Multiple Intelligences, p. 133

Homework Suggestions
Study for **Quiz: Vocabulaire 2**
Cahier de vocabulaire et grammaire, pp. 43–45
HOMETUTOR
Online Practice (**my.hrw.com**)
1.1, 1.2, 1.3, 3.2, 4.2

115I

Chapitre 4 · Lesson Plans

Cultural References

Page numbers referring to material in the Student Edition appear in regular type. For material located in the Teacher's Edition, page numbers appear in **boldface type.**

PEOPLE

POINTS OF INTEREST

PRODUCTS AND ECONOMY

RECIPES

SCHOOL LIFE

SHOPPING

SOCIAL CUSTOMS

SPORTS AND FITNESS

TRADITIONS

TRANSPORTATION

Network, Promote, and Advocate to Increase French Enrollment

Margot M. Steinhart
Dr. Steinhart, President of the American Association of Teachers of French (AATF) and lecturer in French at Northwestern University, taught French in high school for many years. She is national task force co-chair of "Standards for the Learning of French" in Standards for Foreign Language Learning in the 21st Century.

Dear Colleague,

Dickens refers to the French Revolution in the opening line of *A Tale of Two Cities*: "It was the best of times; it was the worst of times." Hyperbole aside, this could describe the status of foreign language study in the United States. Between the publication of Paul Simon's *The Tongue-tied America: Confronting the Foreign Language Crisis* and Thomas Friedman's *The World is Flat,* Americans have grasped incrementally the need to communicate with the rest of the world. Still, only 43.6% of students in Grades 9–12 are enrolled in a foreign language class.

The gradual recognition of foreign languages as part of the core curriculum with national and state standards is a plus, but the commitment accorded foreign language study remains precarious and uneven across the 50 states, making language courses vulnerable to school boards' chopping blocks. In addition, while the Federal Government has identified critical languages to create or expand K–12 programs, French and other most commonly taught languages do not fall within the current definition of "critical languages."

The good news for us in the 21st century is that French remains strongly positioned. For reasons of history, literature, culture, and now globalization, French is identified with ***la Francophonie,*** comprised of 53 nations and governments on five continents. French stands as the most studied foreign language, after English, in the world. In fact, more people use French today than at any time in history.

I'd like to propose that as teachers of world languages and of French that we amass our resources both individually and collectively to maintain and to extend language programs K–12 and, ultimately, to increase enrollment in French classes. This strategy focuses on Networking, Promotion, and Advocacy.

In solidarity,

Margot M. Steinhart

Networking

Networking becomes an invaluable tool when teachers reach beyond the classroom and the school to find solutions to classroom challenges and to collaborate on lesson planning, curriculum development, and special projects. Professional organizations can help fill this role, not only through meetings and conferences, but through more formal mentoring structures. This can even take place on-line in chat rooms, e.g., FLTEACH and BABILLARD of the American Association of Teachers of French (AATF). By attending conferences, one learns about new resources, meets colleagues who want to share, and acquires ideas and materials for one's own classes. By joining professional foreign language organizations, especially those that reflect the interests of French teachers, opportunities become identifiable for scholarships to study in French-speaking countries, for workshops with a special focus, and for professional reading. The web sites for state, regional, and national foreign language associations, as well as those for Title VI National Language Resource Centers, <http://nflrc.msu.edu/>, organize workshops for teachers and offer valuable resources relating to foreign language acquisition.

Promotion

What we do every day with students constitutes promotion of French. It is the cumulative effect of the various initiatives undertaken that creates a reputation for our French program in the school and larger community. What is essential is that our community SEE evidence of that success and that French be taken outside of the classroom INTO the community.

Sometimes teachers create events, but they also take advantage of occasions announced in the school calendar. For example, an open house for incoming students or parent conferences provide opportunities to distribute promotional flyers and to highlight programs through photo displays, PowerPoint, or French promotional clips. When school or community events lend themselves to additional participation, consider how French students or Francophone Club members might be involved, e.g., presentations at meetings of community service clubs, or celebrations, like Homecoming or Mardi Gras.

National French Week (NFW) and **la Fête de la Francophonie** provide instances to celebrate everything French. Requesting a proclamation from the mayor and having it presented at a town meeting is a very public way to validate French studies. Having students present a program, teach a game or song, or introduce French expressions to students at a sending school in the district can attract prospective students. When recruiting students *per se* is discouraged, events planned to coincide with NFW may garner more administrative support. Whatever the event, it is important to invite school administrators and board members, counselors, and local officials. AATF, <www.frenchteachers.org>, has a plethora of ideas that French teachers have developed to promote French.

An effective promotional activity incorporates a learning component and can be linked to the national standards. Many teachers organize excursions to art exhibits and restaurants, trips to French-speaking countries, and immersion days with both instructional and promotional elements. Another way to connect French with the "Communities" standard is through service or fund-raising projects for international organizations like Doctors without Borders or the Red Cross. It is important to take the extra step to collect photographs and write articles for the local and school newspapers, for the parents' bulletins or the principal or headmaster's newsletter about students' experiences. Where available, the French program can be featured on the local cable station, if not the area public stations.

Students need reassurance that their study of French has value beyond their immediate studies or college admission. Incorporate a lesson on career opportunities, using some of the web resources, like <www.monster.com>. Make the connections for students in terms of where French is used and expressions that can enrich their speaking and writing in English.

Advocacy

Language advocacy frequently surfaces in response to a proposed or actual program reduction as a way to influence public policy or to redistribute financial resources. The reasons for such devastating announcements are frequently attributed to failed school referenda, budget cuts, other funding priorities, declining enrollment, teacher retirement, politics of a local school board member or community leader, a bias that language choice is not important or that another language is more useful, or no identified need for foreign languages in the region. Ideally, the French teacher has been networking and knows where to find resources, both people and materials, and has been building community support for the French program. This makes it harder to eliminate a visibly successful French program and easier to find support when the advocacy card needs to be played.

When any of the danger signs mentioned appear, the time is right to align a support team, engaging as many influential people in the community as possible. Parents and students can be very effective supporters, for they are important stakeholders in the decision. Over time, the French teacher should consider building and updating a data base of students who have completed the capstone French course and who can provide effective testimonials or be part of a letter writing campaign to save programs. In addition, professional organizations are poised to provide materials and to supply letters in support of French programs. The AATF web site provides a number of links to data that can be used to produce arguments and talking points for supporting French. State foreign language associations and the Joint National Committee for Languages and the National Council for Languages and International Studies (JNCL-NCLIS) can also provide tips, strategies, and sample models for directing an advocacy campaign.

Being an effective French teacher requires more than being a good teacher. It demands that we observe and research our community, that we identify resources, and that we develop the knowledge and skills to network, promote, and advocate for French. The efficient French teacher sees how to initiate and share responsibilities, for a strong French program benefits students, a whole community, and potentially, the world.

Professional Development

Holt McDougal is dedicated to enabling America's students to study world languages and culture. The educators who developed ***Bien dit!*** know that professional development begins with the instructional resources that teachers use every day. To that end, ***Bien dit!*** Teacher's Editions include:

Differentiated Instruction

ADVANCED LEARNERS	SPECIAL LEARNING NEEDS
Bring several clothing catalogues to class and have students choose a page with an outfit that	**Students with Learning Disabilities/ Dyslexia** Students with learning disabilities

- Instructions for adapting activities to meet the needs of a diverse student population with a wide range of ability levels and interests

Communication

Communication, pp. 187, 189, 191, 193, 199, 201, 203, 205

- Specific suggestions for building the national standards into the instructional program

TPR

TOTAL PHYSICAL RESPONSE

Have students help you gather a variety of clothing items made of various fabrics. Ask individual students to respond to these commands.

- Instructions for using methods, such as TPR, that appeal to specific types of learners

- Ancillaries such as the ***Cahier d'activités*** help teachers learn to use reading strategies to help struggling readers become more effective readers.

The No Child Left Behind (NCLB) legislation considers foreign language a "core academic subject," which means foreign language teachers must be "highly qualified"; therefore states and districts can use their Title II teacher quality grant money on professional development and other initiatives to get their teachers, including foreign language teachers, to become highly qualified in their field.

ACTFL introduced policy directives to increase the international focus of the Department of Education. In response, the Fulbright-Hays Group Projects Abroad includes a request for seminars that develop and improve foreign language and area studies at elementary and secondary schools. Holt Speaker's Bureau Institutes can help local schools and districts increase their focus.

For the first time, the Title VI Undergraduate International Studies and Foreign Language competition has asked for projects that provide in-service training for K-12 teachers in foreign languages and international studies. Holt Professional Development courses can provide teachers with research-based, data-driven teacher education programs that are highly effective in improving performance.

Several Holt Professional Development Workshops are available for foreign language teachers.

Holt Professional Development Workshops

- **TPR Storytelling**
- **Teaching for Proficiency**
- **Culture in the World Languages Classroom**
- **Meeting the Needs of Diverse Learners and Students with Special Needs**
- **Assessment Options for World Languages**
- **Balancing the Four Skills and Culture**
- **The "What, Why, and How" of No Child Left Behind**
- **Teaching and Technology**

Implementing National Standards

Paul Sandrock
World Language Consultant, Wisconsin Department of Public Instruction Madison, Wisconsin

RESEARCH

National Standards in Foreign Language Education Project. (1999) *Standards for Foreign Language Learning in the 21st Century. Lawrence, KS: Allen Press.*

Phillips, June K., ed. (1999) *Foreign Language Standards: Linking Research, Theories, and Practice.* Lincolnwood, IL: National Textbook Company. (ACTFL Foreign Language Education Series)

Sandrock, Paul. (2002) *Planning Curriculum for Learning World Languages.* Madison, WI: Wisconsin Department of Public Instruction.

Shrum, Judith and Eileen Glisan. (2000) *Teacher's Handbook: Contextualized Language Instruction,* 2nd Edition. Heinle & Heinle.

Wiggins, Grant, and Jay McTighe. (1998) *Understanding by Design.* Alexandria, VA: Association for Supervision and Curriculum Development.

To implement the five goals of the national standards—communication, cultures, connections, comparisons, and communities—requires a shift from emphasizing the means to focusing on the ends.

Instead of simply planning a series of activities, today's world language teacher focuses on what and how the student is learning. Rather than teaching and testing the four skills of listening, speaking, reading, and writing in isolation, teachers need to make their instructional decisions based on the three purposes directing the communication (interpersonal, interpretive, and presentational) and within a cultural context. Our standards answer why we are teaching various components of language.

Since the publication of the standards, many states have developed more specific performance standards that provide evidence of the application of the national content standards, and teachers have carried the standards into the classroom. Textbook writers and materials providers are also responding to the shift brought about by the standards, providing an organization, creating a context, and modeling the kind of instruction that leads students to successfully demonstrate the communication strategies envisioned in our standards. Textbooks can bring authentic materials into the classroom, real cultural examples that avoid stereotypes, and a broader exposure to the variety of people who speak the language being studied. Standards provide the ends; teachers use textbooks and materials to help students practice the means.

Assessment is the jigsaw puzzle that shows students what they can do with their new language. If we only test students on the means of vocabulary and grammar, students simply collect random puzzle pieces. We have to test, and students have to practice, putting the pieces together in meaningful and purposeful ways. When they are truly communicating, students will know they've achieved the standards.

Goal	Standards
Communication Communicate in Languages Other Than English	**Standard 1.1 Interpersonal** Students engage in conversations, provide and obtain information, express feelings and emotions, and exchange opinions. **Standard 1.2 Interpretive** Students understand and interpret written and spoken language on a variety of topics. **Standard 1.3 Presentational** Students present information, concepts, and ideas to an audience of listeners or readers on a variety of topics.
Cultures Gain Knowledge and Understanding of Other Cultures	**Standard 2.1 Practices** Students demonstrate an understanding of the relationship between the practices and perspectives of the culture studied. **Standard 2.2 Products** Students demonstrate an understanding of the relationship between the products and perspectives of the culture studied.
Connections Connect with Other Disciplines and Acquire Information	**Standard 3.1 Across Disciplines** Students reinforce and further their knowledge of other disciplines through the foreign language. **Standard 3.2 Added Perspective** Students acquire information and recognize the distinctive viewpoints that are only available through the foreign language and its cultures.
Comparisons Develop Insight into the Nature of Language and Culture	**Standard 4.1 Language** Students demonstrate understanding of the nature of language through comparisons of the language studied and their own. **Standard 4.2 Culture** Students demonstrate understanding of the concept of culture through comparisons of the cultures studied and their own.
Communities Participate in Multilingual Communities at Home and Around the World.	**Standard 5.1 Practical Applications** Students use the language both within and beyond the school setting. **Standard 5.2 Personal Enrichment** Students show evidence of becoming life-long learners by using the language for personal enjoyment and enrichment.

Teaching Comprehension

Kylene Beers, PhD.
Clinical Associate Professor
University of Houston
Houston, Texas

RESEARCH

Baumann, J. 1984
"Effectiveness of a Direct Instruction Paradigm for Teaching Main Idea Comprehension." *Reading Research Quarterly*, 20: 93–108.

Beers, K. 2002.
When Kids Can't Read—What Teachers Can Do. Portsmouth: Heinemann.

Dole, J., Brown, K., and Trathen, W. 1996.
The Effects of Strategy Instruction on the Comprehension Performance of At-Risk Students," *Reading Research Quarterly*, 31: 62–89.

Duffy, G. 2002
"The Case for Direct Explanation of Strategies." *Comprehension Instruction: Research-Based Best Practices.* Eds. C. Block and M. Pressley. New York: Guilford Press. 28–41.

Pearson, P. D. 1984
"Direct Explicit Teaching of Reading Comprehension." *Comprehension Instruction: Perspectives and Suggestions.* Eds. G. Duffy, L. Roehler, and J. Mason. New York: Longman, 222–233

"Comprehension is both a product and a process, something that requires purposeful, strategic effort on the reader's part as he or she predicts, visualizes, clarifies, questions, connects, summarizes, and infers."

—Kylene Beers

When the Text is Tough

"Comprehension is only tough when you can't do it," explained the eleventh grader. I almost dismissed his words until I realized what truth they offered. We aren't aware of all the thinking we do to comprehend a text until faced with a difficult text. Then, all too clearly, we're aware of what words we don't understand, what syntax seems convoluted, what ideas are beyond our immediate grasp. As skilled readers, we know what to do; we slow our pace, re-read, ask questions, connect whatever we do understand to what we don't understand, summarize what we've read thus far, make inferences about what the author is saying. In short, we make that invisible act of comprehension visible as we consciously push our way through the difficult text. At those times, we realize that, indeed, comprehension is tough.

Reading Strategies for Struggling Readers

It's even tougher if you lack strategies that would help you through the difficult text. Many struggling readers believe they aren't successful readers because that's just the way things are (Beers, 2002); they believe successful readers know some secret that they haven't been told (Duffy, 2002). While we don't mean to keep comprehension a secret, at times we do. For instance, though we tell students to "re-read," we haven't shown them how to alter their reading. We tell them to "make inferences," or "make predictions," but we haven't taught them how to do such things. In other words, we tell them what to do, but don't show them how to do it, in spite of several decades of research showing the benefit of direct instruction in reading strategies to struggling readers. (Baumann, 1984; Pearson, P.D., 1984; Dole, et al., 1996; Beers, 2002).

Direct Instruction

Direct instruction means telling students what you are going to teach them, modeling it for them, providing assistance as they practice it, then letting them practice it on their own. It's not saying, "Visualize while you read," but, instead, explaining, "Today, I'm going to read this part aloud to you. I'm going to focus on seeing some of the action in my mind as I read. I'm going to stop occasionally and tell you what I'm seeing and what in the text helped me see that." When we directly teach comprehension strategies to students via modeling and repeated practice, we show students that good readers don't just get it. They work hard to get it. ***Bien dit!*** takes the secret out of comprehension as it provides teachers the support they need to reach struggling readers.

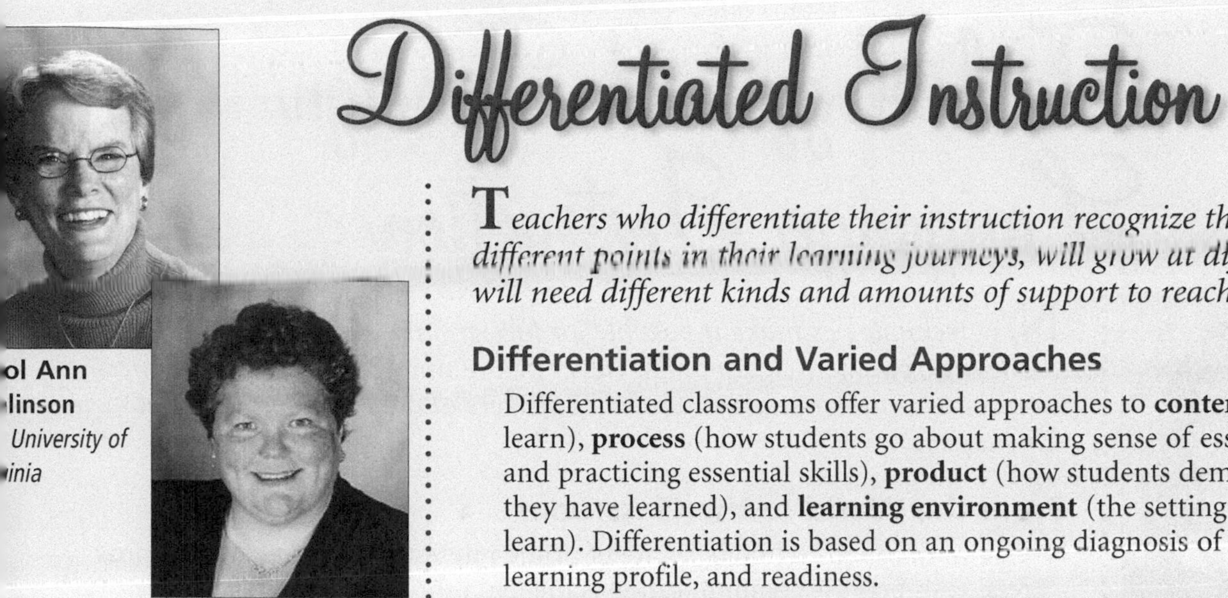

Differentiated Instruction

ol Ann
linson
University of
inia

Cindy Strickland
The University of Virginia

Teachers who differentiate their instruction recognize that students are at different points in their learning journeys, will grow at different rates, and will need different kinds and amounts of support to reach their goals.

Differentiation and Varied Approaches

Differentiated classrooms offer varied approaches to **content** (what students learn), **process** (how students go about making sense of essential knowledge and practicing essential skills), **product** (how students demonstrate what they have learned), and **learning environment** (the setting in which students learn). Differentiation is based on an ongoing diagnosis of student interest, learning profile, and readiness.

Differentiation and the World Language Teacher

World language teachers are natural differentiators for learning profile. We provide opportunities for students to acquire proficiency in the target language through a variety of means: speaking, listening, writing, and reading. Through this variety of approaches, we recognize that students' proficiency in each of these skill areas will vary. Good language teachers work hard to help students improve in areas in which they struggle, and revel in areas of strength.

Systematic differentiation for readiness provides many world language teachers with a bit more of a challenge. Students come to us with a huge range in amount and type of language experience, including, for example, first-year students who have had no exposure to the target language, who have had an exploratory class, who have studied another target language, or who are native speakers.

Key Principles of Differentiated Instruction

There are several key principles to follow when differentiating instruction in the language classroom. First, start by clearly defining what is most essential for students to know, understand, and be able to do in the target language. Second, hold high expectations for all students and make sure that they are engaged in **respectful work.** Third, use **flexible grouping,** an excellent tool to ensure that all students learn to work independently, cooperatively and collaboratively in a variety of settings and with a variety of peers.

A final principle of differentiated instruction is **ongoing assessment.** To this end, the teacher constantly monitors student interest, learning profile, and readiness in order to adjust to the growing and changing learner. Teachers must not assume that a student will have the same readiness or interest in every unit of study or in every skill area. Preassessment is a must, particularly in the areas of knowledge and facility with vocabulary and grammatical constructions.

The Role of the Teacher in Academically Diverse Classrooms

Good teachers have always recognized that "one size fits all" instruction does not serve students well. To be effective, teachers must find ways consistently to **reach more kinds of learners more often**—by recognizing and responding to students' varied readiness levels, by honoring their diverse interests, and by understanding their preferences for how they learn information and practice new skills.

RESEARCH

Tomlinson, C., and Eidson, C. *Design for Differentiation: Curriculum for the Differentiated Classroom,* Grades 5–9. Alexandria, VA: Association for Supervision and Curriculum Development (in press).

Tomlinson, C. 2001. *How to Differentiate Instruction in Mixed-Ability Classrooms,* 2/e. Alexandria, VA: Association for Supervision and Curriculum Development

Tomlinson, C. and Allan, S. 2001. *Leadership for Differentiating Schools and Classrooms.* Alexandria, VA: Association for Supervision and Curriculum Development, 2000.

Winebrenner, S. 1996. *Teaching Kids with Learning Difficulties in the Regular Classroom.* Minneapolis, MN: Free Spirit, 1996.

Technology and Foreign Language Instruction

Robert Ponterio, *Professor of French, SUNY Cortland*

Jean W. LeLoup, *Professor of Spanish, SUNY Cortland*

New technologies make it possible for foreign language teachers to bring the world into their classroom as never before and to make direct connections between their students and the speakers and culture of the target language.

From the World to the Classroom

Communication technologies are of prime interest to foreign language professionals because communication is the main thrust in foreign language teaching (Omaggio Hadley, 2001; Phillips, 1998). The present emphasis on using language, not just learning about language, calls for materials that prepare students for authentic communicative situations and lead them quickly to work with real information in the target language. In addition, the ready access to authentic materials, native speakers, and rich target language input that these new media can provide facilitates the creation of lessons that have tremendous potential in the foreign language classroom for directly addressing many of the goal areas of the national Standards for Foreign Language Learning (Shrum & Glisan, 2000).

The Standards, Cultural Knowledge, and Multimedia

The Standards stress the importance of cultural knowledge as an integral part of language learning; the tri-part examination of cultural products, practices and the perspectives underlying them is greatly enhanced by using Internet materials that help students better connect with different cultural realities (Standards, 1999). Multimedia—by mixing together realia, photos, video, and sounds from the native environment—contributes significantly to creating a culturally and linguistically authentic context for language learning. Multimedia visual materials also offer a window to nonlinguistic cues that are vital to second language comprehension and learning (Binkley, 2003).

Technology Is a Tool

Technology is a powerful tool when properly integrated in the curriculum (LeLoup & Ponterio, 2003). Computers, audio, and video are an adjunct to language learning objectives and not an end in themselves; they offer many benefits for expanding options in the instructional process. Access to the materials through Internet sites can significantly increase the time spent working with the language as well as the quality of homework activities. Electronic materials are easily updated for continued accuracy and adapted to correspond to current lesson topics and themes. Computer-based exercises that offer immediate feedback to the learner reflect a student-centered approach to language instruction that can help reinforce accuracy in the written language and provide for self-paced learning. For example, the use of hypertext allows an individual to find clarification of meaning or to examine an idea in more depth by connecting to additional materials beyond the text. It puts the power to control this exploration squarely in the student's hands. Current writing tools, both assisted writing environments and word processors, help develop the skills needed for communication in the real world (Scott, 1996). Finally, because of its flexibility and ease of use, technology provides the optimal vehicle for creating authentic assessments, which parallels the use of authentic materials and complements a proficiency-based orientation (Terry, 1998).

RESEARCH

Binkley, S. C. (2004). "Using digital video of native speakers to enhance listening comprehension and cultural competence." In Lomicka, L., & Cooke-Plagwitz, J., Eds. *Teaching with Technology.* Boston, MA: Heinle & Heinle; 115–120.

LeLoup, J. W. & Ponterio, R. (2003). *Second Language Acquisition and Technology: A Review of the Research.* ERIC Digest EDO-FL-03-11.

Omaggio Hadley, A. (2001). *Teaching Language in Context.* Boston, MA: Heinle & Heinle.

Phillips, J. K. (1998). "Changing teacher/learner roles in Standards-driven contexts." In Harper, J., Lively, M., & Williams, M., Eds. *The coming of age of the profession: Issues and emerging ideas for the teaching of foreign languages.* Boston, MA: Heinle & Heinle; 3–14.

Scott, V. M. (1996). *Rethinking foreign language writing.* Boston, MA: Heinle & Heinle.

Shrum, J. L., & Glisan, E. W. (2000). *Teacher's Handbook: Contextualized Language Instruction.* Boston, MA: Heinle & Heinle.

Standards for foreign language learning in the 21st century. (1999). Lawrence, KS: Allen Press, Inc.

Terry, R. M. (1998). Authentic tasks and materials for testing in the foreign language classroom. In Harper, J., Lively, M., & Williams, M., Eds. *The coming of age of the profession: Issues and emerging ideas for the teaching of foreign languages.* Boston, MA: Heinle & Heinle; 277-290.

Classroom Management

Nancy Humbach
Associate Professor, Miami University

RESEARCH

Cangelosi, James (1997). *Classroom Management Strategies: Gaining and Maintaining Students' Cooperation.* New York: Addison Wesley Longman. Third Edition.

Danforth, Scot and Joseph R. Boyle (2000). *Cases in Behavior Management.* Upper Saddle River: Pearson Education (Merrill Prentice Hall).

McEwan Landau, Barbara (2004). *The Art of Classroom Management: Building Equitable Learning Communities.* Pearson Education (Merrill Prentice Hall).

McEwan, Barbara (2000). *The Art of-Classroom Management: Effective Practices for Buiding Equitable Learning Communities.* Upper Saddle River: Pearson Education (Merrill Prentice Hall).

Palmer, Parker (1998). *The Courage to Teach: Exploring the Inner Landscape of a Teacher's Life.* San Francisco: Jossey-Bass Publishers.

Schmuck, Richard A. and Patricia A. Schmuck (2001). *Group Processes in the Classroom.* Boston: McGraw Hill. Eighth Edition.

Shrum, Judith and Eileen Glisan. *Teachers' Handbook: Contextualized Language Instruction.* Boston: Heinle and Heinle. Any edition.

Successful classes are created by teachers who are motivated, have high expectations, demonstrate enthusiasm for their students and for content, and who maintain organization, flexibility, and the ability to mediate.

Managing Your Class Successfully

Managing the classroom so that students stay on task, understand the concepts being taught, and have their needs addressed is one of the most daunting challenges facing a teacher. The beginning of the year is the best time to let students know what you expect of them and what they can expect of you. Inform students what they will need to bring to class and discuss with them required behaviors, such as respect for others. For more effective participation, allow students to brainstorm behaviors that would help them learn.

Present your expectations in writing and on your Web site, if you have one, keeping rules and regulations simple and clear. State them in positive terms, such as "Come to class with textbook, paper, etc.," instead of "Don't come to class without…"

Plans and Organization

To keep your class running smoothly, create lesson plans that have a variety of activities, plans for transitions between activities, a varied pace, and attention to time-on-task. Effective lesson plans take into account the ability level of the students. They present a challenge that is within reach of the students but holds their interest, and they include advance organizers, presentations, checks, and evaluations.

Begin class on a positive note by having an activity (some type of advance organizer) on the board, the overhead, or on paper. Such an activity will allow you to take attendance and check homework and still be ready to begin class as the bell rings.

Task-based activities enlist the creativity of students and may be done either alone, in pairs, or in groups. Problem-solving tasks with time limits allow students to be involved actively in learning, as do those that require students to discover solutions or outcomes.

Pair and Group Work

Group work is important in a language class. If you plan well, train students to work in groups, and have a sound evaluation plan, group work can be rewarding and a highly productive part of the learning process. No matter how you establish your groups, the process of moving into groups must be rapid and cause as little disruption as possible. Systematic monitoring is essential for successful pair and group work, evaluation, and teacher feedback.

Be Prepared—But Stay Flexible

No two teaching situations are alike. What works for one teacher or one class may not work in all situations. However, motivation, preparation, interest in the students and in the content, and sensible ground rules for such things as pair and group work can help you maintain a successful class.

Game Bank

Loto!

This game, played much like Bingo, lets students practice numbers, colors, body parts, clothing, or other objects in French.

Materials Index cards (or paper) and markers

Procedure Students prepare their own **Loto!** card by drawing a card similar to a Bingo card with five horizontal and vertical spaces. Students write a number, color a square a certain color, or draw a body part, piece of clothing, or other object in each space. Read a number or one of the other themed vocabulary words in French and record it. Students cover or cross off the spaces as the items in them are called until a player has filled an entire row or column. He or she then says **Loto!** The student who reads the vocabulary back correctly wins. You may laminate the cards for later use with water-based markers, or use paper scraps to cover the numbers.

Cerveau

This game, played like Concentration®, helps students learn and review through concentration and recall. This game can be used to reinforce vocabulary, questions and answers, and verbs.

Materials Index cards

Procedure Have students make three pairs of cards. On a card have them write a question, a verb, or another vocabulary word. On the card's mate, the student writes the answer to the question, draws the action of the verb, or draws the vocabulary item. Divide the class into pairs or small groups. Have one student combine and shuffle all the group's cards together and then lay them out in a grid on the desk, blank side up. Players take turns turning over two cards each. If they match, the player takes them. If they don't, they are returned, face down, to their original place. Play continues until all the cards are paired. The player with the most matches wins.

Catégories

This game is patterned after the game Scattergories®. It should be played in teams and is good for reinforcing vocabulary from various categories.

Materials A timer, index cards, and pencils and paper for scoring

Procedure Make index cards with the letters of the alphabet on them. Write a list of three categories on the board that the class has learned: classes, school supplies, names, descriptive adjectives or other themed vocabulary. Have teams prepare a paper with three columns, one for each category. One team chooses a letter from the stack of index cards and calls out the letter to be used in this round. The timer is set for one minute and the round begins. For each category, teams quickly fill in the answer sheet with vocabulary words that begin with the key letter. When the timer rings, students must stop writing. Have one team read its answers. If any other team has that word, everyone crosses it off their list. The next team reads any words remaining on their lists, and again any duplicates are crossed off all lists. Repeat this process for the remaining teams. The winning team is the one with the highest number of unique, unduplicated words.

Scrabble®

Similar to Scrabble®, this game is excellent for review of all learned vocabulary and verbs.

Materials Heavy paper or card stock.

Procedure Cut the paper into one-inch squares. Leave a third of them blank and write the French alphabet on the rest. Make extra squares with the most common letters: vowels, s, t, etc. A blank may serve as any letter. Place the letters face down in one pile and the blanks in another pile. Each student picks ten letters and five blanks. Using learned vocabulary, students arrange letters and blanks to form as many words as possible on their desk. The student with the most words, and the student with the longest word, are the winners. This game may be played in pairs with students taking turns and building their words off of the already played words on the desk.

Charade

Played like charades, this game reviews active verbs. It is an excellent activity for kinesthetic learners.

Materials Index cards

Procedure Write action verbs or phrases from chapter themes on index cards, (things you like to do, school activities, preparing for a party, preparing and serving food, staying healthy, or vacation activities). Divide the class into teams and give one card to each student. Taking turns, students act out their word or phrase without speaking, while the other team guesses in French. You may consider limiting the time that each team has to guess. As a challenge, have the teams combine a number of students' cards to create sentences, assigning nouns and other necessary parts of speech to individuals. The team acts out its string of words while the other team tries to figure out the sentence that is being presented.

faire de la musculation

aller au ciné

jouer à des jeux vidéo

La patate chaude

This exciting game quickly practices vocabulary and phrases while getting the entire class involved.

Materials A small box, a wind-up timer or battery-operated alarm clock

Procedure Make a **patate chaude** by placing an alarm clock or a timer in a small box. Be sure the alarm or timer ticks loudly. Have students sit in a circle. Call out a category based on a vocabulary category, (**fruits, le petit-déjeuner,** etc.). As you name the category, hand the **patate** to a student who must then say a related vocabulary word. After saying a word, that student then passes the **patate** to the student to the right, who is to name a different item from the category. If a student is left holding the **patate** when the timer goes off, he or she is out of the game. You decide when a category has been exhausted and change it accordingly. The winner is the last student remaining who could think of a new vocabulary word, and pass the **patate** on without getting caught by the buzzer.

Lettres dans le désordre

This game is good for tactile learners. The goal is for students to construct French vocabulary words from scrambled letters.

Materials Small squares of paper for each student

Procedure Divide the class into two teams. Each person on the team finds a different French vocabulary word from the chapter and writes each letter of that word on one of the pieces of paper. After everyone is finished, team members exchange their letters with a person on the other team. Students quickly try to arrange the letters to form the word. The student who unscrambles a word before his or her counterpart wins a point for his or her team.

Un mot de plus

This game helps students build on words and ideas to make complete sentences. The sentences can be odd or funny, but they should be grammatically correct.

Procedure Create any number of teams. Begin a sentence on the board with a word. For example, (**Mon**). Have one player write a word to continue the sentence, (**frère**). The next team's player writes another word, (**a**). Once the sentence becomes complicated, students may add words before or after others. For example, **petit** could go between **mon** and **frère**. Players score one point for each logical contribution.

Dessine-le!

This game provides a thorough review of nouns, verbs, and adjectives and creates team spirit within the class.

Materials Index cards and colored markers

Procedure Divide the class into five equal groups of students. Each group selects 10 vocabulary items from a chapter or various chapters already learned and writes one vocabulary word on each card. A more challenging version can be played with phrases or short sentences. Combine all cards from each group and shuffle. Divide the class into two teams. You will need one scorekeeper and one timekeeper. Give the first team a card with the French word written on it. That team member goes to the board and must illustrate the word within 15 seconds. The next three people in line from that person's team are allowed one guess each. If one of the three people guesses correctly, the team scores a point. If they cannot guess, the question goes to the next person on the other team. The other team is allowed only one guess. If the student shown the card does not know what the French word means, the team defaults its turn, and the opportunity to play the word goes to the other team. ***Dessine-le!*** can be played by the whole class, or a small group, for vocabulary review.

D'une syllabe à un mot

This game provides an opportunity to practice pronunciation and can be used to review vocabulary from any chapter.

Materials Index cards and pens or markers

Procedure Review the definition of a syllable as a short unit of speech. Break up the vocabulary words from the chapter into syllables and have the students write each syllable on an index card using large letters. For example, make three cards for **por-ta-ble,** two cards for **ca-hier,** etc. Shuffle the cards and pass them out among students. Say **"D'une syllabe à un mot"**. Give the students a specific amount of time (one minute), to find other people with whom they can form a word. Tell students to call out **"Mot!"** when they have formed a word. The group must say their word in unison as you point to them. Collect all the index cards, shuffle them, and redistribute to play again.

Le base-ball avec des mots

With this game students will practice the new vocabulary words and expressions and review previously learned vocabulary.

Preparation Develop a list of questions whose answers require the students to use words and phrases from the current and previous chapters. (Examples: **Pour ne pas être stressé (e), je fais ____. Pour avoir de gros muscles, il faut faire ____. Tu dois dormir pour ne pas être ____. Avant de faire de l'exercice, il faut ____.**

Procedure Divide the class into two teams. Assign a student scorekeeper. Draw a baseball diamond with bases on the board. Set a number of innings for playing. The batter is the first player on Team A. You serve as the pitcher and ask the batter a question. If the batter gives a correct answer, he or she moves to first base. The scorekeeper places a mark on first base. If the batter cannot answer, he or she is out. You then ask a question of the second batter on Team A. If the second batter answers correctly, he or she goes to first base. If there is a player on first base, he or she advances to second base and the scorekeeper places a mark on second base. A team scores a run by advancing a player to home plate. Team A continues batting until it has three outs. Then Team B goes to bat. When Team B has three outs, the first inning is over. Teams get one point for each run, and the team with the most points wins.

Enchaînement

This game, which helps students review vocabulary, is good for auditory learners.

Procedure Have all students stand up. Announce a vocabulary theme, (school classes, clothing, household items, etc.). Say a sentence with one word from the theme. For example, **J'étudie les mathématiques à l'école**. The first student then repeats the sentence saying what you said and adding another word that follows the theme. **J'étudie les mathématiques et le français à l'école.** When someone says the "chain" incorrectly, he or she sits down. This sequence continues until no one can add any more words to the sentence. At this time you might select another theme. The winners are the last three students to be left standing.

Why Study French?

French Can Take You around the World!

Margot M. Steinhart, Ph.D.

Chers élèves,

Formidable! You have chosen to learn French, the most frequently studied world language after English, and are becoming a citizen of the world. Your sphere immediately expands to include 175 million French speakers in more than 50 countries and millions of people who have studied French on five continents. And did you know that about 2 million people speak French as a first language in the U.S.?

In addition to learning the language, you will discover the uniqueness of many cultures from around the world. You will have the opportunity to explore Quebec, the Caribbean, West and North Africa, Europe, and the Pacific Ocean islands, to name a few. It is remarkable that through one language, French, the richness of these diverse regions can be learned and experienced. You can connect to the Francophone world through e-mail correspondence or by travel and study experiences.

Browse the flower market in Rennes. It's a visual delight!

Did you select French because it is a language associated with renowned artists, literary giants, medical, scientific, and techno-logical break-through discoveries, and an enviable sense of style? French can also improve your English-language skills since French is more like English than is any other Romance language, such as Italian and Spanish. More than 30% of English vocabulary is derived from French. How many French expressions related to government, law, food, art, music, dance, cinema, literature,

Buy souwère paintings by local artisans in markets all over Senegal.

Take the bullet train from Paris to Nice. It can be fun!

architecture, fashion, or diplomacy do you already know: *coup d'état, bon appétit, faux pas, genre, à la mode, pas de deux, carte blanche, and déjà vu?*

As you plan your future, French can lead to fulfilling careers in many fields: manufacturing, finance, law, government, education, the sciences, journalism, advertising, telecommunications, tourism and hospitality. Your language skills will also benefit you in working with international agencies like the International Red Cross, UNESCO, the World Health Organization, and the International Olympic Committee. Did you know that the majority of U.S. exports are to countries having French as a national language? Exports to bilingual Canada alone are greater than the combined exports to all countries south of the United States. Approximately $1 billion in commercial transactions take place between the U.S. and France each day. In terms of emerging markets, French-speaking Africa occupies an area larger than the U.S.

You undoubtedly chose French for very personal reasons. Imagine yourself as a fluent speaker of the language, communicating in French with people all around the globe, being an international student in a French-speaking country, or attending the Cannes Film Festival. How about serving in the Peace Corps in a Sub-Saharan African country, working with **Médecins sans Frontières** *(Doctors Without Borders)*, or negotiating a business deal for a multinational company?

As you continue your journey as a French speaker, and as you open doors to opportunities that become possible just because you have chosen to communicate in French, let me wish you **Bonne chance!** *(Good luck!)*. May you enjoy the adventure that awaits you.

Bonne Continuation,

Margot M. Steinhart

Discover modern art at the MAMAC museum in Nice!

Why Study French?

Meet French-speaking teens from around the world.

Ride the funicular in Quebec!

Stop at a crêperie in Paris for a tasty treat!

Le monde francophone

Welcome to the French-speaking World

Did you know that French is spoken not only in France but in many other countries in Europe (Belgium, Switzerland, Andorra and Monaco), North America (New England, Louisiana and Quebec province), Asia (Vietnam, Laos and Cambodia), and over twenty countries in Africa? French is also the official language of France's overseas territories like Martinique, Guadeloupe, French Guiana, and Reunion.

As you look at the map, what other places can you find where French is spoken? Can you imagine how French came to be spoken in these places?

La France

Le Québec

La Louisiane

La Martinique

Saint-Pierre-et-Miquelon

QUÉBEC

NOUVELLE-ANGLETERRE

ÉTATS-UNIS

OCÉAN ATLANTIQUE

LOUISIANE

Antilles françaises

HAÏTI

GUYANE FRANÇAISE

OCÉAN PACIFIQUE

Polynésie française

N O E S

Le Maroc
Le Sénégal
Le Mali
Le Viêtnam
BELGIQUE
LUXEMBOURG
SUISSE
FRANCE
ANDORRE
MONACO
TUNISIE
MAROC
ALGÉRIE
MAURITANIE
MALI
NIGER
TCHAD
SÉNÉGAL
GUINÉE
BÉNIN
CÔTE D'IVOIRE
TOGO
RÉPUBLIQUE CENTRAFRICAINE
BURKINA FASO
CAMEROUN
GABON
RÉPUBLIQUE DÉMOCRATIQUE DU CONGO
RUANDA
CONGO
BURUNDI
DJIBOUTI
Mayotte
OCÉAN ATLANTIQUE
OCÉAN INDIEN
MADAGASCAR
Île de la Réunion
VIÊTNAM
LAOS
CAMBODGE
OCÉAN PACIFIQUE
Îles Wallis
Île Futuna
Nouvelle-Calédonie

Map of French-speaking World

Instructions

Directions

Throughout the book, many activities will have directions in French. Here are some of the directions you'll see, along with their English translations.

Complète... avec un mot/une expression de la boîte.
Complete . . . with a word/an expression from the box.

Complète le paragraphe avec...
Complete the paragraph with . . .

Complète les phrases avec la forme correcte du verbe (entre parenthèses).
Complete the sentences with the correct form of the verb (in parentheses).

Indique si les phrases suivantes sont vraies ou fausses. Si la phrase est fausse, corrige-la.
Indicate if the following sentences are true or false. If the sentence is false, correct it.

Avec un(e) camarade, jouez...
With a classmate, act out . . .

Réponds aux questions suivantes.
Answer the following questions.

Réponds aux questions en utilisant...
Answer the questions using . . .

Complète les phrases suivantes.
Complete the following sentences.

Fais tous les changements nécessaires.
Make all the necessary changes.

Choisis l'image qui convient.
Choose the most appropriate image.

Écoute les phrases et indique si...
Listen to the sentences and indicate if . . .

Utilise les sujets donnés pour décrire...
Use the subjects provided to describe . . .

Écoute les conversations suivantes. Choisis l'image qui correspond à chaque conversation.
Listen to the following conversations. Match each conversation with the appropriate image.

Choisis un mot ou une expression de chaque boîte pour écrire...
Choose a word or expression from each box to write . . .

En groupes de..., discutez...
In groups of . . ., discuss . . .

Demande à ton/ta camarade...
Ask your classmate . . .

Suis l'exemple.
Follow the model.

Échangez les rôles.
Switch roles.

Remets... en ordre.
Put in . . . order.

Regarde les images et dis ce qui se passe.
Look at the images and tell what is happening.

Utilise le vocabulaire de... pour compléter...
Use the vocabulary from... to complete...

Suggestions pour apprendre le français

Tips for Learning French

Do you remember everything you learned last year? It's easy to forget your French when you don't use it for a while. Here are some tips to help you in French class this year.

Listen

When someone else is speaking, ask yourself what that person is saying. Listen for specific words or phrases that either support or do not support your guess. If you don't hear or understand a word, don't panic or give up. Try to figure out its meaning from the sentences that follow it.

Speak

Have you ever tried to say something in English, but then you forgot a certain word? Chances are you did not let that stop you. You simply thought of another way of saying the same thing. Use that same trick when speaking French.

With a classmate, practice short conversations on topics you learned about last year. If you can't remember how to say something in French, look in the glossary or ask someone, **"Comment dit-on... ?"** You can also try using words you do know or gestures to explain what you mean.

Read

Sometimes you might feel anxious when you read in French because understanding the entire text seems to be an overwhelming task. One easy way to reduce this anxiety is to break the reading up into parts. With the reading divided into small sections, you can focus all your attention on one section at a time.

If you look up specific words or phrases in an English-French dictionary, be careful about choosing the meaning. Many words can have several different meanings in English or in French. Be sure to look closely at the context, if one is given, before choosing a word.

Write

Before you begin writing, organize your ideas. Write a sentence that states the main idea. Then choose the details that support it. List them in an order that makes sense to you. After you have listed all of your ideas, you can write about the ones that appeal to you most.

One way to make the task of writing easier is to make sure you know most of the words you will need to use. With a classmate, make a list of words you will probably need to complete your task. Then look up the words you don't know in the dictionary. Look at the charts in the back of this book to refresh your memory on important grammar points.

Learning a foreign language is like any other long-term project, such as getting into shape or taking up a new sport: it will take some time to see the results you want. Remember, knowing another language is a valuable asset, and you've already come a long way. Keep up your French and...

Bonne chance! (Good luck!)

Géoculture Overview

Paris

Bienvenue! This section is designed to familiarize the students with the geographic location, history, and cultural practices of the region to be explored. It provides a guide for classroom discussion and discovery of the differences and similarities of the student's own culture and that of the French-speaking world.

50-Minute Lesson Plans

Day 1

Lesson Sequence

Géoculture: Paris, pp. xxii–1

- Ask students what they have heard or read about Paris. Have they or a family member visited Paris? What sights did they visit or would like to visit? Why? **12 min.**
- Go over the photos and captions with students. **10 min.**
- See Map Activities, p. T72. **5 min.**
- Talk about geographic features on the map. Have students compare the infrastructure of Paris to that of a city of comparable size in the U.S. **9 min.**
- Complete **Géo-quiz**. **1 min.**
- Show **Géoculture** video. **3 min.**
- Have students answer **Questions,** p. 1. **10 min.**

Optional Resources

- Background Information, p. T72
- **Savais-tu que...?,** p. 1
- Thinking Critically, p. T71
- Research Online!, p. T71

Homework Suggestions

Online Practice (**my.hrw.com**)

1.2, 2.1, 2.2, 3.1, 4.2

Day 2

Lesson Sequence

Géoculture: Paris, pp. 2–3

- Briefly revisit the main points about geography. **5 min.**
- Go over the photos and captions with students. **8 min.**
- Discuss the discoveries of Léon Foucault and Marie and Pierre Curie. Compare these to the discoveries by American scientists in the nineteenth century. **5 min.**
- Have students answer **As-tu compris?** questions, p. 3. **7 min.**
- Play the Map Game on p. T71 of the interleaf. **25 min.**

Optional Resources

- Advanced Learners, p. T71 ▲
- Special Learning Needs, p. T71 ●
- Interdisciplinary Links, pp. 2–3
- **Prépare-toi pour le quiz,** p. T71

Homework Suggestions

Activité, p. 3

Study for the **Géoculture** quiz.

1.1, 1.2, 1.3, 2.1, 2.2, 3.1, 3.2

90-Minute Lesson Plan

Block 1

Lesson Sequence

Géoculture: Paris, pp. xxii–3

- Ask students what they have heard or read about Paris. Have they or a family member visited Paris? What sights did they visit or would like to visit? Why? **10 min.**
- Go over the photos and captions with students. **20 min.**
- See Map Activities, p. T72. **5 min.**
- Talk about geographic features on the map. Have students compare the infrastructure of Paris to that of a city of comparable size in the U.S. **10 min.**
- Complete **Géo-quiz. 1 min.**
- Show **Géoculture** video. **4 min.**
- Have students answer **Questions,** p. 1. **5 min.**
- Have students answer **As-tu compris?** questions, p. 3. **5 min.**
- Ask students if they have learned anything about Paris that surprised them. Why? **5 min.**
- Play the Map Game on p. T71 of the interleaf. **25 min.**

Optional Resources

- Background Information, p. T72
- **Savais-tu que...?,** p. 1
- Advanced Learners, p. T71 ▲
- Special Learning Needs, p. T71 ●
- Thinking Critically, p. T71
- Research Online!, p. T71
- Interdisciplinary Links, pp. 2–3
- **Prépare-toi pour le quiz,** p. T71

Homework Suggestions

Online Practice (**my.hrw.com**)

Activité, p. 3

Study for the **Géoculture** quiz.

1.1, 1.2, 1.3, 2.1, 3.1, 3.2, 4.2

KEY

▲ Advanced Learners ◆ Slower Pace Learners ● Special Learning Needs

Géoculture

Differentiated Instruction

Advanced Learners

Extension Have students create a timeline of five important events in the history of Paris. Students should do research in the library or on the Internet. They should provide the date and a two-sentence description of each event. Students may want to illustrate the events with photos. Have students present their timeline to the class. 1.3, 3.1

Special Learning Needs

Students with Visual Impairments Students may have trouble seeing how the photos relate to the text on the **Géoculture** pages. Have advanced learners describe the photos in French. The students with visual impairments should ask for clarifications if necessary. 1.2

Thinking Critically

Analysis Ask students to discuss why Napoleon decided to construct **L'Arc de Triomphe.** Can students think of other emperors who ordered the construction of triumphal arches? What was the purpose of these arches? (Napoleon commissioned the arch to commemorate the heroics of his **Grande Armée.** Its design, by Jean Chalgrin, is based on the Arch of Titus in Rome. Among the Roman emperors who commissioned triumphal arches are Titus, Constantine, and Septimus Severus.) 2.2, 3.1

Critical Thinking and Problem Solving

Quiz Preparation/Enrichment

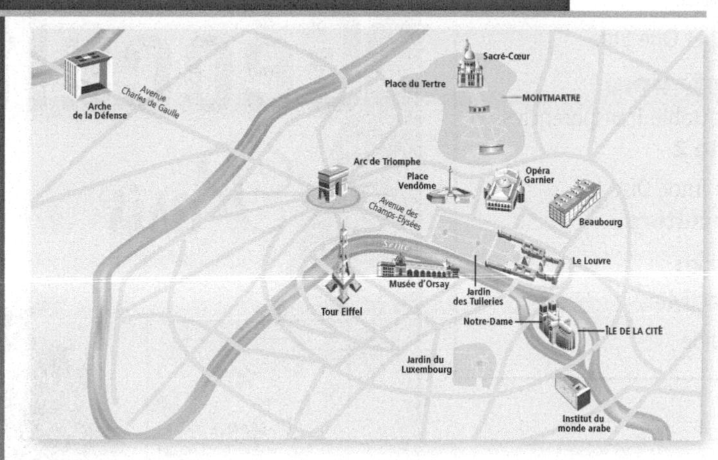

Map Game You will need a large map of Paris on which the districts are numbered and two pins with different-colored heads (or two small different-colored flags). Form two groups and assign each group a pin (or flag). Both pins are placed on the map at **Cimetière du Père Lachaise** in **arrondissement** 20. When a group correctly answers a question asked by the other group, it is allowed to move its pin to **arrondissement** 19. The groups take turns asking and answering questions. When a group answers correctly, it moves its pin until it reaches the **Jardin des Tuileries** in **arrondissement** 1. If a group asks a question that it itself cannot answer, it has to move its pin one **arrondissement** back. **Bonne route!** 1.1, 1.2, 3.1

Prépare-toi pour le quiz

1. Have students find a sight in each **arrondissement.**
2. Have students make a graphic organizer to group museums, parks, churches, plazas, and so on. 1.2

Musées	Parcs	Églises	Places
Le Louvre	Parc Montsouris	Notre-Dame	Place de la Concorde

Research Online!

Tour de Paris Have groups of students design a sightseeing tour of Paris. The tour should include at least five sights that are within walking distance of one another. Students should provide at least one photo or illustration and a brief description of each sight. Have each group present its tour to the class. As an alternative, students may post their tour on their Web site or the Web site of the class. Students should document their sources by noting the URLs of all the sites they consulted. 1.3, 3.1

Resources

Planning:
Lesson Planner
 Teacher One Stop

Presentation:
 Projectable Transparencies
Carte 2
 DVD Tutor, Disc 1
Géoculture

Practice:
Cahier d'activités
Media Guide

Map ACTIVITIES

1. Have students locate Paris on the map of France on page R2. Ask students why they think Paris became the economic and political center of France. (Trade was encouraged because Paris is located on a river, close to two other rivers and the sea. There are no geographic barriers to communication or trade.)
2. Have students find a map of Paris divided into **arrondissements** *(districts)* on the Internet or in a guidebook. Ask them how the **arrondissements** are laid out. (They spiral clockwise from the center.) Tell students that **arrondisse-ment** numbers form the last digits in a district's zip code.

Chapitres 1 et 2

Géoculture

Paris

Géoculture

▲ **La Grande Arche de la Défense**
Cette arche immense est alignée avec l'Arc de Triomphe et le Louvre. À l'intérieur, il y a des bureaux *(offices)*. ❷

◀ **L'Arc de Triomphe**
Napoléon a ordonné la construction de ce monument en 1806. Il se situe au croisement de 12 avenues. ❶

Almanach

Nom des habitants
Les Parisiens

Population
Plus de 2 millions d'habitants

Personnages célèbres
Jacques Chirac, Catherine Deneuve, Édith Piaf, Jean-Paul Sartre

▼ **Les cafés**
Les Parisiens aiment se retrouver au café. Le café de Flore et Les Deux Magots sont deux cafés célèbres à Paris.

Savais-tu que...?

La ville de Paris est divisée en 20 quartiers *(neighborhoods)* appelés «arrondissements».

Background Information

 Geography

Paris lies in a basin ringed by seven hills. The Seine flows from east to west in a seven-mile arc, dividing the city between **la rive gauche** (Left Bank) and **la rive droite** (Right Bank). It then curves north, passing **la Défense.** The **île de la Cité** and **île St-Louis,** two islands in the middle of the Seine, form the heart of the city. The distances of all main roads are measured from **le point zéro des routes de France,** just outside of Notre-Dame on **île de la Cité.**

History

Paris was first settled in the 3rd century BC by a tribe of Celtic Gauls, called the Parisii. The Romans then ruled the city from 52 BC until the 5th century when the Germanic Franks took control. The Frankish king, Clovis I, united Gaul, France's name at the time, and made Paris the capital of his kingdom in 508. Except for two periods during France's history, Paris has been the country's capital. Point out to students the relationship between Paris's early occupants and the names *Paris* and *France.*

Paris

Le Louvre, d'abord forteresse, puis palais royal, est un grand musée aujourd'hui. La pyramide en verre a été construite par l'Américain I.M. Pei. 3

L'Institut du monde arabe symbolise les échanges entre les deux cultures. C'est un bâtiment moderne inspiré par l'architecture arabe traditionnelle. 4

Notre-Dame de Paris Sa construction a commencé en 1163. C'est un chef-d'œuvre de l'art gothique. 5

La place du Tertre, à Montmartre, a conservé une atmosphère de village. C'est le rendez-vous des artistes locaux. 6

Les catacombes Au 18e siècle, on a vidé *(emptied)* certains cimetières parisiens trop pleins et mis les ossements *(bones)* dans le sous-sol de Paris.

Géo-quiz des bureaux 2.2
Qu'est-ce qu'il y a dans la Grande Arche de la Défense?

Connections

Art Link

In the late 19th and early 20th centuries, many important artists lived or worked near the **place du Tertre** in Montmartre. One of the most famous was Pablo Picasso, who, from 1904 to 1909, lived and painted in a building called Le Bateau-Lavoir. Other artists who drew inspiration from and worked in the area are Vincent van Gogh, Henri Matisse, Pierre-Auguste Renoir, Edgar Degas, and Toulouse Lautrec. Show students paintings by these artists and ask them if they recognize any of the works. You might show students several of their works so that they can recognize each artist's style when they see it. 3.1

Cultures

Practices and Perspectives

At the base of the **Arc de Triomphe,** the remains of an unknown soldier from World War I are buried. Every evening at 6:30, people lay wreathes of blue, white, and red on the tomb and relight a torch. This flame symbolizes the sacrifices made by young men who died during the war. Ask students why they think this practice continues even though World War I took place a long time ago. Ask them if they know where there is a similar monument and ceremony in the United States. (Arlington National Cemetery) 2.1, 4.2

Savais-tu que...?

Students might be interested in knowing the following facts about Paris.

- Paris is known as **la Ville lumière,** but few agree on the origin of this nickname. Some say it stems from the many lights that illuminate the city and its monuments, while others claim it is due to Paris's cultural and intellectual energy.
- The Louvre is over 800 years old. Designated a museum in 1793, its collection has over 300,000 works, assembled over five centuries. Some of the most important pieces in its collection are **La Joconde,** or *Mona Lisa,* and the *Venus de Milo.*

Questions

1.2

1. **Comment s'appellent deux cafés célèbres à Paris? (le café de Flore et Les Deux Magots)**
2. **Qui a ordonné la construction de l'Arc de Triomphe? (Napoléon)**
3. **Où est le rendez-vous des artistes locaux? (la place du Tertre)**
4. **Quelle organisation symbolise les échanges entre les cultures arabe et française? (l'Institut du monde arabe)**
5. **Où est-ce qu'on a mis les ossements à Paris au 18e siècle? (dans les catacombes)**

Pre-AP Language Examination

ACTIVITÉ PRÉ-AP PRÉPARATOIRE

Géoculture helps students better understand practices, products, and perspectives of French-speaking cultures and their relationship to one another. It can be used to practice for the **Interpretive Communication** and **Presentational Writing** sections of the AP Language and Culture Exam.

Connections

Language Note

Tennis originated in France, and many of the terms used internationally in today's game are adaptations of borrowed French words. The name *tennis* is probably derived from **tenez,** meaning *catch, here you are,* or *be ready.* The term *service* originates from the fact that royalty thought it demeaning to put the ball in play and had a servant do it. The score *love*, which means that the player has zero points, may be derived from **œuf,** since an egg and the number zero have the same shape. Ask students what they think the origin of the score *deuce* is. Deuce means tied at 40-40, each player having won three points. (It originates from **à deux,** indicating that a player must win two more consecutive points to win the game.) 3.2, 4.1

Connections

Science Link

Since opening its doors in 1986, the **Cité des Sciences et de l'Industrie** has welcomed over 40 million visitors. This popular science park consists of several museums and theaters where visitors can engage in interactive activities related to all aspects of science and technology. Exhibits and films have ranged from the exploration of space and how the brain works to the science of Jules Verne and the digital age. Have students go to the Cité Web site, do one of its Internet activities, and report back to the class what they learned. 1.3, 3.1

Découvre Paris

Sports

Le Tour de France se termine toujours sur les Champs-Élysées en juillet.

Le Tournoi des Six Nations est un championnat de rugby. Les équipes de France, d'Angleterre, d'Écosse, du Pays de Galles *(Wales)*, d'Irlande et d'Italie y participent.

Les Internationaux de France ont lieu chaque année au stade Roland-Garros. C'est un tournoi de tennis sur terre battue *(clay)*.

Sciences

Marie et Pierre Curie ont fait des recherches sur la radioactivité et ont découvert le polonium et le radium. Ils ont reçu le Prix Nobel de physique en 1903.

Le pendule de Foucault En 1851, le physicien Léon Foucault a créé ce pendule pour montrer la rotation de la terre sur son axe.

La Cité des Sciences et de l'Industrie est un musée consacré aux progrès de la technologie.

Interdisciplinary Links

Les sports 1.3, 3.1

Geography Link The **Tour de France** may be one of the greatest and most challenging sporting events in the world. This cycling race takes place every year over three weeks in July, traveling through France and sometimes its neighboring countries. Although the route changes every year, it always ends on the Champs-Élysées in Paris. Have students research the route of the latest tour and plot it on a map of France and neighboring countries if appropriate.

Les sciences 3.1

Science Link When Marie and Pierre Curie discovered radium, they almost immediately saw the possible impact this chemical element could have on medicine. Not only did they find that radium gives off heat and light, but Pierre discovered that it could damage living organisms when he exposed it to his flesh. This meant that new ways to treat cancer and other illnesses might be possible. Have students research radium on the Internet and list several ways it is used today in the field of medicine.

Paris

Activité

1. Les Internationaux de France
2. Marie et Pierre Curie
3. des étoiles
4. au printemps et en automne

Cultures

Practices and Perspectives

Despite having excellent restaurants with some of the richest food, Parisians and the rest of the French manage to stay thin. Parisians eat slowly and have small portions. Ask students if they can think of any social, economic, or cultural reasons why this might be so. Have students discuss their own cultural values regarding portion sizes and time spent eating. 2.1

As-tu compris?

You can use the following questions to check students' comprehension of **Géoculture.**

1. **Qu'est-ce que le pendule de Foucault montre? (la rotation de la terre sur son axe)**
2. **Le Tournoi des Six Nations est un championnat de quel sport? (le rugby)**
3. **Qu'est-ce que le nombre d'étoiles d'un restaurant indique? (la qualité de la cuisine)**
4. **Où est-ce que le Tour de France se termine? (sur les Champs-Élysées)**
5. **Quand est-ce que les couturiers présentent leurs collections? (au printemps et en automne)** 1.2

Assess

Assessment Program

Quiz: Géoculture

Differentiated Practice and Assessment CD-Rom

Online Assessment

my.hrw.com

Test Generator 

Gastronomie

Online Practice

my.hrw.com
Photo Tour

La haute cuisine française
Paris symbolise la haute cuisine française qui est réputée dans le monde entier.

Les chocolatiers de Paris mélangent le chocolat avec des épices, des fruits et même des fleurs pour créer des saveurs nouvelles.

Savais-tu que...?
Il y a plus de restaurants à Paris que dans aucune autre ville de la même grandeur.

Les restaurants parisiens
Chaque année, les meilleurs *(best)* chefs reçoivent des «étoiles» pour la qualité de leur cuisine, avec un maximum de trois étoiles. Il y a plusieurs restaurants «trois étoiles» à Paris.

Mode

Les magasins de luxe
Avec ses parfumeries, ses maroquineries et ses autres magasins spécialisés, Paris est la ville idéale pour faire du shopping!

Les grands bijoutiers
Beaucoup de bijoutiers connus ont leurs magasins sur la place Vendôme, à Paris.

La haute couture
Paris est la capitale de la haute couture. Les grands couturiers y présentent leurs collections deux fois par an, au printemps et en automne.

Activité

2.2

1. **Sports**: Quel tournoi a lieu au stade Roland-Garros?
2. **Sciences**: Qui a découvert le polonium et le radium?
3. **Gastronomie**: Qu'est-ce que les bons chefs reçoivent?
4. **Mode**: Quand est-ce que les couturiers présentent leurs collections?

La gastronomie 3.1

Health Link **Haute cuisine** is a cooking style characterized by complex, rich dishes. It was developed by Marie-Antoine Carême (1784–1833), who reorganized traditional French cooking into a comprehensive whole. Auguste Escoffier (1846–1935) further refined the style, creating a hierarchy of sauces with basic ingredients to use in classic dishes. Have students find recipes for these sauces: **Béchamel, Velouté, Espagnole,** and **Hollandaise.** Then have them determine which sauce is the most healthful and which is the least healthful, based on their fat and caloric content.

La mode 3.2

Economics Link Fashion and luxury goods make up an important sector of the French economy. These high-value items include clothes, cosmetics, perfume, jewelry, furs, and leather goods. Industries producing these goods bring in over 28 billion euros in revenue annually and employ over 234,000 people. Many of them are headquartered in Paris. Have students find out the approximate percentage of the French Gross Domestic Product (France's total earnings) attibutable to fashion and luxury goods.

chapitre 1

Planning Guide

Ma famille et mes copains

Chapter Section		Resources
Vocabulaire 1 • Family, descriptive adjectives **Grammaire 1** • Review of the verbs **avoir** and **être** • Review of adjective agreement **Application 1** • **Un peu plus:** The adjectives **beau**, **nouveau**, **vieux**	pp. 6–9 pp. 10–13 pp. 14–15	Projectable Transparencies: Vocabulaire 1.1, 1.2; Bell Work 1.1, 1.2, 1.3, 1.4 Cahier de vocabulaire et grammaire, pp. 1–6 Grammar Tutor for Students of French Cahier d'activités, pp. 1–3 Media Guide, pp. 1–4, 46–48 **Assessment Program** Quiz: Vocabulaire 1, pp. 3–4 Quiz: Grammaire 1, pp. 5–6 Quiz: Application 1, pp. 7–8
Culture • **Culture appliquée: La cursive** • **Comparaisons et Communauté**	pp. 16–17	Cahier d'activités, p. 4
Vocabulaire 2 • Leisure activities, café foods **Grammaire 2** • Review of **-er** verbs • Review of **-ir** and **-re** verbs **Application 2** • **Un peu plus:** Verbs like **dormir**	pp. 18–21 pp. 22–25 pp. 26–27	Projectable Transparencies: Vocabulaire 1.3, 1.4; Bell Work 1.5, 1.6, 1.7, 1.8 Cahier de vocabulaire et grammaire, pp. 7–12 Grammar Tutor for Students of French Cahier d'activités, pp. 5–7 Media Guide, pp. 1–4, 46–47, 49 **Assessment Program** Quiz: Vocabulaire 2, pp. 9–10 Quiz: Grammaire 2, pp. 11–12 Quiz: Application 2, pp. 13–14
Télé-roman	pp. 28–29	Media Guide, pp. 47, 50
Lecture et écriture	pp. 30–33	Cahier d'activités, p. 8 Reading Strategies and Skills Handbook Intermediate Reader French InterActive Reader **Assessment Program** Quiz: Lecture, p. 15 Quiz: Écriture, p. 16
Prépare-toi pour l'examen • **Résumé de vocabulaire et grammaire** • **Lettres et sons** **Révisions cumulatives**	pp. 34–37 pp. 38–39	Independent Study Guide, pp. 1–3, 33 Media Guide, p. 4 **Assessment Program** Examen: Chapitre 1, pp. 17–22 Examen oral: Chapitre 1, p. 317 Projectable Transparencies: Fine Art, Ch. 1 Cahier d'activités, pp. 4, 9–10
Variations littéraires • **Paris-plage**	pp. 382–383	Reading Strategies and Skills Handbook Intermediate Reader French InterActive Reader

Visit Us Online

my.hrw.com
Online Edition

Pacing Suggestions

	Essential	Recommended	Optional
Vocabulaire 1 • Family, descriptive adjectives • **Flash culture**	✔		
Grammaire 1 • Review of the verbs **avoir** and **être** • Review of adjective agreement • **Flash culture**	✔		
Application 1 • **Un peu plus:** The adjectives **beau**, **nouveau**, **vieux**	✔		
Culture • **Culture appliquée: La cursive** • **Comparaisons et Communauté**		✔	
Vocabulaire 2 • Leisure activities, café foods • **Flash culture**	✔		
Grammaire 2 • Review of **-er** verbs • Review of **-ir** and **-re** verbs • **Flash culture**	✔		
Application 2 • **Un peu plus:** Verbs like **dormir**	✔		
Télé-roman • Épisode 1: **Le Secret de la statuette**			✔
Lecture et écriture • **Le vieux piano, L'enfant à l'harmonica** (Lecture) • **Vacances en famille** (Écriture)		✔	
Prépare-toi pour l'examen		✔	
Révisions cumulatives			✔
Variations littéraires • **Paris-plage**			✔

Technology

Bien dit! Online
- Student Edition with multi-media
- **performance space** recording tool
- Interactive activities with feedback
- Self-tests with feedback
- Cahier d'activités (Interactive workbook)
- Cahier de vocabulaire et grammaire (Interactive workbook)
- Holt Online Assessment

DVD Tutor
- Télé-vocab
- Grammavision
- Télé-roman

@HOMETUTOR
- Interactive games
- Differentiated Practice
- Cultural video

Audio Program
- Student Edition listening activities
- Assessment listening activities
- Songs

Teacher One Stop
- Complete resources
- ExamView Pro Test Generator
- Holt Calendar Planner

Holt McDougal Apps

Interactive Whiteboard Lessons

Differentiated Practice and Assessment CD

For slower pace and advanced learner options, see the Differentiated Practice and Assessment CD.

Planning Guide

Projects

Album de photos

Students will choose photographs of themselves and their friends and create a photo album. Students may use magazine photos if they prefer. 1.3

Suggested Sequence

1. Have students list at least five people, including themselves, whom they want to include in their album. You may wish to have them create a graphic organizer to include words and phrases to describe each person. They should also include the age, two activities, and two likes and dislikes of each person.
2. Have students choose photos, magazine pictures, or draw sketches of each person they are featuring in the album.
3. Students then write drafts of their descriptions. You may wish to have partners exchange drafts for peer editing.
4. Have them assemble their albums with construction paper and the photos and descriptions they created.
5. Have students design and make a cover for their album. They can punch holes in the construction paper and the cover and thread them together to complete the project.

Grading the project

Suggested point distribution (100 points total)

Completion of assignment	25 pts.
Vocabulary use	25 pts.
Presentation/Creativity	25 pts.
Language use	25 pts.

Partner Class Project

Have students write a letter of introduction to an e-mail buddy. (For privacy and security, you might create a series of anonymous, numbered e-mail addresses.) Assign each student the address of an e-mail buddy from his or her class or another class. In their letter of introduction, have students include the following information: a greeting, their name (or class French name), how they are doing, age, birthday, physical description (two adjectives minimum), and personality (three adjectives minimum). They should also mention two things they like and two things they dislike. Remind students to find out the same information from their e-mail buddy by asking questions. 1.1, 1.2

Communication

e-community

e-mail forum:

Location: http://french

Post the following questions on the classroom e-mail forum:

Qu'est-ce que tu as fait hier soir?
As-tu regardé la télé?
As-tu fait tes devoirs?
5.1

All students will contribute to the list and then share the items.

Game Bank
For game ideas, see pages T60–T63.

Loisirs

Every day, Parisians escape the hustle and bustle of Paris by taking a stroll or sitting in one of the city's many parks and gardens. One of the most popular parks is the **Jardin du Luxembourg**. As the day passes, the park fills with children playing, workers enjoying a picnic lunch or snack, and retirees playing chess or **pétanque**, a type of lawn bowling. However, it is on the weekends that the grounds really come alive. Children ride ponies or the 100-year-old carousel and watch the marionette show at the **Grand Guignol**. Teens and adults play tennis, jog, or sit on the many park benches, chatting with friends or reading. As is the case in many of the parks in France, walking or sitting on the grass is forbidden. Have students conduct an Internet search to get more information about this and other famous parks in Paris.

2.1

La cuisine

The neighborhood in Paris called **les Halles** was once full of markets that sold produce to restaurants and stores in the early hours of the morning. Farmers and store managers would gather in cafés before or after work to enjoy a hot bowl of onion soup. **Les Halles** is now a shopping mall, but many cafés in the area have kept the tradition alive and stay open 24 hours a day. Artists often meet there after their evening performances in local theatres or concert halls. Encourage students to make **gratinée des Halles** in their foods class or at home for family and friends.

1.2, 2.2

Gratinée des Halles

pour 6 personnes

4 gros oignons
4 cuillères à soupe de beurre
1 cuillère à soupe d'huile
1 cuillère à soupe de farine
4 tasses de bouillon
1 cuillère à café de sucre
3 tasses de gruyère râpé
1 baguette
sel et poivre

Peler et couper les oignons. Faire cuire les oignons avec le sucre dans le mélange beurre-huile jusqu'à ce qu'ils deviennent bruns. Ajouter la farine et mélanger. Ajouter le bouillon. Saler et poivrer. Laisser cuire pendant 20 minutes. Faire griller la baguette. Mettre le pain grillé dans des bols individuels. Recouvrir de gruyère râpé. Verser la soupe par-dessus, rajouter du fromage râpé et gratiner.

Listening Activity Scripts

Vocabulaire à l'œuvre 1

2 p. 8, CD 1, Tr. 1

1. — Oh, c'est ta famille?
   — Oui. Il y a moi, ma sœur Sonia, son mari, Olivier, mon frère Laurent et ma tante.
2. — Sonia te ressemble beaucoup!
   — Oui, c'est vrai. Elle est grande, mince et brune comme moi, mais elle a les cheveux courts. Elle adore les animaux.
3. — Et Olivier, comment est-il?
   — Il a de beaux yeux verts et il est intelligent. Il n'est pas très sportif.
4. — Quel âge a ton frère?
   — Sept ans. Laurent est petit et sympa, mais il peut être assez pénible.
5. — C'est qui, la femme là?
   — Ma cousine Émilie. Elle est rousse avec les yeux bleus. Elle est un peu timide, mais charmante.

Answers to Activity 2
1. b 2. b 3. b 4. a 5. a

Grammaire à l'œuvre 1

7 p. 10, CD 1, Tr. 2

1. Notre grand-mère est très marrante.
2. Il est timide, Jean-Claude, non?
3. Dans ma famille, nous sommes six. Mon père a quarante ans.
4. Qu'est-ce que tu es pénible alors!
5. Elle n'a pas les cheveux blonds.
6. Karine est brune.

Answers to Activity 7
1. a 2. a 3. b 4. a 5. c 6. c

11 p. 12, CD 1, Tr. 3

1. Dominique est très sportif.
2. Dominique est petite avec les yeux bleus.
3. Dominique est assez jeune.
4. Dominique n'est pas du tout ennuyeuse!
5. Dominique est trop sérieux.
6. Dominique est très grand.
7. Dominique est sympathique.
8. Dominique est toujours heureuse!

Answers to Activity 11
1. a 2. b 3. c 4. b 5. a 6. a 7. c 8. b

Vocabulaire à l'œuvre 2

23 p. 20, CD 1, Tr. 4

1. — Camille, tu veux faire de la photo avec moi après l'école?
   — Oui, je veux bien. J'ai un nouvel appareil photo.
2. — Qu'est-ce que tu as envie de manger ce midi?
   — J'ai envie de manger un croque-monsieur.
3. — Ahmed, est-ce que tu joues bien de la batterie?
   — Assez bien.
   — On cherche quelqu'un qui joue de la batterie pour notre groupe de rock.
4. — Ludivine, ça te dit de faire les magasins cet après-midi?
   — Non, je n'ai pas le temps. Je vais faire de la vidéo avec ma sœur.
5. — Qu'est-ce que tu penses de ma nouvelle raquette?
   — Elle est géniale!

Answers to Activity 23
1. d 2. c 3. e 4. a 5. b

Grammaire à l'œuvre 2

31 p. 24, CD 1, Tr. 5

1. — Bonjour. Ça va?
   — Ça va très bien! J'ai eu dix-huit sur vingt en maths.
2. — Je vais faire les magasins. Tu viens avec moi?
   — Oui. Je bois mon café et j'arrive.
3. — Marine et moi, on va au café. Tu veux venir avec nous?
   — Non, je ne peux pas maintenant. Ma sœur doit arriver dans cinq minutes et nous devons aller à la bibliothèque.
4. — Je peux vous aider?
   — Oui, je voudrais acheter le bleu, s'il vous plaît.
5. — Bonjour, je cherche un livre de grammaire française.
   — Oui, c'est sur l'étagère là-bas.

Answers to Activity 31
1. d 2. e 3. b 4. a 5. c

Application 2

36 p. 26, CD 1, Tr. 6

1. — Salut, Mathias! Ça va? Tu vas où?
   — Je vais à mon cours de guitare. On se retrouve plus tard?
   — Si tu veux. À plus.
2. — J'ai faim. Valentine, tu veux venir avec moi chercher quelque chose à manger?
   — Si tu veux. J'aimerais bien manger un croque-monsieur.
   — Ce n'est pas une mauvaise idée. Mais je crois que je vais plutôt prendre un sandwich au jambon.
3. — Audrey, qu'est-ce que tu fais ce week-end?
   — J'ai un match de tennis samedi matin et après je n'ai rien de prévu. Ça te dit d'aller au cinéma après le match?
4. — Salut. Où est Benjamin?
   — Il fait de la photo au parc avec son nouvel appareil photo.
5. — Salut, Magali. Qu'est-ce que tu vas faire cet après-midi?
   — Je fais du théâtre à la MJC.

Answers to Activity 36
1. c 2. d 3. a 4. e 5. b

Prépare-toi pour l'examen

6 p. 35, CD 1, Tr. 10

— Géraldine, regarde le garçon qui arrive. C'est Marc, le cousin d'Alice. Il est beau, tu ne trouves pas?
— Oui, avec ses yeux bleus et ses cheveux noirs, il est super. Il a quel âge?
— Je ne sais pas, mais je crois qu'il a dix-sept ans, comme mon frère. Ils sont dans la même classe. Écoute, tu veux aller au parc avec moi demain? C'est jeudi et Marc et ses copains jouent au foot au parc tous les jeudis!

Answers to Activity 6
1. b 2. a 3. a 4. b 5. b

Dictée p. 36, CD 1, Tr. 13

1. Ta mère est souvent sérieuse.
2. Nous préférons l'été.
3. Je te présente mon père.
4. Ça te dit de jouer aux échecs?
5. Le garçon parle bien français.

Révisions cumulatives

1 p. 38, CD 1, Tr. 14

1. Ma grande sœur s'appelle Nathalie. Elle est rousse et elle a les cheveux courts. Elle est très marrante.
2. Ma cousine n' est pas très sympa. Elle est petite et elle a les cheveux longs et châtains.
3. Ma petite sœur s'appelle Micheline. Elle a les cheveux longs et blonds. Elle est très sportive.
4. Ma mère est prof de maths. Elle est grande et mince. Elle a les cheveux courts et noirs.

Answers to Activity 1
1. c 2. b 3. d 4. a

50-Minute Lesson Plans

Ma famille et mes copains

Day 1

OBJECTIVE
Describe yourself and ask about others

Core Instruction
Chapter Opener, pp. 4–5
- See Using the Photo, p. 4. **5 min.**
- See Chapter Objectives, p. 4. **5 min.**

Vocabulaire 1, pp. 6–9
- Present **Vocabulaire 1,** pp. 6–7. See Teaching **Vocabulaire,** p. 6. **10 min.**
- Show **Télé-vocab 1. 5 min.**
- Present **Exprimons-nous!,** p. 7. **10 min.**
- Do Activity 1, p. 8. **5 min.**
- Play Audio CD 1, Tr. 1 for Activity 2, p. 8. **5 min.**
- Present **Flash culture,** p. 8. **5 min.**

Optional Resources
- Slower Pace Learners, p. 7 ◆
- Special Learning Needs, p. 7 ●

Homework Suggestions
Cahier de vocabulaire et grammaire, pp. 1–2
@HOMETUTOR
1.2, 4.2

Day 2

OBJECTIVE
*Describe yourself and ask about others; Talk about likes and dislikes; Use the verbs **avoir** and **être***

Core Instruction
Vocabulaire 1, pp. 6–9
- Have students do Bell Work 1.1, p. 6. **5 min.**
- Have students do Activity 3, p. 8. **10 min.**
- See Teaching **Exprimons-nous!,** p. 8. **10 min.**
- Have students do Activities 4–5, p. 9. **15 min.**

Grammaire 1, pp. 10–13
- See Teaching **Grammaire,** p. 10. **5 min.**
- Show **Grammavision 1.1. 5 min.**

Optional Resources
- Advanced Learners, p. 9 ▲
- Multiple Intelligences, p. 9

Homework Suggestions
Study for **Quiz: Vocabulaire 1**
Cahier de vocabulaire et grammaire, p. 3
1.1, 1.2

Day 3

OBJECTIVE
*Use the verbs **avoir** and **être***

Core Instruction
Vocabulaire 1, pp. 6–9
- Review **Vocabulaire 1,** pp. 6–9. **10 min.**
- Give **Quiz: Vocabulaire 1. 20 min.**

Grammaire 1, pp. 10–13
- Have students do Activity 6, p. 10. **5 min.**
- Play Audio CD 1, Tr. 2 for Activity 7, p. 10. **5 min.**
- Have students do Activities 8–10, p. 11. **10 min.**

Optional Resources
- Communities, p. 11
- Slower Pace Learners, p. 11 ◆
- Special Learning Needs, p. 11 ●

Homework Suggestions
Cahier de vocabulaire et grammaire, p. 4
Cahier d'activités, p. 1
Online Practice (**my.hrw.com**)
1.1, 1.2, 1.3, 5.1

Day 4

OBJECTIVE
*Use adjective agreement; Use the adjectives **beau, nouveau, vieux***

Core Instruction
Grammaire 1, pp. 10–13
- Present **Flash culture,** p. 12. **5 min.**
- See Teaching **Grammaire,** p. 12. **10 min.**
- Show **Grammavision 1.2. 5 min.**
- Play Audio CD 1, Tr. 3 for Activity 11, p. 12. **5 min.**
- Do Activities 12–15, pp. 12–13. **15 min.**

Application 1, pp. 14–15
- Do Activity 16, p. 14. **5 min.**
- See Teaching **Un peu plus,** p. 14. **5 min.**

Optional Resources
- Advanced Learners, p. 13 ▲

Homework Suggestions
Study for **Quiz: Grammaire 1**
Cahier de vocabulaire et grammaire, p. 5
Cahier d'activités, p. 2
1.1, 1.2, 1.3, 4.2

Day 5

OBJECTIVE
*Use the adjectives **beau, nouveau, vieux***

Core Instruction
Grammaire 1, pp. 10–13
- Review **Grammaire 1,** pp. 10–13. **10 min.**
- Give **Quiz: Grammaire 1. 20 min.**

Application 1, pp. 14–15
- Have students do Activities 17–21, pp. 14–15. **20 min.**

Optional Resources
- Connections, p. 15
- Communication (TE), p. 15
- Slower Pace Learners, p. 15 ◆
- Multiple Intelligences, p. 15

Homework Suggestions
Study for **Quiz: Application 1**
Cahier de vocabulaire et grammaire, p. 6
Cahier d'activités, p. 3
Online Practice (**my.hrw.com**)
1.1, 1.2, 1.3, 3.1

Day 6

OBJECTIVE
Learn about francophone culture

Core Instruction
Application 1, pp. 14–15
- Review **Application 1,** pp. 14–15. **10 min.**
- Give **Quiz: Application 1. 20 min.**

Culture, pp. 16–17
- See **Culture appliquée** (TE), p. 16. **10 min.**
- See **Comparaisons et communauté** (TE), p. 16. **10 min.**

Optional Resources
- Connections, p. 17
- Cultures, p. 17
- Advanced Learners, p. 17 ▲
- Special Learning Needs, p. 17 ●

Homework Suggestions
Cahier d'activités, p. 4
Online Practice (**my.hrw.com**)
Finish **Culture appliquée** project
1.3, 2.1, 2.2, 3.1, 4.2, 5.1

Day 7

OBJECTIVE
Inquire and respond

Core Instruction
Vocabulaire 2, pp. 18–21
- Have students do Bell Work 1.5, p. 18. **5 min.**
- Present **Vocabulaire 2,** pp. 18–19. See Teaching **Vocabulaire,** p. 18. **10 min.**
- Show **Télé-vocab 2. 5 min.**
- Present **Exprimons-nous!,** p. 19. **10 min.**
- Have students do Activity 22, p. 20. **5 min.**
- Play Audio CD 1, Tr. 4 for Activity 23, p. 20. **5 min.**
- Have students do Activity 24, p. 20. **5 min.**
- Present **Flash culture,** p. 20. **5 min.**

Optional Resources
- TPR, p. 19
- Advanced Learners, p. 19 ▲
- Multiple Intelligences, p. 19

Homework Suggestions
Cahier de vocabulaire et grammaire, pp. 7–8
1.1, 1.2, 1.3, 4.2

Day 8

OBJECTIVE
*Tell when you do something; Use **-er** verbs*

Core Instruction
Vocabulaire 2, pp. 18–21
- See Teaching **Exprimons-nous!,** p. 20. **10 min.**
- Have students do Activities 25–26, p. 21. **20 min.**

Grammaire 2, pp. 22–25
- See Teaching **Grammaire,** p. 22. **10 min.**
- Show **Grammavision 2.1. 5 min.**
- Have students do Activity 27, p. 22. **5 min.**

Optional Resources
- Slower Pace Learners, p. 21 ◆
- Multiple Intelligences, p. 21
- Special Learning Needs, p. 23 ●

Homework Suggestions
Study for **Quiz: Vocabulaire 2**
Cahier de vocabulaire et grammaire, p. 9
Online Practice (**my.hrw.com**)
1.1, 1.2, 1.3

To edit and create your own lesson plans, see the **Teacher One Stop™**

KEY
- ▲ Advanced Learners
- ◆ Slower Pace Learners
- ● Special Learning Needs

50-Minute Lesson Plans

Day 9

OBJECTIVE
Use ***-er*** *verbs*

Core Instruction

Vocabulaire 2, pp. 18–21
- Review **Vocabulaire 2,** pp. 18–21. **10 min.**
- Give **Quiz: Vocabulaire 2. 20 min.**

Grammaire 2, pp. 22–25
- Have students do Activities 28–30, p. 23. **20 min.**

Optional Resources
- French for Spanish Speakers, p. 23
- Communication (TE), p. 23
- Advanced Learners, p. 23 ▲

Homework Suggestions

Cahier de vocabulaire et grammaire, p. 10
Cahier d'activités, p. 5
@HOMETUTOR
Online Practice (**my.hrw.com**)

1.1, 1.2, 1.3, 4.1

Day 10

OBJECTIVE
Use ***-ir*** *and* ***-re*** *verbs*

Core Instruction

Grammaire 2, pp. 22–25
- Do Bell Work 1.7, p. 24. **5 min.**
- Present **Flash culture,** p. 24. **5 min.**
- See Teaching **Grammaire,** p. 24. **5 min.**
- Show **Grammavision 2.2. 5 min.**
- Play Audio CD 1, Tr. 5 for Activity 31, p. 24. **5 min.**
- Have students do Activities 32–35, pp. 24–25. **15 min.**

Application 2, pp. 26–27
- Play Audio CD 1, Tr. 6 for Activity 36, p. 26. **5 min.**
- Do Activity 37, p. 26. **5 min.**

Optional Resources
- Slower Pace Learners, p. 25 ◆
- Multiple Intelligences, p. 25

Homework Suggestions

Study for **Quiz: Grammaire 2**
Cahier de vocabulaire et grammaire, p. 11
Cahier d'activités, p. 6

1.1, 1.2, 1.3, 4.2

Day 11

OBJECTIVE
Use verbs like ***dormir***

Core Instruction

Grammaire 2, pp. 22–25
- Review **Grammaire 2,** pp. 22–25. **10 min.**
- Give **Quiz: Grammaire 2. 20 min.**

Application 2, pp. 26–27
- See Teaching **Un peu plus,** p. 26. **5 min.**
- Have students do Activities 38–41, pp. 26–27. **15 min.**

Optional Resources
- Communication (TE), p. 27
- Advanced Learners, p. 27 ▲
- Special Learning Needs, p. 27 ●

Homework Suggestions

Study for **Quiz: Application 2**
Cahier de vocabulaire et grammaire, p. 12
Cahier d'activités, p. 7
Online Practice (**my.hrw.com**)

1.1, 1.2, 1.3

Day 12

OBJECTIVE
Develop listening and reading skills

Core Instruction

Application 2, pp. 26–27
- Review **Application 2,** pp. 26–27. **10 min.**
- Give **Quiz: Application 2. 20 min.**

Télé-roman, pp. 28–29
- Show **Télé-roman.** See Teaching **Télé-roman,** p. 28. **5 min.**
- Have students answer the **As-tu compris?** questions, p. 29. **15 min.**

Optional Resources
- Connections, p. 28
- Gestures, p. 28
- Communication (TE), p. 29

Homework Suggestions

Online Practice (**my.hrw.com**)

1.1, 1.2, 3.2

Day 13

OBJECTIVE
Develop listening, reading, and writing skills

Core Instruction

Lecture et écriture, pp. 30–33
- See Teaching **Lecture,** p. 30. **35 min.**
- See Teaching **Espace écriture,** p. 32. **15 min.**

Optional Resources
- Applying the Strategies, p. 30
- Considering Genre, p. 30
- Comparisons, p. 31
- Connections, p. 31
- Slower Pace Learners, p. 31 ◆
- Special Learning Needs, p. 31 ●
- Comparisons, p. 32
- Advanced Learners, p. 33 ▲
- Special Learning Needs, p. 33 ●

Homework Suggestions

Cahier d'activités, p. 5
Espace écriture, Activity 3, p. 33

1.2, 1.3, 3.1, 4.1

Day 14

OBJECTIVE
Develop writing skills; Review the chapter

Core Instruction

Lecture et écriture, pp. 30–33
- See Teaching **Espace écriture,** p. 32. **25 min.**

Prépare-toi pour l'examen, pp. 34–36
- Have students do Activities 1–5, pp. 34–35. **25 min.**

Optional Resources
- Writing Assessment, p. 33
- Reteaching, p. 34
- **Proverbes,** p. 34
- Fold-N-Learn, p. 34
- Oral Assessment, p. 35

Homework Suggestions

Online Practice (**my.hrw.com**)

1.2, 1.3, 2.1

Day 15

OBJECTIVE
Review the chapter

Core Instruction

Prépare-toi pour l'examen, pp. 34–36
- Play Audio CD 1, Tr. 10 for Activity 6, p. 35. **5 min.**
- Have students do Activity 7, p. 35. **5 min.**
- Play Audio CD 1, Tr. 11–13 for **Lettres et sons,** p. 36. **10 min.**

Révisions cumulatives, pp. 38–39
- Play Audio CD 1, Tr. 14 for Activity 1, p. 38. **5 min.**
- Have students do Activities 2–6, pp. 38–39. **25 min.**

Optional Resources
- Game, p. 36
- Chapter Review, pp. 36–37
- Online Culture Project, p. 38
- Fine Art Connection, p. 39

Homework Suggestions

Study for Chapter Test
Online Practice (**my.hrw.com**)

1.1, 1.2, 1.3, 2.2, 3.1

Day 16/Test

Core Instruction

Chapter Test 50 min.

Optional Resources

Assessment Program
- Alternative Assessment
- Test Generator
- **Quiz: Lecture**
- **Quiz: Écriture**

Homework Suggestions

Cahier d'activités, pp. 9–10, 102–103
Online Practice (**my.hrw.com**)

90-Minute Lesson Plans

Ma famille et mes copains

Block 1

OBJECTIVE
Describe yourself and talk about others; Talk about likes and dislikes

Core Instruction

Chapter Opener, pp. 4–5
- See Using the Photo, p. 4. **5 min.**
- See Chapter Objectives, p. 4. **5 min.**

Vocabulaire 1, pp. 6–9
- Present **Vocabulaire 1,** pp. 6–7. See Teaching **Vocabulaire,** p. 6. **10 min.**
- Show **Télé-vocab 1. 5 min.**
- Present **Exprimons-nous!,** p. 7. **10 min.**
- Have students do Activity 1, p. 8. **5 min.**
- Play Audio CD 1, Tr. 1 for Activity 2, p. 8. **5 min.**
- Have students do Activity 3, p. 8. **5 min.**
- Present **Flash culture,** p. 8. **10 min.**
- See Teaching **Exprimons-nous!,** p. 8. **10 min.**
- Have students do Activities 4–5, p. 9. **20 min.**

Optional Resources

- Learning Tips, p. 5
- **Proverbes,** p. 6
- Connections, p. 6
- TPR, p. 7
- **Attention!,** p. 7
- Cultures, p. 7
- Slower Pace Learners, p. 7 ◆
- Special Learning Needs, p. 7 ●
- Comparisons, p. 9
- Communication (TE), p. 9
- Advanced Learners, p. 9 ▲
- Multiple Intelligences, p. 9

Homework Suggestions

Study for **Quiz: Vocabulaire 1**
Cahier de vocabulaire et grammaire, pp. 1–3
@HOMETUTOR
Online Practice (**my.hrw.com**)
1.1, 1.2, 1.3, 3.1, 4.2

Block 2

OBJECTIVE
*Use the verbs **avoir** and **être**; Use adjective agreement*

Core Instruction

Vocabulaire 1, pp. 6–9
- Review **Vocabulaire 1,** pp. 6–9. **10 min.**
- Give **Quiz: Vocabulaire 1. 20 min.**

Grammaire 1, pp. 10–13
- See Teaching **Grammaire,** p. 10. **5 min.**
- Show **Grammavision 1.1. 5 min.**
- Have students do Activity 6, p. 10. **5 min.**
- Play Audio CD 1, Tr. 2 for Activity 7, p. 10. **5 min.**
- Have students to Activities 8–10, p. 11. **15 min.**
- Present **Flash culture,** p. 12. **5 min.**
- See Teaching **Grammaire,** p. 12. **5 min.**
- Show **Grammavision 1.2. 5 min.**
- Play Audio CD 1, Tr. 3 for Activity 11, p. 12. **5 min.**
- Have students do Activities 12–13, pp. 12–13. **5 min.**

Optional Resources

- **Attention!,** p. 11
- Communities, p. 11
- Communication (TE), p. 11
- Slower Pace Learners, p. 11 ◆
- Special Learning Needs, p. 11 ●
- Advanced Learners, p. 13 ▲
- Special Learning Needs, p. 13 ●

Homework Suggestions

Study for **Quiz: Grammaire 1**
Cahier de vocabulaire et grammaire, pp. 4–5
Cahier d'activités, pp. 1–2
@HOMETUTOR
Online Practice (**my.hrw.com**)
1.1, 1.2, 1.3, 4.2, 5.1

Block 3

OBJECTIVE
*Use adjective agreement; Use the adjectives **beau, nouveau, vieux;** Learn about francophone culture*

Core Instruction

Grammaire 1, pp. 10–13
- Have students do Activities 14–15, p. 13. **10 min.**
- Review **Grammaire 1,** pp. 10–13. **10 min.**
- Give **Quiz: Grammaire 1. 20 min.**

Application 1, pp. 14–15
- Have students do Activity 16, p. 14. **10 min.**
- See Teaching **Un peu plus,** p. 14. **5 min.**
- Have students do Activities 17–21, pp. 14–15. **15 min.**

Culture, pp. 16–17
- See **Culture appliquée** (TE), p. 16. **10 min.**
- See **Comparaisons et communauté** (TE), p. 16. **10 min.**

Optional Resources

- Teacher to Teacher, p. 13
- Communication (TE), p. 13
- Connections, p. 15
- Communication (TE), p. 15
- Slower Pace Learners, p. 15 ◆
- Multiple Intelligences, p. 15
- Connections, p. 17
- Cultures, p. 17
- Advanced Learners, p. 17 ▲
- Special Learning Needs, p. 17 ●

Homework Suggestions

Study for **Quiz: Application 1**
Cahier de vocabulaire et grammaire, p. 6
Cahier d'activités, pp. 3–4
@HOMETUTOR
Online Practice (**my.hrw.com**)
Finish **Culture appliquée** project
1.1, 1.2, 1.3, 2.1, 2.2, 3.1, 4.2, 5.1

Block 4

OBJECTIVE
Inquire and respond; Tell when you do something

Core Instruction

Application 1, pp. 14–15
- Review **Application 1,** pp. 14–15. **10 min.**
- Give **Quiz: Application 1. 20 min.**

Vocabulaire 2, pp. 18–21
- Present **Vocabulaire 2,** pp. 18–19. See Teaching **Vocabulaire,** p. 18. **10 min.**
- Show **Télé-vocab 2. 5 min.**
- Present **Exprimons-nous!,** p. 19. **5 min.**
- Have students do Activity 22, p. 20. **5 min.**
- Play Audio CD 1, Tr. 4 for Activity 23, p. 20. **5 min.**
- Have students do Activity 24, p. 20. **5 min.**
- Present **Flash culture,** p. 20. **5 min.**
- See Teaching **Exprimons-nous!,** p. 20. **10 min.**
- Have students do Activities 25–26, p. 21. **10 min.**

Optional Resources

- TPR, p. 19
- Cultures, p. 19
- Advanced Learners, p. 19 ▲
- Multiple Intelligences, p. 19
- Comparisons, p. 21
- Communication (TE), p. 21
- Slower Pace Learners, p. 21 ◆
- Multiple Intelligences, p. 21

Homework Suggestions

Study for **Quiz: Vocabulaire 2**
Cahier de vocabulaire et grammaire, pp. 7–9
@HOMETUTOR
Online Practice (**my.hrw.com**)
1.1, 1.2, 1.3, 2.2, 4.2

To edit and create your own lesson plans, see the **Teacher One Stop™**

KEY
- ▲ Advanced Learners
- ◆ Slower Pace Learners
- ● Special Learning Needs

Block 5

OBJECTIVE
Use ***-er*** *verbs; Use* ***-ir*** *and* ***-re*** *verbs*

Core Instruction

Vocabulaire 2, pp. 18–21
- Review **Vocabulaire 2,** pp. 18–21. **10 min.**
- Give **Quiz: Vocabulaire 2. 20 min.**

Grammaire 2, pp. 22–25
- See Teaching **Grammaire,** p. 22. **5 min.**
- Show **Grammavision 2.1. 5 min.**
- Have students do Activities 27–30, pp. 22–23. **20 min.**
- Present **Flash culture,** p. 24. **5 min.**
- See Teaching **Grammaire,** p. 24. **5 min.**
- Show **Grammavision 2.2. 5 min.**
- Play Audio CD 1, Tr. 5 for Activity 31, p. 24. **5 min.**
- Have students do Activities 32–33, pp. 24–25. **10 min.**

Optional Resources
- French for Spanish Speakers, p. 23
- Communication (TE), p. 23
- Advanced Learners, p. 23 ▲
- Special Learning Needs, p. 23 ●
- **Attention!,** p. 25
- Slower Pace Learners, p. 25 ◆
- Multiple Intelligences, p. 25

Homework Suggestions
Study for **Quiz: Grammaire 2**
Cahier de vocabulaire et grammaire, pp. 10–11
Cahier d'activités, pp. 5–6
HOMETUTOR
Online Practice (**my.hrw.com**)
1.1, 1.2, 1.3, 4.1, 4.2

Block 6

OBJECTIVE
Use ***-ir*** *and* ***-re*** *verbs; Use verbs like* ***dormir;*** *Develop listening and reading skills*

Core Instruction

Grammaire 2, pp. 22–25
- Have students do Activities 34–35, p. 25. **10 min.**
- Review **Grammaire 2,** pp. 22–25. **10 min.**
- Give **Quiz: Grammaire 2. 20 min.**

Application 2, pp. 26–27
- Play Audio CD 1, Tr. 6 for Activity 36, p. 26. **5 min.**
- Have students do Activity 37, p. 26. **5 min.**
- See Teaching **Un peu plus,** p. 26. **5 min.**
- Have students do Activities 38–41, pp. 26–27. **15 min.**

Télé-roman, pp. 28–29
- Show **Télé-roman.** See Teaching **Télé-roman,** p. 28. **5 min.**
- Have students answer the **As-tu compris?** questions, p. 29. **15 min.**

Optional Resources
- Communication (TE), p. 25
- Communication (TE), p. 27
- Advanced Learners, p. 27 ▲
- Special Learning Needs, p. 27 ●
- Connections, p. 28
- Gestures, p. 28
- Communication (TE), p. 29

Homework Suggestions
Study for **Quiz: Application 2**
Cahier de vocabulaire et grammaire, p. 12
Cahier d'activités, p. 7
Online Practice (**my.hrw.com**)
1.1, 1.2, 1.3, 3.2

Block 7

OBJECTIVE
Develop listening, reading, and writing skills; Review the chapter

Core Instruction

Application 2, pp. 26–27
- Review **Application 2,** pp. 26–27. **10 min.**
- Give **Quiz: Application 2. 20 min.**

Lecture et écriture, pp. 30–33
- See Teaching **Lecture,** p. 30. **20 min.**
- See Teaching **Espace écriture,** p. 32. **30 min.**

Prépare-toi pour l'examen, pp. 34–36
- Have students do Activities 1–3, p. 34. **10 min.**

Optional Resources
- Applying the Strategies, p. 30
- Considering Genre, p. 30
- Comparisons, p. 31
- Connections, p. 31
- Slower Pace Learners, p. 31 ◆
- Special Learning Needs, p. 31 ●
- Comparisons, p. 32
- Process Writing, p. 33
- Writing Assessment, p. 33
- Advanced Learners, p. 33 ▲
- Special Learning Needs, p. 33 ●
- Reteaching, p. 34
- Fold-N-Learn, p. 34

Homework Suggestions
Study for Chapter Test
Cahier d'activités, p. 8
Espace écriture, Activity 3, p. 33
Online Practice (**my.hrw.com**)
1.2, 1.3, 3.1, 4.1

Block 8

OBJECTIVE
Review and assess the chapter

Core Instruction

Prépare-toi pour l'examen, pp. 34–36
- Have students do Activities 4–5, p. 35. **5 min.**
- Play Audio CD 1, Tr. 10 for Activity 6, p. 35. **5 min.**
- Have students do Activity 7, p. 35. **5 min.**
- Play Audio CD 1, Tr. 11–13 for **Lettres et sons,** p. 36. **5 min.**

Chapter Test 50 min.

Révisions cumulatives, pp. 38–39
- Play Audio CD 1, Tr. 14 for Activity 1, p. 38. **5 min.**
- Have students do Activities 2–5, pp. 38–39. **15 min.**

Optional Resources
- TPRS, p. 34
- **Proverbes,** p. 34
- Oral Assessment, p. 35
- Game, p. 36
- Chapter Review, pp. 36–37
- Teacher to Teacher, p. 37
- Online Culture Project, p. 38
- Fine Art Connection, p. 39

Homework Suggestions
Cahier d'activités, pp. 9–10, 102–103
Online Practice (**my.hrw.com**)
1.1, 1.2, 1.3, 2.1, 2.2, 3.1

Chapter Opener

Meeting the National Standards

Communication
Communication, pp. 8, 9, 11, 13, 15, 21, 23, 25, 27, 29
À ton tour, p. 39

Cultures
Flash culture, pp. 8, 12, 20, 24
Comparaisons, p. 17
Products and Perspectives, pp. 17,19

Connections
Social Studies Link, p. 6
Film Studies Link, p. 15
History Link, p. 17
Visual Learners, p. 28
Language Arts Link, p. 31

Comparisons
Comparaisons, p. 17
Comparing and Contrasting, pp. 9, 21, 31, 32

Communities
Communauté, p. 17
Career Path, p. 11
School link, p. 14

Using the Photo

In this photo, a family strolls across the **pont Alexandre III** in Paris. The bridge was built to celebrate the ratification of the treaty that created the Russian-French alliance. The first stone was laid in 1896. Lavishly decorated lampposts, sculptures, and huge granite pillars adorned with gilded bronze statues line the bridge. Have students compare the architecture of the **pont Alexandre III** with that of a famous bridge in the United States. 4.2

Vocabulaire supplémentaire

Students might use these terms to discuss the photo.

l'aile (f.) *wing*
doré(e) *golden*
le lampadaire *lamppost*
le pilier *pillar*
la sculpture *sculpture*
2.2, 3.1

chapitre 1

Ma famille et mes copains

Objectifs

In this chapter, you will learn to
- describe yourself and ask about others
- talk about your likes and dislikes
- inquire
- tell when you do something

And you will review
- the verbs **avoir** and **être**
- adjective agreement
- the adjectives **beau, nouveau,** and **vieux**
- **-er** verbs
- **-ir** and **-re** verbs
- verbs like **dormir**

Que vois-tu sur la photo?
Où est cette famille?
Qu'est-ce que cette famille fait?
Et toi, qu'est-ce que tu aimes faire avec ta famille?

ACTFL 21st Century Skills

Technology Literacy:	TE: pp. 8, 13, 15 (Global Awareness), 38
Flexibility and Adaptability:	TE: p. 14, 17
Initiative and Self-Direction:	TE: pp. 8, 21 (Global Awareness)
Social and Cross-Cultural Skills:	SE: p. 17; TE: pp. 6, 9, 15, 17, 19, 21, 31, 32
Productivity and Accountability:	TE: pp. 3C, 5, 13, 19, 27, 37
Leadership and Responsibility:	TE: pp. 14, 17, 27

Chapter Opener

Le pont Alexandre III, à Paris

DIGITAL FRENCH

TEACHER TOOLS

- Interactive Whiteboard Lessons
- Generate Success!

ALSO AVAILABLE...

- Online Workbooks
- French InterActive Reader

FRENCH ON THE GO!

- Performance Space
- Holt McDougal French Apps
- *Bien dit!* eTextbook

Learning Tips

Students may need to review the French vocabulary and grammar that they have already studied. You may want to help them do this by providing them with a list of basic words and expressions or by playing a review game in class. Recommend that they make flashcards of the words and expressions that they use most frequently.

VIDEO OPTIONS

- **Télé-vocab 1**
- **Grammavision 1**
- **Télé-vocab 2**
- **Grammavision 2**
- **Télé-roman**

LISTENING PRACTICE

Language Lab and Classroom Activities

Vocabulaire
Activity 2, p. 8, CD 1, Tr. 1
Télé-vocab 1, p. 6, DVD Tutor
Activity 23, p. 20, CD 1, Tr. 4
Télé-vocab 2, p. 18, DVD Tutor

Grammaire
Activity 7, p. 10, CD 1, Tr. 2
Grammavision 1, pp. 10, 12, DVD Tutor
Activity 31, p. 24, CD 1, Tr. 5
Grammavision 2, pp. 22, 24, DVD Tutor

Application
Activity 11, p. 12, CD 1, Tr. 3
Activity 36, p. 26, CD 1, Tr. 6

Prépare-toi pour l'examen
Activity 6, p. 35, CD 1, Tr. 10

Révisions cumulatives
Activity 1, p. 38, CD 1, Tr. 14

Télé-roman
p. 28, DVD Tutor

Lecture
p. 30, CD 1, Tr. 7–8

Variations littéraires
p. 382, CD 1, Tr. 9

Lettres et sons
p. 36, CD 1, Tr. 11–13

Resources

Planning:
Lesson Planner
Teacher One Stop

Presentation:
Projectable Transparencies **Vocabulaire 1.1, 1.2**
DVD Tutor, Disc 1 **Télé-vocab 1**
Interactive Whiteboard Lessons

Practice:
Cahier de vocabulaire et grammaire
Differentiated Practice and Assessment CD-ROM
Independent Study Guide
Media Guide
Projectable Transparencies Bell Work 1.1
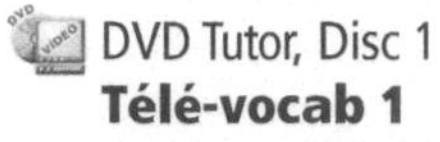
Holt McDougal French Apps

Bell Work

Use Bell Work 1.1 in the *Projectable Transparencies* or write this activity on the board.

List five adjectives in French to describe yourself. 1.2

Connections

Social Studies Link

Students may be surprised to learn that in French, **beau-père** and **belle-mère** can mean *step-father* and *stepmother* as well as *father-in-law* and *mother-in-law.* Share with students that different cultures may use terms for family members in novel ways. For example, some cultures use the same word for both *mother* and *aunt* or may address an uncle who is older differently than one who is younger. Have students research some of these terms used in another culture and create a family tree to present to the class. 3.1

Objectifs
- to describe yourself and ask about others
- to talk about likes and dislikes

Vocabulaire à l'œuvre 1

Télé-vocab

Révisions Ma famille et mes copains

Core Instruction

TEACHING VOCABULAIRE

1. Introduce the vocabulary with transparencies **Vocabulaire 1.1** and **1.2** and model the pronunciation of each word. **(2 min.)**
2. Bring in magazine photos of people and hold them up one at a time, modeling descriptive sentences about each one. **(2 min.)**
3. Ask students about family members. **Ta mère est grande? Ton chat est gros? Ton frère a les yeux bleus? (3 min.)**
4. Ask the class about individual students. **Le chat de... est gros?** Have volunteers answer **oui** or **non** to each question. **(5 min.)**

Télé-vocab 1

For a video presentation of this vocabulary, see the *DVD Tutor.*

Télé-vocab

Et voilà mes copains...

Là, c'est Céline, une copine. Elle est très gentille.

Ça, c'est Marc, un copain de classe. Il est brun et sportif.

Le frère de Céline, Éric, est sérieux et un peu timide.

Online Practice
my.hrw.com
Vocabulaire 1 practice

D'autres mots utiles

le beau-père/la belle-mère	*stepfather/stepmother*
le grand-père	*grandfather*
le chat	*cat*
l'oncle/la tante	*uncle/aunt*
le cousin/la cousine	*cousin*

À la québécoise

In Quebec, you might hear the word **bolle** to describe someone who is intelligent.

Mon frère, c'est une bolle.

Exprimons-nous!

To describe yourself and ask about others	
Comment tu t'appelles? *What's your name?*	**Je m'appelle** Christophe. *My name is . . .*
Tu as quel âge? *How old are you?*	**J'ai** 16 **ans.** *I am . . . years old.*
De quelle couleur sont les yeux d'Aurélie? *What color are . . . ?*	**Ils sont** bleus./**Elle a les yeux** bleus. *They are . . . /She has . . .*
Il/Elle est comment, ton ami(e)? *What is he/she like . . . ?*	**Il/Elle est** petit(e). *He/She is . . .*

Vocabulaire et grammaire, *pp. 1–3* — Online Workbooks

▶ **Vocabulaire supplémentaire,** La famille et les adjectifs descriptifs, **p. R16**

TPR — Total Physical Response

Have students respond to these commands.

Lève la main si tu t'appelles (Jennifer).

Lève les deux mains si tu n'es pas timide.

Lève-toi si tu as un chien.

Assieds-toi si ton chien est petit.

Lève la main si tu as seize ans.

Mets la main sur la tête si ta mère a les yeux verts.

Montre-moi une fille qui a les cheveux blonds et courts.

Cherche un(e) élève qui n'aime pas la musique rap.

Amène-moi un copain (une copine) qui est grand(e) et brun(e).

Viens au tableau si ta grand-mère est sportive.

1.2

Common Error Alert — Attention !

When telling someone's profession in French, students may be inclined to say, **"Mon père est un pharmacien."** The indefinite article is only used after **"C'est"**. **(C'est un pharmacien.)**

Differentiated Instruction

Slower Pace Learners

Draw a four-column chart on the board with the headings "Age," "Hair Color," "Eye Color," and "Personality." Ask students to name the vocabulary words and phrases that belong under each heading. Then make true and false statements about student volunteers. **Il a les cheveux blonds.** Have students give a thumbs-up sign for true statements and a thumbs-down for false statements. Use magazine photos for less positive adjectives (**gros, embêtant, timide**). 1.2

Special Learning Needs

Students with Learning Disabilities Have students prepare to use the phrases in **Exprimons-nous!** by making note cards with the questions and translations on one side and example answers on the other side. Students can use the cards to practice individually or with a partner. When they feel ready, ask students to practice without the note card prompts. 1.2

Proverbes

For French proverbs and activities related to the chapter theme and vocabulary, see **Proverbes,** pp. R6–R7.

Resources

Planning:
Lesson Planner
Teacher One Stop

Presentation:
Projectable Transparencies **Vocabulaire 1.1, 1.2**
DVD Tutor, Disc 1 **Télé-vocab 1**
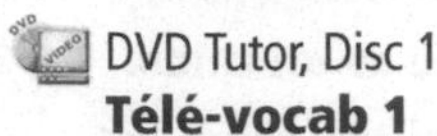
Interactive Whiteboard Lessons

Practice:
Cahier de vocabulaire et grammaire
Differentiated Practice and Assessment CD-ROM
Independent Study Guide
Media Guide
Audio CD 1, Tr. 1
@HOMETUTOR
Holt McDougal French Apps

2 Script

See script on p. 3E.

3 Answers

1. La mère de Napoléon s'appelle Maria Letizia Ramolino.
2. Napoléon a quatre frères et trois sœurs.
3. Napoléon a un fils qui s'appelle Napoléon II.
4. Answers will vary.

Communication

Pair Activity: Presentational

Have partners choose a topic of particular interest to them. Have them set aside 30 minutes per week outside of class to research their topic using authentic resources in French. Ask students to keep a journal or blog in which they summarize what they learn each week. Have them take turns sharing their findings in class. At the end of the class year, you may have students present their most interesting findings in a Powerpoint® presentation or in another multimedia format. 1.3

Flash culture

En France, le dimanche se passe généralement en famille. Après le repas de midi, certaines familles ont pour habitude d'aller se promener en forêt ou dans des parcs. À Paris, on peut se promener au jardin du Luxembourg, au parc Monceau ou le long des quais de la Seine. Dans la région parisienne, l'un des lieux favoris de promenade est la forêt de Fontainebleau.

Qu'est-ce que tu fais le dimanche? Est-ce que tu vas souvent te promener avec les membres de ta famille? 4.2

1 Une grand-mère curieuse 1.2

Lisons Ta grand-mère pose beaucoup de questions au sujet de tes amis. Choisis les réponses logiques.

e **1.** David a quel âge?
c **2.** De quelle couleur sont les cheveux de Marie?
a **3.** Elle est comment, Stéphanie?
d **4.** Il s'appelle comment, ton chat?
b **5.** Comment est Antoine?

a. Très marrante!
b. Un peu timide...
c. Elle est blonde.
d. Minou.
e. Dix-sept ans.

2 Écoutons CD 1, Tr. 1 1.2

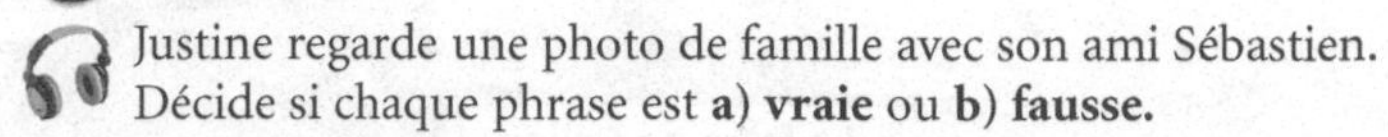

Justine regarde une photo de famille avec son ami Sébastien. Décide si chaque phrase est **a) vraie** ou **b) fausse.**

b **1.** Justine a deux sœurs et deux frères.
b **2.** Sonia a les cheveux longs.
b **3.** Olivier est sportif.
a **4.** Laurent est petit et sympa.
a **5.** Émilie est rousse et un peu timide.

3 L'arbre généalogique de Napoléon 1.2

Écrivons/Parlons Regarde l'arbre généalogique de Napoléon 1er et réponds aux questions.

1. Comment s'appelle la mère de Napoléon?
2. Napoléon a combien de frères et de sœurs?
3. Napoléon a des enfants? Comment s'appellent-ils/elles?
4. Pense à ton arbre généalogique. Qu'est-ce que vous avez en commun, toi et Napoléon?

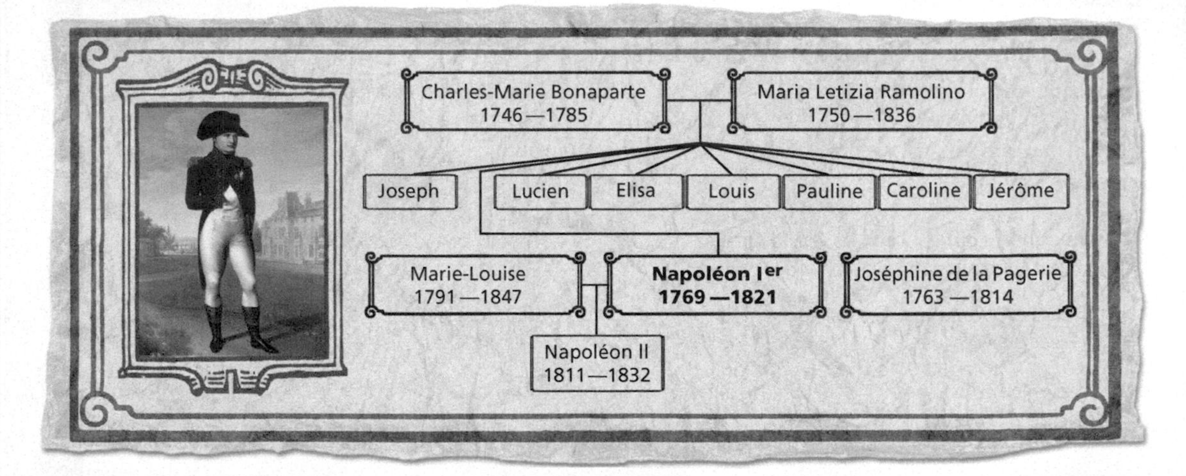

Core Instruction

TEACHING EXPRIMONS-NOUS!

1. Introduce yourself with four statements, making sure one of the statements is false. **Je m'appelle Marie. J'ai 29 ans. J'ai les yeux bleus. Je suis grande. (1 min.)**
2. Ask students which statements are **vrai** and which ones are **faux.** Then, one at a time, describe two or three students in the class and repeat the activity. **(2 min.)**
3. Continue with additional true statements about your friends, family members, or other members of the class and ask students to take notes so that you are able to ask at the end of the activity, **Qui est sportive? Qui n'a pas les cheveux longs? Qui est petit?** Call on students to provide the answers from their notes. **(3 min.)**

To talk about likes and dislikes	
J'adore/J'aime bien le sport. *I love/I really like . . .*	**Moi aussi./Pas moi.** *Me too./Not me.*
Moi, je n'aime pas la musique classique. *I don't like . . .*	**Moi non plus.** *Me neither.*
Je n'aime pas beaucoup voyager. *I don't like . . . very much.*	**Moi si.** *I do.*
Qu'est-ce qu'Arnaud **aime faire?** *What does . . . like to do?*	**Il aime** aller au cinéma. *He likes . . .*

Vocabulaire et grammaire, *pp. 1–3* — Online Workbooks

4 Des correspondants 1.2

Lisons/Écrivons Lis cette annonce sur le site Web du club international de la francophonie et réponds aux questions. Possible answers:

Salut! Je m'appelle Carole et j'ai 15 ans. J'habite en France. Je suis brune aux yeux marron. Je ne suis ni grande ni petite. Je suis intelligente, gentille, marrante et assez sportive. J'aime sortir, aller au cinéma et écouter de la musique. J'adore le rock! Je parle français, anglais et espagnol et j'aime les voyages. J'aimerais correspondre avec des filles ou garçons âgés de 13 à 15 ans! Écrivez-moi vite!

1. Comment s'appelle-t-elle? Elle s'appelle Carole.
2. Quel âge a-t-elle? Elle a 15 ans.
3. De quelle couleur sont ses yeux? Elle a les yeux marron.
4. De quelle couleur sont ses cheveux? Elle a les cheveux bruns.
5. Comment est sa personnalité? Elle est intelligente, gentille, marrante et sportive.
6. Qu'est-ce qu'elle aime? Elle aime le sport et voyager.

Communication

5 Questions personnelles 1.1

Parlons Avec un(e) camarade, parlez des membres de vos familles. Comment sont-ils? Jouez cette scène pour la classe.

MODÈLE —**J'ai deux frères. Marc a treize ans et il est...**

Comparisons

Comparing and Contrasting

Have students exchange e-mails with students in a francophone partner school to find out what kind of music they listen to. Instruct them to write a report comparing French-speaking teens' taste in music to that of American teens. As an alternative, have students research 'top hit' songs on Web sites in francophone countries and compare the songs to those on American lists. Instruct them to choose appropriate songs to compare. 4.2

Communication

Group Activity: Presentational

Have students bring in photos of their real family or pictures cut from magazines. After students describe the members of their own family to a partner or in small groups, have each student present a classmate's family with that classmate's pictures. Remind students to use **son, sa,** and **ses,** as well as the third-person forms of **avoir** and **être.** 1.3

Differentiated Instruction

ADVANCED LEARNERS

3 Ask students to rewrite the questions as if they were talking to Napoleon in person. The following day, ask students to imagine that you are Napoleon and have them ask you their questions. If possible, ask a native French speaker in your community to play the role of Napoleon. 1.1

MULTIPLE INTELLIGENCES

3 Interpersonal After completing the activity, have students create **l'arbre généalogique** for their own or an imaginary family. Ask students to label each family member with the vocabulary they learned in this chapter. Working in pairs, students may then ask each other the questions in the activity regarding their own family. Be prepared to assist students with the French words for stepmother, stepfather, half-brother, or other common family members. 1.1

Assess

Assessment Program
Quiz: Vocabulaire 1
Alternative Assessment
Differentiated Practice and Assessment CD-ROM

Online Assessment
my.hrw.com

Test Generator 

Resources

Planning:
Lesson Planner
Teacher One Stop

Presentation:
DVD Tutor, Disc 1
Grammavision 1.1

Practice:
Grammar Tutor for Students of French, Chapter 1
Cahier de vocabulaire et grammaire
Differentiated Practice and Assessment CD-ROM
Cahier d'activités
Independent Study Guide
Media Guide
Projectable Transparencies
Bell Work 1.2
Audio CD 1, Tr. 2

Bell Work

Use Bell Work 1.2 in the *Projectable Transparencies* or write this activity on the board.

Write five sentences in French that describe a member of your family. 1.2

7 Script

1. Notre grand-mère est très marrante.
2. Il est timide, Jean-Claude, non?
3. Dans ma famille, nous sommes six. Mon père a quarante ans.
4. Qu'est-ce que tu es pénible alors!
5. Elle n'a pas les cheveux blonds.
6. Karine est brune.

Objectifs
- the verbs *avoir* and *être*
- adjective agreement

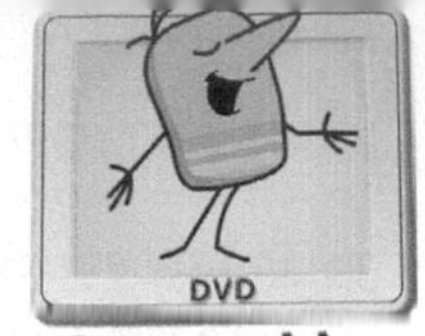

Grammavision

Révisions The verbs *avoir* and *être*

1 In Level 1, you learned how to conjugate verbs according to their subjects. The subject pronouns are **je** (*I*), **tu** (*you*), **il/elle/on** (*he/she/it, "we"*), **nous** (*we*), **vous** (*you*), and **ils/elles** (*they*).

2 The verbs avoir (*to have*) and être (*to be*) are irregular in the present tense.

	avoir	être
je (j')	ai	suis
tu	as	es
il/elle/on	a	est
nous	avons	sommes
vous	avez	êtes
ils/elles	ont	sont

3 To make a sentence negative, place **ne (n')**... before the verb and **pas** after the verb.

—Est-ce que ta sœur est timide?
—Non, elle **n'**est **pas** timide.

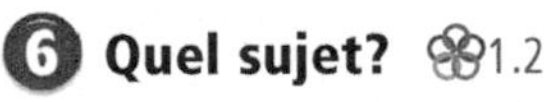
Vocabulaire et grammaire, *pp. 4–5*
Cahier d'activités, *pp. 1–3*

Déjà vu!

Do you remember the difference between **tu** and **vous**?

Use **tu** when . . .
- talking to friends or someone your own age or younger
- talking to someone in your family

Use **vous** when . . .
- addressing an adult, like your teacher
- talking to someone you do not know
- talking to more than one person

6 Quel sujet? 1.2

Lisons Choisis la phrase qui correspond à chaque sujet.

d **1.** Nous — **a.** n'ont pas de frère.
a **2.** Elles — **b.** es gentille!
e **3.** On — **c.** avez les cheveux longs.
f **4.** Je (J') — **d.** sommes timides.
b **5.** Tu — **e.** n'est pas français.
c **6.** Vous — **f.** ai un chien intelligent.

7 Écoutons CD 1, Tr. 2 1.2

Éva parle de sa famille et de ses amis. Écoute les phrases et décide si elle parle de **a) sa personnalité, b) son âge** ou **c) son physique.**

1. a **2.** a **3.** b **4.** a **5.** c **6.** c

Core Instruction

TEACHING GRAMMAIRE

1. Re-introduce the verbs **avoir** and **être** and model the pronunciation with the subject pronouns. Remind students of the **liaison** between a pronoun ending in a consonant and a verb starting with a vowel sound. Discuss the rules for making sentences negative. **(2 min.)**

2. On the board, write a student's first name, a teacher's name, **Maman**, and **mes amis**. Model asking these people about themselves. **Tu es français(e)? Vous êtes intelligent(e)(s)? Tu as un frère? Vous avez de la famille à Paris?** Students decide to whom you are speaking. If students have trouble, go over **Déjà vu** to remind them of the uses of **tu** and **vous. (4 min.)**

Grammavision

For a video presentation of the verbs **avoir** and **être,** see the *DVD Tutor.*

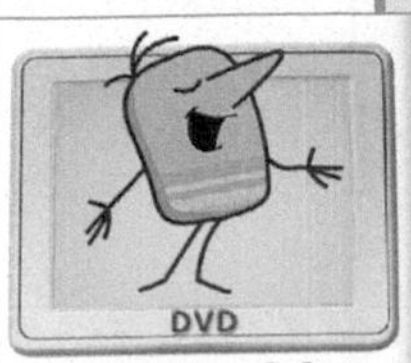

Grammavision

Online Practice
my.hrw.com
Grammaire 1 practice

8 Une conversation téléphonique 1.2

Écrivons Jules et Claudine sont au téléphone. Ils parlent de leurs familles. Complète leur conversation avec les formes correctes des verbes **être** et **avoir**.

JULES Comment ___est 1___ ton père?
CLAUDINE Il ___a 2___ les cheveux très courts et il ___est 3___ grand. Toute ma famille est grande. Et dans ta famille, vous ___êtes 4___ tous petits?
JULES Non. Mes deux frères ___sont 5___ très grands! Pas comme moi!
CLAUDINE Ils ___ont 6___ quel âge?
JULES Seize et treize ans. Nous ___avons 7___ aussi une sœur. Elle ___est 8___ grande aussi. Elle ___est 9___ très pénible!

9 Une journée en famille 1.3

Écrivons/Parlons Voici la famille de Philippe. Comment est sa famille? Utilise **être** et **avoir** et des adjectifs pour décrire sa famille.

MODÈLE **Le frère de Philippe est marrant. Il a les cheveux...**

Digital performance space

Communication

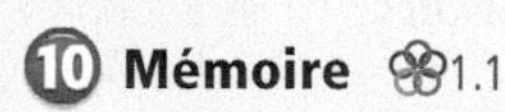

10 Mémoire 1.1

Parlons En groupes de quatre, observez bien chaque personne de votre groupe pendant une minute. Ensuite, fermez les yeux. Le professeur va spécifier une personne du groupe. Tu dois faire une description détaillée de cette personne. Cette personne va dire si la description est correcte ou pas.

MODÈLE **—(yeux fermés) Julie, tu es grande. Tu as les cheveux blonds et...**
—Oui, j'ai les cheveux blonds, mais je n'ai pas...

Differentiated Instruction

SLOWER PACE LEARNERS

Have students practice the forms of **avoir** with a tennis ball. Model **J'ai une balle.** Toss the ball to a student and ask, **Tu as une balle?** The student answers, **Oui, j'ai une balle.** Ask the class, **Il / Elle a une balle?** and have them answer. The student gives the ball to a pair of students. Ask the pair, **Vous avez une balle? (Oui, nous avons une balle.)** Begin again with the verb **être. Je suis sportif(–ive).** (Toss the ball.) **Tu es sportif(–ive)?**, and so on. 1.2

SPECIAL LEARNING NEEDS

7 Students with Auditory Impairments

For students with auditory impairments or difficulty with auditory processing, make this a reading activity instead of a listening activity. Provide the written script. Have students read the script and complete the activity along with the rest of the class. 1.2

COMMON ERROR ALERT
ATTENTION !

Since the article is not used in English, students may need to be reminded to supply the definite article before body parts. **Elle a les cheveux bruns et les yeux bleus.**

Communities

Career Path

Describe to students the **au pair** system in which young men and women live with a family in a French-speaking country and take care of the family's children in exchange for room and board. Have students visit Web sites that match **au pair** with families to find out how to apply to be an **au pair.** Then have partners imagine that they are both **au pair.** One has been placed with a perfect **au pair** family, while the other has been placed with a less-than-perfect family. Have students write an e-mail exchange in which they describe their respective host families. 5.1

Communication

10 Group Work: Presentational

In the same groups of four, have students describe three celebrities, using three descriptors for each celebrity. Then have a student from each group present the celebrities but ask the student to make one mistake that the class should correct. 1.3

Resources

Planning:
Lesson Planner
Teacher One Stop

Presentation:
DVD Tutor, Disc 1
Grammavision 1.2

Practice:
Grammar Tutor for Students of French, Chapter 1
Cahier de vocabulaire et grammaire
Differentiated Practice and Assessment CD-ROM
Cahier d'activités
Independent Study Guide
Media Guide
Projectable Transparencies
Bell Work 1.3
Audio CD 1, Tr. 3
@HOMETUTOR

Bell Work

Use Bell Work 1.3 in the *Projectable Transparencies* or write this activity on the board.

Fill in the blank with the correct form of **avoir** or **être.**

1. **Ma sœur ____ quinze ans.**
2. **Mes deux frères ____ très grands.**
3. **Je (J') ____ très timide.**
4. **Nous ____ un chien très gentil.**
5. **Vous ____ américains ou français?** 1.2

11 Script

See script on p. 3E.

13 Answers

1. Ma grand-mère a des amies ennuyeuses.
2. Nous avons deux chiens gros et intelligents.
3. Célia est petite et toujours heureuse.
4. Les élèves de la classe sont intellectuels et sportifs.
5. Mon chien a les yeux marron.

Révisions Adjective agreement

1 Adjectives are words that describe nouns. They agree with the noun they describe in number and gender.

Marc est grand et Anne est grand**e** aussi.

2 To make most adjectives **feminine**, add an **-e**, unless it already ends in unaccented **-e**. Also note some common changes and exceptions between these masculine and feminine forms.

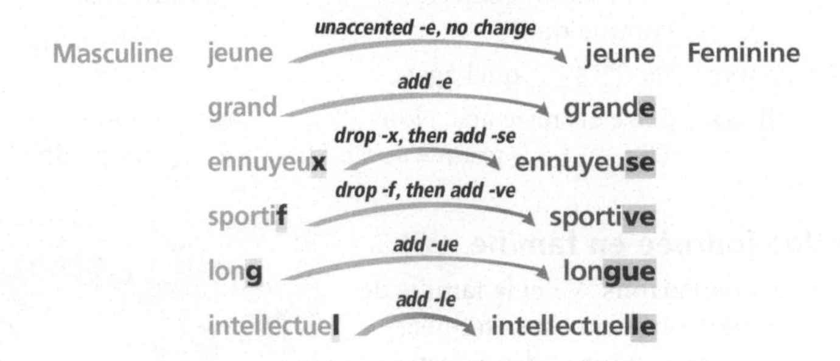

3 To make most adjectives plural, add **-s**, unless it ends in **-eux**.

masculine	grand	grand**s**
	ennuyeux	ennuyeux
feminine	grande	grande**s**
	ennuyeuse	ennuyeuse**s**

4 **Marron** and **orange** do not change form in the feminine or plural.

Martin a les yeux bleu**s** mais sa sœur a les yeux marron.

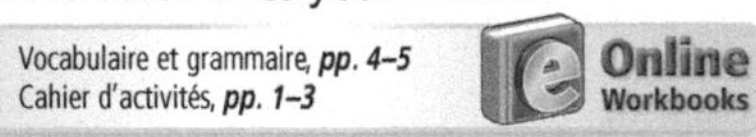

Vocabulaire et grammaire, pp. 4–5
Cahier d'activités, pp. 1–3
Online Workbooks

Flash culture

En France, les enfants appellent leurs parents **maman** et **papa.** Les grands-parents deviennent souvent **papi** et **mamie. Tonton** est utilisé pour les oncles et **tata** ou **tatie** pour les tantes. Les parents aiment aussi donner des petits noms à leurs enfants comme **mon cœur** *(my heart),* **ma petite puce** *(my little flea),* **mon chou** *(my cream puff),* **mon lapin** *(my bunny),* ou encore **mon chaton** *(my kitty cat).* Les **diminutifs** *(nicknames)* sont aussi communs. Par exemple, Pierre devient Pierrot.

Est-ce que tu as un diminutif? Comment est-ce que tu appelles les différents membres de ta famille? 4.2

11 Écoutons CD 1, Tr. 3 1.2

Martin a une tante et un oncle qui s'appellent tous les deux Dominique. Est-ce qu'il parle **a) de son oncle, b) de sa tante** ou **c) est-ce qu'on ne peut pas savoir?**

1. a 2. b 3. c 4. b 5. a 6. a 7. c 8. b

12 La bonne forme 1.2

Lisons Annick parle de sa famille. Complète ses phrases avec la forme correcte de l'adjectif.

1. Ludivine et Théo sont jeunes (jeune).
2. Mon chien n'aime pas jouer. Il est très sérieux (sérieux).
3. Mamie n'aime pas le sport; elle n'est pas sportive (sportif).
4. Mes frères sont très minces (mince).
5. Monica a les cheveux longs (long).

Core Instruction

TEACHING GRAMMAIRE

1. Remind students about adjective agreement and placement of adjectives. **(1 min.)**
2. Go over each point for forming masculine/feminine and singular/plural adjectives. Discuss spelling changes and explain that these types of adjectives are common in French. **(3 min.)**
3. Ask students to imagine you have a twin of the opposite sex. Describe yourself with three adjectives. **Je suis…** Then describe your twin of opposite gender with the same three adjectives. **Il/Elle est… (3 min.)**
4. Finally, describe characteristics you and your twin have in common, modeling plural adjectives. **Nous sommes…** Check comprehension by asking true or false questions. **(4 min.)**

Grammavision

For a video presentation of adjective agreement, see the *DVD Tutor.*

13 Des phrases 1.2

Écrivons Célia décrit sa vie. Fais des phrases complètes. Attention à la forme des adjectifs.

1. ma grand-mère / avoir / des amies / ennuyeux
2. nous / avoir / deux chiens / gros / intelligent / et
3. Célia / être / petit / et / toujours heureux
4. les élèves de la classe / être / intellectuel / sportif / et
5. mon chien / avoir / les yeux / marron

14 Des photos 1.2

Parlons Fais une description des photos. Utilise deux adjectifs pour chaque personne. Les phrases peuvent être affirmatives ou négatives.

MODÈLE Ils sont âgés et intelligents.

1.

2.

3.

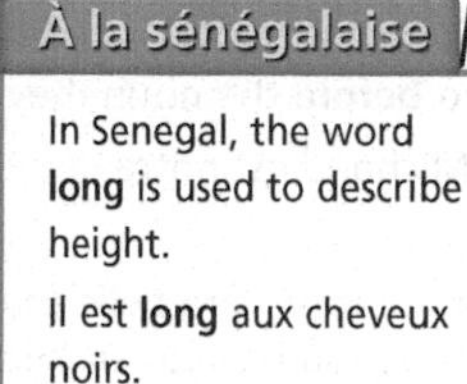

À la sénégalaise

In Senegal, the word **long** is used to describe height.

Il est **long** aux cheveux noirs.

4.

5.

6.

Possible answers:
1. Elle est jeune et elle n'est pas timide.
2. Ils sont petits et sportifs.
3. Il est gros et heureux.
4. Elles sont âgées et heureuses.
5. Il est grand et intelligent.
6. Il est petit et pénible.

Digital performance space

Communication

15 Scénario 1.1

Parlons Choisis une personne de la classe et décris cette personne à ton/ta camarade. Ton/ta camarade va essayer de deviner le nom de la personne. Ensuite, échangez les rôles.

MODÈLE —**Il est grand. Il n'est pas blond.**
—**C'est Morris?**

Teacher to Teacher

Geneviève Delfosse
Thomas Jefferson High School for Science and Technology
Alexandria, VA

This is a good project for the first weeks of school. Students introduce themselves by creating a visual and speaking for one minute. Students are required to use two large paper plates stapled together to form a mobile. Students decorate both sides of the plates with items of their choice that represent their personalities, hobbies, and interests, and use them as a visual when presenting. All the plate mobiles can be hung to decorate the classroom. 1.3

Communication

15 Group Activity: Interpersonal

Have students write their description of the student they chose. They should use at least four descriptors with one in the negative. Then have the students circulate around the room, read their descriptors aloud, and guess one another's chosen student. The students who guess correctly should sign the paper. 1.1

Differentiated Instruction

ADVANCED LEARNERS

Have students go on a photo safari to take pictures of people who represent the different adjectives from **Vocabulaire 1.** (Tell them they must find a chubby animal, not a person, for the adjective **gros.**) This could be done individually with students' own cameras, or with one disposable class camera. In this case, each student would be assigned one adjective. Have students write captions for the photos and present them to the rest of the class. 1.3

SPECIAL LEARNING NEEDS

Students with AD(H)D Before reviewing adjective agreement and placement, ask students to create a grammar rule notebook, note card box, or database. To help students remember and review the rules of grammar, have them copy each rule and example on a page, note card, or data field. Students may use these for future reference and review.

Assess

Assessment Program
Quiz: Grammaire 1
Alternative Assessment
Differentiated Practice and Assessment CD-ROM

Online Assessment
my.hrw.com

Test Generator

Resources

Planning:
Lesson Planner

Teacher One Stop

Practice:
Grammar Tutor for Students of French, Chapter 1
Cahier de vocabulaire et grammaire
Differentiated Practice and Assessment CD-ROM
Cahier d'activités
Independent Study Guide

Projectable Transparencies
Bell Work 1.4

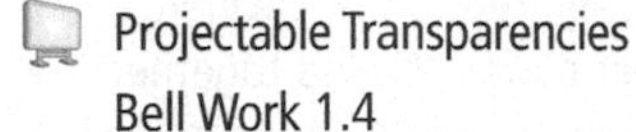

Bell Work

Use Bell Work 1.4 in the *Projectable Transparencies* or write this activity on the board.

Unscramble the words to create sentences. Conjugate the verbs and pay attention to adjective agreement and placement.

1. **avoir / Marie / robe / beau / vert / une**
2. **Ma mère / petit / gentil / blond / être / et**
3. **Céline et Chloé /ennuyeux / filles / ne pas être / des**
4. **Julie / jeune / sportif / fille / être / une**
5. **Nous / grand / et / mince / être** 1.2

Synthèse
• Vocabulaire 1
• Grammaire 1

Application 1

16 Une personne que j'admire 1.3

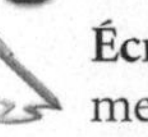

Écrivons Pense à une personne que tu admires beaucoup (un membre de ta famille ou une personne célèbre). Écris un paragraphe pour décrire cette personne et explique pourquoi tu l'admires.

MODÈLE **J'aime beaucoup ma tante Lauren parce qu'elle est très intelligente et très marrante. Elle a... Elle est...**

Un peu plus Révisions

The adjectives *beau, nouveau, vieux*

Beau *(handsome)*, nouveau *(new)*, and vieux *(old)* are placed **before** the noun they describe.

M. Michaud est notre nouveau professeur.

The feminine forms are **belle** *(beautiful)*, **nouvelle**, and **vieille**. If you have a feminine plural noun, just add an **-s**.

Paris est une **vieille** ville.
Où sont les **nouvelles** voitures?

Before a masculine noun that begins with a vowel sound, use **bel, nouvel**, and **vieil**. For masculine plural nouns, use **beaux, nouveaux**, and **vieux**.

Farid est un **nouvel** élève.
Ses chiens sont beaux.

Vocabulaire et grammaire, *p. 6*
Cahier d'activités, *pp. 1–3*

17 Quelle forme choisir? 1.2

Écrivons Complète chaque phrase avec la forme de l'adjectif qui convient.

1. Marcus est un nouvel élève. (nouveau)
2. Mon vieil oncle Jean est très sympathique. (vieux)
3. Ces beaux chats sont à vous? (beau)
4. Julie et Laure sont les nouvelles amies de Céline. (nouveau)
5. Ma grand-mère est vieille, mais très marrante. (vieux)

18 Phrases variées 1.2

Écrivons Récris chaque phrase en ajoutant un adjectif approprié. Mets chaque adjectif à la forme et à la place qui conviennent. Possible answers:

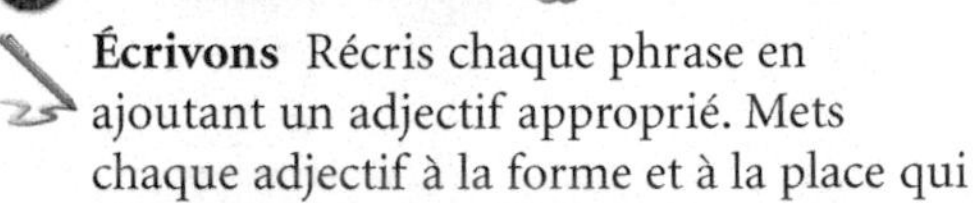

sportif	vieux	beau
gentil	timide	nouveau

MODÈLE C'est ma raquette.
C'est ma nouvelle raquette.

1. Martina est une fille. (Martina est une belle fille.)
2. J'aime les chiens. (J'aime les chiens gentils.)
3. Mon frère est un élève. (Mon frère est un nouvel élève.)
4. Ma tante a un piano. (Ma tante a un vieux piano.)
5. Pierrick est un garçon. (Pierrick est un garçon sportif.)

Communication

School Link

Arrange to have your students participate in weekly tutorial sessions or study groups during which they share their experiences with students in lower levels and help them with their homework assignments and projects. You may have a volunteer keep a log of the material discussed during these sessions. 5.1

Core Instruction

INTEGRATED PRACTICE

1. Have students do Activity 16 to practice adjectives and their agreement. **(5 min.)**
2. Describe the physical characteristics, the age, the likes and dislikes, and the activities of someone well known to most of your students. Give a minimum of five sentences in your explanation. Ask students to try to guess who that person is. **(10 min.)**
3. Introduce **Un peu plus** (see presentation suggestions at right). **(5 min.)**

TEACHING UN PEU PLUS

1. Remind students that they know three "bags" adjectives, describing **b**eauty, **a**ge, **g**oodness, **s**ize, that all precede the noun. **(2 min.)**
2. Show pictures that represent masculine nouns, feminine nouns, and masculine nouns starting with a vowel sound. Ask **oui** or **non** questions. **C'est une nouvelle église? C'est un vieil hôtel? (3 min.)**
3. Continue with integrated practice activities 17–19. **(20 min.)**

Online Practice
my.hrw.com
Application 1 practice

19 À la recherche d'une nouvelle star 1.2, 1.3

a. Lisons Un film va être tourné *(filmed)* près de chez toi et le metteur en scène *(director)* cherche des acteurs. Lis les annonces qu'il a passées dans un magazine. Laquelle te correspond le mieux?

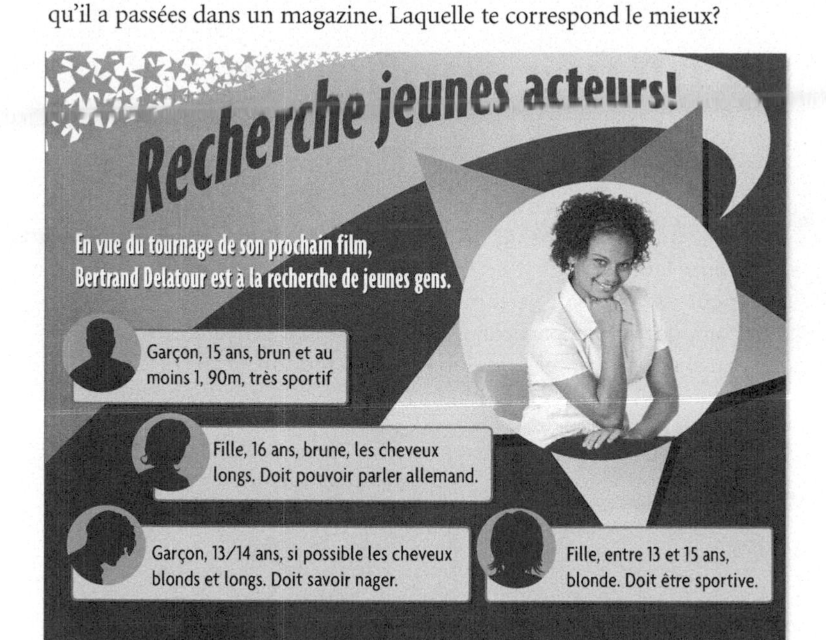

Recherche jeunes acteurs!
En vue du tournage de son prochain film,
Bertrand Delatour est à la recherche de jeunes gens.
Garçon, 15 ans, brun et au moins 1, 90m, très sportif
Fille, 16 ans, brune, les cheveux longs. Doit pouvoir parler allemand.
Garçon, 13/14 ans, si possible les cheveux blonds et longs. Doit savoir nager.
Fille, entre 13 et 15 ans, blonde. Doit être sportive.

b. Écrivons Maintenant, écris une lettre au metteur en scène. Décris pourquoi tu pourrais *(could)* être un acteur (une actrice) dans son nouveau film. Ou bien, tu peux suggérer un ami.

MODÈLE **Bonjour, Monsieur. J'aime le cinéma. J'ai quinze ans et...**

Communication

20 Opinions personnelles 1.1

Parlons Qui est ton acteur (actrice) préféré(e)? Avec ton/ta camarade, fais une description de cette personne. Comment est-il/elle? Mentionne ce qu'il/elle aime faire aussi.

MODÈLE **—Mon acteur préféré est... Il est grand et beau...**

21 Interview 1.1

Parlons C'est la rentrée et tu viens de commencer une nouvelle année à ton lycée. Avec deux ou trois camarades, parlez de ce qui est nouveau dans vos vies (professeurs, sports, amis, CD, etc.).

MODÈLE **—Tu as un nouveau professeur de maths?**

Connections

Film Studies Link

Ask students to name as many actors as they can. Then ask them to name as many movie directors as they can. Explain to students that, in the United States, the stars of a movie receive the most attention from moviegoers, whereas in France, the directors receive as much or even more recognition for their work on a film than the actors. Have each student research and write a short biography of a famous French director. You might choose appropriate classic French films to show throughout the school year. Have students present their directors' biographies before the films are shown. 3.1

Communication

Pair Activity: Presentational

Have students bring in a picture of one or two celebrities (TV, film, or music) and have them describe these people to a partner. In addition to describing the people in the pictures, students should also describe what the celebrities are wearing, using the proper form of **nouveau, beau,** or **vieux** and a color for the articles of clothing or accessories. Remind students to pay attention to proper agreement and placement of the adjectives. 1.3

Differentiated Instruction

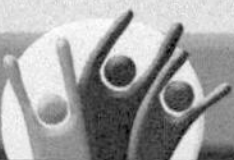

SLOWER PACE LEARNERS

19 On the board, write the salutation and first sentence to help students begin their letter.

Monsieur ou Madame,

Me référant à votre annonce, je me permets de poser ma candidature pour un rôle dans votre nouveau film. Je suis...

You might also provide the letter ending: **Je vous prie d'agréer, Monsieur ou Madame, l'expression de mes sentiments distingués.** 1.3

MULTIPLE INTELLIGENCES

19 Bodily-Kinesthetic After they have written the letter of interest, ask students to create a script for the actual interview. The students may role-play the director of the film and the actor. They should introduce themselves and ask and answer questions about their likes and dislikes and any special talents they have that might apply to this acting position. Have partners present their interviews to the class. 1.3

Assess

Assessment Program
Quiz: Application 1
Audio CD 1, Tr. 15
Alternative Assessment
Differentiated Practice and Assessment CD-ROM

Online Assessment
my.hrw.com

Test Generator 

Resources

Planning:
Lesson Planner
Teacher One Stop

Practice:
Cahier d'activités

Vocabulaire supplémentaire

You might wish to use these terms to discuss the project with students.

copier	*to copy*
former	*to form*
l'alphabet (m.)	*alphabet*
un caractère	*character*
un chiffre	*numeral*
lentement	*slowly*
soigneusement	*carefully*
tenir correctement (le crayon, le stylo)	*to hold correctly (the pencil, the pen)*
droitier/gaucher	*right-handed/left-handed*
lisible	*legible*

Culture

Écrire au tableau

Culture appliquée

La cursive 2.2

En France, les enfants apprennent à écrire en cursive sans avoir appris[1] les caractères d'imprimerie[2]. Ils apprennent aussi à écrire avec un stylo plume[3] et continuent d'utiliser le stylo plume pendant toute leur scolarité. L'écriture de chaque élève change petit à petit pour devenir plus personnelle. Certains adolescents vont même faire des efforts particuliers pour avoir une écriture différente et aussi pour inventer une signature qui leur est propre[4]. Il n'est pas rare qu'ils y passent[5] plusieurs heures.

1. without having learned 2. block letters 3. fountain pen 4. his/her own 5. for them to spend

Ta page d'écriture 2.2

Materials needed:
- a piece of graph paper
- a pencil or pen

It's your turn to play the role of a French student and to try to copy the letters illustrated below. Try to come up with your own signature.

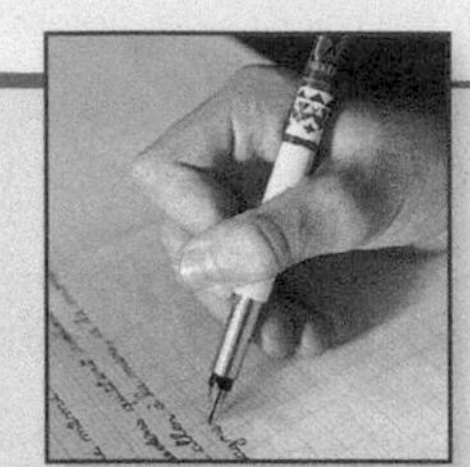

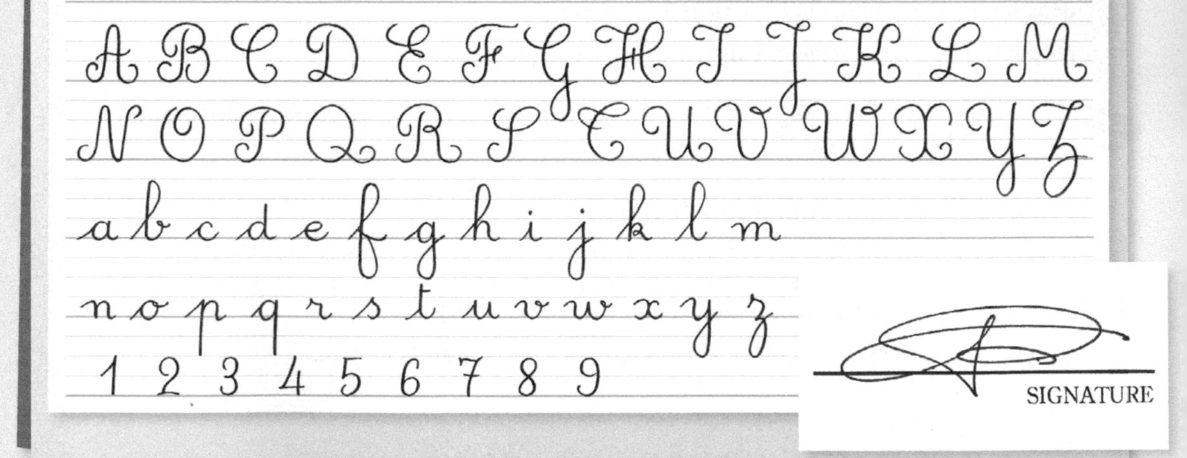

Recherches Comment un élève français écrit-il un essai? Est-ce qu'il utilise un ordinateur ou est-ce qu'il l'écrit à la main? 2.1

Core Instruction

CULTURE APPLIQUÉE

1. Have the class read and discuss the introductory paragraph. **(3 min.)**
2. Ask students to practice writing both upper case and lower case letters, as well as the numbers. **(5 min.)**
3. After the practice, have students write their name, address, and phone number on a piece of graph paper. Ask the class what it was like to re-learn to write the alphabet. **(5 min.)**

COMPARAISONS ET COMMUNAUTÉ

1. Have the class read the first section and decide on the correct answer. Then have students read the information about Moroccan families. **(10 min.)**
2. Have small groups discuss **Et toi? (15 min.)**
3. Read **Communauté et professions** aloud in class. Ask comprehension questions to check understanding. Assign the questions as homework. **(6 min.)**

Comparaisons

La famille au Maroc 4.2

Tu rends visite à une famille qui habite à la campagne au Maroc. Tu t'attends à voir:

a. les parents et les enfants.
b. toute la famille: les parents, les enfants, les grands-parents, les oncles et tantes, etc.
c. les parents uniquement.

Repas en famille

Les Marocains accordent une grande importance à l'unité et à l'honneur de la famille. Dans les zones rurales, parents, enfants, grands-parents, oncles, tantes, frères et sœurs vivent sous le même toit[1] et se partagent[2] le travail. Les couples mariés ont des pièces privées et préparent leurs propres repas. Tous les membres de la famille participent à l'éducation des enfants. Dans les villes, les couples mariés habitent aujourd'hui dans leur propre maison ou appartement.

ET TOI?

1. Qu'est-ce que veut dire «famille étendue» *(extended)* aux États-Unis?
2. Quel est le rôle de la famille dans l'éducation des enfants aux États-Unis?

Communauté et professions

Le français et l'enseignement 5.1

En France, les enfants apprennent à écrire vers 4 ou 5 ans à l'école maternelle[3]. Dans certaines écoles, ils commencent aussi à apprendre une langue étrangère. À quel âge est-ce que les enfants apprennent à écrire dans ta communauté? Est-ce qu'il existe des cours de langue pour les enfants dans ta communauté? Et à l'école primaire, est-ce qu'il y a des cours de langue? Fais des recherches et présente ce que tu as trouvé à la classe.

Classe de langue

1. under the same roof 2. share 3. kindergarten

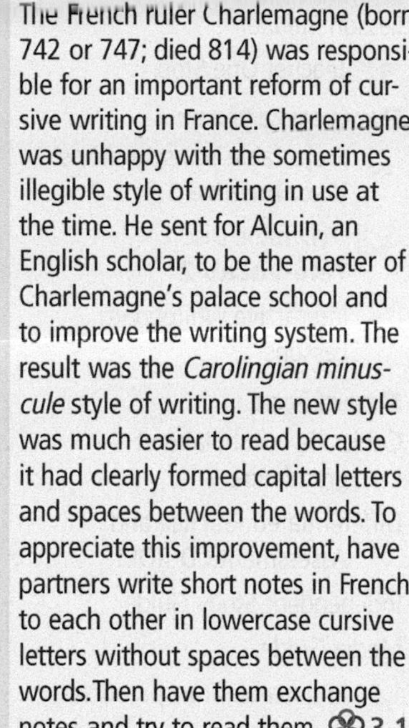

Connections

History Link

The French ruler Charlemagne (born 742 or 747; died 814) was responsible for an important reform of cursive writing in France. Charlemagne was unhappy with the sometimes illegible style of writing in use at the time. He sent for Alcuin, an English scholar, to be the master of Charlemagne's palace school and to improve the writing system. The result was the *Carolingian minuscule* style of writing. The new style was much easier to read because it had clearly formed capital letters and spaces between the words. To appreciate this improvement, have partners write short notes in French to each other in lowercase cursive letters without spaces between the words. Then have them exchange notes and try to read them. 3.1

Cultures

Products and Perspectives

Point out to students that the word **plume,** of **stylo plume,** means *feather.* Fountain pens were originally made from the feathers, or quills, of birds. First used around 700 A.D., quill pens are still in use today, especially by calligraphers who value their flexibility and sharp strokes. You might have students research the origin of the English word *pen* (derived from the Latin word *penna,* meaning "feather"). 2.2

Differentiated Instruction

ADVANCED LEARNERS

Have students write and illustrate a book for children ages three to five years. Students should write their book in French cursive. If possible, have volunteers visit a daycare center to read their books aloud to the children. 1.3, 5.1

SPECIAL LEARNING NEEDS

Students with Learning Disabilities/ Dyslexia Ask students to review and practice the vocabulary for family relationships in **Comparaisons** by designing their own, or an imaginary, family tree. Have students label the family members in French. When completing **Et toi?,** students may indicate on their family tree who lives in the same home and who plays a role in their education. Have students discuss the cultural differences between francophone countries and the United States. 2.1

Language Examination

Culture can be used to practice for the **Interpretive Communication** and **Presentational Writing** sections of the AP Language and Culture Exam as it helps students get acquainted with and reflect on products and practices from the French-speaking world while reading culture-focused passages and answering questions in French.

Resources

Planning:
Lesson Planner
Teacher One Stop

Presentation:
Projectable Transparencies **Vocabulaire 1.3, 1.4**

DVD Tutor, Disc 1 **Télé-vocab 2**
Interactive Whiteboard Lessons

Practice:
Cahier de vocabulaire et grammaire
Differentiated Practice and Assessment CD-ROM
Independent Study Guide
Media Guide
Projectable Transparencies Bell Work 1.5
HOMETUTOR
Holt McDougal French Apps

Bell Work

Use Bell Work 1.5 in the *Projectable Transparencies* or write this activity on the board.

Complete the sentences with the correct form of the adjective in parentheses.

1. **Ma tante a une ____ écharpe. (nouveau)**
2. **Mon cousin a des ____ yeux. (beau)**
3. **Notre chatte est très ____. Elle a onze ans. (vieux)**
4. **Tu as lu *Le* ____ *Automne?* (nouveau)**
5. **J'aime les ____ escaliers. (vieux)** 1.2

Objectifs
- to inquire
- to tell when you do something

Vocabulaire à l'œuvre 2

Télé-vocab

Révisions Après l'école, nous aimons...

faire du théâtre

jouer au tennis

aller au cinéma

faire de la vidéo amateur

jouer au basket-ball

Core Instruction

TEACHING VOCABULAIRE

1. Introduce the vocabulary with transparencies **Vocabulaire 1.3** and **1.4** and model the pronunciation of the words as you point to each person and item. **(2 min.)**
2. Ask for volunteers to mime the activities as you call out the vocabulary words. Model **Exprimons nous!,** identifying the activities. Then ask students if they do these activities. **Mark, tu joues de la batterie? Rachel, tu fais du théâtre? (3 min.)**
3. Ask, **Quand tu vas au café, est-ce que tu aimes boire (manger) une limonade (un croissant)?** If students do not seem to understand *to drink,* make the motion of drinking. Students answer with **oui** or **non.** Repeat, using each of the food and drink items in the presentation. **(3 min.)**

Télé-vocab 2

For a video presentation of this vocabulary, see the *DVD Tutor.*

Télé-vocab

Online Practice
my.hrw.com
Vocabulaire 2 practice

jouer de la musique

la guitare

la batterie

jouer du piano

aller au café

D'autres mots utiles

jouer aux échecs	*to play chess*
lire	*to read*
un coca	*soda*
un chocolat chaud	*hot chocolate*
un croque-monsieur	*toasted cheese sandwich with ham*
un jus de fruit	*fruit juice*
une limonade	*lemon-lime soda*
un sandwich au jambon	*ham sandwich*
une glace	*ice cream*
une tarte aux pommes	*apple tart*

Exprimons-nous!

To inquire	To respond
Il est bon, ton sandwich? *Is . . . any good?*	**Excellent!/Pas mauvais.** *Excellent!/Not bad.*
Est-ce que tu joues bien du piano? *Do you play . . . well?*	**Assez bien.** *Pretty well.*
Tu as envie d'/Ça te dit d'aller au café? *Do you feel like . . . ?*	**Pourquoi pas?** *Why not?*
Tu veux aller jouer au tennis maintenant? *Do you want . . . ?*	Non, **je n'ai pas le temps. Je dois...** *. . . I don't have the time. I have to/must . . .*
Qu'est-ce que tu penses de mon appareil photo? *What do you think of . . . ?*	**Il est génial!** *It's great!*

Vocabulaire et grammaire, *pp. 7–9*

▸ Vocabulaire supplémentaire, Au café, pp. R16–R17

Differentiated Instruction

ADVANCED LEARNERS

After presenting **Exprimons-nous!,** review the days of the week, months of the year, and seasons, using a calendar. On one month, write in activities you do regularly. Tell students an activity you do and how often. Ask individual students if they do the activity and if so, how often. 1.2

MULTIPLE INTELLIGENCES

Logical-Mathematical Using the vocabulary for **un café,** ask students to create a menu for the **café** with prices listed beside each item. Have students work with partners to order meals and create checks with the cost of the meal tallied. Students may research additional food items and their cost before doing the activity. Have students convert the prices to euros. 1.1

TPR
TOTAL PHYSICAL RESPONSE

Have students respond to these commands.

Lève-toi si tu joues du piano.

Lève la main si tu as un appareil photo numérique.

Mets les mains sur la tête si tu fais de la vidéo amateur.

Touche ton nez si tu adores la tarte aux pommes.

Then have some students mime activities. Their classmates will guess the activities.

Tu joues de la guitare?

Tu manges un sandwich?

Tu bois un chocolat chaud?

Finally, have their classmates tell them what activities to mime.

Fais de la photo!

Joue au tennis!

Mange une glace! 1.2

Cultures

Products and Perspectives

Have interested students form groups to compete in a baking contest. All groups might prepare their own version of a **tarte aux pommes,** or you might have them research recipes and prepare a variety of French pastries. Have the groups set up a display table for their entries. The rest of the class will circulate to do taste tests. Have students speak only French during the taste tests. Bakers should encourage their classmates to sample their pastries and ask them for their opinion. 2.2

Resources

Planning:
Lesson Planner
Teacher One Stop

Presentation:
Projectable Transparencies **Vocabulaire 1.3, 1.4**
DVD Tutor, Disc 1 **Télé-vocab 2**
Interactive Whiteboard Lessons

Practice:
Cahier de vocabulaire et grammaire
Differentiated Practice and Assessment CD-ROM
Independent Study Guide
Media Guide
Audio CD 1, Tr. 4
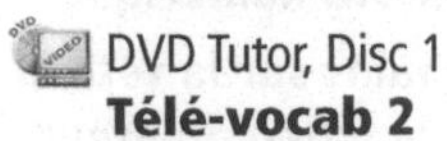
Holt McDougal French Apps

23 Script

1. — Camille, tu veux faire de la photo avec moi après l'école?
— Oui, je veux bien. J'ai un nouvel appareil photo.
2. — Qu'est-ce que tu as envie de manger ce midi?
— J'ai envie de manger un croque-monsieur.
3. — Ahmed, est-ce que tu joues bien de la batterie?
— Assez bien.
— On cherche quelqu'un qui joue de la batterie pour notre groupe de rock.
4. — Ludivine, ça te dit de faire les magasins cet après-midi?
— Non, je n'ai pas le temps. Je vais faire de la vidéo avec ma sœur.
5. — Qu'est-ce que tu penses de ma nouvelle raquette?
— Elle est géniale!

Flash culture

En général, les adolescents français n'ont pas d'activités après l'école. Le mercredi après-midi et le samedi après-midi, ils ne vont pas à l'école et beaucoup d'élèves font du sport. Ils vont en ville pour retrouver leurs copains, pour faire les magasins, ou pour aller au cinéma, à la médiathèque et dans les cafés. Beaucoup d'enfants ont aussi des leçons de musique ou de danse.

Et toi, qu'est-ce que tu aimes faire après l'école? Est-ce que tu aimes les mêmes activités que les élèves français? 4.2

22 Trouve l'intrus 1.2

Lisons Choisis le mot qui ne correspond pas aux autres.

1. a. une batterie b. un piano (c.) un appareil photo d. une guitare
2. a. une raquette (b.) une glace c. une balle d. une batte
3. (a.) aller au café b. un caméscope c. un appareil photo d. faire de la vidéo
4. a. un chocolat chaud (b.) une glace c. une limonade d. un coca
5. (a.) un sandwich au jambon b. une limonade c. un jus de fruit d. un café
6. a. un caméscope (b.) un croque-monsieur c. faire de la vidéo amateur d. un appareil photo

23 Écoutons CD 1, Tr. 4 1.2

Écoute les conversations suivantes. Quelle activité est-ce que chaque personne fait?

d 1. Camille — a. faire de la vidéo amateur
c 2. Yoan — b. jouer au tennis
e 3. Ahmed — c. aller au café
a 4. Ludivine — d. faire de la photo
b 5. Laurent — e. jouer de la musique

24 Tu veux bien... ? 1.2

Écrivons Tu es au café avec des amis. Pour chaque image, écris une conversation logique en utilisant les expressions de la boîte.

Il est bon... ? Est-ce que tu joues bien... ? Elle est bonne... ? Tu veux... ? Tu as envie de/d'... ?

MODÈLE —Il est bon, ton croque-monsieur?
—Oui, excellent!

1.

2.

3.

4.

5.

Entre copains

cool	*cool*
Ça me branche!	*I really like it!*
Ça me botte.	*I'm into it.*
Chouette!	*Great!*
vachement	*really, way*

Core Instruction

TEACHING EXPRIMONS-NOUS!

1. Show students a calendar and indicate the day or the season. Describe an activity you do on a certain day of the week. **Le vendredi, je vais au cinéma. Je dîne au café le dimanche.** Tell them how often you do activities. **Je fais de l'aérobic cinq fois par semaine. (2 min.)**
2. Tell them an activity you do in a certain season. **Je vais à la plage en été. (2 min.)**
3. Ask, **Qu'est-ce que tu fais le lundi?** Ask a different student for each day of the week. Ask the class, **Qui joue au tennis? (... fait du théâtre?)** Continue with, **Combien de fois par semaine est-ce que tu vas au café? (... fais de la photo?) (4 min.)**
4. Finally, ask about common student activities. **Est-ce que tu vas au match tous les vendredis? (4 min.)**

Exprimons-nous!

To tell when you do something

Le lundi, je fais **souvent** de la photo.
On Mondays . . . often . . .

Je joue au foot trois **fois par semaine.**
. . . times a week.

Je joue du piano **tous les mercredis.**
. . . every Wednesday.

Je fais du ski nautique **au printemps** et **en été.**
. . . in spring . . . in summer.

Je fais **rarement** du ski.
. . . rarely . . .

Vocabulaire et grammaire, *pp. 7–9*

Déjà vu!

Do you remember the days of the week and months?

lundi, mardi, mercredi, jeudi, vendredi, samedi, dimanche

janvier, février, mars, avril, mai, juin, juillet, août, septembre, octobre, novembre, décembre

25 Ta journée? 1.2

Écrivons Quand est-ce que tu fais ces activités? Écris des phrases en employant des mots de chaque boîte.

MODÈLE **Je joue au foot tous les vendredis.**

joue	de la photo	le vendredi
fais	du piano	au printemps (en été...)
vais	de la guitare	rarement
	du théâtre	souvent
	au base-ball	de temps en temps
	au cinéma	...fois par semaine
	aux cartes	tous les vendredis
	???	

Communication

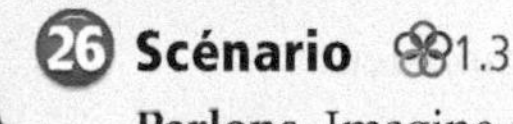

26 Scénario 1.3

Parlons Imagine que tu es un nouvel élève à ton école. Présente-toi à un camarade de classe. Parle-lui de ce que tu aimes et de ce que tu n'aimes pas. Parle aussi de ce que tu fais et de ce que tu ne fais pas après l'école. Ensuite, échangez les rôles.

MODÈLE **—Je m'appelle Christina et j'adore la musique. Je joue de la batterie tous les jours!**

Comparisons

Comparing and Contrasting

Have each student choose an activity and survey their classmates on how often they do the activity. Then have students e-mail a partner class in a French-speaking country to learn how often they do the same activity. Have groups compare their findings and see if they can come up with any generalizations on how teenagers in the French-speaking country spend their time compared to American teenagers. 4.2

Communication

26 Group Activity: Presentational

When partners interview each other, have them also talk about their own classes and what they think about them. Then have partners present their "new classmate" to the class. Presenters should include name, age, what the student does and doesn't do, what classes he or she has, and what his or her opinions are. The class should write down the information as they hear the "new classmates" being introduced. You might ask the class questions about individual students to see if the class can guess who they are. 1.3

Differentiated Instruction

SLOWER PACE LEARNERS

Have groups of three students create a short conversation using as many words and phrases in **Vocabulaire** and **Exprimons-nous!** as possible. Suggest that one student invite another to a **café** to have lunch with a third friend. The first student describes the third friend's appearance and personality. When the friend arrives, he or she turns out to be very materialistic, asking the first two students **"Qu'est-ce que tu penses de mon appareil photo (caméscope, raquette...)?".** 1.3

MULTIPLE INTELLIGENCES

Interpersonal Ask students to make a list of activities they enjoy, such as playing a sport, going to the movies, or listening to music. Each student should list at least ten activities. Have partners interview each other about how often they engage in each activity. Students will use expressions in **Exprimons-nous!** to reply to their partner's questions. 1.1

Assess

Assessment Program

Quiz: Vocabulaire 2

Alternative Assessment

Differentiated Practice and Assessment CD-ROM

Online Assessment
my.hrw.com

Test Generator 

Resources

Planning:
Lesson Planner
Teacher One Stop

Presentation:
DVD Tutor, Disc 1
Grammavision 2.1

Practice:
Grammar Tutor for Students of French, Chapter 1
Cahier de vocabulaire et grammaire
Differentiated Practice and Assessment CD-ROM
Cahier d'activités
Independent Study Guide
Media Guide
Projectable Transparencies
Bell Work 1.6
HOMETUTOR

Bell Work

Use Bell Work 1.6 in the *Projectable Transparencies* or write this activity on the board.

Choose the thing in each group that does not belong.

1. a. jouer aux cartes b. jouer au tennis c. jouer aux échecs
2. a. la batterie b. la glace c. la guitare
3. a. souvent b. tous les jours c. rarement
4. a. une raquette b. un caméscope c. un appareil photo

1.2

Objectifs
- *-er* verbs
- *-ir* and *-re* verbs

Grammaire à l'œuvre 2

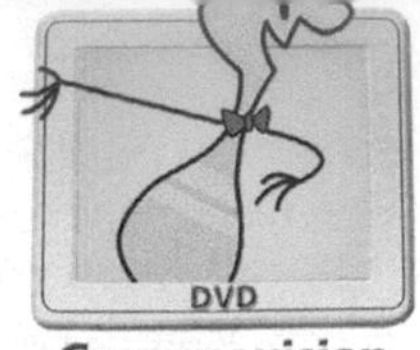

Grammavision

Révisions *-er* verbs

1 Most present-tense verbs ending in **-er** follow a regular pattern.

parler *(to speak)*	
je parl**e**	nous parl**ons**
tu parl**es**	vous parl**ez**
il/elle/on parl**e**	ils/elles parl**ent**

2 Verbs like **acheter** and **préférer** have the following spelling changes:

acheter *(to buy)*	préférer *(to prefer)*
j' ach**è**te	je préf**è**re
tu ach**è**tes	tu préf**è**res
il/elle/on ach**è**te	il/elle/on préf**è**re
nous achetons	nous préférons
vous achetez	vous préférez
ils/elles ach**è**tent	ils/elles préf**è**rent

3 Verbs ending in **-ger** and **-cer,** like **manger** *(to eat),* **voyager** *(to travel),* and **commencer** *(to begin),* have a spelling change in the **nous** form.

Nous ne mang**e**ons pas de pain.

Nous commen**ç**ons la fête?

Do you remember these other regular **-er** verbs?

regarder	*to look at*
aider	*to help*
étudier	*to study*
penser	*to think*
danser	*to dance*

Vocabulaire et grammaire, *pp. 10–11*
Cahier d'activités, *pp. 5–7*

4.1

En anglais

In English, you can tell that an action is happening in the present by using three forms of a verb.

I speak
I am speaking
I do speak

Look at the above examples. Do all the examples mean the same thing?

In French, you use one present tense form to express all three ideas.

Je travaille → *I work, I'm working, I do work*

The meanings vary slightly depending on the context.

27 Qu'est-ce qu'on fait? 1.2

Écrivons Fais des phrases en utilisant un élément de chaque boîte.

MODÈLE Je mange un croque-monsieur.

Je (J')	jouer	les cours à huit heures
Le professeur	manger	très bien français
Mes copains	parler	batterie
Nous, les élèves, nous	commencer	croque-monsieur
Vous, les Français, vous	préférer	faire de la photo

Core Instruction

TEACHING GRAMMAIRE

1. Re-introduce **-er** verb conjugations; model pronunciation with subject pronouns. Emphasize to students that the "shoe" verbs have the same pronunciation; **-ent** on the end of a verb is never pronounced. **(2 min.)**
2. Remind students that **acheter** and **préférer** have spelling changes, except in the **nous** and **vous** forms. For **acheter,** the **e** in the shoe has an **accent grave** (**è**). For **préférer,** the second **e** in the shoe changes from an **accent aigu** (**é**) to an **accent grave** (**è**). **(2 min.)**
3. Remind students that **manger** and **commencer** have spelling changes in the **nous** form to soften the hard **g** and **c** sounds. **(2 min.)**

Grammavision

For a video presentation of **-er** verbs, see the *DVD Tutor.*

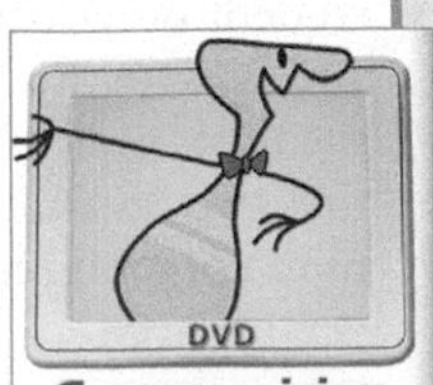

Grammavision

Online Practice
my.hrw.com
Grammaire 2 practice

28 Qu'est-ce qu'ils font? 1.2

Écrivons/Parlons Fais une phrase pour dire ce que chaque personne fait. Utilise les sujets indiqués et des verbes en **-er**.

MODÈLE **Loïc préfère la limonade.**

Loïc

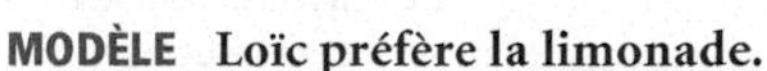
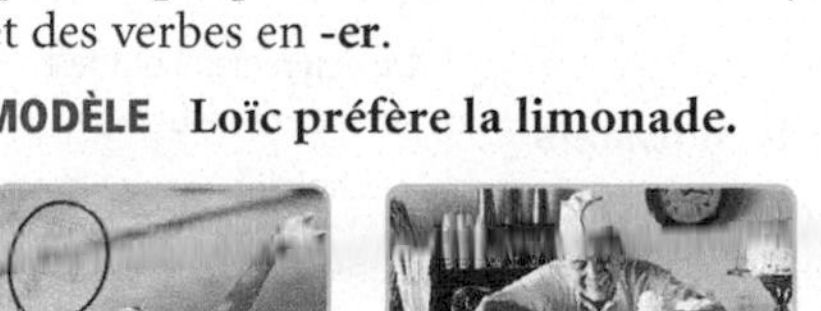

1. Julien

2. Tu

3. Nous

4. Vous

5. Géraldine et Christine

6. Je

29 Lettre à Hugo 1.3

Écrivons Tu as un nouveau correspondant français qui s'appelle Hugo. Écris-lui une lettre pour lui dire ce que tu aimes faire. Utilise des verbes en **-er** et dis quand tu fais les activités mentionnées.

MODÈLE **Salut, Hugo,**
Je m'appelle James et j'ai seize ans. J'aime… Je joue… trois fois par semaine. Avec mes amis, nous...

Communication

30 Questions personnelles 1.1

Parlons D'abord, prépare une liste de huit à dix questions à poser à un(e) camarade sur ses activités et sur les activités de ses amis et de sa famille. Puis, pose tes questions à ton/ta camarade. Ensuite, échangez les rôles.

MODÈLE **—Ashley, est-ce que toi et ta famille, vous voyagez en été?**
—Oui, nous voyageons souvent. Nous adorons aller à Miami. Et toi, tu aimes Miami?
—Je préfère Los Angeles...

Differentiated Instruction

ADVANCED LEARNERS

Share with students René Descartes's famous quote: **Je pense, donc je suis.** Discuss its meaning with students. Then have students come up with a similar statement that sums up who they are, for example, **Je joue au tennis, donc je suis.** Have them use the statement to create a poster, bumper sticker, or T-shirt. 1.3

SPECIAL LEARNING NEEDS

28 Students with Visual Impairments To assist students in your class, assign a partner to describe the photos in the activity. Ask students to listen to the descriptions and complete the sentences orally, in Braille, or in writing. Students may also use their own assistive technology to view the photos or may benefit from an enlarged copy of the photos.

French for Spanish Speakers

Ask Spanish speakers which verbs in Spanish correspond to **–er** verbs, like **parler.** (**–ar** verbs, like **hablar**) If they were to make up a new verb in Spanish, what ending would seem most likely? Ask them to name verbs in Spanish that have been borrowed from English. **(surfear)** Which verb ending do these words have? Why do students think this is? (**–ar** is the default verb form) Ask students how they use present-tense forms in Spanish and how they compare with the use of the present tense in French. (They both correspond to the three uses in English described in **En anglais.**) 4.1

28 Possible Answers

1. Julien joue au tennis.
2. Tu achètes une glace.
3. Nous voyageons en train.
4. Vous achetez un appareil photo.
5. Géraldine et Christine étudient à la bibliothèque..
6. Je mange un sandwich.

Communication

30 Group Activity: Interpersonal

Have students refer to the same list and ask their classmates how often they do the activities. **Combien de fois par... est-ce que...?** Responses should include adverbs or other expressions denoting frequency or time frame. The students should write down the responses they received.

MODÈLE
— Combien de fois par... est-ce que toi et tes amis, vous allez à la plage?
— Nous allons à la plage deux fois par an. 1.1

Resources

Planning:
Lesson Planner
Teacher One Stop

Presentation:

DVD Tutor, Disc 1
Grammavision 2.2

Practice:
Grammar Tutor for Students of French, Chapter 1
Cahier de vocabulaire et grammaire
Differentiated Practice and Assessment CD-ROM
Cahier d'activités
Independent Study Guide
Media Guide
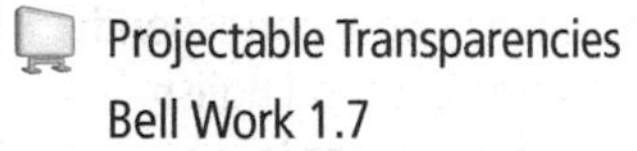
Projectable Transparencies
Bell Work 1.7
Audio CD 1, Tr. 5
@HOMETUTOR

Bell Work

Use Bell Work 1.7 in the *Projectable Transparencies* or write this activity on the board.

Complete the sentences with the correct form of the verb in parentheses.

1. Paul ____ au tennis. (jouer)
2. Nous ____ une tarte aux pommes au café. (manger)
3. Tu ____ jouer aux cartes ou jouer du piano? (préférer)
4. Ils ____ à la bibliothèque après l'école. (étudier)
5. Christian et moi, nous ____ les cours à 8h30. (commencer)

1.2

31 Script

See script on p. 3E.

Révisions -ir and -re verbs

Regular present-tense **-ir** and **-re** verbs follow these patterns.

finir (*to finish*)			
je	fin**is**	nous	fin**issons**
tu	fin**is**	vous	fin**issez**
il/elle/on	fin**it**	ils/elles	fin**issent**

vendre (*to sell*)			
je	vend**s**	nous	vend**ons**
tu	vend**s**	vous	vend**ez**
il/elle/on	vend	ils/elles	vend**ent**

Do you remember these regular **-ir** and **-re** verbs?

choisir	*to choose*
grossir	*to gain weight*
maigrir	*to lose weight*
réussir	*to succeed, pass an exam*
attendre	*to wait for*
descendre	*to go down, to get off/out*
perdre	*to lose*

Vocabulaire et grammaire, *pp. 10–11*
Cahier d'activités, *pp. 5–7*
Online Workbooks

Flash culture

Dans un café, il n'y a généralement pas autant de choix que dans un *coffee shop* américain. Vous pouvez commander **un café noir, un café au lait, un café crème** ou **un cappuccino.** Le café est servi dans de petites tasses et il est très fort. Vous pouvez aussi commander **un chocolat chaud** ou **un jus de fruits.** Il y a aussi des boissons au sirop. Vous pouvez déjeuner dans un café, mais le menu se limite aux sandwichs et au plat du jour.

Et le coffee shop près de chez toi, qu'est-ce qu'il offre? 4.2

31 Écoutons CD 1, Tr. 5 1.2

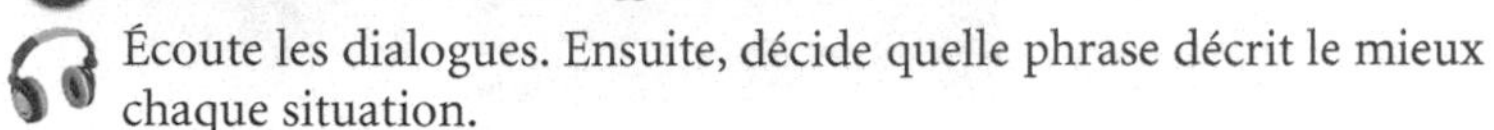

Écoute les dialogues. Ensuite, décide quelle phrase décrit le mieux chaque situation.

1. d
2. e
3. b
4. a
5. c

a. Julien choisit un t-shirt.
b. Farida attend sa sœur.
c. Le libraire (*bookstore employee*) vend des livres.
d. Nicolas réussit à son examen.
e. Claudine finit son café.

32 Questions 1.3

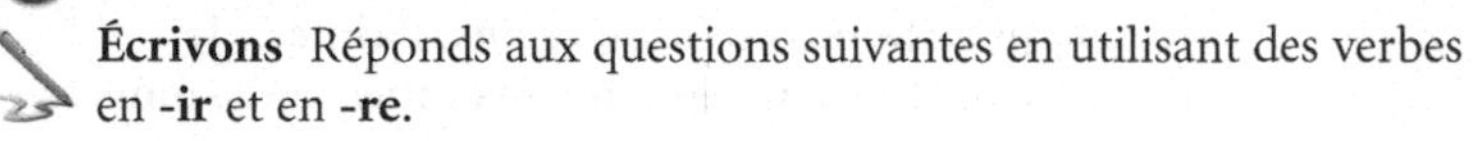

Écrivons Réponds aux questions suivantes en utilisant des verbes en **-ir** et en **-re**.

MODÈLE Quand est-ce que tu finis tes devoirs le soir?
Je finis mes devoirs à huit heures.

1. Qu'est-ce qu'on vend dans un café en France?
2. Qu'est-ce qui arrive aux personnes qui mangent trop?
3. Qu'est-ce qui arrive aux personnes qui ne mangent pas?
4. Où est-ce que tu attends souvent tes amis?
5. Est-ce que vous attendez souvent le professeur?
6. Pour jouer au tennis, tu choisis de porter un jean et une chemise ou un short et un tee-shirt?
7. Est-ce que tu réussis à tes examens?

Core Instruction

TEACHING GRAMMAIRE

1. Re-introduce **-ir** and **-re** verb conjugations; model pronunciation with subject pronouns. **(3 min.)**
2. Individually, ask students five **oui** or **non** questions. **Tu perds souvent ton livre? Tu descends l'escalier pour aller en cours de biologie? Tu grossis pendant les vacances d'hiver? Tu finis tes devoirs le dimanche soir? Tu attends tes amis après les cours? (5 min.)**
3. Then ask the class, **Qui perd souvent son livre?** Students will answer with the name of the correct student. **(5 min.)**

Grammavision

For a video presentation of **-ir** and **-re** verbs, see the *DVD Tutor.*

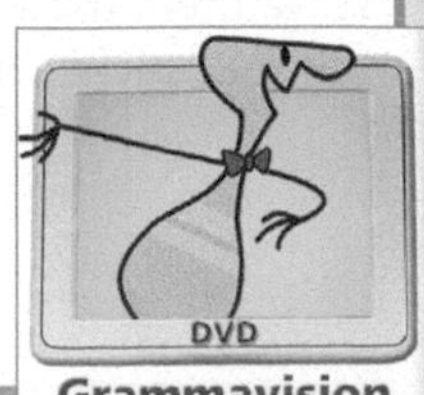

Grammavision

33 Suite logique 1.2

Lisons/Parlons Lis chaque phrase et propose une continuation logique. Utilise des verbes en **-ir** et en **-re**. Possible answers:

MODÈLE Il y a encore 4 pages dans mon livre. (finir)
Tu finis le livre.

1. Gérald a dix raquettes de tennis et il n'aime pas jouer au tennis. Il vend ses raquettes.
2. Noémie mange beaucoup de glace et de sandwichs. Elle grossit.
3. Tu es au café. Tu adores le chocolat. Tu choisis un chocolat chaud.
4. Nous ne mangeons pas beaucoup en été. Nous maigrissons.
5. On est dans le bus et on arrive à l'école. On descend.
6. Ahmed et Nan travaillent dans un magasin de photos. Ils vendent des appareils photo.

34 Qui fait quoi? 1.2

Écrivons/Parlons Décris ce qui se passe sur l'image. Utilise des verbes en **-ir** et en **-re**.

MODÈLE **Mlle Duménil et Mlle Lasti descendent les escaliers.**

Communication

Digital performance space

35 Scénario 1.1

Parlons Tu es au café avec des amis. Choisissez ensemble ce que vous allez prendre. Ensuite, parlez des activités que vous faites en ce moment ou de ce que vous allez faire pendant la journée. Utilisez des verbes en **-er, -ir** et en **-re.**

MODÈLE **—Alors, vous choisissez?**
—Oui, je choisis une limonade.

Grammaire 2

COMMON ERROR ALERT
ATTENTION !

Many **-ir** verbs already have **-is** or **ss** in their stems, which makes it very easy for students to forget to add the **-iss** in the plural forms. They will tend to write **grossons** instead of **grossissons** or **choisez** instead of **choisissez.**

34 Possible Answers

1. Sophie et Natalie attendent le serveur.
2. Ursula choisit une glace.
3. Marc et Gilles finissent leurs sandwichs.
4. M. Ramier vend le café.
5. Amadou attend sa petite amie.

Communication

Group Work: Presentational

Have small groups role-play a conversation between a restaurant server and some guests. Conversations should include inquiring what is available and the prices, ordering something to eat and drink, and paying the check. 1.3

Differentiated Instruction

SLOWER PACE LEARNERS

Form two teams. Have three students from each team go to the board. Call out an **-ir** verb and give students three minutes to write the conjugation with the help of their teammates. The team with the most correct verb forms wins a point. Erase the board and ask another two groups to go up. Give them two minutes to conjugate another **-ir** verb. Rotate team members and repeat with another **–ir** verb, but this time allow only one minute. Repeat with **–re** verbs. 1.3

MULTIPLE INTELLIGENCES

Musical Ask students to create rhythmic patterns or raps with the forms of the **-ir** and **-re** verbs. Students may practice all of the verbs, repeating the rhythmic pattern or rap they create, by pairing the subject with the verb form.

Je (clap) **fin** (clap) **is** (clap)
Tu (clap) **fin** (clap) **is** (clap)
Il (clap) **fin** (clap) **it** (clap) 1.2

Assess

Assessment Program
Quiz: Grammaire 2
Alternative Assessment
Differentiated Practice and Assessment CD-ROM

Online Assessment
my.hrw.com

Test Generator 

Synthèse
- Vocabulaire 2
- Grammaire 2

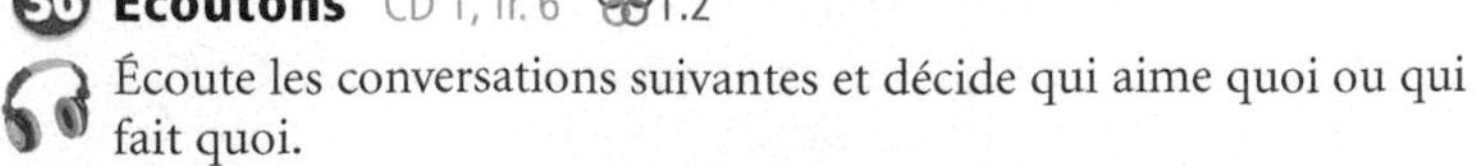

Application 2

36 Écoutons CD 1, Tr. 6 1.2

Écoute les conversations suivantes et décide qui aime quoi ou qui fait quoi.

c **1.** Mathias	**a.** joue au tennis.
d **2.** Valentine	**b.** aime le théâtre.
a **3.** Audrey	**c.** joue de la guitare.
e **4.** Benjamin	**d.** a envie de manger un croque-monsieur.
b **5.** Magali	**e.** fait de la photo.

37 Une journée typique 1.3

Écrivons Décris ce que tu fais typiquement dans la journée. Utilise des verbes variés (**-er**, **-ir** et **-re**).

MODÈLE **J'attends le bus. Quand j'arrive à l'école, je... Après les cours, je joue du piano. Le soir, je finis mes devoirs...**

Un peu plus

Révisions

Verbs like *dormir*

As you learned in Level 1, **dormir, partir,** and **sortir** follow a similar pattern of conjugation.

dormir *(to sleep)*: je dor**s**, tu dor**s**, il/elle/on dor**t**, nous dor**mons**, vous dor**mez**, ils/elles dor**ment**

partir *(to leave)*: je par**s**, tu par**s**, il/elle/on par**t**, nous par**tons**, vous par**tez,** ils/elles par**tent**

sortir *(to go out)*: je sor**s**, tu sor**s**, il/elle/on sor**t**, nous sor**tons**, vous sor**tez**, ils/elles sor**tent**

Vocabulaire et grammaire, *p. 12*
Cahier d'activités, *pp. 5–7*
Online Workbooks

38 Dormir, partir ou sortir? 1.2

Écrivons Complète chaque phrase avec la forme qui convient du verbe **dormir, partir** ou **sortir,** d'après le contexte.

1. Nous sortons souvent le samedi soir.
2. Vous maigrissez et vous êtes fatigués *(tired)*. Vous ne dormez pas assez!
3. Ces deux chiens dorment sur le lit toute la journée!
4. Claudia, tu sors ce soir? Où tu vas?
5. Les Martin partent en vacances en juillet.
6. Je pars pour l'école à huit heures le matin.
7. On dort tard le dimanche matin!

Resources

Planning:
Lesson Planner
Teacher One Stop

Practice:
Grammar Tutor for Students of French, Chapter 1
Cahier de vocabulaire et grammaire
Differentiated Practice and Assessment CD-ROM
Cahier d'activités
Independent Study Guide
Media Guide
Projectable Transparencies
Bell Work 1.8
Audio CD 1, Tr. 6

Bell Work

Use Bell Work 1.8 in the *Projectable Transparencies* or write this activity on the board.

Fill in the blanks with the correct form of **dormlr, partir,** or **sortir.**

1. **Le samedi matin, je ____ jusqu'à onze heures.**
2. **Nous ____ en vacances en Grèce.**
3. **Tu ____ avec tes amis ce soir.**
4. **Je ____ le train à 10h27.**
5. **Mon chat et mon chien ____ sur mon lit.**
6. **Vous ____ les poubelles le lundi matin.** 1.2

36 Script

See script on p. 3F.

39 Possible Answers

1. Oui, je dors beaucoup.
2. Oui, nous sortons le week-end.
3. Non, mes parents sortent rarement le soir.
4. Oui, j'ai un chien et un chat. Oui, ils dorment beaucoup.
5. Oui, je pars en vacances avec ma famille en été.
6. Moi, je pars à sept heures.

Core Instruction

INTEGRATED PRACTICE

1. Have students do Activities 36 and 37 to practice vocabulary and **-er** and **-ir** verbs. **(5 min.)**
2. Tell the class that they are organizing a **fête** for a group of visiting French teenagers. Ask questions. **Paul, tu achètes des boissons? (Oui, j'achète des boissons.)** Remind students of the **nous** form spelling changes in **-ger** and **-cer** verbs. **(5 min.)**

TEACHING UN PEU PLUS

1. Remind students that they know some verbs that look like regular **-ir** verbs, but are conjugated differently. **(1 min.)**
2. Remind students that the stem for the singular uses the first three letters of the infinitive, with endings **-s, -s, -t.** The stem for the plural uses the first four letters of the infinitive and endings are just like **-er** endings. **(2 min.)**
3. Continue with integrated practice Activities 38–40. **(10 min.)**

39 Et toi? 1.3

Parlons Réponds aux questions suivantes en utilisant les verbes **dormir, partir** et **sortir.**

1. Est-ce que tu dors beaucoup le week-end?
2. Est-ce que tes amis et toi, vous sortez le week-end?
3. Est-ce que tes parents sortent souvent le soir?
4. Est-ce que tu as des animaux? Ils dorment beaucoup?
5. Tu pars en vacances en été?
6. Moi, je pars de la maison à six heures le matin. Et toi?

40 Le dimanche 1.3

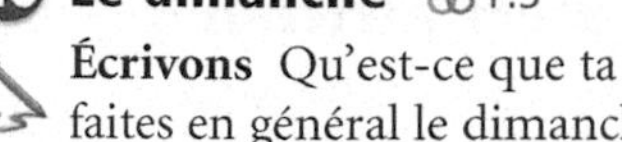

Écrivons Qu'est-ce que ta famille (ou tes amis) et toi, vous faites en général le dimanche? Écris un paragraphe pour décrire vos activités. Utilise le vocabulaire et la grammaire de ce chapitre.

MODÈLE **Je dors beaucoup parce que j'adore dormir! À onze heures, ma famille et moi, nous partons... Après, nous mangeons... Je choisis...**

Online Practice
my.hrw.com
Application 2 practice

Communication

Digital performance space

41 On fait connaissance 1.1

Parlons Imagine que tu rencontres *(meet)* ton/ta camarade de classe pour la première fois. Vous voulez savoir ce que vous aimez. Lisez les questions ci-dessous et répondez-y de manière logique. Ensuite, échangez les rôles.

— **Comment tu t'appelles?**
—
— **Qu'est-ce que tu aimes comme musique?**
—
— **Qu'est-ce que tu aimes faire?**
—
— **Est-ce que tu joues souvent au foot?**
—
— **Ça te dit d'aller au cinéma samedi?**
—

Language Examination

41 Sample answer:

— . . .
— Je m'appelle Cassandra.
— . . .
— J'aime la musique pop-rock et classique.
— . . .
— J'aime jouer aux échecs et au tennis.
— . . .
— Non, je ne joue jamais au foot.
— . . .
— Oui, pourquoi pas?

Differentiated Instruction

ADVANCED LEARNERS

Have students invent a card game or board game that helps students practice the conjugations of **-er, -ir,** and **-re** verbs. Set up stations around the room where students who have created games can teach small groups of students how to play their game. 1.1

SPECIAL LEARNING NEEDS

Students with AD(H)D To help students with AD(H)D focus on learning and have an opportunity to get out of their seats, ask a group to design and assemble a bulletin board or poster of verbs like **dormir**. The students should draw or find pictures showing the definition of **dormir, partir,** and **sortir.** Each verb should be conjugated correctly and a sample sentence given for each form. Other students may add additional verbs to the bulletin board. 1.2

Assess

Assessment Program
Quiz: Application 2
Audio CD 1, Tr. 16
Alternative Assessment
Differentiated Practice and Assessment CD-ROM

Online Assessment
my.hrw.com

Test Generator

Resources

Planning:
Lesson Planner
 Teacher One Stop

Presentation:
DVD Tutor, Disc 1
Télé-roman

Practice:
Media Guide
DVD Tutor, Disc 1
Télé-roman

Connections

Visual Learners

To help students understand the events in this episode of **Télé-roman,** have them create a flow chart of what happens. Guide students through the chart on the board by asking questions and filling in the boxes with simple sentences. In the first box, write what happens in scene 1: **Monsieur Gadio travaille dans son bureau.** Then ask students what happens next. Continue asking questions until students have charted the action of the entire episode. 3.2

Monsieur Gadio travaille dans son bureau.
↓
Monsieur Rigaud arrive dans le bureau de Monsieur Gadio.
↓
Monsieur Rigaud montre une statuette à Monsieur Gadio.

Gestures

Have students observe the body language and facial expression of Mr. Rigaud in scene 8. Ask them whether the expressions correspond to his words. What do they think he really thinks about Mr. Gadio's colleague coming to Dakar? 2.1

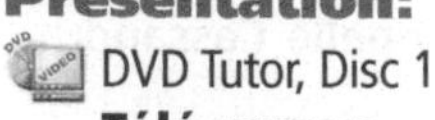

Télé-roman

Le Secret de la statuette *Épisode 1*

STRATÉGIE

Looking for clues A careful viewer looks for clues that can provide insight into where the story is headed. A clue can be something a character says, where a scene takes place, or any important event. Sometimes clues are quite obvious and sometimes they are purposely hidden. As you watch this first episode, look for as many clues as you can. 1.2

À Dakar: le bureau du conservateur du Musée d'art africain...

1 *M. Gadio travaille à son bureau. Quelqu'un tape à la porte.*

2

M. Rigaud Monsieur Gadio? Bonjour. Charles Rigaud. C'est moi qui vous ai téléphoné au sujet de la statuette. Comme je vous l'ai dit au téléphone, je suis responsable d'un groupe d'étudiants en archéologie et nous avons découvert cet objet rare.

3

M. Gadio Très intéressant... C'est une statuette dogon, en effet. Mais ce n'est pas ma spécialité. Je me spécialise en art wolof.

4

M. Rigaud Vous avez peut-être un collègue qui pourrait nous aider...

M. Gadio Oui, j'ai une collègue experte en objets rares de ce type, mais elle habite en France, à Nice. Mme Anne Bondy.

M. Rigaud Alors, gardez la statuette et faites ce que vous pouvez. Bonne journée, M. Gadio, et à bientôt!

Core Instruction

TEACHING TÉLÉ-ROMAN

1. Have students scan the **Télé-roman** text and look at the pictures. **(2 min.)**
2. Play the video in three segments, pausing after scenes 4, 6, and 8. Ask students who the woman in scene 5 is and where she is. Have students compare the different way Mr. Gadio speaks to her and to Mr. Rigaud. What does his language reveal about his relationship with these people? If students have trouble understanding, you might use the captioned version of the episode. **(5 min.)**
3. Play the video again without stopping and ask general comprehension questions. Have volunteers read and act out **Télé-roman.** Have them use gestures they saw in the video. **(10 min.)**
4. Have partners answer the **As-tu compris?** questions on page 29. **(5 min.)**

DVD Tutor 

As an alternative, you might use the captioned version of **Le Secret de la statuette** on DVD.

Visit Us Online
my.hrw.com
Online Edition

M. Gadio téléphone à son amie Anne Bondy.

5

Anne Salif! Quelle surprise! Ça va bien. Et toi?

6

M. Gadio Bien, bien… Dis-moi, j'ai un objet intéressant à te montrer… C'est une longue histoire. C'est une statuette… un objet rare, paraît-il…

Quelques jours plus tard, au bureau du conservateur

7

M. Rigaud Cher M. Gadio! Bonjour. Je passais dans le quartier, alors…

M. Gadio J'ai de très bonnes nouvelles, M. Rigaud. Ma collègue a décidé de venir à Dakar. Elle arrive la semaine prochaine. Comme ça, elle va pouvoir expertiser l'objet ici!

8

M. Rigaud Ah oui?… Elle vient à Dakar? Eh bien… c'est parfait… Écoutez, euh… je repasserai la semaine prochaine, alors. Bon… au revoir.

1.2

AS-TU COMPRIS?

1. Qui est M. Gadio?
2. Qu'est-ce que M. Rigaud veut?
3. Est-ce que M. Gadio peut évaluer la statuette? Pourquoi?
4. À qui est-ce que M. Gadio téléphone? Pourquoi?
5. Qui va venir à Dakar la semaine prochaine?

Prochain épisode:
D'après ce que tu as appris à la fin de cet épisode, est-ce que tu peux deviner ce qui va arriver dans l'épisode 2?

Télé-roman

As-tu compris? Answers

1. Il est conservateur du Musée d'art africain à Dakar.
2. laisser la statuette avec M. Gadio
3. non; ce n'est pas sa spécialité
4. à Mme Bondy; Elle est experte en objets rares, comme la statuette.
5. Mme Anne Bondy

Communication

Pair Activity: Interpersonal

After students have watched **Télé-roman,** have partners practice greeting people, providing information, and making requests. Have partners alternate role-playing Mr. Rigaud and Mr. Gadio. Then have them create a dialog that might have taken place during the rest of the phone conversation between Anne and Mr. Gadio. 1.1

Le Secret de la statuette Episode 1

This **Télé-roman** begins in the office of Salif Gadio, a museum curator in Dakar. A strange man wearing explorer's gear introduces himself as Charles Rigaud. He is a nervous man who constantly pulls on his ear. He wants help authenticating a Dogon statuette. When Mr. Gadio tells him he is not an expert in Dogon artifacts, Rigaud suggests that he ask a colleague. Mr. Gadio agrees to send it to a specialist in France, Anne Bondy. When Rigaud returns a few days later, he seems disappointed to learn that the statuette was not sent because Anne is coming to Dakar instead.

Lecture et écriture

Resources

Planning:

Lesson Planner

Teacher One Stop

Presentation:

Audio CD 1, Tr. 7–8

Practice:

Cahier d'activités

Reading Strategies and Skills Handbook, Chapter 1

Intermediate Reader

French InterActive Reader

Applying the Strategies

For practice with considering genre, have students use the "Sketch to Stretch" strategy from the *Reading Strategies and Skills Handbook.*

READING PRACTICE

STRATEGIES

Strategy: Sketch to Stretch

Reading Skill	When can I use this strategy?		
	Prereading	During Reading	Postreading
Drawing Conclusions			✓
Making Generalizations			✓
Analyzing Cause and Effect			✓
Summarizing			✓

Strategy at a Glance: Sketch to Stretch

- The teacher introduces **Sketch to Stretch** to students by showing and discussing symbolic pictures based on a text.
- After reading a selection, students work independently or with a partner to create their own symbolic sketches. On the back of the sketches, students write why they drew what they did, using evidence from the text to support their opinions.
- Students share their sketches in small groups, allowing others to comment before revealing explanations of their work.

Many students find it difficult to go beyond the reading selection to talk about the theme, or the symbolism, or to express a generalization about the story that can be applied to their lives. But some students who have difficulty talking about a text can express their ideas visually, far beyond what even they themselves imagine. This strategy, **Sketch to Stretch**, gives students the opportunity to formulate images that represent the ideas they cannot otherwise express. For some students, putting ideas into pictures, rather than words, is the best way to express their responses to the text.

This is a postreading strategy in which students think about what a passage or entire selection means to them and then draw symbolic representations of their interpretations of the text. As students discuss the text and decide what to draw, they think about the theme, draw conclusions, form generalizations, recognize cause-and-effect relationships, and summarize.

Considering Genre

Explain to students that genre is a literary category of text, such as poetry, prose, or drama. Ask students to identify the genre of this selection. What characteristics help them identify the genre? Then have partners discuss what this selection would be like if it were written in another genre. Would the effect be the same?

Lecture et écriture

Maurice Carême (1899–1978), instituteur et poète belge, écrit ses premiers poèmes en 1914. Il devient instituteur en 1918. À partir de 1943, il décide de se consacrer[1] à la littérature. Il écrit beaucoup pour les enfants.

STRATÉGIE pour lire

Genre of a text Consider the genre of a text before you read it. Different genres are short stories, novels, poems, essays, and plays. The genre tells you what kind of writing to expect.

A Avant la lecture 3.1

Le poème est un genre littéraire particulier. Pense aux poèmes que tu as déjà lus. Quelles sont leurs caractéristiques? Est-ce qu'ils sont tous en vers[2]? Est-ce qu'ils riment? Est-ce qu'ils ont plusieurs strophes? CD 1, Tr. 7–8

Le vieux piano

Lorsque[3] je vais chez ma cousine,
Elle ouvre son vieux piano.
Malheureusement, il joue faux[4],
Le piano de ma cousine.

5 Mon cousin est sourd comme un pot[5],
Et il sourit[6] dans la cuisine
Lorsqu'il voit taper[7] ma cousine
Sur son vieux piano si faux.

Mais que peut penser la voisine[8] ?
10 Elle doit me trouver bien sot[9]
Lorsque j'écoute ma cousine
Taper sur son vieux piano.

1. dedicate himself **2.** verse **3.** when **4.** out of tune **5.** deaf as a post **6.** smiles **7.** to bang **8.** neighbor **9.** foolish

Core Instruction

TEACHING LECTURE

1. Read **Stratégie** aloud and discuss it with students. **(1 min.)**
2. Have students do **Avant la lecture** orally. Provide examples of well-known poems in English to which students can refer to answer the questions. **(2 min.)**
3. Have students read the poems silently and take note of key words that help them understand the poems. Then have partners work together to do Activities B and C. Discuss with the class what effect these selections would have if they were written in another genre. **(10 min.)**
4. Choose two students to read the poems aloud. Complete Activities D and E orally in class. **(8 min.)**

L'enfant à l'harmonica

Un enfant joue un air
D'harmonica dans la lumière[1].
L'air est si doux[2] que l'on voudrait,
Sur le seuil[3] de la porte,
5 Être sa mère qui paraît[4]
Et lui sourit, accorte[5].
Des gens[6] passent, surpris,
Et regardent l'enfant assis.
Et l'on est si comblé[7] de joie
10 Que l'on a envie, malgré soi[8],
De remercier les cieux[9]
Où l'on dirait que Dieu[10]
Lui-même est venu s'accouder[11]
Pour écouter l'enfant jouer.

1. light 2. soft 3. threshold 4. appears 5. cheerful 6. people 7. filled with 8. despite oneself 9. heavens 10. God 11. to lean on his elbows

Lecture et écriture

Differentiated Instruction

SLOWER PACE LEARNERS

Before class, write the stanzas of **"Le vieux piano"** and sections of **"L'enfant à l'harmonica"** on index cards. Read the poems aloud once. Then form small groups. Give each group an index card and have them discuss the meaning of their section of the poems. Call on each group to give their interpretation. 1.2

SPECIAL LEARNING NEEDS

Students with Learning Disabilities Review the meaning of genre before beginning Activity A and **Stratégie pour lire.** Help students understand genre by providing examples of short stories, novels, poems, essays, and plays. Discuss with students the particular characteristics of each genre and show the examples to the class.

Lecture et écriture

Comparisons

Comparing and Contrasting

Ask students if they see any differences, besides the language, in how the titles are written, compared to poem titles in English. Point out that in English, the first word and last word of titles are capitalized, as well as nouns, verbs, adjectives, adverbs, and, occasionally, other parts of speech. In French, there are several systems for capitalizing titles. In one system, shown by these poems' titles, only the first letter and any proper nouns are capitalized. You might find French books, newspapers, and magazines that use another system of capitalizing titles and have students see if they can figure out the rules. 4.1

Connections

Language Arts Link

Ask students to name the four main purposes authors and poets have for writing. (to entertain, to inform, to persuade, to share an experience) Discuss the poet's purposes in writing **"Le vieux piano"** and **"L'enfant à l'harmonica".** You might ask students to find four poems, short stories, fables, or other literature that reflect the four main purposes. 3.1

Language Examination

ACTIVITÉ PRÉPARATOIRE PRE AP

Through the practice of listening and reading comprehension, as well as essay writing, **Lecture et écriture** helps students prepare for the **Interpretive Reading and Listening** and the **Presentational Writing** sections of the AP Language and Culture Exam.

Additional Practice

For more reading practice, see **Variations littéraires,** pp. 382–383.

Comparisons

Comparing and Contrasting

Read a line from a poem in English that has a strong beat ("LIST-en my CHIL-dren and YOU shall HEAR, of the MIDnight RIDE of PAUL ReVERE."). Point out that in English poetry, certain syllables are given heavier stress to create the rhythm of the poem. Then read the first line of **"Le vieux piano"**, stressing the syllables as if it were an English poem. Then read it normally, without heavy stress. Tell students that French poetry does not place heavy stress on syllables because the French language itself is largely "stress-free." French poetry achieves its rhythm by the number of syllables in each line, rather than by stressing syllables. Have students research French poetry Web sites to find out what the terms **décasyllabe, octosyllabe,** and **alexandrin** mean. (ten-syllable, eight-syllable, and twelve-syllable lines of poetry) 4.1

Compréhension

B Complète chaque phrase en choisissant la bonne réponse. 1.2

Le vieux piano

1. _______ joue du piano.
   a. Le cousin — (b.) La cousine
2. Le piano est en _______ condition.
   a. bonne — (b.) mauvaise
3. Le cousin _______.
   (a.) n'entend *(hear)* pas bien — b. fait la cuisine

L'enfant à l'harmonica

4. L'enfant est _______ la maison.
   (a.) devant — b. dans
5. La mère de l'enfant est _______.
   a. surprise — (b.) contente
6. L'enfant joue très _______.
   (a.) bien — b. mal

C Réponds aux questions suivantes. 1.2

Le vieux piano

1. Qui est sourd? le cousin
2. Qui aime jouer du piano? la cousine
3. Qu'est-ce que la voisine doit penser du narrateur? Elle doit penser que le narrateur est sot.

L'enfant à l'harmonica

4. Qui sort de la maison pour regarder l'enfant? sa mère
5. Qui écoute l'enfant jouer de l'harmonica? les gens
6. Quel sentiment est-ce que les gens éprouvent *(feel)* en écoutant l'enfant jouer de l'harmonica? Ils sont heureux.

Après la lecture

D Look at the characteristics for one of the poems that you recalled in **Avant la lecture**. Which characteristics did you find in each of these new poems? Point out examples of at least two characteristics in each poem. 3.1

E Both poems are about music, an art form meant to be heard. Read the poems aloud. Which sounds repeat themselves? What is the rhyme scheme or pattern of sounds at the end of each line? 3.1

Core Instruction

TEACHING ESPACE ÉCRITURE

1. Discuss **Stratégie pour écrire.** You may wish to model a writing plan for students, making a short list of your friends or relatives and then a cluster diagram to organize adjectives and adverbs. **(5 min.)**
2. Assign a specific number of relatives about whom students are to write. Have students brainstorm with a partner for step 1. Then have them complete steps 2 and 3 individually. If students are not able to complete the assignment in class, you might assign it as homework. **(25 min.)**
3. Have students complete step 4, allowing time for them to answer their partner's letter. **(15 min.)**

Espace écriture

STRATÉGIE pour écrire

A writing plan can help you create an interesting description that has variety and detail. An example of a writing plan would be to list the topics you want to cover, then to use a cluster diagram to organize nouns, adjectives and adverbs related to each topic.

Vacances en famille 1.3

Imagine that you are spending a month with some relatives during the summer. The relatives may be real or imaginary. Write a letter describing your vacation to your best friend back at home. Use the following guidelines to write your letter.

1 Plan

List the names of real or imaginary relatives. For each person, brainstorm:

- physical and personality traits
- things and activities he/she likes or dislikes
- activities you do together
- when or how often you do the activities.

Then, organize the information in a cluster diagram.

grand, brun, yeux verts | gentil, timide | cinéma, football
Kevin

2 Rédaction

Now, write the letter to your best friend, telling about your relatives and what you do together. Describe your relatives and tell what they like and dislike. Then, mention some of the activities you do together and when you usually do them.

3 Correction

Read your draft at least two times. Check for:

- agreement of adjectives and definite articles
- the correct forms of **être, avoir,** and **-er, -ir,** and **-re** verbs.

4 Application

Exchange letters with classmates and read them. With whose family would your classmates most like to spend the summer? Choose a classmate's letter and answer it.

Lecture et écriture

Process Writing

Avant d'écrire Although students may be tempted to write some words or phrases in English in the prewriting activity, encourage them to write their ideas in French. Set a time limit of three to five minutes. Students should build their cluster diagrams beginning with words and progressing to phrases. You may want to play a word association game to show them how to get started.

Writing Assessment

To assess the **Espace écriture,** you can use the following rubric. For additional rubrics, see the *Assessment Program* or refer to the *Generate Success* Rubric Generator.

Writing Rubric	4	3	2	1
Content (Complete—Incomplete)				
Comprehensibility (Comprehensible—Seldom comprehensible)				
Accuracy (Accurate—Seldom accurate)				
Organization (Well-organized—Poorly organized)				
Effort (Excellent effort—Minimal effort)				

18-20: A 16-17: B 14-15: C 12-13: D Under 12: F

Differentiated Instruction

ADVANCED LEARNERS

Modify the writing activity by having students write a poem, or poems, about their two relatives. First, show students how to analyze the rhyme schemes of **"Le vieux piano"** and **"L'enfant à l'harmonica".** (Mark the first line "A" and all the lines that rhyme with it "A", then mark the next line that ends with a different sound "B" and the lines that rhyme with that line as "B", and so forth.) Have students choose one of the rhyme schemes to use in their poem. 1.2

SPECIAL LEARNING NEEDS

Students with Learning Disabilities Prior to beginning **Espace écriture,** create a worksheet with a blank cluster diagram like the one pictured. Make copies of the worksheet for any student who would like to use it when making the writing plan described in **Stratégie pour écrire.** Students may need more than one copy, one for each relative they describe in their letter. Assist students by writing a brief letter based on the diagram in the text.

Assess

Assessment Program
Quiz: Lecture
Quiz: Écriture
Online Assessment my.hrw.com
Test Generator 

Prépare-toi pour l'examen

Resources

Planning:
Lesson Planner
Teacher One Stop

Practice:
Cahier d'activités
Media Guide
DVD Tutor, Disc 1
Projectable Transparencies
Situation, Chapitre 1
Picture Sequences, Chapter 1
Audio CD 1, Tr. 10–13
@HOMETUTOR

French for Spanish Speakers

Ask Spanish speakers to compare the use of accents in French with those in Spanish. Ask them what an accent on a word like **écrire** indicates. (the pronunciation of the letter *e*) Have them compare that with the written accent in the Spanish word **lápiz.** What does the accent in this word indicate? (The stress falls on the first syllable instead of the last.) Spanish and French do share a common use for accents: to distinguish otherwise identical words from each other. 4.1

Reteaching

Begin by asking, **Je suis comment? grand(e)? jeune? amusant(e)?** Next, hold up pictures of people and ask what they are like. **Il/Elle est comment? Ils/Elles sont comment?** Then name or show a photo of a celebrity and ask questions, such as **Il est fort? Il est brun?**

Chapitre 1

Prépare-toi pour l'examen

@HOMETUTOR

1 Vocabulaire 1
- to describe yourself and ask about others
- to talk about your likes and dislikes

pp. 6–9

1 Comment est ton/ta meilleur(e) ami(e)? Réponds aux questions suivantes. 1.3

1. Il/Elle s'appelle comment?
2. Il/Elle a quel âge?
3. Il/Elle a les yeux et les cheveux de quelle couleur?
4. Comment est-il/elle? (Décris sa personnalité.)
5. Qu'est-ce qu'il/elle aime faire?

2 Grammaire 1
- the verbs **avoir** and **être**
- adjective agreement

Un peu plus
- the adjectives **beau, nouveau, vieux**

pp. 10–15

2 Aurélie parle de sa famille. Complète ses phrases avec les formes correctes des verbes **avoir** ou **être**. 1.2

1. Mon père n'est __1__ pas très âgé. Il a __2__ 38 ans.
2. Mes sœurs ont __3__ les yeux marron et les cheveux blonds. Elles sont __4__ très jolies.
3. Je suis __5__ grande et je (j') ai __6__ les cheveux noirs.
4. Mon cousin et moi, nous avons __7__ seize ans. Nous sommes __8__ jeunes! Et vous, vous avez __9__ quel âge?
5. Tu as __10__ quinze ans et ta sœur a __11__ quinze ans aussi?

3 Vocabulaire 2
- to inquire
- to tell when you do something

pp. 18–21

3 D'abord, décris les personnes représentées. Ensuite, dis ce qu'ils/elles ont ou ce qu'ils/elles font. 1.2

Preparing for the Exam

FOLD-N-LEARN
Pinwheel Map Study Aid

1. Have students fold a sheet of paper in thirds from top to bottom, and then from side to side. They should unfold the sheet and, in the center rectangle, draw a circle and write **Chapitre 1.** In the bottom middle rectangle they should draw a circle and, in it, write **Describing.** Students should draw a line to connect the circles.

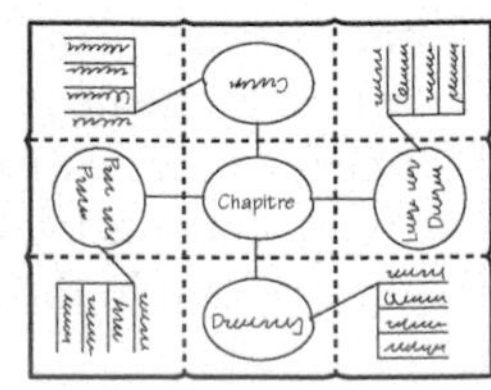

2. In the middle rectangle students should draw a circle and write **Likes and Dislikes.** They should connect this with the center circle, and then continue drawing and labeling circles for the rest of the chapter vocabulary.
3. Ask students to draw a line from each circle to the rectangle to the right. Have them list the vocabulary for the category in the rectangle and draw branch lines to the line from the category. Students should write the English equivalents on the back of each rectangle.

Prépare-toi pour l'examen

Online Assessment
my.hrw.com
Chapter Self-test

4 Écris des phrases complètes. 1.2

1. Je / finir toujours / mes devoirs de français
2. Mes amis et moi / préférer passer le samedi au parc / et nous / attendre le week-end avec impatience
3. Mes parents / manger beaucoup / et ils / grossir facilement
4. Mon ami / aimer étudier / et il / ne jamais perdre ses devoirs
5. Vous / répondre toujours aux questions du professeur

4 Grammaire 2
- -er verbs
- -ir and -re verbs

Un peu plus
- verbs like **dormir**

pp. 22–27

5 Réponds aux questions suivantes. 2.1

1. Qu'est-ce qu'on fait le dimanche en général en France?
2. Donne trois exemples de diminutifs familiaux.

5 Culture
- **Flash culture pp. 8, 12, 20, 24**
- **Comparaisons pp. 16–17**

6 Écoute la conversation entre Michèle et son amie Géraldine et dis si les phrases suivantes sont **a) vraies** ou **b) fausses.** 1.2

CD 1, Tr. 10

b **1.** Marc est le frère d'Alice.
a **2.** Géraldine trouve que Marc est beau.
a **3.** Michèle a un frère.
b **4.** Michèle croit que Marc a dix-huit ans.
b **5.** Marc joue au foot le mardi.

7 C'est la rentrée et tu parles avec un(e) nouvel(le) élève. D'abord, lisez les instructions pour chaque réplique *(exchange)*. Ensuite, créez votre dialogue en utilisant des expressions de ce chapitre et des autres chapitres. 1.1

Élève A:	Salue ton/ta camarade. Présente-toi et demande-lui comment il/elle s'appelle.
Élève B:	Dis comment tu t'appelles.
Élève A:	Demande à ton/ta camarade son âge.
Élève B:	Dis ton âge et pose la même question.
Élève A:	Dis ton âge et pose à ton/ta camarade une question sur sa famille.
Élève B:	Réponds et demande à ton/ta camarade ce qu'il/elle aime faire.
Élève A:	Dis ce que tu aimes faire. Propose à ton/ta camarade de faire quelque chose.
Élève B:	Accepte ou refuse l'invitation.

4 Answers
1. Je finis toujours mes devoirs de français.
2. Mes amis et moi, nous préférons passer le samedi au parc et nous attendons le week-end avec impatience.
3. Mes parents mangent beaucoup et ils grossissent facilement.
4. Mon ami aime étudier et il ne perd jamais ses devoirs.
5. Vous répondez toujours aux questions du professeur.

5 Answers
1. On passe le temps en famille.
2. Maman, papa, mamie, papi, tonton, tatie ou tata

6 Script
See script on p. 3F.

7 Sample conversation:

a. Bonjour. Je m'appelle Jonathan. Comment tu t'appelles?
b. Je m'appelle Margot.
a. Tu as quel âge?
b. J'ai 16 ans? Et toi?
a. J'ai 15 ans. Tu as des frères et sœurs?
b. Non, je suis fille unique. Qu'est-ce que tu aimes faire?
a. J'aime aller au cinéma. Ça te dit d'aller au cinéma avec moi samedi?
b. Non, je n'ai pas le temps.

Additional Speaking Practice

- For additional speaking practice, you might use the *Picture Sequences Transparency* for Chapter 1 found in the *Projectable Transparencies.*
- To assess the speaking activities in this section, you might use the *Generate Success* Rubric Generator or the oral rubrics found in the *Assessment Program.*

Pre-AP Practice

7 This guided conversation activity helps students practice oral exchanges using material from this chapter and previous chapters. The activity helps prepare students for the **Interpersonal Speaking** section of the AP French Language and Culture Exam.

Chapitre 1

Prépare-toi pour l'examen

Grammar Review

For more practice with the grammar topics in this chapter, see the *Grammar Tutor*, the *DVD Tutor*, the *@HomeTutor*, or the *Cahier de vocabulaire et grammaire*.

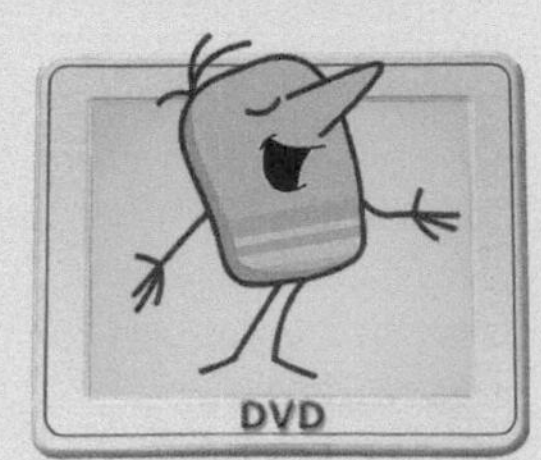

Grammavision

Online Edition

Students might use the online textbook and Performance Space to practice the **Lettres et sons** feature.

Dictée Script

1. Ta mère est souvent sérieuse.
2. Nous préférons l'été.
3. Je te présente mon père.
4. Ça te dit de jouer aux échecs?
5. Le garçon parle bien français.

Game

Téléphone Write five to ten sentences with the vocabulary and structures from the chapter. Form teams of 8–10 and ask each team to stand in a row. Ask the first student in each row to read silently the same sentence. These students will then whisper the sentence to the person behind them, and so on down the row, until the last person hears the sentence. That person writes the sentence on a piece of paper. Give a point to the team whose final sentence was closest to the original. Give 2 points if it was exactly the same. Continue with this game until all the sentences have been read.

1.1

Grammaire 1
- the verbs **avoir** and **être**
- adjective agreement

Un peu plus
- the adjectives **beau, nouveau, vieux**

pp. 10–15

Résumé: Grammaire 1

Here are the forms of the verbs **avoir** *(to have)* and **être** *(to be)*:

avoir: j'**ai**, tu **as**, il/elle/on **a**, nous **avons**, vous **avez**, ils/elles **ont**

être: je **suis**, tu **es**, il/elle/on **est**, nous **sommes**, vous **êtes**, ils/elles **sont**

To make most adjectives **feminine**, add an **-e**. To make most adjectives **plural**, add an **-s**. Masculine adjectives that end in **-eux** do not change form in the plural.

These adjectives have irregular forms:

Masculine before a consonant	Masculine before a vowel (sound)	Feminine	Masculine plural	Feminine plural
beau	bel	belle	beaux	belles
nouveau	nouvel	nouvelle	nouveaux	nouvelles
vieux	vieil	vieille	vieux	vieilles

Grammaire 2
- **-er** verbs
- **-ir** and **-re** verbs

pp. 22–27

Un peu plus
- verbs like **dormir**

Résumé: Grammaire 2

Most verbs ending in -er follow this pattern:

parler: je parle, tu parles, il/elle/on parle, nous parl**ons**, vous parl**ez**, ils/elles parl**ent**

Regular **-ir** and **-re** verbs follow this pattern:

finir: je fin**is**, tu fin**is**, il/elle/on fin**it**, nous fin**issons**, vous fin**issez**, ils/elles fin**issent**

vendre: je vend**s**, tu vend**s**, il/elle/on vend, nous vend**ons**, vous vend**ez**, ils/elles vend**ent**

Verbs like **dormir** *(to sleep)*, **partir** *(to leave)*, and **sortir** *(to go out)* follow a pattern: je dor**s**, tu dor**s**, il/elle/on dor**t**, nous dor**mons**, vous dor**mez**, ils/elles dor**ment**

Lettres et sons

Les accents CD 1, Tr. 11–13

Accent marks are important to the spelling and pronunciation of French words.

- Pronounce **é (accent aigu)** like the *a* in the word *day*: vidéo, caméscope
- Pronounce **è (accent grave)** like the *e* in the English word *jet*: mère, père. However, the **accent grave** over other vowels does not change pronunciation.
- The **cédille** under the letter *c* indicates that it should be pronounced like an *s*: **Ç**a te dit?

Jeux de langue

En été, à la mer, ma mère préfère aller avec mon père et mes frères.

Dictée

1.2

Écris les phrases de la dictée.

Chapter Review

DVD Program

Online Edition

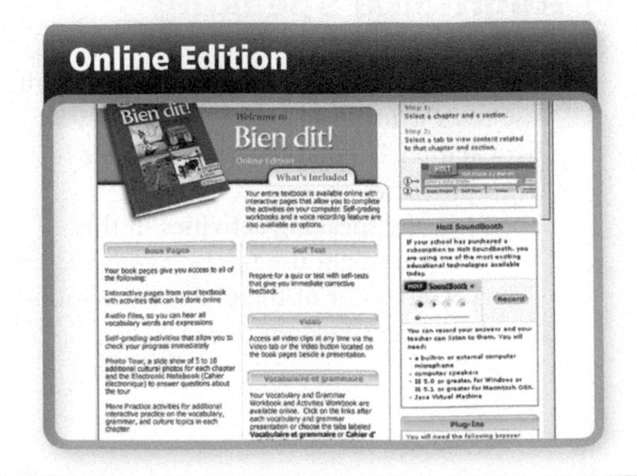

Résumé: Vocabulaire 1

PRACTICE FRENCH WITH HOLT MCDOUGAL APPS!

To describe yourself and ask about others

âgé(e)	*old*
un beau-père/une belle-mère	*stepfather/stepmother*
blond(e)/roux (rousse)	*blond/red-haired*
brun(e)	*brunette*
un chat/un chien	*cat/dog*
des cheveux (m.)	*hair*
un copain	*friend*
court(e)/long(ue)	*short/long*
un cousin (une cousine)	*cousin*
une famille	*family*
un frère/une sœur	*brother/sister*
gentil(le)	*nice*
grand(e)	*tall*
une grand-mère	*grandmother*
un grand-père	*grandfather*
gros(se)	*fat*
intelligent(e)	*intelligent*
marrant(e)	*funny*
marron	*brown*
une mère/un père	*mother/father*
mince	*slim*
un oncle/une tante	*uncle/aunt*
pénible	*annoying*
petit	*short, small*
sérieux (sérieuse)	*serious*
sportif (sportive)	*athletic*
timide	*shy*
vert(e)	*green*
des yeux (m.)	*eyes*
Comment tu t'appelles?	*What is your name?*
Je m'appelle...	*My name is . . .*
Tu as quel âge?	*How old are you?*
J'ai... ans.	*I am . . . years old.*
De quelle couleur sont...?	*What color are . . . ?*
Ils sont...	*They are . . .*
Il/Elle est comment... ?	*What is he/she like . . . ?*
Il/Elle est...	*He/She is . . .*

To talk about likes and dislikes..............See p. 9

Résumé: Vocabulaire 2

To inquire

aller au cinéma	*to go to the movies*
un appareil photo (numérique)	*(digital)camera*
un café	*café/coffee*
un caméscope	*video camera*
un chocolat chaud	*hot chocolate*
un coca/une limonade	*soda/lemon soda*
un croque-monsieur	*toasted cheese sandwich with ham*
faire de la photo	*to do photography*
faire du théâtre	*to do theater/drama*
faire de la vidéo amateur	*to make videos*
une glace	*ice cream*
jouer au basket-ball	*to play basketball*
jouer au tennis	*to play tennis*
jouer aux échecs	*to play chess*
jouer de la batterie	*to play drums*
jouer de la guitare/du piano	*to play guitar/piano*
un jus de fruit	*fruit juice*
lire	*to read*
une limonade	*lemon-lime soda*
une raquette/une balle	*racket/(tennis) ball*
un sandwich au jambon	*ham sandwich*
une tarte aux pommes	*apple tart*
Ça te dit de/d'... ?	*Do you feel like . . . ?*
Tu as envie de/d'...?	*Do you feel like . . . ?*
Est-ce que tu joues bien... ?	*Do you play . . . well?*
Il est bon, ...?	*Is . . . any good?*
Qu'est-ce que tu penses de... ?	*What do you think of . . . ?*
Tu veux...?	*Do you want . . . ?*
Assez bien.	*Pretty well.*
Il est génial!	*It's great!*
Je n'ai pas le temps.	*I don't have the time.*
Pourquoi pas?	*Why not?*

To tell when you do something.............See p. 21

Prépare-toi pour l'examen

Chapitre 1

Prépare-toi pour l'examen

Holt McDougal French Apps

Remind students that they can use the Holt McDougal French Apps to review their vocabulary.

Teacher to Teacher

Sue Mistric
Mount St. Mary Academy
Little Rock, AR

To help students enrich their vocabulary as they continue to study French, use these tips at the beginning of the year and refer to them all year. A good way to build vocabulary is to help students recognize word families. For example, *to skate, skating, skating rink, skate,* and *skater* are all in the same word family. When presenting the verb **patiner,** also present **patinage, patinoire, patin,** and **patineur/patineuse.**

1.2

Projectable Transparency

More Digital Resources

FOR THE STUDENT

- Holt McDougal French Apps
- @HomeTutor
- News and Networking
- Performance Space

FOR THE TEACHER

- Interactive Whiteboard Lessons
- Generate Success!

Assess

Assessment Program

Examen: Chapitre 1

Audio CD 1, Tr. 17–18

Examen oral: Chapitre 1

Alternative Assessment

Differentiated Practice and Assessment CD-ROM

Online Assessment
my.hrw.com

Test Generator 

Chapitre 1

Révisions cumulatives

Resources

Planning:

Lesson Planner

Teacher One Stop

Practice:

Cahier d'activités

Media Guide

Projectable Transparencies **Fine Art, Chapter 1**

Audio CD 1, Tr. 14

Holt McDougal French Apps

1 Script

1. Ma grande sœur s'appelle Nathalie. Elle est rousse et elle a les cheveux courts. Elle est très marrante.
2. Ma cousine n'est pas très sympa. Elle est petite et elle a les cheveux longs et châtains.
3. Ma petite sœur s'appelle Micheline. Elle a les cheveux longs et blonds. Elle est très sportive.
4. Ma mère est prof de maths. Elle est grande et mince. Elle a les cheveux courts et noirs.

2 Answers

1. Oui, elle trouve sa famille américaine sympa.
2. La fille s'appelle Anne.
3. Elle a 15 ans. Elle est grande et mince. Elle est très marrante.
4. Le fils s'appelle Daniel.
5. Il a 18 ans. Il est sérieux, timide et très gentil. Il a les cheveux bruns et les yeux verts. Isabelle pense qu'il est beau.
6. Ils aiment jouer aux échecs.

Révisions cumulatives

1 Écoute Irène parler de sa famille et choisis la photo qui correspond à chaque membre de sa famille. CD 1, Tr. 14 1.2

1. c **2.** b **3.** d **4.** a

a.

b.

c.

d.

2 Isabelle, une jeune Française, passe un mois chez des amis au Texas. Lis la lettre qu'elle envoie à sa copine qui est restée en France. Ensuite, réponds aux questions qui suivent. 1.2

Salut, Amélie!
Comment ça va? Moi, je vais bien et j'adore le Texas! Ma famille américaine est super sympa. Ils sont quatre: les parents, leur fille et leur fils. La fille s'appelle Anne et elle a quinze ans, comme moi. Elle est assez grande et très mince. Elle est très marrante et parle tout le temps! Son frère s'appelle Daniel et il a 18 ans. Il est assez sérieux et un peu timide, mais très gentil. Il a les cheveux noirs et les yeux verts et il est très beau. Nous jouons souvent aux échecs. Et toi? Comment ça va? Écris-moi vite!

À plus.
Isabelle

1. Est-ce qu'Isabelle aime sa famille américaine?
2. Comment s'appelle la fille de la famille?
3. Elle a quel âge? Comment est-elle?
4. Comment s'appelle le fils de la famille?
5. Il a quel âge? Comment est-il?
6. Qu'est-ce qu'Isabelle et Daniel aiment faire?

Online Culture Project

Tell students to imagine they are studying architecture at the **Université Paris-Sorbonne.** Their assignment is to put together a PowerPoint® slide show on the architecture of Paris. Have students search the Web for photos of famous buildings or monuments and write captions in French that tell the name of each structure, the date it was built, and an interesting fact about it. Have students document the URLs of the sites they consult. **2.2, 3.1**

Révisions cumulatives

Online Assessment
my.hrw.com
Cumulative Self-test

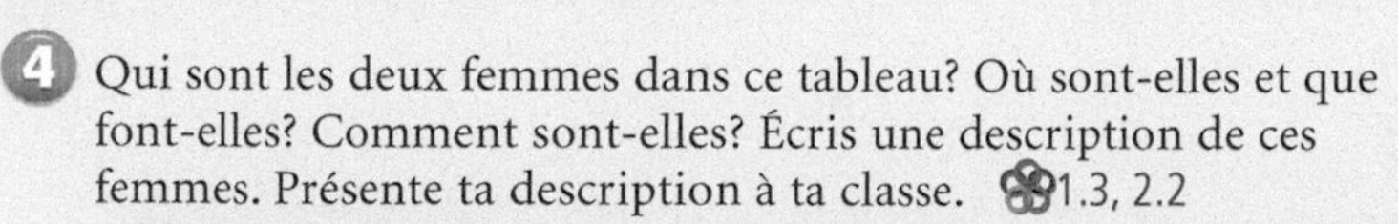

3. Décris une personne célèbre à ton partenaire. Il/Elle va deviner *(guess)* de qui tu parles. 1.1

4. Qui sont les deux femmes dans ce tableau? Où sont-elles et que font-elles? Comment sont-elles? Écris une description de ces femmes. Présente ta description à ta classe. 1.3, 2.2

Renoir, Pierre Auguste, Yvonne et Christine Lerolle au piano, 1897. Oil on canvas, 73 x 92 cm, Musée de l'Orangerie, Paris.

Yvonne et Christine Lerolle au piano **de Pierre Auguste Renoir**

5. Écris une lettre à un(e) élève français(e). Dis comment tu t'appelles. Parle de ton âge, de ton apparence physique et de ta personnalité. Parle aussi de ce que tu aimes faire. 1.3

6. **À ton tour**

Portrait de famille Do a class survey to get to know your classmates better. First, create questions to find out the age of each student in the class, how many brothers and sisters each one has, what each one likes and likes to do, and what each one does on the weekend. Ask each classmate your questions. After everyone has responded, put the information together to report your survey results. 1.1, 1.3

Fine Art Connection

Introduction Pierre Auguste Renoir was born in Limoges, France, in 1841. He is one of the best known painters in the world. Renoir painted landscapes in the soft style characteristic of impressionist painters, but, unlike his friend Claude Monet, he also loved to paint people. He left a great number of portraits, some of which are too detailed to be true impressionist works. In this painting, *Yvonne et Christine Lerolle au piano*, the models are the daughters of painter Henry Lerolle. The two paintings on the wall are by Edgar Degas (*Avant la course* and *Les Danseuses*). Renoir's hands eventually became badly deformed from rheumatoid arthritis. He painted some of his late works sitting in a wheelchair with brushes tied to his wrists.

Analyzing

To help students discuss the painting, you might use the following questions.

1. **Comment est-ce qu'on sait que ce tableau vient de la période impressionniste?**
2. **À votre avis, quel âge ont les deux jeunes femmes? Peut-on en être sûr?**
3. **Est-ce que vous croyez qu'elles aiment jouer du piano?**
4. **Sont-elles d'une famille modeste ou bourgeoise?**
5. **Quels arts et activités est-ce qu'on voit sur ce tableau?** 3.1

Extension

Have students search on the Internet for the painting of Edgar Degas' *Avant la course*, visible on the wall behind the piano players. Are the colors the same as in the original or did Renoir take liberties? Is the original painting more detailed? What color(s) did Renoir use to paint shadows? 2.2, 3.1

ACTFL Performance Standards

The activities in Chapter 1 target the communicative modes as described in the Standards.

Interpersonal	Two-way communication using receptive skills and productive skills	**Communication (SE),** pp. 9, 11, 13, 15, 23, 25, 27 **Communication (TE),** pp. 13, 23, 27 **À ton tour,** p. 39
Interpretive	One-way communication using receptive skills	**Comparaisons,** p. 17 **Télé-roman,** pp. 28–29
Presentational	One-way communication using productive skills	**Communication (SE),** p. 21 **Communication (TE),** pp. 9, 11, 15, 21, 25

chapitre 2

Planning Guide

On fait la fête

Planning Guide

Chapter Section		Resources
Vocabulaire 1 • Holidays, birthday celebrations	pp. 42–45	Projectable Transparencies: Vocabulaire 2.1, 2.2; Bell Work 2.1, 2.2, 2.3, 2.4 Cahier de vocabulaire et grammaire, pp. 13–18 Grammar Tutor for Students of French Cahier d'activités, pp. 11–13 Media Guide, pp. 5–8, 52–54
Grammaire 1 • Direct objects and direct object pronouns • Indirect objects and indirect object pronouns	pp. 46–49	**Assessment Program** Quiz: Vocabulaire 1, pp. 31–32 Quiz: Grammaire 1, pp. 33–34 Quiz: Application 1, pp. 35–36
Application 1 • **Un peu plus:** The verb **offrir**	pp. 50–51	
Culture • **Culture appliquée: Le carnaval** • **Comparaisons et Communauté**	pp. 52–53	Cahier d'activités, p. 14
Vocabulaire 2 • Party preparations and foods	pp. 54–57	Projectable Transparencies: Vocabulaire 2.3, 2.4; Bell Work 2.5, 2.6, 2.7, 2.8 Cahier de vocabulaire et grammaire, pp. 19–24 Grammar Tutor for Students of French Cahier d'activités, pp. 15–17 Media Guide, pp. 5–8, 52–53, 55
Grammaire 2 • Review of the **passé composé** with **avoir** • Review of the **passé composé** with **être**	pp. 58–61	**Assessment Program** Quiz: Vocabulaire 2, pp. 37–38 Quiz: Grammaire 2, pp. 39–40 Quiz: Application 2, pp. 41–42
Application 2 • **Un peu plus:** Negative expressions	pp. 62–63	
Télé-roman	pp. 64–65	Media Guide, pp. 53, 56
Lecture et écriture	pp. 66–69	Cahier d'activités, pp. 18 Reading Strategies and Skills Handbook Intermediate Reader French InterActive Reader **Assessment Program** Quiz: Lecture, p. 43 Quiz: Écriture, p. 44
Prépare-toi pour l'examen • **Résumé de vocabulaire et grammaire** • **Lettres et sons**	pp. 70–73	Independent Study Guide, pp. 4–6, 34 Media Guide, p. 8 **Assessment Program** Examen: Chapitre 2, pp. 45–50 Examen: Chapitre 2, p. 318
Révisions cumulatives	pp. 74–75	Projectable Transparencies: Fine Art, Ch. 2 Cahier d'activités, pp. 14, 19–20
Variations littéraires • **Le Fantôme de l'opéra**	pp. 384–385	Reading Strategies and Skills Handbook Intermediate Reader French InterActive Reader

my.hrw.com
Online Edition

Pacing Suggestions

	Essential	Recommended	Optional
Vocabulaire 1 • Holidays, birthday celebrations • **Flash culture**	✔		
Grammaire 1 • Direct objects and direct object pronouns • Indirect objects and indirect object pronouns • **Flash culture**	✔		
Application 1 • **Un peu plus:** The verb **offrir**	✔		
Culture • **Culture appliquée: Le carnaval** • **Comparaisons et Communauté**		✔	
Vocabulaire 2 • Party preparations and foods • **Flash culture**	✔		
Grammaire 2 • Review of the **passé composé** with **avoir** • Review of the **passé composé** with **être** • **Flash culture**	✔		
Application 2 • **Un peu plus:** Negative expressions	✔		
Télé-roman • Épisode 2: **Le Secret de la statuette**			✔
Lecture et écriture • **Le réveillon en fête** (Lecture) • **Est-ce que tu as tout préparé?** (Écriture)		✔	
Prépare-toi pour l'examen		✔	
Révisions cumulatives			✔
Variations littéraires • **Le Fantôme de l'opéra**			✔

Technology

Bien dit! Online
- Student Edition with multi-media
- **performance space** recording tool
- Interactive activities with feedback
- Self-tests with feedback
- Cahier d'activités (Interactive workbook)
- Cahier de vocabulaire et grammaire (Interactive workbook)
- Holt Online Assessment

DVD Tutor
- Télé-vocab
- Grammavision
- Télé-roman

- Interactive games
- Differentiated Practice
- Cultural video

Audio Program
- Student Edition listening activities
- Assessment listening activities
- Songs

Teacher One Stop
- Complete resources
- ExamView Pro Test Generator
- Holt Calendar Planner

Holt McDougal Apps

Interactive Whiteboard Lessons

Differentiated Practice and Assessment CD

For slower pace and advanced learner options, see the Differentiated Practice and Assessment CD.

Projects

Spectacle de marionnettes

Students work in groups to create puppet shows about holiday celebrations. Each group researches the history, customs, and cultural importance of a different francophone holiday. The presentation tells a story of the celebration. 1.3, 2.1

Suggested Sequence

1. Explain the project and set due dates for research, a written script, and the show.
2. Form groups of four or five. Each group decides which holiday to learn more about and present.
3. Have groups turn in a rough draft of their script. Review and return the scripts.
4. Have students make simple puppets in class and allow the groups time to rehearse their show.
5. Groups present their show to the class.
6. Groups turn in copies of their script and a short paragraph about the celebration they researched. You may wish to make copies of the paragraphs to discuss in class.

Creativity and Innovation

Grading the project

Suggested point distribution (100 points total)

Cultural research	30 pts.
Scripts	20 pts.
Creativity	20 pts.
Puppet show	30 pts.

Partner Class Project

Have students go online to a French-language electronic greeting card Web site and choose a card to send to their key pal. It does not matter if there is a holiday at the time you are doing this activity, as such Web sites have cards for all occasions. In the card, students should tell which are their three favorite holidays and why. They should discuss what they are planning to do for one of those holidays this year, and how they celebrated it last year. They should also find out similar information from their key pal. If they are writing to a key pal in another country, they should also write about one typical holiday in the United States, such as Thanksgiving or the Fourth of July. 1.1, 1.3

Technology Literacy

e-community

e-mail forum:

Location: http://french

Post the following questions on the classroom e-mail forum:

C'est quand, ton anniversaire?

Quelle est ta fête préférée?

5.1

All students will contribute to the list and then share the items.

Game Bank

For game ideas, see pages T60–T63.

Le quatorze juillet

Bastille Day, **la fête nationale,** is celebrated on July 14. It commemorates the storming of the Bastille prison in 1789, the event that symbolized the end of the French monarchy and the beginning of the Republic. It is a French national holiday, and each community celebrates this day with its local parades, dances, and fireworks. In Paris, locals and tourists line up along the Champs-Élysées to watch the spectacular military parade. At night, families get together in their neighborhood to eat, drink, talk, and dance at the **petits bals de quartier.** The most popular **bal** is at the **place de la Bastille,** where the prison used to stand. Late in the evening, revelers watch fireworks displays throughout the city. Have students compare the Bastille Day celebrations in Paris to those of July 4th in their hometown. 2.1

La cuisine

As a yearly tradition in March, a **pot-au-feu,** or **pot-bouille,** is prepared in a small village in the west of France. The tradition dates from over 200 years ago when a villager won a cow during a card game. He decided to give the cow to the poor of the village under one condition: make a gigantic **pot-au-feu** for everyone. Encourage students to make **pot-au-feu** in their foods class or at home for family and friends. 1.2, 2.2

Pot-au-feu

Pour 6 personnes

- **4** livres de viande de bœuf
- **1** cuillère à soupe de gros sel
- **1** gousse d'ail
- **1** oignon
- **1** livre de carottes
- **1** livre de navets
- **3** gros poireaux
- **4** branches de céleri
- **2** livres de pommes de terre
- **1** os à moëlle

Dans une large marmite, mettre la viande et recouvrir d'eau (environ 12 tasses). Faire bouillir. Ajouter le sel. Ajouter tous les légumes, sauf les pommes de terre. Laisser frémir pendant 3 à 4 heures. Ajouter alors les pommes de terre et l'os à moëlle. Laisser cuire pendant 30 minutes. Retirer la viande et les légumes du bouillon. Jeter l'oignon. Filtrer le bouillon. Servir la viande et les légumes chauds. Le bouillon peut servir de sauce.

Listening Activity Scripts

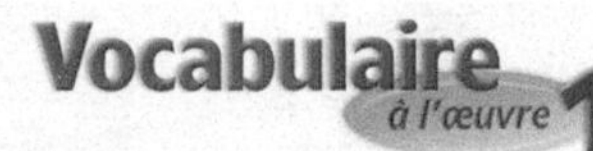

Vocabulaire à l'œuvre 1

1 p. 44, CD 2, Tr. 1

1. — Comment trouves-tu le sapin?
   — Il est beau, et la bûche est délicieuse.
2. — C'est un très joli bouquet de fleurs!
   — Comme toujours, un bouquet de fleurs et une boîte de chocolats pour Maman.
3. — Voilà le gâteau pour Amélie, les bougies, les cadeaux...
   — Cool! À quelle heure commence la soirée?
4. — Qu'est-ce que tu apportes pour le réveillon?
   — Des confettis.
5. — J'adore la foule, le défilé et le feu d'artifice!
   — Moi aussi.

Answers to Activity 1

1. b 2. c 3. e 4. d 5. a

Grammaire à l'œuvre 1

11 p. 49, CD 2, Tr. 2

1. — Bonjour, Pierre. Tu as une idée de cadeau pour ma mère pour la fête des mères?
   — Tu peux leur offrir une boîte de chocolats.
2. — J'espère que tu vas avoir un bon anniversaire, Charles.
   — Merci. Je crois que mes parents vont me donner un chèque-cadeau.
3. — Céline, j'aime beaucoup ces chaussures. Elles te vont très bien.
   — Je les achète pour ma sœur. Je vais les leur donner pour Noël.
4. — Marie, tu envoies une invitation à Monique?
   — Non, je vais lui téléphoner pour l'inviter.
5. — Salut, Charles et Émile! Vous allez envoyer une carte de vœux à votre tante?
   — Oui, nous lui envoyons une carte de vœux tous les ans.

Answers to Activity 11

1. b 2. a 3. b 4. a 5. a

Application 1

18 p. 51, CD 2, Tr. 3

1. — Quel âge a-t-il aujourd'hui?
   — Marc a 16 ans.
2. — Hier, nous avons décoré le sapin.
   — Il est très beau.
3. — Le défilé se passe à deux heures de l'après-midi et il y a un feu d'artifice ce soir. Ça va être chouette.
4. — Je vais offrir un bouquet de fleurs à ma mère.
5. — Est-ce que tu vas acheter une cravate pour ton père?
   — Non, il en a déjà plein.

Answers to Activity 18

1. la fête d'anniversaire
2. Noël
3. la fête nationale
4. la fête des mères
5. la fête des pères

Vocabulaire à l'œuvre 2

21 p. 56, CD 2, Tr. 4

1. — Voilà. Nous avons des chips, des bonbons et des cacahuètes.
   — C'est tout? On n'a pas de biscuits? Et où sont les boissons?
2. — Combien de timbres il faut acheter?
   — Nous avons trente invitations. Alors, il faut acheter trente timbres.
3. — Ça t'ennuie d'emballer ce livre?
   — Bien sûr que non.
4. — Tu pourrais m'aider à décorer le salon?
   — Oui, pas de problème.
5. — Tu peux m'aider à ranger la maison?
   — Pas maintenant. Je dois aller chercher le gâteau.
6. — Regardons les CD… On a un CD de MC Solaar?
   — Je ne sais pas, mais on a Alizée.

Answers to Activity 21

1. c 2. e 3. d 4. f 5. a 6. b

27 p. 58, CD 2, Tr. 5

1. La boum a fini à dix heures.
2. J'attends Serge pour aller acheter un cadeau pour Amandine.
3. Ma mère a préparé des amuse-gueules.
4. Tu as envoyé les invitations, Jonah?
5. Elles emballent les cadeaux de Noël.
6. Est-ce que vous avez invité Laura et Sabine?
7. Je n'ai pas envie de décorer le salon.
8. Tu as passé l'aspirateur?

Answers to Activity 27

1. a 2. b 3. a 4. a 5. b 6. a 7. b 8. a

Application 2

38 p. 63, CD 2, Tr. 6

1. — Tu as déjà emballé les cadeaux?
   — Non, pas encore.
2. — Est-ce qu'il reste des choses à faire?
   — Non, c'est bon. J'ai tout fait.
3. — Tu as pensé à acheter des fleurs?
   — Mais oui! Je les ai achetées ce matin. Elles sont sur la table.
4. — Tu as bien sorti le gâteau du four?
   — Oh zut! J'ai complètement oublié!
5. — As-tu déjà mis les chips dans un bol?
   — Mais oui! Je l'ai fait il y a 20 minutes.
6. — Tu as bien passé l'aspirateur?
   — Non, pas encore. J'ai complètement oublié, mais je vais le faire tout de suite. Ne t'inquiète pas.
7. — Tu as pensé à acheter un cadeau à Léa?
   — Oui, bien sûr. Je l'ai même emballé! Le voilà!

Answers to Activity 38

1. b 2. a 3. a 4. b 5. a 6. b 7. a

Prépare-toi pour l'examen

6 p. 71, CD 2, Tr. 9

Mes amis sont arrivés vers sept heures. Nous avons mangé de la pizza et de la salade et nous avons bu du coca et des jus de fruit. Après, Rachid a joué de la guitare et nous avons chanté. Moi, j'aime bien danser, mais nous n'avons pas dansé parce que mes amis n'aiment pas trop danser.

Answers to Activity 6

Ils ont mangé de la pizza et de la salade, ils ont bu du coca et des jus de fruit, et ils ont chanté. Ils n'ont pas dansé.

Dictée, p. 72, CD 2, Tr. 12

1. — Est-ce que tu étudies la musique?
2. — As-tu vu cette voiture?
3. — Ça m'amuse d'aller au musée.
4. — Je ne mets pas de lunettes de soleil quand il y a des nuages.
5. — Elle allume les bougies à la soirée costumée.

Révisions cumulatives

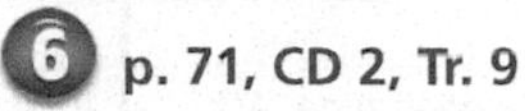

1 p. 74, CD 2, Tr. 13

1. — Tu peux m'aider à ranger le salon?
   — Pas de problème.
2. — Tu as une idée de cadeau pour Olivia?
   — Tu pourrais lui offrir un tee-shirt.
3. — Tu as déjà préparé les amuse-gueules?
   — Oui, c'est bon. Ils sont prêts.
4. — J'ai fini le gâteau.
   — D'accord, je vais chercher les bougies.

Answers to Activity 1

1. d 2. b 3. a 4. c

Listening Activity Scripts

50-Minute Lesson Plans

On fait la fête

Day 1

OBJECTIVE
Wish someone a good time

Core Instruction
Chapter Opener, pp. 40–41
- See Using the Photo, p. 40. **5 min.**
- See Chapter Objectives, p. 40. **5 min.**

Vocabulaire 1, pp. 42–45
- Present **Vocabulaire 1,** pp. 42–43. See Teaching **Vocabulaire,** p. 42. **10 min.**
- Show **Télé-vocab 1. 5 min.**
- Present **Exprimons-nous!,** p. 43. **10 min.**
- Play Audio CD 2, Tr. 1 for Activity 1, p. 44. **5 min.**
- Do Activity 2, p. 44. **5 min.**
- Present **Flash culture,** p. 44. **5 min.**

Optional Resources
- Slower Pace Learners, p. 43 ◆
- Multiple Intelligences, p. 43

Homework Suggestions
Cahier de vocabulaire et grammaire, pp. 13–14
@HOMETUTOR
1.2, 1.3, 2.1, 4.2

Day 2

OBJECTIVE
Wish someone a good time; Ask for and give advice; Use direct object pronouns

Core Instruction
Vocabulaire 1, pp. 42–45
- Do Bell Work 2.1, p. 42. **5 min.**
- Have students do Activity 3, p. 44. **10 min.**
- See Teaching **Exprimons-nous!,** p. 44. **10 min.**
- Have students do Activities 4–5, p. 45. **15 min.**

Grammaire 1, pp. 46–49
- See Teaching **Grammaire,** p. 46. **5 min.**
- Show **Grammavision 1.1. 5 min.**

Optional Resources
- Communication (TE), p. 45
- Advanced Learners, p. 45 ▲
- Special Learning Needs, p. 45 ●

Homework Suggestions
Study for **Quiz: Vocabulaire 1**
Cahier de vocabulaire et grammaire, p. 15
1.1, 1.2, 1.3

Day 3

OBJECTIVE
Use direct object pronouns

Core Instruction
Vocabulaire 1, pp. 42–45
- Review **Vocabulaire 1,** pp. 42–45. **10 min.**
- Give **Quiz: Vocabulaire 1. 20 min.**

Grammaire 1, pp. 46–49
- Have students do Activities 6–9, pp. 46–47. **20 min.**

Optional Resources
- Connections, p. 46
- French for Spanish Speakers, p. 47
- Communication (TE), p. 47
- Slower Pace Learners, p. 47 ◆
- Special Learning Needs, p. 47 ●

Homework Suggestions
Cahier de vocabulaire et grammaire, p. 16
Cahier d'activités, p. 11
Online Practice (**my.hrw.com**)
1.1, 1.2, 1.3, 3.1, 4.1

Day 4

OBJECTIVE
*Use indirect object pronouns; Use the verb **offrir***

Core Instruction
Grammaire 1, pp. 46–49
- Present **Flash culture,** p. 48. **5 min.**
- See Teaching **Grammaire,** p. 48. **5 min.**
- Show **Grammavision 1.2. 5 min.**
- Do Activity 10, p. 48. **5 min.**
- Play Audio CD 2, Tr. 2 for Activity 11, p. 49. **5 min.**
- Do Activities 12–14, p. 49. **15 min.**

Application 1, pp. 50–51
- Do Activity 15, p. 50. **5 min.**
- See Teaching **Un peu plus,** p. 50. **5 min.**

Optional Resources
- Advanced Learners, p. 49 ▲
- Multiple Intelligences, p. 49

Homework Suggestions
Study for **Quiz: Grammaire 1**
Cahier de vocabulaire et grammaire, p. 17
Cahier d'activités, p. 12
1.1, 1.2, 1.3, 2.1, 4.2

Day 5

OBJECTIVE
*Use the verb **offrir***

Core Instruction
Grammaire 1, pp. 46–49
- Review **Grammaire 1,** pp. 46–49. **10 min.**
- Give **Quiz: Grammaire 1. 20 min.**

Application 1, pp. 50–51
- Have students do Activities 16–17, p. 50. **5 min.**
- Play Audio CD 2, Tr. 3 for Activity 18, p. 51. **5 min.**
- Have students do Activities 19–20, p. 51. **10 min.**

Optional Resources
- Communication (TE), p. 51
- Slower Pace Learners, p. 51 ◆
- Special Learning Needs, p. 51 ●

Homework Suggestions
Study for **Quiz: Application 1**
Cahier de vocabulaire et grammaire, p. 18
Cahier d'activités, p. 13
Online Practice (**my.hrw.com**)
1.1, 1.2, 1.3

Day 6

OBJECTIVE
Learn about francophone culture

Core Instruction
Application 1, pp. 50–51
- Review **Application 1,** pp. 50–51. **10 min.**
- Give **Quiz: Application 1. 20 min.**

Culture, pp. 52–53
- See **Culture appliquée** (TE), p. 52. **10 min.**
- See **Comparaisons et communauté** (TE), p. 52. **10 min.**

Optional Resources
- Communities, p. 53
- Cultures, p. 53
- Slower Pace Learners, p. 53 ◆
- Special Learning Needs, p. 53 ●

Homework Suggestions
Cahier d'activités, p. 14
Online Practice (**my.hrw.com**)
Finish **Culture appliquée** project
1.2, 1.3, 2.1, 2.2, 4.2, 5.1

Day 7

OBJECTIVE
Ask for help and respond

Core Instruction
Vocabulaire 2, pp. 54–57
- Do Bell Work 2.5, p. 54. **5 min.**
- Present **Vocabulaire 2,** pp. 54–55. See Teaching **Vocabulaire,** p. 54. **10 min.**
- Show **Télé-vocab 2. 5 min.**
- Present **Exprimons-nous!,** p. 55. **10 min.**
- Play Audio CD 2, Tr. 4 for Activity 21, p. 56. **5 min.**
- Have students do Activities 22–23, p. 56. **10 min.**
- Present **Flash culture,** p. 56. **5 min.**

Optional Resources
- Communities, p. 54
- TPR, p. 55
- Advanced Learners, p. 55 ▲
- Special Learning Needs, p. 55 ●

Homework Suggestions
Cahier de vocabulaire et grammaire, pp. 19–20
1.2, 1.3, 4.2, 5.1

Day 8

OBJECTIVE
*Check if things have been done; Use the **passé composé** with **avoir***

Core Instruction
Vocabulaire 2, pp. 54–57
- See Teaching **Exprimons-nous!,** p. 56. **10 min.**
- Have students do Activities 24–26, p. 57. **20 min.**

Grammaire 2, pp. 58–61
- See Teaching **Grammaire,** p. 58. **10 min.**
- Show **Grammavision 2.1. 5 min.**
- Play Audio CD 2, Tr. 5 for Activity 27, p. 58. **5 min.**

Optional Resources
- Slower Pace Learners, p. 57 ◆
- Multiple Intelligences, p. 57

Homework Suggestions
Study for **Quiz: Vocabulaire 2**
Cahier de vocabulaire et grammaire, p. 21
@HOMETUTOR
Online Practice (**my.hrw.com**)
1.1, 1.2, 1.3

To edit and create your own lesson plans, see the **Teacher One Stop™**

KEY
- ▲ Advanced Learners
- ◆ Slower Pace Learners
- ● Special Learning Needs

Day 9

OBJECTIVE
*Use the **passé composé** with **avoir***

Core Instruction
Vocabulaire 2, pp. 54–57
- Review **Vocabulaire 2,** pp. 54–57. **10 min.**
- Give **Quiz: Vocabulaire 2. 20 min.**

Grammaire 2, pp. 58–61
- Have students do Activities 28–31, pp. 58–59. **20 min.**

Optional Resources
- Communication (TE), p. 59
- Communities, p. 59
- Advanced Learners, p. 59 ▲
- Special Learning Needs, p. 59 ●

Homework Suggestions
Cahier de vocabulaire et grammaire, p. 22
Cahier d'activités, p. 15
HOMETUTOR
Online Practice (**my.hrw.com**)
1.1, 1.2, 1.3, 5.1

Day 10

OBJECTIVE
*Use the **passé composé** with **être**; Use negative expressions*

Core Instruction
Grammaire 2, pp. 58–61
- Do Bell Work 2.7, p. 60. **5 min.**
- Present **Flash culture,** p. 60. **5 min.**
- See Teaching **Grammaire,** p. 60. **5 min.**
- Show **Grammavision 2.2. 5 min.**
- Have students do Activities 32–35, pp. 60–61. **20 min.**

Application 2, pp. 62–63
- Do Activity 36, p. 62. **5 min.**
- See Teaching **Un peu plus,** p. 62. **5 min.**

Optional Resources
- Communication (TE), p. 61
- Slower Pace Learners, p. 61 ◆

Homework Suggestions
Study for **Quiz: Grammaire 2**
Cahier de vocabulaire et grammaire, p. 23
Cahier d'activités, p. 16
1.1, 1.2, 1.3, 4.2

Day 11

OBJECTIVE
Use negative expressions

Core Instruction
Grammaire 2, pp. 58–61
- Review **Grammaire 2,** pp. 58–61. **10 min.**
- Give **Quiz: Grammaire 2. 20 min.**

Application 2, pp. 62–63
- Have students do Activity 37, p. 62. **5 min.**
- Play Audio CD 2, Tr. 6 for Activity 38, p. 63. **5 min.**
- Have students do Activities 39–41, p. 63. **10 min.**

Optional Resources
- Communication (TE), p. 63
- Advanced Learners, p. 63 ▲

Homework Suggestions
Study for **Quiz: Application 2**
Cahier de vocabulaire et grammaire, p. 24
Cahier d'activités, p. 17
Online Practice (**my.hrw.com**)
1.2, 1.3

Day 12

OBJECTIVE
Develop listening and reading skills

Core Instruction
Application 2, pp. 62–63
- Review **Application 2,** pp. 62–63. **10 min.**
- Give **Quiz: Application 2. 20 min.**

Télé-roman, pp. 64–65
- Show **Télé-roman.** See Teaching **Télé-roman,** p. 64. **5 min.**
- Have students answer the **As-tu compris?** questions, p. 65. **15 min.**

Optional Resources
- Connections, p. 64
- Gestures, p. 64
- Communication (TE), p. 65

Homework Suggestions
Online Practice (**my.hrw.com**)
1.2, 1.3, 3.2

Day 13

OBJECTIVE
Develop listening, reading, and writing skills

Core Instruction
Lecture et écriture, pp. 66–69
- See Teaching **Lecture,** p. 66. **35 min.**
- See Teaching **Espace écriture,** p. 68. **15 min.**

Optional Resources
- Applying the Strategies, p. 66
- Recognizing Cognates, p. 66
- Cultures, p. 67
- Connections, p. 67
- Advanced Learners, p. 67 ▲
- Special Learning Needs, p. 67 ●
- Connections, p. 68
- Communities, p. 68
- Slower Pace Learners, p. 69 ◆
- Multiple Intelligences, p. 69

Homework Suggestions
Cahier d'activités, p. 18
Espace écriture, Activity 2, p. 69
1.1, 1.2, 1.3, 2.1, 3.1, 4.1, 5.1

Day 14

OBJECTIVE
Develop writing skills; Review the chapter

Core Instruction
Lecture et écriture, pp. 66–69
- See Teaching **Espace écriture,** p. 68. **25 min.**

Prépare-toi pour l'examen, pp. 70–72
- Have students do Activities 1–5, pp. 70–71. **25 min.**

Optional Resources
- Writing Assessment, p. 69
- Reteaching, p. 70
- Game, p. 70
- Fold-N-Learn, p. 70
- Oral Assessment, p. 71

Homework Suggestions
Online Practice (**my.hrw.com**)
1.1, 1.2, 2.1

Day 15

OBJECTIVE
Review the chapter

Core Instruction
Prépare-toi pour l'examen, pp. 70–72
- Play Audio CD 2, Tr. 9 for Activity 6, p. 71. **5 min.**
- Do Activity 7, p. 71. **5 min.**
- Play Audio CD 2, Tr. 10–12 for **Lettres et sons,** p. 72. **10 min.**

Révisions cumulatives, pp. 74–75
- Play Audio CD 2, Tr. 13 for Activity 1, p. 74. **5 min.**
- Have students do Activities 2–6, pp. 74–75. **25 min.**

Optional Resources
- French for Spanish Speakers, p. 72
- Chapter Review, pp. 72–73
- Online Culture Project, p. 74
- Fine Art Connection, p. 75

Homework Suggestions
Study for Chapter Test
Online Practice (**my.hrw.com**)
1.1, 1.2, 1.3, 2.1, 2.2, 3.2, 4.1

Day 16/Test

Core Instruction
Chapter Test 50 min.

Optional Resources
Assessment Program
- Alternative Assessment
- Test Generator
- **Quiz: Lecture**
- **Quiz: Écriture**

Homework Suggestions
Cahier d'activités, pp. 19–20, 104–105
Online Practice (**my.hrw.com**)

90-Minute Lesson Plans

On fait la fête

Block 1

OBJECTIVE
Wish someone a good time; Ask for and give advice

Core Instruction

Chapter Opener, pp. 40–41
- See Using the Photo, p. 40. **5 min.**
- See Chapter Objectives, p. 40. **5 min.**

Vocabulaire 1, pp. 42–45
- Present **Vocabulaire 1,** pp. 42–43. See Teaching **Vocabulaire,** p. 42. **10 min.**
- Show **Télé-vocab 1. 5 min.**
- Present **Exprimons-nous!,** p. 43. **10 min.**
- Play Audio CD 2, Tr. 1 for Activity 1, p. 44. **10 min.**
- Have students do Activities 2–3, p. 44. **15 min.**
- Present **Flash culture,** p. 44. **5 min.**
- See Teaching **Exprimons-nous!,** p. 44. **10 min.**
- Have students do Activities 4–5, p. 45. **15 min.**

Optional Resources
- Learning Tips, p. 41
- Cultures, p. 42
- TPR, p. 43
- Cultures, p. 43
- **Attention!,** p. 43
- Slower Pace Learners, p. 43 ◆
- Multiple Intelligences, p. 43
- Cultures, pp. 44, 45
- Communication (TE), p. 45
- Advanced Learners, p. 45 ▲
- Special Learning Needs, p. 45 ●

Homework Suggestions
Study for **Quiz: Vocabulaire 1**
Cahier de vocabulaire et grammaire, pp. 13–15
@HOMETUTOR
Online Practice (**my.hrw.com**)

❀ 1.1, 1.2, 1.3, 2.1, 4.2

Block 2

OBJECTIVE
Use direct object pronouns; Use indirect object pronouns

Core Instruction

Vocabulaire 1, pp. 42–45
- Review **Vocabulaire 1,** pp. 42–45. **10 min.**
- Give **Quiz: Vocabulaire 1. 20 min.**

Grammaire 1, pp. 46–49
- See Teaching **Grammaire,** p. 46. **5 min.**
- Show **Grammavision 1.1. 5 min.**
- Have students do Activities 6–9, pp. 46–47. **15 min.**
- Present **Flash culture,** p. 48. **5 min.**
- See Teaching **Grammaire,** p. 48. **10 min.**
- Show **Grammavision 1.2. 5 min.**
- Have students do Activity 10, p. 48. **5 min.**
- Play Audio CD 2, Tr. 2 for Activity 11, p. 49. **5 min.**
- Have students do Activity 12, p. 49. **5 min.**

Optional Resources
- Connections, p. 46
- French for Spanish Speakers, p. 47
- Communication (TE), p. 47
- Slower Pace Learners, p. 47 ◆
- Special Learning Needs, p. 47 ●
- **Attention!,** p. 49
- Comparisons, p. 49
- Advanced Learners, p. 49 ▲
- Multiple Intelligences, p. 49

Homework Suggestions
Study for **Quiz: Grammaire 1**
Cahier de vocabulaire et grammaire, pp. 16–17
Cahier d'activités, pp. 11–12
@HOMETUTOR
Online Practice (**my.hrw.com**)

❀ 1.1, 1.2, 1.3, 2.1, 3.1, 4.2

Block 3

OBJECTIVE
*Use indirect object pronouns; Use the verb **offrir**; Learn about francophone culture*

Core Instruction

Grammaire 1, pp. 46–49
- Have students do Activities 13–14, p. 49. **10 min.**
- Review **Grammaire 1,** pp. 46–49. **10 min.**
- Give **Quiz: Grammaire 1. 20 min.**

Application 1, pp. 50–51
- Have students do Activity 15, p. 50. **5 min.**
- See Teaching **Un peu plus,** p. 50. **5 min.**
- Have students do Activities 16–17, p. 50. **5 min.**
- Play Audio CD 2, Tr. 3 for Activity 18, p. 51. **5 min.**
- Have students do Activities 19–20, p. 51. **10 min.**

Culture, pp. 52–53
- See **Culture appliquée** (TE), p. 52. **10 min.**
- See **Comparaisons et communauté** (TE), p. 52. **10 min.**

Optional Resources
- Communication (TE), p. 49
- **Attention!,** p. 51
- Teacher to Teacher, p. 51
- Communication (TE), p. 51
- Slower Pace Learners, p. 51 ◆
- Special Learning Needs, p. 51 ●
- **Vocabulaire supplémentaire,** p. 52
- Bulletin Board Project, p. 52
- Communities, p. 53
- Cultures, p. 53
- Slower Pace Learners, p. 53 ◆
- Special Learning Needs, p. 53 ●

Homework Suggestions
Study for **Quiz: Application 1**
Cahier de vocabulaire et grammaire, p. 18
Cahier d'activités, pp. 13–14
Online Practice (**my.hrw.com**)
Finish **Culture appliquée** project

❀ 1.1, 1.2, 1.3, 2.1, 2.2, 4.2, 5.1

Block 4

OBJECTIVE
Ask for help and respond; Check if things have been done

Core Instruction

Application 1, pp. 50–51
- Review **Application 1,** pp. 50–51. **10 min.**
- Give **Quiz: Application 1. 20 min.**

Vocabulaire 2, pp. 54–57
- Present **Vocabulaire 2,** pp. 54–55. See Teaching **Vocabulaire,** p. 54. **10 min.**
- Show **Télé-vocab 2. 5 min.**
- Present **Exprimons-nous!,** p. 55. **5 min.**
- Present **Flash culture,** p. 56. **5 min.**
- Play Audio CD 2, Tr. 4 for Activity 21, p. 56. **5 min.**
- Have students do Activities 22–23, p. 56. **5 min.**
- See Teaching **Exprimons-nous!,** p. 56. **10 min.**
- Have students do Activities 24–26, p. 57. **15 min.**

Optional Resources
- Communities, p. 54
- TPR, p. 55
- Cultures, p. 55
- **Proverbes,** p. 55
- Advanced Learners, p. 55 ▲
- Special Learning Needs, p. 55 ●
- Connections, p. 56
- Communication (TE), p. 57
- Connections, p. 57
- Slower Pace Learners, p. 57 ◆
- Multiple Intelligences, p. 57

Homework Suggestions
Study for **Quiz: Vocabulaire 2**
Cahier de vocabulaire et grammaire, pp. 19–21
@HOMETUTOR
Online Practice (**my.hrw.com**)

❀ 1.1, 1.2, 1.3, 2.2, 3.1, 4.2, 5.1

To edit and create your own lesson plans, see the **Teacher One Stop™**

KEY
- ▲ Advanced Learners
- ◆ Slower Pace Learners
- ● Special Learning Needs

Block 5

OBJECTIVE
*Use the **passé composé** with **avoir**; Use the **passé composé** with **être***

Core Instruction

Vocabulaire 2, pp. 54–57
- Review **Vocabulaire 2,** pp. 54–57. **10 min.**
- Give **Quiz: Vocabulaire 2. 20 min.**

Grammaire 2, pp. 58–61
- See Teaching **Grammaire,** p. 58. **10 min.**
- Show **Grammavision 2.1. 5 min.**
- Play Audio CD 2, Tr. 5 for Activity 27, p. 58. **5 min.**
- Have students do Activities 28–31, pp. 58–59. **15 min.**
- Present **Flash culture,** p. 60. **5 min.**
- See Teaching **Grammaire,** p. 60. **5 min.**
- Show **Grammavision 2.2. 5 min.**
- Have students do Activities 32–33, pp. 60–61. **10 min.**

Optional Resources
- Teacher to Teacher, p. 59
- Communication (TE), p. 59
- Communities, p. 59
- Advanced Learners, p. 59 ▲
- Special Learning Needs, p. 59 ●
- Connections, p. 61
- Slower Pace Learners, p. 61 ◆
- Multiple Intelligences, p. 61

Homework Suggestions
Study for **Quiz: Grammaire 2**
Cahier de vocabulaire et grammaire, pp. 22–23
Cahier d'activités, pp. 15–16
@HOMETUTOR
Online Practice (**my.hrw.com**)
1.1, 1.2, 1.3, 3.1, 4.2, 5.1

Block 6

OBJECTIVE
*Use the **passé composé** with **être**; Use negative expressions; Develop listening and reading skills*

Core Instruction

Grammaire 2, pp. 58–61
- Have students do Activities 34–35, p. 61. **10 min.**
- Review **Grammaire 2,** pp. 58–61. **10 min.**
- Give **Quiz: Grammaire 2. 20 min.**

Application 2, pp. 62–63
- Have students do Activity 36, p. 62. **5 min.**
- See Teaching **Un peu plus,** p. 62. **5 min.**
- Have students do Activity 37, p. 62. **5 min.**
- Play Audio CD 2, Tr. 6 for Activity 38, p. 63. **5 min.**
- Have students do Activities 39–41, p. 63. **10 min.**

Télé-roman, pp. 64–65
- Show **Télé-roman.** See Teaching **Télé-roman,** p. 64. **5 min.**
- Have students answer the **As-tu compris?** questions, p. 65. **15 min.**

Optional Resources
- Communication (TE), p. 61
- Communication (TE), p. 63
- Advanced Learners, p. 63 ▲
- Multiple Intelligences, p. 63
- Connections, p. 64
- Gestures, p. 64
- Communication (TE), p. 65

Homework Suggestions
Study for **Quiz: Application 2**
Cahier de vocabulaire et grammaire, p. 24
Cahier d'activités, p. 17
Online Practice (**my.hrw.com**)
1.1, 1.2, 1.3, 3.2

Block 7

OBJECTIVE
Develop listening, reading, and writing skills; Review the chapter

Core Instruction

Application 2, pp. 62–63
- Review **Application 2,** pp. 62–63. **10 min.**
- Give **Quiz: Application 2. 20 min.**

Lecture et écriture, pp. 66–69
- See Teaching **Lecture,** p. 66. **20 min.**
- See Teaching **Espace écriture,** p. 68. **30 min.**

Prépare-toi pour l'examen, pp. 70–72
- Have students do Activities 1–3, p. 70. **10 min.**

Optional Resources
- Applying the Strategies, p. 66
- Recognizing Cognates, p. 66
- Cultures, p. 67
- Connections, p. 67
- Advanced Learners, p. 67 ▲
- Special Learning Needs, p. 67 ●
- Connections, p. 68
- Communities, p. 68
- Process Writing, p. 69
- Writing Assessment, p. 69
- Slower Pace Learners, p. 69 ◆
- Multiple Intelligences, p. 69
- Reteaching, p. 70
- Fold-N-Learn, p. 70

Homework Suggestions
Study for Chapter Test
Cahier d'activités, p. 18
Espace écriture, Activity 2, p. 69
Online Practice (**my.hrw.com**)
1.1, 1.2, 1.3, 2.1, 3.1, 4.1, 5.1

Block 8

OBJECTIVE
Review and assess the chapter

Core Instruction

Prépare-toi pour l'examen, pp. 70–72
- Have students do Activities 4–5, p. 71. **5 min.**
- Play Audio CD 2, Tr. 9 for Activity 6, p. 71. **5 min.**
- Have students do Activity 7, p. 71. **5 min.**
- Play Audio CD 2, Tr. 10–12 for **Lettres et sons,** p. 72. **5 min.**

Chapter Test 50 min.

Révisions cumulatives, pp. 74–75
- Play Audio CD 2, Tr. 13 for Activity 1, p. 74. **5 min.**
- Have students do Activities 2–6, pp. 74–75. **15 min.**

Optional Resources
- Game, p. 70
- Oral Assessment, p. 71
- French for Spanish Speakers, p. 72
- Chapter Review, pp. 72–73
- **Cinquain** Poetry, p. 73
- Online Culture Project, p. 74
- Fine Art Connection, p. 75

Homework Suggestions
Cahier d'activités, pp. 19–20, 104–105
Online Practice (**my.hrw.com**)
1.1, 1.2, 1.3, 2.1, 2.2, 3.2, 4.1

Chapter Opener

Meeting the National Standards

Communication
Communication, pp. 45, 47, 49, 51, 57, 59, 61, 63
À ton tour, p. 75

Cultures
Flash culture, pp. 44, 48, 56, 60
Comparaisons, p. 53
Practices and Perspectives, pp. 42, 43, 45, 53, 67
Products and Perspectives, p. 55

Connections
Math Link, p. 68
Language Arts Link, pp. 46, 61
Visual Learners, p. 64
Home Economics Link, p. 56
Social Studies Link, p. 57
Language to Language, p. 67

Comparisons
Comparaisons, p. 53
Comparing and Contrasting, p. 49

Communities
Communauté, p. 53
School Link, p. 53
Family Link, p. 54, 59
Community Link, p. 68

Using the Photo

On August 25, 2004, Parisians, many dressed in period clothing, celebrated the 60th anniversary of the liberation of Paris during World War II with a reenactment of the raising of the flag and ceremonies honoring the veterans of the war. Ask students to compare our celebration of Veterans Day with the celebration in this photo. 2.1, 4.2

Vocabulaire supplémentaire

Students might use these terms to discuss the photo.

agiter le drapeau *to wave the flag*
le sourire *smile*
la terrasse *terrace*
l'ancien combattant (m.) *veteran*

chapitre 2

On fait la fête

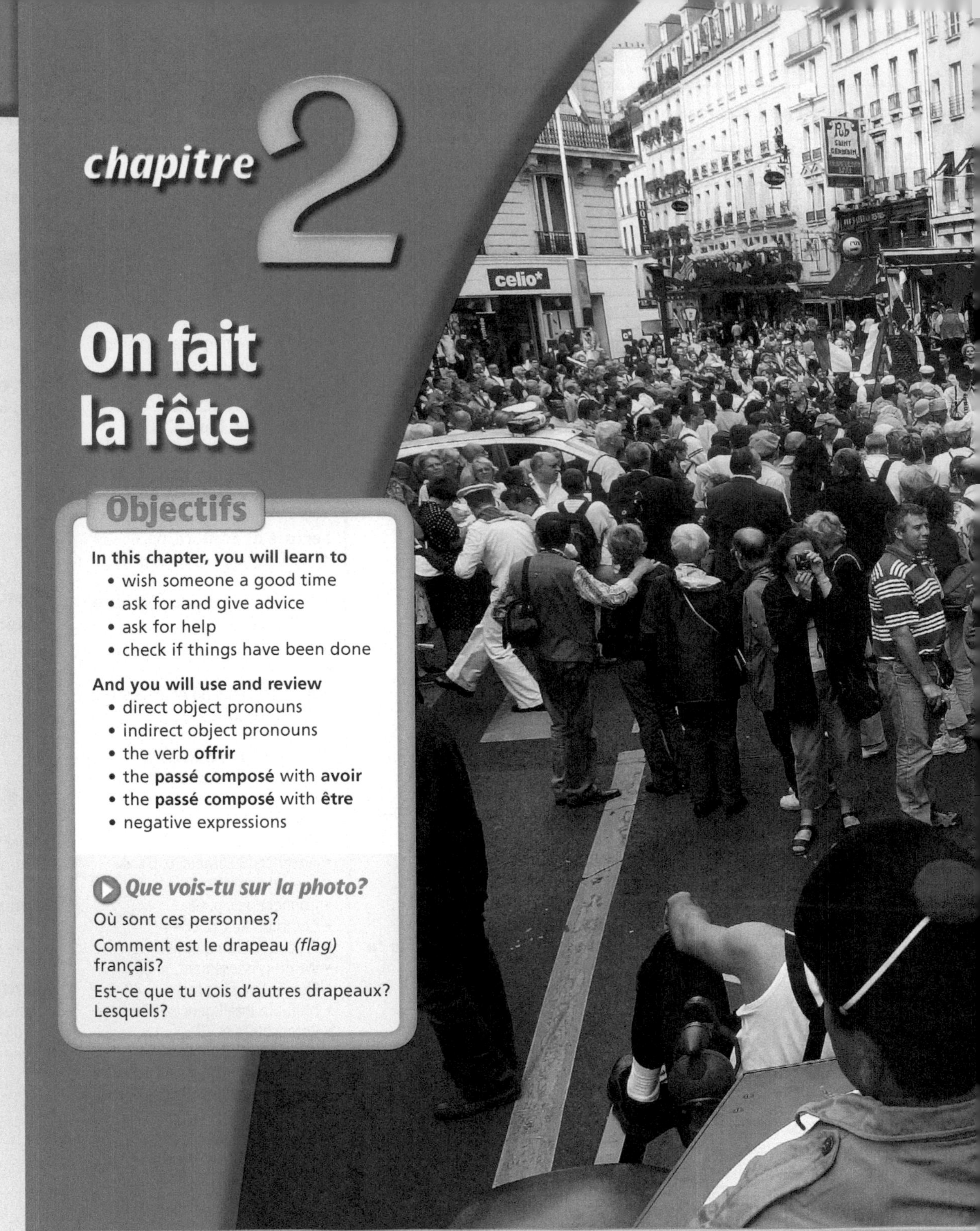

Objectifs

In this chapter, you will learn to
- wish someone a good time
- ask for and give advice
- ask for help
- check if things have been done

And you will use and review
- direct object pronouns
- indirect object pronouns
- the verb **offrir**
- the **passé composé** with **avoir**
- the **passé composé** with **être**
- negative expressions

Que vois-tu sur la photo?
Où sont ces personnes?
Comment est le drapeau *(flag)* français?
Est-ce que tu vois d'autres drapeaux? Lesquels?

ACTFL 21st Century Skills

Creativity and Innovation:	SE: pp. 52, 61; TE: pp. 39C, 43, 45, 49, 52, 53, 54, 56, 61, 63, 67, 70, 73
Technology Literacy:	TE: pp. 39C, 56, 61, 67 (Global Awareness), 75
Initiative and Self-Direction:	TE: pp. 53, 54, 57, 67, 68
Social and Cross-Cultural Skills:	SE: pp. 52, 53; TE: pp. 39D, 40, 43, 45, 49, 52, 55, 67, 74
Productivity and Accountability:	TE: pp. 47, 51, 52, 53, 55, 61, 66
Leadership and Responsibility:	TE: pp. 49, 53 (Global Awareness)

Chapter Opener

Anniversaire commémorant la libération de Paris

DIGITAL FRENCH

TEACHER TOOLS
- Interactive Whiteboard Lessons
- Generate Success!

ALSO AVAILABLE...
- Online Workbooks
- French InterActive Reader

FRENCH ON THE GO!
- Performance Space
- Holt McDougal French Apps
- *Bien dit!* eTextbook

Learning Tips

Tell students that understanding spoken French may be easier if, before they begin listening, they clear their minds and focus their attention on what the speaker says. If they don't hear or understand a word, encourage them not to panic or give up. They should try to figure out its meaning from the other sentences.

VIDEO OPTIONS

- **Télé-vocab 1**
- **Grammavision 1**
- **Télé-vocab 2**
- **Grammavision 2**
- **Télé-roman**

LISTENING PRACTICE

Language Lab and Classroom Activities

Vocabulaire
Activity 1, p. 44, CD 2, Tr. 1
Télé-vocab 1, p. 42, DVD Tutor
Activity 21, p. 56, CD 2, Tr. 4
Télé-vocab 2, p. 54, DVD Tutor

Grammaire
Activity 11, p. 49, CD 2, Tr. 2
Grammavision 1, pp. 46, 48, DVD Tutor
Activity 27, p. 58, CD 2, Tr. 5
Grammavision 2, pp. 58, 60, DVD Tutor

Application
Activity 18, p. 51, CD 2, Tr. 3
Activity 38, p. 63, CD 2, Tr. 6

Prépare-toi pour l'examen
Activity 6, p. 71, CD 2, Tr. 9

Révisions cumulatives
Activity 1, p. 74, CD 2, Tr. 13

Télé-roman
p. 64, DVD Tutor

Lecture
p. 66, CD 2, Tr. 7

Variations littéraires
p. 384, CD 2, Tr. 8

Lettres et sons
p. 72, CD 2, Tr. 10–12

Resources

Planning:
Lesson Planner
Teacher One Stop

Presentation:
Projectable Transparencies **Vocabulaire 2.1, 2.2**

DVD Tutor, Disc 1 **Télé-vocab 1**

Interactive Whiteboard Lessons

Practice:
Cahier de vocabulaire et grammaire
Differentiated Practice and Assessment CD-ROM
Independent Study Guide
Media Guide
Projectable Transparencies Bell Work 2.1
@HOMETUTOR
Holt McDougal French Apps

Bell Work

Use Bell Work 2.1 in the *Projectable Transparencies* or write this activity on the board.

Fill in the blanks using the correct form of the verb in parentheses.

1. **Je ____ (sortir) avec mes amis le samedi soir.**
2. **Nous ____ (dormir) tard le dimanche matin.**
3. **Ils ____ (sortir) de l'école à cinq heures.**
4. **Tu ____ (partir) en vacances avec tes parents tous les étés?**
5. **Vous êtes trop fatigués. Vous ne ____ (dormir) pas assez.** 1.2

Cultures

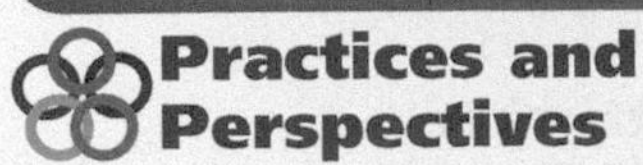

Practices and Perspectives

In French, many people also wish **bonne santé** along with **bonne année.** Ask students why it may be common to express these wishes together. 2.1

Objectifs
- to wish someone a good time
- to ask for and give advice

Vocabulaire à l'œuvre 1

Télé-vocab

Les fêtes en France

La fête nationale

Noël

la carte de vœux

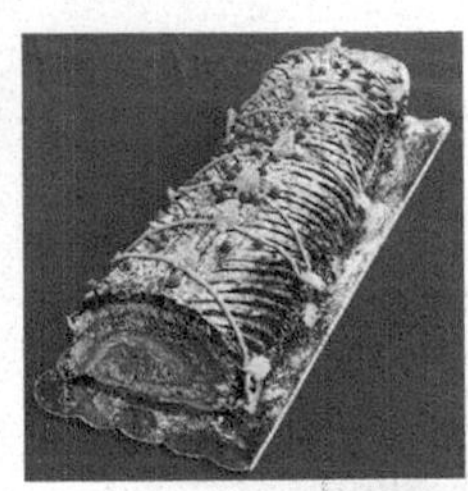
la bûche de Noël

Le nouvel an

Core Instruction

TEACHING VOCABULAIRE

1. Introduce the vocabulary with transparencies **Vocabulaire 2.1** and **2.2.** Model pronunciation of each word and the expressions in **Exprimons-nous! (2 min.)**
2. Ask students yes or no questions about each holiday. **Tu chantes l'hymne national pour la fête des mères? Tu allumes les bougies pour Noël? Tu reçois un chèque-cadeau pour ton anniversaire? (4 min.)**
3. Give the dates of several holidays. Make true or false statements and have students respond. **Noël est au mois de décembre.** (vrai) **La fête nationale pour la France est au mois d'avril.** (faux) **La fête des pères est au mois de mai.** (faux) **(2 min.)**

Télé-vocab 1
For a video presentation of this vocabulary, see the *DVD Tutor.*

Télé-vocab

Vocabulaire 1

L'anniversaire de Léa

les ballons (m.)
le cadeau
les invité(e)s
les bougies (f.)
le bouquet de fleurs
le gâteau

la carte d'anniversaire

Online Practice
my.hrw.com
Vocabulaire 1 practice

D'autres mots utiles

le jour de l'an	*New Year's Day*	un bal populaire	*dance*
la fête des mères/pères	*Mother's Day/ Father's Day*	une boîte de chocolats	*box of chocolates*
le réveillon	*midnight feast*	un chèque-cadeau	*gift card*
l'hymne (m.) national	*national anthem*	allumer	*to light*
		remercier	*to thank*

Exprimons-nous!

To wish someone a good time

J'espère que tu vas passer un joyeux/bon Noël. *I hope you will have . . .*

Amuse-toi bien! *Have fun!*

Bonne soirée! *Have a good evening!*

Profite bien de tes vacances. *Enjoy . . .*

Je te/vous souhaite un bon anniversaire. *I wish you . . .*

Joyeux anniversaire! Happy Birthday!

Vocabulaire et grammaire, *pp. 13–15*

▶ **Vocabulaire supplémentaire**—Les fêtes, **p. R17**

TPR — Total Physical Response

Have students respond to these commands.

Lève-toi si tu aimes les **fêtes.**

Assieds-toi si tu as toujours un sapin de Noël **chez toi.**

Mets une main sur la tête si tu veux un gâteau **pour** ton **anniversaire.**

Lève le doigt si tu aimes recevoir une boîte de chocolats.

Lève la main si tu aimes mieux un bouquet de fleurs.

Lève les deux mains si tu préfères un chèque-cadeau.

Donne un cadeau **à un(e) camarade.**

Viens ici si tu n'aimes pas le feu d'artifice.

Chante l'hymne national **américain.**

Va au tableau et dessine un ballon. 1.2

Cultures

Practices and Perspectives

The French today celebrate the festival of Saint Nicholas on December 6, primarily in the north and in Alsace and Lorraine. In Saint-Nicolas-de-Port and Nancy, where Nicholas is the patron saint, thousands come on pilgrimage for his feast day and have a celebration. Ask students to research Saint Nicholas and celebrations that take place December 6 and share their findings. 2.1

Differentiated Instruction

Slower Pace Learners

Bring an assortment of greeting cards to class and tape them to the board. Make statements that could be found in the cards. **J'espère que tu vas passer un bon anniversaire.** After each statement, ask a student to go to the board and point to the card that matches the statement. 1.2

Multiple Intelligences

Visual Ask students to design, illustrate, and write a greeting card for a holiday of their choice. The outside of the card should have a general holiday greeting and the inside should express personal wishes for an enjoyable holiday. You might have students share their cards and then display them on the classroom bulletin board. 1.3

Common Error Alert — Attention !

Remind students of the difference between **bonsoir** *(good-night)* and **bonne soirée** *(have a good evening)*. It is the same as the difference between **bonjour** and **bonne journée.**

Resources

Planning:
Lesson Planner
Teacher One Stop

Presentation:
Projectable Transparencies **Vocabulaire 2.1, 2.2**

DVD Tutor, Disc 1 **Télé-vocab 1**
Interactive Whiteboard Lessons

Practice:
Cahier de vocabulaire et grammaire
Differentiated Practice and Assessment CD-ROM
Independent Study Guide
Media Guide
Audio CD 2, Tr. 1
HOMETUTOR
Holt McDougal French Apps

1 Script

1. — Comment trouves-tu le sapin?
   — Il est beau, et la bûche est délicieuse.
2. — C'est un très joli bouquet de fleurs!
   — Comme toujours, un bouquet de fleurs pour Maman et une boîte de chocolats.
3. — Voilà le gâteau pour Amélie, les bougies, les cadeaux…
   — Cool! À quelle heure commence la soirée?
4. — Qu'est-ce que tu apportes au réveillon?
   — Des confettis.
5. — J'adore la foule, le défilé et le feu d'artifice!
   — Moi aussi.

Teacher Note

You may wish to give students the terms for these holidays.

Divali	*Diwali*
Hanoukka	*Hanukkah*
La pâque juive	*Passover*
Pâques	*Easter*
Le ramadan	*Ramadan*

1 Écoutons CD 2, Tr. 1 1.2

Des amis parlent de fêtes. Écoute leurs conversations et choisis l'image correcte. 1. b 2. c 3. e 4. d 5. a

a.

b.

c.

d.

e.

2 Faisons la fête! 1.2

Écrivons Complète les phrases suivantes sur les fêtes. Choisis l'expression qui complète le mieux la phrase.

la foule	les décorations	des cartes de vœux
passer	l'hymne national	la fête nationale
remercier	allumer	le gâteau

1. En France, après le dîner, on mange le gâteau.
2. La maison est très belle avec toutes les décorations de Noël.
3. À la fin de l'année, en France on envoie des cartes de vœux aux amis pour dire «Bonne Année».
4. Nous devons remercier nos grands-parents pour les cadeaux de Noël.
5. J'espère que tu vas passer un joyeux Noël.
6. Nous chantons l'hymne national en juillet.
7. La fête nationale française est le 14 juillet, mais aux États-Unis, c'est le 4 juillet.

Flash culture

Les Français célèbrent beaucoup de fêtes. Une fête importante est l'épiphanie, le jour des rois. Le premier dimanche de janvier, les Français mangent une galette des rois. Dans la galette, il y a un petit objet en céramique, la fève. La personne qui trouve la fève dans son gâteau est le roi ou la reine et porte la couronne (crown).

Est-ce que tu célèbres l'épiphanie? Est-ce que tu connais des gens qui la célèbrent? 2.1, 4.2

3 Les vœux 1.2

Écrivons/Parlons Donne tes vœux selon les situations suivantes.

MODÈLE Ce sont les vacances d'été.
Profite bien de tes vacances! Possible answers:

1. C'est l'anniversaire de Ludovic. Joyeux anniversaire!
2. Ton frère sort avec des amis ce soir. Bonne soirée!
3. C'est le 21 décembre. J'espère que tu vas passer un bon Noël.
4. C'est le 31 décembre. Je vous souhaite une bonne année!
5. Ton ami(e) va à une fête d'anniversaire. Amuse-toi bien à la fête!

Core Instruction

TEACHING EXPRIMONS-NOUS!

1. Model the pronunciation of the expressions in **Exprimons-nous! (2 min.)**
2. Using the vocabulary, ask, **Qui offre/reçoit... pour...?** Have students raise their hand to respond. **Qui offre des fleurs pour la fête des mères? Qui reçoit des cadeaux pour Noël? Qui donne une carte d'anniversaire pour un anniversaire? (2 min.)**
3. Name a student and begin an expression for giving advice about a gift. **Tu pourrais lui offrir...** Have volunteers finish the expression by naming a gift they think is appropriate for that student. **...un chèque-cadeau.** Respond to each suggestion. **Bonne idée! (3 min.)**

Exprimons-nous!

To ask for advice	To give advice	To respond
Tu as une idée de cadeau pour... ? *Do you have an idea for a present for . . . ?*	**Tu pourrais lui/leur offrir** un CD. *You could give him (her)/ them . . .*	**Bonne idée!** *Good idea!* **Tu n'as pas une autre idée?** *Don't you have another idea?*
Qu'est-ce que je pourrais offrir à Yann? *What could I get for . . . ?*	**Offre-lui** un jeu vidéo. *Give him/her . . .*	**Il en a déjà plein.** *He already has plenty of them.*

Vocabulaire et grammaire, *pp. 13–15*

4 Scénario 1.1

Parlons Tu demandes des conseils pour des cadeaux. Utilise les expressions dans les boîtes.

MODÈLE —**Tu as une idée de cadeau pour l'anniversaire de ma grand-mère?**
—**Offre-lui...**

ton cousin (il aime le sport)	la fête des mères	une boîte de chocolats
ta mère	son anniversaire	un bouquet de fleurs
ton père	la fête des pères	une cravate
ta copine	Noël	des billets de théâtre
ton frère		un DVD
ta sœur (elle adore la musique)		un chèque-cadeau

Communication

5 Une idée de cadeau 1.1

Parlons Tu veux offrir des cadeaux à trois ami(e)s pour leur anniversaire, mais tu ne sais pas quoi leur offrir. Demande des conseils à ton/ta camarade en utilisant la publicité à droite.

MODÈLE —**Qu'est-ce que je pourrais offrir à... ?**
—**Tu pourrais...**

LE VOILÀ!
LA RÉCRÉ
Jeux vidéo
à partir de
24 €
Casques écouteurs
21,99 €
Bandes dessinées
à partir de 5,50 €
DVD et CD à petits prix!
à partir de 8,50 €
Boule & Bill

Chapitre 2
Vocabulaire 1

Cultures

Practices and Perspectives

French colonists introduced **Mardi gras** to North America in the late 1600s. It became especially popular in the South and is a public holiday in Alabama, Florida, Missouri, and Louisiana. In French, **Mardi gras** means *Fat Tuesday*. It refers to the custom of parading a fat ox through the streets of Paris on Shrove Tuesday, which is the Tuesday before Ash Wednesday. Ask students to compare this to the ancient Roman custom of celebrating before a period of fasting and to brainstorm a list of other holidays people celebrate with feasting or fasting. 2.1

Communication

5 Pair Activity: Interpersonal

Have students write the names of five celebrities, teachers, or friends. Then have partners ask for and give advice about appropriate gifts for the people on their list. Instruct the partners to ask questions to determine the interests of the gift recipient in order to make a more informed suggestion. 1.1

Differentiated Instruction

ADVANCED LEARNERS

5 Have students write a three-frame comic strip entitled **Tu n'as pas une autre idée?** In the first frame, a student asks a classmate for ideas for a birthday present for his or her best friend. In the second frame, the classmate offers a suggestion. The third frame should show why the idea is not a very good one. For example, the classmate suggests a bouquet of flowers, but in the third frame the student's friend is shown walking by a park filled with flowers and sneezing from allergies. 1.3

SPECIAL LEARNING NEEDS

Students with Learning Disabilities/ Dyslexia Have partners act out short conversations using the phrases in **Exprimons-nous!** Each student should ask for advice, give advice, and respond several times. Students can use different names of family members and gift suggestions to continue the activity after they have used the examples given. 1.1

Assess

Assessment Program
Quiz: Vocabulaire 1
Alternative Assessment
Differentiated Practice and Assessment CD-ROM

Online Assessment
my.hrw.com

Test Generator

Resources

Planning:
Lesson Planner
Teacher One Stop

Presentation:
DVD Tutor, Disc 1
Grammavision 1.1

Practice:
Grammar Tutor for Students of French, Chapter 2
Cahier de vocabulaire et grammaire
Differentiated Practice and Assessment CD-ROM
Cahier d'activités
Independent Study Guide
Media Guide
Projectable Transparencies
Bell Work 2.2
@HOMETUTOR

Bell Work

Use Bell Work 2.2 in the *Projectable Transparencies* or write this activity on the board.

Complete the sentences.

1. **Ton sapin de Noël est superbe avec ces ____.**
2. **À Noël, le dessert traditionnel, c'est la ____.**
3. **Nous envoyons des ____ pour souhaiter «bonne année».**
4. **Tu peux m'aider à emballer les ____?**
5. **Pour la fête des mères, tu offres un ____ de fleurs à ta maman.** 1.2

Connections

Language Arts Link

Challenge students to think of an example in English such as, "With this ring, I thee wed," in which the direct object comes before the verb. 4.1

Objectifs
- direct object pronouns
- indirect object pronouns

Direct object pronouns

1. A **direct object** is the person or thing receiving the action of the verb.

   Ils achètent **le gâteau.**

2. **Direct objects** can be nouns or pronouns. To avoid repetition, **direct objects** can be replaced by **direct object pronouns.**

me	*me*	nous	*us*
te	*you* (sing., fam.)	vous	*you* (formal, plural)
le/la	*him/her, it*	les	*them*

3. In the present tense, place the direct object pronoun before the conjugated verb. If there is an infinitive, place it before the infinitive.

   —Ils vont regarder **le défilé?**
   —Oui, ils vont le regarder.

   —Je vous invite tous chez moi.
   —Tu nous invites tous? C'est très gentil!

4. Me, te, le, and la change to m', t', l', and l' before a vowel sound.

   —Ma mère m'envoie une carte d'anniversaire?

Vocabulaire et grammaire, *pp. 16–17*
Cahier d'activités, *pp. 11–13*

En anglais 4.1

In English, direct and indirect object pronouns usually go after the verb.

Alicia sees us.

Can you think of two more sentences using different object pronouns?

In French, object pronouns are usually placed before the verb.

Alicia **nous** regarde.

I see him. We buy them.

6 Où sont les objets directs? 1.2

Lisons Trouve le pronom d'objet direct dans les phrases suivantes.

1. Ces décorations sont belles. On les achète?
   a. ces **b.** on **c.** les (circled)
2. Isabelle va vous inviter chez elle pour le nouvel an.
   a. le **b.** vous (circled) **c.** elle
3. Merci! Ce bouquet de fleurs est vraiment magnifique. Je l'adore!
   a. l' (circled) **b.** ce **c.** je
4. Ces ballons? On les achète pour la soirée de Léa.
   a. on **b.** les (circled) **c.** la
5. À Noël, je vous invite chez moi.
   a. moi **b.** je **c.** vous (circled)

Core Instruction

TEACHING GRAMMAIRE

1. Tell students that direct objects answer *what?* or *whom?* and follow the verb. Remind students that when a pronoun is used to replace the direct object, it comes before the conjugated verb or infinitive. **(2 min.)**
2. Write the object pronouns on the board in two columns of three, the same order as subject pronouns. Make statements or questions with a direct object. **(2 min.)**
3. Have students hold up one to six fingers to indicate which of the pronouns replaces the direct object. **Je prépare la bûche de Noël.** (3) **Paul invite ses amis à la boum.** (6) **(3 min.)**

Grammavision

For a video presentation of direct objects and direct object pronouns, see the *DVD Tutor.*

Online Practice
my.hrw.com
Grammaire 1 practice

7 Trop de répétitions! 1.2

Écrivons/Parlons Réécris les phrases suivantes. Utilise des pronoms d'objet direct pour éviter les répétitions.

MODÈLE La bûche? Nous achetons la bûche à la pâtisserie.
La bûche? Nous l'achetons à la pâtisserie.

1. Coralie et Fabienne? Je vais inviter Coralie et Fabienne à mon anniversaire.
2. Le défilé commence à midi. Nous allons voir le défilé.
3. Cassandra offre une boîte de chocolats à Nadine. Nadine remercie Cassandra.
4. C'est un cadeau parfait. Mon père va beaucoup aimer ce cadeau.
5. Tu pourrais offrir un DVD à Luciane. Elle adore les DVD.
6. Papa a trouvé un joli cadeau pour maman. Il achète ce cadeau.

8 Une très bonne fête! 1.3

Écrivons/Parlons Décris les images suivantes. Utilise des pronoms d'objet direct.

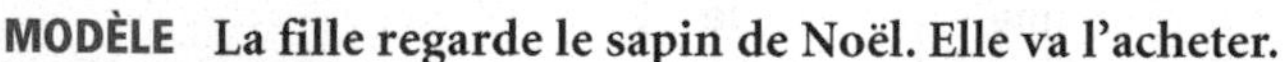

MODÈLE La fille regarde le sapin de Noël. Elle va l'acheter.

1.

2.

3.

4.

9 Scénario 1.1

Parlons Tous les ans, pour le 4 juillet, ton/ta camarade et toi êtes invité(e)s à une fête chez un(e) ami(e). Parlez des choses que vous allez faire et voir le 4 juillet. Utilisez des pronoms d'objet direct pour éviter les répétitions.

MODÈLE **—Joyce, tu aimes les fêtes de Martin?**
—Oui, je les adore. Et toi?
—Moi aussi. À quelle heure est-ce qu'on va regarder le... ?
—On va le regarder...

7 Answers

1. Je vais les inviter à mon anniversaire.
2. Nous allons le voir.
3. Nadine la remercie.
4. Mon père va beaucoup l'aimer.
5. Elle les adore.
6. Il l'achète.

French for Spanish Speakers

Ask students to compare the direct object pronouns in French with those in Spanish. Which are spelled the same? **(me, te, la)** Have students compare placement. (In French and in Spanish the direct object pronoun usually goes before the verb. However, in Spanish, with an infinitive, the speaker has the choice of putting the direct object pronoun either before the conjugated verb or attaching it to the end of the infinitive.) Have students create a chart that compares direct object pronoun placement in French and Spanish.

Français	Español
Je peux *le* voir.	***Lo* puedo ver.** or **Puedo *verlo*.**

4.1

Communication

Pair Activity: Interpersonal

Ask students to imagine they are having guests for Christmas and they want everything to be ready. Have one partner ask a question about the tasks below. The other partner answers with a direct object pronoun. They should alternate asking and answering the questions.

décorer le sapin de Noël
acheter la bûche de Noël
allumer les bougies
préparer le réveillon
acheter les cartes de vœux

1.1

Differentiated Instruction

SLOWER PACE LEARNERS

Play Direct Object Chairs. Write the direct object pronouns on index cards and tape the cards to the seats of ten chairs. Place the chairs in a circle with the seats facing out. Instruct groups of students to walk around the chairs. Say a short sentence. **Je regarde la télé.** Students try to be the first to sit in the chair that has the corresponding direct object pronoun. If the student can repeat the sentence, he or she keeps that card. The game continues until students have collected all the cards. 1.2

SPECIAL LEARNING NEEDS

Students with Language Impairments Ask students to copy grammar rules and examples into a **Grammaire** notebook of their own. Work with students individually to be sure they understand the rule and ask them to create additional examples to show they have mastered the concept. Use **En anglais** to assist students with language impairments in connecting French language structures to those in English. 4.1

Resources

Planning:
Lesson Planner
Teacher One Stop

Presentation:
DVD Tutor, Disc 1
Grammavision 1.2

Practice:
Grammar Tutor for Students of French, Chapter 2
Cahier de vocabulaire et grammaire
Differentiated Practice and Assessment CD-ROM
Cahier d'activités
Independent Study Guide
Media Guide
Projectable Transparencies
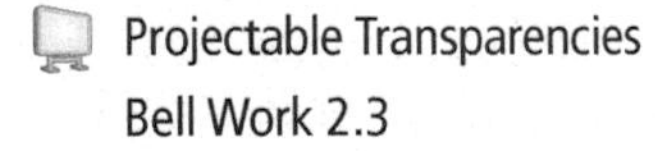
Bell Work 2.3
Audio CD 2, Tr. 2
HOMETUTOR

Bell Work

Use Bell Work 2.3 in the *Projectable Transparencies* or write this activity on the board.

Write the answer to each question using a direct object pronoun.

1. **Tu achètes ces décorations? Oui, je...**
2. **Ta mère va décorer le sapin de Noël? Oui, elle...**
3. **Vous allumez les bougies? Oui, nous...**
4. **Tu nous invites? Oui, je...**
5. **La foule va regarder le feu d'artifice? Oui, elle...** 1.2

⑩ Answers

1. Oui, elle va les lui offrir.
2. Oiu, nous la lui envoyons.
3. Oui, elle les lui donne.
4. Oui, je vais leur téléphoner.

⑪ Script

See script on p. 39E.

Indirect object pronouns

1 An indirect object is the person who benefits from the action of the verb. In French, the indirect object is almost always preceded by **à** and is often used with verbs of giving and receiving **(donner, offrir, envoyer)** and of commmunicating **(parler, téléphoner, dire)**.

Je vais envoyer une invitation à ton cousin.

2 **Indirect object** pronouns are used to avoid repetition. Place the indirect object pronoun before the conjugated verb or infinitive.

me (m')	(*to*) *me*	**nous**	(*to*) *us*
te (t')	(*to*) *you*	**vous**	(*to*) *you*
lui	(*to*) *him, her*	**leur**	(*to*) *them*

Alors, je **vous** envoie une invitation à ma fête.
Tu pourrais **lui** offrir un CD.

3 If you have a sentence with both direct and indirect object pronouns, place the pronouns in the order presented in the chart below.

me	**le**	
te	**l'**	**lui**
nous	**la**	**leur**
vous	**les**	

J'envoie **cette carte** à mon ami.

Je l'envoie à mon ami.	*I'm sending **it** to my friend.*
Je **lui** envoie cette carte.	*I'm sending **him** this card.*
Je la **lui** envoie.	*I'm sending **it** to **him**.*
Je **te** l'envoie.	*I'm sending **it** to **you**.*

Vocabulaire et grammaire, *pp. 16–17*
Cahier d'activités, *pp. 11–13*

Flash culture

Le 14 juillet est le jour de la fête nationale en France. On célèbre la prise de la Bastille en 1789. La Bastille était une prison et elle représentait le pouvoir royal. La prise de la Bastille marque le début de la révolution française. Aujourd'hui, le 14 juillet est un jour férié, marqué par les défilés militaires sur les Champs-Élysées et le discours du Président. Les villes organisent des festivités: souvent il y a un bal populaire et un feu d'artifice.

Qu'est-ce que tu fais le 4 juillet? Qu'est-ce que ta ville organise? 2.1, 4.2

⑩ L'anniversaire de Lucie 1.2

Écrivons La famille de Michel organise une fête. Réponds aux questions en remplaçant les mots soulignés avec des pronoms.

MODÈLE Michel donne les ballons à ses parents?
Oui, il les leur donne.

1. Maman va offrir les fleurs à Lucie?
2. Maman et Papa, vous envoyez l'invitation à oncle Marcel?
3. Sara donne les décorations à Maman?
4. Tu vas téléphoner aux amis de Lucie?

Core Instruction

TEACHING GRAMMAIRE

1. Go over Points 1 and 2. **(2 min.)**
2. Tell students that when a sentence has both a direct and an indirect object, the direct object comes first. Model examples. **(2 min.)**
3. Have students count off by six, each number representing an indirect object pronoun. Write six indirect object pronouns across the board. Make a statement or question with an indirect object. The student whose number represents the corresponding indirect object pronoun moves to the board and stands by that pronoun. **(4 min.)**

Grammavision

For a video presentation of indirect objects and indirect object pronouns, see the *DVD Tutor.*

11 Écoutons CD 2, Tr. 2 1.2

Écoute chaque conversation et décide si la réponse est **a) logique** ou **b) pas logique.** **1.** b **2.** a **3.** b **4.** a **5.** a

12 Des réactions logiques 1.2

Écrivons Complète les conversations suivantes avec des pronoms.

1. Tes amis ont de nouveaux portables?
   Oui, je _______ téléphone tous les jours. leur
2. Tu nous invites à la fête?
   Bien sûr, je _______ envoie une invitation aujourd'hui! vous
3. Tu _______ donnes ce cadeau? me
   Oui, je _______ _______ donne. te, le
4. Elle donne ce cadeau à Ahmed?
   Oui, elle _______ _______ donne. le, lui
5. Alors, Anne et Paul, je _______ téléphone ce soir. Au revoir! vous

13 La boum de Noémie 1.2

Écrivons/Parlons Explique ce qui se passe à la boum de Noémie. Utilise des pronoms d'objet direct et indirect dans tes phrases.

Alain, Noémie

MODÈLE **Il l'invite à danser.**

Possible answers:

1. sa mère, les bougies
Elle les allume.

2. Noémie, Sabine
Elle lui téléphone.

3. le chien, le gâteau
Il le mange.

4. ses amis, un cadeau, à Noémie
Ils lui donnent un cadeau.

Digital performance space

Communication

14 Scénario 1.1

Parlons Deux frères/sœurs cherchent un cadeau pour l'anniversaire de leur mère. Ils/Elles vont au magasin, mais ils/elles ne sont d'accord sur rien. Jouez la scène et puis échangez les rôles.

MODÈLE **—Pourquoi est-ce que tu ne lui achètes pas une boîte de chocolats?**
—Non, elle n'aime pas le chocolat.

COMMON ERROR ALERT
ATTENTION !

As an indirect object, the word **leur** never ends with an **–s.** Students may confuse it with the possessive adjective, which has a plural form **leurs.**

Comparisons

Comparing and Contrasting

Tell students that French birthday candles are usually much longer than those that top American birthday cakes. Have students find pictures of American and French birthday cakes and their recipes and write a paragraph to compare the two. 4.2

Communication

Pair Activity: Interpersonal

Have students think of three people for whom they would like to buy gifts. Students should take turns with a partner asking for gift ideas for those people. The student asking for the suggestions should reject each suggestion and give a reason why. The student making the suggestions should suggest three different things. Partners must use object pronouns in each interchange. 1.1

Differentiated Instruction

ADVANCED LEARNERS

Challenge groups of students to invent a hopscotch game that teaches direct object and indirect object placement. You might help them get started by suggesting they place the pronouns **Je, Tu, Il/Elle/On, Nous, Vous, Ils/Elles** at the near end of the hopscotch grid, with the object pronouns extending out from this starting point. Have groups demonstrate their game to the rest of the class. 1.3

MULTIPLE INTELLIGENCES

Interpersonal Encourage students who easily grasp the grammar concepts to be peer tutors to those who are struggling with the lesson. You might assign students to work in pairs or small groups to assist others. Allow tutors time to explain the presentation and then suggest that partners or other group members echo the presentation to check for comprehension.

Assess

Assessment Program
Quiz: Grammaire1
Alternative Assessment
Differentiated Practice and Assessment CD-ROM

Online Assessment
my.hrw.com

Test Generator 

Resources

Planning:
Lesson Planner
Teacher One Stop

Practice:
Grammar Tutor for Students of French, Chapter 2
Cahier de vocabulaire et grammaire
Differentiated Practice and Assessment CD-ROM
Cahier d'activités
Independent Study Guide
Media Guide
Projectable Transparencies
Bell Work 2.4
Audio CD 2, Tr. 3

Bell Work

Use Bell Work 2.4 in the *Projectable Transparencies* or write this activity on the board.

Fill in the blanks using the correct pronoun.

1. **Vous envoyez une carte de vœux à votre professeur. Il ____ répond.**
2. **Tu as une idée de cadeau pour ton père? Tu pourrais ____ acheter un livre.**
3. **Tu vas donner ce CD à Julien? Oui, je vais ____ ____donner.**
4. **Ces fleurs sont superbes. Je ____ remercie.**
5. **Tu achètes ces ballons? Oui, je ____ achète.** 1.2

18 Script

1. — Quel âge a-t-il aujourd'hui?
   — Marc a seize ans.
2. — Hier, nous avons décoré le sapin.
   — Il est très beau.
3. Le défilé se passe à deux heures de l'après-midi et le soir il y a un feu d'artifice. Ça va être chouette.
4. Je vais offrir un bouquet de fleurs à ma mère.
5. Est-ce que tu vas acheter une cravate pour ton père?
   — Non, il en a déjà plein.

Synthèse
• Vocabulaire 1
• Grammaire 1

Application 1

15 Et toi? 1.3

Parlons/Écrivons Tu fais un sondage sur les fêtes avec tes camarades. Réponds aux questions en utilisant des pronoms.

1. Qu'est-ce que tu vas offrir à ton/ta meilleur(e) ami(e) pour son anniversaire? Pourquoi?
2. Est-ce que tu aimes les feux d'artifice? Pourquoi?
3. Qu'est-ce que tu fais d'habitude le 4 juillet? Tu chantes l'hymne national? Tu vas voir le feu d'artifice?
4. Est-ce que tu aimes décorer le sapin de Noël?
5. Comment est-ce que tu invites tes amis à faire quelque chose? (par lettre? e-mail? téléphone? texto?)

Un peu plus

The verb *offrir*

The verb **offrir** ends in **-ir**, but it is conjugated like an **-er** verb.

offrir *(to give a gift, offer)*	
j' offr**e**	nous offr**ons**
tu offr**es**	vous offr**ez**
il/elle/on offr**e**	ils/elles offr**ent**

Vocabulaire et grammaire, *p. 18*
Cahier d'activités, *pp. 11–13*

16 Qu'est-ce qu'on offre? 1.2

Écrivons Complète les phrases avec la forme correcte du verbe **offrir**.

1. Nous _offrons_ un DVD à Marie-Claire.
2. Tu leur _offres_ encore des chocolats?
3. J'_offre_ toujours des fleurs à ma mère pour la fête des mères.
4. En France, on _offre_ des cadeaux à la Chandeleur?
5. Mes tantes m'_offrent_ toujours des cadeaux super!

17 Ma famille et moi 1.2

Écrivons Fais six phrases complètes pour dire quels cadeaux ces personnes offrent. Utilise la forme correcte du verbe **offrir** et le pronom approprié pour remplacer la personne entre parenthèses.

MODÈLE nous / portables (à toi et ton frère)
Nous vous offrons des portables.

1. je / les bougies (à Marina)
2. ma cousine / une boîte de chocolats (à moi)
3. tes parents / un vélo super (à toi)
4. nous / un bouquet de fleurs (à Pauline et à toi)
5. tu / le ballon de foot (à tes petits frères)
6. vous / une BD (à ma copine et à moi)

Answers:
1. Je lui offre les bougies.
2. Ma cousine m'offre une boîte de chocolats.
3. Tes parents t'offrent un vélo super.
4. Nous vous offrons un bouquet de fleurs.
5. Tu leur offres le ballon de foot.
6. Vous nous offrez une BD.

Core Instruction

INTEGRATED PRACTICE

1. Have students do Activity 15 to practice vocabulary and object pronouns. **(5 min.)**
2. Ask questions that can be answered with a holiday. **Pour quelle fête est-ce que tu offres des fleurs? (3 min.)**
3. Ask questions that require answers with direct or indirect objects. **Paul offre le cadeau à Marie? (5 min.)**
4. Continue with Activities 16–19. **(12 min.)**

TEACHING UN PEU PLUS

1. Remind students that **offrir** looks like an **-ir** verb, but is conjugated like an **-er** verb. Go over **Un peu plus** and model pronunciation. **(2 min.)**
2. Using vocabulary pictures, some of which you keep, some of which you hand out to students, form sentences with **offrir. J'offre la boîte de chocolats à Jean. Vous offrez un DVD à Marie.** Have students follow your directions. **(3 min.)**

18 Écoutons CD 2, Tr. 3 1.2

Quelle fête est-ce? Dis de quelle fête on parle.

Noël	la fête nationale	la fête d'anniversaire
la fête des mères	la fête des pères	

Online Practice
my.hrw.com
Application 1 practice

1. la fête d'anniversaire
2. Noël
3. la fête nationale
4. la fête des mères
5. la fête des pères

19 Festivités du 14 juillet 1.3

Lisons/Écrivons Tu as trouvé cette invitation pour le 14 juillet et tu veux aller aux festivités. Écris un e-mail à ton ami(e) pour l'inviter. Mentionne ce que vous pouvez faire ensemble.

MODÈLE **J'ai reçu cette invitation… On peut…**

Festivités du 14 juillet
Allons enfants de la patrie
Jeudi 13 juillet
22h30 feu d'artifice sur la Grande place
de 21h à 4h bal animé par l'orchestre des Magnifiques
et aussi
manèges pour les petits
barbes à papa
stands restauration et boissons

À l'algérienne

In Algeria and other north African countries, you might hear **faire la nouba** to mean *to celebrate* or *to party.*

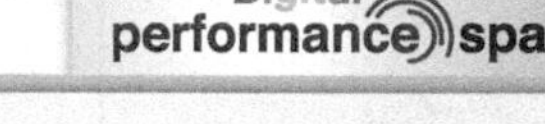

Communication

20 Questions personnelles 1.1

Parlons Quelle fête est-ce que tu préfères? Pourquoi? Qu'est-ce que tu fais d'habitude pour cette fête? Quelles sont les fêtes préférées de tes camarades? Utilise des pronoms d'objet direct et indirect dans tes phrases pour éviter les répétitions.

MODÈLE **J'aime beaucoup Noël. C'est ma fête préférée. J'adore envoyer des cartes de vœux. Ma mère me les...**

COMMON ERROR ALERT
ATTENTION !

Students should be cautioned that only phrases introduced by **à** and followed by a person may be replaced with indirect object pronouns. Compare **je réponds au prof (je lui réponds)** to **je réponds au téléphone (j'y réponds).**

Communication

Group Activity: Interpersonal

Write on the board a list of **-er**, **-ir**, and **-re** verbs that take direct and indirect objects. Then have one student ask another a question with one of the verbs. The other student must answer affirmatively or negatively with an appropriate object pronoun and then ask a question to a third student. Have students continue until they all have had a turn. 1.1

Differentiated Instruction

SLOWER PACE LEARNERS

19 Prepare close-paragraph worksheets about different holidays. Delete direct and indirect object pronouns and chapter vocabulary and list them at the top of the page. Allow students to choose the holiday worksheet they would like to complete. 1.2

SPECIAL LEARNING NEEDS

Students with Dyslexia Ask students to use the conjugation chart for the verb **offrir** to create a poster or notebook page with pictures of gifts they might like. Each picture should have a caption with the correct form of the verb to explain who might give the gift. Students may refer to the poster or pages as they complete the activities. You may wish to display the posters in class. 1.3

Assess

Assessment Program
Quiz: Application 1
Audio CD 2, Tr. 14
Alternative Assessment
Differentiated Practice and Assessment CD-ROM
Online Assessment
my.hrw.com
Test Generator 

Resources

Planning:
Lesson Planner
Teacher One Stop

Practice:
Cahier d'activités

Vocabulaire supplémentaire

You might wish to use these terms to discuss the project with students.

le papier de bricolage	*construction paper*
la colle	*glue*
coller	*to glue*
les ciseaux	*scissors*
les plumes	*feathers*
les paillettes	*sequins*
la perle	*bead*
le ruban	*ribbon*

Bulletin Board Project

Have students work in small groups to research on the Internet or in the library traditional clothing styles in several francophone countries. Assign a different country to each group. The styles may be for daily wear or costumes for festivals or special events such as **Mardi gras.** Have each group write a short paragraph to describe the style of traditional clothing in their assigned country and illustrate their paragraph with an original drawing or a photo from the Web site or a book. Remind students to document the Web sites they visit. Have volunteers create a bulletin board with the articles and entitle it **La Mode traditionnelle.** 1.3, 2.1

Culture

Mardi Gras à Montmartre, Paris

Culture appliquée

Le carnaval 2.1

Mardi Gras est célébré dans toute la France et en particulier à Nice qui a un des plus importants carnavals du monde. D'autres villes francophones (Québec au Canada, Fort-de-France à la Martinique, ou encore La Nouvelle-Orléans en Louisiane) célèbrent le mardi gras et organisent un carnaval. Pendant le carnaval on peut admirer des défilés, de beaux masques, des musiciens, des spectacles et des feux d'artifice. En France, les enfants fêtent le carnaval à l'école en se déguisant. Ils peuvent porter des masques et se maquiller[1]. Dans certaines villes, les lycéens[2] se retrouvent dans le centre-ville pour une bataille de farine[3] et d'œufs après les cours.

1. put on make-up 2. high school students 3. flour

Les masques 2.2

Materials needed:

- construction paper in different colors
- glue
- feathers
- sequins
- beads
- ribbons
- glitter
- a thin stick or elastic band

Step 1 Trace the mask on a sheet of construction paper. Cut out the shape to make the base.

Step 2 Decorate the mask with glitter, sequins, beads, feathers, or other materials.

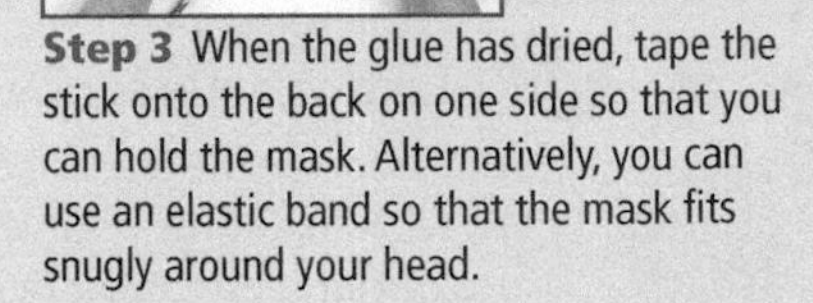
Step 3 When the glue has dried, tape the stick onto the back on one side so that you can hold the mask. Alternatively, you can use an elastic band so that the mask fits snugly around your head.

Recherches Dans quelles autres cultures est-ce qu'on fête le carnaval? Quelles sont les différences et les similarités entre ces célébrations? 2.1

Core Instruction

CULTURE APPLIQUÉE

1. In class, read and discuss the first paragraph. Ask if any students have been to a **Mardi gras** celebration. Ask them to tell what they experienced. **(10 min.)**
2. Place the materials to make the masks at several work stations. If there are not enough supplies for each student, it may be easier to form small groups to work together. Remind students to follow the directions in the text to make their masks. You may wish to display the masks in class. **(25 min.)**

COMPARAISONS ET COMMUNAUTÉ

1. Have students read the introductory question and discuss the answer. **(3 min.)**
2. Ask students to read the second paragraph. Ask if they know of any flowers in our culture that are associated with special occasions. Discuss **Et toi? (5 min.)**
3. Go over **Communauté et professions** with students and have them answer the questions. **(4 min.)**

Online Practice
my.hrw.com
Online Edition

Comparaisons

Marchand de fleurs

Invitation à manger 1.2

Tu es invité(e) à dîner chez ton ami français, Jean-Christophe. Qu'est-ce que tu offres à sa mère?

a. un bouquet de fleurs en plastique
(b.) une douzaine de belles roses
c. un pot de chrysanthèmes

En général, quand on est invité à dîner, on offre des fleurs à la maîtresse de maison[1]. Mais attention, on n'offre pas de chrysanthèmes! Les significations des fleurs ont évolué avec le temps et sont différentes d'une culture à une autre. En France, le chrysanthème est la fleur de la Toussaint (1er novembre), du souvenir et de la commémoration des morts. Certaines personnes superstitieuses pensent qu'offrir des chrysanthèmes porte malheur[2].

4.2

ET TOI?

1. Et dans ta culture, qu'est-ce que le chrysanthème représente?
2. Qu'est-ce que tu offres quand tu es invité(e) à dîner chez quelqu'un?

Communauté et professions

Spécialités pour les fêtes 5.1

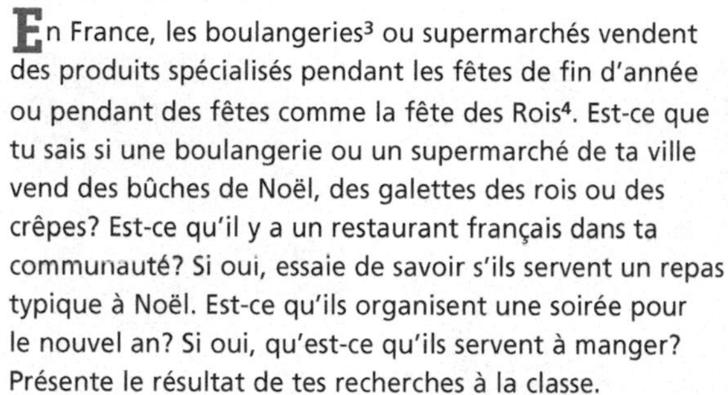

En France, les boulangeries[3] ou supermarchés vendent des produits spécialisés pendant les fêtes de fin d'année ou pendant des fêtes comme la fête des Rois[4]. Est-ce que tu sais si une boulangerie ou un supermarché de ta ville vend des bûches de Noël, des galettes des rois ou des crêpes? Est-ce qu'il y a un restaurant français dans ta communauté? Si oui, essaie de savoir s'ils servent un repas typique à Noël. Est-ce qu'ils organisent une soirée pour le nouvel an? Si oui, qu'est-ce qu'ils servent à manger? Présente le résultat de tes recherches à la classe.

Bûche de Noël

1. hostess 2. bad luck 3. bakeries 4. Epiphany

Differentiated Instruction

SLOWER PACE LEARNERS

Write a question on the board for each sentence of **Le carnaval.** Review the questions with students to give them a purpose for reading and help them anticipate the kinds of information they will find. Then read the paragraph aloud as a class. Pause after each sentence to ask the related question. 1.2

SPECIAL LEARNING NEEDS

Students with Auditory Impairments
Visual representation helps students with auditory impairments to understand abstract concepts, such as cultural differences. Ask students to research the various customs presented in **Culture.** Have students create a collage of pictures or bring books to display in class to show festivals, foods, flowers, and costumes that are traditional in francophone countries. Have students document their sources. 2.1

Communities

School Link

Ask small groups of students to create a plan for a school-wide event to celebrate **Mardi gras.** Students might create posters or other displays to teach classmates about the holiday or plan a **Mardi gras** costume contest or a **Mardi gras** parade. 1.3, 5.1

Cultures

Practices and Perspectives

Have students search the Internet for a Web site that gives advice to travelers who are visiting different countries. Instruct students to choose a francophone country and find information for travelers on its rules of etiquette. Remind students to document the Web sites they use. Have small groups create a humorous conversation in which a visitor to that country unknowingly violates a rule of etiquette. 2.1, 3.2

Language Examination

Culture can be used to practice for the **Interpretive Communication** and **Presentational Writing** sections of the AP Language and Culture Exam as it helps students get acquainted with and reflect on products and practices from the French-speaking world while reading culture-focused passages and answering questions in French.

Resources

Planning:

Lesson Planner

Teacher One Stop

Presentation:

Projectable Transparencies **Vocabulaire 2.3, 2.4**

DVD Tutor, Disc 1 **Télé-vocab 2**

Interactive Whiteboard Lessons

Practice:

Cahier de vocabulaire et grammaire

Differentiated Practice and Assessment CD-ROM

Independent Study Guide

Media Guide

Projectable Transparencies Bell Work 2.5

HOMETUTOR

Holt McDougal French Apps

Bell Work

Use Bell Work 2.5 in the *Projectable Transparencies* or write this activity on the board.

Fill in the blanks with the correct form of **offrir.**

1. **Tu lui ____ toujours des fleurs pour son anniversaire.**
2. **Nous t' ____ souvent des chocolats.**
3. **Pascal et Pauline vous ____ des CD.**
4. **Vous nous ____ ce nouveau DVD?**
5. **Je vais vous ____ cette jolie montre.** 1.2

Communities

Family Link

Stage a "Parent Appreciation" day with a party in class. Have students invite their parents or guardians and purchase or craft a small present for each invitee. Students will conduct all planning and preparation for the party in French. 5.1

Objectifs

- to ask for help
- to check if things have been done

Télé-vocab

On organise une soirée à Paris!

envoyer les invitations (f.)

faire les courses (f.)

ranger la maison

faire le ménage

faire la poussière

emballer les cadeaux

décorer la salle

choisir la musique

préparer les amuse-gueules (m.)

Core Instruction

TEACHING VOCABULAIRE

1. Introduce vocabulary with transparencies **Vocabulaire 2.3** and **Vocabulaire 2.4** and model pronunciation of the expressions in **Exprimons-nous!** as you point to each image. **(2 min.)**
2. Have nine volunteers mime each of the activities. Ask the other students, **Qui fait les courses? Qui range la maison? Qui décore la salle?** They should answer with the correct student's name. **(3 min.)**
3. Number all nine activities on a transparency. (For **faire les courses (pour),** add the five food items on page 55 to that activity.) Have volunteers put the activities in order of importance, in their opinion, for a party. Then model a conversation asking for help and responding to each of the activities. **(3 min.)**

Télé-vocab 2

For a video presentation of this vocabulary, see the *DVD Tutor.*

Télé-vocab

Online Practice
my.hrw.com
Vocabulaire 2 practice

Exprimons-nous!

To ask for help	To respond
Tu peux m'aider à ranger le salon? *Can you help me . . . ?*	Oui, **pas de problème.** *. . . no problem.* **D'accord.** *O.K.* **Désolé(e), je n'ai pas le temps.** *Sorry, I don't have the time.*
Ça t'ennuie de passer l'aspirateur? *Do you mind . . . ?*	**Bien sûr que non.** *Of course not.* **Pas maintenant. Je dois d'abord** finir mes devoirs. *Not right now. First, I need to . . .*

Vocabulaire et grammaire, *pp. 19–21*

Online Workbooks

▶ **Vocabulaire supplémentaire,** Les fêtes, **p. R17**

TPR
Total Physical Response

Have students respond to these commands.

Lève-toi si c'est toi qui fais les courses chez toi.
Assieds-toi si ça t'ennuie de ranger la maison.
Lève le doigt si tu aimes beaucoup les bonbons.
Lève la main si tu aimes les soirées costumées.
Lève les deux mains si c'est toujours toi qui choisis la musique.
Viens ici si tu peux m'aider à nettoyer mon bureau.
Mets la tête sur la table si tu n'as pas le temps de m'aider.

Then have students mime the following activities.

Tu fais la poussière.
Balaye la salle de classe!
Maintenant, tu passes l'aspirateur. 1.2

Cultures
Products and Perspectives

Point out the bowl of peanuts in the photo. Tell students that although both peanuts and butter can be commonly found in France, peanut butter **(beurre de cacahuètes** or **beurre d'arachides)** is somewhat hard to find. Have students do research to find out if any of their favorite snacks would be unavailable to them if they were to travel to France.

2.2

Proverbes

For French proverbs and activities related to the chapter theme and vocabulary, see **Proverbes et expressions,** pp. R6–R7.

Differentiated Instruction

Advanced Learners

Have students write a how-to speech on one of the party preparation activities such as how to prepare a recipe for a party appetizer, how to wrap presents, or how to choose appropriate music for a party. Have students look up vocabulary they will need for their speech. Have them prepare vocabulary lists to give to their classmates prior to delivering their speech. 1.3

Special Learning Needs

Students with Visual Impairments Be sure the pictures in the vocabulary presentation are large enough for students with visual impairments to analyze. If enlargement or assistive technology for magnification is not an option, assign these students a partner who will describe all the pictures in detail.

Resources

Planning:
Lesson Planner
Teacher One Stop

Presentation:
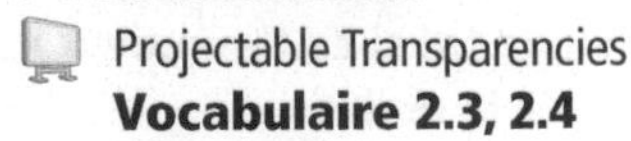
Projectable Transparencies **Vocabulaire 2.3, 2.4**
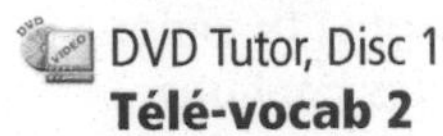
DVD Tutor, Disc 1 **Télé-vocab 2**
Interactive Whiteboard Lessons

Practice:
Cahier de vocabulaire et grammaire
Differentiated Practice and Assessment CD-ROM
Independent Study Guide
Media Guide
Audio CD 2, Tr. 4
HOMETUTOR
Holt McDougal French Apps

21 Script

See script on p. 39E.

22 Answers

1. a organisé
2. ai invité
3. a préparé
4. a nettoyé
5. a décoré
6. chips
7. fruits
8. gâteau
9. eau
10. limonade
11. a choisi

Connections

Home Economics Link

Have students write and video-tape a TV show in French about tips for cleaning your house, creative gift-wrapping techniques, or throwing a theme party. 3.1

Flash culture

Pour Noël et le nouvel an, les Français réveillonnent, c'est-à-dire qu'ils font un grand repas la veille de Noël ou du jour de l'an. On mange du foie gras *(goose or duck liver)*, des huîtres et la bûche de Noël. En général, les adultes ouvrent leurs cadeaux le soir du réveillon, mais les enfants attendent le matin du 25 décembre pour découvrir ce que le père Noël leur a apporté. Les enfants mettent leurs chaussons *(slippers)* au pied du sapin de Noël.

Qu'est-ce que tu fais avec ta famille pendant les fêtes? 4.2

21 Écoutons CD 2, Tr. 4 1.2

Regarde les photos et écoute les conversations. Indique quelle photo correspond à chaque conversation.
1. c 2. e 3. d 4. f 5. a 6. b

a.

b.

c.

d.

e.

f.

22 Mon week-end 1.2

Écrivons Kiné envoie un e-mail à son cousin pour lui raconter la fête qu'elle a donnée. Complète l'e-mail avec les mots appropriés.

a choisi	a organisé	a nettoyé	a décoré	fruits	limonade
ai invité	gâteau	a préparé	chips	eau	CD

On __1__ une fête. J'__2__ quelques amis. Ma mère __3__ les amuse-gueules, mon père __4__ et __5__ le salon. Il y avait des __6__, des __7__ secs et du __8__. Comme boissons, il y avait de l'__9__ minérale et de la __10__. Mon copain Alex __11__ la musique. On s'est vraiment bien amusés!

Entre copains

bouffer	*to eat*
faire la teuf	*to party*
la boum	*party*
la zique	*music*

23 Avant la fête 1.2

Écrivons/Parlons Un(e) ami(e) organise une fête et tu veux aider, mais tu as des choses à faire. Réponds à ses questions.

1. Tu peux m'aider à décorer la salle?
2. Ça t'ennuie de faire la poussière?
3. Tu peux m'aider à emballer les cadeaux?
4. Ça t'ennuie de ranger la maison?
5. Tu peux m'aider à préparer les biscuits?

Core Instruction

TEACHING EXPRIMONS-NOUS!

1. Model the questions and responses. Then repeat the questions and give negative and affirmative responses. **(2 min.)**
2. Ask each student to choose one negative or positive response and write it on a notecard. Tell students that you think you have everything done for your party. **(2 min.)**
3. Begin with a group of four students and ask if things have been done. Each student should read aloud the response he or she has written. Collect the positive responses and see how many tasks have been done. **(3 min.)**
4. Continue with another group of four students until everyone has participated. Determine which group has been most helpful with the preparations. **(8 min.)**

Exprimons-nous!

To check if things have been done	To respond
Tu as déjà préparé les amuse-gueules? *Did you already . . . ?*	Non, **pas encore.** *. . . not yet.*
Est-ce qu'il y a encore des courses à faire? *Are there still . . . ?*	Non, **c'est bon.** *. . . it's all taken care of.*
Tu as bien envoyé les invitations? *Are you sure you . . . ?*	**Mais oui!** Je les ai envoyées la semaine dernière. *But of course!*
Tu as pensé à choisir la musique? *Have you thought of . . . ?*	**J'ai complètement oublié!** *I totally forgot!*

Vocabulaire et grammaire, *pp. 19–21*

24 Qu'est-ce qu'il faut faire? 1.1

Parlons/Écrivons Ton cousin donne une fête chez lui. Regarde la liste pour voir ce qu'il a déjà fait et ce qu'il lui reste à faire. Pose-lui des questions et indique ses réponses.

MODÈLE —**Est-ce que tu as déjà préparé les amuse-gueules?**
—**Oui, c'est bon.**

À faire pour la fête

- ✓ envoyer les invitations
- ✓ décorer le salon
- acheter les boissons
- ✓ préparer les amuse-gueules
- ✓ ranger le salon
- choisir la musique
- emballer les cadeaux
- ✓ mettre les cacahuètes sur la table
- sortir un bol pour les chips

Communication

Digital performance space

25 Scénario 1.1

Parlons C'est l'anniversaire d'un ami. Tu voudrais faire une fête. Tu appelles une copine pour lui demander des idées. Parlez de tous les détails: combien de personnes vous allez inviter, à quelle heure ça va commencer et ce que vous allez manger.

MODÈLE —**Alors, qu'est-ce qu'on prépare comme... ?**
—**Pourquoi pas des... ?**

26 Scénario 1.1

Parlons Ta fête commence dans une heure et tu veux vérifier que tout a été fait. Comme il y a encore beaucoup de choses à faire, tu demandes à tes amis de t'aider. Certains peuvent t'aider mais d'autres ne peuvent pas.

MODÈLE —**Céline, tu as mis les bonbons sur la table?**

Connections

Social Science Link

Have students design an experiment on motivation. For example, students could try to find out if people are more motivated to get a job done when they are tempted by a reward than when they are faced with the threat of punishment. Have students review with you their plans for their experiments before conducting them. You may wish to have students present their results in French to the rest of the class. 3.1

Communication

25 Group Activity: Interpretive

Ask students to imagine they are organizing a party, but nothing is getting done. Have students in small groups take turns asking each other if they are doing the activities listed in the "to-do list" in Activity 24. Ask students to respond negatively with the appropriate object pronoun. You may want to review the present-tense conjugations of **mettre** and **sortir.**

MODÈLE
— **Est-ce que tu envoies les invitations?**
— **Non, je ne les envoie pas.**
1.2

Differentiated Instruction

SLOWER PACE LEARNERS

25 Have students prepare a "talking points" list before they act out their phone conversation to make sure they cover all the topics in the activity. Talking points might include gift ideas, how many people to invite, when the party will start, and what to eat. Under each talking point, have them write questions and vocabulary they might use to discuss each one. Allow them to refer to their talking points as they act out their conversation. 1.2

MULTIPLE INTELLIGENCES

Naturalist Have students describe the preparations needed for a party to be held outdoors. A party in the backyard or park will require different preparations and chores. Drawing a picture with labels, developing a menu, creating a list of supplies, or writing a conversation about the party are alternate ways of practicing the vocabulary and grammar in the chapter. 1.3

Assess

Assessment Program
Quiz: Vocabulaire 2
Alternative Assessment
Differentiated Practice and Assessment CD-ROM

Online Assessment
my.hrw.com

Test Generator 

Resources

Planning:
Lesson Planner
Teacher One Stop

Presentation:
DVD Tutor, Disc 1
Grammavision 2.1

Practice:
Grammar Tutor for Students of French, Chapter 2
Cahier de vocabulaire et grammaire
Differentiated Practice and Assessment CD-ROM
Cahier d'activités
Independent Study Guide
Media Guide
Projectable Transparencies
Bell Work 2.6
Audio CD 2, Tr. 5
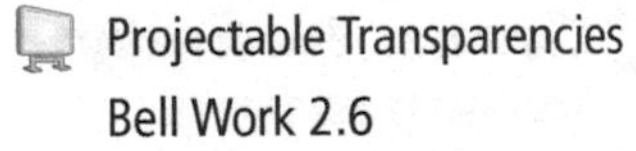

Bell Work

Use Bell Work 2.6 in the *Projectable Transparencies* or write this activity on the board.

Write a question or a response for the following prompts.

1. **J'ai complètement oublié la musique.**
2. **Désolé(e), je n'ai pas le temps de les emballer maintenant.**
3. **Tu as bien envoyé les invitations?**
4. **Ça t'ennuie de préparer les amuse-gueules?**
5. **Tu peux m'aider à faire le ménage?** 1.2

27 Script

See script on p. 39F.

29 Answers

1. On a fait les courses avant...
2. On a décoré la salle avant...
3. On a envoyé les invitations avant...
4. On a acheté les ballons avant...
5. On a nettoyé le salon après...
6. On a préparé les amuse-gueules avant...

Objectifs
- the *passé composé* with *avoir*
- the *passé composé* with *être*

Grammaire à l'œuvre 2

Grammavision

Révisions — The *passé composé* with *avoir*

1 To form the **passé composé**, use a present-tense form of avoir with a past participle. To form the past participle of regular verbs, replace the **-er** ending with **-é,** the **-ir** ending with **-i,** and the **-re** ending with **-u.**

	parler	finir	attendre
j'	ai parlé	ai fini	ai attendu
tu	as parlé	as fini	as attendu
il/elle/on	a parlé	a fini	a attendu
nous	avons parlé	avons fini	avons attendu
vous	avez parlé	avez fini	avez attendu
ils/elles	ont parlé	ont fini	ont attendu

2 Many verbs you know have irregular past participles.

boire **(bu)**	voir **(vu)**	avoir **(eu)**
connaître **(connu)**	vouloir **(voulu)**	être **(été)**
pleuvoir **(plu)**	dire **(dit)**	mettre **(mis)**
pouvoir **(pu)**	écrire **(écrit)**	prendre **(pris)**
savoir **(su)**	faire **(fait)**	offrir **(offert)**

Vocabulaire et grammaire, *pp. 22–23*
Cahier d'activités, *pp. 15–17*

Online Workbooks

Déjà vu!

Remember to use the passé composé to say what happened or to tell what someone did in the past.

Pauline a emballé les cadeaux avant la fête.
Pauline wrapped the presents before the party.

27 Écoutons CD 2, Tr. 5 1.2

Est-ce qu'on parle du **a) passé** ou du **b) présent?**

1. a 2. b 3. a 4. a 5. b 6. a 7. b 8. a

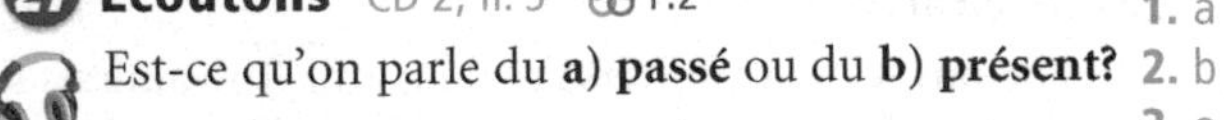

28 Des préparatifs 1.2

Écrivons Fais des phrases pour dire ce que ces personnes ont fait hier avant la boum.

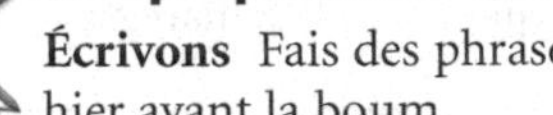

1. Léopold / choisir / musique
2. Jean-Yves et Nora / décorer / salle
3. vous / emballer / cadeau de Claire
4. nous / faire / poussière
5. tu / préparer / amuse-gueules
6. je / écrire / carte pour Claire

1. Léopold a choisi la musique.
2. Jean-Yves et Nora ont décoré la salle.
3. Vous avez emballé le cadeau de Claire.
4. Nous avons fait la poussière.
5. Tu as préparé les amuse-gueules.
6. J'ai écrit une carte pour Claire.

Core Instruction

TEACHING GRAMMAIRE

1. Re-introduce the **passé composé** with **avoir.** Remind students that this tense takes two verbs, **avoir** in the present tense plus the past participle of the main verb. Give examples of forming the past participle of regular verbs, replacing the **-er** ending with **é,** the **-ir** ending with **i,** and the **-re** ending with **u.** Model pronunciation of past participles. **(3 min.)**
2. Remind students that they know several verbs with irregular past participles. Model pronunciation of those in **Grammaire. (2 min.)**
3. Using these verbs, make several statements, either in the present or the **passé composé.** Have students indicate if the statement is in the present by pointing down or in the past by pointing over their shoulder. **(3 min.)**

Grammavision

For a video presentation of the **passé composé** with **avoir,** see the *DVD Tutor.*

Grammavision

Online Practice
my.hrw.com
Grammaire 2 practice

29 Avant ou après la Saint-Sylvestre? 1.2

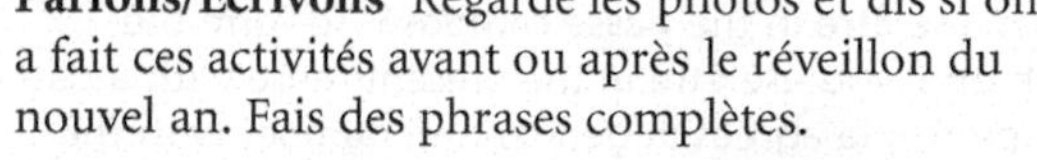
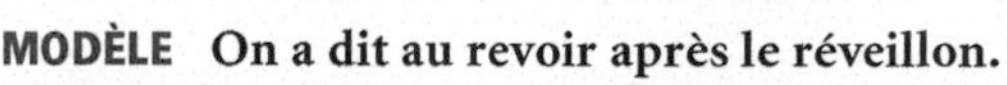

Parlons/Écrivons Regarde les photos et dis si on a fait ces activités avant ou après le réveillon du nouvel an. Fais des phrases complètes.

MODÈLE **On a dit au revoir après le réveillon.**

1.

2.

3.

4.
5.
6.

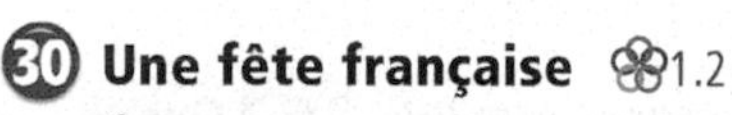

30 Une fête française 1.2

Écrivons Le professeur de français a organisé une petite fête pour ses élèves et il/elle a préparé un repas français! Donne huit détails de cette petite fête.

MODÈLE **Le professeur a acheté des ballons bleus, blancs et rouges. Il/Elle a préparé des sandwiches.**

À la française

In French, you can use the prefix **re-** to mean to redo or to start something again. Can you guess the meaning of the verbs **revenir, reprendre,** and **ressortir**?

Digital performance space

Communication

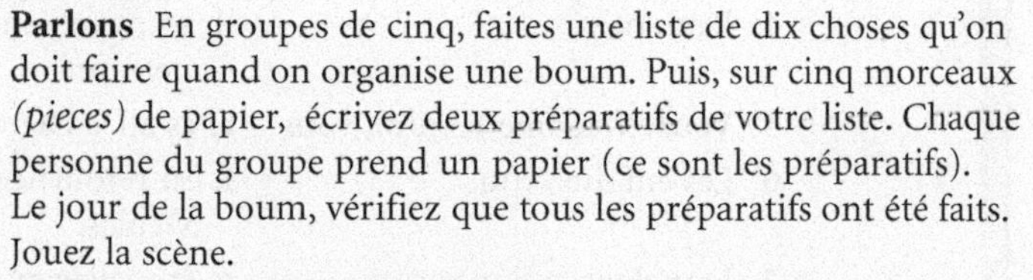

31 Scénario 1.1

Parlons En groupes de cinq, faites une liste de dix choses qu'on doit faire quand on organise une boum. Puis, sur cinq morceaux *(pieces)* de papier, écrivez deux préparatifs de votre liste. Chaque personne du groupe prend un papier (ce sont les préparatifs). Le jour de la boum, vérifiez que tous les préparatifs ont été faits. Jouez la scène.

MODÈLE **—Qui a envoyé les invitations?**
—Moi. J'ai aussi acheté les boissons. Et toi, Loïs?
—J'ai préparé les amuse-gueules et...

Teacher to Teacher

Elaine Bind
McDonogh School
Ownings Mills, MD

To practice the placement of **ne... pas** in the **passé composé,** I paste pictures from magazines onto cards or draw simple pictures that represent different activities. I then put on the board a list of time frames: **été 2008, le week-end dernier, hiver 2006, les vacances, hier soir,** and so on. I hold up a card and specify a time. Students say whether they did or didn't do the activity at that time. 1.2

Communities

Family Link

Have students ask their parents, older siblings, and grandparents what happened the day or the year they were born. Students will use the **passé composé** to report their findings. Students might also use archived newspapers to get information about their birthday or birth year. 5.1

Differentiated Instruction

ADVANCED LEARNERS

Tell students that a useful language skill is to rephrase what someone says to verify their comprehension. Tell students a story in the present tense about a party. Pause after each sentence and have students tell you what happened using the **passé composé. Alors, c'est l'anniversaire de ma grand-mère et j'organise une soirée. (Vous avez organisé une soirée pour votre grand-mère.)** You might tell the whole story first and then have students rephrase it in the **passé composé.** 1.2

SPECIAL LEARNING NEEDS

Students with Auditory Impairments
Students who use American Sign Language to communicate and understand events that happened in the past can use the sign for *past* after the verb instead of changing the form of the verb. Ask the sign language interpreter to assist in explaining the past tense forms of verbs to help students practice each of the forms in the **passé composé.**

Communication

Pair Activity: Interpretive

Copy the blackline master of the vocabulary transparency for each student. Have students number each square 1 through 9. Then have partners play Tic-Tac-Toe. Student B must ask Student A if he or she did each activity. If Student B does not ask the question correctly, Student A gets that square. If Student B asks correctly, Student A must respond negatively to win the square. If not, Student B wins it. 1.2

Resources

Planning:
Lesson Planner
 Teacher One Stop

Presentation:
DVD Tutor, Disc 1
Grammavision 2.2

Practice:
Grammar Tutor for Students of French, Chapter 2
Cahier de vocabulaire et grammaire
Differentiated Practice and Assessment CD-ROM
Cahier d'activités
Independent Study Guide
Media Guide
Projectable Transparencies
Bell Work 2.7
HOMETUTOR

Bell Work

Use Bell Work 2.7 in the *Projectable Transparencies* or write this activity on the board.

Complete each sentence with the **passé composé** of the verb in parentheses.

1. Nous ____ (écrire) nos cartes de vœux ce matin.
2. Tu ____ (voir) son cadeau? Il est super.
3. J' ____ (faire) le ménage cet après-midi.
4. Vous ____ (emballer) leur boîte de chocolats.
5. Marine ____ (mettre) les biscuits sur la table.
6. Les enfants ____ (boire) beaucoup de jus de fruit.

1.2

Révisions The *passé composé* with *être*

1 Some verbs, like **aller,** use **être** in the **passé composé.** To form the **passé composé** with **être,** you use **être** in the present tense with a past participle. The past participle agrees in gender and number with the subject.

aller *(to go)*			
je	suis allé**(e)**	nous	sommes allé**(e)s**
tu	es allé**(e)**	vous	êtes allé**(e)(s)**
il/elle/on	est allé**(e)(s)**	ils/elles	sont allé**(e)s**

Ma mère et ma sœur sont allé**es** à la plage.

2 The following verbs use **être** in the **passé composé.**

arriver **(arrivé)**	partir **(parti)**
descendre **(descendu)**	rentrer **(rentré)**
entrer **(entré)**	rester **(resté)**
monter **(monté)**	retourner **(retourné)**
mourir **(mort)**	sortir **(sorti)**
naître **(né)**	venir **(venu)**
devenir **(devenu)**	

Vocabulaire et grammaire, *pp. 22–23*
Cahier d'activités, *pp. 15–17*

Flash culture

Quand un jour férié tombe un jeudi ou un mardi, les Français prennent souvent le vendredi ou le lundi comme jour de congé. C'est ce qu'on appelle **faire le pont.** Quand il y a un jour férié, les magasins sont en général fermés. Quelques magasins d'alimentation comme les boulangeries sont ouverts le matin seulement (sauf le jour de Noël). Cependant, avant les fêtes de fin d'année, les magasins restent ouverts plus tard.

Est-ce que les magasins dans ta communauté ferment les jours fériés? 4.2

32 L'autre moitié 1.2

Lisons Ton professeur veut savoir ce que tout le monde a fait ce week-end. Complète ses phrases logiquement.

f **1.** Virginie	**a.** êtes montés chez les Monnier?
h **2.** Les élèves	**b.** es resté à la maison?
d **3.** Nous, les filles, nous	**c.** sommes sortis faire les courses.
b **4.** Paul, tu	**d.** sommes rentrées pour nettoyer.
g **5.** Vous, Madame Rimini, vous	**e.** es allée chercher de la glace?
a **6.** Les enfants, vous	**f.** est retournée à la boum de Nicolas.
c **7.** Franck et moi, nous	**g.** êtes allée au bal du 14 juillet?
e **8.** Mila, est-ce que tu	**h.** sont partis en vacances.

Core Instruction

TEACHING GRAMMAIRE

1. Re-introduce the **passé composé** with **être.** To help students remember the verbs conjugated with **être** in the **passé composé,** give them the mnemonic device **DR. & MRS. VANDERTRAMP**. The letters in the names are the first letters of the verbs. (**Devenir, Revenir, Mourir, Rentrer, Sortir, Venir, Aller, Naître, Descendre, Entrer, Rester, Tomber, Retourner, Arriver, Monter, Partir) (4 min.)**
2. Model another way to help remember this group of verbs and past participles by singing the following to the tune of "Ten Little Indians". **Je suis arrivé allé et venu, devenu revenu entré rentré, descendu retourné resté monté, parti sorti tombé né mort. (2 min.)**
3. Remind students that the past participle must agree in number and gender with the subject. **(1 min.)**

Grammavision

For a video presentation of the **passé composé** with **être,** see the *DVD Tutor.*

33 Aujourd'hui, en cours de français 1.3

Parlons/Écrivons Raconte ce qui s'est passé en cours de français aujourd'hui. Utilise le passé composé avec **être.**

MODÈLE Moi, je **suis arrivée en retard.**

1. Moi, je...
2. Le professeur...
3. Ma camarade [nom]...
4. Nous, les élèves, nous...
5. Mon ami [nom]...
6. Les élèves...

34 Hier soir, chez les Durand 1.2

Écrivons Finis les phrases d'après les illustrations pour expliquer ce qui s'est passé hier soir chez les Durand. Utilise les sujets donnés et le passé composé.

MODÈLE **M. et Mme Durand sont restés à la maison.**

M. et Mme Durand

1. Olivia et Karine

2. Alexandre

3. Les amis d'Alexandre

4. Olivia et Karine

Communication

35 Scénario 1.1

Parlons Un riche aristocrate, Monsieur Pleindesous, a disparu hier soir pendant une fête. Une des personnes du groupe joue le rôle du détective. Il/Elle pose des questions à tous les suspects pour savoir ce qu'ils ont fait hier soir et pour savoir ce qui s'est passé à la fête. Les autres personnes jouent le rôle des suspects.

MODÈLE **—Monsieur Pleindesous a disparu. Je suis le détective Nezfin et je dois vous poser quelques questions. Mademoiselle Delor, à quelle heure est-ce que vous êtes entrée dans l'appartement?**
—Euh... vers huit heures. Avant, je suis allée...

34 Possible Answers

1. Olivia et Karine sont parties à l'école.
2. Alexandre est descendu pour ouvrir la porte.
3. Les amis d'Alexandre sont venus chez lui.
4. Olivia et Karine sont rentrées.

Connections

Language Arts Link

Write words that share a common Latin origin with the verbs in the grammar presentation (descendant, entrance, mortician, renaissance, depart . . .) Have students match them to the French verbs. 3.1

Communication

Group Work: Interpersonal

Ask students to write ten verbs in the infinitive (five that take **avoir** and five that take **être**) that reflect what they did yesterday or the past weekend. Then have students in groups of three to four take turns asking one another if they did the activities listed. Students should respond in complete sentences in the **passé composé.** Ask students to write **oui** or **non** after each activity to keep track of their group's responses to see how many activities they have in common. 1.1

Differentiated Instruction

SLOWER PACE LEARNERS

Write a song, either to a familiar tune or to an original melody, that includes verbs that use **être** in the **passé composé.** For example, you might write a song about a day in the life of the sun: **Je suis né, je suis arrivé, je suis monté, c'est une autre journée...** Teach the song to students and sing it as a class, or have students create a music video based on your song. 1.2

MULTIPLE INTELLIGENCES

Visual Learners Ask students to create verb conjugation charts for the verbs that use **être** in the **passé composé.** The charts should look similar to the chart in the presentation with the verb **aller.** Students can use these charts as a reference when completing the activities in **Grammaire 2.**

Assess

Assessment Program
Quiz: Grammaire 2
Alternative Assessment
Differentiated Practice and Assessment CD-ROM

Online Assessment
my.hrw.com

Test Generator 

Resources

Planning:
Lesson Planner
Teacher One Stop

Practice:
Grammar Tutor for Students of French, Chapter 2
Cahier de vocabulaire et grammaire
Differentiated Practice and Assessment CD-ROM
Cahier d'activités
Independent Study Guide
Media Guide
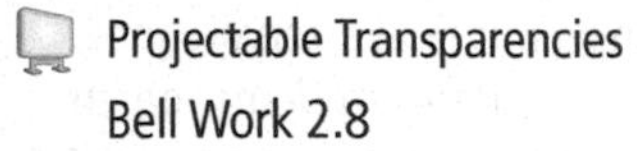
Projectable Transparencies
Bell Work 2.8
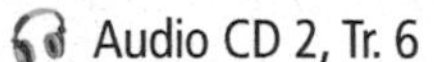
Audio CD 2, Tr. 6

Bell Work

Use Bell Work 2.8 in the *Projectable Transparencies* or write this activity on the board.

Complete each sentence with the logical ending.

1. Mon amie Chloé...
2. Augustin...
3. Pardon, madame, vous...
4. Hier soir, vous...
5. Dis, Corinne, tu...

a. ... êtes venue souvent dans ce musée?
b. ... es retournée voir ce film?
c. ... est restée à la maison.
d. ... êtes sortis au café jusqu'à quelle heure?
e. ... est arrivé en retard à son cours.

1.2

37 Answers

1. La fille ne balaie jamais la cuisine.
2. Il est huit heures et le fils n'est pas encore entré.
3. Les parents ne nettoient pas le salon.
4. La fille n'est plus d'accord pour aider.
5. Le fils ne fait rien.

38 Script

See script on p. 39F.

Synthèse
- Vocabulaire 2
- Grammaire 2

Application 2

36 Une grande occasion 1.3

Écrivons/Parlons Est-ce que tu as déjà organisé une fête pour une occasion spéciale? Décris huit choses que tu as préparées.

MODÈLE **Pour la fête des pères, j'ai préparé le dîner. Ma mère et moi, nous sommes allé(e)s... On a acheté...**

En anglais 4.1

In English, you do not use more than one negative word in a sentence.

I don't have anything to do. I have nothing to do.

Can you think of other negative expressions in English?

In French, you have to use two negative words: **ne** and a negative expression **(rien, jamais...).**

Je **n'**ai **rien** à faire.

I have nothing to do.

no one, never, not yet

Un peu plus

Negative expressions

1. In a sentence, place negative expressions around the conjugated verb. In the **passé composé,** place them around the helping verb.

ne... pas	*not*	Je n'ai pas de cadeau.
ne... pas encore	*not yet*	Je n'ai pas encore acheté de cadeau.
ne... jamais	*never, not ever*	Je n'achète jamais de cadeau.
ne... plus	*no more, no longer*	Je n'achète plus de cadeau.
ne... rien	*nothing, not anything*	Je ne fais rien.
ne... personne	*no one, nobody*	Je ne vois personne.

2. You can use many negative expressions without a complete sentence. Use only the second part of the expression, without the word **ne**.

— Qu'est-ce que ta tante fait pour t'aider? — **Rien.**

Vocabulaire et grammaire, *p. 24*
Cahier d'activités, *pp. 15–17*

37 Des fainéants 1.2

Écrivons Les Laroche font une soirée à Noël, mais la famille ne veut pas faire les préparatifs! Raconte ce qui se passe.

MODÈLE le père / envoyer les invitations / ne... pas
Le père n'envoie pas les invitations.

1. la fille / balayer la cuisine / ne... jamais
2. le fils / entrer / il est huit heures / et / ne.. pas encore
3. les parents / nettoyer le salon / ne... pas
4. la fille / être d'accord pour aider / ne... plus
5. le fils / faire / ne...rien

Core Instruction

INTEGRATED PRACTICE

1. Tell students they are having a class party tomorrow. Ask questions, using verbs with irregular past participles. **Rachel, tu as envoyé les invitations? Oui, j'ai envoyé les invitations. (2 min.)**
2. Have students do Activity 36 to practice the **passé composé. (5 min.)**
3. Present **Un peu plus. (2 min.)**
4. Have students complete the integrated practice Activities. **(15 min.)**

TEACHING UN PEU PLUS

1. Remind students that they have made sentences negative by putting the negative expression around the conjugated verb. Go over **Un peu plus** and model pronunciation. **(2 min.)**
2. Write **pas encore, jamais, rien,** and **personne** on the board. Ask questions and have students point to the appropriate answer. **Tu as voyagé en Europe? Qu'est-ce que tu fais ce week-end? (3 min.)**

Online Practice
my.hrw.com
Application 2 practice

38 Écoutons CD 2, Tr. 6 1.2

Écoute les conversations suivantes et dis **a) ce qui a été fait** ou **b) ce qu'il reste à faire.** 1. b 2. a 3. a 4. b 5. a 6. b 7. a

39 Une soirée vraiment ratée 1.2

Lisons/Écrivons La semaine dernière, tu es allé(e) à une soirée complètement ratée. Tout s'est mal passé! Réponds aux questions de ton ami(e). Utilise des expressions négatives dans tes réponses.

MODÈLE —Est-ce que tu t'es bien amusé(e)?
—Non, je ne me suis pas bien amusé(e).

1. Est-ce que ton copain/ta copine est arrivé(e) pour t'accompagner à la soirée?
2. Tu as mangé des amuse-gueules?
3. Est-ce qu'on a encore dansé après huit heures?
4. Est-ce que tu es resté(e) jusqu'à minuit?
5. Tu as déjà oublié cette soirée?

40 Une fête pour la classe de français 1.3

Écrivons Imagine que tu vas organiser une fête pour la classe de français. Quels amuse-gueules vas-tu préparer? Quels CD vas-tu choisir? Qui va faire les courses?

Communication

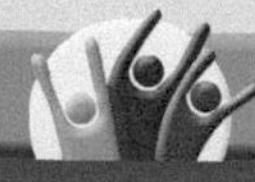

41 Joyeux anniversaire! 1.1

Parlons Avec ton/ta camarade de classe, vous avez décidé d'organiser une fête pour l'anniversaire de votre ami Lucas. Vous parlez des préparatifs pour la fête. Lisez les questions ci-dessous et répondez-y de manière logique. Ensuite, échangez les rôles.

— **Tu as déjà acheté la boisson, les cacahuètes et les chips?**
—
— **Tu peux m'aider à ranger le salon?**
—
— **Est-ce qu'il y a encore des choses à préparer?**
—
— **Tu as pensé au cadeau?**
—
— **Qu'est-ce qu'on pourrait offrir à Lucas?**
—

39 Possible Answers

1. Non, il (elle) n'est jamais arrivé(e).
2. Non, je n'ai rien mangé.
3. Non, on n'a plus dansé après huit heures.
4. Non, je ne suis pas resté(e) jusqu'à minuit.
5. Non, je n'ai pas encore oublié cette soirée.

Language Examination

41 Sample answer:

— ...
— **Oui, c'est bon.**
— ...
— **Pas maintenant. Je dois aller acheter des CD.**
— ...
— **Oui. Il faut décorer le salon.**
— ...
— **Non. J'ai complètement oublié!**
— ...
— **On pourrait lui offrir un livre.**

Differentiated Instruction

ADVANCED LEARNERS

Have students write and perform a skit about two people who are partners in a party-planning business. One asks the other if he or she has done the tasks for different upcoming parties and finds out that none of the tasks have been completed. An argument ensues over which partner does the most work. 1.3

MULTIPLE INTELLIGENCES

Spatial Ask students to draw a floor plan of their house during a party. Have students label each room or area of the house with sentences describing what preparations they made. Students may describe what food they prepared in the kitchen or on the outdoor grill, what music they played in the living room, who greeted guests at the door, and what food they served in the dining room. Ask them to include negative expressions for preparations they did not make. 1.3

Assess

Assessment Program
Quiz: Application 2
Audio CD 2, Tr. 15
Alternative Assessment
Differentiated Practice and Assessment CD-ROM

Online Assessment
my.hrw.com

Test Generator 

Resources

Planning:
Lesson Planner
 Teacher One Stop

Presentation:
 DVD Tutor, Disc 1
Télé-roman

Practice:
Media Guide
DVD Tutor, Disc 1
Télé-roman

Connections

Visual Learners

To help students understand the family relationships in **Télé-roman,** have them draw simple family trees based on the information provided in this episode. As models, draw the framework of two trees similar to the ones below. Then have students fill in the names of each family member, including Monsieur and Madame Gadio, Seydou Gadio, Waly Gadio, Anne Bondy, and Léa Bondy. 3.2

Les Gadio

Monsieur Gadio — Madame Gadio
→ Seydou
→ Waly

Les Bondy

Anne Bondy
→ Léa Bondy

Gestures

Before they read **Télé-roman,** have students look at scenes 2–4. Based on the gestures and body language in these scenes, what do students think is going on? How well do these people know one another? Then call students' attention to the expression on Mr. Gadio's face in scene 6. How has it changed? Ask students what they think might have happened. 2.1

Télé-roman

Le Secret de la statuette *Épisode 2*

STRATÉGIE

Gathering information As you go through a story, you must gather information from characters' conversations. As you watch and read **Episode 2**, write down at least three bits of information that you learn from each conversation. Who are the various characters in the Gadio household? Is it the first time Anne meets the Gadios? What about Léa? Why is Anne in Dakar? What transpires from Salif Gadio's and Anne Bondy's conversation with Inspector Sonko? 1.2

Une semaine plus tard, à Dakar...

1 *Anne Bondy et sa fille Léa arrivent à Dakar.*

2

M. Gadio Anne! Comme je suis content de te revoir!
Anne Bonjour, Salif! Bonjour, Adja. Comment vas-tu?
Mme Gadio Sénégalaisement. Vous avez fait bon voyage?

3

M. Gadio Et voici Léa, je suppose... Bonjour.
Léa Bonjour.

4

M. Gadio Voici Seydou, notre fils aîné.

5

M. Gadio Excusez-moi une minute.

6

M. Gadio C'était le musée. Quelqu'un a volé la statuette!

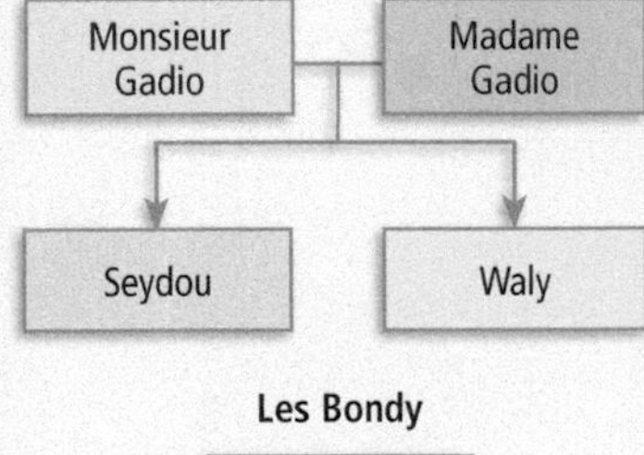

Core Instruction

TEACHING TÉLÉ-ROMAN

1. Have students scan the pictures in **Télé-roman** without reading the text. Have them make predictions about what will happen in this episode. Have them give reasons to support their predictions. **(5 min.)**
2. Freeze-frame the video after the scene at the airport. Ask students where the people are, what their relationship is, and what they might be doing. Then play the video through scene six and ask the same questions about the Gadio family. **(5 min.)**
3. After viewing the entire episode, ask general comprehension questions. Were any of the students' predictions accurate? Were there any surprises in the plot? **(5 min.)**
4. Have partners answer the **As-tu compris?** questions on page 65. **(5 min.)**

DVD Tutor

As an alternative, you might use the captioned version of **Le Secret de la statuette** on DVD.

Visit Us Online

my.hrw.com
Online Edition

Un peu plus tard, au musée...

7

L'inspecteur Sonko Votre assistant a tout vérifié. Ils ont seulement volé la statuette. Elle avait beaucoup de valeur?

8

Anne On ne sait pas. Le but de ma visite à Dakar était de l'expertiser.

9

M. Gadio Comment je vais expliquer tout ça à M. Rigaud, moi?

L'inspecteur Sonko Monsieur qui?

M. Gadio Rigaud. Charles Rigaud. C'est lui qui m'a apporté la statuette.

10

L'inspecteur Sonko Et vous avez son numéro de téléphone ou son adresse?

M. Gadio Ah non! Maintenant que j'y pense, il ne m'a pas donné d'adresse.

L'inspecteur Sonko Ah bon?! C'est curieux, ça. Très curieux!

1.2

AS-TU COMPRIS?

1. Quelles personnes arrivent à Dakar au début de l'épisode?
2. Qui est Seydou?
3. Pourquoi M. Gadio et Anne vont au musée?
4. Qui est Charles Rigaud?
5. Qu'est-ce que l'inspecteur Sonko trouve bizarre?

Prochain épisode:
Est-ce que tu penses que M. Gadio et Anne vont retrouver la statuette à l'épisode 3? Pourquoi ou pourquoi pas?

Télé-roman

As-tu compris? Answers

1. Anne Bondy et sa fille, Léa
2. le fils de M. Gadio
3. quelqu'un a volé la statuette
4. l'homme qui a apporté la statuette à M. Gadio
5. M. Rigaud n'a pas donné son numéro de téléphone ou son addresse à M. Gadio.

Communication

Pair Work: Presentational
After students have seen **Télé-roman,** have them work in groups of four or five to write and act out a scene similar to the first half of this episode. Students should include a variety of greetings and introductions in their scenes. Then have them write a second scene in which the characters are summoned to the scene of an imaginary crime and must answer a series of questions. Have groups write short scripts and assign character roles. Allow time to practice, and then have each group present its scene to the class. 1.3

Le Secret de la statuette Episode 2

In this episode, Anne Bondy arrives in Dakar with her daughter, Léa. They go to Mr. Gadio's home, where they meet his wife and sons, Waly and Seydou. The museum calls to say that someone has stolen the statuette. At the museum, inspector Sonko tells them the only clue found was some sand, which will be sent to a laboratory for analysis. Sonko does not have much time to devote to the case because he is busy trying to solve another crime, a jewel theft. Mr. Gadio gives the inspector Mr. Rigaud's name and then realizes that Rigaud never gave his address.

Lecture et écriture

Resources

Planning:
Lesson Planner
Teacher One Stop

Presentation:
Audio CD 2, Tr. 7

Practice:
Cahier d'activités
Reading Strategies and Skills Handbook, Chapter 2
Intermediate Reader
French InterActive Reader

Applying the Strategies

For practice with recognizing cognates, have students use the "Think Aloud" strategy from the *Reading Strategies and Skills Handbook.*

READING PRACTICE

STRATEGIES

Strategy: Think Aloud

Reading Skill	When can I use this strategy?		
	Prereading	During Reading	Postreading
Monitoring Reading		✓	

Strategy at a Glance: Think Aloud

- The teacher models the **Think Aloud** strategy for students, letting them tally the types of comments the teacher makes (predicting, picturing the text, comparing, commenting, identifying a problem, or fixing a problem) on the **Think Aloud** tally sheet.
- Students practice the strategy with a partner using short and easy texts before using **Think Aloud** with their assignments.
- Students regularly practice the strategy, eventually using it on their own as needed.

Many times students do what they call reading: their eyes travel over the words from left to right and from top to bottom,and they turn pages at the appropriate time. What they don't do is pay any attention to what those words mean. That is where a strategy like **Think Aloud** can help.

The **Think Aloud** strategy helps readers think about how they make meaning. As they read, they carry on a dialog with the text. This is something that good readers do constantly as they read, although they usually do it silently. **Think Aloud** provides a structure for struggling readers to have a dialog with a text; they learn to think about their reading and to monitor what they do and do not understand. As you monitor the comments students make while using this strategy, you will see that the student is actively engaged with the text. As they do it more often, they will learn to do it silently—and that is the goal of the strategy.

Best Use of the Strategy

Use the **Think Aloud** strategy (Davey 1983; Olshavsky 1976-77) to help readers think about how they make meaning. As students read, they pause occasionally to think aloud about predicting what happens next, commenting on the text, picturing the text, making comparisons, identifying problems they are encountering with understanding, and thinking of ways to fix the problems they identify. This oral thinking not only helps the teacher understand why or how a

Recognizing Cognates

Ask students to scan the reading and find one word they think is a cognate. Then have them share their cognates with the class. Remind them that a word that is a cognate for one person may not be recognizable to another. Have students return to **Avant la lecture** after they have read the selection and ask them to use context to verify the cognates and false cognates on their lists.

STRATÉGIE pour lire

Using cognates Remember to look for cognates, words with similar meanings and spellings in two languages, to help you figure out what you're reading. Also watch for false cognates, words that look alike in two languages but that have different meanings.

A Avant la lecture 4.1

Parcours des yeux *(glance at)* l'article suivant et fais une liste des mots qui s'écrivent de la même façon en anglais. Cherche les mots dans un dictionnaire pour découvrir s'ils sont apparentés *(cognates)* ou s'ils sont des faux-amis *(false cognates).*

Le réveillon en fête

CD 2, Tr. 7

C'est bientôt le jour de l'an, et comme tous les ans, vous vous demandez ce que vous allez bien pouvoir faire. C'est le moment de faire le tour de vos options :

Option 1

Papa et maman ont décidé que, cette année, les vacances de fin d'année se passeraient[1] en famille. Vous n'avez pas le choix, vous devez aller chez papi et mamie. Le réveillon se passera à jouer aux cartes ou devant la télé.

Option 2

Vous êtes invité. Pas de problème! La seule chose dont vous avez à vous soucier[2], c'est de trouver la tenue[3] de réveillon idéale. N'oubliez pas de vous renseigner : est-ce une soirée habillée ? ou à thème ?

Option 3

Vous décidez d'aller voir comment on fête le nouvel an dans les autres pays d'Europe. Prenez le car ou le train pour Londres, Barcelone, Amsterdam ou encore Berlin.

Option 4

Vous décidez d'organiser la fête de l'année dont tout le monde parlera pendant des mois. Dans ce cas, mieux vaut être organisé.

1. will be spent 2. to worry about 3. outfit

Core Instruction

TEACHING LECTURE

1. Read **Stratégie** with students. **(1 min.)**
2. Have students do **Avant la lecture** orally in class. You might ask volunteers to write the results of the two tasks on the board. **(3 min.)**
3. Have students read the selection and then work with a partner to do Activities B and C orally. Have partners write down the cognates they find. **(10 min.)**
4. Discuss Activities D and E, making sure all students have a chance to answer and participate. **(12 min.)**

Online Practice
my.hrw.com
Online Edition

Lecture et écriture

Un réveillon qui en jette[1]

Pour organiser la soirée de réveillon parfaite, il vaut mieux tout prévoir[2] à l'avance.

Je m'organise.

Préparez tout la veille pour éviter les surprises de derniers moments. Essayez d'avoir une idée approximative du nombre d'invités pour éviter de tomber court[3] côté boissons et amuse-gueules. Achetez tout ce qu'il faut (boissons, nourriture, assiettes et verres en plastique). N'oubliez pas de pré-programmer la musique avec tous les hits du moment et aussi des plus anciens. Ça évite que quelqu'un passe sa soirée à la sono[4]. Pour tout ça, faites-vous aider par les copains.

Je décore.

Pour le nouvel an, décorez la maison : recyclez les guirlandes lumineuses du sapin de Noël, accrochez des rubans argentés ou dorés au plafond. Les bougies peuvent aussi être de la partie, mais attention où vous les placez : au milieu d'une table est l'endroit idéal.

J'anime.

Pourquoi ne donneriez-vous pas un thème à votre soirée ? Dans ce cas, toute la fête doit être thématisée, pas seulement les costumes. Pour une soirée « bleue », tout le monde doit être en bleu, la déco doit être bleue, les boissons bleues et la nourriture bleue (utiliser des colorants alimentaires[5]). Vous pouvez aussi projeter[6] les films *Bleu* ou *Le Grand Bleu*.

Astuces

Faites une liste pour ne rien oublier. Faites-la relire par un ami.

Les boissons. Jus d'orange, de pomme, de raisin, sodas, limonade, sirop de grenadine, menthe, eau pétillante... Attention d'avoir à boire pour tout le monde. Rien de plus embarrassant que de devoir ne servir que de l'eau à un invité. Pour faire différent, servez les jus de fruit avec des morceaux de fruits coupés dedans.

La nourriture. Prévoyez aussi pour tous les goûts et ne rechignez[7] pas sur la quantité: mini-pizzas, mini-quiches, saucisses à apéritif, cacahuètes, fruits secs, toasts au pâté, rillettes[8], tarama[9], thon-mayonnaise, tomates-cerises, œufs durs... Tout ce qui se grignote[10] facilement. Vous pouvez toujours congeler[11] ce qui n'a pas été mangé. Présentez le tout de façon originale et disposez des plats un peu partout, pas seulement sur une table.

1. to show off 2. to plan 3. to be short of something 4. sound system 5. food coloring 6. show 7. to balk 8. type of meat spread 9. fish dip 10. snack 11. to freeze

Differentiated Instruction

ADVANCED LEARNERS

Have groups of students use the information in the article to prepare a script for a television program hosted by a home entertainment expert. Assign different holidays to different groups for a variety of shows. You might videotape the groups' television programs to share with other classes. 1.3

SPECIAL LEARNING NEEDS

Students with Dyslexia After all students have read Options 1–4, have them get together in groups of four. Assign each group one of the options to translate. When groups finish with their translations, ask a volunteer from each group to read the translation to the class. This will ensure everyone understands each of the Options before moving on to the rest of the reading and writing activities. Configure groups with mixed reading and translation skills. 1.1

Lecture et écriture

Cultures

Practices and Perspectives

Le réveillon began as a huge feast enjoyed with one's family after returning home from midnight mass on Christmas Eve. The dishes served vary by region: In Paris, **foie gras** and oysters are favored. In Alsace, roast goose is traditional. Buckwheat cakes with sour cream are favorites in Brittany. In Burgundy, the main course is turkey garnished with chestnuts. **Le réveillon du nouvel an,** or **Le réveillon de Saint-Sylvestre,** is the French New Year's Eve celebration. You might have students prepare a traditional **réveillon** dish and tell in French the **bonne résolution** they plan to make next New Year's Eve. 2.1

Connections

Language to Language

The word **astuce** means *cleverness* or *skill* from the Latin *astus.* Ask students if they can think of an English word similar to **astuce,** meaning *clever.* (*astute*) Then ask students to explain why **Astuces** is appropriate as a heading in this article. 3.1

Pre-AP Language Examination

Through the practice of listening and reading comprehension, as well as essay writing, **Lecture et écriture** helps students prepare for the **Interpretive Reading and Listening** and the **Presentational Writing** sections of the AP Language and Culture Exam.

Additional Practice

For more reading practice, see **Variations littéraires,** pp. 384–385.

C Answers

1. pour éviter les surprises
2. les hits du moment et des plus anciens
3. les guirlandes lumineuses du sapin de Noël, des rubans, des bougies
4. donner un thème à votre soirée
5. en bleu
6. de l'eau
7. avec des morceaux de fruits coupés dedans
8. un peu partout

Connections

Math Link

Have students imagine they have a budget of 5,000 euros and two plane tickets to the French-speaking country of their choice, where they will stay for **le réveillon.** Have them do research on different countries' **réveillon** celebrations and decide where they will go, who they will take with them, and how they will spend their money. Ask students to present their plans to the class. You might have the class vote on the most exciting or best budgeted **réveillon** celebration plans. 3.1

Communities

Community Link

Invite older French-speaking members of your community to talk to your classes about how they celebrated **le réveillon** when they were children. You might also stage a **réveillon** cooking contest among your students that day and have your guest(s) judge the students' dishes on taste, presentation, and authenticity. 5.1

Compréhension

B Quelle option de l'article correspond le mieux à ce que tu fais dans chaque phrase suivante? 1.2

b **1.** Tu mets une robe que tu aimes beaucoup.
a **2.** Tu regardes la télé.
d **3.** Tu fais une liste de choses que tu dois faire.
c **4.** Tu fais ta valise.
a **5.** Tu parles avec tes parents.

a. option 1
b. option 2
c. option 3
d. option 4

C Réponds aux questions sur les sections «Un réveillon qui en jette» et «Astuces». 1.2

1. Pourquoi est-ce qu'il est important de tout prévoir à l'avance?
2. Quel genre de musique est-ce que tu dois pré-programmer?
3. Qu'est-ce que tu dois utiliser pour décorer la maison?
4. Pour avoir une fête animée, qu'est-ce que l'article suggère?
5. Comment est-ce qu'il faut s'habiller pour une soirée bleue?
6. Qu'est-ce qui peut être embarrassant de servir à un(e) invité(e)?
7. Comment est-ce que tu peux servir les jus pour être différent?
8. Où est-ce que tu dois mettre les plats de nourriture?

Après la lecture

D Quelles sont les deux ou trois recommandations les plus importantes de l'article pour organiser une fête? Est-ce que tu es d'accord ou pas avec l'article? Pourquoi? 1.3

E Imagine that you are planning a party similar to the one described in the paragraph **J'anime.** Decide what type of party you will have, then make a list of the things you need to do and buy to get ready for the party. You and your classmates might even organize and throw the party for the class or French Club. 2.1

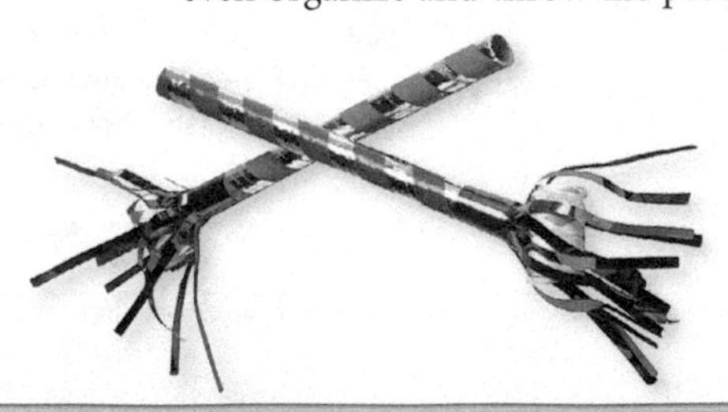

Core Instruction

TEACHING ESPACE ÉCRITURE

1. Read **Stratégie pour écrire** and discuss it with the class. Verify students' understanding of style and point of view. **(2 min.)**
2. Have students complete their charts in step 1 before they begin to write their conversations. **(10 min.)**
3. As students create their conversations, remind them to use expressions they learned in **Exprimons-nous!** in **Vocabulaire 2.** Have them check their use of the **passé composé. (15 min.)**
4. Assign partners for step 3 and have them peer edit each other's conversation as they read aloud. **(10 min.)**
5. Assign step 4 as homework, reminding students to bring props or illustrations to help with their oral presentation. **(2 min.)**

Espace écriture

STRATÉGIE pour écrire

Good use of dialogue makes your writing more natural and interesting for your readers. It also helps you to keep your thoughts well-ordered and to form logical questions and answers. As you put yourself in the role of each speaker, remember to vary your style and point of view.

Est-ce que tu as tout préparé?

You and a friend are giving a party tonight to celebrate a holiday or birthday. You're checking that everything has been done and discussing last-minute preparations. Recreate your conversation, including an account of the cleaning you did, the foods and beverages you prepared, and how you've decorated the house. 1.1

1 Plan

Imagine the type of party you would like to have.

- Create a chart divided into four categories: cleaning, foods and beverages, decorations, and miscellaneous.
- For each category, make a checklist of two or three things that you might have had to do or still might need to do to get ready for the party.

Nettoyer	la salle à manger le salon
Nourriture et boissons	chips, cacahuètes jus d'orange
Décoration	guirlandes
Divers	assiettes en papier

2 Rédaction

- Start creating your conversation by telling your friend that the party will begin soon.
- Next, use the **passé composé** to tell what you did to get ready for the party. Ask if your friend did something from your chart that you didn't mention. Your friend responds and asks if there is anything else to do.

Don't forget to be polite in your requests.

3 Correction

Read with a classmate your conversation aloud, taking roles.

- Check for the correct use of the **passé composé**.
- Make sure the questions and answers are logical.

4 Application

You may wish to act out your conversation for the class, using props or illustrations to make the scene more realistic.

Lecture et écriture

Lecture et écriture

Process Writing

Avant d'écrire Before students begin writing, have them recall what they learned in this chapter and have them make two lists of words and phrases associated with parties. The first list should be party foods and beverages. The second list should be the preparations they need to make for the party. Finally, they should put a check mark next to the tasks they would like to do themselves and a question mark next to those for which they plan to seek help.

Writing Assessment

To assess the **Espace écriture,** you can use the following rubric. For additional rubrics, see the *Assessment Program* or refer to the *Generate Success* Rubric Generator.

Writing Rubric	4	3	2	1
Content (Complete—Incomplete)				
Comprehensibility (Comprehensible—Seldom comprehensible)				
Accuracy (Accurate—Seldom accurate)				
Organization (Well-organized—Poorly organized)				
Effort (Excellent effort—Minimal effort)				

18-20: A 14-15: C Under
16-17: B 12-13: D 12: F

Differentiated Instruction

SLOWER PACE LEARNERS

Work as a class to brainstorm tasks for the chart. Then list on the board or on a transparency verbs in the **passé composé** that relate to each task. Review the expressions in **Exprimons-nous!** in **Vocabulaire 2.** Then have students create their chart and continue with steps 2 through 4. 1.2

MULTIPLE INTELLIGENCES

Musical Ask students to choose one of the four options for New Year's Eve and select the music that would be appropriate for the party. Students should list at least ten musical selections for the type of party they chose. Ask volunteers to share their choices and their reasons for their choices with the class. 1.2

Assess

Assessment Program
Quiz: Lecture
Quiz: Écriture
Online Assessment my.hrw.com
Test Generator 

Prépare-toi pour l'examen

Resources

Planning:
Lesson Planner
Teacher One Stop

Practice:
Cahier d'activités
Media Guide
DVD Tutor, Disc 1
Projectable Transparencies
Situation, Chapitre 2
Picture Sequences, Chapter 2
Audio CD 2, Tr. 9–12
@HOMETUTOR

2 Answers

1. Ortense les achète.
2. Yannick lui téléphone.
3. Corentin les allume.
4. Patricia les achète.
5. Ahmed leur parle.
6. Claire les envoie.

3 Answers

1. envoyer
2. emballer
3. ménage
4. choisir
5. préparer
6. maison
7. faire

Reteaching

Have students invent and name an imaginary holiday, determine a date for it, and write a brief description of how it is celebrated. Have partners present their new holidays to each other.

Game

Mots croisés Students will each need two sheets of graph paper to create a crossword puzzle for a classmate to solve. It should consist of about twenty vocabulary words. They should number the words and write a clue in both English and French. Have each student duplicate the puzzle on another sheet of paper with just the numbers, blank squares, and clues. Partners then exchange and solve the puzzles. 1.1

Chapitre 2

Prépare-toi pour l'examen

@HOMETUTOR

1 Vocabulaire 1
- to wish someone a good time
- to ask for and give advice

pp. 42–45

1 C'est la fête! Pour chaque photo, identifie les éléments indiqués. Ensuite, fais des souhaits pour chaque occasion. 1.2

1.

2.

3.

4.

2 Grammaire 1
- direct object pronouns
- indirect object pronouns

Un peu plus
- the verb **offrir**

pp. 46–51

2 Des amis organisent une fête et chacun a ses responsabilités. Utilise un pronom d'objet dans tes réponses. 1.2

1. Qui achète les amuse-gueules?
2. Qui téléphone à Marc?
3. Qui allume les bougies?
4. Qui achète les décorations?
5. Qui parle à Zoé et André?
6. Qui envoie les invitations?

amuse-gueules - Ortense
acheter les décorations - Patricia
téléphoner à Marc - Yannick
envoyer les invitations - Claire
parler à Zoé et André - Ahmad
allumer les bougies - Corentin

3 Vocabulaire 2
- to ask for help
- to check if things have been done

pp. 54–57

3 Claire demande à Ahmad de l'aider avec les invitations, mais il a déjà beaucoup de choses à faire. Complète leur conversation. 1.2

—Ahmad, tu peux m'aider à __1__ les invitations?
—Désolé, je n'ai pas le temps. Je dois d'abord __2__ les cadeaux, faire le __3__, __4__ la musique et __5__ les amuse-gueules.
—Et moi, je dois ranger la __6__ et __7__ les courses!

Preparing for the Exam

FOLD-N-LEARN
Comparison Chart Study Aid

1. Have students fold a sheet of paper in thirds from top to bottom and in thirds from side to side. They should unfold the sheet, trace all the creases with a pen or pencil, and turn the sheet horizontally.

Chapitre		
Conjugation		
Uses		

2. Ask students to write **Chapitre 2** in the upper left-hand corner, and then in the two rectangles below it, **Conjugation** and **Uses.** Then, have them do the same with another sheet.
3. At the top of one sheet, students should write **avoir** in the upper right-hand rectangle. On the other sheet, they should write **être.** Have them fill in the charts to review the **passé composé** with **avoir** and **être.** On the back, they should write examples in French of the uses.
4. Have students review using their Comparison Chart.

Prépare-toi pour l'examen

Online Assessment
my.hrw.com
Chapter Self-test

4 Samedi, Laure a invité des amis chez elle pour fêter son anniversaire. Complète sa description en mettant les verbes entre parenthèses au **passé composé.** 1.2

Samedi matin, je/j'___1___ (ranger) la maison, mon père ___2___ (faire) le gâteau et ma mère ___3___ (préparer) les amuse-gueules. Après, nous ___4___ (finir) de décorer le salon. Vers deux heures les invités ___5___ (arriver). Sarah et Léontine ___6___ (choisir) la musique et nous ___7___ (danser). Mes amis m'___8___ (donner) des cadeaux super! **1.** ai rangé **2.** a fait **3.** a préparé **4.** avons fini **5.** sont arrivés **6.** ont choisi **7.** avons dansé **8.** ont donné

4 Grammaire 2
- the passé composé with avoir
- the passé composé with être

Un peu plus
- negative expressions

pp. 58–63

5 Réponds aux questions suivantes. 2.1

1. Qu'est-ce que c'est, l'épiphanie? Que font les Français?
2. Quelles sont des traditions observées à Noël en France?
3. Est-ce que les magasins sont ouverts toute l'année? Pourquoi ou pourquoi pas?

5 Culture
- Flash culture pp. 44, 48, 56, 60
- Comparaisons pp. 52–53

6 Marius a aussi fêté son anniversaire samedi dernier. Il parle de sa fête. Fais une liste de trois choses que Marius et ses amis ont faites à la fête et mentionne une chose qu'ils n'ont pas faite. CD 2, Tr. 9 1.2

7 Imagine que ton/ta camarade et toi, vous êtes frère et sœur et c'est l'anniversaire de votre mère. Vous parlez de ce que vous voulez faire. D'abord, lisez les instructions pour chaque réplique *(exchange)*. Ensuite, créez votre dialogue en utilisant des expressions de ce chapitre et des autres chapitres. 1.1

Élève A:	Demande si ton frère ou ta sœur sait quoi offrir à votre mère.
Élève B:	Réponds négativement. Demande si ton frère ou ta sœur a une idée.
Élève A:	Propose un cadeau.
Élève B:	Dis que tu n'es pas d'accord et explique pourquoi. Propose une fête.
Élève A:	Dis que tu aimes cette idée et parle de tout ce que vous devez faire.
Élève B:	Demande à ton frère ou ta sœur de faire certaines corvées.
Élève A:	Dis que tu es d'accord et demande aussi de l'aide pour une corvée.
Élève B:	Réponds positivement.
Élève A:	Remercie ton frère ou ta sœur.

5 Answers
1. le jour des rois; ils mangent une galette des rois.
2. Ils réveillonnent; les enfants mettent leurs chaussons au pied du sapin.
3. Ils sont fermés les jours fériés.

6 Script
Mes amis sont arrivés vers sept heures. Nous avons mangé de la pizza et de la salade et nous avons bu du coca et des jus de fruit. Après, Rachid a joué de la guitare et nous avons chanté. Moi, j'aime bien danser, mais nous n'avons pas dansé parce que mes amis n'aiment pas trop danser.

6 Answer
Ils ont mangé de la pizza et de la salade, ils ont bu du coca et des jus de fruit, et ils ont chanté. Ils n'ont pas dansé.

Language Examination

7 Sample conversation:
- **a.** Tu as une idée de cadeau pour Maman?
- **b.** Non. Et toi?
- **a.** On pourrait lui offrir un DVD.
- **b.** Non, elle en a déjà plein. On pourrait faire une fête.
- **a.** Bonne idée! Il faut envoyer les invitations, faire le ménage, faire les courses,…
- **b.** Ça t'ennuie de faire les courses?
- **a.** Bien sûr que non. Tu peux m'aider à faire le ménage?
- **b.** Oui, pas de problème.
- **a.** Merci.

Additional Speaking Practice

- For additional speaking practice, you might use the *Picture Sequences Transparency* for Chapter 2 found in the *Projectable Transparencies.*
- To assess the speaking activities in this section, you might use the *Generate Success* Rubric Generator or the oral rubrics found in the *Assessment Program.*

Pre-AP Practice

7 This guided conversation activity helps students practice oral exchanges using material from this chapter and previous chapters. The activity helps prepare students for the **Interpersonal Speaking** section of the AP French Language and Culture Exam.

Prépare-toi pour l'examen

Grammaire 1
- direct object pronouns
- indirect object pronouns

Un peu plus
- the verb **offrir**

pp. 46–51

Résumé: Grammaire 1

Direct and indirect object pronouns can be used to avoid repetition. They are usually placed before the verb.

Direct Object	me	te	le/la	nous	vous	les
Indirect Object	me	te	lui	nous	vous	leur

If you use both direct and industrial object pronouns at the same time, place them in the following order:

me, te, nous, vous	le, la, l', les	lui, leur

The verb **offrir** is formed like an **-er** verb: j'offr**e**, tu offr**es**, il/elle/on offr**e**, nous offr**ons**, vous offr**ez**, ils/elles offr**ent**.

Grammaire 2
- the **passé composé** with **avoir**
- the **passé composé** with **être**

Un peu plus
- negative expressions

pp. 58–63

Résumé: Grammaire 2

The **passé composé** is formed with the present tense of a helping verb, **avoir** or **être**, and a past participle. When you use **être** as a helping verb, the past participle agrees with the subject.

parler	j' ai **parlé**
finir	tu as **fini**
descendre	ils sont **descendus**

Negative expressions are placed around the conjugated verb. **ne.. pas** *(not);* **ne... pas encore** *(not yet);* **ne... jamais** *(never, not ever);* **ne... plus** *(no more, no longer);* **ne... rien** *(nothing, not anything):*

Lettres et sons

The sound [y] CD 2, Tr. 10–12

The sound [y] in French does not exist in English. You can hear the sound [y] in words such as **bûche, plus,** and **musique.** To pronounce [y], start by saying [i] as in the English word *me.* Then, round your lips as if you were going to say the English word *moon,* keeping your tongue pressed behind your lower front teeth.

Jeux de langue 1.2

As-tu vu le tutu de tulle de Lili d'Honolulu?

Dictée

Écris les phrases de la dictée.

Grammar Review

For more practice with the grammar topics in this chapter, see the *Grammar Tutor*, the *@HomeTutor*, or the *Cahier de vocabulaire et grammaire*.

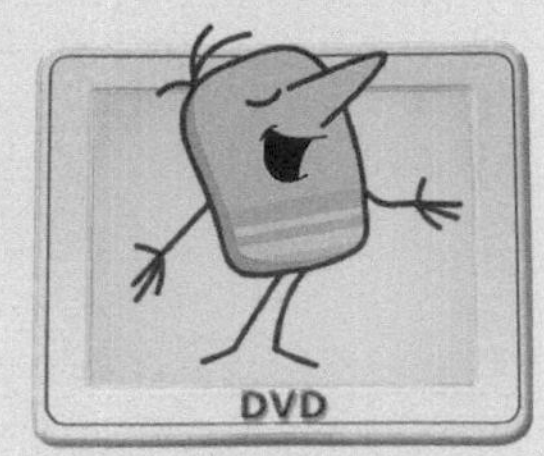

Grammavision

Online Edition

Students might use the online textbook and Performance Space to practice the **Lettres et sons** feature.

Dictée Script

1. Est-ce que tu étudies la musique?
2. As-tu vu cette voiture?
3. Ça m'amuse d'aller au musée.
4. Je ne mets pas de lunettes de soleil quand il y a des nuages.
5. Elle allume les bougies à la soirée costumée.

French for Spanish Speakers

Ask Spanish speakers the translation of negative words in a negative sentence like the French example **Je ne fais rien. (No hago nada.)** Ask students if they recognize any cognates among the negative expressions. (**Jamais** is similar in meaning and spelling to **jamás,** although **nunca** is more commonly used.) Ask students about the position of the negative words in French and Spanish. What do the languages have in common? (Both require that the negative words go around the verb.) 4.1

Chapter Review

DVD Program

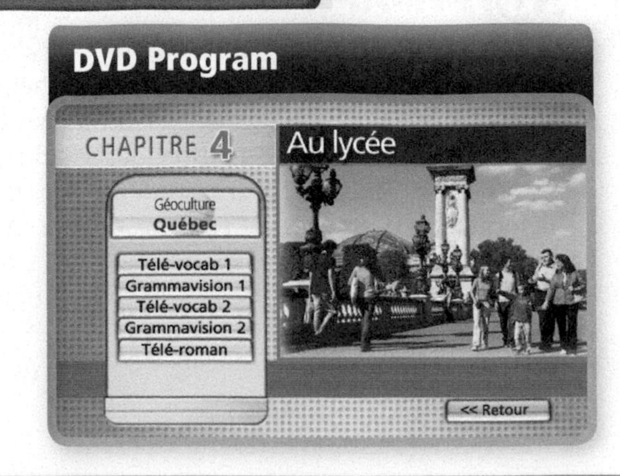

Online Edition

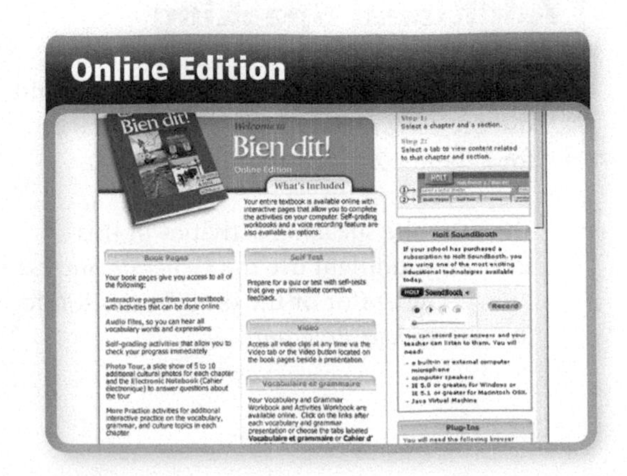

Prépare-toi pour l'examen

Résumé: Vocabulaire 1

PRACTICE FRENCH WITH HOLT MCDOUGAL APPS!

To wish someone a good time

allumer	to light
l'anniversaire (m.)	birthday
un bal populaire	village dance
le ballon/les décorations (f.)	balloon/decorations
une boîte de chocolats	box of chocolates
les bougies (f.)	candles
un bouquet (m.) de fleurs	bouquet of flowers
la boum	party
la bûche de Noël	Yule log
les cadeaux (m.)	presents
une carte d'anniversaire	birthday card
une carte de vœux	greeting card
un chèque-cadeau	gift card
les confettis (m.)	confetti
le défilé	parade
le drapeau	flag
les fêtes (f.)	parties/ holidays
la fête des mères/pères	Mother's/Father's Day
la fête nationale	national holiday
le feu d'artifice	fireworks
la foule	crowd
le gâteau	cake
l'hymne (m.) national	national anthem
l'invité(e)	guest
le jour de l'an/le nouvel an	New Year's Day/New Year's
le Noël	Christmas
remercier	to thank
le réveillon	midnight feast
le sapin de Noël	Christmas tree
Amuse-toi bien...	Have fun . . .
Joyeux anniversaire!	Happy birthday!
Bonne année!	Happy New Year!
Bonne soirée!	Have a good evening!
J'espère que tu vas passer...	I hope that you have . . .
Je te/vous souhaite...	I wish you . . .
Joyeux Noël!	Merry Christmas!
Profite bien de...	Enjoy . . .

To ask for and give advice

Bonne idée!	Good idea!
Offre-lui...	Give him/her . . .
Qu'est-ce que je pourrais offrir à...?	What could I get for . . . ?
Tu as une idée de cadeau... ?	Do you have an idea for a present . . . ?
Tu n'as pas une autre idée?	You don't have another idea?
Tu pourrais lui offrir...	You could give him/her . . .
Il en a déjà plein.	He already has plenty of them.

Résumé: Vocabulaire 2

To ask for help and respond

les amuse-gueules (m.)	snacks
les biscuits (m.)/les chips (f.)	cookies/chips
les bonbons (m.)	sweets/candy
les cacahuètes (f.)	peanuts
choisir la musique	to choose the music
décorer la salle	to decorate the room
emballer les cadeaux (m.)	to wrap presents
envoyer les invitations (f.)	to send the invitations
faire les courses (f.)	to go grocery shopping
faire le ménage/la poussière	to do housework/to dust
les fruits secs (m.)	dried fruit
organiser une soirée	to plan a party
ranger la maison	to prepare/to tidy up the house
une soirée costumée	costume party
Ça t'ennuie de... ?	Would you mind . . . ?
Tu peux m'aider à... ?	Can you help me . . . ?
Bien sûr que non.	Of course not.
D'accord./Pas de problème.	Okay./No problem
Désolé(e), je n'ai pas le temps.	Sorry, I don't have the time.
Pas maintenant. Je dois d'abord...	Not now. First, I have to . . .

To check if things have been done and respond

c'est bon	it's fine (all taken care of)
Est-ce qu'il y a encore... ?	Is there still . . . ?
J'ai complètement oublié!	I completely forgot!
Mais oui!	But of course!
pas encore	not yet
Tu as bien... ?	Are you sure you . . . ?
Tu as déjà... ?	Did you already . . . ?
Tu as pensé à... ?	Have you thought of . . .?

Prépare-toi pour l'examen

Holt McDougal French Apps

Remind students that they can use the Holt McDougal French Apps to review their vocabulary.

Cinquain Poetry

Have students follow these directions to write a cinquain using the vocabulary and grammar in this chapter. Have students share their poems with the class.

Line 1: A one-word noun that gives the poem its title
Line 2: Two adjectives that describe the noun
Line 3: Three verbs that are related to the noun
Line 4: A sentence that expresses a feeling related to the noun
Line 5: A one-word noun that renames the poem

Sample Answer

Le cadeau
Beau, nouveau
J'achète, j'offre, j'envoie
J'adore les anniversaires.
La fête

Projectable Transparency

More Digital Resources

FOR THE STUDENT

Holt McDougal French Apps
@HomeTutor
News and Networking
Performance Space

FOR THE TEACHER

- Interactive Whiteboard Lessons
- Generate Success!

Assess

Assessment Program
Examen: Chapitre 2
Audio CD 2, Tr. 16–17 
Examen oral: Chapitre 2
Alternative Assessment
Differentiated Practice and Assessment CD-ROM
Online Assessment
my.hrw.com
Test Generator

Resources

Planning:
Lesson Planner
Teacher One Stop

Practice:
Cahier d'activités
Media Guide
Projectable Transparencies
Fine Art, Chapter 2
Audio CD 2, Tr. 13

Holt McDougal French Apps

1 Script

1. — Tu peux m'aider à ranger le salon?
   — Pas de problème.
2. — Tu as une idée de cadeau pour Olivia?
   — Tu pourrais lui offrir un tee-shirt.
3. — Tu as déjà préparé les amuse-gueules?
   — Oui, c'est bon. Ils sont prêts.
4. — J'ai fini le gâteau.
   — D'accord, je vais chercher les bougies.

Teacher to Teacher

Jodi Mahlmann
Seven Lakes High School
Katy, TX

My students make human sentences to practice direct object pronouns. I write sentences on strips of paper and cut out each word. **Jean / lave / la / voiture.** Then I assign one word per student and have them stand up in proper order. I assign other students **le, la,** and **les.** I ask the class what the direct object is. **(la voiture)** The student holding the word **la** goes to the appropriate place to replace the student with **la voiture.** The activity continues with different sentences. 1.2

Révisions cumulatives

1 Des amis organisent la fête d'anniversaire d'Olivia. Écoute les conversations et choisis la photo qui correspond à chacune. CD 2, Tr. 13 1.2

1. d **2.** b **3.** a **4.** c

a.

b.

c.

d.

2 Une amie parisienne pense à louer *(to rent)* un salon de réception pour son mariage. Lis la publicité et réponds aux questions. 3.2, 1.2

un véritable paradis au cœur de Paris
Le Bois vert
Pour une fête réussie
Le Bois vert accueille vos repas et réceptions.
Mariage
Anniversaire
Repas d'affaires
salle de réception dans un cadre exceptionnel
terrasses et jardins
Nous proposons :
• buffet chaud • boissons
• desserts • décorations • orchestre

1. Comment s'appelle la salle de réception?
2. Quelles fêtes est-ce qu'ils organisent?
3. Quels services est-ce qu'ils offrent?
4. Et toi, est-ce que tu aimerais louer cette salle de réception? Pourquoi ou pourquoi pas?

1. le Bois vert
2. mariage, anniversaire, repas d'affaires
3. buffet chaud, boissons, desserts, décorations, orchestre
4. Answers will vary

Online Culture Project

Tell students that your school is organizing an international student fair, where information about food, customs, and celebrations across the French-speaking world is presented. Each student should create a poster to represent three celebrations. On their poster have students answer these questions about the celebration: What? Where? When? Why? Students should research francophone celebrations on the Web and document their sources. 1.3, 2.1

Révisions cumulatives

Online Assessment
my.hrw.com
Cumulative Self-test

3 Pose des questions à deux ou trois amis pour savoir ce qu'ils aiment faire pour fêter le nouvel an. Demande-leur où et avec qui ils aiment passer leur anniversaire. Après, dis à la classe ce que tes amis aiment faire. 1.1, 1.3

4 Imagine que tu visites Paris pour la fête nationale avec ta famille. Réponds aux questions suivantes. Ensuite, fais une description de la fête en utilisant le tableau. 1.3, 2.2

1. Décris les couleurs de la scène.
2. Que font les personnes?
3. Quelle est l'atmosphère de la scène?
4. Qu'est-ce que tu fais pendant les fêtes nationales?

Monet, Claude (1840-1926), Rue Montorgueil, Festival of 30 June, 1878. Oil on canvas. Musée des Beaux-Arts, Rouen, France.

La Rue Montorgueil, La Fête du 30 juin 1878 de Claude Monet

5 Choisis une de tes fêtes préférées. Écris une lettre à un(e) ami(e) français(e) et dis-lui ce qu'on fait dans ta région pour célébrer cette fête. 1.3

6 À ton tour

Joyeux anniversaire! You're having a birthday party for a relative and three of your friends are helping you make plans. Decide where and when to have the party, whom to invite, what chores each of you will do, what type of food you want to serve and what games and activities you will do. Act out your conversation for the class. 1.1

Fine Art Connection

Introduction Claude Monet (1840–1926) was born in Paris. He was influenced by Eugène Boudin, one of the first French landscape painters to paint **en plein air.** He later met other famous impressionists, such as Auguste Renoir, Frédéric Bazille, and Alfred Sisley, with whom he shared outdoor painting techniques. Monet painted in many outdoor places, but some of his most famous works were painted in the garden of his Giverny house (Haute-Normandie), which has a beautiful waterlily-covered pond. Toward the end of his life, Monet had become nearly blind and had cataract surgery in both eyes. These cataracts affected the way he saw the world around him, and they gave some of his paintings a very distinctive appearance.

Analyzing

To help students discuss the painting, you might use the following questions.

1. **Comment sait-on que cette rue est en France?**
2. **Est-ce que cette scène pourrait se passer pendant la période actuelle?**
3. **Est-ce que les rues des villes américaines sont parfois décorées comme ça? Quand?**
4. **Est-ce que tu voudrais être dans cette rue? Pourquoi?** 3.2

Extension

Ask students to download a variety of pictures of paintings by Monet from the Internet and compare them. What are their dominant colors? Does the amount of detail vary from one painting to another? Is it possible to know at what point in Monet's life a painting was done just by looking at it? 2.2, 3.1

ACTFL Performance Standards

The activities in Chapter 2 target the communicative modes as described in the Standards.

Interpersonal	Two-way communication using receptive skills and productive skills	**Communication (SE),** pp. 45, 47, 49, 51, 57, 59, 61 **Communication (TE),** pp. 45, 47, 49, 51, 61 **À ton tour,** p. 75
Interpretive	One-way communication using receptive skills	**Comparaisons,** p. 53 **Communication (SE),** p. 63 **Communication (TE),** pp. 57, 59 **Télé-roman,** pp. 64–65
Presentational	One-way communication using productive skills	**Communication (TE),** p. 63

Géoculture Overview

Québec

Bienvenue! This section is designed to familiarize the students with the geographic location, history, and cultural practices of the region to be explored. It provides a guide for classroom discussion and discovery of the differences and similarities of the student's own culture and that of the French-speaking world.

50-Minute Lesson Plans

Day 1

Lesson Sequence

Géoculture: Québec, pp. 76–77

- Ask students to locate Quebec City on the map. Have them make conjectures about the city's climate, its architecture, its economy, and the leisure activities it may offer its inhabitants. Students should base their predictions on the location of Quebec. **12 min.**
- Go over the photos and captions with students. **10 min.**
- See Map Activities, p. 76. **5 min.**
- Discuss Background Information, p. 76. **9 min.**
- Complete **Géo-quiz. 1 min.**
- Show **Géoculture** video. **3 min.**
- Have students answer **Questions,** p. 77. **10 min.**

Optional Resources

- **Savais-tu que...?,** p. 77
- Thinking Critically, p. 75B
- Research Online!, p. 75B

Homework Suggestions

Online Practice (**my.hrw.com**)

1.2, 1.3, 2.2, 3.1, 4.2

Day 2

Lesson Sequence

Géoculture: Québec, pp. 78–79

- Briefly revisit the main points about the geography. **5 min.**
- Go over the photos and captions with students. **8 min.**
- Discuss the festivals and celebrations in Quebec City and have students compare these to festivals and celebrations in their hometown. **5 min.**
- Have students answer **As-tu compris?** questions, p. 79. **7 min.**
- Do **Prépare-toi pour le quiz,** p. 75B. **25 min.**

Optional Resources

- Map Game, p. 75B
- Slower Pace Learners, p. 75B ◆
- Multiple Intelligences, p. 75B
- Interdisciplinary Links, pp. 78–79

Homework Suggestions

Activité, p. 79

Study for the **Géoculture** quiz.

1.1, 1.2, 1.3, 2.2, 3.1, 3.2, 5.1, 5.2

90-Minute Lesson Plan

Block 1

Lesson Sequence

Géoculture: Québec, pp. 76–79

- Ask students to locate Quebec City on the map. Have them make conjectures about the city's climate, its architecture, its economy, and the leisure activities it may offer its inhabitants. Students should base their predictions on the location of Quebec. **10 min.**
- Go over the photos and captions with students. **20 min.**
- See Map Activities, p. 76. **5 min.**
- Discuss Background Information, p. 76. **10 min.**
- Complete **Géo-quiz. 1 min.**
- Show **Géoculture** video. **4 min.**
- Have students answer **Questions,** p. 77. **5 min.**
- Have students answer **As-tu compris?** questions, p. 79. **5 min.**
- Ask students if they would want to live in Quebec City. Why or why not? **5 min.**
- Do **Prépare-toi pour le quiz,** p. 75B. **25 min.**

Optional Resources

- **Savais-tu que ...?,** p. 77
- Slower Pace Learners, p. 75B ◆
- Multiple Intelligences, p. 75B
- Thinking Critically, p. 75B
- Research Online!, p. 75B
- Interdisciplinary Links, pp. 78–79
- Map Game, p. 75B

Homework Suggestions

Online Practice (**my.hrw.com**)

Activité, p. 79

Study for the **Géoculture** quiz.

1.1, 1.2, 1.3, 2.2, 3.1, 3.2, 4.2, 5.1, 5.2

KEY

▲ Advanced Learners ◆ Slower Pace Learners ● Special Learning Needs

Differentiated Instruction

Slower Pace Learners

Additional Practice Provide students a copy of **Géoculture** with specific terms and phrases in the captions left blank. As advanced learners take turns presenting **Géoculture,** students fill in the blanks. If students need clarifications, they may ask the presenters to repeat the captions, to spell difficult terms and phrases, or to use circumlocution and gestures to explain terms and phrases. 1.1, 1.2

Multiple Intelligences

Kinesthetic/Linguistic Have students work in groups of three to create a conversation in which they talk about taking a sightseeing tour of Quebec. The conversation should be between an eager tour guide and two tourists who ask many questions. Students should role-play their sightseeing tours for the class. Encourage students to use props. 1.1, 3.1

Thinking Critically

Observing Ask students to look at the map and circle the area where they think Quebec's Old Town **(Le Vieux-Québec)** is located. Students should explain why they circled a specific location. 3.1

Critical Thinking and Problem Solving

Quiz Preparation/Enrichment

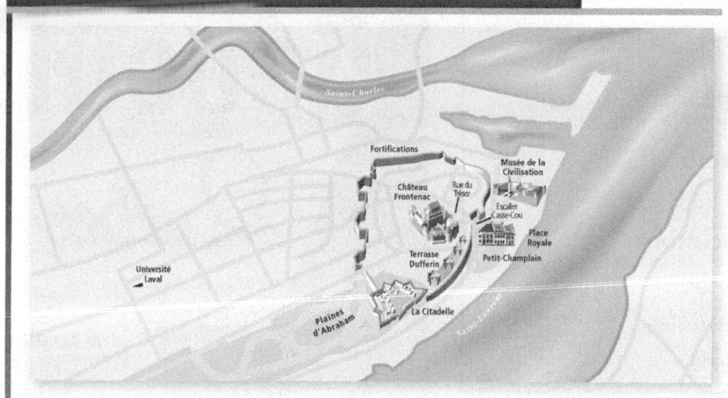

Map Game This game is similar to Scrabble®. Cut heavy paper into one-inch squares. Leave a third of the squares blank and write the French alphabet on the rest. Make extra squares with the most common letters: vowels, *s, t,* and so on. A blank may serve as any letter, as a hyphen, or as an apostrophe. Place the letters face down in one pile and the blanks in another pile. Each student picks fifteen letters and five blanks. Students arrange letters and blanks to form the name of any feature that is shown on the map. Once students have formed a name, they should write it down and reuse the letters and blanks to form new names. The student with the most names is the winner. 3.1

Prépare-toi pour le quiz

1. Students should make a list of the sights featured on the map. Ask students to write next to each sight the street(s) on which it is located and if it is north or south of the St. Lawrence River.
2. Have students describe in a complete sentence three of Quebec's sights.
3. Working in groups, have students plan a two-day trip to Quebec City. They should plan to tour some of its sights, sample its cuisine, attend a festival or celebration, and visit a museum or an art show. You may want to ask groups to present their plans to the class. 1.3, 3.1

Research Online!

L'histoire de Québec The 400th anniversary of the founding of Quebec City by French explorer Samuel de Champlain is July 3, 2008. Students should explore on the Internet or in the library the history of Quebec City. Have students decide on at least three important events in Quebec's history and create a timeline that includes dates and brief descriptions of the events. Students should present their timeline to the class. Have students document their sources by noting the URLs of all the sites they consulted. 1.3, 3.1

Resources

Planning:
Lesson Planner
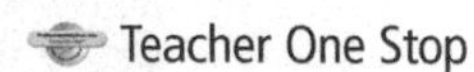
Teacher One Stop

Presentation:

Projectable Transparencies
Carte 5

DVD Tutor, Disc 1
Géoculture

Practice:
Cahier d'activités
Media Guide

Map ACTIVITIES

1. Have students locate Quebec City on a map of Quebec Province and name the two rivers that meet there. (Saint Lawrence and Saint Charles) Then have students trace the Saint Lawrence River north to the Atlantic Ocean and name the bodies of water between its mouth and the ocean. **(Détroit** [Strait] **d'Hongueado, Détroit de Jacques Cartier,** Gulf of Saint Lawrence, Cabot Strait)
2. Ask students why they think Samuel de Champlain decided to establish a colony at Quebec City. (easy access to the Atlantic and the two rivers) Ask students which industries can be attributed to the city's location. **(trafic portuaire, tourisme)**

Chapitres 3 et 4

Géoculture

Québec

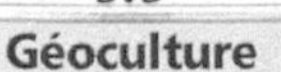
DVD
Géoculture

La Chute Montmorency est plus haute que les chutes du Niagara. En hiver, elle gèle *(freezes)* et on peut l'escalader *(climb)*. 3

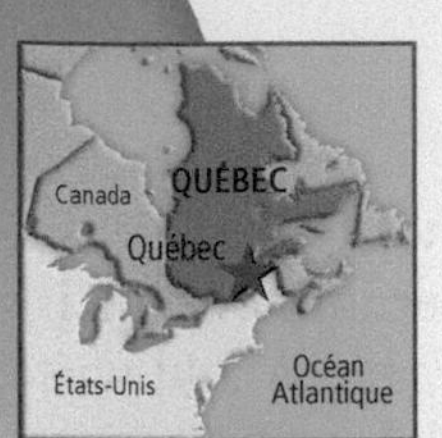

Almanach

Nom des habitants
Les Québécois

Population
Plus de 160.000 habitants

Personnages célèbres
Marie-Claire Blais, Yves Thériault, Félix Leclerc, Guy Laliberté

Économie
industrie alimentaire, textile, trafic portuaire, tourisme

La place Royale C'est ici que Samuel de Champlain a fondé la ville de Québec en 1608. 2

La terrasse Saint-Denis Cette large promenade offre une belle vue du Saint-Laurent. C'est un des lieux de rendez-vous préférés des jeunes Québécois. 1

Université Laval

Savais-tu que...?

La terrasse Saint-Denis était un des endroits favoris des poètes et écrivains.

Background Information

Geography

Quebec City lies where the Saint Lawrence and Saint Charles rivers meet. The historic district of the capital, **Vieux Québec,** is divided into the **Haute-Ville** (Upper Town) and the **Basse-Ville** (Lower Town). The fortified **Haute-Ville** sits on top of **Cap Diamant** (Cape Diamond), while **Basse-Ville** lies below and around the steep cliffs. Montmorency Falls are 272 feet high, 98 feet higher than Niagara Falls. They are located to the east of Quebec City at the mouth of the **Rivière Montmorency** where it drops into the Saint Lawrence River.

History

Battle of the Plains of Abraham This decisive battle altered the course of Canadian history. Up until 1759, the French had ruled over all of Canada, but after the British defeated them at Quebec City, they lost control of the colony to the British.

Battle of Quebec During the American Revolution, the Americans attacked the British at Quebec City, hoping to bring the Canadians in on their side of the war. They were defeated and the Canadians remained loyal to the British.

Québec

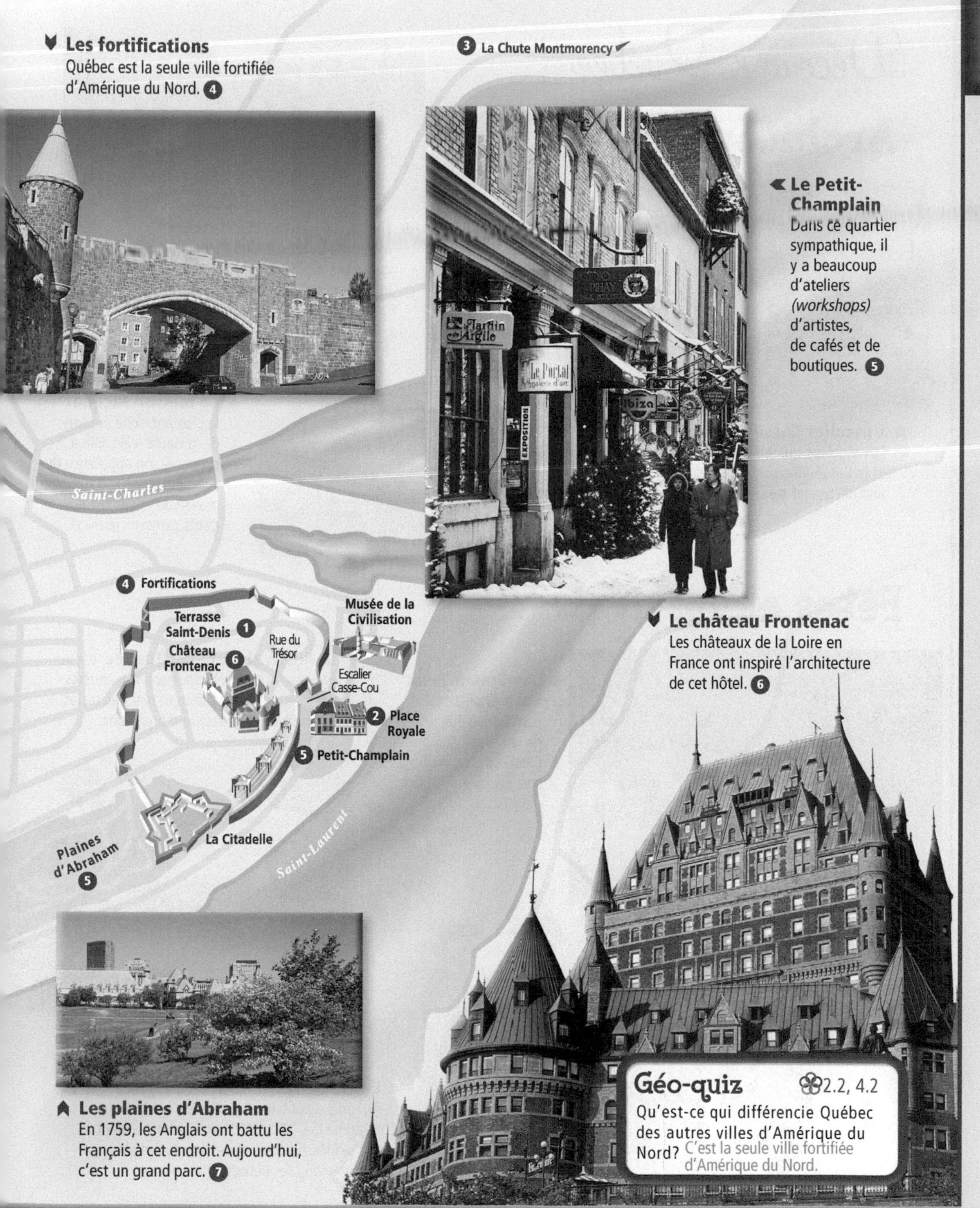

Les fortifications
Québec est la seule ville fortifiée d'Amérique du Nord. 4

Le Petit-Champlain
Dans ce quartier sympathique, il y a beaucoup d'ateliers *(workshops)* d'artistes, de cafés et de boutiques. 5

Le château Frontenac
Les châteaux de la Loire en France ont inspiré l'architecture de cet hôtel. 6

Les plaines d'Abraham
En 1759, les Anglais ont battu les Français à cet endroit. Aujourd'hui, c'est un grand parc. 7

Géo-quiz 2.2, 4.2
Qu'est-ce qui différencie Québec des autres villes d'Amérique du Nord? C'est la seule ville fortifiée d'Amérique du Nord.

Culture

Products and Perspectives

The Château Frontenac was built as a luxury hotel between 1893 and 1924. Designed by New York architect Bruce Price, the hotel reflects the architectural styles of the Middle Ages and the Renaissance. It was here that U.S. President Franklin D. Roosevelt, British Prime Minister Winston Churchill, and Canadian Prime Minister William Lyon Mackenzie King met during WWII to work out their countries' strategies against Hitler. Today, the Château Frontenac is considered to be the national symbol of Quebec. Ask students why they think this might be so. 2.2

Comparisons

Comparing and Contrasting

La terrasse Dufferin is a 425-meter boardwalk at the foot of the Château Frontenac. In the warmer months, people go there to take a walk, watch street performers, or meet friends. In winter, people gather to skate at the outdoor ice rink or go sledding. Ask students if they have ever visited a boardwalk in the United States. If so, ask how it was similar to or different than **la terrasse Dufferin.** You might also ask students where people in their community go to meet friends and do outdoor activities. 4.2

Savais-tu que...?

Students might be interested in knowing the following facts about Quebec City.

- Quebec City is considered the cradle of French civilization in North America. Although most of the inhabitants are bilingual, about 95% can claim French ancestry.
- Tourists who visit Quebec City in the winter can stay in a hotel where everything is made of ice, even the beds. About 350 tons of ice are used each winter to build the Ice Hotel, a huge structure covering 3,000 square meters, that melts in the spring.

Questions 1.2

1. **À quel endroit est-ce que Champlain a fondé la ville de Québec? (à la place Royale)**
2. **Quel sport est-ce qu'on peut faire à la chute Montmorency en hiver? (de l'escalade)**
3. **Comment est-ce que la ville de Québec se différencie de toutes les autres villes en Amérique du Nord? (C'est la seule ville fortifiée.)**
4. **D'où vient l'inspiration pour l'architecture du château Frontenac? (des châteaux de la Loire)**
5. **Où est-ce qu'on peut trouver beaucoup d'ateliers d'artistes et de cafés? (le Petit-Champlain)**

Language Examination

Géoculture helps students better understand practices, products, and perspectives of French-speaking cultures and their relationship to one another. It can be used to practice for the **Interpretive Communication** and **Presentational Writing** sections of the AP Language and Culture Exam.

Cultures

Products and Perspectives

The **Musée de la civilisation** is a 20,000-square-meter contemporary building situated in the heart of Quebec City's historical district. Made of local materials, its roof, dormer windows, and steeples blend in with those of nearby houses and churches. The building's network of stairways and terraces allows visitors in the summertime to discover the city's landscape. In addition to housing several modern exhibition spaces, four existing historical structures have been incorporated into the building. The oldest is a stone embankment dating back to 1751. Have students find photos of the **Musée de la civilisation** and read more about it online. Then ask them how the museum's design reflects Quebec's cultural values and architecture. 2.2

Connections

Science Link

Every July, countries from around the world enter fireworks displays in the **Grands Feux Loto-Québec** competition. To create the colorful effects that might win first prize, technicians use chemistry to manufacture the fireworks and modern computer technology to set them off. Fireworks contain three types of chemical substances: combustibles, which allow shells to ignite and burn; oxidizing agents, which provide oxygen for the burn; and metal salts, which give the bursts color. When the shells are ignited, a chemical reaction occurs, causing them to burst into the air. At the **Grands Feux Loto,** computers coordinate music and lasers with the fireworks. Have students research chemical substances used in fireworks and create a chart in French giving the names of the substances and their purpose. 1.3, 3.1

Découvre Québec

Architecture

L'escalier Casse-Cou
Les escaliers qui relient *(join)* la Haute-Ville et la Basse-Ville sont une des caractéristiques architecturales de Québec.

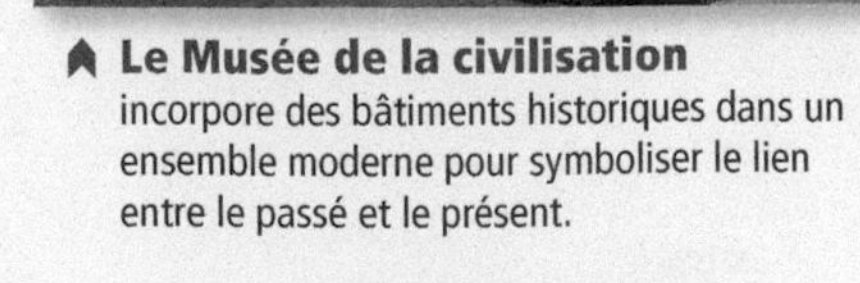

Le Musée de la civilisation
incorpore des bâtiments historiques dans un ensemble moderne pour symboliser le lien entre le passé et le présent.

La maison Jacquet est la plus ancienne maison de la Haute-Ville. Elle a conservé son apparence du 17e siècle avec son toit *(roof)* mansardé et ses fenêtres à petits carreaux *(panes)*.

Fêtes et festivals

Les Grands Feux Loto-Québec ont lieu chaque été au Parc de la Chute-Montmorency. Plusieurs pays participent à ce concours de feux d'artifice.

Le Festival d'été de Québec est un événement culturel important. Des artistes internationaux y présentent des spectacles de musique, de danse et d'animation.

Les Fêtes de la Nouvelle-France
Au mois d'août, les Québécois s'habillent en costume des 17e et 18e siècles et organisent des défilés, des bals et des spectacles pour commémorer les débuts de la colonie.

Interdisciplinary Links

L'architecture  3.2

Social Studies Link Houses from the early period of Quebec City's history, such as **la maison Jacquet,** were built with the region's harsh winters in mind. Their simplicity also reflects the lack of materials and labor available to early settlers. Typical houses of the 17th century were rectangular and had two-sided, sloping roofs made of cedar shingles. They had few windows and one or two chimneys. Ask students how they think these architectural features protected early settlers during Quebec's winters.

Les fêtes et festivals 3.1

Music Link Every July, francophone musicians present hundreds of free concerts during the **Festival d'été de Québec.** They play different types of music, ranging from pop and hip-hop to classical and traditional music. Each year some of them are awarded the **Prix international de la chanson francophone** for their outstanding performances during the festival or their life's work in francophone music. Have students research one of the following past festival participants: Celine Dion, Colette Borky, Robert Charlebois, Louise Forestier, or Michel Rivard.

Gastronomie

La cuisine traditionnelle, servie dans les restaurants du Vieux-Québec, ressemble à la cuisine française. Elle utilise des produits locaux, comme le gibier *(game)*, les légumes secs et le sirop d'érable.

Online Practice
my.hrw.com
Photo Tour

Savais-tu que...?

À l'époque où Québec était une colonie, les carreaux venaient de France. On les choisissait très petits et on les transportait dans des tonneaux de mélasse *(molasses)* pour ne pas les casser.

Les desserts à l'érable
Le sirop d'érable est présent partout dans la cuisine québécoise, par exemple dans ses pâtisseries.

La poutine est un plat populaire québécois. C'est un plat de frites avec du fromage *cheddar* et une sauce au jus de viande.

Arts

La rue du Trésor
En été, les artistes s'installent dans cette rue pour vendre des peintures et des dessins.

La fresque des Québécois représente des endroits caractéristiques de la ville et aussi des personnages importants de l'histoire du Québec.

Activité

2.1, 2.2

1. **Architecture**: Qu'est-ce que l'architecture du Musée de la civilisation symbolise?
2. **Fêtes et festivals**: Qu'est-ce qu'on peut voir pendant le Festival d'été?
3. **Gastronomie**: Qu'est-ce que c'est, la poutine?
4. **Arts**: Qu'est-ce que la fresque des Québécois représente?

Activité

1. le lien entre le passé et le présent
2. des spectacles de musique, de danse et d'animation
3. un plat de frites avec du fromage et une sauce au jus de viande
4. des endroits caractéristiques et des personnages importants

Communities

Traditions

Le temps des sucres occurs each spring. Families spend the day at **cabanes à sucre** *(sugar shacks)* gathering sap from maple trees, making dishes such as **soupe aux pois, omelettes dans le sirop,** and **tartelettes à l'érable,** and folkdancing in the evening. Ask students to name traditions in their area associated with harvesting a particular crop. 5.2

As-tu compris?

You can use the following questions to check students' comprehension of **Géoculture.**

1. **Comment s'appelle la maison la plus ancienne de la Haute-Ville? (la maison Jacquet)**
2. **Qu'est-ce qu'on peut trouver dans la rue du Trésor? (des artistes avec leurs peintures)**
3. **Qu'est-ce que la Fête de la Nouvelle-France commémore? (les débuts de la colonie)**
4. **Quels sont quelques ingrédients de la cuisine du Vieux-Québec? (le gibier, les légumes secs et le sirop d'érable)** 1.2

La gastronomie

3.1, 5.1

Math Link Recipes from Quebec generally use the metric system, while those from the United States use cups, tablespoons, and teaspoons. Have students find a recipe for **tartelettes à l'érable** in French and a recipe conversion chart online. Then have them convert the recipe from the metric system to the traditional U.S. system. You might also have students prepare the tarts to see if their conversions were correct.

L'art

3.2

History Link The **fresque des Québécois** features portraits of important historical figures. Those that influenced both Canadian and world history include explorer Jacques Cartier, Samuel de Champlain, founder of Quebec City, and Louis Jolliet, discoverer of the Mississippi. Other figures of more local impact include Louis de Buade, Count of Frontenac, defender of Quebec City against the British, Catherine de Longpré, an administrator at Quebec City's first hospital, and Félix Leclerc, 'the father' of **québécois** song. Have students research one of these historical figures.

Assess

Assessment Program
Quiz: Géoculture
Differentiated Practice and Assessment CD-ROM

Online Assessment
my.hrw.com

Test Generator 

chapitre 3

Planning Guide

Faisons les courses

Chapter Section		Resources
Vocabulaire 1 • Vegetables, fruits, food preparation **Grammaire 1** • Review of the partitive • The pronoun **y** **Application 1** • **Un peu plus:** Review of question formation	pp. 82–85 pp. 86–89 pp. 90–91	Projectable Transparencies: Vocabulaire 3.1, 3.2; Bell Work 3.1, 3.2, 3.3, 3.4 Cahier de vocabulaire et grammaire, pp. 25–30 Grammar Tutor for Students of French Cahier d'activités, pp. 21–23 Media Guide, pp. 9–12, 60–62 **Assessment Program** Quiz: Vocabulaire 1, pp. 61–62 Quiz: Grammaire 1, pp. 63–64 Quiz: Application 1, pp. 65–66
Culture • **Culture appliquée: Le sirop d'érable** • **Comparaisons et Communauté**	pp. 92–93	Cahier d'activités, p. 24
Vocabulaire 2 • Specialty stores, expressions of quantity **Grammaire 2** • The pronoun **en** • Placement of object pronouns **Application 2** • **Un peu plus:** Review of contractions with **à** and **de**	pp. 94–97 pp. 98–101 pp. 102–103	Projectable Transparencies: Vocabulaire 3.3, 3.4; Bell Work 3.5, 3.6, 3.7, 3.8 Cahier de vocabulaire et grammaire, pp. 31–36 Grammar Tutor for Students of French Cahier d'activités, pp. 25–27 Media Guide, pp. 9–12, 60–61, 63 **Assessment Program** Quiz: Vocabulaire 2, pp. 67–68 Quiz: Grammaire 2, pp. 69–70 Quiz: Application 2, pp. 71–72
Télé-roman	pp. 104–105	Media Guide, pp. 61, 64
Lecture et écriture	pp. 106–109	Cahier d'activités, p. 28 Reading Strategies and Skills Handbook Intermediate Reader French InterActive Reader **Assessment Program** Quiz: Lecture, p. 73 Quiz: Écriture, p. 74
Prépare-toi pour l'examen • **Résumé de vocabulaire et grammaire** • **Lettres et sons** **Révisions cumulatives**	pp. 110–113 pp. 114–115	Independent Study Guide, pp. 7–9, 35 Media Guide, p. 12 **Assessment Program** Examen: Chapitre 3, pp. 75–80 Examen oral: Chapitre 3, p. 319 Projectable Transparencies: Fine Art, Ch. 3 Cahier d'activités, pp. 24, 29–30
Variations littéraires • **Poèmes d'Anne Hébert**	pp. 386–387	Reading Strategies and Skills Handbook Intermediate Reader French InterActive Reader

Planning Guide

Visit Us Online

my.hrw.com
Online Edition

Pacing Suggestions

	Essential	Recommended	Optional
Vocabulaire 1 • Vegetables, fruits, food preparation • **Flash culture**	✔		
Grammaire 1 • Review of the partitive • The pronoun **y** • **Flash culture**	✔		
Application 1 • **Un peu plus:** Review of question formation	✔		
Culture • **Culture appliquée: Le sirop d'érable** • **Comparaisons et Communauté**		✔	
Vocabulaire 2 • Specialty stores, expressions of quantity • **Flash culture**	✔		
Grammaire 2 • The pronoun **en** • Placement of object pronouns • **Flash culture**	✔		
Application 2 • **Un peu plus:** Review of contractions with **à** and **de**	✔		
Télé-roman • Épisode 3: **Le Secret de la statuette**			✔
Lecture et écriture • **Le Petit Nicolas : On a fait le marché avec papa** (Lecture) • **Un plat délicieux** (Écriture)		✔	
Prépare-toi pour l'examen		✔	
Révisions cumulatives			✔
Variations littéraires • **Poèmes d'Anne Hébert**			✔

Technology

Bien dit! Online
- Student Edition with multi-media
- **performance space** recording tool
- Interactive activities with feedback
- Self-tests with feedback
- Cahier d'activités (Interactive workbook)
- Cahier de vocabulaire et grammaire (Interactive workbook)
- Holt Online Assessment

DVD Tutor
- Télé-vocab
- Grammavision
- Télé-roman

HOMETUTOR
- Interactive games
- Differentiated Practice
- Cultural Video

Audio Program
- Student Edition listening activities
- Assessment listening activities
- Songs

Teacher One Stop
- Complete resources
- ExamView Pro Test Generator
- Holt Calendar Planner

Holt McDougal Apps

Interactive Whiteboard Lessons

Differentiated Practice and Assessment CD

For slower pace and advanced learner options, see the Differentiated Practice and Assessment CD.

Projects

Grading the project

Suggested point distribution (100 points total)

Preparation	20 pts.
Language use	30 pts.
Participation/Creativity	30 pts.
Written assignment	20 pts.

e-community

e-mail forum:

Location: http://french

Post the following questions on the classroom e-mail forum:

Qu'est-ce que tu prends au petit-déjeuner?
Au déjeuner?
Au dîner? 5.1

All students will contribute to the list and then share the items.

Jour de marché

Students role-play a marketplace scene, acting as vendors and customers. You might have students do this project after they learn the expressions in **Exprimon-nous!** in **Vocabulaire 2.** 1.1, 1.3, 2.1

Suggested Sequence

1. Explain the project and ask students to brainstorm a list of French foods that may be available locally. Then bring in, or have students bring in, some of these foods.
2. Ask five or six volunteers to be the vendors; the other students will be the customers. Have the vendors make signs for their stands and set up the marketplace. Vendors might ask two or three other classmates to work with them on their stand. Have the customers make paper euros.
3. On "market day," have the vendors set up their stand and clean and cut the foods into portions so everyone can "buy" some. All the shopping, bargaining, and purchasing should be conducted in French.
4. After everyone has shopped and tried some of the foods, have students clean up. Have them write a short paragraph giving their opinions of the foods they tried. You may wish to review with them the phrases for expressing likes and dislikes in Chapter 1.

21st Century **Communication**

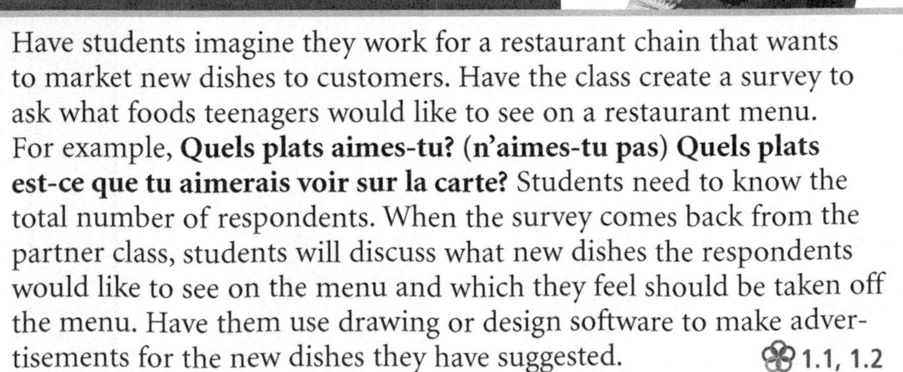

Partner Class Project

Have students imagine they work for a restaurant chain that wants to market new dishes to customers. Have the class create a survey to ask what foods teenagers would like to see on a restaurant menu. For example, **Quels plats aimes-tu? (n'aimes-tu pas) Quels plats est-ce que tu aimerais voir sur la carte?** Students need to know the total number of respondents. When the survey comes back from the partner class, students will discuss what new dishes the respondents would like to see on the menu and which they feel should be taken off the menu. Have them use drawing or design software to make advertisements for the new dishes they have suggested. 1.1, 1.2

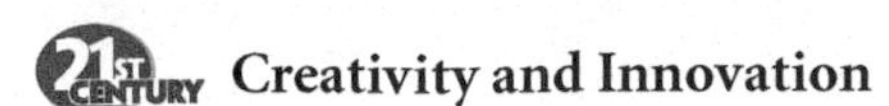

21st Century **Creativity and Innovation**

Game Bank
For game ideas, see pages T60–T63.

Les recettes traditionnelles

The first French settlers in Quebec came mainly from Brittany and Normandy in northwestern France. Faced with very different flora and fauna in the New World, their regional recipes were adapted to native products. Over time, local fruit, vegetables, and meats replaced the traditional ingredients. The settlers hunted wild game, so, for example, the traditional beef stew (**bœuf Bourgignon**) became bear or caribou stew. They learned to cultivate corn, sweet potatoes, and pumpkins from the Native Americans, and they tapped maple trees and produced syrup to use in desserts. The traditional **crème brûlée** with its caramelized sugar topping became **crème brûlée à l'érable.** Today, traditional recipes in Quebec are a blend of French, British, Scottish, and Irish cuisines. Have students find recipes on the Internet or look in cookbooks at a local library for traditional foods in Quebec. Have groups discuss how the recipes may have evolved over time. 2.2

La cuisine

In the 4th century, the Church forbade Christians to eat eggs during the 40 days of Lent. During these forty days, however, the hens kept laying eggs. People began painting the eggs and giving them away as presents. Quebec inherited the Anglo-Saxon tradition of painting eggs for Easter. Encourage students to make **tarte aux œufs** in their foods class or at home for family and friends. 1.2, 2.2

Tarte aux œufs pour 6 personnes

Pâte à tarte
2 tasses de farine
1/2 tasse de sucre
1/2 tasse de beurre
1 œuf

Garniture
3 œufs + un blanc d'œuf
2 tasses de lait
1 tasse de sucre
1 gousse de vanille (ou 1 sachet de sucre vanillé)

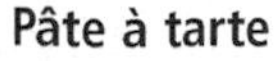

Pâte à tarte
Faire fondre le beurre. Placer la farine dans un saladier. Faire un puits. Y mettre le sucre et l'œuf. Commencer à mélanger doucement. Ajouter le beurre petit à petit. Faire une boule du mélange. Si la boule est trop beurrée, ajouter une ou deux cuillères à soupe de farine.

Garniture
Faire chauffer le lait. Dans un bol, mélanger le sucre, les œufs et le sucre vanillé. Ajouter le lait chaud petit à petit. Rouler la pâte dans le moule et badigeonner avec le blanc d'œuf. Mettre au four chaud pendant deux minutes. Retirer du four. Verser la garniture sur la pâte. Remettre au four à 425° F jusqu'à ce que la tarte soit ferme.

Listening Activity Scripts

Vocabulaire à l'œuvre 1

4 **p. 85, CD 3, Tr. 1**

1. — Camille, tu veux bien aller chercher deux baguettes, s'il te plaît?
   — Oui, j'y vais tout de suite.
2. — Camille, tu pourrais me rapporter du café si tu vas au magasin?
   — D'accord. Il te faut autre chose?
3. — Camille, n'oublie pas d'aller acheter des fruits pour le dessert.
   — Maman, je suis trop occupée. J'ai mon examen de maths demain.
4. — Aujourd'hui, je vais faire une tarte. Rapporte-moi de la farine et des fraises.
   — Je regrette mais je n'ai pas le temps. Je dois finir mes devoirs.
5. — On n'a plus de sucre. Tu pourrais aller m'en chercher un paquet?
   — Oui, papa. Tu n'as besoin de rien d'autre?

Answers to Activity 4
1. a 2. a 3. b 4. b 5. a

Grammaire à l'œuvre 1

8 **p. 86, CD 3, Tr. 2**

1. Moi, j'adore les fraises.
2. Qu'est-ce qu'il y a dans ton sandwich?
3. Tu as envie de manger du poisson ce soir?
4. Martine n'aime pas les légumes.
5. Ajoute du lait, c'est meilleur!
6. Maman a acheté des framboises au marché.
7. Julie, tu veux de l'ail dans ta salade?
8. Une pastèque et un melon, s'il vous plaît.

Answers to Activity 8
1. b 2. b 3. a 4. b 5. a 6. a 7. a 8. b

Application 1

19 **p. 90, CD 3, Tr. 3**

1. Manges-tu souvent des petits pois?
2. Papa et moi, on déteste les carottes!
3. Norbert va apporter une tarte aux cerises pour le déjeuner.
4. Les filles, vous aimez les bananes et les pêches?
5. Madame Touzeau, est-ce que vous voulez du chocolat?
6. C'est facile de faire une quiche au fromage?
7. Ma grand-mère ne mange pas de sel.

Answers to Activity 19
1. a 2. b 3. b 4. a 5. a 6. a 7. b

Vocabulaire à l'œuvre 2

23 **p. 96, CD 3, Tr. 4**

1. J'arrive au magasin à quatre heures du matin pour faire les baguettes et les croissants. Après, je fais les gâteaux et les tartes.
2. Si vous cherchez de délicieuses crevettes, venez chez moi. Mes fruits de mer sont toujours excellents.
3. Je travaille dans un supermarché. Les clients me donnent de l'argent et je mets leurs produits dans un sac en plastique.
4. Je vends du bœuf, du porc, du poulet et du saucisson.
5. Notre magasin n'est pas grand, mais on y trouve de tout—de la farine, du café, des fruits, des légumes et des produits laitiers. Nos clients n'aiment pas les hypermarchés. Ils préfèrent notre petit magasin.

Answers to Activity 23
1. e 2. c 3. d 4. b 5. a

Grammaire à l'œuvre 2

28 p. 98, CD 3, Tr. 5

1. — Antonin, tu veux du pain?
   — Oui, j'en veux bien, merci.
2. — Solène, tu reprends du poulet?
   — Oui, j'en veux. Et des pommes de terre aussi, s'il te plaît.
3. — Émilia, tu veux de la salade?
   — J'en veux bien. Merci.
4. — Quentin, tu aimes le fromage?
   — Oui, j'adore. Tu en as?
5. — Éva, tu prends de la mousse au chocolat?
   — Non, je n'en veux pas. Merci.
6. — Et toi, Magali? Tu n'as presque rien mangé, tu vas reprendre de la mousse au chocolat?
   — Non, merci. Je n'ai plus faim.

Answers to Activity 28
1. a 2. a 3. a 4. a 5. b 6. b

Application 2

39 p. 102, CD 3, Tr. 6

1. Mia achète du poisson et des crevettes.
2. Mia prend un chariot.
3. Mia achète deux tranches de jambon et des steaks.
4. Mia achète des fruits et des légumes.
5. Mia parle à l'épicière.

Answers to Activity 39
Elle est...
1. à la poissonnerie
2. au supermarché
3. à la boucherie-charcuterie
4. au marché
5. à l'épicerie

Prépare-toi pour l'examen

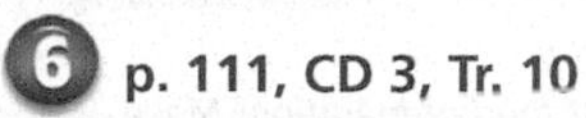

6 p. 111, CD 3, Tr. 10

Ce matin, j'ai fait les courses avec ma mère. D'abord, nous sommes allées à l'épicerie pour acheter des fruits et des légumes. Nous avons acheté des abricots, des cerises, des carottes et des champignons. Nous avons voulu acheter des pommes pour faire une tarte, mais les pommes n'étaient pas belles. Alors, nous avons décidé d'aller acheter un gâteau à la boulangerie-pâtisserie. Ensuite, nous sommes allées à la boucherie-charcuterie où nous avons acheté un poulet et du jambon. Mmmmm...nous allons bien manger ce soir!

Answers to Activity 6
Elle a acheté: des abricots, des cerises, des carottes, des champignons, un gâteau, un poulet et du jambon.
Elle est allée: à l'épicerie, à la boulangerie-pâtisserie et à la boucherie-charcuterie.

Dictée p. 112, CD 3, Tr. 10

1. Je vais prendre un kilo de haricots verts.
2. Tu joues souvent au hockey?
3. Aujourd'hui, c'est le huit mars.
4. Nous attendons dans le hall de l'hôtel.
5. Le héros du roman est très intelligent.

Révisions cumulatives chapitres 1-3

1 p. 114, CD 3, Tr. 14

1. C'est très facile à faire. Il vous faut des œufs, du sel, du poivre, du lait et des légumes.
2. Faites cuire les œufs. Coupez la salade et ajoutez de l'huile et du vinaigre. Mélangez bien. Ajoutez les œufs, le thon et les haricots verts.
3. Il vous faut du sucre, de la farine, des œufs et du beurre—et bien sûr, du chocolat.
4. Coupez les pommes et faites-les cuire pendant cinq minutes. Ajoutez le sucre.

Answers to Activity 1
1. c 2. b 3. d 4. a

50-Minute Lesson Plans

Faisons les courses

Day 1

OBJECTIVE
Ask about food preparation

Core Instruction
Chapter Opener, pp. 80–81
- See Using the Photo, p. 80. **5 min.**
- See Chapter Objectives, p. 80. **5 min.**

Vocabulaire 1, pp. 82–85
- Present **Vocabulaire 1,** pp. 82–83. See Teaching **Vocabulaire,** p. 82. **10 min.**
- Show **Télé-vocab 1. 5 min.**
- Present **Exprimons-nous!,** p. 83. **10 min.**
- Do Activities 1–2, p. 84. **10 min.**
- Present **Flash culture,** p. 84. **5 min.**

Optional Resources
- Advanced Learners, p. 83 ▲
- Special Learning Needs, p. 83 ●
- Slower Pace Learners, p. 85 ◆
- Special Learning Needs, p. 85 ●

Homework Suggestions
Cahier de vocabulaire et grammaire, pp. 25–26
@HOMETUTOR

1.2, 1.3, 4.2

Day 2

OBJECTIVE
Ask about food preparation; Make requests and respond; Use the partitive

Core Instruction
Vocabulaire 1, pp. 82–85
- Do Activity 3, p. 84. **5 min.**
- See Teaching **Exprimons-nous!,** p. 84. **10 min.**
- Play Audio CD 3, Tr. 1 for Activity 4, p. 85. **5 min.**
- Have students do Activities 5–6, p. 85. **15 min.**

Grammaire 1, pp. 86–89
- See Teaching **Grammaire,** p. 86. **10 min.**
- Do Activity 7, p. 86. **5 min.**

Optional Resources
- Multiple Intelligences, p. 87

Homework Suggestions
Study for **Quiz: Vocabulaire 1**
Cahier de vocabulaire et grammaire, p. 27
Online Practice (**my.hrw.com**)

1.1, 1.2, 1.3

Day 3

OBJECTIVE
Use the partitive

Core Instruction
Vocabulaire 1, pp. 82–85
- Review **Vocabulaire 1,** pp. 82–85. **10 min.**
- Give **Quiz: Vocabulaire 1. 20 min.**

Grammaire 1, pp. 86–89
- Show **Grammavision 1.1. 5 min.**
- Play Audio CD 3, Tr. 2 for Activity 8, p. 86. **5 min.**
- Have students do Activities 9–11, p. 87. **10 min.**

Optional Resources
- Communication (TE), p. 87
- Advanced Learners, p. 87 ▲

Homework Suggestions
Cahier de vocabulaire et grammaire, p. 28
Cahier d'activités, p. 21
Online Practice (**my.hrw.com**)

1.1, 1.2, 1.3

Day 4

OBJECTIVE
*Use the partitive; Use the pronoun **y**; Form questions*

Core Instruction
Grammaire 1, pp. 86–89
- Have students do Activity 12, p. 87. **5 min.**
- Present **Flash culture,** p. 88. **5 min.**
- See Teaching **Grammaire,** p. 88. **10 min.**
- Show **Grammavision 1.2. 5 min.**
- Have students do Activities 13–17, pp. 88–89. **15 min.**

Application 1, pp. 90–91
- Do Activity 18, p. 90. **5 min.**
- See Teaching **Un peu plus,** p. 90. **5 min.**

Optional Resources
- Slower Pace Learners, p. 89 ◆
- Special Learning Needs, p. 89 ●

Homework Suggestions
Study for **Quiz: Grammaire 1**
Cahier de vocabulaire et grammaire, p. 29
Cahier d'activités, p. 22

1.1, 1.2, 1.3, 2.2

Day 5

OBJECTIVE
Form questions

Core Instruction
Grammaire 1, pp. 86–89
- Review **Grammaire 1,** pp. 86–89. **10 min.**
- Give **Quiz: Grammaire 1. 20 min.**

Application 1, pp. 90–91
- Play Audio CD 3, Tr. 3 for Activity 19, p. 90. **5 min.**
- Have students do Activities 20–22, p. 91. **15 min.**

Optional Resources
- Communication (TE), p. 91
- Slower Pace Learners, p. 91 ◆
- Special Learning Needs, p. 91 ●

Homework Suggestions
Study for **Quiz: Application 1**
Cahier de vocabulaire et grammaire, p. 30
Cahier d'activités, p. 23
@HOMETUTOR
Online Practice (**my.hrw.com**)

1.1, 1.2, 1.3

Day 6

OBJECTIVE
Learn about francophone culture

Core Instruction
Application 1, pp. 90–91
- Review **Application 1,** pp. 90–91. **10 min.**
- Give **Quiz: Application 1. 20 min.**

Culture, pp. 92–93
- See **Culture appliquée** (TE), p. 92. **10 min.**
- See **Comparaisons et communauté** (TE), p. 92. **10 min.**

Optional Resources
- Cultures, p. 93
- Communities, p. 93
- Advanced Learners, p. 93 ▲
- Multiple Intelligences, p. 93

Homework Suggestions
Cahier d'activités, p. 24
Online Practice (**my.hrw.com**)
Finish **Culture appliquée** project

1.1, 2.1, 2.2, 4.2, 5.1, 5.2

Day 7

OBJECTIVE
Shop for groceries

Core Instruction
Vocabulaire 2, pp. 94–97
- Have students do Bell Work 3.5, p. 94. **5 min.**
- Present **Vocabulaire 2,** pp. 94–95. See Teaching **Vocabulaire,** p. 94. **10 min.**
- Show **Télé-vocab 2. 5 min.**
- Present **Exprimons-nous!,** p. 95. **10 min.**
- Play Audio CD 3, Tr. 4 for Activity 23, p. 96. **5 min.**
- Have students do Activities 24–25, p. 96. **10 min.**
- Present **Flash culture,** p. 96. **5 min.**

Optional Resources
- TPR, p. 95
- Slower Pace Learners, p. 95 ◆
- Multiple Intelligences, p. 95
- Advanced Learners, p. 97 ▲

Homework Suggestions
Cahier de vocabulaire et grammaire, pp. 31–32

1.1, 1.2, 4.2

Day 8

OBJECTIVE
*Ask where things are; Use the pronoun **en***

Core Instruction
Vocabulaire 2, pp. 94–97
- See Teaching **Exprimons-nous!,** p. 96. **10 min.**
- Have students do Activities 26–27, p. 97. **20 min.**

Grammaire 2, pp. 98–101
- See Teaching **Grammaire,** p. 98. **10 min.**
- Show **Grammavision 2.1. 5 min.**
- Play Audio CD 3, Tr. 5 for Activity 28, p. 98. **5 min.**

Optional Resources
- Communication (TE), p. 97
- Multiple Intelligences, p. 97

Homework Suggestions
Study for **Quiz: Vocabulaire 2**
Cahier de vocabulaire et grammaire, p. 33
@HOMETUTOR
Online Practice (**my.hrw.com**)

1.1, 1.2, 1.3

To edit and create your own lesson plans, see the

KEY
- ▲ Advanced Learners
- ◆ Slower Pace Learners
- ● Special Learning Needs

Day 9

OBJECTIVE
*Use the pronoun **en***

Core Instruction
Vocabulaire 2, pp. 94–97
- Review **Vocabulaire 2,** pp. 94–97. **10 min.**
- Give **Quiz: Vocabulaire 2. 20 min.**

Grammaire 2, pp. 98–101
- Have students do Activities 29–33, pp. 98–99. **20 min.**

Optional Resources
- Communication (TE), p. 99
- Advanced Learners, p. 99 ▲
- Special Learning Needs, p. 99 ●

Homework Suggestions
Cahier de vocabulaire et grammaire, p. 34
Cahier d'activités, p. 25
@HOMETUTOR
Online Practice (**my.hrw.com**)

1.1, 1.2, 1.3

Day 10

OBJECTIVE
Use object pronouns

Core Instruction
Grammaire 2, pp. 98–101
- Have students do Bell Work 3.7, p. 100. **5 min.**
- Present **Flash culture,** p. 100. **5 min.**
- See Teaching **Grammaire,** p. 100. **5 min.**
- Show **Grammavision 2.2. 5 min.**
- Have students do Activities 34–37, pp. 100–101. **20 min.**

Application 2, pp. 102–103
- Do Activity 38, p. 102. **5 min.**
- Play Audio CD 3, Tr. 6 for Activity 39, p. 102. **5 min.**

Optional Resources
- Slower Pace Learners, p. 101 ◆
- Multiple Intelligences, p. 101

Homework Suggestions
Study for **Quiz: Grammaire 2**
Cahier de vocabulaire et grammaire, p. 35
Cahier d'activités, p. 26

1.1, 1.2, 2.2

Day 11

OBJECTIVE
*Use contractions with **à** and **de***

Core Instruction
Grammaire 2, pp. 98–101
- Review **Grammaire 2,** pp. 98–101. **10 min.**
- Give **Quiz: Grammaire 2. 20 min.**

Application 2, pp. 102–103
- See Teaching **Un peu plus,** p. 102. **5 min.**
- Have students do Activities 40–43, pp. 102–103. **15 min.**

Optional Resources
- Communication (TE), p. 103
- Advanced Learners, p. 103 ▲
- Special Learning Needs, p. 103 ●

Homework Suggestions
Study for **Quiz: Application 2**
Cahier de vocabulaire et grammaire, p. 36
Cahier d'activités, p. 27
@HOMETUTOR
Online Practice (**my.hrw.com**)

1.1, 1.2, 1.3

Day 12

OBJECTIVE
Develop listening and reading skills

Core Instruction
Application 2, pp. 102–103
- Review **Application 2,** pp. 102–103. **10 min.**
- Give **Quiz: Application 2. 20 min.**

Télé-roman, pp. 104–105
- Show **Télé-roman.** See Teaching **Télé-roman,** p. 104. **5 min.**
- Have students answer the **As-tu compris?** questions, p. 105. **15 min.**

Optional Resources
- Connections, p. 104
- Gestures, p. 104
- Communication (TE), p. 105

Homework Suggestions
Online Practice (**my.hrw.com**)

1.1, 1.2, 3.2

Day 13

OBJECTIVE
Develop listening, reading, and writing skills

Core Instruction
Lecture et écriture, pp. 106–109
- See Teaching **Lecture,** p. 106. **35 min.**
- See Teaching **Espace écriture,** p. 108. **15 min.**

Optional Resources
- Applying the Strategies, p. 106
- Making Inferences, p. 106
- Cultures, p. 107
- Connections, p. 107
- Slower Pace Learners, p. 107 ◆
- Special Learning Needs, p. 107 ●
- Comparisons, p. 108
- Communities, p. 108
- Process Writing, p. 109

Homework Suggestions
Cahier d'activités, p. 28
Espace écriture, Activity 2, p. 109

1.1, 1.2, 2.1, 3.1, 4.2, 5.1

Day 14

OBJECTIVE
Develop writing skills; Review the chapter

Core Instruction
Lecture et écriture, pp. 106–109
- See Teaching **Espace écriture,** p. 108. **25 min.**

Prépare-toi pour l'examen, pp. 110–112
- Have students do Activities 1–5, pp. 110–111. **25 min.**

Optional Resources
- Writing Assessment, p. 109
- Advanced Learners, p. 109 ▲
- Multiple Intelligences, p. 109
- Reteaching, p. 110
- Fold-N-Learn, p. 110
- Oral Assessment, p. 111

Homework Suggestions
Online Practice (**my.hrw.com**)

1.2, 1.3, 2.1, 2.2, 5.1, 5.2

Day 15

OBJECTIVE
Review the chapter

Core Instruction
Prépare-toi pour l'examen, pp. 110–112
- Play Audio CD 3, Tr. 9 for Activity 6, p. 111. **5 min.**
- Have students do Activity 7, p. 111. **5 min.**
- Play Audio CD 3, Tr. 10–12 for **Lettres et sons,** p. 112. **10 min.**

Révisions cumulatives, pp. 114–115
- Play Audio CD 3, Tr. 13 for Activity 1, p. 114. **5 min.**
- Have students do Activities 2–6, pp. 114–115. **25 min.**

Optional Resources
- Chapter Review, pp. 112–113
- Online Culture Project, p. 114
- Fine Art Connection, p. 115

Homework Suggestions
Study for Chapter Test
Online Practice (**my.hrw.com**)

1.1, 1.2, 1.3, 2.2, 3.1, 3.2

Day 16/Test

Core Instruction
Chapter Test 50 min.

Optional Resources
Assessment Program
- Alternative Assessment
- Test Generator
- **Quiz: Lecture**
- **Quiz: Écriture**

Homework Suggestions
Cahier d'activités, pp. 29–30, 106–107
Online Practice (**my.hrw.com**)

50-Minute Lesson Plans

90-Minute Lesson Plans

Faisons les courses

Block 1

OBJECTIVE
Ask about food preparation; Make requests and respond

Core Instruction

Chapter Opener, pp. 80–81
- See Using the Photo, p. 80. **5 min.**
- See Chapter Objectives, p. 80. **5 min.**

Vocabulaire 1, pp. 82–85
- Present **Vocabulaire 1,** pp. 82–83. See Teaching **Vocabulaire,** p. 82. **15 min.**
- Show **Télé-vocab 1. 5 min.**
- Present **Exprimons-nous!,** p. 83. **10 min.**
- Have students do Activities 1–3, p. 84. **15 min.**
- Present **Flash culture,** p. 84. **5 min.**
- See Teaching **Exprimons-nous!,** p. 84. **10 min.**
- Play Audio CD 3, Tr. 1 for Activity 4, p. 85. **5 min.**
- Have students do Activities 5–6, p. 85. **15 min.**

Optional Resources
- Learning Tips, p. 81
- Comparisons, p. 82
- TPR, p. 83
- **Attention!,** p. 83
- Teacher Note, p. 83
- French for Spanish Speakers, p. 83
- Advanced Learners, p. 83 ▲
- Special Learning Needs, p. 83 ●
- Cultures, p. 84
- Communication (TE), p. 85
- Slower Pace Learners, p. 85 ◆
- Special Learning Needs, p. 85 ●

Homework Suggestions
Study for **Quiz: Vocabulaire 1**
Cahier de vocabulaire et grammaire, pp. 25–27
@HOMETUTOR
Online Practice (**my.hrw.com**)
1.1, 1.2, 1.3, 2.2, 4.1, 4.2

Block 2

OBJECTIVE
*Use the partitive; Use the pronoun **y***

Core Instruction

Vocabulaire 1, pp. 82–85
- Review **Vocabulaire 1,** pp. 82–85. **10 min.**
- Give **Quiz: Vocabulaire 1. 20 min.**

Grammaire 1, pp. 86–89
- See Teaching **Grammaire,** p. 86. **5 min.**
- Show **Grammavision 1.1. 5 min.**
- Have students do Activity 7, p. 86. **5 min.**
- Play Audio CD 3, Tr. 2 for Activity 8, p. 86. **5 min.**
- Have students do Activities 9–12, p. 87. **15 min.**
- Present **Flash culture,** p. 88. **5 min.**
- See Teaching **Grammaire,** p. 88. **5 min.**
- Show **Grammavision 1.2. 5 min.**
- Have students do Activities 13–15, pp. 88–89. **10 min.**

Optional Resources
- Cultures, p. 86
- Communication (TE), p. 87
- Advanced Learners, p. 87 ▲
- Multiple Intelligences, p. 87
- Connections, p. 89
- Slower Pace Learners, p. 89 ◆
- Special Learning Needs, p. 89 ●

Homework Suggestions
Study for **Quiz: Grammaire 1**
Cahier de vocabulaire et grammaire, pp. 28–29
Cahier d'activités, pp. 21–22
@HOMETUTOR
Online Practice (**my.hrw.com**)
1.1, 1.2, 1.3, 2.2, 3.2

Block 3

OBJECTIVE
*Use the pronoun **y**; Form questions; Learn about francophone culture*

Core Instruction

Grammaire 1, pp. 86–89
- Have students do Activities 16–17, p. 89. **10 min.**
- Review **Grammaire 1,** pp. 86–89. **10 min.**
- Give **Quiz: Grammaire 1. 20 min.**

Application 1, pp. 90–91
- Have students do Activity 18, p. 90. **5 min.**
- See Teaching **Un peu plus,** p. 90. **5 min.**
- Play Audio CD 3, Tr. 3 for Activity 19, p. 90. **5 min.**
- Have students do Activities 20–22, p. 91. **15 min.**

Culture, pp. 92–93
- See **Culture appliquée** (TE), p. 92. **10 min.**
- See **Comparaisons et communauté** (TE), p. 92. **10 min.**

Optional Resources
- Communication (TE), p. 89
- Communication (TE), p. 91
- Slower Pace Learners, p. 91 ◆
- Special Learning Needs, p. 91 ●
- Cultures, p. 93
- Communities, p. 93
- Advanced Learners, p. 93 ▲
- Multiple Intelligences, p. 93

Homework Suggestions
Study for **Quiz: Application 1**
Cahier de vocabulaire et grammaire, p. 30
Cahier d'activités, pp. 23–24
Online Practice (**my.hrw.com**)
Finish **Culture appliquée** project
1.1, 1.2, 1.3, 2.1, 2.2, 4.2, 5.1, 5.2

Block 4

OBJECTIVE
Shop for groceries; Ask where things are

Core Instruction

Application 1, pp. 90–91
- Review **Application 1,** pp. 90–91. **10 min.**
- Give **Quiz: Application 1. 20 min.**

Vocabulaire 2, pp. 94–97
- Present **Vocabulaire 2,** pp. 94–95. See Teaching **Vocabulaire,** p. 94. **10 min.**
- Show **Télé-vocab 2. 5 min.**
- Present **Exprimons-nous!,** p. 95. **5 min.**
- Play Audio CD 3, Tr. 4 for Activity 23, p. 96. **5 min.**
- Have students do Activities 24–25, p. 96. **10 min.**
- Present **Flash culture,** p. 96. **5 min.**
- See Teaching **Exprimons-nous!,** p. 96. **10 min.**
- Have students do Activities 26–27, p. 97. **10 min.**

Optional Resources
- Teacher Note, p. 94
- TPR, p. 95
- **Attention!,** p. 95
- Cultures, p. 95
- **Proverbes,** p. 95
- Slower Pace Learners, p. 95 ◆
- Multiple Intelligences, p. 95
- Cultures, p. 97
- Communication (TE), p. 97
- Advanced Learners, p. 97 ▲
- Multiple Intelligences, p. 97

Homework Suggestions
Study for **Quiz: Vocabulaire 2**
Cahier de vocabulaire et grammaire, pp. 31–33
@HOMETUTOR
Online Practice (**my.hrw.com**)
1.1, 1.2, 1.3, 2.1, 4.2

To edit and create your own lesson plans, see the **Teacher One Stop™**

KEY
- ▲ Advanced Learners
- ◆ Slower Pace Learners
- ● Special Learning Needs

Block 5

OBJECTIVE
*Use the pronoun **en;** Use object pronouns*

Core Instruction
Vocabulaire 2, pp. 94–97
- Review **Vocabulaire 2,** pp. 94–97. **10 min.**
- Give **Quiz: Vocabulaire 2.** **20 min.**

Grammaire 2, pp. 98–101
- See Teaching **Grammaire,** p. 98. **10 min.**
- Show **Grammavision 2.1.** **5 min.**
- Play Audio CD 3, Tr. 5 for Activity 28, p. 98. **5 min.**
- Have students do Activities 29–33, pp. 98–99. **15 min.**
- Present **Flash culture,** p. 100. **5 min.**
- See Teaching **Grammaire,** p. 100. **5 min.**
- Show **Grammavision 2.2.** **5 min.**
- Have students do Activities 34–35, pp. 100–101. **10 min.**

Optional Resources
- Comparisons, p. 99
- Communication (TE), p. 99
- Advanced Learners, p. 99 ▲
- Special Learning Needs, p. 99 ●
- **Attention!,** p. 100
- French for Spanish Speakers, p. 101
- Slower Pace Learners, p. 101 ◆
- Multiple Intelligences, p. 101

Homework Suggestions
Study for **Quiz: Grammaire 2**
Cahier de vocabulaire et grammaire, pp. 34–35
Cahier d'activités, pp. 25–26
HOMETUTOR
Online Practice (**my.hrw.com**)
1.1, 1.2, 1.3, 2.2, 4.1, 4.2

Block 6

OBJECTIVE
*Use object pronouns; Use contractions with **à** and **de;** Develop listening and reading skills*

Core Instruction
Grammaire 2, pp. 98–101
- Have students do Activities 36–37, p. 101. **10 min.**
- Review **Grammaire 2,** pp. 98–101. **10 min.**
- Give **Quiz: Grammaire 2.** **20 min.**

Application 2, pp. 102–103
- Have students do Activity 38, p. 102. **5 min.**
- Play Audio CD 3, Tr. 6 for Activity 39, p. 102. **5 min.**
- See Teaching **Un peu plus,** p. 102. **5 min.**
- Have students do Activities 40–43, pp. 102–103. **15 min.**

Télé-roman, pp. 104–105
- Show **Télé-roman.** See Teaching **Télé-roman,** p. 104. **5 min.**
- Have students answer the **As-tu compris?** questions, p. 105. **15 min.**

Optional Resources
- Communication (TE), p. 101
- Communication (TE), p. 103
- Advanced Learners, p. 103 ▲
- Special Learning Needs, p. 103 ●
- Connections, p. 104
- Gestures, p. 104
- Communication (TE), p. 105

Homework Suggestions
Study for **Quiz: Application 2**
Cahier de vocabulaire et grammaire, p. 36
Cahier d'activités, p. 27
Online Practice (**my.hrw.com**)
1.1, 1.2, 1.3, 3.2

Block 7

OBJECTIVE
Develop listening, reading, and writing skills; Review the chapter

Core Instruction
Application 2, pp. 102–103
- Review **Application 2,** pp. 102–103. **10 min.**
- Give **Quiz: Application 2.** **20 min.**

Lecture et écriture, pp. 106–109
- See Teaching **Lecture,** p. 106. **20 min.**
- See Teaching **Espace écriture,** p. 108. **30 min.**

Prépare-toi pour l'examen, pp. 110–112
- Have students do Activities 1–3, p. 110. **10 min.**

Optional Resources
- Applying the Strategies, p. 106
- Making Inferences, p. 106
- Cultures, p. 107
- Connections, p. 107
- Slower Pace Learners, p. 107 ◆
- Special Learning Needs, p. 107 ●
- Comparisons, p. 108
- Communities, p. 108
- Process Writing, p. 109
- Writing Assessment, p. 109
- Advanced Learners, p. 109 ▲
- Multiple Intelligences, p. 109
- Reteaching, p. 110

Homework Suggestions
Study for Chapter Test
Cahier d'activités, p. 28
Espace écriture, Activity 2, p. 109
Online Practice (**my.hrw.com**)
1.2, 1.3, 2.1, 3.1, 4.2, 5.1, 5.2

Block 8

OBJECTIVE
Review and assess the chapter

Core Instruction
Prépare-toi pour l'examen, pp. 110–112
- Have students do Activities 4–5, p. 111. **5 min.**
- Play Audio CD 3, Tr. 9 for Activity 6, p. 111. **5 min.**
- Have students do Activity 7, p. 111. **5 min.**
- Play Audio CD 2, Tr. 10–12 for **Lettres et sons,** p. 112. **5 min.**

Chapter Test **50 min.**
Révisions cumulatives, pp. 114–115
- Play Audio CD 3, Tr. 13 for Activity 1, p. 114. **5 min.**
- Have students do Activities 2–6, pp. 114–115. **15 min.**

Optional Resources
- TPRS, p. 110
- Fold-N-Learn, p. 110
- Oral Assessment, p. 111
- Game, p. 112
- Chapter Review, pp. 112–113
- Teacher to Teacher, pp. 113, 114
- Online Culture Project, p. 114
- Fine Art Connection, p. 115

Homework Suggestions
Cahier d'activités, pp. 29–30, 106–107
Online Practice (**my.hrw.com**)
1.1, 1.2, 1.3, 2.1, 2.2, 3.1, 3.2

Chapter Opener

Meeting the National Standards

Communication
Communication, pp. 85, 87, 89, 91, 97, 99, 101, 103
À ton tour, p. 115

Cultures
Flash culture, pp. 84, 88, 96, 100
Comparaisons, p. 93
Practices and Perspectives, pp. 93, 95, 97, 107
Products and Perspectives, pp. 84, 86

Connections
Acquiring Information, p. 89
Visual Learners, p. 104
Math Link, p. 107

Comparisons
Comparaisons, p. 93
Comparing and Contrasting, pp. 82, 99, 108

Communities
Communauté, p. 93
Community Link, p. 93
Family Link, p. 108

Using the Photo

Like these students, many people in Quebec purchase their food from small deli-style grocers which often offer high-quality fresh fruits and vegetables, a variety of fresh breads, and many types of meat. Also available in most corner stores is Quebec's famous maple syrup, **sirop d'érable,** for use on top of pancakes and waffles or boiled down into sweet candies to be sold as gifts. Ask students to describe a specialty store or market near where they live. 4.2

Vocabulaire supplémentaire

Students might use these terms to discuss the photo.

le chariot *cart*
la citrouille *pumpkin*
l'étagère *shelf*
frais *fresh*
le tonneau *barrel*

chapitre 3

Faisons les courses

Objectifs

In this chapter, you will learn to
- ask about food preparation
- make requests
- shop for groceries
- ask where things are

And you will use and review
- the partitive
- the pronoun **y**
- question formation
- the pronoun **en**
- placement of object pronouns
- contractions with **à** and **de**

Que vois-tu sur la photo?
Où sont ces jeunes?
Qu'est-ce qu'ils font?
Et toi, est-ce que tu fais souvent les courses?

ACTFL 21st Century Skills

Communication:	SE: pp. 89, 91, 103, 111; TE: pp. 85, 87, 97, 107
Collaboration:	SE: pp. 87, 115; TE: pp. 85, 87, 97, 107 (Financial Literacy)
Critical Thinking and Problem Solving:	TE: pp. 82, 93, 104, 106, 108, 109
Creativity and Innovation:	SE: p. 115; TE: pp. 85, 87, 93, 95, 103, 109
Information Literacy:	SE: p. 92; TE: pp. 82, 89 (Global Awareness), 91, 93, 95 (Civic Literacy)
Leadership and Responsibility:	TE: pp. 83, 93, 109

Chapter Opener

TEACHER TOOLS
- Interactive Whiteboard Lessons
- Generate Success!

ALSO AVAILABLE...
- Online Workbooks
- French InterActive Reader

FRENCH ON THE GO!
- Performance Space
- Holt McDougal French Apps
- *Bien dit!* eTextbook

- Télé-vocab 1
- Grammavision 1
- Télé-vocab 2
- Grammavision 2
- Télé-roman

Une épicerie, à Québec

LISTENING PRACTICE — Language Lab and Classroom Activities

Vocabulaire
- Activity 4, p. 85, CD 3, Tr. 1
- **Télé-vocab 1,** p. 82, DVD Tutor
- Activity 23, p. 96, CD 3, Tr. 4
- **Télé-vocab 2,** p. 94, DVD Tutor

Grammaire
- Activity 8, p. 86, CD 3, Tr. 2
- **Grammavision 1,** pp. 86, 88, DVD Tutor
- Activity 28, p. 98, CD 3, Tr. 5
- **Grammavision 2,** pp. 98, 100, DVD Tutor

Application
- Activity 19, p. 90, CD 3, Tr. 3
- Activity 39, p. 102, CD 3, Tr. 6

Prépare-toi pour l'examen
- Activity 6, p. 111, CD 3, Tr. 10

Révisions cumulatives
- Activity 1, p. 114, CD 3, Tr. 14

Télé-roman
- p. 104, DVD Tutor

Lecture
- p. 106, CD 3, Tr. 7

Variations littéraires
- p. 386, CD 3, Tr. 8–9

Lettres et sons
- p. 112, CD 3, Tr. 11–13

Resources

Planning:
Lesson Planner
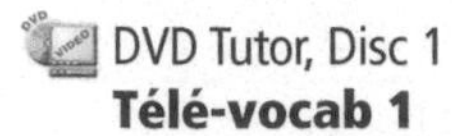
Teacher One Stop

Presentation:
Projectable Transparencies **Vocabulaire 3.1, 3.2**
DVD Tutor, Disc 1 **Télé-vocab 1**
Interactive Whiteboard Lessons

Practice:
Cahier de vocabulaire et grammaire
Differentiated Practice and Assessment CD-ROM
Independent Study Guide
Media Guide
Projectable Transparencies Bell Work 3.1
@HOMETUTOR
Holt McDougal French Apps

Bell Work

Use Bell Work 3.1 in the *Projectable Transparencies* or write this activity on the board.

Answer each question with a negative expression.

1. **Est-ce que tu fais quelque chose ce soir?**
2. **Est-ce que Lucas veut encore danser?**
3. **Est-ce que tes amis sont déjà allés au Japon?**
4. **Est-ce que Juliette a déjà acheté le cadeau pour Astrid?** 1.2

Comparisons

Comparing and Contrasting

The photo features the **École de l'Hôtelier** in Quebec City. Have students research information on both a French and an American culinary school and prepare a presentation to contrast the two schools. 4.2

Objectifs
- to ask about food preparation
- to make requests

Vocabulaire à l'œuvre 1

Télé-vocab

On prépare à manger à Québec!

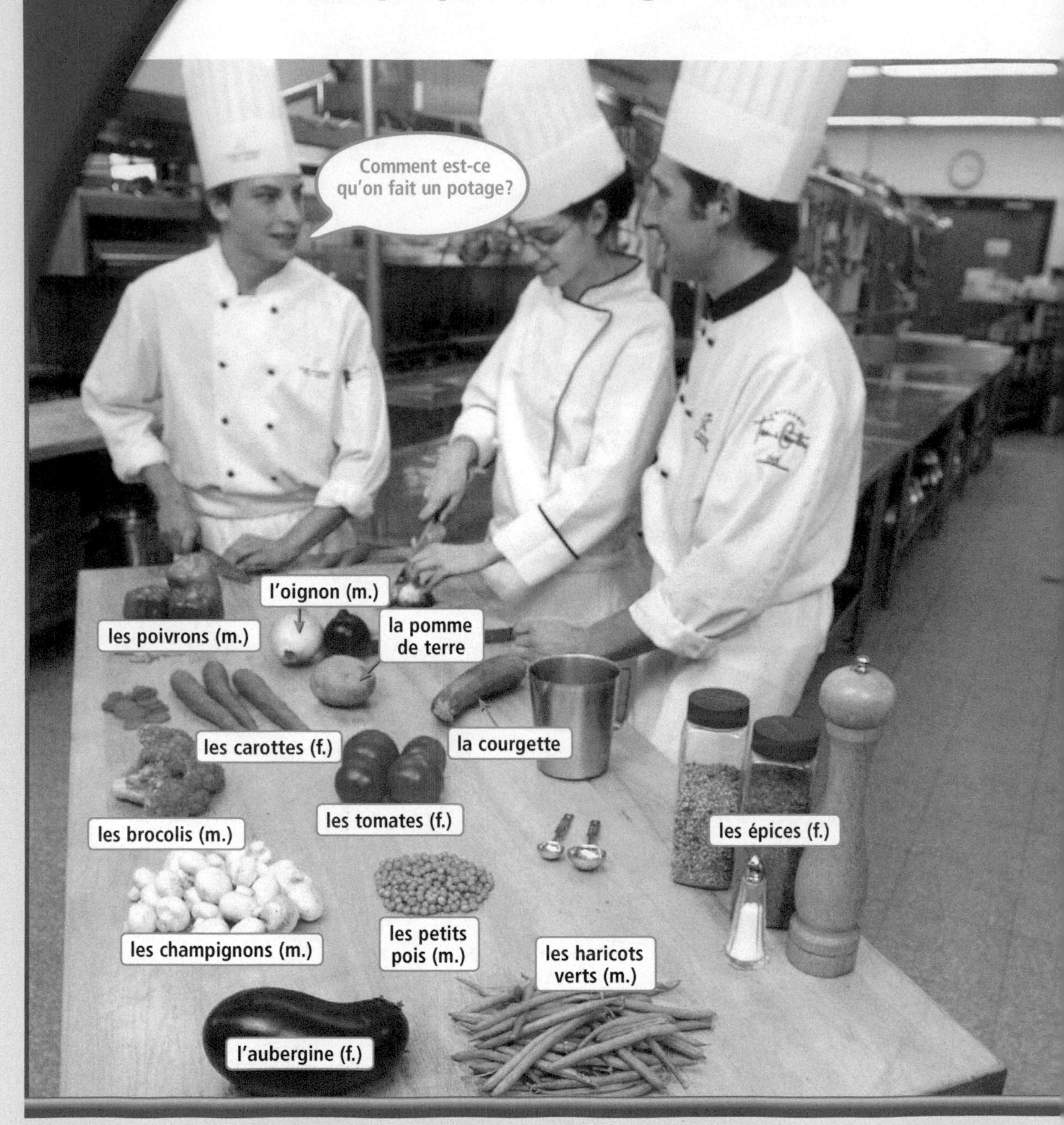

Core Instruction

TEACHING VOCABULAIRE

1. Introduce the vocabulary with transparencies **Vocabulaire 3.1** and **3.2** and model the pronunciation of each word using expressions in **Exprimons-nous! (2 min.)**
2. Ask students about the items. **Est-ce qu'il y a des tomates dans une salade? Le sel et le poivre, sont-ils des fruits? (3 min.)**
3. On the board, draw two columns with the heads **C'est simple** and **C'est compliqué.** Bring in magazine pictures of some common French foods (**mousse au chocolat, omelette, soupe, bœuf bourgignon, glace**). Hold up each picture and ask **C'est simple ou c'est compliqué à faire?** Have students take turns posting the pictures under the correct heading. **(2 min.)**

Télé-vocab 1

For a video presentation of this vocabulary, see the *DVD Tutor.*

Télé-vocab

Les fruits

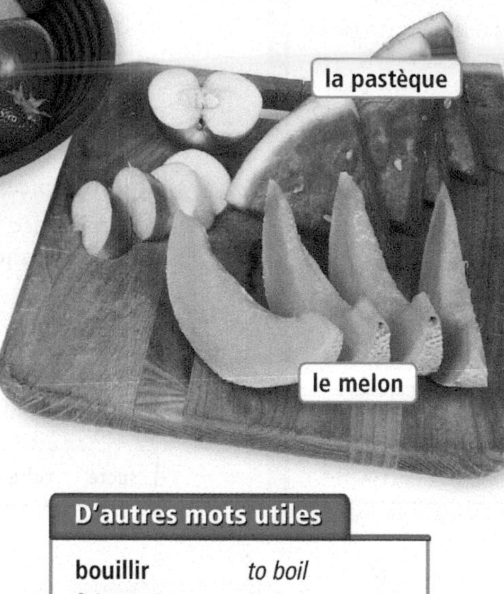

Online Practice
my.hrw.com
Vocabulaire 1 practice

Dans la cuisine

D'autres mots utiles

bouillir	*to boil*
faire cuire	*to bake, to cook*
le four	*oven*
la cuisinière	*stove*
la farine	*flour*
le sucre	*sugar*
la laitue	*lettuce*

Exprimons-nous!

To ask about food preparation	
Comment est-ce qu'on fait une salade? *How do you make . . . ?*	**Coupe** les tomates. **Ajoute** de l'huile d'olive, du sel et du poivre. **Mélange** bien. *Cut . . . Add . . . Stir/Mix . . .*
C'est facile de faire une mousse au chocolat? *Is it easy to make . . . ?*	Oui, **c'est très simple.** *. . . it's very simple.* Non, **c'est compliqué.** *. . . it's complicated.*
Qu'est-ce qu'il y a dans une omelette? *What's in . . . ?*	**Il y a** des œufs, du lait, du sel et du poivre. *There is/are . . .*

Vocabulaire et grammaire, pp. 25–27 Online Workbooks

▸ **Vocabulaire supplémentaire**—Dans la cuisine, **pp. R17–R18**

TPR — Total Physical Response

Have students respond to these commands.

Lève-toi si tu aimes les **fruits.**

Assieds-toi si tu préfères les **légumes.**

Lève le doigt si tu manges souvent du **brocoli.**

Lève la main si tu aimes mieux les **haricots verts.**

Mets une main sur la tête si tu es allergique aux **fraises.**

1.2

Common Error Alert — ATTENTION !

Pronunciation of the words **œuf** and **œufs** is problematic for students. In the singular form the *f* is pronounced. In the plural form the last two letters are silent.

Teacher Note

Point out to students that the infinitive can be used as an imperative in French. They will often see this in recipes, instruction manuals, and so on.

French for Spanish Speakers

Ask Spanish speakers which Spanish words they think may be cognates. **(framboise/frambuesa, fraise/fresa, cerise/cereza, banane/banana)** It may be less obvious to students to see the connection between **poire/pera,** but explain that sometimes they can predict the meaning of French words that have the **oi** [wa] vowel combination if they substitute a Spanish *e* [e] vowel sound. **(loi / foi, ley / fe)** Ask students to guess the cognates of the words **roi** and **voisin.** **(rey** and **vecino)** 4.1

Differentiated Instruction

ADVANCED LEARNERS

Invite a local chef, preferably from a French restaurant, to give a cooking demonstration in your class. Ask the chef to use ingredients in **Vocabulaire 1** if possible. As an alternative, ask volunteers from upper-level classes to present the demonstration. Have students take notes in French on the ingredients and the steps involved in preparing the dish. 1.2

SPECIAL LEARNING NEEDS

Students with Auditory Impairments Ask students who use sign language to share with the class how nouns with gender are organized. Nouns with male gender are signed near the right temple, and nouns with female gender are signed near the right side of the chin. Ask students to teach the class the signs for the words in **Vocabulaire 1.** Fingerspelling the proper French article **(la, le, les)** to indicate gender is a good memory tool.

Vocabulaire 1

Resources

Planning:
Lesson Planner
Teacher One Stop

Presentation:
Projectable Transparencies **Vocabulaire 3.1, 3.2**
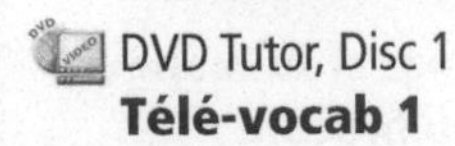
DVD Tutor, Disc 1 **Télé-vocab 1**
Interactive Whiteboard Lessons

Practice:
Cahier de vocabulaire et grammaire
Differentiated Practice and Assessment CD-ROM
Independent Study Guide
Media Guide
Audio CD 3, Tr. 1
@HOMETUTOR
Holt McDougal French Apps

2 Answers

1. sucre
2. œufs
3. cuillerées
4. Couper
5. cuire
6. four

Cultures

Products and Perspectives

Some apple producers in Quebec open their orchards to the public in the fall and allow people to harvest their own apples. **L'autocueillette des pommes** is an enjoyable way to sample many varieties of apples and to celebrate the change of seasons. Ask students if they know of any places in your area where people can pick their own apples or other fruit. 2.2

Flash culture

Les Québécois, comme les Français, utilisent le système métrique pour les mesures. Ils utilisent les mètres et kilomètres pour mesurer les distances et les celcius pour les températures. Ils utilisent les grammes et les kilogrammes pour mesurer les poids. Ils utilisent les litres pour mesurer les liquides.

Est-ce que tu utilises le système métrique? Dans quelles circonstances? 4.2

1 L'intrus 1.2

Lisons Indique le terme qui n'appartient pas à la liste.

1. a. l'abricot (b.) le champignon c. la pêche d. la pastèque
2. (a.) le sucre b. la cuillerée c. la tasse d. la cuisinière
3. a. le poivron b. l'oignon (c.) la pomme d. l'aubergine
4. a. l'ail (b.) la farine c. les épices d. l'huile d'olive
5. a. la cerise b. la framboise (c.) la banane d. la fraise

2 Gâteau aux pommes de grand-mère 1.2

Lisons/Écrivons Tu as décidé de faire un gâteau québécois. Complète la recette en t'aidant des mots de la boîte.

sucre cuire four couper œufs cuillerées

Gâteau aux pommes de grand-mère

3 tasses de farine
1 tasse de ___(1)___
5 pommes
5 ___(2)___
3 ___(3)___ de beurre

Faire fondre *(melt)* le beurre. ___(4)___ les pommes. Faire ___(5)___ pendant 5 min. Beurrer un moule. Verser les pommes dans le moule. Battre les œufs. Ajouter les ingrédients secs. Étendre la pâte dans le moule. Mettre au ___(6)___ 30 min. Servir chaud avec du sirop d'érable.

3 L'école de cuisine 1.3

Écrivons Tu aimes faire la cuisine et ton ami(e) ne fait jamais la cuisine! Choisis un plat (une salade, une pizza, etc.) et écris-lui un e-mail pour expliquer comment on prépare ce plat.

MODÈLE Faire une omelette, c'est facile. Mélange les œufs...

Core Instruction

TEACHING EXPRIMONS-NOUS!

1. Show pictures of items in **Vocabulaire 1.** Tell students what you want to do and ask them to get the pictured item for you. **Je voudrais faire une salade de fruits. Tu veux bien aller m'acheter...? (Tu me rapportes...?)** Have students respond **oui** or **non,** according to whether each item should be added. Model responding favorably or unfavorably to requests. **(5 min.)**
2. Continue with other questions and have students name any other foods that they would include. **Vous n'avez besoin de rien d'autre? Il vous faut autre chose? (5 min.)**

Exprimons-nous!

To make requests	To respond
Tu veux bien aller m'acheter des poires? *Can you/Would you mind . . . ?*	**Oui, j'y vais tout de suite.** *Yes, I'll go there right away.*
Tu me rapportes de la farine? *Can you bring me . . . ?*	**Non, je regrette mais** je n'ai pas le temps. *No, I am sorry but . . .* Désolé(e), **je suis trop occupé(e).** *. . . I'm too busy.*
Rapporte(-moi) de la margarine, s'il te plaît. *Bring (me) . . .*	Oui, d'accord. **Tu n'as besoin de rien d'autre?** *. . . Do you need anything else?*
N'oublie pas d'acheter des cerises. *Don't forget . . .*	Bon. **Il te faut autre chose?** *. . . Do you need anything else?*

Vocabulaire et grammaire, *pp. 25–27* — Online Workbooks

4 Écoutons CD 3, Tr. 1 1.2

Les parents de Camille lui demandent toujours d'aller faire des courses. Écoute les conversations suivantes et décide si Camille **a) accepte** ou **b) refuse.** 1. a 2. a 3. b 4. b 5. a

5 D'accord ou pas d'accord 1.2

Écrivons Les parents de tes amis leur demandent d'aller faire des courses. Écris leurs réponses.

MODÈLE Nicolas, tu peux aller acheter du beurre? (non, finir ses devoirs)
Je n'ai pas le temps. Je dois finir mes devoirs.

1. Karine, rapporte-moi de la farine, s'il te plaît! (oui)
2. Yasmina, tu peux acheter des tomates? (non, étudier)
3. Hugo, va acheter des fraises pour ma tarte. (oui)
4. Romain, peux-tu acheter des champignons? (non, faire les devoirs)
5. Agathe, tu peux me rapporter des pommes de terre du marché? (non, aller à la bibliothèque)

Entre copains

la bouffe	*grub*
bouffer	*to chow*
la flotte	*water*
les nouilles	*noodles*
les patates	*potatoes*

Digital performance space

Communication

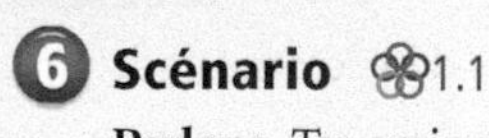

6 Scénario 1.1

Parlons Tes amis et toi préparez une grande «bouffe» pour fêter ton anniversaire. Décidez ensemble ce que vous allez préparer et faites une liste. Ensuite, demandez à deux amis d'aller acheter les ingrédients.

MODÈLE **—J'aime le chocolat. Comment est-ce qu'on fait... ?**

4 Script

1. — Camille, tu veux bien aller chercher deux baguettes, s'il te plaît?
   — Oui, j'y vais tout de suite.
2. — Camille, tu pourrais me rapporter du café si tu vas au magasin?
   — D'accord. Il te faut autre chose?
3. — Camille, n'oublie pas d'aller acheter des fruits pour le dessert.
   — Maman, je suis trop occupée. J'ai mon examen de maths demain.
4. — Aujourd'hui, je vais faire une tarte. Rapporte-moi de la farine et des fraises.
   — Je regrette mais je n'ai pas le temps. Je dois finir mes devoirs.
5. — On n'a plus de sucre. Tu pourrais aller m'en chercher un paquet?
   — Oui, papa. Tu n'as besoin de rien d'autre?

Communication

Pair Activity: Interpersonal

Have students write out a real or imaginary recipe. Then have students tell a partner how to make the dish. The partner should give an opinion of the dish. Have the first student write the partner's name and opinion. Ask students to continue in this manner until they have three opinions about their recipe. 1.1

Differentiated Instruction

SLOWER PACE LEARNERS

2 Activate students' prior knowledge of baking before they begin the activity. Ask them to describe the steps involved in baking a pie. Write the steps on the board. Then, after students have completed the activity, have them compare the steps in the activity recipe with the steps written on the board. 1.3

SPECIAL LEARNING NEEDS

2 Students with Speech Impairments It may be beneficial for students to preview the vocabulary and activity directions. Prior to assigning the activity, go over the directions and words with students personally. With this extra time to practice the words and become familiar and confident about the activity, students will be better able to complete the task.

Assess

Assessment Program

Quiz: Vocabulaire 1

Alternative Assessment

Differentiated Practice and Assessment CD-ROM

Online Assessment
my.hrw.com

Test Generator 

Resources

Planning:
Lesson Planner
Teacher One Stop

Presentation:
DVD Tutor, Disc 1
Grammavision 1.1

Practice:
Grammar Tutor for Students of French, Chapter 3
Cahier de vocabulaire et grammaire
Differentiated Practice and Assessment CD-ROM
Cahier d'activités
Independent Study Guide
Media Guide
Projectable Transparencies
Bell Work 3. 2
Audio CD 3, Tr. 2
HOMETUTOR

Bell Work

Use Bell Work 3.2 in the *Projectable Transparencies* or write this activity on the board.

Choose the food in each group that does not belong.

1. a. petits pois b. courgettes c. fraises
2. a. poivron b. framboises c. cerises
3. a. laitue b. melon c. pastèque
4. a. aubergine b. pomme c. poivron
5. a. pêche b. abricot c. champignon

Cultures

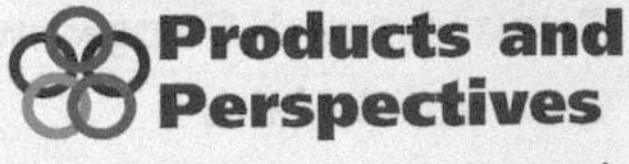

La ratatouille is a traditional vegetable stew in Provence. The word is derived from the verb **touiller,** meaning *to stir.* Can students guess the meaning of **fondre** based on their knowledge of fondue cooking? *(to melt)* 2.2

Objectifs
- the partitive
- the pronoun *y*

Grammaire à l'œuvre 1

Grammavision

Révisions The partitive

1 The **partitive articles** express the idea of *some* or *any,* or a *part/portion* of a whole item.

Masculine	Feminine	Sing word beginning with a vowel	Plural
du sucre	de la farine	de l'huile	des petits pois

—Tu veux **du** gâteau ou **de la** tarte?
—*Do you want (some) cake or (some) pie?*

2 The forms of the partitive change to **de (d')** in a negative sentence and after words of quantity like **beaucoup.**

Il y a **de la** farine, mais il n'y a pas **d'**ail.
Karine mange beaucoup **de** cerises!

3 To talk about a whole item, use the indefinite article **un, une,** or **des.**

Nous achetons **une** tarte aux pommes.

Vocabulaire et grammaire, *pp. 28–29*
Cahier d'activités, *pp. 21–23*

Déjà vu!

The indefinite articles are **un, une,** and **des.** They mean *a, an,* or *some.* The definite articles are **le, la,** and **les.** They mean *the.* To say that you like something, use a definite article.

Ariane achète **une** tarte.
J'aime **les** fraises.

7 Parlons de cuisine 1.2

Lisons Choisis l'article qui convient pour compléter chaque phrase.

1. Marianne et ses amis aiment bien _______ salade.
   a. de la **(b.)** la **c.** les
2. Je mange _______ légumes, mais pas de viande.
   (a.) des **b.** de **c.** un
3. Il y a beaucoup _______épices dans ces légumes.
   a. des **b.** de **(c.)** d'
4. Je vais préparer une tarte et il me faut _______ sucre.
   a. des **(b.)** du **c.** de la
5. Il n'y a pas _______ tomates dans cette salade.
   a. de l' **(b.)** de **c.** une

1. b 2. b 3. a 4. b 5. a 6. a 7. a 8. b

8 Écoutons CD 3, Tr. 2 1.2

Des amis parlent au café. Écoute chaque phrase et dis si **a) il y a un partitif** ou si **b) il n'y a pas de partitif.**

Core Instruction

Teaching Grammaire

1. Re-introduce the partitive. Go over the use of **du, de la, de l',** and **des** to talk about any or some of an item. Remind students to use **de** or **d'** in a negative sentence or after a quantity. **(2 min.)**
2. Give one large note card to each of six students and have them write a partitive article on the card. Ask those six students to come to the front of the room and hold up their card. Show a picture of a vocabulary word and say either **Je mange... (Je ne mange pas...)** or **Je prépare... (Je ne prépare pas...).** Ask volunteers to point to the student who is holding the correct article and to finish your sentence. **(3 min.)**

Grammavision

For a video presentation of the partitive, see the *DVD Tutor.*

Grammavision

Online Practice
my.hrw.com
Grammaire 1 practice

9 Une recette 1.2

Écrivons Ton ami québécois veut préparer une recette française pour sa famille. Complète la recette avec les articles définis, indéfinis ou partitifs qui conviennent.

La ratatouille

Ingrédients: __1__ aubergines, __2__ courgettes, __3__ poivron vert, __4__ poivron rouge, __5__ oignon, __6__ tomates, __7__ ail, __8__ huile d'olive

Préparation: Couper __9__ légumes en morceaux. Faire revenir (*sauté*) __10__ ail et __11__ oignon dans une poêle (*frying pan*). Ajouter __12__ légumes, bien mélanger et cuire 30 minutes. Ajouter __13__ épices, si vous aimez!

1. des
2. des
3. un
4. un
5. un
6. des
7. de l'
8. de l'
9. les
10. l'
11. l'
12. les
13. des

10 Qu'est-ce qu'il faut pour faire... ? 1.2

Écrivons Fais une liste de trois ingrédients dont on a besoin pour préparer chaque plat. Utilise le partitif.

1. un sandwich au jambon
2. une tarte aux fruits
3. un steak frites
4. une omelette
5. une pizza végétarienne
6. une salade

11 Madame Lionnet fait les courses 1.3

Parlons Décris ce que madame Lionnet a acheté au supermarché. Ensuite, essaie de deviner ce qu'elle va préparer pour le dîner ce soir.

MODÈLE Il y a du beurre... À mon avis, madame Lionnet va préparer/servir...

Digital performance space

Communication

12 Interview 1.1

Parlons Qu'est-ce que les élèves de ta classe aiment bien manger? Demande à plusieurs camarades ce qu'ils mangent souvent au petit-déjeuner, au déjeuner et au dîner. Prends des notes, puis compare tes notes avec celles d'autres camarades pour voir quels sont les plats les plus populaires.

**MODÈLE —Norman, qu'est-ce que tu manges au petit-déjeuner?
—Moi, je mange des fruits et je bois du jus d'orange.**

8 Script

1. Moi, j'adore les fraises.
2. Qu'est-ce qu'il y a dans ton sandwich?
3. Tu as envie de manger du poisson ce soir?
4. Martine n'aime pas les légumes.
5. Ajoute du lait, c'est meilleur!
6. Maman a acheté des framboises au marché.
7. Julie, tu veux de l'ail dans ta salade?
8. Une pastèque et un melon, s'il vous plaît.

10 Possible Answers

1. du pain, du jambon, du fromage
2. de la farine, du sucre, des framboises
3. un steak, des pommes de terre, de l'huile
4. des œufs, du fromage, des champignons
5. des tomates, de l'ail, des oignons
6. de la laitue, des carottes, de l'huile

11 Possible Answer

Il y a du beurre, un poulet, de la laitue, des pommes de terre, un oignon, des courgettes, de l'huile, de la farine, du pain, des tomates, de l'ail et des poires. À mon avis, madame Lionnet va préparer une salade, du poulet avec des légumes et des pommes de terre. Elle va aussi faire une tarte aux poires.

Communication

12 Pair Activity: Interpersonal

Ask students what pizza toppings they like. List the toppings with the definite articles on the board. Then have partners role-play ordering a pizza. The student placing the order should use the partitive and the student taking the order should write down exactly what is being ordered. Ask students to also talk about the price. Have partners change roles. 1.1

Differentiated Instruction

ADVANCED LEARNERS

Provide groups of students with copies of simple recipes in English. Have groups translate their recipe into French, leaving a blank space for each partitive and definite article. Make copies of their recipes and distribute them to the class. Have students fill in the articles on their classmates' recipes and exchange to peer check. Then compile all the recipes into a class cookbook. 1.2

MULTIPLE INTELLIGENCES

Linguistic Make a connection between this presentation of the partitive and other situations in which a portion of a whole item would be discussed. Ask students to create a poster that illustrates other uses of the partitive other than with portions of food. They may use sentences that describe part of a book, some of the day, part of the year, preference for some music, or other situations in which the partitive is used. 1.3

Resources

Planning:
Lesson Planner
 Teacher One Stop

Presentation:
DVD Tutor, Disc 1
Grammavision 1.2

Practice:
Grammar Tutor for Students of French, Chapter 3
Cahier de vocabulaire et grammaire
Differentiated Practice and Assessment CD-ROM
Cahier d'activités
Independent Study Guide
Media Guide
Projectable Transparencies
Bell Work 3.3
@HOMETUTOR

Bell Work

Use Bell Work 3.3 in the *Projectable Transparencies* or write this activity on the board.

Fill in the blanks with the appropriate article.

1. J'adore ____ salade de tomates.
2. Les végétariens ne mangent pas ____ viande.
3. Tu prends ____ sucre dans ton café?
4. Lucie prend ____ omelette et ____ coca.
5. Je bois toujours ____ eau minérale pendant mes repas.
6. Mon cousin n'aime pas ____ pêches. 1.2

The pronoun *y*

1 To avoid repeating places and locations, use the pronoun y. It can be used to replace names of places that start with prepositions such as **à, dans, sur, en,** and **chez.**

—Tu peux aller **au supermarché?**
—Bien sûr. J'y vais tout de suite.

—Est-ce que le sucre est **dans la cuisine?**
—Oui, il y est.

2 The pronoun y, like many other pronouns you have learned, goes before the conjugated verb. If there is an infinitive, place y directly before the infinitive.

—Tu aimes aller **au café?**
—Je n'y vais pas souvent, mais de temps et temps, j'aime bien y aller.

Vocabulaire et grammaire, *pp. 28–29*
Cahier d'activités, *pp. 21–23*

Flash culture

La province de Québec a une cuisine qui lui est propre. Les colons français qui se sont implantés dans la province de Québec ont dû adapter leur savoir culinaire aux produits qu'ils ont trouvés sur place. Ils ont découvert le caribou et la morue *(cod)*. Les spécialités québécoises sont la poutine et les cretons (espèce de pâté) entre autres.

Quel type de cuisine a beaucoup d'influence dans ta région? 2.2

13 À remplacer 1.2

Écrivons Identifie la partie de la phrase que le pronom **y** peut remplacer.

MODÈLE D'habitude, on achète les fruits au marché.
au marché

1. Les Girbaud vont toujours à Montréal. à Montréal
2. J'ai mis les abricots sur la table. sur la table
3. Le Café de la Poste? Oui, Salima déjeune souvent dans ce café. dans ce café
4. Tu veux dîner chez moi ce soir? Je vais préparer du poulet. chez moi
5. On mange très bien au Restaurant des Artistes! au Restaurant des Artistes
6. Mon oncle est en France pendant le mois de juin. Il adore la cuisine française. en France

14 Chez nous 1.3

Écrivons/Parlons Réponds aux questions d'après tes habitudes personnelles. Utilise le pronom **y** dans tes réponses.

1. Est-ce que ta famille fait ses courses au supermarché?
2. Est-ce que tu aimes aller au supermarché avec ta famille?
3. Qu'est-ce que vous achetez souvent au supermarché?
4. Est-ce que tu vas souvent au marché?
5. Qu'est-ce qu'on peut acheter au marché aux États-Unis?

Core Instruction

TEACHING GRAMMAIRE

1. Re-introduce the pronoun **y.** Remind students that they have used **y** to replace phrases that begin with **à, dans, en,** and **chez.** Go over the placement of **y** in a sentence with a conjugated verb and with an infinitive. **(2 min.)**
2. Write several sentences that include prepositional phrases on the board or on a transparency. Use the verbs in present, **passé composé,** the future, both the negative and the affirmative. **(2 min.)**
3. Have individuals come up to the board, cross out the prepositional phrase that would be replaced by **y,** and write **y** in the sentence in the correct place. **(4 min.)**

Grammavision

For a video presentation of the pronoun **y,** see the *DVD Tutor.*

15 Qu'est-ce que tu fais ce soir? 1.2

Écrivons Plusieurs de tes camarades t'ont envoyé des textos pour savoir ce que tu fais ce soir. Réponds-leur en utilisant le pronom **y** et les indices donnés.

MODÈLE Oui, je peux y aller ce soir.

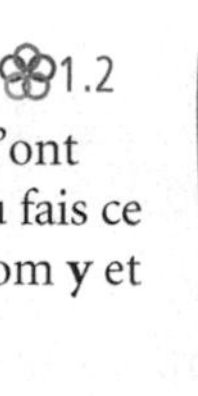
Tu vas au café ce soir?

(oui, pouvoir aller)

Bibliothèque après les cours?

1. (oui, aller) Oui, j'y vais.

Chez Tanguy vers 6:00?

2. (non, pouvoir aller) Non, je ne peux pas y aller.

Céline et toi, ciné à 8:00?

3. (oui, vouloir aller) Oui, nous voulons bien y aller!

Tes parents, restaurant?

4. (pas ce soir, aller) Non, ils n'y vont pas ce soir.

Digital performance space

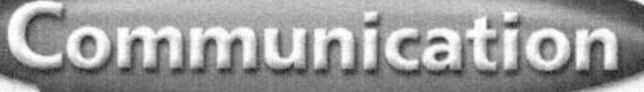
Communication

16 Scénario 1.1

Parlons Formez de petits groupes. Une personne de chaque groupe choisit un magasin ou un endroit *(place)* où elle veut aller. Les autres membres du groupe posent des questions pour essayer de deviner le nom du magasin ou de l'endroit. Utilisez le pronom **y** pour ne pas mentionner le nom.

Souviens-toi! En ville, p. R10

MODÈLE —On y achète des fruits et des légumes?
—Non.

17 Interview 1.1

Parlons Tu fais des sondages pour un magazine pour les consommateurs. Aujourd'hui, tu dois demander où les personnes que tu interviewes font leurs courses et pourquoi elles préfèrent ces endroits. Joue cette scène avec un(e) camarade, puis échangez les rôles. Utilisez le pronom **y** plusieurs fois dans votre conversation.

MODÈLE —Bonjour, madame. Où est-ce que vous aimez faire vos courses?
—J'aime bien aller au marché parce qu'on y trouve... J'aime y acheter...

Connections

Acquiring Information

Ask students how to say the letter *y* in French. **(i grec)** Share with them that the letter *y* hints at the influence of the Greek alphabet on the Latin alphabet, on which French is based. Have students research the history of the alphabet and create a timeline to show its development. 3.2

Communication

17 Pair Activity: Interpersonal

Have partners interview one another about their favorite places in town. Students should answer using the pronoun **y.**

MODÈLE
— Tu vas souvent au cinéma Alamo?
— Oui, j'y vais souvent le samedi. 1.1

Differentiated Instruction

SLOWER PACE LEARNERS

14 Write the question fragments on flashcards, leaving out the words that are to be replaced by **y**. For example, write **Est-ce que ta famille** on one card and **fait ses courses?** on another card. Distribute the cards randomly to students. Write a large **y** on the board. Then read a question as it appears in the activity. Students with the fragments for that question will arrange themselves correctly around the **y** on the board. 1.2

SPECIAL LEARNING NEEDS

14 Students with Learning Disabilities/ Dyslexia To assist students who may have difficulties with the oral responses, have students prepare note cards with the questions and their responses. When learning new concepts, a visual cue, such as the note cards, will be more helpful. 1.2

Assess

Assessment Program
Quiz: Grammaire 1
Alternative Assessment
Differentiated Practice and Assessment CD-ROM

Online Assessment
my.hrw.com

Test Generator 

Resources

Planning:
Lesson Planner
Teacher One Stop

Practice:
Grammar Tutor for Students of French, Chapter 3
Cahier de vocabulaire et grammaire
Differentiated Practice and Assessment CD-ROM
Cahier d'activités
Independent Study Guide
Media Guide
Projectable Transparencies
Bell Work 3.4
Audio CD 3, Tr. 3

Bell Work

Use Bell Work 3.4 in the *Projectable Transparencies* or write this activity on the board.

Answer the following questions using the pronoun **y.**

1. **Quels jours es-tu à l'école?**
2. **Est-ce que tu vas souvent au cinéma?**
3. **Est-ce que tes amis et toi, vous aimez dîner au restaurant?**
4. **Est-ce que tu es déjà allé(e) en France?** 1.2

18 Answers

1. Oui; il y a des œufs, du fromage, des champignons et du lait.
2. Non; il y a du pain, des œufs et du beurre, mais il n'y a pas de jambon.
3. Non; il y a des tomates et de l'huile, mais il n'y a pas de laitue.
4. Non; il y a de la farine, des œufs, du beurre et du lait, mais il n'y a pas de chocolat.
5. Oui; il y a des œufs, du fromage, du lait, du beurre et de la farine.

Synthèse
- Vocabulaire 1
- Grammaire 1

Application 1

18 Qu'est-ce qu'on va préparer? 1.2

Parlons/Écrivons Regarde bien l'illustration. Est-ce que tu peux préparer les plats suivants avec les ingrédients qu'il y a sur l'illustration? Pourquoi ou pourquoi pas?

MODÈLE des pâtes au fromage
Non; Il y a du fromage, mais il n'y a pas de pâtes.

1. une omelette au fromage et aux champignons
2. un croque-monsieur
3. une salade avec des tomates
4. un gâteau au chocolat
5. une quiche au fromage

Un peu plus Révisions

Question formation

1 To ask a yes-no question, simply raise the pitch of your voice. You can also start the question with est-ce que (est-ce qu').

Est-ce que tu es allergique aux œufs?

2 You can also ask a question by inverting a subject pronoun and its verb. Remember to insert -t- before il, elle, or on if the verb ends in a vowel sound.

Est-elle dans la cuisine? Prépare-t-elle une salade?

3 To ask an information question, you can use the question words: **qui** *(who)*; **pourquoi** *(why)*; **que (qu')** *(what)*; **combien de (d')** *(how much/many)*; **quand** *(when)*; **comment** *(how)*; and **où** *(where)*.

Comment est-ce qu'on fait une omelette?

Que manges-tu à midi?

Vocabulaire et grammaire, *pp. 28–30*
Cahier d'activités, *pp. 21–23*

19 Écoutons CD 3, Tr. 3 1.2

Écoute chaque phrase et dis si c'est **a) une question** ou **b) une phrase affirmative.** 1. a 2. b 3. b 4. a 5. a 6. a 7. b

Core Instruction

INTEGRATED PRACTICE

1. Have students do Activity 18 to practice vocabulary and the partitive. **(3 min.)**
2. Name ingredients of a dish and have students guess what the dish is. (**une tarte aux pommes, un sandwich au jambon, le bœuf bourgignon, la glace à la fraise, une salade de fruits, une pizza**) Say, **Dans ce plat, il y a du/de la/des/de l'...,** and so on. **(5 min.)**
3. Introduce **Un peu plus** and complete the integrated practice Activities. **(15 min.)**

TEACHING UN PEU PLUS

1. Remind students that to form **oui** or **non** questions, they can raise their voice at the end of a sentence, put **Est-ce que** at the beginning, or use inversion. Remind students about inserting **–t** between vowels. **(3 min.)**
2. Remind students that to ask for information, they must start the sentence with a question word (**qui, que, comment, où, quand, pourquoi, combien de**) and use either **est-ce que** or inversion to complete the question. **(2 min.)**

Online Practice

my.hrw.com
Application 1 practice

20 Invente les questions! 1.2

Écrivons Lis ces réponses et pour chacune, imagine la question qu'on a posée pour obtenir chaque réponse. Utilise l'intonation, **est-ce que** ou l'inversion.

MODÈLE Du pain, du fromage et du jambon.
Qu'est-ce qu'il y a dans un croque-monsieur?

1. Non merci. Je n'aime pas le chocolat.
2. Parce que je suis allergique aux cerises...
3. Jamais! Elle est végétarienne.
4. Mélange les framboises avec le sucre.
5. Quatre courgettes, s'il vous plaît.
6. Non, j'ai fait une salade avec des tomates.

21 Une lettre à Matthieu 1.3

Écrivons Ton correspondant canadien, Matthieu, va passer l'été chez toi. Ta mère veut savoir ce qu'il aime manger et ce qu'il n'aime pas manger. Écris une lettre à Matthieu et demande-lui ce qu'il aime manger.

MODÈLE **Matthieu,**
Qu'est-ce que tu aimes manger au petit-déjeuner? Tu manges... ou bien est-ce que tu préfères... ?

Communication

Digital performance space

22 Scénario 1.1

Parlons Imagine que tu étudies dans une école à Québec. Voici le menu de la cantine *(cafeteria)*. Avec un(e) camarade, discutez du menu. Dites ce que vous allez manger et ce que vous n'allez pas manger et expliquez pourquoi.

MODÈLE **—Moi, je vais manger à la cantine mardi.**
—Pourquoi?
—Parce qu'il y a de la soupe à l'oignon...

Lycée Hugo Semaine du 21/9—25/9

Lundi	Mardi	Mercredi	Jeudi	Vendredi
Salade de tomates Poulet haricots verts Yaourt	Soupe à l'oignon Steak pommes de terre Tarte aux abricots	Salade verte Poisson sauce aux champignons et riz Pastèque	Carottes en salade Omelette et ratatouille de courgettes et d'aubergines Fromage blanc	Soupe de tomate Poisson, petits pois et carottes Gâteau aux framboises

Application 1

19 Script

1. Manges-tu souvent des petits pois?
2. Papa et moi, on déteste les carottes!
3. Norbert va apporter une tarte aux cerises pour le déjeuner.
4. Les filles, vous aimez les bananes et les pêches?
5. Madame Touzeau, est-ce que vous voulez du chocolat?
6. C'est facile de faire une quiche au fromage?
7. Ma grand-mère ne mange pas de sel.

Communication

Group Activity: Interpersonal

On a sheet of paper, have students write these question words in the following order: **où, que, combien de, quand, comment.** Then have groups of students ask one another questions about their family's grocery shopping and purchases. Have students use the pronoun **y** and other object pronouns whenever possible. Have groups summarize the answers in a graph or chart and present the information to the class.

MODÈLE
— Où est-ce que ta mère fait les courses?
— Elle les fait à...
— Qu'est-ce qu'elle y achète?
— Elle achète... 1.1

Differentiated Instruction

SLOWER PACE LEARNERS

20 Make the activity less open-ended by writing two possible questions per item on the board. Students will choose the more logical question. For example, for **1. Non merci. Je n'aime pas le chocolat.**, write **1. a) Tu veux du chocolat? b) Est-ce que tu as acheté du chocolat?** 1.2

SPECIAL LEARNING NEEDS

Students with AD(H)D Students with attention disorders are better able to learn new material when they experience real-life or hands-on applications. For practice in developing questions that ask for information, ask students to search a current newspaper for an article of interest. Ask them to use the question words in **Un peu plus** to form questions the reporter may have asked while preparing the news story. The questions can then be shared in small groups or with partners. 1.3

Assess

Assessment Program
Quiz: Application 1
Audio CD 3, Tr. 15
Alternative Assessment
Differentiated Practice and Assessment CD-ROM

Online Assessment
my.hrw.com

Test Generator

Resources

Planning:
Lesson Planner
Teacher One Stop

Practice:
Cahier d'activités

Vocabulaire supplémentaire

You might wish to use these terms to discuss the project with students.

les bonbons (m)	*candy*
doux/douce	*sweet*
Ça fond dans la bouche!	*It melts in your mouth!*
la crème de tartre	*cream of tartar*
une pincée de sel	*a pinch of salt*
faire bouillir	*to boil*
le thermomètre à bonbons	*candy thermometer*
le moule à bonbons	*candy mold*
graissé(e)	*greased*
le mélange	*mixture*

Culture appliquée

Le sirop d'érable 2.2

Récolte du sirop d'érable

Le sirop d'érable[1] fait partie de la cuisine québécoise depuis longtemps. Les Amérindiens ont appris aux colons[2] français à récolter[3] l'eau d'érable pour la changer en sucre. Le sirop était utilisé par les Amérindiens comme médicament. La saison de la récolte a lieu au début du printemps et s'appelle «le temps des sucres». Le Québec produit la majorité du sirop d'érable vendu dans le monde.

1. maple syrup 2. settlers 3. collect

Des sucettes au sirop d'érable 2.2

Ingredients

- 2 cups maple syrup
- 1/2 teaspoon cream of tartar
- 1 teaspoon butter
- Pinch of salt
- Candy thermometer
- Candy molds
- Lollipop sticks

Step 1 Boil all the ingredients together until they reach a temperature of 238°F.

Step 2 Pour the mixture into greased candy molds. Set a lollipop stick in the mold. Let it set. Put in the freezer for best results.

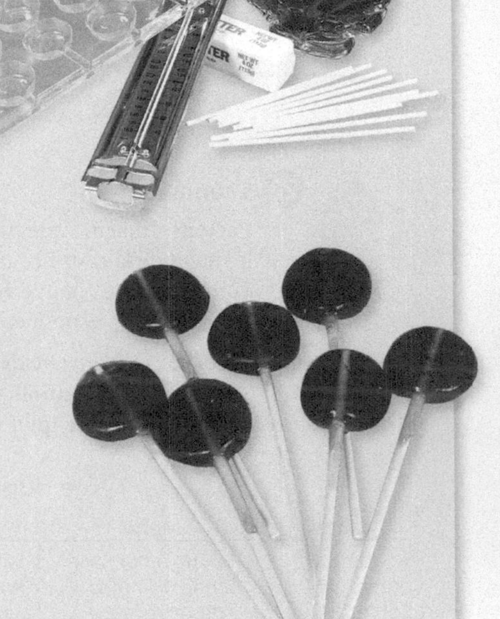

Recherches Fais des recherches pour savoir comment les Amérindiens récoltaient l'eau d'érable. Est-ce que leur technique est différente de la technique utilisée aujourd'hui? 2.1

Core Instruction

CULTURE APPLIQUÉE

1. Ahead of time, ask the culinary arts teacher to trade rooms for the day. Have students bring ingredients and supplies to class.
2. In class, read and discuss the introductory paragraph. **(2 min.)**
3. Make copies of the recipe. Form small groups and assign tasks to each group member. Have each group prepare the recipe. **(20 min.)**
4. Assign **Recherches** as homework. **(5 min.)**

COMPARAISONS ET COMMUNAUTÉ

1. Have a volunteer read the introduction. Discuss the answer to the question. **(1 min.)**
2. Ask students if there are any foods served in their family that are presented or eaten in a special way. Discuss **Et toi?** as a class. **(3 min.)**
3. Have partners read and discuss **Communauté et professions. (8 min.)**

Online Practice
my.hrw.com
Online Edition

Comparaisons

La préparation du couscous

Le couscous 4.2

Tu rends visite à tes amis marocains à Casablanca. Ils ont préparé un couscous. Pour manger le couscous de manière traditionnelle, tu manges avec:

a. la main droite.
b. une fourchette et un couteau.
c. une cuillère.

Au Maroc, le couscous se mange en début d'après-midi. Chaque personne se lave les mains avant le repas. Ensuite, chaque personne s'assied sur des coussins[1] posés par terre autour d'une table basse[2] et ronde. Un grand plat de semoule[3] avec viandes et légumes est posé au centre de la table et on mange avec les doigts. On prend le couscous avec trois doigts et ensuite on en fait une petite boule dans la main. On ne doit utiliser que la main droite, jamais la main gauche. Tout autour du plat, de petites assiettes en terre cuite contiennent les épices. Généralement, on boit du thé à la menthe. Après le repas, chacun se lave les mains, souvent avec de l'eau de fleur d'oranger.

4.2

ET TOI?

1. Quelles spécialités est-ce que tu manges avec les doigts aux États-Unis?
2. Est-ce que tu bois une boisson traditionnelle chez toi? Laquelle?

Communauté et professions

Le français dans les cuisines 5.1

Dans les recettes de cuisine de nombreux mots sont français ou d'origine française. Est-ce que tu connais un chef? Est-ce qu'il y a une école de cuisine près de chez toi? Fais des recherches sur Internet ou à la bibliothèque pour en savoir plus sur le métier de chef. Présente ce que tu as trouvé à la classe.

1. cushions 2. low 3. type of flour made from hard wheat

Des apprentis cuisiniers

Cultures

Practices and Perspectives

In Quebec, the **cabane à sucre** is a special cabin where the sap collected from maple trees is boiled to make syrup. This is a time-consuming task, but a pleasurable one, because people traditionally invite their friends and family members to help, transforming what could be a tedious chore into a chance to socialize and to celebrate the approach of spring. There are also many **cabanes à sucre** that cater to tourists who wish to experience this traditional **québécois** event. Ask students if their family has a traditional task that they do together once a year. 2.1

Communities

Community Link

Have groups of students conduct a candy sale to raise money for a class project, for a field trip, or to donate to charity. Each group could prepare a batch of **sucettes au sirop d'érable** or make other traditional candies of francophone countries that they have researched. Ask students to speak only in French as they organize their sale. 1.1, 5.1

Language Examination

Culture can be used to practice for the **Interpretive Communication** and **Presentational Writing** sections of the Advanced Placement exam as it helps students get acquainted with and reflect on products and practices from the French-speaking world while reading culture-focused passages and answering questions in French.

Differentiated Instruction

ADVANCED LEARNERS

Have students research a list of French cooking terms and their meanings. Have them use the terms to make a poster or decorate a cooking apron, oven mitt, or kitchen towel. Students should write the terms in French and illustrate their meanings. 5.2

MULTIPLE INTELLIGENCES

Visual Ask students to research and review French cookbooks to find differences and similarities in American and French cooking traditions. Students should then create a chart to show the recipes that are similar to and those that are different from American foods. You might have students find unique ingredients, patterns of ingredients, or cooking techniques that appear often in French recipes and report to the class. 2.1

Resources

Planning:
Lesson Planner
Teacher One Stop

Presentation:
Projectable Transparencies
Vocabulaire 3.3, 3.4
DVD Tutor, Disc 1
Télé-vocab 2
Interactive Whiteboard Lessons

Practice:
Cahier de vocabulaire et grammaire
Differentiated Practice and Assessment CD-ROM
Independent Study Guide
Media Guide
Projectable Transparencies
Bell Work 3.5
HOMETUTOR
Holt McDougal French Apps

Bell Work

Use Bell Work 3.5 in the *Projectable Transparencies* or write this activity on the board.

Write the questions for these answers.

1. ______________
Un kilo de fraises, s'il vous plaît.
2. ______________
Non, merci. Je ne prends jamais de café.
3. ______________
Je mange ce sandwich parce que j'ai très faim.
4. ______________
Je vais bien, merci. Et vous? 1.2

Teacher Note

Tell students that they may hear these expressions of quantity as well: **une brique de lait** *(a carton of milk)*; **un sachet d'épices** *(a packet of spices)*.

Objectifs
- to shop for groceries
- to ask where things are

Vocabulaire à l'œuvre 2

Télé-vocab

On fait les courses!

Core Instruction

TEACHING VOCABULAIRE

1. Introduce the vocabulary with transparencies **Vocabulaire 3.3** and **3.4** and model the pronunciation of the words using expressions in **Exprimons-nous!** as you point to each item, person, or store. **Il me faut... Je vais en prendre... (2 min.)**
2. Using the transparency, ask **oui** or **non** questions about the people and the stores: **L'épicière travaille à la crémerie-fromagerie? La boulangère travaille à la boucherie-charcuterie? Le caissier travaille à l'épicerie? (2 min.)**
3. Pointing to the images, ask questions about each. **On achète du jambon à la poissonnerie? On achète du pain à la boulangerie-pâtisserie? On achète un pot de confiture à l'épicerie? (3 min.)**

Télé-vocab 2

For a video presentation of this vocabulary, see the *DVD Tutor.*

Télé-vocab

Online Practice
my.hrw.com
Vocabulaire 2 practice

Au supermarché

Exprimons-nous!

To shop for groceries	
Qu'est-ce qu'il vous faut? *What do you need?*	**Il me faut** un kilo de pommes de terre, s'il vous plaît. *I need . . .*
Combien vous en faut-il? *How many/much do you need?*	**À peu près une livre.** *About one pound.* Un kilo **environ.** *. . . approximately.*
Vous les voulez comment, vos abricots/ vos tomates? *How do you want the . . . ?*	**Bien mûr(e)(s),** s'il vous plaît. *Very ripe / ripe. . .*
C'est cinq euros **le kilo.** *It's . . . per kilo.*	Bon, **je vais en prendre** trois kilos. *. . . I'll take . . .*
Ce sera tout? *Will that be all?*	Oui, **c'est tout pour aujourd'hui,** merci. *. . . that's all for today . . .*

Vocabulaire et grammaire, *pp. 31–33* Online Workbooks

▶ **Vocabulaire supplémentaire—À la boucherie-charcuterie, À la poissonnerie, p. R18**

Vocabulaire 2

TPR
Total Physical Response

Have students help you bring fruits and vegetables to class. Then have students respond to the following commands.

Tu veux bien aller me chercher une banane, **s'il te plaît?**

Rapporte-moi une pomme.

N'oublie pas les tomates.

Tu me rapportes une pomme de terre?

Il me faut aussi une carotte. 1.2

Common Error Alert
Attention !

Sometimes students will mix up the word for a store with the word for the owner. If they are not careful with the ending, **une boulangerie** can easily be confused with **une boulangère.**

Cultures
Practices and Perspectives

Tell students that over the years, there has been much debate on the legal requirements for outdoor commercial signs and store names in Quebec. Have students research the history of the debate from the Canadian Supreme Court ruling of 1988 to more recent legal hearings on Quebec's sign laws and the use of French and English in stores' signage. 2.1

Differentiated Instruction

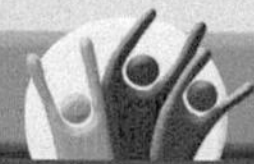

Slower Pace Learners

Bring to class plastic or toy grocery items and empty packages to represent the food items in **Vocabulaire 2.** Form teams of three: two shoppers and one cashier. Give one shopper a shopping list. He or she will say, for example, **Il me faut un paquet de pâtes!** The other shopper will get the item and say **Un paquet de pâtes!** Once they have all the items, they will go to the cashier. The cashier must name each food item and its quantity before bagging the item. 1.1

Multiple Intelligences

Spatial Ask students to design and draw part of a floor plan for a grocery store. The illustrations should indicate where the items are located on aisles in the store. Using the floor plan, have students ask one another where specific items are located in the store. You may give students the option of designing department or specialty store floor plans instead. 1.1

Proverbes

For French proverbs and activities related to the chapter theme and vocabulary, see **Proverbes et expressions,** pp. R6–R7.

Resources

Planning:
Lesson Planner
Teacher One Stop

Presentation:
Projectable Transparencies **Vocabulaire 3.3, 3.4**
DVD Tutor, Disc 1 **Télé-vocab 2**
Interactive Whiteboard Lessons

Practice:
Cahier de vocabulaire et grammaire
Differentiated Practice and Assessment CD-ROM
Independent Study Guide
Media Guide
Audio CD 3, Tr. 4
HOMETUTOR

23 Script

1. J'arrive au magasin à quatre heures du matin pour faire les baguettes et les croissants. Après, je fais les gâteaux et les tartes.
2. Si vous cherchez de délicieuses crevettes, venez chez moi. Mes fruits de mer sont toujours excellents.
3. Je travaille dans un grand magasin. Les clients me donnent de l'argent et je mets leurs produits dans un sac en plastique.
4. Je vends du bœuf, du porc, du poulet et du saucisson.
5. Notre magasin n'est pas grand, mais on y trouve de tout—de la farine, du café, des fruits, des légumes et des produits laitiers. Nos clients n'aiment pas les hypermarchés. Ils préfèrent notre petit magasin.

25 Answers

1. Pour acheter un litre de lait, va à la crémerie-fromagerie.
2. Pour acheter un morceau de pâté, va à la boucherie-charcuterie.
3. Pour acheter deux kilos de farine, va à l'épicerie.
4. Pour acheter une douzaine de crevettes, va à la poissonnerie.
5. Pour acheter une livre de poires, va à l'épicerie.
6. Pour acheter dix tranches de saucisson, va à la boucherie-charcuterie.
7. Pour acheter six croissants, va à la boulangerie-pâtisserie.

23 Écoutons CD 3, Tr. 4 1.2

Regarde les photos et écoute les commentaires. Indique quelle photo correspond à chaque commentaire. **1.** e **2.** c **3.** d **4.** b **5.** a

a.

b.

c.

d.

e.

24 À l'épicerie 1.2

Écrivons Marie-Ève et Denis font les courses. Complète leur conversation en utilisant les expressions de la boîte.

combien	faut	douzaine	kilo
litre	chariot	morceau	sera

DENIS — Bon, qu'est-ce qu'il te ___1___? faut
MARIE-ÈVE — J'ai besoin d'oignons.
DENIS — ___2___ t'en faut-il? Combien
MARIE-ÈVE — Un ___3___. kilo
DENIS — Ce ___4___ tout? sera
MARIE-ÈVE — Non, on achète aussi des produits laitiers: un ___5___ de lait et un ___6___ de fromage. litre morceau
DENIS — Et n'oublie pas qu'il nous faut une ___7___ d'œufs. douzaine

Flash culture

Au Québec, comme aux États-Unis, vous avez le choix entre des sacs en plastique ou des sacs en papier dans les supermarchés. Les caissiers rangent les produits dans les sacs pour vous. En France, les clients doivent ranger eux-mêmes leurs courses dans des sacs. De plus en plus de supermarchés et hypermarchés ne fournissent plus de sacs à leurs clients. Il faut penser à apporter ses propres sacs ou son panier quand on va faire ses courses.

Qui range les courses dans des sacs quand tu vas faire des courses? 4.2

25 Où va-t-on? 1.2

Écrivons Yann va faire les courses pour sa mère. Identifie le magasin de la colonne de droite où Yann peut acheter chaque produit de la colonne de gauche. Dis-lui où il faut aller.

MODÈLE **Pour acheter six croissants, va à la boulangerie-pâtisserie.**

un litre de lait	la boulangerie-pâtisserie
un morceau de pâté	la crémerie-fromagerie
deux kilos de farine	l'épicerie
une douzaine de crevettes	la poissonnerie
une livre de poires	la boucherie-charcuterie
dix tranches de saucisson	
six croissants	

Core Instruction

TEACHING EXPRIMONS-NOUS!

1. On the board or on a transparency, write 12 vocabulary items, four each in three rows. **(3 min.)**
2. Ask **oui** or **non** questions using location words. **La tomate est tout près de la poire? Le beurre est au milieu de la table? Les haricots verts, ça se trouve à gauche des cerises? (2 min.)**
3. Continue modeling the expressions using the corresponding words in **Déjà vu! (2 min.)**

Exprimons-nous!

To ask where things are	
Madame, les produits congelés, s'il vous plaît? *Ma'am, where are the frozen foods, please?*	**Alors,** ils sont **tout près** des fruits, là. *Well . . . right next to . . .*
Où est-ce que je pourrais trouver les épices? *Where could I find . . . ?*	**Si vous allez** tout droit, **au bout du** rayon, vous allez trouver les épices. *If you go . . . at the end of . . .*
Le lait, **ça se trouve où,** s'il vous plaît? *. . . is found where . . . ?*	**Au milieu du** magasin. *In the middle of . . .*

Vocabulaire et grammaire, *pp. 31–33* Online Workbooks

Déjà vu!

You have already learned some words to tell where things are.

devant	*in front of*
derrière	*behind*
entre	*between*
à côté de	*next to*
à droite de	*to the right of*
à gauche de	*to the left of*

26 Où sont les tomates? 1.2

Lisons/Écrivons Une nouvelle épicerie vient d'ouvrir à côté de chez toi. Tu dois acheter différents produits mais tu ne les trouves pas. Complète la conversation logiquement. Possible answers:

Toi —Pardon, où ___1___ les tomates? sont
L'épicier —___2___ du magasin. Au milieu
Toi —Et les œufs?
L'épicier —Les œufs sont ___3___ du beurre. à côté
Toi —Et les champignons, ils sont où?
L'épicier —___4___ les carottes et la salade. Entre
Toi —Maintenant, je cherche l'huile d'olive.
L'épicier —___5___ du sucre. À droite
Toi —Et le sucre, où se trouve-t-il?
L'épicier —___6___ du rayon. Au bout
Toi —Merci.

Communication

Digital performance space

27 Scénario 1.1

Parlons Tu vas au supermarché pour acheter des fruits et des légumes. Comme le magasin est grand, tu ne sais pas où se trouvent les fruits et les légumes que tu veux acheter. Demande à l'employé(e). Complète cette conversation avec ton/ta camarade. Puis, échangez les rôles.

MODÈLE **–Pardon, où est-ce que je pourrais trouver... ?**
–Si vous allez tout droit...

Cultures

Practices and Perspectives

Tell students that some grocery stores in France offer home delivery and online grocery shopping. Have students do research to find grocery stores in their area that may offer these services, or businesses that provide other grocery shopping services. 2.1

Communication

Pair Activity: Interpersonal

Have students write a shopping list of eight to ten items. Then have partners create a conversation in which a parent asks a son or daughter to get an item and the teen asks where to find that item before agreeing to get it right away. Have partners switch roles.

MODÈLE
— Tu me rapportes deux tranches de jambon?
— D'accord, ça se trouve où?
— Ça se trouve à la boucherie-charcuterie.
— J'y vais tout de suite.
1.1

Differentiated Instruction

ADVANCED LEARNERS

25 Make a list of additional food items that can be bought at each place and distribute copies to students. Have students look up any items they do not know and determine where they can be bought. Have partners compare answers. 1.2

MULTIPLE INTELLIGENCES

Bodily-Kinesthetic To practice asking where things are, have several students stand in a group in the classroom. Have other students ask and answer questions about the location of each student in the group. Students can use the questions in **Exprimons-nous!** and the vocabulary in **Déjà vu!** to create their own questions and responses about the location of each person in the group. **—Où est Mark? —Il est entre Jan et Desha.** 1.1

Assess

Assessment Program
Quiz: Vocabulaire 2
Alternative Assessment
Differentiated Practice and Assessment CD-ROM

Online Assessment
my.hrw.com

Test Generator 

Resources

Planning:
Lesson Planner
Teacher One Stop

Presentation:
DVD Tutor, Disc 1
Grammavision 2.1

Practice:
Grammar Tutor for Students of French, Chapter 3
Cahier de vocabulaire et grammaire
Differentiated Practice and Assessment CD-ROM
Cahier d'activités
Independent Study Guide
Media Guide
Projectable Transparencies
Bell Work 3.6
Audio CD 3, Tr. 5
@HOMETUTOR

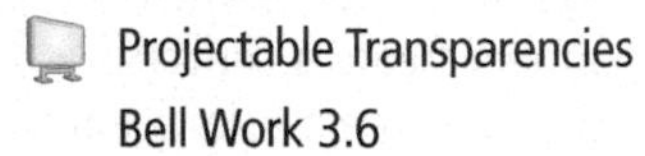

Bell Work

Use Bell Work 3.6 in the *Projectable Transparencies* or write this activity on the board.

List two items that can be purchased at the following stores.

1. la boulangerie-pâtisserie
2. la crémerie
3. la boucherie-charcuterie
4. la poissonnerie
5. l'épicerie 1.2

28 Script

1. — Antonin, tu veux du pain?
 — Oui, j'en veux bien, merci.
2. — Solène, tu reprends du poulet?
 — Oui, j'en veux. Et des pommes de terre aussi, s'il te plaît.
3. — Émilia, tu veux de la salade?
 — J'en veux bien. Merci.
4. — Quentin, tu aimes le fromage?
 — Oui, j'adore. Tu en as?
5. — Éva, tu reprends de la mousse au chocolat?
 — Non, je n'en veux pas. Merci.
6. — Et toi, Magali? Tu n'as presque rien mangé, tu vas reprendre de la mousse au chocolat?
 — Non, merci. Je n'ai plus faim.

Objectifs
- the pronoun *en*
- placement of object pronouns

Grammaire à l'œuvre 2

Grammavision

The pronoun *en*

1. You can replace a form of de + noun with en. It often translates as *some, any, of it,* or *of them.*

 — Tu veux du yaourt? — *Would you like some yogurt?*
 — Non, merci, je n'en veux pas. — *No thanks, I don't want any.*

2. En can also replace nouns that follow un, une, **numbers,** or **expressions of quantity.** In this case, you normally still use un, une, the number, or the expression of quantity in the sentence with en.

 — Tu manges **beaucoup de sandwichs**?
 — Oui, j'en mange beaucoup. J'en prends souvent un à midi.
 — Moi, j'en prends souvent deux!

3. Place en before the infinitive in the sentence if there is one. Otherwise, place it before the conjugated verb.

 Des crevettes? Je vais en acheter.

Vocabulaire et grammaire, *pp. 34–35*
Cahier d'activités, *pp. 25–27*

À la cajun

In Louisiana, you will sometimes hear **une chevrette** instead of **une crevette** for *shrimp.*

28 Écoutons CD 3, Tr. 5 1.2

Magali a invité ses amis pour dîner. Écoute leurs conversations et dis si les invités **a) veulent** ou **b) ne veulent pas** de chaque plat.

1. a 2. a 3. a 4. a 5. b 6. b

29 Il y en a combien? 1.2

Écrivons Dis combien il y a de fruits et de légumes sur la photo. Utilise **en** dans tes phrases.

MODÈLE des champignons?
Il y en a trois.

1. des bananes? Il y en a quatre.
2. des pastèques? Il y en a une.
3. des pommes? Il y en a dix.
4. des cerises? Il y en a beaucoup!
5. des melons? Il y en a deux.
6. des poivrons? Il y en a un.

Core Instruction

TEACHING GRAMMAIRE

1. Tell students that **en** is an object pronoun that replaces **de** + noun. It can also replace nouns that follow **un/une,** numbers, or expressions of quantity; explain that in this case, those words remain in the sentence with **en. (2 min.)**
2. Explain the placement of **en** with a conjugated verb and with an infinitive. **(1 min.)**
3. On the board or on a transparency, write a variety of sentences with phrases starting with **de/du/des**, numbers, and expressions of quantity. Ask individuals to come up, cross out the words that would be replaced by **en,** and write **en** in the sentence in the correct place. **(4 min.)**

Grammavision

For a video presentation of the pronoun **en,** see the *DVD Tutor.*

Grammavision

Online Practice
my.hrw.com
Grammaire 2 practice

30 Dans le bon ordre 1.2

Écrivons Remets les éléments de chaque phrase dans le bon ordre.

1. non merci / en / ne... pas / je / veux
2. adore / les pêches / mange / j' / beaucoup / j' / en / et
3. des petits pois / tu / il y a / veux / en / si
4. nous / avons / en / deux
5. maman / pour le dîner / souvent / prépare / en
6. en / vous / est-ce que / avez / deux

31 Un sondage 1.3

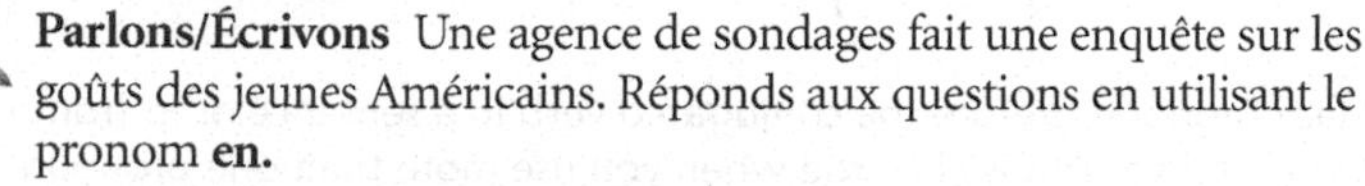

Parlons/Écrivons Une agence de sondages fait une enquête sur les goûts des jeunes Américains. Réponds aux questions en utilisant le pronom **en.**

1. Est-ce que tu aimes manger des fruits au petit-déjeuner?
2. Quel est ton fruit préféré? Tu en manges souvent?
3. Est-ce qu'il y a des légumes que tu ne manges jamais?
4. Est-ce que tu aimes les épices? Tu en mets dans quels plats?
5. Tu manges beaucoup de yaourt?
6. Est-ce que tu manges souvent des œufs? Quand?

32 Nous, les Américains 1.3

Écrivons Un magazine suisse fait une enquête sur les produits typiques qui représentent les pays du monde. À ton avis, qu'est-ce qui représente le mieux les États-Unis? Fais une liste de 4 choses. Utilise le pronom **en** dans tes réponses.

MODÈLE **Le coca, c'est la boisson préférée des Américains. Ils en boivent beaucoup!**

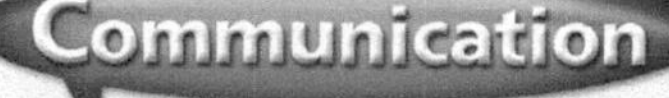

Communication

33 Devinettes 1.1

Parlons Choisis un fruit ou un légume et décris-le à ton/ta camarade. Ne mentionne pas le nom du fruit ou du légume que tu as choisi et utilise **en** dans ta description. Ton/Ta camarade va essayer de deviner de quel fruit ou de quel légume tu parles. Ensuite, échangez les rôles.

MODÈLE **—Il y en a des rouges.**
—Des pommes?
—Non. On en met quelquefois sur des glaces.
—Des cerises?

Grammaire 2

30 Answers

1. Non merci, je n'en veux pas.
2. J'adore les pêches et j'en mange beaucoup.
3. Il y a des petits pois si tu en veux.
4. Nous en avons deux.
5. Maman en prépare souvent pour le dîner.
6. Est-ce que vous en avez deux?

Comparisons

Comparing and Contrasting

Tell students that the French are the world's largest consumers of cheese per capita. Per year, each French person eats about 40 pounds of cheese. Have students research how much cheese the average American eats per year. Students might also find out how the French compare to Americans in their consumption of other food items, such as soft drinks. 4.2

Communication

Pair Activity: Interpersonal

Have each student choose a dish whose ingredients include fruits or vegetables, such as a fruit pie, ice cream, or a vegetable quiche. Have partners take turns naming their dish's ingredients without naming the dish. They should try to guess each other's dish. 1.1

Differentiated Instruction

ADVANCED LEARNERS

Have students write a survey on food preferences. Each question should be in a multiple-choice format. Answer options should all use the pronoun **en.** As an alternative, have students assume the role of a food-industry marketing consultant. Students will conduct group interviews in which they ask other students to discuss their food preferences. 1.3

SPECIAL LEARNING NEEDS

Students with Learning Disabilities For additional practice with the pronoun **en,** ask students to prepare a grocery list that includes the new vocabulary in this chapter. They can use the list to ask a partner questions about which items they would need to purchase on a trip to the grocery store. The list may include such items as **le brocoli, la pêche, la banane,** and **le melon.** The questions may include **Est-ce que tu veux du brocoli?** or **Il y a des bananes?** Responses should include the proper use of **en.** 1.1

Resources

Planning:
Lesson Planner
Teacher One Stop

Presentation:
DVD Tutor, Disc 1
Grammavision 2.2

Practice:
Grammar Tutor for Students of French, Chapter 3
Cahier de vocabulaire et grammaire
Differentiated Practice and Assessment CD-ROM
Cahier d'activités
Independent Study Guide
Media Guide
Projectable Transparencies
Bell Work 3.7
HOMETUTOR

Bell Work

Use Bell Work 3.7 in the *Projectable Transparencies* or write this activity on the board.

Answer the following questions, using the cue and the pronoun **en**.

1. **Tu veux un yaourt? Non,...**
2. **Tu manges beaucoup de chocolat? Oui,...**
3. **Tu vas prendre un steak-frites? Oui,...**
4. **Tu manges des œufs au petit-déjeuner? Non,...**

1.2

COMMON ERROR ALERT
ATTENTION !

If students have been told that **ne** and **pas** go "around the verb," they may have trouble remembering what to do when there is a direct object pronoun preceding the verb. **Ne** and **pas** will surround both the pronoun and the verb. **Je ne le fais pas.**

Placement of object pronouns

1. You have learned that if you have a sentence with both direct and indirect object pronouns, you place the pronouns in a certain order. You can also combine the pronouns y and en with the object pronouns you have learned. Notice the position of these pronouns when used with other object pronouns.

me (m')	le			
te (t')	l'	lui	y	en
nous	la	leur		
vous	les			

2. Place pronouns before the conjugated verb in a sentence or in front of the infinitive. This is also true when you use more than one pronoun at a time.

—Tu peux me donner des fraises?
—Bien sûr. Je t'en donne.
—Vous achetez **les baguettes** à la boulangerie?
—Oui, je **les** y achète.

3. Y and en can be used together in the same sentence, although it is not common. They are used together with the following expression.

Il y a des cerises au marché?
Oui, il y en a.

Vocabulaire et grammaire, *pp. 34–35*
Cahier d'activités, *pp. 25–27*

Flash culture

Au Québec, on peut utiliser un chariot dans les supermarchés comme aux États-Unis, mais c'est différent en France. La plupart des supermarchés ont un système de consigne *(deposit)* pour que les personnes remettent en place les chariots au lieu de les laisser sur le parking. Pour prendre un chariot, le client dépose une pièce d'un euro dans un boîtier *(case)* et le client la reprend quand il remet le chariot en place.

Est-ce que les supermarchés de ta région ont un système pour remettre en place les chariots? 2.2

34 Quel pronom? 1.2

Écrivons Pour chaque phrase, indique quelle partie de la phrase peut être remplacée par des pronoms objets et indique par quel pronom.

MODÈLE Je vais donner la tarte à Marie.
la tarte: la
à Marie: lui

1. Marco va acheter les crevettes à la poissonnerie.
les crevettes: les; à la poissonnerie: y
2. Tu veux bien mettre le sucre sur la table? Merci.
le sucre: le; sur la table: y
3. Tu peux donner des yaourts à Paul?
des yaourts: en; à Paul: lui
4. Est-ce qu'il y a des champignons au marché?
des champignons: en; au marché: y
5. Vous voulez les abricots comment?
les abricots: les
6. Il faut donner le sac en plastique à l'employée.
le sac en plastique: le; à l'employée: lui

Core Instruction

TEACHING GRAMMAIRE

1. Tell students that they will often have more than one object pronoun in a sentence. When **y** and **en** are in the same sentence, they come in the order of **y en,** sounding like a donkey. **(1 min.)**
2. Remind students of the placement and sequence of object pronouns if more than one pronoun is used in a sentence. Suggest students memorize the sequence. **(2 min.)**
3. Write sentences on the board with direct and indirect objects to be replaced by **le/la/les, lui/leur, y, en.** Ask groups of three to copy the sentences and take turns underlining each phrase, determining the correct object pronoun to use and placing it in the sentence. **(5 min.)**

Grammavision

For a video presentation of the placement of object pronouns, see the *DVD Tutor.*

35 Une journée chargée 1.2

Écrivons Refais les phrases en utilisant des pronoms pour remplacer les mots soulignés.

MODÈLE J'achète les pâtes au supermarché.
Je les y achète.

1. Mazarine, tu vas préparer la tarte aux abricots?
2. Tu me donnes des fruits?
3. Vous allez envoyer ces fleurs à Maman?
4. Les Martin ne vont pas acheter d'abricots.
5. Je t'envoie une invitation.
6. Il n'y a pas de jambon.

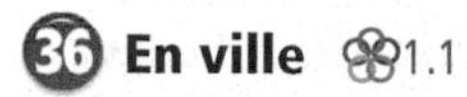

36 En ville 1.1

Écrivons Écris une petite conversation pour accompagner chaque photo. Utilise des pronoms dans tes conversations.

MODÈLE **—Tu peux me rapporter trois baguettes?**
—Oui, j'y vais tout de suite. Je vais en acheter...

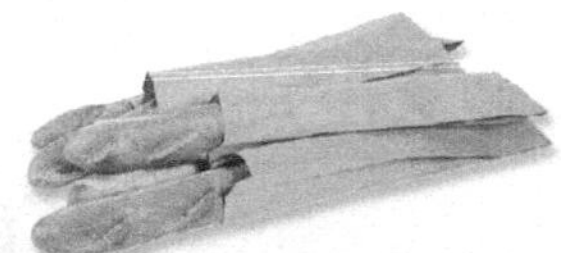

1.

2.

3.

4.

Digital performance space

Communication

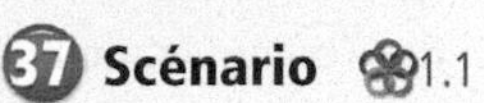

37 Scénario 1.1

Parlons Imagine que ta classe de français va faire un pique-nique à la campagne avec quelques élèves francophones ce week-end. En petits groupes, choisissez ce que vous voulez manger et boire. Ensuite, décidez qui va aller faire les courses et où. Chaque personne du groupe doit faire quelque chose. Essayez d'utiliser des pronoms dans vos réponses.

MODÈLE **—Qu'est-ce qu'on va préparer pour le pique-nique?**
—On fait des sandwichs?
—D'accord. Moi, je vais acheter le pain à la boulangerie. Je peux y acheter aussi...

French for Spanish Speakers

Ask Spanish speakers to compare the pronouns with pronouns in Spanish. What do the languages have in common? (Both place object pronouns before the main verb.) What are some of the differences? (Spanish has no equivalent for the pronouns **y** and **en**; indirect object pronouns in Spanish change from **le/les** to **se** when used with direct object pronouns.) 4.1

35 Answers

1. Mazarine, tu vas la préparer?
2. Tu m'en donnes?
3. Vous allez les lui envoyer?
4. Les Martin ne vont pas en acheter.
5. Je t'en envoie une.
6. Il n'y en a pas.

Communication

Group Work: Interpersonal

Have students imagine they have 200 euros with which to buy gifts. Have them write five sentences with **acheter à** to say what they are going to buy and for whom. Partners should ask each other questions and confirm or deny by responding with two object pronouns. 1.1

Differentiated Instruction

SLOWER PACE LEARNERS

After presenting the placement of object pronouns, hold up flashcards of places **(à la bibliothèque, à la boucherie, à l'épicerie)** or things **(des livres, du jambon, de la confiture)** and have students tell you if the words would be replaced by **y** or **en.** Then work together as a class to write sentences with the flashcard words, first without the pronouns, and then with them. 1.2

MULTIPLE INTELLIGENCES

37 Intrapersonal Students with more introspective strengths may prefer to work alone rather than in a group. Give students the option of completing the activity independently by writing an imaginary conversation. You may also give students the option of completing a scenario of their own creation that will show mastery of the use of pronouns. 1.2

Assess

Assessment Program
Quiz: Grammaire 2
Alternative Assessment
Differentiated Practice and Assessment CD-ROM

Online Assessment
my.hrw.com

Test Generator

Resources

Planning:
Lesson Planner
Teacher One Stop

Practice:
Grammar Tutor for Students of French, Chapter 3
Cahier de vocabulaire et grammaire
Differentiated Practice and Assessment CD-ROM
Cahier d'activités
Media Guide
Independent Study Guide
Projectable Transparencies
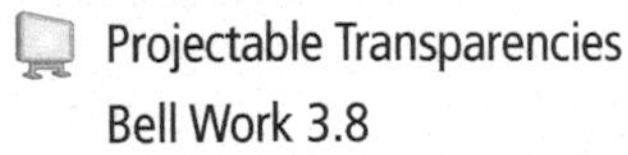
Bell Work 3.8
Audio CD 3, Tr. 6

Bell Work

Use Bell Work 3.8 in the *Projectable Transparencies* or write this activity on the board.

Unscramble the words to make logical sentences.

1. acheter / les / vais / lui / je
2. souvent / vous / donne / il / en
3. en / quelquefois / il / a / y
4. lui / va / on / parler / en
5. allons / préparer / en / leur / nous / un 1.2

39 Script

1. Mia achète du poisson et des crevettes.
2. Mia prend un chariot.
3. Mia achète deux tranches de jambon et des steaks.
4. Mia achète des fruits et des légumes.
5. Mia parle à l'épicière.

39 Answers

1. Elle est à la poissonnerie.
2. Elle est au supermarché.
3. Elle est à la boucherie-charcuterie.
4. Elle est au marché.
5. Elle est à l'épicerie.

Synthèse
- Vocabulaire 2
- Grammaire 2

Application 2

38 Question de goût! 1.2

Écrivons Est-ce que ces personnes ou ces animaux aiment les choses suivantes? Dis s'ils en mangent ou pas et donne un détail supplémentaire (quand ils en mangent, pourquoi ils aiment ou n'aiment pas ça, etc.).

MODÈLE toi / la salade
J'adore la salade. J'en mange souvent au déjeuner.

1. les lapins *(rabbits)* / les carottes
2. mon chien / les framboises
3. toi / les brocolis
4. ton (ta) meilleur(e) ami(e) / les aubergines
5. les Français / les escargots *(snails)*

39 Écoutons CD 3, Tr. 6 1.2

Mia fait des courses en ville ce matin. Écoute chaque phrase et dis où se trouve Mia d'après les choses qu'elle achète ou qu'elle fait.

Un peu plus Révisions

Contractions with *à* and *de*

Remember how to form contractions with **à** and **de**? Here are the forms.

à	de
à + le = au	de + le = du
à + la = à la	de + la = de la
à + l' = à l'	de + l' = de l'
à + les = aux	de + les = des

Je vais à l'épicerie du quartier ou à l'hypermarché au coin de la rue.

Vocabulaire et grammaire, *pp. 34–36*
Cahier d'activités, *pp. 25–27*

40 Le bon choix 1.2

Écrivons Choisis la préposition et l'article ou la contraction qui convient pour compléter chaque phrase.

1. J'adore le marché _______ ville!
   a. du **b.** la **(c.)** de la
2. Sophie va aller _______ supermarché ce matin.
   a. du **(b.)** au **c.** de la
3. Il y a des marchés _______ États-Unis?
   a. à l' **b.** des **(c.)** aux
4. La caissière _______ supermarché est très sympa.
   a. de la **b.** des **(c.)** du
5. Est-ce qu'il y a une boulangerie _______ centre commercial?
   a. du **(b.)** au **c.** à la
6. On ne mange pas très bien à la cantine _______ école!
   a. d' **b.** la **(c.)** de l'

Core Instruction

INTEGRATED PRACTICE

1. Have students do Activities 38–39. **(5 min.)**
2. Give students a list of ingredients needed to prepare a full meal. **(1 min.)**
3. Students should decide where to buy each item. **Où est-ce que tu achètes de la crème fraîche? (J'en achète à la crémerie.)** Continue. **Peux-tu y en trouver? (Oui, je peux y en trouver.) (6 min.)**
4. Present **Un peu plus** and complete the integrated practice Activities. **(10 min.)**

TEACHING UN PEU PLUS

1. Remind students of the required contractions in French for **à** and **de. (1 min.)**
2. Point to a food item on transparency **Vocabulaire 3.2** and have students form a sentence about it. **À la poissonnerie, on trouve du poisson. À l'épicerie, on trouve des boîtes de conserve. (3 min.)**

Online Practice
my.hrw.com
Application 2 practice

41 Un article de journal 1.2

Lisons/Écrivons Voici un article de journal sur les préférences des Français quand ils font leurs courses. Complète l'article avec les articles ou les contractions qui conviennent.

Beaucoup de Français disent qu'ils préfèrent les légumes __1__ marché parce qu'ils sont meilleurs. __2__ marché, les Français achètent aussi souvent leurs fruits. Pour le fromage, ils préfèrent aller __3__ crémerie. Pour les produits congelés, ils préfèrent l'épicerie __4__ quartier. __5__ boulangerie, ils aiment le pain bien chaud et les croissants. Et pour le poisson, ils vont __6__ poissonnerie où ils peuvent parler __7__ poissonnière pour savoir quel poisson acheter.

1. du (au)
2. Au
3. à la
4. du
5. À la
6. à la
7. à la

42 Les préférences des Américains 1.3

Écrivons Écris un paragraphe pour décrire les préférences des Américains quand ils font leurs courses. Utilise l'article de l'activité 41 comme modèle.

MODÈLE **Beaucoup d'Américains font leurs courses à... D'habitude, ils y achètent...**

Communication

Digital performance space

43 À l'épicerie 1.1

Parlons Julien travaille dans une épicerie à Québec et un(e) client(e) lui pose des questions. Avec un(e) camarade, vous allez jouer le rôle de Julien et du/de la client(e). Lisez les questions ci-dessous et répondez-y de manière logique. Ensuite, échangez les rôles.

— **Bonjour. Les yaourts, s'il vous plaît?**
—
— **Merci. Quel est le prix d'un kilo de tomates?**
—
— **Bon, je vais en prendre un kilo, s'il vous paît.**
—
— **Oui, c'est tout pour aujourd'hui, merci. Au revoir.**
—

Communication

Group Work: Interpersonal

Write a list of verbs on the board such as **acheter à, offrir à, donner à, finir, mettre,** or **prendre.** Ask students to use one of the verbs in a sentence with both a direct and indirect object or a reference to a place. Then have them write the corresponding sentence with the pronouns. In small groups, have students read their first sentence aloud. Group members should repeat the sentence with the appropriate object pronouns. 1.1

Activité Pré-AP Préparatoire — Language Examination

43 Sample answer

— . . .
— **Ils sont au milieu du magasin, au bout du rayon.**
— . . .
— **C'est trois euros cinquante le kilo.**
— . . .
— **Ce sera tout?**
— . . .
— **Au revoir.**

Differentiated Instruction

ADVANCED LEARNERS

Have students create their own comic strip that includes the food vocabulary in this chapter. Students should draw the pictures for each frame or take pictures of their classmates who act out the storyline of their comic strip. 1.3

SPECIAL LEARNING NEEDS

41 Students with Dyslexia Students may more easily complete the activity if the paragraph is enlarged and copied for use as a worksheet. You may wish to provide students with a word bank of answer choices. 1.2

Assess

Assessment Program

Quiz: Application 2

Audio CD 3, Tr. 16

Alternative Assessment

Differentiated Practice and Assessment CD-ROM

Online Assessment
my.hrw.com

Test Generator 

Resources

Planning:
Lesson Planner
 Teacher One Stop

Presentation:
 DVD Tutor, Disc 1
Télé-roman

Practice:
Media Guide
 DVD Tutor, Disc 1
Télé-roman

Connections

Visual Learners

To help students better understand the personality of Charles Rigaud, have them diagram what they know about him so far. Start by drawing a circle and writing his name in it. Coming out of the circle, draw several spokes connected to additional circles. In each one, have students write one piece of information about Mr. Rigaud. Encourage students to include as much information as they can in the diagram. 3.2

Gestures

Call students' attention to scene 6. What is the merchant doing? Why is his gesture important to the story? Ask students what they think will happen next. Then have students look at scene 9. Based on their position and the perspective of this image, what might Léa and Seydou be doing? 2.1

Télé-roman

Le Secret de la statuette *Épisode 3*

STRATÉGIE

Comparing attitudes Comparing the characters' attitudes toward an idea or an event can help you to understand their motives and their actions. In **Episode 3**, Seydou and Léa react differently to the mysterious disappearance of the statuette. Who detains the information at the beginning of the episode? Who decides to take action? Do the two characters react in the same way when they find out that Charles Rigaud is on the island? Based on what you learn in the episode, who do you think is the most adventurous? The most cautious? 1.2

Quelques jours plus tard, chez les Gadio...

1

Seydou Tu sais, l'inspecteur Sonko a dit à mon père qu'il n'y a pas de Charles Rigaud à Dakar.

Léa Ah oui? Et alors?

Seydou Eh bien, peut-être que l'homme qui a apporté la statuette à mon père ne s'appelle pas vraiment Charles Rigaud.

2

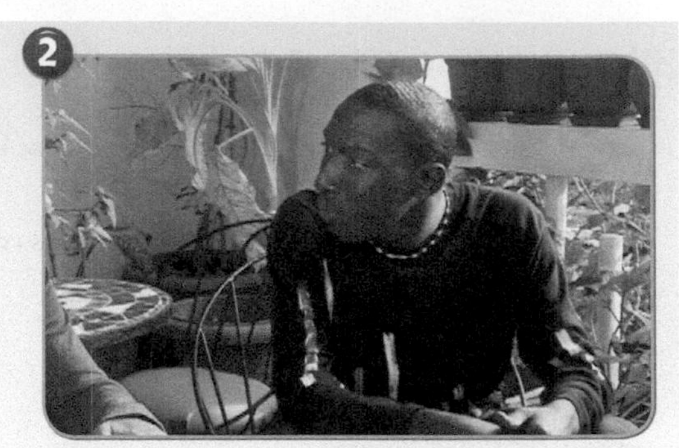

Seydou L'inspecteur Sonko a trouvé quelque chose. Il a fait analyser le sable qu'il a trouvé dans le bureau de mon père. C'est du sable de l'île de Gorée.

3

Léa Alors, on y va?

Seydou Où?

Léa Sur l'île de Gorée. C'est peut-être là que les voleurs se cachent.

Seydou et Léa prennent le bateau pour l'île de Gorée.

Core Instruction

TEACHING TÉLÉ-ROMAN

1. Have students scan the **Télé-roman** text and look at the pictures. **(1 min.)**
2. Play the video, pausing after each scene change. Ask general comprehension questions after each segment. **(5 min.)**
3. Play the video again without stopping. Have volunteers read and act out **Télé-roman.** Have them use gestures and facial expressions they saw in the video. **(5 min.)**
4. Have students work in pairs to answer the **As-tu compris?** questions on page 105. **(5 min.)**

DVD Tutor 

As an alternative, you might use the captioned version of **Le Secret de la statuette** on DVD.

Visit Us Online
my.hrw.com
Online Edition

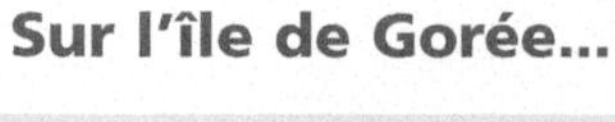

Sur l'île de Gorée...

5 **Seydou** Pardon, monsieur. Nous faisons une petite enquête sur un vol. Est-ce que vous avez remarqué quelque chose de bizarre ces jours-ci?

Le commerçant Attendez un peu! Il y a cet homme qui vient au magasin depuis une semaine ou deux.

6 **Le commerçant** Il a l'air d'un explorateur, avec le chapeau et tout! Il se tire toujours l'oreille, comme ça...

7 **Seydou** Charles Rigaud! Je suis sûr que c'est lui!

Léa Mais pourquoi? C'est pas logique du tout! C'est lui qui a apporté la statuette à ton père et maintenant, il la vole? Ça n'a aucun sens!

8 **Seydou** Bon, on téléphone à l'inspecteur Sonko?

Léa D'abord, je pense qu'on devrait attendre ici. Rigaud va peut-être passer au magasin.

Seydou Bon. D'accord.

9 *Seydou et Léa attendent Charles Rigaud devant le magasin de l'île de Gorée.*

1.2

AS-TU COMPRIS?

1. Qu'est-ce que l'inspecteur Sonko a dit à monsieur Gadio?
2. Pourquoi Seydou et Léa décident d'aller sur l'île de Gorée?
3. Le commerçant décrit un homme. Qui est cet homme?
4. Quand Seydou dit «Charles Rigaud! Je suis sûr que c'est lui!», qu'est-ce qu'il veut dire?
5. Qu'est-que Seydou et Léa décident de faire à la fin de l'épisode?

Prochain épisode: *Peux-tu deviner qui va venir au magasin dans l'épisode 4?*

Télé-roman

As-tu compris? Answers

1. qu'il n'y a pas de Charles Rigaud à Dakar
2. pour chercher les voleurs
3. Charles Rigaud
4. Rigaud a volé la statuette
5. d'attendre Charles Rigaud devant le magasin

Communication

Pair Work: Presentational

After students have seen **Télé-roman,** have them work in pairs to role-play the parts of Léa and Seydou after they learn that Mr. Rigaud has been seen on Île de Gorée. Seydou believes that Mr. Rigaud stole the statuette, but Léa thinks that makes no sense. Students should each present a logical argument in favor of his or her position. 1.3

Le Secret de la statuette Episode 3

In this episode, Seydou tells Léa that the police inspector has learned that there is no Charles Rigaud in Dakar. It is a false name. An analysis of the sand found at the museum revealed that it came from **l'île de Gorée.** Léa and Seydou take a ferry to the island and ask people if they have seen anyone who resembles Rigaud. One merchant remembers seeing a man who fits his description. Seydou is suddenly convinced that Rigaud stole the statuette and wants to call the police. Léa suggests they wait around to see if Rigaud shows up at the store.

Lecture et écriture

Resources

Planning:
Lesson Planner
Teacher One Stop

Presentation:
Audio CD 3, Tr. 7

Practice:
Cahier d'activités
Reading Strategies and Skills Handbook, Chapter 3
Intermediate Reader
French InterActive Reader

Applying the Strategies

For practice with monitoring comprehension, have students use the "Probable Passage" strategy from the *Reading Strategies and Skills Handbook.*

READING PRACTICE

Strategy: Probable Passage

STRATEGIES

Reading Skill	When can I use this strategy?		
	Prereading	During Reading	Postreading
Identifying Purpose	✓		✓
Making Predictions	✓		
Comparing and Contrasting			
Analyzing Chronological Order			✓

Strategy at a Glance: Probable Passage

- The teacher chooses key words or phrases from the text students will read, then develops categories for the words and writes the Probable Passage (a cloze passage with key words omitted).
- Before students read the text, they arrange the key words and phrases in the categories. Then they fill in the blanks in the cloze passage with the key words.
- After students read the text, they discuss how their passages were similar to or different from the actual text.

Many readers struggle because they don't predict what a selection might be about and don't think about what they already know about a topic. These students simply open a book, look at words, and begin turning pages. **Probable Passage** is a strategy that helps stop those poor reading habits by encouraging students to make predictions and to activate their prior knowledge about a topic.

Best Use of the Strategy

Probable Passage (Wood 1984) is a brief preview of a text from which key words and phrases have been omitted. The teacher chooses these key words from the text and presents them to the students. In some cases, it might be necessary to discuss the meaning of the words; many times, students can figure this out for themselves. Students arrange the words in categories according to their probable functions in the story (such as Setting, Characters, or Conflicts), then use the words to fill in the blanks of the Probable Passage. After reading the story, students compare it to their passages and discuss differences. As students work through this process, they use what they know about story structure, think about vocabulary, practice making predictions, and compare their predictions to the story line.

Making Inferences

Have students talk about what it means to make an inference. Have them brainstorm some jobs that require one to make inferences and draw conclusions. (detectives, archeologists, jurors) Give students a few minutes to talk about times when they have had to make inferences. Ask them if they have ever been wrong when making an inference. What information would they have needed in order to have inferred correctly?

Lecture et écriture

Jean-Jacques Sempé

René Goscinny

Jean-Jacques Sempé (1932–) est un des dessinateurs français les plus connus. Il commence à publier des dessins humoristiques vers l'âge de 19 ans. À partir de 1960, *Le Petit Nicolas* prend la forme de romans écrits par **René Goscinny** (1926–1977) et illustrés par Sempé. Goscinny est aussi le scénariste[1] de la bande dessinée *Astérix*.

STRATÉGIE pour lire

Making inferences is drawing conclusions based on evidence that is hinted at, or implied. While you read, pause after each paragraph, or exchange to think about the details the author includes, why they are included, and what those details tell you.

A Avant la lecture 1.3

Lis le titre et regarde les illustrations. D'après toi, qui est le narrateur? Qu'est-ce qu'il fait? Avec qui? Essaie d'imaginer l'histoire à partir des illustrations.

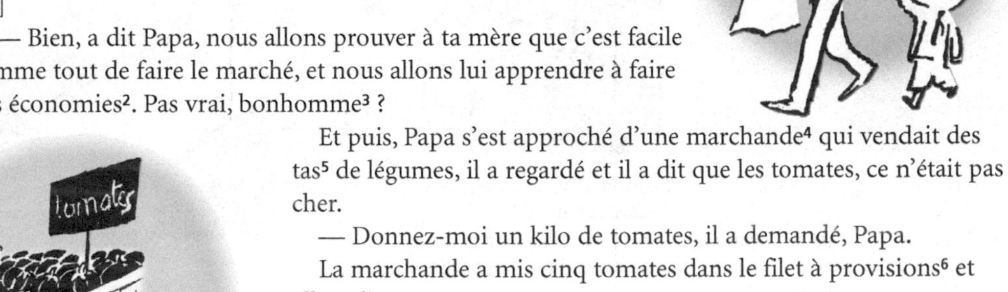

Le Petit Nicolas

CD 3, Tr. 7

On a fait le marché avec papa

[...]

— Bien, a dit Papa, nous allons prouver à ta mère que c'est facile comme tout de faire le marché, et nous allons lui apprendre à faire des économies[2]. Pas vrai, bonhomme[3] ?

Et puis, Papa s'est approché d'une marchande[4] qui vendait des tas[5] de légumes, il a regardé et il a dit que les tomates, ce n'était pas cher.

— Donnez-moi un kilo de tomates, il a demandé, Papa.

La marchande a mis cinq tomates dans le filet à provisions[6] et elle a dit :

— Et avec ça. Qu'est-ce que je vous mets ?

Papa a regardé dans le filet, et puis il a dit :

— Comment ? Il n'y a que cinq tomates dans un kilo ?

— Et qu'est-ce que vous croyez, a demandé la dame, que pour le prix vous aurez une plantation ? Les maris, quand ça vient faire le marché, c'est tous du pareil au même[7].

— Les maris, on se laisse moins rouler[8] que nos femmes, voilà tout ! a dit Papa.

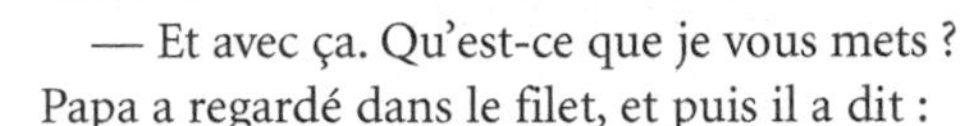

1. writer 2. save money 3. young man 4. saleswoman 5. loads of 6. string bag 7. all the same 8. we are not easy to con

Core Instruction

TEACHING LECTURE

1. Read **Stratégie** aloud with students. **(1 min.)**
2. Have students do Activity A orally in class. If students have not read ***Le Petit Nicolas*** before, tell them he can be compared to our Dennis the Menace or Calvin of "Calvin and Hobbes". **(2 min.)**
3. Assign all parts, including the narrator, and have students read the selection aloud in class. **(14 min.)**
4. Have partners do Activities B and C. **(3 min.)**
5. Assign Activity D as homework. You may wish to give suggestions on using the dialogue in the reading selection and have groups work together to look up words they will need to include in the stage directions. **(3 min.)**

— Répétez-ça un peu, si vous êtes un homme ? a demandé la marchande, qui ressemblait à M. Pancrace, le charcutier de notre quartier.

Papa a dit : « Bon, ça va, ça va » ; il m'a laissé porter le filet et nous sommes partis, pendant que la marchande parlait de Papa à d'autres marchandes.

Et puis, j'ai vu un marchand avec plein de poissons sur sa table et des grosses langoustes[1] :

— Regarde, papa ! Des langoustes ! j'ai crié.

— Parfait, a dit Papa, allons voir ça.

Papa, il s'est approché du marchand, et il a demandé si les langoustes étaient fraîches. Le marchand lui a expliqué qu'elles étaient spéciales. Quant à être fraîches, il pensait que oui, puisqu'elles étaient vivantes[2], et il a rigolé.

— Oui, bon, a dit Papa, à combien la grosse, là, qui remue[3] les pattes ?

Le marchand lui a dit le prix et Papa a ouvert des yeux gros comme tout.

— Et l'autre, là, la plus petite ? a demandé Papa. Le marchand lui a dit le prix de nouveau et Papa a dit que c'était incroyable et que c'était une honte[4].

— Dites, a demandé le marchand, c'est des langoustes ou des crevettes que vous voulez acheter. Parce que ce n'est pas du tout le même prix. Votre femme aurait dû vous prévenir.

— Viens, Nicolas, a dit Papa, nous allons chercher autre chose.

Mais moi, j'ai dit à Papa que ce n'était pas la peine d'aller ailleurs[5], que ces langoustes me paraissaient terribles, avec leurs pattes qui remuaient, et que la langouste c'est drôlement bon.

— Ne discute pas et viens, Nicolas, m'a dit Papa. Nous n'achèterons pas de langouste, voilà tout.

— Mais, Papa, j'ai dit, Maman fait chauffer[6] de l'eau pour les langoustes, il faut en acheter.

— Nicolas, m'a dit Papa, si tu continues, tu iras m'attendre dans la voiture !

Alors, là, je me suis mis à pleurer[7] ; c'est vrai, quoi, c'est pas juste. [...]

— Nous rentrons, a dit Papa, qui avait l'air nerveux et fatigué ; il se fait très tard.

— Mais, Papa, j'ai dit, nous n'avons que cinq tomates. Moi, je crois qu'une langouste...

1. spiny lobster 2. alive 3. is moving 4. it was a scandal 5. somewhere else 6. to boil 7. to cry

Lecture et écriture

Cultures

Practices and Perspectives

There is an increasing number of supermarkets in francophone countries **(supermarchés** or **hypermarchés). Supermarchés en ligne** deliver groceries ordered online. However, many people still prefer to shop at specialty shops and outdoor markets. Have students discuss in small groups the advantages and disadvantages of shopping at **supermarchés, supermarchés en ligne,** specialty shops, and **marchés en plein air.** 2.1

Connections

Math Link

Bring to class a scale that measures in grams, along with three small boxes of oranges, apples, and bananas. Label the price per kilogram of each kind of fruit. Give partners a budget of ten euros. Partners will tell you the amount and kind of fruit for you to weigh **(Deux pommes, s'il vous plaît.),** then figure out how much they owe for that selection. Their goal is to try to come close to their ten-euro budget without going over. Students cannot put back any items once they have selected them. The partners who come closest to ten euros win. 3.1

Differentiated Instruction

SLOWER PACE LEARNERS

Separate the reading into logical sections. Prepare multiple-choice questions that summarize each section. Read the first section aloud to students and have them answer the first multiple-choice question as a class. For example, for the first section a question might be: 1. Papa and Nicolas are going... a. to check out books at the library; b. to shop for clothing; c. to shop for food. 1.2

SPECIAL LEARNING NEEDS

Students with Learning Disabilities/ Dyslexia Using **Stratégie pour lire,** determine places in ***Le Petit Nicolas*** for students to pause as suggested. Allow students to talk to a partner about what they have read. Ask partners to discuss the details, why they are included, and what they know about those details. Have partners report to the class and compare their inferences. 1.1

Activité préparatoire Pre-AP Language Examination

Through the practice of listening and reading comprehension, as well as essay writing, **Lecture et écriture** helps students prepare for the **Interpretive Reading and Listening** and the **Presentational Writing** sections of the Advanced Placement exam.

Additional Practice

For more reading practice, see **Variations littéraires,** pp. 386–387.

Comparisons

Comparing and Contrasting

Assign teams of students to prepare two similar American and French dishes, for example American-style apple pie and **tarte tatin** or chocolate pudding and chocolate mousse. Have a taste testing in class to see which version students prefer. You might also have students analyze the differences between the American and French versions and see if they can make any generalizations about American versus French cuisine. 4.2

Communities

Family Link

Assign students to prepare a French dish for their family, and then interview each member to see how they liked it. Students should write a report in French on their family's opinions. You might have students take pictures of each family member as they take their first bite to use as illustrations in their report. 5.1

Mais Papa ne m'a pas laissé finir, il m'a tiré par la main, et comme ça m'a surpris, j'ai lâché le filet à provision, qui est tombé par terre. C'était gagné. Surtout qu'une grosse dame qui était derrière nous a marché sur les tomates, ça a fait « cruish », et elle nous a dit de faire attention. Quand j'ai ramassé le filet à provisions, ce qu'il y avait dedans, ça ne donnait pas faim.

Compréhension

B Lis les phrases suivantes du texte. Puis, utilise la **Stratégie pour lire** pour déterminer le sens des phrases. 1.2

1. « Comment? Il n'y a que cinq tomates dans un kilo ? »
   - **a.** Il y a beaucoup de tomates.
   - **(b.)** Il n'y a pas assez de tomates.
2. « Répétez ça un peu, si vous êtes un homme ? »
   - **a.** La marchande n'a pas bien compris.
   - **(b.)** La marchande veut se battre (*fight*) avec Papa.
3. « Le marchand lui a dit le prix et Papa a ouvert des yeux gros comme tout. »
   - **(a.)** Les langoustes sont très chères.
   - **b.** Les langoustes sont bon marché.
4. « Quand j'ai ramassé le filet à provisions, ce qu'il y avait dedans, ça ne donnait pas faim. »
   - **a.** Nicolas ne veut pas manger les tomates.
   - **(b.)** Le petit Nicolas n'a plus faim.

C Complète les phrases suivantes en t'aidant de la lecture. 1.2

1. La marchande vend…
2. Papa veut acheter des tomates parce que…
3. Quand le petit Nicolas voit la table du marchand de poisson, il veut…
4. Les langoustes sont fraîches parce qu'elles sont…
5. Le petit Nicolas pleure parce que…
6. Le petit Nicolas a lâché le filet parce que…

Possible answers:
1. des légumes/tomates.
2. les tomates ne sont pas chères.
3. acheter des langoustes.
4. vivantes.
5. papa n'a pas acheté de langoustes.
6. papa l'a tiré par la main.

Après la lecture

D Work with four of your classmates to rewrite the reading selection as a play. Use the dialogue that is already there, but add stage directions and other information the actors might need. Perform the play for the class. 1.3

Core Instruction

TEACHING ESPACE ÉCRITURE

1. Discuss **Stratégie pour écrire.** Have the students look at the recipe and point out the infinitives in the directions. **(2 min.)**
2. Have students bring a simple recipe to class for this assignment. Give them a vocabulary list of common cooking terms. Have them do steps 1 and 2 in class. If students do not complete the activities in class, they should finish as homework. Remind students that after a quantity, **des, de l', de la, du** become **de. (25 min.)**
3. Assign partners for step 3 and have students peer edit their partner's recipe. **(10 min.)**
4. Hand out 3 x 5 index cards or recipe cards, have students copy their recipes, and complete **Application. (5 min.)**

Espace écriture

STRATÉGIE pour écrire

Arranging your ideas chronologically can help you map out a plan for your writing. When you give written instructions, such as recipes, the ordering of elements is crucial.

Un plat délicieux 

It is your turn to organize a dinner for the French Club. You've planned the menu and are giving each guest a recipe for a dish to bring. Write a recipe for a dish. At the bottom of the recipe, add a tip or comment that would help the cook better prepare the recipe.

1 Plan

Choose a dish that can be served at a French Club dinner. List the ingredients needed to prepare the dish. Then, arrange the ingredients in the order they will be needed. Write the quantity needed in front of each ingredient, or use the partitive if an exact quantity is not required.

2 Rédaction

When writing the recipe:

- use infinitives, direct object pronouns, **en**, and **y**
- describe in detail each step in the preparation

At the bottom of the recipe, write a comment or a helpful hint about the preparation.

3 Correction

Exchange your recipe with a classmate. Have your classmate check to make sure that all the steps are in logical order and nothing has been left out. Check for spelling, punctuation, and correct use of the partitive and pronouns.

4 Application

Illustrate your recipe and display it on a poster board in class or compile all the recipes into a class cookbook. Consider testing a few of the recipes in class or at home. You might even have a potluck lunch.

Gratin de poires

(pour 6 personnes)

- 8 poires
- 2 tasses de lait
- 1 tasse de farine
- 1/2 tasse de sucre
- 1 cuillère à soupe de beurre
- 4 cuillères à soupe d'amandes pilées
- 1 cuillère d'extrait de vanille

Dans un bol, mélanger la farine, le sucre, l'extrait de vanille et le lait. Éplucher et couper les poires en lamelles. Beurrer un plat qui va au four. Mettre les poires dans le plat. Verser la pâte sur les poires. Mettre au four à 375°F pendant 30 minutes. Servir tiède.

Lecture et écriture

Lecture et écriture

Process Writing

Avant d'écrire Suggest to students that before they write out their recipe that they illustrate the steps of the recipe first. They can then write steps as captions to go with each picture. This will help students arrange their ideas and give them a visual cue as they think of the correct sequence of commands.

Writing Assessment

To assess the **Espace écriture,** you can use the following rubric. For additional rubrics, see the *Assessment Program* or refer to the *Generate Success* Rubric Generator.

Writing Rubric	4	3	2	1
Content (Complete—Incomplete)				
Comprehensibility (Comprehensible—Seldom comprehensible)				
Accuracy (Accurate—Seldom accurate)				
Organization (Well-organized—Poorly organized)				
Effort (Excellent effort—Minimal effort)				

18-20: A 16-17: B 14-15: C 12-13: D Under 12: F

Differentiated Instruction

ADVANCED LEARNERS

Search the Internet for a French online bookstore. Search the site for books by Jean-Jacques Sempé and René Goscinny. Print reviews that readers have written about several of their books. Distribute the reviews to students. Students should choose one book that they would like to read and write a paragraph summarizing what the book is likely about and why they would like to read it. Alternatively, have students search the Internet themselves for the book reviews.

5.2

MULTIPLE INTELLIGENCES

Bodily Kinesthetic After completing the **Un plat délicieux** activity, ask students to decide on one or two recipes to actually create. Volunteers can take the recipes home, assemble the ingredients, and follow the directions to cook the dish. As an alternative, the recipes can be made at school, if practicable. If the recipes are followed exactly as written, some difficulties may occur. Facilitate a class discussion about what went wrong if the recipe is not entirely successful.

5.1

Assess

Assessment Program
Quiz: Lecture
Quiz: Écriture
Online Assessment my.hrw.com
Test Generator 

Prépare-toi pour l'examen

Resources

Planning:
Lesson Planner
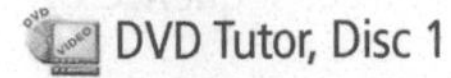
Teacher One Stop

Practice:
Cahier d'activités
Media Guide
DVD Tutor, Disc 1
Projectable Transparencies
Situation, Chapitre 3
Picture Sequences, Chapter 3
Audio CD 3, Tr. 10–13
@HOMETUTOR

② Answer

Lucas va servir du pain, du fromage, du poisson avec des pommes de terre, de la salade, du brocoli, du beurre, une salade de fruits et un gâteau au chocolat.

③ Answer

Lucas va à la boulangerie-pâtisserie pour acheter un gâteau et du pain, à la crémerie-fromagerie pour acheter du fromage et du beurre, au marché pour acheter des fruits et des légumes et à la poissonnerie pour acheter du poisson.

Reteaching

With a loaf of bread, demonstrate **un pain,** and then break off a piece and offer it to students to illustrate the partitive **du pain.**

Chapitre 3

Prépare-toi pour l'examen

@HOMETUTOR

① Vocabulaire 1
- to ask about food preparation
- to make requests

pp. 82–85

① Identifie autant de *(as many)* fruits ou de légumes que tu peux pour chaque catégorie. 1.2

DES LÉGUMES:	DES FRUITS:
1. verts	1. verts
2. rouges	2. rouges
3. orange	3. orange
4. marron	4. jaunes
5. blancs	

② Grammaire 1
- the partitive
- the pronoun y

Un peu plus
- question formation

pp. 86–91

② Lucas prépare du saumon *(salmon)* pour des amis ce soir. Il prépare beaucoup d'autres choses aussi! Regarde la photo et dis ce qu'il va servir. Utilise le partitif. 1.2

③ Vocabulaire 2
- to shop for groceries
- to ask where things are

pp. 94–97

③ Lucas fait ses courses pour le dîner ce soir. Il préfère les petits magasins parce qu'il n'aime pas le supermarché. Regarde de nouveau *(once again)* la photo de l'Activité 2 et dis où Lucas doit aller pour faire ses courses. 1.2

Preparing for the Exam

FOLD-N-LEARN

Pocket Folder Study Aid

1. Have students fold a 2-inch lengthwise flap in a sheet of paper and then a 1/2-inch flap on either end. Glue or tape these flaps where they meet the original 2-inch fold.
2. When the flaps are dry, ask students to fold the paper in half so that the two folded ends meet with the pockets on the inside. Students should label both sides of the pocket folder "Chapter 3 Flashcards".
3. Ask students to use 3x5 index cards to create flashcards for **Vocabulaire 1** and **2** and place them in the left pocket, English side up.
4. Students can review the expressions in Chapter 3 by taking a flashcard, reading the English word or phrase, and trying to recall the French written on the other side. If correct, they should place the card in the right pocket. If not, the card is filed in the left pocket for further review.

Prépare-toi pour l'examen

Online Assessment
my.hrw.com
Chapter Self-test

4 Inès parle de ce qu'elle fait le samedi. Récris ce qu'elle dit en remplaçant les noms en italique par des pronoms. 1.2

Le samedi, je fais les courses avec ma mère. Nous aimons faire *les courses* ensemble. D'abord, nous allons à la boulangerie et nous achetons du pain *à la boulangerie.* Il y a beaucoup *de pain!* Ensuite, nous allons à l'hypermarché. Ils vendent de tout *à l'hypermarché.* Après, nous aimons aller manger dans un café sur la place St. Jean. Nous mangeons souvent *dans ce café.* Le soir, nous préparons le dîner. Quelquefois, mon père nous aide à préparer *le dîner.* Mes grands-parents aiment manger dans leur chambre. Alors, nous servons *le dîner à mes grands-parents* dans leur chambre.

4 Grammaire 2
- the pronoun en
- placement of object pronouns

Un peu plus
- contractions with à and de

pp. 98–103

5 Réponds aux questions suivantes. 2.1, 2.2

1. Quelles sont quelques spécialités québécoises?
2. Si on veut faire les courses au supermarché, quelles sont les différences entre le Québec et la France?

5 Culture
- Flash culture pp. 84, 88, 96, 100
- Comparaisons pp. 92–93

6 Perrine parle des courses qu'elle a faites ce matin. Fais une liste de toutes les choses qu'elle a achetées et des endroits où elle est allée. CD 3, Tr. 10 1.2

7 Dominique (Élève A) et toi, vous préparez à manger pour vos parents ce soir. Toi, tu fais bien la cuisine mais Dominique ne sait pas la faire. Il/Elle te pose des questions et te demande de l'aider. Joue la scène avec un(e) camarade. D'abord, lisez les instructions pour chaque réplique *(exchange).* Ensuite, créez votre dialogue en utilisant des expressions de ce chapitre et d'autres chapitres. 1.1

Élève A:	Demande à ton/ta camarade la recette de la salade de fruits.
Élève B:	Donne à ton/ta camarade la recette de la salade de fruits.
Élève A:	Il te manque des ingrédients. Demande à ton/ta camarade d'aller en acheter.
Élève B:	Tu veux bien aller au magasin. Assure-toi que ta liste d'achats est complète.
Élève A:	Tu veux faire un autre plat et tu en demandes les ingrédients à ton/ta camarade.
Élève B:	Décris les ingrédients pour cette recette.
Élève A:	Dis quels ingrédients ton/ta camarade doit acheter pour ta recette.
Élève B:	Tu te souviens que tu as un cours de guitare dans une demi-heure. Excuse-toi de ne pas pouvoir aller au magasin.

4 Answers

Nous aimons les faire ensemble.
D'abord, nous allons à la boulangerie et nous y achetons du pain.
Il y en a beaucoup!
Ils y vendent de tout.
Nous y mangeons souvent.
Quelquefois, mon père nous aide à le préparer.
Alors, nous le leur servons dans leur chambre.

5 Answers

1. la poutine, les cretons
2. Au Québec, le caissier met les produits dans le sac; en France, les clients doivent ranger leurs courses eux-mêmes.

6 Script

See script on p. 79F.

6 Answers

Elle a acheté des abricots, des cerises, des carottes, des champignons, un gâteau, un poulet et du jambon. Elle est allée à l'épicerie, à la boulangerie-pâtisserie et à la boucherie-charcuterie.

Language Examination

7 Sample conversation

a. Comment est-ce qu'on fait la salade de fruits?

b. Coupe les oranges, les bananes et les pommes. Ajoute du yaourt.

a. Je n'ai pas de pommes. Tu veux bien aller m'acheter des pommes?

b. Oui, d'accord. Tu n'as besoin de rien d'autre?

a. Qu'est-ce qu'il y a dans les crêpes?

b. Il y a des œufs, de la farine et du lait.

a. Tu me rapportes de la farine et du lait?

b. Non, je regrette mais j'ai un cours de guitare dans une demi-heure!

Additional Speaking Practice

- For additional speaking practice, you might use the *Picture Sequences Transparency* for Chapter 3 found in the *Projectable Transparencies.*
- To assess the speaking activities in this section, you might use the *Generate Success* Rubric Generator or the oral rubrics found in the *Assessment Program.*

Pre-AP Practice

7 This guided conversation activity helps students practice oral exchanges using material from this chapter and previous chapters. The activity helps prepare students for the **Interpersonal Speaking** section of the AP French Language and Culture Exam.

Chapitre 3

Prépare-toi pour l'examen

Grammar Review

For more practice with the grammar topics in this chapter, see the *Grammar Tutor*, the *DVD Tutor*, the *@HomeTutor* or the *Cahier de vocabulaire et grammaire*.

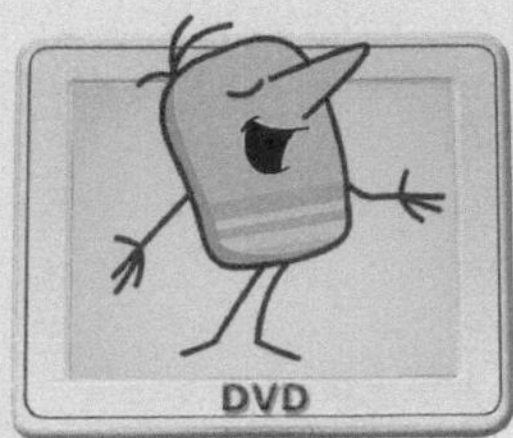

Grammavision

Online Edition

Students might use the online textbook and Performance Space to practice the **Lettres et sons** feature.

Dictée Script

1. Je vais prendre un kilo de haricots verts.
2. Tu joues souvent au hockey?
3. Aujourd'hui, c'est le huit mars.
4. Nous attendons dans le hall de l'hôtel.
5. Le héros du roman est très intelligent.

Game

Des trous Assign vocabulary expressions to teams of five and have them write a sentence with each one on a transparency, leaving blanks where the vocabulary items should be. Project the transparencies one at a time for thirty seconds each. Opposing teams fill in the blanks. They should sit out the round involving the transparency they created. After you show the last transparency, have teams read their answers aloud and either verify or correct them. The team that correctly fills in the most blanks wins. 1.1

Grammaire 1
- the partitive
- the pronoun **y**

Un peu plus
- question formation

pp. 86–91

Résumé: Grammaire 1

To talk about *part of* or *some of* an item, use the partitive articles **du, de la** or **des.** To talk about whole items, use **un, une,** or **des.**

—Tu veux faire **un** gâteau?
—Oui, alors je vais acheter **de la** farine, **du** sucre et **de** l'huile.

Use pronoun **y** to replace phrases beginning with **à, dans, en, sur,** and **chez.**

Tu peux aller **au marché**? Oui, j'y vais tout de suite.

To ask questions, use **est-ce que,** inversion, or a question word.

Est-ce que tu aimes les abricots? **Est-elle** à la crémerie? **Comment** est la quiche?

Grammaire 2
- the pronoun **en**
- placement of object pronouns

Un peu plus
- contractions with **à** and **de**

pp. 98–103

Résumé: Grammaire 2

The pronoun **en** replaces **de + noun.**

—Tu veux **du fromage?** —Non, merci, je n'**en** veux pas.

When replacing nouns that follow an expression of quantity, you still use the expression of quantity with **en.**

—Tu manges **beaucoup de légumes?**
—Oui, j'**en** mange **beaucoup.**

When you use both direct and indirect object pronouns together, they follow a certain order. **Y** and **en** always come last.

Cette pomme? Tiens, je **te la** donne.

Remember that **à + le** contracts to form **au** and **à + les** contracts to form **aux. De + le** contracts to form **du** and **de + les** contracts to form **des.**

Lettres et sons

"h" aspiré CD 3, Tr. 11–13

You've learned that you don't pronounce the letter **h** in French, like in the word **l'hiver.** However, some words begin with an *aspirated h*, or **h aspiré.** This means that you don't make a liaison with the word that comes before. For example: **les haricots, le héros, le hockey.** Since these words begin with **h aspiré,** you do not drop the **e** from the article **le.**

Jeux de langue

Hier, Henri rêvait d'être le héros d'un match de hockey et de monter en hélicoptère.

Dictée 1.2

Écris les phrases de la dictée.

Chapter Review

DVD Program

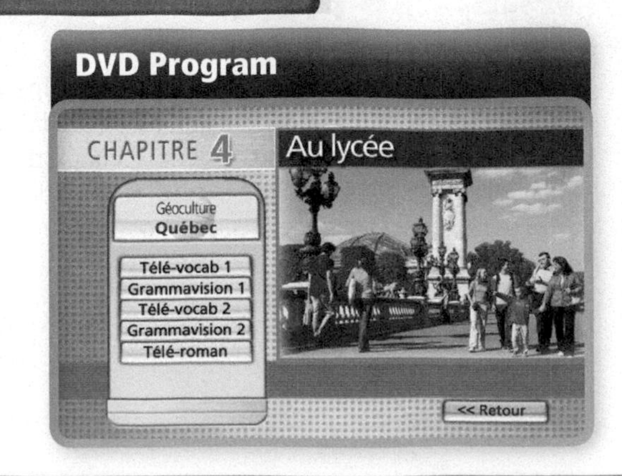

Online Edition

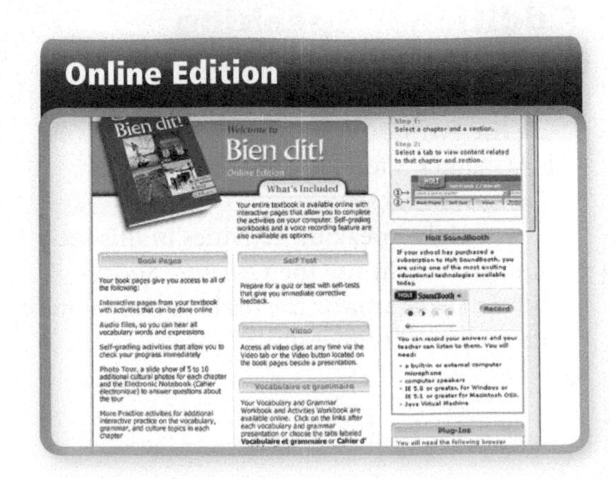

Prépare-toi pour l'examen

Résumé: Vocabulaire 1

PRACTICE FRENCH WITH HOLT MCDOUGAL APPS!

To ask about food preparation

l'abricot (m.)	apricot
l'ail (m.)	garlic
ajouter	to add
l'aubergine (f.)	eggplant
la banane	banana
bouillir	to boil
le brocoli	broccoli
la carotte	carrot
la cerise (f.)	cherry
le champignon	mushroom
la courgette	zucchini
la cuisinière	stove
couper	to cut
une cuillerée à café/à soupe	teaspoon/tablespoon
les épices (f.)	spices
la farine	flour
faire cuire	to bake, to cook
le four	oven
la fraise/la framboise	strawberry/raspberry
les haricots (m.) verts	green beans
l'huile (f.) (d'olive)	(olive) oil
la laitue	lettuce
mélanger	to mix
l'oignon (m.)	onion
la pastèque/le melon	watermelon/melon
la pêche	peach
les petits pois (m.)	peas
la poire	pear
le poivron	bell pepper
la pomme	apple
la pomme de terre	potato
le sucre	sugar
une tasse de...	a cup of. . . .
la tomate	tomato
c'est compliqué	it's complicated
C'est facile de faire...?	Is it easy to make . . . ?
c'est très simple	it's very simple
Comment est-ce qu'on fait... ?	How do you make . . . ?
Qu'est-ce qu'il y a dans...?	What's in . . . ?
Il y a...	There is/There are . . .

To make requests........................see page 85

Résumé: Vocabulaire 2

To shop for groceries

du bœuf (m.)	beef
le/la boucher(-ère)	butcher
la boucherie/la charcuterie	butcher shop/delicatessen
le/la boulanger(-ère)	baker
la boulangerie/la pâtisserie	bakery/pastry shop
le/la caissier(-ière)	cashier
le chariot	shopping cart
les crevettes (f.)/des huîtres (f.)	shrimp/oyster(s)
la crémerie/la fromagerie	dairy market/cheese market
l'épicerie (f.)/l'épicier/l'épicière	grocery store/grocer
les fruits de mer (m.)	seafood
le/la poissonnier(-ière)	fish monger
la poissonnerie	fish market
un sac en plastique	plastic bag
le yaourt	yogurt
à peu près/environ	about/approximately
C'est tout pour aujourd'hui.	That's all for today.
C'est... le kilo.	It's . . . per kilo.
Ce sera tout?	Will that be all?
Combien vous en faut-il?	How many do you need?
Il me faut...	I need . . .
Je vais en prendre...	I'll take . . .
mûr(e)(s)/bien mûr(e)(s)	ripe/very ripe
Qu'est-ce qu'il vous faut?	What do you need?
Vous les voulez comment,...?	How do you want the . . . ?
une boîte (de conserve)	canned food/a box (can) of . . .
une bouteille de...	a bottle of . . .
une douzaine de...	a dozen . . .
un kilo(gramme) de...	a kilogram of . . .
un litre de.../une livre de...	a liter.../a pound of . . .
un morceau de...	a piece of . . .
un paquet (m.) de...	a package of . . .
un pot (m.) de...	a jar of . . .
une tranche de...	a slice of. . .

To ask where things are..................see page 97

Holt McDougal French Apps

Remind students that they can use the Holt McDougal French Apps to review their vocabulary.

Teacher to Teacher

Cindy McDaniel
Rushville Consolidated High School
Rushville, IN

Using laminated pictures of individual foods and drinks, I put together a "meal" of six to eight items for each group of four to five students. Students put their desks together and spread out their "meal" in the center. Each student must offer one of the items to someone else at the table and ask for another item. The other student responds to the offer or request. I then have the groups switch meals so that they practice with many different foods and drinks. 1.1

Projectable Transparency

More Digital Resources

FOR THE STUDENT

- Holt McDougal French Apps
- @HomeTutor
- News and Networking
- Performance Space

FOR THE TEACHER

- Interactive Whiteboard Lessons
- Generate Success!

Assess

Assessment Program

Examen: Chapitre 3

Audio CD 3, Tr. 17–18

Examen oral: Chapitre 3

Alternative Assessment

Differentiated Practice and Assessment CD-ROM

Online Assessment
my.hrw.com

Test Generator

Révisions cumulatives

Resources

Planning:
Lesson Planner
Teacher One Stop

Practice:
Cahier d'activités
Media Guide
Projectable Transparencies
Fine Art, Chapter 3
Audio CD 3, Tr. 14
Holt McDougal French Apps

1 Script

1. C'est très facile à faire. Il vous faut des œufs, du sel, du poivre, des légumes et du fromage.
2. Il vous faut des œufs, du sel, du poivre, du lait et des légumes.
3. Il vous faut du sucre, de la farine, des œufs et du beurre, et bien sûr, du chocolat.
4. Coupez les pommes et faites-les cuire pendant cinq minutes. Ajoutez le sucre.

Teacher to Teacher

Todd Bowen
Barrington HS
Barrington, IL

I use Learning Centers to help students review. Each center is set up with a five-minute activity that practices a skill. The students rotate to each center until they work their way through all activities (usually 5 or 6). I typically offer half-sheet worksheets for structure skills, an additional listening activity, a speaking activity, a vocabulary review, and a culture quiz. Students check the answer key before moving on to the next center. 1.2

chapitres 1-3 Révisions cumulatives

1 Tu écoutes des recettes à la radio à Québec. Écoute ces extraits et choisis la photo qui correspond à chacune des recettes. 1.2

1. c 2. b 3. d 4. a

CD 3, Tr. 14

a.

b.

c.

d.

2 Les légumes et les fruits, sont-ils vraiment importants? Lis les publicités et décide si les phrases suivantes sont **a) vraies** ou **b) fausses**. 1.2, 3.2

Mangez des légumes!

Faites votre plein en vitamines, en fer, en magnésium et en fibre !

Conseils :
• Chaque catégorie de légumes apporte son lot de nutriments. Diversifiez votre consommation de légumes.
• Mangez-les crus ou cuits.
(au moins 5 par jour combinés avec les fruits)

Mangez des fruits!

Faites votre plein de vitamines A et C sans oublier le potassium !

Conseils :
• Les jus de fruit 100 % fruit sont les meilleurs.
• Préférez les fruits nature : ils contiennent plus de fibres que les jus de fruits.
• Mangez des fruits riches en vitamine C.
(au moins 5 par jour combinés avec les légumes)

a **1.** Les fruits nous apportent des vitamines A et C.
b **2.** Les fruits contiennent une forte quantité de sodium.
b **3.** Les jus de fruit contiennent plus de fibres que les fruits.
a **4.** Les légumes nous apportent de nombreuses vitamines et des minéraux.
b **5.** Chaque catégorie de légumes apporte les mêmes nutriments. Vous pouvez donc vous limiter à manger une seule catégorie de légumes.

Online Culture Project

Have students imagine that they want to give their grandfather a gift basket filled with French specialty foods. Ask students to do a Web search for an online shop in Quebec that sells delicatessen foods (**une épicerie**). Students should note the items and the prices of the items they choose. Have students document their sources by referencing the names and URLs of all the sites they consulted.

 3.2

Révisions cumulatives

Online Assessment
my.hrw.com
Cumulative Self-test

3 Tu vas bientôt fêter ton anniversaire! Imagine que tu fais des achats dans une épicerie à Québec. Avec un(e) camarade, créez une conversation entre le/la commerçant(e) et le/la client(e). 1.1

4 Aujourd'hui, c'est le jour du marché. Imagine ce qui se passe dans l'image. Qu'est-ce que les marchands vendent? De quoi parlent les personnes? Est-ce qu'il y a des marchés comme ça aujourd'hui? Écris un paragraphe qui décrit le jour du marché. 1.3, 2.2

La rue des abbesses de Maximilien Luce

5 Écris une lettre à une amie québécoise. Parle de ce que tu manges souvent le matin, à midi et le soir. Dis aussi quand, où et avec qui tu manges. Pose-lui des questions pour tout savoir sur ses habitudes alimentaires *(eating habits)*. 1.3

6 **À ton tour**

Émission de cuisine You will host a cooking show for your classmates. Working with a partner, think of or research a recipe you would like to make. List all the ingredients you will need and their quantities. Then compile the steps needed in order to complete the recipe. You and your partner will present your recipe and demonstrate how to cook your recipe for the class. 1.3

Fine Art Connection

Introduction Maximilien Luce was born into a working-class Parisian family in 1858. His painting was influenced by Impressionism, and he became one of the founders of the Neo-Impressionist movement, along with his friends Camille Pissarro, Georges Seurat, and Paul Signac. Maximilien Luce particularly liked to paint landscapes, especially the streets of the Montmartre area of Paris, which has always been a favorite of artists. He also liked to paint soldiers and workers. The technique he used consists of painting small dots of primary colors to create a visual effect. The small dots blend together to create secondary colors when the painting is viewed from a distance. Artists who used this technique belong to the Pointillist movement.

Analyzing

To help students discuss the painting, you might use the following questions.

1. **Qu'est-ce qu'on vend dans cette rue?**
2. **Est-ce que c'est un bon sujet pour un peintre néo-impressionniste? Pourquoi?**
3. **Quelles sortes de personnages crois-tu que Maximilien Luce aime peindre?**
4. **Qu'est-ce qui changerait sur ce tableau si on le peignait aujourd'hui?**

3.1

Extension

Bring to class prints of works by Maximilien Luce. Hold them at a distance and ask students to describe what they see. Then have students take a very close look and comment on what they see. Ask them to research Pointillism and share their findings.

2.2, 3.1

ACTFL Performance Standards

The activities in Chapter 3 target the communicative modes as described in the Standards.

Interpersonal	Two-way communication using receptive skills and productive skills	**Communication (SE),** pp. 85, 87, 89, 91, 97, 99, 101 **Communication (TE),** pp. 85, 87, 89, 91, 97, 99, 101, 103
Interpretive	One-way communication using receptive skills	**Comparaisons,** p. 93 **Télé-roman,** pp. 104–105
Presentational	One-way communication using productive skills	**Communication (SE),** p. 103 **À ton tour,** p. 115

chapitre 4

Planning Guide

Au lycée

Chapter Section		Resources
Vocabulaire 1 • School places and events **Grammaire 1** • Object pronouns with the **passé composé** • **Quelqu'un, quelque chose, ne... personne, ne... rien, ne... que** **Application 1** • **Un peu plus:** The verb **recevoir**	pp. 118–121 pp. 122–125 pp. 126–127	Projectable Transparencies: Vocabulaire 4.1, 4.2; Bell Work 4.1, 4.2, 4.3, 4.4 Cahier de vocabulaire et grammaire, pp. 37–42 Grammar Tutor for Students of French Cahier d'activités, pp. 31–33 Media Guide, pp. 13–16, 66–68 **Assessment Program** Quiz: Vocabulaire 1, pp. 89–90 Quiz: Grammaire 1, pp. 91–92 Quiz: Application 1, pp. 93–94
Culture • **Culture appliquée: La ringuette** • **Comparaisons et Communauté**	pp. 128–129	Cahier d'activités, pp. 34
Vocabulaire 2 • Computer terms **Grammaire 2** • The verb **suivre** • **Depuis, il y a, ça fait...** **Application 2** • **Un peu plus:** The verb **ouvrir**	pp. 130–133 pp. 134–137 pp. 138–139	Projectable Transparencies: Vocabulaire 4.3, 4.4; Bell Work 4.5, 4.6, 4.7, 4.8 Cahier de vocabulaire et grammaire, pp. 43–48 Grammar Tutor for Students of French Cahier d'activités, pp. 35–37 Media Guide, pp. 13–16, 66–67, 69 **Assessment Program** Quiz: Vocabulaire 2, pp. 95–96 Quiz: Grammaire 2, pp. 97–98 Quiz: Application 2, pp. 99–100
Télé-roman	pp. 140–141	Media Guide, pp. 67, 70
Lecture et écriture	pp. 142–145	Cahier d'activités, pp. 38 Reading Strategies and Skills Handbook Intermediate Reader French InterActive Reader **Assessment Program** Quiz: Lecture, pp. 101 Quiz: Écriture, pp. 102
Prépare-toi pour l'examen • **Résumé de vocabulaire et grammaire** • **Lettres et sons** **Révisions cumulatives**	pp. 146–149 pp. 150–151	Independent Study Guide, pp. 10–12, 36 Media Guide p. 16 **Assessment Program** Examen: Chapitre 4, pp. 103–108 Examen oral: Chapitre 4, p. 320 Projectable Transparencies: Fine Art, Ch. 4 Cahier d'activités, pp. 34, 39–40
Variations littéraires • **L'alouette**	pp. 388–389	Reading Strategies and Skills Handbook Intermediate Reader French InterActive Reader

Visit Us Online

my.hrw.com
Online Edition

Pacing Suggestions

	Essential	Recommended	Optional
Vocabulaire 1 • School places and events • **Flash culture**	✔		
Grammaire 1 • Object pronouns in the **passé composé** • **Quelqu'un, quelque chose, ne... personne, ne... rien, ne... que** • **Flash culture**	✔		
Application 1 • **Un peu plus:** The verb **recevoir**	✔		
Culture • **Culture appliquée: La ringuette** • **Comparaisons et Communauté**		✔	
Vocabulaire 2 • Computer terms • **Flash culture**	✔		
Grammaire 2 • The verb **suivre** • **Depuis, il y a, ça fait...** • **Flash culture**	✔		
Application 2 • **Un peu plus:** The verb **ouvrir**	✔		
Télé-roman • Épisode 4: **Le Secret de la statuette**			✔
Lecture et écriture • **Intermezzo** (Lecture) • **Tout va de travers!** (Écriture)		✔	
Prépare-toi pour l'examen		✔	
Révisions cumulatives			✔
Variations littéraires • **L'alouette**			✔

Technology

Bien dit! Online

- Student Edition with multi-media
- **performance)))space** recording tool
- Interactive activities with feedback
- Self-tests with feedback
- Cahier d'activités (Interactive workbook)
- Cahier de vocabulaire et grammaire (Interactive workbook)
- Holt Online Assessment

DVD Tutor

- Télé-vocab
- Grammavision
- Télé-roman

HOMETUTOR

- Interactive games
- Differentiated Practice
- Cultural video

Audio Program

- Student Edition listening activities
- Assessment listening activities
- Songs

Teacher One Stop™

- Complete resources
- ExamView Pro Test Generator
- Holt Calendar Planner

Holt McDougal Apps

Interactive Whiteboard Lessons

Differentiated Practice and Assessment CD

For slower pace and advanced learner options, see the Differentiated Practice and Assessment CD.

Projects

Le sondage d'activités

Students produce a survey on favorite school and after-school activities. They should include words and phrases from **Vocabulaire 1** and expressions in **Exprimons-nous!** to ask for information. Assign survey dates and a minimum number of respondents. 1.1, 1.3

Suggested Sequence

1. Students choose a topic (their own or from a list of suggestions) and write an outline of the questions to include in the survey.
2. Have students draft their surveys and turn them in for suggestions.
3. On assigned dates, students interview others throughout the school during lunch and before or after classes.
4. Once students have enough information, they organize and evaluate it. You may want to discuss the basics of compiling survey results such as counting answers, grouping data, calculating percentages, and so on.
5. Students present and explain the results of their surveys to the class.

Grading the project

Suggested point distribution (100 points total)

Completion of assignment	30 pts.
Written survey	40 pts.
Oral presentation	30 pts.

e-community

e-mail forum:

Post the following questions on the classroom e-mail forum:

Est-ce que tu passes beaucoup de temps devant ton ordinateur?
Quelles sortes de recherches fais-tu sur Internet?
Que fais-tu quand ton ordinateur plante? 5.1

All students will contribute to the list and then share the items.

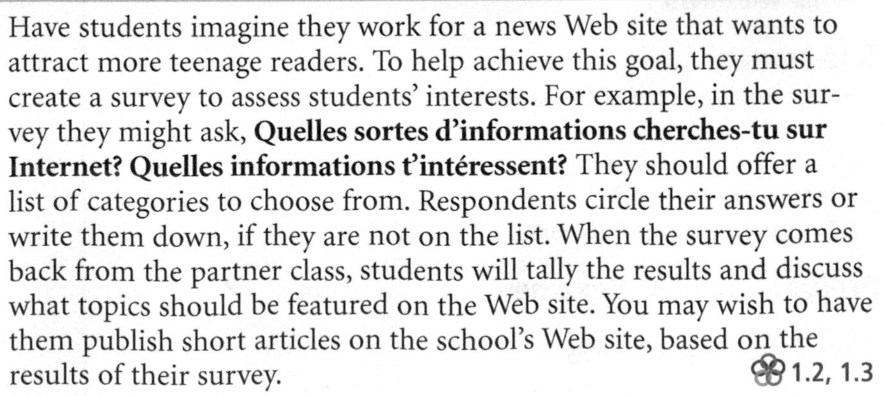

Partner Class Project

Have students imagine they work for a news Web site that wants to attract more teenage readers. To help achieve this goal, they must create a survey to assess students' interests. For example, in the survey they might ask, **Quelles sortes d'informations cherches-tu sur Internet? Quelles informations t'intéressent?** They should offer a list of categories to choose from. Respondents circle their answers or write them down, if they are not on the list. When the survey comes back from the partner class, students will tally the results and discuss what topics should be featured on the Web site. You may wish to have them publish short articles on the school's Web site, based on the results of their survey. 1.2, 1.3

21st Century **Collaboration**

Game Bank
For game ideas, see pages T60–T63.

L'éducation au Québec

The education system in Quebec is derived from the traditional French system. Unlike the school system in France, however, all students in Quebec may choose to participate in many extra-curricular and intramural activities and clubs. Schools in Quebec (those for French-speaking students, who comprise over 80% of the population, and those for English-speaking students) offer similar extra-curricular activities. There are a number of all-school special events that take place each year. Most of these are long-standing traditions. They include cross-country runs and ski meets and marathons. Community service and charitable projects are organized in many schools, especially schools with International Baccalaureate programs. Additionally, ski trips and trips to Europe and the United States are sponsored as extra-curricular activities. Have students research a school in the French school system **(Commission scolaire de la capitale)** and compare the activities it offers to those in schools in Quebec. 1.3, 2.1

La cuisine

The **comté** is a large, round cheese that is usually sold by the slice because of its massive size. It can weigh up to 50 kilos (approximately 110 pounds). To produce a cheese such as **comté,** one needs about 600 liters of milk, which is equivalent to the daily production of 20 cows. Encourage students to make **gratin dauphinois** in their foods class or at home for family and friends. 1.2, 2.2

Gratin dauphinois

pour 6 personnes

- **2** gousses d'ail
- **2** livres de pommes de terre
- **1** tasse de crème fraîche
- **1** tasse de lait
- **1** tasse de comté (ou de gruyère) râpé
- sel
- poivre
- **2** cuillères de beurre
- **1** pincée de noix de muscade

Peler et couper en tranches les pommes de terre. Beurrer un grand plat et y disposer les pommes de terre. Dans un bol, mélanger le lait, la crème fraîche, la muscade, le sel et le poivre. Verser sur les pommes de terre. Parsemer de comté ou de gruyère râpé. Faire cuire au four à 350° F pendant une heure. Servir avec un plat de viande ou de poulet.

Listening Activity Scripts

Vocabulaire à l'œuvre 1

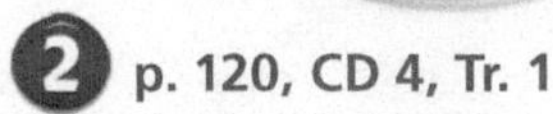

2 p. 120, CD 4, Tr. 1

1. — Alors, ton expérience de physique, tu l'as réussie?
   — Non, je l'ai complètement ratée.
2. — Alors, l'interro de français, ça a marché?
   — Évidemment! C'est le seul cours où j'ai de bonnes notes.
3. — Au fait, est-ce que tu as trouvé le livre que tu cherchais au CDI?
   — Oui, la documentaliste m'a aidée.
4. — Comment s'est passé l'entraînement?
   — Je n'en sais rien. J'ai passé tout l'après-midi en retenue.
5. — Je ne t'ai pas vu à la cantine. Il t'est arrivé quelque chose?
   — J'avais mal à la tête. Je suis allé à l'infirmerie.

Answers to Activity 2
1. b 2. a 3. a 4. b 5. b

Grammaire à l'œuvre 1

11 p. 124, CD 4, Tr. 2

1. — Allô! C'est Samir! Qu'est-ce que tu as fait ce week-end?
2. — C'est Karine. Tu es allée à la compétition, n'est-ce pas? Est-ce que tu as vu quelqu'un là-bas, comme, par exemple... Marc? Appelle-moi!
3. — Salima? C'est Éric. Qu'est-ce qui t'est arrivé au laboratoire? Tout va bien, j'espère!
4. — Coucou! C'est Charlotte. Comment s'est passé la fête d'Annick?
5. — Allô! Salima, ici Charles. Je crois que je t'ai prêté trois livres, et tu m'as rendu seulement deux livres. C'est ça? Appelle-moi.

Answers to Activity 11
1. b 2. a 3. a 4. b 5. a

Application 1

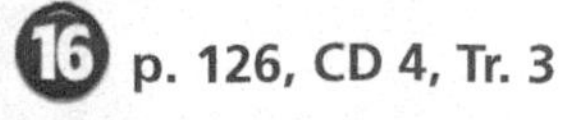

16 p. 126, CD 4, Tr. 3

— Salut, Myriam! Dis-moi, tu sais si Éloïse était en cours ce matin?
— Non, je n'en sais rien. Pourquoi?
— Je ne l'ai pas vue à l'entraînement cet après-midi.
— Tu crois qu'il lui est arrivé quelque chose?
— C'est possible. Tu connais Éloïse! Hier soir, elle m'a dit qu'elle avait une expérience de chimie à préparer.
— Oh, oh! Tu as peut-être raison. Tu devrais téléphoner chez elle.
— J'ai essayé, mais il n'y avait personne.
— Je parie que Charlotte sait quelque chose. C'est sa meilleure amie. On peut lui téléphoner.

Answers to Activity 16
1. Non 2. préparer une expérience de chimie
3. Elle lui suggère de téléphoner à une amie d'Éloïse.

Vocabulaire à l'œuvre 2

24 p. 133, CD 4, Tr. 4

1. — Mégane à l'appareil.
   — Salut, c'est Ivan. Je suis dans la salle d'informatique et ma souris ne marche pas bien.
   — Donne-moi cinq minutes. J'arrive.
2. — Mégane à l'appareil. Qu'est-ce qui se passe?
   — Il faut absolument que j'imprime ce document pour mon cours de géo dans cinq minutes et l'imprimante ne veut pas marcher. Je ne sais pas quoi faire!
   — Est-ce que l'imprimante est branchée?
3. — Mégane à l'appareil.
   — Je ne comprends pas pourquoi mon clavier est différent. Les lettres ne sont pas au même endroit que d'habitude.
   — C'est parce que tu travaille sur l'ordinateur avec le clavier américain. Le clavier est différent.
4. — Mégane à l'appareil.
   — Salut. C'est Justin. J'essaie d'installer un logiciel sur l'ordinateur dans la salle d'informatique, mais rien ne marche.
   — C'est normal! Tu n'as pas le droit d'installer ton propre logiciel, surtout si c'est un jeu!
5. — Mégane à l'appareil.
   — J'étais en train de taper un document quand mon écran est devenu tout vert. Depuis, plus rien ne marche.
   — J'arrive.

Answers to Activity 24
1. b 2. d 3. e 4. a 5. c

Grammaire à l'œuvre 2

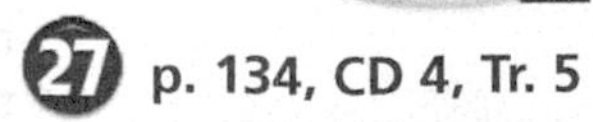

27 p. 134, CD 4, Tr. 5

1. — Nous suivons un cours de maths avec madame Michaud. C'est ennuyeux!
2. — Tu vas suivre un cours d'arts plastiques? Je parie que tu vas beaucoup aimer ça.
3. — Quelle sorte d'ordinateur est-ce que tu me recommandes? Je suis un cours d'informatique cette année.
4. — Sonia et Mina, comment était le cours de géographie que vous avez suivi?
5. — Mathieu et Romain vont suivre un cours de ballet? Ça va être marrant!
6. — Ma sœur a suivi un cours d'informatique et maintenant elle pense qu'elle sait tout au sujet des ordinateurs!

Answers to Activity 27

1. a 2. c 3. a 4. b 5. c 6. b

Grammaire à l'œuvre 2

32 p. 136, CD 4, Tr. 6

1. — Allô, Ordinateurs plantés. C'est Lucie. Je peux vous aider?
   — Bonjour. Je ne peux pas démarrer mon ordinateur depuis ce matin.
2. — Allô, Ordinateurs plantés. C'est Fatima. Est-ce que je peux vous aider?
   — Bonjour. Ça fait trois jours que mon imprimante ne marche pas.
3. — Allô, Ordinateurs plantés. C'est Marc. Est-ce que je peux vous aider?
   — J'ai parlé à Fatima hier. Depuis lundi, je ne peux pas imprimer.
4. — Allô, Ordinateurs plantés. C'est Justine.
   — Il y a huit heures que mon ordinateur télécharge un logiciel! Qu'est-ce qu'on fait pour l'arrêter?
5. — Allô, Ordinateurs plantés. C'est Damien. Je peux vous aider?
   — Bonjour. Mon ordinateur n'arrête pas de planter depuis une semaine! Je ne sais pas quoi faire!
6. — Allô, Ordinateurs plantés. C'est Tran. Quelle est votre question?
   — J'essaie de graver un CD depuis trente minutes, mais ça ne marche pas.

Answers to Activity 32

1. c 2. e 3. d 4. a 5. f 6. b

Application 2

39 p. 139, CD 4, Tr. 7

1. — Salut! Je m'appelle Paul. Ça fait deux ans que je suis élève ici. Je suis des cours de chimie et de physique. J'adore faire des expériences. Vous pouvez toujours me trouver au laboratoire!
2. — Bonjour! Je suis Madeleine. Je suis élève au lycée Charles Baudelaire depuis trois ans. Je suis des cours d'anglais, d'allemand et d'espagnol. Vous pouvez me trouver au laboratoire aussi–le laboratoire de langues!
3. — Salut! Je m'appelle Sophie. Ça fait un an que je suis élève ici. Je suis des cours de maths et d'informatique. Vous pouvez me trouver devant un ordinateur!
4. — Bonjour à tous! Je m'appelle Bernard. Ça fait deux ans que je suis ici. Je suis des cours de maths, d'anglais, d'histoire et de chimie, mais je préfère le sport. Vous pouvez me trouver au gymnase.
5. — Bonjour, tout le monde! Je m'appelle Nathalie. Je suis élève ici depuis quatre ans. Je suis des cours d'histoire, de géographie et de musique. Vous pouvez me trouver dans la salle de musique où j'aime jouer de la guitare.
6. — Salut! Je m'appelle Xavier. Ça fait deux ans que je suis élève au lycée Charles Baudelaire. Je suis des cours d'arts plastiques. Et vous pouvez toujours me trouver... en retenue!

Answers to Activity 39

1. a 2. b 3. b 4. a 5. a 6. b

Prépare-toi pour l'examen

6 p. 147, CD 4, Tr. 10

1. — Je peux t'aider, Anne?
   — Oui. Comment est-ce qu'on fait pour imprimer ce document?
2. — Alors, tu vas acheter un nouvel ordinateur?
   — Oui. Quelle sorte d'ordinateur est-ce que tu me recommandes?
3. — Tu as fini tes devoirs?
   — Non, et je ne sais pas quoi faire. Ça fait trois fois que je perds mon document.
4. — Qu'est-ce que tu veux faire, André?
   — Je voudrais graver un CD.
5. — Qu'est-ce qu'il y a, Magali?
   — Aujourd'hui, tout va de travers. Mon ordinateur n'arrête pas de planter.

Answers to Activity 6

1. d 2. c 3. a 4. b 5. e

Dictée p. 148, CD 4, Tr. 13

1. Est-ce que vous avez un graveur de CD?
2. Qu'est-ce que tu utilises comme navigateur?
3. Je trouve le cours de maths ennuyeux.
4. Elle a quelle sorte d'ordinateur?
5. C'est un professeur généreux.

Révisions cumulatives Chapitres 1-4

1 p. 150, CD 4, Tr. 14

1. — Ça m'énerve. Cet ordinateur n'arrête pas de planter!
   — Calme-toi. Je peux t'aider.
2. — J'ai peur de ne pas réussir cette expérience.
   — C'est vrai que tu n'es pas très fort en chimie.
3. — J'essaie de faire une recherche, mais je ne trouve pas les livres dont j'ai besoin.
   — Demande au documentaliste.
4. — Tu as faim?
   — Pas tellement. Qu'est-ce qu'il y a à la cantine?

Answers to Activity 1

1. d 2. b 3. c 4. a

50-Minute Lesson Plans

Au lycée

Day 1

OBJECTIVE
Ask how something turned out

Core Instruction

Chapter Opener, pp. 116–117
- See Using the Photo, p. 116. **5 min.**
- See Chapter Objectives, p. 116. **5 min.**

Vocabulaire 1, pp. 118–121
- Present **Vocabulaire 1,** pp. 118–119. See Teaching **Vocabulaire,** p. 118. **5 min.**
- Show **Télé-vocab 1. 5 min.**
- Present **Exprimons-nous!,** p. 119. **10 min.**
- Do Activity 1, p. 120. **5 min.**
- Play Audio CD 4, Tr. 1 for Activity 2, p. 120. **5 min.**
- Do Activity 3, p. 120. **5 min.**
- Present **Flash culture,** p. 120. **5 min.**

Optional Resources
- Slower Pace Learners, p. 119 ◆
- Multiple Intelligences, p. 119

Homework Suggestions
Cahier de vocabulaire et grammaire, pp. 37–38

1.2, 1.3, 4.2

Day 2

OBJECTIVE
*Ask how something turned out; Wonder what happened; Use object pronouns with the **passé composé***

Core Instruction

Vocabulaire 1, pp. 118–121
- Do Activity 4, p. 120. **5 min.**
- See Teaching **Exprimons-nous!,** p. 120. **10 min.**
- Do Activities 5–6, p. 121. **15 min.**

Grammaire 1, pp. 122–125
- See Teaching **Grammaire,** p. 122. **10 min.**
- Show **Grammavision 1.1. 5 min.**
- Do Activity 7, p. 122. **5 min.**

Optional Resources
- Advanced Learners, p. 121 ▲
- Special Learning Needs, p. 121 ●

Homework Suggestions
Study for **Quiz: Vocabulaire 1**
Cahier de vocabulaire et grammaire, p. 39

1.1, 1.2, 1.3

Day 3

OBJECTIVE
*Use object pronouns with the **passé composé***

Core Instruction

Vocabulaire 1, pp. 118–121
- Review **Vocabulaire 1,** pp. 118–121. **10 min.**
- Give **Quiz: Vocabulaire 1. 20 min.**

Grammaire 1, pp. 122–125
- Have students do Activities 8–10, p. 123. **15 min.**
- Present **Flash culture,** p. 124. **5 min.**

Optional Resources
- French for Spanish Speakers, p. 123
- Slower Pace Learners, p. 123 ◆
- Special Learning Needs, p. 123 ●

Homework Suggestions
Cahier de vocabulaire et grammaire, p. 40
Cahier d'activités, p. 31
Online Practice (**my.hrw.com**)

1.1, 1.2, 4.1, 4.2

Day 4

OBJECTIVE
*Use **quelqu'un, quelque chose, ne... personne, ne... rien, ne... que***

Core Instruction

Grammaire 1, pp. 122–125
- See Teaching **Grammaire,** p. 124. **10 min.**
- Show **Grammavision 1.2. 5 min.**
- Play Audio CD 4, Tr. 2 for Activity 11, p. 124. **5 min.**
- Have students do Activities 12–15, pp. 124–125. **20 min.**

Application 1, pp. 126–127
- Play Audio CD 4, Tr. 3 for Activity 16, p. 126. **5 min.**
- Do Activity 17, p. 126. **5 min.**

Optional Resources
- Advanced Learners, p. 125 ▲
- Special Learning Needs, p. 125 ●

Homework Suggestions
Study for **Quiz: Grammaire 1**
Cahier de vocabulaire et grammaire, p. 41
Cahier d'activités, p. 32

1.1, 1.2

Day 5

OBJECTIVE
*Use the verb **recevoir***

Core Instruction

Grammaire 1, pp. 122–125
- Review **Grammaire 1,** pp. 122–125. **10 min.**
- Give **Quiz: Grammaire 1. 20 min.**

Application 1, pp. 126–127
- See Teaching **Un peu plus,** p. 126. **5 min.**
- Have students do Activities 18–20, p. 127. **15 min.**

Optional Resources
- Communication (TE), p. 127
- Slower Pace Learners, p. 127 ◆

Homework Suggestions
Study for **Quiz: Application 1**
Cahier de vocabulaire et grammaire, p. 42
Cahier d'activités, p. 33
@HOMETUTOR
Online Practice (**my.hrw.com**)

1.1, 1.2, 1.3

Day 6

OBJECTIVE
Learn about francophone culture

Core Instruction

Application 1, pp. 126–127
- Review **Application 1,** pp. 126–127. **10 min.**
- Give **Quiz: Application 1. 20 min.**

Culture, pp. 128–129
- See **Culture appliquée** (TE), p. 128. **10 min.**
- See **Comparaisons et communauté** (TE), p. 128. **10 min.**

Optional Resources
- Bulletin Board Project, p. 128
- Connections, p. 129
- Comparisons, p. 129
- Slower Pace Learners, p. 129 ◆
- Multiple Intelligences, p. 129

Homework Suggestions
Cahier d'activités, p. 34
Finish **Culture appliquée** project

1.3, 2.1, 2.2, 3.1, 4.2, 5.1

Day 7

OBJECTIVE
Ask for information

Core Instruction

Vocabulaire 2, pp. 130–133
- Have students do Bell Work 4.5, p. 130. **5 min.**
- Present **Vocabulaire 2,** pp. 130–131. See Teaching **Vocabulaire,** p. 130. **10 min.**
- Show **Télé-vocab 2. 5 min.**
- Present **Exprimons-nous!,** p. 131. **10 min.**
- Have students do Activities 21–23, p. 132. **15 min.**
- Present **Flash culture,** p. 132. **5 min.**

Optional Resources
- TPR, p. 131
- Connections, p. 131
- Advanced Learners, p. 131 ▲
- Multiple Intelligences, p. 131

Homework Suggestions
Cahier de vocabulaire et grammaire, pp. 43–44

1.2, 1.3, 3.2, 4.2

Day 8

OBJECTIVE
*Express frustration; Use the verb **suivre***

Core Instruction

Vocabulaire 2, pp. 130–133
- See Teaching **Exprimons-nous!,** p. 132. **10 min.**
- Play Audio CD 4, Tr. 4 for Activity 24, p. 133. **5 min.**
- Have students do Activities 25–26, p. 133. **15 min.**

Grammaire 2, pp. 134–137
- See Teaching **Grammaire,** p. 134. **10 min.**
- Show **Grammavision 2.1. 5 min.**
- Play Audio CD 4, Tr. 5 for Activity 27, p. 134. **5 min.**

Optional Resources
- Communication (TE), p. 133
- Slower Pace Learners, p. 133 ◆
- Multiple Intelligences, p. 133

Homework Suggestions
Study for **Quiz: Vocabulaire 2**
Cahier de vocabulaire et grammaire, p. 45
@HOMETUTOR

1.1, 1.2

To edit and create your own lesson plans, see the **Teacher One Stop™**

KEY
▲ Advanced Learners
◆ Slower Pace Learners
● Special Learning Needs

Day 9

OBJECTIVE
*Use the verb **suivre***

Core Instruction
Vocabulaire 2, pp. 130–133
- Review **Vocabulaire 2,** pp. 130–133. **10 min.**
- Give **Quiz: Vocabulaire 2. 20 min.**

Grammaire 2, pp. 134–137
- Present **Flash culture,** p. 134. **5 min.**
- Have students do Activities 28–31, pp. 134–135. **15 min.**

Optional Resources
- Communication (TE), p. 135
- Advanced Learners, p. 135 ▲
- Special Learning Needs, p. 135 ●

Homework Suggestions
Cahier de vocabulaire et grammaire, p. 46
Cahier d'activités, p. 35
HOMETUTOR
Online Practice (**my.hrw.com**)
1.1, 1.2, 4.2

Day 10

OBJECTIVE
*Use **depuis, il y a, ça fait...***
*Use the verb **ouvrir***

Core Instruction
Grammaire 2, pp. 134–137
- See Teaching **Grammaire,** p. 136. **10 min.**
- Show **Grammavision 2.2. 5 min.**
- Play Audio CD 4, Tr. 6 for Activity 32, p. 136. **5 min.**
- Have students do Activities 33–36, pp. 136–137. **20 min.**

Application 2, pp. 138–139
- Do Activity 37, p. 138. **5 min.**
- See Teaching **Un peu plus,** p. 138. **5 min.**

Optional Resources
- Slower Pace Learners, p. 137 ◆
- Special Learning Needs, p. 137 ●

Homework Suggestions
Study for **Quiz: Grammaire 2**
Cahier de vocabulaire et grammaire, p. 47
Cahier d'activités, p. 36
1.1, 1.2, 1.3

Day 11

OBJECTIVE
*Use the verb **ouvrir***

Core Instruction
Grammaire 2, pp. 134–137
- Review **Grammaire 2,** pp. 134–137. **10 min.**
- Give **Quiz: Grammaire 2. 20 min.**

Application 2, pp. 138–139
- Do Act. 38, p. 138. **5 min.**
- Play Audio CD 4, Tr. 7 for Activity 39, p. 139. **5 min.**
- Have students do Activities 40–41, p. 139. **10 min.**

Optional Resources
- Communication (TE), p. 139
- Slower Pace Learners, p. 139 ◆
- Multiple Intelligence, p. 139

Homework Suggestions
Study for **Quiz: Application 2**
Cahier de vocabulaire et grammaire, p. 48
Cahier d'activités, p. 37
Online Practice (**my.hrw.com**)
1.2, 1.3

Day 12

OBJECTIVE
Develop listening and reading skills

Core Instruction
Application 2, pp. 138–139
- Review **Application 2,** pp. 138–139. **10 min.**
- Give **Quiz: Application 2. 20 min.**

Télé-roman, pp. 140–141
- Show **Télé-roman.** See Teaching **Télé-roman,** p. 140. **5 min.**
- Have students answer the **As-tu compris?** questions, p. 141. **15 min.**

Optional Resources
- Connections, p. 140
- Gestures, p. 140
- Communication (TE), p. 141

Homework Suggestions
Online Practice (**my.hrw.com**)
1.1, 1.2, 3.2

Day 13

OBJECTIVE
Develop listening, reading, and writing skills

Core Instruction
Lecture et écriture, pp. 142–145
- See Teaching **Lecture,** p. 142. **35 min.**
- See Teaching **Espace écriture,** p. 144. **15 min.**

Optional Resources
- Applying the Strategies, p. 142
- Comparisons, p. 143
- Connections, p. 143
- Advanced Learners, p. 143 ▲
- Multiple Intelligences, p. 143
- Cultures, p. 144
- Comparisons, p. 144
- Process Writing, p. 145
- Slower Pace Learners, p. 145 ◆
- Multiple Intelligences, p. 145

Homework Suggestions
Cahier d'activités, p. 38
Espace écriture, Activity 2, p. 145
1.2, 1.3, 2.1, 3.1, 4.2

Day 14

OBJECTIVE
Develop writing skills; Review the chapter

Core Instruction
Lecture et écriture, pp. 142–145
- See Teaching **Espace écriture,** p. 144. **25 min.**

Prépare-toi pour l'examen, pp. 146–148
- Have students do Activities 1–5, pp. 146–147. **25 min.**

Optional Resources
- Writing Assessment, p. 145
- Reteaching, p. 146
- Game, p. 146
- Fold-N Learn, p. 146
- Oral Assessment, p. 147

Homework Suggestions
Online Practice (**my.hrw.com**)
1.1, 1.2, 1.3, 4.2

Day 15

OBJECTIVE
Review the chapter

Core Instruction
Prépare-toi pour l'examen, pp. 146–148
- Play Audio CD 4, Tr. 10 for Activity 6, p. 147. **5 min.**
- Have students do Activity 7, p. 147. **5 min.**
- Play Audio CD 4, Tr. 11–13 for **Lettres et sons,** p. 148. **10 min.**

Révisions cumulatives, pp. 150–151
- Play Audio CD 4, Tr. 14 for Activity 1, p. 150. **5 min.**
- Have students do Activities 2–5, pp. 150–151. **25 min.**

Optional Resources
- Teacher to Teacher, p. 148
- Chapter Review, pp. 148–149
- Online Culture Project, p. 150
- Fine Art Connection, p. 151

Homework Suggestions
Study for Chapter Test
Online Practice (**my.hrw.com**)
1.1, 1.2, 1.3, 2.2, 3.1

Day 16/Test

Core Instruction
Chapter Test 50 min.

Optional Resources
Assessment Program
- Alternative Assessment
- Test Generator
- **Quiz: Lecture**
- **Quiz: Écriture**

Homework Suggestions
Cahier d'activités, pp. 39–40, 108–109
Online Practice (**my.hrw.com**)

90-Minute Lesson Plans

Au lycée

Block 1

OBJECTIVE
Ask how something turned out; Wonder what happened

Core Instruction

Chapter Opener, pp. 116–117
- See Using the Photo, p. 116. **5 min.**
- See Chapter Objectives, p. 116. **5 min.**

Vocabulaire 1, pp. 118–121
- Present **Vocabulaire 1,** pp. 118–119. See Teaching **Vocabulaire,** p. 118. **15 min.**
- Show **Télé-vocab 1. 5 min.**
- Present **Exprimons-nous!,** p. 119. **10 min.**
- Have students do Activity 1, p. 120. **5 min.**
- Play Audio CD 4, Tr. 1 for Activity 2, p. 120. **5 min.**
- Have students do Activities 3–4, p. 120. **10 min.**
- Present **Flash culture,** p. 120. **5 min.**
- See Teaching **Exprimons-nous!,** p. 120. **10 min.**
- Have students do Activities 5–6, p. 121. **15 min.**

Optional Resources
- Learning Tips, p. 117
- **Attention!,** p. 118
- TPR, p. 119
- **Proverbes,** p. 119
- Cultures, p. 119
- Slower Pace Learners, p. 119 ◆
- Multiple Intelligences, p. 119
- Connections, p. 121
- Communication (TE), p. 121
- Advanced Learners, p. 121 ▲
- Special Learning Needs, p. 121 ●

Homework Suggestions
Study for **Quiz: Vocabulaire 1**
Cahier de vocabulaire et grammaire, pp. 37–39
@HOMETUTOR
Online Practice (**my.hrw.com**)
1.1, 1.2, 1.3, 2.1, 3.1, 4.2

Block 2

OBJECTIVE
*Use object pronouns with the **passé composé**; Use **quelqu'un, quelque chose, ne... personne, ne... rien, ne... que***

Core Instruction

Vocabulaire 1, pp. 118–121
- Review **Vocabulaire 1,** pp. 118–121. **10 min.**
- Give **Quiz: Vocabulaire 1. 20 min.**

Grammaire 1, pp. 122–125
- See Teaching **Grammaire,** p. 122. **5 min.**
- Show **Grammavision 1.1. 5 min.**
- Have students do Activities 7–10, pp. 122–123. **20 min.**
- Present **Flash culture,** p. 124. **5 min.**
- See Teaching **Grammaire,** p. 124. **5 min.**
- Show **Grammavision 1.2. 5 min.**
- Play Audio CD 4, Tr. 2 for Activity 11, p. 124. **5 min.**
- Have students do Activities 12–14, pp. 124–125. **10 min.**

Optional Resources
- French for Spanish Speakers, p. 123
- Communication (TE), p. 123
- Slower Pace Learners, p. 123 ◆
- Special Learning Needs, p. 123 ●
- **Attention!,** p. 125
- Special Learning Needs, p. 125 ●

Homework Suggestions
Study for **Quiz: Grammaire 1**
Cahier de vocabulaire et grammaire, pp. 40–41
Cahier d'activités, pp. 31–32
@HOMETUTOR
Online Practice (**my.hrw.com**)
1.1, 1.2, 4.1, 4.2

Block 3

OBJECTIVE
*Use **quelqu'un, quelque chose, ne... personne, ne... rien, ne... que;** Use the verb **recevoir;** Learn about francophone culture*

Core Instruction

Grammaire 1, pp. 122–125
- Have students do Bell Work 4.3, p. 124. **5 min.**
- Have students do Activity 15, p. 125. **5 min.**
- Review **Grammaire 1,** pp. 122–125. **10 min.**
- Give **Quiz: Grammaire 1. 20 min.**

Application 1, pp. 126–127
- Play Audio CD 4, Tr. 3 for Activity 16, p. 126. **5 min.**
- Have students do Activity 17, p. 126. **5 min.**
- See Teaching **Un peu plus,** p. 126. **5 min.**
- Have students do Activities 18–20, p. 127. **15 min.**

Culture, pp. 128–129
- See **Culture appliquée** (TE), p. 128. **10 min.**
- See **Comparaisons et communauté** (TE), p. 128. **10 min.**

Optional Resources
- Communication (TE), p. 125
- Advanced Learners, p. 125 ▲
- Communities, p. 127
- Communication (TE), p. 127
- Slower Pace Learners, p. 127 ◆
- Multiple Intelligences, p. 127
- **Vocabulaire supplémentaire,** p. 128
- Bulletin Board Project, p. 128
- Connections, p. 129
- Comparisons, p. 129
- Slower Pace Learners, p. 129 ◆
- Multiple Intelligences, p. 129

Homework Suggestions
Study for **Quiz: Application 1**
Cahier de vocabulaire et grammaire, p. 42
Cahier d'activités, pp. 33–34
Online Practice (**my.hrw.com**)
Finish **Culture appliquée** project
1.1, 1.2, 1.3, 2.1, 2.2, 3.1, 4.2, 5.1, 5.2

Block 4

OBJECTIVE
Ask for information; Express frustration

Core Instruction

Application 1, pp. 126–127
- Review **Application 1,** pp. 126–127. **10 min.**
- Give **Quiz: Application 1. 20 min.**

Vocabulaire 2, pp. 130–133
- Present **Vocabulaire 2,** pp. 130–131. See Teaching **Vocabulaire,** p. 130. **5 min.**
- Show **Télé-vocab 2. 5 min.**
- Present **Flash culture,** p. 132 **5 min.**
- Present **Exprimons-nous!,** p. 131. **5 min.**
- Have students do Activities 21–23, p. 132. **20 min.**
- See Teaching **Exprimons-nous!,** p. 132. **10 min.**
- Play Audio CD 4, Tr. 4 for Activity 24, p. 133. **5 min.**
- Have students do Activities 25–26, p. 133. **5 min.**

Optional Resources
- TPR, p. 131
- Connections, p. 131
- Advanced Learners, p. 131 ▲
- Multiple Intelligences, p. 131
- Connections, p. 132
- Teacher to Teacher, p. 133
- Communication (TE), p. 133
- Slower Pace Learners, p. 133 ◆
- Multiple Intelligences, p. 133

Homework Suggestions
Study for **Quiz: Vocabulaire 2**
Cahier de vocabulaire et grammaire, pp. 43–45
@HOMETUTOR
Online Practice (**my.hrw.com**)
1.1, 1.2, 1.3, 3.2, 4.2

To edit and create your own lesson plans, see the **Teacher One Stop™**

KEY
▲ Advanced Learners
◆ Slower Pace Learners
● Special Learning Needs

Block 5

OBJECTIVE
*Use the verb **suivre**; Use **depuis, il y a, ça fait...***

Core Instruction

Vocabulaire 2, pp. 130–133
- Review **Vocabulaire 2,** pp. 130–133. **10 min.**
- Give **Quiz: Vocabulaire 2. 20 min.**

Grammaire 2, pp. 134–137
- Present **Flash culture,** p. 134. **5 min.**
- See Teaching **Grammaire,** p. 134. **5 min.**
- Show **Grammavision 2.1. 5 min.**
- Play Audio CD 4, Tr. 5 for Activity 27, p. 134. **5 min.**
- Have students do Activities 28–31, pp. 134–135. **15 min.**
- See Teaching **Grammaire,** p. 136. **5 min.**
- Show **Grammavision 2.2. 5 min.**
- Play Audio CD 4, Tr. 6 for Activity 32, p. 136. **5 min.**
- Have students do Activities 33–34, pp. 136–137. **10 min.**

Optional Resources
- **Attention!,** p. 134
- Communication (TE), p. 135
- Cultures, p. 135
- Advanced Learners, p. 135 ▲
- Special Learning Needs, p. 135 ●
- Slower Pace Learners, p. 137 ◆
- Special Learning Needs, p. 137 ●

Homework Suggestions
Study for **Quiz: Grammaire 2**
Cahier de vocabulaire et grammaire, pp. 46–47
Cahier d'activités, pp. 35–36
HOMETUTOR
Online Practice (**my.hrw.com**)
1.1, 1.2, 2.1, 4.2

Block 6

OBJECTIVE
*Use **depuis, il y a, ça fait...**; Use the verb **ouvrir**; Develop listening and reading skills*

Core Instruction

Grammaire 2, pp. 134–137
- Have students do Activities 35–36, p. 137. **10 min.**
- Review **Grammaire 2,** pp. 134–137. **10 min.**
- Give **Quiz: Grammaire 2. 20 min.**

Application 2, pp. 138–139
- Have students do Activity 37, p. 138. **5 min.**
- See Teaching **Un peu plus,** p. 138. **5 min.**
- Have students do Activity 38, p. 138. **5 min.**
- Play Audio CD 4, Tr. 7 for Activity 39, p. 139. **5 min.**
- Have students do Activities 40–41, p. 139. **10 min.**

Télé-roman, pp. 140–141
- Show **Télé-roman.** See Teaching **Télé-roman,** p. 140. **5 min.**
- Have students answer the **As-tu compris?** questions, p. 141. **15 min.**

Optional Resources
- Communication (TE), p. 137
- French for Spanish Speakers, p. 138
- Communication (TE), p. 139
- Slower Pace Learners, p. 139 ◆
- Multiple Intelligences, p. 139
- Connections, p. 140
- Gestures, p. 140
- Communication (TE), p. 141

Homework Suggestions
Study for **Quiz: Application 2**
Cahier de vocabulaire et grammaire, p. 48
Cahier d'activités, p. 37
Online Practice (**my.hrw.com**)
1.1, 1.2, 1.3, 3.2, 4.1

Block 7

OBJECTIVE
Develop listening, reading, and writing skills; Review the chapter

Core Instruction

Application 2, pp. 138–139
- Review **Application 2,** pp. 138–139. **10 min.**
- Give **Quiz: Application 2. 20 min.**

Lecture et écriture, pp. 142–145
- See Teaching **Lecture,** p. 142. **20 min.**
- See Teaching **Espace écriture,** p. 144. **30 min.**

Prépare-toi pour l'examen, pp. 146–148
- Have students do Activities 1–3, p. 146. **10 min.**

Optional Resources
- Applying the Strategies, p. 142
- Reading with a Purpose, p. 142
- Comparisons, p. 143
- Connections, p. 143
- Advanced Learners, p. 143 ▲
- Multiple Intelligences, p. 143
- Cultures, p. 144
- Comparisons, p. 144
- Process Writing, p. 145
- Writing Assessment, p. 145
- Slower Pace Learners, p. 145 ◆
- Multiple Intelligences, p. 145
- Reteaching, p. 146
- Game, p. 146
- Fold-N-Learn, p. 146

Homework Suggestions
Study for Chapter Test
Cahier d'activités, p. 38
Espace écriture, Activity 2, p. 145
Online Practice (**my.hrw.com**)
1.1, 1.2, 1.3, 2.1, 3.1, 4.2

Block 8

OBJECTIVE
Review and assess the chapter

Core Instruction

Prépare-toi pour l'examen, pp. 146–148
- Have students do Activities 4–5, p. 147. **5 min.**
- Play Audio CD 4, Tr. 10 for Activity 6, p. 147. **5 min.**
- Have students do Activity 7, p. 147. **5 min.**
- Play Audio CD 4, Tr. 11–13 for **Lettres et sons,** p. 148. **5 min.**

Chapter Test 50 min.

Révisions cumulatives, pp. 150–151
- Play Audio CD 4, Tr. 14 for Activity 1, p. 150. **5 min.**
- Have students do Activities 2–5, pp. 150–151. **15 min.**

Optional Resources
- TPRS, p. 147
- Oral Assessment, p. 147
- Teacher to Teacher, p. 148
- Chapter Review, pp. 148–149
- Cinquain Poetry, p. 149
- Online Culture Project, p. 150
- Fine Art Connection, p. 151

Homework Suggestions
Cahier d'activités, pp. 39–40, 108–109
Online Practice (**my.hrw.com**)
1.1, 1.2, 1.3, 2.2, 3.1, 4.2

Chapter Opener

Meeting the National Standards

Communication
Communication, pp. 121, 123, 125, 127, 133, 135, 137, 139
À ton tour, p. 151

Cultures
Flash culture, pp. 120, 124, 132, 134
Comparaisons, p. 129
Practices and Perspectives, p. 119, 135,144

Connections
Science Link, p. 121
Physical Education Link, p. 129
Computer Science Link, p. 131
Language Link, p. 132
Visual Learners, p. 140
Language Arts Link, p. 143

Comparisons
Comparaisons, p. 129
Comparing and Contrasting, pp. 129, 143, 144

Communities
Community Link, p. 127
Communauté, p. 129

Using the Photo

Hockey, the national sport of Canada, was created there around 1837. The National Hockey League's ultimate prize is the Stanley Cup. It is named after Lord Stanley of Preston, Governor General of Canada, who first awarded it in 1892. Today the NHL is comprised of 30 teams, six of which are Canadian. Ask students to research one of the teams and share their findings. 4.2

Vocabulaire supplémentaire

Students might use these terms to discuss the photo.

la crosse de hockey *hockey stick*
le hockeyeur *hockey player*
le hockey sur glace *ice hockey*
le trophée *trophy*
l'entraîneur *coach*

chapitre 4

Au lycée

Objectifs

In this chapter, you will learn to
- ask how something turned out
- wonder what happened
- ask for information
- express frustration

And you will use
- object pronouns with the **passé composé**
- **quelqu'un, quelque chose, ne... personne, ne...rien,** and **ne... que**
- the verb **recevoir**
- the verb **suivre**
- **depuis, il y a,** and **ça fait**
- the verb **ouvrir**

Que vois-tu sur la photo?

Où sont ces jeunes?
Quel sport est-ce que ces joueurs pratiquent?
Et toi, est-ce que tu joues à ce sport?

ACTFL 21st Century Skills

Collaboration:	TE: pp. 115C, 127, 133, 144
Technology Literacy:	SE: p. 144; TE: pp. 115C, 119, 131, 133, 134, 139
Initiative and Self-Direction:	TE: pp. 115C, 117 (Global Awareness), 145
Social and Cross-Cultural Skills:	SE: pp. 128, 129; TE: pp. 115D, 123, 128 (Global Awareness), 129, 134
Productivity and Accountability:	SE: p. 145; TE: pp. 117, 119, 123, 125, 127, 132, 143
Leadership and Responsibility:	TE: pp. 127, 129 (Health Literacy), 131, 133, 139

Chapter Opener

L'équipe de hockey de l'école Cardinal-Roy, à Québec

DIGITAL FRENCH

TEACHER TOOLS

- Interactive Whiteboard Lessons
- Generate Success!

ALSO AVAILABLE...

- Online Workbooks
- French InterActive Reader

FRENCH ON THE GO!

- Performance Space
- Holt McDougal French Apps
- *Bien dit!* eTextbook

Learning Tips

Tell students that often the key to understanding a foreign language is understanding the culture of the country or countries where the language is spoken. The educational systems in French-speaking countries are not the same as in the U.S. The French terminology used for degrees and courses cannot always be literally translated. Encourage students to supplement their language study with cultural information.

VIDEO OPTIONS

- **Télé-vocab 1**
- **Grammavision 1**
- **Télé-vocab 2**
- **Grammavision 2**
- **Télé-roman**

LISTENING PRACTICE

Language Lab and Classroom Activities

Vocabulaire
Activity 2, p. 120, CD 4, Tr. 1
Télé-vocab 1, p. 118, DVD Tutor
Activity 24, p. 133, CD 4, Tr. 4
Télé-vocab 2, p. 130, DVD Tutor

Grammaire
Activity 11, p. 124, CD 4, Tr. 2
Grammavision 1, pp. 122, 124, DVD Tutor
Activity 27, p. 134, CD 4, Tr. 5
Activity 32, p. 136, CD 4, Tr. 6
Grammavision 2, pp. 134, 136, DVD Tutor

Application
Activity 16, p. 126, CD 4, Tr. 3
Activity 39, p. 139, CD 4, Tr. 7

Prépare-toi pour l'examen
Activity 6, p. 147, CD 4, Tr. 10

Révisions cumulatives
Activity 1, p. 150, CD 4, Tr. 14

Télé-roman
p. 140, DVD Tutor

Lecture
p. 142, CD 4, Tr. 8

Variations littéraires
p. 388, CD 4, Tr. 9

Lettres et sons
p. 148, CD 4, Tr. 11–13

Resources

Planning:
Lesson Planner
Teacher One Stop

Presentation:
Projectable Transparencies **Vocabulaire 4.1, 4.2**
DVD Tutor, Disc 1 **Télé-vocab 1**

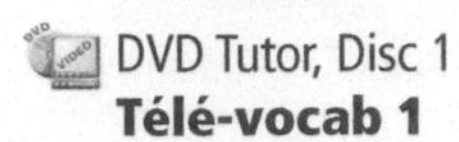

Interactive Whiteboard Lessons

Practice:
Cahier de vocabulaire et grammaire
Differentiated Practice and Assessment CD-ROM
Independent Study Guide
Media Guide
Projectable Transparencies Bell Work 4.1
HOMETUTOR
Holt McDougal French Apps

Bell Work

Use Bell Work 4.1 in the *Projectable Transparencies* or write this activity on the board.

Fill in the blanks with the correct article or contraction.

1. **Ce soir, Sophie va ____ cinéma.**
2. **La caissière ____ supermarché travaille beaucoup.**
3. **La boulangerie ____ quartier est excellente.**
4. **Je vais acheter ____ eau minérale ____ épicerie.**

1.2

COMMON ERROR ALERT
ATTENTION !

Students need to know that **une note** means *a grade*, as in an evaluation. They should not use this word to refer to the student's grade level.

Objectifs
- to ask how something turned out
- to wonder what happened

Vocabulaire à l'œuvre 1

Télé-vocab

Au lycée à Québec

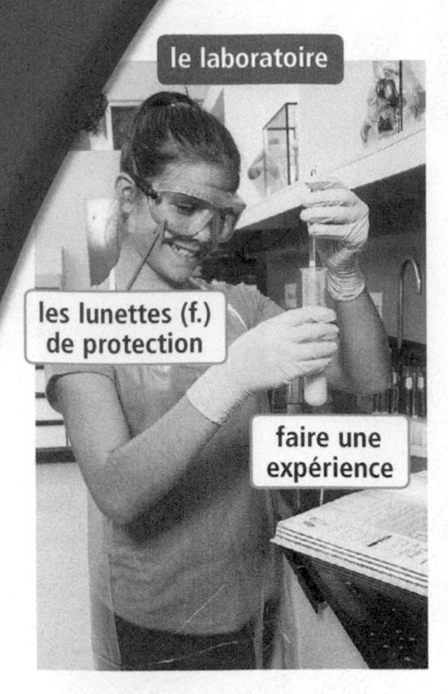

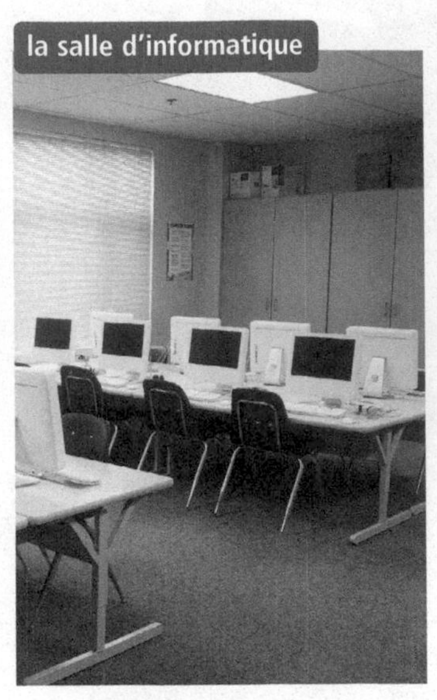

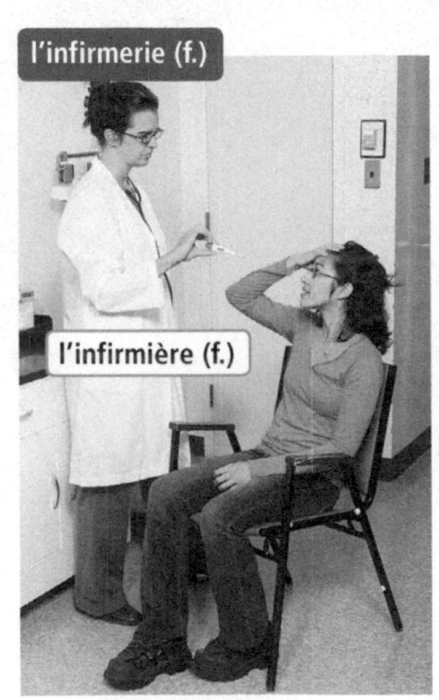

Core Instruction

TEACHING VOCABULAIRE

1. Introduce vocabulary with transparencies **Vocabulaire 4.1** and **4.2** and model pronunciation of each word. Include vocabulary in **D'autres mots utiles** and expressions in **Exprimons-nous! (2 min.)**
2. Make a floorplan of your school. Point to rooms and outside spaces and tell what they are. Then tell what one does in each. **Au laboratoire, on fait des expériences. Dans le gymnase, on a entraînement. (3 min.)**
3. Ask yes or no questions about the school. **Le documentaliste travaille dans le CDI? On déjeune sur le terrain de sport? Y a-t-il des ordinateurs dans la salle d'informatique? (3 min.)**

Télé-vocab 1

For a video presentation of this vocabulary, see the *DVD Tutor.*

Télé-vocab

Le complexe sportif

le gymnase

avoir entraînement (m.)

D'autres mots utiles

être en retenue	*to be in detention*
le conseiller/la conseillère d'éducation	*school counselor*
une note	*grade*
faire des recherches	*to do research*
rater	*to fail*
réussir	*to pass, to succeed*
passer un examen	*to take a test*
une interro(gation)	*quiz, test*

Exprimons-nous!

To ask how something turned out	To respond
Au fait, Élodie est allée à l'entraînement? *By the way . . .*	**Évidemment!** *Obviously!*
Comment s'est passé(e) ton match/ta compétition? *How did . . . go/turn out?*	**Je l'ai gagné(e)!** *I won it!*
Alors, le nouveau documentaliste, il est sympa? *So . . .*	**Je n'en sais rien.** Je ne l'ai pas encore vu. *I don't know anything about it . . .*
Dis-moi, tu as réussi ton expérience de chimie? *Tell me . . .*	Non, je l'ai **complètement** ratée. *. . . completely . . .*

Vocabulaire et grammaire, *pp. 37–39* Online Workbooks

▸ **Vocabulaire supplémentaire**—L'athlétisme, Au gymnase, **p. R19**

Differentiated Instruction

SLOWER PACE LEARNERS

Form small groups. Have each group use a disposable or digital camera to take pictures around the school that illustrate the words in **Vocabulaire.** Have students use the printed pictures to create a bulletin board or load their pictures on a CD to share. 1.3

MULTIPLE INTELLIGENCES

Visual Have students create flashcards that depict the new vocabulary words. The pictures should be labeled in French. On the back of each card, ask students to write sentences in French that describe the images. Partners can exchange flashcards for additional practice. 1.3

TPR
Total Physical Response

Have students respond to these commands.

Lève la main si tu empruntes souvent des livres.

Lève-toi si tu n'as jamais été en retenue.

Mets une main sur la tête si tu connais l'infirmière.

Lève les deux mains si tu aimes parler avec tes amis dans la cour de récréation.

Then have some students mime activities. Their classmates guess where they are and what they are doing.

Elle fait une expérience au laboratoire.

Tu manges à la cantine?

C'est la salle d'informatique?

Tu as entraînement au gymnase ou au terrain de sport! 1.2

Proverbes

For French proverbs and activities related to the chapter theme and vocabulary, see **Proverbes et expressions,** pp. R6–R7.

Cultures

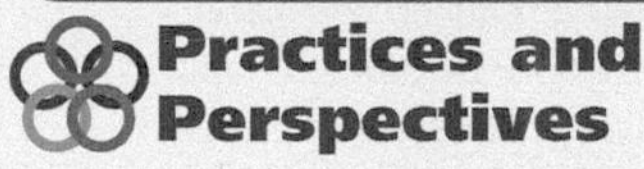

In the United States, many high school athletes compete with an eye toward receiving a full college athletic scholarship. These scholarships also attract Canadian students to American universities, since some Canadian provinces offer limited or no scholarships to their college athletes. Have students research the scholarship policies of Ontario and Quebec provinces and write a paragraph to compare and contrast the two systems. 2.1

Vocabulaire 1

Resources

Planning:
Lesson Planner
Teacher One Stop

Presentation:
Projectable Transparencies **Vocabulaire 4.1, 4.2**

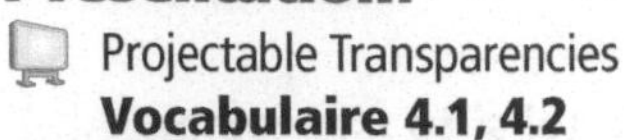

DVD Tutor, Disc 1 **Télé-vocab 1**

Interactive Whiteboard Lessons

Practice:
Cahier de vocabulaire et grammaire
Differentiated Practice and Assessment CD-ROM
Independent Study Guide
Media Guide
Audio CD 4, Tr. 1
@HOMETUTOR
Holt McDougal French Apps

2 Script

1. — Alors, ton expérience de physique, tu l'as réussie?
   — Non, je l'ai complètement ratée.
2. — Alors, l'interro de français, ça a marché?
   — Évidemment! C'est le seul cours où j'ai de bonnes notes.
3. — Au fait, est-ce que tu as trouvé le livre que tu cherchais au CDI?
   — Oui, la documentaliste m'a aidée.
4. — Comment s'est passé l'entraînement?
   — Je n'en sais rien. J'ai passé tout l'après-midi en retenue.
5. — Je ne t'ai pas vu à la cantine. Il t'est arrivé quelque chose?
   — J'avais mal à la tête. Je suis allé à l'infirmerie.

3 Possible Answers

1. Mes amis et moi, nous avons mangé à la cantine.
2. J'ai fait une expérience intéressante au labo.
3. J'ai eu entraînement au gymnase.
4. Après l'école, j'ai eu une compétition d'athlétisme. Je l'ai gagnée!

Flash culture

Au Québec, à la fin du CÉGEP, les élèves doivent passer le DEC (Diplôme d'études collégiales), qui est l'équivalent du bac en France. Certains élèves choisissent de passer le bac international. Un élève qui veut entrer à l'université doit avoir un DEC. Un élève qui choisit une formation technique peut passer son DEC après trois ans et peut entrer sur le marché de l'emploi *(job market)*.

Quel diplôme est-ce que tu obtiens à la fin du lycée? Est-ce que c'est un diplôme spécialisé? 4.2

1 Au lycée 1.2

Écrivons À quelle partie du lycée associes-tu les personnes ou les choses suivantes?

d **1.** la documentaliste	**a.** à la cantine
e **2.** le terrain de foot	**b.** à la cour de récréation
c **3.** une expérience	**c.** au laboratoire
e **4.** une compétition	**d.** au CDI
a **5.** le déjeuner	**e.** au complexe sportif
e **6.** un entraînement	**f.** à la salle d'informatique
d **7.** un livre	**g.** à l'infirmerie
g **8.** les médicaments	
f **9.** les ordinateurs	

2 Écoutons CD 4, Tr. 1 1.2

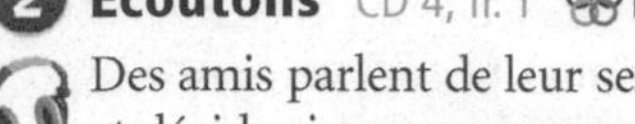

Des amis parlent de leur semaine au lycée. Écoute les conversations et décide si ces personnes ont passé **a) une bonne journée** ou **b) une mauvaise journée.** 1. b 2. a 3. a 4. b 5. b

3 La journée d'Antoine 1.2

Écrivons/Parlons Antoine a passé une journée intéressante. Imagine que tu es Antoine et raconte ce qui s'est passé d'après les images.

MODÈLE **Ce matin, j'ai été en retenue avec madame Roussel.**

1.

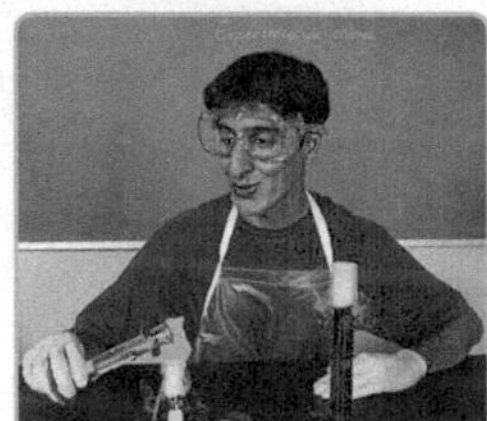

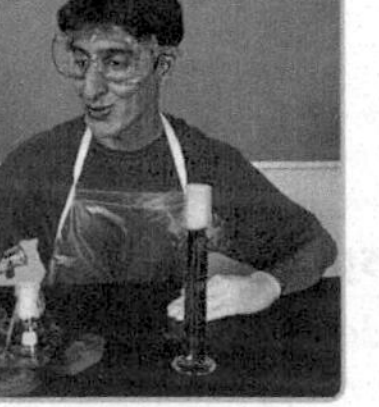

2.

3.

4.

4 Quelle journée! 1.3

Écrivons Tu as passé une très mauvaise journée au lycée. Écris dans ton journal quatre choses qui ne se sont pas bien passées.

MODÈLE **J'ai complètement raté mon interro… Alors…**

Core Instruction

TEACHING EXPRIMONS-NOUS!

1. Model the pronunciation of the expressions in **Exprimons-nous!** Then model a conversation in which one person responds to several questions or statements. **(4 min.)**
2. On eight large notecards, have students write the six responses in **Exprimons-nous!** and two from **Entre copains. (6 min.)**
3. Make statements or ask questions, wondering what happened. Include the new vocabulary in **Entre copains. Est-ce que le prof a raté un cours à l'université? Je parie que Rachel réussit toujours à l'examen de français. Voulez-vous une bonne note en français? Je me demande si Paul a jamais été collé.** Have students hold up the card with the correct response. Ask volunteers to read aloud the appropriate response. **(5 min.)**

Exprimons-nous!

To wonder what happened	To respond
Je me demande si Anne a **encore** perdu son match de tennis. *I wonder if . . . again.*	Non, elle l'a gagné **pour une fois.** *. . . for once.*
Je parie que Mathieu a reçu une bonne note. *I'll bet that . . .*	**Oui, sans doute.** *Yes, without a doubt.* **Tu crois?** *Do you think so?*
Tu crois qu'il est arrivé quelque chose à Martin? *Do you think something happened to . . . ?*	**C'est possible.** *It's possible.* **Tu as peut-être raison.** *You could be right.*
Est-ce que **quelqu'un** est allé à l'entraînement? *. . . someone . . .*	Non, **personne.** *. . . nobody.*

Vocabulaire et grammaire, pp. 37–39

5 La nouvelle élève 1.2

Écrivons/Parlons Julia est une nouvelle élève et elle est très bavarde *(talkative)*. Réponds à ses questions.

MODÈLE —Est-ce que tu sais si Li est déjà allée à la cantine?
—Oui, sans doute.

—Comment s'est passé ton match de tennis?

—(1) ______

—Il est midi. Tu crois qu'il est arrivé quelque chose à Fabien?

—(2) ______

—Est-ce que quelqu'un est allé à la compétition de natation?

—(3) ______

—Je parie qu'Anne-Sophie a eu une bonne note en maths.

—(4) ______

être collé(e)	*to be in detention*
potasser/ bachoter	*to study/ cram*
C'est dingue!	*It's crazy!*
Tu rigoles!	*You must be kidding!*

Communication

Digital performance space

6 Questions personnelles 1.1

Parlons Avec ton/ta camarade, discute de ta semaine et mentionne trois choses qui se sont bien ou mal passées. Pose des questions à ton/ta camarade aussi.

MODÈLE **—J'ai eu une compétition de foot cette semaine.**
—Ah bon? Comment s'est passée ta compétition?

Differentiated Instruction

ADVANCED LEARNERS

Have individual students write a short story in French that includes the words from **Vocabulaire.** The story should be suspenseful or have a surprise ending. Have students read the first half of their stories in small groups. Then pause to lead a discussion of what will happen in the second half. Students should use the expressions in **Exprimons-nous!** 1.1

SPECIAL LEARNING NEEDS

Students with AD(H)D Use newspapers, magazines, or photos to practice the expressions in **Exprimons-nous!** Ask partners to take turns asking and responding to questions about what is shown in the photographs in Activity 3. 1.1

5 Possible Answers

1. Je l'ai gagné!
2. C'est possible.
3. Non, personne.
4. Tu crois?

Connections

Science Link

The expressions in **Exprimons-nous!** are used to speculate what might have happened. Ask students to name the five senses. Then ask if they have ever heard of the "sixth sense," or intuition. Have students write an anecdote about a time when their intuition told them something that turned out to be true and share it with the class. 3.1

Communication

Pair Activity: Interpersonal

Write prompts on the board or on a transparency such as **faire une expérience au labo, déjeuner à la cantine, emprunter un livre au CDI.** Have students take turns asking each other if they do the activity listed at the specified place. Students should respond in a complete sentence with an appropriate object pronoun and the pronoun **y.** 1.1

Assess

Assessment Program
Quiz: Vocabulaire 1
Alternative Assessment
Differentiated Practice and Assessment CD-ROM

Online Assessment
my.hrw.com

Test Generator

Resources

Planning:
Lesson Planner
Teacher One Stop

Presentation:
DVD Tutor, Disc 1
Grammavision 1.1

Practice:
Grammar Tutor for Students of French, Chapter 4
Cahier de vocabulaire et grammaire
Differentiated Practice and Assessment CD-ROM
Cahier d'activités
Independent Study Guide
Media Guide
Projectable Transparencies
Bell Work 4.2
HOMETUTOR

Bell Work

Use Bell Work 4.2 in the *Projectable Transparencies* or write this activity on the board.

Match the action with the correct place.

1. faire des expériences
2. s'amuser avec ses copains
3. rendre un livre
4. s'entraîner
5. déjeuner

a. le CDI
b. le complexe sportif
c. le laboratoire
d. la cantine
e. la cour de récréation 1.2

Objectifs
- object pronouns with the passé composé
- quelqu'un, quelque chose, ne... personne, ne... rien, ne... que

Grammavision

Object pronouns with the *passé composé*

1. You already learned that direct and indirect object pronouns come before the conjugated verb. In the **passé composé,** place object pronouns before the helping verb **avoir** or **être**.

   —Tu as parlé à la **documentaliste?**
   —Oui, je **lui** ai parlé.

2. The pronouns y and en also come before the verb in the **passé composé**.

   Oui, j'y suis allé hier. J'en ai acheté.

3. In the **passé composé,** the past participle agrees with the direct object if the direct object appears *before* the verb.

   Nous avons gagné la **compétition**.

   La **compétition**? Nous l'avons gagn**ée.**
   (Agreement with *preceding* direct object)

Vocabulaire et grammaire, *pp. 40–41*
Cahier d'activités, *pp. 31–33*

Déjà vu!

Do you remember the forms of the direct and indirect object pronouns?
Direct object pronouns:
me, te, le, la, nous, vous, les
Indirect object pronouns:
me, te, lui, nous, vous, leur

7 Les nouveaux lycéens 1.2

Écrivons Yasmina fait visiter le lycée à deux nouveaux élèves. Complète les phrases avec le pronom objet direct et la forme appropriée du verbe **avoir** ou du verbe **être**.

1. —Sandrine, est-ce que tu as essayé le nouvel ordinateur?
   —Oui, je ______ ______ essayé. l'ai
2. —Là bas *(over there)*, c'est le gymnase.
   —Oui, je sais. Je (j') ______ ______ allée hier. y suis
3. —Dis-moi, est-ce que vous avez déjà acheté des cahiers?
   —Oui, nous ______ ______ déjà acheté. en avons
4. —Au fait, vous avez acheté vos lunettes de protection pour le cours de chimie?
   —Non, nous ne ______ ______ pas encore achetées. les avons
5. —Sandrine, est-ce que le prof de sport t'a choisie pour faire partie d'une équipe?
   —Oui, il ______ ______ choisie pour l'équipe de basket. m'a

Core Instruction

TEACHING GRAMMAIRE

1. Remind students that direct and indirect objects go before the conjugated verb in the **passé composé.** Go over Points 1 and 2. Explain agreement of the past participle when there is a preceding direct object. **(2 min.)**
2. On the board or on a transparency, write sentences in the **passé composé** with direct and indirect objects that can be replaced with **le/la/les** and **lui/leur. (3 min.)**
3. Have one group of students cross out the direct or indirect objects. Have the next group put the correct object pronoun in the right place in the sentence. Have the third group of students make the past participle agree, if necessary. **(3 min.)**

Grammavision

For a video presentation of the object pronouns with the **passé composé,** see the *DVD Tutor.*

Grammavision

Online Practice
my.hrw.com
Grammaire 1 practice

8 La dernière fois que... 1.2

Écrivons Complète les phrases suivantes pour expliquer ce qui s'est passé la dernière fois que tu as fait ces choses.

MODÈLE La dernière fois que j'ai participé à un tournoi de golf, je ____ (perdre). **l'ai perdu**

1. La dernière fois que j'ai fait une expérience en chimie, je ____ (réussir.) l'ai réussie
2. La dernière fois que j'ai parlé à Thomas, je ____ (parler) de ce qui s'est passé au laboratoire. lui ai parlé
3. La dernière fois que j'ai offert un cadeau à un de mes profs, je ____ (acheter) un livre. lui ai acheté
4. La dernière fois que j'ai parlé à mes amis, c'est quand je ____ (téléphoner) après la compétition. leur ai téléphoné

À la sénégalaise

In Senegal, you might hear the expression **faire les bancs** *(seat)* to mean **aller à l'école.**

9 Un sondage 1.2

Écrivons Gisèle est allée au CDI. Plus tard, elle a reçu un sondage. Aide-la à répondre au sondage d'après les images.

MODÈLE Où est-ce que vous avez fait vos recherches?
Je les ai faites au CDI.

1.

2.

3.

4.

1. Est-ce que vous avez trouvé les livres que vous cherchiez?
2. Est-ce que vous avez trouvé les magazines que vous cherchiez?
3. Avez-vous demandé de l'aide au documentaliste?
4. Est-ce que le documentaliste vous a aidé(e)?

Communication

Digital performance space

10 Questions personnelles 1.1

Parlons Ton/Ta camarade va te poser des questions au sujet de ce qui s'est passé au lycée la semaine dernière. Ensuite, échangez les rôles.

MODÈLE **—Comment ça s'est passé ton examen de... ?**

French for Spanish Speakers

Ask Spanish speakers to compare the placement of the pronouns in the **passé composé** with the placement of the pronouns in the **perfecto** in Spanish. Ask them to compare the following sentences.
Le musée? Je l'ai visité.
El museo? Lo he visitado.
What do the sentence structures in each language have in common? (Both place object pronouns before the helping verb.) What are some of the differences? (The subject pronoun is not always necessary in Spanish, so **yo** is left out of the Spanish sentence.) 4.1

9 Answers

1. Oui, je les ai trouvés.
2. Non, je ne les ai pas trouvés.
3. Oui, je lui ai demandé de l'aide.
4. Oui, il m'a aidée.

Communication

Pair Activity: Interpersonal

On the board or on a transparency, list items of clothing and related occasions or activities, such as **un costume de clown / pour la soirée costumée** and **des bottes / pour faire du ski.** Using the **passé composé** of **mettre,** partners take turns asking if the other put on the items mentioned. Partners should respond that they did put on the item, using the direct object pronoun and making the necessary changes to the past participle.

MODÈLE
— Tu as mis tes lunettes pour faire une expérience?
— Oui, je les ai mises. 1.1

Differentiated Instruction

SLOWER PACE LEARNERS

9 Write the responses to each question on the board or on a transparency with the words in scrambled order. Have students work as a class or in small groups to write the responses in the correct order. 1.2

SPECIAL LEARNING NEEDS

Students with Language Impairments
Spend extra time with students when presenting a new grammar lesson. Provide additional examples and ask students to create their own examples. Make connections to similarities and differences between English grammar and French grammar in order to enhance understanding and retention of the new material.

Resources

Planning:
Lesson Planner
Teacher One Stop

Presentation:
DVD Tutor, Disc 1
Grammavision 1.2

Practice:
Grammar Tutor for Students of French, Chapter 4
Cahier de vocabulaire et grammaire
Differentiated Practice and Assessment CD-ROM
Cahier d'activités
Independent Study Guide
Media Guide
Projectable Transparencies
Bell Work 4.3
Audio CD 4, Tr. 2
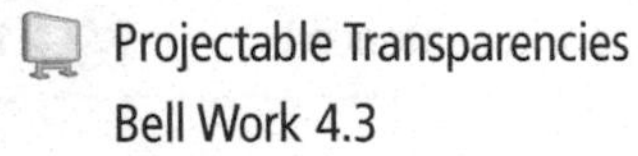

Bell Work

Use Bell Work 4.3 in the *Projectable Transparencies* or write this activity on the board.

Answer the following questions using an object pronoun.

1. **Est-ce que tu as parlé à la documentaliste? Oui, ...**
2. **Est-ce que Benjamin a gagné la compétition? Non, ...**
3. **Élise, est-ce que tu as raté ton examen? Non, ...**
4. **As-tu rendu les livres que tu as empruntés? Oui, ...**
5. **Est-ce que vous avez acheté vos livres de chimie? Oui, ...**

1.2

11 Script

See script on p. 115E.

Flash culture

Au Québec, comme aux États-Unis, les élèves reçoivent leurs livres en prêt pour l'école. Les parents doivent acheter les autres fournitures scolaires en début d'année. En France, ce sont en général les élèves qui achètent leurs propres livres. Ils les achètent directement aux élèves des classes supérieures et revendent leurs livres aux élèves des classes inférieures.

Est-ce qu'il t'arrive d'acheter des livres pour l'école? 4.2

Quelqu'un, quelque chose, ne... personne, ne... rien, ne... que

1. Use **quelqu'un** and **quelque chose** to say *someone* or *something*.

   Quelqu'un fait une expérience dans le laboratoire.

2. You've learned the expressions **ne... personne** and **ne... rien** to say *no one* and *nothing*. Place them around the conjugated verb in a sentence. In the **passé composé**, place **rien** after the form of **avoir** or **être. Personne,** however, comes *after* the past participle in the **passé composé**.

   Je **n'**ai **rien** vu. *I didn't see anything.*
   Je **n'**ai vu **personne**. *I didn't see anyone.*

3. *No one* and *nothing* can also be the subject. Place the word **personne** or **rien** in the subject position and place **ne** before the verb.

   Personne n'est venu et **rien n'**est arrivé.
   Nobody came and nothing happened.

4. **Ne... que (qu')** means *only.* Place **ne...** in front of the verb and **que** before what you are limiting.

   Il **n'**a gagné **que** deux compétitions.
   He won only two competitions.

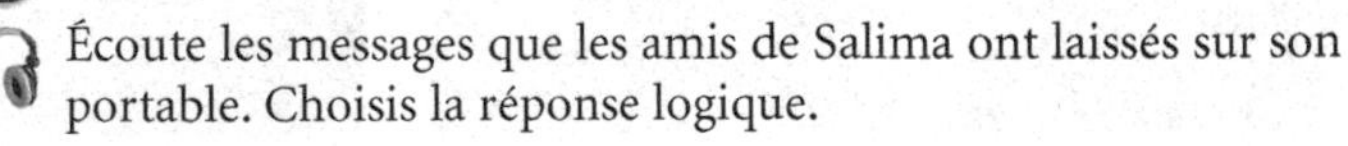

11 Écoutons CD 4, Tr. 2 1.2

Écoute les messages que les amis de Salima ont laissés sur son portable. Choisis la réponse logique.

1. a. Je ne fais rien. **(b.)** Je n'ai rien fait.
2. **(a.)** Je n'ai vu personne. b. Personne ne m'a vu.
3. **(a.)** Il ne m'est rien arrivé. b. Elle n'en sait rien.
4. a. Je ne connais personne. **(b.)** Personne n'est venu.
5. **(a.)** Tu ne m'as prêté que deux livres. b. Tu me prêtes quelques livres.

12 À la foire aux sciences 1.2

Écrivons Remets dans le bon ordre les notes que Rachida a prises pendant son expérience à la foire aux sciences *(science fair)*.

1. 8h à 9h— ma / n'est / à / personne / venu / table
2. 9h à 10h—n'est / rien / arrivé
3. 10h à 11h—personne / n'ai / vu / je
4. 11h à 12h—la table / il n'y a / de l'eau rose / sur / que

Core Instruction

TEACHING GRAMMAIRE

1. Go over Point 1, explaining that the opposites or negatives of **quelqu'un** and **quelque chose** are **ne... personne** and **ne... rien.** Explain that **personne** and **rien** can also be subjects of a sentence with **ne** in front of the conjugated verb. **(2 min.)**
2. Explain that **ne... que** is not a negative expression, so it goes around both verbs if there is more than one. **(1 min.)**
3. Ask students questions that can be answered with **personne** or **rien. Quelqu'un veut parler russe? Voulez-vous quelque chose à faire ce soir? Quelque chose d'intéressant passe à la télé ce soir? (3 min.)**

Grammavision

For a video presentation of **quelqu'un, quelque chose, ne... personne, ne... rien,** and **ne... que,** see the *DVD Tutor.*

13 Tout va de travers! 1.2

Lisons Ça ne va pas aujourd'hui! Choisis les images qui correspondent aux phrases suivantes.

a. Personne n'a réussi.
b. Personne n'est venu.
c. Il n'a rien trouvé.
d. Personne n'a gagné.
e. Ils n'ont rien vu.
f. Rien ne s'est passé.

1. a

2. e

3. b

4. c

5. f

6. d

14 Les opposés 1.2

Écrivons Pierre et Marie ont eu des journées très differentes! Pour chaque événement, décris ce qui est arrivé à Marie.

MODÈLE Pierre a vu quelqu'un. **Marie n'a vu personne.**

1. Pierre a fait beaucoup de choses aujourd'hui.
2. Pierre a vu un film au cinéma.
3. Pierre n'a parlé à personne.
4. Personne n'a vu Pierre.

Communication

Digital performance space

15 Scénario 1.1

Parlons Ton lycée a gagné le grand match et tu es en train de préparer une fête pour célébrer. Imagine cette scène avec tes camarades. Utilise **quelque chose, quelqu'un, rien,** et **ne... que** dans tes conversations.

Souviens-toi! Party preparations, pp. 54-55

MODÈLE **—Est-ce qu'il y a quelqu'un qui peut aller au marché?**
—Moi, je veux bien. J'achète quelque chose... ?

COMMON ERROR ALERT
ATTENTION !

The **ne... que** expression does not seem negative in translation, but when a person says, **Je n'ai que deux sœurs,** it means that he or she does have sisters, but only two of them. Students may mistakenly translate this as "I don't have two sisters."

12 Answers

1. 8h à 9h — Personne n'est venu à ma table.
2. 9h à 10h — Rien n'est arrivé.
3. 10h à 11h — Je n'ai vu personne.
4. 11h à 12h — Il n'y a que de l'eau rose sur la table.

14 Answers

1. Marie n'a rien fait aujourd'hui.
2. Marie n'a rien vu au cinéma.
3. Marie a parlé à quelqu'un.
4. Quelqu'un a vu Marie.

Communication

15 Pair Activity: Interpersonal

Have students write an original question with a verb and an object that is a person or a thing. Verbs might include **voir, rater, rendre, finir, inviter, attendre.** Then have students ask a partner the question. The partner should respond with **ne... personne** or **ne... rien.** Students should use either the present tense or the **passé composé.** 1.1

Differentiated Instruction

ADVANCED LEARNERS

Have students write and perform a courtroom drama or comedy in which falsely accused students are on trial for minor, school-related "crimes" such as returning a book late to the library, not going to football practice, and so on. Students should use the expressions **quelqu'un, quelque chose, ne... personne, ne... rien,** and **ne... que** in their scenes. 1.1

SPECIAL LEARNING NEEDS

13 Students with AD(H)D Allow students to create their own cartoons to illustrate the concepts in the activity. Ask them to use the responses given or develop their own responses to create captions for their cartoons or text bubbles in a comic strip. 1.1

Assess

Assessment Program
Quiz: Grammaire 1
Alternative Assessment
Differentiated Practice and Assessment CD-ROM

Online Assessment
my.hrw.com

Test Generator

Resources

Planning:
Lesson Planner
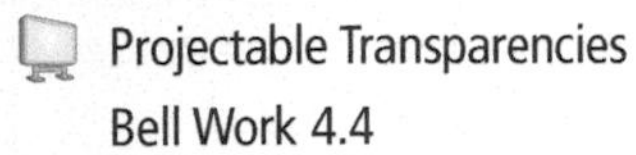
Teacher One Stop

Practice:
Grammar Tutor for Students of French, Chapter 4
Cahier de vocabulaire et grammaire
Differentiated Practice and Assessment CD-ROM
Cahier d'activités
Independent Study Guide
Media Guide
Projectable Transparencies Bell Work 4.4
Audio CD 4, Tr. 3

Bell Work

Use Bell Work 4.4 in the *Projectable Transparencies* or write this activity on the board.

Answer the questions in complete sentences using **ne... rien, ne... personne,** or **ne... que.**

1. **Est-ce que tu as vu quelqu'un ce matin?**
2. **Qu'est-ce que tu as fait hier soir?**
3. **Est-ce qu'il a gagné une ou plusieurs compétitions?**

1.2

16 Script

— Salut, Myriam! Dis-moi, tu sais si Éloïse était en cours ce matin?
— Non, je n'en sais rien. Pourquoi?
— Je ne l'ai pas vue à l'entraînement cet après-midi.
— Tu crois qu'il lui est arrivé quelque chose?
— C'est possible. Tu connais Éloïse! Hier soir, elle m'a dit qu'elle avait une expérience de chimie à préparer.
— Oh, oh! Tu as peut-être raison. Tu devrais téléphoner chez elle.
— J'ai essayé, mais il n'y avait personne.
— Je parie que Charlotte sait quelque chose. C'est sa meilleure amie. On peut lui téléphoner.

Synthèse
• Vocabulaire 1
• Grammaire 1

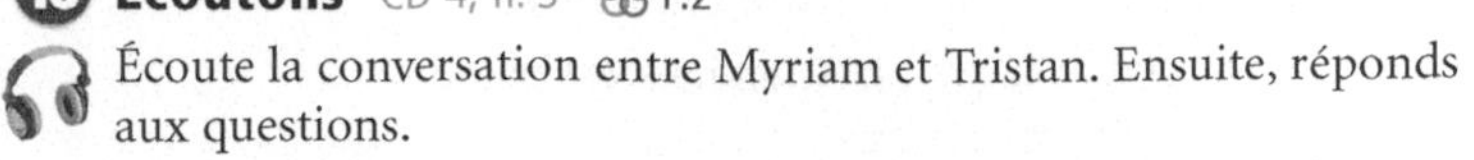

Application 1

16 Écoutons CD 4, Tr. 3 1.2

Écoute la conversation entre Myriam et Tristan. Ensuite, réponds aux questions.

1. Est-ce qu'Éloïse est allée à l'entraînement hier? Non
2. Qu'est-ce qu'Éloïse devait faire hier soir? préparer une expérience de chimie
3. Qu'est-ce que Myriam suggère à Tristan de faire? Elle lui suggère de téléphoner à Éloïse.

17 Au bureau 1.2

Écrivons Tu travailles au bureau administratif de ton lycée. Utilise des pronoms d'objets directs ou indirects et les éléments des boîtes pour répondre aux questions.

MODÈLE Les raquettes? **Je les ai emportées au gymnase.**

mettre emporter envoyer rendre	dans le dans la au à la	laboratoire CDI salle de classe gymnase cantine

1. Les classeurs?
2. Les ballons?
3. La boîte de pommes?
4. Les livres?
5. Les lunettes de protection?

Possible answers:
1. Je les ai mis dans la salle de classe.
2. Je les ai mis dans le gymnase.
3. Je l'ai envoyée à la cantine.
4. Je les ai rendus au CDI.
5. Je les ai mises dans le laboratoire.

Un peu plus

The verb *recevoir*

Notice the vowel change in the forms of **recevoir** *(to receive, to get).*

recevoir (participe passé : reçu)	
je reçois	nous recevons
tu reçois	vous recevez
il/elle/on reçoit	ils/elles reçoivent

Je reçois toujours de bonnes notes en chimie.

Vocabulaire et grammaire, *p. 42*
Cahier d'activités, *pp. 31–33*

Core Instruction

INTEGRATED PRACTICE

1. Have students do Activities 16–17 to practice vocabulary and object pronouns. **(3 min.)**
2. List on the board vocabulary that could pertain to both a **grand lycée** and a **petit lycée: le laboratoire, le CDI, la cantine, la cour de récré, l'infirmière, la salle d'informatique, le terrain de sport. (3 min.)**
3. Ask volunteers to use **quelque chose, quelqu'un, ne... personne, ne... rien,** and **ne... que** to describe their school. **(8 min.)**

TEACHING UN PEU PLUS

1. Remind students that they have seen other verbs with a spelling change such as that in **recevoir. (2 min.)**
2. Have partners tell if they get **bonnes notes** or **mauvaises notes** in each of their classes. **(4 min.)**
3. Continue with integrated practice Activities 18–20. **(8 min.)**

Online Practice
my.hrw.com
Application 1 practice

18 À propos de notes... 1.2

Écrivons Lise et Simon discutent de leurs notes. Complète leur conversation avec les formes du verbe **recevoir** qui conviennent.

—Je parie que je vais __1__ une bonne note en biologie. recevoir
La semaine passée, Émilie __2__ une bonne note et mon expérience est bien meilleure, à mon avis. a reçu

—Tu crois que Lucas et Karim vont __3__ de bonnes notes? recevoir

—C'est possible. Ils __4__ toujours de bonnes notes. reçoivent

—À propos de notes, est-ce que tu __5__ ta note d'histoire? as reçu

—Oui, Li et moi, nous __6__ les meilleures notes de la classe! avons reçu

Digital performance space

Communication

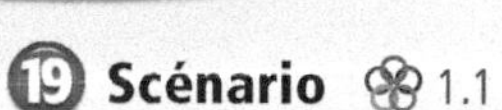

19 Scénario 1.1

Parlons Tu travailles au CDI avec la documentaliste. Lis l'écran et crée une conversation entre toi et la documentaliste.

MODÈLE **—Est-ce qu'Isabelle Chauvet a rendu... ?**
—Non, elle ne l'a pas... Je me demande si quelqu'un...

Fichier Edition Affichage Outils Aide

Centre de Documentation et d'Information — 1 octobre

Numéro d'étudiant	Étudiant	Titre	À rendre	Rendu
107329	Chauvet, Isabelle	Le tennis: le jeu mental	8 octobre	❑
		Jouons au foot!		
		La Chimie pratique	8 octobre	■
		L' Art moderne	14 octobre	❑
102348	Garnier, Valérie	Dessinez des portraits	21 octobre	❑
		L' Histoire de la chimie	21 octobre	❑
103792	Nguyen, Tran			❑
105261	Michaud, Denis	Naviguez sur Internet comme un pro	28 octobre	❑

20 Scénario 1.1

Parlons Ton lycée organise un sondage pour savoir les habitudes des élèves. Avec un(e) camarade, préparez dix questions concernant les élèves pendant le mois dernier. Posez-les à la classe.

MODÈLE **—Êtes-vous souvent allé(e) au CDI?**
—Oui, j'y suis allé au moins dix fois *(times)*.

Communities

Community Link

Have students organize a food, clothing, or toy drive for three local charities. Once items have been collected, have students apportion them among the three charities. Before they pack the items for delivery, have students give a presentation in French in which they describe the items they received and tell which charities will receive which items. 5.2

Communication

Group Activity: Presentational

Have students work in groups of three to prepare a presentation. Have one student mime, with or without visual aids, a school-related activity or a place in the school. The other two students discuss this person, wondering where he or she went and imagining what he or she did there, using object pronouns where necessary. 1.3

Differentiated Instruction

SLOWER PACE LEARNERS

Bring to class a reproduction of Leonardo da Vinci's *Mona Lisa*. Show it to the class and then draw your version on a transparency. Ask students to grade your drawing on a scale of 1–20, with 1 being the lowest grade and 20 the highest. Next, ask several volunteers to draw their own version of the *Mona Lisa* on a transparency. Have the class grade the drawings. Then use the grades you and the students received to practice the forms of **recevoir** with the class. 1.2

MULTIPLE INTELLIGENCES

17 Naturalist Structure the learning in the activity by asking students to create their own questions and answers in settings other than **au bureau,** such as the forest, the beach, or the jungle. Have them research new vocabulary related to those locations. Examples may include **L'éléphant? L'océan? Les arbres?** Their responses should follow the model in the activity. Some students may choose other environmental themes. 1.1

Assess

Assessment Program
Quiz: Application 1
Audio CD 4, Tr. 15
Alternative Assessment
Differentiated Practice and Assessment CD-ROM

Online Assessment
my.hrw.com

Test Generator 

Resources

Planning:
Lesson Planner
Teacher One Stop

Practice:
Cahier d'activités

Vocabulaire supplémentaire

You might wish to use these terms to discuss the project with students.

la patinoire	*ice rink*
le balai	*broom*
la balle	*ball*
faire une passe	*to pass*
frapper	*to hit*
tirer	*to shoot*
marquer un but (Québec: scorer)	*to score a goal*
le score	*the score*
le temps	*period*
une pénalité	*penalty*

Bulletin Board Project

Form small groups and ask students to research on the Internet or in the library foods that might typically be served for lunch in France and Quebec. Remind students to record the Web sites they visit. Have each group create three note cards with an illustration or photo of a food or dish on each card and label the foods in French. Have volunteers create a bulletin board with the note cards and entitle it **Le midi typique.** Finally, have the class compare the foods on the bulletin board to their typical lunch and discuss the similarities and differences. 1.3, 4.2

Culture

Partie de ringuette au Québec

Culture appliquée

La ringuette 2.2

Au Canada, il existe un sport créé spécialement pour les filles, la ringuette. Inventé en 1963, ce sport ressemble au hockey sur glace, mais il n'y a pas de contact physique entre les joueuses. Une équipe de ringuette est composée de cinq joueuses et d'une gardienne de but[1]. L'objectif est de lancer un anneau en caoutchouc[2] avec un bâton dans le but de l'autre équipe. Très populaire au Québec, la ringuette commence à se répandre[3] dans d'autres provinces canadiennes.

1. goal keeper 2. throw a rubber ring 3. to spread

Un mini tournoi de ringuette 2.2

Your class can all play **ringuette**! Instead of an ice rink, you can play outside on the grass or in the gym. Substitute broom handles for the straight sticks used to pass and shoot the rubber ring, which can be replaced with a ball.

Step 1 Divide the class into four teams. Only six players from each team should play at a given time. Choose a **gardien de but**. The other five players will pass the ball to one another and try to hit the ball into the opposing team's goal.

Step 2 Start the game between two teams. If you have enough space, the four teams can play at the same time. The game consists of two 20-minute sessions, but you can make them shorter. Remember, there is no physical contact between players. The team to score the most goals during the game wins.

Step 3 The two highest scoring teams play against each other to determine the final winner.

Recherches Est-ce qu'il existe d'autres sports typiques dans d'autres pays francophones? Lesquels? 2.1

Core Instruction

CULTURE APPLIQUÉE

1. Have the class read and discuss the introductory paragraph and **Recherches** questions. **(3 min.)**
2. Assign groups of five and have students in each group bring in four small brushes and a small ball. Have groups mark off a playing area and goals on a desk. Have students simulate playing the game according to the directions. **(10 min.)**
3. Have groups create a new sport and write in French the basic rules. **(15 min.)**

COMPARAISONS ET COMMUNAUTÉ

1. Have students read the statement and pick one of the choices. Ask, **Pourquoi?** and have students respond. **(5 min.)**
2. Form groups to read **Comparaisons** and discuss the **Et toi?** questions. **(10 min.)**
3. Have volunteers read **Communauté et professions** aloud in class and answer the questions. **(10 min.)**

Online Practice
my.hrw.com
Online Edition

Comparaisons

Repas à la cantine, Nice

On mange où? 1.2

Tu vas au lycée en France mais tu n'as pas assez de temps pour rentrer manger chez toi à midi.

a. Tu achètes un sandwich et un coca dans un distributeur automatique[1].
b. Tu emportes un «sack lunch» comme aux États-Unis.
(c.) Tu manges à la cantine du lycée.

Une journée typique dans un lycée français commence à 8 heures et se termine à 17 heures. Les élèves ont une ou deux heures pour manger le midi. Beaucoup d'élèves qui n'ont pas le temps de rentrer chez eux ou de sortir du lycée pour déjeuner, mangent à la cantine. Ils sont demi-pensionnaires. Leurs parents paient un forfait[2] par mois pour les repas. La cantine est aussi appelée «le réfectoire» ou simplement «le self». De temps en temps, les lycéens aiment aussi aller manger un sandwich au café du coin[3]. Le concept de «sack lunch» n'existe pas en France.

4.2

ET TOI?

1. Qu'est-ce que les élèves de ton lycée font pour déjeuner le midi?
2. Quelles sortes de «cantines» existent dans les lycées aux États-Unis?

Communauté et professions

Être professeur de français 5.1

En France, pour être professeur d'anglais ou toutes autres langues étrangères dans un lycée, il faut faire des études universitaires et ensuite passer un concours, le Capes. Dans ton district, quel diplôme doit-on passer? Est-ce qu'il existe une école spécialisée dans la formation des professeurs? Fais des recherches et présente les résultats à ta classe.

1. vending machine 2. flat rate 3. neighborhood café

Un élève qui apprend le français

Differentiated Instruction

SLOWER PACE LEARNERS

Read the passage aloud to students. Stop after each sentence and make a true or false statement in English about the sentence you just read. For example, **La ringuette** is a sport especially for boys. (false) Have students give a thumbs-up sign for true statements and a thumbs-down sign for false statements. 1.2

MULTIPLE INTELLIGENCES

Musical Ask students to research the musical traditions surrounding school or professional sporting events in Canada or France. Ask students to find out if there are traditional half-time shows where school bands perform and if they do, what types of music they select. Are their traditions similar to American musical traditions, such as songs or cheers for the team or school? Have students share their findings with the class. 2.1

Connections

Physical Education Link

The cold and snowy climate of Canada lends itself to many other winter sports. Have students choose a winter sport that interests them and research how it is practiced in Canada. Students should find information on the history of the sport, special clubs and leagues for the sport, major tournaments and competitions, and how someone interested in the sport can get started. 3.1

Comparisons

Comparing and Contrasting

Have students search the Internet for French school menus (key-words: **restauration, scolaire, menu**) and compare the foods to those served in their own cafeteria. Students might use the information to plan an imaginary campaign to get more healthful food on the school menu. 4.2

Language Examination

Culture can be used to practice for the **Interpretive Communication** and **Presentational Writing** sections of the AP Language and Culture Exam as it helps students get acquainted with and reflect on products and practices from the French-speaking world while reading culture-focused passages and answering questions in French.

Resources

Planning:
Lesson Planner
Teacher One Stop

Presentation:
Projectable Transparencies **Vocabulaire 4.3, 4.4**
DVD Tutor, Disc 1 **Télé-vocab 2**
Interactive Whiteboard Lessons

Practice:
Cahier de vocabulaire et grammaire
Differentiated Practice and Assessment CD-ROM
Independent Study Guide
Media Guide
Projectable Transparencies Bell Work 4.5
@HOMETUTOR
Holt McDougal French Apps

Bell Work

Use Bell Work 4.5 in the *Projectable Transparencies* or write this activity on the board.

Fill in the blanks with the correct form of **recevoir.**

1. **Marie va ____ ses amis pour son anniversaire.**
2. **Hier, nous ____ une lettre de Martinique.**
3. **Pauline et Julien ____ leurs amis chez eux tous les week-ends.**
4. **Vous ____ beaucoup d'e-mail chaque jour?**
5. **Je ____ des cadeaux de tous mes amis à Noël.**
6. **Ma mère ____ le catalogue de ce magasin tous les mois.** 1.2

Objectifs
- to ask for information
- to express frustration

Vocabulaire à l'œuvre 2

Télé-vocab

L'interface d'un ordinateur

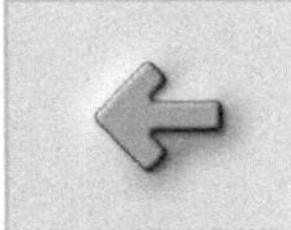
Précédente *Previous*

Suivante *Next*

Actualiser *Refresh*

l'adresse (f).

Recherche *Search*

Favoris *Favorites*

Démarrage *Home*

Courrier *E-mail*

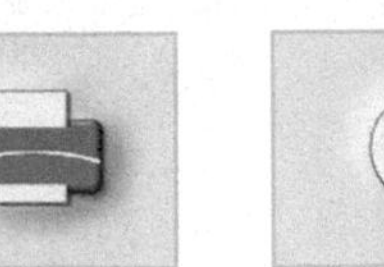
Imprimer *Print*

Arrêter *Stop*

D'autres mots utiles

Fichier	*File*
Édition	*Edit*
Retour	*Return/Enter*
Affichage	*View*
Outils	*Tools*
Aide	*Help*
Accueil	*Home page*
le lien	*(Web) link*
les barres de défilement	*scroll bars*
la fenêtre	*window*

Core Instruction

TEACHING VOCABULAIRE

1. Introduce vocabulary with transparencies **Vocabulaire 4.3** and **4.4** or your classroom computer and model the pronunciation of each word. **(2 min.)**
2. Referring to the transparency or computer, give examples of tasks on the computer, using the new vocabulary. **Je sauvegarde tous les examens que j'écris à l'ordinateur. Quand j'ai le temps, j'aime naviguer sur des sites français. (5 min.)**
3. Ask students all **Exprimons-nous!** questions except the second. They can be answered with **oui** or **non,** the name of a search engine, or a brand of computer. Model the answer to the second question. **(2 min.)**

Télé-vocab 2

For a video presentation of this vocabulary, see the *DVD Tutor.*

Télé-vocab

Un ordinateur (portable)

l'écran
l'imprimante (f.)
la touche
le clavier
la souris

D'autres mots utiles

démarrer	*to start up*	**graver**	*to burn*
naviguer	*to surf, navigate*	**ouvrir une session**	*to start a session*
un navigateur	*browser*	**un logiciel**	*software*
cliquer	*to click*	**un menu déroulant**	*pull-down menu*
télécharger	*to download*	**un graveur de CD/DVD**	*CD/DVD burner*
un moteur de recherche	*search engine*	**une tablette**	*tablet*

Exprimons-nous!

To ask for information

Savez-vous comment démarrer cet ordinateur?
Do you know how to . . . ?

Comment est-ce qu'on fait pour sauvegarder/ouvrir un document?
What do we do to save/open a document?

Qu'est-ce que tu utilises comme tablette?
What do you use for . . . ?

Quelle sorte d'ordinateur est-ce que tu me recommandes?
What type of . . . ?

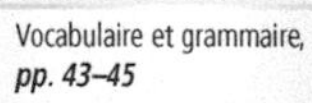

▶ Vocabulaire supplémentaire—Le matériel de bureau, p. R19

TPR
Total Physical Response

Have students respond to these commands.

Lève-toi si tu aimes l'informatique.

Assieds-toi si tu sais naviguer sur Internet.

Lève le doigt si tu sais comment on fait pour graver un CD.

Lève la main si tu télécharges de la musique sur Internet.

Va au tableau et dessine une souris.

Bring a laptop to class if there is no computer in your classroom. Have students gather around and have some of them respond to the following commands.

Démarre l'ordinateur.

Cherche le navigateur et ouvre une session.

Ferme la fenêtre.

Démarre ce logiciel.

Sauvegarde un document.

1.2

Connections
Computer Science Link

Discuss with students the qualities of a good Web site and what they would expect to find on a Web site that promotes tourism in Quebec. Have students search the Internet for sites on Quebec and provide a list of the five best sites they find. Students should write a brief description of each Web site's features, the information it offers, and document the URLs of the sites they visit. 3.1

Differentiated Instruction

Advanced Learners

Give a short lecture in French on the increasing problem of "tech trash" caused by people discarding their used computers and cell phones after they purchase new ones. Have small groups plan an imaginary recycling drive in your community. Instruct students to list everything that would need to be done in order to have a successful event. Have groups share their plans with the class and vote on the best plan. 1.3

Multiple Intelligences

Linguistic Ask students to use the vocabulary from **Un ordinateur** and **D'autres mots utiles** to design a newspaper advertisement for a computer sale at a local store. The advertisement should feature the components included in the purchase (**l'imprimante, la souris, un logiciel**), the capabilities of the computer (**un graveur de CD/DVD, un navigateur**), and the possible uses of the computer by the customer (**sauvegarder, télécharger**). 1.3

Resources

Planning:

Lesson Planner

Teacher One Stop

Presentation:

Projectable Transparencies **Vocabulaire 4.3, 4.4**

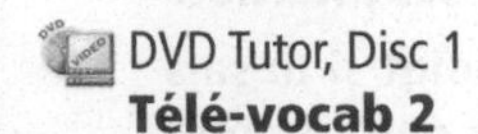

DVD Tutor, Disc 1 **Télé-vocab 2**

Interactive Whiteboard Lessons

Practice:

Cahier de vocabulaire et grammaire

Differentiated Practice and Assessment CD-ROM

Independent Study Guide

Media Guide

Audio CD 4, Tr. 4

@HOMETUTOR

Holt McDougal French Apps

Connections

Language Link

Share with students the fact that expressions often have interesting origins. For example, the expression, "There is more than one way to skin a cat", refers to preparing catfish for cooking. Assign each student an appropriate French idiomatic expression and have them research its origin. Students should then create a poster that illustrates the meaning of the expression and relates its history. 3.2

21 L'intrus 1.2

Écrivons Identifie l'expression qui ne va pas avec les autres.

1. précédente, suivante, sauvegarder
2. le graveur, la fenêtre, le DVD
3. l'écran, les favoris, le clavier
4. la tablette, naviguer, l'adresse
5. ouvrir une session, démarrer, graver
6. outils, aide, logiciel

22 Qu'est-ce qui fait quoi? 1.2

Écrivons Choisis ce qui complète chaque phrase logiquement.

1. On utilise ______ pour choisir des liens.
   a. la souris **b.** un graveur
2. ______ fait une copie d'un document.
   a. Le fichier **b.** L'imprimante
3. Pour regarder toute la page Web, j'utilise ______.
   a. les barres de défilement **b.** le fichier
4. ______ copie un CD.
   a. Une fenêtre **b.** Un graveur
5. ______ indique le site où je suis.
   a. L'adresse **b.** L'imprimante
6. Pour commencer à surfer, il faut ______.
   a. sauvegarder **b.** ouvrir une session
7. ______ permettent de continuer les recherches.
   a. Les liens **b.** Les courriers

Flash culture

La plupart des ordinateurs au Québec ont le même clavier qu'aux États-Unis, le clavier QWERTY. Mais certains ordinateurs sont équipés du clavier qui existe en France, le clavier AZERTY. Les noms QWERTY et AZERTY viennent de l'organisation des touches sur le clavier. Le clavier français commence par les lettres A et Z. Le clavier français a aussi les lettres avec accents.

Quels sont les avantages et inconvénients d'avoir un clavier différent d'une langue à l'autre? 4.2

23 La salle d'informatique 1.2

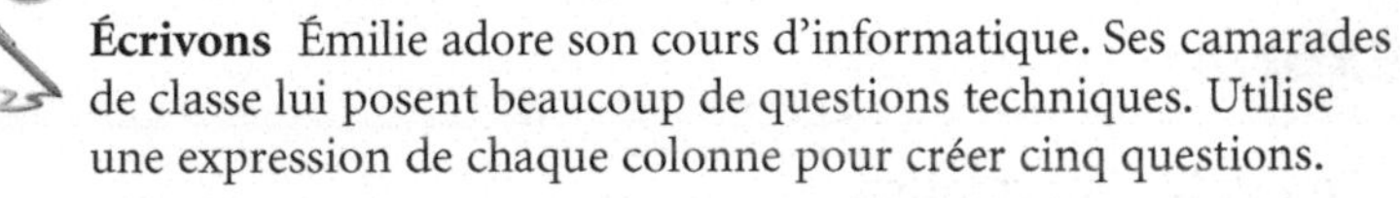

Écrivons Émilie adore son cours d'informatique. Ses camarades de classe lui posent beaucoup de questions techniques. Utilise une expression de chaque colonne pour créer cinq questions.

MODÈLE **Savez-vous comment graver un CD?**

Quelle sorte	comment	ce document?
Comment	tu utilises comme	est-ce que tu me recommandes?
Sais-tu	est-ce qu'on fait pour	aller à l'accueil?
Qu'est-ce que	de clavier	ouvrir une session?
	est-ce qu'on télécharge	logiciel?

Core Instruction

TEACHING EXPRIMONS-NOUS!

1. Model the pronunciation of the expressions. Write on the board or on a transparency four possible responses to the expressions and model the pronunciation of each. **(3 min.)**
2. Tell students you are frustrated by the computer problems you are having today. State your complaint. Ask for volunteers to read aloud one of the responses. Continue until students have responded to each of your problems. **(2 min.)**
3. Call on students to read a complaint to which you respond. **Tout va de travers! Tu as oublié de sauvegarder ton document?** Continue until students have practiced each expression. **(3 min.)**

Exprimons-nous!

To express frustration

Ça m'énerve! Mon ordinateur n'arrête pas de **planter**.
How annoying! . . . crashing.

Tout va de travers depuis que j'ai commencé mes recherches sur Internet. *Everything is going wrong since . . .*

Oh là là! **Rien ne marche** aujourd'hui! *. . . Nothing is working . . . !*

Je ne sais pas quoi faire! Ça fait trois fois que je perds mon document!
I don't know what to do. I lost my document three times already!

Vocabulaire et grammaire, *pp. 43–45*

24 Écoutons CD 4, Tr. 4 1.2

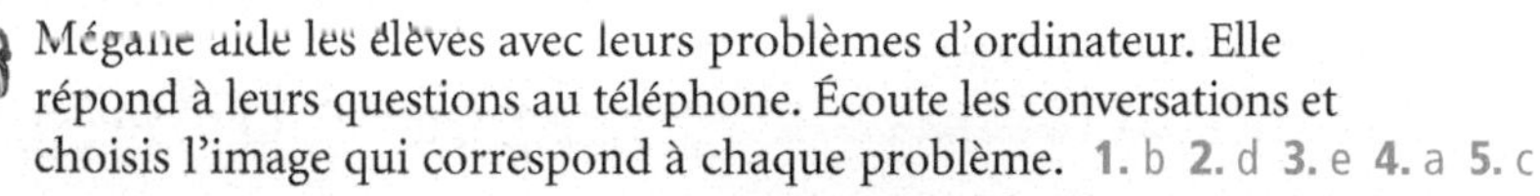

Mégane aide les élèves avec leurs problèmes d'ordinateur. Elle répond à leurs questions au téléphone. Écoute les conversations et choisis l'image qui correspond à chaque problème. **1.** b **2.** d **3.** e **4.** a **5.** c

a.

b.

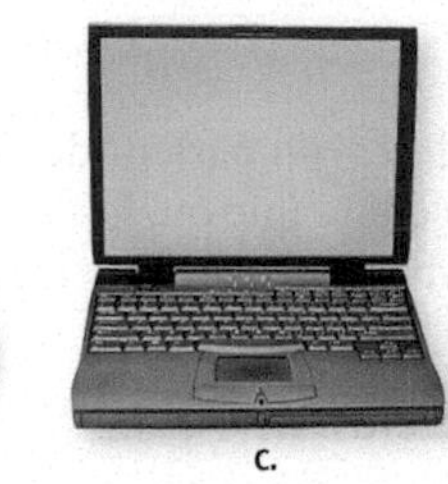
c.

d.

e.

Communication

25 Opinions personnelles 1.1

Parlons Pendant le cours d'informatique, tes amis et toi discutez de ce que vous aimez et de ce que vous n'aimez pas dans la nouvelle salle d'informatique. Suivez le modèle.

MODÈLE **—Tu aimes la nouvelle imprimante?**
—Non. Je ne sais pas comment la démarrer. Et toi?

26 Scénario 1.1

Parlons Il y a un nouvel élève qui ne comprend pas bien les ordinateurs! Il veut faire des recherches pour son projet sur Québec. Explique-lui ce qu'il faut faire. Ensuite, échangez les rôles.

MODÈLE **—D'abord, il faut ouvrir une session.**

24 Script

See script on p. 115E.

Rachel Norwood
Athens Academy
Athens, GA

I have students make a brochure about our school. They use digital cameras and computer software or they may create a brochure by hand with drawings to illustrate the people and places. Be sure students include a map labeled in French, and information such as the library's hours or a typical menu and meal prices in **la cantine.** You might exchange information with a partner school in a French-speaking region. 1.3

Communication

Pair Activity: Interpersonal

Have partners create a conversation. One student has purchased a computer, but has never used one before. The partner gives instructions to type and print a paper for a class and to download an MP3 file and burn it to a CD. Ask volunteers to present their conversation. 1.1

Differentiated Instruction

SLOWER PACE LEARNERS

25 Work together as a class to extend the **Modèle** given. Alternatively, you might write two additional **Modèles** on the board or on a transparency and have students base their conversations on these models. 1.1

MULTIPLE INTELLIGENCES

Intrapersonal Ask students to think of a situation that may have caused them to feel frustrated or confused. Have volunteers identify problems that would cause these feelings, or suggest some to the class. Examples may include learning a new skill, trying to repair a broken object, or losing a competition. After identifying several possible situations, ask students to write a journal entry about a personally frustrating experience. Students do not have to share their journal entry unless they volunteer to do so. 1.3

Assess

Assessment Program
Quiz: Vocabulaire 2
Alternative Assessment
Differentiated Practice and Assessment CD-ROM

Online Assessment
my.hrw.com

Test Generator 

Resources

Planning:
Lesson Planner
 Teacher One Stop

Presentation:
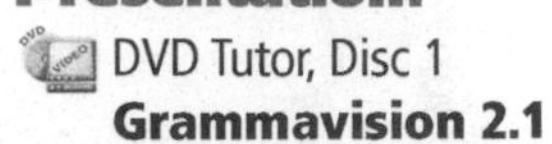 DVD Tutor, Disc 1
Grammavision 2.1

Practice:
Grammar Tutor for Students of French, Chapter 4
Cahier de vocabulaire et grammaire
Differentiated Practice and Assessment CD-ROM
Cahier d'activités
Independent Study Guide
Media Guide
Projectable Transparencies
Bell Work 4.6
Audio CD 4, Tr. 5
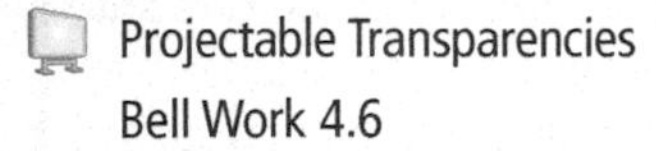

Bell Work

Use Bell Work 4.6 in the *Projectable Transparencies* or write this activity on the board.

Unscramble the words. Then underline the items that do not belong in computer class.

1. VANIEGRU
2. LARÉTÉCHERG
3. RACILVE
4. SEINNT
5. QLICREU
6. GEICOLIL 1.2

COMMON ERROR ALERT / ATTENTION !

When students see **je suis,** they are likely to think that this is the form of **être.** They should be reminded that now they must look at context to determine whether this is a form of the verb **suivre** or **être.**

Objectifs
- the verb **suivre**
- **depuis, il y a, ça fait**

Grammaire à l'œuvre 2

Grammavision

The verb *suivre*

1 The verb suivre *(to follow)* is irregular. You can use suivre to say what courses you are taking.

suivre (participe passé: suivi)			
je	suis	nous	suivons
tu	suis	vous	suivez
il/elle/on	suit	ils/elles	suivent

Je suis un cours d'informatique.

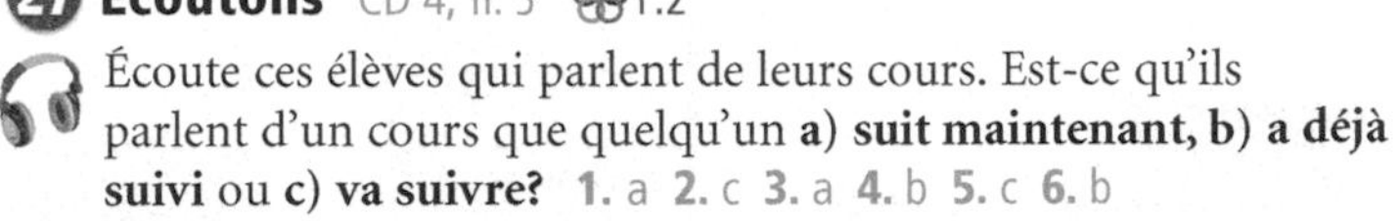
Vocabulaire et grammaire, *pp. 46–47*
Cahier d'activités, *pp. 35–37*
Online Workbooks

27 Écoutons CD 4, Tr. 5 1.2

Écoute ces élèves qui parlent de leurs cours. Est-ce qu'ils parlent d'un cours que quelqu'un **a) suit maintenant, b) a déjà suivi** ou **c) va suivre? 1.** a **2.** c **3.** a **4.** b **5.** c **6.** b

Flash culture

La plupart des sites web canadiens sont en anglais et en français. Il faut donc choisir la langue du site sur la page d'accueil. Si en France on utilise beaucoup de termes anglais pour se référer à l'informatique, les Québécois préfèrent utiliser des termes français. Ils ont créé le terme *courriel* pour remplacer le mot *e-mail*. Le mot courriel a été officiellement adopté par la France mais n'est pas très utilisé. Les Français préfèrent parler d'e-mail ou même de mail. 4.2

Est-ce que tu as visité des sites Web canadiens?

28 Un cours à choisir 1.2

Lisons/Écrivons Complète la conversation qu'Anne et Luke ont avec leur conseiller d'éducation. Utilise les formes correctes du verbe **suivre**.

M. MALONE Bonjour, Anne et Luke. Vous devez choisir un autre cours à __1__, c'est ça? suivre

ANNE Oui, il y a eu une erreur. Nous __2__ le cours d'informatique l'année dernière. avons suivi

M. MALONE Alors, regardez l'écran. Voici vos emplois du temps. Luke, tu __3__ des cours de maths, de chimie et de physique le matin... suis

LUKE Non, c'est l'emploi du temps d'Anne. Moi, je __4__ des cours d'anglais, d'espagnol et d'allemand... suis

M. MALONE Ah! Tu as raison! Anne __5__ ces cours. Est-ce que vous __6__ un cours d'art moderne? Il y a un cours à 9h. Ça vous intéresse? suit suivez

ANNE Oui! Mes copines __7__ ce cours. Et toi, Luke? suivent

LUKE D'accord. Mes copains __8__ ce cours l'automne dernier et ils m'ont dit que c'était génial. ont suivi

Core Instruction

TEACHING GRAMMAIRE

1. Explain that the verb **suivre** is irregular. Remind students that the meaning here is *to take a class*, so **prendre** is not used for this expression. **(2 min.)**
2. Have students put all of their textbooks on their desks. Go around the room, picking up books and asking yes or no questions. **Tu suis un cours de maths? Vous suivez un cours d'histoire? Elles suivent un cours de littérature?**
3. Then ask about individual students' classes. **David suit un cours d'art? Yvette et Jean suivent un cours de chimie? (3 min.)**

Grammavision

For a video presentation of the verb **suivre,** see the *DVD Tutor.*

Grammavision

Online Practice
my.hrw.com
Grammaire 2 practice

29 Je n'aime pas mes cours! 1.2

Écrivons Didier n'aime pas ses cours cette année. Il préfère les cours de ses copains. Remets dans l'ordre les phrases de Didier.

1. année / suivre / ennuyeux / cours / je / très / cette / des
2. et / vous / Iris / un / cours / Camille / d'histoire / suivre
3. d'arts / suivre / cours / Marie / plastiques / un
4. cours / et / Djamel / suivre / d'informatique / un / moi
5. et / Lise / un / musicale / cours / suivre / d'éducation / Raphaël

30 Les fonds d'écran  1.2

Parlons/Écrivons Regarde les écrans de quelques élèves. Quels cours est-ce que chaque élève suit?

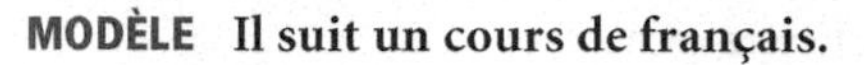

MODÈLE **Il suit un cours de français.**

Il

1. Elle

2. Elles

3. Ils

4. Il

5. Je

6. Nous

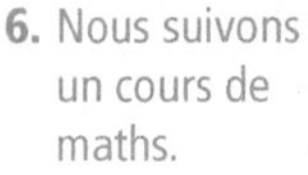

1. Elle suit un cours d'histoire.
2. Elles suivent un cours de géographie.
3. Ils suivent un cours de sport.
4. Il suit un cours de musique.
5. Je suis un cours d'informatique.
6. Nous suivons un cours de maths.

Digital performance space

Communication

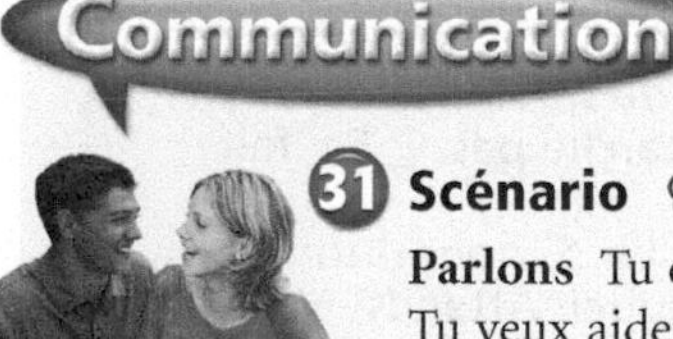

31 Scénario 1.1

Parlons Tu es conseiller (conseillère) d'éducation dans un lycée. Tu veux aider un élève à choisir des cours. Pour commencer, tu dois demander à l'élève quels cours il/elle suit et à quelles heures.

MODÈLE **—Qu'est-ce que tu suis à huit heures... ?**

27 Script

See script on p. 115F.

29 Answers

1. Cette année je suis des cours très ennuyeux.
2. Iris et Camille, vous suivez un cours d'histoire?
3. Marie suit un cours d'arts plastiques.
4. Djamel et moi, nous suivons un cours d'informatique.
5. Lise et Raphaël suivent un cours d'éducation musicale.

Cultures

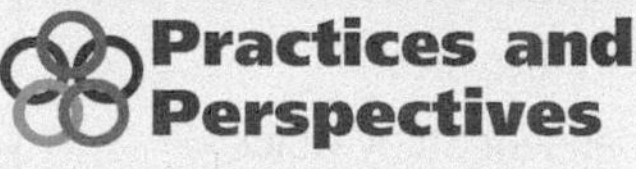

Practices and Perspectives

Explain to students that French children begin studying their first foreign language in **sixième** when they are 11 years old. They begin to study their second foreign language in **quatrième,** at the age of 13. Almost all students choose English as their first or second foreign language. Discuss with students whether it would be easy or difficult to study two languages at the same time.

2.1

Communication

Group Activity: Interpersonal

Have students in groups interview one another about different school subjects. Have students ask about a school subject, using the verb **suivre** in the present tense and respond in the **passé composé,** the present, or **le futur proche,** depending on when they have the class. Students should also use an object pronoun in their responses.

MODÈLE
— Tu suis le cours d'algèbre?
— Non, je l'ai suivi l'année dernière.
— Tu suis le cours d'informatique?
— Non, je vais le suivre l'année prochaine. 1.1

Differentiated Instruction

ADVANCED LEARNERS

Have students research the Web sites of schools in Quebec, France, and a third French-speaking country to find out what classes a typical student their age takes. Have students write a report comparing and contrasting the classes taken by students in the different countries.

4.2

SPECIAL LEARNING NEEDS

Students with Learning Disabilities/ Dyslexia To help students remember the forms of the irregular verb **suivre,** ask them to create a sentence with each subject pronoun. The sentences should describe courses they or their friends are taking. To get them started, use the example, **Je suis un cours d'informatique.** The repetition and extra practice will increase their ability to memorize the irregular conjugations.

1.2

Resources

Planning:
Lesson Planner
Teacher One Stop

Presentation:
DVD Tutor, Disc 1
Grammavision 2.2

Practice:
Grammar Tutor for Students of French, Chapter 4
Cahier de vocabulaire et grammaire
Differentiated Practice and Assessment CD-ROM
Cahier d'activités
Independent Study Guide
Media Guide
Projectable Transparencies
Bell Work 4.7
Audio CD 4, Tr. 6
@HOMETUTOR

Bell Work

Use Bell Work 4.7 in the *Projectable Transparencies* or write this activity on the board.

Fill in the blanks with the correct form of the verb **suivre.**

1. **Quels cours est-ce que vous ____ ce semestre?**
2. **Je ____ un cours de maths et un cours de littérature.**
3. **Et votre frère, est-ce qu'il ____ les mêmes cours que vous?**
4. **Non, nous ne ____ pas les mêmes cours.**
5. **Ses amis et lui ____ un cours d'informatique.** 1.2

32 Script

See script on p. 115F.

Depuis, il y a, ça fait

1 To say *for how long* or *since,* use **depuis.** If you are talking about an action that started in the past and continues in the present, use **depuis** and the present tense.

Elle fait de la recherche **depuis** un an.
She has been doing research for a year.

Il fait du sport **depuis** midi.
He's been playing sports since noon.

2 Two other ways to say *for how long* are **il y a** or **ça fait** and a time expression followed by **que.** These expressions are usually placed at the beginning of the sentence.

Ça fait un an **qu'**elle fait cette recherche.
Il y a un an **qu'**elle fait cette recherche.
She's been doing this research for a year.

Vocabulaire et grammaire, *pp. 46–47*
Cahier d'activités, *pp. 35–37*

En anglais

4.1

In English, we use the expression *has/have been... for/since...* to talk about an action that started in the past and is still going on in the present.

He has been working at the library for 3 years.

What is the difference in meaning between these two sentences?

He has been working at the library for 3 years.

He worked at the library for 3 years.

In French, use the present tense to talk about ongoing actions.

Ça fait trois ans qu'il **travaille** au CDI.

The first sentence implies that he is still working at the library. The second sentence implies that he no longer works at the library.

32 Écoutons CD 4, Tr. 6 1.2

Écoute ces appels que les techniciens du magasin **Ordinateurs plantés** ont reçus. Depuis combien de temps est-ce que ces gens ont des problèmes avec leur ordinateur?

1. c 2. e 3. d 4. a 5. f 6. b

a. huit heures	**c.** depuis ce matin	**e.** trois jours
b. trente minutes	**d.** depuis lundi	**f.** une semaine

33 Une expérience importante 1.2

Lisons/Écrivons Sonia aide un de ses profs à faire une expérience. Complète son e-mail avec **depuis, ça,** ou **il y a.**

1. depuis 2. Ça 3. depuis 4. Il y a 5. Ça 6. Ça

Salut.
Je suis au laboratoire avec le professeur Dufresne. Nous sommes ici __1__ 32 heures! Je ne sais pas quoi faire. __2__ fait quinze ans que le professeur Dufresne travaille avec les chimpanzés. Il travaille ici à l'université __3__ vingt ans, mais s'il rate cette expérience... qui sait? Le pauvre! Tout va de travers pour lui. __4__ dix heures que son ordinateur ne marche pas. __5__ fait trois heures qu'il prend des notes. __6__ fait quatre ans que je travaille avec lui. Si nous ratons l'expérience, je ne sais pas si je veux continuer. Attends! Monsieur Bobo a dit, «Banane!» L'expérience a réussi!

Core Instruction

TEACHING GRAMMAIRE

1. Tell students **depuis** can mean either *since* (starting point) or *for how long* (duration) in the present tense. To put more emphasis on the time frame, **ça fait/il y a** + time period + **que** can be used at the beginning of the sentence. **(2 min.)**
2. Write on the board a list of activities common to your students: **suivre un cours de français, jouer au tennis, faire du théâtre, faire du sport, aller au cinéma. (2 min.)**
3. Have students write how long and since when they have been doing each of the activities. Go around the room and ask individuals questions. Have them point to an appropriate answer on their paper and read it aloud. **(4 min.)**

Grammavision

For a video presentation of **depuis, il y a,** and **ça fait,** see the *DVD Tutor.*

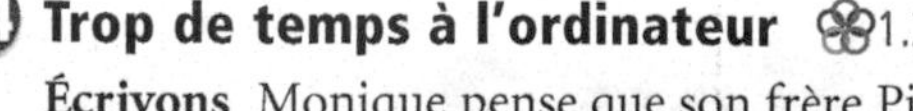

34 Trop de temps à l'ordinateur 1.2

Écrivons Monique pense que son frère Pierre passe trop de temps à son ordinateur. Alors, elle l'observe pour noter le temps qu'il passe à ces activités. Écris des légendes pour chacune de ses observations. Utilise les expressions **depuis, ça fait... que,** et **il y a... que** dans tes légendes.

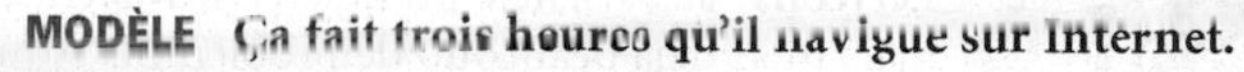

MODÈLE **Ça fait trois heures qu'il navigue sur Internet.**

3 heures

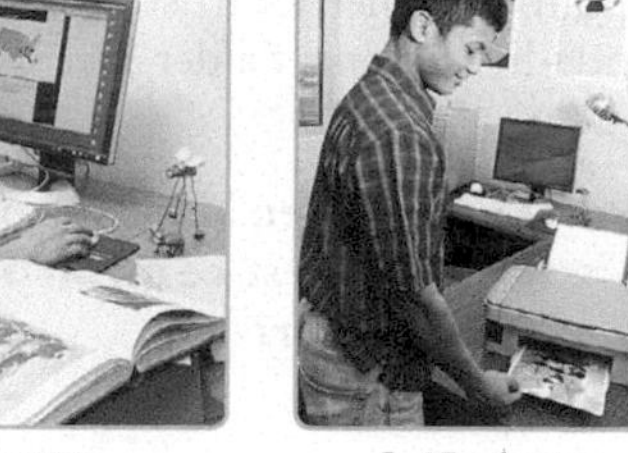

1. deux heures

2. 15 minutes

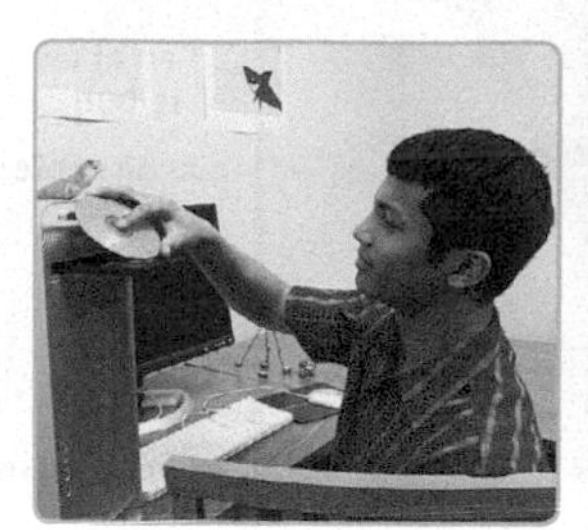

3. une heure

4. 30 minutes

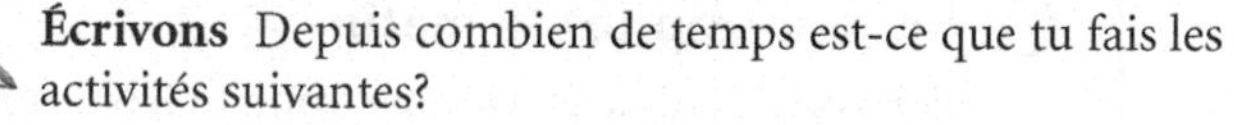

35 Depuis combien de temps... ? 1.2

Écrivons Depuis combien de temps est-ce que tu fais les activités suivantes?

1. Depuis combien de temps est-ce que tu suis des cours de français?
2. Depuis combien de temps est-ce que tu pratiques ton sport préféré?
3. Depuis combien de temps est-ce que tu habites dans cette ville?
4. Depuis combien de temps est-ce que tu vas dans ce lycée?
5. Depuis combien de temps est-ce que tu connais ton/ta meilleur(e) ami(e)?

Communication

Digital performance space

36 Sondage 1.1

Parlons Choisis trois questions de l'activité 35 et fais un sondage parmi tes camarades de classe. Tu peux aussi penser à d'autres questions à leur poser.

MODÈLE **—Depuis combien de temps est-ce que tu habites... ?**
—Ça fait douze ans que j'habite...

34 Possible Answers

1. Il y a deux heures qu'il fait une recherche sur Internet.
2. Ça fait 15 minutes qu'il imprime une photo.
3. Il écoute des CD depuis une heure.
4. Il y a 30 minutes qu'il grave des DVD.

Communication

Group Work: Presentational

Have students create a collage of pictures from magazines, Web sites, or drawings that reflect their activities and interests. Then have students in small groups present their collage and describe what they do. Have classmates ask, **Depuis combien de temps est-ce que tu...?,** to find out how long the student has been doing a particular activity. Students who are presenting should respond appropriately with the new vocabulary. 1.3

Differentiated Instruction

SLOWER PACE LEARNERS

Form three groups and name them **depuis, il y a,** and **ça fait.** Write sentence fragments on the board. **Marie / faire du théâtre / deux ans** First the **depuis** group says their sentence. (**Marie fait du théâtre depuis deux ans.**) Then the **il y a** group says their sentence (**Il y a deux ans que Marie fait du théâtre.**), and finally the **ça fait** group says theirs. (**Ça fait deux ans que Marie fait du théâtre.**) Have groups switch names and repeat. 1.2

SPECIAL LEARNING NEEDS

33 Students with Dyslexia Prior to assigning the activity, review the text of the e-mail. Review all proper nouns and new vocabulary in the paragraph. Assign partners to translate to ensure students comprehend the information before they fill in the blanks. This will help assess students' understanding of the use of **il y a, ça fait,** or **depuis,** without emphasizing reading issues that may complicate choosing the correct answer. 1.2

Assess

Assessment Program
Quiz: Grammaire 2
Alternative Assessment
Differentiated Practice and Assessment CD-ROM

Online Assessment
my.hrw.com

Test Generator 

Resources

Planning:
Lesson Planner
Teacher One Stop

Practice:
Grammar Tutor for Students of French, Chapter 4
Cahier de vocabulaire et grammaire
Differentiated Practice and Assessment CD-ROM
Cahier d'activités
Independent Study Guide
Media Guide
Projectable Transparencies
Bell Work 4.8
Audio CD 4, Tr. 7

Bell Work

Use Bell Work 4.8 in the *Projectable Transparencies* or write this activity on the board.

Answer the questions with **depuis, ça fait... que,** or **il y a... que.**

1. **Depuis combien de temps habites-tu ici?**
2. **Il y a combien de temps que tu connais ton (ta) meilleur(e) ami?**
3. **Ça fait combien de temps que tu es élève?**
4. **Depuis combien de temps suis-tu des cours de français?** 1.2

French for Spanish Speakers

Ask Spanish speakers if they know the word for **ouvrir** in Spanish. **(abrir)** Ask them how they can tell that these words probably came from a similar Latin word. (The consonant combination **–vr** in French is similar to the consonant combination **–br** in Spanish, and both words end in **–ir**). 4.1

Synthèse
- Vocabulaire 2
- Grammaire 2

Application 2

Entre copains

J'en ai ras le bol!	*I'm fed up!*
Je ne capte rien!	*I don't understand a thing!*
J'ai rien pigé!	*I didn't understand a thing!*
J'en ai marre!	*I've had enough!*

37 J'en ai ras le bol! 1.3

Écrivons Tu as acheté un nouvel ordinateur, mais tu as déjà beaucoup de problèmes! Ton ami Ludovic va t'aider. Écris-lui un texto pour exprimer tes frustrations et demande-lui de venir t'aider avec ton ordinateur.

MODÈLE **Ludovic! J'en ai ras le bol! Comment est-ce qu'on démarre l'ordinateur?**

Un peu plus

The verb *ouvrir*

1. A small group of verbs ending in **-ir** are conjugated like **-er** verbs. These verbs include ouvrir *(to open)* and **offrir** *(to offer)*, which you learned in Chapter 2.

ouvrir **(*to open*)**	
j' ouvr**e**	nous ouvr**ons**
tu ouvr**es**	vous ouvr**ez**
il/elle/on ouvr**e**	ils/elles ouvr**ent**

Le CDI ouvre à huit heures et demie.

2. These verbs form the **passé composé** with **avoir** and have irregular past participles.
   ouvrir: j'**ai** ouvert
   offrir: j'**ai offert**

Vocabulaire et grammaire, *p. 48*
Cahier d'activités, *pp. 35–37*

38 Un peu trop tôt le matin 1.2

Écrivons Nadine et Thomas vont au laboratoire pour compléter une expérience. Complète leur conversation avec la forme du verbe **ouvrir** qui convient.

NADINE	Oh, regarde! La salle d'informatique est fermée.
THOMAS	Quand est-ce qu'elle ___1___? ouvre
NADINE	Je ne sais pas. Voilà un professeur! Excusez-moi, monsieur, quand est-ce que vous ___2___ la salle d'informatique? ouvrez
PROF	Nous l'___3___ à neuf heures. ouvrons
THOMAS	Quelle heure il est?
NADINE	Sept heures. Tu veux aller au CDI?
THOMAS	Ils ___4___ le CDI à huit heures. ouvrent
NADINE	Tu as envie d'aller à la cantine?
THOMAS	La cantine ___5___ à sept heures et demie. ouvre
NADINE	Alors, elle va ___6___ dans trente minutes. On peut aller dans la cour en attendant. ouvrir
THOMAS	Bonne idée.

Core Instruction

INTEGRATED PRACTICE

1. Have students do Activity 37 to review vocabulary and grammar in this chapter. **(5 min.)**
2. Introduce **Un peu plus. (3 min.)**
3. Create a list of computer-related verbs: **démarrer, naviguer, sauvegarder, télécharger, graver, planter, ouvrir.** Have students write five questions with these verbs, **suivre,** and **depuis** or **ça fait/il y a** and exchange them with a partner to answer. **(4 min.)**

TEACHING UN PEU PLUS

1. Remind students how to conjugate **-er** verbs and **avoir** in the **passé composé.** Review the verb **offrir** and go over the verb **ouvrir. (2 min.)**
2. Discuss the next gift-giving holiday. Ask students what they will give to whom. **Pour Noël, qu'est-ce que tu offres à ta mère? Qu'est-ce que tes parents t'offrent? (3 min.)**
3. Continue with integrated practice Activities 38–41. **(15 min.)**

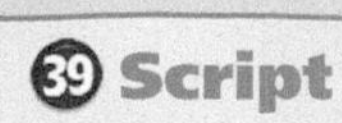

Online Practice
my.hrw.com
Application 2 practice

39 Écoutons CD 4, Tr. 7 1.2

Au lycée Charles Baudelaire, il y a des élèves-orientateurs qui conseillent les nouveaux élèves. Écoute ces élèves-orientateurs et puis décide si les phrases suivantes sont **a) vraies** ou **b) fausses**.

a **1.** Paul est élève au lycée depuis deux ans.
b **2.** Tu peux trouver Madeleine au laboratoire de chimie.
b **3.** Ça fait trois ans que Sophie est élève au lycée.
a **4.** Tu peux trouver Bernard au gymnase.
a **5.** Il y a quatre ans que Nathalie est élève au lycée.
b **6.** Xavier suit des cours d'éducation musicale.

Communication

Digital performance space

40 Scénario 1.1

Parlons Avec un(e) camarade, imagine l'ordinateur du futur. Vous allez le présenter à une foire-exposition (*convention*) sur les nouvelles technologies. Vos camarades de classe vous posent des questions sur votre nouvel ordinateur.

MODÈLE **—Comment est-ce qu'on démarre cet ordinateur?**
—Tu n'utilises que la souris...

41 Comment ça marche? 1.1

Parlons Ton/Ta camarade et toi allez jouer le rôle d'un grand-parent qui ne sait pas utiliser un ordinateur et de son petit-fils/sa petite-fille qui l'aide. D'abord, joue le rôle du grand-parent qui pose les questions ci-dessous et ton/ta camarade va y répondre logiquement. Ensuite, échangez les rôles.

— **Sais-tu comment faire une recherche?**
—
— **Et si je veux aller à la page d'après?**
—
— **Comment est-ce qu'on fait pour envoyer un e-mail?**
—
— **Ça fait trois fois que je perds mon document!**
—

39 Script
See script on p. 115F.

Communication

41 Group Work: Presentational
Have students choose an advertisement for a computer package from a newspaper, magazine, or Web site. Have each student present his or her computer, its features, what software, hardware, and accessories are included, the price, and why he or she recommends this particular computer package. 1.3

Activité Pré-AP Préparatoire — Language Examination

41 Sample answer:
— . . .
— **Il faut utiliser un navigateur.**
— . . .
— **Tu dois cliquer sur "Suivante".**
— . . .
— **Il faut cliquer sur "Courrier".**
— . . .
— **Grand-mère, il faut sauvegarder ton document!**

Differentiated Instruction

SLOWER PACE LEARNERS

38 Have students create a segment for a children's educational TV show that teaches the forms of the verb **ouvrir.** Encourage students to use music, dancing, puppets, or other creative methods to teach the verb forms. You might videotape their segments. 1.3

MULTIPLE INTELLIGENCES

41 **Intrapersonal** Give students the option of creating the entire dialogue themselves. Organize them in groups of two and have them read the directions for context. Have students write their personalized dialogue together and memorize it. Ask volunteers to act out the scene for the class. 1.1

Assess

Assessment Program
Quiz: Application 2
Audio CD 4, Tr. 16
Alternative Assessment
Differentiated Practice and Assessment CD-ROM

Online Assessment
my.hrw.com

Test Generator 

Resources

Planning:
Lesson Planner
 Teacher One Stop

Presentation:
 DVD Tutor, Disc 1
Télé-roman

Practice:
Media Guide
DVD Tutor, Disc 1
Télé-roman

Connections

Visual Learners

To help students understand the characters Léa and Seydou, have them create comparative personality maps. Draw two ovals on the board and label one Léa and the other Seydou. Coming out of each oval, draw several spokes with circles at the ends. Ask students to fill in the circles with personality traits of each character. Ask questions about what each character says and does to elicit several descriptive adjectives. 3.2

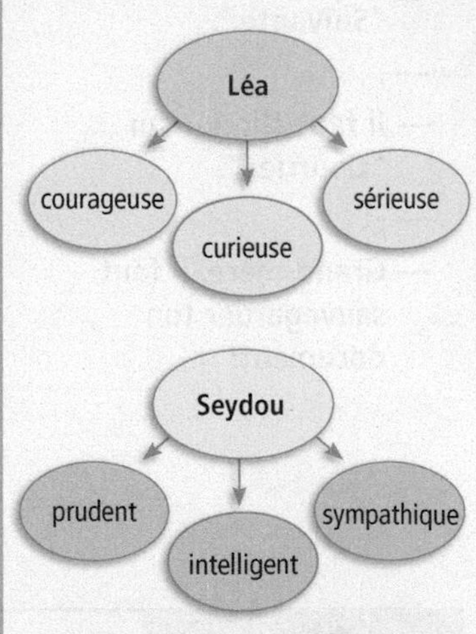

Gestures

Have students look at Seydou's body language in scene 1. What might he be feeling? Then have them look at his gesture in scene 3. Ask students what might have happened to cause his reaction. What are Léa and Seydou doing in scenes 4 and 5? Where is Léa going in scene 10? How does Seydou feel about it? Ask students how they know. 2.1

Télé-roman

Le Secret de la statuette

STRATÉGIE

Understanding subtext Sometimes people don't say exactly what they mean, particularly if they want to hide something. During Rigaud's phone conversation with the mysterious woman, what seems to be her concern? Does Rigaud seem completely satisfied that he got the statuette back? Try to guess what the end of his sentence could be when he says «Mais maintenant que Mme Bondy est à Dakar...» Try also to imagine why the woman on the phone is talking about another plan to send off "the merchandise." 1.2

Devant le magasin de l'île de Gorée...

1

Seydou Dis, Léa, ça fait trois heures qu'on est là. J'en ai marre, moi! On rentre?
Léa Non! Je suis sûre que Rigaud va venir.
Seydou Ben moi, ça m'étonnerait. On perd notre temps!

2 *Charles Rigaud arrive au magasin.*

3

Seydou C'est lui! Regarde! C'est Rigaud!
Léa Qu'est-ce qu'on fait? On le suit?
Seydou Quoi?
Léa Il faut absolument le suivre! Allez, viens!

4 *Léa et Seydou suivent Charles Rigaud dans les rues de Gorée.*

Core Instruction

TEACHING TÉLÉ-ROMAN

1. Have students look at the pictures in **Télé-roman** without reading the text. Have them make predictions about what will happen in this episode. Have them give reasons to support their predictions. **(5 min.)**
2. Play the video in segments, stopping after scenes 3, 7, and 10. Ask general comprehension questions. **(5 min.)**
3. Play the entire episode again without stopping. Were any of the students' predictions accurate? Were there any surprises in the plot? **(5 min.)**
4. Have partners work together to answer the **As-tu compris?** questions on page 141. **(5 min.)**

DVD Tutor

As an alternative, you might use the captioned version of **Le Secret de la statuette** on DVD.

Un peu plus tard, chez Charles Rigaud...

Visit Us Online
my.hrw.com
Online Edition

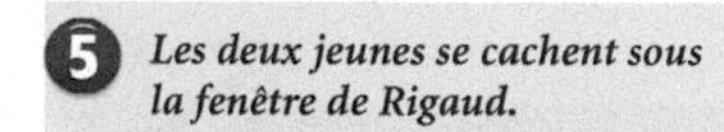

5 Les deux jeunes se cachent sous la fenêtre de Rigaud.

6

7

M. Rigaud Allô?... Oui, madame... J'ai la statuette...
La femme Personne ne se doute de rien?
M. Rigaud Non, non. Personne ne m'a vu. Mais maintenant que Mme Bondy est à Dakar...
La femme Oui, je sais. Il faut trouver une autre solution pour envoyer les... enfin... la marchandise, n'est-ce pas...

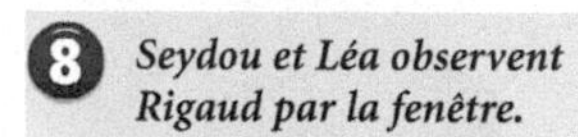

8 Seydou et Léa observent Rigaud par la fenêtre.

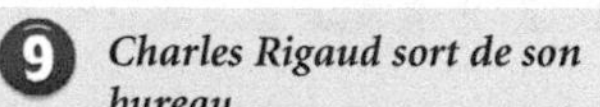

10

Seydou Léa!

1.2

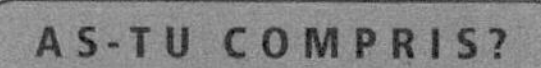

AS-TU COMPRIS?

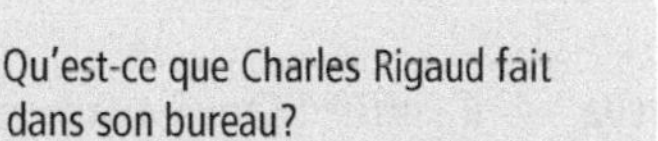

1. Pourquoi Léa et Seydou attendent devant le magasin?
2. Qui arrive au magasin?
3. Où est-ce que Léa et Seydou se cachent?
4. Qu'est-ce que Charles Rigaud fait dans son bureau?
5. Qu'est-ce que Léa décide de faire à la fin de l'épisode?

Prochain épisode:
À ton avis, qu'est-ce que Léa va faire dans le bureau de Charles Rigaud? Est-ce que Seydou va aussi rentrer dans le bureau?

As-tu compris? Answers

1. Ils attendent Charles Rigaud.
2. Rigaud
3. sous la fenêtre de Rigaud
4. Il parle au téléphone.
5. Elle décide d'entrer dans la maison de Rigaud.

Communication

Pair Work: Presentational

After students watch **Télé-roman,** have partners role-play the parts of Léa and Seydou when they see Mr. Rigaud on **l'île de Gorée.** Léa wants to follow him, but Seydou wants to get help (call the police or his father, for example). Partners should each present a logical argument in favor of his or her position. 1.3

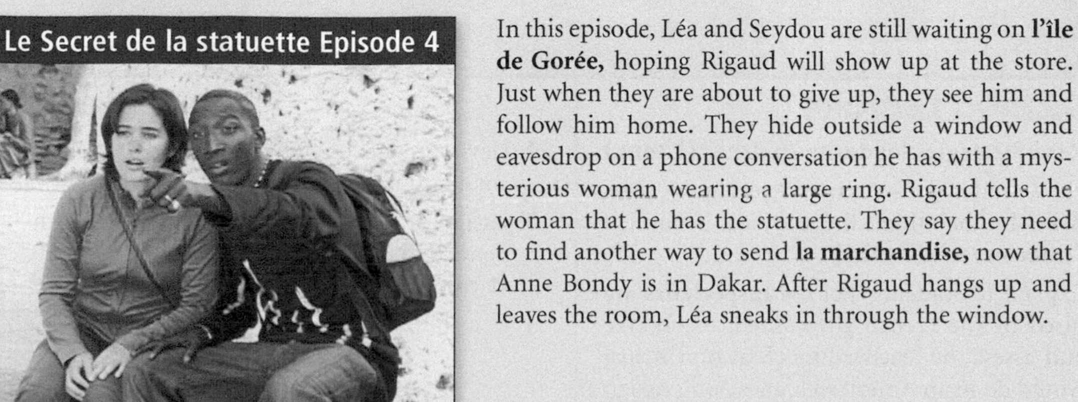

Le Secret de la statuette Episode 4

In this episode, Léa and Seydou are still waiting on **l'île de Gorée,** hoping Rigaud will show up at the store. Just when they are about to give up, they see him and follow him home. They hide outside a window and eavesdrop on a phone conversation he has with a mysterious woman wearing a large ring. Rigaud tells the woman that he has the statuette. They say they need to find another way to send **la marchandise,** now that Anne Bondy is in Dakar. After Rigaud hangs up and leaves the room, Léa sneaks in through the window.

Lecture et écriture

Resources

Planning:
Lesson Planner
Teacher One Stop

Presentation:
Audio CD 4, Tr. 8

Practice:
Cahier d'activités
Reading Strategies and Skills Handbook, Chapter 4
Intermediate Reader
French InterActive Reader

Applying the Strategies

For practice with monitoring comprehension, have students use the "Say Something" strategy from the *Reading Strategies and Skills Handbook.*

READING PRACTICE

STRATEGIES

Strategy: Say Something

Reading Skill	When can I use this strategy?		
	Prereading	During Reading	Postreading
Using Prior Knowledge (Drawing from Your Own Experience)	✓		
Monitoring Reading		✓	

Strategy at a Glance: Say Something

- The teacher models the strategy by "saying something" about a text with a colleague or by reading and discussing a typed **Say Something** dialogue with students.
- Students read a short text, stopping occasionally to discuss the text with a partner. In their conversations, they must make a prediction, ask a question, make a comment, or make a connection.
- Students practice **Say Something** using very short texts before using the strategy with longer assignments.

Often readers are unable to discuss something they have just finished reading because while they were reading, their eyes were merely moving over the words, their minds moving to thoughts of weekend plans, last night's phone conversations, or after-school sports events. They don't focus on what they are reading. To help students break that habit, we need to help them pay attention to what they are reading. **Say Something** is a very simple strategy that keeps readers focused on a text. **Say Something** helps students think about what they are reading by helping them see where they aren't paying attention.

Best Use of the Strategy

Say Something (Horste, Short, and Burke 1988) is a strategy in which students occasionally pause and "say something" to a partner about what they have read. This strategy helps students comprehend what they are reading by helping them to stay focused. Telling students to say something about the text, or giving them specific types of things they can say, keeps them interacting with the text and from that interaction comes meaning.

Getting the Strategy to Work

1. **First, model the strategy.** In order to model the **Say Something** strategy, it is best if you can recruit a colleague to help you demonstrate the strategy. Read aloud each piece of text you will comment on to the students, so they can understand what you

Reading with a Purpose

Have students think about their favorite class and what makes it so enjoyable. How do they feel about what they are learning in that class? Ask them to look for clues as they read that will help them predict whether the students in this reading selection enjoy the class and why.

Lecture et écriture

Jean Giraudoux (1882–1944) est un écrivain français. Il a écrit des nouvelles, des romans *(Siegfried et le Limousin)* et des pièces de théâtre *(La guerre de Troie n'aura pas lieu).*

STRATÉGIE pour lire

The genre of a text Before reading a text, consider its genre. The genre of a text can give you clues about what you are going to read. Take a moment to guess what the genre of the reading is.

A Avant la lecture 1.3

Lis le paragraphe qui présente la pièce et parcours le texte des yeux. Qui sont les personnages principaux? D'après toi, qu'est-ce qui va se passer dans la scène? Pourquoi?

Intermezzo

CD 4, Tr. 8

***Intermezzo** est une comédie. L'histoire se déroule[1] dans un village où des choses étranges se passent depuis que Mlle Isabelle remplace l'institutrice[2]. Mlle Isabelle a décidé de faire cours en plein air[3]. Un inspecteur de l'éducation[4] vient rendre visite à la classe. Il n'aime pas ce qu'il voit. Pour lui, les élèves devraient être assis à un bureau dans une salle de classe. La scène suivante montre Mlle Isabelle, ses élèves et l'inspecteur qui s'affrontent. Les autres personnages, le droguiste, le contrôleur et le maire sont là pour soutenir[5] Mlle Isabelle.*

Acte Premier, scène sixième

ISABELLE — Vous m'avez demandée, monsieur l'Inspecteur ?

L'INSPECTEUR — Mademoiselle, les bruits les plus fâcheux[6] courent sur votre enseignement. Je vais voir immédiatement s'ils sont fondés[7] et envisager la sanction.

ISABELLE — Je ne vous comprends pas, monsieur l'Inspecteur.

L'INSPECTEUR — Il suffit[8] ! Que l'examen commence… Entrez, les élèves… (*Elles rient*) Pourquoi rient-elles ainsi ?

1. happens 2. teacher 3. outside 4. superintendent 5. support 6. upsetting 7. justified 8. That's enough!

Core Instruction

TEACHING LECTURE

1. Read **Stratégie** aloud with students. **(1 min.)**
2. Have students do Activity A orally in class. Ask why they think the selection is entitled **"Intermezzo"**. **(2 min.)**
3. Explain to students that the **inspecteurs** are hired by the French government to observe and assess the teachers, much as a principal would do in an American high school. Assign parts and have students read the selection aloud in class. **(12 min.)**
4. Have students do Activities C and D orally in small groups. **(12 min.)**
5. Assign Activity B as homework. Remind students they are to correct the false statements. **(1 min.)**

Online Practice
my.hrw.com
Online Edition

Isabelle — C'est que vous dites : entrez, et qu'il n'y a pas de porte, monsieur l'Inspecteur.

L'Inspecteur — Cette pédagogie de grand air est stupide… Le vocabulaire des Inspecteurs y perd la moitié de sa force… (*Chuchotements*[1]). Silence, là-bas… La première qui bavarde[2] balaiera la classe, le champ, veux-je dire, la campagne… (*Rires*)… Mademoiselle, vos élèves sont insupportables !

Le Maire — Elles sont très gentilles, monsieur l'Inspecteur, regardez-les.

L'Inspecteur — Elles n'ont pas à être gentilles. Avec leur gentillesse, il n'en est pas une qui ne prétende avoir sa manière spéciale de sourire ou de cligner[3]. J'entends que l'ensemble des élèves montre au maître le même visage sévère et uniforme qu'un jeu de dominos.

Le Droguiste — Vous n'y arriverez pas, monsieur l'Inspecteur.

L'Inspecteur — Et pourquoi ?

Le Droguiste — Parce qu'elles sont gaies.

L'Inspecteur — Elles n'ont pas à être gaies. Vous avez au programme le certificat d'études et non le fou rire[4]. Elles sont gaies parce que leur maîtresse ne les punit pas assez.

Isabelle — Comment les punirais-je ? Avec ces écoles de plein ciel, il ne subsiste presque aucun motif[5] de punir. Tout ce qui est faute dans une classe devient une initiative et une intelligence au milieu de la nature. Punir une élève qui regarde au plafond[6] ? Regardez-le, ce plafond !

Le Contrôleur — En effet, regardons-le.

L'Inspecteur — Le plafond dans l'enseignement, doit être compris de façon à faire ressortir la taille de l'adulte vis-à-vis de la taille de l'enfant[7]. Un maître qui adopte le plein air avoue[8] qu'il est plus petit que l'arbre, moins corpulent[9] que le bœuf, moins mobile que l'abeille[10], et sacrifie la meilleure preuve de sa dignité. *(Rires…)* Qu'y a-t-il encore ?

Le Maire — C'est une chenille[11] qui monte sur vous, monsieur l'Inspecteur !

L'Inspecteur — Elle arrive bien… Tant pis pour elle !

1. whispers 2. talks 3. blink 4. not the "giggles diploma" 5. no reason 6. ceiling 7. That sentence means that "In teaching the teacher is the ultimate authority." 8. confesses 9. stout 10. bee 11. caterpillar

Comparisons

Comparing and Contrasting

Have students brainstorm reasons that teachers may or may not be permitted to hold class outdoors, both in France and the U.S. Are most of their hypotheses based on the culture, the environment, or school policy? Have students research **un lycée général** and **un lycée technologique** for information to refine their hypotheses. 4.2

Connections

Language Arts Link

Show students clips of the movie *Mary Poppins.* If possible, obtain a copy in French with English subtitles. Then discuss in French how Mary Poppins in the movie and Isabelle in the reading are alike. Ask students if teachers who use unusual teaching methods are sometimes more successful than teachers who use traditional techniques. 3.1

Language Examination

Through the practice of listening and reading comprehension, as well as essay writing, **Lecture et écriture** helps students prepare for the **Interpretive Reading and Listening** and the **Presentational Writing** sections of the AP Language and Culture Exam.

Additional Practice

For more reading practice, see **Variations littéraires,** pp. 388–389.

Differentiated Instruction

ADVANCED LEARNERS

Have students create a vocabulary worksheet with the glossed words and phrases from the reading. Give students several formats from which to choose: multiple-choice worksheet, crossword puzzle, seek-and-find puzzle, and so forth. Then have partners exchange and complete each other's worksheet, or make copies to distribute to the entire class. 1.2

MULTIPLE INTELLIGENCES

Musical After they read **"Intermezzo",** ask students to create or find a song that will appropriately express the themes, characters, or humor of the scene. Students may create their own words and music or set new words to a familiar tune or rap. Ask for volunteers to present their creation or selection to the class. Ask students to explain why they chose the music they did. 1.3

Cultures

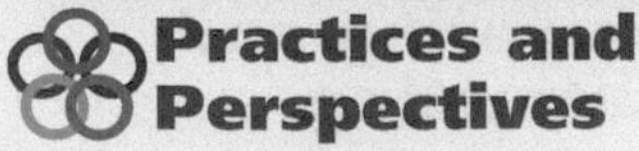

Practices and Perspectives

The French school system is renowned for setting high academic standards and for being very structured and consistent, with teachers generally using traditional teaching methods. However, along with the traditional classroom experience, teachers and their students may go on **classes de découverte.** Similar to an American-style field trip, a **classe de découverte** might be held in any number of locations, including the seashore, the mountains, or the countryside. Students engage in activities to explore nature, the arts and sciences, history and culture, or recreational sports. Have students research the names of organizations that specialize in **classes de découverte** and write letters to request information. 2.1

Comparisons

Comparing and Contrasting

Have students write letters or e-mails via an e-pal organization to students in French-speaking countries or to students in their French partner school. Students should ask questions to find out what the francophone students' teachers and classes are like. Discuss with students the similarities and differences they discover. 4.2

ISABELLE — Oh! monsieur l'Inspecteur... Ne la tuez pas[1] . C'est la *collata azurea.* Elle remplit sa mission de chenille.

L'INSPECTEUR — Mensonge[2]. La mission de la *collata azurea* n'a jamais été de grimper sur les Inspecteurs. (*Sanglots*[3]) Qu'ont-elles maintenant ? Elles pleurent ?

LUCE — Parce que vous avez tué la *collata azurea* !

L'INSPECTEUR — Si c'était un merle[4] qui emportât la *collata azurea,* elles trouveraient son exploit superbe, évidemment, elles s'extasieraient[5].

LUCE — C'est que la chenille est la nourriture du merle !...

LE CONTRÔLEUR — Très juste. La chenille en tant qu'aliment perd toute sympathie

[...]

1. kill 2. That's a lie 3. sobs 4. blackbird 5. would rejoice

Compréhension

B Est-ce que les phrases suivantes sont **a) vraies** ou **b) fausses**? Corrige les phrases fausses. 1.2

1. La scène se passe dans une salle de classe. faux; La scène se passe dehors
2. L'Inspecteur n'a pas une bonne opinion de la classe. vrai
3. Mlle Isabelle n'a jamais besoin de punir ses élèves. vrai
4. L'Inspecteur pense que la routine est importante. vrai
5. La *collata azurea* est le nom scientifique de la chenille. vrai
6. Un oiseau a mangé la chenille. faux; L'Inspecteur l'a tuée.

C Qui dirait *(would say)* les phrases suivantes: l'Inspecteur, Mlle Isabelle ou une élève? 1.2

1. Les hommes doivent contrôler la nature. L'Inspecteur
2. La nature est un bon modèle. Mlle Isabelle
3. L'ordre et la discipline sont très importants. L'Inspecteur
4. Il ne faut pas faire mal aux créatures. Mlle Isabelle ou une élève
5. La créativité et l'initiative sont importantes. Mlle Isabelle
6. L'enseignement, c'est sérieux. L'Inspecteur

Après la lecture

D Est-ce que tu crois qu'une situation telle que celle de la pièce peut arriver en vrai? Pourquoi ou pourquoi pas? Comment se passent les classes dans ton école? Est-ce que vous avez un prof qui ressemble à Mlle Isabelle? Qu'est-ce que vous en pensez? 1.3

Core Instruction

TEACHING ESPACE ÉCRITURE

1. Discuss **Stratégie pour écrire.** Verify that students understand the assignment. Remind them to use expressions and vocabulary from this chapter. **(2 min.)**
2. Assign steps 1 and 2 and allow students to complete them in class. **(25 min.)**
3. Have partners do step 3. It might be helpful to create a rubric for students to use as they edit each other's work. Are "W" questions answered? Are more specifics or details needed? Is the **passé composé** used to say what happened and the present tense used with time expressions? **(6 min.)**
4. For step 4, display the blogs in your room. Assign partners to respond to each other's blog. **(15 min.)**

Espace écriture

STRATÉGIE pour écrire

Answering the five "W" questions (Who? What? Where? When? Why?) can help you clarify your ideas before you begin to write. It can also help you make sure that you don't leave out important information for your readers.

Tout va de travers! 1.3

You are having the most frustrating day ever at school. Write an entry to post on a blog you created about a computer assignment where everything went wrong.

1 Plan

Imagine a research assignment for one of your classes and the things that could go wrong while doing it. To help you explain what went wrong, ask yourself "W" questions.

- What technical problems did you have?
- When did the problems begin?
- Where did they happen?
- Who did you ask for help?
- Why do you think you had these problems?

2 Rédaction

Use the answers to your "W" questions as a guide for writing your blog entry.

- Begin by telling what the assignment is.
- Use the **passé composé** to explain what went wrong.
- Use expressions of time to say when the problems began.

Be as specific and as detailed as you can in your description. Conclude your entry by expressing frustration about the entire experience.

3 Correction

Trade drafts with a classmate. Does your classmate understand what happened? Check the spelling and use of verb tenses.

4 Application

Post your blog entry on the class Web site, or display it on the class bulletin board. Who had the most frustrating experience? Respond to a classmate's posting, expressing sympathy and offering suggestions to resolve his or her computer problems.

Lecture et écriture

Differentiated Instruction

SLOWER PACE LEARNERS

Before students begin **Espace écriture,** work together to think of an introductory sentence or sentences that students can use to get them started. **C'est pas mon jour! Tout va de travers!** Then draw five large squares on the board, arranged vertically. Write one of the "W" questions in each square. Have students suggest possible answers to each question. Finally, work together to think of possible concluding sentences. **J'en ai ras le bol!** 1.2

MULTIPLE INTELLIGENCES

Linguistic Give the option of creating another scenario other than the assignment described in **Tout va de travers!** Ask students to follow the same strategies and steps but allow them to choose the topic of their writing. This will be a more motivating assignment for those who have strong linguistic skills and do not need a writing prompt to create interesting and detailed written compositions. Other students will benefit from the structure of a specific topic. 1.3

Lecture et écriture

Process Writing

Avant d'écrire It might help students to describe the *who, what, where, when,* and *why* if they are given a graphic organizer to complete. A chart is one example of a graphic organizer for this activity. You might also ask students to trace their hand on a piece of paper, and then write the answers for each of the five "w"s on each of the fingers.

Writing Assessment

To assess the **Espace écriture,** you can use the following rubric. For additional rubrics, see the *Assessment Program* or refer to the *Generate Success* Rubric Generator.

Writing Rubric	4	3	2	1
Content (Complete—Incomplete)				
Comprehensibility (Comprehensible—Seldom comprehensible)				
Accuracy (Accurate—Seldom accurate)				
Organization (Well-organized—Poorly organized)				
Effort (Excellent effort—Minimal effort)				

18-20: A 16-17: B 14-15: C 12-13: D Under 12: F

Assess

Assessment Program
Quiz: Lecture
Quiz: Écriture
Online Assessment
my.hrw.com
Test Generator 

Prépare-toi pour l'examen

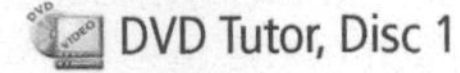

Resources

Planning:
Lesson Planner
Teacher One Stop

Practice:
Cahier d'activités
Media Guide
DVD Tutor, Disc 1
Projectable Transparencies
Situation, Chapitre 4
Picture Sequences, Chapter 4
Audio CD 4, Trs. 10–13
@HOMETUTOR

Reteaching
Write each of the school subjects from **Vocabulaire** on a strip of construction paper or on a transparency. Have students take turns saying which classes they have.

Game
Cercle de mots Have students make two identical sets of flashcards with French words or expressions on one side and the English equivalents on the other. Form two teams and have each team sit in a circle. Give one card to each student. One student on each team begins by showing the English equivalent on his or her card to the teammate on the left. That student gives the French expression. Then he or she shows the English equivalent on his or her card to the student on his or her left. The first team to complete the circle wins. 1.2

4 Answers
1. Il y a (ça fait) trois mois qu'Ousman suit un cours d'informatique.
2. M. Prévost est professeur d'informatique depuis 2001.
3. Ça fait (il y a) deux heures que Sarah travaille dans la salle d'informatique.
4. Il y a (ça fait) cinq heures que Justin navigue sur le Net.
5. Michel utilise ce navigateur depuis un an.

Chapitre 4

Prépare-toi pour l'examen

@HOMETUTOR

1 Vocabulaire 1
- to ask how something turned out
- to wonder what happened

pp. 118–121

1 Lin et ses amis sont au lycée aujourd'hui. Où vont-ils? 1.2

1. Lin va faire une expérience. Il va au laboratoire.
2. Karima va faire des recherches. Elle va au CDI.
3. Marc a faim. Il va à la cantine.
4. Louise va travailler sur l'ordinateur. Elle va à la salle d'informatique.
5. Michel a une compétition de foot. Il va au terrain de sport.

2 Grammaire 1
- object pronouns with the **passé composé**
- **quelqu'un, quelque chose, ne... personne, ne... rien, ne... que**

Un peu plus
- the verb **recevoir**

pp. 122–127

2 Dis qui a fait les choses indiquées, selon les illustrations et le modèle. 1.2

MODÈLE réussir son expérience
David l'a réussie.

1. rater son expérience Victoria l'a ratée.
2. rendre ses livres au CDI Patricia les a rendus (au CDI).
3. gagner son match Caroline l'a gagné.
4. prendre son déjeuner Max et Sara l'ont mangé.

David

Caroline

Victoria

Patricia

Max et Sara

3 Vocabulaire 2
- to ask for information
- to express frustration

pp. 130–133

3 Ahmed aide sa mère qui apprend à travailler sur l'ordinateur. Complète les questions de sa mère avec une expression logique. 1.2

Possible answers:
1. Sais-tu comment ______ cet ordinateur? démarrer.
2. Comment est-ce qu'on fait pour ______ un document? télécharger
3. Je voudrais graver un CD. Où est le ______? graveur de CD
4. Qu'est-ce que tu ______ comme navigateur? utilises
5. J'ai besoin d'une copie de ce document. Où est l'______? imprimante

Preparing for the Exam

FOLD-N-LEARN
Pyramid Study Aid

1. Have students fold the lower left-hand corner across to the opposite edge of a sheet of paper and cut off the tab created by the fold. They should open the paper so that it is a square. Students then fold the lower right-hand corner of the paper diagonally to the opposite corner to form a triangle.

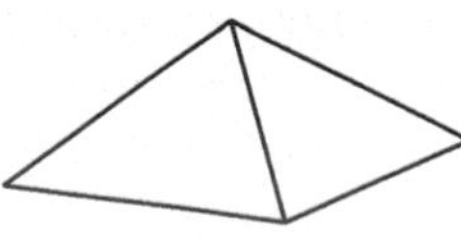

2. Ask students to write in one triangle *"To ask how something turned out"* and then list the words and phrases that accompany that expression. In another triangle they write *"To wonder what happened"* and its phrases and in the third triangle, *"To ask for information"* and *"To express frustration"* and the related phrases.
3. Ask students to cut along the crease to the left of the blank triangle and to stop at the center point. They can tape or glue the blank triangle under another to form a pyramid.
4. Have students review the chapter expressions using the pyramid.

Online Assessment
my.hrw.com
Chapter Self-test

4 Indique depuis combien de temps Ousman et ses amis font ces activités. Utilise **depuis, il y a... que** et **ça fait... que.** 1.2

1. (trois mois) Ousman / suivre un cours d'informatique
2. (2001) M. Prévost / être professeur d'informatique
3. (deux heures) Sarah / travailler dans la salle d'informatique
4. (cinq heures) Justin / naviguer sur le Net
5. (un an) Michel / utiliser ce navigateur

4 Grammaire 2
- the verb **suivre**
- **depuis, il y a, ça fait**

Un peu plus
- the verb **ouvrir**

pp. 134–139

5 Réponds aux questions suivantes. 4.2

1. Dans les lycées au Québec et en France, qui achète les livres?
2. Quelle est la différence entre le clavier français et le clavier américain?

5 Culture
- **Flash culture pp. 120, 124, 132, 134**
- **Comparaisons pp. 128–129**

6 Des élèves sont ensemble dans la salle d'informatique. Écoute chaque conversation et choisis la réponse logique. CD 4, Tr. 10 1.2

1. d **2.** c **3.** a **4.** b **5.** a

a. Il faut sauvegarder plus souvent tes documents.
b. Voilà le graveur de CD.
c. C'est difficile à dire. Il y en a beaucoup de bons.
d. C'est très facile. Tu n'as qu'à démarrer l'imprimante.

7 Imagine que tu viens de participer à une compétition d'athlétisme. Tu discutes avec ton/ta camarade qui vient de faire un match de tennis. D'abord, lisez les instructions pour chaque réplique *(exchange)*. Ensuite, créez votre dialogue en utilisant des expressions que vous avez apprises. 1.1

Élève A:	Salut ton/ta camarade et informe-toi sur son match.
Élève B:	Réponds à ton/ta camarade et informe-toi sur sa compétition.
Élève A:	Réponds et informe-toi sur le match d'un(e) autre camarade.
Élève B:	Dis que tu ne sais pas.
Élève A:	Dis si tu penses que ton autre camarade a gagné ou non.
Élève B:	Dis si tu es d'accord ou pas d'accord.
Élève A:	Demande à ton/ta camarade s'il/si elle a fini un devoir.
Élève B:	Réponds négativement et explique *(explain)* tes problèmes d'ordinateur.

5 Answers

1. au Québec: les écoles
en France: les élèves
2. Le clavier français est AZERTY et le clavier américain est QWERTY.

6 Script

1. — Je peux t'aider, Anne?
— Oui. Comment est-ce qu'on fait pour imprimer ce document?
2. — Alors, tu vas acheter un nouvel ordinateur?
— Oui. Quelle sorte d'ordinateur est-ce que tu me recommandes?
3. — Tu as fini tes devoirs?
— Non, et je ne sais pas quoi faire. Ça fait trois fois que je perds mon document.
4. — Qu'est-ce que tu veux faire, André?
— Je voudrais graver un CD.
5. — Qu'est-ce qu'il y a, Magali?
— Aujourd'hui, tout va de travers. Mon ordinateur n'arrête pas de planter.

Language Examination

7 Sample conversation:

a. **Salut. Comment s'est passé ton match de tennis?**
b. **Je l'ai complètement raté. Comment s'est passé ta compétition?**
a. **Je l'ai gagnée. Je me demande si Chloé a gagné son match de basket.**
b. **Je n'en sais rien.**
a. **Je parie qu'elle l'a gagné.**
b. **Oui, sans doute.**
a. **Alors, tu as fini ton devoir de français?**
b. **Non. Mon ordinateur a planté et j'ai perdu mon document!**

Additional Speaking Practice

- For additional speaking practice, you might use the *Picture Sequences Transparency* for Chapter 4 found in the *Projectable Transparencies.*
- To assess the speaking activities in this section, you might use the *Generate Success* Rubric Generator or the oral rubrics found in the *Assessment Program.*

Pre-AP Practice

7 This guided conversation activity helps students practice oral exchanges using material from this chapter and previous chapters. The activity helps prepare students for the **Interpersonal Speaking** section of the AP French Language and Culture Exam.

Chapitre 4

Prépare-toi pour l'examen

Grammar Review

For more practice with the grammar topics in this chapter, see the *Grammar Tutor*, the *DVD Tutor*, the *@HomeTutor*, or the *Cahier de vocabulaire et grammaire*.

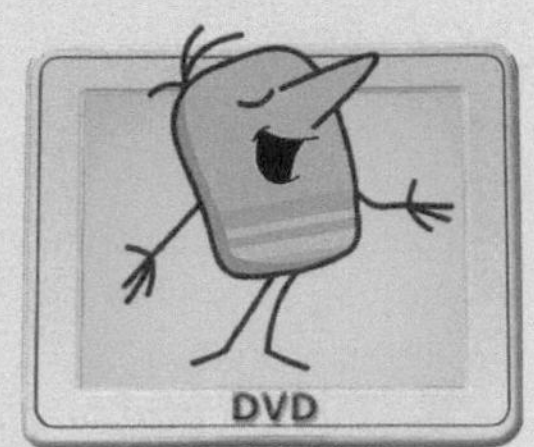

Grammavision

 **Online Edition**

Students might use the online textbook and Performance Space to practice the **Lettres et sons** feature.

Dictée Script

1. Est-ce que vous avez un graveur de CD?
2. Qu'est-ce que tu utilises comme navigateur?
3. Je trouve le cours de maths ennuyeux.
4. Elle a quelle sorte d'ordinateur?
5. C'est un professeur généreux.

Teacher to Teacher

Sandra Behensky
Rock Island High School
Rock Island, IL

I form teams to play a Ladder Game. A member from each team draws a five-rung ladder on the board. Ask a question. Each student at the board tries to be the first to answer correctly. The team who correctly answers first keeps the answer on the rung of the ladder. All other teams erase their answer. A new member of each team goes to the board and answers a new question. Play continues until one team fills all five rungs. 1.2

Grammaire 1
- object pronouns with the **passé composé**
- **quelqu'un, quelque chose, ne... personne, ne... rien, ne... que**

Un peu plus
- the verb **recevoir**

pp. 122–127

Résumé: Grammaire 1

Object pronouns are placed *before* the helping verb in the **passé composé.** Past participles agree with the **direct object** if the **direct object** comes *before* the verb.

Elle a perdu **sa trousse.** Heureusement, Paul l'a trouvé**e**!

For placement of expressions like **ne... personne, ne... rien, ne... que (qu'), quelqu'un,** and **quelque chose,** see page 124.

Here are the forms of the verb **recevoir** *(to receive, to get)*:

je	reç**ois**	nous	recevons
tu	reç**ois**	vous	recevez
il/elle/on	reç**oit**	ils/elles	reç**oi**vent

Grammaire 2
- the verb **suivre**
- **depuis, il y a, ça fait**

Un peu plus
- the verb **ouvrir**

pp. 134–139

Résumé: Grammaire 2

Here are the forms of the verb **suivre** *(to follow* or *to take a class)*:

suivre			
je	suis	nous	suivons
tu	suis	vous	suivez
il/elle/on	suit	ils/elles	suivent

The expressions **depuis, ça fait... que,** and **il y a... que** tell *for how long* someone *has been doing* something.

Here are the forms of **ouvrir** *(to open)*:

ouvrir			
j'	ouvr**e**	nous	ouvr**ons**
tu	ouvr**es**	vous	ouvr**ez**
il/elle/on	ouvr**e**	ils/elles	ouvr**ent**

Lettres et sons

The vowel sounds [ø] and [œ] CD 4, Tr. 11–13

The vowel sound [ø] in **jeu** is represented by the letters **eu.** It is pronounced with the lips rounded and the tongue pressed against the back of the lower front teeth. The vowel sound **[œ]** in the word **moniteur** and **navigateur** is similar to the sound in **neuf** and also represented by the letters **eu.** This sound is more open.

Jeux de langue

Tu veux le moniteur de ma sœur à quelle heure?

Dictée 1.2

Écris les phrases de la dictée.

Chapter Review

DVD Program

Online Edition

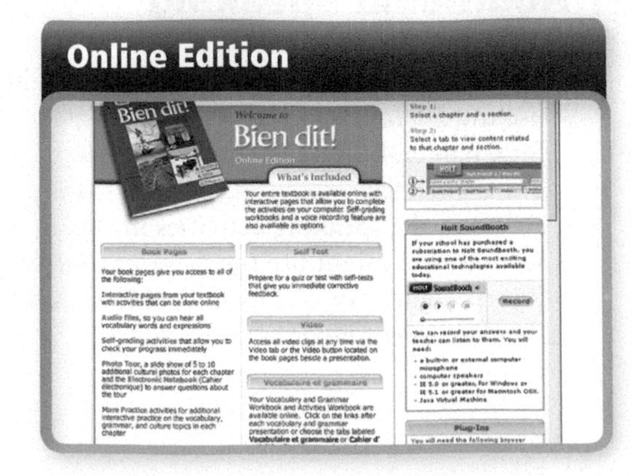

Prépare-toi pour l'examen

Résumé: Vocabulaire 1

PRACTICE FRENCH WITH HOLT MCDOUGAL APPS!

To ask how something turned out

avoir entraînement	*to have practice/training*
la cantine	*cafeteria*
le CDI	*library/resource center*
une compétition	*contest/competition*
le complexe sportif	*sports complex*
le/la conseiller(-ère) d'éducation	*school counselor*
la cour de récré(ation)	*playground, courtyard*
le/la documentaliste	*librarian*
emprunter (un livre)	*to borrow (a book)*
être en retenue	*to be in detention*
faire une expérience	*to do an experiment*
faire des recherches	*to do research*
gagner	*to win*
le gymnase	*gymnasium*
l'infirmier(-ière)	*nurse*
l'infirmerie (f.)	*nurse's office*
l''interro(gation) (f.)	*quiz*
le laboratoire	*laboratory*
les lunettes (f.) de protection	*safety glasses*
une note	*grade*
passer un examen	*to take a test*
la piste (d'athlétisme)	*(athletic) track*
rater	*to fail (an exam, a class)*
rendre (un livre)	*to return (a book)*
réussir	*to pass (an exam)*
la salle d'informatique	*computer room*
le terrain de sport	*sports field*
Au fait,...	*By the way,...*
Comment s'est passé(e)...?	*How did... go?*
complètement	*completely*
Dis-moi,...	*Tell me,...*
évidemment	*obviously*
Je l'ai gagné(e).	*I won it.*
Je n'en sais rien.	*I don't know anything about it.*

To wonder what happened

...quelqu'un...	*...someone...*
Je me demande si	*I wonder if...*
Je parie que...	*I bet...*
Tu crois qu'il est arrivé quelque chose à...?	*Do you think something happened to...?*
...pour une fois.	*...for once.*
Oui, sans doute.	*Yes, without a doubt*
Tu crois?	*You think?*
C'est possible.	*It's possible*
Tu as peut-être raison.	*You could be right.*

Résumé: Vocabulaire 2

To ask for information

l'accueil (m.)/la fenêtre	*home page/window (Internet)*
actualiser/arrêter	*refresh/stop (Internet)*
l'adresse (f.)	*address*
l'affichage (m.)/les outils	*view/tools*
les barres (f.) de défilement	*scroll bars*
le clavier/la touche/le retour	*keyboard/key/return key*
cliquer/la souris	*to click/the mouse*
le courrier	*mail*
le démarrage/démarrer	*home (Internet)/to start up*
l'écran (m.)/le moniteur	*screen/monitor*
l'édition (f.)/le fichier	*edit/file*
les favoris/les liens	*favorites (Internet)/links (Internet)*
graver	*to burn (a CD)*
un graveur de CD/DVD	*CD/DVD burner*
l'imprimante (f.)/imprimer	*printer/to print*
l'interface (f.)	*interface*
un logiciel	*software*
le menu déroulant	*pull-down menu*
le moteur de recherche	*search engine*
le navigateur/naviguer	*browser/to navigate*
la précédente/la suivante	*back (Internet)/forward (Internet)*
rechercher	*to research*
sauvegarder/télécharger	*to save (a document)/to download*
la tablette	*tablet*
Comment est-ce qu'on fait pour... ?	*What do you do to . . . ?*
Qu'est-ce que tu utilises comme... ?	*What do you use as . . . ?*
Quelle sorte de/d'... ?	*What type of . . . ?*
Savez-vous comment... ?	*Do you know how to . . . ?*

To express frustration............................. *see p. 133*

Holt McDougal French Apps

Remind students that they can use the Holt McDougal French Apps to review their vocabulary.

Cinquain Poetry

Have students follow these directions to write a **cinquain** to review the vocabulary and grammar in Chapter 4.

Line 1 A one-word noun that gives the poem its title
Line 2 Two adjectives that describe the noun
Line 3 Three verbs related to the noun
Line 4 A sentence that expresses a feeling related to the noun
Line 5 A noun that renames the poem

Sample Answer

Le lycée
Intéressant, important
Je suis, j'étudie, je réussis,
J'aime bien mes cours.
L'éducation

Projectable Transparency

Situation Au lycée 4

More Digital Resources

FOR THE STUDENT

Holt McDougal French Apps
@HomeTutor
News and Networking
Performance Space

FOR THE TEACHER

- Interactive Whiteboard Lessons
- Generate Success!

Assess

Assessment Program
Examen: Chapitre 4
Audio CD 4, Trs. 17–18
Examen oral: Chapitre 4
Alternative Assessment
Differentiated Practice and Assessment CD-ROM

Online Assessment
my.hrw.com

Test Generator 

Chapitres 1–4

Révisions cumulatives

Resources

Planning:
Lesson Planner
Teacher One Stop

Practice:
Cahier d'activités
Media Guide
Projectable Transparencies
Fine Art, Chapter 4
Audio CD 4, Tr. 14
Holt McDougal French Apps

1 Script

1. — Ça m'énerve. Cet ordinateur n'arrête pas de planter!
— Calme-toi. Je peux t'aider.
2. — J'ai peur de ne pas réussir cette expérience.
— C'est vrai que tu n'es pas très fort en chimie.
3. — J'essaie de faire une recherche, mais je ne trouve pas les livres dont j'ai besoin.
— Demande au documentaliste.
4. — Tu as faim?
— Pas tellement. Qu'est-ce qu'il y a à la cantine?

2 Possible Answer

À droite de la grande cantine, il y a la salle d'informatique, le CDI et le laboratoire. La piste d'athlétisme se trouve à gauche du gymnase. Le stade est à côté du gymnase.

Révisions cumulatives

1 Écoute ces conversations qui ont lieu dans un lycée et choisis la photo qui correspond à chaque conversation. CD 4, Tr. 14 1.2
1. d **2.** b **3.** c **4.** a

a.

b.

c.

d.

2 Regarde ce plan d'un lycée québécois. Ensuite, décris le campus du lycée. 1.2

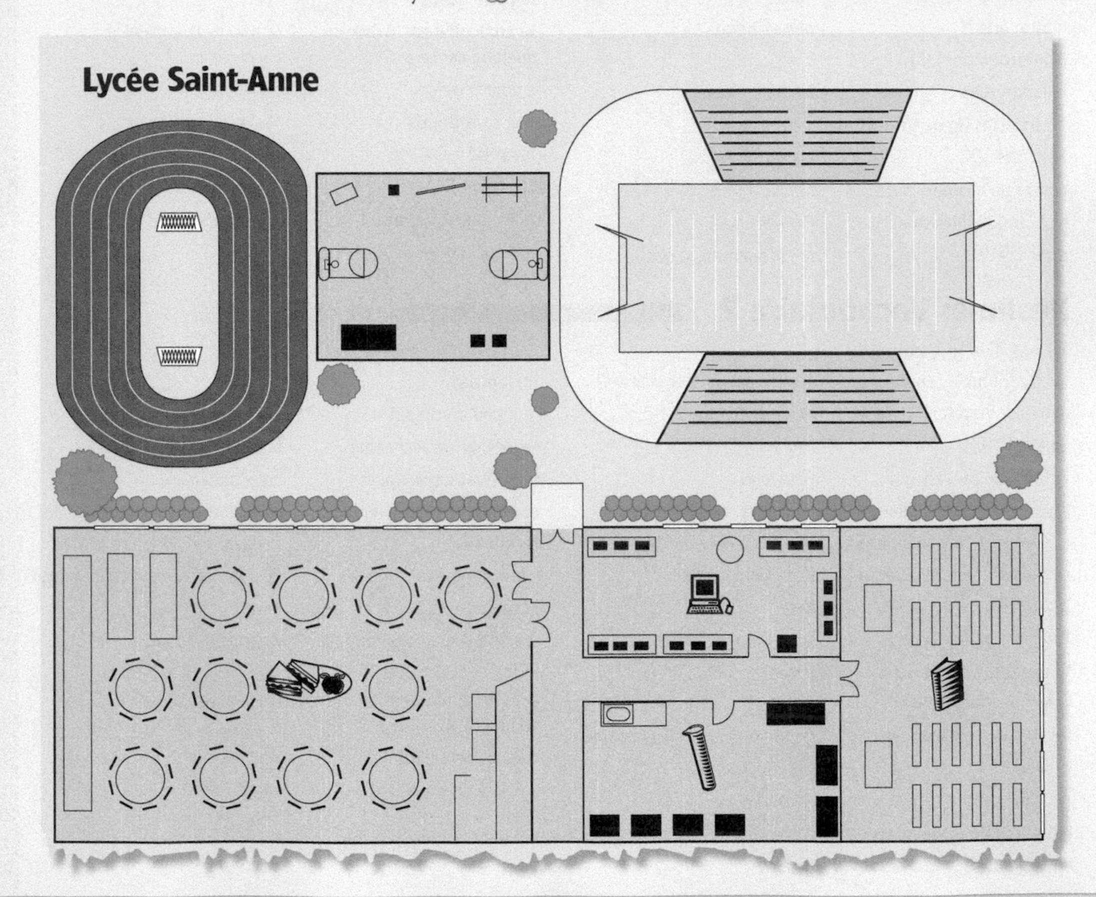

Online Culture Project

Have students do an Internet search for Web sites of schools in the francophone world. Students should choose one school's site and answer these questions. What extra-curricular activities does the school offer? Is there a list of classes? Does the school have computer classes? Have students create a table with the answers. Remind students to document their sources by referencing the names and URLs of all the sites they consulted. 1.3, 2.2

Révisions cumulatives

Online Assessment
my.hrw.com
Cumulative Self-test

3 Regarde l'image et imagine où on est. C'est quelle saison? Que font les jeunes? Est-ce que c'est le passé ou le présent? Est-ce que tu fais partie d'une équipe de ton lycée ou de ta ville? 1.1, 1.3

Le Hockey d'Henri Masson

Masson, Henri (1907-1996) Hockey, 1940. Oil on canvas, 55.6 x 66.3 cm. Musée d'art de Joliette, Quebec. Long Term Loan from Clercs of Saint-Viateur of Joliette.

4 Écris un e-mail à un(e) ami(e) québécois(e). Explique-lui ce qu'il y a dans ton lycée et parle-lui de tes activités scolaires. 1.3

5 À ton tour

Un lycée idéal With a small group of classmates, design the ideal high school. Decide what classes and facilities you would have and where they would be located. Create a map in French of your ideal school and label the areas of your school. Show your drawings to the class and talk about your ideal school. 1.3

Révisions cumulatives

Fine Art Connection

Introduction Henri Léopold Masson was born in Spy, Belgium, in 1907. He emigrated to Canada with his mother in 1921, at the age of fourteen. Henri Masson had studied art in Belgium, but he was an engraver by trade, and he only painted in his free time. At the age of thirty-eight, he gave up his job to teach and paint full time. His favorite subjects, that he painted in the style of naive imagery, were Canadian landscapes, still lifes, and portraits of people involved in everyday activities.

Analyzing

To help students discuss the painting, you might use the following questions.

1. **En quelle saison est-ce que cette scène se passe?**
2. **Que portent les personnages?**
3. **Est-ce que tu crois qu'ils sont des joueurs professionnels? Pourquoi?**
4. **Est-ce que ce sont des garçons ou des filles?**
5. **Est-ce que tu crois que tout le monde s'amuse bien? Pourquoi?** 3.1

Extension

Ask students to find pictures of other works by Henri Léopold Masson. Have them compare their shapes and colors. Masson painted another hockey game that takes place in another environment. Have students compare the colors of the two paintings and the different shapes (round and angular) the artist used to represent the players. Which of the two games is just for fun? 2.2, 3.1

ACTFL Performance Standards

The activities in Chapter 4 target the communicative modes as described in the Standards.

Interpersonal	Two-way communication using receptive skills and productive skills	**Communication (SE),** pp. 121, 123, 125, 127, 133,135, 137,139 **Communication (TE),** pp. 121, 123, 125, 133,135 **À ton tour,** p. 151
Interpretive	One-way communication using receptive skills	**Comparaisons,** p. 129 **Télé-roman,** pp. 140–141 **Communication (SE),** p. 139
Presentational	One-way communication using productive skills	**Communication (TE),** pp. 127, 137, 139

Géoculture Overview

Rennes

Bienvenue! This section is designed to familiarize the students with the geographic location, history, and cultural practices of the region to be explored. It provides a guide for classroom discussion and discovery of the differences and similarities of the student's own culture and that of the French-speaking world.

50-Minute Lesson Plans

Day 1

Lesson Sequence
Géoculture: Rennes, pp. 152–153
- Ask students if they have heard of Rennes. What have they heard? Basing their conjectures on the location of Rennes, students should speculate about the political and economic significance of this city. **10 min.**
- Go over the photos and captions with students. **10 min.**
- See Map Activities, p. 152. **5 min.**
- Discuss Background Information, p. 152. **11 min.**
- Complete **Géo-quiz. 1 min.**
- Show **Géoculture** video. **3 min.**
- Have students answer **Questions,** p. 153. **10 min.**

Optional Resources
- **Savais-tu que...?**, p. 152
- Research Online!, p. 151B

Homework Suggestions
Online Practice (**my.hrw.com**)
1.2, 2.1, 2.2, 3.1, 4.2

Day 2

Lesson Sequence
Géoculture: Rennes, pp. 154–155
- Briefly revisit the main points about the geography. **5 min.**
- Go over the photos and captions with students. **8 min.**
- Ask students to discuss the architecture of Rennes and compare it to that of their hometown. **5 min.**
- Have students answer the **As-tu compris?** questions, p. 155. **7 min.**
- Do the Map Game on p. 151B of the interleaf. **25 min.**

Optional Resources
- Slower Pace Learners, p. 151B ◆
- Multiple Intelligences, p. 151B
- Thinking Critically, p. 151B
- **Savais-tu que...?**, p. 155
- Interdisciplinary Links, pp. 154–155
- **Prépare-toi pour le quiz,** p. 151B

Homework Suggestions
Activité, p. 155
Study for the **Géoculture** quiz.
1.1, 1.2, 1.3, 2.1, 2.2, 3.1, 3.2, 4.2

90-Minute Lesson Plan

Block 1

Lesson Sequence
Géoculture: Rennes, pp. 152–155
- Ask students if they have heard of Rennes. What have they heard? Basing their conjectures on the location of Rennes, students should speculate about the political and economic significance of this city. **10 min.**
- Go over the photos and captions with students. **20 min.**
- See Map Activities, p. 152. **5 min.**
- Discuss Background Information, p. 152. **10 min.**
- Complete **Géo-quiz. 1 min.**
- Show **Géoculture** video. **4 min.**
- Have students answer **Questions,** p. 153. **5 min.**
- Have students answer the **As-tu compris?** questions, p. 155. **5 min.**
- Ask students to discuss the architecture of Rennes and compare it to that of their hometown. **5 min.**
- Do the Map Game on p. 151B. **25 min.**

Optional Resources
- **Savais-tu que ...?**, pp. 152, 155
- Slower Pace Learners, p. 151B ◆
- Multiple Intelligences, p., 151B
- Thinking Critically, p. 151B
- Research Online!, p. 151B
- Interdisciplinary Links, pp. 154–155
- **Prépare-toi pour le quiz,** p. 151B

Homework Suggestions
Online Practice (**my.hrw.com**)
Activité, p. 155
Study for the **Géoculture** quiz.
1.1, 1.2, 1.3, 2.1, 2.2, 3.1, 3.2, 4.2

KEY
▲ Advanced Learners ◆ Slower Pace Learners ● Special Learning Needs

Géoculture

Differentiated Instruction

Slower Pace Learners

Building on Previous Skills Before reading **Géoculture,** students should make lists of terms they would expect to find in descriptions of buildings, festivals, music, and art. As students read **Géoculture,** they should expand their lists with terms they have not included previously. 1.2, 3.1

Multiple Intelligences

Interpersonal Have students work with a partner to discuss the festivals and celebrations in Rennes from the point of view of the composer Yann Tiersen and a band member of Tri Yann. Partners should consider which festivals these musicians would enjoy and why and in which festival(s) these musicians may have participated and why. 1.1, 3.2

Thinking Critically

Comparing and Contrasting Tell students that in Rennes, the metro, with most of its routes underground, started operating in 2002. Ask students why they think that a relatively small city such as Rennes has built a metro system. Have students compare the transit system of Rennes to that of their hometown. Would their hometown or a town of comparable size to Rennes that is close to them agree to build a subway system? Why or why not? 2.2

Critical Thinking and Problem Solving

Quiz Preparation/Enrichment

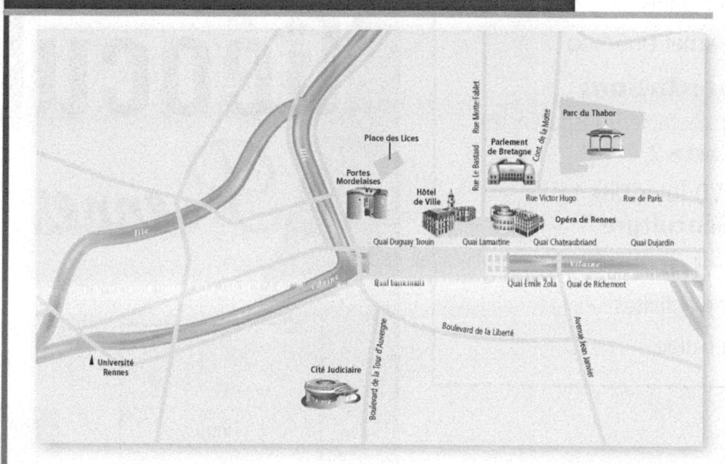

Map Game Students should play this game in pairs. One student chooses a feature that is shown on the map and writes it down. The other student will find this feature by asking a maximum of five yes or no questions. **Est-ce une rue? (non) Est-ce une place? (oui) Est-ce la place des Lices? (oui)** Partners take turns playing this game. They should have at least three turns each. 1.1, 3.1

Prépare-toi pour le quiz

1. Attach the captions of the photos in **Géoculture** to large index cards. Then attach the photos to another set of index cards. Ask students to match the photos with the corresponding captions.
2. Have students locate three sights on the map and describe each sight in two sentences.
3. Partners should create a conversation about the architecture, festivals, celebrations, music, and art of Rennes. They should express their opinions and likes and dislikes. You may want to ask some partners to present their conversation to the class. 1.3, 2.1, 3.1

Research Online!

Événements culturels dans Rennes Rennes has a dynamic cultural life. Have students research a cultural event. They should address the following questions.What kind of event is it? When and where does it take place? Why is the event popular? Is there a similar event taking place in their hometown? Students should present their research to the class. Have students document their sources by noting the URLs of all the sites they consulted. 2.1, 4.2

Géoculture

Resources

Planning:
Lesson Planner
Teacher One Stop

Presentation:
Projectable Transparencies
Carte 2
DVD Tutor, Disc 1
Géoculture

Practice:
Cahier d'activités
Media Guide

Map ACTIVITIES

1. Have students find Rennes on the map of France on page R2. Tell them that Rennes has been a busy crossroads throughout its more than 2,000-year-old history. Have them identify the cities and bodies of water where these roads probably led. (north: **La Manche,** Caen; west: Brest; south: Nantes, **l'Océan Atlantique;** southwest: Tours; east: Orleans, Chartres)
2. Ask students to identify the region where Rennes is located. (Brittany) Then ask them why Rennes might make a better regional capital than some other city. (It is closer to Normandy, the Loire, and Paris.)

Chapitres 5 et 6

DVD
Géoculture

Géoculture
Rennes

L'Ille et la Vilaine
Rennes est au confluent *(junction)* de deux rivières, l'Ille et la Vilaine. 2

La cité judiciaire, construite dans les années 80, est un exemple d'architecture futuriste. 1

Almanach

Nom des habitants
Les Rennais

Population
Plus de 200.000 habitants

Personnages célèbres
Étienne Daho, Paul Féval, Jean-Denis Lanjuinais, La Motte-Piquet, Marie-Charles Vanel

Économie
construction automobile, enseignement, recherche, industrie agroalimentaire

Les Universités de Rennes I et Rennes II
Rennes est une ville universitaire et un centre de recherche scientifique très important. Il y a environ 60.000 étudiants à Rennes.

Université de Rennes

Savais-tu que...?

En 1720, Rennes a été détruite par un incendie qui a duré six jours. Quand on l'a reconstruite, on a interdit l'utilisation du bois *(wood)*. Les bâtiments ont été reconstruits en pierres *(stone)*.

Background Information

Geography

Rennes lies in the eastern portion of Brittany where the Ille and Vilaine rivers meet. The Vilaine flows through the city center in a steep-sided canal that moves underground just before the **place de la République.** The northern part of Rennes contains the city's oldest buildings, while the southern part is very modern. Rennes is the capital of Brittany and the seat of the **département de l'Ille-et-Vilaine,** one of the four administrative districts in the region.

History

Julius Ceasar conquered Condate, the Celtic city that would become Rennes, in 57 BC. The city became an important administrative and trade center of the Roman Empire.

The Great Fire of 1720 destroyed about 900 buildings in the city center. Rennes's present-day layout dates back to the city's reconstruction.

Rennes became the administrative center of the Nazi occupation of Brittany during World War II. The city was finally liberated in August 1944 by the Americans.

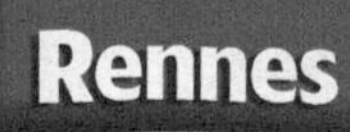

Rennes

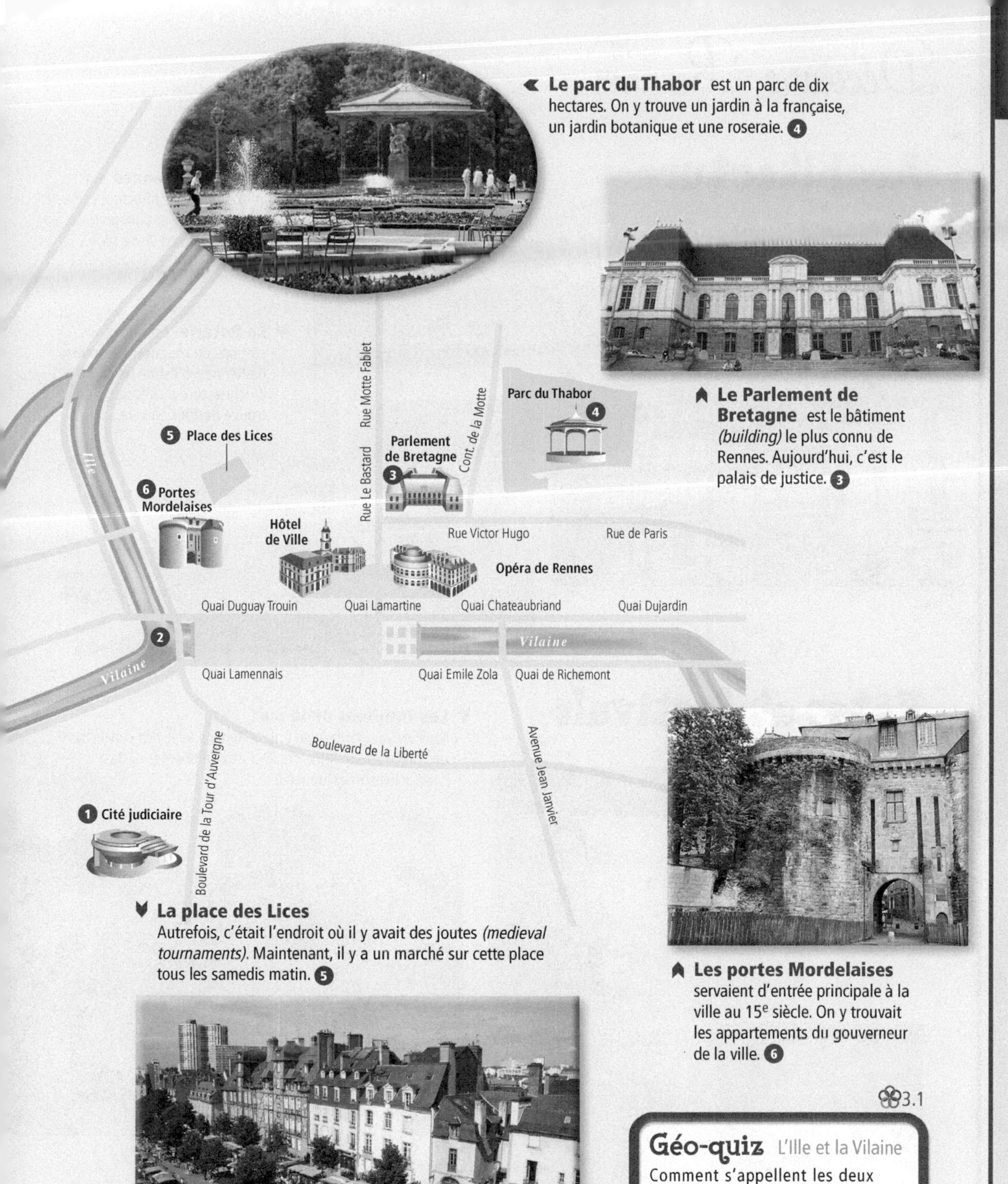

Le parc du Thabor est un parc de dix hectares. On y trouve un jardin à la française, un jardin botanique et une roseraie. (4)

Le Parlement de Bretagne est le bâtiment *(building)* le plus connu de Rennes. Aujourd'hui, c'est le palais de justice. (3)

La place des Lices Autrefois, c'était l'endroit où il y avait des joutes *(medieval tournaments)*. Maintenant, il y a un marché sur cette place tous les samedis matin. (5)

Les portes Mordelaises servaient d'entrée principale à la ville au 15e siècle. On y trouvait les appartements du gouverneur de la ville. (6)

3.1

Géo-quiz L'Ille et la Vilaine
Comment s'appellent les deux rivières qui se rejoignent à Rennes?

Comparisons

Comparing and Contrasting

Rennes has been a university town since the 18th century. Apart from its two main universities, Rennes 1 and Rennes 2, the city is home to some 20 other institutions of higher learning. Rennes 1 and many of the other schools offer degrees in science, biotechnology, electronics, telecommunications, and other cutting-edge technologies. Consequently, the city has become an important research center. Around 25,000 people work for companies in these fields. Ask students if they know of any university towns in the United States associated with high-tech industries and research. 4.2

Connections

Government Link

Although construction of the **Parlement de Bretagne** building did not begin until 1618, the parliament was installed in Rennes in 1561, ten years after its foundation. Today, the **Parlement de Bretagne** houses Rennes's Court of Appeals. The court reviews cases from the lower courts of five **départements** (administrative districts), continuing a tradition established hundreds of years ago. Have students research the French judicial system and report on its structure and hierarchy. 2.2, 3.1

Savais-tu que...?

Students might be interested in knowing the following facts about Rennes.

- High definition television and the Minitel were developed in Rennes. The Minitel is a videotext online service accessible through telephone lines. It is considered one of the most successful precursors to the World Wide Web.
- The Ille and Vilaine rivers form part of a canal that links the English Channel with the Atlantic Ocean. Hundreds of pleasure boats pass through Rennes each year on the canal.
- Rennes's municipal slogan is **Vivre en intelligence.** (Live intelligently.)

Questions

1.2

1. **Où se trouvent les appartements du gouverneur de Rennes? (aux portes Mordelaises)**
2. **Qu'est-ce qui s'est passé en 1720? (un incendie terrible)**
3. **Où est-ce qu'on fait des achats le samedi matin? (à la place des Lices)**
4. **Qu'est-ce qu'on peut voir au parc du Thabor? (un jardin à la française, un jardin botanique, une roseraie)**

Language Examination

Géoculture helps students better understand practices, products, and perspectives of French-speaking cultures and their relationship to one another. It can be used to practice for the **Interpretive Communication** and **Presentational Writing** sections of the AP Language and Culture Exam.

Cultures

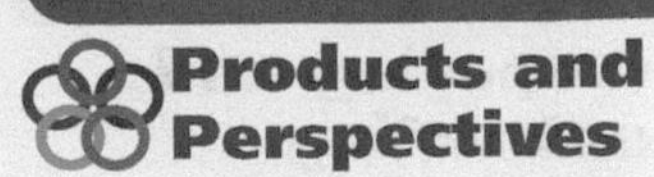

Products and Perspectives

After five years of construction, much opposition, and an expense of 527.17 million euros. Rennes opened a single-line subway system in 2002. The Rennes metro is a driverless, light rail system called **VAL (Véhicule Automatique Léger).** The single line is 9.4 kilometers long, running northwest to southeast. It has 15 stations and, although it was designed to carry 70,000 passengers daily, it often carries thousands more. At least four people man a central command post to run the network, and cameras monitor activity in and around the stations. Rennes is one of the smallest cities in the world to have such a metro system. Ask students why they think some people opposed the construction of the metro. You might have them stage a debate between those who are in favor of the metro and those who are against it. 1.1, 2.2

Comparisons

Comparing and Contrasting

Les Tombées de la nuit is a five-day festival that showcases different types of traditional and contemporary creative expression, including poetry, mime, theater, music, and culinary arts. The festival was originally created in the early 1980s in an effort to capitalize on Brittany's rich cultural heritage and build a new kind of tourism. Over the years it has played an important role in the renaissance of Breton culture. Open-air performances take place in different parts of the city, attracting thousands of spectators each July. Have students name any festivals that they know of in their state or region that promote local culture. Ask them what activities or products the festivals promote and how they compare to **les Tombées de la nuit.** 4.2

Découvre Rennes

Architecture

Les maisons à colombages du vieux quartier de Rennes sont faites de terre *(clay)* et de bois. Ces maisons datent du Moyen Âge.

L'Opéra de Rennes est un exemple d'architecture néoclassique. C'est un des derniers théâtres de ce style en France.

La Poterie est une des stations du tout nouveau métro de Rennes. C'est un exemple de l'architecture moderne qu'on trouve partout en ville.

Fêtes et festivals

Le festival Travelling est le festival du cinéma de Rennes. Chaque année, le public peut découvrir une ville différente à travers les films présentés. Les jeunes réalisateurs peuvent participer à un concours de courts métrages *(short films)*.

Les Tombées de la nuit
Tous les ans, ce festival anime Rennes avec des concerts, des pièces de théâtre, des lectures de poèmes et des spectacles son et lumière.

Les Rencontres transmusicales de Rennes
C'est un festival des musiques du monde. Plusieurs stars de rock, de hip hop et de techno ont commencé leur carrière ici.

Interdisciplinary Links

L'architecture 2.2, 3.1

Architecture Link Archeological discoveries in Rome and Greece in the 18th century created an interest in classical art and literature. Neoclassical architecture grew out of this interest, imitating the forms of Roman and Greek structures. This style was popular in France, where the heros of classical history had inspired people during the French Revolution. Have students research the common elements of neoclassical architecture and explain how the **Opéra de Rennes** reflects this style.

Les fêtes et festivals 3.1, 3.2

Social Studies Link The Travelling film festival has a three-fold purpose: to promote film in Brittany, to educate the public, and to foster cross-cultural communication. Each year the festival features films and workshops that explore the culture of a different city in the world. Past festivals have focused on such cities as Dublin, Algiers, Marseille, and Teheran. The festival also features films for children and competitions aimed at discovering new talent. Have students find out which city is featured this year and what cultural themes the festival will examine.

Musique

Online Practice
my.hrw.com
Photo Tour

Tri Yann Ce groupe a fait connaître la musique celtique traditionnelle bretonne dans le monde entier.

Savais-tu que...?
Rennes est une des plus petites villes au monde à avoir un métro.

Yann Tiersen a composé plusieurs musiques de films, comme celle de *Good bye Lenin* et celle du *Fabuleux destin d'Amélie Poulain*.

Le biniou est la version bretonne de la cornemuse.

Arts

Urbain Huchet est un peintre rennais qui a représenté la région de Pont-Aven dans plusieurs de ses tableaux.

Isidore Odorico a créé les mosaïques de style art déco qui ornent la piscine Saint-Georges et plusieurs autres immeubles. Il a rendu Rennes célèbre pour ses mosaïques modernes.

Activité

2.1, 2.2

1. **Architecture**: De quoi sont faites les maisons à colombages?
2. **Fêtes et festivals**: Qu'est-ce qu'on voit au festival Travelling?
3. **Musique**: Qu'est-ce que Yann Tiersen a composé?
4. **Arts**: Qui a créé de belles mosaïques pour plusieurs bâtiments rennais?

Activité

1. de terre et de bois
2. des films
3. plusieurs musiques de films
4. Isidore Odorico

Connections

Language Note

Many of Tri Yann's songs are based on traditional folk songs in Breton, a Celtic language, originally spoken in Britanny. In recent decades, many French educators and writers have attempted to promote and preserve the language. Have students comment on why they think there is an effort to preserve Breton, why it is not an official language, and whether they think it should be preserved and officially recognized. 3.2

As-tu compris?

You can use the following questions to check students' comprehension of **Géoculture.**

1. **Qui a commencé sa carrière aux Rencontres Transmusicales? (plusieurs stars de rock, de hip hop et de techno)**
2. **Qu'est-ce que le groupe Tri Yann joue comme musique? (la musique celtique traditionnelle bretonne)**
3. **Quel artiste est associé avec la région Pont-Aven? (Urbain Huchet)**

1.2

La musique

3.1

Music Link In the 1950s and 1960s, a revival of traditional Celtic music occurred in Brittany. Festivals and contests featuring traditional Breton songs and dances sprang up everywhere. Bagpipers and other Celtic musicians formed **bagadoù,** groups similar to Scottish pipebands. Over the years, these groups continued to explore Brittany's rich oral tradition and develop technical mastery. They also introduced new elements into their music, creating a new genre. Have students listen to some Breton music on the Internet or at the library and share their impressions with the class.

Les arts

2.2, 3.1

Art Link Mosaics are designs or pictures made by setting small pieces of colored stones, glass, or other material in cement. Although an ancient art form, they were a popular feature in important French buildings, post offices, shops, and swimming pools from the late 19th century until the 1940s. Some of the best mosaicists of that time were of Italian descent, like Isidore Odorico, who produced many beautiful works in Rennes. Have students find designs from Odorico's work in Rennes online and recreate one of them with pieces of colored construction paper and glue.

Assess

Assessment Program
Quiz: Géoculture
Differentiated Practice and Assessment CD-ROM

Online Assessment
my.hrw.com

Test Generator 

Planning Guide

Une journée typique

Chapter Section		Resources
Vocabulaire 1 • Daily routine and activities **Grammaire 1** • Reflexive verbs • **Tout, tous, toute, toutes** **Application 1** • **Un peu plus: S'appeler** and **se lever**	pp. 158–161 pp. 162–165 pp. 166–167	Projectable Transparencies: Vocabulaire 5.1, 5.2; Bell Work 5.1, 5.2, 5.3, 5.4 Cahier de vocabulaire et grammaire, pp. 49–54 Grammar Tutor for Students of French Cahier d'activités, pp. 41–43 Media Guide, pp. 17–20, 74–76 **Assessment Program** Quiz: Vocabulaire 1, pp. 119–120 Quiz: Grammaire 1, pp. 121–122 Quiz: Application 1, pp. 123–124
Culture • **Culture appliquée: La faïence de Quimper** • **Comparaisons et Communauté**	pp. 168–169	Cahier d'activités, pp. 44
Vocabulaire 2 • Daily routine and activities **Grammaire 2** • Reflexive verbs in the **passé composé** • The imperative with reflexive verbs **Application 2** • **Un peu plus:** Reflexive verbs with infinitives	pp. 170–173 pp. 174–177 pp. 178–179	Projectable Transparencies: Vocabulaire 5.3, 5.4; Bell Work 5.5, 5.6, 5.7, 5.8 Cahier de vocabulaire et grammaire, pp. 55–60 Grammar Tutor for Students of French Cahier d'activités, pp. 45–47 Media Guide, pp. 17–20, 74–75, 77 **Assessment Program** Quiz: Vocabulaire 2, pp. 125–126 Quiz: Grammaire 2, pp. 127–128 Quiz: Application 2, pp. 129–130
Télé-roman	pp. 180–181	Media Guide, pp. 75, 78
Lecture et écriture	pp. 182–185	Cahier d'activités, pp. 48 Reading Strategies and Skills Handbook Intermediate Reader French InterActive Reader **Assessment Program** Quiz: Lecture, p. 131 Quiz: Écriture, p. 132
Prépare-toi pour l'examen • **Résumé de vocabulaire et grammaire** • **Lettres et sons** **Révisions cumulatives**	pp. 186–189 pp. 190–191	Independent Study Guide, pp. 13–15, 37 Media Guide, p. 20 **Assessment Program** Examen: Chapitre 5, pp. 133–138 Examen oral: Chapitre 5, p. 321 Examen partiel, pp. 147–154 Projectable Transparencies: Fine Art, Ch. 5 Cahier d'activités, pp. 44, 49–50
Variations littéraires • **Mémoires d'outre-tombe**	pp. 390–391	Reading Strategies and Skills Handbook Intermediate Reader French InterActive Reader

Visit Us Online

my.hrw.com

Online Edition

Pacing Suggestions

	Essential	Recommended	Optional
Vocabulaire 1 • Daily routine and activities • **Flash culture**	✔		
Grammaire 1 • Reflexive verbs • **Tout, tous, toute, toutes** • **Flash culture**	✔		
Application 1 • **Un peu plus:** **S'appeler** and **se lever**	✔		
Culture • **Culture appliquée: La faïence de Quimper** • **Comparaisons et Communauté**		✔	
Vocabulaire 2 • Daily routine and activities • **Flash culture**	✔		
Grammaire 2 • Reflexive verbs in the **passé composé** • The imperative with reflexive verbs • **Flash culture**	✔		
Application 2 • **Un peu plus:** Reflexive verbs with infinitives	✔		
Télé-roman • Épisode 5: **Le Secret de la statuette**			✔
Lecture et écriture • **Comme un roman** (Lecture) • **Vive la variété!** (Écriture)		✔	
Prépare-toi pour l'examen		✔	
Révisions cumulatives			✔
Variations littéraires • **Mémoires d'outre-tombe**			✔

Technology

Bien dit! Online
- Student Edition with multi-media
- **performance space** recording tool
- Interactive activities with feedback
- Self-tests with feedback
- Cahier d'activités (Interactive workbook)
- Cahier de vocabulaire et grammaire (Interactive workbook)
- Holt Online Assessment

DVD Tutor
- Télé-vocab
- Grammavision
- Télé-roman

HOMETUTOR
- Interactive games
- Differentiated Practice
- Cultural video

Audio Program
- Student Edition listening activities
- Assessment listening activities
- Songs

Teacher One Stop™
- Complete resources
- ExamView Pro Test Generator
- Holt Calendar Planner

Holt McDougal Apps

Interactive Whiteboard Lessons

Differentiated Practice and Assessment CD

For slower pace and advanced learner options, see the Differentiated Practice and Assessment CD.

Projects

Une bande dessinée

In groups of four, students will create, write, and illustrate a comic strip of eight frames, entitled **Une journée typique.** All group members will participate in all aspects of the project, but each student will have a specific role. 1.3

Suggested Sequence

1. Form groups and assign the roles of leader/creator, writer, proofreader, and artist.
2. Students create the story and outline what will happen in each frame of the comic strip. Then they sketch illustrations or find pictures in magazines.
3. Have groups turn in a draft, including speech bubbles or captions, for suggestions.
4. Group members work together to rewrite the draft and illustrate each frame of the comic strip on a separate piece of paper.
5. Have groups glue the frames together on poster board. You may wish to display the posters in the classroom and have students vote on the most typical or funniest daily routine.

Creativity and Innovation

Grading the project

Suggested point distribution (100 points total)

Content	30 pts.
Language use	30 pts.
Originality/creativity	20 pts.
Effort/participation	20 pts.

e-community

e-mail forum:

Post the following questions on the classroom e-mail forum:

Est-ce qu'il te faut beaucoup de temps pour te préparer le matin?
À quelle heure est-ce que tu te lèves pour aller à l'école? 5.1

All students will contribute to the list and then share the items.

Partner Class Project

Have students imagine they work for an advertising agency that wants to market a new soap, shampoo, and toothpaste to teens. Students should create a survey to poll their partner class about their daily routine. They should include questions such as, **Préfères-tu prendre une douche ou un bain? Est-ce que tu te laves les cheveux dans la douche? Tu te brosses les dents deux fois par jour ou plus souvent?** When the survey comes back from the partner class, students should create a graph to display the results. 1.3

Communication

Game Bank
For game ideas, see pages T60–T63.

Café, bistro, brasserie

For the past several hundred years, the people of Rennes have been meeting their friends for a meal or drink at a **café, bistro,** or **brasserie.** They meet in cafes to discuss current events, read, or play chess over a cup of coffee or some other beverage. This tradition continues today, the **café** or **bistro** being a place where friends meet to have a drink or light snack and to watch the world go by. The other popular meeting places in Rennes are the **brasseries,** restaurants that specialize in Alsatian **choucroute** (sausage and sauerkraut) and seafood. Have students read *A Moveable Feast*, by Ernest Hemingway or one of George Simenon's books, featuring Detective Maigret, to find out more about the **café, bistro,** and **brasserie** tradition. 2.1

La cuisine

The **galette,** like the **crêpe,** is a traditional food from **Bretagne,** but it is salty instead of sweet. The dough, made from buckwheat, is typically filled with meat, fish, vegetables, or cheese. A type of **galette** particular to Rennes is the **galette saucisse.** A necessity at festivals, public gatherings, and soccer games, it consists of a **galette** wrapped around a sausage. 1.2, 2.2

Galette pour 5 personnes

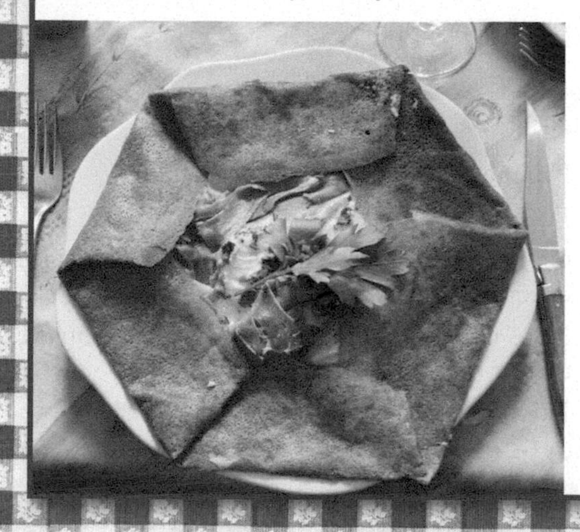

500 g de blé noir
1 pichet d'eau froide
1 œuf
de l'huile

Garniture (au choix)
du jambon
un œuf
une tomate
du fromage
une saucisse
des crevettes

Mélanger le blé noir et l'œuf dans un bol. Ajouter l'eau au fur et à mesure. La pâte devrait être très liquide. Faire chauffer une grande poêle. Mettre un peu d'huile sur un morceau d'essuie-tout et huiler la poêle avec. Verser la pâte dans la poêle. Laisser cuire cinq minutes, puis retourner la galette. Servir immédiatement.

Listening Activity Scripts

Vocabulaire à l'œuvre 1

2 p. 160, CD 5, Tr. 1

1.	Charlotte	Lili, tu te réveilles à quelle heure?
	Lili	Chaque matin, mon réveil sonne à six heures et demie. Je me lève tout de suite.
2.	Charlotte	Et tu t'habilles?
	Lili	Pas tout de suite. D'abord, je prends une douche et je me sèche les cheveux.
3.	Charlotte	Et ensuite?
	Lili	Ensuite, je me maquille.
4.	Charlotte	Et tu prends ton petit-déjeuner?
	Lili	Oui, je prends mon petit-déjeuner en même temps que je finis mes devoirs.
5.	Charlotte	Et après ça?
	Lili	Je me brosse les dents.
6.	Charlotte	Et après?
	Lili	Et enfin je m'habille et je m'en vais!

Answers to Activity 2
1. e **2.** c **3.** a **4.** f **5.** b **6.** d

Grammaire à l'œuvre 1

7 p. 163, CD 5, Tr. 2

1. Aujourd'hui, c'est Nathan qui réveille son petit frère.
2. Ensuite, ils se préparent en même temps dans la salle de bain.
3. Nathan lave les cheveux de son petit frère.
4. Nathan s'habille toujours avant le petit-déjeuner.
5. Nathan prépare un bon petit-déjeuner.
6. Nathan et son petit frère se brossent les dents après le petit-déjeuner.

Answers to Activity 7
1. b **2.** a **3.** b **4.** a **5.** b **6.** a

Application 1

18 p. 167, CD 5, Tr. 3

1. Bonjour. Comment est-ce que tu t'appelles?
2. À quelle heure est-ce que tu te lèves quand tu as cours?
3. Comment s'appelle ton lycée?
4. Et tes meilleurs amis, ils s'appellent comment?
5. Est-ce que tu t'ennuies en cours quelquefois?
6. Et les professeurs, est-ce qu'ils sont ennuyeux, à ton avis?

Answers to Activity 18
1. d **2.** b **3.** e **4.** c **5.** f **6.** a

Vocabulaire à l'œuvre 2

22 p. 172, CD 5, Tr. 4

1. Je prépare mon sac avant d'aller au lycée.
2. Je me déshabille et je me mets en pyjama.
3. Je me mets au lit à dix heures et demie au plus tard.
4. Je prends le bus pour aller au lycée.
5. Après les cours, quand je rentre à la maison, je m'occupe de ma petite sœur.
6. Je range mes affaires avant de me coucher.
7. Je souhaite une bonne nuit à mes parents.

Answers to Activity 22
1. a **2.** b **3.** b **4.** a **5.** a **6.** b **7.** b

Grammaire à l'œuvre 2

32 p. 176, CD 5, Tr. 5

1. Pauline et moi, nous sommes fatigués.
2. J'ai faim ce matin!
3. Oh là là! J'ai cours dans une demi-heure et je suis encore au lit!
4. Nous n'avons pas entendu le réveil et le bus va arriver dans cinq minutes!
5. J'ai mangé beaucoup de gâteau.

Answers to Activity 32
1. e **2.** d **3.** b **4.** f **5.** a

Application 2

 p. 178, CD 5, Tr. 6

1. Il faudrait dire à Monique de se coucher, tu ne crois pas?
2. On pourrait demander à tes cousins de s'occuper de ton petit frère.
3. Il est temps de t'habiller, Karine!
4. Pendant la semaine, tu ne devrais pas te coucher trop tard.
5. Ça te dit d'aller au café?
6. Je voudrais faire la sieste cet après-midi.

Answers to Activity 37

1. c 2. d 3. a 4. e 5. b 6. f

Prépare-toi pour l'examen

6 p. 187, CD 5, Tr. 9

1. Réveille-toi. Il est huit heures.
2. Brosse-toi les dents avant de te coucher.
3. Mets-toi en pyjama.
4. Habille-toi. Le bus arrive bientôt!
5. Couche-toi. Il est tard.
6. Mets-toi au lit.
7. Habille-toi et viens prendre ton petit-déjeuner.

Answers to Activity 6

1. a 2. b 3. b 4. a 5. b 6. b 7. a

Dictée, p. 188, CD 5, Tr. 12

1. Je me lève toujours de bonne heure.
2. Elle se sèche les cheveux avec le sèche-cheveux.
3. Vous vous rasez avec de la crème à raser ou avec du gel douche?
4. Ma mère ne met jamais de rouge à lèvres.
5. Dépêche-toi! Tu vas être en retard

Révisions cumulatives

2 p. 191, CD 5, Tr. 13

Aujourd'hui, j'ai fait beaucoup de choses! D'abord, je me suis levée à huit heures du matin. Je me suis lavé les cheveux et puis je me suis habillée. Maman m'a demandé d'aller à la charcuterie acheter du jambon. Après ça, je suis allée emprunter un livre au CDI. Quand je suis rentrée, j'ai dû m'occuper de mon petit frère. Il est mignon mais très pénible!

Answers to Activity 2

1. c 2. b 3. e 4. d 5. a

50-Minute Lesson Plans

Une journée typique

Day 1

OBJECTIVE
Talk about your routine

Core Instruction
Chapter Opener, pp. 156–157
- See Using the Photo, p. 156. **5 min.**
- See Chapter Objectives, p. 156. **5 min.**

Vocabulaire 1, pp. 158–161
- Present **Vocabulaire 1,** pp. 158–159. See Teaching **Vocabulaire,** p. 158. **10 min.**
- Show **Télé-vocab 1. 5 min.**
- Present **Exprimons-nous!,** p. 159. **10 min.**
- Do Activity 1, p. 160. **5 min.**
- Play Audio CD 5, Tr. 1 for Activity 2, p. 160. **5 min.**
- Do Activity 3, p. 160. **5 min.**

Optional Resources
- Slower Pace Learners, p. 159 ◆

Homework Suggestions
Cahier de vocabulaire et grammaire, pp. 49–50
@HOMETUTOR
1.2, 4.2

Day 2

OBJECTIVE
Express impatience; Use reflexive verbs

Core Instruction
Vocabulaire 1, pp. 158–161
- Present **Flash culture,** p. 160. **5 min.**
- See Teaching **Exprimons-nous!,** p. 160. **10 min.**
- Have students do Activities 4–5, p. 161. **20 min.**

Grammaire 1, pp. 162–165
- See Teaching **Grammaire,** p. 162. **10 min.**
- Have students do Activity 6, p. 162. **5 min.**

Optional Resources
- Communication (TE), p. 161
- Advanced Learners, p. 161 ▲
- Special Learning Needs, p. 161 ●

Homework Suggestions
Study for **Quiz: Vocabulaire 1**
Cahier de vocabulaire et grammaire, p. 51
Cahier d'activités, p. 41
1.1, 1.2, 1.3, 4.2

Day 3

OBJECTIVE
Use reflexive verbs

Core Instruction
Vocabulaire 1, pp. 158–161
- Review **Vocabulaire 1,** pp. 158–161. **10 min.**
- Give **Quiz: Vocabulaire 1. 20 min.**

Grammaire 1, pp. 162–165
- Show **Grammavision 1.1. 5 min.**
- Play Audio CD 5, Tr. 2 for Activity 7, p. 163. **5 min.**
- Have students do Activities 8–10, p. 163. **10 min.**

Optional Resources
- **Attention!,** p. 162
- Communication (TE), p. 163
- Slower Pace Learners, p. 163 ◆
- Multiple Intelligences, p. 163

Homework Suggestions
Cahier de vocabulaire et grammaire, p. 52
Cahier d'activités, p. 42
Online Practice (**my.hrw.com**)
1.1, 1.2

Day 4

OBJECTIVE
*Use **tout, tous, toute, toutes;** Use the verbs **s'appeler** and **se lever***

Core Instruction
Grammaire 1, pp. 162–165
- Present **Flash culture,** p. 164. **5 min.**
- See Teaching **Grammaire,** p. 164. **10 min.**
- Show **Grammavision 1.2. 5 min.**
- Have students do Activities 11–15, pp. 164–165. **20 min.**

Application 1, pp. 166–167
- Do Activity 16, p. 166. **5 min.**
- See Teaching **Un peu plus,** p. 166. **5 min.**

Optional Resources
- Communication (TE), p. 165
- Advanced Learners, p. 165 ▲
- Special Learning Needs, p. 165 ●

Homework Suggestions
Study for **Quiz: Grammaire 1**
Cahier de vocabulaire et grammaire, p. 53
Cahier d'activités, p. 43
1.1, 1.2, 1.3, 4.2 5.1

Day 5

OBJECTIVE
*Use the verbs **s'appeler** and **se lever***

Core Instruction
Grammaire 1, pp. 162–165
- Review **Grammaire 1,** pp. 162–165. **10 min.**
- Give **Quiz: Grammaire 1. 20 min.**

Application 1, pp. 166–167
- Have students do Activity 17, p. 166. **5 min.**
- Play Audio CD 5, Tr. 3 for Activity 18, p. 167. **5 min.**
- Have students do Activities 19–20, p. 167. **10 min.**

Optional Resources
- French for Spanish Speakers, p. 167
- Communication (TE), p. 167
- Slower Pace Learners, p. 167 ◆
- Special Learning Needs, p. 167 ●

Homework Suggestions
Study for **Quiz: Application 1**
Cahier de vocabulaire et grammaire, p. 54
1.1, 1.2, 1.3, 4.1

Day 6

OBJECTIVE
Learn about francophone culture

Core Instruction
Application 1, pp. 166–167
- Review **Application 1,** pp. 166–167. **10 min.**
- Give **Quiz: Application 1. 20 min.**

Culture, pp. 168–169
- See **Culture appliquée** (TE), p. 168. **10 min.**
- See **Comparaisons et communauté** (TE), p. 168. **10 min.**

Optional Resources
- **Vocabulaire supplémentaire,** p. 168
- Communities, p. 169
- Cultures, p. 169
- Advanced Learners, p. 169 ▲
- Multiple Intelligences, p. 169

Homework Suggestions
Cahier d'activités, p. 44
Finish **Culture appliquée** project
1.3, 2.1, 2.2, 4.2, 5.1

Day 7

OBJECTIVE
Say when you do things

Core Instruction
Vocabulaire 2, pp. 170–173
- Do Bell Work 5.5, p. 170. **5 min.**
- Present **Vocabulaire 2,** pp. 170–171. See Teaching **Vocabulaire,** p. 170. **10 min.**
- Show **Télé-vocab 2. 5 min.**
- Present **Exprimons-nous!,** p. 171. **10 min.**
- Have students do Activity 21, p. 172. **5 min.**
- Play Audio CD 5, Tr. 4 for Activity 22, p. 172. **5 min.**
- Have students do Activity 23, p. 172. **5 min.**
- Present **Flash culture,** p. 172. **5 min.**

Optional Resources
- TPR, p. 171
- Advanced Learners, p. 171 ▲
- Multiple Intelligences, p. 171

Homework Suggestions
Cahier de vocabulaire et grammaire, pp. 55–56
1.1, 1.2, 4.2

Day 8

OBJECTIVE
*Make recommendations; Use reflexive verbs in the **passé composé***

Core Instruction
Vocabulaire 2, pp. 170–173
- See Teaching **Exprimons-nous!,** p. 172. **10 min.**
- Have students do Activities 24–26, p. 173. **20 min.**

Grammaire 2, pp. 174–177
- See Teaching **Grammaire,** p. 174. **10 min.**
- Show **Grammavision 2.1. 5 min.**
- Have students do Activity 27, p. 174. **5 min.**

Optional Resources
- Slower Pace Learners, p. 173 ◆
- Multiple Intelligences, p. 173
- Special Learning Needs, p. 175 ●

Homework Suggestions
Study for **Quiz: Vocabulaire 2**
Cahier de vocabulaire et grammaire, p. 57
1.1, 1.2, 1.3

To edit and create your own lesson plans, see the

Teacher One Stop™

KEY

- ▲ Advanced Learners
- ◆ Slower Pace Learners
- ● Special Learning Needs

Day 9

OBJECTIVE

Use reflexive verbs in the ***passé composé***

Core Instruction

Vocabulaire 2, pp. 170–173

- Review **Vocabulaire 2,** pp. 170–173. **10 min.**
- Give **Quiz: Vocabulaire 2. 20 min.**

Grammaire 2, pp. 174–177

- Present **Flash culture,** p. 174. **5 min.**
- Have students do Activities 28–31, p. 175. **15 min.**

Optional Resources

- Communication (TE), p. 175
- Advanced Learners, p. 175 ▲

Homework Suggestions

Cahier de vocabulaire et grammaire, p. 58

Cahier d'activités, p. 45

@HOMETUTOR

Online Practice (**my.hrw.com**)

1.1, 1.2, 1.3, 4.2

Day 10

OBJECTIVE

Use the imperative with reflexive verbs

Core Instruction

Grammaire 2, pp. 174–177

- See Teaching **Grammaire,** p. 176. **10 min.**
- Show **Grammavision 2.2. 5 min.**
- Play Audio CD 5, Tr. 5 for Activity 32, p. 176. **5 min.**
- Do Activities 33–36, pp. 176–177. **20 min.**

Application 2, pp. 178–179

- Play Audio CD 5, Tr. 6 for Activity 37, p. 178. **5 min.**
- Have students do Activity 38, p. 178. **5 min.**

Optional Resources

- Slower Pace Learners, p. 177 ◆
- Multiple Intelligences, p. 177

Homework Suggestions

Study for **Quiz: Grammaire 2**

Cahier de vocabulaire et grammaire, p. 59

Cahier d'activités, p. 46

1.1, 1.2, 1.3

Day 11

OBJECTIVE

Use reflexive verbs with infinitives

Core Instruction

Grammaire 2, pp. 174–177

- Review **Grammaire 2,** pp. 174–177. **10 min.**
- Give **Quiz: Grammaire 2. 20 min.**

Application 2, pp. 178–179

- See Teaching **Un peu plus,** p. 178. **5 min.**
- Have students do Activities 39–42, pp. 178–179. **15 min.**

Optional Resources

- Communication (TE), p. 179
- Advanced Learners, p. 179 ▲
- Multiple Intelligences, p. 179

Homework Suggestions

Study for **Quiz: Application 2**

Cahier de vocabulaire et grammaire, p. 60

Cahier d'activités, p. 47

Online Practice (**my.hrw.com**)

1.1, 1.2, 1.3, 4.2

Day 12

OBJECTIVE

Develop listening and reading skills

Core Instruction

Application 2, pp. 178–179

- Review **Application 2,** pp. 178–179. **10 min.**
- Give **Quiz: Application 2. 20 min.**

Télé-roman, pp. 180–181

- Show **Télé-roman.** See Teaching **Télé-roman,** p. 180. **5 min.**
- Have students answer the **As-tu compris?** questions, p. 181. **15 min.**

Optional Resources

- Connections, p. 180
- Gestures, p. 180
- Communication (TE), p. 181

Homework Suggestions

Online Practice (**my.hrw.com**)

1.2, 1.3, 3.2

Day 13

OBJECTIVE

Develop listening, reading, and writing skills

Core Instruction

Lecture et écriture, pp. 182–185

- See Teaching **Lecture,** p. 182. **35 min.**
- See Teaching **Espace écriture,** p. 184. **15 min.**

Optional Resources

- Applying the Strategies, p. 182
- Using Context, p. 182
- Communities, p. 183
- Slower Pace Learners, p. 183 ◆
- Special Learning Needs, p. 183 ●
- Connections, p. 184
- Process Writing, p. 185

Homework Suggestions

Cahier d'activités, p. 48

Espace écriture, Activity 2, p. 185

1.2, 1.3, 3.1, 5.1

Day 14

OBJECTIVE

Develop writing skills; Review the chapter

Core Instruction

Lecture et écriture, pp. 182–185

- See Teaching **Espace écriture,** p. 184. **25 min.**

Prépare-toi pour l'examen, pp. 186–188

- Have students do Activities 1–5, pp. 186–187. **25 min.**

Optional Resources

- Writing Assessment, p. 185
- Advanced Learners, p. 185 ▲
- Multiple Intelligences, p. 185
- Reteaching, p. 186
- Fold-N-Learn, p. 186
- Oral Assessment, p. 187

Homework Suggestions

Online Practice (**my.hrw.com**)

1.2, 1.3

Day 15

OBJECTIVE

Review the chapter

Core Instruction

Prépare-toi pour l'examen, pp. 186–188

- Play Audio CD 5, Tr. 9 for Activity 6, p. 187. **5 min.**
- Have students do Activity 7, p. 187. **5 min.**
- Play Audio CD 5, Tr. 10–12 for **Lettres et sons,** p. 188. **10 min.**

Révisions cumulatives, pp. 190–191

- Have students do Activity 1, p. 190. **5 min.**
- Play Audio CD 5, Tr. 13 for Activity 2, p. 191. **5 min.**
- Have students do Activities 3–5, p. 191. **20 min.**

Optional Resources

- Online Culture Project, p. 190
- Fine Art Connection, p. 191

Homework Suggestions

Study for Chapter Test

Online Practice (**my.hrw.com**)

1.1, 1.2, 1.3, 2.2, 3.1, 3.2

Day 16/Test

Core Instruction

Chapter Test 50 min.

Optional Resources

Assessment Program

- Alternative Assessment
- Test Generator
- **Quiz: Lecture**
- **Quiz: Écriture**

Homework Suggestions

Cahier d'activités, pp. 49–50, 110–111

Online Practice (**my.hrw.com**)

90-Minute Lesson Plans

Une journée typique

Block 1

OBJECTIVE
Talk about your routine; Express impatience

Core Instruction

Chapter Opener, pp. 156–157
- See Using the Photo, p. 156. **5 min.**
- See Chapter Objectives, p. 156. **5 min.**

Vocabulaire 1, pp. 158–161
- Present **Vocabulaire 1,** pp. 158–159. See Teaching **Vocabulaire,** p. 158. **15 min.**
- Show **Télé-vocab 1. 5 min.**
- Present **Exprimons-nous!,** p. 159. **10 min.**
- Have students do Activity 1, p. 160. **5 min.**
- Play Audio CD 5, Tr. 1 for Activity 2, p. 160. **5 min.**
- Have students do Activity 3, p. 160. **5 min.**
- Present **Flash culture,** p. 160. **5 min.**
- See Teaching **Exprimons-nous!,** p. 160. **10 min.**
- Have students do Activities 4–5, p. 161. **20 min.**

Optional Resources
- Learning Tips, p. 157
- **Proverbes,** p. 158
- TPR, p. 159
- **Attention!,** p. 159
- Connections, p. 159
- Slower Pace Learners, p. 159 ◆
- Multiple Intelligences, p. 159
- Teacher Note, p. 160
- Cultures, p. 161
- Communication (TE), p. 161
- Advanced Learners, p. 161 ▲
- Special Learning Needs, p. 161 ●

Homework Suggestions
Study for **Quiz: Vocabulaire 1**
Cahier de vocabulaire et grammaire, pp. 49–51
@HOMETUTOR
Online Practice (**my.hrw.com**)
1.1, 1.2, 1.3, 2.2, 4.2

Block 2

OBJECTIVE
*Use reflexive verbs; Use **tout, tous, toute, toutes***

Core Instruction

Vocabulaire 1, pp. 158–161
- Review **Vocabulaire 1,** pp. 158–161. **10 min.**
- Give **Quiz: Vocabulaire 1. 20 min.**

Grammaire 1, pp. 162–165
- See Teaching **Grammaire,** p. 162. **5 min.**
- Show **Grammavision 1.1. 5 min.**
- Have students do Activity 6, p. 162. **5 min.**
- Play Audio CD 5, Tr. 2 for Activity 7, p. 163. **5 min.**
- Have students do Activities 8–10, p. 163. **15 min.**
- Present **Flash culture,** p. 164. **5 min.**
- See Teaching **Grammaire,** p. 164. **5 min.**
- Show **Grammavision 1.2. 5 min.**
- Have students do Activities 11–13, pp. 164–165. **10 min.**

Optional Resources
- **Attention!,** p. 162
- Communication (TE), p. 163
- Slower Pace Learners, p. 163 ◆
- Multiple Intelligences, p. 163
- Special Learning Needs, p. 165 ●

Homework Suggestions
Study for **Quiz: Grammaire 1**
Cahier de vocabulaire et grammaire, pp. 52–53
Cahier d'activités, pp. 41–42
@HOMETUTOR
Online Practice (**my.hrw.com**)
1.1, 1.2, 4.2

Block 3

OBJECTIVE
*Use **tout, tous, toute, toutes;** Use the verbs **s'appeler** and **se lever;** Learn about francophone culture*

Core Instruction

Grammaire 1, pp. 162–165
- Have students do Activities 14–15, p. 165. **10 min.**
- Review **Grammaire 1,** pp. 162–165. **10 min.**
- Give **Quiz: Grammaire 1. 20 min.**

Application 1, pp. 166–167
- Have students do Activity 16, p. 166. **5 min.**
- See Teaching **Un peu plus,** p. 166. **5 min.**
- Have students do Activity 17, p. 166. **5 min.**
- Play Audio CD 5, Tr. 3 for Activity 18, p. 167. **5 min.**
- Have students do Activities 19–20, p. 167. **10 min.**

Culture, pp. 168–169
- See **Culture appliquée** (TE), p. 168. **10 min.**
- See **Comparaisons et communauté** (TE), p. 168. **10 min.**

Optional Resources
- Connections, p. 164
- Communication (TE), p. 165
- Advanced Learners, p. 165 ▲
- French for Spanish Speakers, p. 167
- Communication (TE), p. 167
- Slower Pace Learners, p. 167 ◆
- Special Learning Needs, p. 167 ●
- Communities, p. 169
- Cultures, p. 169
- Advanced Learners, p. 169 ▲
- Multiple Intelligences, p. 169

Homework Suggestions
Study for **Quiz: Application 1**
Cahier de vocabulaire et grammaire, p. 54
Cahier d'activités, pp. 43–44
Online Practice (**my.hrw.com**)
Finish **Culture appliquée** project
1.1, 1.2, 1.3, 2.1, 2.2, 3.1, 4.1, 4.2, 5.1

Block 4

OBJECTIVE
Say when you do things; Make recommendations

Core Instruction

Application 1, pp. 166–167
- Review **Application 1,** pp. 166–167. **10 min.**
- Give **Quiz: Application 1. 20 min.**

Vocabulaire 2, pp. 170–173
- Present **Vocabulaire 2,** pp. 170–171. See Teaching **Vocabulaire,** p. 170. **5 min.**
- Show **Télé-vocab 2. 5 min.**
- Present **Exprimons-nous!,** p. 171. **5 min.**
- Have students do Activity 21, p. 172. **5 min.**
- Play Audio CD 5, Tr. 4 for Activity 22, p. 172. **5 min.**
- Have students do Activity 23, p. 172. **5 min.**
- Present **Flash culture,** p. 172. **5 min.**
- See Teaching **Exprimons-nous!,** p. 172. **10 min.**
- Have students do Activities 24–26, p. 173. **15 min**

Optional Resources
- Connections, p. 170
- TPR, p. 171
- **Attention!,** p. 171
- Advanced Learners, p. 171 ▲
- Multiple Intelligences, p. 171
- Communities, p. 173
- Communication (TE), p. 173
- Slower Pace Learners, p. 173 ◆
- Multiple Intelligences, p. 173

Homework Suggestions
Study for **Quiz: Vocabulaire 2**
Cahier de vocabulaire et grammaire, pp. 55–57
@HOMETUTOR
Online Practice (**my.hrw.com**)
1.1, 1.2, 1.3, 3.1, 4.2, 5.2

To edit and create your own lesson plans, see the **Teacher One Stop™**

KEY
- ▲ Advanced Learners
- ◆ Slower Pace Learners
- ● Special Learning Needs

Block 5

OBJECTIVE
*Use reflexive verbs in the **passé composé;** Use the imperative with reflexive verbs*

Core Instruction
Vocabulaire 2, pp. 170–173
- Review **Vocabulaire 2,** pp. 170–173. **10 min.**
- Give **Quiz: Vocabulaire 2. 20 min.**

Grammaire 2, pp. 174–177
- Present **Flash culture,** p. 174. **5 min.**
- See Teaching **Grammaire,** p. 174. **5 min.**
- Show **Grammavision 2.1. 5 min.**
- Have students do Activities 27–31, pp. 174–175. **20 min.**
- See Teaching **Grammaire,** p. 176. **5 min.**
- Show **Grammavision 2.2. 5 min.**
- Play Audio CD 5, Tr. 5 for Activity 32, p. 176. **5 min.**
- Have students do Activities 33–34, pp. 176–177. **10 min.**

Optional Resources
- French for Spanish Speakers, p. 175
- Communication (TE), p. 175
- Advanced Learners, p. 175 ▲
- Special Learning Needs, p. 175 ●
- Slower Pace Learners, p. 177 ◆
- Multiple Intelligences, p. 177

Homework Suggestions
Study for **Quiz: Grammaire 2**
Cahier de vocabulaire et grammaire, pp. 58–59
Cahier d'activités, pp. 45–46
HOMETUTOR
Online Practice (**my.hrw.com**)
1.1, 1.2, 1.3, 4.1, 4.2

Block 6

OBJECTIVE
Use the imperative with reflexive verbs; Use reflexive verbs with infinitives; Develop listening and reading skills

Core Instruction
Grammaire 2, pp. 174–177
- Have students do Activities 35–36, p. 177. **10 min.**
- Review **Grammaire 2,** pp. 174–177. **10 min.**
- Give **Quiz: Grammaire 2. 20 min.**

Application 2, pp. 178–179
- Play Audio CD 5, Tr. 6 for Activity 37, p. 178. **5 min.**
- Have students do Activity 38, p. 178. **5 min.**
- See Teaching **Un peu plus,** p. 178. **5 min.**
- Have students do Activities 39–42, pp. 178–179. **10 min.**

Télé-roman, pp. 180–181
- Show **Télé-roman.** See Teaching **Télé-roman,** p. 180. **5 min.**
- Have students answer the **As-tu compris?** questions, p. 181. **15 min.**

Optional Resources
- Communication (TE), p. 177
- Communication (TE), p. 179
- Advanced Learners, p. 179 ▲
- Multiple Intelligences, p. 179
- Connections, p. 180
- Gestures, p. 180
- Communication (TE), p. 181

Homework Suggestions
Study for **Quiz: Application 2**
Cahier de vocabulaire et grammaire, p. 60
Cahier d'activités, p. 47
Online Practice (**my.hrw.com**)
1.1, 1.2, 1.3, 2.1

Block 7

OBJECTIVE
Develop listening, reading, and writing skills; Review the chapter

Core Instruction
Application 2, pp. 178–179
- Review **Application 2,** pp. 178–179. **10 min.**
- Give **Quiz: Application 2. 20 min.**

Lecture et écriture, pp. 182–185
- See Teaching **Lecture,** p. 182. **20 min.**
- See Teaching **Espace écriture,** p. 184. **30 min.**

Prépare-toi pour l'examen, pp. 186–188
- Have students do Activities 1–3, p. 186. **10 min.**

Optional Resources
- Applying the Strategies, p. 182
- Using Context, p. 182
- Communities, p. 183
- Slower Pace Learners, p. 183 ◆
- Special Learning Needs, p. 183 ●
- Connections, p. 184
- Process Writing, p. 185
- Writing Assessment, p. 185
- Advanced Learners, p. 185 ▲
- Mulitple Intelligences, p. 185
- Reteaching, p. 186
- Fold-N-Learn, p. 186

Homework Suggestions
Study for Chapter Test
Cahier d'activités, p. 48
Espace écriture, Activity 2, p. 185
Online Practice (**my.hrw.com**)
1.2, 1.3, 3.1, 5.1

Block 8

OBJECTIVE
Review and assess the chapter

Core Instruction
Prépare-toi pour l'examen, pp. 186–188
- Have students do Activities 4–5, p. 187. **5 min.**
- Play Audio CD 5, Tr. 9 for Activity 6, p. 187. **5 min.**
- Have students do Activity 7, p. 187. **5 min.**
- Play Audio CD 5, Tr. 10–12 for **Lettres et sons,** p. 188. **5 min.**

Chapter Test 50 min.

Révisions cumulatives, pp. 190–191
- Have students do Activity 1, p. 190. **5 min.**
- Play Audio CD 5, Tr. 13 for Activity 2, p. 191. **5 min.**
- Have students do Activities 3–5, p. 191. **10 min.**

Optional Resources
- TPRS, p. 186
- Oral Assessment, p. 187
- Game, p. 188
- **Proverbes,** p. 188
- Chapter Review, pp. 188–189
- Teacher to Teacher, p. 189
- Online Culture Project, p. 190
- Fine Art Connection, p. 191

Homework Suggestions
Cahier d'activités, pp. 49–50, 110–111
Online Practice (**my.hrw.com**)
1.1, 1.2, 1.3, 2.2, 3.1, 3.2

Chapter Opener

Meeting the National Standards

Communication
Communication, pp. 161, 163, 165, 167, 173, 175, 177, 179
À ton tour, p. 191

Cultures
Flash culture, pp. 160, 164, 172, 174
Comparaisons, p. 169
Products and Perspectives, pp. 161, 169

Connections
Science Link, p. 164
Acquiring Information, p. 159
History Link, p. 170
Visual Learners, p. 180
Language Arts Link, p. 184

Comparisons
Comparaisons, p. 169

Communities
Communauté, p. 169
Community Link, pp. 169, 173, 183

Using the Photo

This family hurries to catch the **VAL (Véhicule Automatique Léger)** in Rennes. Rennes is the third French city to construct and use the **VAL,** or Automated Guided Transit system. Construction began in 1997, and in 2002 riders began making their way across the city in as few as 16 minutes. Most of the nine-kilometer route runs underground. Ask students if they have ever ridden a rapid public transit system and if so, where. How does that system compare to the **VAL?** 4.2

Vocabulaire supplémentaire

Students might use these terms to discuss the photo.

les distributeurs de billets *ticket machines*
le passager/la passagère *passenger*
le quai *platform*
le garde-fou *railing*

chapitre 5

Une journée typique

Objectifs

In this chapter, you will learn to
- talk about your routine
- express impatience
- say when you do things
- make recommendations

And you will use
- reflexive verbs
- **tout, tous, toute, toutes**
- the verbs **s'appeler** and **se lever**
- reflexive verbs in the **passé composé**
- the imperative with reflexive verbs
- reflexive verbs with infinitives

Que vois-tu sur la photo?

Où sont ces personnes?
Qu'est-ce qu'elles font? À ton avis, où est-ce qu'elles vont?
Comment est-ce que tu vas à l'école?

ACTFL 21st Century Skills

Communication:	SE: pp. 161, 165, 173, 191; TE: pp. 155C (Financial Literacy), 169, 177, 181
Collaboration:	TE: pp. 165, 179, 183
Information Literacy:	TE: pp. 164 (Health Literacy), 169 (Civic Literacy), 170, 173, 184, 190
Flexibility and Adaptability:	SE: pp. 167, 182; TE: pp. 155C, 165, 175, 182
Initiative and Self-Direction:	TE: pp. 157, 169 (Global Awareness), 183
Leadership and Responsibility:	TE: pp. 169, 183

Chapter Opener

TEACHER TOOLS
- Interactive Whiteboard Lessons
- Generate Success!

ALSO AVAILABLE...
- Online Workbooks
- French InterActive Reader

FRENCH ON THE GO!
- Performance Space
- Holt McDougal French Apps
- *Bien dit!* eTextbook

Le VAL, métro de Rennes

Learning Tips

In this chapter, students will learn how to talk about their daily routines, giving them more vocabulary to talk about what is relevant to their lives. Encourage students to use this vocabulary to speak in French to classmates outside of class whenever possible.

- **Télé-vocab 1**
- **Grammavision 1**
- **Télé-vocab 2**
- **Grammavision 2**
- **Télé-roman**

LISTENING PRACTICE

Language Lab and Classroom Activities

Vocabulaire
Activity 2, p. 160, CD 5, Tr. 1
Télé-vocab 1, p. 158, DVD Tutor
Activity 22, p. 172, CD 5, Tr. 4
Télé-vocab 2, p. 170, DVD Tutor

Grammaire
Activity 7, p. 163, CD 5, Tr. 2
Grammavision 1, pp. 162, 164, DVD Tutor
Activity 32, p. 176, CD 5, Tr. 5
Grammavision 2, pp. 174, 176 DVD Tutor

Application
Activity 18, p. 167, CD 5, Tr. 3
Activity 39, p. 178, CD 5, Tr. 6

Prépare-toi pour l'examen
Activity 6, p. 187, CD 5, Tr. 9

Révisions cumulatives
Activity 2, p. 191, CD 5, Tr. 13

Télé-roman
p. 180, DVD Tutor

Lecture
p. 182, CD 5, Tr. 7

Variations littéraires
p. 390, CD 5, Tr. 8

Lettres et sons
p. 188, CD 5, Tr. 10–12

Objectifs
- to talk about your routine
- to express impatience

Vocabulaire à l'œuvre 1

Télé-vocab

Resources

Planning:
Lesson Planner
Teacher One Stop

Presentation:
Projectable Transparencies **Vocabulaire 5.1, 5.2**
DVD Tutor, Disc 1 **Télé-vocab 1**
Interactive Whiteboard Lessons

Practice:
Cahier de vocabulaire et grammaire
Differentiated Practice and Assessment CD-ROM
Independent Study Guide
Media Guide
Projectable Transparencies Bell Work 5.1
HOMETUTOR
Holt McDougal French Apps

Bell Work

Use Bell Work 5.1 in the *Projectable Transparencies* or write this activity on the board.

Complete the following sentences with the correct form of **ouvrir** or **offrir.**

1. **À quelle heure ____ la bibliothèque?**
2. **Nous ____ tous les jours à huit heures.**
3. **Qu'est-ce que Thomas ____ à sa mère hier?**
4. **____ cette porte, s'il vous plaît.**
5. **Mes amis ____ toujours des fleurs quand ils sont invités.** 1.2

Proverbes

For French proverbs and activities related to the chapter theme and vocabulary, see **Proverbes et expressions,** pp. R6–R7.

Une journée typique à Rennes

La matinée de Farida

Je me réveille à six heures.

Je prends un bain.

Je me sèche les cheveux et je me brosse.

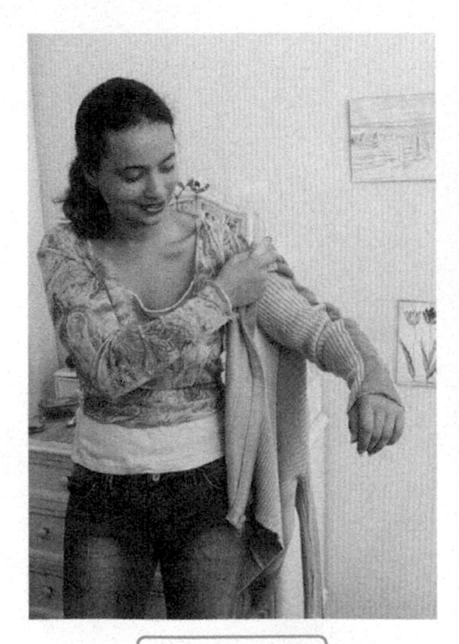
Je m'habille.

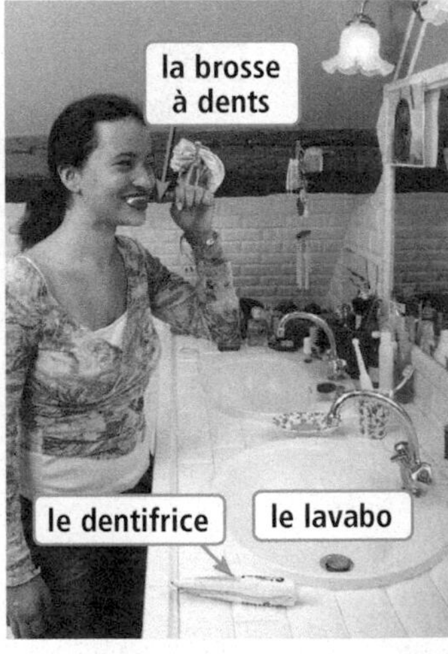

Je me brosse les dents.

Core Instruction

TEACHING VOCABULAIRE

1. Introduce vocabulary with transparencies **Vocabulaire 5.1** and **5.2** and model pronunciation. **(3 min.)**
2. Tell students your basic daily routine, using the vocabulary presented and **D'autres mots utiles,** pantomiming where necessary. **(2 min.)**
3. Repeat your daily routine, giving more details and using expressions from **Exprimons-nous!** Then ask students **oui** or **non** questions about your routine. **(4 min.)**
4. Ask students **oui** or **non** questions about their daily routine. **(3 min.)**

Télé-vocab 1

For a video presentation of this vocabulary, see the *DVD Tutor.*

Télé-vocab

Online Practice
my.hrw.com
Vocabulaire 1 practice

La matinée d'Arthur

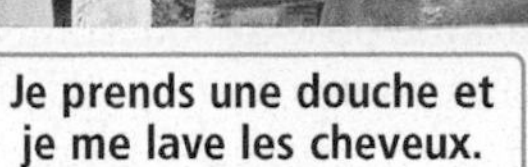

la serviette

le rasoir

Je me rase.

le peigne

Je me peigne.

Exprimons-nous!

To talk about your routine

Je prends mon petit-déjeuner **en premier** et **ensuite,** je m'habille. *. . . first, and then, . . .*

Chaque matin, je me réveille à sept heures. *Every/Each . . .*

Je prends toujours mon petit-déjeuner **avant de** prendre ma douche. *. . . before . . .*

Je me rase **tous les deux** jours. *. . . every other . . .*

Je bois mon café **en même temps que** je m'habille. *. . . at the same time as . . .*

Je m'habille **pendant que** mon père prépare le petit-déjeuner. *. . . while . . .*

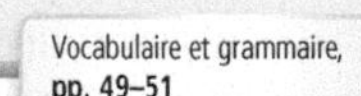

▶ **Vocabulaire supplémentaire,** Les produits de beauté, **p. R19**

le shampooing

le gel douche

la crème à raser

D'autres mots utiles

le déodorant	*deodorant*
se coiffer	*to do one's hair*
le peignoir	*robe*
le robinet	*faucet*
le rasoir électrique	*electric razor*

Vocabulaire 1

TPR — Total Physical Response

Have students respond to these commands.

Lève la main si tu te lèves tout de suite quand ton réveil sonne.

Mets la main sur la tête si tu as pris une douche ce matin.

Lève-toi si tu prends ton petit-déjeuner chaque matin.

Ask students to help you bring toiletries to class. Then have them respond to these commands.

Apporte-moi le savon!

Cherche une brosse à dents.

Montre-moi un peigne.

Finally, have volunteers mime activities while their classmates guess what they are doing.

Il se rase?

Tu prends un bain?

Elle se maquille?  1.2

Common Error Alert — Attention !

Students may find the expression **tous les deux** in the dictionary meaning *both*, but the phrase **tous les deux jours** means *every other day*, not *both days*.

Connections

Acquiring Information

Make students aware of French they may encounter in their everyday life. Have each student bring to class a toiletry item that has directions in both English and French on its label. Individuals will read aloud the French on their label without revealing the item. The rest of the class will guess what the item is. 3.1

Differentiated Instruction

Slower Pace Learners

Bring the toiletry items in **Vocabulaire** to class (toothbrush, toothpaste, bath towel, make-up items, and so on) and place them on a table at the front of the class. Make statements about personal grooming. **Je me brosse les dents.** Call on students to choose the items you will need to carry out that action. You might make it a game by dividing the class into teams and having two students at a time compete to grab as many of the necessary items as they can. 1.2

Multiple Intelligences

Logical-Mathematical After presenting **Exprimons-nous!,** ask students to estimate the time they take for each step in the morning preparations and calculate the total number of minutes. Survey the class to compare the preparation time. There may be significant differences among males and females and between teachers and students to discuss. 3.1

Resources

Planning:
Lesson Planner
Teacher One Stop

Presentation:
Projectable Transparencies **Vocabulaire 5.1, 5.2**
DVD Tutor, Disc 1 **Télé-vocab 1**
Interactive Whiteboard Lessons

Practice:
Cahier de vocabulaire et grammaire
Differentiated Practice and Assessment CD-ROM
Independent Study Guide
Media Guide
Audio CD 5, Tr. 1
@HOMETUTOR
Holt McDougal French Apps

Teacher Note

Point out to students that the verb **se sécher** has a spelling change. **(je me sèche, nous nous séchons)**

2 Script

1. — Lili, tu te réveilles à quelle heure?
   — Chaque matin, mon réveil sonne à six heures et demie. Je me lève tout de suite.
2. — Et tu t'habilles?
   — Pas tout de suite. D'abord, je prends une douche et je me sèche les cheveux.
3. — Et ensuite?
   — Ensuite, je me maquille.
4. — Et tu prends ton petit-déjeuner?
   — Oui, je prends mon petit-déjeuner en même temps que je finis mes devoirs.
5. — Et après ça?
   — Je me brosse les dents.
6. — Et après?
   — Et enfin je m'habille et je m'en vais!

1 Similarités 1.2

Écrivons Indique le terme qui n'appartient pas à la liste.

1. **a.** la brosse **(b.)** le gel douche **c.** le peigne
2. **a.** le gel douche **b.** le savon **(c.)** le robinet
3. **a.** le rouge à lèvres **b.** le maquillage **(c.)** le peignoir
4. **(a.)** un lavabo **b.** une douche **c.** un bain
5. **a.** la baignoire **(b.)** le réveil **c.** le lavabo

2 Écoutons CD 5, Tr. 1 1.2

Charlotte pose des questions à Lili au sujet de sa matinée. Indique quelles photos correspondent aux activités décrites par Lili.
1. e 2. c 3. a 4. f 5. b 6. d

a.

b.

c.

d.

e.

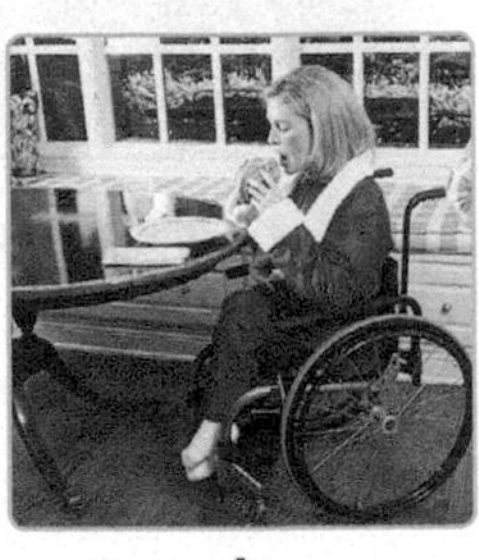
f.

Flash culture

En France, les jeunes vont à l'école à 8 heures ou à 9 heures. Certains rentrent à la maison pour déjeuner et d'autres mangent à la cantine. Ils finissent l'école vers 5 heures. Ensuite, ils font leurs devoirs. Ils dînent vers 8 heures avec leurs parents. Après le dîner, ils ont du temps libre pour jouer sur l'ordinateur, regarder la télé, ou faire autre chose et puis ils vont se coucher.

Comment s'organise ta journée? Est-ce qu'elle ressemble à la journée typique d'un adolescent français? 4.2

3 Ta matinée 1.2

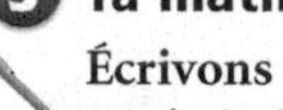

Écrivons Utilise les mots des deux boîtes pour décrire ta matinée. Écris cinq phrases et ajoute des détails.

MODÈLE Chaque matin, je me lève à six heures.

avant de	je me brosse
chaque matin	je m'habille
en même temps que	je me lave
en premier	je me lève
ensuite	je me maquille
pendant que	je prends une douche
	je prends mon petit-déjeuner

Core Instruction

TEACHING EXPRIMONS-NOUS!

1. Write the five expressions on the board or on a transparency. Read each one aloud, and ask students if they would use that expression with **un professeur** or **un copain. (1 min.)**
2. Ask two students to come to the board. Have a card with **professeur** written on one side and **élève** on the other. **(1 min.)**
3. Make a statement that includes a time and one of the phrases in **Vocabulaire** as you show one side of the card. **Il est 7h45 et je prends mon petit-déjeuner en même temps que je m'habille.** Students at the board should point to the appropriate response. Rotate students as you continue. **(5 min.)**

Exprimons-nous!

To express impatience

Dépêche-toi!	*Hurry up!*
Vous allez être en retard.	*You're going to be late.*
Tu es prêt(e)?	*Are you ready?*
Alors, on y va?	*So, shall we go?*
Arrête de traîner!	*Stop dragging your feet/dawdling!*

Vocabulaire et grammaire, pp. 49–51 Online Workbooks

4 Dépêche-toi! 1.2

Lisons Pour chaque situation, choisis la réaction la plus logique.

1. Il est 8h. Ton frère prend son petit-déjeuner. Le bus passe à 8h05.
   (a.) Dépêche-toi! **b.** Tu es prêt?
2. Tu vas à une fête et tu attends ta sœur. Elle se regarde dans le miroir pendant quinze minutes.
   a. Tu vas être en retard. (b.) Tu es prête?
3. En rentrant de l'école, ta sœur s'arrête devant toutes les vitrines de magasin *(store window)*.
   (a.) Arrête de traîner! **b.** Tu vas être en retard.
4. Tes amis et toi, vous allez au cinéma. Tout le monde est prêt.
   a. Arrête de traîner! (b.) Alors, on y va?
5. Ton/Ta meilleur(e) ami(e) a rendez-vous chez le docteur. Comme d'habitude il/elle n'est pas prêt(e).
   a. Alors, on y va? (b.) Tu vas être en retard.

Entre copains

se grouiller, se magner	*to hurry*
se fringuer	*to get dressed*
les fringues	*clothes*

Digital performance space

Communication

5 Scénario 1.1

Parlons Il est huit heures du matin, ton premier cours commence à huit heures vingt et tu es en retard. Ton père/Ta mère est très impatient(e) et dit qu'il faut te dépêcher. Réponds en disant ce que tu fais. Imagine cette conversation avec un(e) camarade. Ensuite, échangez les rôles.

Alors, on y va?	Arrête de traîner!	Attends...	Dépêche-toi!
Désolé(e)...	Pas encore...	Tu es prêt(e)?	Un moment...

MODÈLE —**Tu es prêt(e)?**
—**Pas encore. Je me rase.**

Cultures

Products and Perspectives

Cosmetics and perfumes are France's fourth largest export, after space and aeronautics, beverages, and automobiles. However, although over 200 countries worldwide import French cosmetic products, the French themselves are the world's biggest consumer of beauty products. Every day, almost half a million bath and shower products are sold in France, along with approximately 172,000 bottles of perfume. Ask students if they can think of brand names of any French cosmetics. 2.2

Communication

5 Group Activity: Interpersonal

Have students write down their morning routine. Then have them tell four other classmates their routine. After each statement, students should say whether they do the same thing.

MODÈLE:
— **Chaque matin je me réveille avec un réveil.**
— **Moi aussi, je me réveille avec un réveil.**
— **Ensuite, je prends une douche avec du savon.**
— **Moi non, je prends un bain avec du savon.**
1.1

Differentiated Instruction

ADVANCED LEARNERS

Have groups of students write the script for an episode of an imaginary TV program, called "Teen Swap", in which two teens from two very different families trade places for a week. One family gets up early and has a highly structured routine, while the other family likes to sleep late and has an unstructured routine. Have groups perform their episode for the class. 1.3

SPECIAL LEARNING NEEDS

Students with Auditory/Speech Impairments Help students to comprehend and use the expressions in **Exprimons-nous!** by asking them to create a list of situations in which the expressions would be appropriately used. After they complete the list, ask students to review each situation and choose the response that would possibly be used. The mini conversations can be acted out or written. 1.3

Assess

Assessment Program
Quiz: Vocabulaire 1
Alternative Assessment
Differentiated Practice and Assessment CD-ROM

Online Assessment
my.hrw.com

Test Generator 

Resources

Planning:
Lesson Planner
Teacher One Stop

Presentation:
DVD Tutor, Disc 1
Grammavision 1.1

Practice:
Grammar Tutor for Students of French, Chapter 5
Cahier de vocabulaire et grammaire
Differentiated Practice and Assessment CD-ROM
Cahier d'activités
Independent Study Guide
Media Guide
Projectable Transparencies
Bell Work 5.2
Audio CD 5, Tr. 2
HOMETUTOR

Bell Work

Use Bell Work 5.2 in the *Projectable Transparencies* or write this activity on the board.

Put these verbs in the right order.

1. s'habiller / se lever / se laver
2. se maquiller / s'en aller / prendre une douche
3. se sécher / se peigner / prendre un bain
4. déjeuner / se réveiller / se brosser les dents
5. se peigner / s'habiller / se réveiller 1.2

COMMON ERROR ALERT
ATTENTION !

Once they have learned about reflexives, students will tend to make every verb reflexive. This is especially true for verbs that refer to their daily activities such as **prendre un bain** and **faire la toilette.**

Objectifs
- reflexive verbs
- *tout, tous, toute, toutes*

Reflexive verbs

1 Reflexive verbs are used when the same person performs and receives the action of the verb. The **reflexive pronoun** helps you identify a reflexive verb.

Elle se brosse les cheveux. — *She is brushing her hair.*
Elle **brosse** le chat. — *She is brushing the cat.* (not reflexive)

2 To form a reflexive verb, use the correct form of the verb and the reflexive pronoun that agrees with the subject.

se laver	
je me lave	nous nous lavons
tu te laves	vous vous lavez
il/elle/on se lave	ils/elles se lavent

Je me brosse les cheveux pendant que ma sœur se maquille.

3 Place ne... pas around the reflexive pronoun and verb.

Je ne me peigne pas, je me brosse les cheveux.

Vocabulaire et grammaire, *pp. 52–53*
Cahier d'activités, *pp. 41–43*

En anglais 4.1

In English, to talk about parts of the body, you use possessive pronouns: *I wash my hands; I brush my teeth.*

In French, you often use the definite article **(le, la, l', les)** with body parts.

Je me lave **les** mains et je me brosse **les** dents.

I wash my hands and I brush my teeth.

In these French sentences, how do you know to whom the body part belongs when you see le, la, or les?

From the subject

6 Activités quotidiennes 1.2

Écrivons Choisis la forme correcte du verbe pour compléter chaque phrase.

1. Après le petit-déjeuner, on ______ les dents.
   a. nous brossons **(b.)** se brosse **c.** me brosse
2. Mais non! Mes cousins ne ______ pas.
   (a.) se maquillent **b.** te maquilles **c.** se maquille
3. Après ta douche, tu ______ les cheveux.
   a. vous séchez **b.** se sèche **(c.)** te sèches
4. Le matin, je ______ rapidement.
   (a.) me prépare **b.** nous préparons **c.** se préparent
5. Mon père et moi, nous ______ le soir.
   a. se rase **(b.)** nous rasons **c.** vous rasez

Core Instruction

TEACHING GRAMMAIRE

1. Explain Point 1 to students and give examples of reflexive verb conjugations. **(3 min.)**
2. Using reflexive verbs, model statements about your routine. **Je me réveille tôt. Je me lève à 5h30. (3 min.)**
3. Ask students **oui** or **non** questions about themselves. **Paul, tu te rases le matin? Marie, tu te réveilles avant tes parents? Les filles, vous vous séchez les cheveux avec un sèche-cheveux? (5 min.)**

Grammavision

For a video presentation of reflexive verbs, see the *DVD Tutor.*

Online Practice
my.hrw.com
Grammaire 1 practice

7 Écoutons CD 5, Tr. 2 1.2

Écoute ce qu'on fait chez Nathan aujourd'hui et pour chaque phrase, indique si c'est une action **a) réfléchie** ou **b) non réfléchie.** 1. b 2. a 3. b 4. a 5. b 6. a

8 Dans le bon ordre 1.2

Écrivons Mets les mots dans le bon ordre pour faire des phrases logiques. N'oublie pas de faire tous les changements nécessaires.

1. les cheveux / avec un sèche-cheveux / nous / se sécher / chaque matin
2. se réveiller / à 6h / je / le lundi matin
3. les dents / mes cousines / avant de partir à l'école / se brosser
4. tu / toujours / s'habiller / après le petit-déjeuner
5. ne… pas / Lisa / tous les matins / se maquiller
6. les cheveux / tous les soirs / se peigner / vous

9 Devinettes 1.2

Parlons/Écrivons Que font les personnes suivantes, d'après les photos?

MODÈLE **Nous nous brossons les dents.**

Nous

1. Lætitia

2. Laurie et Nathalie

3. Je

4. Vous

Digital performance space

Communication

10 Interview 1.1

Parlons Prépare une liste de six questions à poser à un(e) camarade de classe au sujet de sa routine. Ensuite, pose tes questions à ton/ta camarade, puis échangez les rôles.

MODÈLE **—Julie, à quelle heure est-ce que tu te réveilles le lundi?**
—Moi, je me réveille à 7h.
—Est-ce que tu te laves le matin ou le soir?

7 Script

See script on p. 155E.

8 Answers

1. Chaque matin, nous nous séchons les cheveux avec un sèche-cheveux.
2. Je me réveille à 6h le lundi matin.
3. Mes cousines se brossent les dents avant de partir à l'école.
4. Tu t'habilles toujours après le petit-déjeuner.
5. Lisa ne se maquille pas tous les matins.
6. Vous vous peignez les cheveux tous les soirs.

9 Answers

1. Lætitia se maquille.
2. Laurie et Nathalie se lavent les cheveux.
3. Je me rase.
4. Vous vous séchez les cheveux.

Communication

10 Pair Activity: Interpersonal

Have partners talk about the morning routine of their mother, father, or sibling. Have them mention three things this person does and three things that this person does not do. Ask students to include the expressions in **Exprimons-nous!** 1.1

Differentiated Instruction

SLOWER PACE LEARNERS

Teach students the forms of **se laver** by singing them to the tune of "Early in the Morning". ("This is the way we wash ourselves, wash ourselves, wash ourselves, [repeat] . . . early in the morning!"). The French version might be: **C'est comme ça que je me lave, que tu te laves, qu'il/elle se lave! que nous nous lavons, que vous vous lavez, qu'ils se lavent, qu'elles se lavent!** Alternatively, have volunteers come up with a rap song that uses the reflexive verb forms. 1.2

MULTIPLE INTELLIGENCES

Visual Visual learners would benefit from visual representations of several reflexive verbs in order to comprehend the difference between performing an action to or for oneself and to or for someone else. Ask students to draw pictures that depict a person brushing his or her own hair and brushing the hair of another person or pet. Give students a list of other situations that require a reflexive verb to distinguish the difference. Ask students to illustrate another verb and share it with a partner. 1.2

Resources

Planning:
Lesson Planner
Teacher One Stop

Presentation:
DVD Tutor, Disc 1
Grammavision 1.2

Practice:
Grammar Tutor for Students of French, Chapter 5
Cahier de vocabulaire et grammaire
Differentiated Practice and Assessment CD-ROM
Cahier d'activités
Independent Study Guide
Media Guide
Projectable Transparencies
Bell Work 5.3
@HOMETUTOR

Bell Work

Use Bell Work 5.3 in the *Projectable Transparencies* or write this activity on the board.

Complete the sentences with the correct reflexive pronoun.

1. Nous ____ réveillons à sept heures tous les matins.
2. Je ____ lève rapidement.
3. Après chaque repas, on ____ brosse les dents.
4. Tu ____ laves les cheveux avec ce shampooing?
5. Les hommes ne ____ maquillent pas, enfin!
6. Vous ____ rasez tous les jours? 1.2

Connections

Science Link

Give students a list of absolute statements related to personal health and hygiene, such as **Tout le monde devrait se brosser les dents trois fois par jour.** Have students research health experts' opinions on these statements. 3.1

Flash culture

Métro, boulot, dodo est l'expression typique pour symboliser la routine de la vie en France. Comme les grandes villes françaises, Rennes a un réseau de transport en commun bien développé. Rennes possède un métro qui traverse la ville en 16 minutes. Trois parcs relais sont à la disposition des automobilistes. On peut garer sa voiture dans un parc relais (parking surveillé et gratuit) et prendre le métro pour aller dans le centre-ville de Rennes.
Comment est le réseau des transports en commun de ta ville? 4.2

tout, tous, toute, toutes

1. To say *all* or *whole*, use tout. The form will agree with the noun in gender and number.

	SINGULAR	PLURAL
MASCULINE	tout	tous
FEMININE	toute	toutes

Toute ma famille se lève tôt.
My whole family gets up early.

2. Tout le monde means *everyone*. It uses the same verb form as **il** and **elle**.

Tout le monde est prêt? *Is everyone ready?*

Vocabulaire et grammaire, *pp. 52–53*
Cahier d'activités, *pp. 41–43*

11 Pas très originaux! 1.2

Écrivons Dans ton école, tout le monde fait la même chose le matin! Complète les phrases avec la forme de **tout** qui convient.

1. ______ les filles se maquillent! Toutes
2. ______ les garcons s'habillent à 7h! Tous
3. ______ le monde se prépare rapidement! Tout
4. ______ la classe prend une douche! Toute
5. ______ les élèves se réveillent à 6h45! Tous
6. ______ les professeurs de français se lavent les cheveux le soir! Tous

12 Points communs 1.2

Écrivons Trouve quelque chose que ces personnes ou ces choses ont en commun *(have in common)*. Utilise une forme de **tout** dans tes phrases.

MODÈLE les baignoires
Toutes les baignoires ont des robinets.

1. les élèves de ton lycée
2. les cours au lycée
3. les salles de bain
4. ta famille
5. le monde
6. tes amis

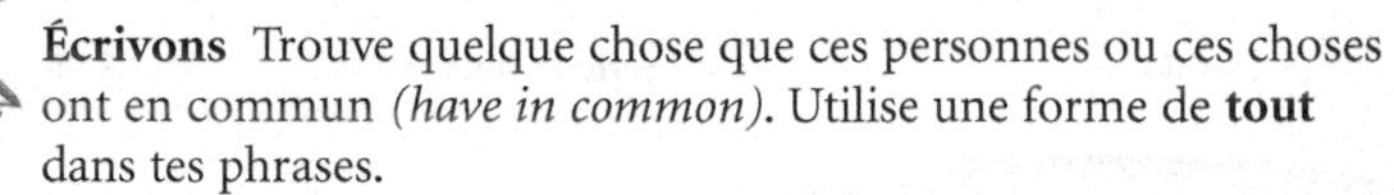

Core Instruction

TEACHING GRAMMAIRE

1. Go over Point 1, explaining the four forms of **tout** and agreement. **(2 min.)**
2. Ask students yes or no questions about themselves, the class, and so on. **Tout le monde parle anglais? Toutes les filles sont blondes? Tous les garçons portent un jean? Toutes les fenêtres sont fermées? (4 min.)**
3. Give each student four slips of paper. On each they will write one form of **tout.** With transparency **Vocabulaire 5.1,** point to a vocabulary word and say either the singular or plural form. The students will then hold up the correct **tout** form that matches the vocabulary word. **(3 min.)**

Grammavision

For a video presentation of **tout, tous, toute,** and **toutes,** see the *DVD Tutor.*

13 Comme c'est bizarre! 1.2

Parlons/Écrivons Décris ces illustrations. Utilise une forme de **tout** dans chaque phrase.

MODÈLE Toute la salle de bain est verte!

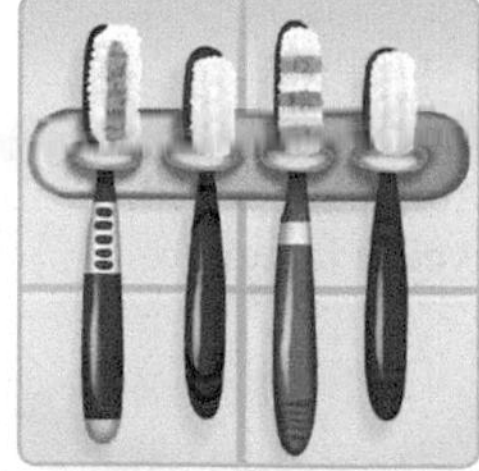
1.

2.

3.

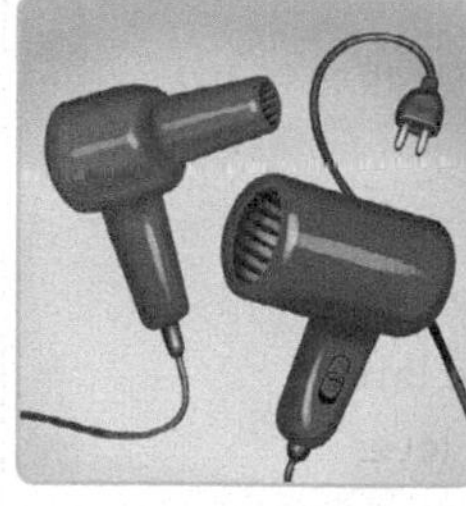
4.

5.

6.

14 Mon premier jour en France 1.3

Écrivons Tu étudies en France et aujourd'hui, c'est ton premier jour au lycée. Dans un e-mail à un(e) ami(e), décris ton nouveau lycée et tes nouveaux camarades.

MODÈLE Tous mes camarades sont... Toute la classe...

Communication

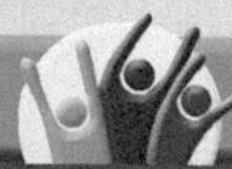

15 Scénario 1.1

Parlons Imagine que tu viens de passer un an dans un lycée à Rennes. Tous tes camarades américains ont des questions à te poser sur la France. Réponds à leurs questions et ensuite, échangez les rôles.

MODÈLE —Est-ce que toutes les salles de bain françaises ont des baignoires?
—Non, il y a aussi des salles de bain avec des douches…

13 Answers

1. Toutes les brosses à dents sont rouges!
2. Toutes les serviettes de bain sont bleues!
3. Tous les peignoirs sont jaunes!
4. Tous les sèche-cheveux sont violets!
5. Tout le maquillage est dans le lavabo!
6. Toute la famille/Tout le monde a les cheveux roux!

Communication

Pair Activity: Interpersonal

Have partners create a conversation in which one student asks questions in an accusing tone with an appropriate verb and a form of **tout.** The other partner responds by accepting blame or blaming someone else, using a form of **tout.** You may want to have students act out their conversation for the class. 1.1

Differentiated Instruction

ADVANCED LEARNERS

14 Find out if there are any francophone clubs such as the **Alliance française** in your area or if a nearby university French department hosts a French conversation table. Either take the entire class to participate in one of their meetings or have individual students go on their own time. Have students use the experience as the basis for their e-mail in the activity. 5.1

SPECIAL LEARNING NEEDS

Students with Dyslexia Ask students to create a chart with **tout, tous, toute, toutes,** and **tout le monde** as five headings across the top. Under each heading students should write at least two expressions in English and then in French that include these words. Students who struggle with new language concepts would be more successful completing this activity in a small group. 1.2

Assess

Assessment Program
Quiz: Grammaire 1
Alternative Assessment
Differentiated Practice and Assessment CD-ROM

Online Assessment
my.hrw.com

Test Generator

Resources

Planning:
Lesson Planner
Teacher One Stop

Practice:
Grammar Tutor for Students of French, Chapter 5
Cahier de vocabulaire et grammaire
Differentiated Practice and Assessment CD-ROM
Cahier d'activités
Independent Study Guide
Media Guide
Projectable Transparencies
Bell Work 5.4
Audio CD 5, Tr. 3

Bell Work

Use Bell Work 5.4 in the *Projectable Transparencies* or write this activity on the board.

Complete the sentences with the correct form of **tout.**

1. **____ ces dentifrices sont bon marché.**
2. **____ les brosses sont en solde.**
3. **____ le monde se lave le matin et le soir.**
4. **____ les serviettes sont marron.**
5. **____ la journée on est en cours.** 1.2

Synthèse
- **Vocabulaire 1**
- **Grammaire 1**

Application 1

16 La routine de ma famille 1.3

Écrivons Écris un paragraphe pour décrire la routine quotidienne de ta famille.

MODÈLE **Mes parents se réveillent à 6h. Moi, je me réveille à 6h30, mais mon frère, il ne se réveille jamais avant 7h…**

Un peu plus

The verbs *s'appeler* and *se lever*

There are spelling changes in all forms of the verbs **s'appeler** and **se lever** except the nous and vous forms.

	s'appeler *(to be named/called)*	**se lever** *(to get up)*
je	m'appe**ll**e	me l**è**ve
tu	t'appe**ll**es	te l**è**ves
il/elle/on	s'appe**ll**e	se l**è**ve
nous	nous appelons	nous levons
vous	vous appelez	vous levez
ils/elles	s'appe**ll**ent	se l**è**vent

Vocabulaire et grammaire, *p. 54*
Cahier d'activités, *pp. 41–43*

Déjà vu!

You already learned to conjugate verbs like **balayer** and **essayer**. When conjugating verbs that end in **-yer**, like **s'ennuyer,** remember to change the **"y"** to **"i"** in all forms except those of **nous** and **vous.**

s'ennuyer
je m'ennuie
tu t'ennuies
il/elle/on s'ennuie
nous nous ennuyons
vous vous ennuyez
ils/elles s'ennuient

17 La famille Martin 1.2

Écrivons Michel parle de sa famille. Lis ses réponses et pour chacune, imagine la question qu'on lui a posée.

MODÈLE Mes parents se lèvent à 8h et moi à 10h.
À quelle heure est-ce que vous vous levez?

1. Ma mère s'appelle Eugénie et mon père s'appelle Henri.
2. Le samedi, mon frère se lève souvent à midi.
3. Mon frère et moi, on ne s'ennuie jamais le samedi après-midi!
4. Non, mes parents font beaucoup de choses intéressantes le samedi.
5. Moi, je m'ennuie parfois le samedi soir.

17 Answers

1. Comment s'appellent tes parents?
2. À quelle heure est-ce que ton frère se lève le week-end?
3. Ton frère et toi, vous vous ennuyez parfois le samedi après-midi?
4. Tes parents s'ennuient le samedi?
5. Est-ce que tu t'ennuies le samedi soir?

Core Instruction

INTEGRATED PRACTICE

1. Go over Activity 16 to review previously presented material. **(8 min.)**
2. Ask the class to describe a typical girl's and a typical boy's routine. List the activities on the board. **(6 min.)**
3. Ask questions about the lists. **Les filles, vous prenez une douche en premier? Les garçons, vous vous rasez chaque matin avec un rasoir électrique? (4 min.)**
4. Introduce **Un peu plus. (4 min.)**

TEACHING UN PEU PLUS

1. Remind students that there are spelling changes in the present-tense "shoe" of **appeler** and **lever.** Point out the double *l* for **appeler** and the **accent grave** for **lever. (2 min.)**
2. Explain to students that they can hear the effect of the spelling changes. Model two sentences with each verb, talking about your friends and family. **(6 min.)**
3. Have students complete Activities 17–20. **(20 min.)**

Online Practice
my.hrw.com
Application 1 practice

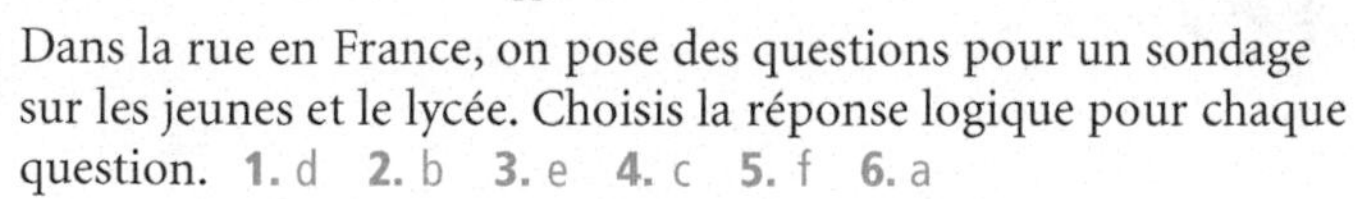

18 Écoutons CD 5, Tr. 3 1.2

Dans la rue en France, on pose des questions pour un sondage sur les jeunes et le lycée. Choisis la réponse logique pour chaque question. **1.** d **2.** b **3.** e **4.** c **5.** f **6.** a

a. Non, au contraire, ils sont très intéressants.
b. D'habitude, à six heures et quart.
c. Ils s'appellent Max et Émilie.
d. Je m'appelle Mégane Besson.
e. Le lycée Victor Hugo.
f. De temps en temps, oui, je m'ennuie.

19 Qu'est-ce que c'est? 1.2

Parlons/Écrivons Igor vient d'arriver à Rennes, mais il ne parle pas très bien le français. Lis les descriptions des choses qu'il veut acheter et dis-lui ce dont *(what)* il a besoin.

MODÈLE —C'est ce que j'emploie quand je me lave la figure.
—Tu as besoin de savon.

1. C'est le liquide que j'utilise quand je me lave les cheveux.
2. Ce sont les deux choses que j'utilise quand je me brosse les dents.
3. C'est le savon que j'utilise quand je prends une douche.
4. Ce sont les deux choses que j'utilise quand je me rase.
5. C'est la cloche *(clock)* qui sonne le matin.
6. C'est ce que j'emploie quand je me sèche les cheveux.

À la française

When you are not sure of a word in French, remember that you can use **circumlocution** to help you communicate. Try to paraphrase **(C'est un(e)...)**, use synonyms **(Ça ressemble à...)**, or describe essential elements **(On l'utilise pour...)**.

Digital performance space

Communication

20 Scénario 1.1

Parlons Imagine que tu es Arthur et tu décris ta routine matinale à un(e) camarade de classe. Ta camarade va te poser des questions. Ajoute des détails. Ensuite, échangez les rôles.

MODÈLE **—À quelle heure tu te lèves... ?**
—Moi, je...

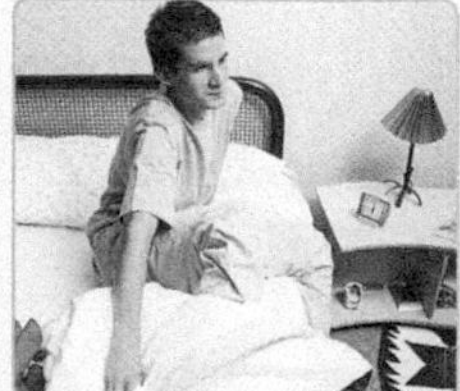

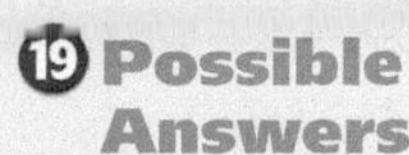

18 Script

See script on p. 155 E.

19 Possible Answers

1. Tu as besoin de shampooing.
2. Tu as besoin d'une brosse à dents et de dentifrice.
3. Tu as besoin de gel douche.
4. Tu as besoin d'un rasoir et de crème à raser.
5. Tu as besoin d'un réveil.
6. Tu as besoin d'un sèche-cheveux.

French for Spanish Speakers

Ask Spanish speakers which Spanish verbs correspond to **s'appeler** and **se lever. (llamarse** and **levantarse)** Ask if both verbs are used in the same way. (**Llamarse** and **s'appeler** both literally mean *to call oneself* and figuratively are used to ask and tell someone's name; **levantarse** and **se lever** are equivalent.) 4.1

Communication

20 Group Activity: Presentational

Ask partners to assume the roles of a celebrity and a reporter. The interview should be about the celebrity's daily routine. Have them present their interview to the class. 1.3

Differentiated Instruction

SLOWER PACE LEARNERS

17 Draw a chart on the board with daily-routine verbs written across the top and different times of the morning (**6h, 6h15, 6h30, 7h,** and so on) listed down the left side of the chart. Fill in the chart with your own family's names to show when each family member does each activity. Then write a model paragraph based on the information. Have students create a chart based on their own family's routine and use the information to write a similar paragraph.

 1.3

SPECIAL LEARNING NEEDS

Students with Learning Disabilities/ Dyslexia Spelling can be challenging for students, and using multi-sensory ways of remembering correct spelling can be helpful. While presenting **Un peu plus,** ask students to spell the words aloud and clap for each letter as they say it chorally or to trace the letters in the air with their fingers as they say each letter. Emphasis on the rhythm of the choral response assists with memory. 1.2

Assess

Assessment Program
Quiz: Application 1
Audio CD 5, Tr. 14
Alternative Assessment
Differentiated Practice and Assessment CD-ROM

Online Assessment
my.hrw.com

Test Generator

Resources

Planning:
Lesson Planner
Teacher One Stop

Practice:
Cahier d'activités

Vocabulaire supplémentaire

You might wish to use these terms to discuss the project with students.

le bord de l'assiette	*edge of the plate*
le centre (le milieu) de l'assiette	*center of the plate*
couper	*to cut*
dessiner	*to draw*
le dessin	*drawing, design*
décalquer le dessin	*to trace the design*
colorer	*to color*
l'atelier de poterie (m.)	*pottery shop*
l'argile (f.)	*potter's clay*
cuire au four	*to fire (pottery) in a kiln*

Culture

Faïence de Quimper

Culture appliquée

La faïence de Quimper 2.2

Si on visite la Bretagne, on peut voir partout[1] les mêmes personnages bretons et décorations sur les assiettes, les nappes et autres accessoires. La faïence[2] de Quimper existe depuis le 15e siècle. Aujourd'hui encore, chaque plat et assiette est fait de manière traditionnelle: peint et vernis[3] à la main et signé. Chaque pièce est donc unique.

1. everywhere 2. earthenware 3. glazed

Art breton 2.2

Materials
- color pencil or markers
- white paper plate
- sheet of paper, glue
- scissors

Step 1 Choose a design to go on the edge of your plate, and then choose a main design for the inside. You might choose a design inspired by a Quimper plate or create your own design. Draw them on a piece of paper and cut them out.

Step 2 Glue the different designs you have cut out as many times as you need on your paper plate.

Step 3 Color your paper plate. You can also go to a ceramic store and reproduce your design on a plate and have it glazed.

Est-ce qu'il y a d'autres types de faïencerie connue en France (porcelaine de Sèvres ou de Malicorne, par exemple)? Qu'est-ce qu'elles ont de particulier? 2.2

Core Instruction

CULTURE APPLIQUÉE

1. Have the class read and discuss the introductory paragraph and take note of glossed words. **(2 min.)**
2. Ahead of time, ask other French teachers or staff if they have any French earthenware or porcelain that you could borrow to share with students. Or, you might ask students to research museum Web sites, books, or encyclopedias to find pictures of French dishware to share with the class. **(10 min.)**

COMPARAISONS ET COMMUNAUTÉ

1. Have students read the introductory statement and discuss the correct answer. Do item 1 of **Et toi?** and have students group themselves by the way they get to school. Have students remain in these groups to read and discuss **Comparaisons. (10 min.)**
2. Have groups discuss the second question in **Et toi? (3 min.)**
3. Ask students to read and discuss **Communauté et professions. (4 min.)**

Comparaisons

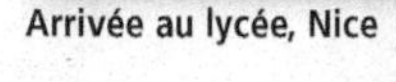
Arrivée au lycée, Nice

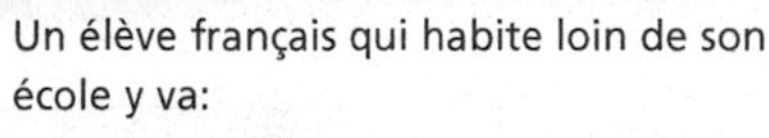

À pied, à vélo ou en bus? 4.2

Un élève français qui habite loin de son école y va:

a. en bus jaune, comme aux États-Unis.
b. à vélo.
c. en bus, en «pedibus» ou en «vélobus».

En France, les départements[1] organisent et financent les transports scolaires. Un ramassage scolaire[2] est organisé quand le trajet[3] est trop long. Beaucoup d'élèves vont aussi à l'école en voiture avec leurs parents. Depuis quelques années, il y a deux nouveaux types de ramassage scolaire: le «pedibus» et le «vélobus». Un adulte, à pied (pedibus) ou à vélo (vélobus), attend les élèves devant un panneau[4]. En chemin[5] vers l'école, le groupe «ramasse» d'autres élèves qui attendent devant d'autres panneaux. À partir de 14 ans, les jeunes peuvent aussi conduire une mobylette ou un scooter pour aller à l'école.

4.2

ET TOI?

1. Comment vas-tu à l'école? À pied, à vélo ou en bus? Ou est-ce que tes parents t'accompagnent?
2. Est-ce qu'il existe des systèmes comme le «pedibus» ou le «vélobus» dans ta région?

Communauté et professions

Le français et les produits de beauté 5.1

As-tu remarqué que de nombreux produits de toilette ou de beauté sont français? Certains ont même des instructions d'utilisation en français. Cherche dans ta salle de bain ou au supermarché de ton quartier les produits de toilette ou de beauté qui sont français ou dont les instructions d'utilisation sont en français. Partage les résultats de tes recherches avec ta classe.

Un salon de beauté

1. French administrative districts 2. school bus service 3. route 4. sign 5. on the way

Communities

Community Link

Have students organize a Bike-to-School Day at your school. Have small groups make posters in both French and English to display around the school. Students might also put together a booth to welcome students and faculty who bike to school that day. They might offer a small reward, such as a button, sticker, or a bottle of water with a message about Bike-to-School Day written in French and English on its label. 5.1

Cultures

Products and Perspectives

The rooster, the national bird of France, is a common emblem not just in the Brittany region, but throughout France. Its image is often used to decorate dinnerware. The connection to the rooster dates back to Roman times when the Latin word for *rooster* also meant *Gaul*, an early name for France. (This connection is also apparent in the Spanish language in which the word for *rooster* is **gallo.**) Napoleon tried to change the national bird from the rooster to the eagle, but the rooster remained a symbol of French pride and tenacity. Have students do research and compare the history of the French national bird to the American national bird, the bald eagle. 2.2

Differentiated Instruction

ADVANCED LEARNERS

Using their project plates, have groups of three students write a conversation between two people who take their plates to a professional appraiser on an antiques appraisal TV show. Have students present their conversations to the class. 1.3

MULTIPLE INTELLIGENCES

Interpersonal After they read **Comparaisons,** ask students to research the transportation support provided to students with disabilities in Canada or France. Students should find out if accessible buses are provided for students by the schools or if students with special needs must provide their own transportation. If the school provides the transportation, do they have separate buses or are the buses all students ride accessible to wheelchairs or other special needs? 2.1

Language Examination

Culture can be used to practice for the **Interpretive Communication** and **Presentational Writing** sections of the AP Language and Culture Exam as it helps students get acquainted with and reflect on products and practices from the French-speaking world while reading culture-focused passages and answering questions in French.

Resources

Planning:
Lesson Planner
Teacher One Stop

Presentation:

Projectable Transparencies
Vocabulaire 5.3, 5.4

DVD Tutor, Disc 1
Télé-vocab 2

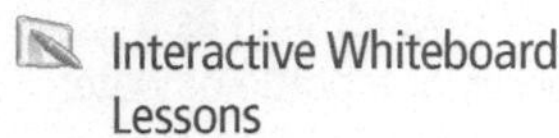

Interactive Whiteboard Lessons

Practice:
Cahier de vocabulaire et grammaire
Differentiated Practice and Assessment CD-ROM
Independent Study Guide
Media Guide
Projectable Transparencies
Bell Work 5.5
HOMETUTOR
Holt McDougal French Apps

Bell Work

Use Bell Work 5.5 in the *Projectable Transparencies* or write this activity on the board.

Answer the following questions.

1. **Comment t'appelles-tu?**
2. **Comment s'appellent tes frères et tes sœurs?**
3. **Tes parents et toi, à quelle heure vous levez-vous?**
4. **Est-ce que tes amis se lèvent tôt?**
5. **Comment s'appelle ton professeur de français?** 1.2

Connections

History Link

The word **bus** is short for **omnibus,** meaning **for everyone.** It is believed to have been coined by a Frenchman who took people by stagecoach to his public baths on the outskirts of Nantes. He dropped people off along the way, thus launching the world's first organized transportation system. Have students research the **omnibus** in Nantes. 3.1

Objectifs
- to say when you do things
- to make recommendations

Vocabulaire à l'œuvre 2

Télé-vocab

Dans la journée...

je prends le bus

je rentre à la maison

je fais mes devoirs

je m'occupe de mon petit frère

je range mes affaires

Core Instruction

TEACHING VOCABULAIRE

1. Introduce the vocabulary with transparencies **Vocabulaire 5.3** and **5.4** and model pronunciation. **(3 min.)**
2. Using as much of the vocabulary as you can, tell about yourself, pointing to the transparency where applicable. **Dans la journée, je... Le soir, je... (2 min.)**
3. Repeat your daily habits, giving more details and using the expressions in **Exprimons-nous!** Ask students **oui** or **non** questions about your habits. **(4 min.)**
4. Ask students similar questions about their daily habits. **(3 min.)**

Télé-vocab 2

For a video presentation of this vocabulary, see the *DVD Tutor.*

Télé-vocab

Online Practice
my.hrw.com
Vocabulaire 2 practice

Le soir...

Je me déshabille...

je me mets en pyjama

je fais ma toilette

je me couche

je m'endors

Exprimons-nous!

To say when you do things

Le lundi, je dois me lever **tôt** pour aller au lycée.

D'habitude, je me lève **de bonne heure.** *. . . early . . .*

Mes parents se couchent **tard.** *. . . late.*

Une fois que je me brosse les dents, je me mets en pyjama. *Once . . .*

Après ça, je vais me coucher. *Afterwards, . . .*

Je dois me coucher à 10 heures **au plus tard.** *. . . at the latest.*

Vocabulaire et grammaire, *pp. 55–57* Online Workbooks

► **Vocabulaire supplémentaire,** Les produits de soins et de beauté, **p. R19**

D'autres mots utiles

aller au lycée/au travail *to go to school/work*
souhaiter une bonne nuit *to say goodnight*
se laver la figure *to wash one's face*
se mettre au lit *to go to bed*
faire la sieste *to take a nap*
une chemise de nuit *nightgown*

TPR
Total Physical Response

Have students respond to these commands.

Lève le doigt si tu prépares ton sac quand c'est l'heure de partir.

Lève-toi si tu te mets au lit de bonne heure.

Touche ton nez si tu rentres à la maison tard.

Viens ici si tu t'occupes de ton petit frère ou de ta petite sœur.

Va au tableau et dessine un pyjama.

Then have students mime the following activities.

Il est temps de ranger tes affaires.

Tu t'endors en classe...

Assieds-toi et fais tes devoirs!

Lave-toi la figure.

Souhaite-nous une bonne nuit et couche-toi par terre.

1.2

Common Error Alert
Attention !

La figure is a false cognate. Students may think it sounds as though it refers to the shape of a person's body, but in French it refers only to the person's face.

Differentiated Instruction

Advanced Learners

Have students write questions for a game in which they guess each other's daily routine. **Complète la phrase: Le week-end, je me lève... de bonne heure? tard? ou pas avant midi?** Then have students pair up with classmates they think they know well. One partner will step out of the room. Read the questions aloud and have Student A answer the way he or she thinks Student B will respond. The partners with the most correct guesses win. 1.1

Multiple Intelligences

Spatial Ask students to draw a simple floor plan of a house on a large sheet of paper or poster board and label each room. In each room have students write phrases presented in **Vocabulaire 1** or **Vocabulaire 2.** The house will be full of activities conducted in each room when complete. The floor plans can be displayed or shared with the class. 1.2

Resources

Planning:
Lesson Planner
Teacher One Stop

Presentation:
Projectable Transparencies
Vocabulaire 5.3, 5.4
DVD Tutor, Disc 1
Télé-vocab 2

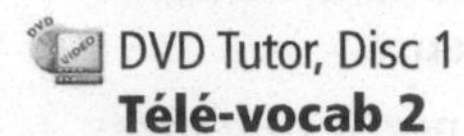

Interactive Whiteboard Lessons

Practice:
Cahier de vocabulaire et grammaire
Differentiated Practice and Assessment CD-ROM
Independent Study Guide
Media Guide
Audio CD 5, Tr. 4
@HOMETUTOR
Holt McDougal French Apps

22 Script

1. Je prépare mon sac avant d'aller au lycée.
2. Je me déshabille et je me mets en pyjama.
3. Je me mets au lit à dix heures et demie au plus tard.
4. Je prends le bus pour aller au lycée.
5. Après les cours, quand je rentre à la maison, je m'occupe de ma petite sœur.
6. Je range mes affaires avant de me coucher.
7. Je souhaite une bonne nuit à mes parents.

23 Possible Answers

1. Il se lève de bonne heure.
2. Il rentre à la maison tard.
3. Il fait la sieste dans la journée.
4. Il fait ses devoirs le soir.
5. Une fois qu'il a fait ses devoirs, il se met en pyjama.
6. Il s'endort à 11h au plus tard.

Flash culture

Le goûter, aussi appelé le «quatre heures» est typique des enfants français. Après l'école, les enfants mangent quelque chose pour «tenir» jusqu'au dîner. Le goûter peut être soit une simple tartine ou un pain au chocolat. Certains jeunes aiment aussi boire un yaourt liquide pour le goûter.

Et toi, est-ce que tu manges quelque chose en rentrant de l'école? Quoi? 4.2

21 En premier… ensuite… 1.2

Lisons Range les activités suivantes par ordre chronologique.

4 **a.** Alors, on dîne en famille vers huit heures.
1 **b.** Après l'école, je rentre à la maison vers quatre heures.
2 **c.** Je prépare le goûter pendant que mon frère s'occupe de notre petite sœur.
5 **d.** Après le dîner, je finis mes devoirs pendant que mes parents lisent le journal.
7 **e.** Je me couche à dix heures au plus tard.
3 **f.** Mes parents rentrent à la maison vers six heures.
6 **g.** Plus tard, je fais ma toilette et me mets en pyjama.

22 Écoutons CD 5, Tr. 4 1.2

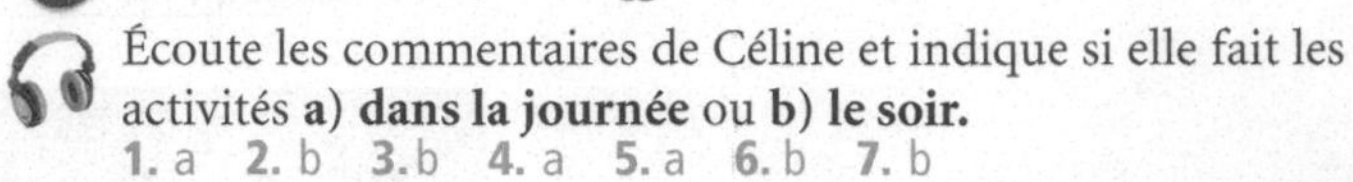

Écoute les commentaires de Céline et indique si elle fait les activités **a) dans la journée** ou **b) le soir.**
1. a **2.** b **3.** b **4.** a **5.** a **6.** b **7.** b

23 La journée de Yann 1.2

Parlons/Écrivons Qu'est-ce que Yann fait la journée et le soir? Décris ses activités en utilisant les expressions de la boîte.

MODÈLE Il s'occupe de son frère.

au plus tard	dans la journée	de bonne heure	le soir
tard	tôt	une fois que	

1.

2.

3.

4.

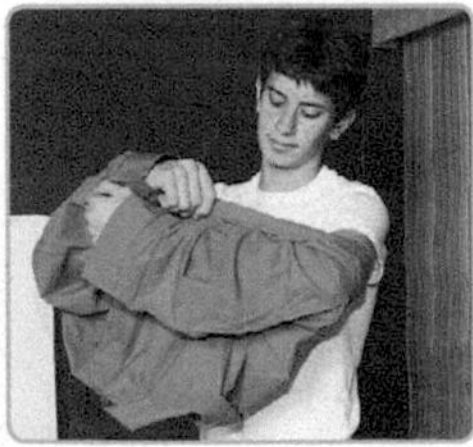

5.

6.

Core Instruction

TEACHING EXPRIMONS-NOUS!

1. Give each student a large index card. Using the expressions, have each student write a recommendation. Tell students to use different infinitive phrases than those in the text. **(4 min.)**
2. Say a time of the day or evening. If a student can respond appropriately with his or her card, he or she raises it. **Il est 3h45.** (Possible response: **C'est l'heure de rentrer à la maison.**) **(6 min.)**
3. Have volunteers write a time in French on the board. Make a recommendation for an activity or habit for each time and have students tell you whether the recommendations are logical. Tell students that these times can be either evening or morning. **(4 min.)**

Exprimons-nous!

To make recommendations

Tu devrais te brosser les dents. *You should . . .*

Va te coucher. **Il est tard.** *Go . . . It's late.*

Il est temps de se préparer.
C'est l'heure d'aller te coucher. *It's time to*

Vocabulaire et grammaire, *pp. 55–57* 

24 Recommandations 1.2

Écrivons/Parlons Tu fais du baby-sitting et l'enfant, qui a quatre ans, est très difficile. Réponds à ses commentaires avec des recommandations utiles.

1. —Je déteste le petit-déjeuner!
   —_____ prendre un petit-déjeuner tous les matins. Tu devrais
2. —Je ne veux pas me préparer pour aller à l'école!
   —Mais _____ de te préparer. Le bus va arriver dans vingt minutes. il est temps *or* c'est l'heure
3. —Je ne veux pas prendre le bus!
   —Tu _____ partir. Le bus ne va pas t'attendre. devrais
4. —_____ faire la sieste après l'école. Alors, plus d'excuses. Tu devrais

Entre copains

le boulot	*job*
pioncer, roupiller	*to snooze*
le plumard	*bed*

25 Des conseils 1.3

Écrivons Une élève française va passer un mois chez toi. Donne-lui cinq conseils qui vont l'aider à profiter de son séjour.

Communication

Digital performance space

26 Interviews 1.1

Parlons Avec un(e) camarade, écrivez cinq questions sur les activités que vous faites dans la journée. Ensuite, interviewez quatre camarades et faites un tableau de leurs réponses.

MODÈLE —**Tu vas au travail après les cours?**
—**Le samedi, tu te lèves de bonne heure?**

Questions	*Camarades de classe* Adèle	Clément	Salima	Bosco
Tu vas au travail?	oui	non	non	oui
Tu te lèves de bonne heure?	oui; à 7 heures	non; à 10 heures	non; vers 8h30	oui; à 6 heures

Chapitre 5
Vocabulaire 2

Communities

Community Link

Tell students about the International Youth Hostel Association which provides inexpensive lodging for young international travelers. Each hostel has a set curfew and a lock-out time that must be observed. Have students research how to apply to be a member of the IYHA and the curfew times of one of the member hostels. 5.2

Communication

26 Pair Activity: Interpersonal

Have students write six activities that they do during a normal day and at what time. Their partner should give them advice related to each of these activities.

MODÈLE
— À 6h30 je prends une douche.
— Tu devrais utiliser du savon.
— À 7h je prépare mon sac.
— Tu devrais mettre tes livres et tes devoirs dans ton sac. 1.1

Differentiated Instruction

SLOWER PACE LEARNERS

25 Draw a large schoolhouse on the board, leaving room to write inside the school. Then have the class suggest things students should do to succeed both in and out of school. Write their ideas for succeeding in school inside the schoolhouse drawing. Write ideas for outside-of-school success outside the drawing. 1.3

MULTIPLE INTELLIGENCES

26 Intrapersonal Give students the option of writing their own responses rather than conducting the interviews in the activity. Have students follow the activity directions but complete the chart with information about themselves and family members with whose routines they are familiar or create characters and invent their responses. 1.3

Assess

Assessment Program
Quiz: Vocabulaire 2
Alternative Assessment
Differentiated Practice and Assessment CD-ROM
Online Assessment
my.hrw.com
Test Generator 

Resources

Planning:
Lesson Planner
Teacher One Stop

Presentation:
DVD Tutor, Disc 1
Grammavision 2.1

Practice:
Grammar Tutor for Students of French, Chapter 5
Cahier de vocabulaire et grammaire
Differentiated Practice and Assessment CD-ROM
Cahier d'activités
Independent Study Guide
Media Guide
Projectable Transparencies
Bell Work 5.6
@HOMETUTOR

Bell Work

Use Bell Work 5.6 in the *Projectable Transparencies* or write this activity on the board.

Match the following words or expressions with their synonyms.

1. se mettre au lit
2. de bonne heure
3. faire sa toilette
4. boulot

a. se nettoyer
b. se coucher
c. tôt
d. travail

1.2

Objectifs
- reflexive verbs in the *passé composé*
- the imperative with reflexive verbs

Grammavision

Reflexive verbs in the *passé composé*

1 All reflexive verbs use **être** in the **passé composé**.

Il **s'est levé** et ensuite il **s'est habillé**.

2 In most cases, the past participle agrees with the reflexive pronoun (and the subject) in gender and number.

se laver			
je	me suis lavé(e)	nous	nous sommes lavé(e)s
tu	t'es lavé(e)	vous	vous êtes lavé(e)(s)
il/elle/on	s'est lavé(e)(s)	ils/elles	se sont lavé(e)s

Julia s'est lev**ée** en premier et ensuite, Théo s'est lev**é**. Nous nous sommes lev**és** après.

3 The past participle only agrees with the reflexive pronoun when it is the direct object of the verb. Sometimes, you can tell it is *not* the direct object if there is another direct object in the sentence.

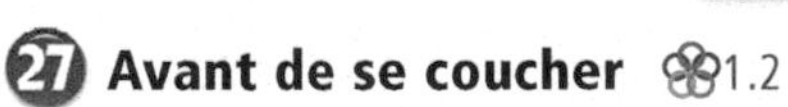

Iris s'est lav**ée.** BUT Iris s'est lavé les cheveux.

Vocabulaire et grammaire, *pp. 58–59*
Cahier d'activités, *pp. 45–47*

Flash culture

Les Français font leurs courses de plus en plus dans des supermarchés et vont de moins en moins dans les petits magasins. Par conséquent, ils font leurs courses de moins en moins souvent. Cependant, la plupart des Français achètent leur pain quotidiennement à leur boulangerie préférée.

Où est-ce que ta famille fait ses courses? 4.2

Une boulangerie à Rennes

27 Avant de se coucher 1.2

Écrivons Voilà ce que les Floret ont fait avant de se coucher. Complète chaque phrase avec un verbe logique au passé composé.

1. Aude _______ avec sa brosse. s'est brossé les cheveux
2. Aude et Frédéric _______ les dents. se sont brossé
3. Madame Floret et Aude _______. Aude a pris une douche et madame Floret a pris un bain. se sont lavées
4. Les enfants _______ et ont mis leurs pyjamas. se sont déshabillés
5. Madame Floret _______ les cheveux avec le sèche-cheveux après son bain. s'est séché
6. Toute la famille _______ vers 11 heures. s'est couchée

Core Instruction

TEACHING GRAMMAIRE

1. Explain to students how to form the **passé composé** of reflexive verbs with **être. (2 min.)**
2. Using reflexive verbs in the **passé composé,** make statements about yourself and other students in class, being sure to use words that cue the past tense. **Hier, Paul s'est levé à 7h. Ce matin, je me suis lavé les cheveux. (3 min.)**
3. Bring in two pictures from magazines that show someone neat and clean and someone dirty or sloppily dressed. Give each a French name and ask **oui** or **non** questions about them. **Paul s'est bien habillé? Marie s'est lavée ce matin? (3 min.)**

Grammavision

For a video presentation of reflexive verbs in the **passé composé,** see the *DVD Tutor.*

Grammavision

Online Practice
my.hrw.com
Grammaire 2 practice

28 Déjà fait! 1.2

Parlons/Écrivons Monsieur Richard demande à ses enfants et à sa femme ce qu'ils font ce matin, mais ils ont déjà fait tout ce qu'il mentionne. Donne les réponses de la famille Richard.

MODÈLE Cyril et Jean, vous vous levez?
Nous nous sommes déjà levés!

1. Chérie, tu te maquilles?
2. Julia et Jean, vous vous réveillez?
3. Julia et Myrna, vous vous habillez?
4. Myrna, tu te laves la figure?
5. Jean et Cyril, vous vous brossez les dents?

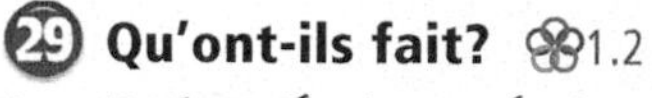

29 Qu'ont-ils fait? 1.2

Parlons/Écrivons Écris ce qui se passe sur les photos. Utilise le sujet donné et un verbe réfléchi au passé composé.

MODÈLE **Les filles se sont maquillées.**

les filles

1. Vous

2. Gérard

3. Moi, je

4. Toi, tu

30 Chez toi hier soir 1.3

Écrivons Écris un paragraphe pour décrire ce que tu as fait hier soir avant de te coucher. Utilise le passé composé.

MODÈLE **Hier soir, j'ai pris un bain... Je me suis lavé...**

Communication

Digital performance space

31 Questions personnelles 1.1

Parlons Fais une liste de six choses que toi et ta famille avez faites à la maison ce matin. Ensuite, prépare six questions à poser à un(e) camarade pour savoir si sa famille a fait les mêmes choses que ta famille.

MODÈLE — **Bryan, est-ce que ton père s'est réveillé à 6h?**
— **Oui, mais ma mère s'est levée à 7h.**

Differentiated Instruction

ADVANCED LEARNERS

Have students create a mystery game about an antique comb that was stolen by one of the overnight guests. On separate cards, students should describe each character and what the person did. One of the cards will be for the "thief". Another card will be for the detective and will include clues to the thief's identity. Distribute the cards to students. The detective should interview each one. Groups should then work together to determine the identity of the thief. 1.1

SPECIAL LEARNING NEEDS

27 Students with Language Impairments/Dyslexia Prior to assigning the activity, you might modify the assignment by making a copy of the page and enlarging the text. Create a word bank of possible verbs that would fit in the blanks and type them on a worksheet. Ask students to use the worksheet to fill in the blanks with the logical verbs in the **passé composé.** 1.2

28 Answers

1. Je me suis déjà maquillée!
2. Nous nous sommes déjà réveillés!
3. Nous nous sommes déjà habillées!
4. Je me suis déjà lavé la figure!
5. Nous nous sommes déjà brossé les dents!

29 Answers

1. Vous vous êtes lavé les mains.
2. Gérard s'est déshabillé.
3. Moi, je me suis lavé la figure.
4. Toi, tu t'es rasé.

French for Spanish Speakers

Ask Spanish speakers to compare **Ne vous couchez pas tard!** with the Spanish equivalent **¡No se acuesten tarde!** Ask students what they notice about the placement of the reflexive pronouns. (Both come before the verb and after the negation words **ne** and **no.**) Ask students the differences in the affirmative forms. (In **Couchez-vous!** the reflexive pronoun goes after the verb and is attached by a hyphen. In **¡Acuéstense!** the reflexive pronoun is part of the word and is also added to the end. A written accent is added to the second syllable to preserve the original stress.) 4.1

Communication

Group Activity: Interpersonal

Have each student write eight sentences to tell what he or she did yesterday after school. Then have students ask a partner if he or she did the same thing. The partner should respond in a complete sentence. Students should write **oui** or **non** after their sentences to represent their partner's answers. 1.1

Resources

Planning:
Lesson Planner
Teacher One Stop

Presentation:
DVD Tutor, Disc 1
Grammavision 2.2

Practice:
Grammar Tutor for Students of French, Chapter 5
Cahier de vocabulaire et grammaire
Differentiated Practice and Assessment CD-ROM
Cahier d'activités
Independent Study Guide
Media Guide
Projectable Transparencies
Bell Work 5.7
Audio CD 5, Tr. 5
@HOMETUTOR

Bell Work

Use Bell Work 5.7 in the *Projectable Transparencies* or write this activity on the board.

Complete the sentences with the correct **passé composé** form of the verbs in parentheses.

1. Jérôme, tu ____ (s'occuper) de ton frère hier?
2. Je ____ (s'endormir) tout de suite.
3. Vous ____ (se réveiller) très tôt.
4. Myriam ____ (se brosser) les cheveux.
5. Nous ____ (s'habiller) rapidement.
6. Julie et Iris ____ (se maquiller) avant de sortir. 1.2

32 Script

See script on p. 155E.

Déjà vu!

You can use **tu, vous,** or **nous** commands. Use the appropriate form of the verb without the pronoun **tu, vous,** or **nous**.

Tu prends ton livre. → **Prends** ton livre.

Vous prenez vos livres. → **Prenez** vos livres.

Nous prenons nos livres. → **Prenons** nos livres.

Remember to drop the final **-s** from the **tu** commands of **-er** verbs.

Tu rentre**s** tôt. → Rentre tôt.

The imperative with reflexive verbs

1 When you make a **negative command** using a reflexive pronoun, place the reflexive pronoun immediately *before* the verb.

Ne **te** lève pas!	*Don't get up!*
Ne **vous** couchez pas tard!	*Don't go to bed late!*
Ne **nous** dépêchons pas!	*Let's not hurry!*

2 When you make an **affirmative command** using a reflexive verb, attach the reflexive pronoun to the *end* of the verb with a hyphen. Notice that **te** becomes **toi** in this situation.

Lève-toi!	*Get up!*
Couchez-vous!	*Go to bed!*
Dépêchons-nous!	*Let's hurry!*

Vocabulaire et grammaire, ***pp. 58–59***
Cahier d'activités, ***pp. 45–47***

32 Écoutons CD 5, Tr. 5 1.2

Trouve la continuation logique à chaque phrase que tu entends. Attention! Toutes les réponses ne vont pas être utilisées!
1. e **2.** d **3.** b **4.** f **5.** a

a. Brosse-toi les dents!
b. Lève-toi!
c. Sèche-toi les mains!
d. Prends ton petit-déjeuner!
e. Couchez-vous!
f. Dépêchez-vous!

33 Six conseils pour une meilleure vie 1.2

Écrivons Madame Rigaudet donne quelques conseils à ses petits-enfants. Complète ses conseils avec l'impératif des verbes entre parenthèses. Il faut choisir logiquement entre la forme affirmative et la forme négative des verbes.

1. Marina, lève-toi tôt tous les jours et fais du sport! (se lever)
2. Georges et Marina, ne vous couchez pas trop tard ce soir! (se coucher)
3. Vous et moi, ____ bien de notre famille et de nos amis. (s'occuper) occupons-nous
4. Georges et Marina, ____ tout le temps! Ce n'est pas bon! (se dépêcher) ne vous dépêchez pas
5. Georges, ____ tous les jours. (se raser) rase-toi
6. Marina, lave-toi les mains avant de passer à table. (se laver)

Core Instruction

TEACHING GRAMMAIRE

1. Read **Déjà vu** aloud with the class and have students review forming commands. Go over Point 1. Explain the word order in affirmative and negative commands and model additional examples with **ne... pas. (3 min.)**
2. Give commands to students to pantomime. Use all three forms and include yourself. **Lavons-nous! Marie, maquille-toi! Séchez-vous les mains! (3 min.)**
3. When the students become more familiar with the verbs and commands, play **Jacques a dit,** using **vous** forms. You might have a small prize for the winner. **(5 min.)**

Grammavision

For a video presentation of the imperative with reflexive verbs, see the *DVD Tutor.*

Grammavision

34 Incroyable! 1.2

Écrivons/Parlons Tout le monde fait des choses bizarres aujourd'hui! Dis-leur ce qu'ils ne doivent pas faire.

MODÈLE **Calypso, ne te couche pas sur la table!**

Calypso

1. Noëlle et Firmin

2. Zelda

3. Nous

4. Maui et Maya

5. Vous

6. Karine

35 Avant l'interro 1.3

Écrivons Tu écris un article pour le journal de ton lycée. À ton avis, qu'est-ce qu'on doit faire pour se préparer avant une interrogation? Donne cinq conseils.

MODÈLE **Ne vous couchez pas tard!**

Communication

36 Scénario 1.1

Parlons Imagine que tu fais du baby-sitting pour une famille française ce soir. Malheureusement, les trois enfants, Hugo, Luc et Florence, sont impossibles! Tu leur demandes de se préparer pour aller au lit, mais ils n'ont pas envie de se coucher et ils ne t'écoutent pas.

MODÈLE — **Hugo, déshabille-toi et couche-toi!**
— **Non, je ne me couche jamais de bonne heure! Je préfère lire.**

Grammaire 2

34 Answers

1. Noëlle et Firmin, ne vous brossez pas les cheveux avec une brosse à dents!
2. Zelda, ne te couche pas à 9h30 du matin!
3. Ne nous dépêchons pas!
4. Maui et Maya, ne vous couchez pas sur mes devoirs!
5. Ne vous rasez pas avec du déodorant!
6. Karine, ne te maquille pas avec mon rouge à lèvres!

Communication

36 Group Work: Interpersonal

Have groups of three students create a conversation involving a parent, an obedient child, and a rebellious child. The parent gives commands to the obedient child who responds (in the present tense) that he or she is doing what is requested. The rebellious child tells the obedient child not to do what the parent says. Have each group present their conversation to the class with no written support.

MODÈLE
— **Tony, lève-toi!**
— **Oui, je me lève.**
— **Ne te lève pas!** 

Differentiated Instruction

SLOWER PACE LEARNERS

Bring props to class that will prompt the command forms of personal grooming verbs such as pajamas for **Habille-toi!**, a messy wig for **Brosse-toi les cheveux!**, and so on. Ask students to dress up in the props and stand in a row for a military-style "inspection." The rest of the class will play the role of "officers" who inspect their "troops," and tell them what they need to do. Then switch roles, with the first group now giving the commands. 1.1

MULTIPLE INTELLIGENCES

Bodily-Kinesthetic After teaching the commands with reflexives, create a set of note cards with an affirmative or negative command written on each card. The English translation could be written on the back of each card. Ask students to take turns selecting a card from the stack and acting out the command. The class will guess the command from the gestures. You might give a list of possible commands and translations and instruct students to respond in French. 1.2

Assess

Assessment Program
Quiz: Grammaire 2
Alternative Assessment
Differentiated Practice and Assessment CD-ROM

Online Assessment
my.hrw.com

Test Generator 

Resources

Planning:
Lesson Planner
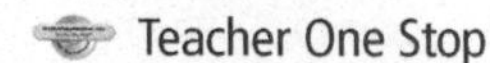
Teacher One Stop

Practice:
Grammar Tutor for Students of French, Chapter 5
Cahier de vocabulaire et grammaire
Differentiated Practice and Assessment CD-ROM
Cahier d'activités
Independent Study Guide
Media Guide
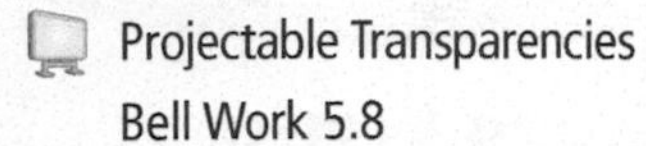
Projectable Transparencies
Bell Work 5.8
Audio CD 5, Tr. 6

Bell Work

Use Bell Work 5.8 in the *Projectable Transparencies* or write this activity on the board.

Use the imperative of the correct verb to complete the sentences.

s'occuper se raser se laver se coucher se lever

1. **Nous sommes très fatigués, alors _____ .**
2. **Tu es très sale! _____ .**
3. **Alice et Sophie, _____ de votre petit frère.**
4. **Tous les matins, vous êtes en retard? _____ plus tôt!**
5. **Tu veux avoir une moustache? _____ !** 1.2

37 Script

See script on p. 155F.

39 Answers

1. Le professeur de français va s'occuper des élèves francophones.
2. Les élèves de la classe vont se dépêcher pour être à l'heure en cours.
3. Nous allons nous coucher de bonne heure pour nous préparer pour l'interro.
4. Vous, les profs, vous allez vous habiller pour la cérémonie.
5. Moi, je vais me réveiller à 6h.
6. Et toi, tu vas te préparer avant de venir à la réunion.

Synthèse
- Vocabulaire 2
- Grammaire 2

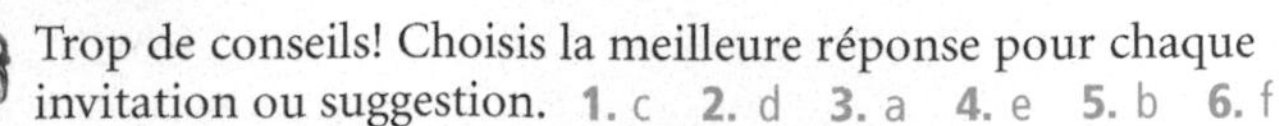

Application 2

37 Écoutons CD 5, Tr. 6 1.2

Trop de conseils! Choisis la meilleure réponse pour chaque invitation ou suggestion. 1. c 2. d 3. a 4. e 5. b 6. f

a. Oui, et je vais préparer mon sac aussi.
b. Oui, mais je dois m'occuper de mon frère.
c. Non, elle va faire ses devoirs.
d. Non, ils doivent étudier.
e. Je me couche assez tôt.
f. Tu ne peux pas. Tu dois faire les courses.

38 Vive les vacances! 1.3

Écrivons Imagine que ta famille et toi, vous partez une semaine à la Guadeloupe! Écris un petit mot à ta famille pour dire à tout le monde ce qu'il faut faire et ne pas faire pour être prêt de bonne heure. Utilise l'impératif.

MODÈLE Claire et Tara: Lavez-vous ce soir.

Un peu plus

Reflexive verbs with infinitives

1. When using a reflexive verb in the infinitive form in a sentence, remember to use the reflexive pronoun that agrees with the subject.

   Moi, je dois **me** lever à huit heures, mais mes sœurs aiment **se** lever tard.

2. Form the immediate future by using a form of the verb aller with the reflexive pronoun plus an infinitive.

   À quelle heure est-ce que vous allez **vous** coucher?

Vocabulaire et grammaire, *p. 60*
Cahier d'activités, *pp. 45–47*

39 Les responsabilités de chacun 1.2

Écrivons Fais des phrases au futur proche avec les éléments donnés.

1. professeur de français / s'occuper / élèves francophones
2. élèves de la classe / se dépêcher / pour être à l'heure en cours
3. nous / se coucher de bonne heure / pour se préparer pour l'interro
4. vous, les profs / s'habiller / pour la cérémonie
5. moi, je / se réveiller / à 6h
6. et toi, tu / se préparer / avant de venir à la réunion

Core Instruction

INTEGRATED PRACTICE

1. Go over Activities 37–38 to review vocabulary and commands. **(5 min.)**
2. Tell students to imagine they are baby-sitting two children who need to get ready for school. What will they say to each of them? to both of them? Encourage students to use commands as well as ask questions. **(6 min.)**
3. Have students role-play what they would say to their baby-sitter. **(4 min.)**
4. Present **Un peu plus** and do Activities 39–42.

TEACHING UN PEU PLUS

1. Remind students that if they use a reflexive verb in the infinitive, they must use the reflexive pronoun that agrees with the subject. The immediate future can be formed this way with **aller. (3 min.)**
2. Ask students questions with reflexive verbs in the infinitive. **À quelle heure est-ce que tu vas te lever? Vous devez vous habiller en robe pour aller à l'église? Paul, il doit s'occuper de son chien? (5 min.)**

Online Practice
my.hrw.com
Application 2 practice

40 Qu'est-ce qu'ils vont donc faire? 1.2

Écrivons D'après toi, qu'est-ce que ces gens vont faire ce soir?

MODÈLE Mademoiselle Laugier s'est réveillée à 4h du matin.
Elle va se coucher de bonne heure.

1. Je n'ai pas eu le temps de prendre une douche ce matin.
2. La fille de Laurence est malade (*sick*).
3. Les enfants Garcia ont écrit sur leurs mains avec des stylos.
4. Tu as mangé du chocolat pour le dessert.
5. Vous êtes très fatigués.

41 Qu'est-ce qui s'est passé la semaine dernière? 1.3

Écrivons Pense à tout ce que tu as fait la semaine dernière et réponds aux questions suivantes.

Qu'est-ce que tu as fait...

1. à 10h samedi matin?
2. à 8h vendredi soir?
3. à midi dimanche?
4. à 7h mercredi matin?
5. à 11 h jeudi soir?
6. à 9h lundi matin?

Communication

42 Routine du matin 1.1

Parlons Avec ton/ta camarade, vous parlez de ce que vous faites le matin typiquement. Lisez les questions ci-dessous et répondez-y de manière logique. Ensuite, échangez les rôles.

— **Tu te lèves à quelle heure?**
—
— **Qu'est-ce que tu fais avant de partir au lycée?**
—
— **À quelle heure tu pars au lycée?**
—
— **Quand est-ce que tu ranges tes affaires?**
—

Application 2

Communication

Group Work: Interpersonal

Have students create a question and answer chain with **devoir** and **aller.** One student asks a classmate if he or she has to do something **(devoir)** related to his or her daily routine. The classmate responds with **aller** and then asks another student a question, using **devoir.** The chain continues until everyone has participated. 1.1

Activité Pré-AP Préparatoire — Language Examination

42 Sample answer:

— . . .
— **Je me lève à 7 heures.**
— . . .
— **Je prends mon petit-déjeuner avant de prendre ma douche. Ensuite, je m'habille.**
— . . .
— **Je pars vers 8 heures.**
— . . .
— **Je range mes affaires avant de me coucher.**

Differentiated Instruction

ADVANCED LEARNERS

Have students create a videotape about a day in the life of an American teenager. Students will share one videotape, each student taping a segment about his or her own daily routine. You might contact a partner school in a French-speaking country to see if they would like to do the same project and then exchange videotapes. 4.2

MULTIPLE INTELLIGENCES

Interpersonal Ask students to use the vocabulary and grammar presented in the chapter to create a simple children's picture book. The book should describe activities a child does during the day and recommendations a parent might make to the child. Have students illustrate their books, share them with the class, and keep them in the classroom as a resource for studying vocabulary. 1.3

Assess

Assessment Program
Quiz: Application 2
Audio CD 5, Tr. 15
Alternative Assessment
Differentiated Practice and Assessment CD-ROM

Online Assessment
my.hrw.com

Test Generator 

Resources

Planning:
Lesson Planner
 Teacher One Stop

Presentation:
 DVD Tutor, Disc 1
Télé-roman

Practice:
Media Guide
DVD Tutor, Disc 1
Télé-roman

Connections

Visual Learners

To help students understand the events of this episode, draw a chart on the board. Write the names of the characters in this episode across the top. Down the left side, have students brainstorm things people do in this episode. Then have them write an X under the name of the character who does each thing. 3.2

	Seydou	Léa	M. Rigaud
se cache près de la fenêtre	X		
entre dans le bureau		X	X
se cache derrière un rideau		X	
met la statuette dans le bureau			X
prend la statuette		X	
oublie son sac		X	
trouve un carnet d'adresse			X

Gestures

Have students look at Léa and Seydou's expressions in scenes 1 and 2. What emotions do they convey? Then direct students' attention to scene 3. What is Léa doing? Why? Ask students to look at Mr. Rigaud in scene 9. What might he be thinking? 2.1

Télé-roman

Le Secret de la statuette *Épisode 5*

STRATÉGIE

Evaluating choices Léa and Seydou have made several choices to get to where they are by the end of **Episode 5**. Go back and write down all the decisions they have made up to this point. Then decide which choices were reasonable and which were foolish or dangerous. Where would you have made a different choice? Why? Does Léa's last action in **Episode 5** seem reasonable to you? What could be the consequences of such an act? 1.2

Chez Charles Rigaud, sur l'île de Gorée...

1

Seydou Léa! Tu es folle! Reviens!

Léa entend Charles Rigaud dans le couloir.

 *Elle décide de se mettre derrière le rideau (curtain).*

 *Rigaud met la statuette dans son bureau.*

5 *Il sort de la pièce.*

Core Instruction

TEACHING TÉLÉ-ROMAN

1. Have students look at the pictures in **Télé-roman** without reading the text. Have them predict what will happen in this episode. **(5 min.)**
2. Play the video in four segments, pausing after scenes 3, 5, 7, and 10. Ask general comprehension questions. Were any of the students' predictions correct? **(5 min.)**
3. Play the video again without stopping. Have volunteers act out **Télé-roman** using gestures and facial expressions they saw in the video. **(5 min.)**
4. Have students read aloud the **As-tu compris?** questions on page 181. Discuss the answers as a class. **(5 min.)**

DVD Tutor 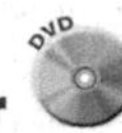

As an alternative, you might use the captioned version of **Le Secret de la statuette** on DVD.

Visit Us Online
my.hrw.com
Online Edition

6 *Après le départ de Rigaud, Léa prend la statuette.*

7 *Seydou et Léa prennent le ferry pour rentrer à Dakar.*

8 *Rigaud revient dans le bureau et découvre que la statuette n'est plus là.*

Rigaud trouve le sac de Léa et son nom dans son carnet d'adresse.

9

M. Rigaud Bondy... Bondy... Ah, mais oui! bien sûr!

10 *Rigaud a une idée... Il donne un coup de téléphone.*

AS-TU COMPRIS?

 1.2

1. Pourquoi est-ce que Léa décide d'entrer dans le bureau de Charles Rigaud?
2. Pourquoi est-ce qu'elle se met derrière le rideau?
3. Où est-ce que Rigaud met la statuette?
4. Qu'est-ce que Léa prend?
5. Comment est-ce que Léa et Seydou rentrent à Dakar?
6. Qu'est-ce que Rigaud trouve sur son bureau? Pourquoi c'est important?

Prochain épisode:
D'après toi, à qui est-ce que Charles Rigaud téléphone à la fin de l'épisode? Pourquoi?

As-tu compris? Answers

1. pour chercher la statuette
2. parce que Rigaud rentre
3. dans son bureau
4. la statuette
5. Ils prennent le ferry.
6. le sac de Léa ; Il trouve son nom, Bondy, dans son carnet d'adresse.

Communication

Group Work: Presentational
After students have seen **Télé-roman,** have them work in small groups to create and act out an alternate version of this episode. In this version, Mr. Rigaud catches Léa hiding behind the curtain, but does not notice Seydou outside the window. Tell students to write a script in which Léa manages to escape and they recover the statuette. Have groups assign character roles. Allow time to practice, and then have each group present its scene to the class. 1.3

Le Secret de la statuette Episode 5

In this episode, Léa is searching Rigaud's office. Seydou is uneasy and wants to leave, but Léa ignores him. Suddenly, she hears Rigaud's voice as he is coming back toward the office. Just in time, she hides behind a curtain. She overhears Rigaud's accomplice call him by his real name, Paul. Rigaud then leaves the room. Léa unlocks a desk drawer, takes the statuette, and flees with Seydou. When Rigaud returns to his office, he sees the open drawer and then discovers Léa's purse, which she has left behind. He recognizes the name Bondy, which is written inside Léa's address book.

Resources

Planning:
Lesson Planner
Teacher One Stop

Presentation:
Audio CD 5, Tr. 7

Practice:
Cahier d'activités
Reading Strategies and Skills Handbook, Chapter 5
Intermediate Reader
French InterActive Reader

Applying the Strategies

For practice with monitoring comprehension, have students use the "Read, Rate, Reread" strategy from the *Reading Strategies and Skills Handbook.*

READING PRACTICE

Using Context

Tell students that they can guess the meaning of many words based on the text around the unknown word in the sentence or paragraph. Context clues are very useful when students come to an unknown word in a sentence. The meaning of words and phrases can often be found just before, just after, or within the sentences they are reading. Remind students to also look for context clues in the illustrations or photos.

Lecture et écriture

Daniel Pennac est né au Maroc en 1944. Il a grandi entre l'Afrique et l'Asie. Après avoir obtenu sa maîtrise de Lettres, il devient professeur dans un collège. En 1985, il publie *Au bonheur des ogres,* premier livre d'une série dont la famille Malaussène est le centre. *Comme un roman* est publié en 1992.

STRATÉGIE pour lire

Using the context When you come across a word that you don't know, use the context of the sentence or passage to figure out the meaning of the word. You can guess an approximate meaning of the word, which is often enough to understand the gist of a text.

A Avant la lecture 1.3

Est-ce que tu aimes lire? Qu'est-ce que tu lis? Pour le plaisir ou pour l'école? Est-ce que tu as les mêmes motivations quand tu lis pour le plaisir et pour l'école?

Comme un roman CD 5, Tr. 7

Est-ce qu'un prof peut conseiller à ses élèves de sauter[1] les pages d'un livre, de ne pas finir un roman et même de ne pas lire? Oui, si c'est le seul moyen pour que[2] ses élèves entrent dans le monde magique des livres. Dans le texte qui suit, l'auteur nous présente un élève typique qui doit lire un texte pour l'école. Il rêve au lieu de lire. Sa mère vient vérifier qu'il est bien en train de lire. Bien sûr il répond qu'il lit.

Le verbe lire ne supporte pas[3] l'impératif. Aversion[4] qu'il partage avec quelques autres : le verbe « aimer »... le verbe « rêver »...

On peut toujours essayer, bien sûr. Allez-y : « Aime-moi ! » « Rêve ! » « Lis ! » « Lis ! Mais lis donc, bon sang[5], je t'ordonne de lire ! »

— Monte dans ta chambre et lis !

Résultat ?

Néant[6].

Il s'est endormi sur son livre. La fenêtre, tout à coup[7], lui a paru immensément[8] ouverte sur quelque chose d'enviable. C'est par là qu'il s'est envolé[9]. Pour échapper[10] au livre. Mais c'est un sommeil vigilant : le livre reste ouvert devant lui. Pour peu que nous ouvrions la porte de sa chambre nous le trouverons assis à son bureau, sagement occupé à lire. Même si nous sommes montés à pas de loup, de la surface de son sommeil il nous aura entendus venir.

1. to skip **2.** so that **3.** doesn't stand **4.** dislike **5.** darn! **6.** no result **7.** suddenly **8.** seemed immensely **9.** flew away **10.** to escape

Core Instruction

TEACHING LECTURE

1. Read **Stratégie** aloud with students. Explain that when they use context in their native language, it is almost an automatic process; they do not always think about it consciously. The more they read in French, the more this will become automatic. **(3 min.)**
2. Have partners do Activity A. **(6 min.)**
3. Have students read the selection silently; then have them do Activity B. Form groups of three and have students compare their answers with those of the others in their group. **(12 min.)**
4. Assign Activity C as homework. **(2 min.)**
5. Have students read aloud in class **Les droits imprescriptibles du lecteur,** pausing to check comprehension. Have students do Activity D orally in class. **(10 min.)**

Lecture et écriture

— Alors, ça te plaît ?

Il ne nous répondra pas non, ce serait un crime de lèse-majesté[1]. Le livre est sacré, comment peut-on ne pas aimer lire ? Non, il nous dira que les descriptions sont trop longues.

Rassuré, nous rejoindrons notre poste de télévision. Il se peut même que cette réflexion suscite un passionnant débat entre nous et les autres nôtres...

— Il trouve les descriptions trop longues. Il faut le comprendre, nous sommes au siècle de l'audiovisuel, évidemment, les romanciers du XIXe avaient tout à décrire...

— Ce n'est pas une raison pour le laisser sauter la moitié des pages !

...

Ne nous fatiguons pas, il s'est rendormi.

Les droits[2] imprescriptibles[3] du lecteur

1. Le droit de ne pas lire.
2. Le droit de sauter des pages.
3. Le droit de ne pas finir un livre.
4. Le droit de relire.
5. Le droit de lire n'importe quoi.
6. Le droit au bovarysme[4] (maladie textuellement transmissible).
7. Le droit de lire n'importe où.
8. Le droit de grappiller[5].
9. Le droit de lire à haute voix.
10. Le droit de nous taire[6].

1. serious crime 2. the rights 3. inalienable 4. from the novel *Madame Bovary* by G. Flaubert 5. to nibble 6. not to say anything

Communities

Community Link

Contact your local public library to see if your students could set up a special French corner, filled with French books, magazines, travel information, and videos. Students might even participate in a monthly book club for members of the community interested in discussing French literature. 5.1

Language Examination

Through the practice of listening and reading comprehension, as well as essay writing, **Lecture et écriture** helps students prepare for the **Interpretive Reading and Listening** and the **Presentational Writing** sections of the AP Language and Culture Exam.

Additional Practice

For more reading practice, see **Variations littéraires,** pp. 390–391.

Differentiated Instruction

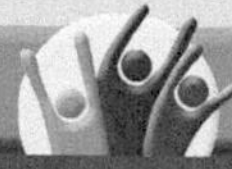

SLOWER PACE LEARNERS

Activate students' prior knowledge by asking them how they feel when someone demands that they do something, whether it is their homework, chores, or even something they enjoy doing. Do they ever pretend to do what they are told when they are actually not cooperating at all? Then ask students to keep this question in mind as they read: What is the boy avoiding doing and why? 1.2

SPECIAL LEARNING NEEDS

Students with Learning Disabilities Assist students in using **Stratégie pour lire** by providing a short English paragraph that contains some words that may be challenging to understand in isolation, but are easy to comprehend in context. Have students read the paragraph and let them discuss how they understood the meaning of the unfamiliar words by using the strategy. 1.2

C Answers

1. Il ne lit pas.
2. Il s'endort.
3. Non, il n'aime pas son livre.
4. Les parents regardent la télévision.
5. Il ne veut pas dire qu'il n'aime pas le livre.

Connections

Language Arts Link

Have students debate the idea, suggested by the reading, that technology is damaging our ability to concentrate and our interest in reading. Students should decide whether they believe this idea is true or false and research information to support their viewpoint. Although they may need to present their debate in English, you might have them summarize in French the information they discovered during their research. 3.1

Compréhension

B Complète les phrases suivantes avec la réponse correcte. 1.2

1. Quand tu sautes les pages…
   a. tu ne lis pas toutes les pages.
   b. tu tournes les pages.
2. «N'importe où» veut dire…
   a. nulle part.
   b. où tu veux.
   c. dans un seul endroit.
3. Deux choses qui partagent des caractéristiques…
   a. sont très différentes.
   b. sont similaires.
   c. sont totalement opposées.
4. Quand on marche à pas de loup, on marche…
   a. en silence.
   b. lentement.
   c. vite.
5. Le sommeil est l'acte de…
   a. rêver.
   b. étudier.
   c. dormir.

C Réponds aux questions suivantes avec des phrases complètes. 1.2

1. Selon l'auteur, qu'est-ce qui se passe quand on ordonne à un enfant de lire?
2. Qu'est-ce que l'enfant fait à son bureau?
3. Est-ce que l'enfant aime son livre?
4. Qui regarde la télévision?
5. Selon le texte, pourquoi est-ce que l'enfant trouve les descriptions trop longues?

Après la lecture

D Est-ce que tu aimes lire? Pourquoi ou pourquoi pas? Est-ce que tu finis toujours les livres que tu commences? Est-ce qu'il t'arrive de sauter des pages? Est-ce que tu es d'accord avec les **droits imprescriptibles du lecteur?** Explique ta réponse. 1.3

Core Instruction

TEACHING ESPACE ÉCRITURE

1. Discuss **Stratégie pour écrire. (1 min.)**
2. Assign steps 1 and 2 as homework. It may help students get started by giving them examples of greetings and general introductory statements. Remind them that even though they do not know this imaginary person, he or she is a peer, and they will use the **tu** form in the letter. **(5 min.)**
3. Have partners complete step 3. Give them a rubric so that they can check each other's verbs, pronouns, agreement, spelling, and punctuation. **(10 min.)**
4. Have students do step 4 in class. Ask the class to choose the most creative letter and the most practical letter. As they are listening, have students make notes of suggestions they would like to follow. As a homework assignment, you might ask them to write themselves a self-help note. **(15 min.)**

Espace écriture

STRATÉGIE pour écrire

Identifying your audience is a primary consideration when you do any type of writing. Having a good idea of who will read what you've written will help you to determine the length, content, and tone of what you write.

Vive la variété! 1.3

Imagine that you write an advice column for the school newspaper. This week you're responding to a letter from a student whose daily routine is so boring that it is affecting the student's school work and overall mood. Write the student a letter in which you recommend several creative and unusual ways to spice up his or her daily routine.

1 Plan

First consider who will be reading your letter—a high school student who is bored and possibly depressed.

- Create a timeline in French of what you imagine to be this student's typical day, from getting up to going to bed.
- Brainstorm ideas about how that student might change his or her daily routine to make the day more fun and interesting.

6h30	Je me lève
8h00	
9h00	
10h00	
11h00	
midi	
13h00	

2 Rédaction

Begin with an appropriate greeting and introductory statement to set the tone and intention of the letter. Use:

- reflexive verbs,
- expressions for saying when you do things,
- expressions for making recommendations. Suggest five changes to the student's daily routine. Refer to your timeline and brainstorming ideas.

To end your letter, explain why the student should make the suggested changes and write an appropriate closing.

3 Correction

Exchange your draft with a classmate who will give you feedback on the appropriateness of the tone and content. Then check for the use of the reflexive verbs and pronouns, agreement, spelling, and punctuation.

4 Application

Read your letter to the class. Which letter has the most creative suggestions? Which one has the most practical suggestions? Which suggestions could you incorporate into your own routine to add variety?

Lecture et écriture

Lecture et écriture

Process Writing

Avant d'écrire Before students begin the **Plan,** suggest that they create a cluster diagram to organize their ideas about the activities in a typical day. A cluster diagram is a useful way for students to see how their suggestions and advice can be related. You might begin a diagram on the board to help students get started.

Writing Assessment

To assess the **Espace écriture,** you can use the following rubric. For additional rubrics, see the *Assessment Program* or refer to the *Generate Success* Rubric Generator.

Writing Rubric	4	3	2	1
Content (Complete—Incomplete)				
Comprehensibility (Comprehensible—Seldom comprehensible)				
Accuracy (Accurate—Seldom accurate)				
Organization (Well-organized—Poorly organized)				
Effort (Excellent effort—Minimal effort)				

18-20: A 16-17: B 14-15: C 12-13: D Under 12: F

Differentiated Instruction

ADVANCED LEARNERS

As an additional writing activity, have students refer to **Les droits imprescriptibles du lecteur** on page 183 and write their own list of ten students' rights, for example: **1. le droit de ne pas être trop ennuyé en cours.** 1.3

MULTIPLE INTELLIGENCES

Interpersonal As a variation on **Vive la variété!,** allow students to change the perspective of the letter. The person asking advice could be a younger child, a college student, or an adult with a career. Changing the recipient of the response letter may make the assignment more motivating, since students are given more choices and greater opportunity to be creative. 1.3

Assess

Assessment Program
Quiz: Lecture
Quiz: Écriture

Online Assessment
my.hrw.com

Test Generator 

Prépare-toi pour l'examen

Resources

Planning:
Lesson Planner
Teacher One Stop

Practice:
Cahier d'activités
Media Guide

DVD Tutor, Disc 1
Projectable Transparencies
Situation, Chapitre 5
Picture Sequences, Chapter 5
Audio CD 5, Tr. 9–12
@HOMETUTOR

2 Answers

1. Marc prend son rasoir et ensuite il se rase.
2. Marie et moi, nous prenons un bain et ensuite nous nous maquillons.
3. Moi, je me lave les cheveux et ensuite je me sèche les cheveux.
4. Marc, il se lave et ensuite il s'habille.
5. Marie et maman, elles se préparent et ensuite elles s'en vont.

3 Answers

1. À quatre heures, il prend le bus.
2. Il rentre à la maison à 4h30.
3. Il se déshabille et se met en pyjama à 10h.
4. Il se met au lit à 10h30.

Reteaching

Ask students how to form the past tense of reflexive verbs. (Use a reflexive pronoun, use **être,** make the past participle agree with the reflexive pronoun, unless the verb is followed by an object.) Demonstrate what you did this morning, using props, and have students say what you did.

Prépare-toi pour l'examen

@HOMETUTOR

1 Vocabulaire 1
- to express impatience
- to talk about your routine

pp. 158–161

1 Des amis parlent de leur routine le matin. Selon ce qu'ils disent, complète leurs phrases logiquement. 1.2

1. Le réveil sonne et je ______. me réveille
2. Je ______ les cheveux avec du shampooing. me lave
3. Avec le sèche-cheveux, je ______. me sèche les cheveux
4. Je prends ma brosse à cheveux et je ______. me brosse les cheveux
5. Je trouve mon maquillage et je ______. me maquille
6. Je prends ma brosse à dents et je ______. me brosse les dents
7. Je prends mon rasoir et je ______. me rase

2 Grammaire 1
- reflexive verbs
- **tout, tous, toute, toutes**

Un peu plus
- the verbs **s'appeler** and **se lever**

pp. 162–167

2 Anne a la visite de sa famille. Anne parle de la routine de sa famille le matin. Dis ce que chaque membre de la famille fait d'abord et ce qu'il fait ensuite. 1.2

MODÈLE papa et maman: se lever / se réveiller
Papa et maman se réveillent et ensuite ils se lèvent.

1. Marc: se raser / prendre son rasoir
2. Marie et moi, nous: prendre un bain / se maquiller
3. moi, je: se laver les cheveux / se sécher les cheveux
4. Marc, il: s'habiller / se laver
5. Marie et maman, elles: se préparer / s'en aller

3 Vocabulaire 2
- to say when you do things
- to make recommendations

pp. 170–173

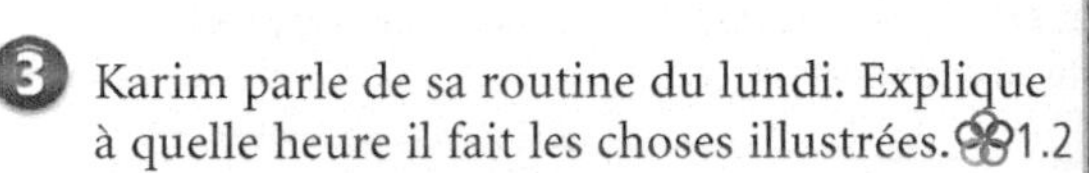

3 Karim parle de sa routine du lundi. Explique à quelle heure il fait les choses illustrées. 1.2

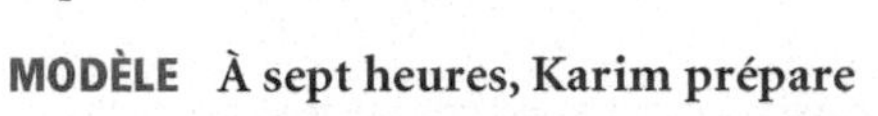

MODÈLE **À sept heures, Karim prépare son sac.**

7h

1. 4h

2. 4h30

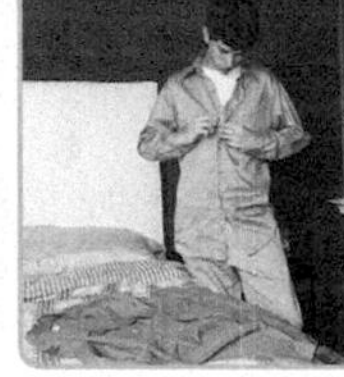

3. 10h

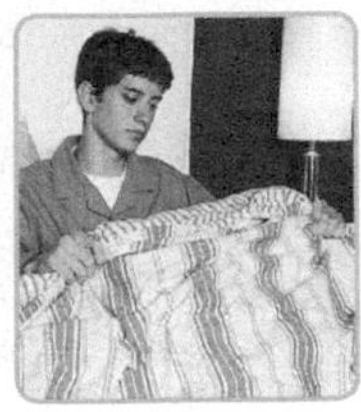

4. 10h30

Preparing for the Exam

FOLD-N-LEARN

Flap Booklet Study Aid

1. Have students fold a sheet of paper into thirds from top to bottom and then unfold the paper. In the middle column of the sheet, ask students to list the French expressions for talking about their routine and saying when they do things.

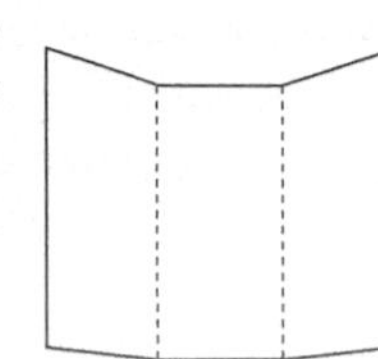

2. In the middle column, students should list the French phrases for expressing impatience and making recommendations.
3. Ask students to write the English equivalent for each French expression in the left-hand column. Have students fold the right hand blank column of the sheet over the middle column.
4. Have students review the chapter expressions with the study aid they have created. They should read each English expression on the left while they try to recall the French equivalent hidden in the middle.

Online Assessment
my.hrw.com
Chapter Self-test

4 La famille Trentin suit la même routine tous les jours. Selon ce que Patricia dit qu'ils font d'habitude, devine ce qu'ils ont fait hier. 1.2

MODÈLE Moi, je m'endors devant la télé. Hier...
je me suis endormie devant la télé.

1. Nous nous réveillons de bonne heure. Hier...
2. Mes parents se lèvent vers six heures. Hier...
3. Moi, je me lève avant sept heures. Hier...
4. Nous nous préparons rapidement. Hier...
5. Je me lave les cheveux le matin. Hier matin...
6. Ma mère se dépêche pour aller au travail. Hier...

4 Grammaire 2
- reflexive verbs in the **passé composé**
- the imperative with reflexive verbs

Un peu plus
- reflexive verbs with infinitives

pp. 174–179

5 Réponds aux questions suivantes. 1.2

1. Comment est une journée typique pour un adolescent français?
2. Quels sont les moyens de transports en commun à Rennes?

5 Culture
- Flash culture **pp. 160, 164, 172, 174**
- Comparaisons **pp. 168–169**

6 Michel s'occupe de son petit frère ce week-end. Est-ce qu'il parle de ce que son frère doit faire **a) le matin** ou **b) le soir?** CD 5, Tr. 9 1.2

1. a 2. b 3. b 4. a 5. b 6. b 7. a

7 Avec ton/ta camarade, imaginez que c'est le matin à la maison. Vous allez jouer les rôles d'une mère et de son fils/sa fille. D'abord, lisez les instructions pour chaque réplique *(exchange)*. Ensuite, créez votre dialogue en utilisant des expressions que vous avez apprises. 1.1

Élève A:	Ton fils/Ta fille est en retard pour l'école. Dis-lui de se dépêcher.
Élève B:	Réponds que tu te prépares. Donne des détails.
Élève A:	Dis (d'une autre manière) à ton fils/ta fille de se dépêcher.
Élève B:	Réponds que tu dois faire autre chose avant de prendre ta douche.
Élève A:	Conseille à ton fils/ta fille de manger avant de partir.
Élève B:	Réponds négativement. Dis ce que tu dois encore faire avant de partir.
Élève A:	Il est 7h45 et vous devez partir immédiatement. Dis-le à ton fils/ta fille.
Élève B:	Demande à ta mère si vous y allez.

Chapitre 5

Prépare-toi pour l'examen

4 Answers

1. ...nous nous sommes réveillés de bonne heure.
2. ...ils se sont levés vers six heures.
3. ...je me suis levée avant sept heures.
4. ...nous nous sommes préparés rapidement.
5. ...je me suis lavé les cheveux.
6. ...elle s'est dépêchée pour aller au travail.

5 Answers

1. Les jeunes vont à l'école à huit heures ou à neuf heures. Ils rentrent à la maison vers cinq heures. Ils font leurs devoirs et puis ils dînent vers huit heures.
2. le métro

6 Script

1. Réveille-toi. Il est huit heures.
2. Brosse-toi les dents avant de te coucher.
3. Mets-toi en pyjama.
4. Habille-toi. Le bus arrive bientôt!
5. Couche-toi. Il est tard.
6. Mets-toi au lit.
7. Habille-toi et viens prendre ton petit-déjeuner.

Language Examination

7 Sample conversation:

a. **Dépêche-toi, Dominique!**
b. **Je prends une douche et je m'habille.**
a. **Arrête de traîner!**
b. **Je dois me brosser les dents avant de prendre ma douche.**
a. **Tu devrais prendre ton petit-déjeuner avant de partir.**
b. **Je n'ai pas le temps. Je dois préparer mon sac.**
a. **C'est l'heure de partir.**
b. **Alors, on y va?**

Additional Speaking Practice

- For additional speaking practice, you might use the *Picture Sequences Transparency* for Chapter 5 found in the *Projectable Transparencies.*
- To assess the speaking activities in this section, you might use the *Generate Success* Rubric Generator or the oral rubrics found in the *Assessment Program.*

Pre-AP Practice

7 This guided conversation activity helps students practice oral exchanges using material from this chapter and previous chapters. The activity helps prepare students for the **Interpersonal Speaking** section of the AP French Language and Culture Exam.

Chapitre 5

Prépare-toi pour l'examen

Grammar Review

For more practice with the grammar topics in this chapter, see the *Grammar Tutor*, the *DVD Tutor*, the *@HomeTutor*, or the *Cahier de vocabulaire et grammaire*.

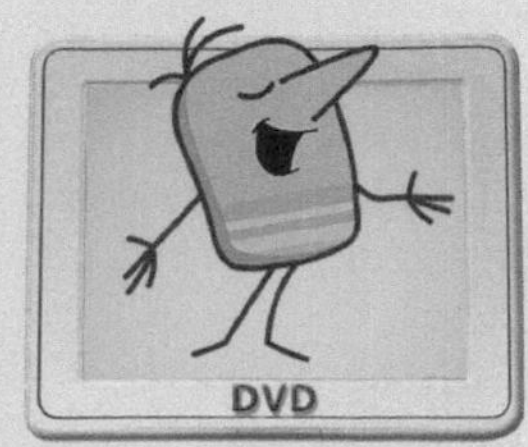

Grammavision

Online Edition

Students might use the online textbook and Performance Space to practice the **Lettres et sons** feature.

Dictée Script

1. Je me lève toujours de bonne heure.
2. Elle se sèche les cheveux avec le sèche-cheveux.
3. Vous vous rasez avec de la crème à raser ou avec du gel douche?
4. Ma mère ne met jamais de rouge à lèvres.
5. Dépêche-toi! Tu vas être en retard.

Game

À toi! Have students form a circle. Call out a sentence containing a reflexive verb. **Nous nous levons à six heures.** Then toss a ball to a student as you call out a different subject **(mon père).** The student catches the ball and says the new sentence. **Mon père se lève à six heures.** Then he or she tosses the ball to another student, calling out another subject. A student who does not respond within five seconds is out, but may get back in by correcting another's error. After several tosses, start a new sentence. 1.1

Grammaire 1
- reflexive verbs
- **tout, tous, toute, toutes**

Un peu plus
- the verbs **s'appeler** and **se lever**

pp. 162–167

Résumé: Grammaire 1

Reflexive pronouns are used when conjugating reflexive verbs. The reflexive pronoun must agree with the subject.

se brosser *to brush (one's hair)*	
je me brosse	nous nous brossons
tu te brosses	vous vous brossez
il/elle se brosse	ils/elles se brossent

Use an appropriate form of **tout** (**tout, tous, toute, toutes**) to say *all* or *the whole.*

When conjugating the verbs **s'appeler, se lever,** and **s'ennuyer,** there are spelling changes in all forms of these verbs, except the **nous** and **vous** forms.

Vous vous appelez comment? Je m'appe**ll**e Bertrand.

Grammaire 2
- reflexive verbs in the **passé composé**
- the imperative with reflexive verbs

Un peu plus
- reflexive verbs with infinitives

pp. 174–179

Résumé: Grammaire 2

With **reflexive verbs,** the **passé composé** is formed using **être**. The past participle agrees with the subject in number and gender, except when the reflexive pronoun is not the direct object of the verb.

Elle s'est lavé**e**. BUT Elle s'est brossé les cheveux.

Negative commands are formed by placing the reflexive pronoun directly before the verb and placing **ne... pas** around the reflexive pronoun and the verb: Ne **te lève** pas tard!

Affirmative commands with reflexive verbs are made by attaching the reflexive pronoun to the *end* of the verb with a hyphen.

Lave-**toi!** Dépêchez-**vous!**

When using **reflexive verbs** in the **infinitive** form, place the **reflexive pronoun** before the infinitive.

Je préfère **me** doucher avant de **me** brosser les dents.

Lettres et sons

The vowel sound [ɛ] CD 5, Tr. 10–12

Listen to the vowels in the word **dépêche.** How are they different? The second vowel represents the vowel sound [ɛ]. To make this sound, hold your mouth in an open, smiling position. Some spellings of this vowel sound are **è, ait, ais,** and **ê.** Try pronouncing these examples: **gel, crème, lèvres.**

Jeux de langue

Un vers vert allait vers un verre en verre vert en faisant des vers.

Dictée 1.2

Écris les phrases de la dictée.

Chapter Review

DVD Program

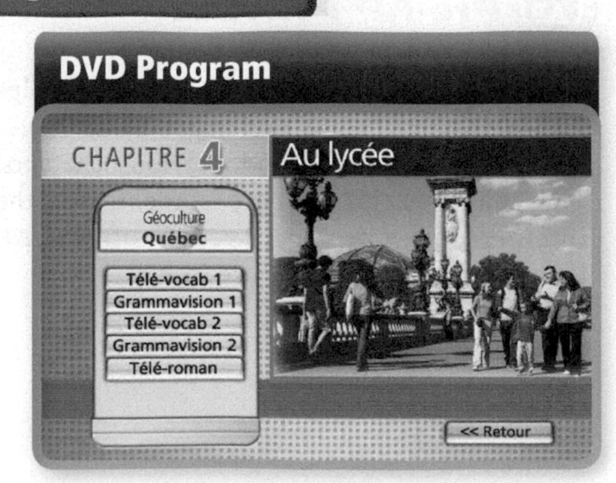

Online Edition

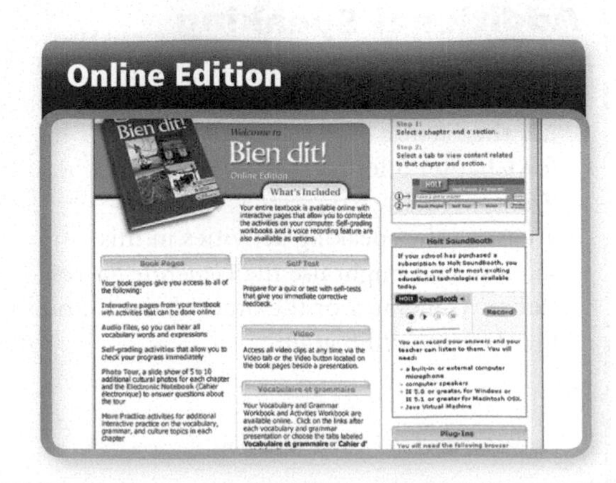

Prépare-toi pour l'examen

Résumé: Vocabulaire 1

PRACTICE FRENCH WITH HOLT MCDOUGAL APPS!

To talk about your routine

la baignoire	*bathtub*
la brosse/la brosse à dents	*brush/toothbrush*
se brosser les cheveux/les dents	*to brush one's hair/teeth*
se coiffer	*to do one's hair*
la crème à raser	*shaving cream*
le dentifrice	*toothpaste*
le déodorant	*deodorant*
la douche	*shower*
s'en aller	*to run along*
le gel douche	*shower gel*
s'habiller	*to get dressed*
le lavabo	*sink*
se laver (les cheveux) (m.)	*to wash (one's hair)*
se lever	*to get up/stand up*
le maquillage	*make-up*
se maquiller	*to put on makeup*
le mascara	*mascara*
la matinée	*morning*
le miroir	*mirror*
le peigne	*comb*
se peigner (les cheveux)	*to comb (one's hair)*
le peignoir	*robe*
prendre un bain/une douche	*to take a bath/shower*
se préparer	*to get ready*
se raser	*to shave*
le rasoir (électrique)	*(electric) razor*
le réveil	*alarm*
le robinet	*faucet*
se réveiller	*to wake up*
le rouge à lèvres	*lipstick*
le savon	*soap*
le sèche-cheveux	*blow-dryer*
se sécher les cheveux (m.)	*to dry one's hair*
la serviette	*towel*
le shampooing	*shampoo*
sonner	*to ring*
avant de	*before*
chaque	*each/every*
en même temps (que)	*at the same time (as)*
en premier	*first/firstly*
ensuite	*then/next*
pendant que	*while/during*
tous les deux (jours)	*every other (day)*

To express impatience

Alors, on y va?	*So, shall we go?*
Arrête de traîner!	*Stop dragging your feet/dawdling!*
Dépêche-toi!	*Hurry up!*
Tu es prêt(e)?	*Are you ready?*
Vous allez être en retard.	*You're going to be late.*

Résumé: Vocabulaire 2

To say when you do things

aller au travail/au lycée	*to go to work/to high school*
se coucher/se mettre au lit	*to go to bed*
se déshabiller/s'endormir	*to get undressed/to fall asleep*
faire la sieste	*to take a nap*
faire sa toilette	*to clean (oneself) up*
faire ses devoirs	*to do one's homework*
la figure	*face*
se mettre en pyjama/en chemise de nuit	*to put on pajamas/a nightgown*
s'occuper (de)	*to take care (of)*
préparer son sac	*to get one's backpack ready*
prendre le bus	*to take the bus*
ranger ses affaires	*to put one's things away*
rentrer à la maison	*to return to the house*
souhaiter une bonne nuit	*to say good night*
au plus tard	*at the latest*
de bonne heure	*bright and early*
tard/tôt	*late/early*
une fois que/après ça	*once/afterwards*
la journée/le soir	*day/evening*

To make recommendations

C'est l'heure de...	*It's time to . . .*
Il est temps de...	*It's time to . . .*
Tu devrais...	*You should . . .*
Va... Il est tard.	*Go . . . It's late.*

Holt McDougal French Apps

Remind students that they can use the Holt McDougal French Apps to review their vocabulary.

Teacher to Teacher

Karen Query
Lincoln High School
Vincennes, IN

I write nine questions on the board, such as **De quelle couleur est ta brosse à dents?** Have students divide a sheet of paper to make a tic-tac-toe grid, then write their answers, one in each box. Students circulate and ask their classmates the questions. If the classmates have the same answer, they sign their name in the box. Continue until everyone has three signatures in a row. 1.1

Projectable Transparency

More Digital Resources

FOR THE STUDENT

Holt McDougal French Apps
@HomeTutor
News and Networking
Performance Space

FOR THE TEACHER

- Interactive Whiteboard Lessons
- Generate Success!

Assess

Assessment Program
Examen: Chapitre 5
Examen oral: Chapitre 5
Examen partie I
Audio CD 5, Tr. 16–17; 18–20
Alternative Assessment
Differentiated Practice and Assessment CD-ROM
Online Assessment
my.hrw.com
Test Generator 

Révisions cumulatives

Resources

Planning:
Lesson Planner
Teacher One Stop

Practice:
Cahier d'activités
Media Guide
Projectable Transparencies
Fine Art, Chapter 5
Audio CD 5, Tr. 13
Holt McDougal French Apps

1 Answers

1. oui, pour éviter la monotonie
2. laisser respirer les autres
3. il faut varier

2 Script

See script on p. 153F.

Teacher to Teacher

Bill Heller
Perry High School
Perry, NY

Have students collect magazine pictures that illustrate as many reflexive verbs as possible from Chapter 5. Divide the class into teams who pool their pictures. Call out a sentence with a reflexive verb, using **il, elle, ils,** or **elles.** The first team to produce an appropriate picture earns two points. Other teams with an appropriate picture earn one point. The team with the most points at the end of the game wins. As an additional assignment, have each team select five of the pictures from their pool and create a story. 1.2

Révisions cumulatives

1 Cet article web décrit *(describes)* comment éviter *(to avoid)* la monotonie de la vie. Lis l'article et réponds aux questions suivantes. 3.2

Espace Bien-être

La routine, l'habitude

Accueil
Forum
Sondage
Chercher

Il est impossible d'éliminer **la routine** de la vie. Le matin on est bien obligé de se lever et d'aller au travail et le soir on est bien obligé de se coucher...

Mais il y a une autre sorte de routine, **un automatisme** qui peut facilement gâcher une vie. Pour une personne qui tous les jours se réveille, déjeune, va au travail, le soir rentre, mange, se brosse les dents et va se coucher... la vie devient ennuyeuse.

Alors, comment ne pas la laisser s'installer, cette routine? Le week-end, partez en famille, mais aussi, laissez respirer les autres. Sortez avec des amis. Ce soir on se fait une soirée. Justement, jeudi il y a un match de foot... En gros, pour que la vie ne devienne pas une habitude, il faut **varier les plaisirs.**

1. Est-il important d'éliminer la routine de la vie? Pourquoi ou pourquoi pas?
2. Dans une famille, il est important de passer du temps en famille, mais il est aussi important de faire quoi?
3. En gros, qu'est-ce qu'on peut faire pour éviter la monotonie?

Online Culture Project

Have students do a Web search for cultural activities offered in Rennes, such as the music festival (**Les Transmusicales, les Tombées de la nuit**) and a cinematic festival (**Travelling**), or activities offered at the **Universités.** Ask students to note the name of the activity, the date(s) and time(s) it takes place, and any other information they can find. When would they be most likely to attend the activity? Have students document the sites they consulted. 1.3, 2.2

Révisions cumulatives

Online Assessment
my.hrw.com
Cumulative Self-test

2 Nadine a passé une journée intéressante. Écoute Nadine et puis mets les évènements de sa journée en ordre. CD 5, Tr. 13 1.2

5 **a.** Elle s'est occupée de son frère.
2 **b.** Elle s'est lavé les cheveux.
1 **c.** Elle s'est levée à huit heures.
4 **d.** Elle est allée au CDI.
3 **e.** Elle est allée à la charcuterie.

3 Regarde l'image suivante et puis réponds aux questions. 3.1

1. Que fait la femme sur l'image? Et l'homme?
2. Fais une description de tout ce que tu vois sur l'image.
3. D'après l'image, imagine la routine quotidienne de cette femme. Comment est sa vie?

Manet, Édouard, Nana, 1877. Oil on canvas, Height: 154.31 cm (60.75in.), Width: 114.94 cm (45.25 in.), Hamburger Kunsthalle Gallery, Hamburg, Germany.

Nana d'Édouard Manet

4 Tu vas partir en week-end avec un(e) ami(e) français(e). Écris-lui un e-mail. Parle de ta routine le matin et le soir. 1.3

5 1.1, 1.3

À ton tour

Trop de conseils! Your friends have problems and you are giving them advice. Your friend Marie never arrives to school on time, Marc is always sleepy in class, Dominique does not do all her homework, and Sylvie wants to do something fun this weekend. With a partner, act out this conversation. Then, present your conversation to the class.

Fine Art Connection

Introduction Édouard Manet was one of the major French painters of the 19th century. He was born into a well-to-do Parisian family in 1832. His father, who was a high-ranking public servant at the Ministry of Justice, wanted him to become a lawyer. Instead, Manet ended up studying with a painter. Although he was at the center of the Impressionist movement, some of Édouard Manet's paintings are much more realistic than those of other Impressionists, and some even consider him a precursor of modern art. Manet painted people in social and leisure activities, often in cafés, restaurants, and concerts.

Analyzing

To help students discuss the painting, you might use the following questions.

1. **Les deux personnages sont-ils riches ou pauvres? Comment est-ce qu'on le sait?**
2. **Que fait la dame devant son miroir?**
3. **Si ce couple va sortir, où est-ce que tu crois qu'il va aller?**
4. **Est-ce que tu trouves cette dame belle? Et le monsieur, est-il beau?**

3.1

Extension

Bring print-outs of these paintings to class: *Le Vieux Musicien, Argenteuil, Le Joueur de fifre,* and *Le Chanteur espagnol.* Have students say which they think are Impressionist works and which are clearly not. 2.2, 3.1

ACTFL Performance Standards

The activities in Chapter 5 target the communicative modes as described in the Standards.

Interpersonal	Two-way communication using receptive skills and productive skills	**Communication (SE),** pp. 161, 163, 165, 167, 173, 175, 177, 179 **Communication (TE),** pp. 161, 163, 165, 173, 175, 177, 179 **À ton tour,** p. 191
Interpretive	One-way communication using receptive skills	**Comparaisons,** p. 169 **Télé-roman,** pp. 180–181
Presentational	One-way communication using productive skills	**Communication (TE),** pp. 167

chapitre 6

Planning Guide

Le bon vieux temps

Chapter Section		Resources
Vocabulaire 1 • Childhood activities **Grammaire 1** • The **imparfait** • The **passé composé** and the **imparfait** **Application 1** • **Un peu plus:** Review of adverb placement	pp. 194–197 pp. 198–201 pp. 202–203	Projectable Transparencies: Vocabulaire 6.1, 6.2; Bell Work 6.1, 6.2, 6.3, 6.4 Cahier de vocabulaire et grammaire, pp. 61–66 Grammar Tutor for Students of French Cahier d'activités, pp. 51–53 Media Guide, pp. 21–24, 80–82 **Assessment Program** Quiz: Vocabulaire 1, pp. 159–160 Quiz: Grammaire 1, pp. 161–162 Quiz: Application 1, pp. 163–164
Culture • **Culture appliquée: Les comptines** • **Comparaisons et Communauté**	pp. 204–205	Cahier d'activités, p. 54
Vocabulaire 2 • Country life **Grammaire 2** • The comparative • The superlative **Application 2** • **Un peu plus:** Irregular comparatives and superlatives	pp. 206–209 pp. 210–213 pp. 214–215	Projectable Transparencies: Vocabulaire 6.3, 6.4; Bell Work 6.5, 6.6, 6.7, 6.8 Cahier de vocabulaire et grammaire, pp. 67–72 Grammar Tutor for Students of French Cahier d'activités, pp. 55–57 Media Guide, pp. 21–24, 80–81, 83 **Assessment Program** Quiz: Vocabulaire 2, pp. 165–166 Quiz: Grammaire 2, pp. 167–168 Quiz: Application 2, pp. 169–170
Télé-roman	pp. 216–217	Media Guide, pp. 81, 84
Lecture et écriture	pp. 218–221	Cahier d'activités, p. 58 Reading Strategies and Skills Handbook Intermediate Reader French InterActive Reader **Assessment Program** Quiz: Lecture, p. 171 Quiz: Écriture, p. 172
Prépare-toi pour l'examen • **Résumé de vocabulaire et grammaire** • **Lettres et sons** **Révisions cumulatives**	pp. 222–225 pp. 226–227	Independent Study Guide, pp. 16–18, 38 Media Guide, p. 24 **Assessment Program** Examen: Chapitre 6, pp. 173–178 Examen oral: Chapitre 6, p. 322 Projectable Transparencies: Fine Art, Ch. 6 Cahier d'activités, pp. 54, 59–60
Variations littéraires • **Saint-Malo, cité corsaire**	pp. 392–393	Reading Strategies and Skills Handbook Intermediate Reader French InterActive Reader

Visit Us Online

my.hrw.com
Online Edition

Pacing Suggestions

	Essential	Recommended	Optional
Vocabulaire 1 • Childhood activities • **Flash culture**	✔		
Grammaire 1 • The **imparfait** • The **passé composé** and the **imparfait** • **Flash culture**	✔		
Application 1 • **Un peu plus:** Review of adverb placement	✔		
Culture • **Culture appliquée: Les comptines** • **Comparaisons et Communauté**		✔	
Vocabulaire 2 • Country life • **Flash culture**	✔		
Grammaire 2 • The comparative • The superlative • **Flash culture**	✔		
Application 2 • **Un peu plus:** Irregular comparatives and superlatives	✔		
Télé-roman • Épisode 6: **Le Secret de la statuette**			✔
Lecture et écriture • **Le matin du monde** (Lecture) • **Un souvenir** (Écriture)		✔	
Prépare-toi pour l'examen		✔	
Révisions cumulatives			✔
Variations littéraires • **Saint-Malo, cité corsaire**			✔

Technology

Bien dit! Online
- Student Edition with multi-media
- **performance)))space** recording tool
- Interactive activities with feedback
- Self-tests with feedback
- Cahier d'activités (Interactive workbook)
- Cahier de vocabulaire et grammaire (Interactive workbook)
- Holt Online Assessment

DVD Tutor
- Télé-vocab
- Grammavision
- Télé-roman

HOMETUTOR
- Interactive games
- Differentiated Practice
- Cultural video

Audio Program
- Student Edition listening activities
- Assessment listening activities
- Songs

Teacher One Stop™
- Complete resources
- ExamView Pro Test Generator
- Holt Calendar Planner

Holt McDougal Apps

Interactive Whiteboard Lessons

Differentiated Practice and Assessment CD

For slower pace and advanced learner options, see the Differentiated Practice and Assessment CD.

Projects

Quand j'étais enfant

Students will create a poster that tells a visual story about their childhood. They write a short report to explain what they have illustrated and why. Students may prefer to create a poster about a celebrity or a historical or fictitious character. 1.3

Suggested Sequence

1. Have students plan what photos, drawings, or magazine pictures they will include in their poster. They might sketch the layout on a piece of paper.
2. Students outline their report that explains the information in the poster.
3. Students begin the layout of the poster, allowing enough space for captions.
4. Students prepare their final version of the poster with the realia they have selected. They should write captions in French for the pictures.
5. Students use their outline to write a report to accompany the poster.
6. Students present their report orally in class. You may wish to display the posters in the classroom.

Grading the project

Suggested point distribution (100 points total)

Originality/design	20 pts.
Written captions	20 pts.
Oral presentation	30 pts.
Language use	30 pts.

Partner Class Project

Ask students to imagine they are the editors of the magazine **La vie à la campagne.** They want to know why their readers (their partner class) prefer country life. Have students create a survey to compare life in the country and in the city. They should include statements such as, **La vie en ville est plus... qu'à la campagne. (La vie à la campagne est moins... qu'en ville.)** The partner class should agree or disagree with each statement and return the survey. Have students tally the results, calculate the percentages of agreement for each question, and discuss the opinions of their partner class. 1.3

Communication

e-community

e-mail forum:

Location: http://french

Post the following questions on the classroom e-mail forum:

Qu'est-ce que tu aimais faire quand tu étais petit(e)?

De quoi avais-tu peur quand tu étais petit(e)?

5.1

All students will contribute to the list and then share the items.

Game Bank

For game ideas, see pages T60–T63.

Le passé celtique de Rennes

The Celtic University, as well as many Celtic circle societies, keeps Celtic traditions alive in the city of Rennes by sponsoring conferences, Celtic weeks, and expositions of Celtic traditions. About one-quarter of the people in Brittany speak Breton, a Celtic language similar to Cornish and Welsh. It is one of the languages taught in schools and is the language spoken at these Celtic events. During the festivals, participants wear traditional costumes of the region and perform dances of the past. The typical Breton dress is a dark color and is topped with a high, stiff lace **coiffe.** Men wear dark pants, white shirts, a vest, and a flat felt hat. Musicians play traditional music on replicas of ancient instruments, such the **biniou,** an instrument that sounds somewhat like a bagpipe, and the **bombarde,** similar to an oboe. Ask students to find illustrations of traditional costumes from the Celtic period in Rennes. 2.1

La cuisine

The Tatin family had a hotel in Lamotte-Beuvron at the turn of the century. One day, while preparing the meal, Isabelle put the dough in the pie dish on top of the apples and created the **tarte tatin** (upside-down tart). Encourage students to make this recipe in their foods class or at home for family and friends. 1.2, 2.2

Tarte Tatin

Pâte à tarte
2 tasses de farine
1/2 tasse de sucre
1/2 tasse de beurre
1 œuf

Garniture
3/4 tasse de beurre
2/3 tasse de sucre
4 pommes épluchées et coupées en lamelles

Pâte à tarte
Faire fondre le beurre. Placer la farine dans un saladier. Faire un puits. Y mettre le sucre et l'œuf. Commencer à mélanger doucement. Ajouter le beurre petit à petit. Faire une boule du mélange. Si la boule est trop beurrée, ajouter une ou deux cuillères à soupe de farine. Laisser reposer pendant que vous préparez les pommes et le reste de la garniture.

Garniture
Allumer le four à 350° F. Placer le beurre dans un moule. Mettre le moule au four pendant 5 minutes. Ajouter le sucre. Mettre de nouveau le moule dans le four pendant 5 minutes. Mélanger de temps en temps. Sortir le moule du four et ajouter les pommes coupées. Rouler la pâte et la placer sur les pommes. Mettre au four pendant 20 à 30 minutes. Retirer du four. Démouler la tarte sur le plat de service. Servir tiède.

Listening Activity Scripts

Vocabulaire à l'œuvre 1

2 p. 196, CD 6, Tr. 1

— Mamie, qu'est-ce que tu aimais faire quand tu étais petite?
— Oh, j'aimais faire beaucoup de choses!
— Mais, quoi?
— J'aimais faire des châteaux de sable sur la plage.
— Est-ce que tu aimais jouer à la poupée?
— Oui, beaucoup! Quand j'avais six ans, ma poupée préférée s'appelait madame Michaud.
— Est-ce que tu aimais sauter à la corde?
— Non, pas tellement, mais j'aimais bien jouer à la marelle.
— Quoi d'autre?
— Oh, quand j'étais plus jeune, j'aimais jouer à chat perché. Mais ce que je préférais, c'était grimper aux arbres.
— Moi, j'adore ça aussi! Tu veux venir grimper aux arbres avec moi, mamie?
— Ah, non, ma petite! À mon âge, ce n'est plus possible! Mais je peux te regarder, d'accord?
— D'accord!

Answers to Activity 2
1. c **2.** e **3.** f **4.** d **5.** b **6.** a

Grammaire à l'œuvre 1

11 p. 200, CD 6, Tr. 2

1. Quand j'étais petite, ma famille et moi, nous allions à la plage tous les étés.
2. D'habitude, nous restions dans un hôtel près de la mer.
3. Toute la famille se levait tôt le matin pour aller sur la plage.
4. Une fois, nous sommes restés chez un ami.
5. Cet été-là, nous avons emmené notre chien avec nous.
6. Je nageais dans la mer pendant que mon petit frère faisait des châteaux de sable.

Answers to Activity 11
1. a **2.** a **3.** a **4.** b **5.** b **6.** a

Application 1

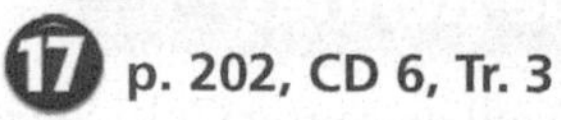

17 p. 202, CD 6, Tr. 3

1. Quand j'étais petit, je jouais rarement au ballon.
2. Quelquefois, j'aimais jouer à la marelle avec ma sœur.
3. Je grimpais souvent aux arbres avec mes amis.
4. Moi, je sautais rarement à la corde. C'était ma sœur qui aimait faire ça.
5. Je regardais toujours des dessins animés le samedi matin.

Answers to Activity 17
1. c **2.** b **3.** a **4.** c **5.** a

Vocabulaire à l'œuvre 2

22 p. 208, CD 6, Tr. 4

1. Regardez le cheval! Qu'est-ce qu'il est beau!
2. Combien de poules est-ce qu'il y a dans la ferme?
3. Vous entendez les canards? Qu'est-ce qu'ils sont bruyants!
4. Je ne vois pas de cochons! Où est-ce qu'ils sont?
5. J'ai peur des vaches! Elles ont l'air dangereuses!

Answers to Activity 22
1. c **2.** e **3.** a **4.** b **5.** d

Grammaire à l'œuvre 2

27 p. 210, CD 6, Tr. 5

1. Moi, je pense que la vie en ville est beaucoup plus stressante que la vie à la campagne.
2. À mon avis, la campagne est moins dangereuse.
3. Je trouve qu'on s'ennuie beaucoup ici. La campagne est moins vivante que la ville.
4. Mais à la campagne, l'air est plus propre et c'est moins pollué!
5. La campagne, c'est moins intéressant que la ville pour les jeunes!
6. C'est tellement bien, la vie à la campagne! Il y a moins de bruit. La campagne est vraiment plus tranquille.

Answers to Activity 27
1. b **2.** b **3.** a **4.** b **5.** a **6.** b

Application 2

38 p. 214, CD 6, Tr. 6

1. Le bruit? Tu parles! Avec tous les animaux de la ferme, c'est encore pire qu'à Paris!
2. L'eau n'est pas très bonne à la ferme. Elle est beaucoup moins bonne qu'en ville.
3. Mes voisins? Ce sont les meilleurs voisins du monde!
4. La salle de bains de la ferme est encore plus petite que celle de mon appartement à Paris.
5. Je préfère la nourriture de la ferme. Elle est meilleure que la nourriture en ville.
6. Mon ami Joseph a les meilleures tomates du monde dans son jardin!

Answers to Activity 38

1. b 2. b 3. a 4. b 5. a 6. a

Prépare-toi pour l'examen

6 p. 223, CD 6, Tr. 9

— Tu es content, toi, ici à la ferme?

— Oui, j'adore. Je trouve la vie à la campagne plus calme et moins stressante que la vie en ville. Et l'air est si pur—il y a beaucoup moins de pollution.

— C'est vrai, je suppose. Pourtant, moi, je préfère la vie en ville. C'est plus intéressant et il y a beaucoup plus de choses à faire.

Answers to Activity 6

À la campagne, la vie est plus calme et moins stressante et il y a moins de pollution.
En ville, la vie est plus intéressante. Il y a plus de choses à faire.

Dictée p. 224, CD 6, Tr. 12

1. La chorale chante bien ensemble.
2. Qu'est-ce que ce chat est méchant!
3. Ma mère m'a acheté un chocolat chaud.
4. Je cherche des chaussures blanches pour mettre avec mes chaussettes.
5. Le cochon a mangé tous les champignons!

Révisions cumulatives *Chapitres 1-6*

1 p. 226, CD 6, Tr. 13

1. Ce matin, je prenais une douche quand le téléphone a sonné.
2. J'ai téléphoné à une amie avant d'entrer dans la douche.
3. Je prenais mon petit-déjeuner quand le bus est arrivé.
4. Ce matin, j'étais en retard. Je suis arrivé en cours à 9h10.

Answers to Activity 1

1. a 2. b 3. c 4. d

50-Minute Lesson Plans

Le bon vieux temps

Day 1

OBJECTIVE
Talk about when you were a child

Core Instruction
Chapter Opener, pp. 192–193
- See Using the Photo, p. 192. **5 min.**
- See Chapter Objectives, p. 192. **5 min.**

Vocabulaire 1, pp. 194–197
- Present **Vocabulaire 1,** pp. 194–195. See Teaching **Vocabulaire,** p. 194. **10 min.**
- Show **Télé-vocab 1. 5 min.**
- Present **Exprimons-nous!,** p. 195. **10 min.**
- Do Activity 1, p. 196. **5 min.**
- Play Audio CD 6, Tr. 1 for Activity 2, p. 196. **5 min.**
- Present **Flash culture,** p. 196. **5 min.**

Optional Resources
- Advanced Learners, p. 195 ▲
- Multiple Intelligences, p. 195

Homework Suggestions
Cahier de vocabulaire et grammaire, pp. 61–62

1.2, 1.3, 2.1

Day 2

OBJECTIVE
*Talk about when you were a child; Tell about an event in the past; Use the **imparfait***

Core Instruction
Vocabulaire 1, pp. 194–197
- Do Activity 3, p. 196. **10 min.**
- See Teaching **Exprimons-nous!,** p. 196. **15 min.**
- Have students do Activities 4–5, p. 197. **15 min.**

Grammaire 1, pp. 198–201
- See Teaching **Grammaire,** p. 198. **5 min.**
- Show **Grammavision 1.1. 5 min.**

Optional Resources
- Slower Pace Learners, p. 197 ◆

Homework Suggestions
Study for **Quiz: Vocabulaire 1**
Cahier de vocabulaire et grammaire, p. 63
Online Practice (**my.hrw.com**)
@HOMETUTOR

1.1, 1.2, 1.3

Day 3

OBJECTIVE
*Use the **imparfait***

Core Instruction
Vocabulaire 1, pp. 194–197
- Review **Vocabulaire 1,** pp. 194–197. **10 min.**
- Give **Quiz: Vocabulaire 1. 20 min.**

Grammaire 1, pp. 198–201
- Present **Flash culture,** p. 198. **5 min.**
- Have students do Activities 6–9, pp. 198–199. **15 min.**

Optional Resources
- Connections, p. 198
- French for Spanish Speakers, p. 199
- Advanced Learners, p. 199 ▲
- Special Learning Needs, p. 199 ●

Homework Suggestions
Cahier de vocabulaire et grammaire, p. 64
Cahier d'activités, p. 51
Online Practice (**my.hrw.com**)
@HOMETUTOR

1.2

Day 4

OBJECTIVE
*Use the **imparfait;** Use the **passé composé** and the **imparfait;** Use adverb placement*

Core Instruction
Grammaire 1, pp. 198–201
- Do Activity 10, p. 199. **10 min.**
- See Teaching **Grammaire,** p. 200. **5 min.**
- Show **Grammavision 1.2. 5 min.**
- Play Audio CD 6, Tr. 2 for Activity 11, p. 200. **5 min.**
- Do Activities 12–15, pp. 200–201. **15 min.**

Application 1, pp. 202–203
- Do Activity 16, p. 202. **5 min.**
- See Teaching **Un peu plus,** p. 202. **5 min.**

Optional Resources
- Slower Pace Learners, p. 201 ◆

Homework Suggestions
Cahier de vocabulaire et grammaire, p. 65
Study for **Quiz: Grammaire 1**

1.1, 1.2, 1.3, 5.1

Day 5

OBJECTIVE
Use adverb placement

Core Instruction
Grammaire 1, pp. 198–201
- Review **Grammaire 1,** pp. 198–201. **10 min.**
- Give **Quiz: Grammaire 1. 20 min.**

Application 1, pp. 202–203
- Play Audio CD 6, Tr. 3 for Activity 17, p. 202. **5 min.**
- Have students do Activities 18–21, pp. 202–203. **15 min.**

Optional Resources
- Communication (TE), p. 203
- Advanced Learners, p. 203 ▲
- Special Learning Needs, p. 203 ●

Homework Suggestions
Study for **Quiz: Application 1**
Cahier de vocabulaire et grammaire, p. 66
Cahier d'activités, pp. 52–53
Online Practice (**my.hrw.com**)

1.1, 1.2, 1.3, 3.2

Day 6

OBJECTIVE
Learn about francophone culture

Core Instruction
Application 1, pp. 202–203
- Review **Application 1,** pp. 202–203. **10 min.**
- Give **Quiz: Application 1. 20 min.**

Culture, pp. 204–205
- See **Culture appliquée** (TE), p. 204. **10 min.**
- See **Comparaisons et communauté** (TE), p. 204. **10 min.**

Optional Resources
- Communities, p. 205
- Cultures, p. 205
- Slower Pace Learners, p. 205 ◆
- Multiple Intelligences, p. 205

Homework Suggestions
Cahier d'activités, p. 54
Online Practice (**my.hrw.com**)
Finish **Culture appliquée** project

2.1, 2.2, 3.1, 4.2, 5.1

Day 7

OBJECTIVE
Compare life in the country and in the city

Core Instruction
Vocabulaire 2, pp. 206–209
- Do Bell Work 6.5, p. 206. **5 min.**
- Present **Vocabulaire 2,** pp. 206–207. See Teaching **Vocabulaire,** p. 206. **10 min.**
- Show **Télé-vocab 2. 5 min.**
- Present **Exprimons-nous!,** p. 207. **10 min.**
- Play Audio CD 6, Tr. 4 for Activity 22, p. 208. **10 min.**
- Have students do Activity 23, p. 208. **5 min.**
- Present **Flash culture,** p. 208. **5 min.**

Optional Resources
- TPR, p. 207
- Slower Pace Learners, p. 207 ◆

Homework Suggestions
Cahier de vocabulaire et grammaire, pp. 67–68

1.2

Day 8

OBJECTIVE
Describe life in the country; Use the comparative with adjectives

Core Instruction
Vocabulaire 2, pp. 206–209
- See Teaching **Exprimons-nous!,** p. 208. **10 min.**
- Have students do Activities 24–26, p. 209. **20 min.**

Grammaire 2, pp. 210–213
- See Teaching **Grammaire,** p. 210. **10 min.**
- Show **Grammavision 2.1. 5 min.**
- Play Audio CD 6, Tr. 5 for Activity 27, p. 210. **5 min.**

Optional Resources
- Advanced Learners, p. 209 ▲
- Multiple Intelligences, p. 209

Homework Suggestions
Study for **Quiz: Vocabulaire 2**
Cahier de vocabulaire et grammaire, p. 69
Cahier d'activités, p. 55
Online Practice (**my.hrw.com**)

To edit and create your own lesson plans, see the

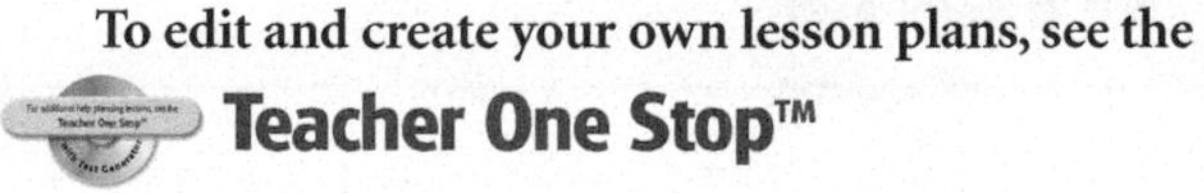

KEY
- ▲ Advanced Learners
- ◆ Slower Pace Learners
- ● Special Learning Needs

Day 9

OBJECTIVE
Use the comparative with adjectives

Core Instruction
Vocabulaire 2, pp. 206–209
- Review **Vocabulaire 2,** pp. 206–209. **10 min.**
- Give **Quiz: Vocabulaire 2. 20 min.**

Grammaire 2, pp. 210–213
- Present **Flash culture,** p. 210. **5 min.**
- Have students do Activities 28–30, pp. 210–211. **15 min.**

Optional Resources
- Slower Pace Learners, p. 211 ◆
- Multiple Intelligences, p. 211

Homework Suggestions
Cahier de vocabulaire et grammaire, p. 70
Cahier d'activités, p. 56
@HOMETUTOR
Online Practice (**my.hrw.com**)

1.1, 1.2, 1.3, 4.2

Day 10

OBJECTIVE
Use the comparative with adjectives; Use the superlative with adjectives; Use irregular comparatives and superlatives

Core Instruction
Grammaire 2, pp. 210–213
- Do Activity 31, p. 211. **5 min.**
- See Teaching **Grammaire,** p. 212. **10 min.**
- Show **Grammavision 2.2. 5 min.**
- Have students do Activities 32–36, pp. 212–213. **20 min.**

Application 2, pp. 214–215
- Do Activity 37, p. 214. **5 min.**
- See Teaching **Un peu plus,** p. 214. **5 min.**

Optional Resources
- Advanced Learners, p. 213 ▲

Homework Suggestions
Study for **Quiz: Grammaire 2**
Cahier de vocabulaire et grammaire, p. 71

1.1, 1.2, 1.3, 5.1

Day 11

OBJECTIVE
Use irregular comparatives and superlatives

Core Instruction
Grammaire 2, pp. 210–213
- Review **Grammaire 2,** pp. 210–213. **10 min.**
- Give **Quiz: Grammaire 2. 20 min.**

Application 2, pp. 214–215
- Play Audio CD 6, Tr. 6 for Activity 38, p. 214. **5 min.**
- Have students do Activities 39–42, pp. 214–215. **15 min.**

Optional Resources
- Communication (TE), p. 215
- Slower Pace Learners, p. 215 ◆
- Special Learning Needs, p. 215 ●

Homework Suggestions
Study for **Quiz: Application 2**
Cahier de vocabulaire et grammaire, p. 72
Cahier d'activités, p. 57
Online Practice (**my.hrw.com**)

1.2

Day 12

OBJECTIVE
Develop listening and reading skills

Core Instruction
Application 2, pp. 214–215
- Review **Application 2,** pp. 214–215. **10 min.**
- Give **Quiz: Application 2. 20 min.**

Télé-roman, pp. 216–217
- Show **Télé-roman.** See Teaching **Télé-roman,** p. 216. **5 min.**
- Have students answer the **As-tu compris?** questions, p. 217. **15 min.**

Optional Resources
- Connections, p. 216
- Gestures, p. 216
- Communication (TE), p. 217

Homework Suggestions
Online Practice (**my.hrw.com**)

1.2

Day 13

OBJECTIVE
Develop listening, reading, and writing skills

Core Instruction
Lecture et écriture, pp. 218–221
- See Teaching **Lecture,** p. 218. **35 min.**
- See Teaching **Espace écriture,** p. 220. **15 min.**

Optional Resources
- Applying the Strategies, p. 218
- Identifying Images, p. 218
- Cultures, p. 219
- Advanced Learners, p. 219 ▲
- Special Learning Needs, p. 219 ●
- Process Writing, p. 221
- Slower Pace Learners, p. 221 ◆
- Multiple Intelligences, p. 221

Homework Suggestions
Cahier d'activités, p. 58
Espace écriture, Activity 2, p. 221

1.2, 1.3, 2.2

Day 14

OBJECTIVE
Develop writing skills; Review the chapter

Core Instruction
Lecture et écriture, pp. 218–221
- See Teaching **Espace écriture** (TE), p. 220. **25 min.**

Prépare-toi pour l'examen, pp. 222–224
- Have students do Activities 1–5, pp. 222–223. **25 min.**

Optional Resources
- Connections, p. 220
- Communities, p. 220
- Writing Assessment, p. 221
- Fold-N-Learn, p. 222
- Oral Assessment, p. 223

Homework Suggestions
Online Practice (**my.hrw.com**)

1.2, 1.3, 2.1, 2.2, 3.1, 5.1

Day 15

OBJECTIVE
Review the chapter

Core Instruction
Prépare-toi pour l'examen, pp. 222–224
- Play Audio CD 6, Tr. 9 for Activity 6, p. 223. **5 min.**
- Have students do Activity 7, p. 223. **5 min.**
- Play Audio CD 6, Tr. 10–12 for **Lettres et sons,** p. 224. **10 min.**

Révisions cumulatives, pp. 226–227
- Play Audio CD 6, Tr. 13 for Activity 1, p. 226. **5 min.**
- Have students do Activities 2–6, pp. 226–227. **25 min.**

Optional Resources
- Reteaching, p. 222
- Game, p. 224
- Chapter Review, pp. 224–225
- Online Culture Project, p. 226
- Fine Art Connection, p. 227

Homework Suggestions
Study for Chapter Test
Online Practice (**my.hrw.com**)

1.1, 1.2, 1.3, 2.1, 2.2, 3.1, 3.2

Day 16/Test

Core Instruction
Chapter Test 50 min.

Optional Resources
Assessment Program
- Alternative Assessment
- Test Generator
- **Quiz: Lecture**
- **Quiz: Écriture**

Homework Suggestions
Cahier d'activités, pp. 59–60, 112–113
Online Practice (**my.hrw.com**)

chapitre 6

90-Minute Lesson Plans

Le bon vieux temps

Block 1

OBJECTIVE
Talk about when you were a child; Tell about an event in the past

Core Instruction

Chapter Opener, pp. 192–193
- See Using the Photo, p. 192. **5 min.**
- See Chapter Objectives, p. 192. **5 min.**

Vocabulaire 1, pp. 194–197
- Present **Vocabulaire 1,** pp. 194–195. See Teaching **Vocabulaire,** p. 194. **10 min.**
- Show **Télé-vocab 1. 5 min.**
- Present **Exprimons-nous!,** p. 195. **10 min.**
- Have students do Activity 1, p. 196. **5 min.**
- Play Audio CD 6, Tr. 1 for Activity 2, p. 196. **5 min.**
- Have students do Activity 3, p. 196. **5 min.**
- Present **Flash culture,** p. 196. **10 min.**
- See Teaching **Exprimons-nous!,** p. 196. **10 min.**
- Have students do Activities 4–5, p. 197. **20 min.**

Optional Resources

- Learning Tips, p. 193
- Proverbs, p. 193
- TPR, p. 195
- Comparisons, p. 195
- Teacher Note, p. 195
- Advanced Learners, p. 195 ▲
- Multiple Intelligences, p. 195
- Communities, p. 197
- Communication (TE), p. 197
- Slower Pace Learners, p. 197 ◆
- Multiple Intelligences, p. 197

Homework Suggestions

Study for **Quiz: Vocabulaire 1**
Cahier de vocabulaire et grammaire, pp. 61–63
@HOMETUTOR
Online Practice (**my.hrw.com**)
1.1, 1.2, 1.3

Block 2

OBJECTIVE
Use the ***imparfait;*** *Use the* ***passé composé*** *and the* ***imparfait***

Core Instruction

Vocabulaire 1, pp. 194–197
- Review **Vocabulaire 1,** pp. 194–197. **10 min.**
- Give **Quiz: Vocabulaire 1. 20 min.**

Grammaire 1, pp. 198–201
- Present **Flash culture,** p. 198. **5 min.**
- See Teaching **Grammaire,** p. 198. **5 min.**
- Show **Grammavision 1.1. 5 min.**
- Have students do Activities 6–10, pp. 198–199. **15 min.**
- See Teaching **Grammaire,** p. 200. **5 min.**
- Show **Grammavision 1.2. 5 min.**
- Play Audio CD 6, Tr. 2 for Activity 11, p. 200. **5 min.**
- Have students do Activities 12–14, pp. 200–201. **15 min.**

Optional Resources

- Connections, p. 198
- French for Spanish Speakers, p. 199
- Communication (TE), p. 199
- Advanced Learners, p. 199 ▲
- Special Learning Needs, p. 199 ●
- **Attention!,** p. 200
- Slower Pace Learners, p. 201 ◆
- Special Learning Needs, p. 201 ●

Homework Suggestions

Study for **Quiz: Grammaire 1**
Cahier de vocabulaire et grammaire, pp. 64–65
Cahier d'activités, pp. 51–52
@HOMETUTOR
Online Practice (**my.hrw.com**)
1.1, 1.2, 1.3, 5.1

Block 3

OBJECTIVE
Use the ***passé composé*** *and the* ***imparfait;*** *Use of adverb placement; Learn about francophone culture*

Core Instruction

Grammaire 1, pp. 198–201
- Have students do Activity 15, p. 201. **10 min.**
- Review **Grammaire 1,** pp. 198–201. **10 min.**
- Give **Quiz: Grammaire 1. 20 min.**

Application 1, pp. 202–203
- See Teaching **Un peu plus,** p. 202. **5 min.**
- Have students do Activity 16, p. 202. **5 min.**
- Play Audio CD 6, Tr. 3 for Activity 17, p. 202. **5 min.**
- Have students do Activities 18–21, pp. 202–203. **15 min.**

Culture, pp. 204–205
- See **Culture appliquée** (TE), p. 204. **10 min.**
- See **Comparaisons et communauté** (TE), p. 204. **10 min.**

Optional Resources

- Communication (TE), p. 201
- Communication (TE), p. 203
- Advanced Learners, p. 203 ▲
- Special Learning Needs, p. 203 ●
- Cultures, p. 204
- **Vocabulaire supplémentaire,** p. 204
- Bulletin Board Project, p. 204
- Communities, p. 205
- Cultures, p. 205
- Slower Pace Learners, p. 205 ◆
- Multiple Intelligences, p. 205

Homework Suggestions

Study for **Quiz: Application 1**
Cahier de vocabulaire et grammaire, p. 66
Cahier d'activités, pp. 53–54
Online Practice (**my.hrw.com**)
Finish **Culture appliquée** project
1.1, 1.2, 1.3, 2.2, 5.1

Block 4

OBJECTIVE
Compare life in the country and in the city; Describe life in the country

Core Instruction

Application 1, pp. 202–203
- Review **Application 1,** pp. 202–203. **10 min.**
- Give **Quiz: Application 1. 20 min.**

Vocabulaire 2, pp. 206–209
- Present **Vocabulaire 2,** pp. 206–207. See Teaching **Vocabulaire,** p. 206. **10 min.**
- Show **Télé-vocab 2. 5 min.**
- Present **Exprimons-nous!,** p. 207. **5 min.**
- Play Audio CD 6, Tr. 4 for Activity 22, p. 208. **5 min.**
- Have students do Activity 23, p. 208. **5 min.**
- Present **Flash culture,** p. 208. **5 min.**
- See Teaching **Exprimons-nous!,** p. 208. **10 min.**
- Have students do Activities 24–26, p. 209. **15 min.**

Optional Resources

- Cultures, p. 206
- TPR, p. 207
- **Attention!,** p. 207
- Communities, p. 207
- Slower Pace Learners, p. 207 ◆
- Special Learning Needs, p. 207 ●
- **Attention!,** p. 208
- Comparisons, p. 208
- Cinquain Poetry, p. 209
- Communication (TE), p. 209
- Advanced Learners, p. 209 ▲
- Multiple Intelligences, p. 209

Homework Suggestions

Study for **Quiz: Vocabulaire 2**
Cahier de vocabulaire et grammaire, pp. 67–69
@HOMETUTOR
Online Practice (**my.hrw.com**)
1.1, 1.2, 1.3, 2.2, 3.1

To edit and create your own lesson plans, see the **Teacher One Stop™**

KEY
- ▲ Advanced Learners
- ◆ Slower Pace Learners
- ● Special Learning Needs

90-Minute Lesson Plans

Block 5

OBJECTIVE
Use the comparative with adjectives; Use the superlative with adjectives

Core Instruction

Vocabulaire 2, pp. 206–209
- Review **Vocabulaire 2,** pp. 206–209. **10 min.**
- Give **Quiz: Vocabulaire 2. 20 min.**

Grammaire 2, pp. 210–213
- Present **Flash culture,** p. 210. **5 min.**
- See Teaching **Grammaire,** p. 210. **5 min.**
- Show **Grammavision 2.1. 5 min.**
- Play Audio CD 6, Tr. 5 for Activity 27, p. 210. **5 min.**
- Have students do Activities 28–31, pp. 210–211. **20 min.**
- See Teaching **Grammaire,** p. 212. **5 min.**
- Show **Grammavision 2.2. 5 min.**
- Have students do Activities 32–34, pp. 212–213. **10 min.**

Optional Resources
- Teacher to Teacher, p. 211
- Communication (TE), p. 211
- Slower Pace Learners, p. 211 ◆
- Multiple Intelligences, p. 211
- Cultures, p. 212
- Advanced Learners, p. 213 ▲
- Multiple Intelligences, p. 213

Homework Suggestions
Study for **Quiz: Grammaire 2**
Cahier de vocabulaire et grammaire, pp. 70–71
Cahier d'activités, pp. 55–56
@HOMETUTOR
Online Practice (**my.hrw.com**)
1.1, 1.2, 2.2

Block 6

OBJECTIVE
Use the superlative with adjectives; Use irregular comparatives and superlatives; Develop listening and reading skills

Core Instruction

Grammaire 2, pp. 210–213
- Have students do Activities 35–36, p. 213. **10 min.**
- Review **Grammaire 2,** pp. 210–213. **10 min.**
- Give **Quiz: Grammaire 2. 20 min.**

Application 2, pp. 214–215
- Have students do Activity 37, p. 214. **5 min.**
- See Teaching **Un peu plus,** p. 214. **5 min.**
- Play Audio CD 6, Tr. 6 for Activity 38, p. 214. **5 min.**
- Have students do Activities 39–42, pp. 214–215. **15 min.**

Télé-roman, pp. 216–217
- Show **Télé-roman.** See Teaching **Télé-roman,** p. 216. **5 min.**
- Have students answer the **As-tu compris?** questions, p. 217. **15 min.**

Optional Resources
- Communication (TE), p. 213
- French for Spanish Speakers, p. 214
- Communication (TE), p. 215
- Slower Pace Learners, p. 215 ◆
- Special Learning Needs, p. 215 ●
- Connections, p. 216
- Gestures, p. 216
- Communication (TE), p. 217

Homework Suggestions
Study for **Quiz: Application 2**
Cahier de vocabulaire et grammaire, p. 72
Online Practice (**my.hrw.com**)
1.1, 1.2, 5.1

Block 7

OBJECTIVE
Develop listening, reading, and writing skills; Review the chapter

Core Instruction

Application 2, pp. 214–215
- Review **Application 2,** pp. 214–215. **10 min.**
- Give **Quiz: Application 2. 20 min.**

Lecture et écriture, pp. 218–221
- See Teaching **Lecture,** p. 218. **20 min.**
- See Teaching **Espace écriture,** p. 220. **30 min.**

Prépare-toi pour l'examen, pp. 222–224
- Have students do Activities 1–3, p. 222. **10 min.**

Optional Resources
- Applying the Strategies, p. 218
- Identifying Images, p. 218
- Cultures, p. 219
- Advanced Learners, p. 219 ▲
- Special Learning Needs, p. 219 ●
- Connections, p. 220
- Communities, p. 220
- Process Writing, p. 221
- Writing Assessment, p. 221
- Slower Pace Learners, p. 221 ◆
- Multiple Intelligences, p. 221
- Reteaching, p. 222
- Fold-N-Learn, p. 222

Homework Suggestions
Study for Chapter Test
Cahier d'activités, p. 58
Espace écriture, Activity 2, p. 221
Online Practice (**my.hrw.com**)
1.2, 1.3, 2.2

Block 8

OBJECTIVE
Review and assess the chapter

Core Instruction

Prépare-toi pour l'examen, pp. 222–224
- Have students do Activities 4–5, p. 223. **5 min.**
- Play Audio CD 6, Tr. 9 for Activity 6, p. 223. **5 min.**
- Have students do Activity 7, p. 223. **5 min.**
- Play Audio CD 6, Tr. 10–12 for **Lettres et sons,** p. 224. **5 min.**

Chapter Test 50 min.

Révisions cumulatives, pp. 226–227
- Play Audio CD 6, Tr. 13 for Activity 1, p. 226. **5 min.**
- Have students do Activities 2–6, pp. 226–227. **15 min.**

Optional Resources
- TPRS, p. 223
- Oral Assessment, p. 223
- Game, p. 224
- Chapter Review, pp. 224–225
- Teacher to Teacher, p. 225
- Online Culture Project, p. 226
- Fine Art Connection, p. 227

Homework Suggestions
Cahier d'activités, pp. 59–60, 112–113
Online Practice (**my.hrw.com**)
1.1, 1.2, 2.2, 3.1

Meeting the National Standards

Communication
Communication, pp. 197, 199, 201, 203, 209, 211, 213, 215
À ton tour, p. 227

Cultures
Flash culture, pp. 196, 198, 208, 210
Comparaisons, p. 205
Practices and Perspectives, p. 219
Products and Perspectives, pp. 205, 206, 212

Connections
History Link, p. 198
Music Link, p. 220
Visual Learners, p. 216

Comparisons
Comparaisons, p. 205
Comparing and Contrasting, pp. 195, 208

Communities
Communauté, p. 205
Community Link, p. 205
Family Link, pp. 197, 220

Using the Photo

In Rennes, children enjoy a ride on the carousel in front of the Opera House. Built in the 19th century, the Opera House was beautifully restored in 1997. The Rennes Opera House hosts some of the finest operas in all of Europe. Locals and visitors to Rennes enjoy not only the opera, but a rich and diverse cultural scene, with music festivals throughout the year. Ask students to describe a musical festival or an opera that they have attended. 1.3

Vocabulaire supplémentaire

Students might use these terms to discuss the photo.

l'ampoule *lightbulb*
le cheval de bois *wooden horse*
taillé *carved*
peindre *to paint*
la barre *pole*

chapitre 6

Le bon vieux temps

Objectifs

In this chapter, you will learn to
- talk about when you were a child
- tell about an event in the past
- compare life in the country and in the city
- describe life in the country

And you will use
- the **imparfait**
- the **passé composé** and the **imparfait**
- adverb placement
- the comparative with adjectives and nouns
- the superlative with adjectives
- irregular comparatives and superlatives

Que vois-tu sur la photo?
Où sont ces jeunes?
Est-ce qu'ils s'amusent?
Et toi, tu aimes les carrousels?

ACTFL 21st Century Skills

Communication:	SE: pp. 197, 201, 202, 211, 215, 221, 227; TE: pp. 191C, 203, 211, 217
Creativity and Innovation:	TE: pp. 195, 197, 207, 209
Information Literacy:	SE: pp. 204, 205; TE: pp. 191D, 195, 198, 204, 205, 207, 209, 212, 219, 226
Technology Literacy:	TE: pp. 191C, 193, 195 (Health Literacy)
Initiative and Self-Direction:	TE: pp. 193, 205, 207, 213, 220
Social and Cross-Cultural Skills:	TE: pp. 204, 205, 206, 207, 219 (Global Awareness), 226, 227

Chapter Opener

Un carrousel devant l'opéra de Rennes

DIGITAL FRENCH

TEACHER TOOLS
- Interactive Whiteboard Lessons
- Generate Success!

ALSO AVAILABLE...
- Online Workbooks
- French InterActive Reader

FRENCH ON THE GO!
- Performance Space
- Holt McDougal French Apps
- *Bien dit!* eTextbook

Learning Tips

It is often difficult for students to follow the rhythm of French speakers. If students have access to the Internet at home, they should try to watch the French news or listen to French radio in order to hear native French speakers. This will also give them more opportunities to hear the language in everyday situations.

VIDEO OPTIONS

- Télé-vocab 1
- Grammavision 1
- Télé-vocab 2
- Grammavision 2
- Télé-roman

LISTENING PRACTICE — Language Lab and Classroom Activities

Vocabulaire
- Activity 2, p. 196, CD 6, Tr. 1
- **Télé-vocab 1,** p. 194, DVD Tutor
- Activity 22, p. 208, CD 6, Tr. 6
- **Télé-vocab 2,** p. 206, DVD Tutor

Grammaire
- Activity 11, p. 200, CD 6, Tr. 2
- **Grammavision 1,** pp. 198, 200, DVD Tutor
- Activity 27, p. 210, CD 6, Tr. 5
- **Grammavision 2,** pp. 210, 212, DVD Tutor

Application
- Activity 17, p. 202, CD 6, Tr. 3
- Activity 38, p. 214, CD 6, Tr. 6

Prépare-toi pour l'examen
- Activity 6, p. 223, CD 6, Tr. 9

Révisions cumulatives
- Activity 1, p. 226, CD 6, Tr. 13

Télé-roman
- p. 216, DVD Tutor

Lecture
- p. 218, CD 6, Tr. 7

Variations littéraires
- p. 392, CD 6, Tr. 8

Lettres et sons
- p. 224, CD 6, Tr. 10–12

Resources

Planning:

Lesson Planner

Teacher One Stop

Presentation:

Projectable Transparencies **Vocabulaire 6.1, 6.2**

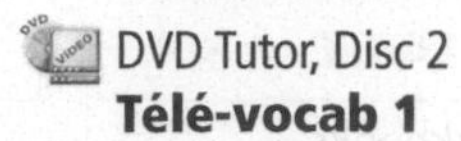

DVD Tutor, Disc 2 **Télé-vocab 1**

Interactive Whiteboard Lessons

Practice:

Cahier de vocabulaire et grammaire

Differentiated Practice and Assessment CD-ROM

Independent Study Guide

Media Guide

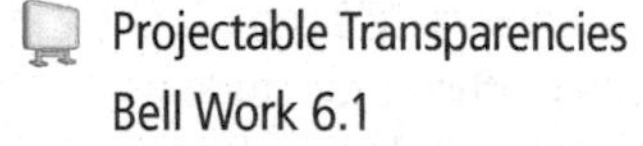

Projectable Transparencies Bell Work 6.1

@HOMETUTOR

Holt McDougal French Apps

Bell Work

Use Bell Work 6.1 in the *Projectable Transparencies* or write this activity on the board.

Say what these people are going to do tomorrow morning.

1. **se réveiller / toi**
2. **se lever / moi**
3. **se laver / nous**
4. **se maquiller / Julie et Sophie**
5. **s'habiller / vous**

1.2

Objectifs

- to talk about when you were a child
- to tell about an event in the past

Vocabulaire à l'œuvre 1

Télé-vocab

Souvenirs d'enfance

Quand j'étais jeune, j'aimais...

faire des châteaux (m.) de sable

jouer à la poupée

sauter à la corde

faire du manège

jouer à chat perché

faire de la balançoire

jouer à la marelle

Proverbes

For French proverbs and activities related to the chapter theme and vocabulary, see **Proverbes et expressions,** pp. R6–R7.

Core Instruction

TEACHING VOCABULAIRE

1. Introduce the vocabulary with transparencies **Vocabulaire 6.1** and **6.2** and model pronunciation. **(2 min.)**
2. Using the expressions in **Exprimons-nous!,** tell what you did when you were younger, pointing to the transparency as you mention each activity. **(3 min.)**
3. Ask students **oui** or **non** questions about their childhood, using the same format. Include the words and phrases in **D'autres mots utiles. (4 min.)**

Télé-vocab 1

For a video presentation of this vocabulary, see the *DVD Tutor.*

Télé-vocab

Et moi, j'aimais...

Online Practice
my.hrw.com
Vocabulaire 1 practice

jouer au train électrique

jouer au ballon

jouer aux petites voitures

jouer aux dames (f.)

grimper aux arbres (m.)

Exprimons-nous!

To talk about when you were a child

Quand j'étais (plus) jeune, j'aimais jouer aux dames. *When I was young (younger) . . .*

Quand j'étais petit(e), j'aimais aller au cirque. *When I was little . . .*

Quand j'avais huit **ans,** j'aimais faire de la balançoire. *When I was . . . years old . . .*

Vocabulaire et grammaire, *pp. 61–63*

D'autres mots utiles

aller au cirque	*to go to the circus*
faire des farces	*to play pranks/ practical jokes*
regarder des dessins animés	*to watch cartoons*
collectionner	*to collect*
jouer aux billes	*to play marbles*
faire de la bascule	*to seesaw*
content(e)/triste	*happy/sad*
obéissant(e)	*obedient*

Vocabulaire 1

TPR

Total Physical Response

Have students respond to these commands.

Lève le doigt si tu faisais du manège quand tu étais petit(e).

Lève la main si tu jouais à la poupée quand tu avais cinq ans.

Lève les deux mains si tu grimpais aux arbres quand tu étais plus jeune.

Lève-toi si tu faisais des farces à tes ami(e)s.

Viens au tableau et dessine une balançoire.

Then have some students mime the following activities.

Joue à la marelle!

Joue au ballon avec Briana.

Saute à la corde!

Joue aux petites voitures par terre!

Joue aux dames avec Jeff.

1.2

Comparisons

Comparing and Contrasting

Many parents worry that their children prefer to stay indoors playing video games rather than be outdoors climbing trees, jumping rope, and playing the other games presented in **Vocabulaire.** Ask students to research on the Internet articles in French magazines about this topic. Have students create a bulletin board that compares the benefits of the activities shown here with those of electronic, computer, and video games. 4.2

Differentiated Instruction

Advanced Learners

Have students create a puppet show whose characters use phrases in **Vocabulaire 1.** For example, students could write a play about grandfather and grandmother puppets who tell their grandchildren what games they used to play when they were young. Have students present their puppet shows to the rest of the class. 1.3

Multiple Intelligences

Visual Allow students to make a small scrapbook or a poster to show a few events in their childhood or in the childhood of a fictitious character. Have them write captions for the photos or illustrations that describe the events. Remind students to use the expressions in **Vocabulaire** and **Exprimons-nous!** in their project. Give students the option of sharing their project with the class. 1.3

Teacher Note

You may wish to explain to students that **jouer à chat perché** is a game of tag, but that a person cannot be tagged while standing on an object such as a chair, table, curb, or even a stone.

Vocabulaire 1

Resources

Planning:
Lesson Planner
Teacher One Stop

Presentation:
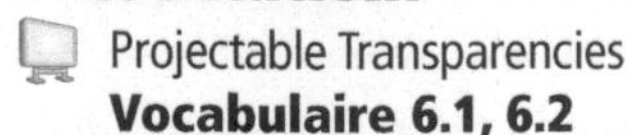
Projectable Transparencies **Vocabulaire 6.1, 6.2**
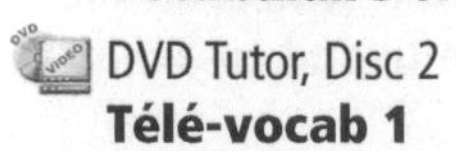
DVD Tutor, Disc 2 **Télé-vocab 1**
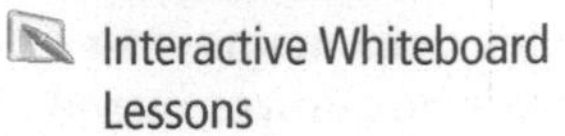
Interactive Whiteboard Lessons

Practice:
Cahier de vocabulaire et grammaire
Differentiated Practice and Assessment CD-ROM
Independent Study Guide
Media Guide
Audio CD 6, Tr. 1
@HOMETUTOR
Holt McDougal French Apps

2 Script

— Mamie, qu'est-ce que tu aimais faire quand tu étais petite?
— Oh, j'aimais faire beaucoup de choses!
— Mais, quoi?
— J'aimais faire des châteaux de sable sur la plage.
— Est-ce que tu aimais jouer à la poupée?
— Oui, beaucoup! Quand j'avais six ans, ma poupée préférée s'appelait madame Michaud.
— Est-ce que tu aimais sauter à la corde?
— Non, pas tellement, mais j'aimais bien jouer à la marelle.
— Quoi d'autre?
— Oh, quand j'étais plus jeune, j'aimais jouer à chat perché. Mais ce que je préférais, c'était grimper aux arbres.
— Moi, j'adore ça aussi! Tu veux venir grimper aux arbres avec moi, mamie?
— Ah, non, ma petite! À mon âge, ce n'est plus possible! Mais je peux te regarder, d'accord?
— D'accord!

Flash culture

Les enfants français aiment jouer aux jeux de société comme jouer aux dames ou aux cartes. Il y a deux jeux de société typiquement français: le jeu des Mille Bornes® et le jeu des petits chevaux. Le jeu des Mille Bornes est basé sur le code de la route. Le jeu des petits chevaux est une course de chevaux.

Quels sont tes jeux préférés? 2.1

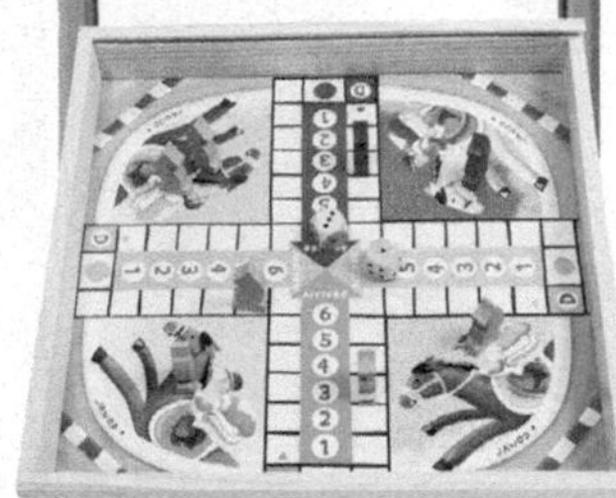
Le jeu des petits chevaux

1 C'est l'intention qui compte 1.2

Écrivons Christian veut choisir un cadeau d'anniversaire pour les six ans de son frère. Alors, il a pensé aux activités qu'il aimait faire à son âge. Complète ses phrases avec des mots de la boîte.

électrique	collectionner	dames
voitures	cirque	dessins animés

1. Quand j'étais petit, j'aimais bien regarder des ______. Peut-être un DVD de Tintin? dessins animés
2. Quand j'avais sept ans, j'aimais ______ les timbres, mais je ne sais pas si René aime faire ça. collectionner
3. Quand j'étais petit, j'aimais jouer aux ______, mais je crois que René aime mieux jouer aux échecs. dames
4. Quand j'étais plus jeune, j'aimais jouer au train ______ (électrique), mais je pense que René aime mieux jouer aux petites ______. voitures
5. Quand j'avais sept ans, j'aimais aller au ______ (cirque). René adore les clowns! Je crois que j'ai trouvé le cadeau idéal.

2 Écoutons CD 6, Tr. 1 1.2

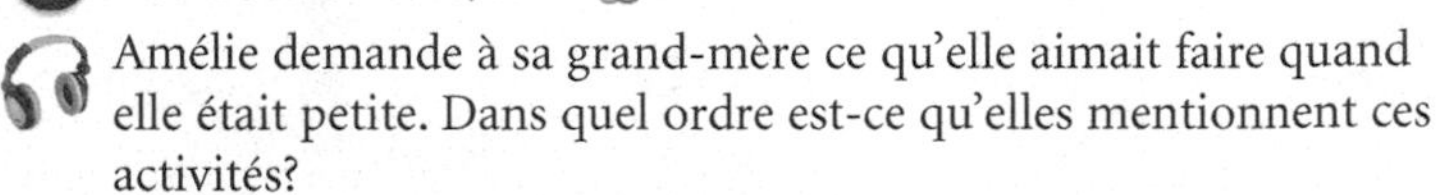

Amélie demande à sa grand-mère ce qu'elle aimait faire quand elle était petite. Dans quel ordre est-ce qu'elles mentionnent ces activités?

6 **a.** grimper aux arbres
5 **b.** jouer à chat perché
1 **c.** faire des châteaux de sable
4 **d.** jouer à la marelle
2 **e.** jouer à la poupée
3 **f.** sauter à la corde

3 Quand j'étais petit(e)... 1.1

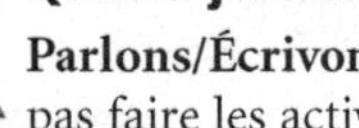

Parlons/Écrivons Dis si tu aimais ou n'aimais pas faire les activités illustrées quand tu étais petit(e).

MODÈLE —**Quand j'étais petit(e), j'aimais sauter à la corde.**

1.

2.

3.

4.

Core Instruction

TEACHING EXPRIMONS-NOUS!

1. Bring in a photo from your childhood or one from a magazine. Tell a story about the photo, using the new vocabulary and expressions in **Exprimons-nous!** Include in your story a series of events. **(3 min.)**
2. Show students a second picture. This time have a different story on a transparency, with the sentences cut apart and mixed up. Ask students to come up one at a time, read a sentence aloud, and then to put it in the correct order. **(3 min.)**
3. Ask a volunteer to read the story aloud after the sentence strips have been arranged in proper order. **(2 min.)**

Exprimons-nous!

To tell about an event in the past

Un jour, **pendant que** je jouais dans le jardin, j'ai vu un petit chat dans un arbre. *. . . while . . .*

Alors que je l'aidais à descendre de l'arbre, il est tombé. *While/When . . .*

À ce moment-là, mon chien est arrivé et a commencé à courir après le chat. *At that moment, . . .*

Heureusement, ma mère a appelé le chien. *Fortunately . . .*

Finalement, le petit chat a pu rentrer chez lui. J'étais content. *Finally . . .*

Vocabulaire et grammaire, *pp. 61–63*

4 Une histoire incroyable 1.2

Lisons La sœur de Marc lui a raconté une histoire incroyable. Remets son histoire dans le bon ordre. c, g, b, f, a, d, e

a. Elle a dit: «Vous devez m'aider! La mer va détruire *(destroy)* mon château!»

b. Alors que je regardais autour de moi, j'ai entendu de nouveau: «Au secours!»

c. Quand j'étais petite, j'aimais beaucoup aller à la plage.

d. J'ai décidé de faire un autre château pour la princesse, loin de la mer.

e. Finalement, la princesse est allée habiter dans son nouveau château.

f. À ce moment-là, j'ai vu une petite princesse à l'une des fenêtres du château de sable!

g. Un jour, pendant que je faisais un château de sable, j'ai entendu quelqu'un appeler: «Au secours!» *(Help!)*

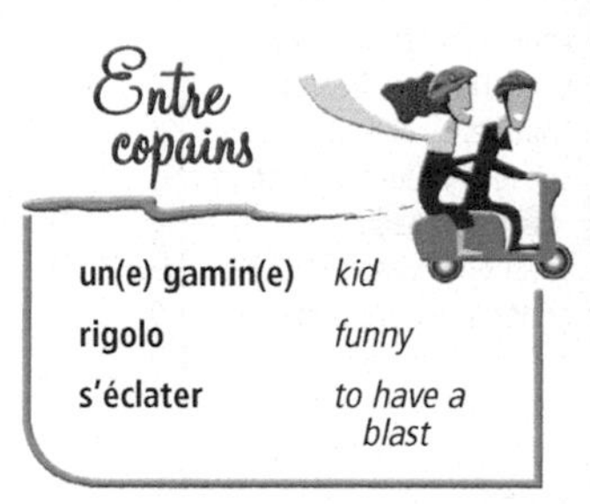

un(e) gamin(e)	*kid*
rigolo	*funny*
s'éclater	*to have a blast*

Communication

5 Scénario 1.1

Parlons Le maire (*mayor*) de ta ville t'a demandé de créer un parc pour les enfants. Avec tes camarades, discutez de quelles activités vous aimiez faire quand vous étiez plus jeunes. Puis, faites un dessin qui montre les activités que votre parc va offrir et présentez votre dessin à la classe.

MODÈLE —Quand j'étais petit(e), j'aimais jouer à la marelle...

Communities

Family Link

Have students interview a grandparent or older neighbor about the games he or she used to play as a child. Students should take notes on the information they learn and either take a photograph or draw a sketch of the person they interviewed. Have students use their notes and the picture to create a poster in French to display in the classroom. 5.2

Communication

5 Group Activity: Interpersonal

Have students make a list of five children's games on a sheet of paper, leaving a few spaces between each. Then have students ask classmates if they did any of the activities last year (in the **passé composé).** Students should respond in a complete sentence with the pronouns **y** or **en** or another appropriate object pronoun. Students should write the names of everyone who answers affirmatively. 1.1

Differentiated Instruction

SLOWER PACE LEARNERS

Help students create a five-sentence anecdote about something that happened to them as a child. Students should use each of the expressions in **Exprimons-nous!** once. Have students practice reading their anecdote aloud to a partner. Then ask volunteers to read their anecdote to the class. 1.3

MULTIPLE INTELLIGENCES

Linguistic Ask students to create a short story like the one in **Exprimons-nous!** Emphasize that the story should follow a logical sequence from beginning to end. Allow students the option of reading their story aloud to the class. Ask volunteers to retell the stories in English as closely as possible and check with the writer for accuracy of translation. 1.3

Assess

Assessment Program

Quiz: Vocabulaire 1

Alternative Assessment

Differentiated Practice and Assessment CD-ROM

Online Assessment
my.hrw.com

Test Generator 

Resources

Planning:
Lesson Planner
Teacher One Stop

Presentation:
DVD Tutor, Disc 2
Grammavision 1.1

Practice:
Grammar Tutor for Students of French, Chapter 6
Cahier de vocabulaire et grammaire
Differentiated Practice and Assessment CD-ROM
Cahier d'activités
Independent Study Guide
Media Guide
Projectable Transparencies
Bell Work 6.2
@HOMETUTOR

Bell Work

Use Bell Work 6.2 in the *Projectable Transparencies* or write this activity on the board.

Fill in the blanks with the correct vocabulary words.

1. **Au bord de la mer, nous faisons des ____ de sable.**
2. **À la campagne, tu aimais ____ aux arbres.**
3. **Mon frère jouait beaucoup avec son train ____.**
4. **Mes parents adoraient ____ des timbres du monde entier.**
5. **Est-ce que tu jouais à la ___ avec tes amies?** 1.2

Connections

History Link

Have students research the history of a popular toy or game and present the information to the class. Students should compare how the toy was used or the game was played then with the way it is used or played today. 3.1

Objectifs
- the *imparfait*
- the *passé composé* and the *imparfait*

Grammaire à l'œuvre 1

Grammavision

The *imparfait*

1 The **imparfait** (imperfect) tense tells *how things were* or what *used to happen repeatedly* in the past. To form the imperfect, drop the **-ons** from the present-tense **nous** form and add these endings.

	parler	finir	vendre
je	parl**ais**	finiss**ais**	vend**ais**
tu	parl**ais**	finiss**ais**	vend**ais**
il/elle/on	parl**ait**	finiss**ait**	vend**ait**
nous	parl**ions**	finiss**ions**	vend**ions**
vous	parl**iez**	finiss**iez**	vend**iez**
ils/elles	parl**aient**	finiss**aient**	vend**aient**

2 Verbs like **manger** and **commencer** that have spelling changes in the **nous** form keep the spelling change in the imperfect, except in the **nous** and **vous** forms.

(nous mang**e**ons) — je mang**e**ais, *but* nous mangions
(nous commen**ç**ons) — je commen**ç**ais, *but* nous commencions

3 **Être** is the only verb that has an irregular stem: **ét-**

Quand j'**ét**ais jeune, j'**ét**ais très timide!

Vocabulaire et grammaire, *pp. 64–65*
Cahier d'activités, *pp. 51–53*

Flash culture

Les bandes dessinées sont très populaires en France. Tout le monde connaît Astérix, Lucky Luke, Tintin et Gaston Lagaffe. Les librairies ont souvent toute une section réservée à la BD. Les enfants commencent en général par lire Boule et Bill. Cela raconte les aventures, une par page, d'un petit garçon, Boule et de son chien, Bill.

Est-ce que tu lis des BD? Lesquelles? 4.2

6 Ah! La jeunesse... 1.2

Écrivons Choisis la forme du verbe qui convient pour compléter les phrases d'après le contexte.

1. Julie, tu ____ jouer à chat perché avec moi cet après-midi?
   (a.) veux **b.** voulais **c.** voulons
2. Quand nous allions à la mer, nous ____ des châteaux de sable.
   a. faisons **(b.)** faisions **c.** faisaient
3. Maman et papa, est-ce que vous ____ danser quand vous étiez jeunes?
   a. aimaient **(b.)** aimiez **c.** aimez
4. Paul et ses copains ____ aux arbres, comme toujours.
   a. grimpez **b.** grimpait **(c.)** grimpaient

Core Instruction

TEACHING GRAMMAIRE

1. Go over Point 1 and model the conjugations. **(3 min.)**
2. Discuss Point 2, pointing out the spelling changes in the **-ger** and **-cer** verbs. Have students give the present tense **nous** form of additional verbs. **(nager, ranger, avancer)** Explain how these spelling changes remain in the **imparfait** except in the **nous** and **vous** forms. **(2 min.)**
3. Go over Point 3, explaining that the stem of **être** is **ét-**, but the **imparfait** endings are the same. Model each form in a sentence. Then describe how the room and your students were yesterday, using the **imparfait. Hier, la salle était allumée. Les élèves écoutaient. Je parlais français. (5 min.)**

Grammavision

For a video presentation of the **imparfait,** see the *DVD Tutor.*

Grammavision

Online Practice
my.hrw.com
Grammaire 1 practice

7 L'enfance 1.2

Écrivons Ursuline discute avec sa grand-mère des activités des enfants d'autrefois *(in the past)*. Complète leur conversation avec les verbes appropriés à l'imparfait.

—Mamie, est-ce que quand tu __1__ petite, il y __2__ des jeux vidéo? étais, avait

—Bien sûr que non! Nous, les filles, nous __3__ à la poupée. On __4__ à la corde aussi. jouions, sautait

—Et les garçons, qu'est-ce qu'ils __5__ faire en général? aimaient

—Eh bien, ils __6__ aux petites voitures ou aux billes. Ils __7__ des trains électriques aussi. Et puis, ils __8__ toujours des farces aux filles! jouaient, avaient, faisaient

8 Les vacances de David 1.2

Écrivons/Parlons Voici des photos des dernières vacances de ton ami David. Invente une légende à l'imparfait pour chaque photo.

MODÈLE **C'était au mois de juillet. On était... Il faisait....**

1.

2.

3.

4.

9 La vie de ma famille il y a dix ans 1.3

Écrivons Qu'est-ce que tu aimais faire quand tu étais petit(e)? Écris un paragraphe pour décrire la vie de ta famille il y a dix ans.

MODÈLE **Ma famille habitait à San Diego. Après l'école, mes frères et moi, nous...**

Digital performance space

Communication

10 Opinions personnelles 1.1

Parlons Imagine que tu travailles pour une compagnie qui fait des jeux pour enfants. Pour créer des idées, les employés parlent des jeux qu'ils aimaient quand ils étaient petits. Jouez cette scène.

MODÈLE **—Alors moi, je jouais toujours à la marelle.**

8 Possible Answers

1. On mangeait souvent au restaurant. Mes parents et moi, nous prenions du poisson, mais mon frère préférait manger de la viande.
2. Les enfants faisaient des châteaux de sable sur la plage. Ils s'amusaient bien.
3. Mon père et ma mère se promenaient sur la plage le soir.
4. Nous nagions dans la mer et nous jouions au ballon sur la plage.

French for Spanish Speakers

Ask Spanish speakers how they would say **quand j'étais jeune. (cuando yo era joven)** Ask what tense **era** is in. **(el imperfecto)** Ask students why they would not use the preterite form **fui** in that sentence. (The period of time referred to in the past, youth, has no determined beginning or ending.) What do they notice about the forms of the imperfect in French? Do they seem to follow a regular pattern? Is this similar to or different than Spanish? (Similar; only three verbs in Spanish are irregular in the imperfect.) 4.1

Communication

Group Activity: Interpersonal

Have students write five sentences about what they used to do with their friends when they were younger. Then have students ask three classmates if they and their friends used to do the same things and write the answer with **ils** as the subject. 1.1

Differentiated Instruction

ADVANCED LEARNERS

9 In their paragraph, have students include both facts and untruths about their life ten years ago. Encourage them to include true, unusual facts and ordinary untruths. Then ask volunteers to read their paragraph aloud. The rest of the class should try to guess which information is true and which is false. 1.3

SPECIAL LEARNING NEEDS

Students with Learning Disabilities/ Dyslexia Ask students to create puzzles by writing subject pronouns, verb stems, and imperfect endings on three strips of paper or three note cards. Students should match a pronoun with a verb stem and verb ending of a variety of verbs. **Je/parl/ais, Tu/parl/ais** Keep each set of puzzles for a verb bundled in envelopes or rubber bands for re-use. Ask students to create more puzzles as they learn new verbs. 1.2

Resources

Planning:
Lesson Planner
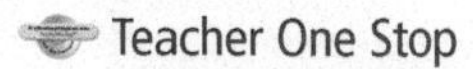
Teacher One Stop

Presentation:
DVD Tutor, Disc 2
Grammavision 1.2

Practice:
Grammar Tutor for Students of French, Chapter 6
Cahier de vocabulaire et grammaire
Differentiated Practice and Assessment CD-ROM
Cahier d'activités
Independent Study Guide
Media Guide
Projectable Transparencies
Bell Work 6.3
Audio CD 6, Tr. 2
HOMETUTOR

Bell Work

Use Bell Work 6.3 in the *Projectable Transparencies* or write this activity on the board.

Fill in the blanks with the correct verbs in the **imparfait.**

1. **Quand j'____ petite, je ____ à la corde.**
2. **Quand ma sœur ____ sept ans, elle ____ à chat perché.**
3. **Quand nous ____ jeunes, nous ____ des dessins animés à la télé.**
4. **À la fête, les enfants ____ du manège.** 1.2

COMMON ERROR ALERT
ATTENTION !

Although certain words or phrases may "trigger" the **imparfait** or **passé composé,** students should be reminded that these are not rules. **Hier** might suggest an isolated event that occurred yesterday **(passé composé),** or it might suggest something that was happening all day long yesterday **(imparfait).**

4.1

En anglais

In English, we use *was/were . . . ing* to talk about something that was going on when something else happened.

What is the difference in meaning between these two sentences?

When Alicia arrived, we were climbing the tree.

When Alicia arrived, we climbed the tree.

In French, use the **imparfait** to talk about something that was going on when something else happened.

In the first sentence, the subjects were in the process of climbing the tree when Alicia arrived. In the second sentence, the subjects started to climb the tree after Alicia arrived.

The *passé composé* and the *imparfait*

1 Use both the **passé composé** and the **imparfait** to talk about the past. Use the **imparfait** to tell how things *were* or what *used to happen* over and over.

Quand j'**étais** jeune, nous **allions** à la plage chaque été.

When I was young, we used to go to the beach every summer.

2 You also use the **imparfait** to give descriptions.

Il **faisait** très beau. Il y **avait** beaucoup de fleurs.

The weather was beautiful. There were a lot of flowers.

3 Use the **passé composé** to say what *happened* or what someone *did* in a set period of time.

Une fois, j'**ai fait** un château de sable incroyable!

4 Sometimes you need to use both the **passé composé** and the **imparfait** in the same sentence. You can tell what was going on **(imparfait)** when another action happened **(passé composé).**

Je **jouais** aux dames quand le téléphone **a sonné.**

Vocabulaire et grammaire, *pp. 64–65*
Cahier d'activités, *pp. 51–53*

11 Écoutons CD 6, Tr 2 1.2

Écoute Nadine qui parle des vacances de sa famille. Est-ce qu'elle parle **a) des choses qu'elle faisait souvent** ou **b) des choses qu'elle a faites une fois** *(one time)*? **1.** a **2.** a **3.** a **4.** b **5.** b **6.** a

12 Une soirée mouvementée 1.2

Souviens-toi! The passé composé, p. 58

Écrivons Hier, il s'est passé beaucoup de choses chez Sonya. Complète les phrases suivantes avec le passé composé ou l'imparfait des verbes entre parenthèses.

1. D'abord, moi, je ______ quand je ______ de la balançoire! (tomber, faire) suis tombée, faisais
2. Puis, mes frères ______ une farce stupide pendant qu'Elsa ______ les dessins animés. (faire, regarder) ont fait, regardait
3. Elsa et moi, nous ______ aux dames après l'école et nous ______. (jouer, se disputer) avons joué, nous sommes disputées
4. Alors que papa ______ dans son bureau, il ______ notre chat dans le jardin. (travailler, voir) travaillait, a vu
5. Mes frères et moi, on ______ dans le jardin quand le petit chat ______ à l'arbre. (s'amuser, grimper) s'amusait, a grimpé
6. Heureusement, papa ______ le petit chat qui ______ de l'arbre sans problème. (aider, descendre) a aidé, est descendu

Core Instruction

TEACHING GRAMMAIRE

1. Go over Points 1–4. Model additional sentences to contrast the differences in use of the **imparfait** and **passé composé.** Read aloud **En anglais,** pausing to have students answer the question and to volunteer additional examples. **(6 min.)**
2. Bring in a photograph or magazine picture about which you can easily tell a story in the past. Use both **imparfait** and **passé composé,** including "specific time" markers in the sentences with the **passé composé.** As you tell the story, have students raise their right hand each time they hear a verb in the **passé composé** and their left hand when they hear a verb in the **imparfait. (4 min.)**
3. Ask **oui** or **non** questions to check comprehension. **(3 min.)**

Grammavision

For a video presentation of the **passé composé** and the **imparfait,** see the *DVD Tutor.*

13 Tout est bien qui finit bien! 1.2

Écrivons/Parlons Justin et sa copine ont passé une journée intéressante au parc la semaine dernière. Raconte ce qui s'est passé, d'après les images suivantes.

MODÈLE **Justin et sa petite amie visitaient le parc quand un cerf-volant est tombé dans un arbre.**

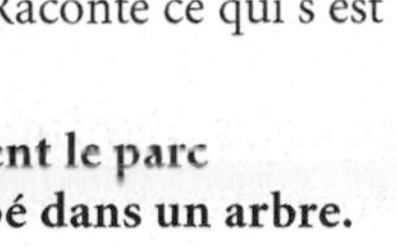

visiter, tomber

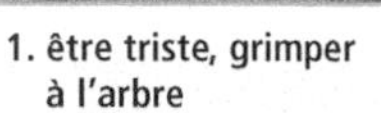

1. être triste, grimper à l'arbre

2. descendre de l'arbre, tomber

3. donner des billets

4. être contents, partir

14 Mon enfance 1.3

Écrivons Réponds aux questions suivantes pour parler de ton enfance (ou de l'enfance d'une autre personne, si tu préfères).

1. Comment étais-tu quand tu avais 8 ans?
2. À quoi est-ce que tu jouais quand tu étais petit(e)?
3. Est-ce que tu aimais grimper aux arbres? Est-ce que tu es tombé(e) un jour?
4. Est-ce que tu préférais jouer aux billes ou à la poupée?
5. Est-ce que tu avais un chien ou un chat? Comment était cet animal?

Communication

15 Scénario 1.3

Parlons En petits groupes, vous allez inventer une histoire au passé. Une personne du groupe commence l'histoire par une phrase ou un morceau de phrase qu'elle invente. Puis, les autres membres du groupe continuent l'histoire, une personne à la fois. L'histoire peut être marrante, bizarre, etc.

MODÈLE ÉLÈVE 1 **Un jour, pendant qu'un enfant rentrait de l'école,...**
ÉLÈVE 2 **... il a vu un magasin de poissons en ville.**
ÉLÈVE 3 **Il adorait les poissons alors...**

11 Script

See script on p. 191E.

13 Possible Answers

1. Le petit garçon était triste, alors Justin a grimpé à l'arbre pour aller chercher le cerf-volant.
2. Alors que Justin descendait de l'arbre, il est tombé et sa petite amie est tombée aussi.
3. Le père du petit garçon a donné des billets de concert à Justin et à sa petite amie.
4. Le petit garçon et son père sont partis. Justin et sa petite amie étaient très contents!

Communication

15 Pair Activity: Presentational

Have students write five sentences to describe a hectic day, real or imaginary. Sentences should start with **pendant que** plus the **imparfait;** a second action in the **passé composé** should interrupt the first. Have partners take turns reading their description aloud. The listener should write his or her partner's sentences in the third person. 1.3

Differentiated Instruction

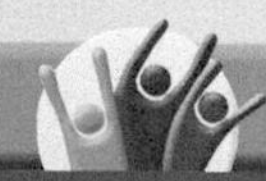

SLOWER PACE LEARNERS

Invent a short fairy tale and write it on the board or on a transparency. Use as much vocabulary from the chapter as possible. Write all the verbs in the infinitive form. Then have students work in small groups to decide if each verb should be in the **imparfait** or **passé composé** and why. 1.2

SPECIAL LEARNING NEEDS

Students with Language Impairments Discuss **En anglais** to emphasize the connection of the **imparfait** with English before asking students to complete Activities 12, 13, and 14. Work closely with students by creating multiple English and French examples to ensure the connection is clear. An appropriate accommodation would be to allow students to use the set of examples as a reference to complete these activities. 1.2

Assess

Assessment Program

Quiz: Grammaire 1

Alternative Assessment

Differentiated Practice and Assessment CD-ROM

Online Assessment
my.hrw.com

Test Generator 

Resources

Planning:
Lesson Planner
Teacher One Stop

Practice:
Grammar Tutor for Students of French, Chapter 6
Cahier de vocabulaire et grammaire
Differentiated Practice and Assessment CD-ROM
Cahier d'activités
Independent Study Guide
Media Guide
Projectable Transparencies
Bell Work 6.4
Audio CD 6, Tr. 3

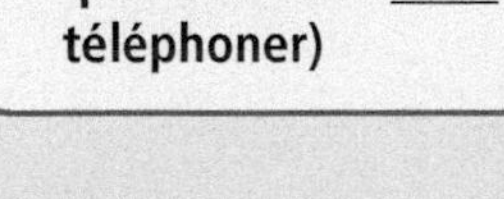

Bell Work

Use Bell Work 6.4 in the *Projectable Transparencies* or write this activity on the board.

Fill in the blanks with the correct verbs in the **imparfait** or the **passé composé**.

1. **Il ____ très beau quand je ____ à la plage. (faire / arriver)**
2. **Quand j' ____ huit ans, je ____ souvent aux arbres, mais un jour je ____. (avoir / grimper / tomber)**
3. **Papa ____ dans son bureau quand Aurélie ____. (être / téléphoner)** 1.2

17 Script

1. Quand j'étais petit, je jouais rarement au ballon.
2. Quelquefois, j'aimais jouer à la marelle avec ma sœur.
3. Je grimpais souvent aux arbres avec mes amis.
4. Moi, je sautais rarement à la corde. C'était ma sœur qui aimait faire ça.
5. Je regardais toujours des dessins animés le samedi matin.

Synthèse
- Vocabulaire 1
- Grammaire 1

Application 1

16 Souvenirs d'enfance 1.2

Écrivons Écris un paragraphe pour raconter un événement important (ou une histoire imaginaire) de ton enfance.

MODÈLE **Un jour, quand j'étais petit(e), ma mère est rentrée avec deux petits chats. Ils étaient...**

Déjà vu!
Do you remember the following adverbs?
souvent
rarement
de temps en temps
beaucoup

Un peu plus Révisions

Adverb placement

1 Generally, place adverbs that tell how much, how often, or how well someone does something *after* the conjugated verb.

Je joue souvent aux dames et hier, j'ai bien joué.

2 **Comme ci comme ça, quelquefois,** and **de temps en temps** are exceptions.

Je joue aux dames **comme ci comme ça. De temps en temps,** je joue avec mon frère. **Quelquefois** je gagne, mais je perds **quelquefois** aussi.

3 Most other adverbs, such as those of time (hier, maintenant) and those ending in **-ment** often go at the beginning or end of the sentence.

Normalement, je passe le samedi avec mes copains.

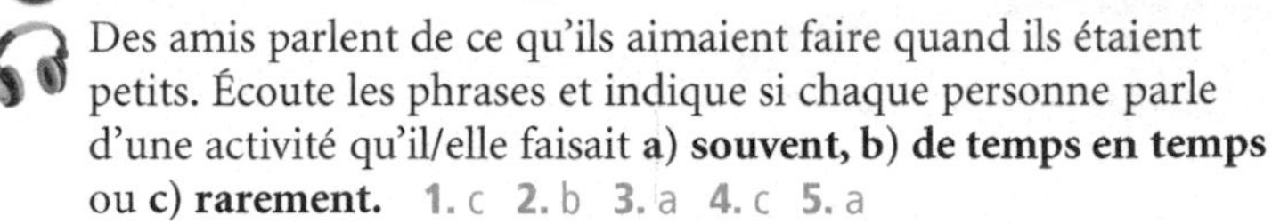

Vocabulaire et grammaire, *p. 66*
Cahier d'activités, *pp. 51–53*

17 Écoutons CD 6, Tr. 3 1.2

Des amis parlent de ce qu'ils aimaient faire quand ils étaient petits. Écoute les phrases et indique si chaque personne parle d'une activité qu'il/elle faisait **a) souvent, b) de temps en temps** ou **c) rarement.** 1. c 2. b 3. a 4. c 5. a

18 Des précisions 1.2

Parlons Complète les phrases avec les adverbes indiqués.

1. La chanteuse a chanté au Super Bowl. (très bien)
2. Les chiens grimpent aux arbres. (assez mal)
3. On est allé sur la planète Jupiter. (ne... jamais)
4. Il a fait beau à Montréal pendant nos vacances. (rarement)
5. Marc jouait au football le dimanche. (souvent)

Core Instruction

INTEGRATED PRACTICE

1. Have students do Activity 16 to review the **passé composé** and **imparfait. (10 min.)**
2. Bring in a child's toy or game. On the board, write five to ten infinitives that could be used in a story about the toy or game. **(2 min.)**
3. As you tell the story, have students choose the appropriate verb in the **imparfait** or the **passé composé** for each sentence. **(8 min.)**
4. Present **Un peu plus** and continue with Activities 17–21. **(10 min.)**

TEACHING UN PEU PLUS

1. Remind students that most shorter adverbs come after the conjugated verb. Adverb phrases and **quelquefois** are exceptions. Adverbs of time and longer adverbs ending in **-ment** go at the beginning or end of a sentence. **(3 min.)**
2. Tell students about yourself, using adverbs in **Un peu plus.** Ask individual students **oui** or **non** questions, using **bien, mal, rarement, souvent, quelquefois, de temps en temps. (6 min.)**

Online Practice
my.hrw.com
Application 1 practice

19 La famille de Tran 1.2

Écrivons Fais des phrases complètes au temps indiqué entre parenthèses pour décrire les activités de la famille de Tran.

1. Tran / mal / jouer au foot / hier (passé composé)
2. La mère de Tran / quelquefois / lire (présent)
3. Lin / comme ci comme ça / jouer aux dames (présent)
4. Sa famille / souvent / aller en vacances à la mer (imparfait)
5. Tran / toujours / être / bon élève au lycée (passé composé)

20 L'interview 1.2

Parlons/Écrivons Une élève francophone veut t'interviewer sur ta jeunesse pour un devoir qu'elle prépare. Utilise des adverbes.

1. Qu'est-ce que tu faisais quand tu avais 6 ans?
2. Est-ce que tu étais content(e) ou triste quand tu étais plus jeune?
3. Qu'est-ce que tu aimais collectionner?

Communication

Digital performance space

21 Questions personnelles 1.1, 3.2

Parlons Lis l'annonce pour un magasin de jouets. Lequel de ces jouets est-ce que tu préférais quand tu étais petit(e)? Demande à ton ou ta camarade lequel de ces jouets il ou elle préférait.

MODÈLE **—Moi, j'aimais... Et toi?**

Au chat perché
Jouets d'autrefois et d'aujourd'hui
Faites découvrir les jouets que vous aimiez à vos enfants
parties de billes à n'en plus finir
dînette avec les poupées
soirée à jouer avec papi et mamie aux jeux de société (dames, petits chevaux, backgammon, mille bornes...)
construction du circuit pour le train électrique avec papa
balançoires • seaux • pelles • bacs à sable et cerfs-volants

18 Answers

1. La chanteuse a très bien chanté au Super Bowl.
2. Les chiens grimpent assez mal aux arbres.
3. On n'est jamais allé sur la planète Jupiter.
4. Il a rarement fait beau à Montréal pendant nos vacances.
5. Marc jouait souvent au football le dimanche.

19 Answers

1. Tran a mal joué au foot hier.
2. La mère de Tran lit quelquefois.
3. Lin joue aux dames comme ci comme ça.
4. Sa famille allait souvent en vacances à la mer.
5. Tran a toujours été bon élève au lycée.

Communication

Pair Activity: Interpersonal

Have students ask a partner what he or she used to do. They should use **quelquefois, rarement, bien, tout le temps,** or **souvent.** The partner should respond using the **imparfait** and the same adverb and add a clause in the **passé composé** that starts with **mais un jour...** Partners should switch roles after they have used all five adverbs. 1.1

Differentiated Instruction

ADVANCED LEARNERS

19 Have students imagine they are twenty five years of age and are remembering back to their teenage years. Have them write a paragraph that describes the activities they used to do and how often they participated in each activity. You may wish to collect the paragraphs, read them aloud, and have the class try to guess who wrote them. 1.3

SPECIAL LEARNING NEEDS

Students with AD(H)D Ask small groups of students to create a bulletin board or a series of posters to depict the three different positions of adverbs explained in **Un peu plus.** All class members can contribute to the display by writing more examples on adhesive notes and placing them in the correct adverb placement category. 1.2

Assess

Assessment Program

Quiz: Application 1

Audio CD 6, Tr. 14

Alternative Assessment

Differentiated Practice and Assessment CD-ROM

Online Assessment
my.hrw.com

Test Generator  

Resources

Planning:
Lesson Planner
Teacher One Stop

Practice:
Cahier d'activités

Vocabulaire supplémentaire

You might wish to use these terms to discuss the project with students.

chanter juste	*to sing in tune*
chanter faux	*to sing off key*
lire la musique	*to read music*
les notes	*notes*
les paroles	*lyrics*
le vers	*verse*
le refrain	*refrain*
chanter en canon	*to sing in a round*
avoir un chat dans la gorge	*to have a frog in one's throat*
racler la gorge	*to clear one's throat*

Bulletin Board Project

In groups of three, have students research **comptines** on the Internet or in the library. Ask each group to choose one song and assign each group member a role: copy the words and music score of the song, illustrate the song, present the song to the class. Have volunteers exhibit the lyrics and illustrations on a bulletin board in the classroom. 1.3

Culture

Une chorale à Versailles

Culture appliquée

Les comptines 2.1, 4.2

Une comptine est une chanson ou un poème pour enfants. La musique de certaines comptines françaises est la même que la musique de comptines américaines. Par exemple, la musique de *Frère Jacques* est la même que celle de *Where is Thumbkin?* La musique de *Twinkle, Twinkle, Little Star* est la même qu'une comptine française du 18e siècle, *Ah! vous dirais-je, maman.*

Paroles et musique CD 11 2.1, 4.2

Below you will find the words and music to *Twinkle, Twinkle, Little Star* and the words to **Ah! vous dirais-je, maman.** Sing the French lyrics to the tune of *Twinkle, Twinkle, Little Star.* In French songs and poems, every syllable is pronounced, including the silent e at the end of a word if it is followed by a consonant.

Ah! vous di - rais je ma-man? Ce qui cau - se mon tour-ment?
Twin-kle, twin-kle, lit - tle star, how I won-der what you are!
Pa - pa veut que je rai-son-ne Comme u- ne gran - de per-son-ne
Up a - bove the world so high, like a dia - mond in the sky.
Moi je dis que les bon-bons Va - lent mieux que la rai - son.
Twin-kle, twin-kle, lit - tle star, how I won-der what you are!

Recherches Fais des recherches pour trouver les paroles françaises de *Jingle Bells.* 2.2

Core Instruction

CULTURE APPLIQUÉE

1. Have the class read and discuss **Les comptines** and **Paroles et musique. (3 min.)**
2. Sing or say the words to "**Ah! vous dirais-je, maman**", remembering to pronounce the mute ***e***. Then have the class sing or say the words with you. **(2 min.)**
3. Assign **Recherches** and ask students to find French and American **comptines** that share the same music. You may wish to give these as extra credit projects. **(2 min.)**

COMPARAISONS ET COMMUNAUTÉ

1. Have students read the introductory question and choose the correct answer. **(1 min.)**
2. Have small groups read **À la ferme** and discuss **Et toi? (4 min.)**
3. In class, read and discuss **Au pair. (2 min.)**
4. If possible, have students contact local organizations that place **au pair** with families or have students research them on the Internet and share their findings. **(15 min.)**

Comparaisons

Une visite d'une ferme d'éveil près de Nantes

À la ferme 4.2

Tu fais du camping à la campagne en France. Tu as besoin de lait et d'œufs, mais tu ne veux pas aller en ville. Où peux-tu faire tes courses?

a. au café du village le plus proche
b. sur le bord[1] de la route
(c.) dans une ferme

En France, pour acheter des produits frais, on peut aller au marché ou directement à la ferme. Il y a plus de 2.200 fermes en France où on peut acheter directement des produits. On y trouve de nombreuses variétés de fruits et de légumes, du lait, de la crème fraîche, du beurre, des fromages (blancs[2], frais, régionaux)... Il existe aussi des «fermes pédagogiques et de découverte». Ce sont des exploitations agricoles[3] qui ouvrent leurs portes au public pour faire découvrir le monde agricole et son environnement.

4.2

ET TOI?

1. Où est-ce que tu fais tes courses en général?
2. Est-ce qu'il y a des «fermes pédagogiques et de découverte» dans ta région? Où?

Communauté et professions

Au pair 5.1

Être au pair peut être une expérience enrichissante, mais il faut s'habituer[4] à la routine des enfants. Les jeunes gens au pair s'occupent des enfants de leur famille d'accueil toute la journée. Est-ce que tu connais quelqu'un qui a été au pair? Est-ce qu'il y a des organisations dans ta région qui organisent le séjour de jeunes gens au pair? Fais des recherches et présente tes résultats à la classe.

Une jeune fille au pair

1. on the side 2. cottage cheese 3. farms 4. to get used to

Communities

Community Link

Have students research additional French **comptines** and choose several to rehearse and present at a community or senior retirement center in your area. Students should be able to explain the meanings of their songs to listeners. 5.1

Cultures

Products and Perspectives

Share with students this quote from Charles de Gaulle that reveals the importance of cheese in French culture: **Comment voulez-vous gouverner un pays qui a deux cent quarante-six variétés de fromage?** *(How can you govern a country that has two hundred and forty-six varieties of cheese?)* Different regions specialize in different kinds of cheese, and there is an official list of French cheeses that are protected under the Protected Designation of Origin policy of the European Union. This designation makes it illegal for a cheese producer to use the name of a French cheese unless it is actually produced in the region. Have each student research one kind of French cheese and report the findings to the class. 2.2

Language Examination

Culture can be used to practice for the **Interpretive Communication** and **Presentational Writing** sections of the AP Language and Culture Exam as it helps students get acquainted with and reflect on products and practices from the French-speaking world while reading culture-focused passages and answering questions in French.

Differentiated Instruction

SLOWER PACE LEARNERS

To help students research **au pair** organizations, have the class write on the board a letter with questions they would like to ask about becoming an **au pair.** Have students copy the letter onto their own paper. Then have partners work together to find the names and addresses of two organizations that match **au pair** with families. Students should send their letter to one of the companies and report back to the class the information they receive. 5.1

MULTIPLE INTELLIGENCES

Musical Ask students to research traditional children's songs and nursery rhymes in French culture. Students may be able to find recordings of French children's music or books of nursery rhymes or poems. Have students read or sing a rhyme or song in class. Ask the class to translate the rhymes into English and compare them to a traditional American song or poem for children. 3.1

Resources

Planning:
Lesson Planner
Teacher One Stop

Presentation:
Projectable Transparencies **Vocabulaire 6.3, 6.4**

DVD Tutor, Disc 2 **Télé-vocab 2**
Interactive Whiteboard Lessons

Practice:
Cahier de vocabulaire et grammaire
Differentiated Practice and Assessment CD-ROM
Independent Study Guide
Media Guide
Projectable Transparencies Bell Work 6.5
@HOMETUTOR
Holt McDougal French Apps

Bell Work

Use Bell Work 6.5 in the *Projectable Transparencies* or write this activity on the board.

Unscramble the words and write the verb in the tense indicated to make a logical sentence.

1. **rarement / Myriam / à la poupée / jouer (imparfait)**
2. **je / aux échecs / comme ci comme ça / hier / jouer (passé composé)**
3. **mes frères / aux billes / de temps en temps / jouer (imparfait)**
4. **toujours / Martine / à la corde / sauter (imparfait)** 1.2

Cultures

Products and Perspectives

Bring samples of French cheeses made from cow, goat, and sheep's milk for students to try. Have them choose their favorite and least favorite cheese. 2.2

Objectifs
- to compare life in the country and in the city
- to describe life in the country

Vocabulaire 2 *à l'œuvre*

DVD Télé-vocab

La vie à la campagne

C'était tellement bien, la vie à la ferme de mes grands-parents.

le paysage
la grange
la poule
le cochon
le champ
le canard
le cheval
le tracteur
le lapin
la vache

Core Instruction

TEACHING VOCABULAIRE

1. Introduce the vocabulary with transparencies **Vocabulaire 6.3** and **6.4** and model pronunciation. **(2 min.)**
2. Describe and compare the animals, using **plus/moins grand... que, plus/moins petit... que. (2 min.)**
3. Display two pictures, one of a city and one of a country scene. Ask students **oui** or **non** questions, including the adjectives in **D'autres mots utiles** and expressions in **Exprimons-nous! La vie à la campagne est plus dangereuse que la vie en ville? L'air est moins pollué à la campagne qu'en ville? (3 min.)**

Télé-vocab 2

For a video presentation of this vocabulary, see the *DVD Tutor.*

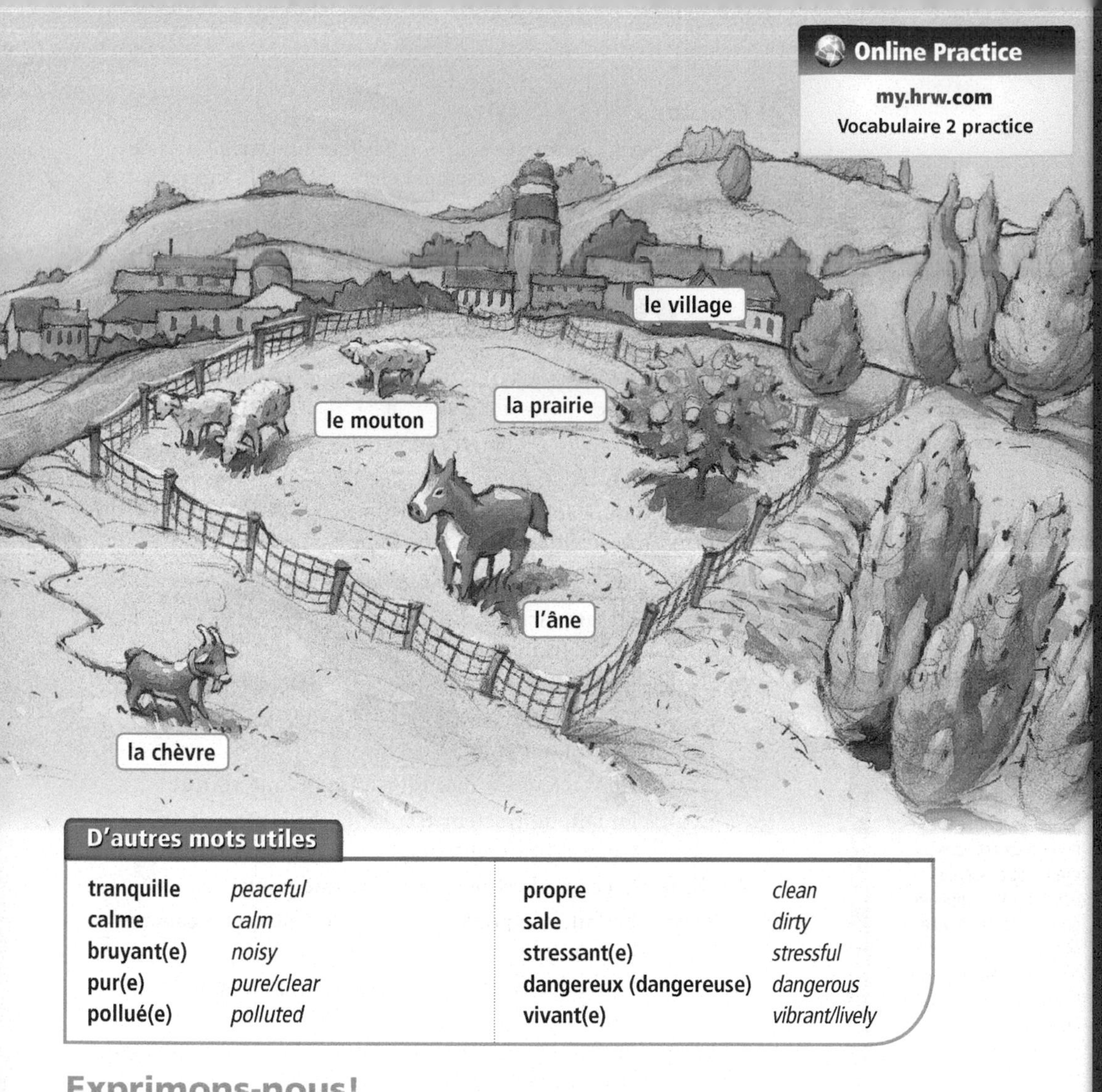

D'autres mots utiles

tranquille	*peaceful*	**propre**	*clean*
calme	*calm*	**sale**	*dirty*
bruyant(e)	*noisy*	**stressant(e)**	*stressful*
pur(e)	*pure/clear*	**dangereux (dangereuse)**	*dangerous*
pollué(e)	*polluted*	**vivant(e)**	*vibrant/lively*

Exprimons-nous!

To compare life in the country and in the city

La vie en ville est **plus** stressante **qu'**à la campagne. *. . . more . . . than . . .*

La campagne, **c'est moins** vivant **que** la ville. *. . . less . . . than . . .*

Il y a plus de bruit à Rennes **que** dans mon village. *There is more . . . than . . .*

La vie à Brest est **différente de** la vie à Saint-Malo. *. . . different from . . .*

J'aime **autant** la vie en ville **qu'**à la campagne. *. . . as much . . . as . . .*

Vocabulaire et grammaire, pp. 67–69 Online Workbooks

▸ **Vocabulaire supplémentaire**—À la campagne, **p. R20**

TPR
Total Physical Response

Have students respond to these commands.

Lève la main si une vache est plus propre qu'un cochon.

Lève-toi si tu aimes autant les tracteurs que les voitures de sport.

Assieds-toi par terre si un âne est moins grand qu'un cheval.

Mets les mains sur les oreilles s'il y a plus de bruit en classe que dans une ferme.

Ask students to bring to class pictures of farm animals. Then have them respond to these commands and suggestions.

Montre-moi un canard.

Amène-moi un mouton.

Va chercher un animal bruyant.

J'aime beaucoup les œufs... 1.2

Common Error Alert
Attention !

Students may have difficulty remembering that **chèvre** is a feminine noun. **La vache** and **la poule** make sense because they are female, and their male equivalents are **le taureau** and **le coq.** The feminine noun **chèvre** refers to both male and female goats.

Differentiated Instruction

Slower Pace Learners

Write the nouns in **Vocabulaire** on index cards, one word per card, and place them in a bag. Write the adjectives on index cards of a different color, also with one word per card. In small groups, have students draw two nouns and one adjective from the bags, and work together to write a logical sentence that compares the nouns. **âne, lapin, bruyant: Un âne est plus bruyant qu'un lapin.** You might also do this activity as a game, with two teams competing to be the first to write a logical sentence. 1.2

Special Learning Needs

Students with AD(H)D Bring to class a collection of children's picture and story books about farm animals. Ask students to translate the text of the books. Have them write the translations on adhesive notes and place them on the appropriate pages of the books. Students can take turns reading the books in French to each other. Ask students to translate the words to the children's song "Old McDonald Had a Farm" and perform it for the class. 1.3

Communities
Community Link

Have students research Jean de La Fontaine's fables that feature the animals in the **Vocabulaire.** Students should either create children's story books based on the fables or write short skits that dramatize the stories and then present their books or stories to elementary or day-care students. 5.1

Resources

Planning:
Lesson Planner
Teacher One Stop

Presentation:
Projectable Transparencies
Vocabulaire 6.3, 6.4

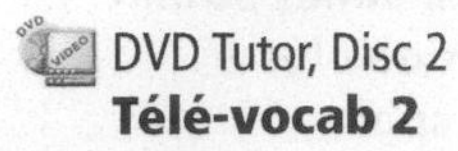

DVD Tutor, Disc 2
Télé-vocab 2

Interactive Whiteboard Lessons

Practice:
Cahier de vocabulaire et grammaire
Differentiated Practice and Assessment CD-ROM
Independent Study Guide
Media Guide
Audio CD 6, Tr. 4
@HOMETUTOR
Holt McDougal French Apps

COMMON ERROR ALERT
ATTENTION !

Students may assume that the verb **manquer** means *to miss.* This will lead them to say incorrectly, **"Je manque mon ami."** instead of **"Mon ami me manque."** *(I miss my friend./ My friend is missing to me.)*

22 Script

1. Regardez le cheval! Qu'est-ce qu'il est beau!
2. Combien de poules est-ce qu'il y a dans la ferme?
3. Vous entendez les canards? Qu'est-ce qu'ils sont bruyants!
4. Je ne vois pas de cochons! Où est-ce qu'ils sont?
5. J'ai peur des vaches! Elles ont l'air dangereuses!

24 Possible Answers

1. Il y a avait un cheval dans le champ.
2. Il y avait des vaches dans la grange.
3. Ce qui était bien, c'était le paysage.
4. Ce qui me manque, c'est les poules.

22 Écoutons CD 6, Tr. 4 1.2

Mademoiselle Chardin et ses élèves visitent une ferme près de leur école. Écoute ce que disent les élèves. De quels animaux est-ce qu'ils parlent? **1.** c **2.** e **3.** a **4.** b **5.** d

a. b.

c.

d.

e.

23 En fait... 1.2

Écrivons Yann habite dans une ferme, mais Jade n'a jamais visité de ferme. Complète les phrases de Yann logiquement.

1. JADE Un cochon est plus sale qu'une vache.
   YANN En fait *(Actually)*, un cochon est ______ sale qu'une vache. (différent, moins)
2. JADE Il n'y a pas de différence entre un cheval et un âne.
   YANN En fait, un âne est ______ d'un cheval. (autant, différent)
3. JADE Un tracteur est moins bruyant qu'une voiture.
   YANN En fait, un tracteur est ______ bruyant qu'une voiture. (différent, plus)
4. JADE Un canard est plus calme qu'une poule.
   YANN En fait, une poule est ______ calme qu'un canard. (moins, plus)
5. JADE La vie à la ferme, c'est moins tranquille que la vie en ville.
   YANN En fait, la vie à la ferme, c'est ______ tranquille que la vie en ville. (plus, autant)

Flash culture

En France, la campagne est de plus en plus populaire. Les Français passent leurs vacances à la campagne pour faire du VTT, de l'escalade et de la randonnée. De nombreux Français préfèrent aussi aller habiter à la campagne que de rester en ville. Mais la campagne doit rester proche de la ville; beaucoup veulent avoir les avantages de la campagne (calme et nature) et les avantages de la ville (travail et commerce).

Est-ce que tu aimes aller à la campagne? Qu'est-ce que tu y fais? 1.2

Exprimons-nous!

To describe life in the country

C'était **tellement** bien, la vie à la ferme!	*. . . really/so . . .*
Il y avait dix poules et six canards.	*There were . . .*
Ce qui était bien, **c'était** le calme.	*What was . . . was . . .*
Ce qui me manque, c'est le paysage.	*What I miss is . . .*

Vocabulaire et grammaire, *pp. 67–69*

Core Instruction

TEACHING EXPRIMONS-NOUS!

1. Hold up the picture of the countryside you displayed for the vocabulary presentation. Modeling the phrases in **Exprimons-nous!**, tell about life in the country. **(2 min.)**
2. Use the same expressions in the negative as you describe the picture of the city. **(4 min.)**
3. Hold up one of these pictures at a time, and make true or false statements about it. Have students tell whether the statement is true **(oui)** or false **(non)**. **Il y avait un cheval dans la grange. Ce qui était bien, c'était les rues sales. Ce qui était bien, c'était le calme de la ville. (5 min.)**

24 C'était tellement bien! 1.2

Écrivons Le grand-père de Justine lui montre des photos de son enfance quand il habitait dans une ferme. Écris ce qu'il dit d'après les photos et utilise les expressions de la boîte.

Il y avait...	Ce qui était bien, c'était...	Ce qui me manque, c'est...

1.

2.

3.

4.

25 À chacun ses goûts 1.2

Parlons/Écrivons Est-ce que tu préfères la vie en ville où à la campagne? Complète les phrases suivantes.

MODÈLE La campagne, c'est moins...
La campagne, c'est moins stressant que la ville.

1. La vie à la campagne, c'est moins...
2. La ville, c'est plus...
3. La campagne, c'est plus...
4. Il y a moins/plus de... en ville.
5. Il y a moins/plus de... à la campagne.

À la française

You can use **assez** *(enough, rather)* and **plutôt** *(rather)* to better describe people or things.

La campagne est assez calme.

Digital performance space

Communication

26 Scénario 1.1

Parlons Tu habites à la campagne, mais tu passes l'été avec ton/ta camarade dans une grande ville. La vie à la campagne te manque beaucoup! Dis à ton/ta camarade ce que tu aimes à la campagne. Il/Elle va essayer de te consoler.

MODÈLE **—C'était tellement bien, la vie à la ferme! Il y avait...**
—Oui, mais la vie en ville, c'est plus....

Differentiated Instruction

ADVANCED LEARNERS

Have students choose an adjective one might use to describe animals (fast, strong, dangerous, poisonous) and do research to find out how different animals compare to each other with respect to that quality. Students should create a graph to chart their data and then discuss their findings with the class. 3.1

MULTIPLE INTELLIGENCES

Naturalist Ask students to use **Vocabulaire 2** and expressions in **Exprimons-nous!** to express their knowledge of and interest in nature by writing descriptive sentences about city and country life. Give students the option of writing prose, poetry, or songs to express their ideas creatively. Matte and display submissions with illustrations or graphics that students select to represent their writing. 1.2

Comparisons

Comparing and Contrasting

Ask students if they can think of any expressions in English that have references to animals. (Never look a gift horse in the mouth.) Have students research similar expressions in French. 4.1

Cinquain Poetry

Have students follow these directions to write a cinquain to describe the countryside.

Line 1 A noun
Line 2 Two adjectives that describe the noun
Line 3 Names of three animals
Line 4 A sentence
Line 5 A word related to the noun

Sample Answer

La campagne
Tranquille, propre
Le cheval, le lapin, le mouton
Ce qui me manque, c'est l'air pur.
Le paysage

Communication

26 Pair Activity: Presentational

Have students write a description of their **ferme idéale** and find or draw a picture to illustrate it. Ask partners to take turns describing their ideal farm. As they listen to their partner, students should draw a picture or layout of the farm that is being described. Then have partners compare pictures. 1.3

Assess

Assessment Program
Quiz: Vocabulaire 2
Alternative Assessment
Differentiated Practice and Assessment CD-ROM

Online Assessment
my.hrw.com

Test Generator

Resources

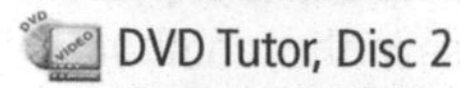

Planning:
Lesson Planner
Teacher One Stop

Presentation:
DVD Tutor, Disc 2
Grammavision 2.1

Practice:
Grammar Tutor for Students of French, Chapter 6
Cahier de vocabulaire et grammaire
Differentiated Practice and Assessment CD-ROM
Cahier d'activités
Independent Study Guide
Media Guide
Projectable Transparencies
Bell Work 6.6
Audio CD 6, Tr. 5
HOMETUTOR

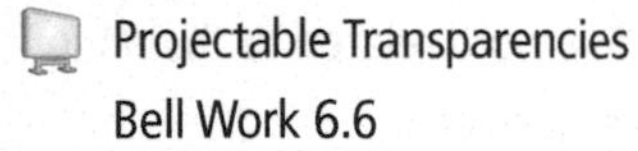

Bell Work

Use Bell Work 6.6 in the *Projectable Transparencies* or write this activity on the board.

Select the logical completion for each sentence.

1. **Dans le champ, il y a plus de poules…**
2. **Une voiture est plus bruyante…**
3. **La vie à la ferme est différente…**
4. **J'aime autant la campagne…**
5. **Ce qui me manque,…**

a. qu'un tracteur.
b. c'est mon cheval.
c. que la ville.
d. que de canards.
e. de la vie en ville. 1.2

27 Script

See script on p. 191E.

Objectifs
- the comparative with adjectives and nouns
- the superlative with adjectives

Grammaire à l'œuvre 2

Grammavision

The comparative with adjectives and nouns

1 You can use these expressions with adjectives to compare things and people. Make the adjective agree with the noun in gender and number. With **c'est,** there is no agreement.

plus + adjective + **que** *more . . . than*
aussi + adjective + **que** *as . . . as*
moins + adjective + **que** *less . . . than*

La ville est **plus** bruyant**e** **que** la campagne.
La ville est **aussi** intéressant**e** **que** la campagne.
La campagne est **moins** pollué**e** **que** la ville.
La ville? C'est **aussi** intéressant **que** la campagne!

2 You can also compare nouns using **plus de, moins de,** and **autant de** before the noun. Remember to use **que/qu'** to continue the comparison.

Il y a **plus de** vaches **que** de canards.
Elle a **moins de** chevaux **que** ses grands-parents.

Vocabulaire et grammaire, *pp. 70–71*
Cahier d'activités, *pp. 55–57*

Flash culture

En France il y a beaucoup de colonies de vacances où les enfants peuvent participer à une grande variété d'activités comme la randonnée, la natation, le kayak, le VTT, l'équitation et parfois des activités spécialisées comme l'art, la musique, le théâtre. Certaines des activités les plus populaires en Bretagne sont la voile et la planche à voile.

Est-ce que tu as déjà été en colonie de vacances? Si oui, est-ce que tu as aimé? Sinon, est-ce que tu aimerais y aller? Pourquoi? 1.3, 4.2

27 Écoutons CD 6, Tr. 5 1.2

On interviewe des personnes. Écoute leurs réponses et indique si chaque personne préfère la vie **a) en ville** ou **b) à la campagne.**

1. b **2.** b **3.** a **4.** b **5.** a **6.** b

28 Les animaux de la ferme 1.2

Écrivons Fais une phrase pour comparer ces animaux qu'on trouve souvent dans les fermes. Utilise **plus... que, moins... que** et **aussi... que.**

MODÈLE lapin / âne / bruyant Possible answers:
Le lapin est moins bruyant que l'âne.

1. poules / canards / gros Les poules sont aussi grosses que les canards.
2. chèvres / moutons / bruyant Les moutons sont moins bruyants que les chèvres.
3. cheval / âne / grand Le cheval est plus grand que l'âne.
4. lapins / poules / calmes Les lapins sont plus calmes que les poules.
5. vaches / cochons / gros Les cochons sont moins gros que les vaches.
6. cochon / cheval / propre Le cheval est plus propre que le cochon.

Core Instruction

TEACHING GRAMMAIRE

1. Go over Points 1 and 2. Tell students that **plus... que, moins... que,** and **aussi... que** are used in comparisons with adjectives. For comparisons of nouns they should use **plus de, moins de,** and **autant de + noun. (3 min.)**
2. Write sentences using the comparatives on the board or on a transparency to model both **que** and **qu'** to complete the comparisons. **(5 min.)**
3. Have the class practice reading the sentences aloud. **(3 min.)**

Grammavision

For a video presentation of the comparative with adjectives and nouns, see the *DVD Tutor.*

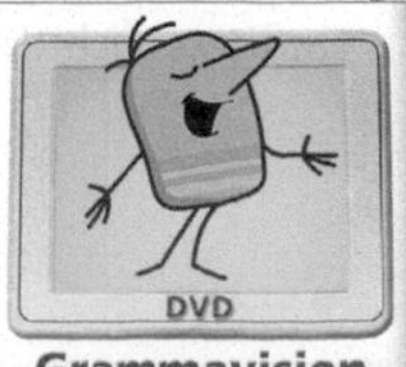

Grammavision

Online Practice
my.hrw.com
Grammaire 2 practice

29 Les photos de Nathalia 4.2

Parlons/Écrivons Nathalia, ta nouvelle correspondante française, t'a envoyé ces photos de son village et de sa famille. Pour chaque photo, fais une comparaison avec l'endroit où tu habites ou avec ta famille.

MODÈLE **Chez Nathalia, la vie est moins stressante que dans ma ville.**

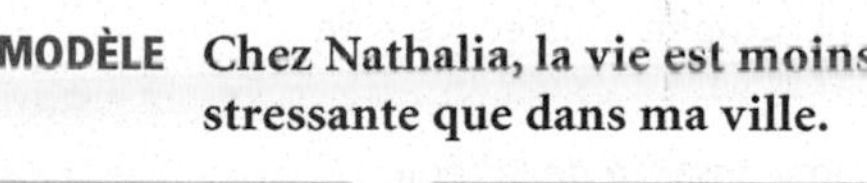

1.

2.

3.

4.

30 Ville ou campagne? 1.3

Écrivons Écris 8 phrases pour donner ton opinion de la vie en ville et de la vie à la campagne et fais des comparaisons entre ces deux endroits. Choisis des adjectifs de la boîte.

joli	pur	calme	stressant	dangereux
vivant	sale	propre	tranquille	intéressant

MODÈLE **Le paysage est plus (moins/aussi) joli à la campagne qu'en ville.**

Communication

Digital performance space

31 Opinions personnelles 1.1

Parlons Imagine que tu vas passer un an dans un pays francophone. Tu vas voir le conseiller/la conseillère du programme d'échanges pour discuter de l'endroit où tu voudrais aller. Il/Elle te demande quel pays francophone tu préfères et si tu veux habiter dans une ville ou à la campagne. Explique-lui tes préférences. Joue cette scène avec un(e) camarade.

MODÈLE **—Alors, Jonathan, est-ce que tu veux aller en France?**
—Non, moi, j'ai envie d'aller au Québec. Le Québec est plus...

Grammaire 2

Teacher to Teacher

Barbara Tentinger
Papillion LaVista High School
Papillion, NE

To review comparatives, we play a simple version of *The Price is Right.*® Have students select items from recent advertisements, glue two pictures to a sheet of construction paper, and label each in French. Then have them glue the advertised prices on the bottom of the page on a flap that can be turned back to be revealed later. Students should include at least a few items that have the same advertised price. Show the pictures to students and have them play by rows. Each row must make a decision. One student from each row states the decision by saying, for example, **Le lait est plus cher que le sucre. Le lait est moins cher que le sucre. Le lait est aussi cher que le sucre.** Each row will pick a new spokesperson for each round. I keep track of points on the board. 1.3

Communication

Group Activity: Interpersonal

Have groups of three compare **cette école avec une autre école** and **votre ville avec une autre ville.** Have Student A start by stating what he or she likes and does not like. Student B asks why and Student A gives his or her comparisons. Student C can agree or disagree, giving his or her own opinion. 1.1

Differentiated Instruction

SLOWER PACE LEARNERS

For practice using the comparative, work as a class to write sentences that compare different school subjects. For example, write sentence-starters, such as **Le français est plus intéressant que...,** and have students complete the sentences either aloud or in writing. 1.2

MULTIPLE INTELLIGENCES

Visual Bring newspapers with sales advertisements and magazines with pictures of people to class. Allow students to cut out pictures and write captions that use the comparative. For example, a student might cut out a picture of two famous people and write that one person wears more make-up than the other or compare a product to another product they believe to be more effective. 1.3

Resources

Planning:
Lesson Planner
 Teacher One Stop

Presentation:
DVD Tutor, Disc 2
Grammavision 2.2

Practice:
Grammar Tutor for Students of French, Chapter 6
Cahier de vocabulaire et grammaire
Differentiated Practice and Assessment CD-ROM
Cahier d'activités
Independent Study Guide
Media Guide
Projectable Transparencies
Bell Work 6.7
HOMETUTOR

Bell Work

Use Bell Work 6.7 in the *Projectable Transparencies* or write this activity on the board.

Form logical sentences using comparisons.

1. **cochon / mouton / gros / +**
2. **cheval / vache / rapide / +**
3. **lapin / canard / bruyant / –**
4. **campagne / ville / intéressant / =**
5. **ville / village / tranquille / –**

1.2

The superlative with adjectives

1 To say *the least* or *the most,* use the following structure. Remember to make the adjective agree in gender and in number with the noun.

le (l') / la (l') / les } **plus/moins** + adjective + **de**

C'est la ville la plus intéressant**e** de la région.

2 When the adjective goes before the noun, use this structure instead.

C'est le plus joli village **de** la région.

Paris est la plus grande ville **de** France.

Vocabulaire et grammaire, *pp. 70–71*
Cahier d'activités, *pp. 55–57*

Déjà vu!

Don't forget that the preposition **de** contracts with **le** and **les** to become **du** and **des.**

C'est la plus grande maison du village.

32 Petit test de culture 1.2

Lisons Connais-tu bien les pays francophones? Trouve la fin de chaque phrase de la colonne de gauche dans la colonne de droite.

d **1.** La tour Eiffel est le monument...	**a.** le plus vivant de Québec.
a **2.** Le quartier du Petit-Champlain est le quartier...	**b.** les plus visités de Paris.
e **3.** Dakar est la ville...	**c.** les plus hautes *(tall)* de France et de Suisse.
c **4.** Les Alpes sont les montagnes...	**d.** le plus célèbre de France.
b **5.** Le musée du Louvre et le musée d'Orsay sont les musées...	**e.** la plus grande du Sénégal.

33 L'agent immobilier 1.2

Écrivons/Parlons Les Mézilla veulent acheter une maison à la campagne. Leur agent leur parle d'une ferme et il exagère beaucoup! Donne les réponses de l'agent en suivant le modèle.

MODÈLE —Est-ce que cette région est dangereuse?
—Non, c'est la région la moins dangereuse!

1. Ce village est calme?
2. Ces champs sont assez sales!
3. Est-ce que l'air est pur dans ce village?
4. L'eau de la rivière est polluée, non?
5. Les voisins *(neighbors)* sont un peu bruyants, non?
6. Et le paysage est joli?

Cultures

Products and Perspectives

Tell students that **gîtes** are privately owned farms, stone houses, or even **châteaux** where the owners accept overnight guests. Have students research two **gîtes** online and compare the amenities they offer. 2.2

Core Instruction

TEACHING GRAMMAIRE

1. Explain that to say *the least* or *the most,* students should use **le/la plus/moins** (adjective) **de.** The position will change according to whether the adjective comes before or after the noun. Model the examples in Point 2. **(2 min.)**
2. Read **Déjà vu!** aloud with students and discuss. **(1 min.)**
3. Talk about your area using comparatives and superlatives. **Notre ville est plus petite que Rennes. Notre état est aussi agricole que la Bretagne. (4 min.)**
4. Ask **oui** or **non** questions with comparatives and superlatives to check student comprehension. **Est-ce que Rennes est la plus petite ville de France? Est-ce que Paris est la plus grande? (2 min.)**

Grammavision

For a video presentation of the superlative with adjectives, see the *DVD Tutor.*

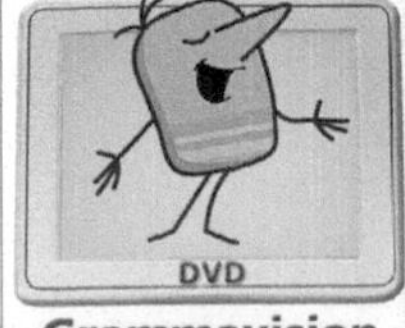

Grammavision

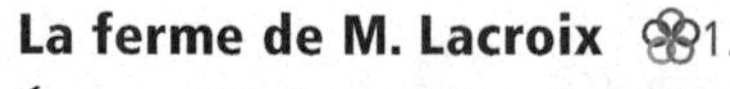

34 La ferme de M. Lacroix 1.2

Écrivons/Parlons Décris les animaux de la ferme de M. Lacroix en utilisant le superlatif.

MODÈLE **Les lapins sont les plus mignons de la ferme.**

1. le cheval, méchant

2. la poule, grand

3. la chèvre, bruyant

4. les cochons, sale

5. le mouton, petit

6. les vaches, calme

35 Ma région francophone préférée 1.3

Écrivons Quelle région francophone est-ce que tu trouves la plus intéressante? Pourquoi? Écris un paragraphe dans lequel tu décris cette région en détail. Utilise le superlatif.

MODÈLE **J'aime beaucoup Tahiti. Je pense que Tahiti a les plus belles plages du monde.**

Entre copains

un patelin	*little town*
mortel(le)	*boring*
la cambrousse	*country*

Communication

36 Interview 1.1

Parlons En France, il y a une émission (program) de télé-réalité qui s'appelle «La ferme aux célébrités». Des stars vont habiter à la campagne. Tu dois interviewer des célébrités qui veulent participer. Tu leur poses des questions sur ce qu'elles pensent de la vie à la campagne. Ensuite, joue cette scène pour ta classe.

MODÈLE **—Alors, qu'est-ce que vous pensez de la vie à la campagne?**
—J'adore! Je trouve que la campagne est l'endroit le moins stressant.

Grammaire 2

33 Possible Answers

1. Oui, c'est le village le plus calme!
2. Non, ce sont les champs les moins sales!
3. Oui, c'est l'air le plus pur!
4. Non, c'est l'eau la moins polluée!
5. Non, ce sont les voisins les moins bruyants!
6. Oui, c'est le plus joli paysage!

34 Answers

1. Le cheval est le plus méchant de la ferme.
2. La poule est la plus grande de la ferme.
3. La chèvre est la plus bruyante de la ferme.
4. Les cochons sont les plus sales de la ferme.
5. Le mouton est le plus petit de la ferme.
6. Les vaches sont les plus calmes de la ferme.

Communication

Group Work: Interpersonal

Have students draw a grid with three columns and three rows. In each square they should write a complete sentence with the superlative, using both **moins** and **plus.** Have students circulate and give their opinions. When students disagree and say the opposite, they sign the square. They must get three signatures in a row, up, down, across, or diagonal. You may wish to teach **à mon avis, je suis d'accord,** and **je ne suis pas d'accord.** 1.1

Differentiated Instruction

ADVANCED LEARNERS

Have volunteers visit your local Humane Society and ask permission to help bring attention to the dogs and cats up for adoption. Students should take a picture of one of the dogs or cats and ask the workers for information about the animal's background and personality. Have students write a caption in French and in English using superlatives to describe the pet and then create a bulletin board encouraging adoption of the animals. 5.1

MULTIPLE INTELLIGENCES

Bodily Kinesthetic Ask students to stand up and form a line in order of youngest to oldest, for example. Students should find their place in line by asking each other's age in French. Have each student use the superlative or comparative structure to describe a classmate compared to another in the line. **Sarah est plus âgée que Jenny.** 1.1

Assess

Assessment Program

Quiz: Grammaire 2

Alternative Assessment

Differentiated Practice and Assessment CD-ROM

Online Assessment
my.hrw.com

Test Generator 

Resources

Planning:
Lesson Planner
Teacher One Stop

Practice:
Grammar Tutor for Students of French, Chapter 6
Cahier de vocabulaire et grammaire
Differentiated Practice and Assessment CD-ROM
Cahier d'activités
Independent Study Guide
Media Guide
Projectable Transparencies
Bell Work 6.8
Audio CD 6, Tr. 6

Bell Work

Use Bell Work 6.8 in the *Projectable Transparencies* or write this activity on the board.

Complete these sentences with a logical superlative.

1. **Québec est la ville... d'Amérique du Nord.**
2. **L'avenue des Champs-Élysées est... de Paris.**
3. **Versailles est le château... de France.**
4. **Le Mont-Blanc est le sommet... d'Europe.**
5. **Genève est la ville... de Suisse.** 1.2

French for Spanish Speakers

Ask students to compare **bon(ne)/meilleur(e)** with the equivalents **bueno(a)/mejor.** (The spelling and consonant sounds are similar.) Ask students to compare **Cette école est la meilleure de la ville.** with the equivalent. **Esta escuela es la mejor de la ciudad.** (The superlatives both precede the noun.) 4.1

Synthèse
- Vocabulaire 2
- Grammaire 2

Application 2

37 Rat des villes ou rat des champs? 1.3

Écrivons En France, aujourd'hui, de plus en plus de jeunes choisissent de quitter les villes pour aller habiter à la campagne. Pourquoi, à ton avis? Écris un paragraphe pour essayer d'expliquer ce phénomène.

MODÈLE **À mon avis, les jeunes Français ont envie d'habiter à la campagne parce que c'est plus calme. Il y a...**

Un peu plus

Irregular comparatives and superlatives

1. The comparative and superlative forms of **bon** and **mauvais** are irregular.

good	→ *better*	→ *best*
bon(ne)(s)	→ meilleur(e)(s)	→ le (la, les) meilleur(e)(s)

bad	→ *worse*	→ *the worst*
mauvais(e)(s)	→ pire(s)	→ le (la, les) pire(s)

Moi, je pense que la vie à la campagne est meilleure que la vie en ville.

2. Notice that it is common to use **moins bon(ne)(s)** rather than **pire(s).**

Et moi, je trouve que la vie à la campagne est **pire / moins bonne** que la vie en ville.

3. Meilleur(e)(s) and **pire(s)** go before the noun.

L'été que j'ai passé chez mes grands-parents était le meilleur **(le pire)** été de ma vie.

Vocabulaire et grammaire, *p. 72*
Cahier d'activités, *pp. 55–57*

38 Écoutons CD 6, Tr. 6 1.2

Patrice a quitté Paris pour aller habiter à la campagne il y a quelques mois. Écoute ses commentaires et indique si Patrice est **a) content** ou **b) pas content** de chaque chose qu'il mentionne.
1. b 2. b 3. a 4. b 5. a 6. a

39 Les titres dans la presse 1.2

Écrivons Complète ces titres avec les comparatifs et les superlatifs de la boîte.

les meilleurs	la moins bonne	les pires
plus mauvaise	meilleure	

1. Bravo aux poulets de Bresse: ce sont les meilleurs poulets de France!
2. Été chaud: la qualité de l'air va être plus mauvaise en juillet qu'en juin!
3. Attention sur la route: les pires accidents arrivent toujours en août!
4. Concours de cuisine: le canard du pauvre maire de Rochefort est ____ spécialité (f.) de la région, d'après les juges! la moins bonne
5. Conclusion du Professeur Hildrez: la vie à la campagne est meilleure pour la santé que la vie en ville.

Core Instruction

INTEGRATED PRACTICE

1. Have students do Activities 37 and 38 to review vocabulary, comparatives, and superlatives. **(12 min.)**
2. Bring in pictures to illustrate the vocabulary. Put each picture and a blank piece of paper on a separate desk. Have students circulate and write one adjective to describe each picture. Then compare the two pictures, using the adjectives students wrote. **(12 min.)**

TEACHING UN PEU PLUS

1. Remind students that they have learned the adjectives **bon(ne)(s)** and **mauvais(e)(s).** Go over Point 1. **(2 min.)**
2. Explain that **meilleur** and **pire** go before the nouns, like **bon** and **mauvais. (1 min.)**
3. Call on students to share either **Mon meilleur/pire souvenir était... (5 min.)**
4. Continue with integrated practice Activities 39–42. **(15 min.)**

Online Practice
my.hrw.com
Application 2 practice

40 Pour le meilleur et pour le pire 1.2

Parlons/Écrivons Selon le contexte, utilise un superlatif ou un comparatif des adjectifs **bon** ou **mauvais** pour parler des choses suivantes.

MODÈLE la cuisine de la cantine du lycée / la cuisine des restaurants de ma ville
La cuisine de la cantine du lycée est plus mauvaise que la cuisine des restaurants de ma ville.

1. regarder les dessins animés / lire un roman
2. les hamburgers / la pizza
3. tes dernières vacances
4. ta note à ton dernier examen de français
5. ton équipe de football / l'équipe de football d'une autre école

41 Question de goût 1.3

Écrivons À ton avis, quels sont les meilleurs livres? Les meilleurs films? Les meilleurs groupes de musique? Et les moins bons? Écris un petit paragraphe dans lequel tu donnes ton opinion des livres, des films et des groupes dont on parle beaucoup en ce moment.

MODÈLE **Moi, je pense que le meilleur livre...**

Digital performance space

Communication

42 Souvenirs d'enfance 1.1

Parlons Avec ton/ta camarade vous discutez des jeux que vous aimiez quand vous étiez petits. Lisez les questions ci-dessous et répondez-y de manière logique. Ensuite, échangez les rôles.

— **À quoi est-ce que tu aimais jouer quand tu étais petit(e)?**
—
— **Où est-ce que tu aimais aller?**
—
— **Est-ce que tu aimais faire de la balançoire?**
—
— **Est-ce que tu allais souvent à la campagne?**
—

Application 2

38 Script
See script on p. 191E.

Communication

Group Work: Interpersonal
Have partners each write a topic and an adjective, such as **joueur de basket/bon.** Have them each ask and answer two questions about the topic, using superlatives. 1.1

Language Examination

42 Sample answer:
— . . .
— J'aimais jouer aux petites voitures.
— . . .
— J'aimais aller au cirque.
— . . .
— Oui, mais je préférais grimper aux arbres.
— . . .
— Oui, j'allais voir mes grands-parents à la campagne.

Differentiated Instruction

SLOWER PACE LEARNERS

Have students practice irregular comparatives and superlatives by creating a "Best Of" survey for your city. List different categories, (Best Shopping Mall, Best Pizza, Best Fast-Food Restaurant, Best Movie Theater) and have students write down their favorites. Then use their responses to create a chart on the board with the headings **Bon, Meilleur(e), Le/La Meilleur(e),** and **Mauvais(e), Pire, Le/La Pire.** 1.1

SPECIAL LEARNING NEEDS

40 Students with AD(H)D Have students list five items to compare. Have them then use the **superlatif** or **comparatif** to explain their preferences. Using their creativity may be motivating and assist in holding their attention as they complete the activity. 1.2

Assess

Assessment Program
Quiz: Application 2
Audio CD 6, Tr. 15
Alternative Assessment
Differentiated Practice and Assessment CD-ROM
Online Assessment
my.hrw.com
Test Generator

Resources

Planning:
Lesson Planner
 Teacher One Stop
Presentation:
 DVD Tutor, Disc 2
Télé-roman
Practice:
Media Guide
 DVD Tutor, Disc 2
Télé-roman

Connections

Visual Learners

To help students better understand the series of events in this episode of **Télé-roman,** have them create a flowchart of the action. Guide students through the chart, starting with what happens in scene 1. 3.2

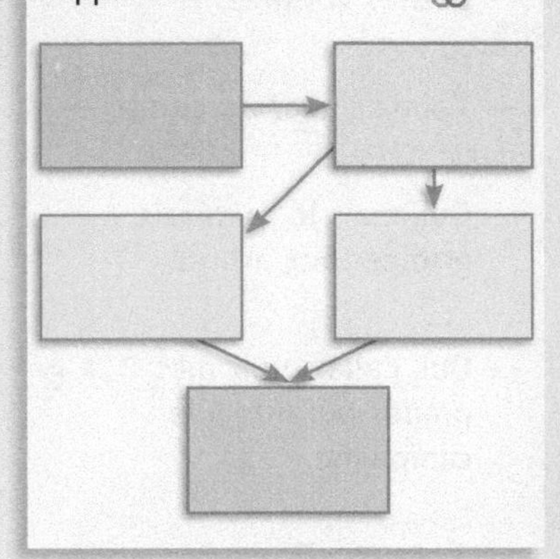

Gestures

Have students look at Anne in scene 1. Why might she be talking on the phone and looking at her watch? Point out that in scene 2, she has her purse in her hand. Where might she be going? Then direct students' attention to the parents' facial expressions in scenes 5 and 6. What might they be thinking and feeling? Finally, have students notice Mr. Rigaud's expression in scene 9. What do students think he has in mind? Ask them what they think will happen next. 2.1

Télé-roman

Le Secret de la statuette *Épisode 6*

STRATÉGIE

Making deductions Making deductions based on what unfolds in the story is an important skill. The characters themselves make deductions as they learn more about their situation. You may or may not agree with their deductions because you may have more information than they have. Think about the information you have gathered in **Episodes 5 and 6** and make a list of deductions. For instance, based on what you know, decide whether Anne Bondy is making the right choice by getting into the black car. 1.2

Chez les Gadio, Anne Bondy reçoit un coup de téléphone...

1 **Anne** Très bien. Dites à l'inspecteur Sonko que j'y serai dans quinze minutes. Merci, monsieur. Au revoir.

2 **Anne** Je vais retrouver l'inspecteur Sonko. Il veut me montrer quelque chose. Tu peux le dire à Salif quand il rentrera?
Mme Gadio Bien sûr, Anne. À plus tard.

Un peu plus tard...

3 **Seydou** Vous ne devinerez jamais ce qui nous est arrivé! Mais d'abord... regardez un peu ce que nous avons!

4 **Léa** On a découvert que Rigaud habite à Gorée. On l'a suivi chez lui... Bref, on a repris la statuette!

Core Instruction

TEACHING TÉLÉ-ROMAN

1. Have students read through **Télé-roman** and study the photos. Assign the parts of the characters to students, and before showing the video, have them act out the episode in class. **(10 min.)**
2. Play the video in its entirety. Ask general comprehension questions. In what ways was the video different from the class performance? If necessary, play the video again. **(8 min.)**
3. As a homework assignment, have students answer the **As-tu compris?** questions on page 217. **(2 min.)**

DVD Tutor

As an alternative, you might use the captioned version of **Le Secret de la statuette** on DVD.

5 **M. Gadio** Mais vous êtes fous!

6 **Mme Gadio** Les enfants, c'était très dangereux, ce que vous avez fait, vous savez.

Pendant ce temps, dans les rues de Dakar...

7 *Anne Bondy attend l'inspecteur Sonko.*

8

L'homme inconnu Madame Bondy?
Anne Oui, c'est moi.
L'homme inconnu L'inspecteur Sonko m'a demandé de venir vous chercher et de vous amener au poste de police.

9 *Anne monte dans la voiture noire de Charles Rigaud.*

1.2

AS-TU COMPRIS?

1. Pourquoi est-ce qu'Anne Bondy part de chez les Gadio?
2. Qu'est-ce que Léa et Seydou disent aux parents de Seydou?
3. Quelle est la réaction des parents de Seydou? Pourquoi?
4. Pourquoi est-ce qu'Anne monte dans la voiture noire?
5. Qui est dans cette voiture?

Prochain épisode:
D'après ce que tu vois à la fin de l'épisode, est-ce que tu penses que la voiture noire va vraiment au poste de police?

As-tu compris? Answers

1. Elle reçoit un coup de téléphone; elle va retrouver l'inspecteur Sonko.
2. Ils ont découvert que Rigaud habite à Gorée et ils ont repris la statuette.
3. Ils sont fâchés; c'était très dangereux.
4. L'homme inconnu lui dit qu'il l'amène au poste de police pour parler avec l'inspecteur.
5. Charles Rigaud

Communication

Pair Work: Presentational
After students have watched **Télé-roman,** have them work with a partner to write a short scene in which a parent is upset with a child for doing something dangerous. The parent should confront the child and ask for an explanation. The child should explain his or her motives and try to reassure the parent in some way. Have partners take turns playing the parent and the child.
1.3

Le Secret de la statuette Episode 6

In this episode, Anne Bondy tells Mrs. Gadio that she received a call from the police and that she is going to meet inspector Sonko. Later, Seydou and Léa come home with the statuette and recount their story. Seydou's parents become very upset and worried. Meanwhile, Anne is waiting for inspector Sonko on a street of Dakar. A man she doesn't recognize arrives in a black car and tells Anne that he will take her to the police station. As the car leaves, we discover that Rigaud is at the wheel. She doesn't know what to do, but then decides to get into the car.

Lecture et écriture

Resources

Planning:
Lesson Planner
Teacher One Stop

Presentation:
Audio CD 6, Tr. 7

Practice:
Cahier d'activités
Reading Strategies and Skills Handbook, Chapter 6
Intermediate Reader
French InterActive Reader

Applying the Strategies

For practice with monitoring comprehension, have students use the "Text Reformulation" strategy from the *Reading Strategies and Skills Handbook.*

READING PRACTICE

STRATEGIES

Strategy: Text Reformulation

Reading Skill	When can I use this strategy?		
	Prereading	During Reading	Postreading
Understanding Text Structure			✓
Analyzing Cause-and-Effect Relationships			✓

Strategy at a Glance: Text Reformulation

- The teacher introduces **Text Reformulation** by having students reformulate a text they have read into a patterned story, such as an ABC story, or into another genre.
- The teacher models several types of reformulations.
- Either the teacher or the students choose which type of reformulation to do based on the desired learning objectives.

Sometimes by transforming a text into a different format—one that is more familiar or friendlier—students can understand it better. An example: reformulating an expository text structure to fit the narrative structure; in other words, taking what might be a difficult, even dry, expository text and retelling it as a story.

Text Reformulation, or **Story Recycling,** is a strategy in which students transform a text into another type of text.

Best Use of the Strategy

When students are having difficulty understanding a text, use the **Text Reformulation** (Feathers 1993), or **Story Recycling,** strategy to show them how to better understand the text by turning it into another type of text that is more familiar to them. Whether students turn expository texts into narratives, poems into newspaper articles, or short stories into patterned stories such as ABC books, reformulating texts encourages students to talk about the original texts.

Identifying Images

Tell students that poets use language to evoke certain images and emotions. The pictures the words create in the readers' minds are part of what makes a poem come to life. Have students look over the poem and note the images the poet uses.

Lecture et écriture

Jules Supervielle (1884-1960), écrivain français, est né à Montevideo en Uruguay. Il a partagé sa vie entre la France et l'Uruguay. Ses premiers poèmes sont traditionnels (*Brumes du passé,* 1900; *Comme des voiliers,* 1910). *L'Homme de la pampa* est un roman fantastique publié en 1923. Il a aussi écrit *Le Voleur d'enfants, L'Enfant de la haute mer* et *La Belle au bois* (pièce de théâtre).

STRATÉGIE pour lire

Using images and symbols Poets use imagery and symbols to express a message. In order to understand the main idea of a poem, you might ask yourself what images and symbols the words express.

A Avant la lecture 1.3

Le poème est sur la nature aux premières heures de la journée. Quelles impresssions as-tu quand tu te réveilles très tôt le matin? Fais une liste des mots et des images que tu peux associer avec les thèmes suivants: la nature et les animaux, le silence et le bruit, la terre et l'espace *(earth and space).* CD 6, Tr. 7

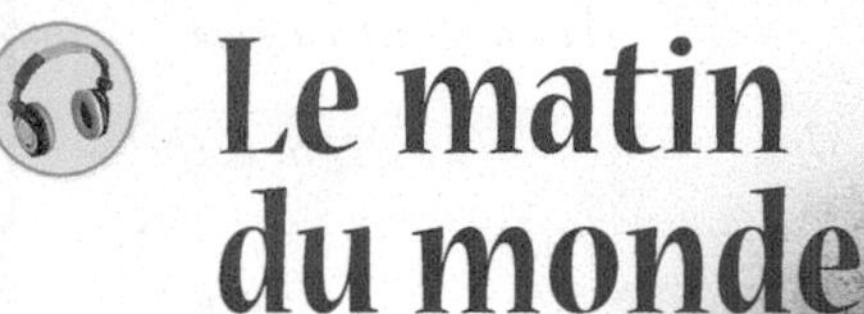

Le matin du monde

Alentour[1] naissaient mille bruits[2]
Mais si pleins[3] encor de silence
Que l'oreille croyait ouïr[4]
Le chant de sa propre innocence

Tout vivait en se regardant,
Miroir était le voisinage[5],
Où chaque chose allait rêvant[6]
A l'éclosion[7] de son âge.

Les palmiers[8] trouvant une forme
Où balancer leur plaisir pur
Appelaient de loin les oiseaux
Pour leur montrer leurs dentelures[9].

1. All around 2. a thousand sounds were being born 3. full 4. that the ear thinks it hears 5. neighborhood 6. dreaming 7. birth 8. palm trees 9. jagged outlines

Core Instruction

TEACHING LECTURE

1. Go over **Stratégie** with students. **(1 min.)**
2. Have students do Activity A orally in class. List the words on the board or on a transparency and then cover them before students read the poem. **(5 min.)**
3. Have students take turns reading the poem aloud in class. **(3 min.)**
4. Have students close their book. Read aloud Activity C. Have students explain in French why they chose the word they did. **(6 min.)**
5. Have students work with a partner to do Activities B and D. **(10 min.)**
6. As a class, do Activity E. **(10 min.)**

Online Practice
my.hrw.com
Online Edition

Un cheval blanc découvrait l'homme[1]
Qui s'avançait à petit bruit,
Avec la Terre autour de lui
Tournant pour son cœur astrologue

Le cheval bougeait[2] les naseaux[3]
Puis hennissait[4] comme en plein ciel[5],
Et tout entouré d'irréel
S'abandonnait à son galop.

Dans la rue des enfants, des femmes,
A de beaux nuages pareils[6],
S'assemblaient pour chercher leur âme[7]
Et passaient de l'ombre[8] au soleil.

Mille coqs[9] traçaient de leurs chants
Les frontières[10] de la campagne
Mais les vagues[11] de l'océan
Hésitaient entre vingt rivages[12]

L'heure était si riche en rameurs[13],
En nageuses phosphorescentes
Que les étoiles[14] oublièrent
Leurs reflets dans les eaux parlantes.

1. man 2. moved 3. nostrils 4. neighed 5. sky 6. similar 7. soul 8. shadows 9. roosters 10. borders 11. waves 12. shores 13. rowers 14. stars

Lecture et écriture

Lecture et écriture

Cultures

Practices and Perspectives

Share with students that poets and other writers often "write what they know." Their choice of topic, theme, point of view, and language is greatly influenced by their own experience and their environment. Assign each student a different francophone country and ask them to find a poem that reflects in some way the country the poet is from. Have students present the poem they find and explain how it reflects the poet's background. 2.1

Language Examination

Activité Pré-AP Préparatoire

Through the practice of listening and reading comprehension, as well as essay writing, **Lecture et écriture** helps students prepare for the **Interpretive Reading and Listening** and the **Presentational Writing** sections of the AP Language and Culture Exam.

Additional Practice

For more reading practice, see **Variations littéraires,** pp. 392–393.

Differentiated Instruction

ADVANCED LEARNERS

Assign each student a stanza of the poem. Ask students to memorize their stanza and be able to paraphrase it in English. Then have students present the poem in its entirety to another class or at a school function, meeting, or open house. 1.3

SPECIAL LEARNING NEEDS

Students with Learning Disabilities/ Dyslexia Give copies of the poem to students who may experience difficulties with the reading. Ask students to highlight key vocabulary words that may be difficult as you review the words and their meanings. This accommodation may enable students to read the poem independently or follow along more easily with oral reading. 1.2

Lecture et écriture

Connections

Music Link

Play for students a recording of a song that was originally a poem. Then have partners work together to set each other's poem to music. Invite students to perform their songs *a cappella* for the class, or ask if any students who play a musical instrument would be willing to accompany their classmates. 3.1

Communities

Family Link

Have students share their poem with a family member and then, either with the whole class, in small groups, or with a partner, they should talk about the experience of sharing the poem. As an alternative, students might prefer to describe the experience in a journal entry. 5.1

Compréhension

B Choisis la réponse correcte. 1.2

1. Comment était le matin?
   (a.) plein de bruits et de silence **b.** noir et froid
2. Qu'est-ce que les palmiers appellent?
   a. des formes (b.) des oiseaux
3. Qu'est-ce que le cheval a découvert?
   a. la terre (b.) l'homme
4. À quoi ressemblent *(look like)* les enfants et les femmes?
   (a.) à des nuages **b.** au soleil
5. Qu'est-ce que les vagues faisaient? Elles. . .
   (a.) essayaient de choisir un rivage. **b.** cherchaient l'océan.

C Quel est l'intrus *(the odd one)*? 1.2

1. bruit	chant	silence	(palmier)
2. miroir	(galop)	image	reflet
3. (vague)	enfant	femme	homme
4. oiseau	cheval	(étoile)	coq
5. océan	(ciel)	vague	rivage
6. nuage	ciel	étoile	(oreille)

D Trouve les mots du poème qui évoquent les thèmes suivants. 1.2

Possible answers:

MODÈLE la naissance et l'enfance

naissaient	**éclosion**
innocence	**pur**
découvrait	**enfants**

1. la nature et les animaux palmier, oiseaux, cheval, coqs
2. le silence et le bruit bruits, silence, oreille, ouïe, chant, hennissait
3. la terre et l'espace voisinage, terre, astrologue, plein ciel, rue, nuages, soleil, frontières

Après la lecture 1.3

E Dans **Avant la lecture,** tu as fait une liste de mots associés à différents thèmes. Compare ta liste avec celle que tu viens de faire dans l'activité D. Est-ce qu'il y a des mots en commun? Est-ce que tu aurais utilisé *(would have used)* les mots de la même manière que Supervielle? Pourquoi ou pourquoi pas?

Core Instruction

TEACHING ESPACE ÉCRITURE

1. Discuss **Stratégie pour écrire** and **Un souvenir.** Even though some examples are given, it may help students to brainstorm different topics for this poem before beginning to write. **(5 min.)**
2. Have students do step 1 in class. Circulate to monitor students' work, especially their choices for activities and events in the **imparfait** and **passé composé. (15 min.)**
3. Pair students with different abilities and have them do steps 2 and 3. **(12 min.)**
4. Randomly choose several poems from which to make transparencies. Have volunteers read the poems as described in step 4. **(5 min.)**

Lecture et écriture

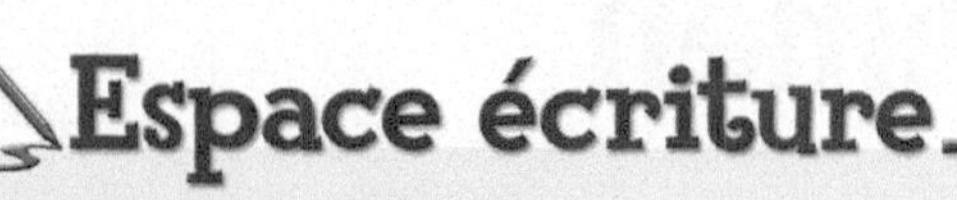

Espace écriture

STRATÉGIE pour écrire

Writing poems Poets use a variety of techniques to express emotion and meaning. They use **symbols,** objects that represent something other than what they are, and **imagery,** words or phrases that appeal to the senses. They also use direct and indirect comparisons. Direct comparisons, such as "He's a teddy bear," are called **metaphors,** and indirect comparisons, such as "He's **like** a teddy bear" are called **similes.**

Un souvenir 1.3

Think about a landscape that you have seen and really enjoyed. What made the landscape so special? Think about what you were like as a child and what you used to do. How would you describe the landscape or your childhood? Write a poem about those memories. You may also want to write about your favorite pet.

1 Plan

Draw three columns on a sheet of paper.

- In the left column, list the things you will describe using the imperfect.
- In the middle column, list events. For each event or activity that took place, use the preterite.
- In the right column, write metaphors, comparisons, similes, or words and phrases that you can use as symbols for the ideas in the first two columns.

description (imparfait)	activités (passé composé)	images et symboles
Il faisait beau.	Je suis allé au lac.	L'eau était bleue comme le ciel.

2 Rédaction

Write your poem in the past, taking care to use vivid language that creates images. Be sure to use some of the symbols, metaphors, and similes from your pre-writing. Revise your poem.

3 Correction

Trade poems with a couple of classmates. Ask your classmates what they think your poem is about. Then, ask them if they can picture your landscape, if they can explain what they think your childhood was like, what was important to you, and how you felt. Also have your classmates check your spelling and use of the preterite and imperfect.

4 Application

Scan your poem so that it can be projected. Read or recite your poem to the class as they view it on a screen.

Lecture et écriture

Process Writing

Avant d'écrire After students complete the prewriting activity, they may want to make a list of synonyms that they could use to describe their childhood activities. This will help them to avoid using the same words repeatedly as they begin to write. After they have completed their drafts, ask them to reread what they have written to ensure that the synonyms they have chosen work well in context.

Writing Assessment

To assess the **Espace écriture,** you can use the following rubric. For additional rubrics, see the *Assessment Program* or refer to the *Generate Success* Rubric Generator.

Writing Rubric	4	3	2	1
Content (Complete—Incomplete)				
Comprehensibility (Comprehensible—Seldom comprehensible)				
Accuracy (Accurate—Seldom accurate)				
Organization (Well-organized—Poorly organized)				
Effort (Excellent effort—Minimal effort)				

18-20: A 16-17: B 14-15: C 12-13: D Under 12: F

Differentiated Instruction

SLOWER PACE LEARNERS

Provide additional structure to help students write their poems. Ask them to describe what things were like and give background details in the first stanza of their poems. In the second stanza, ask them to talk about events, and in the last stanza, ask them to use the techniques in **Stratégie pour écrire.** You might also provide a sentence starter for the first line of each stanza to help students begin their poems. 1.2

MULTIPLE INTELLIGENCES

Spatial Prior to writing the poem required in **Espace écriture,** ask students to first create an illustration of the scene or pet and label it in French. The representation of their ideas may assist those who have spatial or visual strengths to translate their idea into writing. You may wish to display the poems and illustrations in the classroom. 1.3

Assess

Assessment Program
Quiz: Lecture
Quiz: Écriture
Online Assessment
my.hrw.com
Test Generator 

Prépare-toi pour l'examen

Resources

Planning:
Lesson Planner
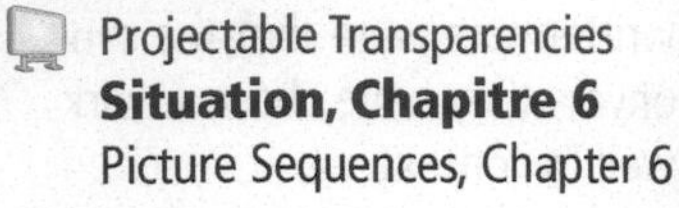
Teacher One Stop

Practice:
Cahier d'activités
Media Guide
DVD Tutor, Disc 2
Projectable Transparencies
Situation, Chapitre 6
Picture Sequences, Chapter 6
Audio CD 6, Tr. 9–12
@HOMETUTOR

1 Answers

1. J'aimais mieux jouer aux billes / sauter à la corde.
2. J'aimais mieux jouer au train électrique / faire de la balançoire.
3. J'aimais mieux jouer au ballon / jouer aux échecs.
4. J'aimais mieux jouer à la poupée / collectionner des timbres.

2 Answers

1. Mes grands-parents (ne) passaient (pas) souvent beaucoup de temps chez moi.
2. Moi, je (ne) jouais (pas) souvent avec des copains.
3. Mon meilleur ami (Ma meilleure amie) (ne) venait (pas) souvent chez moi.
4. Mes amis et moi nous (n') allions (pas) souvent au zoo.
5. Ma famille et moi (ne) regardions (pas) souvent (de) des dessins animés.

3 Possible Answer

Il y avait un tracteur, une vache et des cochons. Il y avait un cheval, un âne, une poule, des canards et un lapin.

Reteaching

Show students magazine pictures of young children. Ask them to describe the activities in the photos using **Quand j'étais plus jeune,...** Then ask volunteers to add another sentence beginning with **À ce moment-là,...**

Chapitre 6

Prépare-toi pour l'examen

@HOMETUTOR

1 Vocabulaire 1
- to talk about when you were a child
- to tell about an event in the past

pp. 194–197

1 Quand tu étais petit(e), quelle activité aimais-tu mieux faire? 1.3

MODÈLE J'aimais mieux grimper aux arbres.

1.

2.

3.

4.

2 Grammaire 1
- the **imparfait**
- the **passé composé** and the **imparfait**

Un peu plus
- adverb placement

pp. 198–203

2 Quand tu étais petit(e), est-ce que ces personnes faisaient souvent les choses indiquées? 1.3

1. mes grands-parents: passer beaucoup de temps chez moi
2. moi, je: jouer avec des copains
3. mon meilleur ami (ma meilleure amie): venir souvent chez moi
4. mes amis et moi: aller au zoo
5. ma famille et moi: regarder des dessins animés

3 Vocabulaire 2
- to compare life in the country and in the city
- to describe life in the country

pp. 206–209

3 Quand Yann était petit, il allait souvent à la ferme de ses grands-parents. Qu'est-ce qu'il y avait? 1.2

Preparing for the Exam

FOLD-N-LEARN
Flap Chart Study Aid

1. Have students fold a sheet of paper from top to bottom and then from side to side. Ask them to unfold the sheet so they see the two sections formed by the crease of the first fold.
2. Ask students to cut along the top-to-bottom fold, starting at the top of the sheet, as far as the fold in the middle to form two flaps.
3. Have students write expressions in French for talking about when they were children and telling about an event in the past. On the right flap, ask students to write expressions in French for comparing life in the country and the city. They should write the English equivalents in the sections under the flaps.
4. Have students review the chapter expressions with the flap charts they have created.

4 Préfères-tu la vie à la campagne ou la vie en ville? Complète ces phrases avec **plus... que, aussi... que, moins... que, plus de...**, **autant de...** ou **moins de...** et les mots donnés entre parenthèses pour exprimer ton opinion. 1.3

1. (intéressant) La vie à la campagne / la vie en ville
2. (stressant) La vie à la campagne / la vie en ville
3. (calme) La vie à la campagne / la vie en ville
4. (arbres) Il y a / à la campagne qu'en ville
5. (pollution) Il y a / à la campagne qu'en ville

5 Réponds aux questions suivantes. 2.1, 2.2

1. À quels jeux est-ce que les jeunes Français jouent?
2. Quelles bandes dessinées sont populaires?
3. Qu'est-ce qu'on peut faire dans une colonie de vacances en France?

6 Loïc et Renaud parlent de la vie en ville et de la vie à la campagne. Écoute leur conversation. Selon Loïc et Renaud, quels sont les avantages de la vie à la campagne et de la vie en ville? CD 6, Tr. 9 1.2

7 Avec ton/ta camarade, vous discutez de la ville et de la campagne. Vous n'êtes pas d'accord sur ce qui est mieux. D'abord, lisez les instructions pour chaque réplique *(exchange)*. Ensuite, créez votre dialogue en utilisant des expressions que vous avez apprises. 1.1

Élève A:	Parle de ton week-end à la campagne. Dis que tu as aimé.
Élève B:	Dis que tu n'aimes pas la campagne. Explique pourquoi.
Élève A:	Compare (positivement) la campagne à la ville.
Élève B:	Explique pourquoi tu préfères la ville.
Élève A:	Explique pourquoi toi, tu n'aimes pas la ville.
Élève B:	Parle des choses qu'on peut faire en ville.
Élève A:	Réponds en disant ce qu'on peut faire à la campagne.
Élève B:	Conclus qu'il y a des différences entre les deux.

Online Assessment
my.hrw.com
Chapter Self-test

4 Grammaire 2
- the comparative with adjectives and nouns
- the superlative with adjectives

Un peu plus
- irregular comparatives and superlatives

pp. 210–215

5 Culture
- Flash culture **pp. 196, 198, 208, 210**
- Comparaisons **pp. 204–205**

Prépare-toi pour l'examen

Prépare-toi pour l'examen

5 Answers
1. des jeux de société
2. Astérix, Lucky Luke, Tintin, Gaston Lagaffe
3. la randonnée, la natation, le kayak, le VTT, l'équitation, la voile

6 Script
See script on p. 191F.

6 Answer
À la campagne, la vie est plus calme et moins stressante et il y a moins de pollution.
En ville, la vie est plus intéressante. Il y a plus de choses à faire.

7 Sample conversation:

a. **Je suis allé(e) à la campagne ce week-end. C'était génial!**
b. **Je déteste la campagne. C'est trop tranquille.**
a. **La campagne, c'est tellement moins stressant que la ville.**
b. **Mais la ville est plus vivante.**
a. **Oui, mais la ville est bruyante et polluée.**
b. **En ville, on peut aller au cinéma, au concert. On peut faire les magasins.**
a. **Mais à la campagne, on peut faire des randonnées, des pique-niques,...**
b. **C'est vrai. La vie en ville est différente de la vie à la campagne!**

Additional Speaking Practice

- For additional speaking practice, you might use the *Picture Sequences Transparency* for Chapter 6 found in the *Projectable Transparencies.*
- To assess the speaking activities in this section, you might use the *Generate Success* Rubric Generator or the oral rubrics found in the *Assessment Program.*

Pre-AP Practice

7 This guided conversation activity helps students practice oral exchanges using material from this chapter and previous chapters. The activity helps prepare students for the **Interpersonal Speaking** section of the AP French Language and Culture Exam.

Chapitre 6

Prépare-toi pour l'examen

Grammar Review

For more practice with the grammar topics in this chapter, see the *Grammar Tutor*, the *DVD Tutor*, the *@HomeTutor*, or the *Cahier de vocabulaire et grammaire.*

Grammavision

 **Online Edition**

Students might use the online textbook and Performance Space to practice the **Lettres et sons** feature.

Dictée Script

1. La chorale chante bien ensemble.
2. Qu'est-ce que ce chat est méchant!
3. Ma mère m'a acheté un chocolat chaud.
4. Je cherche des chaussures blanches pour mettre avec mes chaussettes.
5. Le cochon a mangé tous les champignons!

 **Game**

Course de relais Have students form two teams. In two columns on the board, write several sentences with blanks where the verbs should be. Precede each sentence with the infinitive. **(faire) Tu _____ du vélo.** One student from each team goes to the board to write the **imparfait** form of the verb in one of the sentences. The next team member goes to the board when the preceding player is seated. A student may correct a teammate's mistake or fill in a new blank. When all sentences are completed on one side, the last student on that team says, **Fini!** The team with the most correct verbs wins. 1.2

Grammaire 1
- the **imparfait**
- the **passé composé** and the **imparfait**

Un peu plus
- adverb placement

pp. 198–203

Résumé: Grammaire 1

To form the **imparfait**, drop the **-ons** from the present-tense **nous** form and add these endings: **-ais, -ais, -ait, -ions, -iez, -aient.** The verb **être** has an irregular stem: **ét-.**

The **imparfait** is used to describe *conditions in the past* or *what used to happen over and over.* The **passé composé** is used to tell about *past specific events that happened at a specific time.*

Adverbs telling *how much, how often,* and *how well* something is done go after the conjugated verb. Most adverbs of time, and some ending in -ment, can go at the beginning or end of the sentence.

Grammaire 2
- the comparative with adjectives and nouns
- the superlative with adjectives

Un peu plus
- irregular comparatives and superlatives

pp. 210–215

Résumé: Grammaire 2

To compare adjectives: La campagne est plus calme que la ville.

plus / **aussi** / moins } + **adjective** + **que** + **noun**

To form the superlative, use the following construction. The structure will change slightly depending on whether the adjective goes before or after the verb.

le, l' / la, l' / les } **plus** / moins + **adjective** + de + **noun**

C'est le **plus beau village** du **monde.**
C'est la plage la moins **polluée** du **monde.**

In order to say *better/best* or *worse/worst,* use the comparative and superlative forms of **bon** and mauvais, which are irregular (see page 214). The superlative forms of **bon** and mauvais go in front of the noun.

Lettres et sons

The combination ch CD 6, Tr. 10–12 1.2

In French, **ch** is usually pronounced like the English *sh,* as in the word *shower.* You have learned some words in this chapter that are pronounced like this: **cheval, cochon, chat.** In some cases, **ch** is pronounced like *k,* as in: **chorale, archéologie.**

Jeux de langue

Les chaussettes de l'archi-duchesse sont-elles sèches?

Dictée

Écris les phrases de la dictée.

Chapter Review

DVD Program

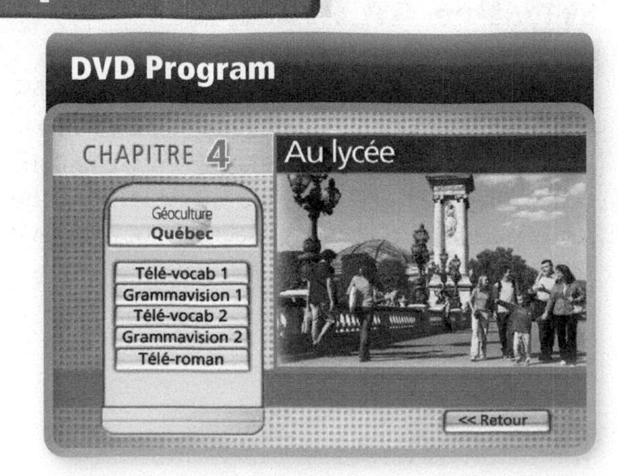

Online Edition

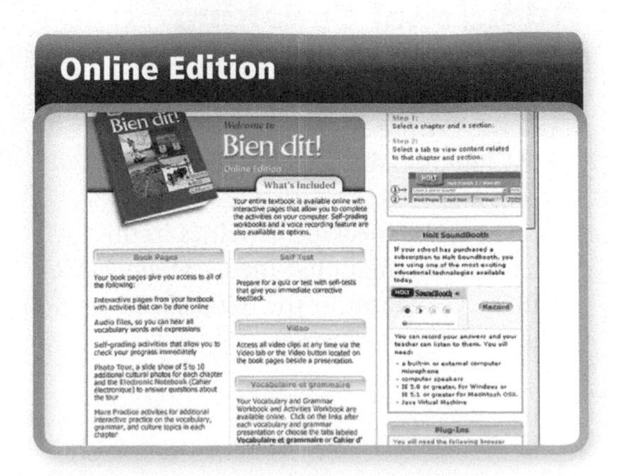

Prépare-toi pour l'examen

Résumé: Vocabulaire 1

PRACTICE FRENCH WITH HOLT MCDOUGAL APPS!

To talk about when you were a child

aller au cirque (m.)	*to go to the circus*
collectionner	*to collect*
content(e)/triste	*happy/sad*
faire de la balançoire	*to swing*
faire de la bascule	*to seesaw*
faire des châteaux (m.) de sable	*to make sandcastles*
faire des farces (f.)	*to play practical jokes*
faire du manège	*to go on a carousel*
grimper aux arbres (m.)	*to climb trees*
jouer au ballon	*to play ball*
jouer aux billes (f.)	*to play marbles*
jouer à chat perché	*to play a game similar to tag*
jouer aux dames (f.)	*to play checkers*
jouer à la marelle	*to play hopscotch*
jouer à la poupée	*to play dolls*
jouer aux petites voitures	*to play with matchbox cars*
jouer au train électrique	*to play with electric trains*
obéissant(e)	*obedient*
regarder des dessins animés	*to watch cartoons*
sauter à la corde	*to jump rope*
les souvenirs d'enfance	*childhood memories*
Quand j'avais... ans,...	*When I was . . . years old, . . .*
Quand j'étais petit(e),...	*When I was little, . . .*
Quand j'étais (plus) jeune,...	*When I was young (younger), . . .*

To tell about an event in the past

à ce moment-là	*at that moment*
alors que	*while*
finalement	*finally*
heureusement	*fortunately*
pendant que	*while/during*

Résumé: Vocabulaire 2

To compare life in the country and the city

l'âne (m.)	*donkey*
bruyant(e)	*noisy*
calme	*calm*
la campagne	*countryside*
le canard	*duck*
le champ	*field*
le cheval	*horse*
la chèvre	*goat*
le cochon	*pig*
dangereux(-euse)	*dangerous*
la ferme	*farm*
la grange	*barn*
le lapin	*rabbit*
le mouton	*sheep*
le paysage	*landscape*
pollué(e)	*polluted*
la poule	*chicken*
la prairie	*meadow*
propre	*clean*
pur(e)	*clear*
sale	*dirty*
stressant(e)	*stressful*
le tracteur	*tractor*
tranquille	*peaceful*
la vache	*cow*
la vie	*life*
le village	*village*
vivant(e)	*vibrant*
autant que	*as much as*
différent(e) de	*different from*
plus... que	*more . . . than*
plus de... que	*more of . . . than*
moins... que	*less . . . than*

To describe life in the country

Ce qui était..., c'était...	*What was . . . was . . .*
Ce qui me manque, c'est...	*What I miss is . . .*
Il y avait...	*There were . . .*
tellement	*so/so much*

Holt McDougal French Apps

Remind students that they can use the Holt McDougal French Apps to review their vocabulary.

Teacher to Teacher

Nancy Rodman
The Blake School
Minneapolis, MN

Students get the impression that feelings are always expressed by the **imparfait** in past-tense narration. To practice the use of the **passé composé** to express a change in a state of mind, have students brainstorm situations in which they "got scared" versus situations when they "were scared." Write examples on the board. For homework, they write a short paragraph, describing a scary situation in the past. 1.3

Projectable Transparency

More Digital Resources

FOR THE STUDENT

Holt McDougal French Apps
@HomeTutor
News and Networking
Performance Space

FOR THE TEACHER

- Interactive Whiteboard Lessons
- Generate Success!

Assess

Assessment Program

Examen: Chapitre 6
Audio CD 6, Tr. 16–17

Examen oral: Chapitre 6
Alternative Assessment
Differentiated Practice and Assessment CD-ROM

Online Assessment
my.hrw.com

Test Generator 

Chapitres 1–6
Révisions cumulatives

Resources

Planning:
Lesson Planner
Teacher One Stop

Practice:
Cahier d'activités
Media Guide
Projectable Transparencies **Fine Art, Chapter 6**
Audio CD 6, Tr. 13
Holt McDougal French Apps

1 Script

1. Ce matin, je prenais une douche quand le téléphone a sonné.
2. J'ai téléphoné à une amie avant d'entrer dans la douche.
3. Je prenais mon petit-déjeuner quand le bus est arrivé.
4. Ce matin, j'étais en retard. Je suis arrivé en cours à 9h10.

Révisions cumulatives

1 Des amis parlent de leur matinée. Pour chaque phrase, choisis l'illustration qui correspond. CD 6, Tr. 13 1.2
1. a **2.** b **3.** c **4.** d

a.

b.

c.

d.

2 Voilà une publicité web pour un centre de vacances. Lis la publicité et réponds aux questions qui suivent. 3.2

Centre de vacances—Animaux de la Ferme

piscine
monter à cheval
tir à l'arc

Pourquoi envoyer vos enfants à la campagne?

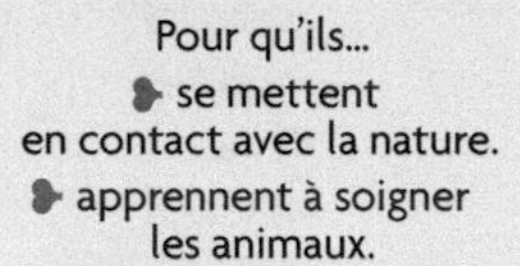

Pour qu'ils...
- se mettent en contact avec la nature.
- apprennent à soigner les animaux.
- passent du temps en plein air.
- apprennent à s'amuser sans télévision, ordinateur.

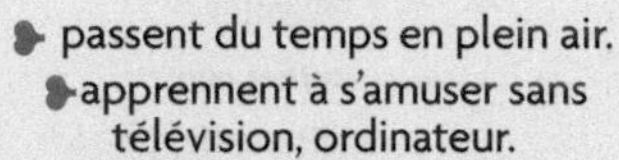

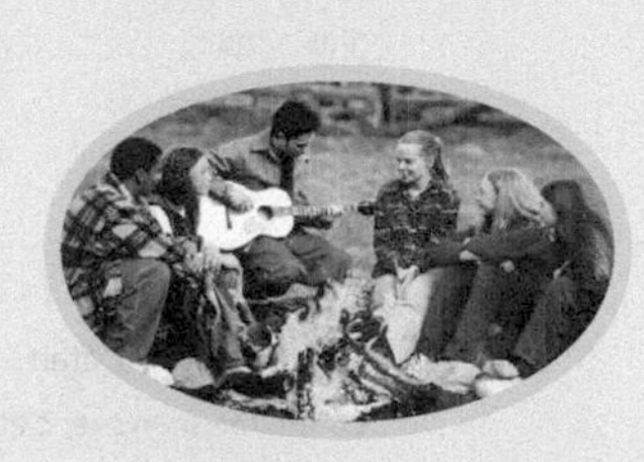

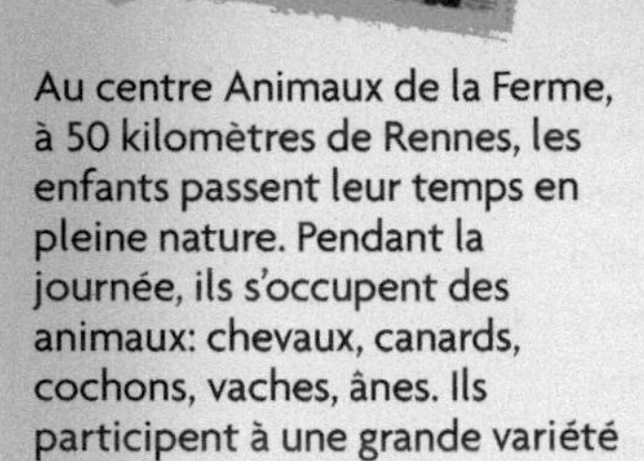

Au centre Animaux de la Ferme, à 50 kilomètres de Rennes, les enfants passent leur temps en pleine nature. Pendant la journée, ils s'occupent des animaux: chevaux, canards, cochons, vaches, ânes. Ils participent à une grande variété d'activités de plein air:
- chasse au trésor,
- tir à l'arc,
- piscine,
- monter à cheval,
- feu de camp.

1. Comment s'appelle ce centre de vacances? Animaux de la Ferme
2. Quelles sont les activités proposées aux enfants?
3. Est-ce que tu aimerais ce centre de vacances? Pourquoi ou pourquoi pas?

2. chasse au trésor, tir à l'arc, piscine, monter à cheval, feux de camp, promenades dans la nature

Online Culture Project

Ask students to research online items they may have collected over the years, such as dolls, sports cards, stamps, or coins. If some students are not collectors, have them imagine a collection they might like or talk with a relative who started a collection as a young child. Have students research French collectables and compare them to their own. Remind students to document each of the sites they consult. 1.3, 2.2

3 Avec deux ou trois amis, parlez de ce que vous aimiez faire quand vous étiez petit(e)s. Après, dites à la classe les différences et les similarités que vous avez trouvées. 1.1

Online Assessment
my.hrw.com
Cumulative Self-test

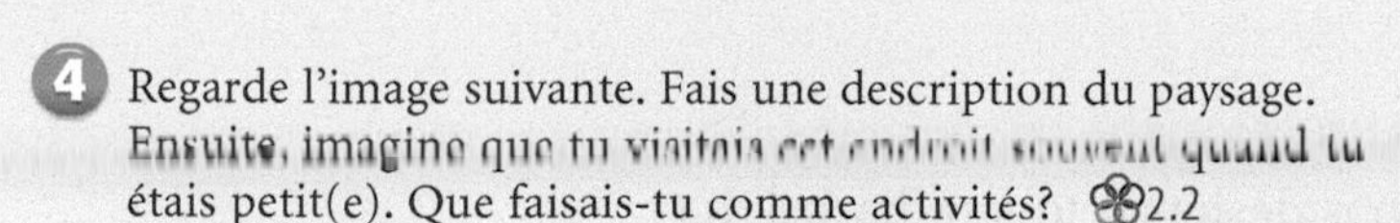

4 Regarde l'image suivante. Fais une description du paysage. Ensuite, imagine que tu visitais cet endroit souvent quand tu étais petit(e). Que faisais-tu comme activités? 2.2

Gauguin, Paul (1848-1903), Landscape in Pont-Aven, France. Canvas, Private Collection.

Paysage de Pont-Aven **de Paul Gauguin**

5 Ta correspondante française veut savoir comment ta vie a changé depuis ta jeunesse. Écris-lui une lettre. Parle de ce que tu faisais et aimais faire quand tu étais enfant et de ce que tu fais et aimes faire maintenant. 1.3

6 À ton tour

Une colonie de vacances! Your class is going to host a weekend camp for French children in your area. Plan the camp. Decide where it will be and what activities you will offer. Create a schedule of activities from the time the children wake up to bedtime. Then create a brochure advertising your camp. 1.3

Chapitres 1–6

Révisions cumulatives

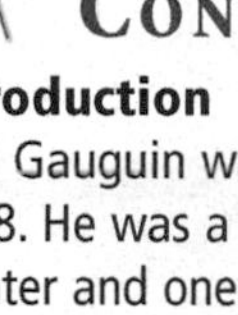

Fine Art Connection

Introduction Eugène Henri Paul Gauguin was born in Paris in 1848. He was a Post-Impressionist painter and one of the precursors of modern art. In Paris, he painted with the great painters Cézanne, Pissarro, and his friend, Vincent Van Gogh. For Gauguin, Pont-Aven represented a vivid contrast to Paris, and he often painted scenes that represented this simple and tranquil lifestyle. He was fascinated by the art of Africa and Asia, and some of his paintings are painted in the Cloisonnist style, with areas of color separated by black outlines. Gauguin spent the later years of his life in Tahiti and the Marquesas islands, where he painted many primitive-style portraits.

Analyzing

To help students discuss the painting, you might use the following questions.

1. **Qu'est-ce qu'on voit sur le tableau?**
2. **Est-ce qu'il est agréable à regarder? Pourquoi?**
3. **À ton avis, quel est l'objet orange en bas du tableau?**
4. **Que font les deux dames?**
5. **Quelle saison crois-tu que c'est?** 3.1

Extension

Have students research the traditional costume of women in Brittany and bring in photos to make a presentation. They might also compare other paintings by Gauguin ***(La Belle Angèle, Femmes bretonnes au tournant, Femme bretonne et oie près de l'eau, Bretonnes dansant).***

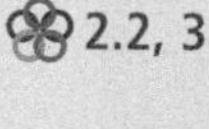
2.2, 3.1

ACTFL Performance Standards

The activities in Chapter 6 target the communicative modes as described in the Standards.

Interpersonal	Two-way communication using receptive skills and productive skills	**Communication (SE),** pp. 197, 199, 203, 209, 211, 213, 215 **Communication (TE),** pp. 197, 199, 203, 211, 213, 215
Interpretive	One-way communication using receptive skills	**Comparaisons,** p. 205 **Télé-roman,** pp. 216–217
Presentational	One-way communication using productive skills	**Communication (SE),** p. 201 **Communication (TE),** pp. 201, 209 **À ton tour,** p. 227

Géoculture Overview

Dakar

Bienvenue! This section is designed to familiarize the students with the geographic location, history, and cultural practices of the region to be explored. It provides a guide for classroom discussion and discovery of the differences and similarities of the student's own culture and that of the French-speaking world.

50-Minute Lesson Plans

Day 1

Lesson Sequence

Géoculture: Dakar, pp. 228–229

- Ask students what they know about Dakar and Senegal. Have they or a family member visited Dakar? Do students have any stereotypes about Dakar, Senegal, or Africa in general? **10 min.**
- Go over the photos and captions with students. **10 min.**
- See Map Activities, p. 228. **5 min.**
- Discuss Background Information, p. 228. **10 min.**
- Complete **Géo-quiz. 1 min.**
- Show **Géoculture** video. **4 min.**
- Have students answer **Questions,** p. 229. **10 min.**

Optional Resources

- **Savais-tu que...?,** p. 229
- Advanced Learners, p. 227B ▲
- Thinking Critically, p. 227B
- Research Online!, p. 227B

Homework Suggestions

Online Practice (**my.hrw.com**)

1.2, 1.3, 2.1, 3.1, 3.2, 4.2

Day 2

Lesson Sequence

Géoculture: Dakar, pp. 230–231

- Briefly revisit the main points about the geography. **5 min.**
- Go over the photos and captions with students. **8 min.**
- Ask students if they have seen any of the movies mentioned in the **Cinéma** feature. Would they like to see any of these movies? Why or why not? **5 min.**
- Have students answer the **As-tu compris?** questions, p. 231. **7 min.**
- Do **Prépare-toi pour le quiz**, p. 227B. **25 min.**

Optional Resources

- Special Learning Needs, p. 227B ●
- Map Game, p. 227B
- Interdisciplinary Links, pp. 230–231

Homework Suggestions

Activité, p. 231

Study for the **Géoculture** quiz.

1.1, 1.2, 1.3, 2.1, 3.1, 3.2, 4.2, 5.2

90-Minute Lesson Plan

Block 1

Lesson Sequence

Géoculture: Dakar, pp. 228–231

- Ask students what they know about Dakar and Senegal. Have they or a family member visited Dakar? Do students have any stereotypes about Dakar, Senegal, or Africa in general? **10 min.**
- Go over the photos and captions with students. **20 min.**
- See Map Activities, p. 228. **5 min.**
- Discuss Background Information, p. 228. **10 min.**
- Complete **Géo-quiz. 1 min.**
- Show **Géoculture** video. **4 min.**
- Have students answer **Questions,** p. 229. **5 min.**
- Have students answer the **As-tu compris?** questions, p. 231. **5 min.**
- Ask students if they have seen any of the movies mentioned in the **Cinéma** feature. Would they like to see any of these movies? Why or why not? **5 min.**
- Do **Prépare-toi pour le quiz,** p. 227B. **25 min.**

Optional Resources

- **Savais-tu que...?,** p. 229
- Advanced Learners, p. 227B ▲
- Special Learning Needs, p. 227B ●
- Thinking Critically, p. 227B
- Research Online!, p. 227B
- Interdisciplinary Links, pp. 230-231
- Map Game, p. 227B

Homework Suggestions

Online Practice (**my.hrw.com**)

Activité, p. 231

Study for the **Géoculture** quiz.

1.1, 1.2, 1.3, 2.1, 3.1, 3.2, 4.2, 5.2

KEY

▲ Advanced Learners ◆ Slower Pace Learners ● Special Learning Needs

Géoculture

Differentiated Instruction

Advanced Learners

Challenge Give advanced learners the opportunity to present the **Géoculture** feature to the class. They should include the information presented in the **Almanach,** as well as brief descriptions of the sights that are introduced. Encourage students to use visual aids such as maps, posters, or PowerPoint® presentations. 1.3, 3.1

Special Learning Needs

Students with Dyslexia Students may find it difficult to understand the captions. Ask the class to scan the photos for visual clues. Then have advanced learners read the text, stressing the terms that are most descriptive of the photo. The class should underline the stressed terms, asking for clarifications if necessary. Encourage students to use the underlined terms in a sentence that describes the corresponding photo. 1.1

Thinking Critically

Observing From the 16th to the 19th centuries, **L'île de Gorée** and later Dakar were major centers of the Atlantic slave trade. Millions of enslaved Africans were transported from **L'île de Gorée.** Ask students why **L'île de Gorée** was suited as a hub for transportation. 3.1

Quiz Preparation/Enrichment

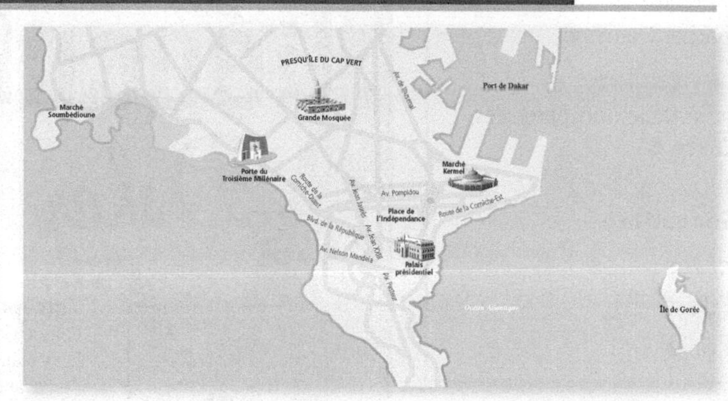

Map Game Have groups of three create a crossword puzzle using the names of features indicated on the map. The puzzles should have at least five horizontal and five vertical fields.

[1]K	E	R	[2]M	E	L
			E		
			D		
			I		
			N		
			A		

horizontal:

1. nom d'un marché

vertical:

2. nom de la vieille ville

Terms that consist of two or more words should be written without spaces between words. Have groups exchange and solve the puzzles. 1.1, 3.1

Prépare-toi pour le quiz

1. Have students draw an outline map of Dakar.
2. Students should label the map. They should include markets, important buildings, squares, and neighborhoods. 1.2, 3.1

Research Online!

Les marchés de Dakar Dakar has many large markets: **marché Sandaga, marché Kermel, marché Tilène, marché de Soumbédioune, marché Castors,** and many more. Have students research at least three markets. They should report on the location and size of each market and the products or produce sold. Have students compare these markets to the markets and shops in their hometown. Students should document their sources by noting the URLs of all the sites that they consulted. 2.1, 4.2

Géoculture

Resources

Planning:
Lesson Planner
Teacher One Stop

Presentation:

Projectable Transparencies **Carte 4**

DVD Tutor, Disc 2 **Géoculture**

Practice:
Cahier d'activités
Media Guide

Map ACTIVITIES

1. Have students locate Dakar on the map of **l'Afrique francophone** on page R4. Then have them look at the map of **le monde francophone** on page R3. Ask students to guess which of the following is closest to Dakar and which is furthest away: France, New York City, South Africa, or Brazil (all are about the same distance from Dakar, but France is the closest and South Africa the furthest: 2,377 miles from Le Havre, France; 3,400 from New York; 3,600 from Capetown, South Africa; 2,800 from Rio de Janeiro, Brazil).
2. Given its location, ask students what role they think Dakar plays in world trade. (It is an international port and the gateway to West Africa.)

Chapitres 7 et 8

Géoculture
Dakar

Géoculture

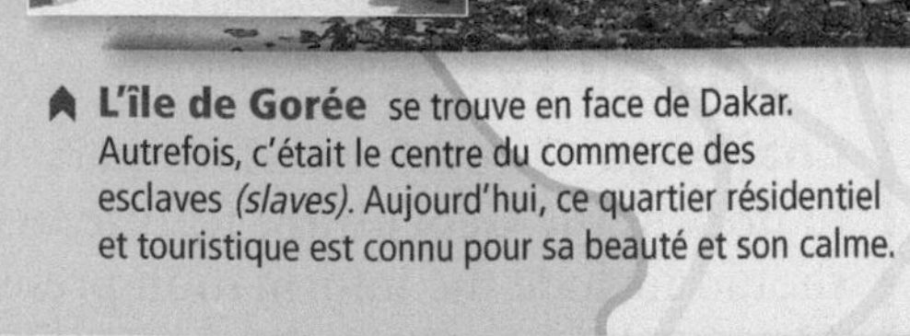
L'île de Gorée se trouve en face de Dakar. Autrefois, c'était le centre du commerce des esclaves *(slaves)*. Aujourd'hui, ce quartier résidentiel et touristique est connu pour sa beauté et son calme.

La place de l'Indépendance se trouve dans le vieux quartier français, le Plateau. C'est le cœur *(heart)* de Dakar où il y a beaucoup d'hôtels, de restaurants et d'entreprises. 2

4 Marché Soumbédioune

Almanach

Nom des habitants
Les Dakarois

Population
919.683 (commune, 2002)
2.411.528 (région, 2002)

Personnages célèbres
Birago Diop,
Youssou N'Dour,
Ousmane Sow

Industries
port maritime,
centre administratif,
raffinerie de pétrole,
industries alimentaires,
tourisme

Au marché Kermel, on peut acheter des produits alimentaires africains et européens, des fleurs et des produits de l'artisanat. 1

Savais-tu que...?

Un Sénégalais sur quatre habite dans la région de Dakar.

Background Information

Geography

Dakar is Senegal's capital and largest city. It is located on the **Cap Vert** peninsula, at the westernmost point of continental Africa. The Atlantic Ocean surrounds the city on three sides and suburbs of the city lie to the east. Dakar has a deep, natural harbor protected by limestone cliffs and a system of breakwaters, making it one of the busiest ports in Africa. **L'île de Gorée** is located at the entrance to the harbor, about two and one-half miles off the coast.

History

Île de Gorée Although the Portuguese had visited the island in 1444, the Dutch established the first permanent European settlement in 1617. They named the island *Goede Reede*, which means "good harbor." This name corrupted into Gorée. The French took possession of Gorée in 1677.

Dakar Louis Faidherbe, govenor of Senegal, founded Dakar on the site of a fishing village in 1857. Dakar became the government seat of French West Africa in 1903, then the capital of Senegal when the country gained independence in 1960.

Dakar

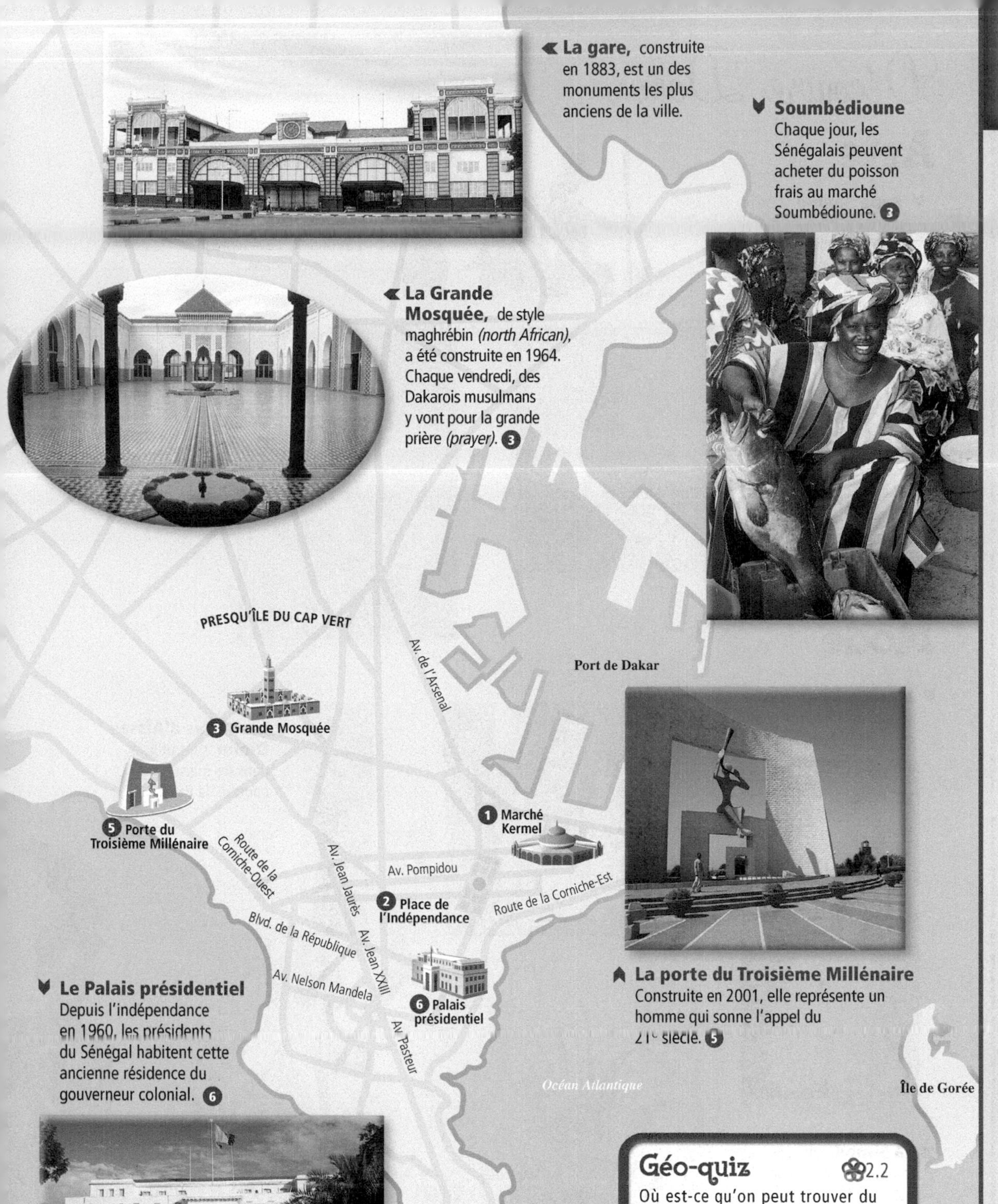

La gare, construite en 1883, est un des monuments les plus anciens de la ville.

Soumbédioune Chaque jour, les Sénégalais peuvent acheter du poisson frais au marché Soumbédioune. 3

La Grande Mosquée, de style maghrébin *(north African)*, a été construite en 1964. Chaque vendredi, des Dakarois musulmans y vont pour la grande prière *(prayer)*. 3

La porte du Troisième Millénaire Construite en 2001, elle représente un homme qui sonne l'appel du 21e siècle. 5

Le Palais présidentiel Depuis l'indépendance en 1960, les présidents du Sénégal habitent cette ancienne résidence du gouverneur colonial. 6

Géo-quiz 2.2
Où est-ce qu'on peut trouver du poisson frais? au marché Soumbédioune

Culture

Practices and Perspectives

Over 90% of the Senegalese people are Muslim. Although the teachings and practices they follow are similar to those elsewhere, the Muslims of Senegal may also be followers of **marabouts,** leaders who are part priest, fortune teller, and mystic. Or, they may belong to a **confrérie,** or brotherhood, that helps them both spiritually and in the material world. One of the largest brotherhoods is the **Mourides.** Many small merchants belong to the **Mourides,** and receive protection from larger retailers who are also members of the brotherhood. Have students research the **Mourides** to find out what their beliefs, customs, and traditions are. 2.1, 3.2

Comparisons

Comparing and Contrasting

Bargaining is an essential part of shopping in Dakar's markets. It involves more than negotiating a price. If a buyer expresses interest, he or she has commited to a lengthy interaction in which many other subjects are discussed before a final price is reached. Have students compare their own interactions with merchants to the bargaining exchange in Dakar. Is establishing a relationship with salespeople important in a transaction? 2.1, 3.2, 4.2

Savais-tu que...?

Students might be interested in knowing the following facts about Dakar.

- In the early 19th century, the original inhabitants of Dakar, the Lébou, were among the first in Africa to establish a system of government resembling a modern republic. It still exists today and is recognized by the government of Senegal.
- There are several theories about the origin of Dakar's name. One claims that it comes from **daxaar** which means *tamarind tree* in Wolof, one of the native languages. Another claims that it comes from a Lébou word meaning *refuge*.

Questions 1.2

1. **Qu'est-ce que l'île de Gorée était autrefois? (un centre du commerce des esclaves)**
2. **Où est le cœur de Dakar? (la place de l'Indépendance)**
3. **Qu'est-ce qu'on achète au marché Kermel? (des produits alimentaires, des fleurs, de l'artisanat)**
4. **Où est-ce qu'on trouve du poisson frais? (au marché Soumbédioune)**
5. **Quand est la grande prière à la Grande Mosquée? (le vendredi)**

Language Examination

Géoculture helps students better understand practices, products, and perspectives of French-speaking cultures and their relationship to one another. It can be used to practice for the **Interpretive Communication** and **Presentational Writing** sections of the AP Language and Culture Exam.

Cultures

Products and Perspectives

Pape Sambe, known as Papisto Boy, paints murals as a way to express his devotion to a Sufi saint. He also paints because he wants to give courage to Dakar's workers and teach them world history. Scenes from his murals include important figures and events in Senegal's history, such as the defeat of Lat Dior, a Senegalese leader who opposed the French in the 19th century. They also include international historical figures, such as Nelson Mandela and Malcolm X, religious figures, and singers. His largest and most famous mural covers two hundred meters and is painted on the exterior of a factory yard in Belaire, the community where he lives. Have students research Pape Sambe's murals and report on who he feels are some of the most influential people in world history. 2.2, 3.2

Comparisons

Comparing and Contrasting

Collé Ardo Sow began her career as a model in Paris. She took up fashion design while there, graduating from the **Institut de coupe et de haute couture de Paris.** She moved back to Dakar and created her own label in 1984. Shortly after beginning her business, a friend asked her to create an outfit out of **pagne,** a traditional West African fabric. The outfit she created received rave reviews at fashion shows. Ardo Sow soon began selling her African influenced creations in stores worldwide. She became known as the ambassador of Senegalese design, particularly after the airline Air Afrique commissioned her to create their uniforms. Ask students which American designers they consider to be "ambassadors of American design" and why. 4.2

Découvre Dakar

Arts

Pape Sambe a peint plusieurs fresques murales à Dakar. Celle-ci représente deux personnages de l'histoire sénégalaise: Lat Dior et le Général Faidherbe.

Dak'Art a pour but la promotion de la création africaine actuelle. Le gouvernement sénégalais patronne cet événement tous les deux ans.

Ousmane Sow est devenu sculpteur tard dans la vie. Il crée de grandes sculptures faites de terre et de matériaux de récupération.

Mode

Mariam Diop crée des vêtements de haute couture qui combinent tradition et modernité.

Les tissus d'Aïssa Dione sont utilisés dans les maisons de couture de Paris.

La Simod, ou la Semaine internationale de la mode, est un événement où tous les stylistes d'Afrique montrent leurs collections.

Interdisciplinary Links

Les arts 3.2

Art Link Most of Ousmane Sow's sculptures, like the *Nouba*, the *Maasai*, and *Little Big Horn*, are giant human figures poised for action or engaged in battle. They have few adornments and their texture is rough. Sow uses steel frames stuffed with straw to create his sculptures. He covers the frames with pieces of jute, paints them with a special mixture, and dries them in the open air. Have students find photos of Sow's sculptures online and report how they think Sow's sculpturing techniques contribute to the themes of his work.

La mode 3.1

Math Link Aïssa Dione began to develop furnishing fabrics after her grandmother introduced her to the weaving techniques of the Mandinka tribe in 1985. However, to create the fabric she desired, she needed a bigger loom. The traditional Mandinka loom produced cloth only 20 cms wide. Dione developed a new loom that could produce 90-cm wide fabric. Later, she also developed one that produces 140-cm wide cloth. Have students calculate how much 90-cm wide cloth they would need to make an 18" × 18" × 1" seat cushion.

Fêtes et festivals

Online Practice
my.hrw.com
Photo Tour

Le Festival du film de quartier permet aux jeunes réalisateurs du monde entier de présenter leur première œuvre audiovisuelle.

Le Festival international de danse Kaay Fecc présente des spectacles de danses traditionnelles et contemporaines.

Savais-tu que...?

Le *griot* joue plusieurs rôles dans la société africaine: historien, musicien, poète et conteur. Il transmet la connaissance et les traditions oralement.

Africa Fête réunit des musiciens de toute l'Afrique pour offrir des concerts divers. Ce festival montre l'universalité des cultures africaines.

Cinéma

Moussa Sene Absa est metteur en scène et acteur de cinéma. Ses films *Tableau Ferraille* et *Madame Brouette* ont reçu des prix dans des festivals internationaux.

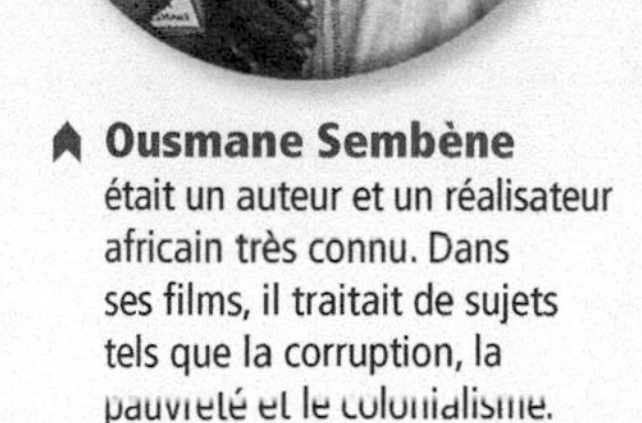

Ousmane Sembène était un auteur et un réalisateur africain très connu. Dans ses films, il traitait de sujets tels que la corruption, la pauvreté et le colonialisme.

Activité

2.1, 2.2

1. **Arts**: Comment sont les sculptures d'Ousmane Sow?
2. **Mode**: Qu'est-ce que c'est que la Simod?
3. **Fêtes et festivals**: Qu'est-ce qu'on peut voir au festival Kaay Fecc?
4. **Cinéma**: De quoi est-ce qu'Ousmane Sembène parlait dans ses films?

Dakar

Activité

1. grandes, faites de terre et de matériaux de récupération
2. un événement où tous les stylistes d'Afrique montrent leurs collections
3. des spectacles de danse traditionnelles et contemporaines
4. la corruption, la pauvreté et le colonialisme

Communities

Traditions

Griots are part historian, storyteller, and musician, passing on history and culture from generation to generation. Some **griots** help preserve family memories. Others are associated with a particular clan or village. The **griot's** role is usually passed on from father to son. Have students imagine they are **griots** and write a song in French about an event or tradition that they think should be passed on to the next generation.
1.3, 2.1, 5.1

As-tu compris?

You can use the following questions to check students' comprehension of the **Géoculture.**

1. **Qu'est-ce que Pape Sambe a peint? (des fresques murales)**
2. **Quel genre de vêtements crée Collé Ardo Sow? (haute couture et prêt-à-porter)**
3. **Quel est le métier de Moussa Sene Absa? (Il est acteur et metteur en scène.)** 1.2

Les fêtes et festivals

3.1

Dance Link The **Festival Kaay Fecc,** which means "come dance" in Wolof, was created to support the training of dancers and choreographers and give them a place to showcase their art. Dance companies from all over the world come to Dakar for this eight-day event. They offer and participate in traditional and contemporary dance workshops that are free and open to the general public. Have students research a traditional Senegalese dance or if possible, have them invite a community member to teach Senegalese dances at their own **Kaay Fecc** festival.

Le cinéma

3.2, 5.2

Social Sciences Link Ousmane Sembène is often considered the father of sub-Saharan African film. He produced short and feature-length films that include dramas, documentaries, and satirical comedies. His film ***La noire de...*** was the first feature ever produced by a sub-Saharan African and was honored at the 1967 Cannes Film Festival. He has made several films in Wolof, Senegal's primary native language, in an effort to reach a wider audience. Suggest that students watch one of Sembène's films and report what they learn about life in Senegal.

Assess

Assessment Program
Quiz: Géoculture
Differentiated Practice and Assessment CD-ROM

Online Assessment
my.hrw.com

Test Generator 

Planning Guide

Un week-end en plein air

Chapter Section	Resources
Vocabulaire 1 pp. 234–237 • Camping equipment and activities **Grammaire 1** pp. 238–241 • The **passé composé** and the **imparfait** • **être en train de** **Application 1** pp. 242–243 • **Un peu plus:** verbs with **être** and **avoir** in the **passé composé**	Projectable Transparencies: Vocabulaire 7.1, 7.2; Bell Work 7.1, 7.2, 7.3, 7.4 Cahier de vocabulaire et grammaire, pp. 73–78 Grammar Tutor for Students of French Cahier d'activités, pp. 61–63 Media Guide, pp. 25–28, 88–90 **Assessment Program** Quiz: Vocabulaire 1, pp. 189–190 Quiz: Grammaire 1, pp. 191–192 Quiz: Application 1, pp. 193–194
Culture pp. 244–245 • **Culture appliquée: Le parc national de la Langue de Barbarie** • **Comparaisons et Communauté**	Cahier d'activités, p. 64
Vocabulaire 2 pp. 246–249 • Nature, outdoors, animals and activities **Grammaire 2** pp. 250–253 • The future **Application 2** pp. 254–255 • **Un peu plus:** The verb **courir**	Projectable Transparencies: Vocabulaire 7.3, 7.4; Bell Work 7.5, 7.6, 7.7, 7.8 Cahier de vocabulaire et grammaire, pp. 79–84 Grammar Tutor for Students of French Cahier d'activités, pp. 65–67 Media Guide, pp. 25–28, 88–89, 91 **Assessment Program** Quiz: Vocabulaire 2, pp. 195–196 Quiz: Grammaire 2, pp. 197–198 Quiz: Application 2, pp. 199–200
Télé-roman pp. 256–257	Media Guide, pp. 89, 92
Lecture et écriture pp. 258–261	Cahier d'activités, p. 68 Reading Strategies and Skills Handbook Intermediate Reader French InterActive Reader **Assessment Program** Quiz: Lecture, p. 201 Quiz: Écriture, p. 202
Prépare-toi pour l'examen pp. 262–265 • **Résumé de vocabulaire et grammaire** • **Lettres et sons** **Révisions cumulatives** pp. 266–267	Independent Study Guide, pp. 19–21, 39 Media Guide, p. 28 **Assessment Program** Examen: Chapitre 7, pp. 203–208 Examen oral: Chapitre 7, p. 323 Projectable Transparencies: Fine Art, Ch. 7 Cahier d'activités, pp. 64, 69–70
Variations littéraires pp. 394–395 • **Les poèmes de Léopold Sédar Senghor**	Reading Strategies and Skills Handbook Intermediate Reader French InterActive Reader

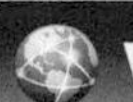

Visit Us Online

my.hrw.com
Online Edition

Pacing Suggestions

	Essential	Recommended	Optional
Vocabulaire 1 • Camping equipment and activities • **Flash culture**	✔		
Grammaire 1 • The **passé composé** and the **imparfait** • **être en train de** • **Flash culture**	✔		
Application 1 • **Un peu plus:** verbs with **être** and **avoir** in the **passé composé**	✔		
Culture • **Culture appliquée: Le parc national de la Langue de Barbarie** • **Comparaisons et Communauté**		✔	
Vocabulaire 2 • Nature, outdoors, animals and activities • **Flash culture**	✔		
Grammaire 2 • The future • **Flash culture**	✔		
Application 2 • **Un peu plus:** The verb **courir**	✔		
Télé-roman • Épisode 7: **Le Secret de la statuette**			✔
Lecture et écriture • **Comment guérir la peur** (Lecture) • **Il était une fois...** (Écriture)		✔	
Prépare-toi pour l'examen		✔	
Révisions cumulatives			✔
Variations littéraires • **Les poèmes de Léopold Sédar Senghor**			✔

Technology

Bien dit! Online

- Student Edition with multi-media
- **performance)) space** recording tool
- Interactive activities with feedback
- Self-tests with feedback
- Cahier d'activités (Interactive workbook)
- Cahier de vocabulaire et grammaire (Interactive workbook)
- Holt Online Assessment

DVD Tutor

- Télé-vocab
- Grammavision
- On rappe!
- Télé-roman

- Interactive games
- Differentiated Practice
- Cultural Video

Audio Program

- Student Edition listening activities
- Assessment listening activities
- Songs

Teacher One Stop™

- Complete resources
- ExamView Pro Test Generator
- Holt Calendar Planner

Holt McDougal Apps

Interactive Whiteboard Lessons

Differentiated Practice and Assessment CD

For slower pace and advanced learner options, see the Differentiated Practice and Assessment CD.

Projects

Vidéo album

In groups, students will record a video album of an imaginary camping trip in a francophone country. A series of pictures, similar to a slide show with narration, will be recorded on video. Each group will create ten illustrations to describe the trip. The first should show the location of the campground on a map of the country. 1.3, 3.1

Suggested Sequence

1. Each group chooses a national or regional park in any francophone country, department, or province as the site of their camping trip.
2. Students select or draw their "photos" and mount each one on a separate piece of paper. Students then write a one- or two-sentence caption for each one.
3. When the photos and captions are finished, students videotape their albums. Students should tape the photos to the wall and focus the camera on only one photo at a time. Group members take turns reading aloud the captions.
4. Each group presents its video to the class. You may wish to have the class vote on the most exciting, most memorable, or most disastrous camping trip.

21st Century Technology Literacy

Grading the project

Suggested point distribution (100 points total)

Originality/design	20 pts.
Written captions	20 pts.
Oral presentation	30 pts.
Language use	30 pts.

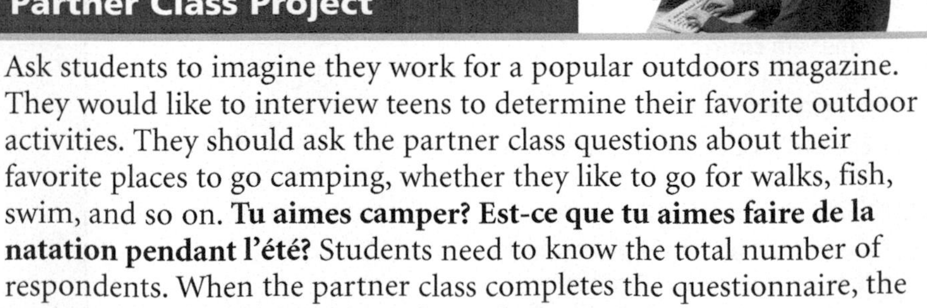

Partner Class Project

Ask students to imagine they work for a popular outdoors magazine. They would like to interview teens to determine their favorite outdoor activities. They should ask the partner class questions about their favorite places to go camping, whether they like to go for walks, fish, swim, and so on. **Tu aimes camper? Est-ce que tu aimes faire de la natation pendant l'été?** Students need to know the total number of respondents. When the partner class completes the questionnaire, the students should discuss the results and use a word processing progam to create a pie chart or a bar graph that represents the information. They can post these to share with their partner class. 1.3

21st Century Communication

e-community

e-mail forum:

Location: http://french

Post the following questions on the classroom e-mail forum:

Est-ce que tu aimes faire des activités en plein air?

Avec qui est-ce que tu fais du camping? 5.1

All students will contribute to the list and then share the items.

Game Bank
For game ideas, see pages T60–T63.

Lac Rose de Retba

Lac Rose de Retba lies about 40 kilometers north of Dakar and is separated from the ocean by less than a kilometer. The water contains a high level of salt, which accumulates on the lake bottom. This salty crust is 'harvested' daily by local men and women, just as they have done for centuries. Shea butter protects their skin from the effects of the salt water as they stand in the salty water up to their waists. They crack the crusts of salt at the bottom of the shallow lake with spears and load it onto their **pirogues** (flat boats). The women fill baskets that they balance on their head and empty the salt into piles at the edge of the lake. Each mound of salt is identified with the mark of its owner. The women then use the salt to preserve fish. With the ocean so close, fish caught by the crews of men can be preserved with no loss of quality. Ask students to think of other traditional methods of preserving food. 2.1

La cuisine

Bell peppers originated in the Americas. They actually belong to the fruit category. Green, yellow, and red bell peppers are the same species at different stages of maturity. Red peppers are the sweetest, yellow peppers the juiciest, and green peppers the fruitiest, but most bitter. The best time to eat bell peppers is between May and October. Encourage students to make **salade créole** in their foods class or at home for family and friends. 1.2, 2.2

Salade créole

Salade
2 poivrons rouges
2 poivrons verts
1 oignon
3 branches de céleri
2 tomates
1/2 tasse d'olives vertes

Vinaigrette
8 cuillères à soupe d'huile d'olive
2 cuillères à soupe de vinaigre blanc
1 gousse d'ail hachée
basilic
sel, poivre

Salade
Couper les légumes. Les mélanger dans un saladier. Mettre au frigidaire jusqu'au moment de servir.

Vinaigrette
Mélanger l'huile d'olive, le vinaigre, l'ail, le sel, le poivre et le basilic. Verser la vinaigrette sur la salade au moment de servir.

Listening Activity Scripts

Vocabulaire à l'œuvre 1

1 p. 236, CD 7, Tr. 1

— Salut, Doudou! Ça s'est bien passé, ton week-end?
— Euh, non.
— Qu'est-ce qui s'est passé?
— Bon, j'allais faire du camping. Avant de partir, mon père m'a dit, «N'oublie pas ta gourde et les boîtes de conserve!» Alors, qu'est-ce que j'ai fait? J'ai oublié ma gourde!
— Oh, là, là! Mais tu as emporté les boîtes de conserve?
— Oui, mais j'ai oublié mon ouvre-boîte! Alors, je n'ai pas pu manger!
— Dommage!
— Heureusement, j'ai pensé à emporter une bouteille isotherme, mais j'ai oublié la lanterne.
— Oh, non!
— Et figure-toi que je suis parti sans allumettes!

Answers to Activity 1
1. b **2.** a **3.** b **4.** a **5.** a

Grammaire à l'œuvre 1

10 p. 240, CD 7, Tr. 2

1. Doudou est allé au terrain de camping.
2. Marianne et Isabelle sont en train d'allumer le feu de camp.
3. Papa était en train de monter la tente quand il a trouvé les allumettes.
4. Oui, on a acheté les boîtes de conserve.
5. J'ai mis de la crème solaire.
6. Mes parents sont en train de sortir les lanternes.

Answers to Activity 10
1. a **2.** b **3.** b **4.** a **5.** a **6.** b

Application 1

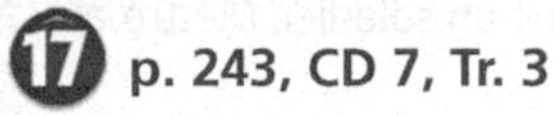

17 p. 243, CD 7, Tr. 3

1. Est-ce que tu montes la tente?
2. Les filles, vous descendez les sacs de la voiture?
3. Tes camarades sortent de la voiture?
4. Tu me passes la gourde?
5. Tes parents ont sorti les sacs?

Answers to Activity 17
1. a **2.** a **3.** b **4.** a **5.** b

Vocabulaire à l'œuvre 2

20 p. 248, CD 7, Tr. 4

1. Un jour Madame Araignée avait faim. Alors, elle a décidé d'aller à la pêche.
2. Elle allait au lac quand elle a rencontré un lézard. Elle lui a expliqué où elle allait et pourquoi. Le lézard a dit: «Comment est-ce que vous allez attraper un poisson? C'est ridicule!»
3. Finalement, Madame Araignée est arrivée au lac. Là, elle a vu des pélicans qui pêchaient. Ils étaient de très bons pêcheurs.
4. Madame Araignée a commencé à pêcher, elle aussi. D'abord, elle a fait un fil. Mais, il n'y avait pas de poisson!
5. Alors, elle s'est fait une toile, exactement comme les toiles qu'elle faisait pour attraper les mouches. Puis, elle a jeté sa toile dans le lac.
6. Madame Araignée a retiré sa toile. Il y avait beaucoup de poissons dans la toile! Les flamants roses et les pélicans ne riaient plus.

Answers to Activity 20
1. e **2.** a **3.** d **4.** c **5.** f **6.** b

Grammaire à l'œuvre 2

25 p. 250, CD 7, Tr. 5

1. Pendant la randonnée de ce matin, mes amis ont vu des tortues dans le lac.
2. Ce soir, on mettra de la lotion anti-moustiques parce qu'il y a beaucoup de moustiques ici!
3. Cet après-midi, les guides nous parleront des oiseaux qu'on peut voir dans ce parc.
4. On s'est promenés sur les sentiers et on a observé les arbres et les animaux.
5. Plus tard, mes amis et moi, nous nous baignerons près de la cascade.
6. Quand je finirai ce devoir sur le parc, je le rendrai à mon professeur.

Answers to Activity 25
1. a **2.** b **3.** b **4.** a **5.** b **6.** b

Application 2

37 p. 254, CD 7, Tr. 6

1. Quand Lucien était petit, son grand-père et lui allaient souvent à la pêche.
2. Tu courras, tu courras, mais tu ne m'attraperas pas!
3. Regarde! Ce lézard court après une mouche!
4. La prochaine fois que je ferai du camping, j'emporterai de la lotion anti-moustiques.
5. Nous étions en train de monter la tente quand il a commencé à pleuvoir.

Answers to Activity 37

1. b 2. c 3. a 4. c 5. b

Prépare-toi pour l'examen

6 p. 263, CD 7, Tr. 10

— Tu sais, je viens de faire du camping avec des amis.

— Oui, je sais. Vous vous êtes bien amusés?

— Bof, pas trop.

— Mais pourquoi?

— D'abord, vendredi, nous avions à peine fini de monter la tente quand il a commencé à pleuvoir. Nous voulions faire du vélo, mais comme il pleuvait, nous n'avons pas pu. Il était impossible de faire un feu de camp. Tout ce qu'il y avait à manger, c'était des haricots froids.

— Et samedi?

— Samedi il a fait assez beau. Le matin, nous sommes allés au lac pour pêcher. J'ai pêché pendant deux heures, mais je n'ai rien attrapé. Thomas a attrapé trois gros poissons. Nous rentrions au camp quand soudain un serpent a traversé le sentier juste devant nous. Nous avons couru si vite que Thomas a perdu ses poissons. Une fois de plus il n'y avait rien à manger!

Answers to Activity 6

1. pleuvait
2. du vélo
3. beau, à la pêche
4. attrapé, trois
5. serpent, poissons

Dictée, p. 264, CD 7, Tr. 13

1. Mets le désinfectant dans la trousse de premiers soins.
2. La prochaine fois, je vais me promener dans les bois.
3. Le serpent a traversé le sentier.
4. L'oiseau se baigne dans la piscine!
5. Ma sœur est souvent paresseuse.

Révisions cumulatives *chapitres 1-7*

1 p. 266, CD 7, Tr. 14

1. Je n'arrive pas à allumer ce feu. Tu n'as pas de briquet?
2. Aïe ! Je me suis coupé la main. Elle est où, la trousse de premiers soins ?
3. Regarde les beaux poissons que j'ai attrapés ce matin. Allume le feu et je les ferai cuire.
4. Alors, c'est fait. Nous avons monté la tente et trouvé les sacs de couchage. Et voilà la lampe de poche. Tout est prêt pour la nuit.

Answers to Activity 1

1. b 2. b 3. a 4. a

50-Minute Lesson Plans

Un week-end en plein air

Day 1

OBJECTIVE
Say what happened

Core Instruction
Chapter Opener, pp. 232–233
- See Using the Photo, p. 232. **5 min.**
- See Chapter Objectives, p. 232. **5 min.**

Vocabulaire 1, pp. 234–237
- Present **Vocabulaire 1,** pp. 234–235. See Teaching **Vocabulaire,** p. 234. **10 min.**
- Show **Télé-vocab 1. 5 min.**
- Present **Exprimons-nous!,** p. 235. **10 min.**
- Play Audio CD 7, Tr. 1 for Activity 1, p. 236. **5 min.**
- Have students do Activities 2–3, p. 236. **10 min.**

Optional Resources
- Slower Pace Learners, p. 235 ◆
- Special Learning Needs, p. 235 ●

Homework Suggestions
Cahier de vocabulaire et grammaire, pp. 73–74
1.2, 1.3

Day 2

OBJECTIVE
*Describe circumstances; Use the **passé composé** and the **imparfait***

Core Instruction
Vocabulaire 1, pp. 234–237
- Present **Flash culture,** p. 236. **5 min.**
- See Teaching **Exprimons-nous!,** p. 236. **10 min.**
- Have students do Activities 4–5, p. 237. **20 min.**

Grammaire 1, pp. 238–241
- See Teaching **Grammaire,** p. 238. **10 min.**
- Show **Grammavision 1.1. 5 min.**

Optional Resources
- Advanced Learners, p. 237 ▲

Homework Suggestions
Study for **Quiz: Vocabulaire 1**
Cahier de vocabulaire et grammaire, p. 75
Online Practice (**my.hrw.com**)
@HOMETUTOR
1.1, 1.2, 4.1

Day 3

OBJECTIVE
*Use the **passé composé** and the **imparfait***

Core Instruction
Vocabulaire 1, pp. 234–237
- Review **Vocabulaire 1,** pp. 234–237. **10 min.**
- Give **Quiz: Vocabulaire 1. 20 min.**

Grammaire 1, pp. 238–241
- Have students do Activities 6–9, pp. 238–239. **20 min.**

Optional Resources
- French for Spanish Speakers, p. 239
- Slower Pace Learners, p. 239 ◆
- Multiple Intelligences, p. 239

Homework Suggestions
Cahier de vocabulaire et grammaire, p. 76
Cahier d'activités, p. 61
Online Practice (**my.hrw.com**)
1.1, 1.2, 1.3, 4.2

Day 4

OBJECTIVE
*Use **être en train de***

Core Instruction
Grammaire 1, pp. 238–241
- Present **Flash culture,** p. 240. **5 min.**
- See Teaching **Grammaire,** p. 240. **10 min.**
- Show **Grammavision 1.2. 5 min.**
- Play Audio CD 7, Tr. 2 for Activity 10, p. 240. **5 min.**
- Do Activities 11–14, pp. 240–241. **20 min.**

Application 1, pp. 242–243
- Do Activity 15, p. 242. **5 min.**

Optional Resources
- Advanced Learners, p. 241 ▲
- Special Learning Needs, p. 241 ●

Homework Suggestions
Study for **Quiz: Grammaire 1**
Cahier de vocabulaire et grammaire, p. 77
Cahier d'activités, p. 62
1.2, 1.3

Day 5

OBJECTIVE
*Use verbs with **être** or **avoir** in the **passé composé***

Core Instruction
Grammaire 1, pp. 238–241
- Review **Grammaire 1,** pp. 238–241. **10 min.**
- Give **Quiz: Grammaire 1. 20 min.**

Application 1, pp. 242–243
- See Teaching **Un peu plus,** p. 242. **5 min.**
- Have students do Activity 16, p. 242. **5 min.**
- Play Audio CD 7, Tr. 3 for Activity 17, p. 243. **5 min.**
- Have students do Activities 18–19, p. 243. **5 min.**

Optional Resources
- Slower Pace Learners, p. 243 ◆
- Special Learning Needs, p. 243 ●

Homework Suggestions
Study for **Quiz: Application 1**
Cahier de vocabulaire et grammaire, p. 78
Cahier d'activités, p. 63
1.1, 1.2, 1.3

Day 6

OBJECTIVE
Learn about francophone culture

Core Instruction
Application 1, pp. 242–243
- Review **Application 1,** pp. 242–243. **10 min.**
- Give **Quiz: Application 1. 20 min.**

Culture, pp. 244–245
- See **Culture appliquée** (TE), p. 244. **10 min.**
- See **Comparaisons et communauté** (TE), p. 244. **10 min.**

Optional Resources
- Connections, p. 245
- Communities, p. 245
- Advanced Learners, p. 245 ▲
- Multiple Intelligences, p. 245

Homework Suggestions
Cahier d'activités, p. 64
Online Practice (**my.hrw.com**)
Finish **Culture appliquée** project
1.2, 2.2, 3.1, 4.2, 5.1

Day 7

OBJECTIVE
Tell what you will do

Core Instruction
Vocabulaire 2, pp. 246–249
- Do Bell Work 7.5, p. 246. **5 min.**
- Present **Vocabulaire 2,** pp. 246–247. See Teaching **Vocabulaire,** p. 246. **10 min.**
- Show **Télé-vocab 2. 5 min.**
- Present **Exprimons-nous!,** p. 247. **10 min.**
- Play Audio CD 7, Tr. 4 for Activity 20, p. 248. **5 min.**
- Have students do Activities 21–22, p. 248. **15 min.**

Optional Resources
- TPR, p. 247
- Slower Pace Learners, p. 247 ◆
- Multiple Intelligences, p. 247
- Advanced Learners, p. 249 ▲
- Multiple Intelligences, p. 249

Homework Suggestions
Cahier de vocabulaire et grammaire, pp. 79–80
1.2, 1.3, 4.2

Day 8

OBJECTIVE
Wonder what will happen; Use the future

Core Instruction
Vocabulaire 2, pp. 246–249
- Present **Flash culture,** p. 249. **5 min.**
- See Teaching **Exprimons-nous!,** p. 248. **10 min.**
- Have students do Activities 23–24, p. 249. **15 min.**

Grammaire 2, pp. 250–253
- See Teaching **Grammaire,** p. 250. **10 min.**
- Show **Grammavision 2.1. 5 min.**
- Play Audio CD 7, Tr. 5 for Activity 25, p. 250. **5 min.**

Optional Resources
- Communication (TE), p. 249

Homework Suggestions
Study for **Quiz: Vocabulaire 2**
Cahier de vocabulaire et grammaire, p. 81
@HOMETUTOR
1.1, 1.2

To edit and create your own lesson plans, see the **Teacher One Stop™**

KEY
- ▲ Advanced Learners
- ◆ Slower Pace Learners
- ● Special Learning Needs

Day 9

OBJECTIVE
Use the future

Core Instruction
Vocabulaire 2, pp. 246–249
- Review **Vocabulaire 2,** pp. 246–249. **10 min.**
- Give **Quiz: Vocabulaire 2. 20 min.**

Grammaire 2, pp. 250–253
- Have students do Activities 26–29, pp. 250–251. **20 min.**

Optional Resources
- Communication (TE), p. 251
- Advanced Learners, p. 251 ▲
- Multiple Intelligences, p. 251

Homework Suggestions
Cahier de vocabulaire et grammaire, p. 82
Cahier d'activités, p. 65
@HOMETUTOR
Online Practice (**my.hrw.com**)
1.1, 1.2

Day 10

OBJECTIVE
*Use the future of irregular verbs; Use the verb **courir***

Core Instruction
Grammaire 2, pp. 250–253
- Present **Flash culture,** p. 252. **5 min.**
- See Teaching **Grammaire,** p. 252. **5 min.**
- Show **Grammavision 2.2. 5 min.**
- Have students do Activities 30–34, pp. 252–253. **20 min.**

Application 2, pp. 254–255
- Have students do Activities 35–36, p. 254. **10 min.**
- See Teaching **Un peu plus,** p. 254. **5 min.**

Optional Resources
- Slower Pace Learners, p. 253 ◆
- Special Learning Needs, p. 253 ●

Homework Suggestions
Study for **Quiz: Grammaire 2**
Cahier de vocabulaire et grammaire, p. 83
Cahier d'activités, p. 66
1.1, 1.2, 1.3, 4.2

Day 11

OBJECTIVE
*Use the verb **courir***

Core Instruction
Grammaire 2, pp. 250–253
- Review **Grammaire 2,** pp. 250–253. **10 min.**
- Give **Quiz: Grammaire 2. 20 min.**

Application 2, pp. 254–255
- Play Audio CD 7, Tr. 6 for Activity 37, p. 254. **5 min.**
- Have students do Activities 38–40, p. 255. **15 min.**

Optional Resources
- Communication (TE), p. 255
- Special Learning Needs, p. 255 ●

Homework Suggestions
Study for **Quiz: Application 2**
Cahier de vocabulaire et grammaire, p. 84
Cahier d'activités, p. 67
Online Practice (**my.hrw.com**)
1.1, 1.2, 1.3

Day 12

OBJECTIVE
Develop listening and reading skills

Core Instruction
Application 2, pp. 254–255
- Review **Application 2,** pp. 254–255. **10 min.**
- Give **Quiz: Application 2. 20 min.**

Télé-roman, pp. 256–257
- Show **Télé-roman.** See Teaching **Télé-roman,** p. 256. **5 min.**
- Have students answer the **As-tu compris?** questions, p. 257. **15 min.**

Optional Resources
- Connections, p. 256
- Gestures, p. 256
- Communication (TE), p. 257

Homework Suggestions
Online Practice (**my.hrw.com**)
1.2, 1.3, 1.1.2, 1.3

Day 13

OBJECTIVE
Develop listening, reading, and writing skills

Core Instruction
Lecture et écriture, pp. 258–261
- See Teaching **Lecture,** p. 258. **35 min.**
- See Teaching **Espace écriture,** p. 260. **15 min.**

Optional Resources
- Applying the Strategies, p. 258
- Summarizing, p. 258
- Cultures, p. 259
- Connections, p. 259
- Slower Pace Learners, p. 259 ◆
- Special Learning Needs, p. 259 ●

Homework Suggestions
Cahier d'activités, p. 68
Espace écriture, Activity 2, p. 261
1.2, 1.3, 2.1, 3.1

Day 14

OBJECTIVE
Develop writing skills; Review the chapter

Core Instruction
Lecture et écriture, pp. 258–261
- See Teaching **Espace écriture,** p. 260. **25 min.**

Prépare-toi pour l'examen, pp. 262–264
- Have students do Activities 1–5, pp. 262–263. **25 min.**

Optional Resources
- Communities, p. 260
- Connections, p. 260
- Process Writing, p. 261
- Writing Assessment, p. 261
- Advanced Learners, p. 261 ▲
- Multiple Intelligences, p. 261
- Fold-N-Learn, p. 262

Homework Suggestions
Online Practice (**my.hrw.com**)
1.2, 1.3, 3.1, 5.1

Day 15

OBJECTIVE
Review the chapter

Core Instruction
Prépare-toi pour l'examen, pp. 262–264
- Play Audio CD 7, Tr. 10 for Activity 6, p. 263. **5 min.**
- Have students do Activity 7, p. 263. **5 min.**
- Play Audio CD 7, Tr. 11–13 for **Lettres et sons,** p. 264. **10 min.**

Révisions cumulatives, pp. 266–267
- Play Audio CD 7, Tr. 14 for Activity 1, p. 266. **5 min.**
- Have students do Activities 2–6, pp. 266–267. **25 min.**

Optional Resources
- Online Culture Project, p. 266
- Fine Art Connection, p. 267

Homework Suggestions
Study for Chapter Test
Online Practice (**my.hrw.com**)
1.1, 1.2, 1.3, 2.1, 3.1, 3.2

Day 16/Test

Core Instruction
Chapter Test 50 min.

Optional Resources
Assessment Program
- Alternative Assessment
- Test Generator
- **Quiz: Lecture**
- **Quiz: Écriture**

Homework Suggestions
Cahier d'activités, pp. 69–70, 114–115
Online Practice (**my.hrw.com**)

90-Minute Lesson Plans

Un week-end en plein air

Block 1

OBJECTIVE
Say what happened; Describe circumstances

Core Instruction

Chapter Opener, pp. 232–233
- See Using the Photo, p. 232. **5 min.**
- See Chapter Objectives, p. 232. **5 min.**

Vocabulaire 1, pp. 234–237
- Present **Vocabulaire 1,** pp. 234–235. See Teaching **Vocabulaire,** p. 234. **10 min.**
- Show **Télé-vocab 1. 5 min.**
- Present **Exprimons-nous!,** p. 235. **10 min.**
- Play Audio CD 7, Tr. 1 for Activity 1, p. 236. **5 min.**
- Have students do Activities 2–3, p. 236. **15 min.**
- Present **Flash culture,** p. 236. **5 min.**
- See Teaching **Exprimons-nous!,** p. 236. **10 min.**
- Have students do Activities 4–5, p. 237. **20 min.**

Optional Resources

- Learning Tips, p. 233
- Connections, p. 234
- TPR, p. 235
- Language Note, p. 235
- Communities, p. 235
- Slower Pace Learners, p. 235 ◆
- Special Learning Needs, p. 235 ●
- **Attention!,** p. 237
- Teacher to Teacher, p. 237
- Communication (TE), p. 237
- Advanced Learners, p. 237 ▲
- Multiple Intelligences, p. 237

Homework Suggestions

Study for **Quiz: Vocabulaire 1**
Cahier de vocabulaire et grammaire, pp. 73–75
HOMETUTOR
Online Practice (**my.hrw.com**)
1.1, 1.2, 1.3, 3.1, 4.1

Block 2

OBJECTIVE
*Use the **passé composé** and the **imparfait;** Use **être en train de***

Core Instruction

Vocabulaire 1, pp. 234–237
- Review **Vocabulaire 1,** pp. 234–237. **10 min.**
- Give **Quiz: Vocabulaire 1. 20 min.**

Grammaire 1, pp. 238–241
- See Teaching **Grammaire,** p. 238. **5 min.**
- Show **Grammavision 1.1. 5 min.**
- Have students do Activities 6–9, pp. 238–239. **15 min.**
- Present **Flash culture,** p. 240. **5 min.**
- See Teaching **Grammaire,** p. 240. **10 min.**
- Show **Grammavision 1.2. 5 min.**
- Play Audio CD 7, Tr. 2 for Activity 10, p. 240. **5 min.**
- Have students do Activities 11–12, pp. 240–241. **10 min.**

Optional Resources

- **Attention!,** p. 238
- Connections, p. 238
- French for Spanish Speakers, p. 239
- Communication (TE), p. 239
- Slower Pace Learners, p. 239 ◆
- Multiple Intelligences, p. 239
- Special Learning Needs, p. 241 ●

Homework Suggestions

Study for **Quiz: Grammaire 1**
Cahier de vocabulaire et grammaire, pp. 76–77
Cahier d'activités, pp. 61–62
HOMETUTOR
Online Practice (**my.hrw.com**)
1.1, 1.2, 1.3, 3.1, 4.1, 4.2

Block 3

OBJECTIVE
*Use **être en train de;** Use verbs with **être** or **avoir** in the **passé composé;** Learn about francophone culture*

Core Instruction

Grammaire 1, pp. 238–241
- Have students do Activities 13–14, p. 241. **10 min.**
- Review **Grammaire 1,** pp. 238–241. **10 min.**
- Give **Quiz: Grammaire 1. 20 min.**

Application 1, pp. 242–243
- Have students do Activity 15, p. 242. **5 min.**
- See Teaching **Un peu plus,** p. 242. **5 min.**
- Have students do Activity 16, p. 242. **5 min.**
- Play Audio CD 7, Tr. 3 for Activity 17, p. 243. **5 min.**
- Have students do Activities 18–19, p. 243. **10 min.**

Culture, pp. 244–245
- See **Culture appliquée** (TE), p. 244. **10 min.**
- See **Comparaisons et communauté** (TE), p. 244. **10 min.**

Optional Resources

- Teacher Note, p. 241
- Communication (TE), p. 241
- Advanced Learners, p. 241 ▲
- Comparisons, p. 242
- Communication (TE), p. 243
- Slower Pace Learners, p. 243 ◆
- Special Learning Needs, p. 243 ●
- **Vocabulaire supplémentaire,** p. 244
- Connections, p. 245
- Communities, p. 245
- Advanced Learners, p. 245 ▲
- Multiple Intelligences, p. 245

Homework Suggestions

Study for **Quiz: Application 1**
Cahier de vocabulaire et grammaire, p. 78
Cahier d'activités, pp. 63–64
Online Practice (**my.hrw.com**)
Finish **Culture appliquée** project
1.1, 1.2, 1.3, 2.2, 3.1, 4.1, 4.2, 5.1

Block 4

OBJECTIVE
Tell what you will do; Wonder what will happen

Core Instruction

Application 1, pp. 242–243
- Review **Application 1,** pp. 242–243. **10 min.**
- Give **Quiz: Application 1. 20 min.**

Vocabulaire 2, pp. 246–249
- Present **Vocabulaire 2,** pp. 246–247. See Teaching **Vocabulaire,** p. 246. **10 min.**
- Show **Télé-vocab 2. 5 min.**
- Present **Exprimons-nous!,** p. 247. **5 min.**
- Play Audio CD 7, Tr. 4 for Activity 20, p. 248. **5 min.**
- Have students do Activities 21–22, p. 248. **10 min.**
- Present **Flash culture,** p. 249. **5 min.**
- See Teaching **Exprimons-nous!,** p. 248. **10 min.**
- Have students do Activities 23–24, p. 249. **10 min.**

Optional Resources

- **Proverbs,** p. 246
- TPR, p. 247
- Communities, p. 247
- Slower Pace Learners, p. 247 ◆
- Multiple Intelligences, p. 247
- Communication (TE), p. 249
- Advanced Learners, p. 249 ▲
- Multiple Intelligences, p. 249

Homework Suggestions

Study for **Quiz: Vocabulaire 2**
Cahier de vocabulaire et grammaire, pp. 79–81
HOMETUTOR
Online Practice (**my.hrw.com**)
1.1, 1.2, 1.3, 4.1, 5.1

To edit and create your own lesson plans, see the **Teacher One Stop™**

KEY
▲ Advanced Learners
◆ Slower Pace Learners
● Special Learning Needs

Block 5

OBJECTIVE
Use the future; Use the future of irregular verbs

Core Instruction

Vocabulaire 2, pp. 246–249
- Review **Vocabulaire 2,** pp. 246–249. **10 min.**
- Give **Quiz: Vocabulaire 2. 20 min.**

Grammaire 2, pp. 250–253
- See Teaching **Grammaire,** p. 250. **5 min.**
- Show **Grammavision 2.1. 5 min.**
- Play Audio CD 7, Tr. 5 for Activity 25, p. 250. **5 min.**
- Have students do Activities 26–29, pp. 250–251. **20 min.**
- Present **Flash culture,** p. 252. **5 min.**
- See Teaching **Grammaire,** p. 252. **5 min.**
- Show **Grammavision 2.2. 5 min.**
- Have students do Activities 30–32, pp. 252–253. **10 min.**

Optional Resources
- **Attention!,** p. 251
- French for Spanish Speakers, p. 251
- Communication (TE), p. 251
- Advanced Learners, p. 251 ▲
- Multiple Intelligences, p. 251
- Communities, p. 253
- Slower Pace Learners, p. 253 ◆
- Special Learning Needs, p. 253 ●

Homework Suggestions
Study for **Quiz: Grammaire 2**
Cahier de vocabulaire et grammaire, pp. 82–83
Cahier d'activités, pp. 65–66
HOMETUTOR
Online Practice (**my.hrw.com**)
1.1, 1.2, 4.1, 4.2, 5.1

Block 6

OBJECTIVE
Use the future of irregular verbs; Use the verb ***courir;*** *Develop listening and reading skills*

Core Instruction

Grammaire 2, pp. 250–253
- Have students do Activities 33–34, p. 253. **10 min.**
- Review **Grammaire 2,** pp. 250–253. **10 min.**
- Give **Quiz: Grammaire 2. 20 min.**

Application 2, pp. 254–255
- Have students do Activities 35–36, p. 254. **10 min.**
- See Teaching **Un peu plus,** p. 254. **5 min.**
- Play Audio CD 7, Tr. 6 for Activity 37, p. 254. **5 min.**
- Have students do Activities 38–40, p. 255. **10 min.**

Télé-roman, pp. 256–257
- Show **Télé-roman.** See Teaching **Télé-roman,** p. 256. **5 min.**
- Have students answer the **As-tu compris?** questions, p. 257. **15 min.**

Optional Resources
- Communication (TE), p. 253
- Communication (TE), p. 255
- Advanced Learners, p. 255 ▲
- Special Learning Needs, p. 255 ●
- Connections, p. 256
- Gestures, p. 256
- Communication (TE), p. 257

Homework Suggestions
Study for **Quiz: Application 2**
Cahier de vocabulaire et grammaire, p. 84
Cahier d'activités, p. 67
Online Practice (**my.hrw.com**)
1.1, 1.2, 1.3, 5.2

Block 7

OBJECTIVE
Develop listening, reading, and writing skills; Review the chapter

Core Instruction

Application 2, pp. 254–255
- Review **Application 2,** pp. 254–255. **10 min.**
- Give **Quiz: Application 2. 20 min.**

Lecture et écriture, pp. 258–261
- See Teaching **Lecture,** p. 258. **20 min.**
- See Teaching **Espace écriture,** p. 260. **30 min.**

Prépare-toi pour l'examen, pp. 262–264
- Have students do Activities 1–3, p. 262. **10 min.**

Optional Resources
- Applying the Strategies, p. 258
- Summarizing, p. 258
- Cultures, p. 259
- Connections, p. 259
- Slower Pace Learners, p. 259 ◆
- Special Learning Needs, p. 259 ●
- Communities, p. 260
- Connections, p. 260
- Process Writing, p. 261
- Writing Assessment, p. 261
- Advanced Learners, p. 261 ▲
- Multiple Intelligences, p. 261
- Fold-N-Learn, p. 262

Homework Suggestions
Study for Chapter Test
Cahier d'activités, p. 68
Espace écriture, Activity 2, p. 261
Online Practice (**my.hrw.com**)
1.2, 1.3, 2.1, 3.1, 5.1

Block 8

OBJECTIVE
Review and assess the chapter

Core Instruction

Prépare-toi pour l'examen, pp. 262–264
- Have students do Activities 4–5, pp. 262–263. **5 min.**
- Play Audio CD 7, Tr. 10 for Activity 6, p. 263. **5 min.**
- Have students do Activity 7, p. 263. **5 min.**
- Play Audio CD 7, Tr. 11–13 for **Lettres et sons,** p. 264. **5 min.**

Chapter Test 50 min.

Révisions cumulatives, pp. 266–267
- Play Audio CD 7, Tr. 14 for Activity 1, p. 266. **5 min.**
- Have students do Activities 2–6, pp. 266–267. **15 min.**

Optional Resources
- Reteaching, p. 262
- **Proverbs,** p. 262
- Game, p. 262
- Oral Assessment, p. 263
- Teacher to Teacher, p. 264
- Chapter Review, pp. 264–265
- Online Culture Project, p. 266
- Fine Art Connection, p. 267

Homework Suggestions
Cahier d'activités, pp. 69–70, 114–115
Online Practice (**my.hrw.com**)
1.1, 1.2, 1.3, 2.1, 2.2, 3.1, 3.2

Meeting the National Standards

Communication
Communication, pp. 237, 239, 241, 243, 249, 251, 253, 255
À ton tour, p. 267

Cultures
Flash culture, pp. 236, 240, 249, 252
Comparaisons, p. 245
Practices and Perspectives, p. 259

Connections
History Link, p. 234
Social Studies Link, p. 259
Science Link, pp. 245, 260

Comparisons
Comparaisons, p. 245
Comparing and Contrasting, p. 242

Communities
Communauté, p. 245
School Link, pp. 253, 260
Community Link, pp. 245, 247

Using the Photo

The fishing industry is important to the Senegalese, supplying fish to France, Spain, and the rest of Europe. Local fishermen go out to sea in traditional wooden canoes, called **pirogues,** to supply the coastal population with the traditional meal of fish and rice. Fish accounts for 75% of the protein intake of most Senegalese. Ask students if they have ever been fishing in the ocean and if so, to describe the experience. 1.3

Vocabulaire supplémentaire

Students might use these terms to discuss the photo.

la baie *bay*
le filet de pêche *net*
gilet de sauvetage *life jacket*
lancer *to cast*
la proue *boat bow*

chapitre 7

Un week-end en plein air

Objectifs

In this chapter, you will learn to
- say what happened
- describe circumstances
- tell what you will do
- wonder what will happen

And you will use
- the **passé composé** and the **imparfait**
- **être en train de**
- the future
- the verb **courir**

Que vois-tu sur la photo?
Où sont ces personnes?
Qu'est-ce qu'elles font?
Et toi, est-ce que tu aimes pêcher?

 **ACTFL 21st Century Skills**

Collaboration:	SE: p. 267; TE: pp. 231C, 260
Creativity and Innovation:	SE: pp. 244, 261; TE: pp. 237 (Health Literacy), 245, 247, 249, 261
Technology Literacy:	SE: p. 267; TE: pp. 231C, 241, 260, 266
Flexibility and Adaptability:	TE: pp. 237, 245, 247, 260
Productivity and Accountability:	TE: pp. 233, 235, 239, 251, 260, 261
Leadership and Responsibility:	TE: pp. 237, 245, 247, 253, 260

Des pêcheurs à Dakar

DIGITAL FRENCH

TEACHER TOOLS
- Interactive Whiteboard Lessons
- Generate Success!

ALSO AVAILABLE...
- Online Workbooks
- French InterActive Reader

FRENCH ON THE GO!
- Performance Space
- Holt McDougal French Apps
- *Bien dit!* eTextbook

Learning Tips

Have students look up information in French about Dakar on the Internet. Internet sites in French will provide familiar words in context as well as valuable cultural information. Have them practice discussing the information with classmates. Remind them that their classmates are just learning too, so everyone will make mistakes.

VIDEO OPTIONS

- **Télé-vocab 1**
- **Grammavision 1**
- **Télé-vocab 2**
- **Grammavision 2**
- **Télé-roman**

LISTENING PRACTICE

Language Lab and Classroom Activities

Vocabulaire
Activity 1, p. 236, CD 7, Tr. 1
Télé-vocab 1, p. 234, DVD Tutor
Activity 20, p. 248, CD 7, Tr. 4
Télé-vocab 2, p. 246, DVD Tutor

Grammaire
Activity 10, p. 240, CD 7, Tr. 2
Grammavision 1, pp. 238, 240, DVD Tutor
Activity 25, p. 250, CD 7, Tr. 5
Grammavision 2, pp. 250, 252, DVD Tutor

Application
Activity 17, p. 243, CD 7, Tr. 3
Activity 37, p. 254, CD 7, Tr. 6

Prépare-toi pour l'examen
Activity 6, p. 263, CD 7, Tr. 10

Révisions cumulatives
Activity 1, p. 266, CD 7, Tr. 14

Télé-roman
p. 256, DVD Tutor

Lecture
p. 258, CD 7, Tr. 7

Variations littéraires
p. 394, CD 7, Tr. 8–9

Lettres et sons
p. 264, CD 7, Tr. 11–13

Resources

Planning:

Lesson Planner

Teacher One Stop

Presentation:

Projectable Transparencies **Vocabulaire 7.1, 7.2**

DVD Tutor, Disc 2 **Télé-vocab 1**

Interactive Whiteboard Lessons

Practice:

Cahier de vocabulaire et grammaire

Differentiated Practice and Assessment CD-ROM

Independent Study Guide

Media Guide

Projectable Transparencies Bell Work 7.1

HOMETUTOR

Holt McDougal French Apps

Bell Work

Use Bell Work 7.1 in the *Projectable Transparencies* or write this activity on the board.

Complete the sentences with the following comparative or superlative.

les pires	**meilleures**
le meilleur	**plus mauvais**

1. **Le poulet est bon, mais les frites sont ____ .**
2. **«Chez Mimi» est ____ restaurant de la ville.**
3. **L'air est ____ l'été que l'hiver.**
4. **Ce sont ____ vacances que j'ai jamais eues.** 1.2

Connections

History Link

Point out the red cross on the first-aid kit in the photo. Share with students that the symbol of the red cross originated with the creation of the Red Cross organization **(La Croix-Rouge)** in Geneva, Switzerland. Have students research the history and mission of **La Croix-Rouge.** 3.1

Objectifs
- to say what happened
- to describe circumstances

Vocabulaire à l'œuvre 1

Télé-vocab

On fait du camping à Dakar!

la bouteille isotherme

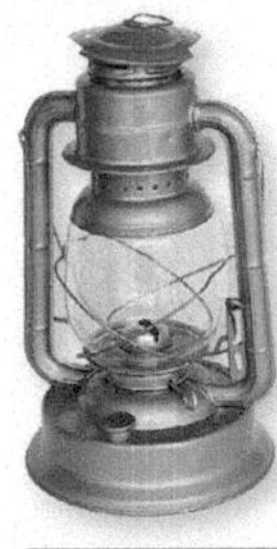
la lanterne

les boîtes (f.) de conserve

Core Instruction

TEACHING VOCABULAIRE

1. Introduce the vocabulary with transparencies **Vocabulaire 7.1** and **7.2** and model pronunciation. **(2 min.)**
2. Have students take turns answering your questions as you point to the item. **J'ai froid. Que faut-il faire? Je suis perdu(e). Que faut-il regarder? Il fait nuit. De quoi est-ce que j'ai besoin? (4 min.)**
3. Tell students a story about your real or imaginary camping trip, using the expressions in **Exprimons-nous! Figurez-vous que je campais avec ma nièce. Alors, elle avait très peur des moustiques. À ce moment-là, Olivia cherchait la trousse de premiers soins. Heureusement, la tente était déjà montée. Bref, nous sommes parties acheter des boîtes de conserve. (3 min.)**

Télé-vocab 1

For a video presentation of this vocabulary, see the *DVD Tutor.*

Télé-vocab

Online Practice
my.hrw.com
Vocabulaire 1 practice

la crème solaire

la lotion anti-moustiques

l'allume-gaz (m.)

le réchaud

la boîte d'allumettes

la trousse de premiers soins

la lampe de poche

la gourde

la boussole

Exprimons-nous!

To say what happened

Figure-toi que pendant que je campais, j'ai décidé de faire un feu. *Imagine that . . .*

Alors, j'ai cherché la boîte d'allumettes. Pas d'allumettes! *So, . . .*

À ce moment-là, j'ai entendu une voiture. C'était mon père. *At that moment, . . .*

Heureusement, il avait un briquet! *Fortunately, . . .*

Bref, on a pu faire un feu de camp et on n'a pas eu froid. *In short, . . .*

Vocabulaire et grammaire, *pp. 73–75*

▶ **Vocabulaire supplémentaire**—Le camping, **p. R20**

D'autres mots utiles

allumer	*to light*
un briquet	*lighter*
camper	*to camp*
un camping	*campsite*
un sac de couchage	*sleeping bag*
un ouvre-boîte	*can opener*
une moustiquaire	*mosquito net*
un désinfectant	*disinfectant*

TPR
Total Physical Response

Have students respond to these commands.

Lève-toi si tu aimes camper.

Assieds-toi si tu sais monter et démonter une tente.

Mets la main sur la tête si tu as une bouteille isotherme chez toi.

Lève le doigt si tu as déjà fait un feu de camp.

Lève les deux mains si tu es en train d'apprendre le français.

Then have some students mime the following activities.

Ouvre une boîte de conserve.

Allume le réchaud avec une allumette.

Maintenant, utilise un briquet.

Assieds-toi dans un fauteuil pliant.

Mets de la crème solaire.

Language Note

- Tell students that **se promener** has spelling changes like **se lever.**
- Explain to students that the prefix **dé-** can change the meaning of a verb. **(monter, démonter)** Have students guess the meaning of **débloquer, décolorer,** and **délacer.**

Differentiated Instruction

Slower Pace Learners

Have students write a set of quiz questions or clues in English about each of the **Vocabulaire** items. ("This is something you sit on." **un fauteuil pliant**) Then have partners ask one another as many questions as possible in three minutes. Allow students to look at their book the first time they do this activity. Have them try it again without looking at the book. 1.2

Special Learning Needs

Students with Language Impairments Make copies of the illustrations depicting the vocabulary words in the chapter. Ask students to cut out the pictures and paste each picture on a note card. Have students write the French word on the back of each note card. Allow students to use the note cards to study the vocabulary with a partner. 1.2

Vocabulaire 1

Resources

Planning:
Lesson Planner
Teacher One Stop

Presentation:
Projectable Transparencies **Vocabulaire 7.1, 7.2**

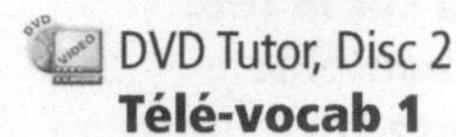

DVD Tutor, Disc 2 **Télé-vocab 1**
Interactive Whiteboard Lessons

Practice:
Cahier de vocabulaire et grammaire
Differentiated Practice and Assessment CD-ROM
Independent Study Guide
Media Guide
Audio CD 7, Tr. 1
@HOMETUTOR
Holt McDougal French Apps

1 Script

— Salut, Doudou! Ça s'est bien passé, ton week-end?
— Euh, non.
— Qu'est-ce qui s'est passé?
— Bon, j'allais faire du camping. Avant de partir, mon père m'a dit, «N'oublie pas ta gourde et les boîtes de conserve!» Alors, qu'est-ce que j'ai fait? J'ai oublié ma gourde!
— Oh, là, là! Mais tu as emporté les boîtes de conserve?
— Oui, mais j'ai oublié mon ouvre-boîte! Alors, je n'ai pas pu manger!
— Dommage!
— Heureusement, j'ai pensé à emporté une bouteille isotherme, mais j'ai oublié la lanterne.
— Oh, non!
— Et figure-toi que je suis parti sans allumettes!

1 Écoutons CD 7, Tr. 1 1.2

Doudou a fait du camping le week-end passé. Écoute sa conversation avec son ami Youssou. Est-ce qu'il **a) a oublié les objets représentés** ou est-ce qu'il **b) les a pris avec lui?**

1. a

2. b

3. a

4. b

5. b

Flash culture

On peut faire du camping ou encore dormir à la belle étoile au Sénégal. Il existe des campements qui sont souvent des bungalows à louer. On peut aussi faire du camping avec une tente. Dans tous les cas, il est conseillé de camper en groupe.

Où est-ce que tu peux faire du camping dans ta région? Quelles sortes de commodités sont proposées? 4.1

2 Pauvre Seydou! 1.2

Lisons Seydou fait du camping avec ses amis et il n'est pas très bien préparé. Choisis les réponses logiques.

c **1.** —Dis, Marius, tu pourrais me prêter ta gourde?
e **2.** —Anselme, il me faut une lampe de poche.
a **3.** —Noah, tu peux me prêter ton briquet pour allumer un feu de camp?
d **4.** —Amadou, tu pourrais me prêter ton sac de couchage?
b **5.** —Taki, il me faut la trousse de premiers soins.

a. —Ne me dis pas que tu as froid! Il fait chaud!
b. —Voilà. Il te faut le désinfectant aussi?
c. —Tiens. Mais ne bois pas toute mon eau!
d. —Non, j'en ai besoin pour dormir ce soir.
e. —Mais, pourquoi? Il est deux heures de l'après-midi!

3 Les conseils du garde-forestier 1.2

Écrivons Un garde-forestier (*park ranger*) parle à Aminata de quelque chose qui lui est arrivé pendant qu'il faisait du camping. Complète son histoire avec les mots de la boîte.

Possible answers: **1.** Pendant **2.** À ce moment-là **3.** Alors **4.** Heureusement **5.** Bref

À ce moment-là	Bref	Pendant
Heureusement	Figurez-vous	Alors

Je faisais du camping dans le parc. Il faisait très froid et je marchais sur le terrain de camping. ___1___ que je traversais un petit lac, la glace s'est rompue (*broke*)! ___2___, je suis tombé dans le lac! ___3___, j'ai perdu toutes mes affaires de camping. ___4___, j'avais un briquet dans ma poche. J'ai fait un feu. ___5___, on ne doit pas faire du camping tout seul en hiver!

Core Instruction

TEACHING EXPRIMONS-NOUS!

1. If you have your own camping photos, bring them to class. If not, borrow a camping magazine or have a student bring his or her photos. Using expressions in **Exprimons-nous!**, model a camping story to accompany these pictures. **(3 min.)**

2. After telling your story, ask true or false questions about the pictures. **(2 min.)**

3. Tell students to think about what habitually happens in class. Model sentences using the new expressions and the **imparfait. J'étais en train de corriger des devoirs quand Paul m'a posé une question. Au moment où je commençais à expliquer, l'alarme a sonné. (3 min.)**

Exprimons-nous!

To describe circumstances

J'étais en train de monter la tente quand Pauline m'a appelé(e).
I was in the process of (middle of) . . .

Je venais d'allumer le feu quand mes copains sont arrivés.
I had just . . .

Au moment où je prenais la photo de Julien, je suis tombé(e).
As . . .

J'étais **sur le point de** partir quand ils m'ont téléphoné.
. . . about to . . .

Vocabulaire et grammaire, *pp. 73–75*

4 Attention au lion! 1.2

Écrivons/Parlons Pendant que toi et ta famille faisiez du camping, un lion est entré dans le terrain de camping. Écris quatre phrases pour décrire ce que tu faisais au moment où le lion est arrivé.

MODÈLE J'étais en train d'allumer la lanterne quand...

J'étais en train de...	démonter la tente	le lion est arrivé
Je venais de...	faire la cuisine	je l'ai vu
J'étais sur le point de...	allumer la lanterne	j'ai vu le lion avec une boîte de conserve
Au moment où...	mettre de la crème solaire	j'ai entendu un bruit
	faire un feu	le lion est venu vers ma tente

Communication

5 Scénario 1.1

Parlons Tu fais du camping avec tes amis. Un garde-forestier arrive et vous dit que quelqu'un a vu une personne en train de donner à manger aux animaux. C'est interdit (*forbidden*) dans le parc. Il demande à chaque personne ce qu'il/elle faisait à ce moment-là. En groupes de quatre, donnez vos alibis.

MODÈLE **—Je cherche la personne qui a... Qu'est-ce que vous faisiez à... ?**
—J'étais en train de...

Differentiated Instruction

ADVANCED LEARNERS

Have the class plan an imaginary camping trip. Have students organize committees or have them work together to plan a list of supplies, food, and activities, and to research information about camp sites in your area. 1.1

MULTIPLE INTELLIGENCES

Naturalist Ask students to use the new vocabulary and phrases in **Exprimons-nous!** to write a short story about the environment or an animal habitat around an imaginary camp site. The story may include animals, plants, trees, weather, and other features of the natural world. Have students illustrate their stories, share them with the class, and then display them in the room. 1.3

COMMON ERROR ALERT
ATTENTION !

Students may confuse **la gourde** (*the canteen*) with **la cantine** (*the cafeteria*).

Teacher to Teacher

Pam Seccombe
Nathan Hale High School
West Allis, WI

To practice camping equipment vocabulary, I give one half of the students each a card with a place and a season. Those students form an inside circle facing out. The remaining students form an outside circle facing in. A student on the inside circle will say, **Je vais au Sénégal en été, qu'est-ce que j'emporte?** The partner in the outside circle must provide three suggestions. The outside circle then moves to the right. At some point, I have the circles switch places. 1.1

Communication

Group Activity: Presentational

Have groups of three role-play a scene in an outfitting store. Students A and B play the role of first-time campers. Student C is the salesperson who tries to sell as much as he or she can. 1.3

Assess

Assessment Program
Quiz: Vocabulaire 1
Alternative Assessment
Differentiated Practice and Assessment CD-ROM

Online Assessment
my.hrw.com

Test Generator

Resources

Planning:
Lesson Planner
Teacher One Stop

Presentation:

DVD Tutor, Disc 2
Grammavision 1.1

Practice:
Grammar Tutor for Students of French, Chapter 7
Cahier de vocabulaire et grammaire
Differentiated Practice and Assessment CD-ROM
Cahier d'activités
Independent Study Guide
Media Guide
Projectable Transparencies
Bell Work 7.2
@HOMETUTOR

Bell Work

Use Bell Work 7.2 in the *Projectable Transparencies* or write this activity on the board.

Unscramble the words to write logical sentences.

1. monté / Les / tente / ont / parents / la
2. feu / a / de / Théo / un / camp / fait
3. perdu / poche / Mathilde / lampe / a / sa / de
4. J' / conserves / deux / ai / boîtes / ouvert /de
5. réchaud / d' / La / allumettes / à / boîte / est / du / côté 1.2

COMMON ERROR ALERT
ATTENTION !

Students may rely on cue words and phrases until they get a feel for the difference between setting the scene **(imparfait)** and the action **(passé composé).**

Objectifs
- the *passé composé* and the *imparfait*
- *être en train de*

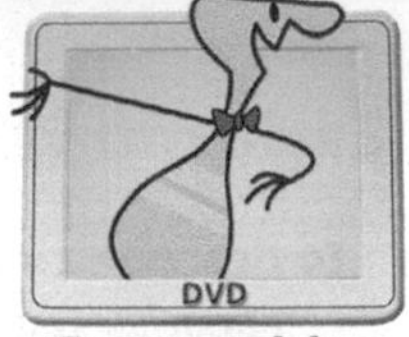

Grammavision

The *passé composé* and the *imparfait*

You know that you use the **passé composé** to tell what happened and the **imparfait** to tell what things used to be like and what people used to do. Here are some additional ways to use these tenses.

USE THE IMPARFAIT TO:	USE THE PASSÉ COMPOSÉ TO:
give background information	tell what happened on a specific occasion
set the scene, explain the circumstances	tell about events happening within a specified period of time in the past Il a travaillé à Dakar pendant trois ans.
explain what you used to do repeatedly, often after expressions like souvent, tous les jours, d'habitude	talk about a change or reaction to something, often after words like soudain *(suddenly)*, à ce moment-là, au moment où

Il **faisait** très beau ce jour-là. D'abord, on **a déjeuné**. Ensuite, on **a fait** un feu de camp.

Vocabulaire et grammaire, *pp. 76–77*
Cahier d'activités, *pp. 61–63*

Déjà vu!
Remember that you can tell what was going on while something else happened by using both the **passé composé** and the **imparfait.**
Nadine **montait** sa tente quand elle **a trouvé** sa boussole.

6 Un week-end catastrophique 1.2

Écrivons Noémie raconte son week-end à Victor. Complète leur conversation avec **l'imparfait** ou le **passé composé** des verbes entre parenthèses.

—Je/J' ___1___ (aller) faire du camping. D'abord, quand nous ___2___ (arriver), il n'y ___3___ (avoir) plus de place au camping.
—Alors, qu'est-ce que vous ___4___ (faire)?
—Nous ___5___ (décider) de monter nos tentes dans la forêt. Mais pendant que je ___6___ (monter) ma tente, on ___7___ (entendre) le guide du parc. Il nous ___8___ (dire) que c'était interdit de monter sa tente dans la forêt, alors on ___9___ (démonter) nos tentes!
—Et qu'est-ce que vous ___10___ (faire)?
—Il ne ___11___ (faire) pas beau, alors on ___12___ (rentrer).

Answers: 1. suis allée 2. sommes arrivés 3. avait 4. avez fait 5. avons décidé 6. montais 7. a entendu 8. a dit 9. a démonté 10. avez fait 11. faisait 12. est rentrés

Core Instruction

TEACHING GRAMMAIRE

1. Tell students the **imparfait** is used to give background information, set the scene, or tell about something done repeatedly. Contrast these uses with those of the **passé composé. (2 min.)**
2. Have a list on the board or on a transparency of seven to ten verbs that could easily be used in a camping trip story. Start narrating a story. Pause and point to a verb before you use it. Have students indicate if it should be in the **imparfait** (wavy motion with the hand) or **passé composé** (chopping motion with the hand). **(4 min.)**

Grammavision

For a video presentation of the **passé composé** and the **imparfait,** see the *DVD Tutor.*

Grammavision

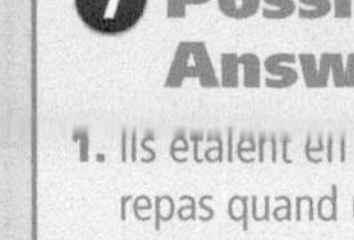

Online Practice
my.hrw.com
Grammaire 1 practice

7 En camp de vacances 1.2

Parlons/Écrivons Adrien a travaillé dans un camp de vacances l'été dernier. Décris ce qui s'est passé. Pour chaque illustration, utilise un verbe au passé composé et un verbe à l'imparfait.

MODÈLE **Ils montaient leur tente quand leurs copains sont arrivés.**

1.

2.

3.

4.

8 Les vacances de mon enfance 1.3

Écrivons Où est-ce que tu passais tes vacances quand tu étais petit(e)? Qu'est-ce que tu faisais? Est-ce que tu t'amusais bien en général? Raconte les vacances de ton enfance et décris un événement important dont tu te souviens.

Souviens-toi! Childhood activities, pp. 194–195

MODÈLE **Quand j'étais petit(e), je passais toujours mes vacances chez mes grands-parents.**

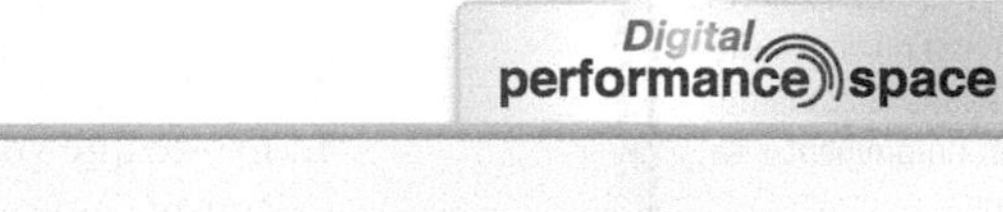

Communication

9 Questions personnelles 1.1

Parlons Imagine que tu travailles pour une compagnie qui fabrique (*makes*) du matériel de camping. Tu dois faire un sondage pour connaître les habitudes des jeunes. Prépare dix questions à poser à tes camarades. Compare tes réponses avec celles d'un(e) autre camarade.

MODÈLE **—La dernière fois que tu as fait du camping, où est-ce que tu es allé(e)?**
—Je suis allé(e) au Grand Canyon.
—Est-ce que tu as pris ta tente?

Grammaire 1

7 Possible Answers

1. Ils étaient en train de préparer le repas quand une fille est tombée.
2. Pendant qu'ils faisaient une randonnée, ils ont perdu leur gourde.
3. Ils allaient allumer le feu de camp quand quelqu'un a sorti une boîte d'allumettes.
4. Au moment où ils démontaient leur tente, il a commencé à pleuvoir.

French for Spanish Speakers

Ask Spanish speakers if the same circumstances apply for using the **passé composé** and the **imparfait** as for using the **pretérito** and the **imperfecto.** (yes) Have students come up with a list of equivalent trigger words for the **passé composé/pretérito** and for the **imparfait/imperfecto.** To get them started, have them complete a story in both languages. **Quand j'étais petit(e), j'allais souvent au bureau de ma mère. Un jour… Cuando era joven, iba a menudo a la oficina de mi madre. Un día…** Then have students create a graphic organizer or other visual aid to share with the class. 4.1

Communication

Pair Activity: Presentational

Have partners tell a story that takes place in the past. One starts a sentence using the **imparfait** and the other finishes the sentence in the **passé composé.** You may want to review key words or phrases that call for the use of the **imparfait** and those that elicit the **passé composé.** Call on partners to present their stories to the class. 1.3

Differentiated Instruction

SLOWER PACE LEARNERS

8 As a class, finish the **Modèle** on the blackboard, making up the details of the vacation. Then discuss each verb and why it is in either the **imparfait** or the **passé composé.** Have students write about their own vacation by changing the details in the **Modèle.** 1.3

MULTIPLES INTELLIGENCES

Linguistic Ask students to copy the grammar chart on page 238 of the uses of the **passé composé** and the **imparfait.** In each box students should write a sentence that shows the correct use of these verb forms. Students may exchange their charts to see if they understand their partner's sentences. 1.2

Resources

Planning:
Lesson Planner
 Teacher One Stop
Presentation:
DVD Tutor, Disc 2
Grammavision 1.2
Practice:
Grammar Tutor for Students of French, Chapter 7
Cahier de vocabulaire et grammaire
Differentiated Practice and Assessment CD-ROM
Cahier d'activités
Independent Study Guide
Media Guide
Projectable Transparencies
Bell Work 7.3
Audio CD 7, Tr. 2
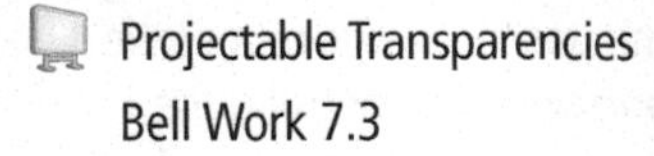

Bell Work

Use Bell Work 7.3 in the *Projectable Transparencies* or write this activity on the board.

Fill in the blanks with the **passé composé** or **imparfait.**

1. Il ____ (faire) beau, alors, nous ____ (aller) faire du camping.
2. On ____ (faire) une randonnée et on ____ (s'arrêter) une fois.
3. Alors que je ____ (monter) la tente, soudain Marine ____. (crier)
4. Nous ____ (entendu) quelque chose… c' ____ (être) un insecte! 

10 Script

See script on p. 231E.

Teacher Note

14 You may wish to give students the words for the acronym OVNI: **Objet volant non identifié.**

Être en train de

1 Use the expression être en train de (d') to emphasize that someone is doing something at a particular moment. Follow it with an infinitive.

Il est en train de faire un feu.
He's making (in the process of making) a fire.

2 To use this expression when talking about the past, use the **imparfait.**

Ils **étaient en train de** démonter la tente quand il a commencé à pleuvoir.
They were in the process of taking down the tent when it started to rain.

Vocabulaire et grammaire, *pp. 76–77*
Cahier d'activités, *pp. 61–63*

Flash culture

Les sports nautiques sont populaires au Sénégal. On peut pratiquer la voile, la plongée sous-marine, le jet-ski, le ski nautique et encore le surf. La plongée sous-marine est une des activités les plus intéressantes. Elle est pratiquée sur la presqu'île du Cap Vert dont les fonds sont assez riches pour être explorés. Il y a aussi quelques sites intéressants sur la Petite Côte et notamment à La Somone.

Est-ce que tu as déjà fait de la plongée? Est-ce que tu aimerais en faire? Pourquoi? 4.2

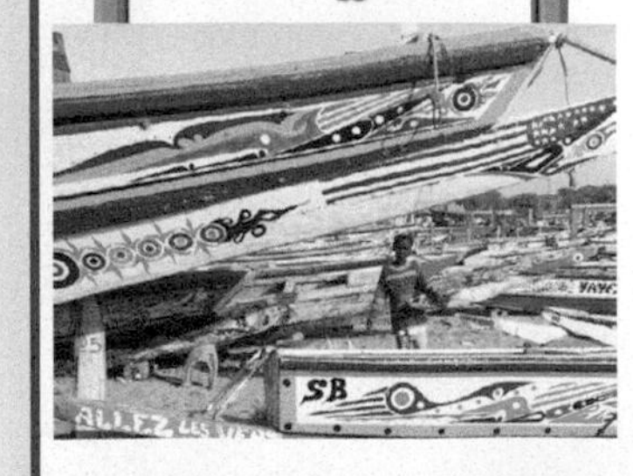

10 Écoutons CD 7, Tr. 2 1.2

Écoute les phrases suivantes et décide si **a) on a déjà fait quelque chose** ou **b) on est en train de faire quelque chose.**
1. a 2. b 3. b 4. a 5. a 6. b

11 Un élève très pénible! 1.2

Écrivons Tu fais du camping avec un groupe d'élèves francophones. Un des élèves pose des questions pour s'assurer que tout se passe bien. Donne les réponses de ces personnes en utilisant l'expression **être en train de** + infinitif.

MODÈLE Vous sortez les lanternes de vos sacs?
Oui, nous sommes en train de sortir les lanternes de nos sacs!

1. Gérald, est-ce que tu mets de la crème solaire?
2. Est-ce que les filles cherchent la trousse de premiers soins?
3. Est-ce que Sophie lave la bouteille isotherme?
4. Est-ce que vous cherchez un allume-gaz pour allumer le feu de camp?
5. Est-ce que Farid et Aminata ouvrent des boîtes de conserve pour le dîner?
6. Et toi, est-ce que tu montes les tentes?
7. Vous allumez les lanternes?
8. Est-ce que Sophie ouvre son sac de couchage?

Core Instruction

TEACHING GRAMMAIRE

1. Tell students that **être en train de** is always followed by an infinitive. It means *in the middle of.* In the past tense, **être** will always be in the **imparfait. (1 min.)**
2. Move around the classroom, telling what you are doing by using **être en train de. Je suis en train de parler français. Je suis en train d'écrire au tableau. (2 min.)**
3. Make two lists of five to seven verbs each. Ask students to name one verb in each list. Say a sentence in the past tense with those two verbs. **camper/perdre: J'étais en train de camper en France, quand j'ai perdu mon passeport. monter/entendre: Paul était en train de monter la tente, quand il a entendu une grenouille. (3 min.)**

Grammavision

For a video presentation of **être en train de (d'),** see the *DVD Tutor.*

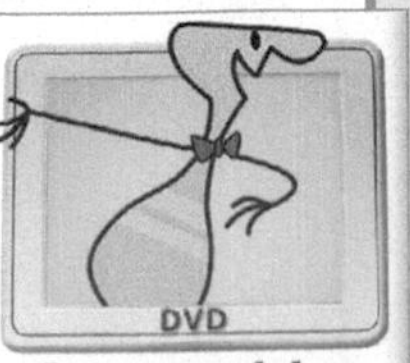

12 Un vol au Camping Forestier 1.2

Parlons/Écrivons Il y a eu un vol *(theft)* au Camping Forestier! Le lieutenant de police Molinart te demande ce que tous les campeurs faisaient au moment du vol. Réponds d'après les images en utilisant l'expression **être en train de** et les sujets donnés.

MODÈLE **Madame Riverain était en train de faire une randonnée.**

Madame Riverain

1. Mes amis et moi

2. Toi, tu

3. Lucie

4. Vous

13 Une aventure incroyable 1.3

Écrivons Imagine que pendant tes dernières vacances, il s'est passé quelque chose de vraiment incroyable *(unbelievable)* (tu as rencontré une star, tu as trouvé un trésor...). Écris un paragraphe pour raconter cette aventure.

MODÈLE **Il s'est passé quelque chose de super la semaine dernière. J'étais en train de monter ma tente quand...**

Communication

14 Interview 1.1

Parlons Un/Une jeune étudiant(e) *(college student)* est allé(e) faire du camping. Il/Elle dit qu'il/elle a vu un OVNI *(UFO)*. Alexis Sensation, reporter pour un journal de Dakar, pose des questions pour obtenir plus de détails: comment était l'OVNI, ce que l'étudiant(e) faisait à ce moment-là, ce qu'il/elle a fait quand il/elle l'a vu, etc. Joue cette scène avec un(e) camarade.

MODÈLE **—Bonjour. Je m'appelle Alexis Sensation et je suis reporter pour le journal *L'Incroyable*. Alors, qu'est-ce que vous faisiez quand vous avez vu l'OVNI?**
—Moi, j'étais en train de chercher ma boussole...

Grammaire 1

11 Possible Answers

1. Oui, je suis en train de mettre de la crème solaire!
2. Oui, elles sont en train de chercher la trousse de premiers soins!
3. Oui, elle est en train de laver la bouteille isotherme!
4. Oui, nous sommes en train de chercher un allume-gaz pour allumer le feu de camp!
5. Oui, ils sont en train d'ouvrir des boîtes de conserve pour le dîner!
6. Oui, je suis en train de monter les tentes!
7. Oui, nous sommes en train d'allumer les lanternes!
8. Oui, elle est en train d'ouvrir son sac de couchage!

12 Answers

1. Mes amis et moi étions en train de faire une promenade.
2. Toi, tu étais en train de monter la tente.
3. Lucie était en train de faire des photos.
4. Vous étiez en train de faire un feu de camp.

Communication

14 Pair Activity: Presentational

In advance, have students find a large magazine photo or advertisement of one or more people outdoors or camping. Then, based on the photo, have partners tell a story in the past. Have them include at least five details using the **imparfait** and the **passé composé.** 1.3

Differentiated Instruction

ADVANCED LEARNERS

12 Have students create a conversation based on the situation in the activity. Have students play the role of police lieutenant Molinart and the people he interviews about the theft. You might have students videotape their conversations. 1.1

SPECIAL LEARNING NEEDS

Students with Learning Disabilities When presenting **être en train de (d'),** work closely with students who need extra help. Give several English examples of the use of the expressions taught and work with students to translate the examples into French. Finally, work with students to create original French sentences that use the expressions. 1.2

Assess

Assessment Program
Quiz: Grammaire 1
Alternative Assessment
Differentiated Practice and Assessment CD-ROM

Online Assessment
my.hrw.com

Test Generator 

Resources

Planning:
Lesson Planner
Teacher One Stop

Practice:
Grammar Tutor for Students of French, Chapter 7
Cahier de vocabulaire et grammaire
Differentiated Practice and Assessment CD-ROM
Cahier d'activités
Independent Study Guide
Media Guide
Projectable Transparencies
Bell Work 7.4
Audio CD 7, Tr. 3

Bell Work

Use Bell Work 7.4 in the *Projectable Transparencies* or write this activity on the board.

Answer the questions using the expression **être en train de.**

1. **Ils démontent la tente? Oui, ils...**
2. **Vous préparez les bouteilles isothermes? Oui, nous...**
3. **Clément range le fauteuil pliant? Non, il...**
4. **Tu mets de la lotion anti-moustiques? Oui, je...**
5. **Louise cherche la trousse de premiers soins? Non, elle...** 1.2

Synthèse
- Vocabulaire 1
- Grammaire 1

Application 1

15 Les moments importants dans ma vie 1.3

Écrivons Réponds aux questions suivantes en utilisant l'imparfait et l'expression **être en train de** dans tes réponses.

1. Qu'est-ce que ton/ta meilleur(e) ami(e) et toi, vous faisiez quand vous vous êtes rencontré(e)s pour la première fois?
2. Est-ce qu'on t'a déjà annoncé une bonne nouvelle (une très bonne note, etc.)? Qu'est-ce que tu étais en train de faire?
3. Pendant tes dernières vacances, est-ce qu'il s'est passé quelque chose d'intéressant, de marrant ou de bizarre? Raconte.

Un peu plus

Verbs with *être* or *avoir* in the passé composé

1. You know that the verbs **sortir, passer, monter,** and **descendre** usually use **être** as the helping verb in the **passé composé.** The past participle agrees with the subject.

   Elle **est** sorti**e** de la maison. Sa copine **est** monté**e** dans la voiture.

2. However, when these verbs have a direct object, they use avoir as the helping verb in the **passé composé.** The past participle does not agree with the subject unless the direct object comes before the verb.

   Elle a sorti la tente de son sac? Oui, elle l'a sorti**e.**

   Elles ont sorti la lanterne de la voiture.

Vocabulaire et grammaire, *p. 78*
Cahier d'activités, *pp. 61–63*

16 Le bon choix 1.2

Écrivons Choisis le verbe correct pour compléter les phrases.

1. Les garçons _______ leurs tentes en moins de deux minutes!
   a. sont montés **b.** ont monté **c.** sont montées
2. Tu _______ la trousse de premiers soins à ton frère, Yvan?
   a. as passé **b.** es passé **c.** a passé
3. Nous _______ dans la voiture pour partir.
   a. sont montées **b.** sommes montés **c.** avons monté
4. Vous _______ les fauteuils pliants de la voiture, les filles?
   a. êtes sorties **b.** avez sortis **c.** avez sorti
5. Ils _______ un excellent week-end dans ce camping.
   a. ont passé **b.** sont passés **c.** ont passés

Comparisons

Comparing and Contrasting

Tell students that there is another past tense, called the **passé simple,** that does not use **être** or **avoir** as an auxilliary verb. The passé simple is only used in formal writing. Ask students if they know any examples in English of language that is only used in formal writing (for example, the wording of legal documents). 4.1

Core Instruction

INTEGRATED PRACTICE

1. Have students do Activity 15 to review grammar and vocabulary in this chapter. **(3 min.)**
2. List ten of the new vocabulary words on the board. Ask small groups to write on a transparency a camping story with that vocabulary and verbs in the infinitive form. **(10 min.)**
3. Call on individuals to rewrite the verb forms either in the **imparfait** or **passé composé. (6 min.)**

TEACHING UN PEU PLUS

1. Remind students that **descendre, monter, passer,** and **sortir** are conjugated with **être** in the **passé composé,** except when there is a direct object. **(2 min.)**
2. Model each of the above verbs in a sentence with **être,** then with **avoir. Je suis sorti(e) de la salle de classe. J'ai sorti la crème solaire du sac à dos. (2 min.)**
3. Continue with integrated practice Activities 16–19. **(15 min.)**

my.hrw.com
Application 1 practice

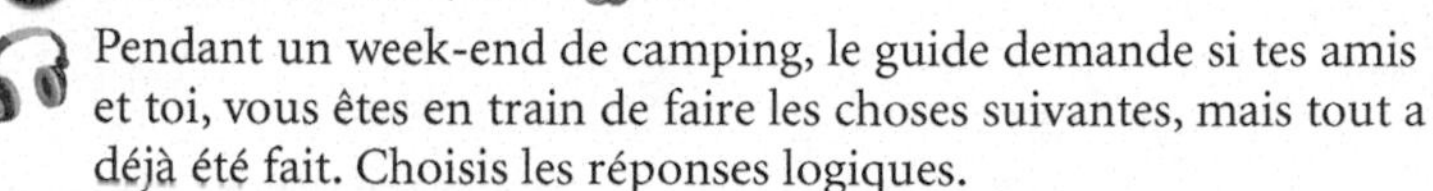

17 Écoutons CD 7, Tr. 3 1.2

Pendant un week-end de camping, le guide demande si tes amis et toi, vous êtes en train de faire les choses suivantes, mais tout a déjà été fait. Choisis les réponses logiques.

1. **(a.)** Je l'ai déjà montée. **b.** Oui, je suis monté.
2. **(a.)** Nous les avons déjà descendus. **b.** Oui, les filles sont descendues ce matin.
3. **a.** Oui, ils ont sorti leurs sacs à dos. **(b.)** Oui, ils sont déjà sortis.
4. **(a.)** Je te l'ai déjà passée. **b.** Oui, je suis passée par le camping.
5. **a.** Oui, ils sont sortis de la voiture. **(b.)** Oui, ils ont sorti les sacs.

18 Les activités de ce matin 1.2

Écrivons Regarde ce que ces personnes ont fait ce matin et écris une légende pour chaque image.

MODÈLE Madame Dialo est passée à la pharmacie.

Madame Dialo / passer

1. Jacqueline et Léa / monter

2. Nos amis / sortir

3. Léopold / monter

4. Isabelle / sortir

Digital performance space

19 Scénario 1.1

Parlons Imagine que ta classe va faire un voyage au Sénégal. Vous allez faire du camping. Il faut vérifier que tous les préparatifs ont été faits. Joue la scène avec un(e) camarade. Utilisez la liste de préparatifs.

MODÈLE —Julian, tu es passé à la pharmacie?

Préparatifs à faire
- *acheter une trousse de premiers soins*
- ✓ *supermarché: eau, boîtes de conserve*
- ✓ *descendre chercher les fauteuils pliants*
- *sortir les trois réchauds*
- *acheter des briquets ou des allumettes*
- ✓ *sortir les tentes et les sacs de couchage*
- *passer au magasin de camping pour acheter des bouteilles isothermes*
- ✓ *monter tous les sacs dans le bus*

17 Script

1. Est-ce que tu montes la tente?
2. Les filles, vous descendez les sacs de la voiture?
3. Tes camarades sortent de la voiture?
4. Tu me passes la gourde?
5. Tes parents ont sorti les sacs?

18 Answers

1. Jacqueline et Awa sont montées dans le bus.
2. Nos amis sont sortis au restaurant.
3. Léopold a monté les sacs.
4. Isabelle a sorti son chien.

Communication

Group Activity: Interpersonal

In small groups, have students imagine that they are a family going on a camping trip. Have one or two students assume the role of parents and the other students the role of the children. The parents ask the children if they took certain supplies out of the car and completed other camp set-up activities. The children respond affirmatively or negatively with an object pronoun. 1.1

Differentiated Instruction

SLOWER PACE LEARNERS

Bring in two cardboard boxes that are large enough for you to get inside. Designate one as the "house" and one as the "car." Place camping items inside each box. Then carry out different actions using verbs that use both **être** and **avoir:** go in and out of the house, get in and out of the car, take a backpack out of the car, and so on. After each action, ask students questions about what you just did. **Est-ce que je suis sorti(e) de la maison?** 1.1

SPECIAL LEARNING NEEDS

Students with AD(H)D Before doing Activities 16–18, ask students to work in small groups to review the infinities that use **être** and **avoir.** Then have them practice forming the past participles and review agreement. Have students conjugate several verbs in the **passé composé** and write them in their notebooks to use as a reference. 1.3

Assess

Assessment Program
Quiz: Application 1
Audio CD 7, Tr. 15
Alternative Assessment
Differentiated Practice and Assessment CD-ROM
Online Assessment
my.hrw.com
Test Generator 

Resources

Planning:
Lesson Planner
Teacher One Stop
Practice:
Cahier d'activités

Vocabulaire supplémentaire

You might wish to use these terms to discuss the project with students.

vivre seul(e)	*to live alone*
vivre en meute	*to live in a pack*
le régime	*diet*
le territoire	*territory*
chasser	*to hunt*
s'occuper des petits	*to take care of the young*
le mâle	*the male*
la femelle	*the female*
un mammifère	*mammal*
un reptile	*reptile*
un amphibie	*amphibian*

Parc national de la Langue de Barbarie

Culture appliquée

Le parc national de la Langue de Barbarie 2.2

Au sud de Saint-Louis au Sénégal se trouve le parc national de la Langue de Barbarie. Le parc a été créé[1] en 1976 et il couvre[2] environ 2.000 hectares[3] entre le fleuve Sénégal et l'océan Atlantique. Le parc national de la Langue de Barbarie est un sanctuaire d'oiseaux. On peut y observer des pélicans, des flamants roses et beaucoup d'autres oiseaux migrateurs chaque année.

1. was created 2. covers 3. about 5,000 acres

Parc national 2.2, 3.1

Research a national park or animal reserve in Senegal either on the Internet or at the library. Create a topographical map using markers or clay and poster-board.

Materials
- poster board
- scissors
- markers or colored pencils
- clay
- glue

Step 1 Draw an outline of the area on your poster board and indicate in blue where there are bodies of water.

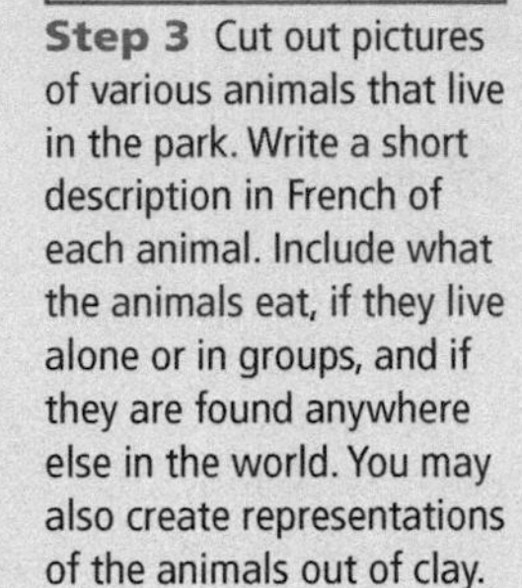

Step 2 Label all the important geographical features, such as mountains, canyons, and so on.

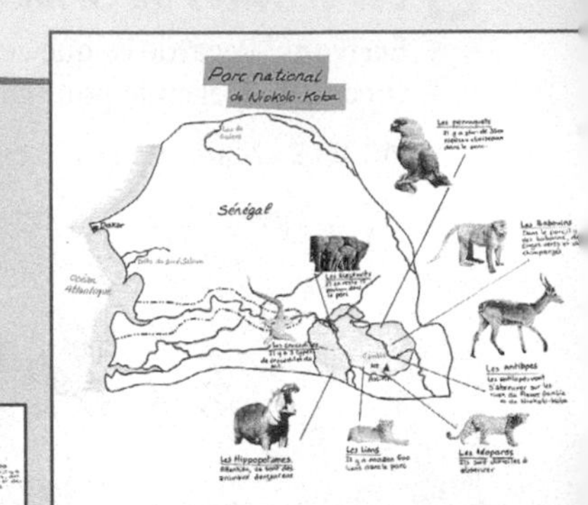

Step 3 Cut out pictures of various animals that live in the park. Write a short description in French of each animal. Include what the animals eat, if they live alone or in groups, and if they are found anywhere else in the world. You may also create representations of the animals out of clay.

Recherches Est-ce qu'il y a des animaux qui vivent seulement au Sénégal? Lesquels? 2.2, 3.1

Core Instruction

CULTURE APPLIQUÉE

1. Have the class read and discuss the introductory paragraph, making note of glossed words. **(2 min.)**
2. Have students research information for the **parc national** project. In their research, students should find answers to the questions in **Recherches. (30 min.)**
3. You may wish to have students work with partners to create their maps. Have students complete the project as homework. **(10 min.)**

COMPARAISONS ET COMMUNAUTÉ

1. Have the class read the introduction to **Le camping** and choose the correct answer. **(1 min.)**
2. Form groups of three or four to read the text and answer **Et toi? (3 min.)**
3. As a class, read and answer the questions in **Communauté et professions.** Make a student-generated list on the board or on a transparency of places in your area that might interest a group of French teenagers. **(6 min.)**

Comparaisons

Un terrain de camping en France

Le camping 4.2

Tu veux faire du camping en France. Tu peux planter ta tente:

a. où tu veux en ville ou à la campagne.
b. seulement dans un parc naturel.
c. sur un terrain de camping.

En France, le camping est très réglementé[1]. Le camping sauvage[2] est officiellement interdit[3]. On peut camper sur une propriété privée si le propriétaire[4] est d'accord. Il existe un classement[5] des terrains de camping comme pour les hôtels (d'une étoile à quatre étoiles). Les terrains de camping sont généralement bien équipés: électricité, eau chaude, toilettes et piscine. Récemment, une nouvelle formule est apparue: le camping en ferme d'accueil[6]. Les personnes qui souhaitent faire du camping en milieu naturel sont accueillies dans une ferme.

4.2

ET TOI?

1. Est-ce que tu peux faire du «camping sauvage» aux États-Unis? Quelles sont les règles?
2. Connais-tu des campings en ferme d'accueil dans ta région? Où?

Communauté et professions

Le français dans le monde du tourisme 4.2, 5.1

Pour être guide touristique, il est souvent conseillé de savoir parler une langue étrangère, le français par exemple. Existe-t-il dans ta ville ou dans ton état un lieu touristique? Les guides parlent-ils le français? Quelles sont les conditions requises pour être guide dans ta ville ou dans ton état? Fais des recherches et présente ce que tu as trouvé à la classe.

Un guide à Chicago

1. regulated 2. camping on unauthorized sites 3. forbidden 4. owner
5. ranking 6. host/B&B farm

Connections

Science Link

Ask students to research the French names of birds native to your area. Have students create a checklist of the birds and go on a bird-watching expedition. You might award a small prize to students who check off the most names of birds on their list or who give the best report of their observations. 3.1

Communities

Community Link

Have students research a site in your area (such as a park, campground, or nature preserve) and prepare a speech they would give as a tour guide for French-speaking tourists. Assign groups and have students imagine they are on a field trip to the site. Have students take turns role-playing the guides. 5.1

Language Examination

Culture can be used to practice for the **Interpretive Communication** and **Presentational Writing** sections of the AP Language and Culture Exam as it helps students get acquainted with and reflect on products and practices from the French-speaking world while reading culture-focused passages and answering questions in French.

Differentiated Instruction

ADVANCED LEARNERS

Have students imagine that part of the school grounds will be set aside as a nature preserve. Have students plan the preserve, design the landscape, and include in the plan bird feeders, bird houses, and so on. Assign groups to create plaques in French and English to identify the different types of trees and plants, and birds and other wildlife that are likely to visit the preserve. 1.3

MULTIPLE INTELLEGENCES

Visual As an alternative or in addition to the poster project, have students create a tri-fold brochure about the park. Have them fold a piece of paper into thirds to create panels to include maps, pictures, and descriptions of geographical features of the park. The brochure may also include descriptions of the area that would encourage people to travel to this location. 1.2

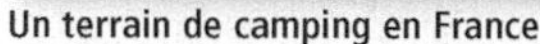

Resources

Planning:
Lesson Planner
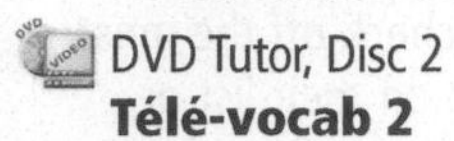 Teacher One Stop

Presentation:
Projectable Transparencies **Vocabulaire 7.3, 7.4**
DVD Tutor, Disc 2 **Télé-vocab 2**
Interactive Whiteboard Lessons

Practice:
Cahier de vocabulaire et grammaire
Differentiated Practice and Assessment CD-ROM
Independent Study Guide
Media Guide
Projectable Transparencies Bell Work 7.5
@HOMETUTOR
Holt McDougal French Apps

Bell Work

Use Bell Work 7.5 in the *Projectable Transparencies* or write this activity on the board.

Fill in the blanks with the **passé composé** of the verbs in parentheses.

1. **En arrivant au camping, nous ____ (monter) la tente.**
2. **Ahmed ____ (sortir) les sacs de couchage.**
3. **Tu ____ (passer) dix minutes à mettre de la crème anti-moustiques.**
4. **Nous ____ (descendre) au village pour acheter du pain.**
5. **Le matin, je ____ (sortir) de la tente la première.**

1.2

Proverbes

For French proverbs and activities related to the chapter theme and vocabulary, see **Proverbes et expressions**, pp. R6–R7.

Objectifs
- to tell what you will do
- to wonder what will happen

Télé-vocab

À la pêche à Dakar

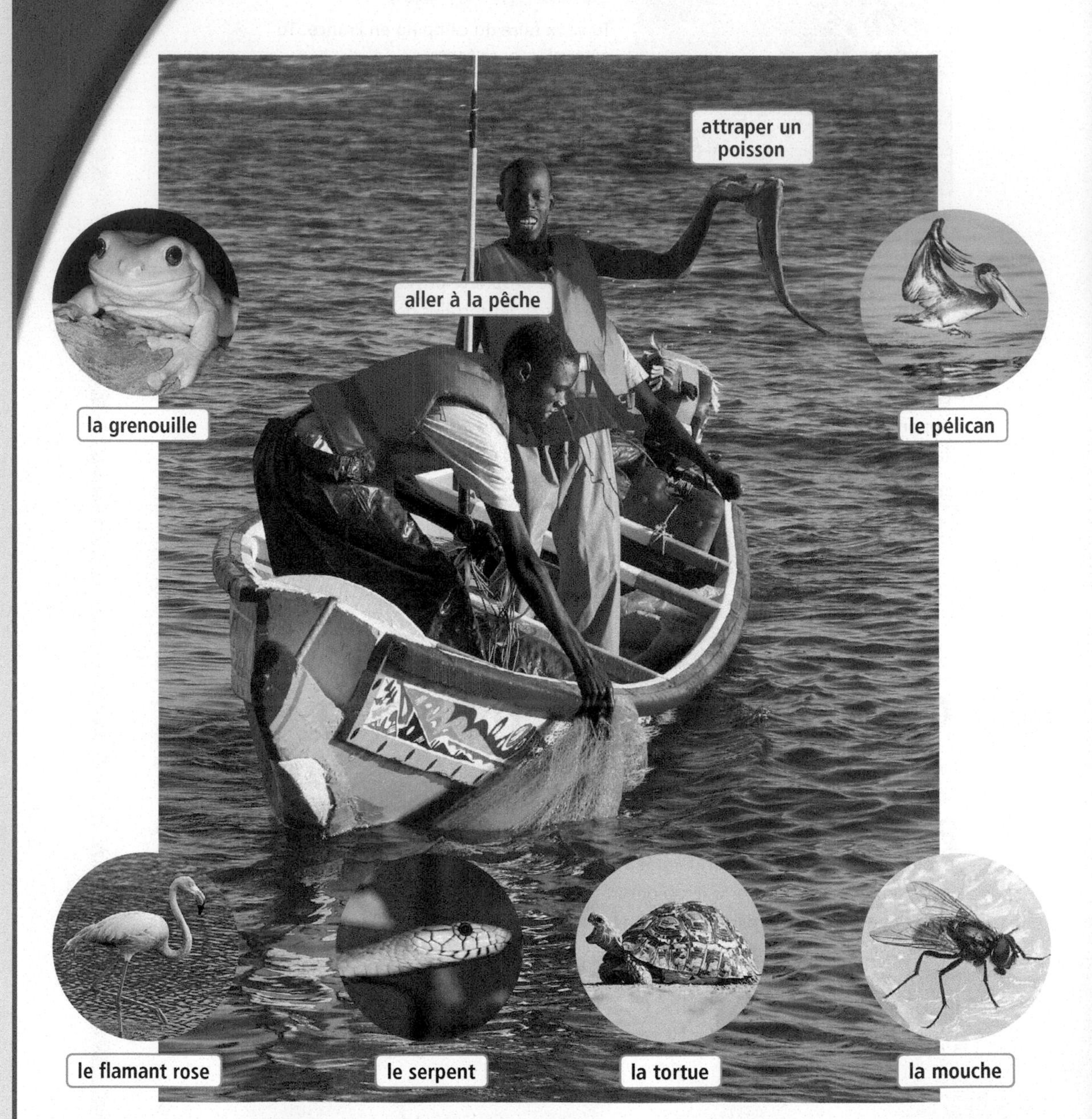

Core Instruction

TEACHING VOCABULAIRE

1. Go over the vocabulary by pointing to each item on transparencies **Vocabulaire 7.3** and **7.4** and modeling the pronunciation. **(2 min.)**
2. Point to items and have students take turns answering your questions. **Qu'est-ce qui est plus rapide, une tortue ou une mouche? Qu'est-ce qui chante le mieux, une araignée ou un oiseau? (2 min.)**
3. Tell students about your next trip or vacation, using expressions in **Exprimons-nous! Tout à l'heure, je vais appeler l'agence de voyages. L'été prochain, je vais aller en Russie. Nous achèterons nos billets d'avion bientôt. (2 min.)**

Télé-vocab 2

For a video presentation of this vocabulary, see the *DVD Tutor.*

Télé-vocab

Online Practice
my.hrw.com
Vocabulaire 2 practice

Exprimons-nous!

To tell what you will do

Tout à l'heure, nous allons nous baigner dans le lac.
Later (today), . . .

Après-demain, je vais aller à la pêche.
The day after tomorrow, . . .

Je vais **bientôt** partir en vacances.
. . . soon . . .

Je vais aller à la campagne l'été **prochain.**
. . . next . . .

La prochaine fois, je vais emporter une lampe de poche.
Next time, . . .

Vocabulaire et grammaire, pp. 79–81  Online Workbooks

▸ **Vocabulaire supplémentaire—**La nature, **p. R20**

D'autres mots utiles

se promener	*to take a stroll*
un moustique	*mosquito*
une toile d'araignée	*spider web*
une forêt	*forest*
se baigner	*to swim, take a dip in the water*
un fleuve	*river (big)*
la rivière	*river (small)*

Vocabulaire 2

TPR
Total Physical Response

Have students respond to these commands.

Lève le doigt si tu te promènes parfois dans la forêt.

Assieds-toi par terre si tu aimes écouter les oiseaux.

Lève la main si tu as déjà attrapé des poissons dans la rivière.

Mets les mains sur les yeux si tu as peur des araignées.

Lève-toi si tu te baignes souvent.

Then have students mime the following situations.

Il y a un serpent sous ta chaise.

Tu vois un moustique sur ton bras.

Tu es une grenouille, viens ici.

Donne-moi une fleur.

Tu es à la pêche.  1.2

Communities
Community Link

Have students prepare a class field guide to the animals, birds, and insects native to your area. Each student will choose one or more species on which to become an "expert" and will research their behavior and habitat. They will then prepare a report for the field guide that includes a drawing or picture of the animal, bird, or insect they researched. 5.1

Differentiated Instruction

SLOWER PACE LEARNERS

Bring a yoga book to class and show students some of the yoga poses that are named for animals, such as the Lion position. Then work as a class to create yoga poses for each of the animals in **Vocabulaire 2.** Have students create posters to illustrate the poses with labels in French. You may wish to display the posters in the room and have volunteers demonstrate the poses. 1.2

MULTIPLE INTELLIGENCES

Naturalist Ask students to research and draw a natural habitat for animals, insects, and plants. The drawing should accurately picture and label in French the living things found in the environment. Examples of possible habitats include a rain forest, ocean, desert, or mountains. Have students present their research and drawings to the class. 1.3

Vocabulaire 2

Resources

Planning:
Lesson Planner
Teacher One Stop

Presentation:

Projectable Transparencies **Vocabulaire 7.3, 7.4**

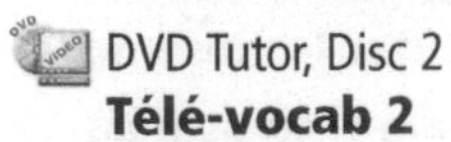

DVD Tutor, Disc 2 **Télé-vocab 2**

Interactive Whiteboard Lessons

Practice:
Cahier de vocabulaire et grammaire
Differentiated Practice and Assessment CD-ROM
Independent Study Guide
Media Guide
Audio CD 7, Tr. 4
@HOMETUTOR
Holt McDougal French Apps

20 Script

1. Un jour Madame Araignée avait faim. Alors, elle a décidé d'aller à la pêche.
2. Elle allait au lac quand elle a rencontré un lézard. Elle lui a expliqué où elle allait et pourquoi. Le lézard a dit: «Comment est-ce que vous allez attraper un poisson? C'est ridicule!»
3. Finalement, Madame Araignée est arrivée au lac. Là, elle a vu des pélicans qui pêchaient. Ils étaient de très bons pêcheurs.
4. Madame Araignée a commencé à pêcher, elle aussi. D'abord, elle a fait un fil. Mais, il n'y avait pas de poisson!
5. Alors, elle s'est fait une toile, exactement comme les toiles qu'elle faisait pour attraper les mouches. Puis, elle a jeté la toile dans le lac.
6. Madame Araignée a retiré sa toile. Il y avait beaucoup de poissons dans la toile! Les flamants roses et les pélicans ne riaient plus.

20 Écoutons CD 7, Tr. 4 1.2

Écoute l'histoire de Madame Araignée et mets les images dans le bon ordre. 1. e 2. a 3. d 4. c 5. f 6. b

a.

b.

c.

d.

e.

f.

21 Une camarade de pêche pénible 1.2

Écrivons Awa va à la pêche pour la première fois avec son frère Ousmane. Complète leur conversation.

tout à l'heure	bientôt	après-demain
prochain	la prochaine fois	demain

AWA Deux heures et pas de poisson!?
OUSMANE Patience, hein? Tu vas __1__ (bientôt) attraper un poisson.
AWA Ça, c'est le huitième poisson que tu attrapes et moi, rien! Le week-end __2__ (prochain), je vais aller me baigner. Je n'aime pas pêcher! Attends... Attends... Regarde mon beau poisson! Dis, on peut aller à la pêche __3__ (demain)?
OUSMANE Non, je dois travailler. Mais __4__ (après-demain), j'irai à la pêche.
AWA Chouette! __5__ (La prochaine fois), je vais attraper plus de poissons que toi!

À la cajun

In Louisiana, you might hear different names for some animals. For example, an alligator can be **un cocodril** and a bullfrog is **un ouaouaron.**

22 Des vacances formidables 1.3

Écrivons Vous allez faire du camping dans la forêt. Décris ce que tu vas faire et ce que tu vas voir.

Core Instruction

TEACHING EXPRIMONS-NOUS!

1. Gather several vacation pictures or bring a travel magazine to class. Ask students questions about the pictures, using the expressions in **Exprimons-nous!** and the new vocabulary. **Tu crois que je vais attraper un poisson? Est-ce qu'il va y avoir d'autres touristes là-bas? (2 min.)**
2. Ask **oui** or **non** questions about students using the same vocabulary. **Est-ce qu'il va y avoir une nouvelle voiture dans le garage de Daniel? Est-ce que tu sais si Rachel a peur des araignées? Tu crois que Paul a des tortues chez lui? (2 min.)**

Exprimons-nous!

To wonder what will happen

Je me demande si on va attraper beaucoup de poissons. *I wonder if . . .*

Tu crois qu'on va voir les flamants roses? *Do you think that . . . ?*

Est-ce qu'il va y avoir un orage? *Is there going to be . . . ?*

Est-ce que tu sais si on va pouvoir se promener? *Do you know if . . . ?*

Vocabulaire et grammaire, *pp. 79–81*

23 Des animaux exotiques 1.2

Écrivons Aminata et Ahmed rendent visite à Marius, un ami d'Aminata qui adore les animaux et les insectes. Ahmed a peur de *(is scared)* ces créatures. Complète sa partie de la conversation.

MODÈLE —**Je me demande si Marius a des araignées.**
—Oui, je suis certaine qu'il en a beaucoup.

1. — _______ ?
   — Oui, je crois qu'il en a un.
2. — _______ ?
   — Oui, mais calme-toi. Ils ne sont pas trop grands.
3. — _______ ?
   —Non, je ne sais pas si on peut leur donner à manger.
4. — _______ .
   —Non, il ne se baigne pas dans la piscine!
5. — _______ .
   — Oui, probablement. Marius les aime beaucoup.
6. — _______ .
   —Je ne sais pas si Marius en a une.

Flash culture

Le Sénégal compte 700 km de côtes environ. L'océan le long des côtes de l'Afrique occidentale est très riche en poissons. La pêche est l'industrie qui rapporte le plus au Sénégal. La pêche sportive rapporte aussi beaucoup d'argent au Sénégal. Plusieurs types de pêche sont pratiqués selon les régions : pêche au lancer, dite surf-casting, pêche à la traîne *(trolling)* ou pêche au gros *(sports fishing)*.

Où peux-tu pêcher près de chez toi? Quels types de poissons? 4.2

Communication

Digital performance space

24 Scénario 1.1

Parlons Tu vas faire du camping pour la première fois. Ton/Ta camarade a souvent fait du camping. Tu veux savoir ce que tu devrais emporter et aussi ce que tu vas peut-être voir dans la forêt.

MODÈLE —**Je me demande si je devrais emporter une gourde.**
—**Oui, tu devrais emporter une gourde.**

23 Possible Answers

1. Tu crois qu'il a un lézard?
2. Est-ce qu'il va y avoir des serpents?
3. Est-ce que tu sais si on pourra donner à manger aux serpents?
4. Je me demande si le lézard se baigne dans la piscine.
5. Est-ce qu'il va y avoir des poissons?
6. Est-ce que tu sais si Marius a une tortue?

Communication

24 Group Activity: Interpersonal

Tell the class that they are going on a camping trip to a place they have never visited. Divide the class into two groups. One student in each group starts by wondering out loud if a certain thing will be there. The student to the left answers that it will be there and then wonders about another item. The third student verifies that the last two things mentioned will be there, and the circle continues. The objective is to see if the last person in the circle can include each thing mentioned.

MODÈLE
— Je me demande si on va voir un lézard.
— Oui, on va voir un lézard. Tu crois qu'on va voir un pélican?
— Oui, on va voir un lézard et un pélican. Est-ce que tu sais si on va voir...
1.1

Differentiated Instruction

ADVANCED LEARNERS

20 Have students write their own animal fable and illustrate it with six drawings, one drawing per sheet of paper. Then have them scramble their drawings and exchange them with a partner's drawings. Have students take turns reading their fable aloud while their partner puts the drawings in the correct order. 1.3

MULTIPLE INTELLIGENCES

20 Spatial As a follow-up to the activity, ask small groups to create a story or cartoon that has a sequence of events. Have each group draw or write on a note card each event in the series. Allow other groups to unscramble the note cards to re-create the story in the correct sequence. Group members can then take turns to retell the story. 1.3

Assess

Assessment Program
Quiz: Vocabulaire 2
Alternative Assessment
Differentiated Practice and Assessment CD-ROM

Online Assessment
my.hrw.com

Test Generator 

Resources

Planning:
Lesson Planner
Teacher One Stop

Presentation:
DVD Tutor, Disc 2
Grammavision 2.1

Practice:
Grammar Tutor for Students of French, Chapter 7
Cahier de vocabulaire et grammaire
Differentiated Practice and Assessment CD-ROM
Cahier d'activités
Independent Study Guide
Media Guide
Projectable Transparencies
Bell Work, 7.6
Audio CD 7 Tr. 5

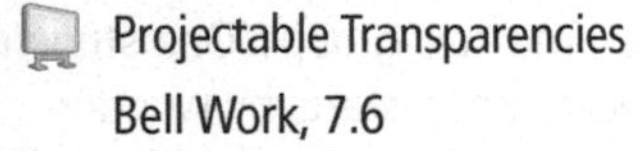

Bell Work

Use Bell Work 7.6 in the *Projectable Transparencies* or write this activity on the board.

Select the correct completion for each sentence.

1. On va à la pêche pour l'attraper, c'est...
2. Il chante pour notre plaisir, c'est...
3. Il est très long et plutôt mince, c'est...
4. Elle se promène avec sa maison, c'est...
5. Il est tout rose, c'est...

a. un oiseau
b. un serpent
c. un poisson
d. un flamant rose
e. une tortue

1.2

See script on p. 231F.

Objectifs
- the future
- the future of irregular verbs

Grammaire à l'œuvre 2

Grammavision

The future

1 The future tense tells what *will* happen. For most verbs, use the infinitive as the stem and add the future endings. Drop the **-e** from verbs ending in **-re** before adding the endings.

	parler	finir	vendre
je	parler**ai**	finir**ai**	vendr**ai**
tu	parler**as**	finir**as**	vendr**as**
il/elle/on	parler**a**	finir**a**	vendr**a**
nous	parler**ons**	finir**ons**	vendr**ons**
vous	parler**ez**	finir**ez**	vendr**ez**
ils/elles	parler**ont**	finir**ont**	vendr**ont**

Nous nous **baignerons** dans le lac. *We will swim in the lake.*

2 Many of the irregular present-tense verbs are regular in the future.

boire	je boir**ai**	mettre	je mettr**ai**
connaître	je connaîtr**ai**	ouvrir	j'ouvrir**ai**
dire	je dir**ai**	suivre	je suivr**ai**

Vocabulaire et grammaire, *pp. 82–83*
Cahier d'activités, *pp. 65–67*

4.1

En anglais

In English, we use the present tense after the word *when*, even when the action is going to take place in the future.

When I **get** *to the lake, I* **will** *swim.*

When does the action in both parts of the sentence take place, now or in the future?

In French, use the future tense after the word **quand** if the action is going to take place in the future.

Quand j'arriverai au lac, je me baignerai.

In the future

25 Écoutons CD 7, Tr. 5 1.2

Malik prépare un devoir sur un parc de sa région. Pour chaque phrase, dis s'il parle **a) de quelque chose qui est déjà arrivé** ou **b) de quelque chose qui arrivera.**

1. a **2.** b **3.** b **4.** a **5.** b **6.** b

26 Les explications du guide 1.2

Écrivons Complète les explications du guide d'un parc naturel avec le futur des verbes entre parenthèses.

1. Ce soir, je vous parlerai (parler) des arbres et des fleurs.
2. Le groupe finira (finir) la randonnée à onze heures.
3. Nous mettrons (mettre) de la crème solaire avant de nager.
4. Les enfants, vous me suivrez (suivre) bien sur les sentiers.
5. Noémie, tu me le diras (dire) si tu es fatiguée.

Core Instruction

TEACHING GRAMMAIRE

1. Tell students that to form the future tense of **-ir** and **-er** verbs, they use the entire infinitive as the future stem. For **-re** verbs, they drop the **-e**, so that the stem ends in **r**. The endings are similar to the verb **avoir: -ai, -as, -a, -ons, -ez, -ont. (2 min.)**
2. Ask individuals about their immediate plans. **David, tu parleras français au lycée demain? Rachel, dîneras-tu avec ta famille vers six heures? (3 min.)**
3. Ask questions about the future. **Voyagerons-nous sur la planète Mars? Parmi vous, y a-t-il quelqu'un qui écrira un roman? Qui travaillera en France? (3 min.)**

Grammavision

For a video presentation of the future, see the *DVD Tutor.*

Grammavision

Online Practice
my.hrw.com
Grammaire 2 practice

27 À chacun sa tâche 1.2

Parlons/Écrivons La famille Dongala est partie le week-end dans le parc naturel du Djoudj. Au camping, tout le monde doit aider. Dis comment ces personnes aideront, d'après les images. Utilise le futur et les sujets indiqués.

MODÈLE **Aïssata ouvrira les boîtes de conserve.**

Aïssata

1. Les garçons

2. Toi, Amadou, tu

3. Nous

4. Aïssata et toi, vous

28 Suite logique 1.2

Écrivons Imagine que tu vas passer des vacances dans un parc national avec ta famille. Finis les phrases pour expliquer ce que vous allez faire dans ces situations. Utilise le futur.

MODÈLE Si on n'arrive pas à monter nos tentes, on **dormira dans la voiture.**

1. Quand nous arriverons au parc, nous ______.
2. Si nous avons faim, mes parents ______.
3. Le soir, mon père ______.
4. S'il fait très chaud, nous ______.
5. Après la randonnée, on ______.
6. Si on n'a plus de boîtes de conserve, moi, je (j') ______.

Entre copains

avoir la frousse	*to be scared*
une bestiole	*a small animal/insect*

Digital performance space

Communication

29 Scénario 1.1

Parlons Tu vas aller rendre visite à Aminata, ta correspondante sénégalaise. Avec sa famille, vous allez faire une randonnée dans le parc national du Niokolo-Koba. Tu téléphones à Aminata pour avoir plus de détails sur cette randonnée.

MODÈLE **—Aminata, je suis très content(e) de venir te voir au Sénégal et j'ai envie de faire une randonnée dans le parc national. On emportera... ?**

27 Possible Answers

1. Les garçons monteront la tente.
2. Toi, Amadou, tu attraperas des poissons.
3. Nous ouvrirons les fauteuils pliants.
4. Aïssata et toi, vous parlerez avec le guide.

French for Spanish Speakers

Ask Spanish speakers to compare the regular future-tense endings in French and in Spanish. Ask students to say aloud the forms of **hablar** in the future. Which endings are the most similar to French? **(hablaré** and **hablará)** Which ending looks similar but is pronounced differently? **(Tu parleras** and **tú hablarás,** but the final **–s** is silent in French.)

4.1

Communication

Group Activity: Interpersonal

In groups, ask students to each write a question in this format: **Qu'est-ce que tu feras si tu** + present tense? Then have each group member pose his or her question. Students should respond with **si** + present tense, followed by a clause in the future. Each of the other members repeats the response in the **il/elle** form.

1.1

Differentiated Instruction

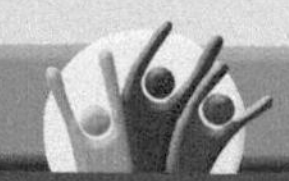

ADVANCED LEARNERS

As an ongoing project, have students compile the verb structures they have learned so far onto one compact study sheet. As an alternative, have them create a mechanical verb-tense guide, for example, a "verb dial" that presents different forms of regular verbs with a twist of the dial.

1.2

MULTIPLE INTELLIGENCES

Bodily-Kinesthetic To review **le futur,** ask students to conjugate each verb. Have students repeat each conjugation chorally a second time and clap as they say each syllable. Repeat the activity for each verb. You might have the class do this activity any time new verbs are introduced.

Je (clap) **parl** (clap) **er** (clap) **ai** (clap)

Tu (clap) **parl** (clap) **er** (clap) **as** (clap)

Il (clap) **parl** (clap) **er** (clap) **a** (clap) **...**

1.2

Resources

Planning:
Lesson Planner
Teacher One Stop

Presentation:
DVD Tutor, Disc 2
Grammavision 2.2

Practice:
Grammar Tutor for Students of French, Chapter 7
Cahier de vocabulaire et grammaire
Differentiated Practice and Assessment CD-ROM
Cahier d'activités
Independent Study Guide
Media Guide
Projectable Transparencies
Bell Work 7.7
HOMETUTOR

Bell Work

Use Bell Work 7.7 in the *Projectable Transparencies* or write this activity on the board.

Complete each sentence with the future of the verb in parentheses.

1. Quand nous ____ (arriver) à la plage, nous ____. (se baigner)
2. S'il fait très chaud, je ____ (boire) de la limonade.
3. Vous ____ (pêcher) peut-être un gros poisson!
3. Le soir, les garçons ____ (monter) la tente.
4. Maxime ____ (ouvrir) sûrement des boîtes de conserve.
5. Nous ____ (rire) autour du feu de camp.
6. Tu ne ____ (dormir) pas beaucoup. 1.2

The future of irregular verbs

1 All verbs in French use the same endings in the future tense, but some verbs have an irregular stem.

aller	ir-	j'i**rai**, tu ir**as**...
avoir	aur-	j'aur**ai**, tu aur**as**...
devoir	devr-	je devr**ai**, tu devr**as**...
être	ser-	je ser**ai**, tu ser**as**
faire	fer-	je fer**ai**, tu fer**as**...
pouvoir	pourr-	je pourr**ai**, tu pourr**as**...
venir	viendr-	je viendr**ai**, tu viendr**as**...
voir	verr-	je verr**ai**, tu verr**as**...
vouloir	voudr-	je voudr**ai**, tu voudr**as**...

2 Verbs with spelling changes in the present tense like **appeler** and **acheter** also have spelling changes in the future.

J'**achèterai** une carte téléphonique et j'**appellerai** mes parents.

Vocabulaire et grammaire, *pp. 82–83*
Cahier d'activités, *pp. 65–67*

Flash culture

Le nom «Sénégal» viendrait du mot Wolof «sunu gal» qui signifie «pirogue». De nos jours, les pirogues sont toujours utilisées pour la pêche. Elles sont décorées de couleurs vives et portent le nom d'une personnalité, d'un saint ou d'un héros local. Des courses de pirogues ont lieu régulièrement au Sénégal. La plus connue est celle qui se déroule à Saint-Louis au mois de février.

D'où vient le nom de ta ville? De ta région? De ton état? 4.2

30 Les deux font la paire 1.2

Lisons Associe l'infinitif qui correspond au verbe au futur dans chaque phrase de la colonne de gauche.

e **1.** Nicolas fera du bateau sur la rivière.
b **2.** Les oiseaux viendront passer l'hiver ici.
a **3.** Dans la forêt, nous verrons des serpents.
d **4.** Nadine, toi, tu iras voir les flamants roses.
c **5.** Après-demain, nous serons près du parc.

a. voir
b. venir
c. être
d. aller
e. faire

31 Projets d'avenir 1.2

Écrivons Complète les descriptions des projets d'avenir *(futur)* de ces personnes avec le futur. Utilise les verbes de la boîte.

appeler voir acheter se baigner vouloir être

1. Moi, je (j')______ une jolie maison en Bretagne. achèterai
2. Lucas ______ habiter au Maroc. voudra
3. Les Dioula ______ leur fille Mariame. appelleront
4. Moi, je ______ pharmacienne. serai
5. Nous ______ dans la rivière avec nos amis. nous baignerons

Core Instruction

TEACHING GRAMMAIRE

1. Tell students that some of the more common irregular verbs have an irregular future stem, but the same future endings as the regular verbs. **(1 min.)**

2. Write the infinitives of the nine irregular verbs on the board. Say a sentence with one of the verbs in the future. Have students guess the infinitive. Continue giving students sentences until they can recognize all infinitives. **(2 min.)**

3. Write the names of all students on little slips of paper and put them into a hat. Draw a name and make a future prediction for that student. Students respond **oui** or **non,** to indicate if it might happen. **(3 min.)**

Grammavision

For a video presentation of the future of irregular verbs, see the *DVD Tutor.*

32 L'été prochain 1.2

Écrivons/Parlons Utilise un élément de chaque colonne pour dire ce que ces personnes feront peut-être l'été prochain.

Moi, je	avoir	un beau voyage
Le professeur de français	pouvoir	passer beaucoup de temps avec des amis
Mes parents	être	peut-être en France
Mes amis et moi, nous	faire	travailler
Vous, les professeurs, vous	devoir	un billet d'avion pour le Sénégal
Toi, [nom de ton (ta) meilleur(e) ami(e)], tu	acheter	le temps d'aller à la pêche

33 Demain 1.2

Écrivons Explique ce que ces personnes feront demain, d'après les photos. Utilise le futur des verbes donnés et les sujets indiqués.

MODÈLE **Henri fera ses devoirs.**

Henri / faire

1. Moi, je (j') / aller
Moi, j'irai au cinéma.

2. Charlotte / appeler
Charlotte appellera des amis au téléphone.

3. Vous / devoir
Vous devrez travailler.

4. Nous / acheter
Nous achèterons un chemisier.

Communication

Digital performance space

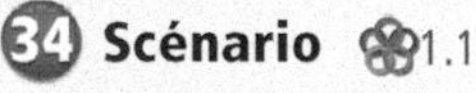

34 Scénario 1.1

Parlons Imagine que tu peux savoir ce qui va se passer dans l'avenir. Tous tes amis veulent que tu leur parles de leur avenir! Donne tes prédictions pour l'avenir d'un(e) camarade. Ensuite, échangez les rôles.

MODÈLE **—Alors, à mon avis, tu iras habiter en France.**
—Ah oui? Et qu'est-ce que je ferai en France?
—Tu travailleras dans un parc.

COMMON ERROR ALERT — ATTENTION !

Pouvoir, vouloir, and **devoir** are often taught together due to their similarities in the present tense. Students may incorrectly assume that their irregular future stems are also similar. The stem of **pouvoir** becomes **pourr-.** The stem of **vouloir** becomes **voudr-,** and the stem of **devoir** becomes **devr-.**

Communities

School Link

Have students raise money for a nonprofit wildlife organization by creating "fortune balloons." Students write fortunes in French with an English translation on slips of paper. After inserting the fortunes in the balloons, they fill the balloons with air. Students might set up a table in the cafeteria at lunchtime to sell their balloons. 5.1

Communication

34 Group Work: Interpersonal

Have each student write a question in the **futur simple,** such as **Qu'est-ce que tu feras quand tu...?** to ask the future plans of a classmate. Then have students circulate and ask their question of as many different students as possible. The interviewer should report the respondent's answer in the **il/elle** form. 1.1

Differentiated Instruction

SLOWER PACE LEARNERS

Write the infinitives of the verbs with irregular stems on one set of cards and their corresponding stems on another set. Distribute the cards randomly to students. Have them find the student who has the stem that goes with their infinitive or vice versa. They should then work together to write six sentences with their verb in the future tense, one sentence for each of the pronouns: **je, tu, il/elle/on, nous, vous, ils/elles.** 1.2

SPECIAL LEARNING NEEDS

32 Students with Dyslexia Allow students to copy each of the phrases or words in the puzzle sections of the activity. Ask them to manipulate the parts of the sentences to form the correct combinations. You may wish to give each student the cards needed to create only two or three of the sentences at a time. 1.2

Assess

Assessment Program
Quiz: Grammaire 2
Alternative Assessment
Differentiated Practice and Assessment CD-ROM

Online Assessment
my.hrw.com

Test Generator 

Resources

Planning:

Lesson Planner

Teacher One Stop

Practice:

Grammar Tutor for Students of French, Chapter 7

Cahier de vocabulaire et grammaire

Differentiated Practice and Assessment CD-ROM

Cahier d'activités

Independent Study Guide

Media Guide

Projectable Transparencies Bell Work 7.8

Audio CD 7, Tr. 6

Bell Work

Use Bell Work 7.8 in the *Projectable Transparencies* or write this activity on the board.

Complete each sentence with the future tense of the verb in parentheses.

1. Vous ____ (aller) dans un pays exotique?
2. Oui, et ma sœur ____ (venir) avec nous.
3. Nous ____ (voir) des pélicans.
4. Mes parents ____ (faire) du bateau.
5. Les plus jeunes ____ (pouvoir) rester sur la plage.
6. Tu ____ (être) dans un hôtel sympa?
7. Oui, il y ____ (avoir) des flamants roses dans les jardins. 1.2

See script on p. 231F.

Synthèse
- Vocabulaire 2
- Grammaire 2

Application 2

35 Des prédictions 1.3

Écrivons Comment est-ce que tu imagines la vie de ces personnes dans plusieurs années? Complète les phrases suivantes avec deux possibilités au futur pour chacune.

MODÈLE Dans cinq ans, j'**irai à l'université et je ferai des études de physique.**

1. Dans cinq ans, je (j') ______.
2. Dans cinq ans, mon/ma meilleur(e) ami(e) ______.
3. Dans dix ans, mes parents ______.
4. Dans quinze ans, vous, monsieur /madame [nom de ton professeur de français], vous ______.
5. Dans vingt ans, ma famille et moi, nous ______.
6. Dans vingt-cinq ans, tous les élèves de la classe ______.
7. Dans dix ans, le président ______.
8. Dans trente ans, je ______.

36 Un voyage idéal 1.3

Écrivons Tu iras en vacances avec ta famille. Décris l'endroit idéal. Est-ce qu'il y aura des lacs, des montagnes, des animaux?

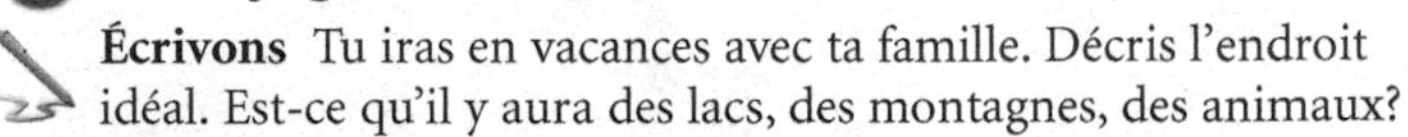

MODÈLE Quand on arrivera près du lac, on verra de grandes forêts. Il y aura...

Un peu plus

The verb **courir** is irregular.

courir *(to run)*	
je **cours**	nous **courons**
tu **cours**	vous **courez**
il/elle/on **court**	ils/elles **courent**

The past participle of courir is couru:
Martin a couru cinq kilomètres.

The future stem for courir is courr-:
Nous courrons très vite samedi.

Vocabulaire et grammaire, *p. 84*
Cahier d'activités, *pp. 65–67*
Online Workbooks

37 Écoutons CD 7, Tr. 6 1.2

Écoute les phrases suivantes et décide si chaque phrase est **a) au présent, b) au passé** ou **c) au futur.**

1. b 2. c 3. a 4. c 5. b

Core Instruction

INTEGRATED PRACTICE

1. Have students do Activities 35 and 36 to review previously taught material. **(10 min.)**
2. Give students sentences and ask them to decide if the situation is **probable** or **peu probable. Le lézard aura la même taille que le flamant rose. Le serpent sera plus grand que l'arbre. (3 min.)**
3. Introduce **Un peu plus** and continue with Activities 37–40. **(15 min.)**

TEACHING UN PEU PLUS

1. Remind students that **courir** is irregular in the present tense. Its past participle is **couru;** its future stem is **courr-. (1 min.)**
2. Give several sentences with the verb **courir** in various tenses. Have students indicate if the verb is in the present by pointing down, in the past by pointing behind, or in the future by pointing ahead. **(5 min.)**

Online Practice
my.hrw.com
Application 2 practice

38 Entraînement dans la nature 1.2

Écrivons Des athlètes se préparent pour les Jeux olympiques. Un journaliste de sport les interviewe au sujet de leur entraînement. Complète l'interview avec les formes correctes du verbe **courir**.

—Alors, Patrick, qu'est-ce que vous faites pour vous entraîner?
—Eh bien, moi, je __1__ (cours) dix kilomètres tous les matins.
—Dix kilomètres! C'est beaucoup!
—Non, pas tellement. On __2__ (court) souvent beaucoup plus que ça!
—Ah bon. Et vous? Vous __3__ (courez) aussi tous les jours?
—Oui, nous __4__ (courons) le matin et le soir, nous nageons dans le lac.
—Et ces jeunes garçons?
—Ils ne __5__ (courent) pas souvent, je crois... Attendez, on peut demander à Paul. Paul, tu __6__ (cours) pour t'entraîner?
—Non, je n'aime pas ça. Je préfère faire du vélo tout terrain.

39 Opinions personnelles 1.3

Écrivons À ton avis, comment sera la vie en 2500? Est-ce qu'il y aura beaucoup de changements?

Communication

Digital performance space

40 On va camper! 1.1

Parlons Avec ton/ta camarade, vous vous préparez à aller camper. L'un(e) de vous n'a jamais campé et n'est pas sûr(e) de ce qu'il faut emporter *(take along)*. Lisez les questions ci-dessous et répondez-y de manière logique. Ensuite, échangez les rôles.

— **Il va faire froid la nuit. Qu'est-ce que je dois emporter?**
—
— **Et si on veut faire un feu de camp?**
—
— **J'aimerais faire la cuisine. C'est possible?**
—
— **Je crois qu'il va y avoir des moustiques. Qu'est-ce qu'on prend?**
—

Communication

Group Work: Interpersonal
Have students form small groups. The groups are to imagine that they are going on a campout. Ask two students in each group to explain what the group will do at the campground. The others should agree and say that they will do the tasks or refuse and give an excuse (in the future). 1.1

Pre-AP Language Examination

40 Sample answer:
— . . .
— **Il faut prendre ton sac de couchage.**
— . . .
— **Il faut prendre des allumettes ou un briquet.**
— . . .
— **Oui, on peut prendre un réchaud.**
— . . .
— **On peut prendre de la lotion anti-moustiques.**

Differentiated Instruction

ADVANCED LEARNERS

39 Extend the activity by having students write a letter to their future self, in which they tell at least five things they plan to do next year. Have them seal their letter in an envelope, stamp it, and address it to themselves in care of a person who will likely be at the same address (a parent or an aunt or uncle, for example). Collect their letters and then set up a "tickler file" to remind yourself to mail students' letters to them next year. 5.2

SPECIAL LEARNING NEEDS

38 Students with Learning Disabilities/ Dyslexia To accommodate students with learning or reading challenges, review the conjugation of the verb **courir.** Make copies of the activity in large type to make the sentences easier to read. Allow students to fill in the blanks using the copy as a worksheet. Review student answers as a class and check for understanding. 1.2

Assess

Assessment Program
Quiz: Application 2
Audio CD 7, Tr. 16
Alternative Assessment
Differentiated Practice and Assessment CD-ROM
Online Assessment
my.hrw.com
Test Generator

Resources

Planning:
Lesson Planner
 Teacher One Stop

Presentation:
 DVD Tutor, Disc 2
Télé-roman

Practice:
Media Guide
DVD Tutor, Disc 2
Télé-roman

Connections

Visual Learners

To help students understand the complicated events of this episode, have them trace what happens from the time Anne leaves the Gadio home until she returns. Draw a series of ovals with directional arrows, similar to the diagram below. Fill in the first and last ovals as shown. Then have students fill in the remaining ovals with the events that occur in between. Guide students by asking questions about what happens. 3.2

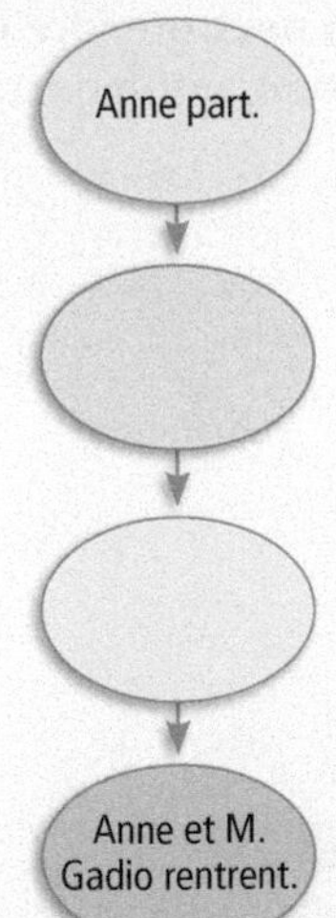
Anne part.
Anne et M. Gadio rentrent.

Gestures

Have students look at Léa's expression in scene 2 and Mr. Gadio's expression in scene 4. What emotions do they reveal? Then direct your students' attention to scene 7. Ask students what Mr. Rigaud might be telling Mr. Gadio to do. 2.1

Télé-roman

Le Secret de la statuette *Épisode 7*

STRATÉGIE

Getting confirmation As a story unfolds, it is important to decide whether the deductions and connections you have made are correct. This allows you to move forward in understanding the story. List the events from **Episode 7**. Then, find your list of deductions from **Episodes 5** and **6** and compare the two lists. Were your deductions right? If they are not completely confirmed, decide whether they might still turn out to be true, or whether you can discard them. 1.2

Quelques heures plus tard, Anne n'est toujours pas rentrée...

1

M. Gadio À quelle heure Anne est partie, Adja?
Mme Gadio Il y a plusieurs heures, c'est sûr.
M. Gadio Je vais téléphoner à l'inspecteur Sonko.

2

Léa Qu'est-ce qui s'est passé? Où est ma mère?

3

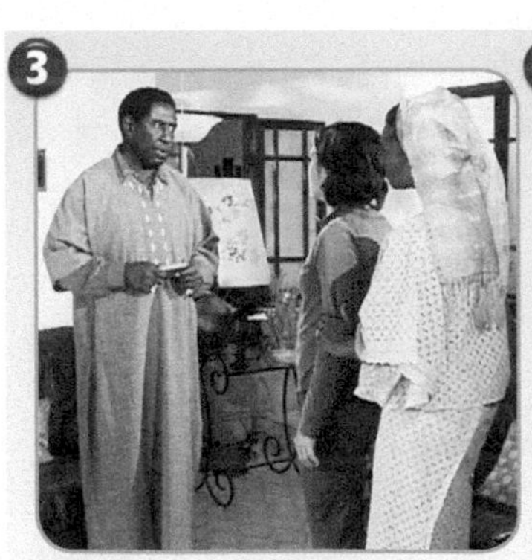

M. Gadio L'inspecteur ne lui a jamais téléphoné. Il pense que c'est Rigaud qui l'a appelée...

4

M. Gadio Allô?... Allô?... Allô!... Ici Salif Gadio, oui! Qui est à l'appareil?... Oui, je comprends. À cinq heures là-bas. Ne lui faites pas de mal, je vous en prie!

5

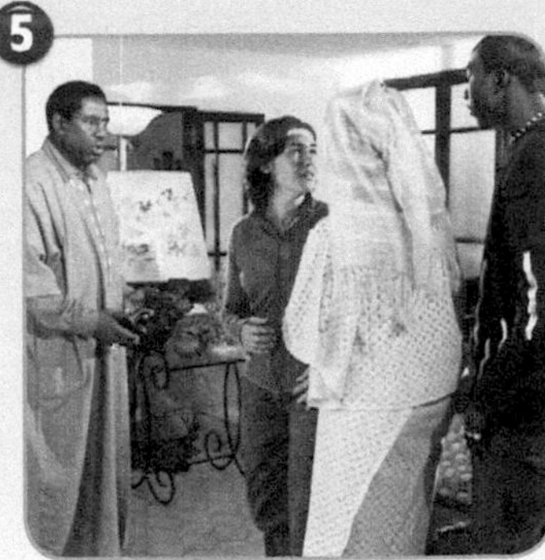

M. Gadio L'inspecteur avait raison. Rigaud a bien kidnappé ta mère, Léa. Il veut la statuette en échange... Je dois aller seul au rendez-vous pour échanger Anne contre la statuette.

Core Instruction

TEACHING TÉLÉ-ROMAN

1. Have students scan **Télé-roman. (1 min.)**
2. Play the video, stopping periodically to assess comprehension. **(8 min.)**
3. Play the video a second time. Have students practice the parts of the characters. For scenes one through five, form groups of four. For scenes six through ten, form groups of three. Encourage students to use facial expressions and gestures to emphasize the action in the scene. **(8 min.)**
4. In the same groups, have students answer the **As-tu compris?** questions on page 257. **(5 min.)**

DVD Tutor 

As an alternative, you might use the captioned version of **Le Secret de la statuette** on DVD.

Visit Us Online
my.hrw.com
Online Edition

M. Gadio rencontre Charles Rigaud

6

M. Rigaud Vous êtes venu seul, j'espère.
M. Gadio Oui, oui! Je suis seul!

7

M. Rigaud Apportez la statuette ici...
Posez la statuette par terre et retournez à votre voiture.

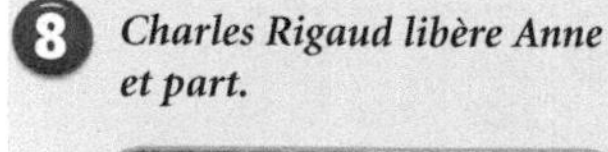

8 *Charles Rigaud libère Anne et part.*

9

M. Gadio Anne! Ça va? Tu es blessée?
Anne Non, non, ça va. Je n'ai rien.

10

M. Gadio Tu sais, Sonko ne t'a pas téléphoné.
Anne Oui, bien sûr, maintenant je le sais. Est-ce que Sonko sait ce qui s'est passé?
M. Gadio Non. Je lui téléphonerai quand on arrivera à la maison.

1.2

AS-TU COMPRIS?

1. Qui est-ce que Léa et les Gadio attendent au début de l'épisode?
2. Est-ce que c'est l'inspecteur de police qui a téléphoné à Anne?
3. Pourquoi est-ce que M. Gadio va retrouver Charles Rigaud?
4. Qu'est-ce que Charles Rigaud reprend?
5. Qu'est-ce que M. Gadio fera quand il arrivera à la maison?

Prochain épisode:
D'après toi, où est-ce que M. Gadio et Anne vont aller? Qui va être content(e) de revoir sa mère?

Le Secret de la statuette Episode 7

In this episode, the Gadio family and Léa are waiting anxiously for Anne to return. When they learn that inspector Sonko never called or asked her to meet him, they realize that she may have been kidnapped. Mr. Gadio then receives a call from Rigaud, who wants to exchange Anne for the statuette. Gadio and Rigaud meet and make the exchange without incident. Rigaud drives away with the statuette, as Mr. Gadio makes sure that Anne is okay. She is shaken but unharmed. They decide to call inspector Sonko when they get back to the house.

Télé-roman

As-tu compris? Answers

1. Anne
2. non, c'était Rigaud
3. pour échanger Anne contre la statuette
4. la statuette
5. Il téléphonera à l'inspecteur.

Communication

Pair Work: Presentational
After students have watched **Télé-roman,** have them work with a partner to create and present a scene in which Mr. Gadio negotiates with Mr. Rigaud on the phone for Anne's release. Allow time to practice and then have partners present their scene to the class. 1.3

Lecture et écriture

Resources

Planning:
Lesson Planner
Teacher One Stop

Presentation:
Audio CD 7, Tr. 7

Practice:
Cahier d'activités
Reading Strategies and Skills Handbook, Chapter 7
Intermediate Reader
French InterActive Reader

Applying the Strategies

For practice with monitoring comprehension, have students use the "Anticipation Guide" strategy from the *Reading Strategies and Skills Handbook.*

READING PRACTICE

STRATEGIES

Strategy: Anticipation Guide

Reading Skill	When can I use this strategy?		
	Prereading	During Reading	Postreading
Making Predictions	✓		
Using Prior Knowledge	✓		
Analyzing Cause and Effect Relationships		✓	
Analyzing Persuasive Techniques			✓
Making Generalizations			✓

Strategy at a Glance: Anticipation Guide

- The teacher writes the Anticipation Guide, a set of generalizations based on issues in the text and designed to promote discussion and predictions about the selection.
- Students mark whether they agree or disagree with each statement, then discuss their responses.
- While students read, they take notes on the issues in the guide as those issues are revealed in the text.
- After reading, students look at their responses again to see whether they still agree or disagree with the statements.

Both younger and older children do it. They constantly ask what's going on and where they are being taken. They ask what the doctor is going to do before the doctor does it, and they plan what they'll say when they are approaching parents with special requests. Adults do it. We pick up travel brochures before we travel, study maps before we make a car trip, and check out the checkbook before we make a purchase. We all do it—we try to anticipate what's going to happen before it actually happens.

Good readers consciously try to anticipate what a text is about before they begin reading. They look at the cover, art, title, genre, author, headings, graphs, charts, length, print size, inside flaps, and back cover. Some students read the bibliographic information on the copyright page. They ask friends, "Is this any good?" They do anything to find out something about a text before they begin reading.

Struggling readers, on the other hand, often don't do that; they are told to read something, and once the text is in hand, they just begin. They often skip titles and background information, hardly ever read book jackets, and rarely look through the text

Summarizing

Remind students that a summary expresses the main idea of a passage, but does not go into specific details. As they read, they will come across important information that they can state in their own words. These ideas, rather than isolated words, are the basis of their summary. By restating the main points of the selection, students can identify the basic meaning of the passage.

Lecture et écriture

STRATÉGIE pour lire

Focusing on ideas When you read in French, it is important to focus on ideas instead of isolated words. 1. Read a portion of the text without looking up any words. 2. Reread the same passage and ask yourself what you understand. 3. Repeat steps 1 and 2 as you read to the end of the text. 4. Read the story a third time, pausing to see if you can summarize what you have read.

A Avant la lecture CD 7, Tr. 7 1.3

Le texte suivant est une légende du Sénégal. Avant de lire le texte, regarde les illustrations et le titre. Est-ce que tu peux deviner le sujet du texte? À l'aide des illustrations, écris trois ou quatre phrases pour raconter l'histoire.

COMMENT GUÉRIR LA PEUR[1]

Il était une fois[2] un homme qui marchait seul dans la brousse[3]. Il a marché si longtemps qu'il a été tenaillé par la faim[4]. Il s'est arrêté dans un village. Là, on lui a donné à manger, il s'est régalé même copieusement[5] et a renoncé à poursuivre sa route. Après avoir épousé[6] une jeune femme du village, il y a élu domicile[7] et n'a plus songé[8] à repartir.

Un jour, après un bon repas, le vieux s'est aventuré dans la brousse, qui, malheureusement, était infestée de fauves[9], surtout de lions.

1. How to cure fear 2. Once upon a time 3. bush 4. he was gnawed by hunger 5. he had a delicious and rich meal 6. wed 7. he chose to make it his home 8. thought 9. wild cats

Core Instruction

TEACHING LECTURE

1. Read **Stratégie** aloud with the students. Go over each step. **(2 min.)**
2. Have students do Activity A individually. Ask them to apply the strategy to this introductory paragraph and then ask volunteers to share the main ideas. **(10 min.)**
3. Have the students read the legend without a dictionary and do Activities B and C in class. **(15 min.)**
4. Form groups of three or four to read and discuss Activity D. When students complete the activity, have each group report its answers to the class. **(15 min.)**

Le vieux n'en savait rien. À peine s'était-il éloigné[1] que le roi de la forêt a surgi[2] en poussant un long rugissement[3]. Le lion s'est approché, le vieux alors s'est engouffré[4] dans un buisson épineux[5]. Le lion l'a cherché, en vain ; il n'a pas réussi à retrouver l'homme. Cependant, il est resté aux aguets[6] pendant une semaine, puis, dégoûté, s'en est allé. Et le vieux est resté seul dans son buisson, complètement abasourdi[7] de son sort. Un chasseur[8] est venu à passer par là. L'homme a entendu son pas[9] et a demandé :

— Qui va là ?
— C'est moi.
— Qui êtes-vous ?
— Je suis un chasseur à la recherche de gibier[10].
— Ami chasseur, veux-tu me porter secours[11] pour me tirer d'ici ?
— Mais comment as-tu fait pour entrer là-dedans ?
— C'est une peur bleue[12] qui m'y a conduit.
— Eh bien ! c'est une peur bleue qui t'en sortira bientôt !
— Et que vas-tu faire ?
— Tu le sauras le moment venu.

Et le chasseur a commencé à entasser de la paille[13] sèche sur le buisson. Tout à coup, il a mis le feu en plusieurs endroits du buisson. Pris de frayeur[14], le vieux s'est élancé[15] et, d'un violent coup de tête dans les épines, s'est mis hors de danger.
Le chasseur l'a accueilli[16] avec un large sourire. Ils se sont embrassés et se sont liés d'amitié.

(Raconté par Amsata Dieye) COPANS Jean et COUTY Philippe. Contes wolofs *du Baol.*

1. He had barely stepped away 2. appeared 3. roar 4. rushed 5. thorny bush 6. on the watch 7. astounded 8. hunter 9. steps 10. game 11. help 12. fright 13. straw 14. fright 15. rushed out 16. welcomed

Differentiated Instruction

SLOWER PACE LEARNERS

As you play the audio recording of the reading, act out what is happening in the story, or coach volunteers to act it out. Stop the recording at logical breaks in the action and discuss with students what has happened so far in the story. Alternatively, play the recording, pausing at logical breaks, and have students illustrate the story as they listen to it. 1.2

SPECIAL LEARNING NEEDS

Students with Learning Disabilities/ Dyslexia Before the lesson, make copies of the reading selection. When reviewing **Avant la lecture,** allow students with word-level reading challenges to scan the text of the reading and highlight the words they know. This prereading activity can be an additional accommodation for **Stratégie pour lire.** 1.2

Cultures

Practices and Perspectives

Explain to students that many African cultures had an oral storytelling tradition long before they had a written language. In Senegal, individuals, called **griots,** were chosen to preserve and pass on to the next generation a group's culture and history through storytelling and music. Discuss with students the benefits and possible drawbacks of passing on information through storytelling and songs. You might also have students research the role of the **griot** in present-day Senegalese culture. 2.1

Connections

Social Studies Link

Describe to students the theory of "learned helplessness," in which people who try to escape a difficult situation and are unsuccessful eventually give up trying. Discuss with students whether they believe the man in the story may have been a victim of learned helplessness. Ask students if they themselves have ever faced a situation that seemed hopeless, only to find out they could be successful after all. 3.1

Language Examination

Through the practice of listening and reading comprehension, as well as essay writing, **Lecture et écriture** helps students prepare for the **Interpretive Reading and Listening** and the **Presentational Writing** sections of the AP Language and Culture Exam.

Additional Practice

For more reading practice, see **Variations littéraires,** pp. 394–395.

Lecture et écriture

Communities

School Link

Have students organize an imaginary French-immersion camping trip with a French class from another school. Have students plan activities and write a list of camping equipment and food that each camper should bring. Then have students e-mail their lists to their partner class and ask them to decide who will be responsible for bringing each item. You might ask small groups of students to translate into French their favorite campfire story or song or cooking instructions for the different foods and share those as well. 5.1

Connections

Science Link

In some parts of the United States, campers might encounter hazards such as bears, poisonous snakes, poison oak, and so forth. Have students research the hazards that campers face in France, Senegal, or another francophone country. Then have them create a guide to prepare people for camping in the francophone country of their choice. Or, they might prepare such a guide for French speakers camping in the United States. 3.1

Compréhension

B Remets dans l'ordre la légende. 1.2 2, 4, 1, 5, 6, 7, 3, 8

1. Un lion a surgi.
2. L'homme s'est installé dans un village et s'est marié.
3. Un chasseur est arrivé.
4. L'homme est parti se promener.
5. L'homme a eu peur et s'est caché dans un buisson.
6. Le lion est parti.
7. L'homme ne pouvait pas sortir du buisson.
8. Le chasseur a aidé l'homme à sortir du buisson.

C Choisis la meilleure réponse aux questions suivantes. 1.2

1. Où est-ce que l'histoire se passe?
   (a.) dans la brousse **b.** dans la jungle
2. Pourquoi est-ce que l'homme s'est arrêté dans le village?
   a. Il avait peur. **(b.)** Il avait faim.
3. Quand l'homme est parti se promener, qu'est-ce qu'il a vu dans la brousse?
   (a.) un lion **b.** un buisson épineux
4. Pourquoi est-ce que l'homme s'est mis dans le buisson? Parce que/qu'...
   (a.) il a eu peur du lion. **b.** le chasseur lui a fait peur.
5. Pourquoi est-ce que l'homme est resté si longtemps dans le buisson?
   (a.) Il ne pouvait pas sortir du buisson.
   b. Il avait honte *(was ashamed)*.
6. Comment est-ce que l'homme est sorti du buisson?
   a. Le chasseur a coupé le buisson.
   (b.) Le chasseur a mis le feu au buisson.

Après la lecture

D Cette histoire est une fable sénégalaise. Une fable est une histoire qui donne une leçon. Quelle est la leçon ou la morale de cette fable? Est-ce que tu connais d'autres histoires, citations ou proverbes qui ont la même morale ou qui ont un thème similaire? Compare-les avec cette fable. 3.1

Core Instruction

TEACHING ESPACE ÉCRITURE

1. Read and discuss **Stratégie pour écrire** and **Il était une fois.** **(4 min.)**
2. Bring in a variety of magazines from which students can choose an illustration for their story or allow students to create their own. Referring to their illustrations, students should answer the questions in step 1. **(15 min.)**
3. Assign step 2 as homework. **(1 min.)**
4. Assign partners for step 3 and have students peer edit their partner's story. **(15 min.)**
5. For step 4, have volunteers read their stories to the class, showing the illustrations. After they read their story, students should ask the class what they think will happen to the characters in the future. **(20 min.)**

Espace écriture

STRATÉGIE pour écrire

When beginning a story, one of the writer's most important tasks is to **create the setting.** A well-written setting includes vivid, concise details, establishes the tone and mood of a story, and may foreshadow events. For example, a storm can suggest conflict of some sort, while a calm lake on a sunny day may suggest tranquility and happiness.

Il était une fois... 1.3

You're writing a short story for a French outdoor magazine about some friends who went on a camping trip and had a hair-raising adventure. Create an engaging setting. Then, narrate the events of your story. Use specific and vivid details to help your readers "see" the story and keep them engaged.

1 Plan

Look for an illustration that matches the setting of your story. Looking at it, decide what to describe.

- How will you depict the surroundings?
- What kind of mood do you want to create?
- What are your characters thinking and doing?

Organize these details to grab the reader's attention. Then, brainstorm the events. Decide on an ending.

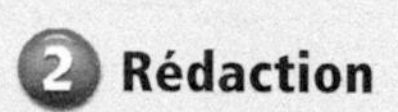

2 Rédaction

Set the scene, using the **imparfait:**

- to describe the surroundings (location, time, weather)
- to explain background circumstances thoughts and motivations).

Then, use the **passé composé:**

- to narrate the events of your story,
- tell what your characters did
- explain what happened to them.

Make sure the events in your story follow a logical order and that you have included details to create suspense and maintain the reader's interest.

3 Correction

Trade stories with a classmate. Does the beginning of your story grab his/her attention? Can he/she visualize the setting? Ask your classmate to check for the correct use of the **imparfait** and the **passé composé**.

4 Application

Attach your final draft to the illustration you found. Post your stories on the wall or hold a storytelling session to read the stories to the class.

Process Writing

Avant d'écrire As students write, have them add transitional phrases between each major turn in the story; they should also make use of as much of the new vocabulary and grammar as possible. When they exchange papers with a partner, ask that they check for all essential elements and suggest any necessary rewriting. Before they read their stories to the class, have students practice the pronunciation of any difficult words.

Writing Assessment

To assess the **Espace écriture,** you can use the following rubric. For additional rubrics, see the *Assessment Program* or refer to the *Generate Success* Rubric Generator.

Writing Rubric	4	3	2	1
Content (Complete—Incomplete)				
Comprehensibility (Comprehensible—Seldom comprehensible)				
Accuracy (Accurate—Seldom accurate)				
Organization (Well-organized—Poorly organized)				
Effort (Excellent effort—Minimal effort)				

18-20: A 16-17: B 14-15: C 12-13: D Under 12: F

Differentiated Instruction

ADVANCED LEARNERS

Instruct students to memorize the highlights of their story. Then darken the classroom as much as possible and sit in a circle around a pile of miniature Christmas tree lights or other light source and have students tell their stories around the "campfire." Have students vote on the scariest, funniest, and strangest story and on the best storyteller. 1.3

MULTIPLE INTELLIGENCES

Visual When they have completed Activity B, ask students to draw a comic strip with eight panels to depict the order of events in the legend. The captions for each frame of the comic strip should be the sentence taken from items one through eight but rearranged in logical order. You may wish to have students share the comic strips and then display them in class. 1.2

Assess

Assessment Program
Quiz: Lecture
Quiz: Écriture
Online Assessment
my.hrw.com
Test Generator

Chapitre 7

Prépare-toi pour l'examen

Resources

Planning:
Lesson Planner
Teacher One Stop

Practice:
Cahier d'activités
Media Guide
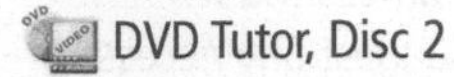
DVD Tutor, Disc 2
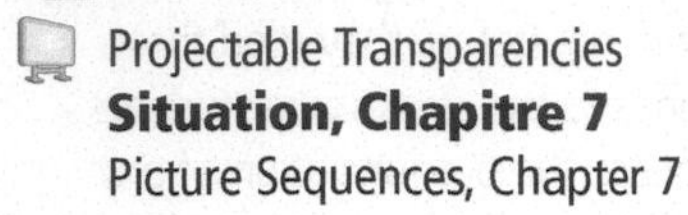
Projectable Transparencies
Situation, Chapitre 7
Picture Sequences, Chapter 7
Audio CD 7, Tr. 10–13
@HOMETUTOR

Reteaching

Review context clues for the **passé composé** and **imparfait.** Have students list them on the board. For example, clues for the **passé composé** include **un jour, une fois, ensuite,** and **finalement;** for the **imparfait,** clues include **quand j'étais jeune, chaque été, toujours, souvent,** and **de temps en temps.**

Proverbes

For French proverbs and activities related to the chapter theme and vocabulary, see **Proverbes et expressions,** pp. R6–R7.

Game

Je m'en souviens! One student begins by saying, **Je vais faire du camping. J'emporte une boussole.** The next student must repeat what was said and add another item. **Je vais faire du camping. J'emporte une boussole et une tente.** The game continues in this manner until someone makes a mistake. The student who makes a mistake is out. Start a new round when someone makes a mistake, but the students who are out stay out. The winner is the last one remaining.

1.1

Chapitre 7

Prépare-toi pour l'examen

@HOMETUTOR

1 Vocabulaire 1
- to say what happened
- to describe circumstances

pp. 234–237

2 Grammaire 1
- the passé **composé** and the **imparfait**
- **être en train de**

Un peu plus
- verbs with **être** or **avoir** in the **passé composé**

pp. 238–243

3 Vocabulaire 2
- to tell what you will do
- to wonder what will happen

pp. 246–249

4 Grammaire 2
- the future
- the future of irregular verbs

Un peu plus
- the verb **courir**

pp. 250–255

1 Imagine que tu as fait du camping ce week-end près de la plage. Écris deux ou trois phrases pour décrire ton week-end. 1.3

2 Alexia parle d'un week-end qu'elle a passé dans un camping. Complète sa description en mettant les verbes au passé composé ou à l'imparfait. 1.2

Le week-end dernier, je/j'__1__ (faire du camping) avec des amies. Nous __2__ (arriver) à la plage vers deux heures. Il __3__ (faire) très beau. La mer __4__ (être) bleue et claire et nous __5__ (décider) de nous baigner. Nous __6__ (mettre) de la crème solaire et nous __7__ (entrer) dans l'eau. L'eau __8__ (être) très agréable.

1. ai fait 2. sommes arrivées 3. faisait 4. était 5. avons décidé 6. avons mis 7. sommes entrées 8. était

3 Noah pêche avec son père. Qu'est-ce que tu vois? 1.2

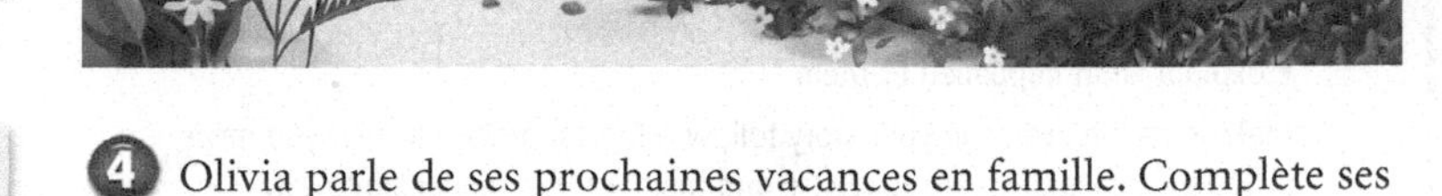

4 Olivia parle de ses prochaines vacances en famille. Complète ses phrases avec le futur d'un verbe de la boîte. 1.2

aller voir partir rentrer faire dormir

Nous __1__ du camping dans la forêt. Nous y __2__ beaucoup de choses intéressantes. Mes parents __3__ à la pêche. Nous __4__ sous une tente. Nous __5__ le 5 juillet et nous __6__ à la maison le 10 juillet. Et ta famille et toi, où __7__-vous en vacances?

Preparing for the Exam

FOLD-N-LEARN

Flap Booklet Study Aid

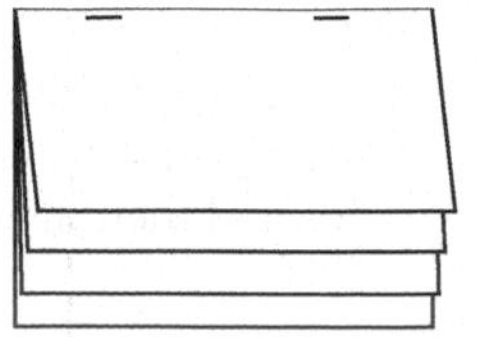

1. Have students lay one sheet of paper on top of another and slide the top sheet up so that one inch of the bottom sheet is showing. They should fold down the top of each sheet so that they have three one-inch flaps underneath the top sheet.
2. On the top page, have students write **En plein air.** On the three one-inch tabs below ask them to write **On fait du camping, La nature,** and **Les activités.**
3. Have students write all the French words and expressions in this chapter under each category on all three pages of the booklet. On the back of each page, they should write the English equivalent for each French expression.
4. Have students review the chapter expressions with the flap booklets they have created.

Online Assessment
my.hrw.com
Chapter Self-test

5 Réponds aux questions suivantes. 2.1, 2.2

1. Comment sont les campements au Sénégal?
2. Quels sont des sports nautiques populaires au Sénégal?
3. Comment est-ce que l'océan influence la vie des Sénégalais?

5 Culture
- Flash culture pp. 236, 240, 249, 252
- Comparaisons pp. 244–245

6 Jérôme raconte son week-end en forêt à Philippe. Écoute leur conversation et complète les phrases qui suivent. CD 7, Tr. 10 1.2

1. Vendredi, Jérôme et ses amis n'ont pas pu faire un feu de camp parce qu'il pleuvait.
2. Ils ont voulu faire du vélo mais ils n'ont pas pu à cause de la pluie.
3. Samedi, il a fait beau et ils sont allés à la pêche.
4. Jérôme n'a rien attrapé. Mais Thomas a attrapé trois poissons.
5. Les garçons ont eu peur quand un serpent a traversé le sentier. Ils ont couru et Thomas a perdu ses poissons.

7 Ton/Ta camarade et toi avez fait du camping le week-end dernier. Vous racontez votre aventure à un(e) autre camarade. Ajoutez *(add)* des détails terrifiants pour impressionner votre ami(e). D'abord, lisez les instructions pour chaque réplique *(exchange)*. Ensuite, créez votre dialogue en utilisant des expressions que vous avez apprises. 1.1

Élève A:	Dis que vous êtes allé(e)s faire du camping et où vous êtes allé(e)s.
Élève B:	Dis ce que vous faisiez quand quelque chose est arrivé.
Élève A:	Ajoute un détail à l'histoire.
Élève B:	Parle de quelque chose d'autre qui s'est passé.
Élève A:	Ajoute un autre détail à l'histoire.
Élève B:	Parle d'autre chose qui s'est passé pendant une action.
Élève A:	Finis l'histoire de votre aventure.
Élève B:	Dis ce que vous ferez la prochaine fois.

Prépare-toi pour l'examen

Prépare-toi pour l'examen

4 Answers
1. ferons
2. verrons
3. iront
4. dormirons
5. partirons
6. rentrerons
7. irez

5 Answers
1. Il y a souvent des bungalows à louer ou des tentes.
2. la voile, la plongée sous-marine, le jet-ski, le ski nautique, le surf
3. La pêche est l'industrie la plus importante.

6 Script
See script on p. 231F.

7 Sample conversation:

a. **Alex et moi, nous sommes allé(e)s faire du camping en forêt!**
b. **Figure-toi qu'au moment où on montait la tante, j'ai vu un serpent.**
a. **Heureusement, il est parti dans la forêt.**
b. **À ce moment-là, on a vu une grande toile d'araignée.**
a. **Alors, on a monté la tante loin de la toile d'araignée.**
b. **J'étais sur le point d'allumer un feu quand il a commencé à pleuvoir.**
a. **Bref, on a passé la journée dans la tante!**
b. **La prochaine fois, on ira à l'hôtel!**

Additional Speaking Practice
- For additional speaking practice, you might use the *Picture Sequences Transparency* for Chapter 7 found in the *Projectable Transparencies.*
- To assess the speaking activities in this section, you might use the *Generate Success* Rubric Generator or the oral rubrics found in the *Assessment Program.*

Pre-AP Practice
7 This guided conversation activity helps students practice oral exchanges using material from this chapter and previous chapters. The activity helps prepare students for the **Interpersonal Speaking** section of the AP French Language and Culture Exam.

Chapitre 7

Prépare-toi pour l'examen

Grammar Review

For more practice with the grammar topics in this chapter, see the *Grammar Tutor*, the *DVD Tutor*, the *@HomeTutor*, or the *Cahier de vocabulaire et grammaire*.

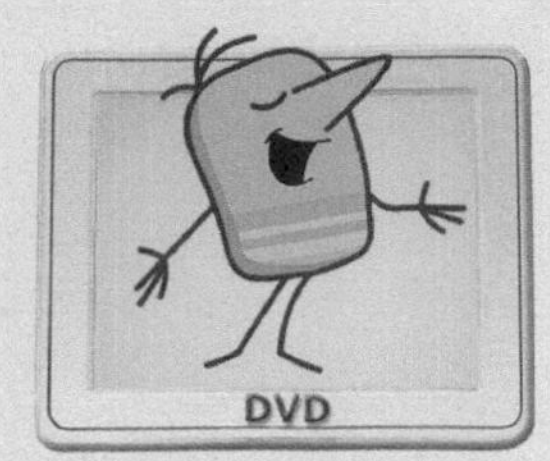

Grammavision

Online Edition

Students might use the online textbook and Performance Space to practice the **Lettres et sons** feature.

Dictée Script

1. Mets le désinfectant dans la trousse de premiers soins.
2. La prochaine fois, je vais me promener dans les bois.
3. Le serpent a traversé le sentier.
4. L'oiseau se baigne dans la piscine!
5. Ma sœur est souvent paresseuse.

Teacher to Teacher

Todd Losié
Renaissance High School
Detroit, MI

To practice the **passé composé** and the **imparfait,** I show students a short video segment. Have half the class take notes about what the scene and people looked like **(imparfait),** and have the other half take notes on the actions they observed **(passé composé).** Students should write eight to ten sentences on their observations. Pair an **"imparfait** student" with a **"passé composé** student" and have them write a summary of the video segment. 1.3

Grammaire 1
- the **passé composé** and the **imparfait**
- **être en train de**

Un peu plus
- verbs with **être** or **avoir** in the **passé composé**

pp. 238–243

Résumé: Grammaire 1

Use the **imparfait** to give background information, set the scene, and tell what someone used to do repeatedly.

Use the **passé composé** to tell what happened on a specific occasion and to tell the order of past events.

À ce moment-là, j'ai entendu un bruit.

Use **être en train de** to tell what someone is or was doing at a specific time.

Use **être** as the helping verb with the verbs **sortir, passer, monter,** and **descendre** and make the past participle agree with the subject. However, if there is a direct object, use **avoir.** With **avoir,** the past participle agrees with a preceding direct object, never the subject.

Elle **est** sortie de la tente. *(no direct object)*
Elle **a** sorti la gourde de la tente. *(direct object)*
Elle **l'a** sortie de la tente. *(direct object precedes the verb)*

Grammaire 2
- the future
- the future of irregular verbs

Un peu plus
- the verb **courir**

pp. 250–255

Résumé: Grammaire 2

To form the future, add **-ai, -as, -a, -ons, -ez,** or **-ont** to the future stem. Some verbs with irregular stems in the future tense are found on page 252.

The verb **courir** *(to run)* is irregular. The past participle of this verb is **couru,** and the future stem is **courr-.**

courir *(to run)*			
je	**cours**	nous	**courons**
tu	**cours**	vous	**courez**
il/elle/on	**court**	ils/elles	**courent**

Lettres et sons

La lettre s CD 7, Tr. 11–13

As you learned in Level 1, the letter **s** can be pronounced either as **s** or z in French. If the letter **s** appears between two vowels, like in **oiseau,** you will hear the **z** sound. If the letter **s** is doubled, as in **poisson,** you use the **s** sound. If it appears at the end of a word, like in **le bois,** you do not pronounce the **s**.

Jeux de langue

—Bonjour Madame Sans-Souci. Combien sont ces soucis-ci?
—Six sous, ces soucis-ci.
—Six sous?! C'est trop cher, Madame Sans-Souci. Et l'oiseau?

Dictée 1.2

Écris les phrases de la dictée.

Chapter Review

DVD Program

Online Edition

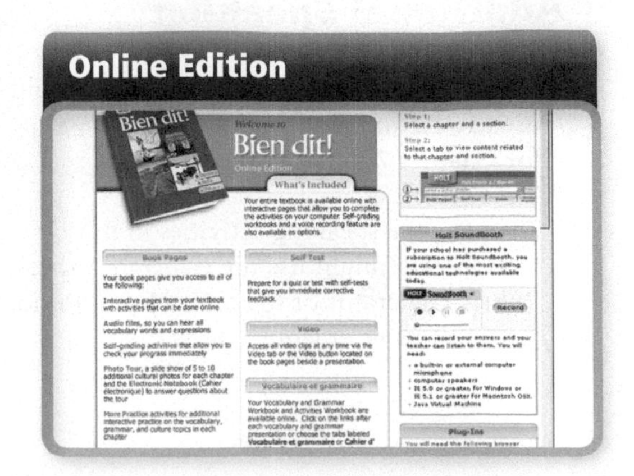

Prépare-toi pour l'examen

Résumé: Vocabulaire 1

PRACTICE FRENCH WITH HOLT MCDOUGAL APPS!

To say what happened

un allume-gaz	*gas lighter*
allumer	*to light*
la boîte d'allumettes	*box of matches*
la boîte de conserve	*can of food*
la boussole	*compass*
la bouteille isotherme	*thermos*
le briquet	*lighter*
camper	*to camp out*
le camping	*camping*
la crème solaire	*sunscreen*
démonter la tente	*to take down the tent*
le désinfectant	*disinfectant*
faire un feu de camp	*to make a campfire*
le fauteuil pliant	*folding chair*
la gourde	*canteen*
la lampe de poche	*flashlight*
la lanterne	*lantern*
la lotion anti-moustiques	*mosquito repellent*
monter la tente	*to pitch a tent*
la moustiquaire	*mosquito net*
un ouvre-boîte	*can opener*
le réchaud	*camping stove*
un sac de couchage	*sleeping bag*
la trousse de premiers soins	*first-aid kit*
le terrain de camping	*campground*
à ce moment-là	*at that moment*
bref	*in short*
Figure-toi que...	*Imagine that . . .*
heureusement	*fortunately*

To describe circumstances

au moment où	*at the time (when) / as*
J'étais en train de...	*I was in the middle of . . .*
Je venais de (d')...	*I had just . . .*
sur le point de	*about to*

Résumé: Vocabulaire 2

To tell what you will do

aller à la pêche	*to go fishing*
l'araignée (f.)	*spider*
l'arbre (m.)	*tree*
attraper un poisson	*to catch a fish*
se baigner	*to swim*
le bois	*woods*
le flamant rose	*flamingo*
la fleur	*flower*
le fleuve	*river (bigger)*
la forêt	*forest*
la grenouille	*frog*
l'insecte (m.)	*insect*
le lézard	*lizard*
la mouche	*fly*
le moustique	*mosquito*
la nature	*nature*
l'oiseau (m.)	*bird*
le pélican	*pelican*
se promener	*to take a stroll*
la rivière	*river (smaller)*
le sentier	*path*
le serpent	*snake*
la toile d'araignée	*spider web*
la tortue	*turtle*
après-demain	*day after tomorrow*
bientôt	*soon*
la prochaine fois	*next time*
prochain(e)	*next*
tout à l'heure	*later (today)*

To wonder what will happen

Est-ce qu'il va y avoir... ?	*Is there going to be . . . ?*
Est-ce que tu sais si... ?	*Do you know if . . . ?*
Je me demande si... ?	*I wonder if . . . ?*
Tu crois que (qu')... ?	*Do you think that . . . ?*

Holt McDougal French Apps

Remind students that they can use the Holt McDougal French Apps to review their vocabulary.

Projectable Transparency

Situation En forêt 7

More Digital Resources

FOR THE STUDENT

Holt McDougal French Apps
@HomeTutor
News and Networking
Performance Space

FOR THE TEACHER

- Interactive Whiteboard Lessons
- Generate Success!

Assess

Assessment Program

Examen: Chapitre 7

Audio CD 7, Tr. 17–18

Examen oral: Chapitre 7

Alternative Assessment

Differentiated Practice and Assessment CD-ROM

Online Assessment
my.hrw.com

Test Generator 

Révisions cumulatives

Resources

Planning:
Lesson Planner
Teacher One Stop

Practice:
Cahier d'activités
Media Guide
Projectable Transparencies
Fine Art, Chapter 7
Audio CD 7, Tr. 14

Holt McDougal French Apps

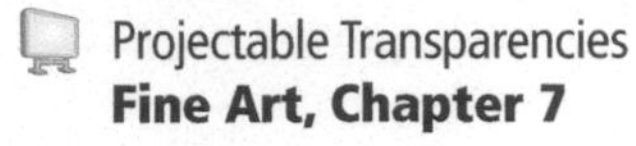

1 Script

1. Je n'arrive pas à allumer ce feu. Tu n'as pas de briquet?
2. Aïe! Je me suis coupé la main. Elle est où, la trousse de premiers soins?
3. Regarde les beaux poissons que j'ai attrapés ce matin. Allume le feu et je les ferai cuire.
4. Alors, c'est fait. Nous avons monté la tente et trouvé les sacs de couchage. Et voilà la lampe de poche. Tout est prêt pour la nuit.

2 Answers

1. entre mars et mai; on aura la meilleure possibilité de voir des animaux
2. en train ou en avion
3. Ils peuvent voir des animaux.
4. Ils sont menacés par l'extinction.

Révisions cumulatives

1 Des amis font du camping. Pour chaque phrase, décide si **a) les choses vont bien** ou **b) les choses ne vont pas bien.** CD 7, Tr. 14
1. b 2. b 3. a 4. a
1.2

2 Lis cet article sur le parc naturel Niokolo-Koba au Sénégal et réponds aux questions qui suivent. 1.2

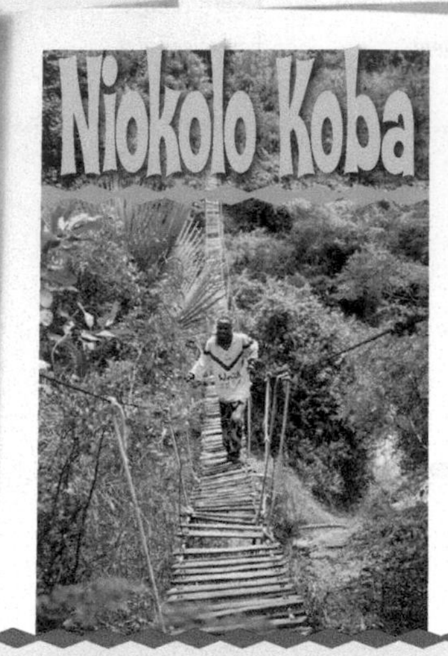

Le parc naturel Niokolo Koba, situé au sud-est de Dakar, est l'une des réserves d'animaux les plus importantes de l'Afrique. Nous vous conseillons de le visiter entre mars et mai, quand, malgré la chaleur, vous aurez la meilleure possibilité de voir des animaux. Le point de départ des excursions est Tambacounda. Vous pourrez y aller en train ou en avion de Dakar. Dans la région, vous trouverez tout ce dont vous aurez besoin: campements, hôtels, voitures de tourisme à louer, guides...

Tout le parc est accessible au touriste. À part les éléphants, les panthères et les chimpanzés, menacés par l'extinction et aujourd'hui rares dans le parc, vous verrez de tout: des hippopotames, des lions, des antilopes, des gazelles, des crocodiles, des hyènes, des buffles...

1. Pendant quels mois est-ce que l'auteur vous conseille de visiter le parc? Pourquoi?
2. Comment est-ce que les touristes peuvent aller au parc?
3. Qu'est-ce que les touristes peuvent faire dans le parc?
4. Pourquoi est-ce que les éléphants, les panthères et les chimpanzés y sont rares?

Online Culture Project

Have students do a Web search for facts about the geography of Senegal. Ask them to describe Senegal in a two-minute Power Point® slide show. They should include five slides with information about Senegal's geographic features. The captions should include the location and name of each geographic feature, large cities in the area, agricultural products that are grown there, and the kinds of animals that might be found there. Have students document the names and URLs of the sites they consulted. 1.3, 3.2

Online Assessment
my.hrw.com
Cumulative Self-test

3 Avec deux amis, imaginez que l'été prochain, vous irez passer un mois en Afrique et vous visiterez une réserve naturelle. Faites des projets. Décidez ce que vous emporterez et ce que vous ferez. Utilisez le futur. Après, parlez de vos projets à la classe. 1.1

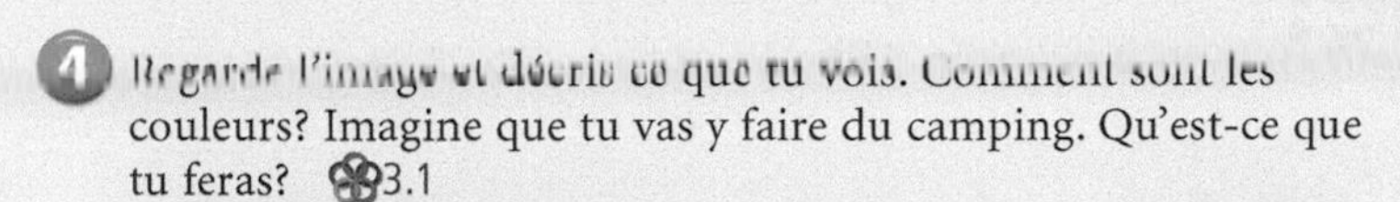
4 Regarde l'image et décris ce que tu vois. Comment sont les couleurs? Imagine que tu vas y faire du camping. Qu'est-ce que tu feras? 3.1

Metzinger, Jean (1883-1956) © ARS, NY. Colorful landscape with aquatic birds. Musée d'Art Moderne de la Ville de Paris, Paris, France.

de Jean Metzinger

5 Un(e) ami(e) français(e) veut faire du camping avec toi. Écris-lui un e-mail. Explique-lui pourquoi tu aimes ou tu n'aimes pas faire du camping. 1.3

6 **À ton tour**

Bulletin du lycée Your class is going to create a newsletter about what will happen this month at your school. Work in small groups and have each group write about a different topic, such as school events, games, field trips to local parks, and so on. Then put all your material together to form the newsletter. When you are finished, post the newsletter on your school web site. You might work with students taking other languages in your school to do the same. 1.3

ACTFL Performance Standards

The activities in Chapter 7 target the communicative modes as described in the Standards.

Interpersonal	Two-way communication using receptive skills and productive skills	**Communication (SE),** pp. 237, 239, 241, 243, 249, 251, 253, 255 **Communication (TE),** pp. 243, 249, 251, 253, 255
Interpretive	One-way communication using receptive skills	**Comparaisons,** p. 245 **Communication (SE),** p. 255 **Télé-roman,** pp. 256–257
Presentational	One-way communication using productive skills	**Communication (TE),** pp. 237, 239, 241 **À ton tour,** p. 267

Fine Art Connection

Introduction Jean Metzinger was born in Nantes in 1883. Although he is known mainly for his Cubist paintings, Metzinger first experimented with Neo-Impressionism and Fauvism. The painting on this page is typical of the works he painted in the years following his arrival in Paris in 1903, when Henri Matisse and the Fauvist movement were most popular. Fauvists commonly used bright colors and simplified lines to express their pleasure of experiencing nature.

Analyzing

To help students discuss the painting, you might use the following questions.

1. **Quels types de paysages est-ce qu'on voit sur ce tableau?**
2. **Quels animaux est-ce qu'il y a? Combien est-ce qu'on en voit?**
3. **Est-ce qu'il y a aussi des personnes?**
4. **Est-ce que tu penses que ce tableau est réaliste? Pourquoi ou pourquoi pas?**
5. **Est-ce que tu crois que Jean Metzinger aimait ce paysage?** 3.1

Extension

Ask students to download Fauvist paintings of landscapes from the Internet and to bring printouts to class. Are they all as harmonious as Jean Metzinger's painting? What do students think of the colors that were used? What emotions was each artist trying to express? As an interesting comparison, some students may also want to present pictures of Metzinger's later Cubist works. 2.2, 3.1

chapitre 8

Planning Guide

Es-tu en forme?

Chapter Section		Resources
Vocabulaire 1 • Parts of the body, illnesses and injuries **Grammaire 1** • The subjunctive **Application 1** • **Un peu plus:** More expressions with the subjunctive	pp. 270–273 pp. 274–277 pp. 278–279	Projectable Transparencies: Vocabulaire 8.1, 8.2; Bell Work 8.1, 8.2, 8.3, 8.4 Cahier de vocabulaire et grammaire, pp. 85–90 Grammar Tutor for Students of French Cahier d'activités, pp. 71–73 Media Guide, pp. 29–32, 94–96 **Assessment Program** Quiz: Vocabulaire 1, pp. 217–218 Quiz: Grammaire 1, pp. 219–220 Quiz: Application 1, pp. 221–222
Culture • **Culture appliquée: L'awalé** • **Comparaisons et Communauté**	pp. 280–281	Cahier d'activités, p. 74
Vocabulaire 2 • Healthful life style **Grammaire 2** • The conditional • **Si** clauses French InterActive Reader **Application 2** • **Un peu plus:** The conditional to make polite requests	pp. 282–285 pp. 286–289 pp. 290–291	Projectable Transparencies: Vocabulaire 8.3, 8.4; Bell Work 8.5, 8.6,8.7, 8.8 Cahier de vocabulaire et grammaire, pp. 91–96 Grammar Tutor for Students of French, Cahier d'activités, pp. 75–77 Media Guide, pp. 29–32, 94–95, 97 **Assessment Program** Quiz: Vocabulaire 2, pp. 223–224 Quiz: Grammaire 2, pp. 225–226 Quiz: Application 2, pp. 227–228
Télé-roman	pp. 292–293	Media Guide, pp. 95, 98
Lecture et écriture	pp. 294–297	Cahier d'activités, p. 78 Reading Strategies and Skills Handbook Intermediate Reader French InterActive Reader **Assessment Program** Quiz: Lecture, p. 229 Quiz: Écriture, p. 230
Prépare-toi pour l'examen • **Résumé de vocabulaire et grammaire** • **Lettres et sons** **Révisions cumulatives**	pp. 298–301 pp. 302–303	Independent Study Guide, pp. 22–24, 40 Media Guide, p. 32 **Assessment Program** Examen: Chapitre 8, pp. 231–236 Examen oral: Chapitre 8, p. 324 Projectable Transparencies: Fine Art, Ch. 8 Cahier d'activités, pp. 74, 79–80
Variations littéraires • **La mendiante et l'écolière**	pp. 396–397	Reading Strategies and Skills Handbook Intermediate Reader French InterActive Reader

Planning Guide

Visit Us Online

my.hrw.com
Online Edition

Pacing Suggestions

	Essential	Recommended	Optional
Vocabulaire 1 • Parts of the body, illnesses and injuries • **Flash culture**	✔		
Grammaire 1 • The subjunctive • **Flash culture**	✔		
Application 1 • **Un peu plus:** More expressions with subjunctive	✔		
Culture • **Culture appliquée: L'awalé** • **Comparaisons et Communauté**		✔	
Vocabulaire 2 • Healthful life style • **Flash culture**	✔		
Grammaire 2 • The conditional • **Si** clauses • **Flash culture**	✔		
Application 2 • **Un peu plus:** The conditional to make polite requests	✔		
Télé-roman • Épisode 8: **Le Secret de la statuette**			✔
Lecture et écriture • **Mange bien!** (Lecture) • **Je lui ai dit, «Tu ferais bien de te reposer».** (Écriture)		✔	
Prépare-toi pour l'examen		✔	
Révisions cumulatives			✔
Variations littéraires • **La mendiante et l'écolière**			✔

Technology

Bien dit! Online
- Student Edition with multi-media
- **performance space** recording tool
- Interactive activities with feedback
- Self-tests with feedback
- Cahier d'activités (Interactive workbook)
- Cahier de vocabulaire et grammaire (Interactive workbook)
- Holt Online Assessment

DVD Tutor
- Télé-vocab
- Grammavision
- Télé-roman

HOMETUTOR
- Interactive games
- Differentiated Practice
- Cultural video

Audio Program
- Student Edition listening activities
- Assessment listening activities
- Songs

Teacher One Stop™
- Complete resources
- ExamView Pro Test Generator
- Holt Calendar Planner

Holt McDougal Apps

Interactive Whiteboard Lessons

Differentiated Practice and Assessment CD

For slower pace and advanced learner options, see the Differentiated Practice and Assessment CD.

Projects

Grading the project

Suggested point distribution (100 points total)

Originality/design	20 pts.
Written captions	20 pts.
Oral presentation	30 pts.
Language use	30 pts.

e-community

e-mail forum:

Location: http://french

Post the following questions on the classroom e-mail forum:

Est-ce que tu t'es déjà cassé le bras?

Qu'est-ce que tu fais pour être en bonne forme? 5.1

All students will contribute to the list and then share the items.

Le plan de bonne santé

Students will put together a fitness program to be advertised by a fictitious health center. In groups, they develop a welcome letter for new members, an outline of an exercise program, a handout of nutritional information, and a brief description of two seminars to be offered. 1.3

Suggested Sequence

1. Form groups of four and have students make an outline of what to include in their program. You may want to provide magazines or advertisements for ideas.
2. Students conduct Internet and/or library research to gather information. Encourage them to make their program appealing to potential clients and to use realia for each part of their program.
3. Each group prepares a rough draft of its program and gives it to another group to peer-edit. Peer editors should check spelling, grammar, and correct usage of French.
4. Students finalize their program, either as a poster or a brochure.
5. Have groups present their project to the class and ask students which health center they would most likely attend.

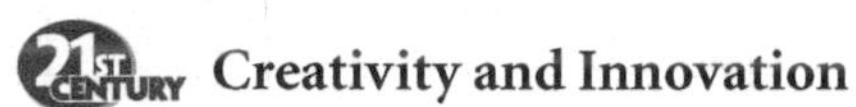

21st Century **Creativity and Innovation**

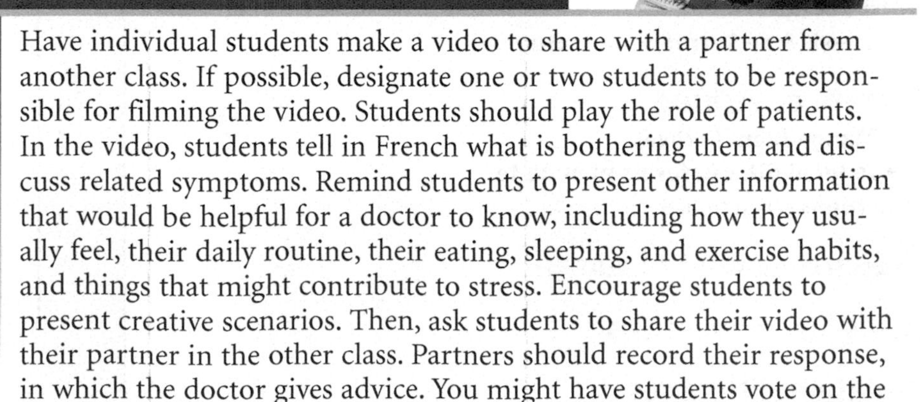

Partner Class Project

Have individual students make a video to share with a partner from another class. If possible, designate one or two students to be responsible for filming the video. Students should play the role of patients. In the video, students tell in French what is bothering them and discuss related symptoms. Remind students to present other information that would be helpful for a doctor to know, including how they usually feel, their daily routine, their eating, sleeping, and exercise habits, and things that might contribute to stress. Encourage students to present creative scenarios. Then, ask students to share their video with their partner in the other class. Partners should record their response, in which the doctor gives advice. You might have students vote on the most creative scenarios. 1.3

21st Century **Technology Literacy**

Game Bank

For game ideas, see pages T60–T63.

La lutte sénégalaise

La lutte sénégalaise is a traditional wrestling match and a national sporting event that sparks passion throughout **Sénégal.** Following a series of highly regulated matches, a winner is determined. Originally performed during the festivities at the end of harvest, the contest has evolved into a professional, televised spectacle. Many of the traditional ceremonies surrounding the matches have been preserved. Contestants undergo ritual baths, **gris-gris.** To intimidate his opponent, a contestant chants and performs ritual dances, chanting and dancing to the rhythm of a tom-tom according to the ancient rules. Female fans dance during the match, waving scarves to ward off bad luck and to aid in the victory of their favorite contestant. Have students research another sport in **Sénégal** and compare it to **la lutte.** 2.1

La cuisine

Creole cuisine is a blend of traditional French, African, and Indian cooking styles. In addition to this rich heritage, creole dishes utilize ingredients native to the Caribbean region. Encourage students to try this recipe in their foods class or at home for family and friends. 1.2, 2.2

Gâteau créole **pour 6 à 8 personnes**

Garniture
5–6 bananes
1/2 tasse de sucre roux
1/2 tasse de noix de coco râpées
1 cuillère à café de cannelle
1 pincée de sel
1 cuillère à café d'extrait de vanille
le jus d'un citron
1/2 tasse de compote de pommes

Pâte brisée
2 tasses de farine
1/2 tasse de sucre
1/2 tasse de beurre
1 œuf

Pâte brisée
Faire fondre le beurre. Placer la farine dans un grand bol. Faire un puits. Y mettre le sucre et l'œuf. Commencer à mélanger doucement. Ajouter le beurre petit à petit. Faire une boule. Si la boule est trop beurrée, ajouter un peu de farine. Étaler la pâte dans un moule. Faire cuire au four pendant 20 minutes.

Garniture
Mélanger tous les ingrédients sauf les bananes. Étaler la pâte obtenue dans le moule sur la pâte brisée. Éplucher les bananes et les couper en rondelles. Disposer celles-ci dans le moule. Faire cuire au four à 400° F pendant 30 minutes.

Listening Activity Scripts

Vocabulaire à l'œuvre 1

2 p. 272, CD 8, Tr. 1

1. — Qu'est-ce que tu as, Joséphine?
   — Je jouais au foot et je me suis foulé la cheville. Je ne peux pas marcher.
2. — Tu n'a pas bonne mine aujourd'hui, Lucas.
   — Je ne me sens pas très bien. J'ai de la fièvre, je crois.
3. — Fatima, qu'est-ce qui s'est passé?
   — Je faisais une expérience en cours de chimie et je me suis brûlé la main.
4. — Tu as l'air fatigué, Georges.
   — Oui, j'ai mal dormi et je suis très fatigué. Je ne me sens pas bien.
5. — Tu as mauvaise mine, Mélodie.
   — Oui, je crois que je suis malade. Je tousse et j'éternue.
6. — Félix, ça n'a pas l'air d'aller!
   — Je jouais au volley et je suis tombé. Je crois que je me suis cassé la jambe.

Answers to Activity 2
1. b **2.** a **3.** b **4.** a **5.** a **6.** b

Grammaire à l'œuvre 1

8 p. 274, CD 8, Tr. 2

1. Nous ne nous sentons pas très bien. Nous avons mal à la gorge et nous avons beaucoup de fièvre.
2. Mon frère et moi, nous avons tous les deux mal aux dents!
3. Je me suis foulé la cheville en jouant au foot.
4. Je suis tellement fatiguée, mais je n'aime ni les fruits ni les légumes.
5. Notre amie ne peut pas sortir avec nous parce qu'elle est malade.

Answers to Activity 8
1. c **2.** a **3.** d **4.** e **5.** b

Application 1

20 p. 278, CD 8, Tr. 3

1. Corinne n'est pas en forme aujourd'hui. Elle a mal au cœur.
2. Il est important que vous mangiez plus de légumes!
3. Marc, je veux que tu désinfectes ton doigt tout de suite!
4. J'ai mal dormi et ce matin, j'ai de la fièvre et j'ai le nez qui coule.
5. Mon frère est allé chez le médecin parce qu'il avait mal au cou.

Answers to Activity 20
1. b **2.** a **3.** a **4.** b **5.** b

Vocabulaire à l'œuvre 2

24 p. 284, CD 8, Tr. 4

1. — Allô! Ici le docteur Bonne Santé! Quelle est ta question?
   — Je m'appelle Chloé et je suis au régime. Tout ce que je mange, c'est des carottes. Qu'est-ce que vous pensez de ce régime?
   — Chloé, je crois que c'est mauvais comme régime. Les carottes sont bonnes pour la santé, mais tu devrais avoir un régime équilibré.
2. — Le docteur Bonne Santé! Tu t'appelles comment?
   — Je m'appelle Luc. Je suis tout le temps fatigué.
   — À quelle heure est-ce que tu te couches?
   — À minuit.
   — À minuit! Bon, tu n'as qu'à te coucher plus tôt! Il ne faut pas se priver de sommeil.
3. — Allô! Tu parles au docteur Bonne Santé! Ton nom et ta question?
   — Je m'appelle Philippe et j'ai mal partout! Chaque jour je fais deux cents pompes et cinq cents abdominaux. En plus, je fais du jogging pendant deux heures.
   — Philippe, il faut faire de l'exercice, mais trop, c'est trop! Tu ferais bien de faire de l'exercice un jour et de te reposer le jour suivant.
4. — Le docteur Bonne Santé! Quelle est ta question?
   — Je m'appelle, Salima. Ma question, c'est: est-ce que je peux perdre du poids si je mange du beurre, du gâteau, de la glace, de la viande, des frites...
   — À mon avis, non. Il ne faut pas manger trop de matières grasses.
5. — Ici le docteur Bonne Santé! Ton nom et ta question?

Je m'appelle Christophe. Mon chien Médor ne mange que le soir. Alors, je me demande si je devrais sauter le petit-déjeuner et le déjeuner moi aussi.
— Christophe, absolument pas! Il ne faut pas sauter de repas. Il faut manger au mois trois fois par jour.

6. — Le docteur Bonne Santé! Je t'écoute!
— Bonjour, docteur. Je m'appelle Pauline et j'étudie pour le bac. Alors, je suis très stressée! Qu'est-ce que je peux faire pour me relaxer?
— Tu peux faire du yoga, Pauline. C'est un excellent moyen de se relaxer. Mes amis, c'est tout pour aujourd'hui! À demain!

Answers to Activity 24
1. c **2.** b **3.** f **4.** a **5.** d **6.** e

Grammaire à l'œuvre 2

34 p. 288, CD 8, Tr. 5

1. Si on allait faire du yoga aujourd'hui?
2. Si Pauline avait plus de temps, elle préparerait des repas avec des produits biologiques.
3. Si vous voulez perdre du poids, vous devriez manger plus léger!
4. On va aller à la piscine. Si on téléphonait à Margot?
5. Si nous voulions être en forme, nous pourrions faire des pompes.
6. Et si on faisait de la musculation après l'école?

Answers to Activity 34
1. a **2.** b **3.** b **4.** a **5.** b **6.** a

Application 2

39 p. 290, CD 8, Tr. 6

1. Bonjour. Je voudrais savoir ce que je pourrais faire pour perdre du poids. J'ai un régime équilibré et je mange léger.
2. Mes enfants mangent trop de sucre. Vous auriez un conseil?
3. Mon mari consomme trop de matières grasses. Qu'est-ce qu'il pourrait manger s'il voulait avoir un régime plus équilibré?
4. Dans ma famille, nous sommes toujours fatigués mais nous avons un régime équilibré. Qu'est-ce que vous suggéreriez si nous voulions être plus en forme?

Answers will vary.

Prépare-toi pour l'examen

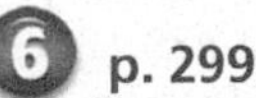

6 p. 299, CD 8, Tr. 9

1. J'ai grossi depuis l'année dernière. Est-ce qu'il faut que je mange plus de matières grasses?
2. Pour maigrir, il faut que je fume et que je saute des repas?
3. Je suis très stressé. Je pense faire du yoga. C'est une bonne idée?
4. J'ai décidé de manger équilibré, de prendre des vitamines et de faire plus d'exercice. Je fais bien, non?

Answers to Activity 6
1. b **2.** b **3.** a **4.** a

Dictée p. 300, CD 8, Tr. 12

1. Hier, ma sœur a eu mal au cœur.
2. Les œufs, c'est bon pour la santé.
3. Il ne faut pas manger trop de bœuf.
4. Chaque année il m'envoie une carte de vœux.
5. Lætícia a deux sœurs.

Révisions cumulatives Chapitres 1-8

1 p. 302, CD 8, Tr. 13

1. Frédéric s'est cassé la jambe en faisant du ski. Tu sais, il n'est vraiment pas sportif.
2. Anne a très mal aux dent. Elle est allée chez le dentiste.
3. Michel s'est fait mal en travaillant à la maison. Il s'est coupé.
4. Pauvre Sophie! Elle a de la fièvre. Où est l'aspirine?

Answers to Activity 1
1. b **2.** a **3.** d **4.** c

chapitre 8

50-Minute Lesson Plans

Es-tu en forme?

50-Minute Lesson Plans

Day 1

OBJECTIVE
Ask and tell how you feel

Core Instruction
Chapter Opener, pp. 268–269
- See Using the Photo, p. 268. **5 min.**
- See Chapter Objectives, p. 268. **5 min.**

Vocabulaire 1, pp. 270–273
- Present **Vocabulaire 1,** pp. 270–271. See Teaching **Vocabulaire,** p. 270. **10 min.**
- Show **Télé-vocab 1. 5 min.**
- Present **Exprimons-nous!,** p. 271. **10 min.**
- Have students do Activity 1, p. 272. **5 min.**
- Play Audio CD 8, Tr. 1 for Activity 2, p. 272. **5 min.**
- Present **Flash culture,** p. 272. **5 min.**

Optional Resources
- Slower Pace Learners, p. 271 ◆
- Multiple Intelligences, p. 271

Homework Suggestions
Cahier de vocabulaire et grammaire, pp. 85–86

1.2, 2.2, 4.2

Day 2

OBJECTIVE
Ask and tell how you feel; Describe symptoms and give advice; Use the subjunctive of regular verbs

Core Instruction
Vocabulaire 1, pp. 270–273
- Have students do Activities 3–5, p. 272. **10 min.**
- See Teaching **Exprimons-nous!,** p. 272. **10 min.**
- Have students do Activities 6–7, p. 273. **20 min.**

Grammaire 1, pp. 274–277
- See Teaching **Grammaire,** p. 274. **5 min.**
- Show **Grammavision 1.1. 5 min.**

Optional Resources
- Advanced Learners, p. 273 ▲
- Special Learning Needs, p. 273 ●

Homework Suggestions
Study for **Quiz: Vocabulaire 1**
Cahier de vocabulaire et grammaire, p. 87
Online Practice (**my.hrw.com**)

1.1, 1.2, 1.3, 5.1

Day 3

OBJECTIVE
Use the subjunctive of regular verbs

Core Instruction
Vocabulaire 1, pp. 270–273
- Review **Vocabulaire 1,** pp. 270–273. **10 min.**
- Give **Quiz: Vocabulaire 1. 20 min.**

Grammaire 1, pp. 274–277
- Play Audio CD 8, Tr. 2 for Activity 8, p. 274. **5 min.**
- Have students do Activities 9–11, p. 275. **15 min.**

Optional Resources
- **Attention!,** p. 275
- Slower Pace Learners, p. 275 ◆
- Multiple Intelligences, p. 275

Homework Suggestions
Cahier de vocabulaire et grammaire, p. 88
Cahier d'activités, p. 71
Online Practice (**my.hrw.com**)
@HOMETUTOR

1.1, 1.2, 1.3

Day 4

OBJECTIVE
Use the subjunctive of regular verbs; Use the subjunctive of irregular verbs; Use more expressions with the subjunctive

Core Instruction
Grammaire 1, pp. 274–277
- Do Activity 12, p. 275. **5 min.**
- Present **Flash culture,** p. 276. **5 min.**
- See Teaching **Grammaire,** p. 276. **5 min.**
- Show **Grammavision 1.2. 5 min.**
- Have students do Activities 13–17, pp. 276–277. **20 min.**

Application 1, pp. 278–279
- Do Activity 18, p. 278. **5 min.**
- See Teaching **Un peu plus,** p. 278. **5 min.**

Optional Resources
- Advanced Learners, p. 277 ▲

Homework Suggestions
Study for **Quiz: Grammaire 1**
Cahier de vocabulaire et grammaire, p. 89
Cahier d'activités, p. 73

1.1, 1.2, 1.3, 4.2

Day 5

OBJECTIVE
Use more expressions with the subjunctive

Core Instruction
Grammaire 1, pp. 274–277
- Review **Grammaire 1,** pp. 274–277. **10 min.**
- Give **Quiz: Grammaire 1. 20 min.**

Application 1, pp. 278–279
- Do Activity 19, p. 278. **5 min.**
- Play Audio CD 8, Tr. 3 for Activity 20, p. 278. **5 min.**
- Have students do Activities 21–23, pp. 278–279. **10 min.**

Optional Resources
- Communication (TE), p. 279
- Slower Pace Learners, p. 279 ◆
- Multiple Intelligences, p. 279

Homework Suggestions
Study for **Quiz: Application 1**
Cahier de vocabulaire et grammaire, p. 90
Cahier d'activités, p. 73
Online Practice (**my.hrw.com**)

1.1, 1.2, 1.3, 3.2

Day 6

OBJECTIVE
Learn about francophone culture

Core Instruction
Application 1, pp. 278–279
- Review **Application 1,** pp. 278–279. **10 min.**
- Give **Quiz: Application 1. 20 min.**

Culture, pp. 280–281
- See **Culture appliquée** (TE), p. 280. **10 min.**
- See **Comparaisons et communauté** (TE), p. 280. **10 min.**

Optional Resources
- Communities, p. 281
- Cultures, p. 281
- Advanced Learners, p. 281 ▲
- Multiple Intelligences, p. 281

Homework Suggestions
Cahier d'activités, p. 74
Online Practice (**my.hrw.com**)
Finish **Culture appliquée** project

1.3, 2.1, 2.2, 4.2, 5.1

Day 7

OBJECTIVE
Complain about health and give advice

Core Instruction
Vocabulaire 2, pp. 282–285
- Do Bell Work 8.5, p. 282. **5 min.**
- Present **Vocabulaire 2,** pp. 282–283. See Teaching **Vocabulaire,** p. 282. **10 min.**
- Show **Télé-vocab 2. 5 min.**
- Present **Exprimons-nous!,** p. 283. **10 min.**
- Play Audio CD 8, Tr. 4 for Activity 24, p. 284. **5 min.**
- Have students do Activities 25–26, p. 284. **10 min.**
- Present **Flash culture,** p. 284. **5 min.**

Optional Resources
- Advanced Learners, p. 283 ▲
- Multiple Intelligences, p. 283
- Slower Pace Learners, p. 285 ◆

Homework Suggestions
Cahier de vocabulaire et grammaire, pp. 91–92

1.2, 1.3, 4.2, 5.2

Day 8

OBJECTIVE
Sympathize with someone; Use the conditional

Core Instruction
Vocabulaire 2, pp. 282–285
- See Teaching **Exprimons-nous!,** p. 284. **15 min.**
- Do Activities 27–28, p. 285. **15 min.**

Grammaire 2, pp. 286–289
- See Teaching **Grammaire,** p. 286. **10 min.**
- Show **Grammavision 2.1. 5 min.**
- Do Activity 29, p. 286. **5 min.**

Optional Resources
- Communication (TE), p. 285
- Special Learning Needs, p. 285 ●

Homework Suggestions
Study for **Quiz: Vocabulaire 2**
Cahier de vocabulaire et grammaire, p. 93
@HOMETUTOR
Online Practice (**my.hrw.com**)

1.1, 1.2

To edit and create your own lesson plans, see the **Teacher One Stop™**

KEY
- ▲ Advanced Learners
- ◆ Slower Pace Learners
- ● Special Learning Needs

50-Minute Lesson Plans

Day 9

OBJECTIVE
Use the conditional

Core Instruction
Vocabulaire 2, pp. 282–285
- Review **Vocabulaire 2,** pp. 282–285. **10 min.**
- Give **Quiz: Vocabulaire 2. 20 min.**

Grammaire 2, pp. 286–289
- Have students do Activities 30–32, p. 287. **20 min.**

Optional Resources
- Communication (TE), p. 287
- Advanced Learners, p. 287 ▲
- Multiple Intelligences, p. 287

Homework Suggestions
Cahier de vocabulaire et grammaire, p. 94
Cahier d'activités, p. 75
@HOMETUTOR
Online Practice (**my.hrw.com**)

1.1, 1.2, 1.3

Day 10

OBJECTIVE
*Use **si** clauses*

Core Instruction
Grammaire 2, pp. 286–289
- Present **Flash culture,** p. 288. **5 min.**
- See Teaching **Grammaire,** p. 288. **5 min.**
- Show **Grammavision 2.2. 5 min.**
- Do Activity 33, p. 288. **5 min.**
- Play Audio CD 8, Tr. 5 for Activity 34, p. 288. **5 min.**
- Have students do Activities 35–38, pp. 288–289. **15 min.**

Application 2, pp. 290–291
- Play Audio CD 8, Tr. 6 for Activity 39, p. 290. **5 min.**
- Do Activity 40, p. 290. **5 min.**

Optional Resources
- Slower Pace Learners, p. 289 ◆

Homework Suggestions
Study for **Quiz: Grammaire 2**
Cahier de vocabulaire et grammaire, p. 95
Cahier d'activités, p. 76

1.1, 1.2, 1.3

Day 11

OBJECTIVE
Use the conditional to make polite requests

Core Instruction
Grammaire 2, pp. 286–289
- Review **Grammaire 2,** pp. 286–289. **10 min.**
- Give **Quiz: Grammaire 2. 20 min.**

Application 2, pp. 290–291
- See Teaching **Un peu plus,** p. 290. **5 min.**
- Have students do Activities 41–44, pp. 290–291. **15 min.**

Optional Resources
- Communication (TE), p. 291
- Advanced Learners, p. 291 ▲
- Multiple Intelligences, p. 291

Homework Suggestions
Study for **Quiz: Application 2**
Cahier de vocabulaire et grammaire, p. 96
Cahier d'activités, p. 77
Online Practice (**my.hrw.com**)

1.1, 1.2, 5.1

Day 12

OBJECTIVE
Develop listening and reading skills

Core Instruction
Application 2, pp. 290–291
- Review **Application 2,** pp. 290–291. **10 min.**
- Give **Quiz: Application 2. 20 min.**

Télé-roman, pp. 292–293
- Show **Télé-roman.** See Teaching **Télé-roman,** p. 292. **5 min.**
- Have students answer the **As-tu compris?** questions, p. 293. **15 min.**

Optional Resources
- Connections, p. 292
- Gestures, p. 292
- Communication (TE), p. 293

Homework Suggestions
Online Practice (**my.hrw.com**)

1.1, 1.2, 1.3

Day 13

OBJECTIVE
Develop listening, reading, and writing skills

Core Instruction
Lecture et écriture, pp. 294–297
- See Teaching **Lecture,** p. 294. **35 min.**
- See Teaching **Espace écriture,** p. 296. **15 min.**

Optional Resources
- Applying the Strategies, p. 294
- Using Background Knowledge, p. 294
- Communities, p. 295
- Connections, p. 295
- Slower Pace Learners, p. 295 ◆
- Special Learning Needs, p. 295 ●
- Process Writing, p. 297

Homework Suggestions
Cahier d'activités, p. 78
Espace écriture, Activity 2, p. 297

1.2, 1.3, 3.1, 5.1

Day 14

OBJECTIVE
Develop writing skills; Review the chapter

Core Instruction
Lecture et écriture, pp. 294–297
- See Teaching **Espace écriture,** p. 296. **25 min.**

Prépare-toi pour l'examen, pp. 298–300
- Have students do Activities 1–5, pp. 298–299. **25 min.**

Optional Resources
- Comparisons, p. 296
- Cultures, p. 296
- Writing Assessment, p. 297
- Advanced Learners, p. 297 ▲
- Special Learning Needs, p. 297 ●
- Fold-N-Learn, p. 298

Homework Suggestions
Online Practice (**my.hrw.com**)

1.2, 1.3, 4.2

Day 15

OBJECTIVE
Review the chapter

Core Instruction
Prépare-toi pour l'examen, pp. 298–300
- Play Audio CD 8, Tr. 9 for Activity 6, p. 299. **5 min.**
- Do Activity 7, p. 299. **5 min.**
- Play Audio CD 8, Tr. 10–12 for **Lettres et sons,** p. 300. **10 min.**

Révisions cumulatives, pp. 302–303
- Play Audio CD 8, Tr. 13 for Activity 1, p. 302. **5 min.**
- Have students do Activities 2–5, pp. 302–303. **25 min.**

Optional Resources
- Reteaching, p. 298
- Game, p. 300
- Online Culture Project, p. 302
- Fine Art Connection, p. 303

Homework Suggestions
Study for Chapter Test
Online Practice (**my.hrw.com**)

1.1, 1.2, 1.3, 2.2

Day 16/Test

Core Instruction
Chapter Test 50 min.

Optional Resources
Assessment Program
- Alternative Assessment
- Test Generator
- **Quiz: Lecture**
- **Quiz: Écriture**

Homework Suggestions
Cahier d'activités, pp. 79–80, 116–117
Online Practice (**my.hrw.com**)

90-Minute Lesson Plans

Es-tu en forme?

Block 1

OBJECTIVE
Ask and tell how you feel; Describe symptoms and give advice

Core Instruction

Chapter Opener, pp. 268–269
- See Using the Photo, p. 268. **5 min.**
- See Chapter Objectives, p. 268. **5 min.**

Vocabulaire 1, pp. 270–273
- Present **Vocabulaire 1,** pp. 270–271. See Teaching **Vocabulaire,** p. 270. **10 min.**
- Show **Télé-vocab 1. 5 min.**
- Present **Exprimons-nous!,** p. 271. **10 min.**
- Have students do Activity 1, p. 272. **5 min.**
- Play Audio CD 8, Tr. 1 for Activity 2, p. 272. **5 min.**
- Have students do Activities 3–5, p. 272. **15 min.**
- Present **Flash culture,** p. 272. **5 min.**
- See Teaching **Exprimons-nous!,** p. 272. **10 min.**
- Have students do Activities 6–7, p. 273. **20 min.**

Optional Resources

- Learning Tips, p. 269
- **Attention!,** p. 270
- TPR, p. 271
- French for Spanish Speakers, p. 271
- Slower Pace Learners, p. 271 ◆
- Multiple Intelligences, p. 271
- Comparisons, p. 272
- Communication (TE), p. 273
- Communities, p. 273
- Advanced Learners, p. 273 ▲
- Special Learning Needs, p. 273 ●

Homework Suggestions

Study for **Quiz: Vocabulaire 1**
Cahier de vocabulaire et grammaire, pp. 85–87
@HOMETUTOR
Online Practice (**my.hrw.com**)
1.1, 1.2, 1.3, 2.2, 4.1, 4.2, 5.1

Block 2

OBJECTIVE
Use the subjunctive of regular verbs; Use the subjunctive of irregular verbs

Core Instruction

Vocabulaire 1, pp. 270–273
- Review **Vocabulaire 1,** pp. 270–273. **10 min.**
- Give **Quiz: Vocabulaire 1. 20 min.**

Grammaire 1, pp. 274–277
- See Teaching **Grammaire,** p. 274. **5 min.**
- Show **Grammavision 1.1. 5 min.**
- Play Audio CD 8, Tr. 2 for Activity 8, p. 274. **5 min.**
- Have students do Activities 9–12, p. 275. **15 min.**
- Present **Flash culture,** p. 276. **5 min.**
- See Teaching **Grammaire,** p. 276. **5 min.**
- Show **Grammavision 1.2. 5 min.**
- Have students do Activities 13–15, pp. 276–277. **15 min.**

Optional Resources

- **Attention!,** p. 275
- Communication (TE), p. 275
- Slower Pace Learners, p. 275 ◆
- Multiple Intelligences, p. 275
- Connections, p. 276
- Teacher to Teacher, p. 277
- Advanced Learners, p. 277 ▲
- Special Learning Needs, p. 277 ●

Homework Suggestions

Study for **Quiz: Grammaire 1**
Cahier de vocabulaire et grammaire, pp. 88–89
Cahier d'activités, pp. 71–72
@HOMETUTOR
Online Practice (**my.hrw.com**)
1.1, 1.2, 1.3, 3.1, 4.2

Block 3

OBJECTIVE
Use the subjunctive of irregular verbs; Use more expressions with the subjunctive; Learn about francophone culture

Core Instruction

Grammaire 1, pp. 274–277
- Have students do Activities 16–17, p. 277. **10 min.**
- Review **Grammaire 1,** pp. 274–277. **10 min.**
- Give **Quiz: Grammaire 1. 20 min.**

Application 1, pp. 278–279
- Have students do Activity 18, p. 278. **5 min.**
- See Teaching **Un peu plus,** p. 278. **5 min.**
- Have students do Activity 19, p. 278. **5 min.**
- Play Audio CD 8, Tr. 3 for Activity 20, p. 278. **5 min.**
- Have students do Activities 21–23, pp. 278–279. **10 min.**

Culture, pp. 280–281
- See **Culture appliquée** (TE), p. 280. **10 min.**
- See **Comparaisons et communauté** (TE), p. 280. **10 min.**

Optional Resources

- Communication (TE), p. 277
- French for Spanish Speakers, p. 279
- Communication (TE), p. 279
- Slower Pace Learners, p. 279 ◆
- Multiple Intelligences, p. 279
- **Vocabulaire supplémentaire,** p. 280
- Bulletin Board Project, p. 280
- Communities, p. 281
- Cultures, p. 281
- Teacher to Teacher, p. 281
- Advanced Learners, p. 281 ▲
- Multiple Intelligences, p. 281

Homework Suggestions

Study for **Quiz: Application 1**
Cahier de vocabulaire et grammaire, p. 90
Cahier d'activités, pp. 73–74
Online Practice (**my.hrw.com**)
Finish **Culture appliquée** project
1.1, 1.2, 1.3, 2.1, 2.2, 3.2, 4.1, 4.2, 5.1

Block 4

OBJECTIVE
Complain about health and give advice; Sympathize with someone

Core Instruction

Application 1, pp. 278–279
- Review **Application 1,** pp. 278–279. **10 min.**
- Give **Quiz: Application 1. 20 min.**

Vocabulaire 2, pp. 282–285
- Present **Vocabulaire 2,** pp. 282–283. See Teaching **Vocabulaire,** p. 282. **10 min.**
- Show **Télé-vocab 2. 5 min.**
- Present **Exprimons-nous!,** p. 283. **5 min.**
- Play Audio CD 8, Tr. 4 for Activity 24, p. 284. **5 min.**
- Have students do Activities 25–26, p. 284. **15 min.**
- Present **Flash culture,** p. 284. **5 min.**
- See Teaching **Exprimons-nous!,** p. 284. **10 min.**
- Have students do Activities 27–28, p. 285. **5 min.**

Optional Resources

- **Proverbes,** p. 282
- TPR, p. 283
- Cultures, p. 283
- Advanced Learners, p. 283 ▲
- Multiple Intelligences, p. 283
- Communication (TE), p. 285
- Communities, p. 285
- Slower Pace Learners, p. 285 ◆
- Special Learning Needs, p. 285 ●

Homework Suggestions

Study for **Quiz: Vocabulaire 2**
Cahier de vocabulaire et grammaire, pp. 91–93
@HOMETUTOR
Online Practice (**my.hrw.com**)
1.1, 1.2, 1.3, 2.1, 4.2, 5.1, 5.2

To edit and create your own lesson plans, see the **Teacher One Stop™**

KEY
- ▲ Advanced Learners
- ◆ Slower Pace Learners
- ● Special Learning Needs

Block 5

OBJECTIVE
Use the conditional; Use ***si*** *clauses*

Core Instruction

Vocabulaire 2, pp. 282–285
- Review **Vocabulaire 2,** pp. 282–285. **10 min.**
- Give **Quiz: Vocabulaire 2. 20 min.**

Grammaire 2, pp. 286–289
- See Teaching **Grammaire,** p. 286. **5 min.**
- Show **Grammavision 2.1. 5 min.**
- Have students do Activities 29–32, pp. 286–287. **15 min.**
- Present **Flash culture,** p. 288. **5 min.**
- See Teaching **Grammaire,** p. 288. **5 min.**
- Show **Grammavision 2.2. 5 min.**
- Have students do Activity 33, p. 288. **5 min.**
- Play Audio CD 8, Tr. 5 for Activity 34, p. 288. **5 min.**
- Have students do Activities 35–36, pp. 288–289. **10 min.**

Optional Resources
- Communities, p. 286
- Communication (TE), p. 287
- Connections, p. 287
- Advanced Learners, p. 287 ▲
- Multiple Intelligences, p. 287
- **Attention!,** p. 288
- Comparisons, p. 289
- Slower Pace Learners, p. 289 ◆
- Special Learning Needs, p. 289 ●

Homework Suggestions
Study for **Quiz: Grammaire 2**
Cahier de vocabulaire et grammaire, pp. 94–95
Cahier d'activités, pp. 75–76
HOMETUTOR
Online Practice (**my.hrw.com**)
1.1, 1.2, 1.3, 3.1, 4.2, 5.1

Block 6

OBJECTIVE
Use ***si*** *clauses; Use the conditional to make polite requests; Develop listening and reading skills*

Core Instruction

Grammaire 2, pp. 286–289
- Have students do Activities 37–38, p. 289. **10 min.**
- Review **Grammaire 2,** pp. 286–289. **10 min.**
- Give **Quiz: Grammaire 2. 20 min.**

Application 2, pp. 290–291
- Play Audio CD 8, Tr. 6 for Activity 39, p. 290. **5 min.**
- Have students do Activity 40, p. 290. **5 min.**
- See Teaching **Un peu plus,** p. 290. **5 min.**
- Have students do Activities 41–44, pp. 290–291. **15 min.**

Télé-roman, pp. 292–293
- Show **Télé-roman.** See Teaching **Télé-roman,** p. 292. **5 min.**
- Have students answer the **As-tu compris?** questions, p. 293. **15 min.**

Optional Resources
- Communication (TE), p. 289
- Communication (TE), p. 291
- Advanced Learners, p. 291 ▲
- Multiple Intelligences, p. 291
- Connections, p. 292
- Gestures, p. 292
- Communication (TE), p. 293

Homework Suggestions
Study for **Quiz: Application 2**
Cahier de vocabulaire et grammaire, p. 96
Cahier d'activités, p. 77
Online Practice (**my.hrw.com**)
1.1, 1.2, 1.3, 5.1

Block 7

OBJECTIVE
Develop listening, reading, and writing skills; Review the chapter

Core Instruction

Application 2, pp. 290–291
- Review **Application 2,** pp. 290–291. **10 min.**
- Give **Quiz: Application 2. 20 min.**

Lecture et écriture, pp. 294–297
- See Teaching **Lecture,** p. 294. **20 min.**
- See Teaching **Espace écriture,** p. 296. **30 min.**

Prépare-toi pour l'examen, pp. 298–300
- Have students do Activities 1–3, p. 298. **10 min.**

Optional Resources
- Applying the Strategies, p. 294
- Using Background Knowledge, p. 294
- Communities, p. 295
- Connections, p. 295
- Slower Pace Learners, p. 295 ◆
- Special Learning Needs, p. 295 ●
- Comparisons, p. 296
- Cultures, p. 296
- Process Writing, p. 297
- Writing Assessment, p. 297
- Advanced Learners, p. 297 ▲
- Special Learning Needs, p. 297 ●
- Fold-N-Learn, p. 298

Homework Suggestions
Study for Chapter Test
Cahier d'activités, p. 78
Espace écriture, Activity 2, p. 297
Online Practice (**my.hrw.com**)
1.2, 1.3, 2.1, 3.1, 4.2, 5.1

Block 8

OBJECTIVE
Review and assess the chapter

Core Instruction

Prépare-toi pour l'examen, pp. 298–300
- Have students do Activities 4–5, p. 299. **5 min.**
- Play Audio CD 8, Tr. 9 for Activity 6, p. 299. **5 min.**
- Have students do Activity 7, p. 299. **5 min.**
- Play Audio CD 8, Tr. 10–12 for **Lettres et sons,** p. 300. **5 min.**

Chapter Test 50 min.

Révisions cumulatives, pp. 302–303
- Play Audio CD 8, Tr. 13 for Activity 1, p. 302. **5 min.**
- Have students do Activities 2–5, pp. 302–303. **15 min.**

Optional Resources
- Reteaching, p. 298
- TPRS, p. 298
- Oral Assessment, p. 299
- Game, p. 300
- Chapter Review, pp. 300–301
- **Proverbes,** p. 301
- Online Culture Project, p. 302
- Fine Art Connection, p. 303

Homework Suggestions
Cahier d'activités, pp. 79–80, 116–117
Online Practice (**my.hrw.com**)
1.1, 1.2, 1.3, 2.1, 2.2, 3.1, 3.2

Chapter Opener

Meeting the National Standards

Communication
Communication, pp. 273, 275, 277, 279, 285, 287, 289, 291
À ton tour, p. 303

Cultures
Flash culture, pp. 272, 276, 284, 288
Comparaisons, p. 281
Practices and Perspectives, pp. 283, 296
Products and Perspectives, p. 281

Connections
Language Arts Link, p. 276
Health Link, pp. 287, 295

Comparisons
Comparaisons, p. 281
Comparing and Contrasting, pp. 272, 289, 296

Communities
Communauté, p. 281
Family Link, p. 285
Community Link, pp. 273, 281, 286
School Link, p. 295

Using the Photo

The Door of the Millennium, inaugurated in 2001 in West Dakar, features three doors of increasing size with a statue of a woman playing the traditional West African side-blown horn. The pedestrian walkway around the monument is **la promenade des lions.** The monument was created by Senegalese architect Pierre Atepa Goudiaby. Have students speculate on the meaning of the three doors in the monument.

 2.2

Vocabulaire supplémentaire

Students might use these terms to discuss the photo.

le pavé *paving stone*
la promenade *walkway*
doré(e) *golden*
la statue *statue*
la trompette *musical horn*

chapitre 8

Es-tu en forme?

Objectifs

In this chapter, you will learn to
- ask and tell how you feel
- describe symptoms and give advice
- complain about health and give advice
- sympathize with someone

And you will use
- the subjunctive
- the conditional
- **si** clauses

Que vois-tu sur la photo?

Où sont ces jeunes?
Qu'est-ce qu'ils font?
Et toi, est-ce que tu fais souvent du jogging? Qu'est-ce que tu fais pour rester en forme *(stay in shape)*?

ACTFL 21st Century Skills

Collaboration:	TE: pp. 267C, 283, 287 (Health Literacy), 291
Critical Thinking and Problem Solving:	TE: pp. 268, 271, 272, 292, 294, 296
Creativity and Innovation:	TE: pp. 267C, 280, 284, 285 (Health Literacy), 296, 300, 303
Information Literacy:	SE: pp. 280, 281; TE: pp. 267C, 267D (Global Awareness), 280, 281, 283, 289, 296, 297, 302
Initiative and Self-Direction:	TE: pp. 269, 287, 283, 286 (Health Literacy)
Leadership and Responsibility:	TE: pp. 273, 281, 283 (Health Literacy), 286, 287, 295

Chapter Opener

DIGITAL FRENCH my.hrw.com
ONLINE STUDENT EDITION with...

performance space
News Networking
@HOMETUTOR

- Audio Resources
- Video Resources

PRACTICE FRENCH WITH HOLT MCDOUGAL APPS!

Des joggers devant la porte du Troisième Millénaire, à Dakar

DIGITAL FRENCH

TEACHER TOOLS
- Interactive Whiteboard Lessons
- Generate Success!

ALSO AVAILABLE...
- Online Workbooks
- French InterActive Reader

FRENCH ON THE GO!
- Performance Space
- Holt McDougal French Apps
- *Bien dit!* eTextbook

Learning Tips

When school is out, students should continue practicing French. In addition to French-language films and radio broadcasts, students can use the materials around them. For example, you may encourage them to explore Web sites in French.

VIDEO OPTIONS

- **Télé-vocab 1**
- **Grammavision 1**
- **Télé-vocab 2**
- **Grammavision 2**
- **Télé-roman**

LISTENING PRACTICE

Language Lab and Classroom Activities

Vocabulaire
Activity 2, p. 272, CD 8, Tr. 1
Télé-vocab 1, p. 270, DVD Tutor
Activity 24, p. 284, CD 8, Tr. 4
Télé-vocab 2, p. 282, DVD Tutor

Grammaire
Activity 8, p. 274, CD 8, Tr. 2
Grammavision 1, pp. 274, 276, DVD Tutor
Activity 34, p. 288, CD 8, Tr. 5
Grammavision 2, pp. 286, 288, DVD Tutor

Application
Activity 20, p. 278, CD 8, Tr. 3
Activity 39, p. 290, CD 8, Tr. 6

Prépare-toi pour l'examen
Activity 6, p. 299, CD 8, Tr. 9

Révisions cumulatives
Activity 1, p. 302, CD 8, Tr. 13

Télé-roman
p. 292, DVD Tutor

Lecture
p. 294, CD 8, Tr. 7

Variations littéraires
p. 396, CD 8, Tr. 8

Lettres et sons
p. 300, CD 8, Tr. 10–12

Resources

Planning:
Lesson Planner
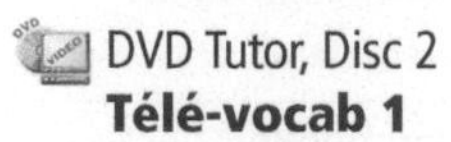 Teacher One Stop

Presentation:
Projectable Transparencies **Vocabulaire 8.1, 8.2**
DVD Tutor, Disc 2 **Télé-vocab 1**
Interactive Whiteboard Lessons

Practice:
Cahier de vocabulaire et grammaire
Differentiated Practice and Assessment CD-ROM
Independent Study Guide
Media Guide
Projectable Transparencies Bell Work 8.1
HOMETUTOR
Holt McDougal French Apps

Bell Work

Use Bell Work 8.1 in the *Projectable Transparencies* or write this activity on the board.

Fill in the blanks with the correct form of the verb **courir.**

1. **Tu viens ____ avec moi?**
2. **Non, hier j'____ avec Jean et je suis fatigué.**
3. **Tu ____ souvent avec lui?**
4. **Oui, nous ____ tous les week-ends.**
5. **Bon, alors cet après-midi, je ____ seul!** 1.2

COMMON ERROR ALERT
ATTENTION !

The question **Qu'est-ce que tu as?** may be interpreted in different ways. Intonation and context may be the only way a student can tell whether this is simply asking what someone has or if it is showing concern by asking the person what is wrong.

Objectifs
- to ask and tell how you feel
- to describe symptoms and give advice

Vocabulaire à l'œuvre 1

Télé-vocab

Le corps

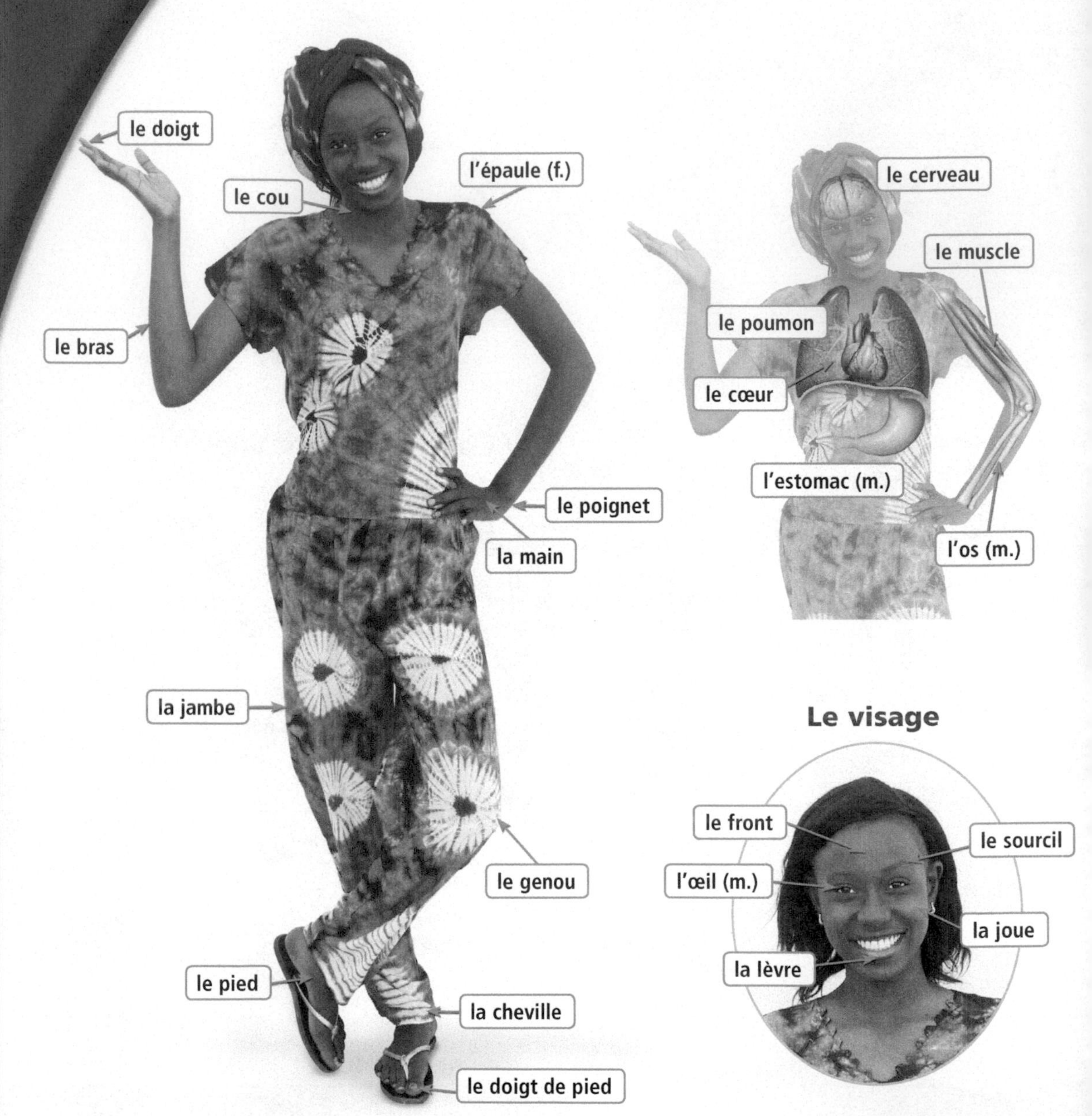

Core Instruction

TEACHING VOCABULAIRE

1. Introduce the vocabulary with transparencies **Vocabulaire 8.1** and **8.2** and model pronunciation. **(2 min.)**
2. Model the expressions in **Exprimons-nous!,** using facial expressions and gestures to help convey meaning. **(3 min.)**
3. Form four groups, each in a corner of the room. Give each group a roll of bathroom tissue. One student in each group will be the "wrappee" and the others will take turns being the "wrapper." Tell them where someone is hurt. **Cet/cette élève a mal au genou.** Each group decides which part should be wrapped. The group with the most correctly wrapped parts wins. **(10 min.)**

Télé-vocab 1

For a video presentation of this vocabulary, see the *DVD Tutor.*

Télé-vocab

Online Practice
my.hrw.com
Vocabulaire 1 practice

Je me suis fait mal.

se fouler le poignet

se casser le pied

Je suis malade.

éternuer

avoir de la fièvre

Déjà vu!
You have already learned several body parts. What do these words mean?
la bouche
la gorge
le nez
les dents
les oreilles
les yeux

D'autres mots utiles

prendre la température	*to take a temperature*	**se brûler**	*to burn oneself*
avoir la grippe	*to have the flu*	**être fatigué(e)**	*to be tired*
tousser	*to cough*	**le dentiste**	*dentist*
se blesser	*to injure oneself*	**le médecin**	*doctor*
		le dos	*back*

Exprimons-nous!

To ask and tell how you feel

Qu'est-ce que tu as? *What's wrong?* **Qu'est-ce qu'il y a?** *What's wrong?*	**Je ne me sens pas bien.** *I don't feel well.* **Je me sens mal.** *I feel sick.*
Ça n'a pas l'air d'aller. *You don't seem to be doing well.* **Tu n'as pas bonne mine** aujourd'hui. *You don't look good . . .* **Tu as mauvaise mine.** *You look bad.*	Non, **je ne suis pas en forme.** *. . ., I'm not in good shape.* Oui, je crois que je suis **malade.** *. . . sick.*
Tu as l'air fatigué(e). *You seem . . .*	Oui, **j'ai mal dormi.** *. . ., I slept badly.*

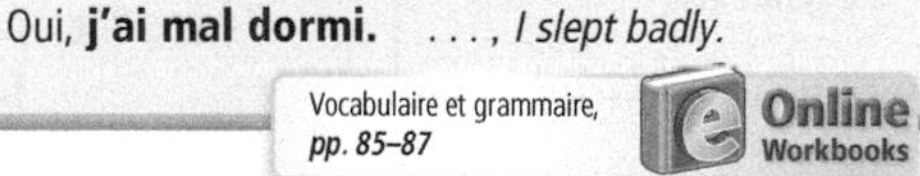

▸ Vocabulaire supplémentaire, Le corps humain, p. R20

Chapitre 8
Vocabulaire 1

TPR
Total Physical Response

Have students respond to these commands.

Mets les doigts **sur** le front **si tu n'as pas** de fièvre.

Montre du doigt ton œil **si tu ne crois pas au Père Noël.**

Lève le bras **si tu as** des muscles.

Mets la main **sur** le cœur.

Touche tes chevilles.

Lève les sourcils **si** tu es **fatigué(e).**

Then have some students mime the following situations for their classmates to guess their ailments.

Tu as mal à l'estomac.

Tu t'es cassé la jambe.

Tu es chez le dentiste.

Tu t'es brûlé(e).

Tu tousses et **tu** éternues.

Tu ne te sens pas très bien.

1.2

French for Spanish Speakers

Ask Spanish speakers to compare the French words for parts of the body with the equivalent words in Spanish. Have them make a list of the cognates that are most similar. (for example, **la main/la mano, le bras/el brazo, le pied/el pie**) Besides having similar spelling, how else are these words alike? (They all share the same gender in both languages.) Which words are most alike in pronunciation? (**le pied/el pie**) Which cognates are pronounced very differently? (possible answer, **le bras/el brazo**) 4.1

Differentiated Instruction

SLOWER PACE LEARNERS

Have students draw a body outline on a sheet of paper and the names of the body parts on individual adhesive notes. Have partners race to see who can be first to place all the notes in the correct position on their body outline. Students should keep the outlines and notes to review the vocabulary. 1.2

MULTIPLE INTELLIGENCES

Bodily-Kinesthetic Bring to class large sheets of butcher paper. Ask partners to trace or draw a life-size outline of a person's body. Have them use markers to label external and internal body parts. You may wish to display the figures in class as references during the chapter activities. 1.2

Vocabulaire 1

Resources

Planning:
Lesson Planner
Teacher One Stop

Presentation:
Projectable Transparencies **Vocabulaire 8.1, 8.2**
DVD Tutor, Disc 2 **Télé-vocab 1**
Interactive Whiteboard Lessons

Practice:
Cahier de vocabulaire et grammaire
Differentiated Practice and Assessment CD-ROM
Independent Study Guide
Media Guide
Audio CD 8, Tr. 1
HOMETUTOR
Holt McDougal French Apps

2 Script

1. — Qu'est-ce que tu as, Joséphine?
— Je jouais au foot et je me suis foulé la cheville. Je ne peux pas marcher.
2. — Tu n'a pas bonne mine aujourd'hui, Lucas.
— Je ne me sens pas très bien. J'ai de la fièvre, je crois.
3. — Fatima, qu'est-ce qui s'est passé?
— Je faisais une expérience en cours de chimie et je me suis brûlé la main.
4. — Tu as l'air fatigué, Georges.
— Oui, j'ai mal dormi et je suis très fatigué. Je ne me sens pas bien.
5. — Tu as mauvaise mine, Mélodie.
— Oui, je crois que je suis malade. Je tousse et j'éternue.
6. — Félix, ça n'a pas l'air d'aller!
— Je jouais au volley et je suis tombé. Je crois que je me suis cassé la jambe.

Comparisons

Comparing and Contrasting

After discussing **Entre copains,** ask students if they know equivalents in English of these slang words in French. What purpose do students think slang words serve in a language? 4.1

Flash culture

Au Sénégal, la population a accès à des soins courants *(routine care)*. L'assurance maladie est obligatoire pour tous les salariés permanents et leurs familles. Comme en France, il y a des centres médicaux privés et publics au niveau local, régional et national.

Est-ce qu'il existe un système d'assurance maladie accessible à tous dans ton état? 4.2

Entre copains

une guibole	*leg*
un panard	*foot*
le bide	*tummy*
un pif	*nose*
ramasser une gamelle	*to fall flat on one's head*

1 L'intrus 1.2

Écrivons Identifie l'expression qui ne va pas avec les autres.

1. la jambe, le genou, (la grippe)
2. se fouler le poignet, se brûler le doigt, (avoir l'air fatigué(e))
3. le cœur, (le front), le poumon
4. (le sourcil), la cheville, le doigt de pied
5. tousser, éternuer, (se blesser)

2 Écoutons CD 8, Tr. 1 1.2

Écoute ces conversations entre l'infirmière et des étudiants. Est-ce que chaque personne **a) est malade** ou **b) s'est fait mal** *(hurt himself/herself)*? **1.** b **2.** a **3.** b **4.** a **5.** a **6.** b

3 Devinettes 1.2 Possible answers:

Écrivons Complète les phrases suivantes logiquement.

1. On dit «à tes souhaits» *(bless you!)* quand tu éternues.
2. Il faut aller chez le dentiste pour se faire soigner *(care for)* les dents.
3. Le médecin prend ma température quand j'ai de la fièvre.
4. Pierre travaille trop et il ne dort pas beaucoup. Alors, il est toujours fatigué.
5. Ne touche pas le four ou tu vas te brûler!

4 J'ai mal à... 1.2

Parlons/Écrivons Qu'est-ce qui te fait mal si...

MODÈLE tu as mangé trop de pizza? **l'estomac** Possible answers:

1. tu as joué au volley-ball toute la journée? les bras
2. tu as dansé jusqu'à minuit? les pieds
3. tu as passé la nuit à étudier? la tête
4. tu es allé(e) chez le dentiste? les dents
5. tu tousses beaucoup? la gorge
6. tu as fait du jogging pendant deux heures? les jambes

5 Je ne suis pas en forme! 1.3

Écrivons Ton/Ta camarade t'a invité(e) à sa fête, mais tu ne vas pas bien de tout! Écris-lui un e-mail et explique-lui comment tu te sens. Demande des conseils.

MODÈLE **Magali,**
Je me sens mal. J'ai mal dormi et...

Core Instruction

TEACHING EXPRIMONS-NOUS!

1. Hand out large note cards to students. Form two groups. Have students in one group each write a description of a different symptom on their card and the other write advice on theirs, including phrases in **D'autres mots utiles.** Remind students to use infinitive phrases rather than the subjunctive. **(5 min.)**
2. One student at a time stands up and shows his or her symptom card as you read it aloud. A student with an advice card that is appropriate stands up and reads it aloud. **(2 min.)**
3. Continue until there are no cards left, or until no one can match the symptom with the advice. **(5 min.)**

Exprimons-nous!

To describe symptoms	To give advice
J'ai mal aux dents/**à la** tête/**à l'**estomac. *I have a(n) . . . ache.*	**Je te conseille de** prendre des comprimés. *I advise you to . . .*
Je me suis coupé le doigt. *I cut my . . .*	**Il est important que** tu le **désinfectes.** *It is important that . . . disinfect . . .*
J'ai le nez qui coule. *I have a runny nose.*	**Il faut que** tu achètes un médicament. *It is necessary that . . .*
J'ai mal au cœur. *I'm nauseated.*	**Tu dois** boire de l'eau **gazeuse.** *You must . . . carbonated*

Vocabulaire et grammaire, *pp. 85–87* Online Workbooks

6 Les premiers soins 1.1

Écrivons Tu joues le rôle d'un(e) malade et tu te plains (*complain*) des maladies représentées. Un(e) ami(e) te donne des conseils. Écris ces conversations.

aller chez le médecin	acheter un médicament	se coucher plus tôt
aller chez le dentiste	prendre un comprimé	boire de l'eau gazeuse

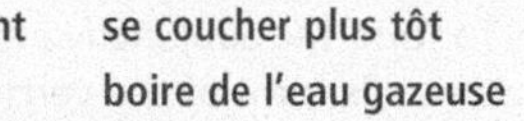

MODÈLE **—J'ai mal à la tête!**
—Je te conseille de prendre un comprimé.

1.

2.

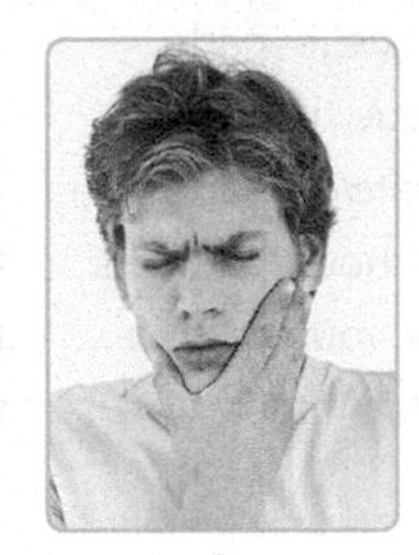
3.

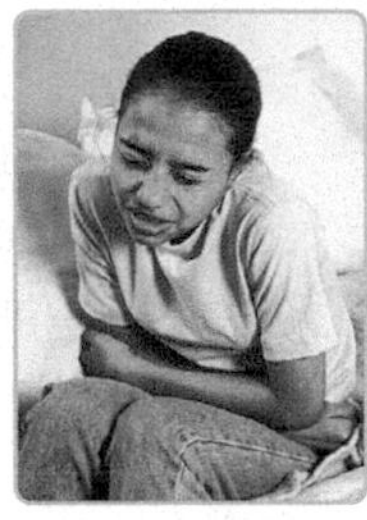
4.

Digital performance space

Communication

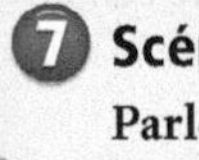

7 Scénario 1.1

Parlons En groupes, jouez cette scène. Toi et ton/ta camarade êtes malades. Vous arrivez à l'infirmerie et il n'y a qu'un lit dans le bureau. Essaie de convaincre l'infirmier(-ère) que c'est toi le/la plus malade. L'infirmier(-ère) vous donne des conseils.

MODÈLE **—Monsieur, je me sens mal. J'ai le nez qui coule...**
—Mais, monsieur, moi aussi, j'ai le nez qui coule et...

Chapitre 8

Vocabulaire 1

6 Possible Answers

1. — J'ai mal à la gorge!
   — Tu dois aller chez le médecin.
2. — J'ai le nez qui coule.
   — Il faut que tu achètes un médicament.
3. — J'ai mal aux dents.
   — Je te conseille d'aller chez le dentiste.
4. — J'ai mal à l'estomac!
   — Tu dois boire de l'eau gazeuse.

Communities

Community Link

Have students choose an African country and research the health challenges currently faced by that country and the names of organizations that are working to meet those challenges. Students might wish to create posters and display them in the community to raise awareness. 5.1

Communication

7 Group Activity: Interpersonal

On a sheet of paper, have students write the description of an imaginary ailment they have. Then have each student ask five classmates what is wrong and write their names and their problems. Then have groups compare answers. 1.1

Differentiated Instruction

ADVANCED LEARNERS

Have students research the names of additional ailments and injuries and prepare a French-English first-aid booklet. You might also have them put together a first-aid kit for the classroom with all the items inside labeled in French. 1.3, 5.1

SPECIAL LEARNING NEEDS

Students with AD(H)D Ask partners to role-play a scene in a medical clinic. They should take the parts of a patient and a doctor or nurse and use as much of the new vocabulary as possible. The medical staff person should ask questions about the patient's well-being and the patient should respond with statements about his or her health problems. The doctor or nurse should then give advice. Have partners switch roles. 1.1

Assess

Assessment Program

Quiz: Vocabulaire 1

Alternative Assessment

Differentiated Practice and Assessment CD-ROM

Online Assessment

my.hrw.com

Test Generator 

Resources

Planning:
Lesson Planner
Teacher One Stop

Presentation:
DVD Tutor, Disc 2
Grammavision 1.1

Practice:
Grammar Tutor for Students of French, Chapter 8
Cahier de vocabulaire et grammaire
Differentiated Practice and Assessment CD-ROM
Cahier d'activités
Independent Study Guide
Media Guide
Projectable Transparencies Bell Work 8.2
Audio CD 8, Tr. 2
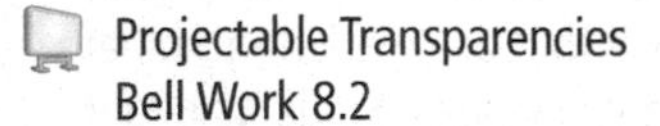

Bell Work

Use Bell Work 8.2 in the *Projectable Transparencies* or write this activity on the board.

Choose a logical ending to complete each sentence.

1. **J'ai pris ma température;...**
2. **J'ai mal dormi, alors...**
3. **Je suis tombé et...**
4. **Je me suis coupé le doigt et...**
5. **J'ai mangé trop de gâteau, alors...**

a. **je me suis foulé la cheville.**
b. **je dois le désinfecter.**
c. **j'ai de la fièvre.**
d. **j'ai mal à l'estomac.**
e. **je suis fatigué.** 1.2

8 Script

See script on p. 267E.

Objectifs
- the subjunctive of regular verbs
- the subjunctive of irregular verbs

Grammavision

The subjunctive of regular verbs

1 The verb tenses you have learned so far, such as the present tense and the **passé composé,** belong to the *indicative* mood. There is another mood called the *subjunctive mood.* In certain situations, you must use the subjunctive.

2 Use the subjunctive with expressions of necessity, such as **il faut que** and **il est important que.** The verb that follows an expression like **il faut que** will be in the subjunctive.

Il faut que vous parliez au médecin.

3 To form the subjunctive of regular verbs, drop the **-ent** of the present-tense **ils** form of the verb and add the following endings.

	parler ils parlent	finir ils finissent	vendre ils vendent
que je	parle	finisse	vende
que tu	parles	finisses	vendes
qu'il/elle/on	parle	finisse	vende
que nous	parlions	finissions	vendions
que vous	parliez	finissiez	vendiez
qu'ils/elles	parlent	finissent	vendent

Il est important qu'elle finisse ses médicaments.

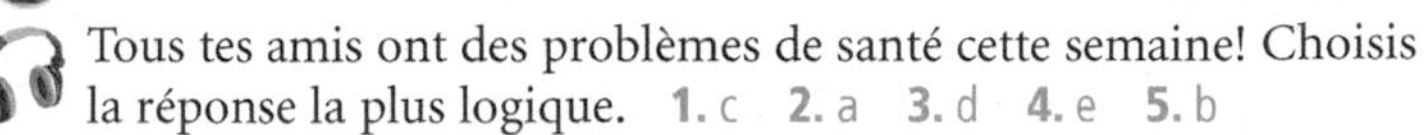

3.1

En anglais

In English, there are different ways to express necessity:

It is important that he get enough sleep!

You must eat right!

In French, if you want to use an expression of necessity, you need to follow the expression with the subjunctive or an infinitive.

Il faut qu'il se couche tôt.

Il faut se coucher tôt.

What is the difference between the two sentences? In what situation do you think that you use a sentence with the infinitive?

The second sentence has an infinitive. You can use an infinitive when you do not have a specific subject in mind.

8 Écoutons CD 8, Tr. 2 1.2

Tous tes amis ont des problèmes de santé cette semaine! Choisis la réponse la plus logique. 1. c 2. a 3. d 4. e 5. b

a. Il faut que vous téléphoniez au dentiste.
b. Il faut qu'elle se couche tôt.
c. Il faut que vous parliez au médecin.
d. Il ne faut pas que tu marches.
e. Il faut que tu manges mieux.

Core Instruction

TEACHING GRAMMAIRE

1. Go over Points 1 and 2. Model examples of sentences with the subjunctive. **(2 min.)**
2. Go over Point 3. Explain that the subjunctive gets its stem from the **ils** form of the verb, with the **-ent** dropped. **(2 min.)**
3. Using regular **-er, -ir,** and **-re** verbs, talk about what it is necessary to do in certain health situations, using as much of the new vocabulary as possible. **Si vous vous coupez la main, il faut que vous vous désinfectiez. Si vous êtes fatigué(s), il est important que vous dormiez plus. (2 min.)**

Grammavision

For a video presentation of the subjunctive of regular verbs, see the *DVD Tutor.*

Grammavision

Online Practice
my.hrw.com
Grammaire 1 practice

9 Souhaits et conseils 1.2

Écrivons Utilise les éléments donnés pour faire des phrases au subjonctif.

1. il faut que / les enfants / se laver / souvent / les mains
2. il est important / que / son fils / manger / des légumes
3. il est important que / nous / parler / au médecin / demain
4. il faut que / tu / finir / toute la soupe
5. il est important que / vous / téléphoner / au dentiste

10 Que faut-il faire? 1.2

Parlons/Écrivons Dis ce que ces personnes doivent faire. Utilise **il faut que (il ne faut pas que)** et le subjonctif dans chaque phrase.

Nathalie

MODÈLE Il faut que Nathalie désinfecte son doigt.

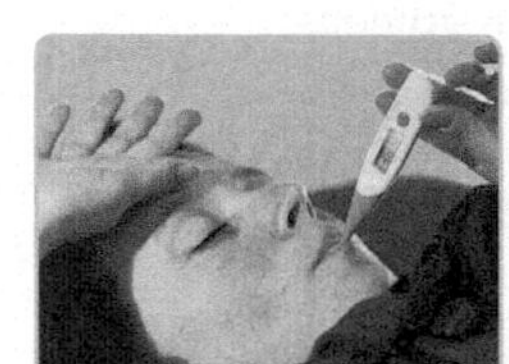
1. Raoul

2. vous

3. je

4. nous

11 Un petit mot 1.3

Écrivons Ton ami Jonathan n'est pas en forme et il est stressé. Écris-lui un petit mot pour lui donner quelques conseils. Utilise **il faut que, il est important que** et le subjonctif.

MODÈLE Il est important que tu manges...

À la québécoise

In Quebec, you might hear the expression **magané** or **abîmé** *(damaged)* to describe someone in poor health.

12 Scénario 1.1

Parlons Marco, un petit garçon, a la grippe. Il demande à ses parents ce qu'il faut faire. Ses parents lui donnent des conseils.

finir les comprimés	manger des fruits	se coucher tôt

MODÈLE —Maman, j'ai mal à la gorge et...
—Il faut que tu te couches....

9 Answers

1. Il faut que les enfants se lavent souvent les mains.
2. Il est important que son fils mange des légumes.
3. Il est important que nous parlions au médecin demain.
4. Il faut que tu finisses toute la soupe.
5. Il est important que vous téléphoniez au dentiste.

10 Possible Answers

1. Il faut que Raoul achète des médicaments.
2. Il faut que vous choisissiez les fruits.
3. Il faut que je téléphone au dentiste.
4. Il faut que nous nous reposions.

COMMON ERROR ALERT
ATTENTION !

Students may need to be reminded that in order for the subjunctive to be used, there must be both a dependent clause and a change of subject. They may say incorrectly, **Je veux que je sois,** instead of simply, **Je veux être.**

Communication

12 Group Activity: Interpretive

Before class, prepare enough index cards for half of the class with a subject pronoun and an expression using a regular verb on one side and on the back, a complete sentence using the prompts. Then have half of the class form a circle, facing out with the cards showing the prompts. The remaining students form an outside circle and use either **Il est important que...** or **Il faut que...** with the subjunctive in response to the prompts. The inside circle verifies the sentence and the outside circle rotates to the left. After finishing the round, both circles exchange places and begin again. 1.2

Differentiated Instruction

SLOWER PACE LEARNERS

To provide daily practice with the subjunctive to express need, label one part of the board "**Il faut que je...**" Each day, have volunteers write on the board their name and one thing they need to do that day after school. Help students with unknown vocabulary words. Use the list to practice the subjunctive forms by asking students what they and their classmates need to do. 1.1

MULTIPLE INTELLIGENCES

10 Visual As an alternative to using the images given in the activity, allow students to create their own illustrations to elicit sentences with **il faut que.** Students may be more motivated to participate in the assignment when allowed to be creative and show their artistic abilities. Have students share their illustrations and sentences with the class. 1.3

Resources

Planning:
Lesson Planner
Teacher One Stop

Presentation:
DVD Tutor, Disc 2
Grammavision 1.2

Practice:
Grammar Tutor for Students of French, Chapter 8
Cahier de vocabulaire et grammaire
Differentiated Practice and Assessment CD-ROM
Cahier d'activités
Independent Study Guide
Media Guide
Projectable Transparencies Bell Work 8.3

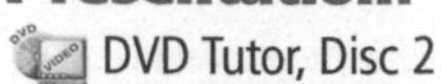

Bell Work

Use Bell Work 8.3 in the *Projectable Transparencies* or write this activity on the board.

Fill in the blanks with the subjunctive of the verbs in parentheses.

Le docteur a dit: Il faut que...

1. **vous ____ (préparer) des repas équillibrés.**
2. **vos enfants ____ (manger) des légumes.**
3. **toi, Astrid, tu ____ (dormir) plus.**
4. **Nicolas ____ (finir) ses comprimés.**
5. **nous ____ (se téléphoner) la semaine prochaine.**

1.2

Connections

Language Arts Link

Ask students what clause to add to correct this sentence grammatically: "She do the job well." ("It is important that she do the job well.") "That clauses" are one of the few situations in English that use the subjunctive. 3.1

The subjunctive of irregular verbs

1 Some verbs, like the ones below, have two stems to which you add the subjunctive endings. The stem for **nous** and **vous** comes from the **nous** form of the present tense. The other stem comes from the **ils/elles** form.

boire	que je **boiv**e	que nous **buv**ions que vous **buv**iez
devoir	que je **doiv**e	que nous **dev**ions que vous **dev**iez
prendre	que je **prenn**e	que nous **pren**ions que vous **pren**iez
venir	que je **vienn**e	que nous **ven**ions que vous **ven**iez
voir	que je **voi**e	que nous **voy**ions que vous **voy**iez

2 These verbs are irregular in all forms of the subjunctive.
Il faut que j'aille chez le docteur.

	aller	être	avoir	faire
que je (j')	aille	sois	aie	fasse
que tu	ailles	sois	aies	fasses
qu'il/elle/on	aille	soit	ait	fasse
que nous	allions	soyons	ayons	fassions
que vous	alliez	soyez	ayez	fassiez
qu'ils/elles	aillent	soient	aient	fassent

Vocabulaire et grammaire, *pp. 88–89*
Cahier d'activités, *pp. 71–73*

Flash culture

Au Sénégal, on peut aller dans une clinique ou dans un hôpital, mais les médecins ne font pas de visite à domicile comme en France. En effet, en France, les médecins font des consultations à domicile si les personnes sont trop malades pour se déplacer. Au Sénégal, on achète les médicaments dans une pharmacie, signalée d'une croix verte.
Est-ce qu'il y a des médecins qui font des consultations à domicile dans ta ville? 4.2

L'Hôpital militaire de Ouakam

13 L'intrus 1.2

Écrivons Pour chaque groupe de verbes, indique quel verbe n'est pas au subjonctif.

1. aies	ayons	(avez)	aient
2. boive	buvions	(buvez)	boives
3. ayons	ayez	aie	(ai)
4. (allez)	ailles	aillent	alliez
5. soient	soyons	(sommes)	sois
6. (allons)	aille	allions	ailles
7. (fais)	fasse	fassions	fassent

Core Instruction

TEACHING GRAMMAIRE

1. Tell students that there are also verbs with irregular forms in the subjunctive. Some have the same stem for all six forms. Some have one stem for the "shoe" and another for the **nous** and **vous** forms, while other forms are all different. Model pronunciation. **(3 min.)**
2. List the nine infinitives on the board. Read aloud sentences with irregular subjunctives. Have students tell you which infinitive you use in each sentence. **(2 min.)**
3. Talk about yourself, using the subjunctive. Tell students what you must do after school today, using all irregular subjunctives. **Il faut que je fasse la lessive. Il est important que j'aille au supermarché. (2 min.)**

Grammavision

For a video presentation of the subjunctive of irregular verbs, see the *DVD Tutor.*

Grammavision

14 Les parents de Pascal et Denis 1.2

Écrivons Les parents de Pascal et Denis parlent de leurs souhaits. Complète les phrases avec le subjonctif du verbe.

1. Plus tard, il faut que vous soyez (être) médecins.
2. Il faut que Denis ait (avoir) de meilleures notes au lycée!
3. Pascal, nous voulons que tu ailles (aller) à l'université.
4. Il faut que vous fassiez (faire) vos devoirs!
5. Il est important que Denis et Pascal aillent (aller) à la bibliothèque plus souvent.
6. Il faut que j'aie (avoir) une conversation sérieuse avec Denis!

15 À faire aujourd'hui 1.3

Parlons/Écrivons Regarde la liste des choses que ta famille doit faire aujourd'hui, puis fais cinq phrases pour dire aux personnes de ton choix ce qu'il faut faire. Utilise le subjonctif et des sujets différents.

Souviens-toi! La famille, pp. 6–7

courses
médicaments
dentiste
chien
gymnase
bibliothèque

MODÈLE **Maman, il faut que tu ailles au supermarché...**

16 De très mauvaises habitudes 1.3

Écrivons Pense à (ou invente) six mauvaises habitudes que ta famille, tes amis et toi avez. Note chaque mauvaise habitude, puis écris ce qu'il faut faire pour la changer. Utilise le subjonctif et des sujets différents.

MODÈLE **Je ne fais jamais de sport. Il faut que je sois plus sportif (sportive).**

Communication

Digital performance space

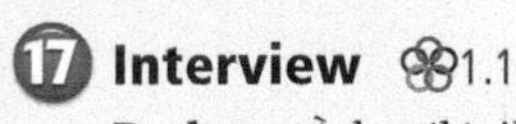

17 Interview 1.1

Parlons À la télé, il y a une nouvelle émission sur la santé. Un médecin donne des conseils: comment rester en forme, que faire quand on est malade, etc. Avec un(e) camarade, inventez une conversation entre l'animateur (animatrice) de l'émission et le médecin. Jouez cette scène pour la classe.

MODÈLE **—Bonjour, Docteur. Je voudrais savoir quels conseils vous avez pour une personne qui n'est pas...**
—Alors, il faut que cette personne soit plus active...

Teacher to Teacher

Dena Hooley
Mt. Vernon City Schools
Mt. Vernon, OH

To teach the subjunctive, I draw a picture of "King Indicative" in his castle. He wants, desires, and commands his subjects. His castle is protected by the moat of **que.** His subjects live in Subjunctiveville. We talk about how requests originate with the King, have an addition of **que,** and then show the reaction of the subjects. I have students tell me this formula for subjunctive sentences: indicative + **que** + subjunctive. 1.2

Communication

17 Group Activity: Presentational

Form groups of four or five to role-play a panel discussion. In each group, assign the roles of moderator and doctors. Have the moderator pose questions about health problems, keeping in shape, and so on, and the doctors take turns giving advice. Have groups present their discussions to the class. 1.3

Differentiated Instruction

ADVANCED LEARNERS

Have students create an exercise verb card for each of the irregular verbs presented in **Grammaire.** For example, one card could have students conjugate the verb **boire** in the subjunctive while doing sit-ups. Place the cards around the room to create exercise/verb stations. In small groups, have students travel from one station to the next and do both the oral and the physical activity. 1.2

SPECIAL LEARNING NEEDS

Students with Auditory/Language Impairments Ensure that students understand the concept of the subjunctive of irregular verbs. Work with a small group or individually with students who may have difficulty understanding the topic. Students who use sign language or have auditory or language impairments may not have a thorough understanding of standard English tenses and will need extra support, examples, and practice to fully comprehend the use of the subjunctive.

Assess

Assessment Program
Quiz: Grammaire 1
Alternative Assessment
Differentiated Practice and Assessment CD-ROM

Online Assessment
my.hrw.com

Test Generator 

Synthèse
- Vocabulaire 1
- Grammaire 1

Application 1

18 Les qualités d'un bon médecin 1.3

Écrivons À ton avis, quelles qualités un bon médecin doit-il avoir? Fais une liste de cinq qualités. Utilise le subjonctif dans tes phrases.

MODÈLE **Il faut qu'il écoute les malades. Il est important...**

Un peu plus

More expressions with the subjunctive

You've used the subjunctive after expressions of necessity **(il faut que, il est important que)**. Another such expression is **il est nécessaire que**.

You also use the subjunctive to express certain requests and with certain emotions.

Je veux que... (Je ne veux pas que...)
Je suis content(e) que...
Je suis triste que...
Il est bon que...

There are more uses with the subjunctive that you will learn about in Level 3.

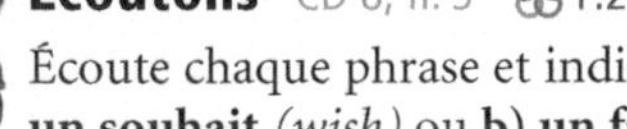

19 Le bon choix 1.2

Lisons Complète les phrases de façon logique.

1. ______ que Marina soit malade.
   (a.) Je suis triste **b.** Il est bon
2. Nous sommes tombés dans le lac. ______ que nous tombions malades!
   a. Je veux (b.) Je ne veux pas
3. Natasha mange des bonbons. ______ qu'elle se brosse les dents.
   a. Il n'est pas bon (b.) Il est nécessaire
4. ______ qu'Alex aille chercher ses médicaments.
   (a.) Il faut **b.** Je suis triste
5. Tu n'es pas en forme. ______ que tu commences à faire plus d'exercice.
   (a.) Il faut **b.** Je ne veux pas

20 Écoutons CD 8, Tr. 3 1.2

Écoute chaque phrase et indique si on exprime **a) une opinion ou un souhait** *(wish)* ou **b) un fait** *(fact)*. **1.** b **2.** a **3.** a **4.** b **5.** b

21 Ma vie 1.3

Parlons/Écrivons Finis chaque phrase en utilisant le subjonctif.

MODÈLE Je suis triste que mon meilleur ami... **n'habite pas dans cette ville.**

1. Mes parents sont contents que je (j')...
2. Il faut que les élèves du cours de français...
3. Il est important que mon/ma petit(e) ami(e)...
4. Je suis content(e) que vous, mes camarades de classe, vous...

Resources

Planning:
Lesson Planner
Teacher One Stop

Practice:
Grammar Tutor for Students of French, Chapter 8
Cahier de vocabulaire et grammaire
Differentiated Practice and Assessment CD-ROM
Cahier d'activités
Independent Study Guide
Media Guide
Projectable Transparencies
Bell Work 8.4
Audio CD 8, Tr. 3

Bell Work

Use Bell Work 8.4 in the *Projectable Transparencies* or write this activity on the board.

Complete the following sentences. Be sure to use the correct subjunctive form of the verb in parentheses.

1. **Il est nécessaire que vous (boire)...**
2. **Il faut que vos amis (venir)...**
3. **Il est important que je (faire)...**
4. **Je voudrais que tu (aller)...**
5. **Nous aimerions qu'il (être)...**
6. **Il faut que nous (avoir)...** 1.2

20 Script

1. Corinne n'est pas en forme aujourd'hui. Elle a mal au cœur.
2. Il est important que vous mangiez plus de légumes!
3. Marc, je veux que tu désinfectes ton doigt tout de suite!
4. J'ai mal dormi et ce matin, j'ai de la fièvre et j'ai le nez qui coule.
5. Mon frère est allé chez le médecin parce qu'il avait mal au cou.

Core Instruction

INTEGRATED PRACTICE

1. Have students do Activity 18 to review vocabulary and the subjunctive. **(10 min.)**
2. Tell the class that your family is very accident prone. Tell what accident each person has had. Then tell what advice you gave. **Ma mère s'est brûlé la main. Maman, il faut que tu fasses attention! Mon frère s'est blessé le genou. (2 min.)**
3. Present **Un peu plus** and then continue with Activities 19–23. **(15 min.)**

TEACHING UN PEU PLUS

1. Remind students that they have used the subjunctive to express necessity and requests and after certain emotions. **(1 min.)**
2. Write the three expressions of necessity plus several emotions and requests on the board. Talk about yourself, the students, or someone they know, varying the expressions and the verbs. **Il est important que vous ayez vos devoirs avec vous. Je suis content(e) que Paul arrive à l'heure. (3 min.)**

Online Practice
my.hrw.com
Application 1 practice

22 Préparatifs de voyage 1.1, 3.2

Lisons/Écrivons Ton/Ta correspondant(e) francophone va aller faire un safari-photo en République centrafricaine. D'abord, lis la brochure que l'agence de voyages lui a donnée. Ensuite, donne des conseils de santé mentionnés dans la brochure à ton/ta correspondant(e).

MODÈLE **Je suis contente que tu ailles faire un safari... Tu sais, il faut que...**

- prenez rendez-vous chez votre médecin avant de partir pour être sûr(e) que vous êtes assez en forme pour faire ce voyage
- préparez-vous bien physiquement (randonnée ou autre sport) pendant plusieurs mois avant de partir
- reposez-vous bien avant le voyage
- ne buvez jamais d'eau non purifiée (achetez toujours de l'eau en bouteille)
- buvez beaucoup d'eau pendant la journée
- lavez-vous souvent les mains
- emportez de la lotion anti-moustiques

Communication

23 Scénario 1.1

Parlons Imagine que toi et ton/ta camarade allez faire un voyage dans un pays tropical. Vous discutez de ce que vous devez faire avant le voyage et de ce que vous pensez faire là-bas. Utilise les éléments de la boîte, ou d'autres idées si tu préfères, et le subjonctif.

avoir un passeport	aller chez le médecin avant de partir
acheter des médicaments	demander un visa
écrire des cartes à nos familles	bien dormir le soir avant le voyage

MODÈLE **—Il est nécessaire que nous ayons des passeports.**
—Oui, et moi, il faut que je demande un visa.

Application 1

French for Spanish Speakers

Ask Spanish speakers if they can think of Spanish equivalents of the expressions in **Un peu plus. (je veux que/quiero que)** Do these expressions take the subjunctive in Spanish? (yes) Ask students why the subjunctive is used after expressions of emotion or requests. (The subjunctive describes situations that may not reflect reality, but rather feelings or desires.) 4.1

Communication

Group Activity: Interpretive
Have each student write a sentence about a bad habit, unhealthful practice, or bad behavior on a sheet of paper. Then in groups, have each student read aloud the sentence he or she wrote and have another student make a request, suggestion, or express an emotion, using the subjunctive that would address the behavior of the reader.

MODÈLE
— Je mange beaucoup de pizza.
— Je veux que tu manges plus de fruits et de légumes et que tu ne choisisses pas de pizza.
1.2

Differentiated Instruction

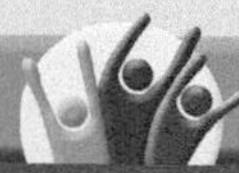

SLOWER PACE LEARNERS

22 Prepare students for the activity by reading the brochure aloud with the class and asking questions about it to check comprehension. Then, as a class, rewrite each piece of advice in the brochure using **Il faut que...** or **Il est nécessaire que...** and the subjunctive. You may wish to keep the sentences on the board for students to refer to as they do **Scénario.** 1.1

MULTIPLE INTELLIGENCES

Interpersonal Ask students to interview their classmates about times they were ill, injured, or were taken to the doctor. Have students translate the scenarios into a short story about the nature of the illness, the visit to the doctor, and the medical advice they were given. Have students share their stories with the class. 1.3

Assess

Assessment Program
Quiz: Application 1
Audio CD 8, Tr. 14
Alternative Assessment
Differentiated Practice and Assessment CD-ROM

Online Assessment
my.hrw.com

Test Generator 

Resources

Planning:
Lesson Planner
Teacher One Stop

Practice:
Cahier d'activités

Vocabulaire supplémentaire

You might wish to use these terms to discuss the project with students.

les fèves (f.)	*beans*
les cailloux (m.)	*pebbles*
les graines (f.)	*seeds*
la rangée	*row*
le trou	*hole*
répartir	*to distribute*
capturer	*to capture*
C'est à toi!	*It's your turn!*
C'est ton tour!	*It's your turn!*
un jeu de société	*boardgame*

Bulletin Board Project

Have groups of students choose one board game to illustrate in French. They should replicate the game board on poster paper, translating into French the directions on all the playing squares. If the game involves instruction cards, groups should translate a representative sample. Have groups exchange and edit their games. Then have groups present their game to the class. Have the class choose the best examples and ask volunteers to post those on a classroom bulletin board. 1.2, 1.3

Language Examination

Culture can be used to practice for the **Interpretive Communication** and **Presentational Writing** sections of the AP Language and Culture Exam as it helps students get acquainted with and reflect on products and practices from the French-speaking world while reading culture-focused passages and answering questions in French.

Une partie d'awalé

Culture appliquée

L'awalé 2.1

L'awalé est le plus célèbre des jeux de réflexion[1] africains. Il est similaire au backgammon. L'awalé était déjà joué en Égypte il y a plusieurs milliers d'années. Il est toujours joué dans toute l'Afrique, en particulier en Afrique de l'ouest. Il est commun que les enfants apprennent à compter[2] en jouant à l'awalé avant même d'apprendre à compter à l'école. C'est un jeu qui développe la mémoire.

1. strategy 2. to count

Une partie d'awalé 2.1

Originally played with seeds that were "sowed" in cups on a game board, **awalé** can also be played with pebbles or marbles. An empty egg carton can be used instead of a ready-made game board.

Materials

- an **awalé** board or an empty carton of a dozen eggs
- two paper cups for captured seeds
- 48 pebbles, marbles, or large seeds

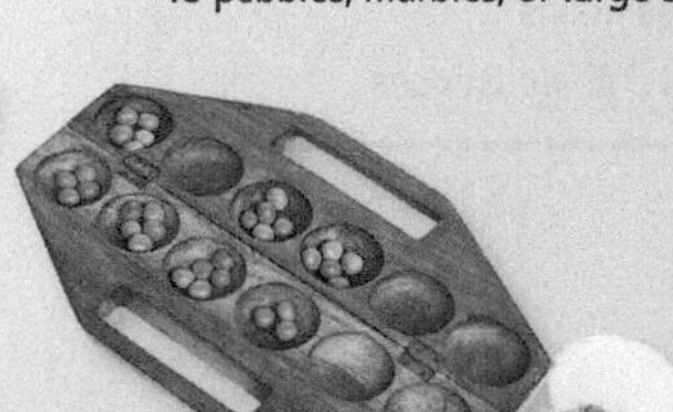

The rules

Step 1. Place 4 "seeds" in each cup of the egg carton "game board". Players sit on opposite sides of the board and play from the six cups in front of them.

Step 2. Player A takes all the seeds from one of his cups and "sows" them to the right, putting one in each cup. Player B then does the same. If a player gets to the last cup on his side, he goes across and continues sowing seeds in his opponent's cups, counterclockwise. Play continues with each player taking turns.

Step 3. If the last seed sowed falls into an opponent's cup containing only 1 or 2 seeds, a player captures those 2 or 3 seeds. If this is also true for the next-to-last seed sowed, the player captures those seeds, too. Players can capture the seeds of several cups at a time. For example, if the last 3 seeds fall in 3 consecutive cups, each containing 1 or 2 seeds, all those seeds are captured. However, if the last 3 seeds fall into 3 cups containing 2, 4, and 2 seeds, only seeds in the last cup are captured.

Step 4. Play continues until one player has no seeds left, and the opponent cannot reach the other side of the board in one move. The player with the most captured seeds wins. (Rules may vary from region to region.)

Le nom du jeu «awalé» est différent d'un pays d'Afrique à un autre. Fais des recherches pour trouver ses autres noms. 2.1

Core Instruction

CULTURE APPLIQUÉE

1. Read **L'awalé** aloud in class. **(10 min.)**
2. Have half of the class bring in an egg carton; have the other half bring in two paper cups. You will also need to provide the dried beans. **(2 min.)**
3. Read aloud the directions for the game, and check for comprehension. Have students agree on how to determine the end of a match and begin play. **(20 min.)**
4. Assign **Recherches** as homework. **(2 min.)**

COMPARAISONS ET COMMUNAUTÉ

1. Have students read the introductory statement and choose the correct completion. **(1 min.)**
2. Have students read **Comparaisons** and answer and discuss **Et toi? (6 min.)**
3. Read **Communauté et professions** aloud in class. Have students do research to see if there is a group in your area that goes to third-world countries to do medical work and then present their findings. **(20 min.)**

Online Practice
my.hrw.com
Online Edition

Comparaisons

Malade en France 1.2

Si tu as un simple rhume en France, il vaut mieux:

a. aller à l'hôpital.
b. consulter un spécialiste.
c. aller à la pharmacie.

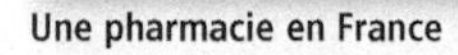

Une pharmacie en France

En France, les pharmaciens ont le droit[1] de donner des conseils[2] médicaux. Si ton problème n'est pas très grave[3], le pharmacien te conseillera un médicament en vente libre (sans ordonnance[4]) ou décidera si tu dois consulter un docteur. Les docteurs français font aussi des visites à domicile[5]. En cas d'urgence, on peut aller dans n'importe quel hôpital. On peut aussi appeler le SAMU (Service d'aide médicale d'urgence) ou SOS Médecins 24 heures sur 24 pour une intervention médicale rapide. Les frais médicaux sont remboursés par la Sécurité sociale (système d'assurance maladie[6] pour les Français et les gens résidant en France).

4.2

ET TOI?

1. Est-ce que ton docteur fait des visites à domicile? Est-ce que les pharmaciens américains conseillent les patients?
2. Compare les services médicaux en France avec ceux des États-Unis. Lesquels préfères-tu?

Communauté et professions

Le français dans le monde médical 5.1

As-tu entendu parler de *Médecins sans frontières?* C'est une organisation française qui fournit une aide médicale (médecins, infirmiers, médicaments...) dans le monde entier. Le personnel médical de MSF est composé de volontaires qui viennent du monde entier et qui doivent pouvoir parler une langue étrangère, par exemple le français. Fais des recherches sur *Médecins sans frontières* ou une autre organisation humanitaire. Présente ce que tu as trouvé à ta classe.

Un volontaire de Médecins sans frontières

1. right 2. advice 3. serious 4. without prescription 5. house calls 6. health insurance

Communities

Community Link

Have students create several **awalé** games. Ask volunteers to visit a nearby hospital to teach the game to young patients. You might also have them research a traditional African song sung in French to share with the children. 5.1

Cultures

Products and Perspectives

Prepare a worksheet with clues about famous French scientists who made important contributions to medical research, for example, the "father of microbiology" who developed a vaccine for rabies, Louis Pasteur. Have students work in teams to research the answers. Then have each team choose one of the scientists and prepare a short scene about an important moment in the person's life. 2.2

Teacher to Teacher

Lynn Payne
Hidden Valley Middle School
Roanoke, VA

I have students create a travel brochure of Dakar with pictures and captions in simple French. The cover of the brochure has a title and a small map. The first panel of the brochure contains three "sights to see." The middle panel is for "things to do." On the third panel, students are to list hotels and restaurants with Senegalese foods, which can be obtained from the Internet. Finally, on the back of the brochure, students put pictures of festivals and special holidays in Senegal. 1.3

Differentiated Instruction

ADVANCED LEARNERS

Have students write directions in French for their favorite board game. Each week, have a different student teach the rest of the class in French how to play his or her game. Alternatively, you might set aside one day as a game day and set up different stations around the room where students teach small groups to play their game. 1.3

MULTIPLE INTELLIGENCES

Naturalist Ask students to research the use of herbs and homeopathic medicines in France or Canada. They should also determine if the plants used for medicinal purposes are indigenous to the geographical area or if they are imported. Ask students to present their findings to the class. 1.3, 2.1

Resources

Planning:
Lesson Planner
Teacher One Stop

Presentation:
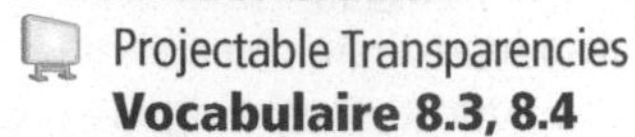
Projectable Transparencies **Vocabulaire 8.3, 8.4**

DVD Tutor, Disc 2 **Télé-vocab 2**
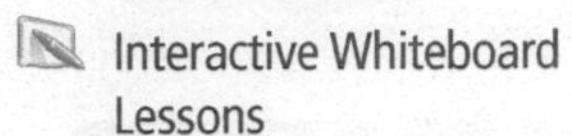
Interactive Whiteboard Lessons

Practice:
Cahier de vocabulaire et grammaire
Differentiated Practice and Assessment CD-ROM
Independent Study Guide
Media Guide
Projectable Transparencies Bell Work 8.5
@HOMETUTOR
Holt McDougal French Apps

Bell Work

Use Bell Work 8.5 in the *Projectable Transparencies* or write this activity on the board.

Find a logical expression to start each sentence.

Il faut **Il n'est pas bon**
Je veux **Je suis contente**
Je suis triste

1. **...que tu sois malade.**
2. **...que vous mangiez trop de sucre.**
3. **...que nous finissions nos exercices.**
4. **...que tu sois en forme.**
5. **...que mes amis viennent chez moi.** 1.2

Proverbes

For French proverbs and activities related to the chapter theme and vocabulary, see **Proverbes et expressions**, pp. R6–R7.

Objectifs
- to complain about health and give advice
- to sympathize with someone

Vocabulaire à l'œuvre 2

DVD
Télé-vocab

En pleine forme à Dakar!

Pour être en forme, il faut faire de l'exercice.
faire de la musculation
faire du yoga

faire des abdominaux (m.)

faire des pompes (f.)

Il faut se ménager aussi...

manger léger
avoir un régime équilibré

se reposer

se relaxer

Core Instruction

TEACHING VOCABULAIRE

1. Introduce vocabulary with transparencies **Vocabulaire 8.3** and **8.4** and model pronunciation. **(2 min.)**
2. Tell students what you have to do to take care of yourself physically and mentally. **Il faut que je fasse de la musculation. Il est important que je me repose. (2 min.)**
3. If possible, find pictures of people with health problems or use the Situation transparencies. Write the complaints in **Exprimons-nous!** below each picture. Display each picture, read the complaint, and then model advice. **(3 min.)**

Télé-vocab 2

For a video presentation of this vocabulary, see the *DVD Tutor.*

DVD
Télé-vocab

Online Practice
my.hrw.com
Vocabulaire 2 practice

Pour rester en forme, <u>il ne faut pas...</u>

se priver de sommeil
fumer
consommer trop de matières grasses
sauter des repas (m)

D'autres mots utiles

se peser	*to weigh oneself*	être en bonne santé	*to be healthy*
se nourrir	*to feed oneself*	prendre des vitamines (f.)	*to take vitamins*
faire un régime	*to go on a diet*	les produits (m.) bio(logiques)	*organic products*
perdre/prendre du poids	*to lose/to gain weight*		

Exprimons-nous!

To complain about health	To give advice
Je suis fatigué(e). *I'm . . .*	**Tu n'as qu'à** te reposer. *All you have to do is . . .*
Je suis au régime. *I'm on a diet.*	**Tu devrais** prendre des vitamines. *You should . . .*
J'ai mal partout. *I ache everywhere.*	**Pourquoi tu ne** vas **pas** chez le docteur? *Why don't you . . . ?*
J'ai grossi. *I gained weight.*	**Tu ferais bien de** manger léger. *You would do well to/You should . . .*
Je suis stressé(e). *I'm stressed.*	**Il faudrait que** tu fasses du yoga. *You should . . .*

Vocabulaire et grammaire, *pp. 91–93* — Online Workbooks

▶ **Vocabulaire supplémentaire,** Les problèmes de santé, **p. R21**

TPR — TOTAL PHYSICAL RESPONSE

Have students respond to these commands.

Lève la main si tu es en **bonne santé.**

Montre tes bras si tu fais de **la musculation.**

Lève le doigt si tu prends **des vitamines.**

Mets la tête dans les mains si tu es stressé(e).

Lève-toi si tu manges léger.

Then have some students mime the following situations.

Tu suis un cours de yoga.

Tu fais des abdominaux.

Fais-moi dix pompes!

Repose-toi.

Tu es malade parce que tu **fumes.**

Tu as mal partout.  1.2

Cultures — Practices and Perspectives

Tell students that although many traditional French foods, such as croissants and **foie gras,** tend to be high-calorie and high-fat, most French people stay quite slim. French nutritionists credit this to the fact that the French tend to eat smaller portions than Americans do. Have students research other differences between French and American eating habits. 2.1

Differentiated Instruction

ADVANCED LEARNERS

Have students host an after-school aerobics class in French that includes the exercises presented in **Vocabulaire.** Students should research the vocabulary they will need to lead the class and find a suitable place to hold it. Review the music they intend to use for the class to make sure it is appropriate for a school environment. 5.2

MULTIPLE INTELLIGENCES

Intrapersonal Ask students to create a personal journal of their meals and physical activities. The journal can be about themselves or a fictious person. Using the new vocabulary and expressions, ask students to set goals for increasing their energy and improving their health. 1.3

Resources

Planning:
Lesson Planner
Teacher One Stop

Presentation:
Projectable Transparencies **Vocabulaire 8.3, 8.4**
DVD Tutor, Disc 2 **Télé-vocab 2**
Interactive Whiteboard Lessons

Practice:
Cahier de vocabulaire et grammaire
Differentiated Practice and Assessment CD-ROM
Independent Study Guide
Media Guide
Audio CD 8, Tr. 4
@HOMETUTOR
Holt McDougal French Apps

24 Script

See script on p. 267E.

Communities

Family Link

Have students create greeting cards using the expressions in **Exprimons-nous!** and send them to friends and family members. You might have them research **cartes virtuelles** on the Internet for ideas. 5.1

24 Écoutons CD 8, Tr. 4 1.2

Écoute ces appels au programme «Docteur Bonne Santé», un programme radio qui répond aux questions de santé des adolescents. Puis, associe les adolescents avec le conseil que le médecin leur donne. **1.** c **2.** b **3.** f **4.** a **5.** d **6.** e

a. b. c. d. e. f.

Flash culture

Tout comme aux États-Unis, les clubs de gym ou les salles de fitness existent au Sénégal. Les salles de sport se présentent aussi bien dans les zones résidentielles que dans les zones populaires. Les hommes et les femmes y vont pour rester en forme. La fréquentation des salles de sports est influencée par les films américains.

Qu'est-ce que tu fais pour rester en forme? Où vas-tu pour faire du sport? 4.2

25 Tu n'as qu'à... 1.2

Écrivons Julien donne des conseils à ses amis. Mets les mots dans le bon ordre.

1. de / bien / perdre / tu / du / poids / ferais
   Tu ferais bien de perdre du poids.
2. relaxer / n'as / te / tu / qu'à
   Tu n'as qu'à te relaxer.
3. tu / pas / au / pourquoi / gymnase / vas / ne
   Pourquoi tu ne vas pas au gymnase?
4. reposes / faudrait / tu / il / te / que
   Il faudrait que tu te reposes.
5. faut / se / ne / sommeil / pas / priver / il / de
   Il ne faut pas se priver de sommeil.

26 Des conseils 1.3

Écrivons/Parlons Ton/Ta meilleure ami(e) ne fait pas d'exercice, n'a pas de régime équilibré et il/elle est toujours stressé(e). Quels conseils est-ce que tu voudrais lui donner?

MODÈLE Pour te nourrir, tu n'as qu'à **manger des produits biologiques.**

1. Pour perdre du poids, tu n'as qu'à...
2. Pour te relaxer, tu devrais...
3. Pour être en bonne forme, tu ferais bien de...
4. Pour prendre du muscle, tu ferais bien de...
5. Pour te relaxer, tu ferais bien de ne pas...

Core Instruction

TEACHING EXPRIMONS-NOUS!

1. Use the same pictures you displayed for **Vocabulaire,** but this time, after you read the complaint, sympathize with the person. **(1 min.)**
2. Using transparency **Vocabulaire 8.1,** have students come up, point to a body part, and tell what is wrong. Sympathize with the students. **(3 min.)**
3. Model a conversation with the expressions in **Entre copains,** sympathizing with each complaint. **(2 min.)**

Exprimons-nous!

To sympathize with someone	
Ce n'est pas grave.	*It's not serious.*
Ne t'en fais pas!	*Don't worry!*
Ça va aller mieux.	*It's going to get better.*
Mon/Ma pauvre!	*Poor thing!*
Je te plains.	*I feel sorry for you.*

Entre copains

Je suis crevé(e).	*I'm exhausted.*
Je suis nase.	*I'm exhausted.*
J'ai pas la pêche.	*I don't feel good.*
J'en ai marre!	*I'm fed up!*

27 Mon pauvre! 1.2

Parlons/Écrivons Imagine que les personnes suivantes sont tes amis et ils ont les symptômes suivants. Donne-leur des conseils.

MODÈLE **—Je ne me sens pas très bien. J'ai de la fièvre.**
—Ma pauvre! Tu devrais prendre un comprimé.

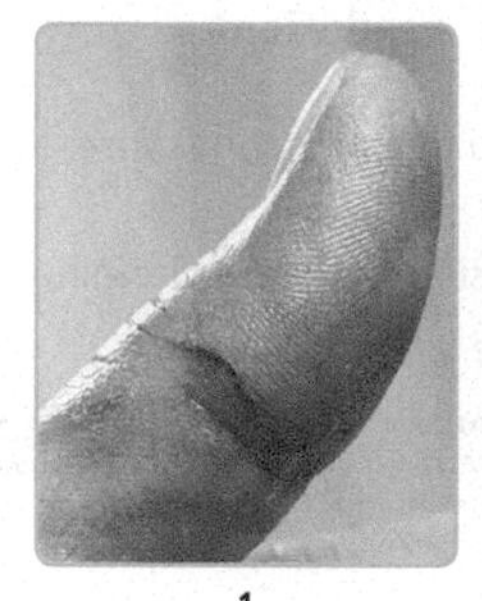
1.

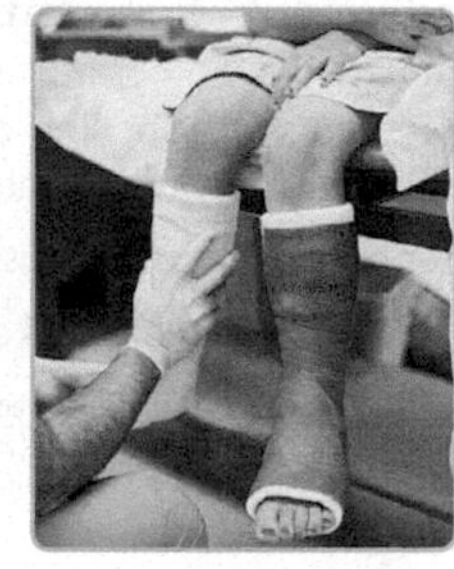
2.

3.

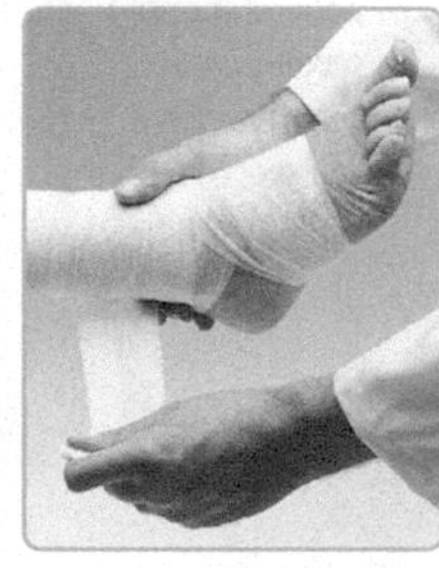
4.

Communication

Digital performance space

28 Scénario 1.1

Parlons Maintenant, tu es «Docteur Bonne Santé». Écoute les problèmes de santé des gens qui t'appellent. Donne-leur des conseils. Joue cette scène en groupes de trois ou quatre.

MODÈLE **—Je m'appelle Josh et j'ai grossi. Qu'est-ce que je peux faire?**
—Ne t'en fais pas, Josh. Tu n'as qu'à faire de l'exercice et manger léger.

27 Possible Answers

1. — Je me suis coupé le doigt.
   — Ce n'est pas grave.
2. — Je me suis cassé la jambe.
   — Ça va aller mieux.
3. — J'ai mal aux dents!
   — Je te plains. Pourquoi tu ne vas pas chez le dentiste?
4. — Je me suis foulé la cheville.
   — Tu ferais bien de ne plus faire de yoga.

Communication

Pair Activity: Interpersonal
Review adverbs of frequency, using the expression **Combien de fois est-ce que...?** Group students in pairs and have each ask the other how often he or she does healthful or unhealthful things. Partners' answers should include adverbs of frequency. 1.1

Differentiated Instruction

SLOWER PACE LEARNERS

24 Stop the audio recording after each teenager speaks. Have students guess the advice that the doctor might give, based on what the teenager says. Then play what the doctor says and have students listen to confirm their guesses. 1.2

SPECIAL LEARNING NEEDS

Students with Learning Disabilities Ask students to create a children's booklet in French about good health and fitness advice. Have students draw or cut the illustrations of healthful foods and physical activity from magazines or newspapers. You may wish to keep the booklets in the classroom so students can refer to them as study aids. 1.2

Assess

Assessment Program
Quiz: Vocabulaire 2
Alternative Assessment
Differentiated Practice and Assessment CD-ROM

Online Assessment
my.hrw.com

Test Generator 

Objectifs
- the conditional
- *si* clauses

Grammaire à l'œuvre 2

Grammavision

Resources

Planning:
Lesson Planner
Teacher One Stop

Presentation:
DVD Tutor, Disc 2
Grammavision 2.1

Practice:
Grammar Tutor for Students of French, Chapter 8
Cahier de vocabulaire et grammaire
Differentiated Practice and Assessment CD-ROM
Cahier d'activités
Independent Study Guide
Media Guide
Projectable Transparencies
Bell Work 8.6
@HOMETUTOR

Bell Work

Use Bell Work 8.6 in the *Projectable Transparencies* or write this activity on the board.

Unscramble the words to make logical sentences.

1. **reposes / faut / tu / souvent / Il / que / te**
2. **musculation / de / faire / Je / la / devrais**
3. **équilibré / ayons / un / nous / Il / que / régime / faudrait**
4. **bien / ferais / vitamines / Tu / de / des / prendre**
5. **qu'à / yoga / Ils / faire / n'ont / du** 1.2

Communities

Community Link

Have students investigate one of the healthful options in **Vocabulaire** available in your area, such as yoga classes, weight management programs, or stores that carry organic foods. Have them use verbs in the conditional to discuss their findings. 5.1

The conditional

1 The conditional **(le conditionnel)** tells what *would* happen. The conditional uses the infinitive as the stem for most verbs. The endings are the same as those of the **imparfait.** Drop the **-e** from verbs ending in **–re** before adding the endings.

	parler	finir	vendre
je	parler**ais**	finir**ais**	vendr**ais**
tu	parler**ais**	finir**ais**	vendr**ais**
il/elle/on	parler**ait**	finir**ait**	vendr**ait**
nous	parler**ions**	finir**ions**	vendr**ions**
vous	parler**iez**	finir**iez**	vendr**iez**
ils/elles	parler**aient**	finir**aient**	vendr**aient**

2 Verbs that have irregular stems and spelling changes in the future tense have the same stems in the conditional.

Tu devrais bien manger. Tu pourrais aussi prendre des vitamines.
You should eat well. You could also take vitamins.

Déjà vu!

Do you remember the stems of verbs that are irregular in the future?

aller (ir-)	**pouvoir** (pourr-)
avoir (aur-)	**savoir** (saur-)
devoir (devr-)	**venir** (viendr-)
être (ser-)	**voir** (verr-)
faire (fer-)	**vouloir** (voudr-)

Vocabulaire et grammaire, *pp. 94–95*
Cahier d'activités, *pp. 75–77*

29 Pour être en bonne santé 1.2

Écrivons Qu'est-ce que ces personnes feraient si elles voulaient être en bonne santé, d'après toi? Écris six phrases en utilisant le conditionnel et un élément de chaque colonne.

MODÈLE Moi, je prendrais des vitamines.

Moi, je	manger	des vitamines
(à ton ami[e]) Tu	faire	plus d'eau
Le professeur	prendre	au club de sport
Nous, les élèves, nous	aller	des pompes
Vous, les parents, vous	avoir	léger
Les jeunes	boire	un régime équilibré

Core Instruction

TEACHING GRAMMAIRE

1. Go over Point 1. Tell students the conditional is formed with the infinitive as the stem, plus the imperfect endings. For **-re** verbs, the **e** is dropped from the infinitive. All conditional stems end in **-r.** **(1 min.)**
2. Point out that the stem of irregular verbs is the same in the future and in the conditional. Go over the verbs in Point 2. **(2 min.)**
3. Model giving advice to a sibling. **Tu devrais maigrir. Tu pourrais manger léger. Tu devrais faire du yoga. Tu pourrais dépenser moins d'argent. (2 min.)**

Grammavision

For a video presentation of the conditional, see the *DVD Tutor.*

Grammavision

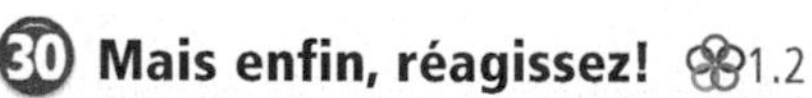

Online Practice

my.hrw.com

Grammaire 2 practice

30 Mais enfin, réagissez! 1.2

Écrivons/Parlons Les personnes sur ces illustrations ne sont pas du tout en forme! Qu'est-ce qu'elles feraient ou ne feraient pas pour aller mieux, d'après toi? Utilise les sujets indiqués et le conditionnel.

MODÈLE **Irina irait voir le dentiste!**

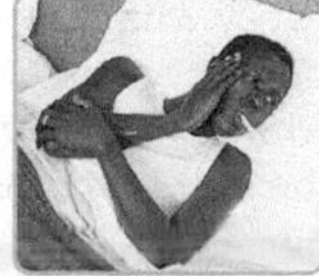
Idrissa

1. Nous

2. Je

3. Elle

4. Vous

31 Ma lettre à Amadou 1.3

Écrivons Amadou, ton correspondant sénégalais, va venir te rendre visite cet été. Écris-lui un e-mail pour lui suggérer des activités que vous pourriez faire ensemble. Attention! Amadou est un athlète et il est très en forme. Il adore le sport et il veut rester en bonne santé, alors propose des activités appropriées.

MODÈLE **Cher Amadou,**
Il y a un club de sport super dans ma ville. On pourrait y aller pour faire du yoga.

Communication

32 Scénario 1.1

Parlons Un(e) jeune Français(e) a décidé de changer ses habitudes pour être en meilleure forme. Il/Elle essaie de convaincre un(e) ami(e) de faire du sport avec lui/elle et de changer leurs habitudes. Son ami(e) n'a pas envie de changer! Avec un(e) camarade, inventez une conversation entre ces deux personnes et jouez la scène pour la classe.

MODÈLE **—On pourrait manger des produits biologiques?**
—Pas question! Moi, j'aimerais mieux manger des sandwichs et des frites!

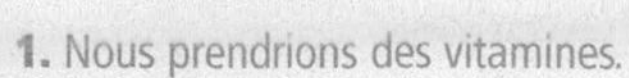

30 Possible Answers

1. Nous prendrions des vitamines.
2. Je me coucherais plus tôt.
3. Elle ne boirait plus de café.
4. Vous ne sauteriez pas de repas.

Connections

Health Link

Invite an emergency medical technician, nurse, or doctor to class to give a lecture on first-aid. Have students take notes in French and then create a quiz entitled **Qu'est-ce que tu ferais?** The quiz items should ask what the quiz-taker would do in different medical emergencies. 3.1

Communication

Group Activity: Interpersonal

On a slip of paper, have students write a request in the **futur simple.** They should circulate and express their request to three classmates. As their classmates hear their request (or desire), they should respond in the conditional, saying that they would do what was requested and then giving an excuse in the present tense, starting with **mais.**

MODÈLE
— Est-ce que tu m'achèteras un nouveau CD?
— Je t'achèterais un nouveau CD mais je n'ai pas d'argent. 1.1

Differentiated Instruction

ADVANCED LEARNERS

Have small groups plan their ideal health club. They should design the floor plan and decide on the exercise equipment they will have and the exercise classes they will offer. Ask them to present their plans to the rest of the class, who will play the role of bankers deciding whether to grant the groups' business loans. In their presentations, students should use the conditional form at least ten times. 1.3

MULTIPLE INTELLIGENCES

Bodily-Kinesthetic As an aid to learning the conditional, use physical movement when reviewing the conjugations. Assign a pronoun to each student. As you read the forms of a verb, point to students who should stand up and state the verb form that agrees with their assigned pronoun, and then sit down. Repeat the process several times with several verbs until students respond quickly and fluently. The physical activity may improve memorization skills. 1.2

Resources

Planning:
Lesson Planner
 Teacher One Stop

Presentation:
DVD Tutor, Disc 2
Grammavision 2.2

Practice:
Grammar Tutor for Students of French, Chapter 8
Cahier de vocabulaire et grammaire
Differentiated Practice and Assessment CD-ROM
Cahier d'activités
Independent Study Guide
Media Guide
Projectable Transparencies Bell Work 8.7
Audio CD 8, Tr. 5
@HOMETUTOR

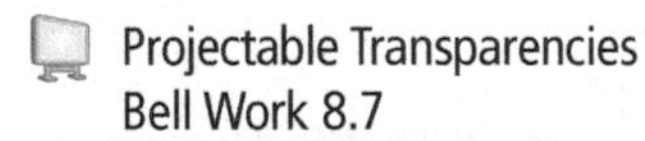

Use Bell Work 8.7 in the *Projectable Transparencies* or write this activity on the board.

Choose the correct verb to complete the sentences.

devraient voudriez pourrions viendrais irions

1. **David et toi ____ venir ce soir?**
2. **Nous ____ au cinéma.**
3. **Tu ____ seul?**
4. **Tes amis ____ nous rejoindre.**
5. **Nous ____ aller au café après.** 1.2

COMMON ERROR ALERT
ATTENTION !

The structure **si on + imparfait** may look like an incomplete if. . . then. . . construction to some students. The question mark at the end may help to serve as a reminder that this is a way to extend an invitation to someone.

Si clauses

1 To say what someone *would* do *if* things were different, use two clauses, an "if" clause and a "result" clause. The "if" clause will start with **si** *(if)* and will be in the **imparfait**. The "result" clause will be in the **conditional**. Either clause can come first.

Si tu **voulais** être en bonne santé, tu **ferais** de l'exercice.
If you wanted to be in good health, you would exercise.
Tu **achèterais** des légumes **si** tu **voulais** bien manger.
You would buy vegetables if you wanted to eat well.

2 You can also use **si** + **on** + **imparfait** to invite someone to something.

Si on faisait de l'exercice? *How about exercising?*

Vocabulaire et grammaire, *pp. 94–95*
Cahier d'activités, *pp. 75–77*

Flash culture

La cuisine sénégalaise est l'une des meilleures d'Afrique. Le riz et le poisson sont les principales sources de nourriture. L'arachide (cacahuète) est la principale culture, son huile remplace le beurre et parfume viandes et poissons. Sur les marchés, on vend des biscuits recouverts de beurre d'arachide et des arachides grillées.

Comment est-ce que la nourriture sénégalaise se compare à la nourriture américaine? 4.2

33 Le bon choix 1.2

Lisons Choisis la forme qui convient pour compléter les phrases.

1. Si nous ______ au gymnase samedi?
   a. allions (circled) **b.** irions
2. Si Monica ______ des abdominaux, elle serait plus en forme.
   a. ferait **b.** faisait (circled)
3. Nous ______ faire un régime si nous voulions perdre du poids.
   a. devrions (circled) **b.** devions
4. Si tu voulais, tu ______ faire de la musculation avec Paul.
   a. pouvais **b.** pourrais (circled)
5. Si les filles faisaient du yoga, elles ______ moins stressées.
   a. étaient **b.** seraient (circled)

34 Écoutons CD 8, Tr. 5 1.2

Écoute chaque phrase et indique s'il s'agit **a) d'une invitation** ou **b) d'une action conditionnelle.** 1. a 2. b 3. b 4. a 5. b 6. a

35 Des si, toujours des si... 1.2

Lisons Complète les phrases avec l'imparfait et le conditionnel des verbes entre parenthèses. Attention à l'ordre des verbes!

1. (vouloir; fumer) Si tu voulais être en forme, tu ne fumerais pas!
2. (perdre; faire) Noémie perdrait du poids si elle faisait un régime.
3. (aller; être) Si vous étiez vraiment malade, vous iriez voir le médecin!
4. (manger; maigrir) Si je mangeais plus léger, je maigrirais!
5. (manger; être) Nous serions en forme si nous mangions mieux!

Core Instruction

TEACHING GRAMMAIRE

1. Go over Point 1. Tell students that **si** will begin the *if* clause and will be in the imperfect, and the other clause will be in the conditional tense. **(2 min.)**
2. Go over Point 2 and model additional sentences. **(2 min.)**
3. Draw two columns on the board, one headed **si** and the other headed **résultat.** Write a list of verbs under each heading. Have students pick one verb from each column and form a sentence with the two verbs. **Si je voulais perdre du poids, je mangerais moins. Si vous étudiiez le soir, vous sauriez les réponses en cours. (3 min.)**

Grammavision

For a video presentation of **si** clauses, see the *DVD Tutor.*

Grammavision

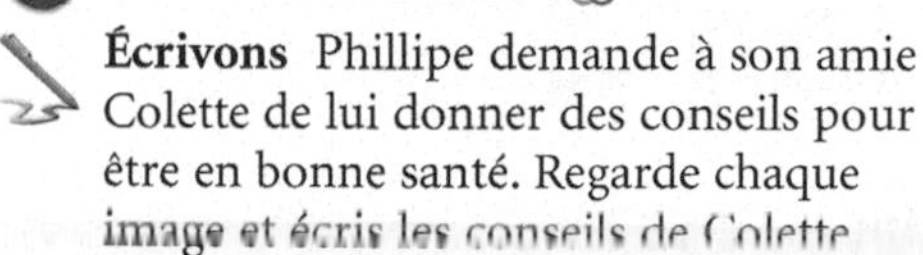

36 De bons conseils 1.2

Écrivons Phillipe demande à son amie Colette de lui donner des conseils pour être en bonne santé. Regarde chaque image et écris les conseils de Colette.

MODÈLE **Si tu voulais faire un régime, tu devrais manger des fruits et des légumes...**

1.

2.

3.

4.

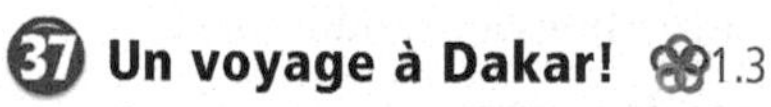

37 Un voyage à Dakar! 1.3

Écrivons Si ta classe de français gagnait un voyage d'une semaine à Dakar ou une autre ville francophone, qu'est-ce que vous feriez? Où iriez-vous? Qu'est-ce que vous visiteriez? Pourquoi? Utilise des phrases avec **si** et le conditionnel.

MODÈLE **Si la classe gagnait un voyage à Dakar, nous serions très contents!**

Communication

38 Questions personnelles 1.1

Parlons Crée un petit sondage pour savoir ce que tes camarades pensent qu'ils pourraient faire pour être plus en forme. Prépare 6 à 8 questions sur les sports qu'ils voudraient faire, les choses qu'ils voudraient manger ou ne plus manger, les mauvaises habitudes qu'ils voudraient changer, etc. Ensuite, circule dans la classe et pose tes questions à des camarades. Enfin, compare leurs réponses avec les réponses des autres élèves.

MODÈLE **—Cindy, qu'est-ce que tu voudrais faire comme sport si tu voulais être plus en forme?**
—Moi, j'aimerais essayer le yoga.

34 Script

See script on p. 267F.

36 Possible Answers

1. Si tu voulais perdre du poids, tu mangerais léger.
2. Si tu voulais être en bonne santé, tu ferais des pompes.
3. Si tu voulais prendre du muscle, tu ferais de la musculation.
4. Si tu ne voulais pas être fatigué, tu boirais du jus d'orange.

Comparisons

Comparing and Contrasting

Have students research policies on smoking in public places in France. Ask students to compare these policies to ordinances in your city or state and share their findings with the class. 4.2

Communication

38 Group Activity: Interpersonal

Have students write five questions that they would like to ask their classmates. **Qu'est-ce que tu ferais si tu + imparfait?** Students should skip several lines between each question. Then in small groups, have students ask one another the questions. The students should answer, using **Si + imparfait + conditional.** The students asking the questions should repeat the responses in the **il/elle** form. 1.1

Differentiated Instruction

SLOWER PACE LEARNERS

37 Allow students to write their paragraph about a city with which they are familiar. They may find it easier to think of activities they would like to do there. You might also work as a class to write **si...** sentence starters on the board for students to use in their paragraph. **Si nous avions assez d'argent... S'il faisait beau... Si nous restions au moins une semaine...** 1.3

SPECIAL LEARNING NEEDS

Students with Language Impairments

When reviewing the **si** clauses, work closely with students to check for understanding of the "if" clause and the "result" clause. Create a chart by dividing a piece of paper in half. The first column should have examples of "if" clauses and the second column should have examples of "result" clauses. Use the chart as a reference to help students understand when to use each type of clause.

Assess

Assessment Program

Quiz: Grammaire 2

Alternative Assessment

Differentiated Practice and Assessment CD-ROM

Online Assessment
my.hrw.com

Test Generator 

Resources

Planning:
Lesson Planner
Teacher One Stop

Practice:
Grammar Tutor for Students of French, Chapter 8
Cahier de vocabulaire et grammaire
Differentiated Practice and Assessment CD-ROM
Cahier d'activités
Independent Study Guide
Media Guide
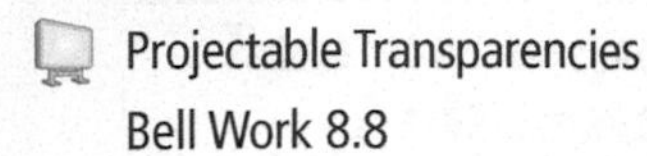
Projectable Transparencies
Bell Work 8.8
Audio CD 8, Tr. 6

Bell Work

Use Bell Work 8.8 in the *Projectable Transparencies* or write this activity on the board.

Complete each sentence with the correct form of the verbs.

1. Si tu ____ (manger) bien, tu ____ (aller) mieux.
2. Elle ____ (perdre) du poids si elle ____ (faire) du yoga.
3. Nous ____ (être) moins stressés si nous ____ (dormir) plus.
4. Si vous ____ (aller) au gym, vous ____ (faire) de la musculation.
5. J'____ (acheter) une nouvelle voiture si j'____ (avoir) de l'argent. 1.2

39 Script

See script on p. 267F.

Synthèse
- Vocabulaire 2
- Grammaire 2

Application 2

39 Écoutons CD 8, Tr. 6 1.2

Imagine que tu es nutritionniste et que tu as une émission à la radio. Plusieurs personnes téléphonent pour te demander des conseils. Choisis toutes les réponses logiques.

Vous devriez...

a. faire une promenade tous les jours
b. faire du jogging
c. manger des fruits
d. manger du poulet ou du poisson
e. manger moins de matières grasses
f. prendre des vitamines

40 Un programme de remise en forme 1.3

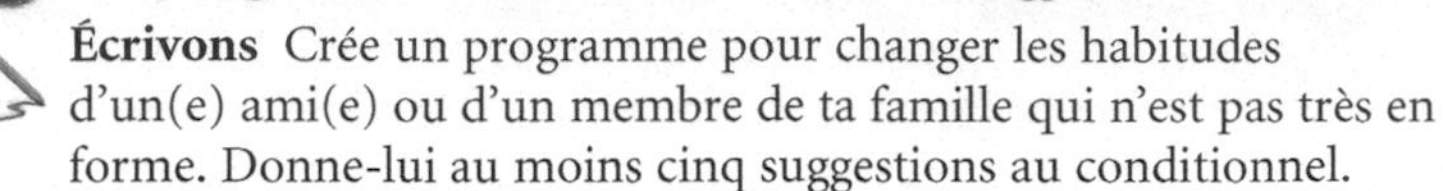

Écrivons Crée un programme pour changer les habitudes d'un(e) ami(e) ou d'un membre de ta famille qui n'est pas très en forme. Donne-lui au moins cinq suggestions au conditionnel.

MODÈLE **Programme pour mon amie Karen:**
1. Tu ne devrais plus sauter de repas parce que c'est mauvais pour la santé.

Un peu plus

The conditional to make polite requests

The conditional (le conditionnel de politesse) can be used to make a request or offer sound more polite.

Pourrais-tu m'aider?
Could you help me?
Est-ce que vous voudriez faire du yoga?
Would you like to do yoga?

Vocabulaire et grammaire, *p. 96*
Cahier d'activités, *pp. 75–77*
Online Workbooks

41 Des questions 1.2

Écrivons Vous entendez ces conversations au gymnase. Choisis le verbe qui convient et fais tous les changements nécessaires.

manger	pouvoir	vouloir
aimer	faire	essayer

1. Pourrais -je t'aider à faire de la musculation?
2. M. Durand, vous voudriez faire un régime?
3. Sasha aimerait -il faire du sport avec nous?
4. Vous pensez que vos enfants feraient une promenade avec Magali?
5. Lucas, mangerais -tu au restaurant biologique avec nous?
6. Essaierions -nous ces boissons aux vitamines?

Core Instruction

INTEGRATED PRACTICE

1. Have students do Activities 39 and 40 to review previously taught material.
2. Tell students that you and your family are trying to be healthier. Tell them your goals or write them on the board. **Si nous faisions de l'exercice, nous serions en forme. Si nous buvions moins de boissons sucrées, nous n'irions pas tant chez le dentiste. (2 min.)**
3. Present **Un peu plus** and continue with Activities 41–44. **(20 min.)**

TEACHING UN PEU PLUS

1. Remind students that they have used the conditional to make polite requests. **(1 min.)**
2. Model requests that you might make of a person on the street. **Sauriez-vous où se trouve Notre-Dame? Auriez-vous l'heure? Connaîtriez-vous un bon restaurant pas trop cher? Où ferait-on du jogging le matin? (3 min.)**

Online Practice
my.hrw.com
Application 2 practice

42 Soyons polis! 1.2

Parlons/Écrivons Reformule les questions suivantes en utilisant le conditionnel pour les rendre plus polies.

MODÈLE Peux-tu me montrer comment faire des pompes?
Pourrais-tu me montrer comment faire des pompes?

1. Luc et Ronan peuvent-ils aller jouer au tennis avec nous?
2. Conduirez-vous les enfants à leur cours de danse?
3. Leslie, tu m'achètes des médicaments à la pharmacie?
4. Carole veut-elle faire plus d'exercice?
5. Devons-nous attendre le prof de yoga?
6. Tu peux passer à la pharmacie? Il me faut des vitamines.

42 Answers

1. Luc et Ronan pourraient-ils aller jouer au tennis avec nous?
2. Conduiriez-vous les enfants à leur cours de danse?
3. Leslie, tu m'achèterais des médicaments à la pharmacie?
4. Carole voudrait-elle faire plus d'exercice?
5. Devrions-nous attendre le prof de yoga?
6. Tu pourrais passer à la pharmacie? Il me faut des vitamines.

43 Le grand marathon 1.3

Écrivons Tu as décidé de participer à un marathon dans six mois, alors bien sûr, tu dois t'entraîner. Écris une lettre à la personne qui organise le marathon pour lui demander des conseils. Utilise le conditionnel pour être plus poli(e).

MODÈLE **Cher Monsieur,**
Je vais faire le marathon dans six mois et je voudrais... Pourriez-vous me dire...

À la française

When you hurt yourself accidentally, say **Aïe!** *(Ow!)* or **Ouille!** *(Ouch!)*. When you have finished doing something physically difficult, say **Ouf!** *(Whew!)*

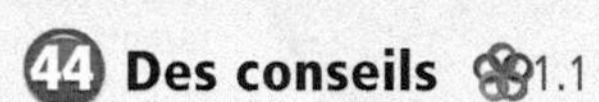

Digital performance space

Communication

44 Des conseils 1.1

Parlons Ton/Ta camarade et toi parlez entre les cours. L'un(e) de vous ne se sent pas bien et l'autre lui pose des questions sur sa santé. Lisez les questions ci-dessous et répondez-y de manière logique et détaillée. Ensuite, échangez les rôles.

— **Ça n'a pas l'air d'aller. Qu'est-ce qu'il y a?**
—
— **Tu crois que tu as de la fièvre?**
—
— **Quels sont tes symptômes?**
—
— **Tu devrais prendre des médicaments.**
—

Communication

Group Work: Interpersonal
Have partners take turns using a **si** clause or another expression to ask for and give advice. 1.1

Language Examination

44 Sample answer:

— . . .
— **Je ne me sens pas bien. je crois que je suis malade.**
— . . .
— **Je ne sais pas. Je n'ai pas pris ma température.**
— . . .
— **J'ai mal à la tête et j'ai le nez qui coule.**
— . . .
— **D'accord. Je vais à la pharmacie.**

Differentiated Instruction

ADVANCED LEARNERS

Have students write five questions they would ask a personal trainer. Then have partners arrange a convenient time to call each other for advice on getting in shape. Alternatively, you might arrange with a French teacher in your area to field phone calls. 5.1

MULTIPLE INTELLIGENCES

43 Logical-Mathematical Ask students to imagine what the organizers would advise runners to do during the six-month preparation for the marathon. Have students create a schedule and training regimen for nutrition and exercise to prepare for the marathon. Have them include mileage and time trials in the training schedule. 1.3

Assess

Assessment Program
Quiz: Application 2
Audio CD 8, Tr. 15
Alternative Assessment
Differentiated Practice and Assessment CD-ROM

Online Assessment
my.hrw.com

Test Generator 

Resources

Planning:
Lesson Planner
Teacher One Stop

Presentation:

DVD Tutor, Disc 2
Télé-roman

Practice:
Media Guide

DVD Tutor, Disc 2
Télé-roman

Connections

Visual Learners

To help students unravel the web of deceit woven by Mr. Rigaud in **Télé-roman,** have them create a Venn diagram. Guide them through the diagram on the board. First, draw an oval and label it **vrai.** Have students write what they know to be true about Mr. Rigaud and the statuette. Then draw an oval for what they now know to be untrue and label it **faux.** Label the overlapping part with a question mark and list elements of the story that remain a mystery. 3.2

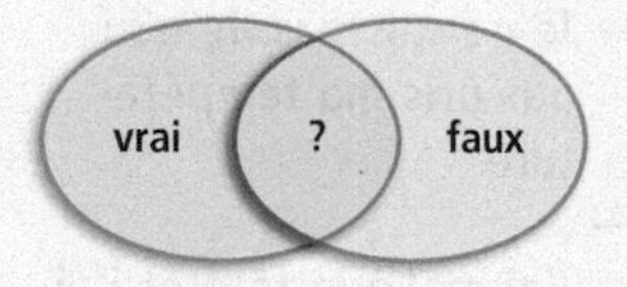

Gestures

Have students look at Seydou's expression in scene 6. What emotion does it convey? What might he be saying? Then call students' attention to Anne and Mr. Gadio's expressions in scenes 7 and 8. What do they think Anne is doing on the computer? What might Mr. Gadio be thinking? 2.1

Télé-roman Le Secret de la statuette *Épisode 8*

STRATÉGIE

Following the plot The plot is the sequence of actions in a story. Go back to the past seven episodes and write down at least two plot developments from each as well as for Episode 8. For example, in Episode 1: (1) Charles Rigaud gives a statuette to Mister Gadio. (2) Mister Gadio calls his French friend Anne Bondy, to tell her about the statuette. Keeping track of the plot will help you to understand the overall storyline, and might give you ideas about how the story will end. 1.2

Le lendemain matin...

1

Anne Alors, il y a du nouveau dans l'enquête? Vous avez des nouvelles de l'inspecteur Sonko?

M. Gadio Eh bien, hier soir, après notre retour, je l'ai appelé et je lui ai raconté l'aventure des enfants à Gorée et ton kidnapping...

Il est tout de suite allé à Gorée, mais il n'a rien trouvé. Rigaud est parti sans laisser de traces.

3 *L'inspecteur Sonko a aussi prévenu les autres postes de police du pays. Il nous téléphonera s'il y a du nouveau.*

Core Instruction

TEACHING TÉLÉ-ROMAN

1. Have students look at the pictures in **Télé-roman** without reading the text. Have them predict what will happen in this episode. **(5 min.)**
2. Play the video, pausing after each scene change. Ask general comprehension questions. Were any of the students' predictions correct? **(5 min.)**
3. Play the video again without stopping. Have volunteers act out **Télé-roman** with the gestures and facial expressions they saw in the video. **(5 min.)**
4. Have partners answer the **As-tu compris?** questions on page 293. **(5 min.)**

DVD Tutor

As an alternative, you might use the captioned version of **Le Secret de la statuette** on DVD.

Visit Us Online
my.hrw.com
Online Edition

Plus tard, ce jour-là, chez les Gadio...

4

Seydou Tu sais, cette histoire de statuette volée est vraiment bizarre. Tu penses que la police va la retrouver?

Léa Je ne sais pas. Si on oubliait un peu toute cette histoire?

5

Seydou Oui, bonne idée. Tu voudrais aller faire un tour quelque part?

Léa Oui. Pourquoi pas?

6

Seydou Il y a un concert de Didier Awadi. C'est un chanteur hip-hop célèbre. Je vais regarder sur Internet s'il y a encore des places.

Au musée...

7

Anne Tu sais, Salif, il y a quelque chose de bizarre au sujet de cette statuette...

M. Gadio Ah oui, c'est sûr! Rigaud me l'apporte lui-même. Et puis, il la vole. C'est une histoire de fous!

8

M. Gadio En tout cas, moi, j'ai l'impression que cette statuette cache quelque chose.

1.2

AS-TU COMPRIS?

1. Où est-ce que l'inspecteur Sonko est allé?
2. Est-ce que l'inspecteur Sonko a trouvé Charles Rigaud?
3. Qu'est-ce que Léa voudrait faire?
4. Qu'est-ce que Seydou propose de faire?
5. Pourquoi l'histoire de la statuette est bizarre?

Prochain épisode:
M. Gadio pense que la statuette «cache quelque chose». Est-ce que tu es d'accord? Si oui, quel est le secret de la statuette, d'après toi?

As-tu compris? Answers

1. au bureau de Rigaud à Gorée
2. non
3. oublier l'histoire de la statuette
4. d'aller à un concert de Didier Awadi, un chanteur hip-hop.
5. parce que Rigaud a apporté la statuette à M. Gadio et puis il l'a volée

Communication

Pair Work: Interpersonal

After students have watched **Télé-roman,** have them work with a partner to recount something exciting or mysterious that happened in the past. Tell students that they can tell a true story that happened to them or someone they know or make one up. Remind them to use connecting words, such as **d'abord, puis, après,** and **finalement.** Partners should react to the story and ask questions about any details they do not understand. Have partners exchange roles. 1.1

Le Secret de la statuette Episode 8

In this episode, Anne has just arrived at the Gadio's after being exchanged for the statuette. She does not feel well and decides to go to bed to recover from her ordeal. Meanwhile, inspector Sonko goes to Rigaud's home on **l'île de Gorée,** but finds no trace of Rigaud or the statuette. A few days later, Léa and Seydou decide to go to a concert to forget about what happened. Meanwhile, Mr. Gadio and Anne discuss the mysterious statuette. They wonder why Rigaud would bring it to them only to steal it back. Mr. Gadio says he is sure it is hiding something.

Lecture et écriture

Resources

Planning:
Lesson Planner
Teacher One Stop

Presentation:
Audio CD 8, Tr. 7

Practice:
Cahier d'activités
Reading Strategies and Skills Handbook, Chapter 8
Intermediate Reader
French InterActive Reader

Applying the Strategies

For practice with monitoring comprehension, have students use the "It Says. . . I Say. . ." strategy from the *Reading Strategies and Skills Handbook.*

READING PRACTICE

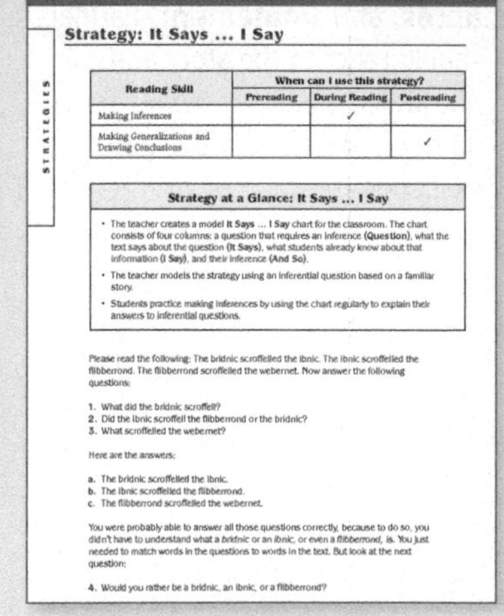

Strategy: It Says … I Say

STRATEGIES

Reading Skill	When can I use this strategy?		
	Prereading	During Reading	Postreading
Making Inferences		✓	
Making Generalizations and Drawing Conclusions			✓

Strategy at a Glance: It Says … I Say

- The teacher creates a model **It Says … I Say** chart for the classroom. The chart consists of four columns: a question that requires an inference (**Question**), what the text says about the question (**It Says**), what students already know about that information (**I Say**), and their inference (**And So**).
- The teacher models the strategy using an inferential question based on a familiar story.
- Students practice making inferences by using the chart regularly to explain their answers to inferential questions.

Please read the following: The bridnic scroffelled the ibnic. The ibnic scroffelled the flibberrond. The flibberrond scroffelled the webernet. Now answer the following questions:

1. What did the bridnic scroffell?
2. Did the ibnic scroffell the flibberrond or the bridnic?
3. What scroffelled the webernet?

Here are the answers:

a. The bridnic scroffelled the ibnic.
b. The ibnic scroffelled the flibberrond.
c. The flibberrond scroffelled the webernet.

You were probably able to answer all those questions correctly, because to do so, you didn't have to understand what a *bridnic* or an *ibnic*, or even a *flibberrond*, is. You just needed to match words in the questions to words in the text. But look at the next question:

4. Would you rather be a bridnic, an ibnic, or a flibberrond?

Using Background Knowledge

Before students begin the reading, have them guess what information the text will contain. This will help them prepare mentally and activate what they already know about a subject. They can then better understand what they read. Have them discuss what they think the reading is about, based on their background knowledge. After students have read the selection, ask them if having an idea of the text's theme makes them feel more comfortable reading in French.

Lecture et écriture

STRATÉGIE pour lire

Using background knowledge can give you a head start on understanding a text. First look at the images and familiar words to determine what the text is about. Then as you read, use what you know about the topic to help you identify its main ideas and guess the meaning of unfamiliar vocabulary.

A Avant la lecture 1.3

Qu'est-ce que tu dois faire pour être en forme? Est-ce que la pyramide alimentaire américaine est familière? Écris ce que tu sais sur une feuille de papier.

Mange bien !

Pour bien vivre, mange de tout
Pour bien manger, équilibre ton alimentation
Pour l'équilibre, fais une activité physique

CD 8, Tr. 7

Mathilde Dauxais est nutritionniste à Paris. Elle recommande, pour être en bonne santé et en pleine forme, une alimentation simple et variée.

Pour bien commencer ta journée[1], prends un bon petit déjeuner : un grand verre de jus de fruit, un bol de chocolat au lait ou un thé, une tartine de confiture ou des céréales. Si tu as très faim, tu peux manger un œuf, mais pas tous les jours !

À midi, le déjeuner est ton repas principal. En entrée, tu peux commencer avec une salade de tomates ou des carottes râpées[2], continuer avec un steak ou une escalope de dinde[3], du riz et des légumes verts, puis prendre un yaourt ou du fromage. Tu peux terminer ton repas avec un dessert sympa : une crème caramel, une glace ou un fruit. Comme boisson, de l'eau c'est très bien. Tu peux aussi boire une limonade, mais pas trop souvent.

Quatre heures, c'est l'heure du goûter. Un petit pain au chocolat, une banane ou une pomme avec un verre de lait ou un jus de fruit, c'est parfait !

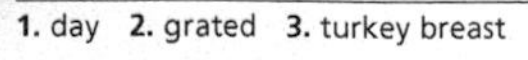

1. day 2. grated 3. turkey breast

Core Instruction

TEACHING LECTURE

1. Read **Stratégie** with students. Have them guess what they think the article is about. **(3 min.)**
2. Have students do **Avant la lecture** individually. Write the results of their pyramids on the board. **(3 min.)**
3. Have students read the article to themselves. **(4 min.)**
4. Have partners do Activities B and C. **(10 min.)**
5. Divide the class into two groups. Have one group discuss why the recommendations would be easy to follow and the other discuss why they would not. **(6 min.)**
6. Assign the last two questions in Activity E as homework. Tell students to write a paragraph of at least six sentences. **(2 min.)**

Le soir, au dîner, mange léger. Une soupe de légumes, un filet de poisson ou une tranche de jambon et des pâtes, une salade verte, un fruit cuit et un yaourt, c'est suffisant. Comme boisson, de l'eau. Tu ne dois pas boire de boissons avec du sucre ou de la caféine si tu veux bien dormir.

Et n'oublie pas de faire du sport tous les jours : du jogging, de la natation, du tennis, du football, du basket, de la danse, du yoga… ou une grande promenade avec ton chien !

La pyramide alimentaire française

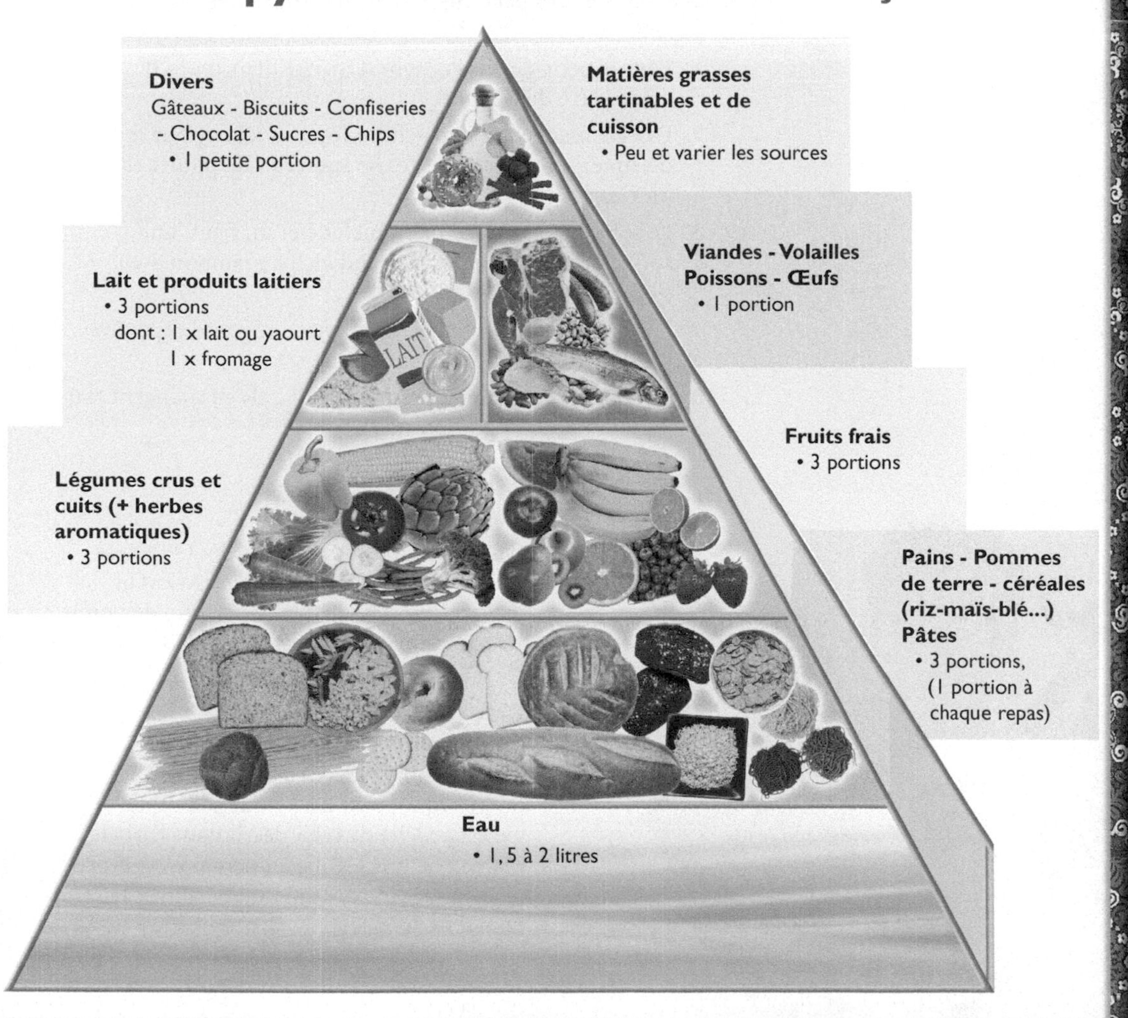

Communities

School Link

Have students use the information in the article to create posters in French that promote healthful eating habits. Students can ask permission to display their posters in the school cafeteria. As an alternative, have small groups work together to build a model of the French food pyramid to display.

 5.1

Connections

Health Link

Tell students that people often snack on unhealthful foods because they are simply not paying attention to what they eat. Have students keep a food journal for a week and then write a report comparing what they ate to the recommendations in the article.

3.1

Through the practice of listening and reading comprehension, as well as essay writing, **Lecture et écriture** helps students prepare for the **Interpretive Reading and Listening** and the **Presentational Writing** sections of the AP Language and Culture Exam.

Differentiated Instruction

SLOWER PACE LEARNERS

Help students activate their background knowledge by creating a chart with the headings *Good* and *Bad* across the top and the words *Breakfast, Lunch, Snack,* and *Dinner* listed down the left side. Have students fill in the chart with foods they should and should not eat at each meal. After they have read the article, ask students how closely their charts matched the advice of the nutritionist.

1.2

SPECIAL LEARNING NEEDS

Students with Dyslexia As an addition to **Stratégie pour lire,** students may benefit from highlighting the visual clues, quotes, headings, and formats before reading the passage. Help students understand or translate the highlighted words before they read independently. Then have students refer to the highlighted cues as they read to better understand the meaning.

1.2

Additional Practice

For more reading practice, see **Variations littéraires,** pp. 396–397.

Lecture et écriture

B Possible Answers

1. Il faut bien manger et faire du sport.
2. Il ne faut pas manger trop de sucre et de matières grasses.
3. Il faut manger des légumes.
4. Le repas le plus important est le déjeuner.
5. Elle recommande de l'eau.
6. Je dois en faire une tous les jours.

Comparisons

Comparing and Contrasting

In France, hospitals are government funded, and health insurance is provided to everyone. In the United States, hospitals are generally privately owned, and individuals or their employers are responsible for health insurance. Have students research the advantages and disadvantages of both systems. You might have students take sides and stage a debate over which system is best. 4.2

Cultures

Practices and Perspectives

There are many idiomatic expressions in French that refer to body parts. Some of these, such as **avoir le cœur sur la main** *(to be very generous)* and **avoir l'estomac dans les talons** *(to be very hungry)*, may sound like serious health problems. Have students write and perform a humorous skit in which a doctor, who is just learning French, tries to give advice to people who say they are suffering from these unusual "ailments." 2.1

Pendant la lecture

B Réponds aux questions suivantes. 1.2

1. Pour avoir une vie équilibrée, qu'est-ce qu'il faut faire?
2. Qu'est-ce qu'il ne faut pas manger trop souvent?
3. Qu'est-ce qu'il faut manger le plus souvent, des fruits ou des légumes?
4. Quel est le repas le plus important de la journée?
5. Quelle boisson est-ce que Mme Dauxais recommande?
6. Quand est-ce que tu dois faire une activité physique?

C Est-ce que Mme Dauxais penserait que les choix alimentaires des personnes suivantes sont bons? Réponds par **oui** ou **non**. 1.2

1. Pour le petit-déjeuner, Robert mange deux œufs, des toasts et un verre de lait. non
2. Pascale mange la même chose tous les jours pour le déjeuner: une salade verte, un morceau de poulet et du riz. non
3. Le soir, Sylvie mange une omelette et un fruit, une soupe et une salade ou un sandwich au jambon avec des crudités. oui
4. Pour le dîner, chez Alain, on mange un grand repas avec tous les groupes alimentaires. non
5. Thomas et Frédéric adorent les fruits. Ils en mangent tous les jours pour le goûter. oui

Après la lecture

D Quel est le message de l'article? Qu'est-ce que tu as écrit sur ta liste dans **Avant la lecture?** Est-ce que tu as beaucoup de points en commun avec l'article? Lesquels? 1.2

E Est-ce que tu penses que les recommandations mentionnées dans l'article sont difficiles à suivre? Pourquoi ou pourquoi pas? Est-ce que ton mode de vie est proche de celui décrit dans l'article? Est-ce que ton régime alimentaire est proche de celui décrit par la pyramide alimentaire? Que dois-tu changer? 1.3

Core Instruction

TEACHING ESPACE ÉCRITURE

1. Read and discuss **Stratégie pour écrire** and **Je lui ai dit...** as a class. **(5 min.)**
2. Have students do step 1. Remind them to use the subjunctive or the conditional. **(20 min.)**
3. Have partners do step 2. **(15 min.)**
4. Have students work with a different partner to do step 3. **(6 min.)**
5. You may wish to post the records in the classroom. Have students select the most interesting set of patients and the most innovative advice. **(4 min.)**

Espace écriture

STRATÉGIE pour écrire

Providing specific details can give clarity and plausibility to a report or story. The details you add provide concrete examples which help your readers understand what you have written and make your writing more vivid and interesting.

Je lui ai dit, «Tu ferais bien de te reposer». 1.3

You're a physician keeping personal records of your patients' problems and the recommendations you give them. Recreate today's chart with several patients' detailed complaints, symptoms, or accounts of accidents, followed by your diagnosis and advice or prescriptions.

1 Plan

Imagine six different accidents or conditions that prompt patients to visit your office, and make a list of them in French. Match words and expressions from the chapter's vocabulary to each accident or condition. Next to each, write two sentences with advice you might give to your patients, using the subjunctive or the conditional tense.

Nom	Symptômes	Conseils
Mireille		
Pascal		
Corinne		
Anne		
Jean		
Alain		

2 Rédaction

Now make a chart like one a doctor might keep on a clipboard, with headings such as **nom, symptômes,** and **conseils.** For each condition or accident, provide interesting and specific details. Then provide your diagnosis, followed by your medical or health advice. Use the sentences you wrote earlier: **Thierry s'est foulé la cheville quand il jouait au football. Je lui ai dit, «Il faut que vous vous reposiez. Ne faites pas de sport pendant huit semaines».**

3 Correction

Trade drafts with a classmate and make suggestions that might improve the thoroughness and detail of the conditions. Check for diagnoses that are appropriate. Check for correct use and forms of the subjunctive and the **passé composé, imparfait,** and conditional tenses.

4 Application

You may wish to provide a title in the form of an invented letterhead for your office. Display the records on a bulletin board for comparison. Which doctors had the most interesting set of patients? Who gave the most innovative advice?

Process Writing

Avant d'écrire Before students begin writing, have them brainstorm the kinds of complaints that people have when they go to a doctor's office. Encourage them to think back to information they gathered from activities they did in class to come up with their list. As they write, make sure that they are using the vocabulary and grammar studied in this chapter. When students have finished the activity, have them proofread what they have written for organization, style, and content.

Writing Assessment

To assess the **Espace écriture,** you can use the following rubric. For additional rubrics, see the *Assessment Program* or refer to the *Generate Success* Rubric Generator.

Writing Rubric	4	3	2	1
Content (Complete—Incomplete)				
Comprehensibility (Comprehensible—Seldom comprehensible)				
Accuracy (Accurate—Seldom accurate)				
Organization (Well-organized—Poorly organized)				
Effort (Excellent effort—Minimal effort)				

18-20: A
16-17: B
14-15: C
12-13: D
Under 12: F

Differentiated Instruction

ADVANCED LEARNERS

As an alternative writing activity, have students interview their own doctor about ailments and injuries students have come to see him or her about recently and the advice he or she gave them. Have students write a report in French based on the interview. 1.3

SPECIAL LEARNING NEEDS

Students with AD(H)D Ask students to research the latest food pyramid adopted by American nutritionists. They should then compare the American with the French food pyramid in a paragraph written in French. The comparison should include similarities and differences found in the two recommendations and the student's opinion as to which one is the most healthful. 4.2

Assess

Assessment Program
Quiz: Lecture
Quiz: Écriture
Online Assessment
my.hrw.com
Test Generator 

Prépare-toi pour l'examen

Resources

Planning:
Lesson Planner
Teacher One Stop

Practice:
Cahier d'activités
Media Guide
DVD Tutor, Disc 2
Projectable Transparencies
Situation, Chapitre 8
Picture Sequences, Chapter 8
Audio CD 8, Tr. 9–12
@HOMETUTOR

1 Possible Answers

1. Amadou a mal à la tête. Il a de la fièvre et il est fatigué. Il doit rester au lit et prendre des comprimés.
2. Aminata a mal à l'estomac et mal au cœur. Il est important qu'elle boive de l'eau gazeuse et qu'elle dorme beaucoup.

Reteaching

Write **Il faut que je _____ mes devoirs** on the board. Ask a volunteer to fill in the blank **(fasse)** and explain how to form the subjunctive. Then have students express their intentions **(Je dois finir mes études.)** as you write their sentences on the board. Have the class change each sentence, using **Il faut que...**

4 Answers

1. Moi, je ferais plus souvent de l'exercise.
2. Ma famille ne mangerait pas beaucoup de matières grasses.
3. Mes amis et moi, nous irions plus souvent au gymnase.
4. Mon meilleur ami / Ma meilleure amie ne fumerait pas.
5. Mes amis mangeraient plus de fruits.

Chapitre 8

Prépare-toi pour l'examen

@HOMETUTOR

1 Vocabulaire 1
- to ask and tell how you feel
- to describe symptoms and give advice

pp. 270–273

1 Amadou et Aminata sont malades. Imagine comment chacun se sent *(feels)*. Ensuite, dis ce que chacun doit faire. 1.2

1. Amadou

2. Aminata

2 Grammaire 1
- the subjunctive of regular verbs
- the subjunctive of irregular verbs

Un peu plus
- more expressions with the subjunctive

pp. 274–279

2 Ton ami a la grippe. Donne-lui des conseils avec **il faut que tu...** et les verbes suivants. 1.2

1. aller chez le médecin Il faut que tu ailles chez le médecin.
2. rester au lit Il faut que tu restes au lit.
3. dormir beaucoup Il faut que tu dormes beaucoup.
4. prendre des médicaments Il faut que tu prennes des médicaments.
5. finir tous tes médicaments Il faut que tu finisses tous tes médicaments.
6. boire beaucoup d'eau Il faut que tu boives beaucoup d'eau.
7. prendre des vitamines Il faut que tu prennes des vitamines.
8. ne... pas sortir ce soir Il ne faut pas que tu sortes ce soir.

3 Vocabulaire 2
- to complain about health and to give advice
- to sympathize with someone

pp. 282–285

3 Qu'est-ce qu'il faut faire dans les circonstances données? Qu'est-ce qu'il ne faut pas faire? Écris au moins deux phrases pour chaque circonstance. 1.2

1. pour être en bonne santé
2. pour perdre du poids
3. pour devenir plus fort *(get stronger)*
4. pour être moins stressé

Preparing for the Exam

FOLD-N-LEARN

Four-Flap Study Aid

1. Have students fold a sheet of paper in half twice, from side to side and from top to bottom. Have them unfold the paper and turn it sideways. Then ask them to fold the right and left edges to meet at the center.
2. Ask students to cut along the middle creases to form four flaps. They should not cut past the folded edges of the long flaps.
3. On the upper left flap, ask students to list the parts of the body in **Vocabulaire 1** and on the upper right flap expressions to tell how they feel and to describe symptoms. On the lower right flap, have students write expressions to complain about health, to give advice, and to talk about dietary habits. They should write the English equivalents under each flap.
4. Have students review with the booklets.

4 Dis si ces personnes devraient faire ou ne pas faire les choses indiquées s'ils voulaient faire plus attention à leur santé. 1.2

MODÈLE à ton ami(e) (sauter des repas)
Si tu voulais faire plus attention à ta santé, tu ne sauterais pas de repas.

1. moi, je (faire plus souvent de l'exercice)
2. ma famille (manger beaucoup de matières grasses)
3. mes amis et moi (aller plus souvent au gymnase)
4. mon meilleur ami / ma meilleure amie (fumer)
5. mes amis (manger plus de fruits)

5 Réponds aux questions suivantes. 2.1, 2.2

1. Qu'est-ce que la France et le Sénégal ont en commun en ce qui concerne la médecine?
2. Décris la nourriture sénégalaise.

6 Samuel voudrait être en bonne santé et il te pose des questions. Donne-lui de bons conseils en répondant à ses questions par **a) oui** ou **b) non.** CD 8, Tr. 9 1.2 **1.** b **2.** b **3.** a **4.** a

7 Avec un(e) camarade, vous allez jouer les rôles d'un(e) jeune qui ne se sent pas bien et d'un docteur. D'abord, lisez les instructions pour chaque réplique *(exchange)*. Ensuite, créez votre dialogue en utilisant des expressions que vous avez apprises. 1.1

Élève A:	Dis bonjour au/à la patient(e). Fais une observation sur son apparence et demande-lui ce qu'il/elle a.
Élève B:	Explique tes symptômes au docteur.
Élève A:	Questionne le/la patient(e) sur ses habitudes (comment il/elle mange, dort, etc.)
Élève B:	Parle au docteur de tes habitudes.
Élève A:	Donne des conseils au/à la patient(e) sur de meilleures habitudes à prendre.
Élève B:	Pose une question au docteur sur ce que tu dois faire comme sport.
Élève A:	Réponds au/à la patient(e) et rassure-le/la *(reassure him/her)*.
Élève B:	Remercie le docteur et dis-lui au revoir.

Online Assessment
my.hrw.com
Chapter Self-test

4 Grammaire 2
- the conditional
- si clauses

Un peu plus
- the conditional to make polite requests

pp. 286–291

5 Culture
- **Flash culture** **pp. 272, 276, 284, 288**
- **Comparaisons** **pp. 280–281**

Prépare-toi pour l'examen

Prépare-toi pour l'examen

5 Answers

1. Il existe un système d'assurance maladie accessible à tous.
2. Les Sénégalais mangent beaucoup de poisson, de riz et de cacahuètes.

6 Script

1. J'ai grossi depuis l'année dernière. Est-ce qu'il faut que je mange plus de matières grasses?
2. Pour maigrir, il faut que je fume et que je saute des repas?
3. Je suis très stressé. Je pense faire du yoga. C'est une bonne idée?
4. J'ai décidé de manger équilibré, de prendre des vitamines et de faire plus d'exercice. Je fais bien, non?

7 Sample conversation:

a. **Bonjour. Tu n'as pas l'air d'aller. Qu'est-ce qu'il y a?**
b. **Je suis fatigué(e). J'ai mal à l'estomac. Je crois que je suis malade.**
a. **Qu'est-ce que tu manges en général? Est-ce que tu fais du sport? Est-ce que tu dors bien?**
b. **Je mange des hamburgers et des frites et j'aime jouer à des jeux vidéo. Je dors mal.**
a. **Tu devrais manger léger et tu ferais bien de faire de l'exercice.**
b. **Quel sport est-ce que je devrais faire?**
a. **Il faudrait que tu fasses de la musculation et du yoga. Ça va aller mieux.**
b. **Merci, docteur. Au revoir.**

Additional Speaking Practice

- For additional speaking practice, you might use the *Picture Sequences Transparency* for Chapter 8 found in the *Projectable Transparencies.*
- To assess the speaking activities in this section, you might use the *Generate Success* Rubric Generator or the oral rubrics found in the *Assessment Program.*

Pre-AP Practice

7 This guided conversation activity helps students practice oral exchanges using material from this chapter and previous chapters. The activity helps prepare students for the **Interpersonal Speaking** section of the AP French Language and Culture Exam.

Chapitre 8

Prépare-toi pour l'examen

Grammar Review
For more practice with the grammar topics in this chapter, see the *Grammar Tutor*, the *DVD Tutor*, the *@HomeTutor*, or the *Cahier de vocabulaire et grammaire*.

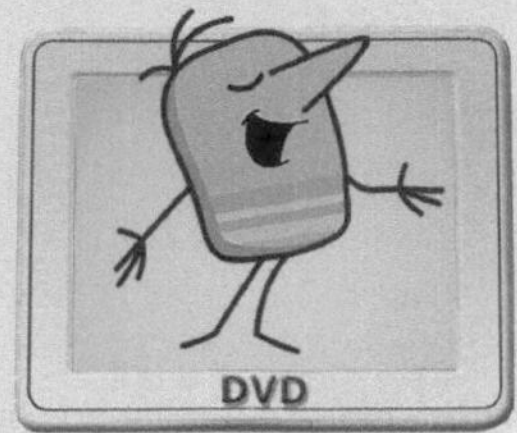

Grammavision

Online Edition
Students might use the online textbook and Performance Space to practice the **Lettres et sons** feature.

Dictée Script

1. Hier, ma sœur a eu mal au cœur.
2. Les œufs, c'est bon pour la santé.
3. Il ne faut pas manger trop de bœuf.
4. Chaque année il m'envoie une carte de vœux.
5. Lætica a deux sœurs.

Game
Le monstre The rose technique is fun and a useful way to practice vocabulary. Ask students to draw a monster using the body parts in the **Vocabulaire** (with two heads, three arms, and so on). Tell them not to let other students see what they draw. Then have them describe their monster to a partner, holding the drawing so the partner cannot see it. The student draws the monster his or her partner describes. Partners should then compare the two monsters and evaluate description, comprehension, and creative interpretation. 1.1

Grammaire 1
- the subjunctive of regular verbs
- the subjunctive of irregular verbs

Un peu plus
- more expressions with the subjunctive

pp. 274–279

Résumé: Grammaire 1

Use the **subjunctive** when talking about something that is a *necessity*, such as after the phrases **il faut que, il est nécessaire que** and **il est important que.**

To form the subjunctive of most verbs, drop the **-ent** from the **ils** form of a present-tense verb and add these endings:

	parler	finir	vendre
je	parl**e**	finiss**e**	vend**e**
tu	parl**es**	finiss**es**	vend**es**
il/elle/on	parl**e**	finiss**e**	vend**e**
nous	parl**ions**	finiss**ions**	vend**ions**
vous	parl**iez**	finiss**iez**	vend**iez**
ils/elles	parl**ent**	finiss**ent**	vend**ent**

Some verbs have different subjunctive stems for the **nous** and **vous** forms. See page 276 to see how these verbs are formed in the subjunctive.

The verbs **aller, être, avoir,** and **faire** all have irregular forms in the subjunctive. See page 276 for a table showing these forms.

Grammaire 2
- the conditional
- **si** clauses

Un peu plus
- the conditional to make polite requests

pp. 286–291

Résumé: Grammaire 2

Use the **conditional** to tell what *would* happen.

To form the conditional, add these endings to the future stem: **-ais, -ais, -ait, -ions, -iez, -aient**

parler → je parler**ais**
vendre → elle vendr**ait**
aller → ils ir**aient**

To tell what someone would do if things were different, use a **si** clause with a verb in the **imparfait** and a result clause with a verb in the **conditional.**

Si j'étais riche, j'achèterais une nouvelle voiture.

The expression **si + on + imparfait** is useful for inviting someone to do something or for making a suggestion: **Si on allait voir un film?**

Lettres et sons

The symbols œ and æ CD 8, Tr. 10–12

These symbols are a combination of two letters and you will sometimes see the letters written separately. Notice the sounds in the words **cœur, sœur,** and **Lætica.**

Jeux de langue
Le cœur de ma sœur ne meurt jamais!

Dictée 1.2
Écris les phrases de la dictée.

Chapter Review

DVD Program

Online Edition

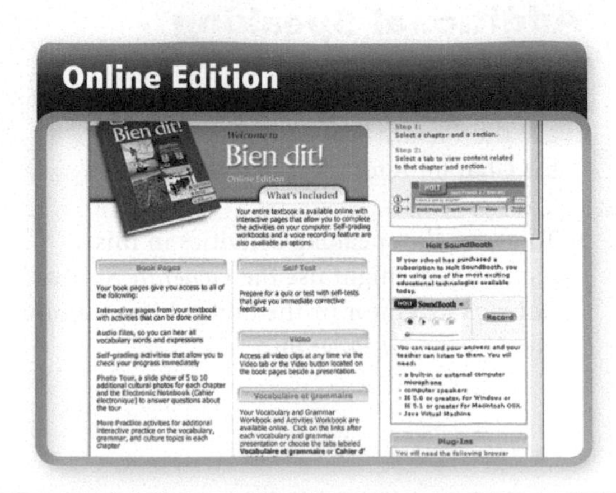

Prépare-toi pour l'examen

Résumé: Vocabulaire 1

PRACTICE FRENCH WITH HOLT MCDOUGAL APPS!

To ask and tell how you feel

avoir la grippe/de la fièvre	*to have the flu/a fever*
se blesser	*to injure oneself*
le bras	*arm*
se brûler	*to burn oneself*
se casser	*to break (one's leg)*
le cerveau	*brain*
la cheville	*ankle*
le cœur	*heart*
le corps	*body*
le cou	*neck*
le dentiste	*dentist*
le doigt (de pied)	*finger (toe)*
le dos	*back*
l'épaule (f.)	*shoulder*
l'estomac (m.)	*stomach*
éternuer	*to sneeze*
être fatigué(e)	*to be tired*
se fouler	*to twist (one's ankle/wrist)*
le front	*forehead*
le genou	*knee*
la jambe	*leg*
la joue	*cheek*
la lèvre	*lip*
la main	*hand*
malade	*sick*
le médecin	*doctor*
le muscle	*muscle*
l'œil (m.)	*eye*
l'os (m.)	*bone*
le pied	*foot*
le poignet	*wrist*
le poumon	*lung*
prendre la température	*to take a temperature*
le sourcil	*eyebrow*
tousser	*to cough*
le visage	*face*
Ça n'a pas l'air d'aller.	*You don't seem to be doing well.*
J'ai mal dormi.	*I slept badly.*
Je me sens mal.	*I feel ill.*
Je ne me sens pas bien.	*I don't feel well.*
Non, je ne suis pas en forme.	*No, I'm not in good shape.*
Qu'est-ce que tu as?	*What's wrong?*
Qu'est-ce qu'il y a?	*What's wrong?*
Tu n'as pas bonne mine...	*You don't look good . . .*
Tu as mauvaise mine.	*You look bad.*
Tu as l'air...	*You seem . . .*

To describe symptoms and give advice, see p. 273

Résumé: Vocabulaire 2

To complain and give advice

avoir un régime équilibré	*to have a balanced diet*
consommer trop de matières grasses	*to consume/eat too many fatty foods*
être en bonne santé	*to be healthy*
faire des abdominaux (m.)	*to do abdominal exercises*
faire de l'exercice (m.)	*to exercise*
faire de la musculation	*to lift weights*
faire des pompes (f.)	*to do push ups*
faire un régime	*to go on a diet*
faire du yoga	*to do yoga*
fumer	*to smoke*
manger léger	*to eat light*
se nourrir	*to feed oneself*
perdre/prendre du poids	*to lose/to gain weight*
se peser	*to weigh oneself*
prendre des vitamines (f.)	*to take vitamins*
se priver de sommeil	*to deprive oneself of sleep*
les produits (m.) bio(logiques)	*organic products*
se relaxer/se reposer	*to relax/to rest*
sauter des repas (m.)	*to skip meals*
Il faudrait que tu...	*You should...*
J'ai mal partout.	*I ache everywhere.*
Je suis au régime.	*I'm on a diet.*
Pourquoi tu ne (n')... pas... ?	*Why don't you . . . ?*
Tu ferais bien de...	*You would do well to . . .*
Tu n'as qu'à...	*All you have to do is . . .*

To sympathize with someone, see p. 285

Holt McDougal French Apps

Remind students that they can use the Holt McDougal French Apps to review their vocabulary.

Proverbes

For French proverbs and activities related to the chapter theme and vocabulary, see **Proverbes et expressions,** pp. R6–R7.

Projectable Transparency

Situation Je ne me sens pas bien! 8

More Digital Resources

FOR THE STUDENT

Holt McDougal French Apps
@HomeTutor
News and Networking
Performance Space

FOR THE TEACHER

- Interactive Whiteboard Lessons
- Generate Success!

Assess

Assessment Program

Examen: Chapitre 8

Audio CD 8, Tr. 16–17

Examen oral: Chapitre 8

Alternative Assessment

Differentiated Practice and Assessment CD-ROM

Online Assessment
my.hrw.com

Test Generator 

Resources

Planning:
Lesson Planner
Teacher One Stop

Practice:
Cahier d'activités
Media Guide
Projectable Transparencies
Fine Art, Chapter 8
Audio CD 8, Tr. 13
Holt McDougal French Apps

1 Script

1. Frédéric s'est cassé la jambe en faisant du ski. Tu sais, il n'est vraiment pas trop sportif.
2. Anne a très mal aux dents. Elle est allée chez le dentiste.
3. Michel s'est fait mal en travaillant à la maison. Il s'est coupé.
4. Pauvre Sophie! Elle a de la fièvre. Où est l'aspirine?

2 Answers

1. à toute personne en bonne santé, de 2 ans et plus
2. Elles sont une source d'énergie importante.
3. Answers will vary.

Révisions cumulatives

CD 8, Tr. 13 1.2

1 C'est une journée difficile pour Justine et ses amis. Pour chaque phrase, choisis la photo qui convient. **1.** b **2.** a **3.** d **4.** c

a.

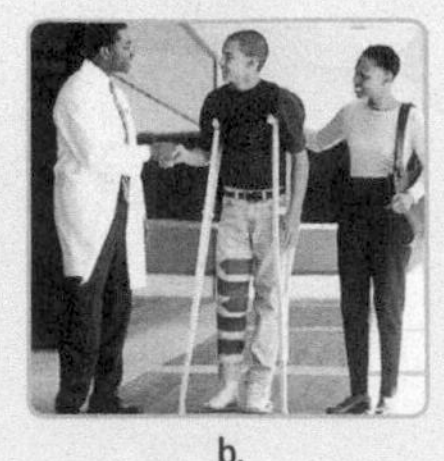
b.

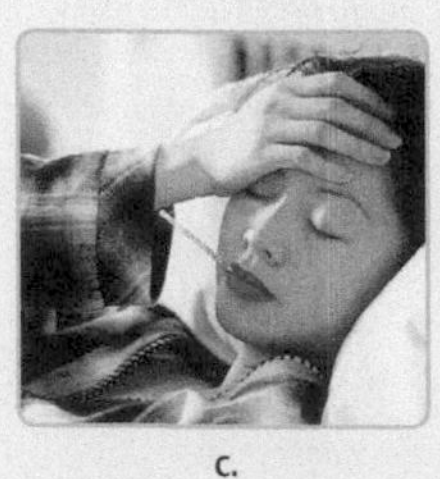
c.

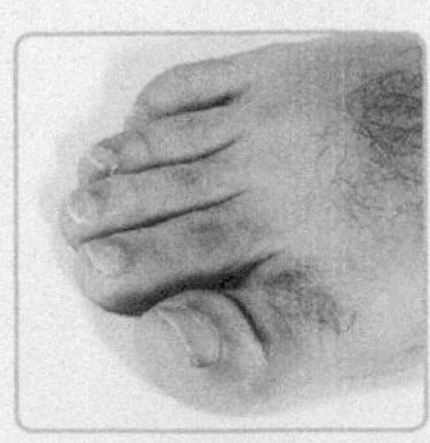
d.

2 Voilà un article Web sur la pyramide de l'équilibre alimentaire. Lis l'article et réponds aux questions qui suivent. 3.2

Choisissez les bonnes proportions pour une meilleure santé avec la pyramide de l'équilibre alimentaire.

- La pyramide de l'équilibre alimentaire s'adresse à toute personne en bonne santé, de 2 ans et plus.
- Ce modèle donne de l'importance aux groupes alimentaires qui se situent à la base de cette pyramide, et en particulier au groupe principal, celui des céréales sous toutes leurs formes : pain, céréales en grains, riz, pâtes alimentaires, etc.
- Le pain, le riz, les pâtes et les céréales sous diverses formes sont des aliments de base parce qu'ils sont une source d'énergie importante.
- Les céréales apportent aussi des vitamines, des minéraux et des fibres.

1. À qui est-ce que la pyramide alimentaire s'adresse?
2. Pourquoi est-il important de manger des céréales?
3. Compare la pyramide française à la pyramide alimentaire américaine.

Online Culture Project

Ask students to choose one city featured in their textbook (Paris, Quebec, Rennes, Dakar, or Nice). They should research online the health facilities or fitness centers in that city. What types of advice about healthful habits do their Web sites offer? Ask students to list the types of services the facilities offer, such as weight-training or aerobic workouts and instruction. Have students document their research with the URLs of the sites they visit. 1.3, 2.2

3 Regarde la scène et décris ce qui se passe. Qui est malade? Imagine les conversations et en petits groupes, jouez la scène pour la classe. 1.1, 2.2

Un souwère **du Sénégal**

4 Imagine que tu as décidé d'améliorer *(to improve)* ta santé. Crée un programme indiquant tes buts *(goals)* et ce que tu devrais et ne devrais pas faire. 1.3

Buts	Actions	Limitations
Je voudrais être moins stressé.	Je devrais faire du yoga.	Il ne faut pas que je me prive de sommeil.

5 **À ton tour**

Un sondage Create a survey to find out about the habits of your classmates. Ask about their classes, their daily routines, and their eating habits. Print the survey and have everyone in the class fill it out. Finally, analyze the results and post them in the classroom. 1.3

Révisions cumulatives

Fine Art Connection

Introduction Reverse-glass painting is a relatively new art form that came from Asian and Islamic countries in the late 19th century. It is now a popular form of artistic expression in urban Senegal. In the Wolof language, these glass paintings are named **souwères** (from the French **sous-verre).** They originally depicted only religious themes or scenes from the country's cultural and historical heritage. They are now evolving to showcase the daily life and concerns of Senegalese city dwellers.

Analyzing

To help students discuss the painting, you might use the following questions.

1. **Où sont ces personnages et pourquoi sont-ils là?**
2. **Qu'est-ce qu'il a, l'homme en gris (à gauche)?**
3. **Quel métier fait la femme en blanc?**
4. **Comment sait-on que cette œuvre d'art est africaine?** 3.1

Extension

Ask students to research the techniques and history of reverse-glass painting and to make a presentation. They should download pictures of reverse-glass paintings from Senegal and other countries from the Internet and bring them to class for a discussion. As a project, students with artistic inclinations may also want to attempt painting a picture in reverse order (details first) on a piece of glass.

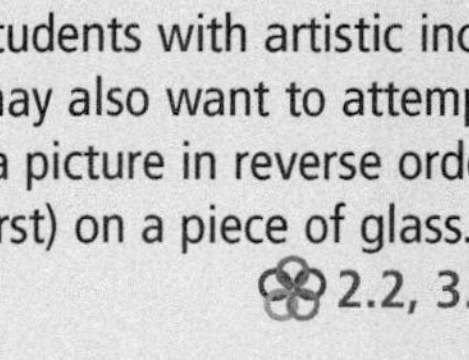

ACTFL Performance Standards

The activities in Chapter 8 target the communicative modes as described in the Standards.

Interpersonal	Two-way communication using receptive skills and productive skills	**Communication (SE),** pp. 273, 275, 277, 279, 285, 287, 289, 291 **Communication (TE),** pp. 273, 285, 287, 289, 291 **À ton tour,** p. 303
Interpretive	One-way communication using receptive skills	**Comparaisons,** pp. 280–281 **Communication (TE),** p. 275, 279 **Télé-roman,** pp. 292–293
Presentational	One-way communication using productive skills	**Communication (TE),** p. 277

Géoculture Overview

Nice

Bienvenue! This section is designed to familiarize the students with the geographic location, history, and cultural practices of the region to be explored. It provides a guide for classroom discussion and discovery of the differences and similarities of the student's own culture and that of the French-speaking world.

50-Minute Lesson Plans

Day 1

Lesson Sequence

Géoculture: Nice, pp. 304–305

- Have students locate Nice on the map. Can students guess what Nice's major industries are? Students should explain why they chose certain industries. **10 min.**
- Go over the photos and captions with students. **10 min.**
- See Map Activities, p. 304. **5 min.**
- Discuss Background Information, p. 304. **10 min.**
- Complete **Géo-quiz. 1 min.**
- Show **Géoculture** video. **4 min.**
- Have students answer **Questions,** p. 305. **10 min.**

Optional Resources

- **Savais-tu que...?,** p. 305
- Thinking Critically, p. 303B
- Research Online!, p. 303B

Homework Suggestions

Online Practice (**my.hrw.com**)

1.2, 1.3, 2.1, 2.2, 3.1, 3.2, 4.1, 4.2

Day 2

Lesson Sequence

Géoculture: Nice, pp. 306–307

- Briefly revisit the main points about the geography. **5 min.**
- Go over the photos and captions with students. **8 min.**
- Ask students if they have sampled or prepared any of the dishes introduced in the **Gastronomie** feature. If not, would they like to sample or prepare one of the dishes mentioned? Why or why not? **5 min.**
- Have students answer the **As-tu compris?** questions, p. 307. **7 min.**
- Do the Map Game on p. 303B. **25 min.**

Optional Resources

- Advanced Learners, p. 303B ▲
- Multiple Intelligences, p. 303B
- **Prépare-toi pour le quiz,** p. 303B
- Interdisciplinary Links, pp. 306–307

Homework Suggestions

Activité, p. 307
Study for the **Géoculture** quiz.

1.1, 1.2, 1.3, 2.1, 2.2, 3.1, 3.2, 4.2

90-Minute Lesson Plan

Block 1

Lesson Sequence

Géoculture: Nice, pp. 304–307

- Have students locate Nice on the map. Can students guess what Nice's major industries are? Students should explain why they chose certain industries. **10 min.**
- Go over the photos and captions with students. **20 min.**
- See Map Activities, p. 304. **5 min.**
- Discuss Background Information, p. 304. **10 min.**
- Complete **Géo-quiz. 1 min.**
- Show **Géoculture** video. **4 min.**
- Have students answer **Questions,** p. 305. **5 min.**
- Have students answer the **As-tu compris?** questions, p. 307. **5 min.**
- Ask students if they have sampled or prepared any of the dishes introduced in the **Gastronomie** feature. If not, would they like to sample or prepare one of the dishes mentioned? Why or why not? **5 min.**
- Do the Map Game on p. 303B. **25 min.**

Optional Resources

- **Savais-tu que ...?,** p. 305
- Advanced Learners, p. 303B ▲
- Multiple Intelligences, p. 303B
- Thinking Critically, p. 303B
- Research Online!, p. 303B
- Interdisciplinary Links, pp. 306–307
- **Prépare-toi pour le quiz,** p. 303B

Homework Suggestions

Online Practice (**my.hrw.com**)
Activité, p. 307
Study for the **Géoculture** quiz.

1.1, 1.2, 1.3, 2.1, 2.2, 3.1, 3.2, 4.1, 4.2

KEY

▲ Advanced Learners ◆ Slower Pace Learners ● Special Learning Needs

Géoculture

Differentiated Instruction

Advanced Learners

Extension Ask advanced learners to report on the architecture of Nice. They may want to use the architecture feature in **Géoculture** as a starting point and research in the library or on the Internet other architectural styles found in Nice. Encourage students to include brief descriptions (including dates) and illustrations of architectural styles. 1.3, 3.1

Multiple Intelligences

Intrapersonal Have students imagine that they are exchange students in Nice. Ask them to write a letter to their best friend in the United States, describing their experiences in, and feelings about, Nice. They should ask themselves questions. What do I like about Nice? What is my favorite food? What festival(s) do I like and why? Would I be happy living permanently in Nice? Students should write at least ten sentences. 1.1, 3.1

Thinking Critically

Drawing Inferences Ask students why one of the major streets of Nice is called **promenade des Anglais.** (The English began arriving for their winter vacations around 1730. The **promenade des Anglais** was built, along with other amenities, for the visitors. Even Queen Victoria visited regularly from 1895 to 1899.) Do students know places in the United States that are popular winter retreats for people who want to escape the cold winters at home? 2.1, 4.2

Quiz Preparation/Enrichment

Map Game Form groups of three to four students. Each group creates a Word Search puzzle. Students should hide within the grid terms they find on the map. Terms should be hidden horizontally, vertically, diagonally, backwards, or forwards. They should be treated as one word, without spaces in between words. Hyphens should be considered letters. There should be at least ten terms. Each group should make a copy of their grid on which all "hidden" terms are shaded in. Each group should complete the Word Search of another group. 1.1, 3.1

Prépare-toi pour le quiz

1. Students should draw a map of Nice, indicating major streets and sights and other geographic features.
2. Have students work in pairs. One partner describes a sight and the other guesses the sight described. Students should have at least three turns describing sights.
3. Ask students to imagine that they are working for the tourist bureau in Nice. Their assignment is to write an article entitled **Découvrez Nice!** In this article students invite readers to visit Nice and explore its sights, art, cuisine, and festivals. 3.1

Research Online!

L'histoire de Nice Students should create an illustrated tour through the history of Nice. They should make a timeline that includes dates and brief descriptions of five important events in the history of Nice. The timeline should have pictures that illustrate events. Students should document their Internet sources by noting the names and the URLs of all the sites they consulted. Have students present their tour to the class. 1.3, 3.1

Resources

Planning:
Lesson Planner
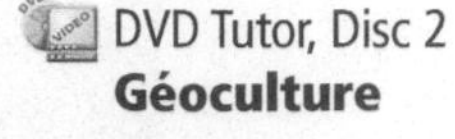 Teacher One Stop

Presentation:
Projectable Transparencies
Carte 2
DVD Tutor, Disc 2
Géoculture

Practice:
Cahier d'activités
Media Guide

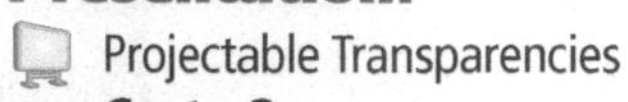

Map ACTIVITIES

1. Have students locate Nice on the map of France on page R2. Ask students to name the mountain range to the northwest of Nice, the body of water to the south, and the country to the east. **(les Alpes, la mer Méditerranée, l'Italie)**
2. Tell students that Nice is known for its subtropical climate. Ask them why they think Nice has such a mild climate. (protected by mountains to the north and the sea to the south)
3. Ask students if they know both the French and English names for the coast where Nice is located. **(la Côte d'Azur,** the French Riviera) Have them find and name the two coastal cities on either side of Nice. (Cannes, Monaco)

Chapitres 9 et 10

Géoculture

Nice

DVD
Géoculture

Les ruines romaines
Sur une colline au nord de la ville se trouve le site archéologique où l'on peut visiter des ruines romaines. 3

Le port Lympia
Les maisons du port de Nice sont de style italien. Nice a été une possession italienne jusqu'en 1860. 2

7 La Cathédrale orthodoxe russe

Boulevard Gambetta

Le musée d'Art moderne et d'art contemporain (MAMAC)
On y trouve toutes les tendances de l'art contemporain de la deuxième moitié *(half)* du 20e siècle. De ses terrasses, on a une très belle vue de Nice. 1

Promenade des Anglais 6

Baie des Anges

Almanach

Nom des habitants
Les Niçois

Population
Plus de 340.000 habitants

Personnages célèbres
Arman, Joseph Garibaldi, Yves Klein, François Payard

Industries
Tourisme, trafic portuaire, informatique, hautes technologies

Savais-tu que...?
Les Niçois ont leur propre langue: le nissard.

Background Information

Geography

Nice is located on the Mediterranean Sea in southeast France, about 20 miles from the Italian border. Overlooking the **baie des Anges,** the city was built below the Estérel and Mercantour mountains (part of the Alps). Nice covers 28 square miles and is the 5th largest city in France. **Vieux Nice** and the port are in the southeastern part of the city, while the modern sections extend out from **Place Masséna,** the central square, to the north and west behind the **promenade des Anglais.**

History

Greeks from Marseilles founded Nice around 350 BC. They named the city Nikaia, from the Greek word "nike," meaning *victory.* In the first century, the city became part of the Roman Empire. Cimiez, the wealthy residential area north of Nice, was the site of the province's capital.

Nice was annexed by France in 1860 after being ruled by various royal houses from Italy and France for centuries.

Mussolini, Italy's dictator during World War II, claimed and occupied Nice from 1940 to 1945.

Nice

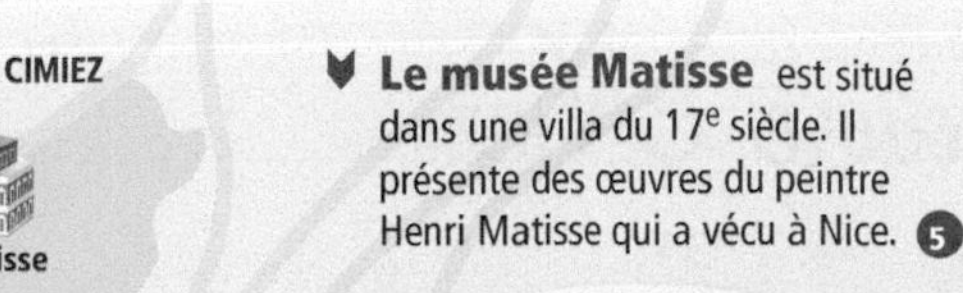

Le musée Matisse est situé dans une villa du 17e siècle. Il présente des œuvres du peintre Henri Matisse qui a vécu à Nice. 5

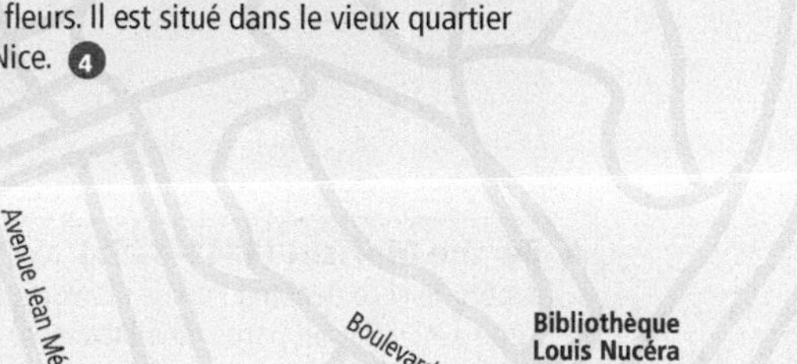

Le cours Saleya est apprécié pour ses terrasses, ses restaurants et son marché aux fleurs. Il est situé dans le vieux quartier de Nice. 4

La promenade des Anglais
C'est un Anglais, Lewis Way, qui a fait construire cette promenade le long de la baie des Anges au 19e siècle. Aujourd'hui, «la Prom» fait le bonheur des amateurs de roller. 6

La cathédrale orthodoxe russe
En 1860, beaucoup de Russes vivaient à Nice. Leur impératrice a initié la construction de cette église typiquement russe. 7

Géo-quiz

3.1

La promenade des Anglais longe une baie. Comment s'appelle cette baie? la baie des Anges

Comparisons

Language Note

Romance languages, like French, Spanish, and Italian, descend from vulgar Latin, the language spoken by common people in the Roman Empire. **Le nissard,** the local language of Nice, also evolved from vulgar Latin. Nissard is not just a regional dialect; it has its own vocabulary and grammar. Many street signs in Nice and the surrounding area appear in both French and Nissard. Write these Nissard words on the board and have students guess their French translations: *detestà, aimà, countent, famihamilha, amic/amiga/amigui.* **(détester, aimer, content, famille, ami[e])** Ask students which words have cognates in English. Finally, have students devise some grammar rules for Nissard, based on the examples and what they know about languages. 3.2, 4.1

Cultures

Products and Perspectives

English tourists began arriving in Nice during the second half of the 18th century, lured by the city's mild climate. The English church raised funds to build **la promenade des Anglais.** Stretching almost three miles along the coast, it is lined with palm trees, cafés, hotels, and apartments. Locals and tourists alike go there daily to jog, walk, roller blade, and relax. Ask students why they think this street has come to symbolize Nice. 2.2

Language Examination

Géoculture helps students better understand practices, products, and perspectives of French-speaking cultures and their relationship to one another. It can be used to practice for the **Interpretive Communication** and **Presentational Writing** sections of the AP Language and Culture Exam.

Savais-tu que...?

Students might be interested in knowing the following facts about Nice.

- The beaches in Nice are covered with smooth, round pebbles, not sand. Some of the beaches are free while others are **plages concédées** (private), where bathers must rent a chair or mattress to use on the beach.
- Nice is home to Europe's largest science and technology park, Sophia Antipolis. Over 1,000 international hi-tech companies conduct research there.
- Nice is the second most popular tourist destination in France after Paris.

Questions

1.2

1. **Pourquoi est-ce que le cours Saleya est apprécié? (pour ses terrasses, ses restaurants, son marché aux fleurs)**
2. **À qui est-ce que Nice appartenait avant 1860? (à l'Italie)**
3. **De quelle époque est l'art du MAMAC? (de la seconde moitié du 20e siècle)**
4. **Qu'est-ce qu'on peut faire sur la promenade des Anglais? (du roller)**
5. **Qui a initié la construction d'une cathédrale orthodoxe russe? (l'impératrice de Russie)**

Cultures

Products and Perspectives

In the 1950's, post-war consumerism and mass production led a number of artists like Arman to seek new forms of expression that dealt with the harsh realities of modern life. They founded an artistic movement called **nouveau réalisme.** Many of Arman's sculptures consisted of everyday objects that had been destroyed or accumulated into piles. Among his most famous collections were ***Accumulations, Déstructions, Poubelles,*** and ***Colères.*** Show students pictures of Arman's sculptures. Ask students to explain what they think Arman is saying about modern society in each sculpture and why he chose the particular objects featured. 2.2, 3.2

Comparisons

Comparing and Contrasting

Le Carnaval de Nice is a two-week celebration before the traditional Catholic fast of Lent. Dating back to the Middle Ages, it includes parades, balls, concerts, fireworks shows, and more. The celebration begins on a Saturday with a flower parade. A Carnival parade usually consists of 20 floats based on that year's theme; over 100 **grosses têtes,** people wearing giant heads of **papier mâché;** and street theater and music groups. All the floats and "big heads" are made by volunteer craftsman, called **carnavaliers.** On the last evening of Carnival, the effigy of His Majesty King Carnival is burned. Have students research **Mardi Gras** traditions in the United States and compare them to those in Nice. 4.2

Découvre Nice

Arts

Arman (1928–2005) utilise des objets de la vie quotidienne pour créer des sculptures et des monuments publics.

Bundle of Clarinets. 1976. Soldered clarinets. Dimensions: 43 x 63 x 32.5 cm. Inv. AM1986-349. Musee National d'Art Moderne, Centre Georges Pompidou, Paris, France.

Yves Klein (1928–1962) a inventé la couleur IKB (*International Klein Blue*). Pendant une période de sa vie, il n'a utilisé que cette couleur dans toutes ses œuvres.

Yves Klein, Blue Sponge, 1959. Dry pigment in synthetic resin on sponge with metal rod and stone base. 39 x 12 x 10 inches (99.06 x 30.48 x 25.4 cm). Solomon R. Guggenheim Museum, New York. Gift Mrs. Andrew P. Fuller, 1964. 64.1752.

Berthe Morisot (1841–1895) a peint le port de Nice pendant l'un de ses voyages. Cette artiste faisait partie du mouvement impressionniste.

Fêtes et festivals

Le Carnaval de Nice anime la ville pendant les deux semaines qui précèdent le Carême.

La Bataille de fleurs est le défilé qui commence les festivités du Carnaval. On y offre des milliers de fleurs aux spectateurs.

Le Nice Jazz Festival a lieu en juillet. On peut assister à des concerts de jazz dans les arènes gallo-romaines et parmi les champs d'oliviers.

Interdisciplinary Links

Les arts 3.1

Art Link Berthe Morisot was one of the few recognized female painters of her time. Painter Édouard Manet introduced Morisot to a circle of young painters who later became known as the impressionists. She herself became a member of that movement. Although a lot of her paintings depict interior scenes, her teacher, famous painter Jean-Baptiste Corot, encouraged Morisot to paint outdoor scenes as well. She distinguished herself by applying large, light-colored touches to the canvas, which gives her works a delicate and fluid style.

Les fêtes et festivals 3.1

Math Link A **Bataille des fleurs** parade usually includes 20 floats, interspersed with different types of musical groups and marching bands. Each float is hand-decorated with some 4,000 local and foreign blossoms, such as carnations, roses, and gladiolas. Models generally sit on top of each float, tossing to spectators up to 60 pounds of flowers each during one parade. Have students calculate how many flowers would be used to decorate floats and how many pounds of flowers would be thrown during a 20-float parade.

Architecture

« **Le château de l'Anglais** est un exemple d'architecture Belle Époque. Construit en 1856, son style mélange des caractéristiques classiques avec celles des palais de l'Inde.

Online Practice

my.hrw.com
Photo Tour

Savais-tu que...?

Nice est la ville française qui a le plus grand nombre d'hôtels après Paris et son aéroport est le deuxième aéroport de France après celui de Paris.

« **La Bibliothèque Louis Nucéra** Inaugurée en 2002, la bibliothèque Louis Nucéra est constituée de la Tête Carré, sculpture monumentale qui accueille l'administration et la Bibliothèque Louis Nucéra.

« **Le Palais Lascaris** a été construit au milieu du 17e siècle par une famille italienne. Son architecture est de style baroque.

Gastronomie

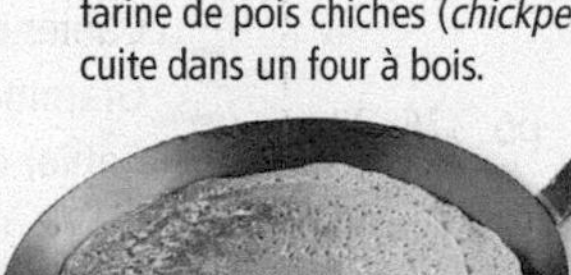

La socca est une crêpe à la farine de pois chiches (*chickpeas*) cuite dans un four à bois.

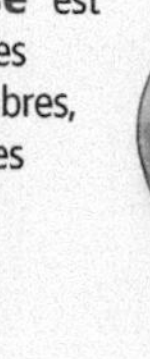

La salade niçoise est faite avec du thon, des tomates, des concombres, des poivrons verts, des œufs durs, des olives noires de Nice et des anchois (*anchovies*).

Les fleurs de courgettes farcies sont une spécialité de Nice. On les prépare avec du fromage, puis on les passe dans une pâte à beignet et ensuite on les frit (*fry*).

Activité

2.1, 2.2

1. **Art**: Qu'est-ce qu'Yves Klein a inventé?
2. **Fêtes et festivals**: Qu'est-ce qui se passe pendant la Bataille de fleurs?
3. **Architecture**: Quel est le style du château de l'Anglais?
4. **Gastronomie**: Quels sont les ingrédients de la salade niçoise?

Connections

Thinking Critically

Socca is a thin pancake made of chickpea flour and served hot in a paper cone. People in Nice eat **socca** like Parisians eat a **croissant** or **pain au chocolat.** One story about the origin of **socca** claims that Italian artisans brought it to France. Another claims that when an invading army of Turks retreated, they left behind the chickpea flour pancakes they had been making. Ask students which of the stories seems more plausible and why.

2.2, 3.2

Activité Answers

1. la couleur IKB
2. On offre des milliers de fleurs aux spectateurs.
3. Belle Époque
4. du thon, des tomates, des concombres, des poivrons verts, des œufs durs, des olives noires et des anchois

As-tu compris?

You can use the following questions to check students' comprehension of **Géoculture.**

1. **De quel mouvement artistique Berthe Morisot faisait partie? (le mouvement impressionniste)**
2. **Quand est le Carnaval de Nice? (les deux semaines avant le Carême)**
3. **Qu'est-ce que c'est que la socca? (une crêpe à la farine de pois chiches)**

1.2

La gastronomie

3.1

Health Link **Niçoise,** or **à la niçoise,** is a term used to describe dishes that are prepared in the traditional style of Nice. Typical ingredients of these dishes include anchovies, garlic, black olives, and tomatoes. Olive oil, instead of butter, and fresh vegetables are also generally used in their preparation. **Salade niçoise** is perhaps the best known of these traditional dishes. Have students find out why many people consider **niçoise** cooking to be much more healthful than traditional French cooking.

L'architecture

3.1

History Link **La Belle Époque** was a period of French history that began around 1890 and lasted until World War I. Many considered it a golden era of beauty, peace, and artistic and scientific innovation. It gave birth to the cinema, cabaret, two artistic styles, Art Nouveau and Impressionism, and the new technologies of electricity and wireless communication. It was also a period of indulgence that eventually led to the rise of socialism and working class militancy. Have students research **la Belle Époque** and create a poster to highlight the era's acheivements.

Assess

Assessment Program
Quiz: Géoculture

Differentiated Practice and Assessment CD-ROM

Online Assessment
my.hrw.com

Test Generator 

Planning Guide

On s'amuse!

Chapter Section		Resources
Vocabulaire 1 • Movies, books	pp. 310–313	Projectable Transparencies: Vocabulaire 9.1, 9.2; Bell Work 9.1, 9.2, 9.3, 9.4 Cahier de vocabulaire et grammaire, pp. 97–102 Grammar Tutor for Students of French Cahier d'activités, pp. 81–83 Media Guide, pp. 33–36, 102–104
Grammaire 1 • Relative pronouns **qui, que** and **dont** • Present participles	pp. 314–317	
Application 1 • **Un peu plus:** Review of **c'est** and **il/elle est**	pp. 318–319	**Assessment Program** Quiz: Vocabulaire 1, pp. 247–248 Quiz: Grammaire 1, pp. 249–250 Quiz: Application 1, pp. 251–252
Culture • **Culture appliquée: Le Festival de Cannes** • **Comparaisons et Communauté**	pp. 320–321	Cahier d'activités, p. 84
Vocabulaire 2 • Television programs, music	pp. 322–325	Projectable Transparencies: Vocabulaire 9.3, 9.4; Bell Work 9.5, 9.6,9.7, 9.8 Cahier de vocabulaire et grammaire, pp. 103–108 Grammar Tutor for Students of French Cahier d'activités, pp. 85–87 Media Guide, pp. 33–36, 102–103, 105
Grammaire 2 • Interrogative pronouns • Demonstrative pronouns	pp. 326–329	
Application 2 • **Un peu plus:** Review of comparatives and superlatives	pp. 330–331	**Assessment Program** Quiz: Vocabulaire 2, pp. 253–254 Quiz: Grammaire 2, pp. 255–256 Quiz: Application 2, pp. 257–258
Télé-roman	pp. 332–333	Media Guide, pp. 103, 106
Lecture et écriture	pp. 334–337	Cahier d'activités, p. 88 Reading Strategies and Skills Handbook Intermediate Reader French InterActive Reader **Assessment Program** Quiz: Lecture, p. 259 Quiz: Écriture, p. 260
Prépare-toi pour l'examen • **Résumé de vocabulaire et grammaire** • **Lettres et sons**	pp. 338–341	Independent Study Guide, pp. 25–27, 41 Media Guide, p. 36 **Assessment Program** Examen: Chapitre 9, pp. 261–266 Examen oral: Chapitre 9, p. 325
Révisions cumulatives	pp. 342–343	Projectable Transparencies: Fine Art, Ch. 9 Cahier d'activités, pp. 84, 89–90
Variations littéraires • **La littérature au cinéma**	pp. 398–399	Reading Strategies and Skills Handbook Intermediate Reader French InterActive Reader

Visit Us Online
my.hrw.com
Online Edition

Pacing Suggestions

	Essential	Recommended	Optional
Vocabulaire 1 • Movies, books • **Flash culture**	✔		
Grammaire 1 • Relative pronouns **qui, que** and **dont** • Present participles • **Flash culture**	✔		
Application 1 • **Un peu plus:** Review of **c'est** and **il/elle est**	✔		
Culture • **Culture appliquée: Le Festival de Cannes** • **Comparaisons et Communauté**		✔	
Vocabulaire 2 • Television programs, music • **Flash culture**	✔		
Grammaire 2 • Interrogative pronouns • Demonstrative pronouns • **Flash culture**	✔		
Application 2 • **Un peu plus:** Review of comparatives and superlatives	✔		
Télé-roman • Épisode 9: **Le Secret de la statuette**			✔
Lecture et écriture • **Génération télé** (Lecture) • **Les gros succès et les navets de l'année** (Écriture)		✔	
Prépare-toi pour l'examen		✔	
Révisions cumulatives			✔
Variations littéraires • **La littérature au cinéma**			✔

Technology

Bien dit! Online
- Student Edition with multi-media
- **performance space** recording tool
- Interactive activities with feedback
- Self-tests with feedback
- Cahier d'activités (Interactive workbook)
- Cahier de vocabulaire et grammaire (Interactive workbook)
- Holt Online Assessment

DVD Tutor
- Télé-vocab
- Grammavision
- Télé-roman

@HOMETUTOR
- Interactive games
- Differentiated Practice
- Cultural video

Audio Program
- Student Edition listening activities
- Assessment listening activities
- Songs

Teacher One Stop™
- Complete resources
- ExamView Pro Test Generator
- Holt Calendar Planner

Holt McDougal Apps

Interactive Whiteboard Lessons

Differentiated Practice and Assessment CD

For slower pace and advanced learner options, see the Differentiated Practice and Assessment CD.

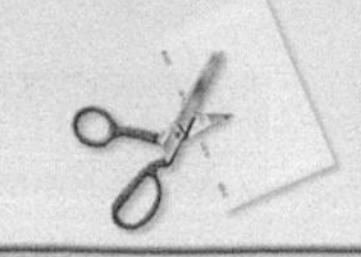

Projects

Guide d'amusement

Students make an entertainment guide for their community. They create or research local events and write descriptions of them in French. Students may look for ideas in magazines, newspapers, brochures, or on the Internet. 1.3

Suggested Sequence

1. In groups of three, students create entertainment guides that include short descriptions of at least six local events. Each group member is responsible for writing two descriptions and peer-editing the others.
2. Show a newspaper entertainment guide to explain the project. Students should include films, concerts, plays, exhibits, and sports. Encourage students to create events of their own.
3. As a group, students prepare a rough draft of their guide and peer-edit it by exchanging with another group. They might sketch the layout of the guide for clarity.
4. Students may include photos from magazines to illustrate the events described. The final product may be folded like a brochure, put together in booklet form, or be a single-page poster.

 Creativity and Innovation

Grading the project

Suggested point distribution (100 points total)

Vocabulary use .... 40 pts.
Appearance.............. 20 pts.
Creativity................ 20 pts.
Grammar and language use .... 20 pts.

Partner Class Project

Have students imagine they work for a magazine that is preparing an article comparing what students liked a year ago with what they like now. They should create a survey that polls their partner class on what was popular last year. **Quels films étaient populaires l'année dernière? Quelle sorte de musique est-ce que tu aimais?** When the survey comes back from the partner class, students should use a drawing or design program to create a poster to show the results. 

 Technology Literacy

e-community

e-mail forum:

Location: http://french

Post the following questions on the classroom e-mail forum:

Quel est ton artiste, musicien ou écrivain préféré?

Qu'est-ce que tu penses de ses tableaux, de sa musique ou de ses livres? 5.1

All students will contribute to the list and then share the items.

Game Bank
For game ideas, see pages T60–T63.

Traditions

Carnaval

Carnaval, the word coming from *carne levare* (away with meat), is a traditional time of celebration before the fasting of Lent. It is known for excesses of food and entertainment. The Nice **Carnaval** is today one of the most famous of such celebrations in the world. **Carnaval** began in Nice in the year 1294 and was perpetuated in the late 1890s by the Count of Nice. Today, during **Carnaval,** there are grand balls, exhibitions, entertainment on the streets, musical events, and parades. Around 120,000 square meters of decorations and over 150,000 small colored lights set the scene for the parades. The **bataille des fleurs,** with hundreds of participants, is the most elaborate parade. It features the **grosses têtes,** or large heads, made of **papier mâché,** and large floats, decorated completely by hand with thousands of flowers. Ask students what practices are observed at the beginning of Lent in their town. 2.1

La cuisine

Herbes de Provence is a mixture of different herbs that grow naturally on the dry land of Provence. The blend may vary from producer to producer. Thyme and rosemary are always included. Then, some combination of the following herbs are added: summer savory, marjoram, oregano, sage, basil, fennel, tarragon, lavender, and bay leaf. **Herbes de Provence** is usually sold pre-packaged and is available in gourmet food stores. Encourage students to make **omelette provençale** in their foods class or at home for family and friends. 1.2, 2.2

Omelette provençale

pour 8 personnes

8 œufs
1/2 tasse de lait
1 oignon
3 tomates
2 cuillères à soupe d'huile d'olive
persil
thym
herbes de Provence
sel
poivre

Éplucher et couper l'oignon en petits morceaux. Faire cuire l'oignon dans une poêle avec l'huile d'olive. Laver et couper les tomates en tranches. Dans un bol, mélanger les œufs, le lait et les différentes herbes (herbes de Provence, persil, thym), le sel et le poivre. Ajouter les tomates. Une fois que l'oignon est cuit, l'ajouter aux œufs, puis verser le tout dans la poêle qui a servi à cuire l'oignon. Laisser cuire pendant 5 à 10 minutes. Servir.

Traditions

Listening Activity Scripts

Vocabulaire à l'œuvre 1

1 p. 312, CD 9, Tr. 1

1. — Chloé, je ne sais pas quoi louer!
   — Est-ce que tu as vu ce film de science-fiction?
   — Non, pas encore.
   — C'est une bonne adaptation du roman.
2. — Chloé, tu as vu ce film de guerre?
   — Oui, je l'ai vu. C'est pas génial. En fait, c'est déprimant.
3. — Est-ce que tu sais si ce film a des sous-titres?
   — Oui, il a des sous-titres. Le film est très ennuyeux.
4. — Est-ce que tu peux me recommander un bon film classique?
   — Oui, j'ai beaucoup aimé celui-ci. J'adore Humphrey Bogart!
5. — Chloé, tu as vu ce film d'horreur?
   — Oui. Je l'ai vu.
   — Comment tu l'as trouvé?
   — C'est pas mal, sans plus.
6. — Est-ce que tu me recommandes ce film d'aventures?
   — Oui, il y a plein de rebondissements. Le héros sauve la vie de l'héroïne et puis l'héroïne sauve la vie du héros.

Answers to Activity 1

1. a **2.** b **3.** b **4.** a **5.** b **6.** a

Grammaire à l'œuvre 1

10 p. 317, CD 9, Tr. 2

1. Je ris beaucoup en regardant un film comique.
2. Je vais retrouver Margot et Céléstine au café et ensuite, on va au ciné.
3. J'ai vu qu'il y avait un film de Spielberg en passant devant le ciné.
4. Je lis toujours en mangeant.
5. Je regarde un film à la télé et après je vais me coucher.
6. Je lis toujours le roman avant de voir l'adaptation au cinéma.

Answers to Activity 10

1. a **2.** b **3.** a **4.** a **5.** b **6.** b

Application 1

15 p. 318, CD 9, Tr. 3

1. Tu as lu *Une journée au parc?* C'est trop déprimant!
2. *Le grand monstre?* Ce n'est pas génial.
3. Je viens de voir *Le mystère de la statuette.* Malheureusement, ça n'a rien à voir avec le roman.
4. Ce roman est plein de rebondissements. Je te le recommande.
5. *Léa et Laurent* est vraiment une histoire passionnante!

Answers to Activity 15

1. c **2.** e **3.** b **4.** a **5.** d

Vocabulaire à l'œuvre 2

20 p. 324, CD 9, Tr. 4

1. — Bonjour, je suis Jean-Pierre Clément de Chaîne Ado. Tu t'appelles comment?
   — Je m'appelle Denis.
   — Qu'est-ce que tu aimes regarder à la télé, Denis?
   — Oh, j'aime les sitcoms et les jeux.
2. — Bonjour! Jean-Pierre Clément de Chaîne Ado. Et toi, tu t'appelles... ?
   — Amadou.
   — Amadou, qu'est-ce que tu aimes regarder à la télé?
   — J'aime les spots publicitaires.
3. — Salut! Je m'appelle Jean-Pierre Clément avec Chaîne Ado. Tu t'appelles comment?
   — Je m'appelle Karine.
   — Qu'est-ce que tu aimes regarder à la télé, Karine?
   — J'aime les documentaires.
   — Tu as vu l'émission sur les tortues de mer?
   — Oui! Je ne rate jamais les documentaires sur les animaux.
4. — Bonjour. Je suis Jean-Pierre Clément de Chaîne Ado. Comment tu t'appelles?
   — Marc.
   — Marc, est-ce que tu aimes regarder «Le Monde du Sport»?
   — Non, je déteste les reportages sportifs.

5. Salut! Je m'appelle Jean-Pierre Clément de Chaîne Ado. Tu t'appelles comment?
 — Je m'appelle Zita.
 — Zita, est-ce que tu aimes regarder les vidéoclips?
 — Oui, j'adore les vidéoclips.
 — Quels vidéoclips est-ce que tu préfères?
 — Oh, je préfère les vidéos de pop et de techno.

Answers to Activity 20

1. b **2.** a **3.** a **4.** b **5.** b

Grammaire à l'œuvre 2

32 **p. 328, CD 9, Tr. 5**

1. — C'est celui qui joue dans *Mission impossible.*
 — Ah, oui, je sais de qui tu parles maintenant.
2. — Dominique Martin?
 — Oui, c'est celle qui présente les informations sur France 3.
3. — Je ne connais pas ce chanteur.
 — Mais si! C'est celui dont nous avons regardé les vidéoclips hier.
4. — Ceux que je préfère, moi, c'est ceux qui jouent dans des films comiques.
 — Moi aussi.
5. — De qui est-ce que vous parlez?
 — De l'actrice qui joue dans Catwoman, celle qui est très belle.
6. — Les héroïnes du film sont vraiment super!
 — Lesquelles? Celles du film d'aventures?

Answers to Activity 32

1. a **2.** b **3.** a **4.** c **5.** b **6.** d

Application 2

37 **p. 330, CD 9, Tr. 6**

1. Le nouveau documentaire d'Henri Doussard est le plus intéressant de tous.
2. Ce présentateur est vraiment moins marrant que celui de TF1.
3. Moi, je trouve le vidéoclip de ce groupe pire que celui de l'autre groupe.
4. Je pense que cette émission-là est plus intelligente.
5. Le deuxième jeu est meilleur que le premier.
6. C'est le soap le plus stupide de tous!

Answers to Activity 37

1. a **2.** b **3.** b **4.** a **5.** a **6.** b

Prépare-toi pour l'examen

 **p. 339, CD 9, Tr. 9**

— Alors, qu'est-ce qu'on fait ce soir?
— Je suis un peu fatigué. Restons à la maison. Nous pouvons regarder la télé.
— Ah non, il n'y a jamais rien de bien à la télé. C'est ennuyeux.
— Mais regarde! Ce soir il y a un documentaire sur la technologie d'aujourd'hui.
— Hmmm... Oui, ça a l'air intéressant. Et il y a aussi ce film de science-fiction basé sur un des livres de Jules Verne.
— J'ai déjà vu ce film et il ne m'a pas emballé. Ça n'a rien à voir avec le roman.
— C'est dommage—le roman est à ne pas manquer! Bon, d'accord. Restons à la maison et regardons ton documentaire.

Answers to Activity 6

1. b **2.** b **3.** a **4.** a

Dictée, p. 340, CD 9, Tr. 12

1. Les animaux au zoo sont drôles.
2. Il fait très beau aujourd'hui.
3. Tu préfères le hip-hop ou le rock?
4. J'adore les gâteaux au chocolat.
5. C'est un roman historique.

Révisions cumulatives chapitres 1-9

 **p. 342, CD 9, Tr. 13**

1. Tu veux aller voir le nouveau film de Jugnot? Ça passe au cinema Rex et il y a une séance à 18h30.
2. Tu as vu son dernier film? C'était plein de rebondissements et il y avait beaucoup de suspense.
3. Tu as vu le documentaire sur la mer à la télé hier soir? Ça ne m'a pas emballé.
4. Je ne te conseille pas cette nouvelle série. Elle n'est pas géniale.
5. J'aime beaucoup ce film. C'est un classique.
6. Ce film est l'histoire d'un homme et une femme qui se marient et qui partent vivre aux États-Unis.

Answers to Activity 1

1. c **2.** a **3.** b **4.** b **5.** a **6.** c

50-Minute Lesson Plans

On s'amuse

Day 1

OBJECTIVE
Describe a movie or book

Core Instruction
Chapter Opener, pp. 308–309
- See Using the Photo, p. 308. **5 min.**
- See Chapter Objectives, p. 308. **5 min.**

Vocabulaire 1, pp. 310–313
- Present **Vocabulaire 1,** pp. 310–311. See Teaching **Vocabulaire,** p. 310. **10 min.**
- Show **Télé-vocab 1. 5 min.**
- Present **Exprimons-nous!,** p. 311. **10 min.**
- Play Audio CD 9, Tr. 1 for Activity 1, p. 312. **5 min.**
- Do Activity 2, p. 312. **5 min.**
- Present **Flash culture,** p. 312. **5 min.**

Optional Resources
- Advanced Learners, p. 311 ▲
- Multiple Intelligences, p. 311

Homework Suggestions
Cahier de vocabulaire et grammaire, pp. 97–98

1.2, 1.3, 4.2

Day 2

OBJECTIVE
*Describe a movie or book; Ask for and give information; Use the relative pronouns **qui, que,** and **dont***

Core Instruction
Vocabulaire 1, pp. 310–313
- Have students do Activity 3, p. 312. **10 min.**
- See Teaching **Exprimons-nous!,** p. 312. **10 min.**
- Have students do Activity 4, p. 313. **15 min.**

Grammaire 1, pp. 314–317
- See Teaching **Grammaire,** p. 314. **10 min.**
- Show **Grammavision 1.1. 5 min.**

Optional Resources
- Slower Pace Learners, p. 313 ◆
- Special Learning Needs, p. 313 ●

Homework Suggestions
Study for **Quiz: Vocabulaire 1**
Cahier de vocabulaire et grammaire, p. 99
Online Practice (**my.hrw.com**)

1.1, 1.2

Day 3

OBJECTIVE
*Use the relative pronouns **qui, que,** and **dont***

Core Instruction
Vocabulaire 1, pp. 310–313
- Review **Vocabulaire 1,** pp. 310–313. **10 min.**
- Give **Quiz: Vocabulaire 1. 20 min.**

Grammaire 1, pp. 314–317
- Have students do Activities 5–8, pp. 314–315. **15 min.**
- Present **Flash culture,** p. 316. **5 min.**

Optional Resources
- Advanced Learners, p. 315 ▲
- Special Learning Needs, p. 315 ●

Homework Suggestions
Cahier de vocabulaire et grammaire, p. 100
Cahier d'activités, p. 81
Online Practice (**my.hrw.com**)
@HOMETUTOR

1.1, 1.2, 1.3, 4.2

Day 4

OBJECTIVE
*Use present participles; Use **C'est** and **il/elle est***

Core Instruction
Grammaire 1, pp. 314–317
- See Teaching **Grammaire,** p. 316. **5 min.**
- Show **Grammavision 1.2. 5 min.**
- Do Activity 9, p. 316. **5 min.**
- Play Audio CD 9, Tr. 2 for Activity 10, p. 317 **5 min.**
- Have students do Activities 11–13, p. 317. **20 min.**

Application 1, pp. 318–319
- Do Activity 14, p. 318. **5 min.**
- See Teaching **Un peu plus,** p. 318. **5 min.**

Optional Resources
- Slower Pace Learners, p. 317 ◆
- Advanced Learners, p. 319 ▲

Homework Suggestions
Study for **Quiz: Grammaire 1**
Cahier de vocabulaire et grammaire, p. 101
Cahier d'activités, p. 82

1.1, 1.2, 1.3

Day 5

OBJECTIVE
*Use **C'est** and **il/elle est***

Core Instruction
Grammaire 1, pp. 314–317
- Review **Grammaire 1,** pp. 314–317. **10 min.**
- Give **Quiz: Grammaire 1. 20 min.**

Application 1, pp. 318–319
- Play Audio CD 9, Tr. 3 for Activity 15, p. 318. **5 min.**
- Have students do Activities 16–19, pp. 318–319. **15 min.**

Optional Resources
- French for Spanish Speakers, p. 319
- Communication (TE), p. 319
- Special Learning Needs, p. 319 ●

Homework Suggestions
Study for **Quiz: Application 1**
Cahier de vocabulaire et grammaire, p. 102
Cahier d'activités, p. 83
Online Practice (**my.hrw.com**)

1.1, 1.2, 1.3, 4.1

Day 6

OBJECTIVE
Learn about francophone culture

Core Instruction
Application 1, pp. 318–319
- Review **Application 1,** pp. 318–319. **10 min.**
- Give **Quiz: Application 1. 20 min.**

Culture, pp. 320–321
- See **Culture appliquée** (TE), p. 320. **10 min.**
- See **Comparaisons et communauté** (TE), p. 320. **10 min.**

Optional Resources
- Communities, p. 321
- Comparisons, p. 321
- Slower Pace Learners, p. 321 ◆
- Multiple Intelligences, p. 321

Homework Suggestions
Cahier d'activités, p. 84
Online Practice (**my.hrw.com**)
Finish **Culture appliquée** project

1.3, 2.1, 2.2, 4.2, 5.1

Day 7

OBJECTIVE
Ask about preferences

Core Instruction
Vocabulaire 2, pp. 322–325
- Do Bell Work 9.5, p. 322. **5 min.**
- Present **Vocabulaire 2,** pp. 322–323. See Teaching **Vocabulaire,** p. 322. **10 min.**
- Show **Télé-vocab 2. 5 min.**
- Present **Exprimons-nous!,** p. 323. **5 min.**
- Play Audio CD 9, Tr. 4 for Activity 20, p. 324. **5 min.**
- Have students do Activities 21–22, p. 324. **15 min.**
- Present **Flash culture,** p. 324. **5 min.**

Optional Resources
- Slower Pace Learners, p. 323 ◆
- Multiple Intelligences, p. 323
- Advanced Learners, p. 325 ▲

Homework Suggestions
Cahier de vocabulaire et grammaire, pp. 103–104
@HOMETUTOR

1.1, 1.2, 1.3, 4.2

Day 8

OBJECTIVE
Recommend or advise against a something; Use the interrogative pronouns

Core Instruction
Vocabulaire 2, pp. 322–325
- See Teaching **Exprimons-nous!,** p. 324. **10 min.**
- Have students do Activities 23–25, p. 325. **20 min.**

Grammaire 2, pp. 326–329
- See Teaching **Grammaire,** p. 326. **10 min.**
- Show **Grammavision 2.1. 5 min.**
- Have students do Activity 26, p. 326. **5 min.**

Optional Resources
- Communication (TE), p. 325
- Multiple Intelligences, p. 325

Homework Suggestions
Study for **Quiz: Vocabulaire 2**
Cahier de vocabulaire et grammaire, p. 105
Online Practice (**my.hrw.com**)

1.1, 1.2, 1.3

To edit and create your own lesson plans, see the **Teacher One Stop™**

KEY
▲ Advanced Learners
◆ Slower Pace Learners
● Special Learning Needs

50-Minute Lesson Plans

Day 9

OBJECTIVE
Use the interrogative pronouns

Core Instruction
Vocabulaire 2, pp. 322–325
- Review **Vocabulaire 2,** pp. 322–325. **10 min.**
- Give **Quiz: Vocabulaire 2. 20 min.**

Grammaire 2, pp. 326–329
- Have students do Activities 27–30, pp. 326–327. **20 min.**

Optional Resources
- Communication (TE), p. 327
- Slower Pace Learners, p. 327 ◆
- Special Learning Needs, p. 327 ●

Homework Suggestions
Cahier de vocabulaire et grammaire, p. 106
Cahier d'activités, p. 85
HOMETUTOR
Online Practice (**my.hrw.com**)
1.1, 1.2

Day 10

OBJECTIVE
Use demonstrative pronouns; Use comparatives and superlatives

Core Instruction
Grammaire 2, pp. 326–329
- Present **Flash culture,** p. 328. **5 min.**
- See Teaching **Grammaire,** p. 328. **5 min.**
- Show **Grammavision 2.2. 5 min.**
- Do Activity 31, p. 328. **5 min.**
- Play Audio CD 9, Tr. 5 for Activity 32, p. 328. **5 min.**
- Have students do Activities 33–35, pp. 328–329. **15 min.**

Application 2, pp. 330–331
- Do Activity 36, p. 330. **5 min.**
- See Teaching **Un peu plus,** p. 330. **5 min.**

Optional Resources
- Advanced Learners, p. 329 ▲

Homework Suggestions
Study for **Quiz: Grammaire 2**
Cahier de vocabulaire et grammaire, p. 107
Cahier d'activités, p. 86
1.1, 1.2, 1.3, 3.2, 4.2

Day 11

OBJECTIVE
Use comparatives and superlatives

Core Instruction
Grammaire 2, pp. 326–329
- Review **Grammaire 2,** pp. 326–329. **10 min.**
- Give **Quiz: Grammaire 2. 20 min.**

Application 2, pp. 330–331
- Play Audio CD 9, Tr. 6 for Activity 37, p. 330. **5 min.**
- Have students do Activities 38–41, pp. 330–331. **15 min.**

Optional Resources
- Communication (TE), p. 331
- Slower Pace Learners, p. 331 ◆
- Multiple Intelligences, p. 331

Homework Suggestions
Study for **Quiz: Application 2**
Cahier de vocabulaire et grammaire, p. 108
Cahier d'activités, p. 87
Online Practice (**my.hrw.com**)
1.1, 1.2, 1.3, 2.1

Day 12

OBJECTIVE
Develop listening and reading skills

Core Instruction
Application 2, pp. 330–331
- Review **Application 2,** pp. 330–331. **10 min.**
- Give **Quiz: Application 2. 20 min.**

Télé-roman, pp. 332–333
- Show **Télé-roman.** See Teaching **Télé-roman,** p. 332. **5 min.**
- Have students answer the **As-tu compris?** questions, p. 333. **15 min.**

Optional Resources
- Connections, p. 332
- Gestures, p. 332
- Communication (TE), p. 333

Homework Suggestions
Online Practice (**my.hrw.com**)
1.1, 1.2

Day 13

OBJECTIVE
Develop listening, reading, and writing skills

Core Instruction
Lecture et écriture, pp. 334–337
- See Teaching **Lecture,** p. 334. **35 min.**
- See Teaching **Espace écriture,** p. 336. **15 min.**

Optional Resources
- Applying the Strategies, p. 334
- Finding the Main Idea, p. 334
- Communities, p. 335
- Connections, p. 335
- Advanced Learners, p. 335 ▲
- Special Learning Needs, p. 335 ●
- Comparisons, p. 336
- Connections, p. 336
- Process Writing, p. 337

Homework Suggestions
Cahier d'activités, p. 88
Espace écriture, Activity 2, p. 337
1.2, 1.3, 3.1, 4.1, 4.2

Day 14

OBJECTIVE
Develop writing skills; Review the chapter

Core Instruction
Lecture et écriture, pp. 334–337
- See Teaching **Espace écriture,** p. 336. **25 min.**

Prépare-toi pour l'examen, pp. 338–340
- Have students do Activities 1–5, pp. 338–339. **25 min.**

Optional Resources
- Writing Assessment, p. 337
- Slower Pace Learners, p. 337 ◆
- Special Learning Needs, p. 337 ●
- Fold-N-Learn, p. 338
- Reteaching, p. 338
- Oral Assessment, p. 339

Homework Suggestions
Online Practice (**my.hrw.com**)
1.2, 1.3, 4.2

Day 15

OBJECTIVE
Review the chapter

Core Instruction
Prépare-toi pour l'examen, pp. 338–340
- Play Audio CD 9, Tr. 9 for Activity 6, p. 339. **5 min.**
- Have students do Activity 7, p. 339. **5 min.**
- Play Audio CD 9, Tr. 10–12 for **Lettres et sons,** p. 340. **10 min.**

Révisions cumulatives, pp. 342–343
- Play Audio CD 9, Tr. 13 for Activity 1, p. 342. **5 min.**
- Have students do Activities 2–6, pp. 342–343. **25 min.**

Optional Resources
- TPRS, p. 338
- Online Culture Project, p. 342
- Fine Art Connection, p. 343

Homework Suggestions
Study for Chapter Test
Online Practice (**my.hrw.com**)
1.1, 1.2, 1.3, 2.2

Day 16/Test

Core Instruction
Chapter Test 50 min.

Optional Resources
Assessment Program
- Alternative Assessment
- Test Generator
- **Quiz: Lecture**
- **Quiz: Écriture**

Homework Suggestions
Cahier d'activités, pp. 89–90, 118–119
Online Practice (**my.hrw.com**)

90-Minute Lesson Plans

On s'amuse

Block 1

OBJECTIVE
Describe a movie or book; Ask for and give information

Core Instruction

Chapter Opener, pp. 308–309
- See Using the Photo, p. 308. **5 min.**
- See Chapter Objectives, p. 308. **5 min.**

Vocabulaire 1, pp. 310–313
- Present **Vocabulaire 1,** pp. 310–311. See Teaching **Vocabulaire,** p. 310. **10 min.**
- Show **Télé-vocab 1. 5 min.**
- Present **Exprimons-nous!,** p. 311. **10 min.**
- Play Audio CD 9, Tr. 1 for Activity 1, p. 312. **10 min.**
- Have students do Activities 2–3, p. 312. **15 min.**
- Present **Flash culture,** p. 312. **5 min.**
- See Teaching **Exprimons-nous!,** p. 312. **10 min.**
- Have students do Activity 4, p. 313. **15 min.**

Optional Resources

- Learning Tips, p. 309
- **Attention!,** p. 310
- TPR, p. 311
- Cultures, p. 311
- Advanced Learners, p. 311 ▲
- Multiple Intelligences, p. 311
- **Attention!,** p. 313
- Communication (TE), p. 313
- Slower Pace Learners, p. 313 ◆
- Special Learning Needs, p. 313 ●

Homework Suggestions

Study for **Quiz: Vocabulaire 1**
Cahier de vocabulaire et grammaire, pp. 97–99
@HOMETUTOR
Online Practice (**my.hrw.com**)
1.1, 1.2, 1.3, 2.2, 4.2

Block 2

OBJECTIVE
Use the relative pronouns ***qui, que,*** *and* ***dont;*** *Use present participles*

Core Instruction

Vocabulaire 1, pp. 310–313
- Review **Vocabulaire 1,** pp. 310–313. **10 min.**
- Give **Quiz: Vocabulaire 1. 20 min.**

Grammaire 1, pp. 314–317
- See Teaching **Grammaire,** p. 314. **5 min.**
- Show **Grammavision 1.1. 5 min.**
- Have students do Activities 5–8, pp. 314–315. **15 min.**
- Present **Flash culture,** p. 316. **5 min.**
- See Teaching **Grammaire,** p. 316. **5 min.**
- Show **Grammavision 1.2. 5 min.**
- Have students do Activity 9, p. 316. **5 min.**
- Play Audio CD 9, Tr. 2 for Activity 10, p. 317. **5 min.**
- Have students do Activities 11–12, p. 317. **10 min.**

Optional Resources

- Communication (TE), p. 315
- Communities, p. 315
- Advanced Learners, p. 315 ▲
- Special Learning Needs, p. 315 ●
- **Attention!,** p. 316
- Cinquaine Poetry, p. 342
- Slower Pace Learners, p. 317 ◆
- Multiple Intelligences, p. 317

Homework Suggestions

Study for **Quiz: Grammaire 1**
Cahier de vocabulaire et grammaire, pp. 100–101
Cahier d'activités, pp. 81–83
@HOMETUTOR
Online Practice (**my.hrw.com**)
1.1, 1.2, 1.3, 5.1

Block 3

OBJECTIVE
Use present participles; Use ***C'est*** *and* ***il/elle est;*** *Learn about francophone culture*

Core Instruction

Grammaire 1, pp. 314–317
- Have students do Activity 13, p. 317. **10 min.**
- Review **Grammaire 1,** pp. 314–317. **10 min.**
- Give **Quiz: Grammaire 1. 20 min.**

Application 1, pp. 318–319
- Have students do Activity 14, p. 318. **5 min.**
- See Teaching **Un peu plus,** p. 318. **5 min.**
- Play Audio CD 9, Tr. 3 for Activity 15, p. 318. **5 min.**
- Have students do Activities 16–19, pp. 318–319. **15 min.**

Culture, pp. 320–321
- See **Culture appliquée** (TE), p. 320. **10 min.**
- See **Comparaisons et communauté** (TE), p. 320. **10 min.**

Optional Resources

- Communication (TE), p. 317
- Language Note, p. 319
- French for Spanish Speakers, p. 319
- Communication (TE), p. 319
- Advanced Learners, p. 319 ▲
- Special Learning Needs, p. 319 ●
- **Vocabulaire supplémentaire,** p. 320
- Connections, p. 320
- Communities, p. 321
- Comparisons, p. 321
- Slower Pace Learners, p. 321 ◆
- Multiple Intelligences, p. 321

Homework Suggestions

Study for **Quiz: Application 1**
Cahier de vocabulaire et grammaire, p. 102
Cahier d'activités, p. 84
Online Practice (**my.hrw.com**)
Finish **Culture appliquée** project
1.1, 1.2, 1.3, 2.1, 2.2, 3.1, 4.1, 4.2, 5.1

Block 4

OBJECTIVE
Ask about preferences; Recommend or advise against something

Core Instruction

Application 1, pp. 318–319
- Review **Application 1,** pp. 318–319. **10 min.**
- Give **Quiz: Application 1. 20 min.**

Vocabulaire 2, pp. 322–325
- Present **Vocabulaire 2,** pp. 322–323. See Teaching **Vocabulaire,** p. 322. **10 min.**
- Show **Télé-vocab 2. 5 min.**
- Present **Exprimons-nous!,** p. 323. **5 min.**
- Play Audio CD 9, Tr. 4 for Activity 20, p. 324. **5 min.**
- Have students do Activities 21–22, p. 324. **10 min.**
- Present **Flash culture,** p. 324. **5 min.**
- See Teaching **Exprimons-nous!,** p. 324. **5 min.**
- Have students do Activities 23–25, p. 325. **15 min.**

Optional Resources

- **Proverbs,** p. 322
- Connections, p. 323
- Slower Pace Learners, p. 323 ◆
- Multiple Intelligences, p. 323
- **Proverbs,** p. 324
- Communication (TE), p. 325
- Cultures, p. 325
- Advanced Learners, p. 325 ▲
- Multiple Intelligences, p. 325

Homework Suggestions

Study for **Quiz: Vocabulaire 2**
Cahier de vocabulaire et grammaire, pp. 103–105
@HOMETUTOR
Online Practice (**my.hrw.com**)
1.1, 1.2, 1.3, 2.2, 3.1, 4.2

To edit and create your own lesson plans, see the

KEY
- ▲ Advanced Learners
- ◆ Slower Pace Learners
- ● Special Learning Needs

Block 5

OBJECTIVE
Use the interrogative pronouns; Use the demonstrative pronouns

Core Instruction

Vocabulaire 2, pp. 322–325
- Review **Vocabulaire 2,** pp. 322–325. **10 min.**
- Give **Quiz: Vocabulaire 2. 20 min.**

Grammaire 2, pp. 326–329
- See Teaching **Grammaire,** p. 326. **10 min.**
- Show **Grammavision 2.1. 5 min.**
- Have students do Activities 26–30, pp. 326–327. **15 min.**
- Present **Flash culture,** p. 328. **5 min.**
- See Teaching **Grammaire,** p. 328. **5 min.**
- Show **Grammavision 2.2. 5 min.**
- Have students do Activity 31, p. 328. **5 min.**
- Play Audio CD 9, Tr. 5 for Activity 32, p. 328. **5 min.**
- Have students do Activity 33, p. 328. **5 min.**

Optional Resources
- Communities, p. 326
- Connections, p. 327
- Communication (TE), p. 327
- Slower Pace Learners, p. 327 ◆
- Special Learning Needs, p. 327 ●
- French for Spanish Speakers, p. 329
- Communication (TE), p. 329
- Special Learning Needs, p. 329 ●

Homework Suggestions
Study for **Quiz: Grammaire 2**
Cahier de vocabulaire et grammaire, pp. 106–107
Cahier d'activités, pp. 85–86
@HOMETUTOR
Online Practice (**my.hrw.com**)
1.1, 1.2, 3.1, 4.1, 4.2, 5.1

Block 6

OBJECTIVE
Use the demonstrative pronouns; Use comparatives and superlatives; Develop listening and reading skills

Core Instruction

Grammaire 2, pp. 326–329
- Have students do Activities 34–35, p. 329. **10 min.**
- Review **Grammaire 2,** pp. 326–329. **10 min.**
- Give **Quiz: Grammaire 2. 20 min.**

Application 2, pp. 330–331
- Have students do Activity 36, p. 330. **5 min.**
- See Teaching **Un peu plus,** p. 330. **5 min.**
- Play Audio CD 9, Tr. 6 for Activity 37, p. 330. **5 min.**
- Have students do Activities 38–41, pp. 330–331. **15 min.**

Télé-roman, pp. 332–333
- Show **Télé-roman.** See Teaching **Télé-roman,** p. 332. **5 min.**
- Have students answer the **As-tu compris?** questions, p. 333. **15 min.**

Optional Resources
- Advanced Learners, p. 329 ▲
- Communication (TE), p. 331
- Slower Pace Learners, p. 331 ◆
- Multiple Intelligences, p. 331
- Connections, p. 332
- Gestures, p. 332
- Communication (TE), p. 333

Homework Suggestions
Study for **Quiz: Application 2**
Cahier de vocabulaire et grammaire, p. 108
Cahier d'activités, p. 87
Online Practice (**my.hrw.com**)
1.1, 1.2, 1.3, 2.1, 3.2

Block 7

OBJECTIVE
Develop listening, reading, and writing skills; Review the chapter

Core Instruction

Application 2, pp. 330–331
- Review **Application 2,** pp. 330–331. **10 min.**
- Give **Quiz: Application 2. 20 min.**

Lecture et écriture, pp. 334–337
- See Teaching **Lecture,** p. 334. **20 min.**
- See Teaching **Espace écriture,** p. 336. **30 min.**

Prépare-toi pour l'examen, pp. 338–340
- Have students do Activities 1–3, p. 338. **10 min.**

Optional Resources
- Applying the Strategies, p. 334
- Finding the Main Idea, p. 334
- Communities, p. 335
- Connections, p. 335
- Advanced Learners, p. 335 ▲
- Special Learning Needs, p. 335 ●
- Comparisons, p. 336
- Connections, p. 336
- Process Writing, p. 337
- Writing Assessment, p. 337
- Slower Pace Learners, p. 337 ◆
- Special Learning Needs, p. 337 ●
- Fold-N-Learn, p. 338

Homework Suggestions
Study for Chapter Test
Cahier d'activités, p. 88
Espace écriture, Activity 3, p. 337
Online Practice (**my.hrw.com**)
1.2, 1.3, 3.1, 4.1, 4.2

Block 8

OBJECTIVE
Review and assess the chapter

Core Instruction

Prépare-toi pour l'examen, pp. 338–340
- Have students do Activities 4–5, p. 339. **5 min.**
- Play Audio CD 9, Tr. 9 for Activity 6, p. 339. **5 min.**
- Have students do Activity 7, p. 339. **5 min.**
- Play Audio CD 9, Tr. 10–12 for **Lettres et sons,** p. 340. **5 min.**

Chapter Test 50 min.

Révisions cumulatives, pp. 342–343
- Play Audio CD 9, Tr. 13 for Activity 1, p. 342. **5 min.**
- Have students do Activities 2–6, pp. 342–343. **15 min.**

Optional Resources
- Reteaching, p. 338
- TPRS, p. 338
- Oral Assessment, p. 339
- Game, p. 340
- Chapter Review, pp. 340–341
- Teacher to Teacher, p. 341
- Online Culture Project, p. 342
- Fine Art Connection, p. 343

Homework Suggestions
Cahier d'activités, pp. 89–90, 118–119
Online Practice (**my.hrw.com**)
1.1, 1.2, 1.3, 2.2, 4.2

Chapter Opener

Meeting the National Standards

Communication
Communication, pp. 313, 315, 317, 319, 321, 325, 327, 329, 331
À ton tour, p. 343

Cultures
Flash culture, pp. 312, 316, 324, 328
Comparaisons, p. 321
Products and Perspectives, pp. 311, 325

Connections
Film Studies Link, p. 320
Music Link, p. 323
Science Link, p. 327
Visual Learners, p. 332
Social Studies Link, p. 335
Language Arts Link, p. 336

Comparisons
Comparaisons, p. 321
Comparing and Contrasting, pp. 321, 336

Communities
Communauté, p. 321
School Link, pp. 315, 321, 326
Community Link, p. 335

Using the Photo

FNAC is the largest French retailer of cultural products and consumer electronics. The store also sells music, DVDs, computers, software, games, cameras, and telecommunications equipment. FNAC was founded in 1954 in Paris as a co-op to buy and sell photo supplies. Today the company has stores in France and worldwide, including Brazil and Taiwan. Have students browse the FNAC Web site and compare prices of books and products from large U.S. retailers. 1.3

Vocabulaire supplémentaire

Students might use these terms to discuss the photo.

l'étagère *book shelf*
l'étalage *display*
le succès de librairie *best seller*
la jaquette *book jacket*

chapitre 9

On s'amuse!

Objectifs

In this chapter, you will learn to
- describe a movie or a book
- ask for and give information
- ask about preferences
- recommend and advise against something

And you will use
- the relative pronouns **qui, que,** and **dont**
- present participles
- **c'est** and **il/elle est**
- interrogative pronouns
- demonstrative pronouns
- comparatives and superlatives

Que vois-tu sur la photo?

Où sont les personnes?
Qu'est-ce qu'elles font?
Et toi, où vas-tu pour acheter des livres, des CD ou des DVD?

ACTFL 21st Century Skills

Communication:	SE: pp. 315, 319, 325, 329, 337, 343; TE: pp. 311, 315, 319, 325, 336
Collaboration:	TE: pp. 307C, 321
Creativity and Innovation:	SE: p. 320; TE: pp. 320, 321, 323, 331, 335, 342
Media Literacy:	SE: pp. 321, 336; TE: pp. 307C, 308, 313, 321, 325, 336
Technology Literacy:	TE: pp. 307C, 309, 311, 320, 321, 325, 336
Social and Cross-Cultural Skills:	SE: pp. 321, 328, 336; TE: pp. 307D (Global Awareness), 311, 313, 321, 335, 336, 342

Chapter Opener

La FNAC®, à Nice

TEACHER TOOLS
- Interactive Whiteboard Lessons
- Generate Success!

ALSO AVAILABLE...
- Online Workbooks
- French InterActive Reader

FRENCH ON THE GO!
- Performance Space
- Holt McDougal French Apps
- *Bien dit!* eTextbook

Learning Tips

One of the best ways to learn a language is by listening to and communicating with native speakers. If students do not know any native speakers, encourage them to watch French films and to listen to French radio programs on the Internet.

- **Télé-vocab 1**
- **Grammavision 1**
- **Télé-vocab 2**
- **Grammavision 2**
- **Télé-roman**

LISTENING PRACTICE

Language Lab and Classroom Activities

Vocabulaire
Activity 1, p. 312, CD 9, Tr. 1
Télé-vocab 1, p. 310, DVD Tutor
Activity 20, p. 324, CD 9, Tr. 4
Télé-vocab 2, p. 322, DVD Tutor

Grammaire
Activity 10, p. 317, CD 9, Tr. 2
Grammavision 1, pp. 314, 316, DVD Tutor
Activity 32, p. 328, CD 9, Tr. 5
Grammavision 2, pp. 326, 328, DVD Tutor

Application
Activity 15, p. 318, CD 9, Tr. 3
Activity 37, p. 330, CD 9, Tr. 6

Prépare-toi pour l'examen
Activity 6, p. 339, CD 9, Tr. 9

Révisions cumulatives
Activity 1, p. 342, CD 9, Tr. 13

Télé-roman
p. 332, DVD Tutor

Lecture
p. 334, CD 9, Tr. 7

Variations littéraires
p. 398, CD 9, Tr. 8

Lettres et sons
p. 340, CD 9, Tr. 10–12

Resources

Planning:
Lesson Planner
Teacher One Stop

Presentation:

Projectable Transparencies **Vocabulaire 9.1, 9.2**
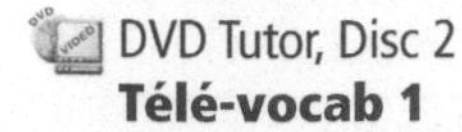
DVD Tutor, Disc 2 **Télé-vocab 1**
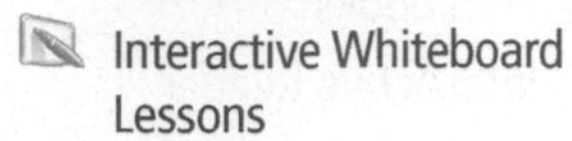
Interactive Whiteboard Lessons

Practice:
Cahier de vocabulaire et grammaire
Differentiated Practice and Assessment CD-ROM
Independent Study Guide
Media Guide
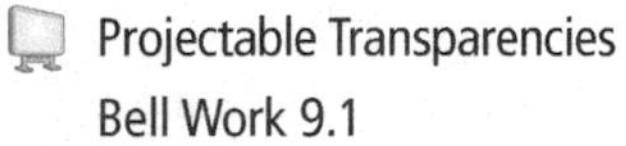
Projectable Transparencies Bell Work 9.1
HOMETUTOR
Holt McDougal French Apps

Bell Work

Use Bell Work 9.1 in the *Projectable Transparencies* or write this activity on the board.

Rewrite these sentences to sound more polite by changing the verbs to the conditional.

1. **Pouvez-vous m'aider?**
2. **Je veux avoir un régime équilibré.**
3. **Vos enfants ne doivent pas boire du coca.**
4. **Il faut acheter des légumes frais.**
5. **Vous faites les courses avec moi?** 1.2

COMMON ERROR ALERT
ATTENTION !

Students may be confused by the fact that the definite article shortens before **héroïne** but not before **héro. Le héro** has an aspirated *h*. The *h* in **l'héroïne** is silent. Most dictionaries indicate whether an *h* is aspirated or silent. Otherwise there is no obvious way to tell.

Objectifs
- to describe a movie or book
- to ask for and give information

Télé-vocab

Les genres de film

un film classique

un film d'aventures

un film d'action

un film d'horreur

un film de science-fiction

un film étranger

un film de guerre

un film d'espionnage

un film comique / une comédie

Core Instruction

TEACHING VOCABULAIRE

1. Show transparencies **Vocabulaire 9.1** and **9.2** and model pronunciation. **(1 min.)**
2. Bring in the movie page from a current newspaper. Point to each movie ad, say the title, and tell what type it is. **C'est un film d'aventures. C'est un film comique. (2 min.)**
3. Bring in a variety of books from the library and identify the genre. **C'est un roman classique. C'est un recueil de poésie. (1 min.)**
4. Have each student bring in a video or DVD cover. Using the expressions in **Exprimons-nous!**, ask individual students yes or no questions about each one. **C'est une histoire passionnante? C'est trop ennuyeux? (3 min.)**

Télé-vocab 1

For a video presentation of this vocabulary, see the *DVD Tutor*.

Télé-vocab

Online Practice
my.hrw.com
Vocabulaire 1 practice

Les genres littéraires

un roman policier

un roman classique

un roman fantastique

un roman d'amour

un recueil de poésie

une pièce de théâtre

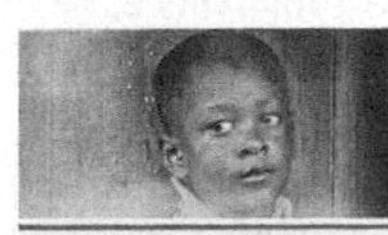
L'enfant noir
Camara Laye
J'étais enfant et je jouais près de la case de mon père. Quel âge avais-je en ce temps-là ? Je ne me rappelle pas exactement. Je devais être très jeune encore : cinq ans, six ans peut-être. Ma
PRESSES POCKET

une autobiographie

D'autres mots utiles

le personnage principal	*main character*
le héros	*hero*
l'héroïne (f.)	*heroine*
un acteur	*actor*
une actrice	*actress*
un dessin animé	*cartoon (film)*
un drame	*drama*
les sous-titres (m.)	*subtitles*
un metteur en scène	*director*

Exprimons-nous!

To describe a movie or book	
C'est drôle/amusant. *It's funny/amusing.*	**C'est trop long/ennuyeux/déprimant.** *It's too long/boring/depressing.*
Il y a plein de rebondissements. *It's full of twists.*	**Il n'y a pas d'histoire.** *There's no story.*
Il y a beaucoup de suspense. *There's a lot of suspense.*	**Ce n'est pas mal, sans plus.** *It's just O.K.*
C'est une histoire passionnante. *It's an exciting story.*	**Ce n'est pas génial.** *It's not great.*
C'est une bonne **adaptation du** roman. *It's a . . . adaptation of the . . .*	**Ça n'a rien à voir avec** le roman. *It has nothing to do with . . .*

Vocabulaire et grammaire, pp. 97–99
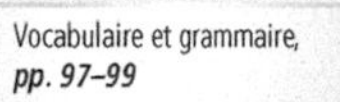

▶ Vocabulaire supplémentaire—Le cinéma, p. R21

TPR
Total Physical Response

Have students respond to these commands.

Lève la main si tu aimes les films d'espionnage.

Touche ta joue si tu préfères les films de guerre.

Croise les bras si tu lis des romans policiers.

Lève-toi si *Shrek* est un film de science-fiction.

Touche ton nez si *La panthère rose* est un film comique.

Place library books and DVDs on a table. Have students respond to these commands.

Va chercher un roman historique.

Apporte-moi un roman d'amour.

Montre-moi une pièce de théâtre.

Je voudrais lire une histoire passionnante.

Choisis un film en version originale. 1.2

Cultures

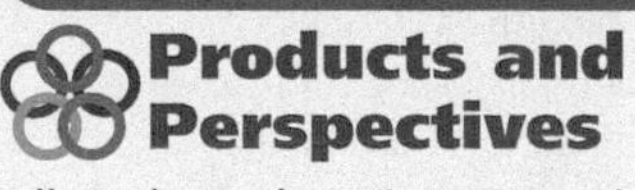
Products and Perspectives

Tell students that Victor Hugo is one of France's most acclaimed writers. ***Les Misérables,*** published in 1862, tells the story of Jean Valjean, who is sent to prison for 19 years for stealing a loaf of bread. Once he is paroled, he cannot find lodging because of his convict status. Finally, a bishop takes him in. Valjean steals his silverware and is caught, but the bishop rescues him by saying it was a gift to Valjean. From that point on, Valjean lives the rest of his life trying to redeem himself. You may wish to show the 1998 film version starring Liam Neeson (rated PG-13). 2.2

Differentiated Instruction

ADVANCED LEARNERS

Bring four videotapes or DVDs of movies to class. Hold them up and have students write the title of the one they would like to see. Then group students according to the movie they prefer. Have each group prepare a list of reasons why they would like to see the movie they picked, as well as a list of reasons they would not like to see the other three movies. Then have each group critique another group's choice and defend their own. 1.3

MULTIPLE INTELLIGENCES

Linguistic Ask students to imagine they are movie or literature critics and to write a review of a book they have read or a movie they have seen. The review should include the genre of the film or book, a summary of the plot, a description of the main character, and a critique of the content. Ask students to share their reviews in small groups. 1.3

Vocabulaire 1

Resources

Planning:
Lesson Planner
Teacher One Stop

Presentation:
Projectable Transparencies **Vocabulaire 9.1, 9.2**
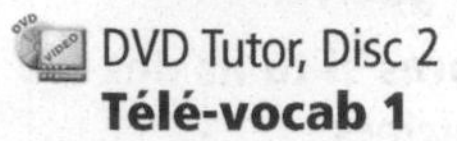
DVD Tutor, Disc 2 **Télé-vocab 1**
Interactive Whiteboard Lessons

Practice:
Cahier de vocabulaire et grammaire
Differentiated Practice and Assessment CD-ROM
Independent Study Guide
Media Guide
Audio CD 9, Tr. 1
@HOMETUTOR
Holt McDougal French Apps

1 Script

1. — Chloé, je ne sais pas quoi louer!
— Est-ce que tu as vu ce film de science-fiction?
— Non, pas encore.
— C'est une bonne adaptation du roman.
2. — Chloé, tu as vu ce film de guerre?
— Oui, je l'ai vu. C'est pas génial. En fait, c'est déprimant.
3. — Est-ce que tu sais si ce film a des sous-titres?
— Oui, il a des sous-titres. Le film est très ennuyeux.
4. — Est-ce que tu peux me recommander un bon film classique?
— Oui, j'ai beaucoup aimé celui-ci. J'adore Humphrey Bogart!
5. — Chloé, tu as vu ce film d'horreur?
— Oui. Je l'ai vu.
— Comment tu l'as trouvé?
— C'est pas mal, sans plus.
6. — Est-ce que tu recommandes ce film d'aventures?
— Oui, il y a plein de rebondissements. Le héros sauve la vie de l'héroïne et puis l'héroïne sauve la vie du héros.

Entre copains

le cinoche	*movie theater*
Ça casse pas des briques.	*It's not great.*
un polar	*detective story (book)*
un navet	*dud, flop (film)*
Ça a fait un tabac.	*It was a hit.*

1. drame
2. long
3. personnages
4. héros
5. héroïne
6. amour
7. acteur
8. actrice

Flash culture

En France, la majorité des films étrangers sont doublés, c'est-à-dire que des acteurs doublent les voix des acteurs étrangers. Les spectateurs peuvent voir un film étranger en français sans avoir à lire les sous-titres. Beaucoup de cinémas montrent aussi les films étrangers dans leur version originale (V.O.), c'est-à-dire dans la langue originale de tournage du film. Les mentions V.F. (version française-doublée) ou V.O. sont inscrites sur les guides de cinéma et dans les salles de cinéma.

Est-ce que tu as vu un film français en V.O.? 4.2

1 Écoutons CD 9, Tr. 1 1.2 **1.** a **2.** b **3.** b **4.** a **5.** b **6.** a

Chloé travaille dans un magasin de vidéos. Est-ce que Chloé **a) recommande** ou **b) ne recommande pas** chaque film?

2 Un revue 1.2

Écrivons Juliette écrit la critique d'un film pour le journal de son lycée. Complète sa critique avec les mots de la boîte.

amour	adaptation	acteur	personnages	héroïne
drame	actrice	héros	long	histoire

Le __1__ *Deux Personnes, un cœur* est mauvais et beaucoup trop __2__. Les __3__ principaux ne sont pas trop intéressants. Le __4__ Thierry est un jeune homme qui ne sait pas quoi faire de sa vie. L' __5__, Cécile est amoureuse de Thierry, mais elle est trop timide pour lui parler. Elle lui recommande des romans d' __6__ comme *Je t'aime toujours*. Thierry ne comprend pas ce qu'elle fait. À la fin du film, Thierry part pour les États-Unis et Cécile reste en France. Bref, il n'y a vraiment pas d'histoire. En plus, l' __7__ qui joue le rôle de Thierry et l'__8__ qui joue le rôle de Cécile ne sont pas très bons.

3 À la librairie 1.2

Écrivons Théo entend ces conversations à la librairie. De quels genres littéraires est-ce que les personnes parlent?

MODÈLE —Tu aimes la musique de Nathalie Chantout? Tu devrais lire son livre *Ma vie et mes rêves.*
une autobiographie

1. —Un homme tombe amoureux d'une femme. C'est tout!
—Oh, mais c'est très romantique! un roman d'amour
2. —Le détective dit, «C'est vous, le meurtrier *(killer)* de Mme Dupont!"
—Ne m'en dis pas plus! Je ne l'ai pas encore lu!» un roman policier
3. —C'était cool quand le professeur est devenu une grenouille!
—Oui, j'ai trouvé ça très drôle! un roman fantastique
4. —Tu vas acheter *Madame Bovary?*
—Non, c'est trop long! un roman historique
5. —Ce livre a tous les poèmes d'Edgar Allan Poe!
—Je n'aime pas ses poèmes. Ils sont déprimants. un recueil de poésie

Core Instruction

TEACHING EXPRIMONS-NOUS!

1. Find on the Internet a movie schedule in French and make a transparency of it. Model the pronunciation of **Exprimons-nous!** expressions as you point to a corresponding film title. **(3 min.)**
2. Using the same transparency, give information about a film and have students guess to which one you are referring. **Il y a un nouveau film au Varsity. C'est avec Harrison Ford. La séance est à 19h10. (3 min.)**
3. Play a game of reverse 20 questions. Describe a film, one sentence at a time, going from vague to precise in your description. Have a small prize for the student who guesses it first. **C'est l'histoire d'une famille à Paris. Ça parle des vidéocassettes qu'ils reçoivent par courrier. C'est avec Daniel Auteuil. (3 min.)**

Exprimons-nous!

To ask for information	To give information
Qu'est-ce qu'on joue au... ? *What's playing . . . ?*	**Il y a** le nouveau film de Jugnot. *There's . . .*
C'est avec qui? *Who's in it?*	**C'est avec** Juliette Binoche. *It's with . . .*
Ça passe où? *Where's it playing?*	**Ça passe au** Majestic. *It's playing at . . .*
Ça commence à quelle heure? *What time does it start?*	**La séance est à** 20h10. *The showing is at . . .*
Qu'est-ce que tu as lu d'intéressant récemment? *What have you read that's interesting . . . ?*	Je viens de finir **le dernier** Pennac. *. . . the latest . . .*
De quoi ça parle? *What's it about?*	**Ça parle d'/C'est l'histoire d'**un garçon... *It's about . . .*
Qu'est-ce que ça raconte? *What's it about?*	**C'est basé sur** une histoire vraie. *It's based on a . . . .*

Vocabulaire et grammaire, pp. 97–99 — Online Workbooks

Digital performance space

Communication

4 Scénario 1.1

Parlons Avec un(e) camarade, discutez des films suivants.

MODÈLE —**Qu'est-ce qu'on joue au cinéma Bijoux?**
—**Il y a le nouveau film de...**

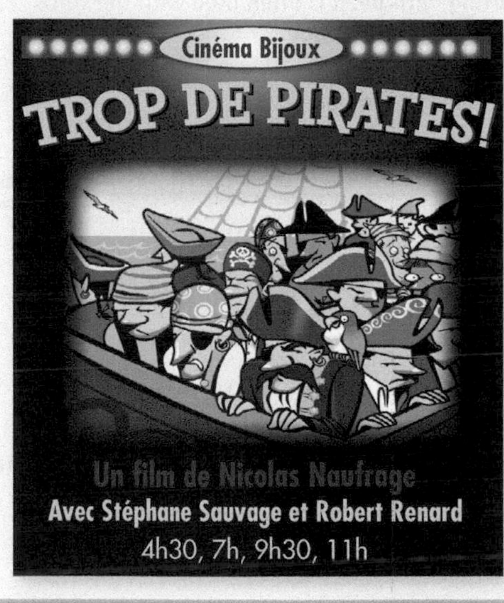

Cinéma Bijoux
TROP DE PIRATES!
Un film de Nicolas Naufrage
Avec Stéphane Sauvage et Robert Renard
4h30, 7h, 9h30, 11h

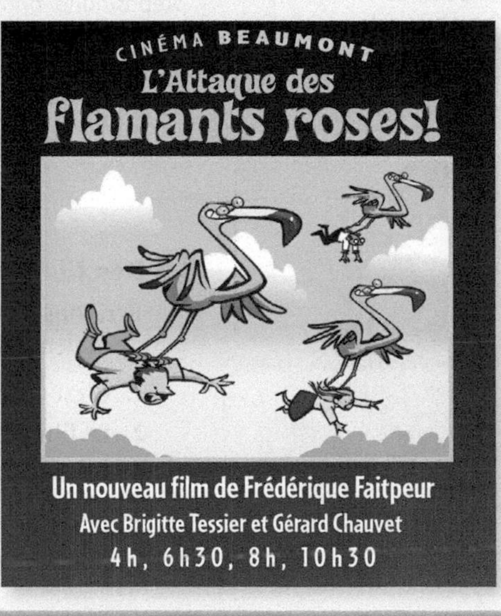

CINÉMA BEAUMONT
L'Attaque des
flamants roses!
Un nouveau film de Frédérique Faitpeur
Avec Brigitte Tessier et Gérard Chauvet
4h, 6h30, 8h, 10h30

COMMON ERROR ALERT — ATTENTION !

The word **personnage** refers to a literary character. Students will often use **caractère** because of its similarity to English. **Caractère** refers to a person's nature or temperament.

Communication

4 Group Activity: Interpersonal

Have students interview three classmates about a movie they saw or something they read recently. The interviewers should find out what kind of film, book, or magazine it is, what it is about, what the student's opinion is, and whether he or she would recommend it. 1.1

Communication

Pair Work: Interpersonal

Have students use the Internet to find French reviews of movies they've seen. Have partners compare and contrast their reviews and discuss whether or not they agree with the reviews. 3.2

Differentiated Instruction

SLOWER PACE LEARNERS

Bring newspaper movie listings to class. Have students form groups of four. Ask each student to write one of the **Exprimons-nous!** questions about movies on a piece of paper. Give each group a movie listing. Have the student with the **Qu'est-ce qu'on joue au cinéma** question read it aloud and choose a student to answer it. Group members repeat the process with the rest of the questions. Students should then pass their question to the student on their right and discuss another movie listing. 1.1

SPECIAL LEARNING NEEDS

Students with Learning Disabilities To help students understand the concept of genres, schedule a class period in the school library. Tour the library and point out examples of different genres to the students. If possible, display examples of these works in French.

Assess

Assessment Program

Quiz: Vocabulaire 1

Alternative Assessment

Differentiated Practice and Assessment CD-ROM

Online Assessment
my.hrw.com

Test Generator 

Resources

Planning:
Lesson Planner
 Teacher One Stop

Presentation:
DVD Tutor, Disc 2
Grammavision 1.1

Practice:
Grammar Tutor for Students of French, Chapter 9
Cahier de vocabulaire et grammaire
Differentiated Practice and Assessment CD-ROM
Cahier d'activités
Independent Study Guide
Media Guide
Projectable Transparencies
Bell Work 9.2
@HOMETUTOR

Bell Work

Use Bell Work 9.2 in the *Projectable Transparencies* or write this activity on the board.

Match these remarks with the films they refer to.

1. Regardes-tu quelquefois de vieux films?
2. C'était très drôle et nous avons beaucoup ri.
3. Tu as vu le dernier James Bond? Il est super.
4. Je ne veux pas aller voir ce film. J'ai peur!
5. Ça se passe en Normandie, le 6 juin 1944.
6. J'ai regardé ce film italien en version originale.

a. un film comique
b. un film d'espionnage
c. un film étranger
d. un film de guerre
e. un film classique
f. un film d'horreur  1.2

Objectifs
- the relative pronouns *qui, que,* and *dont*
- present participles

Grammavision

The relative pronouns *qui, que,* and *dont*

1 Use clauses that begin with qui or **que** (*that, which, who,* or *whom*) to describe something or someone you have already mentioned.

Le livre qui est sur mon bureau est un roman policier.
J'ai vu un nouveau film **que** j'ai beaucoup aimé.

2 Qui *(that, which, who)* is the *subject* of the clause and is followed by a verb.

C'est un film qui est basé sur une histoire vraie.

3 **Que (qu')** *(that, which, whom)* is the *object* of the clause. It is followed by a **subject** and a verb.

C'est un film **qu'on** joue au cinéma Rex.

If the **passé composé** follows **que**, the past participle will agree with the noun **que** represents.

La pièce de théâtre **qu'**on a vu**e** hier était amusante!

4 The relative pronoun dont *(that, whom, whose)* replaces a prepositional phrase starting with **de**. It is often used with the verbs you see in the ***Déjà vu!*** section on this page.

C'est un film. Tout le monde parle de ce film.
C'est un film dont tout le monde parle.
It's a film that everyone is talking about.

Vocabulaire et grammaire, *pp. 100–101*
Cahier d'activités, *pp. 81–83*
Online Workbooks

Déjà vu!

Do you remember these expressions that are often followed by the preposition **de**?

parler de
avoir besoin de
avoir envie de
avoir peur de

5 Des films 1.2

Écrivons Jérémy parle des films qu'il a vus récemment. Complète ses phrases avec **qui, que** ou **dont**.

1. C'est un film étranger _____ j'ai vu avec des amis. que
2. Le film _____ je parle est un film de science-fiction. dont
3. J'aime beaucoup l'acteur _____ joue dans ce film comique. qui
4. C'est une adaptation d'un roman _____ j'ai lu en cours. que
5. L'héroïne, _____ le père est mort, cherche sa mère. dont

Core Instruction

TEACHING GRAMMAIRE

1. Go over Points 1 through 3 and explain that **qui** is the subject in the second clause and is followed by a verb. **Que** is the object in the second clause and is followed by a subject and a verb. **(2 min.)**
2. Go over Point 4. Give additional examples of sentences in which **dont** replaces a prepositional phrase that starts with **de. (2 min.)**
3. Referring to a current newspaper, talk about the films that are now playing, using **qui, que,** and **dont** in your sentences. **Julia Roberts, c'est une actrice qui joue dans beaucoup de bons films. Le film qui passe au Varsity, c'est un film que j'aimerais voir avec ma nièce. Le nouveau film de Steven Spielberg, c'est un film dont tout le monde parle. (3 min.)**

Grammavision

For a video presentation of the relative pronouns **qui, que,** and **dont,** see the *DVD Tutor.*

Grammavision

Online Practice
my.hrw.com
Grammaire 1 practice

6 Des affiches de film 1.3

Parlons/Écrivons Regarde les posters de ces films. Donne ton opinion sur chaque film. Utilise un pronom relatif. Si tu ne connais pas ces films, tu peux parler d'autres films.

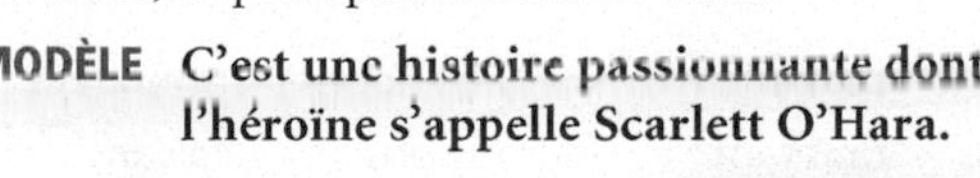

MODÈLE **C'est une histoire passionnante dont l'héroïne s'appelle Scarlett O'Hara.**

1.

2.

3.

7 Mon roman préféré 1.3

Écrivons Quel est ton roman préféré? Écris un paragraphe pour résumer l'histoire et pour expliquer pourquoi ce roman est ton roman préféré. Utilise des pronoms relatifs pour relier tes phrases.

MODÈLE **Mon roman préféré est... C'est un livre qui...**

8 Scénario 1.1

Parlons Tu as envie d'aller au cinéma ce week-end. D'abord, choisis un film que tu voudrais voir. Demande à un(e) camarade s'il/elle veut y aller avec toi. Tu lui racontes un peu l'histoire et tu lui parles des acteurs et des critiques que le film a reçues. Ton/Ta camarade n'est pas très enthousiaste. Jouez cette scène avec ton/ta camarade.

MODÈLE **—Julie, j'ai envie d'aller voir le nouveau film de science-fiction...**
—Je n'aime pas trop la science-fiction. De quoi ça parle?
—C'est un film que...

Communities

School Link

Have students write a movie and/or book review in French and English for the school newspaper. You might have students create a class newspaper entirely in French that includes both movie and book reviews. 5.1

Communication

Pair Activity: Interpersonal

Prepare enough index cards for half of the class. On each card, write two sentences that could be combined as a complex sentence with a relative pronoun. **Je vois les chiens. Les chiens sont sympas. Les chiens que je vois sont sympas.** Make sure that **qui, que,** and **dont** will all be used. Have partners work together. One reads the two sentences and his or her partner combines the sentences into a single complex sentence with the appropriate relative pronoun. Have partners switch roles. 1.1

Differentiated Instruction

ADVANCED LEARNERS

Have students create movie titles that include the relative pronouns **qui, que,** or **dont.** Have students read the titles aloud and have the class vote on the most creative and most humorous titles. You might also have students create a movie poster for one of their titles. 1.2

SPECIAL LEARNING NEEDS

Students with Auditory/Language Impairments Students may need additional help to understand the relative pronoun presentation. Review each rule and give several examples of the rule with English translations. Assign partners or small groups to do the activities together to ensure that one partner or group member has a good understanding of the concept and can assist those who have difficulties.

Resources

Planning:
Lesson Planner
Teacher One Stop

Presentation:
DVD Tutor, Disc 2
Grammavision 1.2

Practice:
Grammar Tutor for Students of French, Chapter 9
Cahier de vocabulaire et grammaire
Differentiated Practice and Assessment CD-ROM
Cahier d'activités
Independent Study Guide
Media Guide
Projectable Transparencies
Bell Work 9.3
Audio CD 9, Tr. 2
@HOMETUTOR

Bell Work

Use Bell Work 9.3 in the *Projectable Transparencies* or write this activity on the board.

Fill in the blanks with **qui, que,** or **dont.**

1. Ce film ____ tout le monde parle est drôle.
2. J'aime l'actrice ____ joue dans ce film.
3. Ça n'a rien à voir avec le livre ____ j'ai lu.
4. C'est le film ____ on a besoin quand on est triste.
5. Le film de science-fiction ____ nous avons vu est super.
6. Je ne connais pas l'acteur ____ joue dans ce film.

1.2

4.1

En anglais

In English, the *–ing* form of a verb can be used with the verb *to be* to say what is happening at a particular moment (present progressive).

We are leaving.

In what other circumstances do we use the –ing form in English?

In French, the present participle is not used to express present progressive time. Instead, the present tense is used.

We are leaving.

Nous partons.

gerunds (Singing is my favorite activity!)

Flash culture

En France la taxe sur les produits s'appelle la TVA (taxe sur la valeur ajoutée). Elle est incluse dans le prix. La TVA est de 19,6 %. Cependant, la TVA sur les livres est seulement de 5,5 %. Certains produits alimentaires, dits de première nécessité (lait, farine, sucre...) ont une TVA réduite à 2,1 %.

Quelle est la taxe sur les produits dans ton état? 4.2

Present participles

1 To form the **present participle**, remove the **-ons** from the **nous** form of the verb and add the ending **-ant.**

écouter nous écoutons + **-ant** = écout**ant**

nous sortons → **sortant**	nous attendons → **attendant**
nous finissons → **finissant**	nous faisons → **faisant**
nous prenons → **prenant**	nous allons → **allant**

2 **Être, avoir,** and **savoir** have irregular present participles.

être → **étant**
avoir → **ayant**
savoir → **sachant**

L'acteur **étant** très célèbre, il y avait une foule!

3 Use **en** or **tout en + present participle** to say that someone is doing something *while* doing something else.

Ils ont quitté le cinéma **tout en parlant** du film.
They left the theater (while) talking about the film.

Je vais acheter le billet **en arrivant** au cinéma.
I will buy the ticket as I arrive at the movie theater.

4 You can also use the present participle as an adjective to describe someone or something. It will agree with the noun being described.

C'est une histoire **passionnante**.
It's an exciting story.

Vocabulaire et grammaire, *pp. 100–101*
Cahier d'activités, *pp. 81–83*

9 Le week-end de Ludivine 1.2

Lisons Ludivine parle de ce qu'elle a fait ce week-end. Indique si dans ses phrases, il y a un participe présent **(oui)** ou pas **(non).** S'il y a un participe présent, indique l'infinitif du verbe.

1. En allant au cinéma, j'ai vu Natasha et je l'ai invitée à venir avec moi. oui; aller
2. Le film que nous avons vu était une bonne adaptation d'un roman célèbre. non
3. Il y a beaucoup de suspense et les acteurs sont formidables. non
4. Tout en regardant le film, j'ai pensé au roman. oui; regarder
5. On a quitté le cinéma tout en discutant du film. oui; discuter

Core Instruction

TEACHING GRAMMAIRE

1. Go over Points 1 and 2 and emphasize that the present participle always translates as *–ing.* Point out that only **avoir, être,** and **savoir** have irregular present participles. **(1 min.)**
2. Ask students yes or no questions about movies and their movie experiences. **En regardant un film, mangez-vous du popcorn? Connaissant déjà la fin, aimez-vous voir un film plus qu'une fois? Ayant votre propre argent de poche, préférez-vous aller au ciné ou louer des DVD? (2 min.)**
3. Go over Points 3 and 4 and provide additional examples. **(3 min.)**

Grammavision

For a video presentation of present participles, see the *DVD Tutor.*

10 Écoutons CD 9, Tr. 2 **1.** a **2.** b **3.** a **4.** a **5.** b **6.** b 1.2

Écoute les personnes suivantes. Dis si elles font les actions **a) simultanément** ou **b) l'une après l'autre.**

11 Des commentaires 1.2

Écrivons Complète chaque phrase avec la forme qui convient du participe présent du verbe donné entre parenthèses.

1. Ces films de guerre sont vraiment ______ (déprimer)! déprimants
2. En ______ (adapter) ce livre pour le cinéma, Mondrieu a vraiment eu une bonne idée. adaptant
3. Avec les films en v.o., on doit lire les sous-titres tout en ______ (regarder) le film. regardant
4. Cette autobiographie est vraiment ______ (passionner). passionnante
5. ______ (être) passionné d'histoire, mon père achète souvent des romans historiques. Étant

12 Deux choses à la fois 1.3

Parlons Fais des phrases pour expliquer ce que tu fais en même temps que les activités illustrées par ces photos.

MODÈLE **J'écoute souvent de la musique en faisant mes devoirs.**

1.

2.

3.

4.

Digital performance space

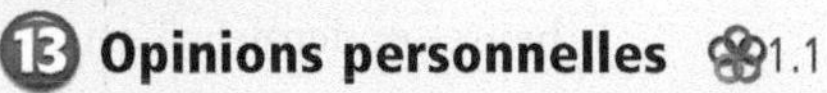

13 Opinions personnelles 1.1

Parlons En petits groupes, organisez un débat sur les différents genres de films et sur ce qu'ils apportent *(they bring)* aux personnes qui les voient. Utilisez des participes présents dans la conversation.

MODÈLE **—Moi, j'aime bien les films étrangers parce qu'en les regardant, on apprend...**
—Oui, et en écoutant les acteurs parler...

10 Script

1. Je ris beaucoup en regardant un film comique.
2. Je vais retrouver Margot et Célestine au café et ensuite, on va au ciné.
3. J'ai vu qu'il y avait un film de Spielberg en passant devant le ciné.
4. Je lis toujours en mangeant.
5. Je regarde un film à la télé et après je vais me coucher.
6. Je lis toujours le roman avant de voir l'adaptation au cinéma.

COMMON ERROR ALERT
ATTENTION !

Students might make a mistake when they use **qui** and **que** as relative pronouns. They know that in questions **qui** refers to people and **que** to things. As relative pronouns, both **qui** and **que** may refer to people or things.

Communication

Pair Activity: Interpersonal

Have students write five questions that begin with **Qu'est-ce que tu fais en** + present participle. Have partners interview each other and write their responses. 1.1

Differentiated Instruction

SLOWER PACE LEARNERS

Before class, write an anecdote about something that happened once when you were at the movies. Use five present participles in your anecdote. Read your story to the class. Have students either raise their hand when they hear a present participle or write down each one they hear. Repeat until students have identified all the present participles. 1.2

MULTIPLE INTELLIGENCES

Bodily-Kinesthetic Create a list of activities that can be demonstrated in class whose description requires the use of the present participle. (He is jumping while holding a book.) Write the activities on slips of paper for students to take turns selecting. Ask students to act out the activity. The class should describe what each student is doing. 1.2

Assess

Assessment Program
Quiz: Grammaire 1
Alternative Assessment
Differentiated Practice and Assessment CD-ROM

Online Assessment
my.hrw.com

Test Generator 

Chapitre 9

Application 1

Resources

Planning:
Lesson Planner
Teacher One Stop

Practice:
Grammar Tutor for Students of French, Chapter 9
Cahier de vocabulaire et grammaire
Differentiated Practice and Assessment CD-ROM
Cahier d'activités
Independent Study Guide
Media Guide
Projectable Transparencies
Bell Work 9.4
Audio CD 9, Tr. 3

Bell Work

Use Bell Work 9.4 in the *Projectable Transparencies* or write this activity on the board.

Link the sentences using **en + participe présent.**

1. **J'écoute de la musique. Je vais à l'école.**
2. **Je parle avec mes sœurs. Je mange avec elles.**
3. **Je regarde un film étranger. Je lis les sous-titres.**
4. **J'achète mon billet. J'arrive au cinéma.**
5. **Je ne parle pas au téléphone. Je conduis.**

1.2

15 Script

1. Tu as lu *Une journée au parc?* C'est trop déprimant!
2. *Le grand monstre?* Ce n'est pas génial.
3. Je viens de voir *Le mystère de la statuette.* Malheureusement, ça n'a rien à voir avec le roman.
4. Ce roman est plein de rebondissements. Je te le recommande.
5. *Léa et Laurent* est vraiment une histoire passionnante!

Synthèse
- Vocabulaire 1
- Grammaire 1

Application 1

14 Ma critique 1.3

Écrivons Écris une critique d'un film que tu as vu récemment. Utilise des pronoms relatifs et des participes présents.

MODÈLE **J'ai vu un film français en DVD. Ce film était en version originale, alors en le regardant... L'acteur qui...**

Un peu plus — Révisions

C'est and il/elle est

1. Use **c'est** and **ce sont** with a noun to identify *who* or *what*. **C'est** can also be used with adjectives to describe something general.

   C'est une histoire vraie. **Ce sont** des acteurs.

   Faire de la vidéo? **C'est** amusant.

2. Identify or describe someone or something with **il/elle est** followed by an adjective.

   Juliette Binoche? **Elle est** belle!

3. When talking about someone's profession or nationality, use either **c'est** or **il/elle est.** If you use **c'est,** you need to use an article.

   C'est un acteur. **Il est** acteur.

   C'est un Français. **Il est** français.

Vocabulaire et grammaire, *p. 102*
Cahier d'activités, *pp. 81–83*

15 Écoutons CD 9, Tr. 3 1.2

Des amis parlent de films et de livres. Qu'est-ce que ces personnes pensent des films et des livres mentionnés?

1. c **a.** Plein de rebondissements
2. e **b.** Ça n'a rien à voir avec le roman.
3. b **c.** C'est trop déprimant.
4. a **d.** C'est une histoire passionnante!
5. d **e.** Ce n'est pas génial.

16 Des descriptions 1.2

Écrivons Complète chaque phrase avec **c'est, ce sont, il est, elle est, ils sont** ou **elles sont.**

1. ______ un acteur de cinéma. C'est
2. ______ française et elle a joué dans beaucoup de films célèbres. Elle est
3. Ces romans? ______ des romans fantastiques. Ce sont
4. Oui, ______ très long, ce film! Trois heures et demie! il est
5. ______ tous les deux au théâtre avec leurs amis. Ils sont

Core Instruction

INTEGRATED PRACTICE

1. Have students complete Activity 14 to review vocabulary, relative pronouns, and present participles. **(10 min.)**
2. Have each student write on a note card one sentence about a movie or book. The sentence should include **qui, que, dont,** or a present participle as an adjective. ***L'enfant noir* est une autobiographie d'un jeune homme qui quitte sa famille.** Have students exchange cards and read the sentences aloud. **(4 min.)**

TEACHING UN PEU PLUS

1. Have students review what they know about nouns and adjectives. Remind students when to use **il/elle est** or **ils/elles sont. (2 min.)**
2. Go over each Points 1–3. **(1 min.)**
3. Write a list of world leaders or well-known professionals on the board. Tell each person's nationality or profession. **Jacques Chirac? C'est l'ancien président français. Lance Armstrong? Il est cycliste. (2 min.)**

Online Practice
my.hrw.com
Application 1 practice

17 C'est quoi? 1.2

Écrivons/Parlons Donne une description des choses suivantes.

MODÈLE le personnage principal d'un film d'horreur
C'est un homme grand qui...

1. l'héroïne d'un roman d'amour
2. l'histoire d'un film d'action
3. les héros des romans policiers
4. des acteurs comiques
5. un film ennuyeux

18 Ma dernière sortie 1.3

Écrivons Raconte ta dernière sortie au cinéma ou au théâtre. Utilise un participe présent dans au moins cinq phrases.

MODÈLE **Je suis allé(e) voir un film...**
En arrivant au cinéma, on a acheté les billets...

Digital performance space

Communication

19 Scénario 1.1

Lisons/Parlons Le professeur de français va montrer un film français à la classe. Les élèves doivent choisir le film. En groupes, lisez les résumés des deux films français que le professeur propose. Ensuite, parlez de ces films. Choisissez un film que tout le groupe a envie de regarder.

MODÈLE **—Moi, je voudrais voir *Le Grand Bleu* parce que c'est un film dont on m'a parlé. Et j'adore...**

Jules et Jim

Juste avant la guerre de 14–18, Jim, un Français, et Jules, un Allemand, deviennent amis et tombent tous les deux amoureux de la même femme qui s'appelle Catherine. Malheureusement, les trois amis sont séparés par la guerre...
Un grand classique du cinéma français à voir absolument.

Le Grand Bleu

Depuis l'enfance, Jacques Mayol et Enzo Molinari se battent pour le record de plongée en apnée. C'est l'aventure de deux hommes liés à la mer. Un jour, Jacques rencontre Johana, une Américaine qui ne comprend pas sa passion pour la mer.
Un film culte pour découvrir un autre monde, le monde de la mer.

French for Spanish Speakers

Ask Spanish speakers which pronouns they would use for **c'est/il/elle est** in Spanish sentences similar to those in **Un peu plus.** (none; The sentence in Spanish would begin with the verb. **C'est une histoire vraie. Es una historia verdadera.)** Have students compare sentences giving nationalities and professions with structures in Spanish. What would the sentences **C'est une Espagnole./ Elle est espagnole.** be in Spanish? (**Es española.** for both sentences) 4.1

Language Note

Explain to students that in French, World War I is referred to as **la guerre de 14–18.**

Communication

Group Activity: Interpretive
Have each student list three objects and three adjectives to describe each object. In small groups, have a student describe one of his or her objects using **il/elle est...,** and an adjective. The other group members try to guess the object saying **C'est un(e)...** Students should give one adjective at a time until the group guesses the object. 1.2

Differentiated Instruction

ADVANCED LEARNERS

14 Have students use their film critiques to create a scene of a television show that reviews movies. Ask students to bring in a videotape or DVD of the film they critique so that they can show a short clip of the movie to accompany their presentation. You might have students work with a partner. Encourage them to disagree with each other's opinion of their film. 1.1

SPECIAL LEARNING NEEDS

Students with AD(H)D Ask students to create a bulletin board or poster to demonstrate the difference between **c'est** and **il/elle est** as described in **Un peu plus.** Examples of each of the uses described should be included in the display. Students should use the visual display to present a lesson to the class. You might encourage classmates to add examples during the lesson. 1.2

Assess

Assessment Program
Quiz: Application 1
Audio CD 9, Tr. 14
Alternative Assessment
Differentiated Practice and Assessment CD-ROM

Online Assessment
my.hrw.com

Test Generator 

Resources

Planning:
Lesson Planner
Teacher One Stop

Practice:
Cahier d'activités

Vocabulaire supplémentaire

You might wish to use these terms to discuss the project with students.

le concours d'affiche	*poster contest*
le maître de cérémonie	*master of ceremonies*
le jury	*jury*
un long métrage	*full-length film*
un court métrage	*short film*
la sélection officielle	*official selection*
la salle de projection	*projection room*
la zone Palais des Festivals	*area of Cannes where the festival is held*
le badge d'identité	*identity badge*

Connections

Film Studies Link

Have groups of students create short videos for a **festival de cinéma.** Suggest that students dramatize a chapter reading they especially like, a promotional video tour of your town, or an original script. Each group should prepare a script with stage directions and production notes, cast the characters, and plan the location in which to shoot the video. Encourage students to rehearse with the final script and props before filming. Have students present their film to the class. After seeing all of the films, have the class vote on best actor, best actress, and best film, and award the winners the **Palme d'or.**

 3.1

Culture

La distribution de la Palme d'or

Culture appliquée

Le Festival de Cannes 2.1

Chaque année, la ville de Cannes accueille[1] des vedettes[2], des cinéastes[3] et des journalistes du monde entier pour le plus grand festival de cinéma du monde. Le premier Festival de Cannes a eu lieu en 1946. Aujourd'hui, parallèlement au festival, il y a aussi des concerts et des expositions[4]. Le prix le plus prestigieux du cinéma, la *Palme d'or*, est accordé[5] au meilleur film de l'année.

1. welcomes 2. superstars 3. filmmakers 4. exhibitions 5. awarded

L'affiche du festival 2.1

Every year for the **Festival international du film de Cannes,** judges select a new design for the official poster. For this project, you will create your own poster promoting either the Cannes Film Festival or an imaginary French film festival held in your town.

Materials needed:
- poster board
- pencil
- markers
- construction paper
- scissors
- glue

Step 1 Divide the class into groups of 2 or 3 students. Each group brainstorms ideas for the poster board. Plan your design by sketching it on a piece of paper.

Step 2 Sketch in pencil your design on the poster board. Color your design with markers. Don't forget to include the name and year of the festival in French.

Step 3 Present your poster to the class. Once all the posters have been presented, the class should vote on the best poster!

Recherches Quel film a gagné la Palme d'or l'année dernière? De quel pays était-il? Quel est le sujet du film? Est-ce que tu voudrais le voir? Pourquoi ou pourquoi pas? 2.2

Core Instruction

CULTURE APPLIQUÉE

1. Have students read **Le Festival de Cannes** aloud. Discuss film festivals in the U.S. and other countries (Sundance, Ebertfest, Toronto International, Kingston Candian). **(5 min.)**
2. Assign step 1 as homework. The next day, provide materials for the students to complete steps 2 and 3 in class. **(30 min.)**
3. The next class period, number the posters and have students vote for their favorite. **(10 min.)**

COMPARAISONS ET COMMUNAUTÉ

1. Have groups read **Comparaisons** and discuss **Et toi?** Ask students what surprised them most about TV in France. **(6 min.)**
2. Have students research local businesses that use interpreters or translators. Discuss the jobs and required training. **(5 min.)**
3. Read **Communauté et professions** aloud in class. Have students discuss other industries in which knowing French might be helpful or required. **(5 min.)**

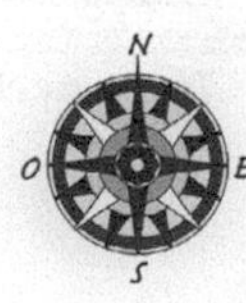

Comparaisons

Un adolescent regardant la télé à Rennes

La télévision en France 4.2

Si tu veux regarder la télévision en France, tu as le choix entre:

a. seulement trois chaînes.
b. seulement des chaînes payantes.
ⓒ quelques chaînes gratuites[1] et des centaines de chaînes payantes.

En France, il y a cinq chaînes de télévision gratuites: TF1, France 2, France 3, France 5/Arte et M6. La première chaîne payante avec décodeur[2], Canal+, existe depuis 1984. Canal+ diffuse essentiellement des films. Canal+ est «en clair»[3] quelques heures par jour. Le câble et la télévision numérique terrestre (TNT)[4] sont de plus en plus populaires et permettent d'avoir accès à des centaines de chaînes. D'autre part, la publicité à la télévision en France est très réglementée: 8 à 12 minutes par heure avant ou après une émission, mais pas pendant.

ET TOI?

1. Est-ce qu'il y a des chaînes de télévision gratuites aux États-Unis? Lesquelles?
2. Quelle est la fréquence de la publicité à la télévision américaine? Quel système préférerais-tu?

Communauté et professions

Être traducteur[5] ou interprète 5.1

Si un film français a du succès aux États-Unis, les acteurs peuvent être invités à donner des interviews. Un interprète sera là pour traduire ce qu'ils disent. Si le film est tiré d'un roman, ce dernier sera sans doute traduit en anglais. C'est le travail du traducteur. Est-ce que tu connais un traducteur ou un interprète? Qu'est-ce qu'il faut faire pour devenir traducteur ou interprète? Fais des recherches et présente ce que tu as trouvé à la classe.

Pendant une conférence internationale

1. free 2. decoder (like a cable box) 3. free (unscrambled) 4. digital TV
5. translator

Communities

School Link

Have students present a French film festival at your school. Help them choose appropriate films with English subtitles. Then have students create posters and judging cards for the audiences. You might have volunteers imagine they are the films' directors, present their film, and give an acceptance speech if their film wins any awards. 5.1

Comparisons

Comparing and Contrasting

Locate two American movies, for example, a western and a love story, in which the script is dubbed by French actors and actresses. Show selected scenes and ask students if the movies are more or less effective with French voices than with American ones. 4.2

Communication

Pair Work: Interpersonal

Students research show business careers that interest them. In pairs, students each choose one job and write an imaginary resume in French. Each student studies their partner's resume and prepares interview questions. Using their own rubric, students interview their partner and decide if he or she is right for the job. 1.2

Differentiated Instruction

SLOWER PACE LEARNERS

Students who are unfamiliar with the Cannes Film Festival might choose to create a poster about an imaginary film festival. Point out to students that film festivals often focus on one genre of film, for example, a wildlife or a horror film festival, or a festival celebrating the work of one director or actor. To help students come up with design ideas for their poster, encourage them to think of their favorite type of film or their favorite actor.

MULTIPLE INTELLIGENCES

Musical In addition to, or as an alternative to the poster assignment, ask students to select a soundtrack to go with the theme of the film festival they plan to describe. After selecting the songs, students should write, in French, the reason they selected each song to express the theme. You might wish to have students present the songs and posters to the class. 3.1

Language Examination

Culture can be used to practice for the **Interpretive Communication** and **Presentational Writing** sections of the Advanced Placement exam as it helps students get acquainted with and reflect on products and practices from the French-speaking world while reading culture-focused passages and answering questions in French.

Objectifs
- to ask about preferences
- to recommend or advise against something

Télé-vocab

Les émissions télé

un reportage sportif

une émission de variétés

les informations (f.)

un feuilleton

le bulletin météo(rologique)

un documentaire

un spot publicitaire

une série (un sitcom)

un jeu

Resources

Planning:
Lesson Planner
Teacher One Stop

Presentation:
Projectable Transparencies **Vocabulaire 9.3, 9.4**
DVD Tutor, Disc 2 **Télé-vocab 2**
Interactive Whiteboard Lessons

Practice:
Cahier de vocabulaire et grammaire
Differentiated Practice and Assessment CD-ROM
Independent Study Guide
Media Guide
Projectable Transparencies Bell Work 9.5
HOMETUTOR
Holt McDougal French Apps

Bell Work

Use Bell Work 9.5 in the *Projectable Transparencies* or write this activity on the board.

Fill in the blanks with **c'est, ce sont, il/elle est,** or **ils/elles sont.**

1. **Jugnot? ____ un acteur français. ____ très amusant.**
2. **Audrey Tautou? ____ française et ____ très jolie. En plus, ____ une très bonne actrice.**
3. **____ un film plein de rebondissements.**
4. **Oh, ____ deux actrices américaines? Non, ____ françaises.**

1.2

Proverbes

For French proverbs and activities related to the chapter theme and vocabulary, see **Proverbes et expressions,** pp. R6–R7.

Core Instruction

TEACHING VOCABULAIRE

1. Show transparencies **Vocabulaire 9.3** and **9.4** and model pronunciation. **(1 min.)**
2. Bring in the TV section from a current newspaper. Choose a show, give its name, and tell what type it is. **(2 min.)**
3. Have a list of popular television shows on the board, several from each category. Ask individual students about their TV watching habits. They should respond by naming a show and its category. **(3 min.)**
4. Hand out a large note card to each student, who should then write one question modeled on those in **Exprimons-nous!** Remind students to use **vous** and to vary the questions. Collect the cards and respond appropriately to each question. **(5 min.)**

Télé-vocab 2

For a video presentation of this vocabulary, see the *DVD Tutor.*

Télé-vocab

Online Practice
my.hrw.com
Vocabulaire 2 practice

Vocabulaire 2

Les genres de musique

le jazz	*jazz*
le rock	*rock*
le rap	*rap*
la pop	*pop*
le hip-hop	*hip-hop*
le reggae	*reggae*
le blues	*blues*
la country	*country*
la techno	*techno*

D'autres mots utiles

les vidéoclips	*music videos*
un présentateur	*(male) newscaster*
une présentatrice	*(female) newscaster*
un animateur	*(male) host*
une animatrice	*(female) host*
une vedette	*star*
en direct	*live*
une chaîne	*channel*
un programme télé	*t.v. program*
une télécommande	*remote control*

Exprimons-nous!

To ask about preferences	To respond
Qu'est-ce que tu aimes regarder à la télé? *What do you like to watch on television?*	**Ce que je préfère, c'est** les vidéoclips. *What I prefer is . . .*
Lequel de ces feuilletons **est-ce que tu préfères?** *Which of . . . do you prefer?*	**Celui avec** Laurie Halle. *The one with . . . .*
Tu as suivi les Jeux olympiques? *Did you follow . . . ?*	Non, **je déteste** regarder le sport à la télé. *. . . I hate . . .*
Tu as vu le concert hip-hop de... ? *Did you see . . . ?*	Oui! **Je ne rate jamais** ce type de concert. *I never miss . . .*

Vocabulaire et grammaire, *pp. 103–105*

TPR — Total Physical Response

Have students respond to these commands.

Lève la main si tu regardes les informations tous les soirs.

Assieds-toi si tu recommandes le dernier film de Harry Potter.

Lève le doigt si tu as un feuilleton préféré.

Lève les bras si tu ne rates jamais les reportages sportifs.

Lève-toi si tu aimes le rap.

Then have some students mime the following situations.

Tu utilises la télécommande pour changer de chaîne.

Tu es une vedette de cinéma.

Tu chantes une chanson mais il n'y a pas de son.

Tu regardes un documentaire qui est ennuyeux à mourir.

Connections

Music Link

Have students choose one of the genres of music in **Vocabulaire** and research its history. Students should create a poster in French to present the information they find. Students might also include on their poster a biography and photo or drawing of a musical artist known for that style of music. 3.1

Differentiated Instruction

SLOWER PACE LEARNERS

Write a list of the names that represent a variety of TV programs and a list of musical groups and artists for each of the music genres. Divide the class into two teams. Place a bell on a table at the front of the class and have a student from each team stand by the table. Say a name from one of the two lists. The first student to hit the bell and correctly guess the name of the program type or music genre wins a point for his or her team. Continue with the rest of the names on the lists. 1.2

MULTIPLE INTELLIGENCES

Linguistic Ask students to write a review of three television shows they have seen recently. Using the vocabulary and expressions in **Exprimons-nous!,** students should tell the type of show it is and give their personal opinion of it. The review should conclude with a recommendation to others about whether they should watch the show. You may wish to have students share their reviews in small groups or with the class. 1.3

Resources

Planning:
Lesson Planner
 Teacher One Stop

Presentation:
Projectable Transparencies **Vocabulaire 9.3, 9.4**
DVD Tutor, Disc 2 **Télé-vocab 2**
Interactive Whiteboard Lessons

Practice:
Cahier de vocabulaire et grammaire
Differentiated Practice and Assessment CD-ROM
Independent Study Guide
Media Guide
Audio CD 9, Tr. 4
@HOMETUTOR
Holt McDougal French Apps

20 Script

See script on p. 307E.

22 Possible Answers

1. J'aime la pop, mais ce que je préfère, c'est le jazz.
2. J'aime la country, mais ce que je préfère, c'est le reggae.
3. J'aime le hip-hop, mais ce que je préfère, c'est le rock.
4. J'aime la techno, mais ce que je préfère, c'est le rap.

Flash culture

Depuis 2005, les Français ont accès à un grand nombre de chaînes à la télé. Certaines sont des chaînes publiques comme France 2, France 3, France 4. D'autres sont des chaînes privées par câble et par satellite. Certaines chaînes privées comme TF1, M6 et Direct 8 sont gratuites D'autres chaînes privées sont payantes. La télé en France donne accès à beaucoup de chaînes étrangères en langue étrangère.

Est-ce que la télévision en France est similiaire à la télévision aux États-Unis? 4.2

20 Écoutons CD 9, Tr. 4 1.2 1. b 2. a 3. a 4. b 5. b

Chaîne Ado, une chaîne de télévision, fait un sondage pour connaître les préférences des adolescents. Écoute les interviews et décide si chaque phrase est **a) vraie** ou **b) fausse.**

1. Denis aime regarder les sitcoms et les feuilletons.
2. Amadou aime regarder les spots publicitaires.
3. Karine ne rate jamais les documentaires sur les animaux.
4. Marc déteste regarder le bulletin météo.
5. Zita aime les vidéoclips de country.

21 À la télé 1.2

Écrivons Sonia rend visite à son grand-père. Il voudrait regarder la télévision. Complète leur conversation avec les mots de la boîte.

émission de variétés	documentaire	informations	jeu
série	reportage sportif	vidéoclips	

SONIA Bon, à six heures, il y a *Le monde aujourd'hui.*
GRAND-PÈRE Non, je n'aime pas regarder les __1__ (informations).
SONIA Il y a aussi *Venez chanter ce soir.*
GRAND-PÈRE Qu'est-ce que c'est que ça?
SONIA C'est une __2__ (émission de variétés). On danse, on chante...
GRAND-PÈRE Est-ce qu'il n'y a pas de __3__ (reportages sportifs)? Je voudrais savoir si les Bleus ont gagné leur match.
SONIA Non. Mais à sept heures il y a le __4__ (jeu) *Qui veut gagner beaucoup d'argent?*, la __5__ (série) *Guillaume et Gigi* et un __6__ (documentaire) sur les lézards d'Australie.

22 Les vidéoclips 1.1

Parlons/Écrivons Quel genre de musique est-ce que tu préfères? Pourquoi ou pourquoi pas?

MODÈLE **—J'aime... mais ce que je préfère...**

1.

2.

3.

4.

Core Instruction

TEACHING EXPRIMONS-NOUS!

1. Briefly review the types of television programs by asking students questions about transparency **Vocabulaire 9.2. (2 min.)**
2. Using the expressions in **Exprimons-nous!**, act out both sides of a conversation in which people make recommendations or advise against seeing a show. **(3 min.)**
3. Have students go to the board and each write either the best or the worst thing they have seen on television this week, including videos and commercials. Read each one aloud and state your opinion, either recommending it or advising against it. **(2 min.)**
4. Ask students yes or no questions about each of the shows, using the expressions in **Exprimons-nous! Tu trouves que ce feuilleton est ennuyeux à mourir? Tu trouves que cette publicité est à ne pas manquer? (3 min.)**

Exprimons-nous!

To recommend something	To advise against something
Je te recommande cette série. Elle est super. *I recommend . . .*	Ce jeu **ne vaut vraiment pas le coup.** *. . . isn't worth your time.*
Le vidéoclip de Zazi est **à ne pas manquer.** *. . . is not-to-be-missed.*	Ce film **ne m'a pas emballé(e).** *. . . didn't thrill me*
Qu'est-ce qu'elle est bien, cette pub! *What a great/awesome . . . !*	Ce sitcom **est ennuyeux à mourir.** *. . . bores me to death.*
C'est le meilleur jeu télévisé **que** j'aie jamais vu! *It's the best . . . that . . .*	**Je ne te conseille pas** ce reportage... *I don't recommend . . .*

Vocabulaire et grammaire, pp. 103–105 — Online Workbooks

23 À mon avis! 1.2

Écrivons Écris cinq expressions logiques en utilisant les mots des boîtes.

J'aime bien	cette série!	Ça ne vaut pas le coup.
Je ne te recommande pas	ce film d'aventures.	C'est à ne pas manquer.
Qu'est-ce qu'elle est bien,	le vidéoclip de MC Solaar.	Il/Elle est drôle!
C'est	ce documentaire.	Il ne m'a pas emballé.
Je déteste	ennuyeux à mourir.	Je ne te conseille pas....

24 Je te recommande... 1.3

Écrivons/Parlons Ton/Ta correspondant(e) te rend visite. Il/Elle ne connaît pas bien les émissions télé américaines. Recommande-lui deux ou trois émissions et dis-lui pourquoi tu les aimes.

MODÈLE **—Je te recommande l'émission *The Apprentice*®! C'est à ne pas manquer! Il y a...**

Entre copains

le clip	*(music) video clip*
la pub	*ad, commercial*
Ça craint.	*It stinks.*

Digital performance space

Communication

25 Sondage 1.1

Parlons Fais un sondage auprès de tes camarades de classe pour savoir quelles émissions de télé ils aiment regarder et le genre de vidéoclips qu'ils préfèrent. En groupes, présentez les résultats à votre classe.

MODÈLE **—Qu'est-ce que tu aimes regarder à la télé?**
—J'aime regarder les jeux.

Chapitre 9
Vocabulaire 2

Cultures

Products and Perspectives

There has been concern that American culture may unduly influence that of other countries, especially that of American TV. However, although American TV programs are popular in France, the most popular films and shows are those made in France. Ask students if they would regularly enjoy watching TV shows from France, or any other country, or if they would rather enjoy watching American shows, with the occasional chance to watch a French movie or a French news broadcast on TV. 2.2

Communication

25 Pair Activity: Interpretive

Have each student write descriptions of three television programs. Students should describe the type of program, the stars or hosts of the show, its time slot on TV, and what the show is about. Then in small groups, have students try to guess the title of the show by hearing only one clue at a time. 1.2

Differentiated Instruction

ADVANCED LEARNERS

25 Have partners write a humorous conversation about what it is like to watch TV with one of their own family members or a friend who has a different taste in TV programs. Have partners present their conversation to the class. 1.3

MULTIPLE INTELLIGENCES

Musical Allow students to write a list of their favorite songs from each of the genres of music listed on page 323. After they complete their list of songs, ask them to write a script in French as though a disc jockey were introducing and critiquing the songs. If possible, ask students to tape the script and songs and present it to the class. 1.3

Assess

Assessment Program
Quiz: Vocabulaire 2
Alternative Assessment
Differentiated Practice and Assessment CD-ROM

Online Assessment
my.hrw.com

Test Generator

Resources

Planning:
Lesson Planner
 Teacher One Stop

Presentation:
DVD Tutor, Disc 2
Grammavision 2.1

Practice:
Grammar Tutor for Students of French, Chapter 9
Cahier de vocabulaire et grammaire
Differentiated Practice and Assessment CD-ROM
Cahier d'activités
Independent Study Guide
Media Guide
Projectable Transparencies
Bell Work 9.6
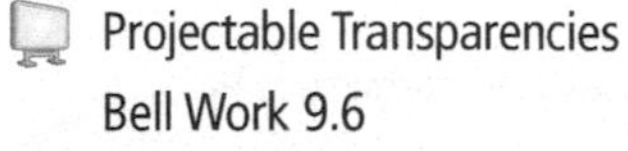

Bell Work

Use Bell Work 9.6 in the *Projectable Transparencies* or write this activity on the board.

Unscramble the words to make logical sentences.

1. **recommande / te / informations / 20 heures / regarder / je / de / les / à**
2. **table / télé / programme / la / le / sur / est**
3. **frère / sportifs / suit / tous / reportages / mon / les**
4. **Clémentine / variété / animatrice/ est / de / émission / une / dans**
5. **manquer / MC Solaar / vidéoclip / ne / à / ce / de / est / pas** 1.2

Communities

School Link

Have students choose an issue, such as whether the school should be year-round or be on a nine-month program, and conduct a poll to find out which students and teachers prefer. They should chart the results in French. 5.1

Objectifs
- interrogative pronouns
- demonstrative pronouns

Grammavision

Interrogative pronouns

The interrogative pronoun **lequel** (*which (one(s))*) asks a question that refers back to someone or something previously named. The form of **lequel** agrees with the person or thing previously named.

	MASCULINE	FEMININE
SINGULAR	lequel	laquelle
PLURAL	lesquel**s**	lesquelle**s**

Il y a **un jeu et un soap** à la télé. **Lequel** préfères-tu regarder?

Vocabulaire et grammaire, *pp. 106–107*
Cahier d'activités, *pp. 85–87*

Déjà vu!

Remember to use **quel (quels, quelle, quelles)** when you want to say *which* or *what* in front of a noun or the word **est** or **sont**.

Quelles émissions aimes-tu regarder?

Quelle est ta série préférée?

26 De quoi parle-t-on? 1.2

Lisons De quel programme est-ce qu'on parle?

1. Laquelle est-ce que tu regardes?
   a. la série **b.** les informations
2. Je ne sais pas laquelle passe sur cette chaîne.
   a. les reportages **b.** la série
3. Lesquels sont les plus intéressants, à ton avis?
   a. les vidéoclips **b.** le soap
4. Lesquelles passent le mardi?
   a. les documentaires **b.** les émissions de variétés
5. Lequel as-tu regardé?
   a. le bulletin météo **b.** la série

27 Besoin de précisions 1.2

Écrivons Tu regardes la télé avec un ami. Demande à ton ami de te dire exactement ce qu'il veut voir.

MODÈLE Je veux regarder les vidéoclips. **Lesquels?**

1. J'ai envie de regarder cette chaîne. Laquelle?
2. Et toi, tu veux voir le reportage sportif? Lequel?
3. Moi, je n'aime pas ces émissions de variétés. Lesquelles?
4. La série que j'ai vue hier est géniale. Laquelle?
5. Et si on regardait les informations? Lesquelles?

Core Instruction

TEACHING GRAMMAIRE

1. Tell students that **lequel** asks *which one?* Point out that there are four forms: feminine singular, feminine plural, masculine singular, masculine plural. **(1 min.)**
2. Use transparency **Vocabulaire 9.2.** Point to two genres of literature or film. Ask a variety of questions so that all students have a chance to answer. **Lequel est plus intéressant, un roman d'amour ou un roman fantastique? Laquelle est plus réaliste, une autobiographie ou une pièce de théâtre? Lesquels sont plus chers à acheter, les films classiques ou les films étrangers? (3 min.)**

Grammavision

For a video presentation of interrogative pronouns, see the *DVD Tutor.*

Grammavision

Online Practice
my.hrw.com
Grammaire 2 practice

28 Chez les Durand 1.2

Écrivons Coralie et Marc choisissent ce qu'ils vont regarder à la télé. Complète leur conversation avec la forme correcte du pronom **lequel**.

—Coralie, on regarde cette chaîne?
___1___? France 3? Laquelle
—Non, TF1. Je n'aime pas le jeu qui passe sur France 3.
—___2___? Lequel
—Ce jeu-là, avec les deux présentateurs sympas.
—Des présentateurs sympas? ___3___? Lesquels
—Je ne sais pas leurs noms. Si on regardait les informations?
—___4___? Les informations régionales ou nationales? Lesquelles
—Les informations nationales.
—Non, moi, je préfère regarder cette émission de variétés.
—___5___? L'émission qui passe sur France 2? Laquelle

29 Ils ont tout en double! 1.2

Écrivons Tu passes une soirée chez les Azaoui. Pose des questions au sujet des objets des illustrations en utilisant une forme du pronom **lequel**.

Rachid / chercher

MODÈLE L'émission? Laquelle tu cherches, Rachid?

1. Madame Azaoui / vouloir

2. Monsieur Azaoui / ne pas trouver

3. Samia / vouloir lire

4. Rachid / utiliser

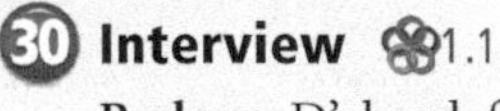

Communication

30 Interview 1.1

Parlons D'abord, fais une liste des types d'émissions que tu regardes. Pour chaque type d'émissions, note les noms de deux ou trois émissions que tu aimes. Interviewe tes camarades pour voir s'ils regardent les mêmes émissions que toi.

MODÈLE —Moi, j'aime le jeu... Et toi, Steven?
—Moi aussi, mais je préfère un autre jeu.
—Ah oui? Lequel?

29 Answers

1. La télécommande? Laquelle vous voulez, madame Azaoui?
2. Le DVD? Lequel vous ne trouvez pas, monsieur Azaoui?
3. Le livre? Lequel tu veux lire, Samia?
4. Le lecteur de CD? Lequel tu utilises, Rachid?

Connections

Science Link

Ask students if they think people are happier with a choice when they can change their mind or when they choose, knowing the decision is final? Have students conduct an experiment to find out the answer. Students might set up a choice in class and/or conduct interviews with people who have been in both situations. 3.1

Communication

Group Activity: Interpersonal

Have each student draw five columns on a sheet of paper. They should label the first column **Nom,** the second **les snacks,** the third **faire du sport,** the fourth **la pizza,** and the fifth **les films.** Have students circulate and ask classmates if they like one of the categories. They should respond in a complete sentence. Students then ask what specific item they like by using an appropriate form of **lequel,** and fill in their chart.

MODÈLE
— Tu aimes les snacks?
— Oui, bien sûr!
— Lesquels?
— Oh, j'aime les bonbons et les chips. 1.1

Differentiated Instruction

SLOWER PACE LEARNERS

For practice using the interrogative pronoun **lequel,** have students write pairs of celebrity names. Then have partners ask each other which one in each pair they prefer. Encourage students to give reasons for their preferences. To practice the plural form, have students compare film genres. **Lesquels préfères-tu, les films d'espionnage ou les films comiques?** 1.1

SPECIAL LEARNING NEEDS

Students with Learning Disabilities Bring several catalogs or sales advertisements from the newspaper to class. Ask partners to practice using the interrogative pronoun **lequel** by asking each other which items they prefer among the choices. 1.1

Resources

Planning:
Lesson Planner
Teacher One Stop

Presentation:
DVD Tutor, Disc 2
Grammavision 2.2

Practice:
Grammar Tutor for Students of French, Chapter 9
Cahier de vocabulaire et grammaire
Differentiated Practice and Assessment CD-ROM
Cahier d'activités
Independent Study Guide
Media Guide
Projectable Transparencies
Bell Work 9.7
Audio CD 9, Tr. 5
HOMETUTOR

Bell Work

Use Bell Work 9.7 in the *Projectable Transparencies* or write this activity on the board.

Ask your friend to be more specific. Use **lequel, laquelle, lesquels,** or **lesquelles.**

1. **Je veux voir le feuilleton à la télé.**
2. **Je n'aime pas les émissions de variétés.**
3. **Et toi, tu as envie de voir ce documentaire?**
4. **Cette nouvelle série est vraiment super!** 1.2

32 Script

See script on p. 307F.

33 Answers

1. Celui qui a beaucoup de suspense.
2. Celui qui joue le rôle du personnage principal.
3. Celles qui jouent dans des films populaires.
4. Ceux qui jouent dans des films amusants.

Demonstrative pronouns

1. The demonstrative pronouns celui, **celle,** ceux, and **celles** refer back to someone or something already named.

   Tu aimes **les drames?** Celui qu'on passe ce soir est super!
   Do you like dramas? The one they're showing tonight is great!

2. The gender of the demonstrative pronoun will match the person or thing already named.

	MASCULINE	FEMININE
SINGULAR	celui	celle
PLURAL	ceux	celles

3. To distinguish *this one* from *that one*, and *these* from *those*, use **-ci** and **-là.**

   Regarde les jeux. Celui**-ci** est bon, mais celui**-là** est ennuyeux.

Vocabulaire et grammaire, *pp. 106–107*
Cahier d'activités, *pp. 85–87*

Flash culture

Toutes les chaînes de télévision doivent respecter des règlements précis établis par le Conseil Supérieur de l'Audiovisuel. Par exemple, la véracité des informations, le respect et la dignité des personnes et la protection des enfants. Il y a aussi des critères pour la publicité. La publicité pour l'alcool *(alcohol)*, les cigarettes et la plupart des médicaments est interdite.

Est-ce qu'il existe un organisme qui régit la télévision aux États-Unis? 4.2

31 Les goûts de Nathalie 1.2

Lisons Tu as demandé à ton amie quelles émissions elle aimait. Associe les éléments des deux colonnes.

d **1.** les émissions de variétés
b **2.** sa présentatrice préférée
c **3.** son jeu favori
a **4.** les sitcoms

a. ceux qui sont amusants
b. celle qui est sur France 2
c. celui qui passe à 18h sur M6
d. celles qui ont des vedettes internationales

32 Écoutons CD 9, Tr. 5 1.2 1. a 2. b 3. a 4. c 5. b 6. d

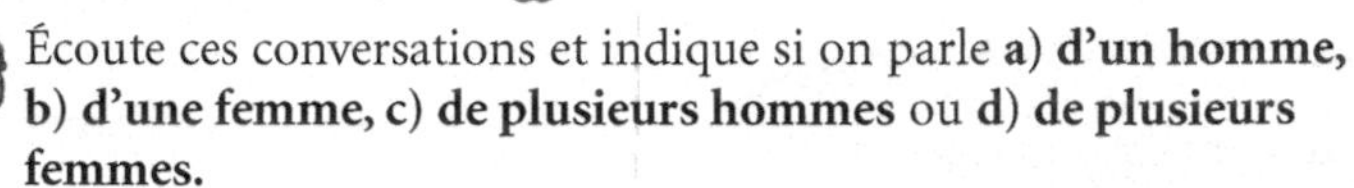

Écoute ces conversations et indique si on parle **a) d'un homme, b) d'une femme, c) de plusieurs hommes** ou **d) de plusieurs femmes.**

33 Devinettes 1.2

Parlons/Écrivons Trouve les réponses aux devinettes *(riddles)* suivantes. Utilise une forme de **celui** dans tes réponses.

MODÈLE les émissions qui passent à la télé au moment où elles sont filmées **Celles qui sont en direct?**

1. le film d'aventures
2. le héros d'un film
3. une actrice célèbre
4. les acteurs comiques

Core Instruction

TEACHING GRAMMAIRE

1. Point out that **celui** has four forms: feminine singular, masculine singular, (this/that one) feminine plural, and masculine plural (these/those). **(1 min.)**
2. Using **celui/celle-ci** and **celui/celle-là,** ask questions about individual students in class. **Qui aime les documentaires—cette fille-là ou cette fille-ci? (3 min.)**
3. Have volunteers answer the questions. Then ask others to tell whether the volunteers guessed correctly. **(3 min.)**

Grammavision

For a video presentation of demonstrative pronouns, see the *DVD Tutor.*

Grammavision

34 Mes préférences à moi 1.3

Écrivons Écris 2 phrases pour expliquer tes préférences en ce qui concerne les choses suivantes en donnant quelques détails. Utilise des pronoms démonstratifs.

MODÈLE mon sitcom préféré
C'est celui qui passe à 18h30. J'adore...

1. mon film préféré
2. mon actrice préférée
3. mes émissions de télé préférées
4. mes vidéoclips préférés
5. ma présentatrice préférée
6. mon spot publicitaire préféré

À la québécoise

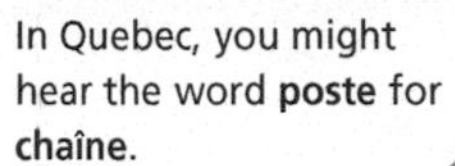

In Quebec, you might hear the word **poste** for **chaîne.**

Digital performance space

Communication

35 Scénario 1.1, 3.2

Parlons Imagine que tu habites avec une famille française cette année. Aujourd'hui, ton «frère»/ta «sœur» français(e) et toi, vous regardez la télé. Discutez des émissions qui vont passer ce soir. Ensemble, essayez de choisir 2 ou 3 programmes que vous allez regarder. Joue cette scène avec un(e) camarade.

MODÈLE **—Tu as envie de regarder le jeu?**
—Lequel?
—Celui qui passe à 16h45.

Vendredi le 18 novembre

16.45	**Le maillon faible** (jeu)
17.15	**Téléfoot** (reportage sportif)
17.45	**À prendre ou à laisser** (jeu)
18.15	**Informations régionales et météo**
19.50	**Musique** (vidéoclips)
20.00	**Journal télévisé** (informations nationales)
20.20	**Bulletin météorologique**
20.25	**Attention danger!** (film d'action)
22.00	**Karen Sisco** (série)
23.00	**Les animaux d'Afrique** (documentaire)

Grammaire 2

French for Spanish Speakers

Ask Spanish speakers to compare the demonstrative pronouns with equivalent forms in Spanish. How are the French forms different from the Spanish ones? (In French, **–ci** and **–là** are added to designate distance from the speaker; in Spanish, different words are used to convey this, such as **éste** for **celui-ci** and **ése** for **celui–là.**) Have students make a chart to compare the forms and then ask if there are any words in one language that the other does not have. (French does not have a word that corresponds to **aquél.**) Ask students how they would translate **aquél** in French. **(celui-là)** 4.1

Communication

Group Work: Interpersonal

Have partners create a conversation between a parent and a child, a store clerk and a client, or two friends who discuss an item. Have them use interrogative and demonstrative pronouns to refer to the item.

MODÈLE
— Johnny, tu as mis les boîtes de conserve dans ton sac à dos?
— Lesquelles?
— Celles qui sont...  1.1

Differentiated Instruction

ADVANCED LEARNERS

34 After students have completed the activity, have them work with a partner to guess each other's answers. One will say, for example, **Mon film préféré, c'est celui avec Johnny Depp.** The other must ask a question, using the demonstrative adjective again, before guessing. **—Celui avec Orlando Bloom? —Oui! —C'est *Pirates of the Caribbean?*** 1.1

SPECIAL LEARNING NEEDS

Students with Learning Disabilities Bring copies of the local television and movie schedules from the newspaper or Internet. After reviewing **Déjà vu!** and the demonstrative pronoun **celui,** ask partners to practice using the demonstrative pronouns to compare television shows or movies. Have partners write their sentences on the board. 1.3

Assess

Assessment Program
Quiz: Grammaire 2
Alternative Assessment
Differentiated Practice and Assessment CD-ROM

Online Assessment
my.hrw.com

Test Generator 

Resources

Planning:
Lesson Planner
Teacher One Stop

Practice:
Grammar Tutor for Students of French, Chapter 9
Cahier de vocabulaire et grammaire
Differentiated Practice and Assessment CD-ROM
Cahier d'activités
Independent Study Guide
Media Guide
Projectable Transparencies
Bell Work 9.8
Audio CD 9, Tr. 6

Bell Work

Use Bell Work 9.8 in the *Projectable Transparencies* or write this activity on the board.

Complete each sentence with the demonstrative pronoun **celui, celle, ceux,** or **celles.**

1. **Ses émissions préférées sont ____ qui passent le matin.**
2. **Le présentateur le plus connu est ____ sur TF1.**
3. **Les jeux télévisés que je regarde sont ____ du dimanche soir.**
4. **Les acteurs plus comiques sont ____ qui jouent les rôles secondaires.** 1.2

37 Script

1. Le nouveau documentaire d'Henri Doussard est le plus intéressant de tous.
2. Ce présentateur est vraiment moins marrant que celui de TF1.
3. Moi, je trouve le vidéoclip de ce groupe pire que celui de l'autre groupe.
4. Je pense que cette émission-là est plus intelligente.
5. Le deuxième jeu est meilleur que le premier.
6. C'est le soap le plus stupide de tous!

Synthèse
- Vocabulaire 2
- Grammaire 2

Application 2

36 Une lettre à ma correspondante 1.3

Écrivons Pour ton cours, tu dois faire un exposé sur ce que les jeunes francophones aiment regarder à la télé. Écris un e-mail à Sylvie, ta correspondante québécoise, pour lui demander ce qu'elle regarde à la télé et quelles émissions elle préfère.

MODÈLE **Chère Sylvie,**
Est-ce qu'au Canada, vous aimez bien les sitcoms? Lesquels? Moi, j'aime...

Un peu plus Révisions

Comparatives and superlatives

1. To compare things , use:

plus + *adjective* + que	*more . . . than*
aussi + *adjective* + que	*as . . . as*
moins + *adjective* + que	*less . . . than*

2. To say *the least . . .* or *the most . . .* use:

le/la/les + plus/moins + *adjective* + de OR
le/la/les + noun + le/la/les + plus/moins + *adjective* + de

3. The superlative forms of **bon** and **mauvais** are irregular:

bon(ne)(s)	**meilleur(e)(s)**	**le (la, les) meilleur(e)(s)**
mauvais(e)(s)	**pire**	**le (la, les) pire(s)**

Vocabulaire et grammaire, *p. 108*
Cahier d'activités, *pp. 85–87*

37 Écoutons CD 9, Tr. 6 1.2

Écoute ces commentaires et indique s'ils sont **a) positifs** ou **b) négatifs.**

1. a 2. b 3. b 4. a 5. a 6. b

38 Chacun ses goûts! 1.3

Écrivons/Parlons Que penses-tu des choses suivantes? Fais des phrases comparatives pour en donner ton opinion personnelle.

MODÈLE les films d'aventures / les films d'horreur
Les films d'aventures sont plus intéressants que les films d'horreur.

1. le jazz / le hip-hop
2. le cinéma / la télé
3. les jeux télévisés / les émissions de variétés
4. les soaps / les séries
5. les jeux / les feuilletons
6. la musique country / la techno
7. les romans policiers / les pièces de théâtre
8. les recueils de poésie / les romans historiques

Core Instruction

INTEGRATED PRACTICE

1. Have students complete Activity 36 to review the vocabulary related to television and forms of **lequel** and **celui. (10 min.)**
2. Form five groups. Have each group write a list of music videos, series, soaps, local channels, or sportscasts. Ask, **De toutes ces chaînes, laquelle préfères-tu? De tous ces reportages sportifs, lequel préfères-tu?** Ask the group to give the response aloud. **(3 min.)**
3. Continue with Activities 37–41. **(20 min.)**

TEACHING UN PEU PLUS

1. Go over Points 1 and 2 and remind students of adjective agreement. **(2 min.)**
2. Point out that **bon** and **mauvais** are irregular. **(1 min.)**
3. Ask questions about TV shows, using comparisons and superlatives. **Quelle est la pire publicité que tu aies vue cette année? Quelle est la meilleure émission que tu aies regardée cette semaine? Quel est le plus mauvais sitcom? (3 min.)**

Online Practice
my.hrw.com
Application 2 practice

39 Pour le meilleur et pour le pire 1.2

Parlons/Écrivons Donne ton opinion sur les sujets suivants en utilisant des superlatifs. Attention aux accords!

MODÈLE actrice / + / beau
Nicole Kidman est la plus belle actrice.

1. film / + / bon
2. spot publicitaire / + / marrant
3. films / + / intéressant
4. musique / – / bon
5. vedettes / + / célèbre
6. émissions / mauvais

40 La meilleure chaîne de télé 1.3

Écrivons À ton avis, quelle est la meilleure chaîne de télé? Écris un paragraphe pour donner ton opinion sur ce sujet. Utilise des comparatifs et des superlatifs.

MODÈLE **Moi, je préfère la chaîne... parce qu'il y a plus de films policiers. J'aime aussi les documentaires sur cette chaîne. Ils sont les plus intéressants...**

Communication

41 Côté musique 1.1

Parlons Avec ton/ta camarade vous parlez des programmes télé. Lisez les questions ci-dessous et répondez-y de manière logique. Ensuite, échangez les rôles.

— **Qu'est-ce que tu aimes regarder à la télé?**
—
— **Tu as suivi le dernier match de foot avec les Rangers?**
—
— **Et tu as vu le concert hip-hop sur la chaîne 5 hier soir?**
—
— **Lequel des animateurs de télé est-ce que tu préfères?**
—

Communication

Group Work: Interpersonal

Review the expressions for agreeing and disagreeing. Then have partners ask each other's favorite film within a certain genre. They then agree or disagree, compare films, and make judgments about the films they discuss, using comparatives and superlatives. 1.1

Pre-AP Language Examination

41 Sample answer:

— . . .
— **Ce que je préfère, c'est les sitcoms.**
— . . .
— **Oui! Je ne rate jamais les matchs de foot.**
— . . .
— **Non, je déteste le hip-hop.**
— . . .
— **Celui de Star Académie®.**

Differentiated Instruction

SLOWER PACE LEARNERS

To have students practice comparatives and superlatives, bring in magazines that feature actors and actresses. Show students two photos and ask which actor or actress is more handsome or beautiful, more intelligent, nicer, more talented, and so on. 2.1

MULTIPLE INTELLIGENCES

41 Visual Give students the option of illustrating the dialogue once they have completed the activity. Students may be more motivated to participate if they are able to use their drawing talents and imagination to visually represent what is being discussed. Ask volunteers to share their work with the class. 1.3

Assess

Assessment Program
Quiz: Application 2
Audio CD 9, Tr. 15
Alternative Assessment
Differentiated Practice and Assessment CD-ROM

Online Assessment
my.hrw.com

Test Generator

Resources

Planning:
Lesson Planner
 Teacher One Stop

Presentation:
DVD Tutor, Disc 2
Télé-roman

Practice:
Media Guide
DVD Tutor, Disc 2
Télé-roman

Connections

Visual Learners

To help students understand what happens in this episode, have them map the events that occur. Guide students through the map on the board. First, draw a rectangle and label it **Léa et Seydou.** Draw lines extending from the rectangle for each of these categories: where? with whom? why? what happens? Then have students write answers for each of these questions, based on **Télé-roman.** 3.2

Gestures

Have students look at Khadim's gesture in scene 8. Who or what might he be pointing out? Then direct students' attention to scene 9. What is Mr. Rigaud doing? What else is happening in this scene? (He is having car trouble.) Ask students what they think will happen next. 2.1

Télé-roman Le Secret de la statuette *Épisode 9*

STRATÉGIE

Predicting As you near the end of a story, you naturally start making predictions about what is going to happen. Based on what you know, make a prediction about the following people and situations: Charles Rigaud and his attempt to send the statuette to France; Inspector Sonko and his attempt to catch Charles Rigaud; Anne Bondy and her eagerness to evaluate the statuette; M. Gadio and his attempt to solve the mystery behind the statuette; the mysterious woman who talked to Rigaud on the phone. 1.2

Le lendemain matin...

1 **Seydou** Bonjour, Léa. Tu as bien dormi?
Léa Bonjour, Seydou. Oui, très bien, merci.

2 **Seydou** Qu'est-ce que tu veux faire aujourd'hui? On pourrait aller au cinéma, si tu veux.
Léa Bof... Je préférerais visiter la ville.

3 **Seydou** Alors, ce matin, on pourrait se promener. Je vais téléphoner à mon copain Khadim pour lui donner rendez-vous. Il est très sympa.

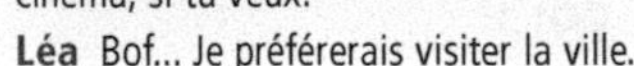

Dans l'après-midi, Léa et Seydou retrouvent Khadim...

4 **Khadim** Salamaleikum.
Seydou Leikumsalam. Je te présente Léa, mon amie française.

5 **Khadim** Nanga def?
Léa Mangui... fi rek.
Khadim Très bien!

Core Instruction

TEACHING TÉLÉ-ROMAN

1. Play **Télé-roman** in segments, stopping after scenes 3, 5, 7, and 9 to ask general comprehension questions. **(10 min.)**
2. Play the video again without stopping. Ask students what they think will happen in the final episode. **(5 min.)**
3. Have students read aloud the **As-tu compris?** questions on page 333. Call on volunteers to answer the questions, and discuss the answers as a class. **(5 min.)**

DVD Tutor

As an alternative, you might use the captioned version of **Le Secret de la statuette** on DVD.

Visit Us Online
my.hrw.com
Online Edition

6

Khadim Alors, quel est l'endroit que tu préfères à Dakar?

Léa L'île de Gorée! C'est l'endroit dont je me souviendrai toujours.

7

Léa Je trouve ça très joli. Les maisons, le musée de la mer, la plage, ... tout!

8

Khadim Eh! Regardez cet homme, là-bas, habillé en explorateur!

9 *Les trois jeunes observent Charles Rigaud qui est au bout de la rue.*

1.2

AS-TU COMPRIS?

1. Qu'est-ce que Seydou propose d'abord comme activité?
2. Qu'est-ce que Seydou et Léa décident de faire ce matin?
3. À qui est-ce que Seydou va téléphoner?
4. Pourquoi Léa aime l'île de Gorée?
5. Qui est-ce que Khadim voit à la fin de l'épisode?

Prochain épisode: *D'après la fin de cet épisode, comment est-ce que tu crois que l'histoire va finir?*

Télé-roman

As-tu compris? Answers

1. d'aller au ciné
2. de visiter la ville, se promener
3. à son copain, Khadim
4. Elle la trouve jolie. Elle aime les maisons, le musée de la mer, la plage,... tout.
5. un homme habillé en explorateur, Charles Rigaud

Communication

Pair Work: Interpersonal

After students have watched **Télé-roman,** have partners tell each other about a visit to another city. Remind them to use the **passé composé** and the **imparfait** and to take turns asking and answering questions. They should tell where they went, what they did, what their favorite part of the visit was, and why. As an alternative, have partners tell each other about an imaginary trip to a place they would like to visit.

1.1

Le Secret de la statuette Episode 9

In this episode, Léa and Seydou discuss the concert they attended. Léa wants to see Dakar, so Seydou offers to show her around. After the tour, Seydou introduces Léa to his friend, Khadim. They tell him about the different places they visited. Léa says she especially likes **l'île de Gorée.** Khadim notices a very strange-looking man dressed up like an explorer. Léa and Seydou recognize right away that it is Rigaud. His car has broken down and he is talking to someone on the phone.

Resources

Planning:

Lesson Planner

Teacher One Stop

Presentation:

Audio CD 9, Tr. 7

Practice:

Cahier d'activités

Reading Strategies and Skills Handbook, Chapter 9

Intermediate Reader

French InterActive Reader

Applying the Strategies

For practice with monitoring comprehension, have students use the "Tea Party" strategy from the *Reading Strategies and Skills Handbook.*

READING PRACTICE

STRATEGIES

Strategy: Tea Party

Reading Skill	When can I use this strategy?		
	Prereading	During Reading	Postreading
Making Predictions	✓		
Using Prior Knowledge	✓		

Strategy at a Glance: Tea Party

- The teacher selects quotations from the text, writes each quotation on a separate card, and distributes one to each student. Students share their quotations in order to form an idea about the subject of the text.
- Each student reads his or her quotation to another student, who responds by also reading a quotation.
- Small groups of students discuss the meaning of the quotations and use the passages to predict what the text will be about.

Tea Party is a strategy that helps readers become engaged with a text before they begin reading the entire selection. Students discuss the meaning of selected quotations from the story, how the passages might relate to each other, and then make predictions about the text based on the quotations.

Best Use of the Strategy

This prereading strategy gives students language to first think about and then to talk about what the text is about and concepts and ideas that may be introduced in the text. In addition, the quotations stimulate students' curiosity about the text and helps them focus on what they are reading.

Getting the Strategy to Work

1. **Select and distribute quotations from the text.** Select a text, choose 10–12 quotations from it, and prepare a list of individual quotations that can be cut into slips. (Be sure to make a master list and copies before cutting the slips. It would be helpful to number the slips or put them on different colors of paper in order to group students later for discussion.) Distribute a slip of paper to each student and ask them to share their quotations in order to form an idea about the reading selection. Have students practice reading their quotations to themselves before they share them with others. Offer to help anyone who is having problems with his or her quotation.

Finding the Main Idea

Discuss **Stratégie** with students. Tell them that gathering supporting details will give them a better understanding of a reading. These details clarify and expand the main idea, and are helpful when the reader is not quite sure what the main idea is. Ask students what they expect to read about when the main idea of a text is "television."

Lecture et écriture

STRATÉGIE pour lire

Recognizing the main idea When you read something, it's important to separate the main idea from the supporting details. Sometimes the main idea is clearly stated, but other times it is just implied. Listing key words as you read can help you find the main idea and determine which details support it.

A Avant la lecture 1.3

Quand est-ce que tu regardes la télévision? Et tes amis, est-ce qu'ils la regardent souvent? Pendant que tu lis l'article suivant prends des notes et essaie de dégager *(to draw)* l'idée principale du texte.

Génération télé

CD 9, Tr. 7

La télé, tu as grandi avec, elle fait partie des meubles[1] mais ce n'est pas l'essentiel !

Tes parents te répètent tous les jours ou presque[2] que tu regardes trop la télé, que tu devrais sortir, faire autre chose. Ils ne s'en rendent pas compte[3], mais c'est ce que tu fais : tu sors, tu vois tes copains. Pour toi, la télé, c'est quand il n'y a rien de mieux[4] à faire. En fait, ce sont tes parents qui la regardent le plus, en moyenne trois heures et demie contre deux heures pour toi.

La télé, quand tu l'allumes, c'est plus par habitude que pour la regarder, un peu comme la radio que tu écoutes sans écouter. Elle est en bruit de fond[5] pendant que tu bosses tes maths ou que tu surfes sur le Net. Quand tu t'assoies devant, tu deviens le roi du zapping[6]. En général, tu n'es pas accro[7] à un programme en particulier, sauf peut-être à une ou deux émissions, celles dont tout le monde parle à la récré. Histoire de rester dans le vent[8].

Car, la télé, c'est aussi un super-sujet de conversation avec les copains. Vous pouvez parler pendant des heures du dernier épisode de la série en vogue. Vous êtes aussi des pros pour vous remémorer les émissions cultes de votre enfance. Tout ça, en affirmant que la télé c'est nul.

Aussi, quand tu regardes la télé, c'est pour te vider la tête[9], pas pour te cultiver. Tu préfères regarder les séries américaines ou des sitcoms. Seuls les films et quelques séries réussissent encore à capter[10] ton attention.

1. part of the furniture 2. almost 3. realize 4. there is nothing better 5. background noise 6. surfing 7. addicted 8. to stay in the loop 9. to clear your head 10. to capture 11. friends 12. to stay in the loop

Maxime, 17 ans

La télé sport

« Je regarde la télé en rentrant du lycée et après le dîner, mais rarement le vendredi soir ou le week-end parce que je sors avec mes potes[11]. Ce que je regarde ? Le sport. Surtout le foot, le basket et le tennis. Je regarde rarement les séries, sauf si au lycée tout le monde commence à parler d'une série, alors j'essaie de la regarder pour rester dans le coup[12]. »

Core Instruction

TEACHING LECTURE

1. Have students read and discuss **Stratégie. (2 min.)**
2. Read Activity A aloud. Have students read **Génération télé** individually. Ask them to take notes as they read and list words to help determine the main idea. After they finish, have students write the main idea of the article in one sentence, using French. **(20 min.)**
3. Have volunteers read aloud the three students' quotes. Have partners do Activities B and C. **(5 min.)**
4. Have students do Activity D as a class. **(3 min.)**
5. Have groups of students discuss the questions in Activity E. **(6 min.)**

Online Practice
my.hrw.com
Online Edition

Lecture et écriture

Salomé, 16 ans

Branchée télé

« Je me réveille avec la télé et m'endors avec la télé. Ça a toujours été comme ça. Mes parents sont pareils[1]. Le matin, je regarde M6 et les clips vidéo. Le soir, après l'école, je l'allume plus par habitude que pour la regarder. Elle est là en bruit de fond pendant que je fais mes devoirs. Je ne suis pas accro à une émission ou une série, juste à la télé. »

Emma, 18 ans

Sans plus

« Je regarde la télé mais sans plus. En fait, ça ne fait pas longtemps qu'on a la télé à la maison. Quand j'étais petite, notre télé a cassé[2] et mes parents ont décidé de ne pas en racheter une tout de suite. Le « pas tout de suite » a duré 12 ans. J'ai pris l'habitude de faire autre chose, alors la plupart du temps j'oublie qu'on a la télé maintenant. Quand je la regarde, c'est pour les infos et les documentaires. Certaines séries sont marrantes aussi. »

1. the same 2. broke

Lecture et écriture

Communities

Community Link

Tell students that in addition to the publicly and privately owned television stations in France, there are also a limited number of non-profit, public-access channels, such as **Zalea,** that allow private citizens and groups to create and broadcast their own programs. Have students research public-access TV in your area and find out if they could create a French-language program of their own. 5.1

Connections

Social Studies Link

Have groups of students use the reading as the basis of an imaginary TV documentary on teenagers and their television viewing habits. Have one student read **Génération télé** as a narrative account of mini-scenes that other members of the group act out. Three students play Maxime, Salomé, and Emma being interviewed. Assign students to interview others around the school about their viewing habits and to provide a translation of the interviews in French. 3.1

Language Examination

Through the practice of listening and reading comprehension, as well as essay writing, **Lecture et écriture** helps students prepare for the **Interpretive Reading and Listening** and the **Presentational Writing** sections of the AP Language and Culture Exam.

Differentiated Instruction

ADVANCED LEARNERS

Challenge students to stop watching TV for one week. Have students keep a daily journal in French of their experience. They should tell how they are dealing with "TV withdrawal" and describe the activities they do instead. 1.3

SPECIAL LEARNING NEEDS

Students with Dyslexia Students with reading challenges may benefit by highlighting the main idea and supporting details while reading. Before discussing **Stratégie pour lire,** make copies of the text. Create a method of marking the main idea and supporting details. For example, underlining the main idea and circling supporting details, or highlighting the main idea in one color and the supporting details in another color. 1.2

Additional Practice

For more reading practice, see **Variations littéraires,** pp. 398–399.

Comparisons

Comparing and Contrasting

Share with students that many American TV shows are broadcast in France. Have them choose a TV show they strongly like or dislike and then search the Internet to see if the program has a French-language Web site. If so, have them read any comments about the program posted by French viewers and compare them with their own opinion. If not, have them share their opinions in small groups. 4.2

Connections

Language Arts Link

Have groups of students write a synopsis of an imaginary new situation comedy, soap opera, or detective show. Have the groups present their pilot to their classmates, who will play the role of TV executives deciding on next season's line-up of shows. You might videotape the pilot episodes.

3.1

LES 15-19 ANS ET LA TÉLÉ

94% ont la télé.

64% ont un lecteur DVD et 80% ont un magnétoscope.

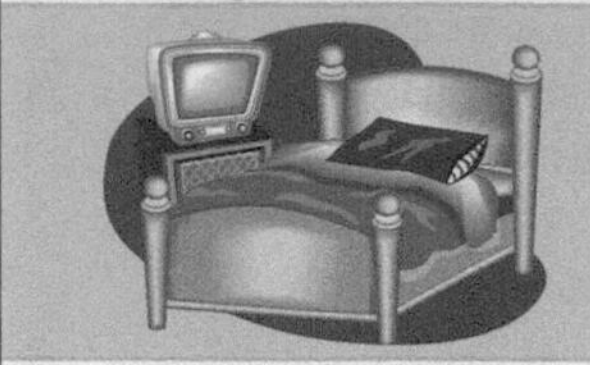

22% ont une télé dans leur chambre.

Statistiques Médiamétrie, France, 2003

Compréhension

B Est-ce que les phrases suivantes sont **a) vraies** ou **b) fausses?** Corrige les phrases fausses. 1.2

1. Les jeunes sortent plus qu'ils ne regardent la télé. a
2. En général, les enfants regardent plus la télé que leurs parents. b; Les parents regardent plus la télé que leurs enfants.
3. Les jeunes ont souvent la télé allumée pendant qu'ils font autre chose. a
4. En général, les jeunes pensent que la télé est très intéressante. b; Ils pensent que c'est nul.
5. Maxime ne regarde jamais les séries. b; Maxime regarde les séries dont on parle à l'école.
6. Chez Salomé, la télé est presque toujours allumée. a

C Remets dans l'ordre de l'article les idées principales suivantes. 1.2 3, 4, 2, 1

1. On regarde la télé pour se reposer.
2. Les jeunes parlent souvent de la télé.
3. Regarder la télé n'est pas l'activité préférée des jeunes.
4. Les jeunes ne sont pas très attachés à la télé ni à la majorité des programmes.

D Choisis l'idée de l'article qui correspond aux commentaires des personnes suivantes. 1.2

c **1.** Maxime
a **2.** Salomé
b **3.** Emma

a. On n'allume pas la télé pour la regarder, mais pour avoir un bruit de fond.
b. Regarder la télé n'est pas l'activité préférée des jeunes.
c. On ne regarde que les programmes dont tout le monde parle à l'école.

Après la lecture

E Reprends les réponses que tu as données dans **Avant la lecture.** Compare tes réponses avec les notes que tu as prises pendant ta lecture. Est-ce que tu penses que les adolescents français ont la même attitude envers la télé que toi et tes amis? Quelles sont les similarités et les différences? Est-ce que tu penses que l'étiquette «**Génération télé**» est aussi vraie pour ta génération? Pourquoi? Pourquoi pas? 1.3

Core Instruction

TEACHING ESPACE ÉCRITURE

1. Read and discuss **Stratégie pour écrire.** You may want to give a few examples of sentences with **qui, que,** and **dont** to refresh students' memory. **(2 min.)**
2. Before beginning, you might write a student-generated list of movies and TV shows on the board. Have each student choose two, so you will be able to read a variety of reviews. Have partners read the introduction and do step 1. **(6 min.)**
3. Have students complete step 2. **(15 min.)**
4. Have students work in pairs to do step 3. You might have students review the corresponding grammar rules to help them peer edit. **(10 min.)**
5. Assign the poster in step 4 as homework. **(1 min.)**

Lecture et écriture

Espace écriture

STRATÉGIE pour écrire

Using conjunctions and relative pronouns helps your writing flow more smoothly and allows for more varied, natural-sounding sentences. Conjunctions such as **et, ou,** and **mais** can join choppy sentences into longer, more interesting ones. The relative pronouns **que, qui,** and **dont** serve the same purpose. They can join two or more clauses to make a more sophisticated and elegant sentence.

Les gros succès et les navets de l'année 1.3

You're writing an article in which you review a movie that you saw this year. For your review, you need to include the genre of the film, the actors who starred in it, a brief summary of what it was about, and your opinion of it. Provide examples from the film that support your opinions.

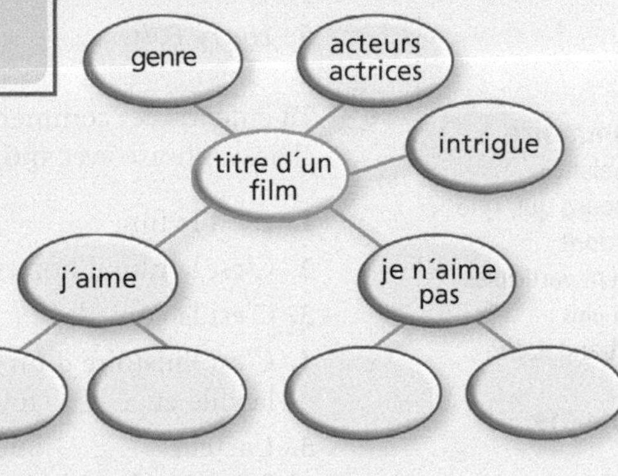

1 Plan

Choose a film to review. Use a cluster diagram to organize the facts about the film and your opinions of it. In the center circle, write the title of the film. Then, in adjoining circles above the center circle, write the facts about the film: the genre, the main actors, and a brief summary of the plot. In two circles that also connect to the center circle, write **"J'aime..."** and **"Je n'aime pas..."** Then, in circles that join those two, write what you like and don't like about the film.

2 Rédaction

Use the cluster diagram to write about the film and your opinion of it. Begin by stating the purpose of your article including the name of the film, the genre and the names of the actors. Give your opinion of the film and support this opinion with examples from the **"J'aime"** and **"Je n'aime pas..."** circles.

3 Correction

Ask a classmate to read your article. Have you provided all the information about the film that the reader needs? Have you supported your opinions?

4 Application

Make a poster with your article and images from a magazine or the Internet that illustrate your reviews. Display it in your classroom. Do you and your classmates agree with each other's reviews? Discuss why or why not.

Process Writing

Avant d'écrire Remind students that graphic organizers can help them remember details of the programs or movies they may otherwise forget to include. By connecting the circles in the diagram, students can see their writing plan more clearly. Ask students to recall what they have learned about writing in chronological order before they begin the list of main events.

Writing Assessment

To assess the **Espace écriture,** you can use the following rubric. For additional rubrics, see the *Assessment Program* or refer to the *Generate Success* Rubric Generator.

Writing Rubric	4	3	2	1
Content (Complete—Incomplete)				
Comprehensibility (Comprehensible—Seldom comprehensible)				
Accuracy (Accurate—Seldom accurate)				
Organization (Well-organized—Poorly organized)				
Effort (Excellent effort—Minimal effort)				

18-20: A 16-17: B 14-15: C 12-13: D Under 12: F

Differentiated Instruction

SLOWER PACE LEARNERS

Rather than writing the full article, have students create a poster of their cluster diagram to present the information about the best and worst movies or television shows of the year. Have students decorate their poster with magazine photos of the actors and actresses they discuss and photos or drawings that illustrate their opinions. For example, a photo of a skunk might illustrate their opinion of the worst movie or TV show. 1.3

SPECIAL LEARNING NEEDS

Students with Learning Disabilities When reviewing **Stratégie pour écrire,** give examples of the use of conjunctions and relative pronouns in English to help students improve their writing. When students have a clear understanding of the use of conjunctions and relative pronouns, introduce French examples. Once the connections to prior learning have been made, students with learning challenges may apply the concept in their own writing.

Assess

Assessment Program
Quiz: Lecture
Quiz: Écriture
Online Assessment my.hrw.com
Test Generator 

Prépare-toi pour l'examen

Resources

Planning:
Lesson Planner
Teacher One Stop

Practice:
Cahier d'activités
Media Guide
DVD Tutor, Disc 2
Projectable Transparencies
Situation, Chapitre 9
Picture Sequences, Chapter 9
Audio CD 9, Tr. 9–12
@HOMETUTOR

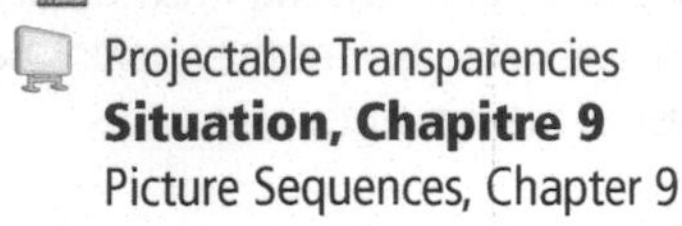

1 Possible Answers

1. un film d'aventures
2. un film de science-fiction
3. un film de guerre
4. un film comique / fantastique
5. un film d'aventures / fantastique

5 Possible Answers

1. v.o.: le film est dans la langue originale
   v.f.: le film est doublé en français
2. Il y a quelques chaînes gratuites et plusieurs chaînes payantes.

Reteaching

Have students describe a film, book, TV show, video game, or song without saying what it is and ask the rest of the class to guess what genre they are describing. **(un film, un roman, une émission de télé,** and so on)

Chapitre 9

Prépare-toi pour l'examen

@HOMETUTOR

1 Vocabulaire 1
- to describe a movie or book
- to ask for and give information

pp. 310–313

1 Ton ami français voudrait louer un de ces films américains. Pour chacun, dis-lui le genre du film et ce que tu en penses. Si tu ne connais pas un des films, essaie d'identifier le genre et dis que tu ne l'as jamais vu. 1.3

1. *Indiana Jones and the Raiders of the Lost Ark*
2. *Star Wars*
3. *Saving Private Ryan*
4. *Shrek*
5. *Harry Potter*

2 Grammaire 1
- the relative pronouns **qui, que** and **dont**
- present participles

Un peu plus
- **c'est** and **il/elle est**

pp. 314–319

2 Tu entends ces commentaires devant le cinéma. Complète chaque phrase avec **qui, que** ou **dont.** 1.2

1. C'est le film _______ on joue au cinéma Bijoux. qu'
2. C'est le film d'horreur _______ tout le monde parle. dont
3. C'est la comédie _______ j'ai vue hier soir. que
4. C'est l'histoire d'un groupe de Zombies _______ attaquent la ville et _______ tout le monde a peur. qui dont
5. L'acteur _______ joue le rôle principal dans ce film s'appelle Stéphane Sauvage. qui

3 Vocabulaire 2
- to ask about preferences
- to recommend or advise against something

pp. 322–325

3 Un groupe d'amis parlent de ce qu'ils aiment et n'aiment pas. Lis leurs réponses et dis quelle sorte d'émission télé chacun préfère regarder. 1.2

SARAH Je lis le journal tous les jours parce que j'aime savoir ce qui se passe dans le monde. les informations

ÉMILE J'aime jouer aux cartes, aux dames... à toute sorte de jeux! les jeux télévisés

PHILIPPE J'adore le sport, surtout le foot. J'aime savoir les résultats de chaque match. les reportages sportifs

LILIANE Comme je travaille en plein air *(outdoors)*, je veux savoir exactement quel temps il va faire chaque jour. les bulletins météo

ROSE Moi, j'aime tout ce qui est musique! les vidéoclips

MARC Moi, j'aime un peu de tout: la musique, la danse, les blagues *(jokes)*... les émissions de variétés

Preparing for the Exam

FOLD-N-LEARN

Booklet Study Aid

1. Have students fold a sheet of paper in half from top to bottom, then from side to side. Have them unfold the sheet and cut a slit along the shorter crease from each edge almost to the longer crease.

2. Ask students to fold the sheet back into fourths in the same order as Step 1. Ask them to write **Chapitre 9** on the cover.
3. On each page, ask students to write the categories from **Vocabulaire 1** and **2,** such as **Les genres de film.** Below each category they should write the French words and expressions and the English equivalents in separate columns.
4. Have students review the chapter vocabulary by flipping through the booklet and selecting an expression. Ask them to cover the English equivalent and try to recall it by looking at the French expression.

Prépare-toi pour l'examen

4 La famille de Karima parle des émissions à la télé. Complète leur conversation avec les formes correctes de **lequel** ou **celui.** 1.2

KARIMA Je voudrais voir ce feuilleton à la télé ce soir.

AHMAD ___1___? Lequel

KARIMA ___2___ qui commence à huit heures. Celui

AHMAD Non, je veux regarder mes deux séries préférées!

KARIMA Ce sont ___3___, tes séries préférées? lesquelles

AHMAD ___4___ qui commencent à huit heures sur Canal plus. Celles

5 Réponds aux questions suivantes. 4.2

1. Quelle est la différence entre **v.o.** et **v.f.**?
2. Comment est la télévision française?

6 Écoute la conversation de Monsieur et Madame Renault et indique si chaque phrase est **a) vraie** ou **b) fausse.** CD 9, Tr. 9 1.2

b **1.** M. Renault voudrait sortir ce soir.
b **2.** Mme Renault aime beaucoup regarder la télé.
a **3.** M. Renault suggère un documentaire.
a **4.** M. et Mme Renault décident de regarder le documentaire.

7 Avec ton/ta camarade, vous parlez d'aller au cinéma ce soir. D'abord, lisez les instructions pour chaque réplique *(exchange)*. Ensuite, créez votre dialogue en utilisant des expressions que vous avez apprises. 1.1

Élève A:	Propose à ton/ta camarade d'aller au cinéma.
Élève B:	Réponds positivement. Demande quel film ton/ta camarade veut voir.
Élève A:	Réponds et parle un peu du film.
Élève B:	Demande où vous pouvez voir ce film.
Élève A:	Réponds.
Élève B:	Demande l'heure de la séance.
Élève A:	Propose deux possibilités.
Élève B:	Suggère une séance.

Online Assessment
my.hrw.com
Chapter Self-test

4 Grammaire 2
- the interrogative pronoun **lequel**
- the demonstrative pronoun **celui**

Un peu plus
- the comparative and superlative

pp. 326–331

5 Culture
- **Flash culture** **pp. 312, 316, 324, 328**
- **Comparaisons** **pp. 320–321**

6 Script

— Alors, qu'est-ce qu'on fait ce soir?
— Je suis un peu fatigué. Restons à la maison. Nous pouvons regarder la télé.
— Ah non, il n'y a jamais rien de bien à la télé. C'est ennuyeux.
— Mais regarde! Ce soir il y a un documentaire sur la technologie d'aujourd'hui.
— Hmmm... Oui, ça a l'air intéressant. Et il y a aussi ce film de science-fiction basé sur un des livres de Jules Verne.
— J'ai déjà vu ce film et il ne m'a pas emballé. Ça n'a rien à voir avec le roman.
— C'est dommage—le roman est à ne pas manquer! Bon, d'accord. Restons à la maison et regardons ton documentaire.

Language Examination

7 Sample conversation:

a. Ça te dit d'aller au cinéma ce soir?
b. Oui. Qu'est-ce que tu veux aller voir?
a. «Les Aventures de Tintin». Je crois que c'est une bonne adaptation de la bande dessinée.
b. Ça passe où?
a. Ça passe au cinéma le Cinoche.
b. Ça commence à quelle heure?
a. Il y a une séance à 19h50 et une à 22h30.
b. On y va à 19h50?

Additional Speaking Practice

- For additional speaking practice, you might use the *Picture Sequences Transparency* for Chapter 9 found in the *Projectable Transparencies.*
- To assess the speaking activities in this section, you might use the *Generate Success* Rubric Generator or the oral rubrics found in the *Assessment Program.*

Pre-AP Practice

7 This guided conversation activity helps students practice oral exchanges using material from this chapter and previous chapters. The activity helps prepare students for the **Interpersonal Speaking** section of the AP French Language and Culture Exam.

Prépare-toi pour l'examen

Grammar Review
For more practice with the grammar topics in this chapter, see the *Grammar Tutor*, the *DVD Tutor*, the *@HomeTutor*, or the *Cahier de vocabulaire et grammaire.*

Grammavision

 **Online Edition**
Students might use the online textbook and Performance Space to practice the **Lettres et sons** feature.

Dictée Script
1. Les animaux au zoo sont drôles.
2. Il fait très beau aujourd'hui.
3. Tu préfères le hip-hop ou le rock?
4. J'adore les gâteaux au chocolat.
5. C'est un roman historique.

Teacher to Teacher

Jon Baker
Westmoore High School
Oklahoma City, OK

To give students practice asking for and giving information, I find an interesting article in the local or school newpaper and assign partners the roles of the reporter and the interviewee. They answer these questions and then role-play an interview. What questions must the reporter have asked? How might the interviewee have answered differently? If you would have interviewed someone else, whom? What would you have asked and what would that person have said? 1.1

Grammaire 1
- the relative pronouns **qui, que** and **dont**
- present participles

Un peu plus
- **c'est** and **il/elle est**

pp. 314–319

Résumé: Grammaire 1

The relative pronouns **qui, que, dont**
- **Qui** is the **subject** of the clause. **Que** is the **object** of the clause.
- Dont replaces phrases beginning with the preposition de.

To form the present participle, drop the **-ons** from the present tense form of the verb and add **-ant**. Verbs with irregular present participles are: **être (étant), avoir (ayant)**, and **savoir (sachant).**

Use **c'est (ce sont)** with a noun to identify who or what something is. Use **il/elle est** with an adjective when there is no identifying noun. When describing someone's profession or nationality, use **c'est** with an article or **il/elle est** without an article.

Grammaire 2
- the interrogative pronoun **lequel**
- the demonstrative pronoun **celui**

Un peu plus
- the comparative and superlative

pp. 326–331

Résumé: Grammaire 2

Use a form of **lequel** *(which one(s))* when asking about something or someone previously named.

	Masculine	Feminine
Singular	lequel	laquelle
Plural	lesquel**s**	lesquelle**s**

Use a form of the pronoun **celui** *(this one, that one, these, those)* when telling about someone or something specific that has already been named. Add **-ci** and **-là** to distinguish between ***this one/these*** and ***that one/those.***

	Masculine	Feminine
Singular	celui	celle
Plural	ceux	celles

To compare things, use **plus/aussi/moins** + **adjective** + **que.**
Use **le/la/les plus/moins** + **adjective** + **de** to say *the most...* or *the least...*
The adjectives **bon** and **mauvais** are irregular; see page 330.

Lettres et sons

The sounds **[o]** and **[ɔ]** CD 9, Tr. 10–12 1.2

The sound [o] is similar to the vowel sound in the English word *boat*. It is usually spelled with **au, eau (beau), ô (drôle),** and sometimes **o (vidéo).** The sound **[ɔ]** is between the vowel sounds in the English words *boat* and *bought*. It is usually spelled with **o (historique).**

Jeux de langue
Ce beau petit garçon a un bateau trop drôle.

Dictée
Écris les phrases de la dictée.

Chapter Review

DVD Program

Online Edition

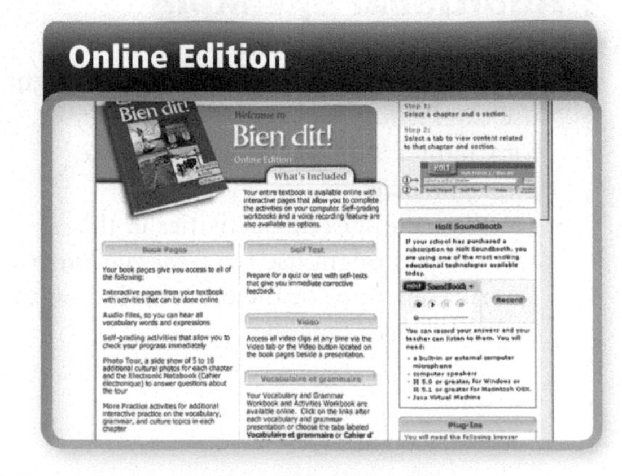

Résumé: Vocabulaire 1

PRACTICE FRENCH WITH HOLT MCDOUGAL APPS!

To describe a movie or a book

un acteur/une actrice	actor/actress
une (auto)biographie	(auto)biography
un dessin animé	cartoon (film)
un drame	drama
un film classique	classic movie
un film comique/une comédie	a comedy
un film d'action/d'aventures	action/adventure movie
un film d'espionnage	spy movie
un film d'horreur	horror movie
un film de guerre/étranger	war movie/foreign film
un film de science-fiction	science-fiction movie
le héros/l'héroïne	hero/heroine
le metteur en scène	director
le personnage principal	main character
une pièce de théâtre	play
un recueil de poésie	poetry collection
un roman classique	classic novel
un roman d'amour	romance novel
un roman fantastique	fantasy novel
un roman policier	mystery novel
les sous-titres (m.)	subtitles
C'est drôle/amusant.	It's funny/amusing.
C'est une...adaptation de...	It's a . . . adaptation of . . .
C'est une histoire passionnante.	It's an exciting story.
Il y a beaucoup de suspense.	There's a lot of suspense.
Il y a plein de rebondissements.	It's full of twists.
Ça n'a rien à voir avec...	It has nothing to do with . . .
Ce n'est pas génial.	It's not great.
Ce n'est pas mal, sans plus.	It's just O.K.
C'est trop long/ennuyeux/déprimant.	It's too long/boring/depressing.
Il n'y a pas d'histoire.	There's no story.

To ask for and give information

Ça commence à quelle heure?	At what time does it begin?
Ça passe où?	Where is it playing?
C'est avec qui?	Who's in it?
De quoi ça parle?	What's it about?
Qu'est-ce qu'on joue... ?	What's playing... ?
Qu'est-ce que tu as lu d'intéressant...?	What have you read . . . that's interesting?
Qu'est-ce que ça raconte?	What's it about?
Ça parle de.../C'est basé sur...	It's about . . . /It's based on . . .
Ça passe au.../C'est avec...	It's playing at . . . /It's with . . .
C'est l'histoire de...	It's the story of . . .
La séance est à...	The showing is at . . .
... le dernier...	. . . the latest . . .

Résumé: Vocabulaire 2

To ask about preferences

un animateur/une animatrice	disc jockey
le blues/la country/le jazz	blues/country/jazz
le bulletin météo(rologique)	weather report
une chaîne/une télécommande	station/remote control
un documentaire/un jeu	documentary/game
une émission de variétés	variety show
en direct	live
un feuilleton	soap opera
le hip-hop/le rap/le reggae	hip-hop/rap/reggae
les informations (f.)	news
la pop/le rock/la techno	pop/rock/techno
un présentateur/une présentatrice	newscaster
un reportage sportif	sports report
une série	series
un spot publicitaire	commercial
une vedette	star
un vidéoclip	music video
Tu as suivi... ?	Did you follow . . . ?
Tu as vu...sur... ?	Did you see . . . on . . .
Ce que je préfère, c'est...	What I prefer is/are . . .
...je déteste...	. . . I hate. . . .
Je ne rate jamais...	I never miss . . .

To recommend or advise against something............*See pp. 325*

Chapitre 9

Prépare-toi pour l'examen

Holt McDougal French Apps

Remind students that they can use the Holt McDougal French Apps to review their vocabulary.

Game

Quel film? Have students think of a film or television show and write three clues about it. Form two teams. A player from one team gives the first clue about his or her film. **(C'est l'histoire d'une femme qui...)** If the opposing team does not guess the title, the player's team wins a point, and the player gives a second clue. Continue until the opposing team guesses the movie or program title. 1.1

Projectable Transparency

More Digital Resources

FOR THE STUDENT

Holt McDougal French Apps
@HomeTutor
News and Networking
Performance Space

FOR THE TEACHER

- Interactive Whiteboard Lessons
- Generate Success!

Assess

Assessment Program

Examen: Chapitre 9

Audio CD 9, Tr. 16–17

Examen oral: Chapitre 9

Alternative Assessment

Differentiated Practice and Assessment CD-ROM

Online Assessment
my.hrw.com

Test Generator 

Révisions cumulatives

Resources

Planning:
Lesson Planner
Teacher One Stop

Practice:
Cahier d'activités
Media Guide
Projectable Transparencies
Fine Art, Chapter 9
Audio CD 9, Tr. 13

Holt McDougal French Apps

1 Script

1. Tu veux aller voir le nouveau film de Jugnot? Ça passe au cinema Rex et il y a une séance à 18h30.
2. Tu as vu son dernier film? C'était plein de rebondissements et il y avait beaucoup de suspense.
3. Tu as vu le documentaire sur la mer à la télé hier soir? Ça ne m'a pas emballé.
4. Je ne te conseille pas cette nouvelle série. Elle n'est pas géniale.
5. J'aime beaucoup ce film. C'est un classique.
6. Ce film est l'histoire d'un homme et une femme qui se marient et qui partent vivre aux États-Unis.

Cinquain Poetry

Have students follow these directions to write a **cinquain** to display on the bulletin board.

Line 1 A noun
Line 2 Two adjectives that describe the noun
Line 3 Three participles related to the noun
Line 4 Four adverbs related to the noun
Line 5 A noun that is a synonym for line one

Sample Answer
Une discussion
Passionnante, longue
Parlant, écoutant, pensant
Souvent, trop, vite, mal
Un débat

Révisions cumulatives

1 Des amis parlent des émissions et des films qu'ils ont vus. Écoute les conversations et décide si on donne **a) une bonne critique, b) une mauvaise critique** ou **c) une description sans critique.** CD 9, Tr. 13 1.2 **1.** c **2.** a **3.** b **4.** b **5.** a **6.** c

2 Voici le programme de télé. Lis le programme et puis réponds aux questions suivantes. 1.2

18.10 Star Academy ★★★

Star Academy Demi-finale

19.05 A prendre ou à laisser
19.50 A vrai dire
19.55 Météo
20.00 Journal
20.35 Portrait d'expert
20.38 A livre ouvert
20.40 Le résultat des courses
20.42 Météo
20.45 Trafic info
20.48 Euro millions
20.50 Téléréalité 2 HEURES 25

ARTE

18.15 La Provence
19.00 La Cuisine Sénégalaise
19.45 Arte info
20.00 Le journal de la culture
20.10 Arte Météo
20.15 La clinique du professeur Mao
20.40 1 HEURE 55 ★★ Charade, Film d'espionnage, EU 1963
22.30 Attention mesdames et messieurs
22.35 Samir et ses frères
23.30 Tracks

K22

18.50 Les chemins de l'étrange Dans le temps
19.50 Météo
20.04 La minute de l'immobilier
20.05 Tout le sport

20.39 Conso le dise
20.40 Infos locales / Kaamelott

☆ 1 BLANK STAR A la rigueur
★ 1 STAR A voir
★★ 2 STARS A enregistrer
★★★ 3 STARS A conserver

1. On peut savoir la météo sur quelle(s) chaîne(s)?
2. Ma meilleure amie adore le sport, alors elle ne manque pas quelle émission sur quelle chaîne?
3. Que pensent les critiques du film Charade?
4. Et toi, quelle(s) émission(s) regarderais-tu?

Online Culture Project

Have students do a Web search for the top ten French films or top ten books in France. They should list the titles and the directors or authors. Ask students to note any online sites that sell these films or books. In what formats are they available? Remind students to document their sources. If possible, have students print photos from the film sites or of book jackets to show as they present their lists to the class. 1.3, 2.2

Révisions cumulatives

Online Assessment
my.hrw.com
Cumulative Self-test

3 Avec deux ou trois amis, parlez de plusieurs films qu'on passe maintenant dans votre région. Décidez quel film vous voulez voir et faites des projets pour aller le voir ensemble. 1.1

4 Regarde l'image et décris ce qui se passe dans la scène. Est-ce qu'on est dans le passé ou le présent? Si tu pouvais visiter cet endroit, que ferais-tu? 1.2

Gogh, Vincent van (1853-1890). Drawbridge at Arles with a group of washerwomen (Pont de Langlois, Arles, France), 1888. Oil on canvas, Rijksmuseum Kroeller-Mueller, Otterlo, The Netherlands.

Pont de Langlois **de Vincent Van Gogh**

5 Écris la critique d'un film que tu as vu ou d'un livre que tu as lu. Dis de quoi ça parle et pourquoi tu l'aimes ou tu ne l'aimes pas. 1.3

6 **À ton tour**

Les divertissements Your class is in charge of the entertainment section of a French club newsletter. As a class, create several articles on activities going on in your school or area and put them together to form the feature for the newsletter. 1.3

ACTFL Performance Standards

The activities in Chapter 9 target the communicative modes as described in the Standards.

Interpersonal	Two-way communication using receptive skills and productive skills	**Communication (SE),** pp. 313, 315, 317, 319, 325, 327, 329 **Communication (TE),** pp. 313, 315, 317, 327, 329, 331 **À ton tour,** p. 343
Interpretive	One-way communication using receptive skills	**Comparaisons,** p. 321 **Communication (TE),** p. 319, 325 **Télé-roman,** pp. 332–333
Presentational	One-way communication using productive skills	**Communication (SE),** p. 331

Fine Art Connection

Introduction Vincent van Gogh was born in 1853 in a small Dutch town, where his father was a minister. He worked for an art dealer before studying theology. Around 1886, van Gogh met famous painters such as Camille Pissarro, Henri de Toulouse-Lautrec, and Paul Gauguin, in Paris. During that period, he produced mainly post-impressionist works. In 1888, he settled in Arles, where he discovered the luminous landscapes of the Provence area of Southern France. Many of van Gogh's paintings are pointillist works, painted with small dots of color. He was also a precursor of fauvism and of expressionism.

Analyzing

To help students discuss the painting, you might use the following questions.

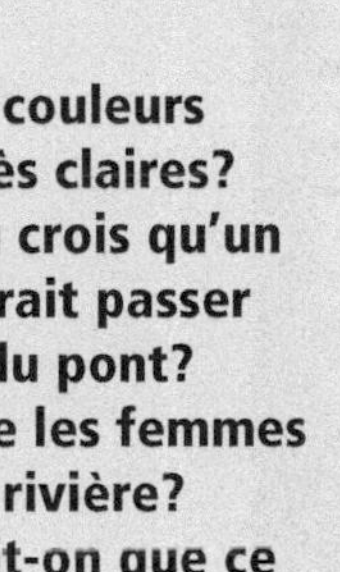

1. **Quel temps fait-il sur cette scène?**
2. **Pourquoi les couleurs sont-elles très claires?**
3. **Est-ce que tu crois qu'un bateau pourrait passer au-dessous du pont?**
4. **Qu'est-ce que les femmes font dans la rivière?**
5. **Comment sait-on que ce tableau n'a pas été peint l'année dernière?** 3.1

Extension

Van Gogh painted several versions of ***Le pont (de) Langlois***. Ask students to do an Internet search and to bring printouts of these paintings to class. Have them compare the different angles and colors. Several countries have printed postage stamps that depict those paintings. Students may want to bring in printouts of the stamps as well and group them by version or by country of origin. 2.2, 3.1

Planning Guide

Partons en vacances!

Chapter Section		Resources
Vocabulaire 1 • Vacation destinations and activities, nationalities **Grammaire 1** • Review of object pronouns and conditional	pp. 346–349 pp. 350–353	Projectable Transparencies: Vocabulaire 10.1, 10.2; Bell Work 10.1, 10.2, 10.3, 10.4 Cahier de vocabulaire et grammaire, pp. 109–114 Grammar Tutor for Students of French Cahier d'activités, pp. 91–93 Media Guide, pp. 37–40, 108–110
Application 1 • **Un peu plus:** Review of **si** clauses	pp. 354–355	**Assessment Program** Quiz: Vocabulaire 1, pp. 275–276 Quiz: Grammaire 1, pp. 277–278 Quiz: Application 1, pp. 279–280
Culture • **Culture appliquée: Le tourisme à Nice** • **Comparaisons et Communauté**	pp. 356–357	Cahier d'activités, p. 94
Vocabulaire 2 • Vacation preparations **Grammaire 2** • Review of the subjunctive • Review of **passé composé** and **imparfait**	pp. 358–361 pp. 362–365	Projectable Transparencies: Vocabulaire 10.3, 10.4; Bell Work 10.5, 10.6, 10.7, 10.8 Cahier de vocabulaire et grammaire, pp. 115–120 Grammar Tutor for Students of French Cahier d'activités, pp. 95–97 Media Guide, pp. 37–40, 108–109, 111
Application 2 • **Un peu plus:** Review of **être en train de**	pp. 366–367	**Assessment Program** Quiz: Vocabulaire 2, pp. 281–282 Quiz: Grammaire 2, pp. 283–284 Quiz: Application 2, pp. 285–286
Télé-roman	pp. 368–369	Media Guide, pp. 109, 112
Lecture et écriture	pp. 370–373	Cahier d'activités, p. 98 Reading Strategies and Skills Handbook Intermediate Reader French InterActive Reader **Assessment Program** Quiz: Lecture, p. 287 Quiz: Écriture, p. 288
Prépare-toi pour l'examen • **Résumé de vocabulaire et grammaire** • **Lettres et sons** **Révisions cumulatives**	pp. 374–377 pp. 378–379	Independent Study Guide, pp. 28–30, 42 Media Guide, p. 40 **Assessment Program** Examen: Chapitre 10, pp. 289–294 Examen oral: Chapitre 10, p. 326 Examen final, pp. 303–310 Projectable Transparencies: Fine Art, Ch. 10 Cahier d'activités, pp. 94, 99–100
Variations littéraires • **Mondo et autres histoires**	pp. 400–401	Reading Strategies and Skills Handbook Intermediate Reader French InterActive Reader

Visit Us Online

my.hrw.com
Online Edition

Pacing Suggestions

	Essential	Recommended	Optional
Vocabulaire 1 • Vacation destinations and activities, nationalities	✔		
Grammaire 1 • Review of object pronouns and conditional • **Flash culture**	✔		
Application 1 • **Un peu plus:** Review of **si** clauses	✔		
Culture • **Culture appliquée: Le tourisme à Nice** • **Comparaisons et Communauté**		✔	
Vocabulaire 2 • Vacation preparations • **Flash culture**	✔		
Grammaire 2 • Review of the subjunctive • Review of **passé composé** and **imparfait** • **Flash culture**	✔		
Application 2 • **Un peu plus:** Review of **être en train de**	✔		
Télé-roman • Épisode 10: **Le Secret de la statuette**			✔
Lecture et écriture • **En sortant de l'école** (Lecture) • **Vos vacances de rêves** (Écriture)		✔	
Prépare-toi pour l'examen		✔	
Révisions cumulatives			✔
Variations littéraires • **Mondo et autres histoires**			✔

Technology

Bien dit! Online
- Student Edition with multi-media
- **performance space** recording tool
- Interactive activities with feedback
- Self-tests with feedback
- Cahier d'activités (Interactive workbook)
- Cahier de vocabulaire et grammaire (Interactive workbook)
- Holt Online Assessment

DVD Tutor
- Télé-vocab
- Grammavision
- Télé-roman

- Interactive games
- Differentiated Practice
- Cultural video

Audio Program
- Student Edition listening activities
- Assessment listening activities
- Songs

Teacher One Stop
- Complete resources
- ExamView Pro Test Generator
- Holt Calendar Planner

Holt McDougal Apps

Interactive Whiteboard Lessons

Differentiated Practice and Assessment CD

For slower pace and advanced learner options, see the Differentiated Practice and Assessment CD.

Planning Guide

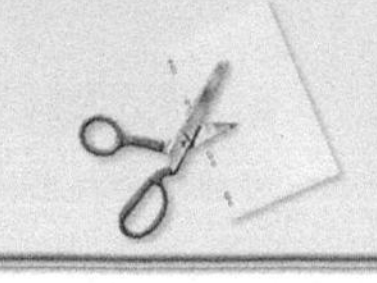

Projects

Le monde du voyageur

Students create travel posters. The posters will depict an airport, a train station, or a vacation scene. Items will be labeled and each person in the scene will have a speech bubble. 1.3

Suggested Sequence

1. In groups of three, students choose the location for their scenes and begin drawing pictures to illustrate them. They should research locations in French-speaking countries for inspiration. The scenes may tell a story or simply show people doing different things.
2. Students plan the layout of the illustrations and labels. Have them label as many items as possible, such as clothing, travel items, objects in the scene, activities, and so on. Remind students to check their spelling.
3. Have students write speech bubbles for the people shown. They might choose to demonstrate greeting or seeing people off, giving advice, or other appropriate functions.
4. Have students edit one another's work. They should make any corrections in labels or language use. Each group then adds the final touches to complete the poster.

Creativity and Innovation

Grading the project

Suggested point distribution
(100 points total)

Completion of project	30 pts.
Appearance	20 pts.
Creativity	20 pts.
Language use	30 pts.

e-community

e-mail forum:

Location: http://french

Post the following questions on the classroom e-mail forum:

Qu'est-ce que tu aimes faire pendant un voyage? Visiter des musées? Faire des randonnées? Te baigner dans la mer? 5.1

All students will contribute to the list and then share the items.

Partner Class Project

Have students imagine that they work for a resort hotel that would like to offer activities and tours to encourage teenagers to visit their establishment. They should ask the partner class questions about the activities they enjoy while on vacation to find out what activities the hotel might offer to younger travelers. **Qu'est-ce que tu aimes faire pendant les vacances? Quelles activités est-ce que les hôtels n'offrent pas à leurs jeunes clients?** Students need to know the total number of respondents. When the survey comes back from the partner class, have students discuss the results and determine what activities the resort hotel should offer young visitors. They should use a word processing program or some type of drawing software to create a brochure that explains all of the new activities the resort will offer. 1.3

Communication

Game Bank
For game ideas, see pages T60–T63.

Le tourisme à Nice

Nice is a very popular getaway destination for tourists. But tourism actually began in Nice in the 19th century with the annual migration of British aristocrats. For that reason, the main walk along the Mediterranean is appropriately named **la promenade des Anglais.** Aristocrats from Russia, Europe, and America soon gave "the season" its elegant international flair. Tourists and locals alike still enjoy the traditional **promenade** along Nice's seaside boulevard. In the winter, tourists flock to Nice for its mild climate and to experience **Carnaval.** During the summer, tourists arrive in Nice from all over the world to take advantage of the three miles of beaches, water sports, restaurants, and tours of parks, museums, and cathedrals. Ask students to compare and contrast a tourist attraction in Nice with one in another francophone destination. 2.1

La cuisine

Basil has 4,000 years of history and traditions. It is used in many culinary dishes that originate in Provence. This vegetable soup relies on crushed basil for its distinct flavor. Encourage students to try this recipe in their foods class or at home for family and friends. 1.2, 2.2

Soupe au pistou

Soupe
12 tasses d'eau
1 tasse de haricots blancs
1 tasse de haricots rouges
1 gros oignon coupé en morceaux
2 carottes pelées et coupées en morceaux
2 courgettes coupées en dés
4 tomates pelées et coupées en dés
1 tasse de farfalle (ou macaroni)

Pistou
3 gousses d'ail
3 tasses de feuilles de basilic
1 cuillère à café de sel
4–6 cuillères à soupe d'huile d'olive
1/2 tasse de gruyère râpé (ou parmesan)

Soupe
Mettre tous les légumes dans une marmite avec l'eau. Quand l'eau bout, réduire le feu et laisser mijoter pendant 1 heure. Ajouter les pâtes et laisser cuire jusqu'à ce que les pâtes soient prêtes (environ 10 minutes).

Pistou
Piler dans un mortier les feuilles de basilic et les gousses d'ail. Ajouter l'huile d'olive petit à petit jusqu'à l'obtention d'une pâte. Ajouter le gruyère râpé. Servir la soupe avec le pistou. Pour transformer la soupe en plat principal, vous pouvez ajouter du lard ou des saucisses au moment de la cuisson.

Listening Activity Scripts

Vocabulaire à l'œuvre 1

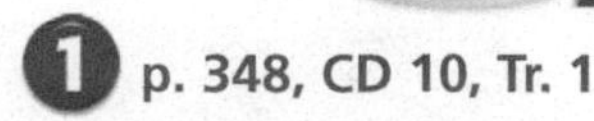

1 p. 348, CD 10, Tr. 1

1. — Sophie, qu'est-ce que tu vas faire pendant les vacances?
   — Pas grande chose. Je reste chez moi.
2. — Bernard, ça t'arrive d'aller au bord de la mer?
   — Oui, j'y vais souvent avec ma famille.
   — Tu fais de la planche à voile quand tu y vas?
   — Oui, j'en fais souvent. J'adore!
3. — Salut, Camille! Qu'est-ce tu fais de beau pendant tes vacances?
   — Ça dépend, mais ce que je voudrais faire c'est aller à la montagne faire du ski.
4. — Samir, qu'est-ce que tu aimes faire pendant les vacances d'été?
   — Ça dépend, mais ce que je préfère c'est aller à la campagne.
5. — Mégane, qu'est-ce que tu aimes faire pendant tes vacances?
   — Moi, j'aime bien monter à cheval.

Answers for Activity 1

1. d **2.** c **3.** a **4.** e **5.** b

Grammaire à l'œuvre 1

11 p. 352, CD 10, Tr. 2

1. Nicolas irait au Sénégal s'il pouvait.
2. Maya et Diego rendent visite à leurs grands-parents en Espagne.
3. Joséphine et Lucas viendraient peut-être avec nous en juillet, non?
4. Nous avons envie de visiter les Pays-Bas.
5. Vous allez partir en Grèce cet été! Quelle chance!
6. Et toi, Ahmed, tu aimerais aller où pour les vacances?

Answers for Activity 11

1. a **2.** b **3.** a **4.** a **5.** b **6.** a

Application 1

19 p. 354, CD 10, Tr. 3

1. Si tu vas en Allemagne, tu dois absolument visiter Berlin! C'est super!
2. Christophe, si on allait faire du voilier cet après-midi?
3. Si tu demandais un plan à l'office de tourisme, tu ne te perdrais plus.
4. Ça serait vraiment génial de monter au sommet de la montagne.
5. Si j'étais toi, je mettrais de la crème solaire avant d'aller à la plage.
6. Et si vous veniez voir le spectacle son et lumière au château avec nous?

Answers for Activity 19

1. a **2.** c **3.** a **4.** b **5.** a **6.** c

Vocabulaire à l'œuvre 2

23 p. 360, CD 10, Tr. 4

1. Je dois aller à New York, mais je ne connais rien de New York. Je vais aller à la librairie acheter un guide.
2. Il faut absolument que je pense à changer de l'argent.
3. Et je ne dois pas oublier mon passeport!
4. Finalement, il faut que je fasse ma valise. Il ne faut pas que j'oublie mon appareil photo et mes lunettes de soleil.

Answers for Activity 23

1. a **2.** d **3.** c **4.** b

Grammaire à l'œuvre 2

28 p. 362, CD 10, Tr. 5

Salut Julie! C'est Noémie. Alors, presque prête? Il y a encore quelques petites choses qu'on doit faire. Moi, il faut que j'aille à l'agence de voyages pour aller chercher les billets d'avion. Je me suis renseignée pour le visa. Il n'est pas nécessaire qu'on en ait un. Par contre, il faut que j'achète un guide. Je vais aller à la librairie aujourd'hui. Et il vaut mieux qu'on ait un plan aussi. Ah! J'allais oublier! Il faut que tu ailles changer de l'argent aussi. Il ne faut pas que nous partions avec des euros seulement. Bon, c'est tout. Ciao! À lundi!

Answers for Activity 28

aller chercher les billets à l'agence, acheter un guide, trouver un plan, changer de l'argent

Application 2

39 p. 366, CD 10, Tr. 6

1. J'étais en train de préparer ma trousse de toilette quand ma mère a téléphoné.
2. Le cousin de Jérémy a décidé de faire ses devoirs quand Jérémy était en train de s'informer sur Internet.
3. Hier, Marina a vu son chien dans la rue pendant que nous étions en cours de géographie.
4. Vous étiez en train de prendre un café quand vous avez retrouvé votre guide dans votre sac à dos.

Answers for Activity 40

1. a 2. b 3. a 4. b

Prépare-toi pour l'examen

p. 375, CD 10, Tr. 9

Chloé — Tu sais quoi? Demain je pars en vacances!

Henri — Et tu vas où?

Chloé — Je vais en colonie de vacances.

Henri — Tu aimes ça? Moi, je préfère partir en vacances avec ma famille. Nous partons en voiture. Nous faisons ce que nous voulons, nous nous arrêtons où nous voulons, nous voyons quelque chose de nouveau tous les jours…

Chloé — Ah, non! Moi, je préfère aller en colonie de vacances. Quand je voyage avec ma famille, mes parents veulent que je m'occupe de ma petite sœur et que je passe tout mon temps en famille. En colonie de vacances, il y a beaucoup d'autres jeunes. Et on s'amuse bien! On se baigne, on fait des randonnés, on fait de la voile… C'est le paradis sur terre!

Answers for Activity 6

1. Il aime faire ce qu'il veut et voir quelque chose de nouveau tous les jours.
2. Ses parents veulent qu'elle s'occupe de sa petite sœur et qu'elle passe tout son temps en famille.
3. Il y a beaucoup d'autres jeunes et on s'amuse bien.

Dictée p. 376, CD 10, Tr. 12

1. Le lundi, j'ai anglais.
2. Il a les cheveux bruns.
3. Tu m'as emprunté un livre?
4. Quel est ton parfum de glace préféré?
5. Quelqu'un veut acheter cette voiture?

Révisions cumulatives *chapitres 1-10*

p. 378, CD 10, Tr. 13

1. Ce que je préfère, c'est me baigner.
2. J'adore faire du ski!
3. Mon rêve, ce serait de passer toute la journée à la plage.
4. Si je pouvais, je descendrais dans un hôtel de luxe, je mangerais dans les meilleurs restaurants, et je passerais tout mon temps dans des musées.
5. Moi, j'adore faire de l'escalade.
6. J'aime faire des visites guidées pour découvrir tous les monuments historiques.
7. J'adore faire de la voile!

Answers for Activity 1

1. b 2. c 3. b 4. a 5. c 6. a 7. b

50-Minute Lesson Plans

Partons en vacances!

Day 1

OBJECTIVE
Ask about a vacation and respond

Core Instruction
Chapter Opener, pp. 344–345
- See Using the Photo, p. 344. **5 min.**
- See Chapter Objectives, p. 344. **5 min.**

Vocabulaire 1, pp. 346–349
- Present **Vocabulaire 1,** pp. 346–347. See Teaching **Vocabulaire,** p. 346. **10 min.**
- Show **Télé-vocab 1. 5 min.**
- Present **Exprimons-nous!,** p. 347. **10 min.**
- Play Audio CD 10, Tr. 1 for Activity 1, p. 348. **5 min.**
- Have students do Activity 2, p. 348. **10 min.**

Optional Resources
- Slower Pace Learners, p. 347 ◆
- Multiple Intelligences, p. 347

Homework Suggestions
Cahier de vocabulaire et grammaire, pp. 109–110
@HOMETUTOR

1.2, 1.3

Day 2

OBJECTIVE
Say what you would do if you could; Review object pronouns

Core Instruction
Vocabulaire 1, pp. 346–349
- Do Bell Work 10.1, p. 346. **5 min.**
- Have students do Activity 3, p. 348. **5 min.**
- See Teaching **Exprimons-nous!,** p. 348. **10 min.**
- Have students do Activities 4–6, p. 349. **20 min.**

Grammaire 1, pp. 350–353
- See Teaching **Grammaire,** p. 350. **5 min.**
- Show **Grammavision 1.1. 5 min.**

Optional Resources
- Communication (TE), p. 349
- Advanced Learners, p. 349 ▲
- Multiple Intelligences, p. 349

Homework Suggestions
Study for **Quiz: Vocabulaire 1**
Cahier de vocabulaire et grammaire, p. 111
Online Practice (**my.hrw.com**)

1.1, 1.2, 1.3, 5.2

Day 3

OBJECTIVE
Review object pronouns

Core Instruction
Vocabulaire 1, pp. 346–349
- Review **Vocabulaire 1,** pp. 346–349. **10 min.**
- Give **Quiz: Vocabulaire 1. 20 min.**

Grammaire 1, pp. 350–353
- Present **Flash culture,** p. 350. **5 min.**
- Have students do Activities 7–10, pp. 350–351. **15 min.**

Optional Resources
- French for Spanish Speakers, p. 351
- Communication (TE), p. 351
- Slower Pace Learners, p. 351 ◆
- Special Learning Needs, p. 351 ●

Homework Suggestions
Cahier de vocabulaire et grammaire, p. 112
Cahier d'activités, p. 91
Online Practice (**my.hrw.com**)

1.1, 1.2, 1.3, 4.1, 4.2

Day 4

OBJECTIVE
Review the conditional

Core Instruction
Grammaire 1, pp. 350–353
- Present **Flash culture,** p. 352. **5 min.**
- See Teaching **Grammaire,** p. 352. **5 min.**
- Show **Grammavision 1.2. 5 min.**
- Play Audio CD 10, Tr. 2 for Activity 11, p. 352. **5 min.**
- Have students do Activities 12–16, pp. 352–353. **20 min.**

Application 1, pp. 354–355
- Have students do Activities 17–18, p. 354. **10 min.**

Optional Resources
- Communication (TE), p. 353
- Advanced Learners, p. 353 ▲
- Multiple Intelligences, p. 353

Homework Suggestions
Study for **Quiz: Grammaire 1**
Cahier de vocabulaire et grammaire, p. 113
Cahier d'activités, p. 92

1.1, 1.2, 1.3, 4.2

Day 5

OBJECTIVE
*Review **si** clauses*

Core Instruction
Grammaire 1, pp. 350–353
- Review **Grammaire 1,** pp. 350–353. **10 min.**
- Give **Quiz: Grammaire 1. 20 min.**

Application 1, pp. 354–355
- See Teaching **Un peu plus,** p. 354. **5 min.**
- Play Audio CD 10, Tr. 3 for Activity 19, p. 354. **5 min.**
- Have students do Activities 20–22, pp. 354–355. **10 min.**

Optional Resources
- Communication (TE), p. 355
- Slower Pace Learners, p. 355 ◆
- Multiple Intelligences, p. 355

Homework Suggestions
Study for **Quiz: Application 1**
Cahier de vocabulaire et grammaire, p. 114
Cahier d'activités, p. 93
Online Practice (**my.hrw.com**)

1.1, 1.2, 1.3, 3.2

Day 6

OBJECTIVE
Learn about francophone culture

Core Instruction
Application 1, pp. 354–355
- Review **Application 1,** pp. 354–355. **10 min.**
- Give **Quiz: Application 1. 20 min.**

Culture, pp. 356–357
- See **Culture appliquée** (TE), p. 356. **10 min.**
- See **Comparaisons et communauté** (TE), p. 356. **10 min.**

Optional Resources
- Connections, p. 357
- Comparisons, p. 357
- Advanced Learners, p. 357 ▲
- Multiple Intelligences, p. 357

Homework Suggestions
Cahier d'activités, p. 94
Online Practice (**my.hrw.com**)
Finish **Culture appliquée** project.

1.3, 2.1, 2.2, 3.1, 4.2, 5.1

Day 7

OBJECTIVE
Express necessity

Core Instruction
Vocabulaire 2, pp. 358–361
- Do Bell Work 10.5, p. 358. **5 min.**
- Present **Vocabulaire 2,** pp. 358–359. See Teaching **Vocabulaire,** p. 358. **10 min.**
- Show **Télé-vocab 2. 5 min.**
- Present **Exprimons-nous!,** p. 359. **5 min.**
- Have students do Activities 24–25, p. 360. **15 min.**
- Play Audio CD 10, Tr. 4 for Activity 23, p. 360. **5 min.**
- Present **Flash culture,** p. 360. **5 min.**

Optional Resources
- Advanced Learners, p. 359 ▲
- Multiple Intelligences, p. 359

Homework Suggestions
Cahier de vocabulaire et grammaire, pp. 115–116
@HOMETUTOR
Online Practice (**my.hrw.com**)

1.2, 4.2, 5.2

Day 8

OBJECTIVE
Ask what has been done; Review the subjunctive

Core Instruction
Vocabulaire 2, pp. 358–361
- See Teaching **Exprimons-nous!,** p. 360. **10 min.**
- Have students do Activities 26–27, p. 361. **20 min.**

Grammaire 2, pp. 362–365
- See Teaching **Grammaire,** p. 362. **10 min.**
- Show **Grammavision 2.1. 5 min.**
- Play Audio CD 10, Tr. 5 for Activity 28, p. 362. **5 min.**

Optional Resources
- Communication (TE), p. 361
- Slower Pace Learners, p. 361 ◆
- Multiple Intelligences, p. 361

Homework Suggestions
Study for **Quiz: Vocabulaire 2**
Cahier de vocabulaire et grammaire, p. 117
@HOMETUTOR
Online Practice (**my.hrw.com**)

1.1, 1.2

To edit and create your own lesson plans, see the **Teacher One Stop™**

KEY
- ▲ Advanced Learners
- ◆ Slower Pace Learners
- ● Special Learning Needs

Day 9

OBJECTIVE
Review the subjunctive

Core Instruction
Vocabulaire 2, pp. 358–361
- Review **Vocabulaire 2,** pp. 358–361. **10 min.**
- Give **Quiz: Vocabulaire 2. 20 min.**

Grammaire 2, pp. 362–365
- Have students do Activities 29–32, p. 363. **20 min.**

Optional Resources
- Communication (TE), p. 363
- Advanced Learners, p. 363 ▲
- Special Learning Needs, p. 363 ●

Homework Suggestions
Cahier de vocabulaire et grammaire, p. 118
Cahier d'activités, p. 95
@HOMETUTOR
Online Practice (**my.hrw.com**)

1.1, 1.2, 1.3

Day 10

OBJECTIVE
Review the ***passé composé*** *and the* ***imparfait****; Review* ***être en train de***

Core Instruction
Grammaire 2, pp. 362–365
- Present **Flash culture,** p. 364. **5 min.**
- See Teaching **Grammaire,** p. 364. **5 min.**
- Show **Grammavision 2.2. 5 min.**
- Have students do Activities 33–37, pp. 364–365. **25 min.**

Application 2, pp. 366–367
- Do Activity 38, p. 366. **5 min.**
- See Teaching **Un peu plus,** p. 366. **5 min.**

Optional Resources
- Communication (TE), p. 365
- Slower Pace Learners, p. 365 ◆
- Multiple Intelligences, p. 365

Homework Suggestions
Study for **Quiz: Grammaire 2**
Cahier de vocabulaire et grammaire, p. 119
Cahier d'activités, p. 96

1.1, 1.2, 1.3, 4.2

Day 11

OBJECTIVE
Review ***être en train de***

Core Instruction
Grammaire 2, pp. 362–365
- Review **Grammaire 2,** pp. 362–365. **10 min.**
- Give **Quiz: Grammaire 2, 20 min.**

Application 2, pp. 366–367
- Play Audio CD 10, Tr. 6 for Activity 39, p. 366. **5 min.**
- Have students do Activities 40–42, p. 367. **15 min.**

Optional Resources
- Communication (TE), p. 367
- Advanced Learners, p. 367 ▲
- Multiple Intelligences, p. 367

Homework Suggestions
Study for **Quiz: Application 2**
Cahier de vocabulaire et grammaire, p. 120
Cahier d'activités, p. 97
Online Practice (**my.hrw.com**)

1.2, 1.3, 2.1

Day 12

OBJECTIVE
Develop listening and reading skills

Core Instruction
Application 2, pp. 366–367
- Review **Application 2,** pp. 366–367. **10 min.**
- Give **Quiz: Application 2, 20 min.**

Télé-roman, pp. 368–369
- Show **Télé-roman.** See Teaching **Télé-roman,** p. 368. **5 min.**
- Have students answer the **As-tu compris?** questions, p. 369. **15 min.**

Optional Resources
- Connections, p. 368
- Gestures, p. 368
- Communication (TE), p. 369

Homework Suggestions
Online Practice (**my.hrw.com**)

1.2, 1.3, 3.2

Day 13

OBJECTIVE
Develop listening, reading, and writing skills

Core Instruction
Lecture et écriture, pp. 370–373
- See Teaching **Lecture,** p. 370. **35 min.**
- See Teaching **Écriture,** p. 372. **15 min.**

Optional Resources
- Applying the Strategies, p. 370
- Analyzing Figurative Language, p. 370
- Cultures, p. 371
- Slower Pace Learners, p. 371 ◆
- Multiple Intelligences, p. 371
- Connections, p. 372
- Cultures, p. 372
- Process Writing, p. 373
- Advanced Learners, p. 373 ▲
- Special Learning Needs, p. 373 ●

Homework Suggestions
Cahier d'activités, p. 98
Espace écriture, Activity 3, p. 373

1.2, 1.3, 2.2, 3.1

Day 14

OBJECTIVE
Develop writing skills; Review the chapter

Core Instruction
Lecture et écriture, pp. 370–373
- See Teaching **Écriture,** p. 372. **25 min.**

Prépare-toi pour l'examen, pp. 374–376
- Have students do Activities 1–5, pp. 374–375. **25 min.**

Optional Resources
- Communities, p. 373
- Writing Assessment, p. 373
- Reteaching, p. 374
- Fold-N-Learn, p. 374

Homework Suggestions
Online Practice (**my.hrw.com**)

1.2, 1.3, 5.1

Day 15

OBJECTIVE
Review the chapter

Core Instruction
Prépare-toi pour l'examen, pp. 374–376
- Play Audio CD 10, Tr. 9 for Activity 6, p. 375. **5 min.**
- Have students do Activity 7, p. 375. **5 min.**
- Play Audio CD 10, Tr. 10–12 for **Lettres et sons,** p. 376. **10 min.**

Révisions cumulatives, pp. 378–379
- Play Audio CD 10, Tr. 13 for Activity 1, p. 378. **5 min.**
- Have students do Activities 2–6, pp. 378–379. **25 min.**

Optional Resources
- TPRS, p. 375
- Online Culture Project, p. 378
- Fine Art Connection, p. 379

Homework Suggestions
Study for Chapter Test
Online Practice (**my.hrw.com**)

1.1, 1.2, 1.3, 2.2, 3.1, 3.2

Day 16/Test

Core Instruction
Chapter Test 50 min.

Optional Resources
Assessment Program
- Alternative Assessment
- Test Generator
- **Quiz: Lecture**
- **Quiz: Écriture**

Homework Suggestions
Cahier d'activités, pp. 99–100, 120–123
Online Practice (**my.hrw.com**)

90-Minute Lesson Plans

Partons en vacances!

Block 1

OBJECTIVE
Ask about a vacation and respond; Say what you would do if you could

Core Instruction

Chapter Opener, pp. 344–345
- See Using the Photo, p. 344. **5 min.**
- See Chapter Objectives, p. 344. **5 min.**

Vocabulaire 1, pp. 346–349
- Present **Vocabulaire 1,** pp. 346–347. See Teaching **Vocabulaire,** p. 346. **10 min.**
- Show **Télé-vocab 1. 5 min.**
- Present **Exprimons-nous!,** p. 347. **10 min.**
- Play Audio CD 10, Tr. 1 for Activity 1, p. 348. **5 min.**
- Have students do Activities 2–3, p. 348. **20 min.**
- See Teaching **Exprimons-nous!,** p. 348. **10 min.**
- Have students do Activities 4–6, p. 349. **20 min.**

Optional Resources

- Learning Tips, p. 345
- **Attention!,** p. 346
- TPR, p. 347
- Teacher to Teacher, p. 347
- Slower Pace Learners, p. 347 ◆
- Multiple Intelligences, p. 347
- Connections, p. 348
- **Attention!,** p. 349
- Communication (TE), p. 349
- Advanced Learners, p. 349 ▲
- Multiple Intelligences, p. 349

Homework Suggestions

Study for **Quiz: Vocabulaire 1**
Cahier de vocabulaire et grammaire, pp. 109–111
@HOMETUTOR
Online Practice (**my.hrw.com**)
1.2, 1.3, 5.2

Block 2

OBJECTIVE
Review object pronouns; Review the conditional

Core Instruction

Vocabulaire 1, pp. 346–349
- Review **Vocabulaire 1,** pp. 346–349. **10 min.**
- Give **Quiz: Vocabulaire 1. 20 min.**

Grammaire 1, pp. 350–353
- Present **Flash culture,** p. 350. **5 min.**
- See Teaching **Grammaire,** p. 350. **5 min.**
- Show **Grammavision 1.1. 5 min.**
- Have students do Activities 7–10, pp. 350–351. **10 min.**
- Present **Flash culture,** p. 352. **5 min.**
- See Teaching **Grammaire,** p. 352. **5 min.**
- Show **Grammavision 1.2. 5 min.**
- Play Audio CD 10, Tr. 2 for Activity 11, p. 352. **5 min.**
- Have students do Activities 12–15, pp. 352–353. **15 min.**

Optional Resources

- Connections, p. 350
- French for Spanish Speakers, p. 351
- Communication (TE), p. 351
- Slower Pace Learners, p. 351 ◆
- Special Learning Needs, p. 351 ●
- Cultures, p. 353
- Advanced Learners, p. 353 ▲
- Multiple Intelligences, p. 353

Homework Suggestions

Study for **Quiz: Grammaire 1**
Cahier de vocabulaire et grammaire, pp. 112–113
Cahier d'activités, pp. 91–92
@HOMETUTOR
Online Practice (**my.hrw.com**)
1.1, 1.2, 1.3, 2.1, 3.2, 4.2

Block 3

OBJECTIVE
*Review the conditional; Review **si** clauses; Learn about francophone culture*

Core Instruction

Grammaire 1, pp. 350–353
- Have students do Bell Work 10.3, p. 352. **5 min.**
- Have students do Activity 16, p. 353. **5 min.**
- Review **Grammaire 1,** pp. 350–353. **10 min.**
- Give **Quiz: Grammaire 1. 20 min.**

Application 1, pp. 354–355
- Have students do Activities 17–18, p. 354. **10 min.**
- See Teaching **Un peu plus,** p. 354. **5 min.**
- Have students do Activities 20–22, pp. 354–355. **15 min.**

Culture, pp. 356–357
- See **Culture appliquée** (TE), p. 356. **10 min.**
- See **Comparaisons et communauté** (TE), p. 356. **10 min.**

Optional Resources

- Communication (TE), p. 353
- Communication (TE), p. 355
- Slower Pace Learners, p. 355 ◆
- Multiple Intelligences, p. 355
- **Vocabulaire supplémentaire,** p. 356
- Bulletin Board Project, p. 356
- Connections, p. 357
- Comparisons, p. 357
- Advanced Learners, p. 357 ▲
- Multiple Intelligences, p. 357

Homework Suggestions

Study for **Quiz: Application 1**
Cahier de vocabulaire et grammaire, p. 114
Cahier d'activités, pp. 93–94
Online Practice (**my.hrw.com**)
Finish **Culture appliquée** project.
1.1, 1.2, 1.3, 2.1, 2.2, 3.1, 3.2, 4.2, 5.1, 5.2

Block 4

OBJECTIVE
Express necessity; Ask what has been done

Core Instruction

Application 1, pp. 354–355
- Review **Application 1,** pp. 354–355. **10 min.**
- Give **Quiz: Application 1. 20 min.**

Vocabulaire 2, pp. 358–361
- Present **Vocabulaire 2,** pp. 358–359. See Teaching **Vocabulaire,** p. 358. **10 min.**
- Show **Télé-vocab 2. 5 min.**
- Present **Exprimons-nous!,** p. 359. **5 min.**
- Play Audio CD 10, Tr. 4 for Activity 23, p. 360. **5 min.**
- Have students do Activities 24–25, p. 360. **10 min.**
- Present **Flash culture,** p. 360. **5 min.**
- See Teaching **Exprimons-nous!,** p. 360. **10 min.**
- Have students do Activities 26–27, p. 361. **10 min.**

Optional Resources

- TPR, p. 359
- **Attention!,** p. 359
- Connections, p. 359
- Advanced Learners, p. 359 ▲
- Multiple Intelligences, p. 359
- Communities, p. 360
- Connections, p. 361
- Communication (TE), p. 361
- Slower Pace Learners, p. 361 ◆
- Multiple Intelligences, p. 361

Homework Suggestions

Study for **Quiz: Vocabulaire 2**
Cahier de vocabulaire et grammaire, pp. 115–117
@HOMETUTOR
Online Practice (**my.hrw.com**)
1.1, 1.2, 3.2, 4.2, 5.1, 5.2

To edit and create your own lesson plans, see the **Teacher One Stop™**

KEY
- ▲ Advanced Learners
- ◆ Slower Pace Learners
- ● Special Learning Needs

Block 5

OBJECTIVE
*Review the subjunctive; Review the **passé composé** and the **imparfait***

Core Instruction

Vocabulaire 2, pp. 358–361
- Review **Vocabulaire 2,** pp. 358–361. **10 min.**
- Give **Quiz: Vocabulaire 2. 20 min.**

Grammaire 2, pp. 362–365
- See Teaching **Grammaire,** p. 362. **5 min.**
- Show **Grammavision 2.1. 5 min.**
- Play Audio CD 10, Tr. 5 for Activity 28, p. 362. **5 min.**
- Have students do Activities 29–32, p. 363. **15 min.**
- Present **Flash culture,** p. 364. **5 min.**
- See Teaching **Grammaire,** p. 364. **5 min.**
- Show **Grammavision 2.2. 5 min.**
- Have students do Activities 33–35, pp. 364–365. **15 min.**

Optional Resources
- Communication (TE), p. 363
- Advanced Learners, p. 363 ▲
- Special Learning Needs, p. 363 ●
- Slower Pace Learners, p. 365 ◆
- Multiple Intelligences, p. 365

Homework Suggestions
Study for **Quiz: Grammaire 2**
Cahier de vocabulaire et grammaire, pp. 118–119
Cahier d'activités, pp. 95–96
@HOMETUTOR
Online Practice (**my.hrw.com**)
1.1, 1.2, 1.3, 4.2

Block 6

OBJECTIVE
*Review the **passé composé** and the **imparfait;** Review **être en train de;** Develop listening and reading skills*

Core Instruction

Grammaire 2, pp. 362–365
- Have students do Activities 36–37, p. 365. **10 min.**
- Review **Grammaire 2,** pp. 362–365. **10 min.**
- Give **Quiz: Grammaire 2. 20 min.**

Application 2, pp. 366–367
- Have students do Activity 38, p. 366. **5 min.**
- See Teaching **Un peu plus,** p. 366. **5 min.**
- Play Audio CD 10, Tr. 6 for Activity 39, p. 366. **5 min.**
- Have students do Activities 40–42, p. 367. **15 min.**

Télé-roman, pp. 368–369
- Show **Télé-roman.** See Teaching **Télé-roman,** p. 368. **5 min.**
- Have students answer the **As-tu compris?** questions, p. 369. **15 min.**

Optional Resources
- Communication (TE), p. 365
- Communication (TE), p. 367
- Advanced Learners, p. 367 ▲
- Multiple Intelligences, p. 367
- Connections, p. 368
- Gestures, p. 368
- Communication (TE), p. 369

Homework Suggestions
Study for **Quiz: Application 2**
Cahier de vocabulaire et grammaire, p. 120
Cahier d'activités, p. 97
Online Practice (**my.hrw.com**)
1.1, 1.2, 1.3, 2.1, 3.2

Block 7

OBJECTIVE
Develop listening, reading, and writing skills; Review the chapter

Core Instruction

Application 2, pp. 366–367
- Review **Application 2,** pp. 366–367. **10 min.**
- Give **Quiz: Application 2. 20 min.**

Lecture et écriture, pp. 370–373
- See Teaching **Lecture,** p. 370. **20 min.**
- See Teaching **Écriture,** p. 372. **30 min.**

Prépare-toi pour l'examen, pp. 374–376
- Have students do Activities 1–3, p. 374. **10 min.**

Optional Resources
- Applying the Strategies, p. 370
- Analyzing Figurative Language, p. 370
- Cultures, p. 371
- Slower Pace Learners, p. 371 ◆
- Multiple Intelligences, p. 371
- Connections, p. 372
- Cultures, p. 372
- Process Writing, p. 373
- Communities, p. 373
- Writing Assessment, p. 373
- Advanced Learners, p. 373 ▲
- Special Learning Needs, p. 373 ●
- Reteaching, p. 374
- Fold-N-Learn, p. 374
- Oral Assessment, p. 375

Homework Suggestions
Study for Chapter Test
Cahier d'activités, p. 98
Espace écriture, Activity 3, p. 373
Online Practice (**my.hrw.com**)
1.2, 1.3, 2.2, 3.1, 5.1

Block 8

OBJECTIVE
Review and assess the chapter

Core Instruction

Prépare-toi pour l'examen, pp. 374–376
- Have students do Activities 4–5, p. 375. **5 min.**
- Play Audio CD 10, Tr. 9 for Activity 6, p. 375. **5 min.**
- Have students do Activity 7, p. 375. **5 min.**
- Play Audio CD 10, Tr. 10–12 for **Lettres et sons,** p. 376. **5 min.**

Chapter Test 50 min.

Révisions cumulatives, pp. 378–379
- Play Audio CD 10, Tr. 13 for Activity 1, p. 378. **5 min.**
- Have students do Activities 2–6, pp. 378–379. **15 min.**

Optional Resources
- TPRS, p. 375
- Game, p. 376
- Chapter Review, pp. 376–377
- French for Spanish Speakers, p. 377
- Online Culture Project, p. 378
- Fine Art Connection, p. 379

Homework Suggestions
Cahier d'activités, pp. 99–100, 120–123
Online Practice (**my.hrw.com**)
1.1, 1.2, 1.3, 2.2, 3.1, 3.2

Chapter Opener

Meeting the National Standards

Communication
Communication, pp. 349, 351, 353, 355, 361, 363, 365, 367
À ton tour, p. 379

Cultures
Flash culture, pp. 350, 352, 360, 364
Comparaisons, p. 357
Practices and Perspectives, p. 353
Products and Perspectives, pp. 371, 372

Connections
Music Link, p. 348
Acquiring Information, pp. 350, 359, 361
History Link, p. 357
Language Arts Link, p. 372

Comparisons
Comparaisons, p. 357
Comparing and Contrasting, p. 357

Communities
Communauté, p. 357
Community Link, pp. 360, 373

Using the Photo

The 10th century **Château de Nice** was razed by Louis XIV. However, many tourists trek up the castle hill to view the **baie des Anges** and the old town of Nice from this spectacular vantage point. Others enjoy the view by going up the **ascenseur.** The **tour Bellanda** is today home to the Naval Museum. Have students find photos of the **tour Ballanda** on the Internet, and then look for it in the photo in their text. 1.3

Vocabulaire supplémentaire

Students might use these terms to discuss the photo.

faire de la voile *to go sailing*
la jetée *pier*
les jumelles *binoculars*
le port (nautique) *sea port*
le voilier *sail boat*

chapitre 10

Partons en vacances!

Objectifs

In this chapter, you will learn to
- ask about a vacation
- say what you would do if you could
- express necessity
- ask about what has been done

And you will use and review
- object pronouns
- the conditional
- **si** clauses
- the subjunctive
- the **passé composé** and the **imparfait**
- **être en train de**

Que vois-tu sur la photo?

Où sont ces adolescents?
Qu'est-ce qu'ils font?
Qu'est-ce que tu aimes faire quand tu es en vacances ou quand tu voyages?

ACTFL 21st Century Skills

Communication:	SE: pp. 349, 351, 353, 366, 373, 379; TE: pp. 347, 355, 367 (Financial Literacy), 369
Collaboration:	TE: pp. 343C, 355, 357, 373
Information Literacy:	SE: pp. 356, 357; TE: pp. 344, 349, 353, 357, 359
Technology Literacy:	TE: pp. 343C, 347, 349, 355, 360 (Civic Literacy), 365, 371, 373
Initiative and Self-Direction:	TE: pp. 345, 349, 355, 357
Productivity and Accountability:	TE: pp. 343C, 345, 349, 351, 359, 365

Chapter Opener

Vue de Nice de la colline du Château

TEACHER TOOLS
- Interactive Whiteboard Lessons
- Generate Success!

ALSO AVAILABLE...
- Online Workbooks
- French InterActive Reader

FRENCH ON THE GO!
- Performance Space
- Holt McDougal French Apps
- *Bien dit!* eTextbook

Learning Tips

Encourage students to continue practicing French on their vacation break. In addition to French-language films and radio broadcasts, students can use the materials around them. For example, you may suggest that students explore Web sites in French.

- **Télé-vocab 1**
- **Grammavision 1**
- **Télé-vocab 2**
- **Grammavision 2**
- **Télé-roman**

LISTENING PRACTICE — Language Lab and Classroom Activities

Vocabulaire
Activity 1, p. 348, CD 10, Tr. 1
Télé-vocab 1, p. 346, DVD Tutor
Activity 23, p. 360, CD 10, Tr. 4
Télé-vocab 2, p. 358, DVD Tutor

Grammaire
Activity 11, p. 352, CD 10, Tr. 2
Grammavision 1, pp. 350, 352, DVD Tutor
Activity 28, p. 362, CD 10, Tr. 5
Grammavision 2, pp. 362, 364, DVD Tutor

Application
Activity 19, p. 354, CD 10, Tr. 3
Activity 39, p. 366, CD 10, Tr. 6

Prépare-toi pour l'examen
Activity 6, p. 375, CD 10, Tr. 9

Révisions cumulatives
Activity 1, p. 378, CD 10, Tr. 13

Télé-roman
p. 368, DVD Tutor

Lecture
p. 370, CD 10, Tr. 7

Variations littéraires
p. 400, CD 10, Tr. 8

Lettres et sons
p. 376, CD 10, Tr. 10–12

Resources

Planning:
Lesson Planner
Teacher One Stop

Presentation:
Projectable Transparencies **Vocabulaire 10.1, 10.2**
DVD Tutor, Disc 2 **Télé-vocab 1**
Interactive Whiteboard Lessons

Practice:
Cahier de vocabulaire et grammaire
Differentiated Practice and Assessment CD-ROM
Independent Study Guide
Media Guide
Projectable Transparencies Bell Work 10.1
HOMETUTOR
Holt McDougal French Apps

Bell Work

Use Bell Work 10.1 in the *Projectable Transparencies* or write this activity on the board.

Use the comparative to give your opinion on the following.

1. **Les romans policiers / les romans d'espionnage (être intéressant)**
2. **La musique classique / le jazz (être agréable)**
3. **les jeux télévisés / les jeux vidéo (être amusant)**
4. **la télévision / le cinéma (aimer bien)**
5. **les plage françaises / les plages américaines (être bon)** 1.2

COMMON ERROR ALERT
ATTENTION !

English has only one verb meaning *to visit.* Some students will use the cognate **visiter** instead of distinguishing between *visiting a place* **(visiter)** and *visiting a person* **(rendre visite à).**

Objectifs
- to ask about a vacation
- to say what you would do if you could

Vocabulaire à l'œuvre 1

Télé-vocab

Dans le sud de la France, on peut aller...

Au bord de la mer

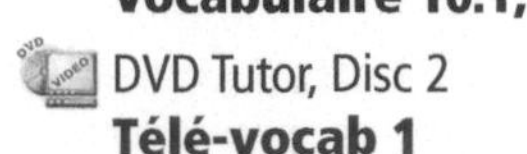

la plage

faire de la planche à voile

À la montagne

faire de l'escalade (f.)

À la campagne

faire une randonnée

En ville

faire une visite guidée

l'office (m.) du tourisme

D'autres mots utiles

le bateau	*boat*	**monter à cheval**	*to go horseback riding*
aller en colonie de vacances	*to go to summer camp*	**faire de la voile**	*to go sailing*
un spectacle son et lumière	*a sound and light show*	**un château**	*castle*

Core Instruction

TEACHING VOCABULAIRE

1. Present the vocabulary with transparencies **Vocabulaire 10.1** and **10.2** and model pronunciation. **(2 min.)**
2. Ask students, **Où aimes-tu aller en vacances?** Have volunteers name a destination as you point to it on the transparency. **(2 min.)**
3. Ask the class to respond to your questions with a show of hands. **Qui a voyagé à l'étranger? Qui voudrait visiter l'Espagne? Qui a fait un séjour en Angleterre?** Include all countries at least once in your questions. **(3 min.)**
4. Ask students the first two questions in **Exprimons-nous! (2 min.)**
5. Ask students the last two questions, changing the activities, the locations, and the seasons. **(2 min.)**

Télé-vocab 1
For a video presentation of this vocabulary, see the *DVD Tutor.*

Télé-vocab

Online Practice
my.hrw.com
Vocabulaire 1 practice

On peut aussi visiter les pays d'Europe.

Fiona est anglaise.

Massimo est italien.

Ana est portugaise.

Kristian est allemand.

Petra est espagnole.

D'autres mots utiles

rendre visite à	*to visit (a person)*	**faire un voyage organisé**	*to take an organized trip*
visiter (un endroit)	*to visit (a place)*	**un itinéraire**	*itinerary/route*
faire un séjour à l'étranger	*to stay (trip) abroad*		

Exprimons-nous!

To ask about a vacation	To respond
Qu'est-ce que tu aimes faire **pendant les vacances?** .... *during your vacation?*	**Ça dépend,** mais ce que je préfère, c'est me baigner. *That depends...*
Qu'est-ce que tu fais de beau pendant tes vacances? *What exciting things are you doing . . . ?*	Rien. **Je reste chez moi.** *. . . I am staying home.*
Tu fais de la planche à voile quand tu vas au bord de la mer? *Do you . . .?*	Oui. **J'en fais** souvent. *I go / I do that. . . .*
Ça t'arrive d'aller à la montagne en été? *Do you ever . . . ?*	Oui, **j'y vais** tous les étés. *. . . , I go there. . .*

Vocabulaire et grammaire, *pp. 109–111* — Online Workbooks

▶ **Vocabulaire supplémentaire,** Quelques pays, **p. R21**

TPR
Total Physical Response

Have students respond to these commands.

Lève-toi si tu voudrais faire un séjour à l'étranger.

Lève le doigt si tu allais en colonie de vacances quand tu étais plus jeune.

Lève la main si tu préfères aller en vacances à la plage.

Assieds-toi si tu rends souvent visite à tes grands-parents.

Viens ici si ton rêve serait de faire le tour du monde.

Then have students mime activities. Their classmates will guess what they are doing.

visiter un musée
monter à cheval
faire de l'escalade
faire de la planche à voile

1.2

Differentiated Instruction

Slower Pace Learners

Bring in postcards or have students draw their own that show the vacation settings in **Vocabulaire: le bord de la mer, à la montagne, à la campagne,** and **en ville.** Then describe in French real or imaginary vacations you took in these settings. Have students hold up the postcard that shows where your vacation took place.

1.2

Multiple Intelligences

Spatial Ask students to create a timeline of trips or vacations they have taken during the last five years or more. Have them indicate the times they visited people or places and events they attended. They might include visiting relatives out-of-town, going to a theme park, taking a vacation, going camping, or traveling to a sporting event. Have students present their timelines with a sentence in French about each entry. You may wish to display the timelines in the classroom.

1.3

Teacher to Teacher

Laura Grable
Riverhead Middle School
Riverhead, NY

As a group, we decide on possible answers to the question **Qu'est-ce que tu vas faire cet été?** I have students come up with ten places they might visit and activities they might do. Each student then surveys his or her classmates by asking the question and keeping a tally of the answers. The students then summarize the results in a bar graph. I ask them to be prepared to do a mini-presentation of the results of their survey. Students get to display their graphs in a prominent place in the classroom.

1.1, 3.1

Vocabulaire 1

Resources

Planning:
Lesson Planner
Teacher One Stop

Presentation:
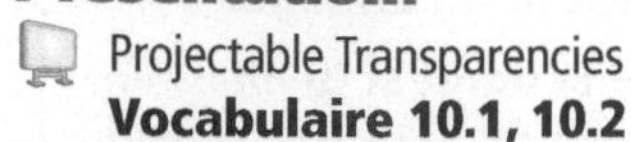
Projectable Transparencies **Vocabulaire 10.1, 10.2**

DVD Tutor, Disc 2 **Télé-vocab 1**
Interactive Whiteboard Lessons

Practice:
Cahier de vocabulaire et grammaire
Differentiated Practice and Assessment CD-ROM
Independent Study Guide
Media Guide
Audio CD 10, Tr. 1
@HOMETUTOR
Holt McDougal French Apps

1 Script

1. — Sophie, qu'est-ce que tu vas faire pendant les vacances?
— Pas grande chose. Je reste chez moi.
2. — Bernard, ça t'arrive d'aller au bord de la mer?
— Oui, j'y vais souvent avec ma famille.
— Tu fais de la planche à voile quand tu y vas?
— Oui, j'en fais souvent. J'adore!
3. — Salut, Camille! Qu'est-ce tu fais de beau pendant tes vacances?
— Ça dépend, mais ce que je voudrais faire c'est aller à la montagne faire du ski.
4. — Samir, qu'est-ce que tu aimes faire pendant les vacances d'été?
— Ça dépend, mais ce que je préfère c'est aller à la campagne.
5. — Mégane, qu'est-ce que tu aimes faire pendant tes vacances?
— Moi, j'aime bien monter à cheval.

Connections

Music Link

Ask students if they can name any songs that express a strong wish. Then have groups of students work together to write a song with the expressions in **Exprimons-nous!** 3.1

Déjà vu!

To say *in* or *to* a country, use:
- **au** with masculine countries
- **en** with feminine countries
- **aux** with countries with plural names

Je vais **en** France

To say *from* a country, use:
- **du** with masculine countries
- **de** with feminine countries
- **des** with countries with plural names

Martine vient **des** États-Unis.

1 Écoutons CD 10, Tr. 1 1.2

Leïla demande à ses amis ce qu'ils font pendant les vacances pour lui donner des idées. Qu'est-ce que chaque personne aime faire?
1. d 2. c 3. a 4. e 5. b

a. aller à la montagne	**d.** rester à la maison
b. monter à cheval	**e.** aller à la campagne
c. faire de la planche à voile	**f.** faire une randonnée

2 Qu'est-ce que tu fais pendant les vacances? 1.2

Écrivons Complète la conversation entre Annick et Nicolas qui parlent de leurs vacances.

la randonnée	la planche à voile	à la montagne	sommet
l'escalade	pendant tes vacances	au bord de la mer	

—Salut, Nicolas! Qu'est-ce que tu fais __1__? pendant tes vacances

—Bon, en juillet, je vais __2__. à la montagne

—Ça t'arrive de faire de __3__? l'escalade

—Oui, j'en fais souvent. Une fois, je suis allé jusqu'au __4__ du mont Blanc. sommet

—Oh là là! C'est difficile, ça! Ce que je préfère, c'est faire de __5__ à la campagne. la randonnée

—Et en août, je vais __6__ pour faire du bateau et de __7__. au bord de la mer / la planche à voile

3 Un examen de géographie 1.2

Écrivons Juliette étudie pour un examen de géographie. Aide-la en écrivant les pays où les villes suivantes se trouvent.

1. Londres se trouve en ______. Angleterre
2. Rome se trouve en ______. Italie
3. Berlin se trouve en ______. Allemagne
4. Oslo se trouve en ______. Norvège

Exprimons-nous!

To say what you would do if you could

Si je pouvais, **je partirais en vacances.**	*. . . I would go on vacation.*
Je voudrais **faire le tour du monde.**	*. . . to travel around the world.*
Mon rêve, ce serait de visiter toute l'Europe.	*My dream would be to . . .*
J'aimerais **tellement** aller à l'étranger!	*. . . really . . .*

Vocabulaire et grammaire, *pp. 109–111*

Core Instruction

TEACHING EXPRIMONS-NOUS!

1. Using the sentences given as models, tell students what you would like to do, where you would like to go, and what your dream is. **Si je pouvais, j'irais au Portugal en mars. Je voudrais voyager en bateau sur la Seine. Mon rêve, ce serait de visiter l'Irlande. J'aimerais tellement voir l'Amazone. (2 min.)**
2. As students take turns naming a place they would like to visit, comment on their choices. **Ah Paul! Si tu pouvais, tu visiterais la Norvège! Rachel, tu voudrais voyager en France! Eric, ton rêve, ce serait d'aller en Angleterre! (3 min.)**

4 J'aimerais tellement... ! 1.3

Écrivons Dis ce que tu aimerais faire en utilisant les expressions suivantes.

MODÈLE —Je voudrais monter au sommet du mont Blanc et...

Je voudrais... Mon rêve, ce serait de... J'aimerais tellement...	monter au sommet du (de la) visiter faire un séjour d'un an à habiter à/en rendre visite à aller faire	mont Blanc tour Eiffel la France l'Italie Paris de la voile un château mon acteur préféré mon actrice préférée à l'étranger

5 Si je pouvais... ! 1.2

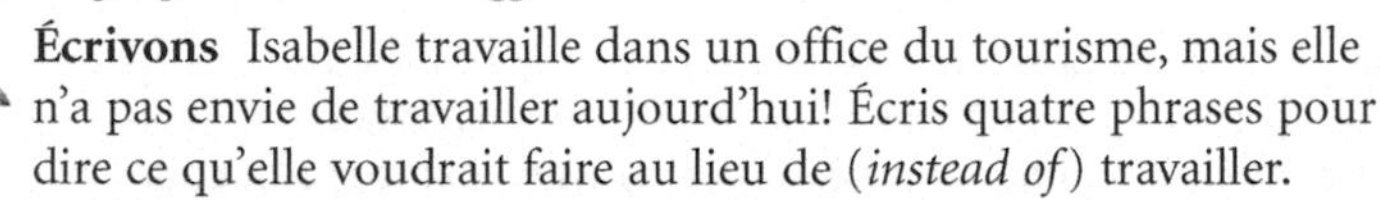

Écrivons Isabelle travaille dans un office du tourisme, mais elle n'a pas envie de travailler aujourd'hui! Écris quatre phrases pour dire ce qu'elle voudrait faire au lieu de (*instead of*) travailler.

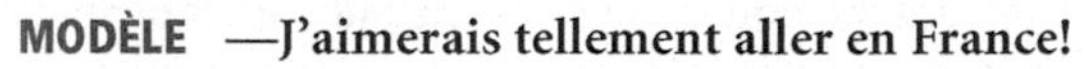

MODÈLE —J'aimerais tellement aller en France!

1.

2.

3.

4.

Communication

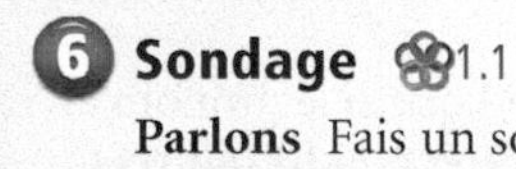

6 Sondage 1.1

Parlons Fais un sondage pour savoir ce que tes camarades font d'habitude en vacances et ce qu'ils/elles aimeraient faire s'ils/elles le pouvaient.

MODÈLE —Qu'est-ce que tu fais d'habitude pendant les vacances?
—D'habitude, je rends visite à mes grands-parents.

5 Possible Answers

1. Je voudrais faire de la planche à voile.
2. Mon rêve, ce serait de faire de l'escalade.
3. J'aimerais tellement faire une randonnée!
4. Si je pouvais, je ferais une visite guidée!

Communication

Group Activity: Presentational

As a homework assignment, have small groups research a francophone country and find out what one could do there, places of interest, cities to visit, and so on. Then have them make a sales pitch with a Powerpoint® presentation, a poster, or a video-taped commercial to entice the audience to visit their country. 1.3

COMMON ERROR ALERT
ATTENTION !

Students may assume that **Je reste chez moi** means *I am resting at home.* The verb **rester** means *to stay* or *to remain.* The idea of resting would be expressed with **se reposer** or **se relaxer.**

Differentiated Instruction

ADVANCED LEARNERS

4 After students have completed the activity, have them write a plan of action for achieving their dream. Students might need to research how much money it would cost to fulfill their dream or if they would need special training in order to achieve it. 5.2

MULTIPLES INTELLIGENCES

Logical-Mathematical Using the new vocabulary, ask students to plan a vacation on a set budget. Have students plan where they would go, how they would travel, sleeping arrangements, meals, and sightseeing. Ask them what they would plan with $500 and what they would plan with $5,000. Have students present their budgets and plans to the class. 1.3

Assess

Assessment Program

Quiz: Vocabulaire 1

Alternative Assessment

Differentiated Practice and Assessment CD-ROM

Online Assessment

my.hrw.com

Test Generator 

Resources

Planning:
Lesson Planner
Teacher One Stop

Presentation:

DVD Tutor, Disc 2
Grammavision 1.1

Practice:
Grammar Tutor for Students of French, Chapter 10
Cahier de vocabulaire et grammaire
Differentiated Practice and Assessment CD-ROM
Cahier d'activités
Independent Study Guide
Media Guide
Projectable Transparencies
Bell Work 10.2
@HOMETUTOR

Bell Work

Use Bell Work 10.2 in the *Projectable Transparencies* or write this activity on the board.

Complete the sentences with the nationalities of these people.

1. **Travis habite à New York. Il est...**
2. **Donatella est de Rome. Elle est...**
3. **Gudrun et Konnie sont nées à Berlin. Elles sont...**
4. **Mes amis sont de Lisbonne. Ils sont...**
5. **Moi, je suis de Paris. Je suis...** 1.2

Connections

Acquiring Information

Point out that if the gender of something is not known, English-speakers have the option of using the word *it*. Have students research how French-speakers handle situations in which gender is difficult to discern. 3.2

Objectifs
- review of object pronouns
- review of the conditional

Grammaire à l'œuvre 1

Grammavision

Révisions Object pronouns

1 Object pronouns are used to avoid repetition. A direct object is the person or thing receiving the action of the verb. An indirect object is the person who benefits from the action of the verb. A noun that is an indirect object is almost always preceded by **à**.

Direct object	me	te	se	le, la, l'	nous	vous	les
Indirect object	me	te	se	lui	nous	vous	leur

2 Object pronouns are placed before the verb (or infinitive). In the **passé composé,** they go before the helping verb **avoir** or **être**.

Je vais lui envoyer cette carte. Je l'ai envoyée à ma cousine.

3 Use **y** to replace prepositional phrases of place or location. Use en to replace indefinite articles or partitives + nouns. When a noun is preceded by a number or a quantity expression like **beaucoup**, use en before the verb to replace the noun, and place the number or quantity expression after the verb.

— Tu vas **en France**? — Tu as une valise?
— Oui, j'y vais. — Non, j'en ai trois!

4 If you have a sentence with both direct and indirect object pronouns, place the pronouns in order according to the chart below.

me, te, se, nous, vous	le, la, l', les	lui, leur	y	en

Vocabulaire et grammaire, *pp. 112–113*
Cahier d'activités, *pp. 91–93*

Online Workbooks

Flash culture

Avec 75 millions de visiteurs étrangers, la France est la première destination mondiale, devant l'Espagne et les États-Unis. La France attire les touristes grâce à sa richesse culturelle et à la qualité de sa nourriture. Mais seulement 10 % des Français partent en vacances à l'étranger. Ils préfèrent l'Espagne, l'Italie, le Maroc, la Tunisie et la Turquie.

Est-ce que tu es déjà parti(e) en vacances à l'étranger? Si oui, où? 4.2

7 En vacances 1.2

Lisons Dans chaque phrase, indique si le pronom en caractères gras est un pronom d'objet **a) direct** ou **b) indirect.**

a **1.** —Je **l'**ai donnée à maman.
b **2.** —On va **leur** en envoyer une d'Écosse.
a **3.** —Oui, nous **les** adorons!
b **4.** —On **vous** envoie un e-mail de la campagne lundi.
b **5.** —Sophie **nous** a téléphoné de la mer.

Core Instruction

TEACHING GRAMMAIRE

1. Go over Points 1 and 2. As you read aloud the examples, point out the position of the object pronouns and the uses of **y** and **en.** Explain the order if there is more than one pronoun in a sentence. **(4 min.)**
2. Write all object pronouns on the board or on a transparency. Say a word or phrase that could be replaced by a pronoun and have students say the correct one. **(2 min.)**
3. Write three incomplete sentences on the board that could end with a direct or indirect object. Each time you add a new object, have a student come up, erase it, and replace it with the correct pronoun in the correct place in the sentence. **(3 min.)**

Grammavision

For a video presentation of object pronouns, see the *DVD Tutor.*

Grammavision

Online Practice
my.hrw.com
Grammaire 1 practice

8 Une amie curieuse 1.3

Écrivons/Parlons Une amie française te pose des questions sur tes voyages. Réponds-lui en utilisant les pronoms qui conviennent pour remplacer les mots en caractères gras.

1. Tu as déjà fait **un voyage organisé**?
2. Est-ce que tu achètes souvent **des cadeaux à ta mère?**
3. Tu vas souvent **à la montagne**?
4. Tu envoies **des cartes postales à tes amis** quand tu voyages?
5. Tu téléphones souvent **à ton ami(e)** quand tu es en vacances?
6. Tu prends **ton appareil photo** quand tu voyages?

9 Des photos 1.1

Parlons/Écrivons Yvan a passé ses vacances en France et il montre ses photos à un camarade. Écris leurs conversations, suivant le modèle. Utilise des pronoms qui correspondent aux photos.

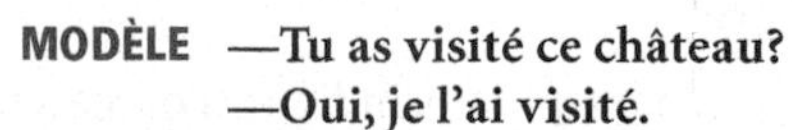

MODÈLE —**Tu as visité ce château?**
—**Oui, je l'ai visité.**

1.

2.

3.

4.

Digital performance space

Communication

10 Opinions personnelles 1.1

Parlons La famille Martin essaie de décider où passer les vacances d'été, mais personne n'est d'accord! Tout le monde veut aller dans un endroit différent et faire des activités différentes. En groupe de quatre, jouez cette scène. Utilisez des pronoms.

MODÈLE —**Moi, j'ai envie d'aller à la mer pour faire du bateau.**
—**Ah non! On y est allés l'année dernière et moi, le bateau, je n'aime pas tellement en faire.**

8 Answers

1. Tu en as déjà fait un?
2. Est-ce que tu lui en achètes souvent?
3. Tu y vas souvent?
4. Tu leur en envoies quand tu voyages?
5. Tu lui téléphones souvent quand tu es en vacances?
6. Tu le prends quand tu voyages?

9 Possible Answers

1. — Tu as visité la tour Eiffel?
   — Oui, je l'ai visitée.
2. — Tu as rendu visite à tes amis?
   — Oui, je leur ai rendu visite.
3. — Tu as mangé des escargots?
   — Oui, j'en ai beaucoup mangé.
4. — Tu es allé à la plage?
   — Oui, j'y suis allé.

French for Spanish Speakers

Ask Spanish speakers to compare the placement of object pronouns in French and in Spanish. What is similar? (In both, the object pronouns go before the verb.) What is different? (In Spanish, the indirect object pronouns **le** and **les,** which correspond to **lui** and **leur,** must be changed to **se** when they precede the direct object pronouns **lo/la/los/las.**) 4.1

Differentiated Instruction

SLOWER PACE LEARNERS

Divide the class into teams. Read aloud, to one student at a time, five sentences in which one word can be replaced by a pronoun. **Je vais lire le livre. Je vais le lire.** Each student has one minute to try to say the five sentences, using object pronouns. Each correct sentence earns one point for his or her team. For the second round, read five sentences in which two words can be replaced by object pronouns. **Je donne le livre à Sophie. Je le lui donne.** 1.2

SPECIAL LEARNING NEEDS

Students with Auditory/Speech Impairments Help students with language challenges to understand the pronoun presentation. Work with a small group of students to develop and discuss examples before reviewing object pronouns. Ask students to write in their journal five sentences in English that include object pronouns. Check these examples for mastery of the concept in English before continuing with French examples. 1.2

Communication

Group Activity: Interpersonal
Have students write a question that includes both a direct and an indirect object. You may want to provide a list of verbs.Then have students write both an affirmative and a negative answer that includes two object pronouns. Have students circulate and ask their question. Those students that answer correctly should sign their name. 1.1

Resources

Planning:
Lesson Planner
Teacher One Stop

Presentation:
DVD Tutor, Disc 2
Grammavision 1.2

Practice:
Grammar Tutor for Students of French, Chapter 10
Cahier de vocabulaire et grammaire
Differentiated Practice and Assessment CD-ROM
Cahier d'activités
Independent Study Guide
Media Guide
Projectable Transparencies
Bell Work, 10.3
Audio CD 10, Tr. 2
@HOMETUTOR

Bell Work

Use Bell Work 10.3 in the *Projectable Transparencies* or write this activity on the board.

Answer the questions and replace the underlined words with the appropriate pronouns.

1. Tu vas souvent en Italie?
2. Tu aimes aller au bord de la mer?
3. Est-ce que tu fais du bateau?
4. As-tu envoyé cette lettre à ton professeur?
5. Tu as acheté beaucoup de souvenirs? 1.2

11 Script

1. Nicolas irait au Sénégal s'il pouvait.
2. Maya et Diego rendent visite à leurs grands-parents en Espagne.
3. Joséphine et Lucas viendraient peut-être avec nous en juillet, non?
4. Nous avons envie de visiter les Pays-Bas.
5. Vous allez partir en Grèce cet été! Quelle chance!
6. Et toi, Ahmed, tu aimerais aller où pour les vacances?

Révisions The conditional

1 To form the conditional, use the infinitive as the stem for most verbs and add these endings.

parler	
je parler**ais**	nous parler**ions**
tu parler**ais**	vous parler**iez**
il/elle/on parler**ait**	ils/elles parler**aient**

2 Use the conditional to say what *would* happen if things were different. You can also use it to make polite requests.

Est-ce que je pourr**ais** changer de l'argent ici?

These verbs have irregular stems in the future and conditional.

être	*ser-*
aller	*ir-*
avoir	*aur-*
devoir	*devr-*
faire	*fer-*
pouvoir	*pourr-*
savoir	*saur-*
venir	*viendr-*
voir	*verr-*
vouloir	*voudr-*

Vocabulaire et grammaire, *pp. 112–113*
Cahier d'activités, *pp. 91–93*

11 Écoutons CD 10, Tr. 2 1.2

On parle de voyages. Pour chaque phrase, indique si on parle **a) d'un souhait** *(wish)* ou **b) de quelque chose qui est certain.**
1. a 2. b 3. a 4. a 5. b 6. a

12 Ah! Si seulement... 1.2

Écrivons Complète les phrases avec la forme correcte du conditionnel pour expliquer ce que ces personnes feraient si elles pouvaient voyager cet été.

1. Nous _aimerions_ (aimer) faire de la planche à voile.
2. Ludivine _ferait_ (faire) du camping à Tahiti avec ses amis.
3. Moi, je (j') _irais_ (aller) faire un voyage organisé en Italie.
4. Les Azouzi _viendraient_ (venir) en France.
5. Vous _iriez_ (aller) voir des pièces de théâtre à New York.

13 Les vacances idéales de tous 1.2

Écrivons D'après toi, qu'est-ce que ces personnes feraient si elles pouvaient choisir leurs vacances idéales? Fais des phrases en utilisant un élément de chaque colonne et le conditionnel.

Moi, je	aller	les grands monuments de Paris
Le prof de français	visiter	faire un séjour à ???
Nous, les élèves de la classe, nous	voir	un voyage organisé
Ma famille	faire	la Suisse
	vouloir	

Flash culture

Les Français ont cinq semaines de congés payés *(paid vacation)* tous les ans. La majorité des Français partent en vacances et vont visiter une autre région. Grâce à la grande diversité géographique de la France, les vacanciers ont beaucoup d'options: la mer, la montagne, la campagne et les villes.

Combien de jours de vacances ont les Américains en moyenne? Qu'est-ce qu'ils font? 4.2

La promenade des Anglais, à Nice

Core Instruction

TEACHING GRAMMAIRE

1. Remind students that the conditional is formed with the future stem and the imperfect endings. Point out that most future and conditional stems are the infinitive. **(2 min.)**
2. Write on the board or on a transparency the beginning of a sentence using the imperfect tense. **Si j'avais le temps...** Complete the sentence with the conditional. Have volunteers do the same, each time with a different verb, using regular and irregular verbs. **(2 min.)**
3. Continue by writing the beginning of a sentence that pertains to the students. **Si vous alliez en France...** Have students complete the sentence. **(3 min.)**

Grammavision

For a video presentation of the conditional, see the *DVD Tutor.*

Grammavision

14 Si nous allions à Tahiti... 1.2

Parlons Si ta famille et toi, vous alliez à Tahiti pour les vacances, qu'est-ce que chaque personne ferait? Décris vos activités, d'après les photos. Utilise le conditionnel et des verbes différents dans chaque phrase.

MODÈLE **On ferait du bateau.**

On

1. Nous

2. Mon père

3. Maman et toi, vous

4. Toi, tu

15 Un voyage de rêve 1.3

Écrivons Si on t'offrait un voyage en Europe, où est-ce que tu irais? Dans quels pays et dans quelles villes est-ce que tu aimerais passer quelques jours? Qu'est-ce que tu y ferais? Écris un paragraphe pour décrire ce voyage.

MODÈLE **Si on m'offrait un voyage en Europe, j'irais d'abord en France. Mes amis et moi, on...**

À la française

French speakers tend to use **on** more often than **nous** in informal speech. To emphasize *we*, you can say **Nous, on...**

Digital performance space

Communication

16 Scénario 1.1

Parlons Imagine que tu travailles dans une agence de voyages à Nice. Un(e) client(e) vient d'entrer dans l'agence et c'est à toi de l'aider avec ses projets de voyage. Tu lui poses des questions pour mieux connaître les préférences de sa famille. Joue cette scène avec un(e) camarade. Ensuite, échangez les rôles.

MODÈLE **—Bonjour, madame (monsieur). Je peux vous aider?**
—Oui, je voudrais partir en vacances une semaine avec ma famille, mais nous ne savons pas trop où aller. Vous auriez des suggestions?

14 Possible answers

1. Nous nagerions dans la mer.
2. Mon père irait à la pêche.
3. Maman et toi, vous achèteriez des légumes au marché.
4. Toi, tu ferais du vélo.

Cultures

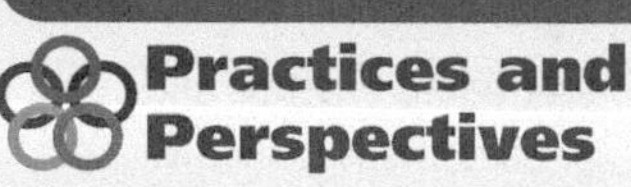

Practices and Perspectives

Have students visit French travel Web sites to find out where the French go on vacation. Do they travel mainly within France or do they prefer to travel abroad? When they vacation abroad, what are their favorite destinations? Students might also research the places in the United States most visited by the French. 2.1

Communication

Pair Activity: Interpersonal

Write a list of places on the board. **(au bord de la mer, à la montagne, en ville)** Then, in pairs, have students take turns asking what his or her partner would do at a particular place. **Qu'est-ce que tu ferais à la montagne?** They should answer in the conditional. You may have partners write their conversation for accountability. 1.1

Differentiated Instruction

ADVANCED LEARNERS

Have students write questions that raise the question of ethics in different situations. **Si tu trouvais de l'argent dans une valise, qu'est-ce que tu ferais?** Then have students discuss the questions as a class or in small groups to see if they can agree on what would be the right thing to do. 1.1

MULTIPLE INTELLIGENCES

Intrapersonal Ask students to practice use of **le conditionnel** by writing personal responses to the following situations. What would you do on an international trip if you lost your passport? What could happen if you were lost on a road trip? What should you do if you find someone else's passport? 1.3

Assess

Assessment Program

Quiz: Grammaire 1

Alternative Assessment

Differentiated Practice and Assessment CD-ROM

Online Assessment
my.hrw.com

Test Generator 

Resources

Planning:
Lesson Planner
Teacher One Stop

Practice:
Grammar Tutor for Students of French, Chapter 10
Cahier de vocabulaire et grammaire
Differentiated Practice and Assessment CD-ROM
Cahier d'activités
Independent Study Guide
Media Guide
Projectable Transparencies
Bell Work 10.4
Audio CD 10, Tr. 3

Bell Work

Use Bell Work 10.4 in the *Projectable Transparencies* or write this activity on the board.

Fill in the blanks with the conditional of the verbs in parentheses.

1. Nous ____ (pouvoir) aller à Tahiti.
2. J'____ (aller) au bord de la mer.
3. Tu ____ (faire) du bateau.
4. Nos amis ____ (venir) avec nous.
5. Edouard et toi, vous ____ (voir) des poissons exotiques.
6. Nous ____ (devoir) voyager plus souvent. 1.2

19 Script

1. Si tu vas en Allemagne, tu dois absolument visiter Berlin! C'est super!
2. Christophe, si on allait faire du voilier cet après-midi?
3. Si tu demandais un plan à l'office de tourisme, tu ne te perdrais plus.
4. Ça serait vraiment génial de monter au sommet de la montagne.
5. Si j'étais toi, je mettrais de la crème solaire avant d'aller à la plage.
6. Et si vous veniez voir le spectacle son et lumière au château avec nous?

Synthèse
- Vocabulaire 1
- Grammaire 1

Application 1

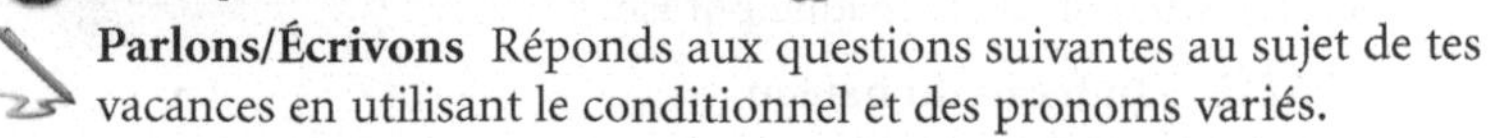

17 Mes prochaines vacances 1.3

Parlons/Écrivons Réponds aux questions suivantes au sujet de tes vacances en utilisant le conditionnel et des pronoms variés.

1. Où est-ce que tu voudrais passer tes prochaines vacances?
2. Avec qui est-ce que tu aimerais partir?
3. Qu'est-ce que vous feriez là-bas? Vous visiteriez des endroits connus? Vous feriez du sport? Lesquels?
4. Quel temps ferait-il pendant ton séjour, à ton avis?
5. Écrirais-tu des cartes postales à tes amis et à ta famille?

18 Des conseils 1.3

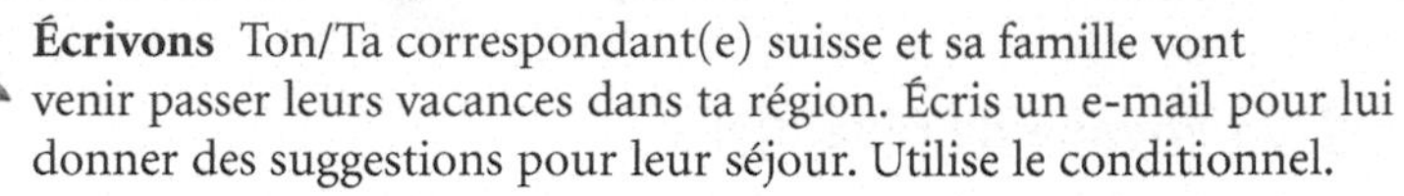

Écrivons Ton/Ta correspondant(e) suisse et sa famille vont venir passer leurs vacances dans ta région. Écris un e-mail pour lui donner des suggestions pour leur séjour. Utilise le conditionnel.

MODÈLE **Alors, pour votre voyage, vous devriez venir en hiver parce que dans le Colorado, vous pourriez faire...**

Un peu plus Révisions

si clauses

Si clauses are used...

- to make a suggestion using the present tense in both clauses.

  Si tu veux aller en France, tu as besoin d'un passeport.

- to express hopes or wishes, to give advice, or to tell what *would happen* if the situation were different. Use **si** with the imperfect in one clause; use the conditional in the result clause.

  Ça serait sympa **si je pouvais** y aller.

- to give an invitation or to say *how about...* by using **si + l'imparfait.**

  Si on faisait du camping?

Vocabulaire et grammaire, *pp. 114*
Cahier d'activités, *pp. 91–93*

Online Workbooks

19 Écoutons CD 10, Tr. 3 1.2

Écoute chaque phrase et indique si c'est **a) une suggestion ou un conseil, b) un désir ou un souhait,** ou **c) une invitation.** 1. a 2. c 3. a 4. b 5. a 6. c

20 Ça serait comme ça 1.3

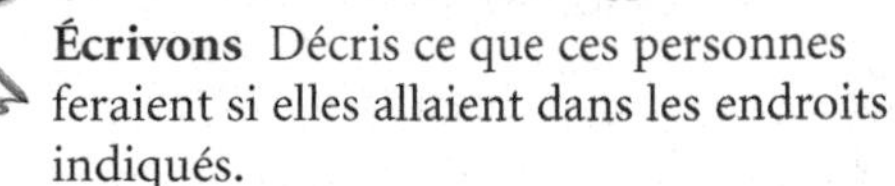

Écrivons Décris ce que ces personnes feraient si elles allaient dans les endroits indiqués.

MODÈLE Laetitia / aller en Angleterre
Si Laetitia allait en Angleterre, elle boirait du thé.

1. Nous / passer les vacances en Suisse
2. Mes amis / voyager en Grèce
3. Tu / visiter le Canada
4. Nathalie / se promener à New York
5. Vous / faire un séjour en Afrique

Core Instruction

INTEGRATED PRACTICE

1. Have students do Activities 17–18 to review the conditional and pronouns. **(10 min.)**
2. Model **si** sentences with the **imparfait** and the **conditionnel. Rachel, si tu faisais une visite au Portugal, tu irais en colonie de vacances. Paul, si tu allais à la montagne, tu monterais à cheval. (6 min.)**
3. Present **Un peu plus** and have students complete Activities 19–22. **(20 min.)**

TEACHING UN PEU PLUS

1. Remind students that if **si** clauses are used to make a suggestion, both parts of the sentence are in the present tense. Point out the use of the **imparfait** and the **conditionnel** in the **si** clause. **(2 min.)**
2. Write two lists of infinitives on the board or on a transparency. Have students take turns choosing one verb from each list and forming a **si** sentence. **Si vous visitiez le Canada, vous verriez ses beaux paysages. (3 min.)**

my.hrw.com
Application 1 practice

21 Réponse à tout 1.2

Parlons/Écrivons Réagis à ce que tes amis francophones disent en utilisant des phrases avec **si** et les éléments de la boîte.

passer les vacances à la Martinique	visiter Barcelone
faire un séjour à Québec	acheter un croque-monsieur
aller au musée du Louvre	aller en colonie de vacances

MODÈLE Ma petite cousine ne sait pas quoi faire cet été.
Si elle allait en colonie de vacances?

1. Il est midi et Céline a très faim.
2. Je voudrais passer des vacances à la mer.
3. Marie a envie de rencontrer de jeunes Canadiens.
4. On fait des études d'art.
5. Mes parents vont visiter l'Espagne cette année.

Digital performance space

Communication

22 Opinions personnelles 1.1, 3.2

Parlons Un(e) élève français(e) a envie de faire un séjour dans un pays anglophone. Voici deux brochures. Aide ton ami(e) à choisir un séjour. Joue la scène avec un(e) camarade.

MODÈLE **—Si j'étais toi, je choisirais le séjour à Cambridge.**

Séjours linguistiques

PROGRAMMES JUNIORS (14-17 ANS)

Cambridge, Angleterre

Centre de cours
- Cours du lundi au vendredi de 9h à 12h00
- Centre-ville, accès en bus facile

Logement (au choix)
- En résidence: chambres individuelles, salles de bains partagées, salle de télé
- Dans une famille d'accueil

Loisirs
- Tour guidé de la ville, visite des célèbres collèges, cinéma, cours de théâtre, sports (football, volley-ball, cricket, piscine, bowling), week-end à Londres ou à Oxford

Boston, USA

Centre de cours
- En centre-ville, près de Beacon Hill
- 10 leçons d'anglais par semaine

Logement
- En chambres doubles meublées tout confort à l'université de Suffolk: salle de bains, bureau, air conditionné, bibliothèque, salle d'ordinateurs avec accès Internet, salle de télé avec DVD, cafétéria

Loisirs
- Promenades en ville, cinéma, promenade en bateau, activités sportives, excursions à New York, à Montréal, aux chutes du Niagara et à Washington

21 Possible Answers

1. Si elle achetait un croque-monsieur?
2. Si tu passais les vacances à la Martinique?
3. Si elle faisait un séjour à Québec?
4. Si vous alliez au musée du Louvre?
5. S'ils visitaient Barcelone?

Communication

22 Pair Activity: Interpersonal

Have students write a question with a **si** clause with the **imparfait** and the **conditionnel. Si tu faisais la cuisine tous les jours, qu'est-ce que tu ferais?** Then have one student call on another and ask his or her question. That student responds and then asks his or her question of another classmate. This chain continues until everyone has had a chance. Encourage students to be creative. 1.1

Differentiated Instruction

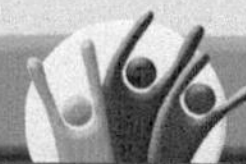

SLOWER PACE LEARNERS

20 Before students begin the activity, brainstorm as a class things that could be done in each country if someone were to go there. Write their ideas on the board with the verbs in the infinitive for students to use as they complete the activity. 1.2

MULTIPLE INTELLIGENCES

Linguistic Ask students to select a French-speaking country they would like to visit and have them write an e-mail in French to the visitor or tourism bureau in that country. The letter should request information about specific interests such as sports, landmarks, beaches, camping facilities, or museums. Have students share the responses with the class. 1.3

Assess

Assessment Program
Quiz: Application 1
Audio CD 10, Tr. 14
Alternative Assessment
Differentiated Practice and Assessment CD-ROM

Online Assessment
my.hrw.com

Test Generator 

Resources

Planning:
Lesson Planner
Teacher One Stop

Practice:
Cahier d'activités

Vocabulaire supplémentaire

You might wish to use these terms to discuss the project with students.

les loisirs culturels (m.)	*cultural activities*
les loisirs sportifs (m.)	*sports activities*
les loisirs jeunes (m.)	*activities for kids*
les loisirs de plein air (m.)	*outdoor activities*
l'hébergement (m.)	*lodging*
la gastronomie	*cuisine*
le patrimoine	*heritage of an area*
les séjours organisés	*guided visits*
les attractions naturelles	*natural attractions*
Comment se rendre à...	*How to get to...*

Bulletin Board Project

Have students create a tourist's handbook. In groups of two or three, have students create a list of phrases that would be useful to tourists in the destinations they chose in **Culture appliquée**. Each group should come up with ten phrases. Ask volunteers to compile the phrases, categorize and alphabetize them, and post the handbook on the bulletin board with their advertisements. Go over all entries as a class.
1.3, 5.2

Culture

L'office du tourisme à Nice

Culture appliquée

Le tourisme à Nice 2.1

Nice est une ville très touristique qui compte beaucoup de choses à visiter. Par exemple il y a l'Opéra et la maison où le peintre Henri Matisse a vécu pendant vingt ans. En été, toutes sortes de festivals ont lieu comme le Nice Jazz Festival en juillet. Il y a aussi une grande sélection de boutiques et de marchés où on peut acheter des produits provençaux[1] et d'autres souvenirs.

1. from Provence

Les destinations s'affichent 2.1

Summer break will soon be here! For this project you will advertise five or six tourist destinations in the francophone world on your classroom or school bulletin board.

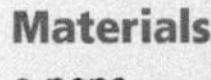

Materials
- pens
- scissors
- glue
- travel magazines
- postcards

Step 1 As a class, make a list of interesting places tourists might like to visit in the francophone world. Choose five or six sites. You can go back to the **Géoculture** pages for ideas. Break into small groups and assign a location to each group.

Step 2 Do some research on the location. What can you visit? What activities are offered? What products are particular to the area? On a piece of paper, make a list of all the things you find. Each member of the group can research a particular aspect of the region.

Step 3 Design the basic outline of your poster. Don't forget to cut out photos from magazines or print them from the Internet. You can also use postcards. Invent an interesting title and write captions for the photos. Glue the photos to your ad.

Step 4 You may also want to write a small paragraph in French advertising the area to potential visitors. Post your ad on the bulletin board of your class or school.

Quelles sont les destinations favorites des Français pour les vacances? 2.1

Core Instruction

CULTURE APPLIQUÉE

1. Read **Le tourisme à Nice** aloud in class. Ask if any students have visited Nice and if so, what sites they visited. **(5 min.)**
2. Do step 1 in class. **(10 min.)**
3. Reserve the media center or computer lab to complete steps 2 and 3. Assign looking for and printing pictures for the poster (in step 3) as homework. **(30 min.)**
4. Assign step 4 as homework and have groups complete the posters the next day. **(20 min.)**

COMPARAISONS ET COMMUNAUTÉ

1. Have partners read **Comparaisons** and answer **Et toi?** Ask students what surprised them most about vacations in France. **(6 min.)**
2. Read **Communauté et professions** aloud in class and discuss. Make a list on the board or on a transparency of 15–20 tourist attractions in your area. Have the class create a sub-list of employees who may need to know French, and for what specific reasons. **(20 min.)**

Online Practice
my.hrw.com
Online Edition

Comparaisons

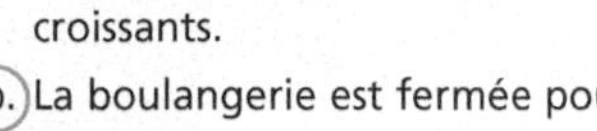

En vacances! ❀4.2

Tu visites la France en août. Un matin, tu veux acheter des croissants pour tes amis à la boulangerie. Surprise!

a. La boulangerie ne vend pas de croissants.
(b.) La boulangerie est fermée pour un mois.
c. La boulangerie n'est pas encore ouverte.

La plage de Nice

Les Français ont cinq semaines de congés[1] payés par an. En général, ils partent en vacances en juillet et en août, pendant les «grandes vacances[2]» scolaires. Les petits commerces de quartier (boulangerie, boucherie) ferment à tour de rôle[3] pendant ces deux mois. Dans les grandes villes, il y a toujours une boulangerie ou une boucherie ouverte. Les supermarchés, eux, ne ferment pas. À l'inverse, au bord de la mer et dans les régions touristiques, les magasins qui sont fermés presque toute l'année sont ouverts tous les jours et même parfois[4] tard le soir.

❀4.2

ET TOI?

1. Combien de jours de vacances est-ce que les Américains ont en général? À ton avis c'est assez?
2. Est-ce qu'il y a aux États-Unis des magasins qui sont ouverts ou fermés selon la saison?

Communauté et professions

Le français et le tourisme ❀5.1

Les métiers du tourisme sont nombreux: employé dans un office du tourisme, employé dans un hôtel, guide... Savoir parler français peut être un avantage au moment d'un entretien[5]. Fais des recherches pour savoir ce que les sites touristiques de ta région attendent[6] de leur employés. Présente les résultats de tes recherches à la classe.

Une réceptionniste dans un hôtel

1. vacation 2. summer vacation 3. take turns 4. sometimes 5. interview 6. expect

Connections

History Link

It is often claimed that Nice was once a part of Italy. However, Nice was under the control of Sardinia when it was made a part of France in 1860. In addition, Italy was not declared a unified country until 1861. Have students research the circumstances surrounding the transfer of Nice to France and write a conversation between Victor Amadeus III, ruler of the Kingdom of Sardinia, and Napoleon III, who agreed to help Sardinia fight against Austria in return for Nice and Savoy. ❀3.1

Comparisons

Comparing and Contrasting

Tourists and locals flock to the shops and restaurants of Nice's **Vieille Ville.** With its narrow, winding streets and ancient, red-tiled buildings, the area has the feel of a medieval village. Find photos on the Internet or postcards of **la Vieille Ville** and have students compare it to historic shopping districts in your area or to ones they have visited elsewhere. Also, have them compare the experience of shopping in a historic district to shopping at a modern mall. ❀4.2

Differentiated Instruction

ADVANCED LEARNERS

As an ongoing project, have students create an **office de tourisme** in a corner of your classroom or in a section of the school library. Students should send e-mails to tourism offices in the countries or cities featured in their book and request brochures and other literature. Have students organize the information in file folders for each country or city. ❀2.2

MULTIPLE INTELLIGENCES

Musical Ask students to research musical events in French-speaking countries and find out which musicians are scheduled to perform in the next few months. Students should then research the artists and their music.They might present examples of the music or descriptions of the music to the class. Have the class give their opinions or reviews of the music. ❀1.3

Language Examination

Culture can be used to practice for the **Interpretive Communication** and **Presentational Writing** sections of the AP Language and Culture Exam as it helps students get acquainted with and reflect on products and practices from the French-speaking world while reading culture-focused passages and answering questions in French.

Resources

Planning:
Lesson Planner
Teacher One Stop

Presentation:
Projectable Transparencies **Vocabulaire 10.3, 10.4**
DVD Tutor, Disc 2 **Télé-vocab 2**
Interactive Whiteboard Lessons

Practice:
Cahier de vocabulaire et grammaire
Differentiated Practice and Assessment CD-ROM
Independent Study Guide
Media Guide
Projectable Transparencies Bell Work 10.5
HOMETUTOR
Holt McDougal French Apps

Bell Work

Use Bell Work 10.5 in the *Projectable Transparencies* or write this activity on the board.

Fill in the blanks with the **imparfait** or the **conditionnel** of the verbs in parentheses.

1. **S'il ____ (faire) beau, je ____ (faire) de la voile.**
2. **Si Maryse ____ (aller) en colonie de vacances, elle ____ (aller) en Bretagne.**
3. **Si nous ____ (être) sur la plage, nous ____ (jouer) au volley.**
4. **Si Marc ____ (passer) l'été en montagne, il ____ (pouvoir) faire des randonnées.**

1.2

Proverbes

For French proverbs and activities related to the chapter theme and vocabulary, see **Proverbes et expressions**, pp. R6–R7.

Objectifs
- to express necessity
- to ask what has been done

Vocabulaire à l'œuvre 2

Télé-vocab

Avant de partir en voyage...

Core Instruction

TEACHING VOCABULAIRE

1. Present the vocabulary with transparencies **Vocabulaire 10.3** and **10.4** and model pronunciation. **(2 min.)**
2. Have students take turns miming the vocabulary words. Have the rest of the class guess the words. **(2 min.)**
3. Using the expressions in **Exprimons-nous!**, make true and false statements about traveling and have students reply accordingly. **J'ai besoin de faire une réservation si je voyage en été. Je dois absolument avoir un passeport avant d'aller en Floride. Il faut que je change de l'argent avant de voyager au Sénégal. (3 min.)**

Télé-vocab 2

For a video presentation of this vocabulary, see the *DVD Tutor*.

Télé-vocab

Vocabulaire 2

Dans ma valise, je mets...

un pull

un appareil photo

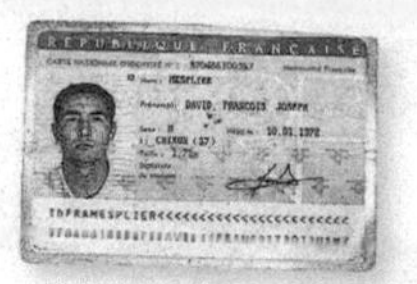
un permis de conduire

des lunettes (f.) de soleil

un passeport

une trousse de toilette

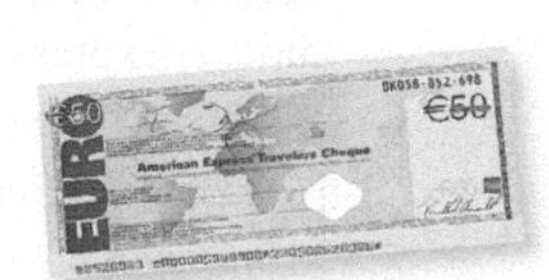

des chèques (m.) de voyage

un sac à dos

D'autres mots utiles

faire une demande de visa	*to apply for a visa*
se faire vacciner	*to get vaccinated*
louer (une maison, une voiture)	*to rent*
partir en voyage	*to leave on a trip*

Exprimons-nous!

To express necessity

Il faut que je me fasse vacciner avant de partir au Sénégal.
I have to . . . .

J'ai besoin d'emporter mon passeport.
I need to . . .

Il ne faut surtout pas oublier nos chèques de voyage.
We especially must not . . .

Je dois absolument changer de l'argent.
I must absolutely . . .

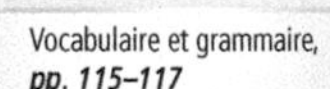

TPR — Total Physical Response

Have students respond to these commands.

Lève les mains si tes parents font des réservations sur Internet.

Dessine des lunettes de soleil.

Assieds-toi par terre si tu mets un pull en hiver.

Mets une main sur la tête si tu as une trousse de toilette.

Lève le pied s'il faut que tu aies un sac à dos pour aller en cours.

Then have some students mime the following activities.

Apporte-moi un billet d'un dollar.

Fais ta valise.

Donne-moi une pièce.

Tu utilises un appareil photo.

Montre-moi ton permis de conduire. 1.2

Common Error Alert — Attention !

Un plan is not a cognate. It does not mean *a plan*, which would be **un projet** in French. It does mean *map*, but specifically a *city map*. A world map would be called **une carte**.

Differentiated Instruction

Advanced Learners

Have students prepare a general checklist for Americans traveling overseas. They might want to choose a specific country and research other preparations that should be done before traveling there and etiquette tips on how to behave properly while visiting the country. 5.2

Multiple Intelligences

Linguistic Ask students to use the vocabulary and expressions in **Exprimons-nous!** to create their own matching vocabulary game. Have students draw two columns on a piece of paper and list the French in one column and the English translations in the second column. Have them exchange papers and complete each other's puzzle. As an alternative, students might create crossword puzzles or seek and find puzzles to exchange with classmates. 1.2

Connections

Acquiring Information

Tell students that if they wish to travel abroad with their canine companions, they will need to find out the travel requirements for their dogs as well as for themselves. Have students research information on the records, vaccinations, and quarantines for dogs required by different French-speaking countries. 3.2

Resources

Planning:
Lesson Planner

Teacher One Stop

Presentation:
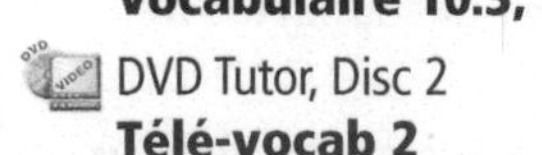
Projectable Transparencies **Vocabulaire 10.3, 10.4**
DVD Tutor, Disc 2 **Télé-vocab 2**
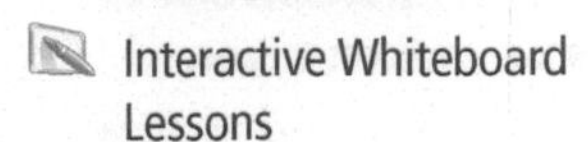
Interactive Whiteboard Lessons

Practice:
Cahier de vocabulaire et grammaire
Differentiated Practice and Assessment CD-ROM
Independent Study Guide
Media Guide
Audio CD 10, Tr. 4
@HOMETUTOR
Holt McDougal French Apps

23 Script

1. Je dois aller à New York, mais je ne connais rien de New York. Je vais aller à la librairie acheter un guide.
2. Il faut absolument que je pense à changer de l'argent.
3. Et je ne dois pas oublier mon passeport!
4. Finalement, il faut que je fasse ma valise. Il ne faut pas que j'oublie mon appareil photo et mes lunettes de soleil.

Communities

Community Link

Tell students that the United States Embassy provides American travelers in France a great variety of services and information. The embassy itself is located in Paris, but there are offices throughout France, including two consulates in Marseilles and Strasbourg and five American presence posts in Bordeaux, Lille, Lyon, Rennes, and Toulouse. Have students research the kinds of services and information the embassy and its offices can provide. 5.1

23 Écoutons CD 10, Tr. 4 1.2

Écoute Marie-Alice qui fait des préparatifs pour son voyage à New York. Puis, mets les images dans le bon ordre.
1. a **2.** d **3.** c **4.** b

a.

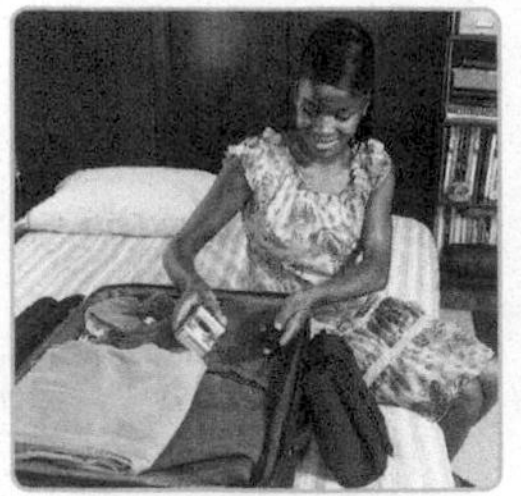
b.

c.

d.

24 Méli-mélo! 1.2

Écrivons Complète la conversation de Mathieu et Anne avec les mots et expressions de la boîte.

me fasse vacciner	m'informe	agence de voyages
brochures	billet d'avion	itinéraires
me renseigner	louer	

—Salut, Mathieu! Qu'est-ce que tu fais?
—Salut, Anne! Je __1__ (m'informe) sur Internet sur le Sénégal.
—J'y suis allée l'année passée. Qu'est-ce que tu veux savoir?
—Je veux savoir s'il faut que je __2__ (me fasse vacciner).
—Oui, c'est une bonne idée. Tu ne veux pas être malade pendant ton voyage. Tu as acheté un guide sur le Sénégal?
—Non, mais je vais __3__ (me renseigner) dans une __4__ (agence de voyages).
—C'est bien. Ils auront des __5__ (brochures) et des __6__ (itinéraires) de train. Ils pourront te renseigner si tu veux __7__ (louer) une voiture.

25 Voyage en Grèce 1.2

Parlons/Écrivons Tu vas partir en Grèce. Tu as demandé conseil à un employé d'une agence de voyages. Fais une liste de cinq ou six choses que tu dois faire avant ton voyage.

Souviens-toi! Les vêtements et les accessoires, p. R15

MODÈLE Je dois acheter des lunettes de soleil....

Flash culture

Beaucoup de familles voyagent pendant les vacances scolaires. L'année scolaire commence au début du mois de septembre. Il y a quatre périodes de vacances : la Toussaint, une semaine et demie à la fin du mois d'octobre; Noël, deux semaines; les vacances d'hiver, deux semaines au mois de février ; les vacances de printemps, deux semaines au mois d'avril. Les grandes vacances d'été commencent fin juin.

Est-ce que tu penses avoir plus ou moins de vacances qu'un élève français? 4.2

Core Instruction

TEACHING EXPRIMONS-NOUS!

1. Give each student four index cards. Instruct students to write one of these phrases on each card. **Mais oui! Mais si! Évidemment! Non!** Tell them you are checking to make sure everyone is ready for the class trip. **(2 min.)**
2. Ask questions and have students respond by holding up the appropriate card. **Tu n'as pas encore fait ta valise? Tu t'es déjà informé sur Internet? Tu as bien pensé à chercher ton billet d'avion à l'agence de voyages? (4 min.)**
3. On another card, have students write an infinitive phrase of a different activity with words in **Vocabulaire.** Remind students they can also use **mettre... dans ma valise. (3 min.)**
4. Ask questions, such as **Tu as bien pensé à...? Tu vas...? Tu n'as pas oublié de...?** as you point to a picture. The student who has the corresponding phrase on his or her card should read it aloud. **(4 min.)**

Exprimons-nous!

To ask what has been done	To respond
Tu as bien pensé à prendre ton caméscope? *Did you make sure you thought of . . . ?*	Non! **Tu as bien fait de me le rappeler.** *It's a good thing you reminded me.*
Tu as **déjà** fait les réservations? *. . . already . . . ?*	**Évidemment que** je les ai faites. *Obviously . . .*
Tu n'as pas oublié d'acheter un guide? *You didn't forget to . . .?*	**Ah, mais si!** J'ai complètement oublié. *Ah, yes!*

Vocabulaire et grammaire, *pp. 115–117* 

26 Tu as bien pensé à prendre... ? 1.2

Écrivons/Parlons Noémie a gagné un voyage en Italie. Elle raconte la bonne nouvelle à son ami Cédric. Écris les questions que Cédric lui pose. Possible answers:

MODÈLE **—Tu as bien pensé à acheter un guide?**
—Non! Tu as bien fait de me le rappeler.

1. —....? Tu as déjà fait une réservation d'avion?
—Oui, évidemment que je l'ai faite! Je pars demain à 8h30.
2. —....? Tu as bien pensé à prendre ton appareil photo?
—Non! Tu as bien fait de me le rappeler. Il faut que je le prenne si je veux faire des photos de la tour de Pise!
3. —....? Tu n'as pas oublié de faire une réservation d'hôtel?
—Ah, mais si! J'ai oublié! Je dois absolument m'informer sur Internet pour trouver le nom d'un hôtel à Rome.
4. —....? Tu as bien pensé à acheter un plan?
—Évidemment que je l'ai acheté! Je ne veux pas me perdre à Rome!
5. —....? Tu as déjà fait ta valise?
—Non, pas encore. Je vais la faire juste avant de partir. Je vais aussi prendre ma trousse de toilette.

Communication

27 Scénario 1.1

Parlons Ta classe de français va partir en France. Avant de partir, ton/ta prof de français te demande si tu as fait tous les préparatifs. Tu n'as encore rien préparé! Jouez cette scène avec un(e) camarade, puis échangez les rôles.

MODÈLE **—Tu as bien pensé à faire une réservation d'avion?**
—Non, Madame! Vous avez bien fait de me rappeler.

Connections

Acquiring Information

Bring to class guidebooks to France. Have students skim each book, then write a paragraph comparing and contrasting the information given in two or more of the guides. Students should explain which book they would buy if they were going on a trip to France. 3.2

Communication

27 Group Activity: Interpersonal

Have students think about a country that they would like to visit this summer. Then, in small groups, have students tell where they are going. The group members should make recommendations and suggestions which are appropriate to the locale about what to pack, prepare for, and see. Students can accept or reject the suggestions, or ask for additional information. 1.1

Differentiated Instruction

SLOWER PACE LEARNERS

27 Write a humorous scene as a worksheet, leaving out some of the words and phrases. Have students complete the worksheet and then use it as a script as they perform the scene. 1.1

MULTIPLE INTELLIGENCES

Visual Ask students to draw a cartoon that shows a situation where the phrases in **Exprimons-nous!** could be used as a caption. It might be a picture of a couple driving away from their home with the suitcases still in the driveway with the caption, **Tu n'as pas oublié de...** or a picture of a person getting out of the car to go back into the house with the caption, **Non! Tu as bien fait de me le rappeler.** 1.2

Assess

Assessment Program
Quiz: Vocabulaire 2
Alternative Assessment
Differentiated Practice and Assessment CD-ROM

Online Assessment
my.hrw.com

Test Generator 

Resources

Planning:
Lesson Planner
Teacher One Stop

Presentation:
DVD Tutor, Disc 2
Grammavision 2.1

Practice:
Grammar Tutor for Students of French, Chapter 10
Cahier de vocabulaire et grammaire
Differentiated Practice and Assessment CD-ROM
Cahier d'activités
Independent Study Guide
Media Guide
Projectable Transparencies
Bell Work 10.6
Audio CD 10, Tr. 5
@HOMETUTOR

Bell Work

Use Bell Work 10.6 in the *Projectable Transparencies* or write this activity on the board.

Match each description to make logical sentences.

1. Je m'informe sur Internet et je cherche...
2. Nous faisons une réservation...
3. Préparez votre passeport et faites...
4. Je fais ma valise et je n'oublie pas...
5. C'est une bonne idée d'emporter...

a. une demande de visa.
b. d'hôtel à Moscou.
c. un appareil photo.
d. ma trousse de toilette.
e. les sites des compagnies aériennes. 1.2

Objectifs
- review of the subjunctive
- review of the **passé composé** and the **imparfait**

Grammavision

Révisions The subjunctive

1 To form the subjunctive of most verbs, drop the **-ent** of the present-tense **ils** form of the verb and add these endings:

visiter	
je visit**e**	nous visit**ions**
tu visit**es**	vous visit**iez**
il/elle/on visit**e**	ils/elles visit**ent**

2 Use the subjunctive with expressions of necessity and obligation.

Il (ne) faut (pas) que... *It's (not) necessary that . . .*
Il (n') est (pas) nécessaire que... *It's (not) necessary that . . .*

3 Some verbs, like **boire, devoir,** and **venir,** have two stems. The stem for the **nous** and **vous** forms come from the **nous** form of the present tense. The other stem comes from the **ils/elles** form.

que je **boiv**e, que nous **buv**ions
que je **vienn**e, que nous **ven**ions

4 The verbs **aller, être, avoir,** and **faire** are irregular in all forms of the subjunctive.

aller **aille, ailles, aille, allions, alliez, aillent**
être **sois, sois, soit, soyons, soyez, soient**
avoir **aie, aies, aie, ayons, ayez, aient**
faire **fasse, fasses, fasse, fassions, fassiez, fassent**

Vocabulaire et grammaire, *pp. 118–119*
Cahier d'activités, *pp. 95–97*

En anglais

In English, you use an infinitive after an expression beginning with *it's . . .* if it's something that should be done by people in general.

It's necessary for you to go to the airport.

Can you think of another example when we use it's + an infinitive in English?

In French, you use an infinitive after these expressions if it's something that should be done by people in general. Otherwise, you use que + the subjunctive.

Il est nécessaire que tu ailles à l'aéroport.

28 Écoutons CD 10, Tr. 5 1.2

Noémie et Julie partent en voyage demain. Écoute le message que Noémie a laissé. Regarde la liste et dis ce qu'elles doivent encore faire.

s'informer sur Internet
acheter un guide
aller chercher les billets à l'agence
réserver les chambres d'hôtel
trouver un plan
changer de l'argent
demander un visa

Core Instruction

TEACHING GRAMMAIRE

1. Remind students that the subjunctive is used after expressions of obligation and necessity. The stem for regular verbs comes from the **-ent** form, with the endings **-e, -es, -e, -ons, -ez, -ent. (2 min.)**
2. Remind students that the verbs **aller, avoir, être,** and **faire** are irregular in the subjunctive. **(1 min.)**
3. Tell students that you are going to Nice for a week. Tell them what you have to do before leaving. **Il faut que je fasse mes valises. Il est nécessaire que quelqu'un nourrisse mon chat. Il faut que je prenne mon passeport. (2 min.)**

Grammavision

For a video presentation of the subjunctive, see the *DVD Tutor.*

Grammavision

Online Practice
my.hrw.com
Grammaire 2 practice

29 Préparatifs de voyage 1.2

Écrivons Explique ce que ces personnes doivent faire pour préparer leurs voyages en utilisant le subjonctif des verbes entre parenthèses.

1. Il faut que Sonya aille (aller) faire ses réservations.
2. Il faut que je sois (être) à la gare à huit heures.
3. Il est nécessaire que nous ayons (avoir) tous un passeport.
4. Il faut que vous partiez (partir) pour l'aéroport tout de suite!
5. Il est nécessaire qu'ils achètent (acheter) un guide de ce pays.

30 Nécessaire ou pas? 1.2

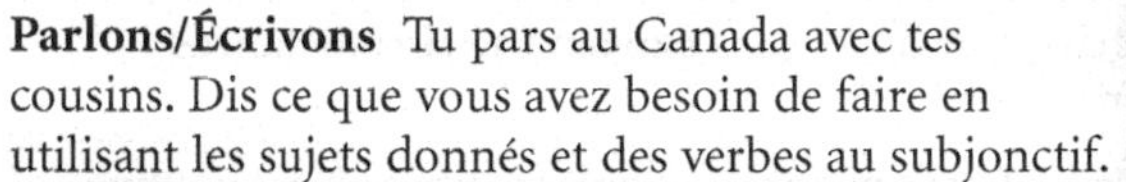

Parlons/Écrivons Tu pars au Canada avec tes cousins. Dis ce que vous avez besoin de faire en utilisant les sujets donnés et des verbes au subjonctif.

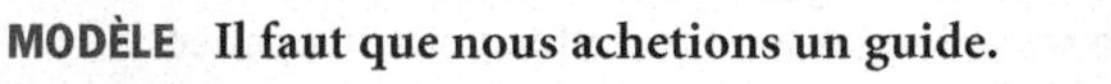

MODÈLE **Il faut que nous achetions un guide.**

Nous

1. Je

2. Mes cousins

3. Ma cousine

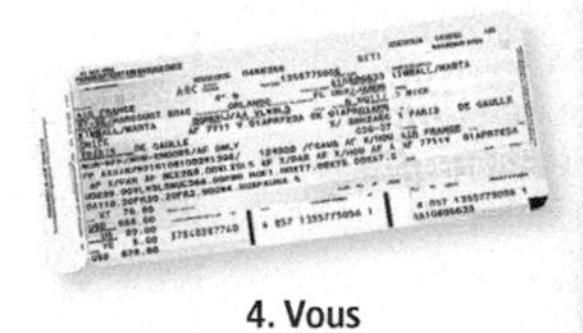
4. Vous

31 Ma liste de préparatifs 1.3

Écrivons Fais une liste de six préparatifs que ta famille et toi, vous devrez faire avant de partir en voyage dans le pays francophone de ton choix. Utilise des verbes variés et le subjonctif.

MODÈLE **Pour aller au Sénégal: Il est nécessaire que nous nous fassions vacciner. Il ne faut pas que...**

Communication

Digital performance space

32 Scénario 1.1

Parlons Hector n'a jamais fait de voyage à l'étranger. Cet été, il va passer ses vacances en Europe. Hector te demande des conseils pour préparer son voyage. Joue cette scène avec un(e) camarade.

MODÈLE **—Dis, est-ce qu'il est nécessaire que je prenne... ?**
—Oui, bien sûr, mais il n'est pas nécessaire que tu...

28 Script

Salut, Julie! C'est Noémie. Alors, presque prête? Il y a encore quelques petites choses qu'on doit faire. Moi, il faut que j'aille à l'agence de voyages pour aller chercher les billets d'avion. Je me suis renseignée pour le visa. Il n'est pas nécessaire qu'on en ait un. Par contre, il faut que j'achète un guide. Je vais aller à la librairie aujourd'hui. Et il vaut mieux qu'on ait un plan aussi. Ah! J'allais oublier! Il faut que tu ailles changer de l'argent aussi. Il ne faut pas que nous partions avec des euros seulement. Bon, c'est tout. Ciao! À lundi!

28 Answers

aller chercher les billets à l'agence, acheter un guide, trouver un plan, changer de l'argent

30 Possible Answers

1. Il faut que je prenne mon passeport.
2. Il est nécessaire que mes cousins n'oublient pas leur carte bancaire.
3. Il faut que ma cousine emporte son appareil photo.
4. Il est nécessaire que vous alliez chercher les billets d'avion.

Communication

Group Activity: Interpersonal

Teach the expressions **Qu'est-ce que tu me conseilles?**, **J'ai un petit problème,** and **Je t'écoute.** Have students think of an imaginary problem at home, work, or school. In groups, have students take turns discussing their problems. Group members should give suggestions, using the subjunctive. Students should accept or reject the advice. 1.1

Differentiated Instruction

ADVANCED LEARNERS

32 Have students prepare a list of questions they have about traveling abroad. If possible, invite a travel agent to your class to answer the students' questions or have students e-mail their questions to another teacher who has sponsored student trips abroad. Have students use the questions they asked and the responses as the basis for their conversation. 1.3

SPECIAL LEARNING NEEDS

Students with Language Impairments
Use a multi-sensory approach to review the irregular verbs in the subjunctive. Clap after each word you say and have the class repeat the word and the clap after you.

Je (clap) **sois** (clap),
Tu (clap) **sois** (clap)... 1.2

Resources

Planning:
Lesson Planner
 Teacher One Stop

Presentation:
DVD Tutor, Disc 2
Grammavision 2.2

Practice:
Grammar Tutor for Students of French, Chapter 10
Cahier de vocabulaire et grammaire
Differentiated Practice and Assessment CD-ROM
Cahier d'activités
Independent Study Guide
Media Guide
Projectable Transparencies
Bell Work 10.7
@HOMETUTOR

Bell Work

Use Bell Work 10.7 in the *Projectable Transparencies* or write this activity on the board.

Unscramble the words and conjugate the verbs in the subjunctive to make logical sentences.

1. **Il faut que / réservations / faire / tu / des**
2. **Il est nécessaire que / être / midi / aéroport / nous / à / avant / l'**
3. **Il faut que / passeport / avoir / un / tu**
4. **Il faut que / valises / nous / moins / prendre / de**
5. **Il est important qu' / lunettes / acheter / soleil / des / ils / de** 1.2

33 Answers

1. est arrivés
2. a fait
3. a fait
4. j'ai fait
5. J'étais
6. a neigé
7. suis rentré
8. était
9. J'ai bu
10. j'ai pris

Flash culture

Les vacances d'hiver et de printemps ne tombent pas en même temps partout en France. Le pays est divisé en trois zones qui ont des dates de vacances différentes. Cela évite *(avoid)* que tout le monde ne parte en même temps en vacances. La période des vacances est alors plus longue pour les hôtels et les restaurants et on évite le surnombre sur les routes et dans les stations de sports d'hiver.

Est-ce que toutes les écoles de ton état sont en vacances en même temps? 4.2

Révisions — The *passé composé* and the *imparfait*

When talking about the past, remember that the **imparfait** and the **passé composé** have different uses.

Use the passé composé to:	Use the imparfait to:
tell what happened on a specific occasion	say how things used to be and what people, places, and things were generally like
tell the sequence of events	set the scene and give background information
talk about a change or a reaction to something	explain the circumstances surrounding an event
talk about an event that began or ended while something else was going on	say what was going on when something else happened

Le jour de notre arrivée, il **faisait** très beau et la plage **était** magnifique. Les gens **se baignaient** et **faisaient** de la planche à voile. Tout le monde **s'amusait**. Je **lisais** un roman quand soudain il **a commencé** à pleuvoir. Nous **avons** tous **couru** vers la porte de l'hôtel. Nous **avons passé** le reste de l'après-midi dans l'hôtel. Nous **avons joué** aux cartes et **nous avons beaucoup parlé**.

Vocabulaire et grammaire, *pp. 118–119*
Cahier d'activités, *pp. 95–97*

33 La carte postale de Maxime 1.2

Lisons Lis la carte postale de ton ami Maxime et choisis le temps correct de chaque verbe.

On (arrivait / est arrivés) en Suisse il y a deux jours. C'est super! Hier, il (faisait / a fait) très beau, alors on (faisait / a fait) du ski toute la matinée. Moi, l'après-midi, je (j') (faisais / ai fait) une randonnée dans la montagne. Je (J') (étais / ai été) très content. Vers quatre heures, tout d'un coup, il (neigeait / a neigé), alors je (rentrais / suis rentré) à l'hôtel. Le salon (était/ a été) plein de monde. Je (J') (buvais, ai bu) un bon chocolat chaud et je (j') (prenais / ai pris) des photos de la neige par la fenêtre.

Maxime

Core Instruction

TEACHING GRAMMAIRE

1. Remind students that the **imparfait** and **passé composé** are past tenses. The **passé composé** tells what happened; the **imparfait** sets the scene and gives background information. **(2 min.)**
2. Tell about the last trip you took, real or imaginary. Use one sentence with two imperfects and two with the **passé composé** to remind students of the difference. **L'été passé quand j'étais à San Francisco, il faisait frais. Un jour nous avons pris le petit-déjeuner, ensuite nous sommes allés faire un tour des maisons victoriennes. Pendant le voyage aux îles, j'ai écouté le guide et j'ai regardé l'eau de la baie. (2 min.)**

Grammavision

For a video presentation of the **passé composé** and the **imparfait**, see the *DVD Tutor.*

34 C'est dans le passé, tout ça! 1.2

Écrivons Réécris les phrases de Juliette au passé. Choisis entre le passé composé et l'imparfait, selon le contexte.

1. Je vais chez le docteur pour me faire vacciner.
2. Nous faisons de la voile ce matin.
3. Les enfants perdent leur argent!
4. Il fait très beau, alors nous allons à la plage.

35 Que s'est-il passé? 1.2

Parlons Explique ce qui est arrivé à ces personnes aujourd'hui.

MODÈLE **Elle lisait le guide quand son amie a trouvé la tour Eiffel.**

Elle

1. Paul et Hervé

2. Nous

3. Amélie

4. Je

36 Ça s'est passé comme ça! 1.3

Écrivons Raconte (ou invente) comment ces événements de ta vie se sont passés. Utilise le passé composé et l'imparfait.

MODÈLE rencontrer mon/ma petit(e) ami(e)
Je faisais un voyage organisé quand j'ai rencontré...

1. décider d'apprendre le français
2. rencontrer mon/ma meilleur(e) ami(e)
3. voir quelqu'un qui est célèbre
4. recevoir une bonne nouvelle

37 Interview 1.1

Parlons Tu fais un reportage sur les différents pays ou régions où les élèves passent leurs vacances. Prépare une liste de 8 à 10 questions. Pose des questions sur les régions qu'ils ont visitées et sur les préparatifs qu'ils ont faits.

MODÈLE **—Où est-ce que tu es allé en vacances, Thomas?**

34 Answers

1. Je suis allée chez le docteur pour me faire vacciner.
2. Nous avons fait de la voile ce matin.
3. Les enfants ont perdu leur argent!
4. Il faisait très beau, alors nous sommes allés à la plage.

35 Possible Answers

1. Paul et Hervé faisaient du ski quand il a commencé à neiger.
2. Nous préparions le repas quand notre ami est arrivé.
3. Amélie se promenait en ville quand elle a perdu son passeport.
4. Je parlais à l'agent de voyages quand on lui a téléphoné.

Communication

Group Work: Presentational

As a homework assignment, have students look up the necessary vocabulary to tell a ghost story. Then in groups or as a class, have students take turns telling their story. The stories should be about two minutes in length and include the **passé composé** and the **imparfait.** Encourage the class to ask questions to get more details about the story, or to ask hypothetical questions with the **conditionnel.** 1.3

Differentiated Instruction

SLOWER PACE LEARNERS

Distribute copies of the chart on page 364 with the uses of the **passé composé** and the **imparfait** with enough room in each square for students to write in examples. Provide partners a French comic book or copies of French online newspapers or magazines. Ask them to find one example of the **passé composé** and one example of the **imparfait** for each of the uses in the chart and write them in their chart. 1.2

MULTIPLE INTELLIGENCES

33 Naturalist As an alternative or in addition to the activity, allow students to make their own postcard with a picture they have drawn or downloaded from the Internet. The message they write on the other side should include the **imparfait** and **passé composé.** You might display the completed postcards after students have presented them to the class. 1.3

Assess

Assessment Program
Quiz: Grammaire 2
Alternative Assessment
Differentiated Practice and Assessment CD-ROM

Online Assessment
my.hrw.com

Test Generator 

Resources

Planning:
Lesson Planner
Teacher One Stop

Practice:
Grammar Tutor for Students of French, Chapter 10
Cahier de vocabulaire et grammaire
Differentiated Practice and Assessment CD-ROM
Cahier d'activités
Independent Study Guide
Media Guide
Projectable Transparencies
Bell Work 10.8
Audio CD 10, Tr. 6

Bell Work

Use Bell Work 10.8 in the *Projectable Transparencies* or write this activity on the board.

Fill in the blanks with the **passé composé** or the **imparfait** of the verbs in parentheses.

1. **Tous les ans, nous ____ (aller) en Italie.**
2. **Tu ____ (faire) de la voile le matin.**
3. **L'hiver dernier, je ____ (faire du ski) à Chamonix.**
4. **Loïc ____ (trouver) un livre intéressant sur les voiliers.**
5. **Nous ____ (visiter) Rome quand nous ____ (perdre) notre argent.** 1.2

Synthèse
- Vocabulaire 2
- Grammaire 2

Application 2

38 Un petit bonjour de Québec 1.3

Écrivons Imagine que tu passes tes vacances à Québec. Écris une carte postale à un(e) camarade de la classe. Décris ce que tu as fait depuis ton arrivée en utilisant le passé composé et l'imparfait.

MODÈLE **Ma mère et moi, nous sommes arrivé(e)s à Québec jeudi. Il faisait très beau et on a décidé de se promener...**

Un peu plus — Révisions

être en train de

Remember that to tell *what was going on* when *something else happened*, you can use the expression **être en train de.** When talking about the past, this expression is almost always in the **imparfait.**

Ils **étaient en train de** prendre des photos de la tour Eiffel quand il a commencé à pleuvoir.

Vocabulaire et grammaire, *p. 120*
Cahier d'activités, *pp. 95–97*

39 Écoutons

Écoute chaque phrase et choisis l'événement qui est arrivé en premier. CD 10, Tr. 6 1.2

1

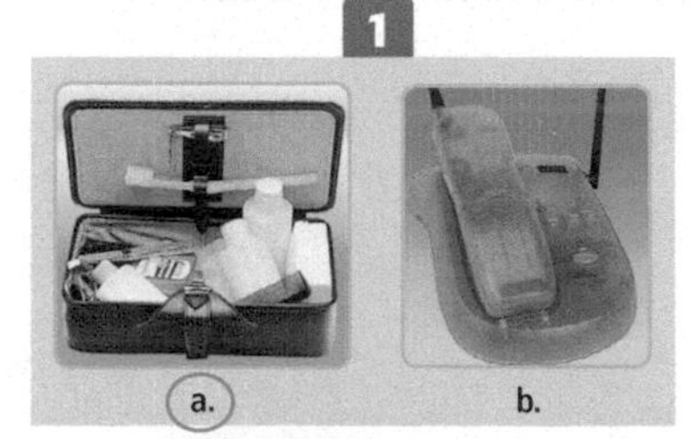

a. b.

2

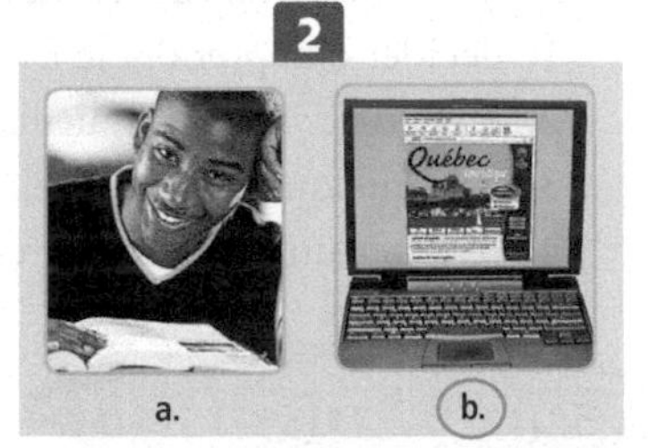

a. b.

3

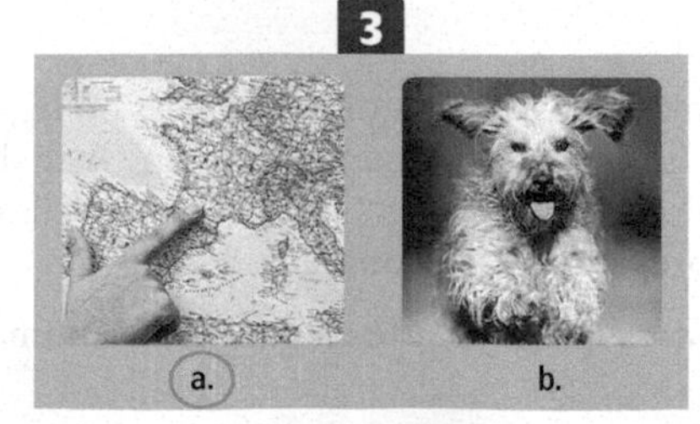

a. b.

4

a. b.

Core Instruction

INTEGRATED PRACTICE

1. Have students do Activity 38 to review the **imparfait** and **passé composé.** **(5 min.)**
2. Write **Il faut que, Il est necessaire que, Vous avez besoin de, Nous devons,** and **Mes amis oublient que** on the board. Have students use the expressions to create a sentence with the subjunctive or with the infinitive. **(4 min.)**
3. Present **Un peu plus** and have students complete Activities 39–42. **(20 min.)**

TEACHING UN PEU PLUS

1. Go over **Un peu plus** and remind students of the use of **être en train de.** **(3 min.)**
2. Have partners each choose a country and brainstorm things that might occur on a trip to those countries. Ask students to create sentences with **être en train de.** **(6 min.)**
3. Have volunteers read aloud their sentences and see if the class can guess the countries they chose. **(4 min.)**

39 Script

1. J'étais en train de préparer ma trousse de toilette quand ma mère a téléphoné.
2. Le cousin de Jérémy a décidé de faire ses devoirs quand Jérémy était en train de s'informer sur Internet.
3. Hier, Marina a vu son chien dans la rue pendant que nous étions en cours de géographie.
4. Vous étiez en train de prendre un café quand vous avez retrouvé votre guide dans votre sac à dos.

my.hrw.com
Application 2 practice

40 Hold-up à la banque 1.2

Parlons/Écrivons Il y a eu un hold-up à la banque! Décris ce que ces personnes faisaient quand c'est arrivé. Utilise **être en train de** et l'imparfait.

1. M. Duchemin: commander des chèques de voyage
2. Je: changer de l'argent
3. Les employés: travailler
4. Nous: compter nos pièces
5. Vous: ranger vos billets

41 Actions logiques 1.3

Écrivons Hier, toutes ces personnes ont fait des préparatifs pour les vacances. À ton avis, qu'est-ce que chaque personne était en train de faire quand elle était à l'endroit indiqué? Possible answers:

MODÈLE Monsieur et Madame Laroche / à la banque
Ils étaient en train de changer de l'argent.

1. Tu / à la librairie Tu étais en train de regarder les guides.
2. Vous / au supermarché Vous étiez en train d'acheter de la crème solaire.
3. Moi, je / chez le docteur Moi, j'étais en train de me faire vacciner.
4. Elsa / à l'agence de voyages Elsa était en train de louer une voiture.
5. Nous / au téléphone Nous étions en train de faire des réservations.

Digital performance space

Communication

42 Bientôt les vacances! 1.1

Parlons Ton/Ta camarade et toi allez jouer les rôles d'un(e) lycéen(ne) et d'un(e) journaliste qui lui pose des questions sur ses vacances. Lisez les questions ci-dessous et répondez-y de manière logique. Ensuite, échangez les rôles.

— **Qu'est-ce que tu fais pendant les vacances?**
—
— **Qu'est-ce que tu aimes faire en vacances?**
—
— **Dans quel pays d'Europe est-ce que tu aimerais aller et pourquoi?**
—
— **Et si tu étais très riche, qu'est-ce que tu ferais?**
—

40 Answers

1. M. Duchemin était en train de commander des chèques de voyage.
2. J'étais en train de changer de l'argent.
3. Les employés étaient en train de travailler.
4. Nous étions en train de compter nos pièces.
5. Vous étiez en train de ranger vos billets.

42 Sample answer:

— . . .
— **Je vais à la montagne tous les étés.**
— . . .
— **J'aime faire de l'escalade et monter à cheval.**
— . . .
— **J'aimerais aller en Suisse pour y faire de l'escalade.**
— . . .
— **Mon rêve, ce serait de faire le tour du monde.**

Differentiated Instruction

ADVANCED LEARNERS

Have students take snapshots of classmates in the middle of various activities in class and around the school. Have them develop the pictures and use them to create a bulletin board. For each photo, they should write a caption using the expression **être en train de. Justin était en train de déjeuner à la cantine.** 2.1

MULTIPLE INTELLIGENCES

Logical-Mathematical Ask students to choose a destination for an imaginary vacation to a French-speaking country. Have them create a "To Do List" with the estimated cost of each item required for the trip. Students will need to research the cost of passports, plane tickets, special clothing or equipment (for sports activities or weather), luggage, insurance, and any other items they determine necessary for their trip. In small groups, have students compare the total cost of their vacations. 1.3, 3.1

Assess

Assessment Program
Quiz: Application 2
Audio CD 10, Tr. 15
Alternative Assessment
Differentiated Practice and Assessment CD-ROM
Online Assessment
my.hrw.com
Test Generator 

Resources

Planning:
Lesson Planner
Teacher One Stop

Presentation:

DVD Tutor, Disc 2
Télé-roman

Practice:
Media Guide
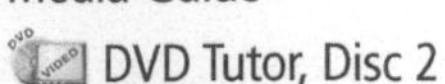
DVD Tutor, Disc 2
Télé-roman

Connections

Visual Learners

To help students understand the events leading up to the conclusion of **Télé-roman,** have them create a concept map that guides them through the history of the statuette. Draw a series of progressively smaller rectangles, similar to the diagram below. Write **Le Secret de la statuette** in the top rectangle. In each of the remaining rectangles, trace the history of the statuette by writing what happens to the statuette in the course of **Télé-roman.** Ask questions and fill in the boxes until the entire story has been charted. 3.2

Gestures

Have students look at scene 3. Ask them to describe what is going on. Then direct students' attention to scenes 8–10. In scene 8, the characters address one another in Wolof. Tell students to infer from the gestures and body language what they might be saying. What is happening in the last scene of the story? 2.1

Télé-roman Le Secret de la statuette

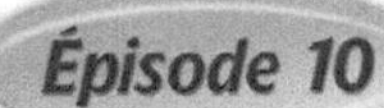
Épisode 10

STRATÉGIE

Putting the pieces together At the end of the story, all the pieces of the puzzle are put together. Imagine you are Léa or Seydou and you are writing an article on the story of the statuette. Go back to each episode and write down the important details. Once you have watched the final episode, you will be able to fully explain in your article why M. Gadio and Anne Bondy were chosen by Rigaud and his boss to carry out their scheme. Try to write a factual report that fairly describes the motivations of all sides. 1.2

Quelques jours plus tard, chez les Gadio...

1 **Mme Gadio** Regardez qui est là! L'inspecteur Sonko. Et il a une surprise pour nous!
L'inspecteur Sonko Je vous apporte quelque chose...

2 **Léa** Alors, racontez-nous tout!
L'inspecteur Sonko Quand j'ai reçu le coup de téléphone de Seydou, je n'étais pas loin de là où était Rigaud... J'ai pu arrêter Rigaud avant qu'il quitte Dakar.

3 **L'inspecteur Sonko** Rigaud a tout avoué. Il s'appelle en fait Paul Delille et il est recherché pour trafic de bijoux.

4 **L'inspecteur Sonko** Et Rigaud nous a donné le nom et l'adresse de son chef de gang. Elle habite à Nice.
Anne Madame Dufresne?! Mais c'est ma bijoutière!

5 **L'inspecteur Sonko** Mais nous ne savons toujours pas pourquoi cette statuette a tant de valeur pour ces trafiquants. Alors, qu'est-ce que vous en pensez?

Core Instruction

TEACHING TÉLÉ-ROMAN

1. Have students skim **Télé-roman** and look at the pictures. Assign the parts of the characters to students, and, before showing the video, have them act out the scene in class. **(10 min.)**
2. Play the entire video without stopping. Ask general comprehension questions. In what ways was the video different from the class performance? If necessary, play the video again. **(8 min.)**
3. As homework, have students write the answers to the **As-tu compris?** questions on page 369. **(2 min.)**

DVD Tutor

As an alternative, you might use the captioned version of **Le Secret de la statuette** on DVD.

Visit Us Online
my.hrw.com
Online Edition

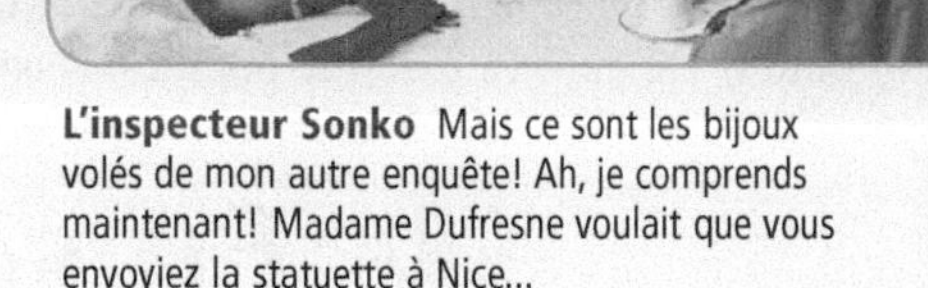

6 **Anne** Euh... Pour vous dire la vérité,... c'est une copie... Tiens, qu'est-ce que c'est que...

7 **L'inspecteur Sonko** Mais ce sont les bijoux volés de mon autre enquête! Ah, je comprends maintenant! Madame Dufresne voulait que vous envoyiez la statuette à Nice...

M. Gadio Eh oui, bien sûr! C'est pourquoi Rigaud ne voulait pas vraiment qu'Anne vienne à Dakar. Il voulait que la statuette aille à Nice.

C'est le moment du départ...

8 **Seydou** Ba beneen yon, inch'Allah!
Léa Dieureudieuf.
Mme Gadio Bravo!

9 **Waly** Pardon, monsieur. J'ai un objet rare que je voudrais vous montrer...
M. Gadio Non, non. Merci!

10 *Anne et Léa Bondy repartent pour la France.*

1.2

AS-TU COMPRIS?

1. Quelle est la surpise de l'inspecteur Sonko?
2. Qui est madame Dufresne?
3. Qu'est-ce qu'il y a dans la statuette?
4. Pourquoi est-ce que Rigaud voulait envoyer la statuette à Anne?
5. Qui fait une blague à la fin de l'histoire?

As-tu compris? Answers

1. Il a arrêté Rigaud.
2. des bijoux volés
3. Il voulait que la statuette aille à Nice avec des bijoux volés.
4. pour les faire arriver chez la bijoutière sans être notées par la police
5. Waly

Communication

Pair Work: Presentational

After students have watched **Télé-roman,** have them work with a partner to create and present a dialog between Inspector Sonko and Mr. Rigaud, based on the photograph in scene 3. Allow time to practice and then have partners present their scene to the class. 1.3

Le Secret de la statuette Episode 10

In this episode, Inspector Sonko arrives at the Gadio home with the statuette. Anne inspects it as Sonko recounts what happened. Sonko arrested Rigaud, who is really Paul Delille, a man wanted for trafficking stolen jewels. Delille's accomplice is Anne's jeweler in Nice. Anne says the statuette is a fake. She then discovers some jewels hidden inside. Sonko recognizes the stolen jewels he has been looking for. Finally, it all makes sense. Delille's plan was to have Mr. Gadio send the statuette containing the jewels to France, where the jeweler could retrieve them without the risk of getting caught smuggling. Anne and Léa say goodbye to the Gadios. Just before they leave for the airport, Waly plays a trick on his father.

Lecture et écriture

Resources

Planning:
Lesson Planner
Teacher One Stop

Presentation:
Audio CD 10, Tr. 7

Practice:
Cahier d'activités
Reading Strategies and Skills Handbook, Chapter 10
Intermediate Reader
French InterActive Reader

Applying the Strategies

For practice with monitoring comprehension, have students use the "Most Important Word" strategy from the *Reading Strategies and Skills Handbook.*

READING PRACTICE

STRATEGIES

Strategy: Most Important Word

Reading Skill	When can I use this strategy?		
	Prereading	During Reading	Postreading
Identifying the Main Idea			✓
Making Generalizations			✓
Summarizing			✓

Strategy at a Glance: Most Important Word

- After reading a text, students discuss their responses to the theme of the work.
- Students decide either independently or in small groups what they think the Most Important Word in the text is, basing their answers on evidence from the reading.
- Students share and explain their choices.

Many times when you ask students to find the main idea of a story, or to make a generalization, or simply, "What did the story mean to you?", they can't do it, because they find the question too broad. One strategy that students can use to help them answer the question is **Most Important Word. Most Important Word** is a postreading strategy in which students decide which word in a text they think is the most important based on specific evidence in the text. As students decide which word is the most important, they begin to formulate their responses to the question: "What did the story mean to you?" **Most Important Word** leads to revealing discussions that encourage students to use this skill while they read and later reflect on what they have read.

Best Use of the Strategy

Most Important Word (Bleich 1975) is a good strategy to help students identify the theme of a reading and to make generalizations about it by breaking down the selection and deciding which word in the text carries the message that speaks to them.

Analyzing Figurative Language

Tell students that figurative language is language that is based on imaginative comparisons and is not literally true. The author uses these descriptions to put pictures in readers' minds. Have students read the poem aloud and visualize the descriptions of the sea. Tell students that each time they read the poem they will get more meaning and pleasure from it.

Lecture et écriture

Jacques Prévert (1900–1977) est un poète français. Il a aussi écrit les scénarios et les dialogues de grands films classiques du cinéma français. Le poème suivant est tiré du recueil ***Histoires.***

A Avant la lecture 1.3

Regarde les illustrations sur ces pages et celle de la page 372. Quels éléments sont personnifiés? De quoi va parler le poème, à ton avis?

STRATÉGIE pour lire

Personification is another technique used by poets. Personification is a type of comparison in which something that is not human is given human abilities, reactions, and characteristics. Other techniques used by poets are alliteration, onomatopoeia and symbols.

En sortant de l'école

de Jacques Prévert CD 10, Tr. 7

En sortant de l'école
nous avons rencontré[1]
un grand chemin de fer[2]
qui nous a emmenés[3]
5 tout autour de la terre[4]
dans un wagon doré
Tout autour de la terre
nous avons rencontré
la mer qui se promenait
10 avec tous ses coquillages[5]
ses îles parfumées
et puis ses beaux naufrages[6]
et ses saumons fumés[7]
Au-dessus de la mer
15 nous avons rencontré
la lune[8] et les étoiles[9]
sur un bateau à voiles
partant pour le Japon
et les trois mousquetaires des cinq doigts de la main
20 tournant la manivelle[10] d'un petit sous-marin[11]
plongeant au fond[12] des mers
pour chercher des oursins[13]

1. met 2. traintrack 3. took us 4. around the world 5. seashells 6. shipwrecks 7. smoked salmon 8. moon 9. stars 10. crank 11. submarine 12. bottom 13. sea urchins

Core Instruction

TEACHING LECTURE

1. Go over **Stratégie** with students. **(1 min.)**
2. Have volunteers read the first 13 lines of the poem aloud in class. **(1 min.)**
3. On the board or on a tranparency, label three columns **les images? quoi? répétition?** (See Activity A.) Have students make suggestions for each of the columns. **(5 min.)**
4. Allow time in class for students to finish reading the poem silently. **(3 min.)**
5. Have partners do Activities B and C. **(5 min.)**
6. Come back together as a class to discuss Activity D. **(6 min.)**

Revenant sur la terre
nous avons rencontré
25 sur la voie[1] de chemin de fer
une maison qui fuyait[2]
fuyait tout autour de la terre
fuyait tout autour de la mer
fuyait devant l'hiver
30 qui voulait l'attraper[3]
Mais nous sur notre chemin de fer
on s'est mis à rouler[4]
rouler derrière l'hiver
et on l'a écrasé[5]
35 et la maison s'est arrêtée
et le printemps nous a salués
C'était lui le garde barrière[6]
et il nous a bien remerciés
et toutes les fleurs de toute la terre
40 soudain[7] se sont mises à pousser[8]
pousser à tort et à travers[9]
sur la voie de chemin de fer
qui ne voulait plus avancer
de peur de les abîmer[10]
45 Alors on est revenu à pied
à pied tout autour de la terre
à pied tout autour de la mer
tout autour du soleil
de la lune et des étoiles
50 À pied à cheval en voiture et en bateau à voiles.

1. track 2. was running away 3. wanted to catch it 4. we started to roll 5. we ran over (winter) 6. gate keeper 7. suddenly 8. to grow 9. wildly 10. to smash

Cultures

Products and Perspectives

Jacques Prévert, one of France's most beloved poets, wrote in a simple, yet effective style. Bring several examples of his poetry to class and have students choose their favorite to memorize and present to the class. Students might also make a class tape recording of their favorite Prévert poems. 1.3, 2.2

Pre-AP Language Examination

Through the practice of listening and reading comprehension, as well as essay writing, **Lecture et écriture** helps students prepare for the **Interpretive Reading and Listening** and the **Presentational Writing** sections of the AP Language and Culture Exam.

Additional Practice

For more reading practice, see **Variations littéraires,** pp. 400–401.

Differentiated Instruction

SLOWER PACE LEARNERS

Prepare flashcards with drawings that illustrate the poem. Shuffle the cards. Have volunteers stand in a line at the front of the class, each one holding a card. Read the poem aloud. Stop after the first scene depicted on the cards. Students should choose which card scene has been described. The student who holds that card moves to the front of the line. Continue reading the rest of the poem until all the students and their cards are lined up in the correct sequence. 1.2

MULTIPLE INTELLIGENCES

Intrapersonal Review **Stratégie pour lire** with the class and give several English examples of personification. Ask students to write a journal entry in which they describe things that represent themselves, such as an animal, car, or plant that may take on the student's personality, characteristics, or skills. 1.3

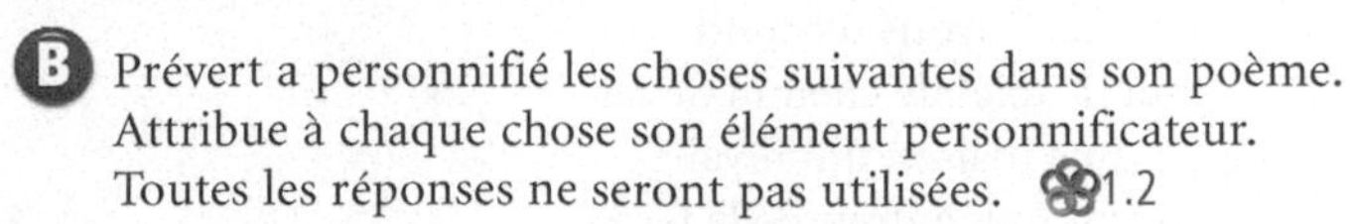

Compréhension

B Prévert a personnifié les choses suivantes dans son poème. Attribue à chaque chose son élément personnificateur. Toutes les réponses ne seront pas utilisées. 1.2

f	**1.** la mer	**a.** conduire
e	**2.** la maison	**b.** rencontrer quelqu'un
c	**3.** l'hiver	**c.** attraper quelque chose
d	**4.** le printemps	**d.** parler
g	**5.** le chemin de fer	**e.** fuir
		f. se promener
		g. avoir peur de faire mal

C Complète les phrases suivantes d'après le poème que tu viens de lire. 1.2

1. Après l'école, le narrateur a fait un voyage...
2. Il voyageait en...
3. La première chose qu'il a vue était...
4. Après, il est parti pour le Japon sur...
5. Les trois mousquetaires sont...
6. Sur le chemin de fer il y avait...
7. L'hiver voulait...
8. Le printemps a dit merci parce que...
9. Le chemin de fer n'a pas avancé parce que...
10. Alors, le narrateur...

Après la lecture

D Est-ce que tu as aimé ce poème? Qu'est-ce que tu as aimé? Qu'est-ce que tu n'as pas aimé? Si tu devais écrire un poème sur le voyage, quelles images est-ce que tu utiliserais? Écris un court poème sur le voyage en utilisant ces images. 1.3

B Answers

1. autour de la terre.
2. train.
3. la mer (des coquillages, des îles, des naufrages, des saumons).
4. un bateau à voiles.
5. le narrateur et ses amis.
6. une maison.
7. attraper la maison qui fuyait.
8. le chemin de fer a écrasé l'hiver.
9. il y avait des fleurs sur la voie.
10. est revenu à pied.

Connections

Language Arts Link

Have students write a poem or short story in French using personification. Students should use one of the objects from **Vocabulaire 1** or **Vocabulaire 2** as the subject of their poem. For example, students could write a story from the point of view of a suitcase that gets routed to the wrong destination during an airplane trip. 3.1

Cultures

Products and Perspectives

Share with students that when a hotel or restaurant in France is called "three-star," this is a reference to the rating system established by **Le Guide Michelin,** the oldest guide book of its kind in France. A three-star restaurant is considered exceptionally good, a two-star, excellent, and a one-star, very good. Have students include a list of restaurants and hotels in their brochures and assign each one a Michelin rating based on a list of criteria they develop.

Core Instruction

TEACHING ESPACE ÉCRITURE

1. Discuss **Stratégie pour écrire** and **Vos vacances de rêve. (2 min.)**
2. Do step 1 as a class, writing suggestions on the board or on a transparency. Encourage students to come up with a variety of vacation spots. **(5 min.)**
3. Assign step 2 as homework. Provide old travel or *National Geographic* magazines that students may cut up for pictures. **(2 min.)**
4. Have partners do step 3. **(6 min.)**
5. Do step 4 in class. Have each student decide on a destination other than his or her own. **(6 min.)**

Espace écriture

STRATÉGIE pour écrire

Always define your purpose for writing. You may want to explain something to someone, to relate something or to persuade someone to do something. Whatever your purpose is, it will influence the tone, language, and organization of your writing.

Vos vacances de rêve 1.3

Create a brochure advertising a vacation destination. The place may be a realistic location or a fanciful one. Your brochure should grab the attention of readers, tell them what activities they can do and what sights to visit, and provide them with a checklist of things that they need for their trip.

1 Plan

Imagine the ideal vacation spot. Brainstorm words to describe:

- what the place looks like
- what kinds of activities there are
- what sights to see and to visit
- what is needed to get ready for the trip

Next, think about what vocabulary expressions you should use to persuade your readers. Don't forget to find photos to illustrate your brochure.

ÉVASION

Vous avez besoin de vacances?

Vous voulez passer un week-end loin de tout.

Venez nous rejoindre au club vacances.

2 Rédaction

Begin with a "catchy" title and introduction. Then describe the activities and sights. Use some expressions of necessity. Conclude your brochure with a checklist of things your readers should do before leaving for this destination.

3 Correction

Ask a classmate to read your brochure, checking for the correct use of **si** clauses and the subjunctive. Does your classmate think that this destination would be a fun place to spend a vacation? What changes could you make to your brochure to make it more appealing?

4 Application

Post your illustrated brochure in class or on the bulletin board. Read each other's brochures and answer your classmates' questions trying to convince them to visit the destination you featured.

Lecture et écriture

Differentiated Instruction

ADVANCED LEARNERS

As an alternative activity, have students create a video for French-speakers that promotes tourism to your area. Students will make a list of sites to videotape and write a script. Students should use the conditional throughout their video. **Si vous visitiez notre ville, vous pourriez...** You might have students send a copy of their video to a partner school or tourism office in a French-speaking country. 1.2

SPECIAL LEARNING NEEDS

Students with Visual Impairments An alternative to creating a brochure would be to allow students to record an advertisement for the tourist destination they select. Ask them to write the script that includes all of the components required in **Stratégie pour écrire** for the advertisement before recording it. The oral description can replace the photo in the brochure. You may wish to play the advertisements for the class. 1.3

Lecture et écriture

Process Writing

Avant d'écrire Before students begin writing, give them time to brainstorm locations, sites, and activities. They should create a web graphic organizer with these ideas and then later connect the adjectives they come up with in the **Plan.** Remind students to use the vocabulary and expressions they learned in this chapter.

Communities

Community Link

Discuss with students the attractions of your city that might interest French-speaking tourists. Then have them come up with a catchy nickname or motto for your city that encourages people to visit. 5.1

Writing Assessment

To assess the **Espace écriture,** you can use the following rubric. For additional rubrics, see the *Assessment Program.* or refer to the *Generate Success* Rubric Generator.

Writing Rubric	4	3	2	1
Content (Complete—Incomplete)				
Comprehensibility (Comprehensible—Seldom comprehensible)				
Accuracy (Accurate—Seldom accurate)				
Organization (Well-organized—Poorly organized)				
Effort (Excellent effort—Minimal effort)				

18-20: A 16-17: B 14-15: C 12-13: D Under 12: F

Assess

Assessment Program
Quiz: Lecture
Quiz: Écriture
Online Assessment
my.hrw.com
Test Generator 

Prépare-toi pour l'examen

Resources

Planning:
Lesson Planner
Teacher One Stop

Practice:
Cahier d'activités
Media Guide
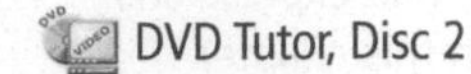
DVD Tutor, Disc 2
Projectable Transparencies
Situation, Chapitre 10
Picture Sequences, Chapter 10
Audio CD 10, Tr. 9–12
@HOMETUTOR

1 Possible Answers

1. Elle va aller au bord de la mer. Elle va se baigner et faire de la planche à voile.
2. Elle va faire des randonnées et du camping.
3. Il va visiter la tour Eiffel et faire une visite guidée du Louvre.
4. Ils vont monter à cheval à la campagne.
5. Ils vont faire du roller sur la promenade des Anglais.

3 Possible Answers

1. Il faut que j'achète une carte.
2. J'ai besoin de m'informer sur Internet.
3. Je dois absolument me faire vacciner.
4. Il faut que je fasse mes valises!

Reteaching

Have pairs of students review expressions for talking about vacations. Students can take turns asking and answering what they do on vacation (present tense), what they did last summer **(passé composé** and **imparfait**), and what they need to do this summer (subjunctive).

Chapitre 10

Prépare-toi pour l'examen

@HOMETUTOR

1 Vocabulaire 1
- to ask about a vacation
- to say what you would do if you could

pp. 346–349

1 Marion et ses amis parlent de ce qu'ils vont faire pendant leurs vacances cet été. Selon l'endroit où ils vont aller, dis toutes les choses qu'ils vont probablement faire. 1.2

1. Marion va étudier à Dakar pour six mois.
2. Aminata va à Québec avec sa famille.
3. Serge va passer deux semaines à Paris.
4. Antoine et son frère vont en colonie de vacances près de la ville de Rennes.
5. Amadou et sa famille vont passer dix jours à Nice.

2 Grammaire 1
- review of object pronouns
- review of the conditional

Un peu plus
- review of **si** clauses

pp. 350–355

2 Qu'est-ce que tes amis et les membres de ta famille aimeraient faire? Dis s'ils feraient les choses indiquées s'ils pouvaient. 1.3

1. mes parents: faire le tour du monde
2. je: aller à la plage
3. mes amis et moi, nous: partir en vacances
4. mon/ma meilleur(e) ami(e): aller en colonie de vacances
5. le/la prof de français: visiter la France
6. tu (à ton meilleur ami): rendre visite à tes grands-parents
7. vous (à tes camarades de classe): rester chez vous pendant les vacances

3 Vocabulaire 2
- to express necessity
- to ask what has been done

pp. 358–361

3 Imagine que tu pars bientôt pour le Sénégal. Dis à un ami ce que tu dois faire pour préparer ton voyage. Base tes phrases sur les illustrations qui suivent. 1.2

1.

2.

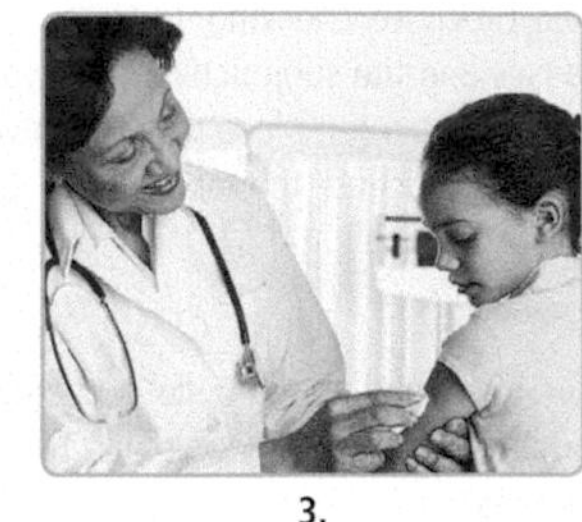
3.

4.

Preparing for the Exam

FOLD-N-LEARN

Pleated Fan Study Aid

1. Have students fold a sheet of paper in thirds from top to bottom and in half lengthwise. They then fold the sheet in half from side to side, fold it in half again, and open the sheet.
2. Ask students to write at the center top of the first row an **–er** verb. Have them write below the verb *singular forms* and label the four columns at the bottom of that first row: conditional, **l'imparfait, passé composé,** and subjunctive. Students should write the three singular conjugated verb forms in the second, fourth, and sixth rows.
3. Have students turn the paper face down, fold down the top row, write the infinitive again, and below that, *plural forms.* Then ask students to write the plural forms in the second, fourth, and sixth rows.
4. Ask students to follow the same steps with two more sheets for **–ir** and **–re** verbs. They can review by opening the folds one by one.

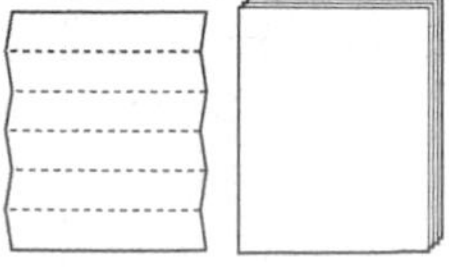

4 Julie prépare un voyage à Nice. Donne-lui des conseils. Utilise les expressions **il faut que** et **il est nécessaire que.** 1.2

Possible answers:

1. Je n'ai pas encore réservé de chambre d'hôtel. Il faut que tu fasses une réservation.
2. Je n'ai pas encore de visa. Il n'est pas nécessaire que tu aies de visa.
3. Je n'ai pas d'euros. Il est nécessaire que tu changes de l'argent.
4. Je voudrais prendre beaucoup de photos. Il ne faut pas que tu oublies ton appareil photo.
5. Je ne sais pas où j'ai mis mon passeport. Il ne faut pas que tu perdes ton passeport.

5 Réponds aux questions suivantes. 1.2

1. Qu'est-ce que les Français aiment faire pendant les vacances?
2. Quelles sont les quatre périodes de vacances en France?

6 Chloé et Henri parlent de leurs vacances. Écoute leur conversation et réponds aux questions qui suivent. CD 10, Tr. 9 1.2

1. Pourquoi est-ce qu'Henri aime voyager en famille?
2. Pourquoi est-ce que Chloë n'aime pas beaucoup voyager en famille?
3. Pourquoi est-ce qu'elle aime aller en colonie de vacances?

7 Imagine que tu pars en vacances avec ton/ta camarade. Vous préparez votre voyage et vous vérifiez si l'un(e) et l'autre, vous avez pensé à tout ce qu'il faut faire. D'abord, lisez les instructions pour chaque réplique *(exchange)*. Ensuite, créez votre dialogue en utilisant des expressions que vous avez apprises. 1.1

Élève A:	Demande à ton/ta camarade s'il/si elle a pensé à faire une chose.
Élève B:	Réponds positivement. Demande si ton/ta camarade a fait autre chose.
Élève A:	Réponds négativement. Dis que tu vas le faire.
Élève B:	Parle de quelque chose que tu dois faire.
Élève A:	Parle de quelque chose que vous ne devez pas oublier.
Élève B:	Parle de ce que tu dois mettre dans ta valise.
Élève A:	Recommande à ton/ta camarade d'autres choses à mettre dans sa valise.
Élève B:	Remercie ton/ta camarade pour la suggestion.

Online Assessment

my.hrw.com

Chapter Self-test

4 Grammaire 2

- review of the subjunctive
- review of the **passé composé** and the **imparfait**

Un peu plus

- review of **être en train de**

pp. 362–367

5 Culture

- **Flash culture** **pp. 350, 352, 360, 364**
- **Comparaisons** **pp. 356–357**

Prépare-toi pour l'examen

Prépare-toi pour l'examen

5 Answers

1. visiter une autre région française
2. la Toussaint, Noël, les vacances d'hiver et les vacances de printemps

6 Script

See script on p. 343F.

6 Answers

1. Il aime faire ce qu'il veut et voir quelque chose de nouveau tous les jours.
2. Ses parents veulent qu'elle s'occupe de sa petite sœur et qu'elle passe tout son temps en famille.
3. Il y a beaucoup d'autres jeunes et on s'amuse bien.

7 Sample conversation:

a. **Tu as déjà acheté un guide de Nice?**

b. **Oui, je l'ai acheté hier. Est-ce que tu as pensé à faire les réservations pour l'hôtel?**

a. **Non, il faut que je fasse les réservations cet après-midi.**

b. **Je dois absolument acheter les billets de train aujourd'hui.**

a. **Il ne faut surtout pas oublier notre argent.**

b. **J'ai besoin d'emporter mon appareil photo, ma trousse de toilette et deux pulls.**

a. **Il faut que tu emportes tes lunettes de soleil et ton sac à dos aussi.**

b. **Tu as bien fait de me le rappeler!**

Additional Speaking Practice

- For additional speaking practice, you might use the *Picture Sequences Transparency* for Chapter 10 found in the *Projectable Transparencies.*
- To assess the speaking activities in this section, you might use the *Generate Success* Rubric Generator or the oral rubrics found in the *Assessment Program.*

Pre-AP Practice

7 This guided conversation activity helps students practice oral exchanges using material from this chapter and previous chapters. The activity helps prepare students for the **Interpersonal Speaking** section of the AP French Language and Culture Exam.

Prépare-toi pour l'examen

Grammar Review
For more practice with the grammar topics in this chapter, see the *Grammar Tutor*, the *DVD Tutor*, the *@HomeTutor*, or the *Cahier de vocabulaire et grammaire.*

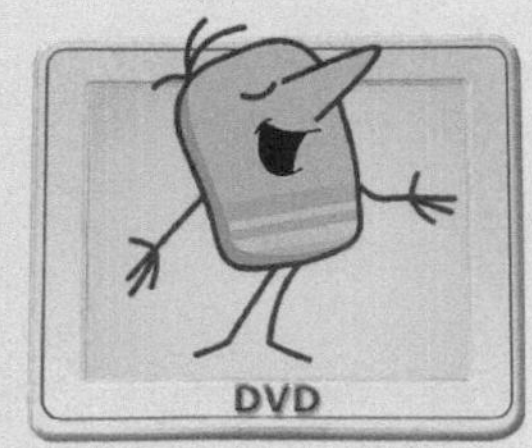

Grammavision

Online Edition
Students might use the online textbook and Performance Space to practice the **Lettres et sons** feature.

Dictée Script
1. Le lundi, j'ai anglais.
2. Il a les cheveux bruns.
3. Tu m'as emprunté un livre?
4. Quel est ton parfum de glace préféré?
5. Quelqu'un veut acheter cette voiture?

Game
Il faut que... Start a chain activity by telling what you need to do to prepare for the trip. **(Je vais en Suisse. Il faut que j'achète un manteau.)** Students continue by repeating your statements and adding others. **(Je vais en Suisse. Il faut que j'achète un manteau et que je trouve mon passeport.)** When a student fails to repeat all the previous statements, he or she is out. Start a new chain when someone makes a mistake. The winner is the last one remaining. 1.2

Grammaire 1
- review of object pronouns
- review of the conditional

Un peu plus
- review of *si* clauses

pp. 350–355

Résumé: Grammaire 1

- The direct object pronouns are: **me, te, se, le/la, nous, vous,** and **les.**
- The indirect object pronouns are: **me, te, se, lui, nous, vous,** and **leur.**

Double object pronouns are placed in the following order.

me, te, se, nous, vous	le, la, l', les	lui, leur	y	en

Use **y** to replace prepositional phrases. **En** is used to replace phrases beginning with **de** and expressions of quantity.

To form the **conditional**, add the appropriate endings (**-ais, -ais, -ait, -ions, -iez, -aient**) to the future stem.

You can use clauses beginning with **si** in a variety of situations:
- for making suggestions (**Si on allait au marché?**)
- for telling what would happen under different circumstances (**Si on avait beaucoup d'argent, on ferait le tour du monde.**)

Grammaire 2
- review of the subjunctive
- review of the **passé composé** and the **imparfait**

Un peu plus
- review of **être en train de**

pp. 362–367

Résumé: Grammaire 2

Form the subjunctive of most French verbs by dropping the **–ent** from the **ils** form and adding the endings: **-e, -es, -e, -ions, -iez, -ent.** The subjunctive is used after expressions of necessity and obligation.

Use the **passé composé** to:
- tell what happened at a **specific point in time.**

Use the **imparfait** to:
- tell **how things used to be** and **what people and things were like**
- give **background information,** and to **set the scene.**

Use the expression **être en train de** to tell *what was going on* when *something else happened.*

Lettres et sons

The nasal sound [œ̃] CD 10, Tr. 10–12

You have already learned how to distinguish between the nasal sounds in the following words: **an, on,** and **copain.** There is one additional nasal sound, the **[œ̃]** sound, that can be heard in words like **un, lundi,** and **brun.**

Jeux de langue
Un enfant brun et son copain marchant dans les embruns mangeaient un morceau de pain brun à la confiture.

Dictée 1.2
Écris les phrases de la dictée.

Chapter Review

DVD Program

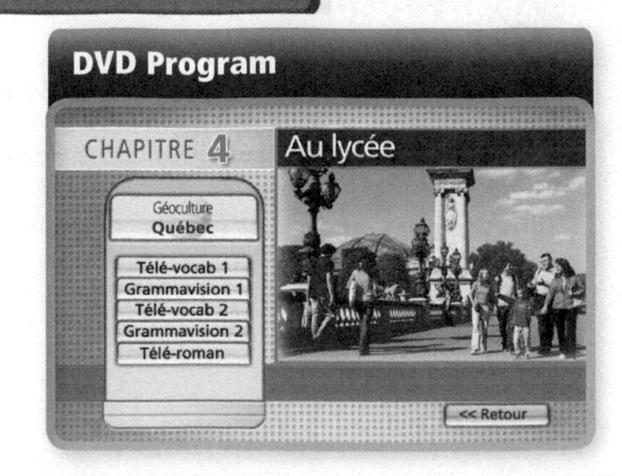

Online Edition

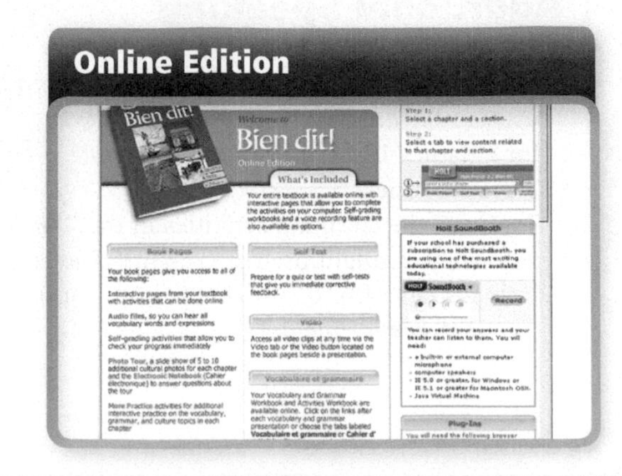

Prépare-toi pour l'examen

Résumé: Vocabulaire 1

PRACTICE FRENCH WITH HOLT MCDOUGAL APPS!

To ask about a vacation

au bord de la mer	*at the seashore*
à la campagne	*in the countryside*
à la montagne	*in the mountains*
en ville	*in the city*
le bateau	*boat*
un château	*castle*
un gilet de sauvetage	*life jacket*
l'office du tourisme (m.)	*tourist center*
la plage	*beach*
le sentier	*path*
le sommet	*peak*
un spectacle son et lumière	*a sound and light show*
la vallée	*valley*
l'Allemagne (f.)	*Germany*
l'Angleterre (f.)	*England*
la Belgique	*Belgium*
le Danemark	*Denmark*
l'Espagne (f.)	*Spain*
la Grèce	*Greece*
l'Italie (f.)	*Italy*
le Portugal	*Portugal*
la Suisse	*Switzerland*
la Norvège	*Norway*
allemand(e)	*German*
anglais(e)	*English/British*
espagnol(e)	*Spanish*
italien(ne)	*Italian*
portugais(e)	*Portuguese*
à l'étranger	*abroad*
aller en colonie de vacances	*to go to summer camp*
faire de l'escalade	*to mountain climb*
faire de la planche à voile	*to windsurf*
faire un séjour	*to stay/to sojourn*
faire une randonnée	*to go hiking*
faire une visite guidée	*to take a guided tour*
monter à cheval	*to horseback ride*
rendre visite à (une personne)	*to visit (a person)*
visiter (un endroit)	*to visit (a place)*
Ça dépend...	*That depends . . .*
Ça t'arrive de/d'	*Do you ever . . . ?*
J'en fais...	*I go . . .*
... j'y vais ...	*. . . I go there . . .*
Je reste chez moi.	*I stay home.*
pendant les vacances (f.)	*during vacation*
Qu'est-ce que tu fais de beau... ?	*What interesting things do you do . . . ?*

To say what you would do if you could . *see p. 348*

Résumé: Vocabulaire 2

To express necessity

acheter un guide	*to buy a guidebook*
un appareil photo	*photo camera*
un billet	*ticket*
une brochure	*brochure*
changer de l'argent (m.)	*to change money*
des chèques de voyage (m.)	*traveller's checks*
faire sa valise	*to pack one's suitcase*
faire une demande de visa	*to apply for a visa*
faire une réservation d'hôtel/de billet de train/d'avion	*to make a hotel/train ticket/airline ticket reservation*
un itinéraire	*itinerary/route*
des lunettes de soleil (f.)	*sunglasses*
un passeport	*passport*
un permis de conduire	*driver's license*
une pièce	*coin*
un plan	*map*
se faire vacciner	*to get vaccinated*
s'informer sur Internet	*to inquire on the Internet*
se renseigner dans une agence de voyages	*to get information at a travel agency*
le site d'une compagnie aérienne	*airline website*
une trousse de toilette	*vanity case*
Il faut que ...	*I have to . . .*
Il ne faut surtout pas...	*We especially must not . . .*
J'ai besoin de/d'...	*I need to . . .*
Je dois absolument...	*I absolutely must . . .*

To ask what has been done .... *see p. 361*

Holt McDougal French Apps

Remind students that they can use the Holt McDougal French Apps to review their vocabulary.

French for Spanish Speakers

Ask Spanish speakers about **être en train de.** Is there an equivalent expression in Spanish that conveys the same idea of immediacy or of being in the middle of an ongoing activity? (Yes, in Spanish this would be conveyed by a form of **estar** + gerund form of the verb. For example, **je suis en train de lire** would be **estoy leyendo.**) Have students translate **Il était en train de prendre des photos. (Estaba sacando fotos.)** 4.1

Projectable Transparency

More Digital Resources

FOR THE STUDENT

Holt McDougal French Apps
@HomeTutor
News and Networking
Performance Space

FOR THE TEACHER

- Interactive Whiteboard Lessons
- Generate Success!

Assess

Assessment Program
Examen: Chapitre 10
Examen oral: Chapitre 10
Examen final
Audio CD 10, Tr. 16–17; 18–20
Alternative Assessment
Differentiated Practice and Assessment CD-ROM
Online Assessment
my.hrw.com
Test Generator 

Révisions cumulatives

Resources

Planning:
Lesson Planner
Teacher One Stop

Practice:
Cahier d'activités
Media Guide
Projectable Transparencies
Fine Art, Chapter 10
Audio CD 10, Tr. 13
Holt McDougal French Apps

1 Script

1. Ce que je préfère, c'est me baigner.
2. J'adore faire du ski!
3. Mon rêve, ce serait de passer toute la journée à la plage.
4. Si je pouvais, je descendrais dans un hôtel de luxe, je mangerais dans les meilleurs restaurants, et je passerais tout mon temps dans des musées.
5. Moi, j'adore faire de l'escalade.
6. J'aime faire des visites guidées pour découvrir tous les monuments historiques.
7. J'adore faire de la voile!

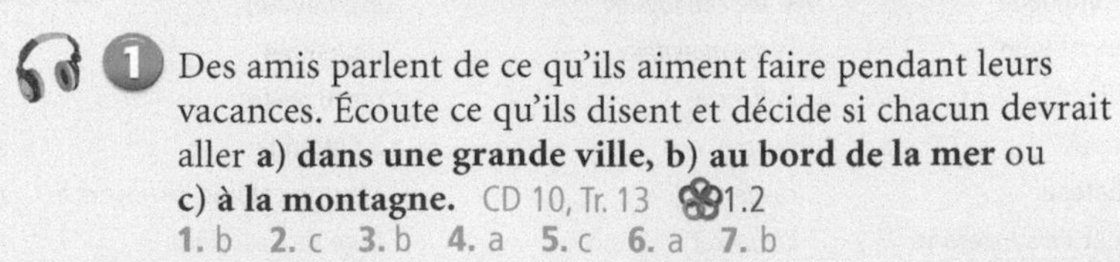

1 Des amis parlent de ce qu'ils aiment faire pendant leurs vacances. Écoute ce qu'ils disent et décide si chacun devrait aller **a) dans une grande ville, b) au bord de la mer** ou **c) à la montagne.** CD 10, Tr. 13 1.2
1. b 2. c 3. b 4. a 5. c 6. a 7. b

2 Une agence de voyages qui se spécialise dans le tourisme pour jeunes te propose ces séjours. Lis la description de chaque séjour. Décide quel séjour tu choisirais et dis pourquoi. 1.3, 3.2

ALLEZ, LES JEUNES!

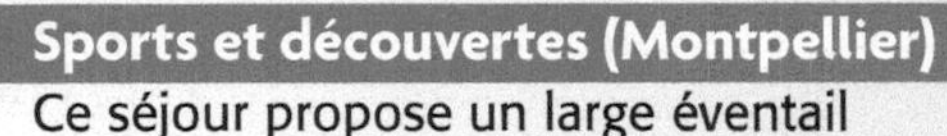

Séjours ECCO.
Contactez-nous à www.hmhpub.ecco.com.

Sports et découvertes (Montpellier)
Ce séjour propose un large éventail d'activités : escalade, tir à l'arc, trampoline, arts martiaux, tennis, danse, baignade au lac, kayak...
- Dates : du 15/04 au 29/04
- Âges : de 11 à 17 ans
- Prix : à partir de 424,00 € / pers

Vedettes! (Lyon)
Danser, chanter, rapper, monter un spectacle, tout cela est possible pendant ce séjour. Chacun rentrera avec un CD ou un DVD de sa première expérience.
- Dates : du 03/07 au 21/07
- Âges : de 6 à 15 ans
- Prix : à partir de 369,00 € / pers

Surf, Snow Blade et Ski! (Noël)
Ce séjour est pensé pour les adolescents de 14 à 16 ans. Au programme ski ou surf tous les jours, piscine, patinoire, veillée raclette...
Contactez-nous pour plus d'informations.

Online Culture Project

Have students create a tourism brochure for Nice. They should include five attractions, such as concerts, exhibitions, festivals, or landmarks, such as parks, churches, monuments, or historic buildings. Ask students to include the name of each attraction and a brief description. They might also include information on unique locations such as cheese shops, confectioners, and **pâtisseries.** Have students print pictures from the Web sites or draw their own to illustrate their brochures and document the sites they visit. 1.3

Révisions cumulatives

Online Assessment
my.hrw.com
Cumulative Self-test

3 Avec deux amis, imaginez que vous allez partir en week-end. Décidez où vous allez aller et ce que vous allez faire comme activité (sports, loisirs)? Ensuite, faites une liste de tout ce qu'il faut faire pour préparer votre voyage. Créez une conversation dans laquelle vous parlez du voyage. Présentez votre conversation à la classe. 1.1

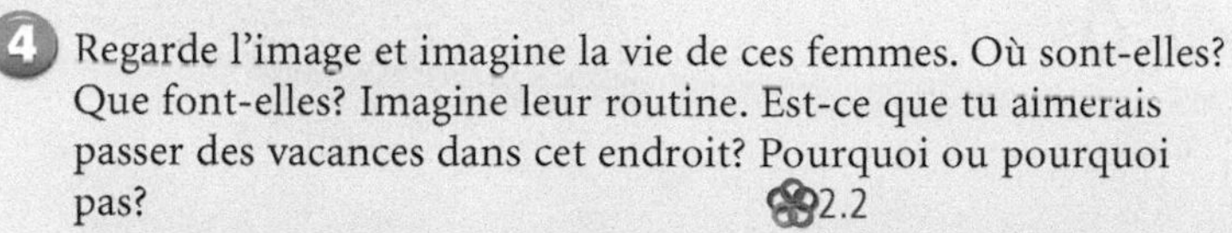

4 Regarde l'image et imagine la vie de ces femmes. Où sont-elles? Que font-elles? Imagine leur routine. Est-ce que tu aimerais passer des vacances dans cet endroit? Pourquoi ou pourquoi pas? 2.2

***Scène du jardin en Bretagne* de Pierre Auguste Renoir**

5 Imagine que tu es en vacances et que tu envoies une carte postale à un(e) de tes camarades de classe. Parle-lui de ce que tu fais pendant tes vacances. 1.3

6 À ton tour

Chez moi, on... Students from a **lycée** in Nice are coming to your area for a two-week visit. Create a brochure in French about your area, recommending places to go and things to do. Include information about your school as well. 1.3

ACTFL Performance Standards

The activities in Chapter 10 target the communicative modes as described in the Standards.

Interpersonal	Two-way communication using receptive skills and productive skills	**Communication (SE),** 349, 351, 353, 355, 361, 363, 365 **Communication (TE),** pp. 351, 353, 355, 361, 363
Interpretive	One-way communication using receptive skills	**Comparaisons,** p. 357 **Télé-roman,** pp. 368–369
Presentational	One-way communication using productive skills	**Communication (SE),** p. 367 **Communication (TE),** pp. 349, 365, 367 **À ton tour,** p. 379

Fine Art Connection

Introduction Pierre Auguste Renoir was born in Limoges, France, in 1841. He was one of the central figures of the impressionist movement and remains one of the best known painters in the world. Renoir painted landscapes in the soft style characteristic of impressionist painters, but, unlike his friend Claude Monet, he also loved to paint people. His paintings of gardens, like the one shown here, display great richness of colors and suggestion of depth. In scenes such as the one in *Scène du jardin en Bretagne*, Renoir knew how to express sweet comfort and optimism.

Analyzing

To help students discuss the painting, you might use the following questions.

1. **Qu'est-ce qu'on voit dans ce tableau?**
2. **Est-ce qu'il y a un autre personnage que les deux femmes?**
3. **Que fait la femme sur la droite?**
4. **Quelles couleurs le peintre a-t-il utilisées?**
5. **Quelle impression est-ce que les couleurs donnent?**

3.1

Extension

Ask students to find other paintings by Pierre Auguste Renoir on the Internet or at the library. Have them bring copies of their favorite painting to class. Organize students in groups of 4 or 5 and have them compare their paintings. They should try to find common characteristics between the works they are sharing. 2.2, 3.1

Meeting the National Standards

Cultures
Products and Perspectives, pp. 383, 385, 389, 391, 393, 395, 401

Connections
Social Studies Link, p. 387

Comparisons
Comparing and Contrasting, pp. 397, 399

Using the Illustration

Have students look at the illustration to predict what types of readings they will find in **Variations littéraires.** Also, ask them to guess from what countries the readings come. Then, have them look at the table of contents to see if any of their predictions were correct.

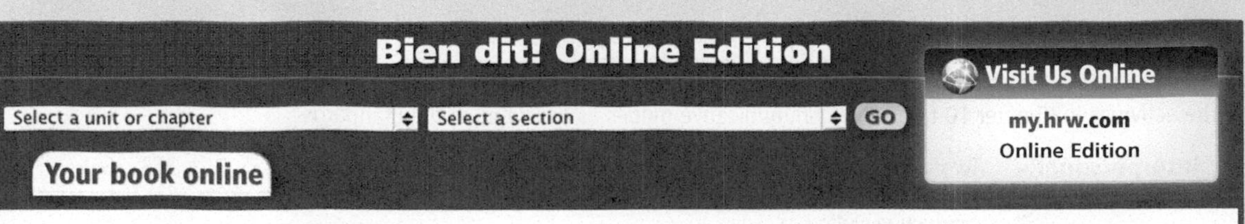

All of the texts in **Variations littéraires** have been recorded and can be found in the online edition of this textbook at **my.hrw.com.**

- Response and feedback: performance space
- Complete video and audio programs
- Interactive activities with feedback
- Recorded vocabulary and readings
- Interactive workbooks
- Graded assessment

Variations littéraires

Teacher Note

The readings in this section of ***Bien dit!*** represent the five different locations presented in the textbook, from Paris to Nice. There are informative readings as well as literary texts. These location-based readings feature:

- high student-interest subject matter
- cultural information about the francophone world
- beautiful illustrations that aid student understanding of the text

The difficulty increases somewhat in going from Chapter 1 to Chapter 10, but all of them are accessible to a Level 2 student. These readings are meant to be fun—and to give students greater insight into the many cultures they encounter as they make their way through ***Bien dit!***

Using the Strategies

With every reading in **Variations littéraires,** there are strategies designed to help students more easily understand the text. Some are pre-reading strategies that suggest techniques that students can apply before reading the text:

- using cognates
- using prior knowledge and experiences
- using text organizers
- determining the main idea
- anticipating content

Some of the strategies will be useful to students as they are reading the text:

- monitoring comprehension
- making inferences
- analyzing chronological order
- looking for metaphors
- using root words

Make sure students use the suggested strategy to make each optional reading more accessible and more enjoyable.

Resources

Presentation:

Audio CD 1, Tr. 9

Practice:

Reading Strategies and Skills Handbook

Intermediate Reader

French InterActive Reader

Applying the Strategies

You might have students use the "Tea Party" strategy from the *Reading Strategies and Skills Handbook* to help them start thinking about the text before reading.

READING PRACTICE

STRATEGIES

Strategy: Tea Party

Reading Skill	When can I use this strategy?		
	Prereading	During Reading	Postreading
Making Predictions	✓		
Using Prior Knowledge	✓		

Strategy at a Glance: Tea Party

- The teacher selects quotations from the text, writes each quotation on a separate card, and distributes one to each student. Students share their quotations in order to form an idea about the subject of the text.
- Each student reads his or her quotation to another student, who responds by also reading a quotation.
- Small groups of students discuss the meaning of the quotations and use the passages to predict what the text will be about.

Tea Party is a strategy that helps readers become engaged with a text before they begin reading the entire selection. Students discuss the meaning of selected quotations from the story, how the passages might relate to each other, and then make predictions about the text based on the quotations.

Best Use of the Strategy

This prereading strategy gives students language to first think about and then to talk about what the text is about and concepts and ideas that may be introduced in the text. In addition, the quotations stimulate students' curiosity about the text and helps them focus on what they are reading.

Getting the Strategy to Work

1. **Select and distribute quotations from the text.** Select a text, choose 10–12 quotations from it, and prepare a list of individual quotations that can be cut into slips. (Be sure to make a master list and copies before cutting the slips. It would be helpful to number the slips or put them on different colors of paper in order to group students later for discussion.) Distribute a slip of paper to each student and ask them to share their quotations in order to form an idea about the reading selection. Have students practice reading their quotations to themselves before they share them with others. Offer to help anyone who is having problems with his or her quotation.

Prereading

Discuss **Stratégie** (anticipating) with students. Tell them that a text will be easier to understand if they are able to formulate some impressions and expectations before they start reading.

Paris

Paris Plages

Aucune voiture sur les berges[1] de la Seine en plein cœur de Paris, entre le tunnel des Tuileries et le pont Henri IV, mais du sable, de l'eau, de la verdure[2], des transats[3], des palmiers et des parasols. Chaque été, Paris Plages reprend ses quartiers d'été[4]. Son objectif : offrir au plus grand nombre la possibilité de se détendre[5] et de s'amuser gratuitement[6]. CD 1, Tr. 9

STRATÉGIE

Before reading a text, you can use **images and titles** to anticipate its content. Briefly look over pictures and section titles, and then skim the text and guess what this reading is about.

Vive la plage !

Trois plages sont proposées aux visiteurs. La première est en lattes de bois[7]. La deuxième est toute en herbe[8]. La troisième est une plage de sable fin[9]. On peut se détendre et faire la sieste[10] en regardant passer les bateaux-mouches[11] grâce à 200 transats et 40 hamacs.

À vos pinceaux[12] !

Si vous aimez la peinture, des artistes sont là pour vous aider à peindre à l'aquarelle[13] une scène de Paris Plages sur un papier format carte postale.

Le Marais
Rue de Rivoli
Quartier Saint-Paul
Le Louvre
Q. du Louvre
Q. de l'Hôtel de Ville
Pont Neuf
Île de la Cité
Île St-Louis
Notre-Dame
Quartier Latin

CALENDRIER	HORAIRES D'OUVERTURE	HORAIRES DES ACTIVITÉS
du 21 juillet au 20 août	de 7h à minuit	de 9h à 22h30 Prix : gratuit

1. banks 2. greenery 3. deck chairs 4. summer headquarters 5. to relax 6. for free 7. wooden decks 8. grass 9. fine sand 10. to take a nap 11. river boats 12. paintbrushes 13. watercolor

Core Instruction

VARIATIONS LITTÉRAIRES

1. On the board or on a transparency, write the headings of each of the paragraphs in the text. Ask students how the photographs and drawings surrounding the text relate to each heading. **(3 min.)**
2. Have students skim the text and supply two or three words or expressions from each section that relate to the heading. **(4 min.)**
3. Form three groups. Have each group read two of the sections in detail. As they read, they should pick out three key facts from their reading and have a group secretary write them down. **(5 min.)**
4. Have a representative from each group share the facts with the rest of the class. **(5 min.)**
5. Have students read through the entire text and answer the **Après la lecture** questions. **(5 min.)**

Pas de plage... sans châteaux de sable[1] !
Face à la Conciergerie, un espace châteaux de sable permet aux tout-petits de jouer aux architectes. Un sculpteur professionnel construit, en sable, des personnages et les principaux monuments de la capitale.

Tous au sport !
Des activités sportives gratuites et encadrées[2] par des professionnels sont proposées, aussi bien pour les débutants que pour les initiés : frisbee®, beach volley, badminton, exercices de relaxation, roller, trampoline, escalade[3]... On peut aussi jouer à la pétanque au boulodrome[4].

Que d'eau !
Il y a un bassin de baignade avec cabines de bains[5] pour se changer et une pataugeoire[6] pour les moins de cinq ans. Des brumisateurs[7] sont également répartis le long de la Seine. Chacun peut aussi se désaltérer[8] gratuitement à l'une des sept fontaines.

APRÈS la lecture 1.2, 1.3

1. Quel est le but de Paris Plages?
2. Quelles sont les différentes sortes de plage?
3. Sur quoi peut-on faire la sieste à Paris Plages?
4. Parmi les sports cités, lequel se joue avec un ballon? Lequel se joue avec des boules?
5. Quelles activités t'intéressent?

1. sand castle 2. directed 3. rock climbing 4. area to play **pétanque** 5. beach hut 6. wading pool 7. water sprays 8. quench your thirst

Differentiated Instruction

ADVANCED LEARNERS

Ask students to write a radio or television advertisement for the **Paris-Plage** events. They should use the information given in the reading as well as any other information they may find in an Internet search. They might make an audio or videotape of their ad to be presented to the class. 1.3

SPECIAL LEARNING NEEDS

Students with Speech Impairments It may be difficult for students with speech impairments to speak in class. They may feel more comfortable working in small groups where they need only express their ideas to two or three other students. By appointing a group secretary, speech-impaired students can have their thoughts heard without having to speak in front of the entire class.

Variations littéraires

Answers

1. offrir au plus grand nombre la possibilité de se détendre et de se distraire gratuitement
2. en lattes de bois, toute en herbe, de sable fin
3. 200 transats et 40 hamacs
4. beach volley; pétanque
5. Answers will vary.

Cultures

Products and Perspectives

The **Paris-Plage** events were begun in 2002 at a cost of a million euros. This annual celebration has been extremely popular, in spite of the one rather obvious omission. . . a place to swim! (The Seine River is not suitable for swimmers.) The beach is not the only option for fun; there are a number of other annual summer events in Paris. Ask students what special events your city offers in the summer to attract tourists. 2.2

Postreading

Have partners make up a conversation in which one person invites the other to **Paris-Plage,** and they discuss the various activities in which they plan to participate. They may act out their conversation for the rest of the class.

Language Examination

Through the practice of listening and reading comprehension, **Variations littéraires** helps students prepare for the **Interpretive Reading and Listening** and the **Presentational Writing** sections of the AP Language and Culture Exam.

Resources

Presentation:

Audio CD 2, Tr. 8

Practice:

Reading Strategies and Skills Handbook

Intermediate Reader

French InterActive Reader

Applying the Strategies

You may want to use the "Sketch to Stretch" strategy from the *Reading Strategies and Skills Handbook* to encourage students to examine the text more closely.

READING PRACTICE

STRATEGIES

Strategy: Sketch to Stretch

Reading Skill	When can I use this strategy?		
	Prereading	During Reading	Postreading
Drawing Conclusions			✓
Making Generalizations			✓
Analyzing Cause and Effect			✓
Summarizing			✓

Strategy at a Glance: Sketch to Stretch

- The teacher introduces **Sketch to Stretch** to students by showing and discussing symbolic pictures based on a text.
- After reading a selection, students work independently or with a partner to create their own symbolic sketches. On the back of the sketches, students write why they drew what they did, using evidence from the text to support their opinions.
- Students share their sketches in small groups, allowing others to comment before revealing explanations of their work.

Many students find it difficult to go beyond the reading selection to talk about the theme, or the symbolism, or to express a generalization about the story that can be applied to their lives. But some students who have difficulty talking about a text can express their ideas visually, far beyond what even they themselves imagine. This strategy, **Sketch to Stretch,** gives students the opportunity to formulate images that represent the ideas they cannot otherwise express. For some students, putting ideas into pictures, rather than words, is the best way to express their responses to the text.

This is a postreading strategy in which students think about what a passage or entire selection means to them and then draw symbolic representations of their interpretations of the text. As students discuss the text and decide what to draw, they think about the theme, draw conclusions, form generalizations, recognize cause-and-effect relationships, and summarize.

Prereading

Discuss **Stratégie** (cognates) with students. This may be a good opportunity to remind students to be aware of three types of cognates. Direct cognates look very similar to their English counterparts **(fantôme).** Indirect cognates resemble related words of similar origin (**avion,** *airplane/aviation).* False cognates resemble English words but have nothing in common with them **(comment).**

Le Fantôme de l'Opéra

Avez-vous déjà vu *Le Fantôme de l'Opéra* ? C'est inspiré par le roman *Le Fantôme de l'Opéra* de Gaston Leroux. CD 2, Tr. 8

STRATÉGIE

Using cognates can be especially helpful with a challenging text. Before you read this passage, skim it for cognates. Use what you know about the story to help you guess their meaning.

Gaston Leroux (1868–1927) a été avocat[1], journaliste et écrivain. Il a écrit une série de romans[2] policiers (*Le Mystère de la chambre jaune, Le Parfum de la dame en noir*) dont le personnage principal, Joseph Rouletabille, ressemble[3] un peu à Sherlock Holmes. Mais, Gaston Leroux est plus connu pour son roman, *Le Fantôme de l'Opéra,* qui est inspiré par des incidents étranges mais réels qui ont eu lieu[4] à l'opéra Garnier.

GASTON LEROUX

Le Fantôme de l'Opéra

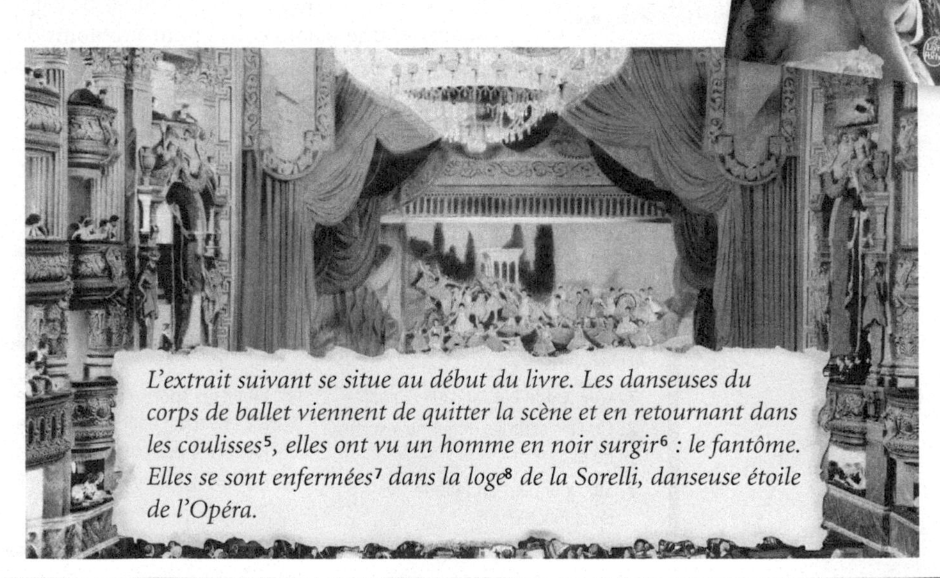

L'extrait suivant se situe au début du livre. Les danseuses du corps de ballet viennent de quitter la scène et en retournant dans les coulisses[5], elles ont vu un homme en noir surgir[6] : le fantôme. Elles se sont enfermées[7] dans la loge[8] de la Sorelli, danseuse étoile de l'Opéra.

1. lawyer 2. novels 3. looks like 4. took place 5. backstage 6. suddenly appear 7. locked themselves 8. dressing room

Core Instruction

VARIATIONS LITTÉRAIRES

1. Read the biographical information about Gaston Leroux with students. While reading, make a list on the board of any direct (**journaliste**), indirect (**tard,** *late/tardy),* or false (**roman**) cognates. **(3 min.)**
2. Have students read the excerpt from the novel, ***Le Fantôme de l'Opéra,*** and note any cognates that will help their comprehension. Remind students that if a cognate adds confusion to the sentence, it is very likely a false cognate. **(7 min.)**
3. Discuss any words that students identified as indirect or false cognates. **(4 min.)**
4. Have students answer the **Après la lecture** questions. **(5 min.)**

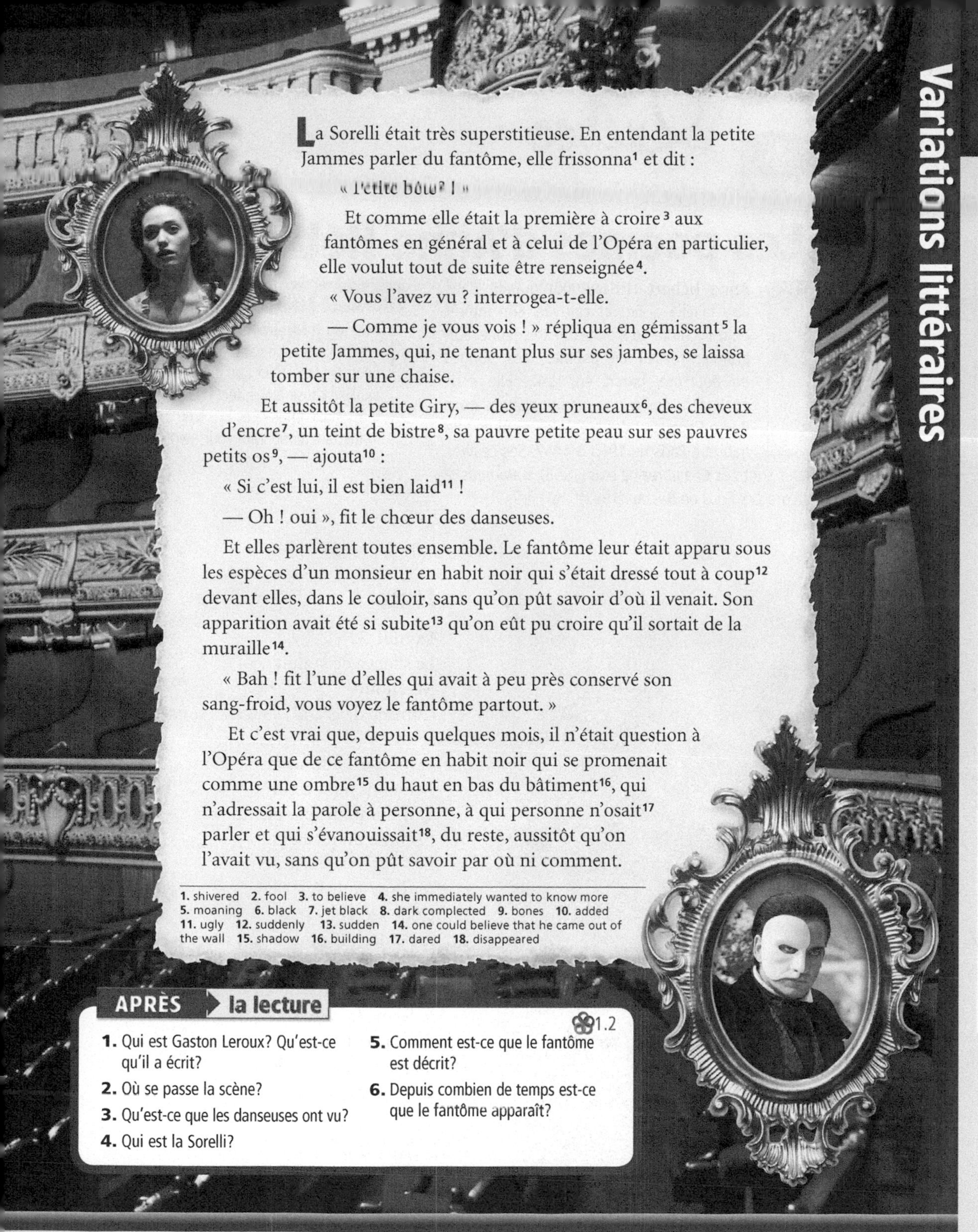

La Sorelli était très superstitieuse. En entendant la petite Jammes parler du fantôme, elle frissonna[1] et dit :

« Petite bête[2] ! »

Et comme elle était la première à croire[3] aux fantômes en général et à celui de l'Opéra en particulier, elle voulut tout de suite être renseignée[4].

« Vous l'avez vu ? interrogea-t-elle.

— Comme je vous vois ! » répliqua en gémissant[5] la petite Jammes, qui, ne tenant plus sur ses jambes, se laissa tomber sur une chaise.

Et aussitôt la petite Giry, — des yeux pruneaux[6], des cheveux d'encre[7], un teint de bistre[8], sa pauvre petite peau sur ses pauvres petits os[9], — ajouta[10] :

« Si c'est lui, il est bien laid[11] !

— Oh ! oui », fit le chœur des danseuses.

Et elles parlèrent toutes ensemble. Le fantôme leur était apparu sous les espèces d'un monsieur en habit noir qui s'était dressé tout à coup[12] devant elles, dans le couloir, sans qu'on pût savoir d'où il venait. Son apparition avait été si subite[13] qu'on eût pu croire qu'il sortait de la muraille[14].

« Bah ! fit l'une d'elles qui avait à peu près conservé son sang-froid, vous voyez le fantôme partout. »

Et c'est vrai que, depuis quelques mois, il n'était question à l'Opéra que de ce fantôme en habit noir qui se promenait comme une ombre[15] du haut en bas du bâtiment[16], qui n'adressait la parole à personne, à qui personne n'osait[17] parler et qui s'évanouissait[18], du reste, aussitôt qu'on l'avait vu, sans qu'on pût savoir par où ni comment.

1. shivered **2.** fool **3.** to believe **4.** she immediately wanted to know more **5.** moaning **6.** black **7.** jet black **8.** dark complected **9.** bones **10.** added **11.** ugly **12.** suddenly **13.** sudden **14.** one could believe that he came out of the wall **15.** shadow **16.** building **17.** dared **18.** disappeared

APRÈS la lecture

1.2

1. Qui est Gaston Leroux? Qu'est-ce qu'il a écrit?
2. Où se passe la scène?
3. Qu'est-ce que les danseuses ont vu?
4. Qui est la Sorelli?
5. Comment est-ce que le fantôme est décrit?
6. Depuis combien de temps est-ce que le fantôme apparaît?

Variations littéraires

Answers

1. avocat, journaliste, écrivain; des romans policiers
2. dans les caulisses de l'opéra
3. un homme en noir
4. la danseuse étoile de l'Opéra
5. des yeux pruneaux, des cheveux d'encre, un teint de bistre, sa pauvre petite pau sur ses pauvres petits os, bien laid
6. depuis quelques mois

Cultures

Products and Perspectives

The **Opéra Garnier** in Paris is named after the architect who designed it. Completed in 1875, it is known for its ornate exterior and the elegant marble and onyx staircases in its lobby. In 1964, the famous artist Marc Chagall painted a mural depicting scenes from various operas which covers the original ceiling in the main auditorium. Curiously, there is also a lake beneath the building, a fact that Gaston Leroux uses in his novel. Have students research the building and bring photographs from books or images from Web sites to share with the class and discuss its architectural aspects. 2.2

Postreading

Even though some students may be familiar with the movie or Broadway version of the story, ask them to use their imagination to explain who the Phantom might be. Where did he come from, and why does he inhabit the **Opéra?** Have them share their theory with the rest of the class.

Language Examination

Through the practice of listening and reading comprehension, **Variations littéraires** helps students prepare for the **Interpretive Reading and Listening** and the **Presentational Writing** sections of the AP Language and Culture Exam.

Differentiated Instruction

SLOWER PACE LEARNERS

Students may feel overwhelmed as reading selections become longer. You might give these students a list of questions to answer while they read. The questions should follow the order of the story and require students to supply specific details. Depending on the ability level of the students, you might use multiple-choice questions. Students will then read with a specific purpose and may succeed in focusing their attention more closely on the selection. 1.2

MULTIPLE INTELLIGENCES

Spacial/Visual You might ask students with artistic abilities to make a painting, clay sculpture, or **papier-mâché** model of what they think the Phantom might look like. Tell them to be creative and try not to be influenced by what they may have seen in the movies or on stage. As an alternative, students might create a blueprint or a diorama of the opera house. 1.3

Resources

Presentation:

Audio CD 3, Tr. 8–9

Practice:

Reading Strategies and Skills Handbook

Intermediate Reader

French InterActive Reader

Applying the Strategies

The "Text Reformulation" strategy, from the *Reading Strategies and Skills Handbook*, may be an effective tool to apply to this reading. Turning these poems into narratives may help students understand the ideas that the poet is trying to convey.

READING PRACTICE

STRATEGIES

Strategy: Text Reformulation

Reading Skill	When can I use this strategy?		
	Prereading	During Reading	Postreading
Understanding Text Structure			✓
Analyzing Cause-and-Effect Relationships			✓

Strategy at a Glance: Text Reformulation

- The teacher introduces **Text Reformulation** by having students reformulate a text they have read into a patterned story, such as an ABC story, or into another genre.
- The teacher models several types of reformulations.
- Either the teacher or the students choose which type of reformulation to do based on the desired learning objectives.

Sometimes by transforming a text into a different format—one that is more familiar or friendlier—students can understand it better. An example: reformulating an expository text structure to fit the narrative structure; in other words, taking what might be a difficult, even dry, expository text and retelling it as a story.

Text Reformulation, or **Story Recycling,** is a strategy in which students transform a text into another type of text.

Best Use of the Strategy

When students are having difficulty understanding a text, use the **Text Reformulation** (Feathers 1993), or **Story Recycling,** strategy to show them how to better understand the text by turning it into another type of text that is more familiar to them. Whether students turn expository texts into narratives, poems into newspaper articles, or short stories into patterned stories such as ABC books, reformulating texts encourages students to talk about the original texts.

Prereading

Discuss **Stratégie** (inference) with students. When reading poetry, we often have to infer what the poet is expressing. Ask students what techniques poets use to suggest to us, rather than tell us directly, what they feel.

Québec

Les poèmes d'Anne Hébert

Anne Hébert (1916–2000) grandit dans une famille aisée[1] et cultivée. Son intérêt pour l'écriture se manifeste[2] très jeune. Son premier recueil de poèmes, *Les Songes en équilibre*, paraît en 1942. Elle écrit également des textes radiophoniques pour Radio-Canada et des scénarios de films. Elle habite à Paris de 1965 à 1997. Ses œuvres les plus connues sont *Les Chambres de bois* (1958), *Kamouraska* (1970), ou encore *Les Fous de Bassan* (1982). CD 3, Tr. 8–9

STRATÉGIE

Making inferences Often in poetry, the author states the cause and not the effect, or states the effect and not the cause. To analyze cause-and-effect relationships, you must make inferences by using information in the text along with your own experience.

Nuit

La nuit
Le silence de la nuit
M'entoure[3]
Comme de grands courants sous-marins[4].

5 Je repose[5] au fond[6] de l'eau muette et glauque[7].
J'entends mon cœur
Qui s'illumine et s'éteint
Comme un phare[8].

Rythme sourd[9]
10 Code secret
Je ne déchiffre aucun mystère.

À chaque éclat[10] de lumière
Je ferme les yeux
Pour la continuité de la nuit
15 La perpétuité du silence
Où je sombre[11].

1. well-to-do 2. showed itself 3. surrounds me
4. underwater currents 5. rest 6. at the bottom
7. silent and dull blue-green 8. lighthouse
9. deaf 10. sparkle 11. sink

Core Instruction

VARIATIONS LITTÉRAIRES

1. Read and discuss the biographical material about Anne Hébert with the class. **(3 min.)**
2. Ask students which French word they expect to see in a simile. **(comme)** Have the class read **"Nuit"** while listening to the recording. Ask students to find the two similes in the poem. To what does the poet compare the silence of the night? To what does she compare the beating of her heart? (Hearing the pulsing of her heartbeat is like seeing the flashing light of a beacon.) Tell students to observe the mixture of sensory images in the poem. **(6 min.)**
3. What other poetic devices are students familiar with? Have them read **"Nos mains au jardin"** while playing the recording. What imagery or symbolism can students find in this poem? **(6 min.)**
4. Have students answer the **Après la lecture** questions. **(5 min.)**

Nos mains au jardin

Nous avons eu cette idée
De planter nos mains au jardin

Branches des dix doigts[1]
Petits arbres d'ossements[2]
5 Chère plate-bande[3].
Tout le jour

Nous avons attendu l'oiseau[4] roux
Et les feuilles fraîches
À nos ongles[5] polis.

10 Nul oiseau
Nul printemps
Ne se sont pris au piège[6] de nos mains coupées.

Pour une seule fleur[7]
Une seule minuscule étoile[8] de couleur
15 Un seul vol d'aile[9] calme
Pour une seule note pure
Répétée trois fois.

Il faudra[10] la saison prochaine
Et nos mains fondues[11] comme l'eau.

1. fingers 2. bones 3. flower bed 4. bird 5. fingernails 6. trapped 7. a flower 8. star 9. a flap of a wing 10. we'll have to 11. melted

APRÈS la lecture

1.2, 1.3

La nuit

1. À quoi «le silence de la nuit» est-il comparé?
2. À quoi le «cœur» est-il comparé?
3. Trouve les mots qui parlent de la mer.

Nos mains au jardin

1. Comment est la nature?
2. Que forment les doigts?
3. Qu'est-ce qu'il faut attendre?

Variations littéraires

Answers

1. aux grands courants sous-marins
2. à un phare
3. (l'eau) muette et glauque

1. comme une main
2. les branches
3. la saison prochaine; le printemps

Connections

Social Studies Link

Anne Hébert's writing career spanned a period of almost 60 years, during which she produced novels, stories, plays, and poems. Her first poems were published in the 1960s when her native province of **Québec** was going through a period of social change. This era, now known as the "Quiet Revolution," eventually led to the Separatist movement in **Québec.** Ask students to research social changes that were occurring in the United States during this same period. 3.1

Postreading

Form small groups. Give each group a paper with the name of one poetic device (rhyme, alliteration, assonance, simile, metaphor, oxymoron, onomatopoeia, hyperbole). Make sure students understand what each device is and then give them several minutes to write one example of that device in French. When they have finished, tell them to pass the paper to another group. Continue until each group has written one example of each device. Share the answers with the class.

Differentiated Instruction

SLOWER PACE LEARNERS

Students may have trouble grasping the symbolic language of poetry. Before they read, have them make a chart of concrete words to look for in each poem. (in **"Nuit"**, words referencing sound and sight; in **"Nos mains au jardin"**, nature and the human body) Explain that the poet's objective is not to tell the reader what he or she thinks, but to use words in a special way to create a mood that the reader can feel. 1.2

MULTIPLE INTELLIGENCES

Linguistic Have students choose one of the two poems by Anne Hébert and memorize it. Ask volunteers to recite their poem for the class. This could be conducted as a departmental recitation contest. As an alternative, have students write their own poem in French to recite. Have the rest of the class choose the student with the best delivery and interpretation. 1.3

Through the practice of listening and reading comprehension, **Variations littéraires** helps students prepare for the **Interpretive Reading and Listening** and the **Presentational Writing** sections of the AP Language and Culture Exam.

Variations littéraires

Resources

Presentation:

Audio CD 1, Tr. 9

Practice:

Reading Strategies and Skills Handbook

Intermediate Reader

French InterActive Reader

Applying the Strategies

You may want to use the "Retellings" strategy from the *Reading Strategies and Skills Handbook* to help students determine the main ideas in this reading selection.

READING PRACTICE

Strategy: Retellings

Strategy at a Glance: Retellings

Best Use of the Strategy

Getting the Strategy to Work

Prereading

Discuss **Stratégie** (metaphors) with students. Give them two or three examples of a metaphor and ask them to come up with a few others. Remind students that although we tend to associate metaphors with poetry, they may occur in any kind of writing. Explain that novelists often use imagery to enrich their prose.

Québec

L'alouette

Gabrielle Roy (1909–1983) est d'abord institutrice[1] dans l'ouest canadien. En 1937, elle part étudier l'art dramatique en France et en Angleterre. Elle écrit ses premiers articles. Elle rentre au Canada juste avant la Deuxième Guerre mondiale. Elle travaille à Montréal comme journaliste et écrivain. Son premier roman, *Bonheur d'occasion,* est publié en 1945. Elle passe le reste de sa vie à écrire.

CD 4, Tr. 9

STRATÉGIE

Look for metaphor (a direct comparison of one thing to another) to help you understand a text where you know they are used. For instance, the title of this story is a metaphor: Nil is called «l'alouette» (the lark) because he, like the bird, sings very well.

L'histoire « L'alouette » est issue du recueil autobiographique Ces Enfants de ma vie. « L'alouette » est un jeune immigré ukrainien doté d'une voix[2] magnifique, et qui apporte le bonheur à ceux qui l'entendent chanter.

Assez souvent je priais[3] mes petits élèves de chanter ensemble. Un jour, au milieu de leurs voix plutôt ternes, j'en distinguai une, claire, frémissante[4], étonnamment juste[5]. Je fis cesser le groupe[6] pour laisser Nil continuer seul. La ravissante voix et de quel prix pour moi qui n'eus[7] jamais beaucoup d'oreille pour la musique !

Dès lors je demandai :

— Donne le ton[8], veux-tu, Nil ?

Il le donnait sans se faire prier ni s'enorgueillir[9], enfant né pour chanter comme d'autres pour faire la moue[10].

Partait alors à sa remorque[11] ma volée de passereaux[12] que Nil entraînait[13] tant bien que mal et, avant longtemps, plutôt bien que mal, car, outre son brillant talent, il possédait celui de paraître[14] en donner aux autres. On écoutait Nil chanter et on se croyait tous capables de chanter.

1. a primary school teacher 2. a voice 3. asked 4. quivering 5. pure 6. asked the group to stop 7. never had 8. to give the pitch 9. to boast 10. to pout 11. in his path 12. my flock of passerines (type of bird) 13. led 14. seem

Core Instruction

VARIATIONS LITTÉRAIRES

1. Read and discuss with the class the biographical information about Gabrielle Roy and the introductory paragraph. **(3 min.)**
2. Ask individual students to read aloud, four or five lines at a time. In order to assure that all students understand, stop after each student reads and have a second student summarize the section in his or her own words. Encourage other students to ask questions or add to the summary. **(10 min.)**
3. Have students answer the **Après la lecture** questions. **(5 min.)**

Variations littéraires

Variations littéraires

L'heure du chant dans ma classe m'attira[1] l'envie des maîtresses des classes avoisinantes[2].

— Que se passe-t-il ? Tous les jours, à présent, de ta classe, c'est un concert.

Il n'y avait rien à comprendre puisque je n'avais guère jusque-là brillé comme maîtresse de chant.

Notre vieil inspecteur des écoles, au cours de sa visite, en fut[3] tout stupéfait.

— Comment se fait-il ! Vos élèves chantent mille fois mieux que ceux des années passées !

Puis il cessa de me guetter[4] pour me demander plutôt de faire chanter encore une fois mes enfants, et la première chose que je sus[5], il était parti au loin d'une rêverie heureuse où il ne paraissait même plus se souvenir qu'il était inspecteur des écoles.

APRÈS la lecture

1.2

1. Qu'est-ce que l'institutrice demande aux enfants de faire?
2. Qui est Nil?
3. Comment Nil est-il appelé? Pourquoi?
4. Pourquoi est-ce que l'inspecteur est étonné quand il entend les enfants chanter?
5. Pourquoi l'inspecteur demande-t-il à l'institutrice de faire chanter les enfants?

1. brought out 2. neighboring 3. was 4. watch 5. knew

Answers

1. de chanter ensemble
2. un jeune immigré ukrainien
3. l'alouette; il chante très bien.
4. Les élèves chantent mieux que ceux des années passées.
5. Il oublie qu'il est inspecteur quand les enfants chantent.

Cultures

Products and Perspectives

Women have played an important role in the Canadian literary world. Like Anne Hébert, Gabrielle Roy had a long and prolific writing career. She was a journalist and novelist who also wrote short stories and some children's books. Ask students if they are familiar with any famous American women writers who have had an influence on our society. 2.2

Postreading

Ask students to think about someone they admire and what they consider to be his or her greatest talent. Give them time to write a short paragraph in French describing this person. Ask volunteers to share with the class what they have written.

Language Examination

Through the practice of listening and reading comprehension, **Variations littéraires** helps students prepare for the **Interpretive Reading and Listening** and the **Presentational Writing** sections of the AP Language and Culture Exam.

Differentiated Instruction

ADVANCED LEARNERS

Ask students to imagine they are one of the people in **L'alouette** (the teacher, the principal, a student in the class, another teacher in the school). Have them talk to the rest of the class about Nil's talent and their reaction to it. What emotions do they feel when he sings? How does his talent affect their lives? 1.3

MULTIPLE INTELLIGENCES

Musical Have students with musical talent learn the song **"L'Alouette"** and teach it to the class. If the class already knows that song, have them try **"Auprès de ma blonde"**, which contains the names of several other birds. This is a good way to have students learn some new vocabulary words. You might ask students who play instruments to accompany their classmates as they sing. 1.3

Resources

Presentation:

Audio CD 5, Tr. 8

Practice:

Reading Strategies and Skills Handbook

Intermediate Reader

French InterActive Reader

Applying the Strategies

Students may find it helpful to use the "Read, Rate, and Reread" strategy from the *Reading Strategies and Skills Handbook* for this text since it is longer than previous reading selections.

READING PRACTICE

STRATEGIES

Strategy: Read, Rate, Reread

Reading Skill	When can I use this strategy?		
	Prereading	During Reading	Postreading
Making Inferences		✓	
Identifying the Main Idea		✓	✓
Determining the Writer's Purpose			✓

Strategy at a Glance: Read, Rate, Reread

- Students read a short text three times, rating their understanding of the text and writing down any questions they have after each reading.
- After the third reading, students discuss with a partner or in a small group any unanswered questions. Then students rate their understanding a fourth and final time.
- As a class, students discuss how their ratings changed between readings, as well as asking any questions they still have.

Many struggling readers don't think reading the same passage or text again does them any good. That is partly because they operate under the misconception that other readers read something once, read it somewhat effortlessly, and "get it" every time, the first time. Rereading doesn't look any different from reading, so struggling readers don't see how many times proficient readers pause, loop back a few sentences, reread up to a point, reflect, start over completely, and then perhaps proceed slowly. Moreover, as we discuss texts with students, we rarely bring up the issue of *how* to understand; we are too busy focusing on *what* students understand. Therefore, struggling readers don't hear teachers or other students talk about the words—or even chapters—that they sometimes reread several times before formulating a meaning. We need to help these students understand that rereading is something good readers do and that it is an important strategy to use when trying to understand a text.

Best Use of the Strategy

Use this strategy to offer students concrete evidence that comprehension does improve with repeated reading. We often tell students that rereading will increase their understanding of a text, but struggling readers need proof. They have years of evidence that reading does not work; therefore, they reason, why would rereading work any better? The structure provided by the **Read, Rate, Reread** strategy (Blau 1992)— the rating and questioning —provides the proof.

Prereading

Discuss **Stratégie** (analyzing chronological order) with students. Make a list on the board or on a transparency of any expressions of time that students can think of. Remind students to look for these expressions as they read the selection.

Rennes

Mémoires d'outre-tombe

François René de Chateaubriand (1768–1848) se destine d'abord à une carrière militaire, mais, après le choc de la Révolution Française (1789), il s'exile en Amérique puis en Angleterre[1]. En 1806, il voyage en Orient. Il commence ensuite une carrière diplomatique et politique. À la fin de sa vie il écrit son chef-d'œuvre autobiographique, les *Mémoires d'outre-tombe*[2], commencé en 1809 et publié après sa mort. CD 5, Tr. 8

STRATÉGIE

In a narrative, **analyzing chronological order** helps you understand the text's structure and, as a consequence the order of events. While you read, try to note the expressions of time.

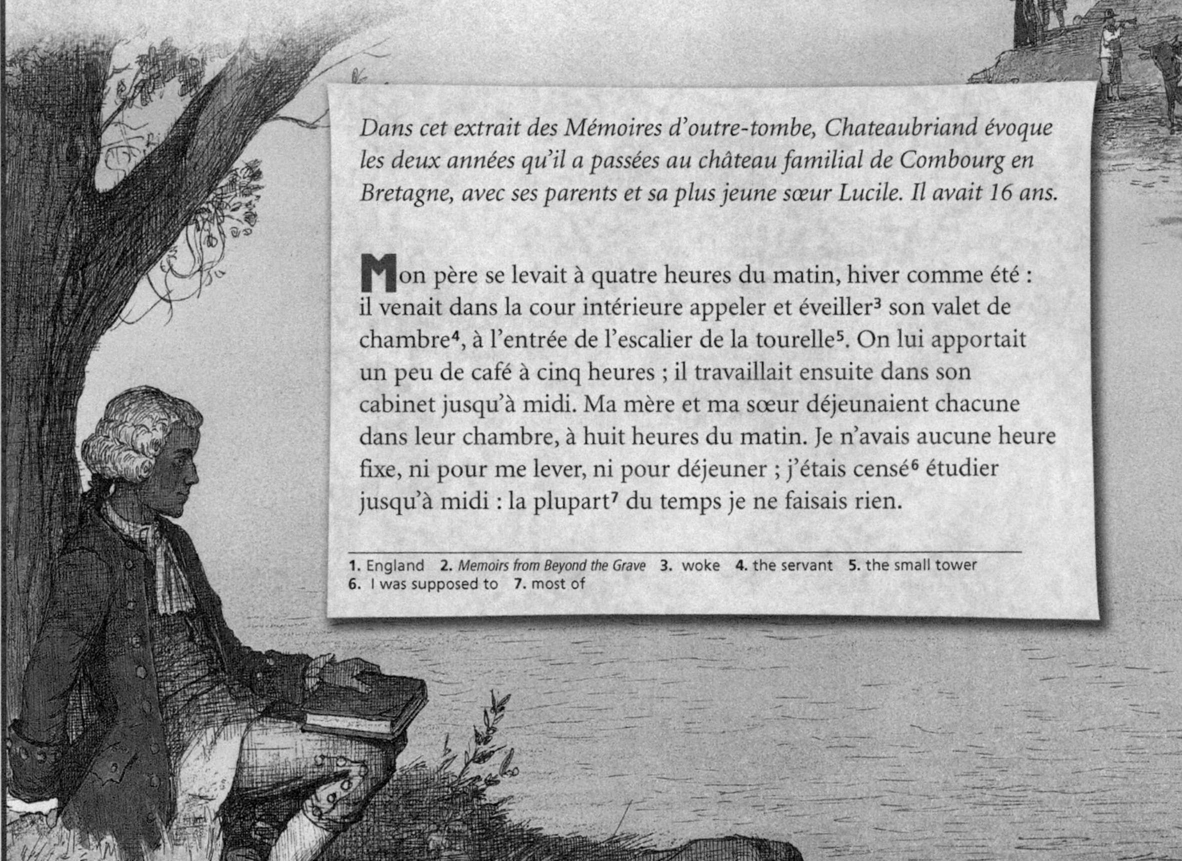

Dans cet extrait des Mémoires d'outre-tombe, Chateaubriand évoque les deux années qu'il a passées au château familial de Combourg en Bretagne, avec ses parents et sa plus jeune sœur Lucile. Il avait 16 ans.

Mon père se levait à quatre heures du matin, hiver comme été : il venait dans la cour intérieure appeler et éveiller[3] son valet de chambre[4], à l'entrée de l'escalier de la tourelle[5]. On lui apportait un peu de café à cinq heures ; il travaillait ensuite dans son cabinet jusqu'à midi. Ma mère et ma sœur déjeunaient chacune dans leur chambre, à huit heures du matin. Je n'avais aucune heure fixe, ni pour me lever, ni pour déjeuner ; j'étais censé[6] étudier jusqu'à midi : la plupart[7] du temps je ne faisais rien.

1. England **2.** *Memoirs from Beyond the Grave* **3.** woke **4.** the servant **5.** the small tower
6. I was supposed to **7.** most of

Core Instruction

VARIATIONS LITTÉRAIRES

1. Have students read the biographical paragraph about Chateaubriand. **(4 min.)**
2. Form small groups of three or four students. Provide each group with a paper that lists the hours of the day from 4 a.m. to 10 p.m. As students read, have them fill in the activities that Chateaubriand mentions next to the times when they would occur. This will help students to pick out the main activities and keep them in the proper order. **(10 min.)**
3. Have students answer the **Après la lecture** questions. **(5 min.)**

À onze heures et demie, on sonnait le dîner que l'on servait à midi. La grand'salle était à la fois salle à manger et salon : on dînait et l'on soupait à l'une de ses extrémités du côté de l'est ; après les repas, on se venait placer à l'autre extrémité du côté de l'ouest, devant une énorme cheminée. La grand'salle était boisée[1], peinte en gris blanc et ornée de vieux portraits depuis le règne de François Ier jusqu'à celui de Louis XIV[2] ; parmi ces portraits, on distinguait ceux de Condé et de Turenne[3] : un tableau représentant Hector tué par Achille sous les murs de Troie[4], était suspendu au-dessus de la cheminée.

Le dîner fait, on restait ensemble, jusqu'à deux heures. Alors, si l'été, mon père prenait le divertissement de la pêche, visitait ses potagers[5], se promenait dans l'étendue du vol du chapon[6] ; si l'automne et l'hiver, il partait pour la chasse[7], ma mère se retirait dans la chapelle, où elle passait quelques heures en prières[8]. Cette chapelle était un oratoire sombre, embelli de bons tableaux des plus grands maîtres[9], qu'on ne s'attendait guère[10] à trouver dans un château féodal, au fond de la Bretagne. J'ai aujourd'hui, en ma possession, une *Sainte Famille* de l'Albane[11], peinte sur cuivre[12], tirée de cette chapelle : c'est tout ce qui me reste de Combourg.

Mon père parti et ma mère en prières, Lucile s'enfermait[13] dans sa chambre ; je regagnais ma cellule[14], où j'allais courir les champs.

À huit heures, la cloche annonçait le souper. Après le souper, dans les beaux jours, on s'asseyait sur le perron[15]. Mon père, armé de son fusil[16], tirait des chouettes[17] qui sortaient des créneaux à l'entrée de la nuit. Ma mère, Lucile et moi, nous regardions le ciel, les bois, les derniers rayons du soleil, les premières étoiles[18]. À dix heures, on rentrait et l'on se couchait.

1. panelled with wood 2. François I (1494–1547) and Louis XIV (1638–1715) were French kings 3. generals of the French king Louis XIV 4. from Homer's The Iliad 5. the vegetable gardens 6. about an acre 7. hunting 8. prayers 9. the master 10. one would hardly expect to 11. an Italian painter 12. copper 13. locked herself up 14. cell 15. the steps of the front door 16. rifle 17. shot owls 18. stars

APRÈS la lecture

1.2, 1.3

1. Quel âge avait Chateaubriand dans ce passage?
2. Combien de repas sont évoqués? Lesquels?
3. Qu'est-ce que Chateaubriand et sa famille faisaient l'après-midi?
4. Quel objet de ce château Chateaubriand a-t-il conservé?
5. Que pensez-vous du mode de vie décrit dans le texte?

Differentiated Instruction

SLOWER PACE LEARNERS

In order to help students organize the ideas in this long text, it might be helpful to supply them with a numbered list of the activities mentioned in the reading. As an alternative, write each activity on a note card. Students can write the hour on the appropriate card and then arrange the cards in chronological order. 1.2

SPECIAL LEARNING NEEDS

Students with Visual Impairments This text is very compact, with long paragraphs and few breaks. Provide students who are visually impaired with a copy of the text in a larger font and perhaps double-spaced. If possible, move footnotes to the margin next to the line in which the word appears to make it easier for students to refer to them.

Variations littéraires

Answers

1. Il avait 16 ans.
2. trois; le déjeuner, le dîner, le souper
3. Ils restaient ensemble jusqu'à deux heures. Son père allait à la pêche, visitait ses potagers et se promenait l'été. L'automne et l'hiver, son père allait à la chasse pendant que sa mère priait dans la chapelle.
4. une peinture de la *Sainte Famille*
5. Answers will vary.

Cultures

Products and Perspectives

In 1791, Chateaubriand spent five months in America. When he returned to France, he published his novel, ***Atala,*** about the Natchez tribe in Louisiana. This interest in exotic themes is one characteristic of the Romantic literary movement with which Chateaubriand is associated. Ask students to investigate Washington Irving, who lived in Spain and wrote about the Moors and the Alhambra. 2.2

Postreading

Ask students their reactions to the daily life of the family. Do they think that Chateaubriand was happy with his life at the **château**? What was his relationship with his family? Is the lack of emotion a reflection of Chateaubriand's feelings, or simply his writing style?

Language Examination

Through the practice of listening and reading comprehension, **Variations littéraires** helps students prepare for the **Interpretive Reading and Listening** and the **Presentational Writing** sections of the AP Language and Culture Exam.

Resources

Presentation:

Audio CD 1, Tr. 6

Practice:

Reading Strategies and Skills Handbook

Intermediate Reader

French InterActive Reader

Applying the Strategies

Have students use the "Think Aloud" strategy from the *Reading Strategies and Skills Handbook* to encourage them to monitor their own reading.

READING PRACTICE

STRATEGIES

Strategy: Think Aloud

Reading Skill	When can I use this strategy?		
	Prereading	During Reading	Postreading
Monitoring Reading		✓	

Strategy at a Glance: Think Aloud

- The teacher models the **Think Aloud** strategy for students, letting them tally the types of comments the teacher makes (predicting, picturing the text, comparing, commenting, identifying a problem, or fixing a problem) on the **Think Aloud** tally sheet.
- Students practice the strategy with a partner using short and easy texts before using **Think Aloud** with their assignments.
- Students regularly practice the strategy, eventually using it on their own as needed.

Many times students do what they call reading: their eyes travel over the words from left to right and from top to bottom, and they turn pages at the appropriate time. What they don't do is pay any attention to what those words mean. That is where a strategy like **Think Aloud** can help.

The **Think Aloud** strategy helps readers think about how they make meaning. As they read, they carry on a dialog with the text. This is something that good readers do constantly as they read, although they usually do it silently. **Think Aloud** provides a structure for struggling readers to have a dialog with a text; they learn to think about their reading and to monitor what they do and do not understand. As you monitor the comments students make while using this strategy, you will see that the student is actively engaged with the text. As they do it more often, they will learn to do it silently—and that is the goal of the strategy.

Best Use of the Strategy

Use the **Think Aloud** strategy (Davey 1983; Olshavsky 1976-77) to help readers think about how they make meaning. As students read, they pause occasionally to think aloud about predicting what happens next, commenting on the text, picturing the text, making comparisons, identifying problems they are encountering with understanding, and thinking of ways to fix the problems they identify. This oral thinking not only helps the teacher understand why or how a

Prereading

Discuss **Stratégie** (prior knowledge and experiences) with students. Ask them what they know about the province of **Bretagne** where Saint-Malo is located. What can students tell about the city from the pictures they see on these pages? Ask if they know what a *corsair* or *privateer* is. (pirate; armed private ship or sailor on such a ship) Any facts that they know ahead of time will help their comprehension of an unfamiliar topic.

Saint-Malo, cité corsaire

Son nom CD 6, Tr. 6

La ville de Saint-Malo doit son nom à un moine gallois[1], Mac Low, et son surnom[2] de « cité corsaire[3] » aux nombreux corsaires qui y ont habité.

Sa devise

Longtemps indépendante, Saint-Malo est rattachée au royaume de France en 1493. Mais selon leur devise[4], « Ni Français, ni Breton, Malouin suis », les Malouins revendiquent[5] leur liberté.

STRATÉGIE

Use prior knowledge and experiences to help you understand a new text. Scan the images, captions, and headings to determine the subject matter, then think of what you already know about the topics.

Les corsaires Un corsaire était un marin[6] qui avait reçu le droit d'attaquer des bateaux ennemis, par le roi. Les règles[7] étaient strictes :

- Un marin ne pouvait pas se déclarer corsaire. Le roi ou le prince devait lui donner une lettre de marque[8]. Cette lettre le protégeait s'il était fait prisonnier. Il était considéré comme soldat par ses ennemis et il ne pouvait pas être pendu[9].
- Les corsaires ne pouvaient pas attaquer n'importe quel navire[10]. Le navire attaqué devait être un navire ennemi en temps de guerre[11].
- Le butin[12] était partagé avec l'État.

Les corsaires de Saint-Malo les plus connus sont René Duguay-Trouin (1673–1736) et Surcouf (1773–1827).

Station balnéaire
On peut profiter des plages et aussi faire de la voile, du kayak de mer et même de la plongée sous-marine.

1. a Welsh monk 2. nickname 3. a privateer was a "pirate" commissioned by the King and was protected by him 4. a motto 5. claim 6. sailor 7. rules 8. letter authorizing one to make its own justice 9. hung 10. ship 11. time of war 12. bounty

Core Instruction

VARIATIONS LITTÉRAIRES

1. Before class, post eight large pieces of paper from a flip chart on the wall. Title each paper with the heading from one of the sections of this reading selection. **(3 min.)**
2. Have students read the text one section at a time, either individually or in groups. At the end of each section, pause to have students come up and write any key words or phrases that they think are significant to the meaning of the section on the appropriate paper. **(15 min.)**
3. Discuss any vocabulary or concepts that are unclear to students. **(5 min.)**
4. Have students answer the **Après la lecture** questions. **(5 min.)**

Saint-Malo, c'est aussi ...

Le port
Au 17e siècle, Saint-Malo était le plus grand port de France grâce au commerce avec les Amériques, les Indes, la Chine et l'Afrique. Aujourd'hui, c'est un des points de départ des ferrys pour l'Angleterre, aussi des croisières sur vieux gréements[1]. C'est aussi d'où part la Course du Rhum, une course de bateaux, en solitaire, dont l'arrivée est à la Guadeloupe.

Le Grand Aquarium, ouvert depuis 1996, comprend[2] plus de 500 espèces animales et un sous-marin[3] qui emporte les visiteurs au fond des mers[4].

ANECDOTE

Pendant la Seconde Guerre mondiale[5], la cité malouine a été détruite à plus de 80%. Elle a été reconstruite à l'identique. Le chantier[6] a pris fin en 1962.

Les remparts[7] ont été construits[8] par l'ingénieur militaire Vauban pour protéger la ville de la flotte[9] anglaise.

APRÈS la lecture

1.2, 3.1

1. D'où vient le nom de Saint-Malo?
2. Qui étaient les corsaires?
3. Qui sont les plus célèbres corsaires de Saint-Malo?
4. Qui a fait construire les remparts de Saint-Malo?
5. Qu'est-ce que tu peux faire à Saint-Malo?

1. old ships 2. includes 3. submarine 4. bottom of the sea 5. World War II 6. reconstruction 7. outer walls 8. were built 9. fleet

Differentiated Instruction

SLOWER PACE LEARNERS

Students may be overwhelmed when faced with two pages of reading, even though it consists of smaller paragraphs. To encourage students, have them skim through the reading and find all the cognates they can. This may reassure students that they already know a large number of words in the reading. 1.2

MULTIPLE INTELLIGENCES

Visual-Spatial Have students use the Internet to gather more information about the city of Saint-Malo and the surrounding area. Ask students to use the information to create a travel brochure to entice people to visit the area, or to plan a trip itinerary that a travel agent might offer to his or her clients. 1.3

Variations littéraires

Answers

1. Le nom vient d'un moine gallois qui s'appelait Mac Low.
2. Les corsaires étaient des marins qui avaient reçu du roi le droit d'attaquer des bateaux ennemis.
3. René Duguay-Trouin et Surcouf
4. l'ingénieur militaire Vauban
5. On peut aller à l'aquarium et à la plage, faire de la voile, du kayak de mer et de la plongée sous-marine.

Cultures

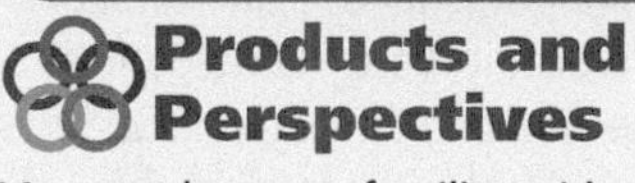

Products and Perspectives

Most students are familiar with the stereotypical pirate that they see in the movies or read about in books: the outlaw pirates who generally sailed the Caribbean. They may not realize that governments sanctioned piracy, especially during wartime. In addition to the famous corsairs of Saint-Malo, one of the best-known privateers was Britain's Sir Francis Drake. Privateers even aided the Colonies during the American Revolution by raiding British ships carrying gunpowder and arms. Have students research one of these privateers on the Internet or in the library and share their findings with the class. 2.2

Postreading

Have students use the information they have gleaned from the reading to create a travel poster that would encourage tourists to visit Saint-Malo.

Language Examination

Through the practice of listening and reading comprehension, **Variations littéraires** helps students prepare for the **Interpretive Reading and Listening** and the **Presentational Writing** sections of the AP Language and Culture Exam.

Resources

Presentation:

Audio CD 7, Tr. 8–9

Practice:

Reading Strategies and Skills Handbook

Intermediate Reader

French InterActive Reader

Applying the Strategies

Have students use the "Most Important Word" strategy from the *Reading Strategies and Skills Handbook* after reading the poems. Choosing the word they think is most important will help students reflect on what they have read.

READING PRACTICE

STRATEGIES

Strategy: Most Important Word

Reading Skill	When can I use this strategy?		
	Prereading	During Reading	Postreading
Identifying the Main Idea			✓
Making Generalizations			✓
Summarizing			✓

Strategy at a Glance: Most Important Word

- After reading a text, students discuss their responses to the theme of the work.
- Students decide either independently or in small groups what they think the Most Important Word in the text is, basing their answers on evidence from the reading.
- Students share and explain their choices.

Many times when you ask students to find the main idea of a story, or to make a generalization, or simply, "What did the story mean to you?", they can't do it, because they find the question too broad. One strategy that students can use to help them answer the question is **Most Important Word. Most Important Word** is a postreading strategy in which students decide which word in a text they think is the most important based on specific evidence in the text. As students decide which word is the most important, they begin to formulate their responses to the question: "What did the story mean to you?" **Most Important Word** leads to revealing discussions that encourage students to use this skill while they read and later reflect on what they have read.

Best Use of the Strategy

Most Important Word (Bleich 1975) is a good strategy to help students identify the theme of a reading and to make generalizations about it by breaking down the selection and deciding which word in the text carries the message that speaks to them.

Prereading

Discuss **Stratégie** (determining the main idea) with students. Tell them to keep the title of the poem in mind as they read. Sometimes the title reveals the main idea of a poem. Sometimes it is only a hint and students need to look deeper into the poem to really understand what the poet is trying to convey.

Dakar

Les poèmes de Léopold Sédar Senghor

Léopold Sédar Senghor (1906–2001) fait ses études à Dakar puis à Paris. En 1933, il obtient[1] la nationalité française et enseigne le français au lycée. Avec Aimé Césaire et Gontran Damas, il établit les fondements[2] de *la négritude*. En 1945, il devient député du Sénégal. En 1960, il est élu président de la République du Sénégal. Il est réélu cinq fois de suite. Il est élu à l'Académie française en 1983. Parmi ses recueils de poèmes, on peut citer *Chants d'ombre* (1945), *Hosties noires* (1948) et *Nocturnes* (1961). CD 7, Tr. 8-9

STRATÉGIE

In each poem, there is a main idea and relevant details that illustrate this idea. **Determining the main idea helps you understand the overall meaning of the poem.**

Et nous baignerons mon amie...

(pour khalam[3])

Et nous baignerons mon amie dans une présence africaine.
Des meubles[4] de Guinée et du Congo, graves et polis sombres et sereins.
Des masques primordiaux et purs aux murs[5], distants mais si présents !
Des tabourets[6] d'honneur pour les hôtes héréditaires, pour les Princes du Pays-Haut.
5 Des parfums fauves[7], d'épaisses[8] nattes[9] de silence
Des coussins[10] d'ombre et de loisirs, le bruit d'une source de paix[11].
Des paroles classiques ; loin, des chants alternés comme les pagnes[12] du Soudan[13].
Et puis lampe amicale, ta bonté[14] pour bercer[15] l'obsession de cette présence
Noir blanc et rouge oh ! rouge comme le sol d'Afrique.

1. acquires **2.** foundations **3.** a type of African guitar that accompanies a poem like this when it is read. **4.** furniture **5.** walls **6.** stools **7.** musky **8.** thick **9.** mats **10.** cushions **11.** peace **12.** fabric **13.** Sudan, an African country **14.** kindness **15.** to rock

Core Instruction

VARIATIONS LITTÉRAIRES

1. Read the biographical information about Senghor with the class. Explain to students the basic concept of **Négritude. (3 min.)**
2. Have students read along as they listen to the audio recording of the poem **"Et nous baignerons mon amie". (2 min.)**
3. Have students name as many items as they can find in the poem that show African influence. **(4 min.)**
4. Have students answer the **Après la lecture** questions. **(5 min.)**

Je suis seul

Je suis seul[1] dans la plaine
Et dans la nuit
Avec les arbres recroquevillés[2] de froid
Qui, coudes au corps[3], se serrent[4] les uns tout contre les autres.

5 Je suis seul dans la plaine
Et dans la nuit
Avec les gestes de désespoir[5] pathétique des arbres
Que leurs feuilles ont quittés pour des îles[6] d'élection.

Je suis seul dans la plaine
10 Et dans la nuit.
Je suis la solitude des poteaux télégraphiques[7]
Le long des routes[8]
Désertes.

1. lonely, alone 2. curled up 3. elbows to body 4. squeeze up 5. despair 6. islands 7. telegraph poles 8. along the roads

APRÈS la lecture

1.2, 1.3

Et nous baignerons mon amie

1. Quels autres pays sont mentionnés?
2. À quoi ressemble la décoration de la maison?
3. Qu'est-ce que la décoration représente?

Je suis seul

4. Comment sont les arbres?
5. Où sont parties les feuilles des arbres?
6. Qu'est-ce que les feuilles représentent?

Variations littéraires

Answers

1. la Guinée, le Congo, le Soudan
2. à la culture africaine
3. l'Afrique
4. Les arbres sont recroquevillés de froid et serrés les uns contre les autres.
5. Les feuilles sont parties aux îles.
6. Answers will vary.

Cultures

Products and Perspectives

Négritude was a literary and artistic movement that originated in the 1930s with an emphasis on maintaining the individuality of Black culture in the African colonies that were dominated by the French. Sénghor and his friends, Césaire and Damas, were influenced by the writings of Richard Wright and Langston Hughes. Ask students if they are familiar with these American writers or any present-day authors who celebrate Black culture in their works. 2.2

Postreading

Ask students to choose one of the two poems and write a short paragraph in French about the emotional effect it had on them. What techniques did the poet use to create the mood of the poem and evoke those emotions?

Differentiated Instruction

ADVANCED LEARNERS

Ask students to write a short poem in French that evokes a particular emotional reaction. Tell them that their poem does not necessarily have to rhyme. Encourage them to make use of some of the poetic devices that they have learned about, such as personification, simile, metaphor, alliteration, and so on. 1.3

SPECIAL LEARNING NEEDS

Students with Language Impairments Students may have difficulty expressing themselves verbally. They may not know how to communicate their reactions to the poems they have read. Ask students instead to draw a picture that illustrates the poem of their choice and the emotions that it evokes in them. Tell them to include specific details from the poem in their drawing to show that they understood what they read. 1.2

Language Examination

Through the practice of listening and reading comprehension, **Variations littéraires** helps students prepare for the **Interpretive Reading and Listening** and the **Presentational Writing** sections of the AP Language and Culture Exam.

Resources

Presentation:

Audio CD 8, Tr. 8

Practice:

Reading Strategies and Skills Handbook

Intermediate Reader

French InterActive Reader

Applying the Strategies

Have students use the "Logographic Cues" strategy from the *Reading Strategies and Skills Handbook* to help organize the information in this reading selection.

READING PRACTICE

STRATEGIES

Strategy: Logographic Cues

Reading Skill	When can I use this strategy? Prereading	During Reading	Postreading
Understanding Text Structure	✓	✓	✓
Analyzing Chronological Order		✓	✓
Making Generalizations and Understanding Text Structure		✓	✓

Strategy at a Glance: Logographic Cues

- Logographs are graphic representations of ideas. The **Logographic Cues** strategy uses simple pictures that represent or symbolize key ideas in a text.
- Students can use logographs to identify textual elements or organize and remember information.

Dr. Kylene Beers explains the **Logographic Cues** strategy with the following story:

I sat in the train station in Chaumont, France, wondering why I had taken Latin instead of French in high school and college. At that moment, I wanted to know if my train to Dijon was leaving when I thought it was. Blank stares and pitying shakes of the head were all I received when people realized that I was limited to English. Finally, I took out my map of the region, drew a train, circled my destination, and wrote the date and time of my departure. Underneath it all I put a big question mark. The clerk behind the window finally understood my question: Is the train from Chaumont to Dijon still departing today from this station at 3:48? "Oui," she said, nodding her head.

Hours later, as I sat on the train, I realized that although I couldn't read French words, I *could* read musical notation, numbers, and international signs. I could read information that was presented logographically, but not information presented alphabetically. A Logographic Cue was worth a million French words.

"And why not?" I thought. Our first understanding of written language is a logographic understanding. Three- and four-year-olds who recognize their names in print rarely do so because they attach sounds to letters; instead, they simply recognize the shape of their printed names. Logographs, or picture cues, remain helpful when students are confronted with an alphabetic principle or text that they don't understand.

Prereading

Discuss **Stratégie** (using text organizers) with students. Explain to them that there are many ways to organize and classify material. What is effective for one student may not work well for another. Encourage students to find a system that works for them and make use of it when they read detailed material.

Dakar

La mendiante et l'écolière

Fatou Diome est née en 1968 au Sénégal. Elle est étudiante à l'université de Dakar quand elle rencontre son futur mari qui est français. Ils s'installent en France en 1994, où elle continue ses études de Lettres[1]. Son premier recueil[2] de nouvelles[3], *La Préférence Nationale*, est publié en 2001. Ses histoires sont en grande partie autobiographiques. Son premier roman *Le ventre de l'Atlantique* est publié en 2003. En Alsace, Fatou Diome est à la fois étudiante en doctorat de Lettres, présentatrice d'émissions littéraires à la télévision et écrivain. CD 8, Tr. 8

STRATÉGIE

When a text presents a lot of material, **using text organizers** helps you classify, summarize, and therefore understand information. For instance, you can create a chart such as a spider to organize the information about different characters.

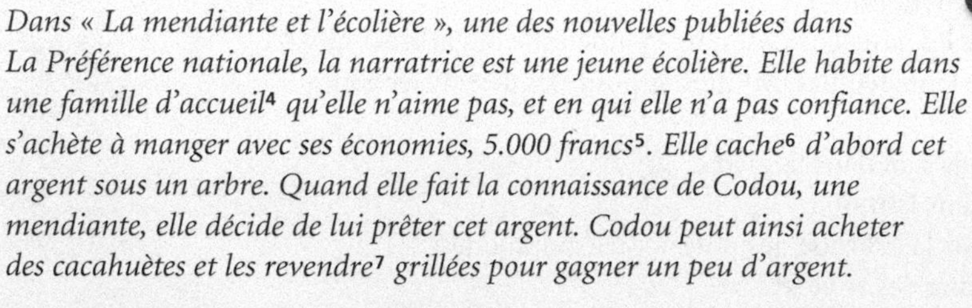

Dans « La mendiante et l'écolière », une des nouvelles publiées dans La Préférence nationale, la narratrice est une jeune écolière. Elle habite dans une famille d'accueil[4] qu'elle n'aime pas, et en qui elle n'a pas confiance. Elle s'achète à manger avec ses économies, 5.000 francs[5]. Elle cache[6] d'abord cet argent sous un arbre. Quand elle fait la connaissance de Codou, une mendiante, elle décide de lui prêter cet argent. Codou peut ainsi acheter des cacahuètes et les revendre[7] grillées pour gagner un peu d'argent.

Foundiougne était le centre actif d'une région agricole. Les paysans[8] y venaient vendre leur récolte d'arachides[9], ce qui rendait le commerce des cacahuètes florissant[10] : il suffisait d'avoir du bois, du sel et un peu d'argent pour y participer. Comme Codou ne manquait que de ce dernier élément, je proposai de lui prêter mes 5 000 F avec lesquels elle achèterait deux sacs d'arachides au marché pour apprêter[11] les cacahuètes. Quant au[12] point de vente, il était tout trouvé puisque Codou habitait en face du collège, il lui suffisait de se tenir[13] devant chez elle pour intercepter la clientèle captive des collégiens dont l'unique goûter, souvent, consistait en un cornet[14] de cacahuètes.

1. Literature and Linguistics **2.** collection **3.** short stories **4.** host family **5.** 5.000 francs CFA (about 9 dollars) **6.** hides **7.** resell **8.** peasants **9.** peanuts **10.** flourishing **11.** prepare **12.** as far as **13.** all she had to do was to stand **14.** cone

Core Instruction

VARIATIONS LITTÉRAIRES

1. Read and discuss with the class the biographical information about Fatou Diome and the introduction to the story. **(4 min.)**
2. Have the students read the story carefully and make use of the many reading strategies they have learned. **(8 min.)**
3. Discuss the two women in the story. What do they have in common? How are they different? You might want to make a chart or Venn diagram on the board or on a transparency to illustrate the comparisons. **(5 min.)**
4. Have students answer the **Après la lecture** questions. **(5 min.)**

Pour le remboursement, nous avions passé un contrat oral : il était convenu qu'elle me donnerait tous les jours de classe, à l'heure du déjeuner, deux cornets de cacahuètes pour la contre-valeur[1] de 20 F, plus trois pièces de 10 F pour l'achat d'un quart de pain. Dès que Codou eut commencé[2] son petit commerce, je lui laissai un carnet[3] où je consignais soigneusement le montant versé[4] ainsi que la valeur restante[5]. Avec ses petits bénéfices[6], Codou nourrissait sa famille ; elle avait même réussi à renouveler[7] son stock d'arachides et sa mendicité[8] n'était plus qu'un triste souvenir.

Je marchais. 4 950 F, me répétais-je, après-demain ça fera 5 000 F de remboursement. C'est la fin[9], oui, la faim. J'étais presque contente en arrivant chez Codou de n'avoir pu acheter mon quart de baguette. Les 30 F rescapés[10] me feraient encore trois cornets de thiaf[11].

— Mais où est ton pain, me questionna Codou.

— La boulangerie est fermée, dis-je.

— Oh petite, dit-elle navrée[12], il fallait hâter le pas[13], tu es toujours rêveuse. Tiens voilà tes deux cornets de thiaf, et un troisième pour compenser ton bout de pain ; mais ne le compte[14] pas, je te l'offre.

— Où est le carnet, lui demandai-je après l'avoir remerciée, je vais noter les 20 F d'aujourd'hui et je te rends les 30 F du pain pour...

— Ne t'en fais pas[15] petite, on ne note rien aujourd'hui, reprit-elle fermement.

— Mais si mame Codou, rétorquai-je[16], d'ailleurs dans deux jours tu ne me devras plus rien[17]. Tu m'as déjà rendu 50 F x 99 moins les 30 F du pain ce qui fait...

— Arrête donc petite, dit-elle en faisant de sa main incurvée une béquille pour sa voix[18], je ne sais ni lire ni écrire, mais je sais combien ça fait. Sache[19] qu'il y a des choses que l'école des Blancs ne t'apprendra jamais à évaluer. Et puisque personne n'a inventé une mesure pour l'amitié, tes cornets de cacahuètes et tes sous pour le pain t'attendront toujours chez moi. À demain petite, je ferai de beaux cornets de thiaf avec notre petit carnet.

APRÈS la lecture

1.2, 1.3

1. Que mangent les collégiens au goûter?
2. Que mange la narratrice au déjeuner d'habitude?
3. Que mange-t-elle ce jour-là?
4. Est-ce que Codou est toujours mendiante?
5. Pourquoi est-ce que la narratrice dit «C'est la fin, oui, la faim»?
6. Pourquoi est-ce que la narratrice veut son petit carnet?
7. Selon Codou, qu'est-ce qui n'a pas de prix?

1. exchange value 2. as soon as Codou started 3. notebook 4. I carefully put down the sum she had paid me 5 remaining 6. profits 7. renew 8. begging 9. end 10. saved 11. grilled peanuts (slang) 12. sorry 13. to hurry 14. don't count it 15. Don't worry 16. I answered back 17. you won't owe me anything any more 18. cupping her hand over her mouth 19. let me tell you

Variations littéraires

Answers

1. Ils mangent un cornet de cacahuètes.
2. Elle mange deux cornets de cacahuètes et un quart de pain.
3. Elle mange trois cornets de cacahuètes sans pain.
4. Non, la mendicité n'est qu'un "triste souvenir" pour elle.
5. Elle commence à tirer profit de son commerce avec Codou.
6. Elle veut noter ce qu'elle doit à Codou.
7. C'est l'amitié qui n'a pas de prix.

Comparisons

Comparing and Contrasting

In her 2003 novel, ***Le ventre de l'Atlantique,*** Fatou Diome touches on the theme of immigration. France has a large population of immigrants from its former colonies in North Africa. There has been unrest and rioting throughout the country in protest against poverty, unemployment, and crime in the housing projects in the suburbs of the big cities of France. What immigration problems are students aware of in the United States, and how do they compare?

4.2

Postreading

Have students write a short essay about the deal that the two women made and how each one profited from it. In their opinion, which one of the two women gained more from the deal?

Differentiated Instruction

ADVANCED LEARNERS

This reading selection has an obvious moral about the value of friendship being more important than money. Have students write a fable that conveys the same moral. Remind them that the main characters in a fable are usually animals that speak or act like human beings.

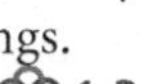

1.3

SPECIAL LEARNING NEEDS

Students with Learning Disabilities Students may be better able to understand the financial deal that the women made if you demonstrate it as a simple algebra problem. You might use play money to show the 5,000 F that the student loaned to her friend and the 50 F that she got back each day. They should then be able to calculate that the loan would be paid off after 100 days.

3.1

Language Examination

Through the practice of listening and reading comprehension, **Variations littéraires** helps students prepare for the **Interpretive Reading and Listening** and the **Presentational Writing** sections of the AP Language and Culture Exam.

Resources

Presentation:

Audio CD 9, Tr. 8

Practice:

Reading Strategies and Skills Handbook

Intermediate Reader

French InterActive Reader

Applying the Strategies

You may want to use the "Say Something" strategy from the *Reading Strategies and Skills Handbook* to help keep students focused on their reading.

READING PRACTICE

Strategy: Say Something

STRATEGIES

Reading Skill	When can I use this strategy?		
	Prereading	During Reading	Postreading
Using Prior Knowledge (Drawing from Your Own Experience)	✓		
Monitoring Reading		✓	

Strategy at a Glance: Say Something

- The teacher models the strategy by "saying something" about a text with a colleague or by reading and discussing a typed **Say Something** dialogue with students.
- Students read a short text, stopping occasionally to discuss the text with a partner. In their conversations, they must make a prediction, ask a question, make a comment, or make a connection.
- Students practice **Say Something** using very short texts before using the strategy with longer assignments.

Often readers are unable to discuss something they have just finished reading because while they were reading, their eyes were merely moving over the words, their minds moving to thoughts of weekend plans, last night's phone conversations, or after-school sports events. They don't focus on what they are reading. To help students break that habit, we need to help them pay attention to what they are reading. **Say Something** is a very simple strategy that keeps readers focused on a text. **Say Something** helps students think about what they are reading by helping them see where they aren't paying attention.

Best Use of the Strategy

Say Something (Horste, Short, and Burke 1988) is a strategy in which students occasionally pause and "say something" to a partner about what they have read. This strategy helps students comprehend what they are reading by helping them to stay focused. Telling students to say something about the text, or giving them specific types of things they can say, keeps them interacting with the text and from that interaction comes meaning.

Getting the Strategy to Work

1. **First, model the strategy.** In order to model the **Say Something** strategy, it is best if you can recruit a colleague to help you demonstrate the strategy. Read aloud each piece of text you will comment on to the students, so they can understand what you

Prereading

After reading an entire text, students will sometimes say, "I didn't understand it." Discuss **Stratégie** (monitoring comprehension) with them. Remind students that asking themselves questions as they read helps them to stay focused. This strategy also helps them realize exactly which passages they do not understand.

La littérature au cinéma

CD 9, Tr. 8

Les Trois Mousquetaires d'Alexandre Dumas, *Le Bossu* de Paul Féval, *Le Hussard sur le toit* de Jean Giono ou encore *Un long dimanche de fiançailles* de Sébastien Japrisot sont connus du large public grâce à leurs adaptations au cinéma. Certains auteurs français, comme Jules Verne ou Marcel Pagnol sont tout particulièrement appréciés du grand écran. Une des adaptations cinématographiques les plus réussies est celle de la pièce *Cyrano de Bergerac* par Jean-Paul Rappeneau (1990), avec Gérard Depardieu dans le rôle principal.

STRATÉGIE

Monitoring your comprehension of a text enables you to make adjustments when necessary. Ask yourself "W" questions (*who, what, when, where* and *why*) about the text as you read. Then re-read or use a dictionary to answer the question before going on.

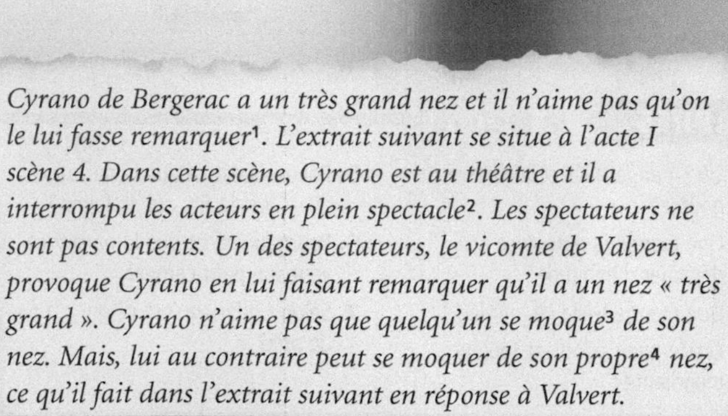

Cyrano de Bergerac a un très grand nez et il n'aime pas qu'on le lui fasse remarquer[1]. L'extrait suivant se situe à l'acte I scène 4. Dans cette scène, Cyrano est au théâtre et il a interrompu les acteurs en plein spectacle[2]. Les spectateurs ne sont pas contents. Un des spectateurs, le vicomte de Valvert, provoque Cyrano en lui faisant remarquer qu'il a un nez « très grand ». Cyrano n'aime pas que quelqu'un se moque[3] de son nez. Mais, lui au contraire peut se moquer de son propre[4] nez, ce qu'il fait dans l'extrait suivant en réponse à Valvert.

1. notice 2. in the middle of the show 3. makes fun 4. own

Core Instruction

VARIATIONS LITTÉRAIRES

1. Read the introductory paragraph with the class. Ask students if they are familiar with any of the movies, authors, actors, or directors mentioned. **(2 min.)**
2. Ask students what they know about the story of Cyrano de Bergerac. Have students discuss their background knowledge as a prereading strategy. **(3 min.)**
3. Have students read the paragraph that sets the scene. **(2 min.)**
4. Have individual students do their best to read aloud Cyrano's insults in the suggested tone. **(5 min.)**
5. Have students answer the **Après la lecture** questions. **(5 min.)**

Variations littéraires

CYRANO

Ah ! non ! c'est un peu court, jeune homme !
On pouvait dire… Oh ! Dieu !... bien des choses en somme[1]…
En variant le ton, — par exemple, tenez :
Agressif : « Moi, monsieur, si j'avais un tel nez,
Il faudrait sur le champ que je me l'amputasse[2] ! »
Amical : « Mais il doit tremper[3] dans votre tasse :
Pour boire, faites-vous fabriquer un hanap[4] ! »
Descriptif : « C'est un roc ! ... c'est un pic[5].. . c'est un cap[6] !
Que dis-je, c'est un cap ? ... c'est une péninsule ! »
Curieux : « De quoi sert cette oblongue capsule ?
D'écritoire[7], monsieur, ou de boîte à ciseaux ? »
Gracieux : « Aimez-vous à ce point les oiseaux
Que paternellement vous vous préoccupâtes[8]
De tendre ce perchoir[9] à leurs petites pattes ? » [. . .]
— Voilà ce qu'à peu près[10], mon cher, vous m'auriez dit,
Si vous aviez un peu de lettres et d'esprit[11] :
Mais d'esprit, ô[12] le plus lamentable des êtres,
Vous n'en eûtes[13] jamais un atome, et de lettres
Vous n'avez que les trois qui forment le mot : sot[14] ! [. . .]

1. all in all, in short 2. amputated it 3. to dip 4. goblet 5. peak (mountain) 6. cape (land) 7. writing case 8. preoccupied 9. perch 10. (just) about 11. education and wit 12. oh! 13. had 14. fool

APRÈS la lecture

1.2, 1.3

1. Quels romans ont été réalisés au cinéma?
2. Quelle pièce de théâtre est-ce que Jean-Paul Rappeneau a adapté au cinéma? Qui est l'acteur principal?
3. D'après toi, est-ce que Cyrano aime qu'on parle de son nez? Pourquoi?
4. Connais-tu d'autres œuvres littéraires qui ont été adaptées au cinéma?

Differentiated Instruction

SLOWER PACE LEARNERS

Students may have difficulty reading longer texts. For them, using movies in the classroom can be an effective tool for learning. Many students today are very familiar with Disney animated films. If they already know the plot and most of the dialog in English, students can listen to the French dialog and make connections with what they already know. 1.2

MULTIPLE INTELLIGENCES

Interpersonal Students often excel in peer-teaching activities. You might pair these students with slower pace students who have difficulty understanding this text. Since this reading selection is written in verse, sentences are not always in the typical subject-verb order, making it difficult to understand. Students working with a partner may be better able to decipher the meaning. 1.2

Variations littéraires

Answers

1. *Les Trois Mousquetaires, Le Bossu, Le Hussard sur le toit, Un long dimanche de fiançailles*
2. *Cyrano de Bergerac*; Gérard Depardieu
3. Answers will vary.
4. Answers will vary.

Comparisons

Comparing and Contrasting

There was an actual Cyrano de Bergerac on whose life Edmond Rostand loosely based his play. The real Cyrano was a dramatist who also wrote several fictional accounts of travels to the Sun and the Moon. Although Rostand's hero is legendary, he does not really have much in common with Cyrano the man. Can students name any American historical figures who have become legendary due to stories that have been told about their lives? 4.2

Postreading

Have groups of students act out their favorite passage in the reading. You might ask one student to play the role of moderator, who introduces and sets the scene for the presentation.

Language Examination

Through the practice of listening and reading comprehension, **Variations littéraires** helps students prepare for the **Interpretive Reading and Listening** and the **Presentational Writing** sections of the AP Language and Culture Exam.

Variations littéraires

Resources

Presentation:

Audio CD 10, Tr. 8

Practice:

Reading Strategies and Skills Handbook

Intermediate Reader

French InterActive Reader

Applying the Strategies

The "Save the Last Word for Me" strategy from the *Reading Strategies and Skills Handbook* will help students get involved in the selection and find personal meaning in it.

READING PRACTICE

STRATEGIES

Strategy: Save the Last Word for Me

Reading Skill	When can I use this strategy?		
	Prereading	During Reading	Postreading
Comparing and Contrasting			✓
Determining the Main Idea			✓

Strategy at a Glance: Save the Last Word for Me

- After reading a text, students prepare a **Last Word** card: they write their favorite passage from the text on the front of the card; on the back of the card, they write why they like that passage.
- In small groups, students take turns reading their selected passages. The others in the group give their response to the passage.
- After everyone has finished making comments, each student reads his or her comments about the passage, thus having the "last word" about the passage.

Some readers struggle through texts, and when they have finished, they have nothing to say about what they have read. Maybe it's because they never seem to get it right. No one wants to be told continually that their answers are wrong, so rather than speak up in class about what they have read, they just proclaim that they have nothing to say. They either can't answer the question ("What do you want to say about the story?") or they risk an answer, only to discover that their answer is wrong. Eventually, they learn to distrust their own responses, and finally, they don't even bother to form them. When that happens, these readers must be convinced to trust their ability to form responses and to recognize that all readers—including good readers—constantly refine their responses based on what they already know, what they learn from the text, and from others. A strategy that helps readers learn to trust their own responses while learning from others' responses is called **Save the Last Word for Me**. This strategy requires students to choose a portion of a text that they particularly like and to copy that text onto the front of a note card. On the back of the card, they explain what that sentence or passage means to them. Next, students get into small groups and share their passages. The listeners respond to the passage by saying what it means to them. After everyone has finished making comments, the student who wrote the comment turns the card over and shares what he or she has written. At that point, no one can refute, add to, change, or argue with what is said. The last word belongs to that student. Students are willing to participate in **Save the Last Word for Me** because it allows each voice to be heard and, at the same time, gives each participant the opportunity to be the authority.

Prereading

Discuss **Stratégie** (root words) with students. This is a strategy that requires practice, much like identifying indirect cognates. Some students will just skip over unfamiliar words; others will immediately consult their dictionary. Tell students that if they can learn to identify root words and their derived forms, it will greatly increase their comprehension and decrease their need for a dictionary.

Nice

Mondo et autres histoires

Jean-Marie Le Clézio est né à Nice en 1940. Il commence à écrire vers l'âge de huit ans et publie son premier roman, *Le procès-verbal*, en 1963. Son œuvre[1] est composée de romans, d'histoires pour enfants et d'essais. Elle compte plus de trente volumes dont son chef-d'œuvre *Désert* (1980). « Mondo » provient du recueil de contes *Mondo et autres histoires* (1978). CD 10, Tr. 8

STRATÉGIE

Using root words to expand vocabulary When you know one word, you can often guess the meaning of a related word. These derived forms often have a similar meaning. For example, **le pêcheur** means *the fisherman*. You can guess that the meaning of the verb **pêcher** is *to fish*.

Mondo est un petit garçon d'une dizaine d'années arrivé un jour dans la ville. Personne ne sait d'où il vient, ni pourquoi il est là. Il vit libre et seul, et se cache[2] la nuit pour ne pas être emporté par l'Assistance publique ou par la police. Pendant ses promenades, il parle avec des habitants ; certains sont mêmes devenus ses amis. Dans cet extrait, il discute avec Giordan le Pêcheur.

Un jour, pas très loin en mer, ils avaient vu un grand cargo noir qui glissait[3] sans bruit.

« Comment s'appelle-t-il ? » demandait Mondo.

Giordan le Pêcheur mettait sa main en visière et plissait ses yeux[4].

« *Erythrea* », disait-il ; puis il s'étonnait un peu :

« Tu n'as pas de bons yeux. »

« Ce n'est pas cela », disait Mondo. « Je ne sais pas lire. »

« Ah bon ? » disait Giordan.

Ils regardaient longuement le cargo qui passait.

« Qu'est-ce que ça veut dire, le nom du bateau ? » demandait Mondo.

« Erythrea ? C'est un nom de pays, sur la côte d'Afrique, sur la mer Rouge. »

« C'est un joli nom », disait Mondo. « Ça doit être un beau pays.»

1. His work 2. hides 3. glided along 4. shaded his eyes with his hand and squinted

Core Instruction

VARIATIONS LITTÉRAIRES

1. Read the biography of Jean-Marie Le Clézio with the class. **(2 min.)**
2. Have a student read aloud the introductory paragraph. **(2 min.)**
3. Form groups of three. Ask one student in each group to read the part of Mondo, another to be Giordan le Pêcheur, and a third to read the narrative material. Give each group a chance to read part of the story aloud. **(8 min.)**
4. Have students answer the **Après la lecture** questions. **(5 min.)**

Mondo réfléchissait un instant.

« Et la mer là-bas s'appelle la mer Rouge ? »

Giordan le Pêcheur riait :

« Tu crois que là-bas la mer est vraiment rouge ? »

« Je ne sais pas », disait Mondo.

« Quand le soleil se couche, la mer devient rouge, c'est vrai. Mais elle s'appelle comme ça à cause des hommes qui vivaient là autrefois[1]. »

Mondo regardait le cargo qui s'éloignait[2].

« Il va sûrement là-bas, vers l'Afrique. »

« C'est loin », disait Giordan le Pêcheur. « Il fait très chaud là-bas, il y a beaucoup de soleil et la côte est comme le désert. »

« Il y a des palmiers ? »

« Oui, et des plages de sable[3] très longues. Dans la journée, la mer est très bleue, il y a beaucoup de petits bateaux de pêche avec des voiles en forme d'aile[4], ils naviguent le long de la côte, de village en village. »

« Alors on peut rester assis sur la plage et regarder passer les bateaux ? On reste assis à l'ombre[5], et on se raconte des histoires en regardant les bateaux sur la mer ? »

« Les hommes travaillent, ils réparent les filets[6] et ils clouent[7] des plaques de zinc sur la coque[8] des bateaux échoués dans le sable. Les enfants vont chercher des brindilles[9] sèches et ils allument des feux sur la plage pour faire chauffer la poix qui sert à colmater les fissures des bateaux[10]. »

Giordan le Pêcheur ne regardait plus sa ligne maintenant. Il regardait au loin, vers l'horizon, comme s'il cherchait à voir vraiment tout cela.

1. in the past 2. moved away 3. sand 4. wing 5. in the shade 6. the nets 7. nail down 8. hull 9. twigs 10. to heat the pitch which is used to fill in cracks in the boats

APRÈS la lecture

1.2, 1.3

1. Est-ce que Mondo voit bien?
2. Où va le grand cargo noir?
3. Selon les personnages, pourquoi la « mer Rouge » s'appelle-t-elle ainsi?
4. Pourquoi est-ce que le pêcheur « ne regardait plus sa ligne? »
5. À ton avis, qu'est-ce que Mondo aide le pêcheur à faire?

Variations littéraires

Answers

1. Mondo voit bien, mais il ne sait pas lire.
2. Il va vers l'Afrique.
3. La mer Rouge s'appelle ainsi à cause des hommes qui vivaient là autrefois.
4. Il rêve du pays qu'il vient de décrire.
5. Answers will vary.

Cultures

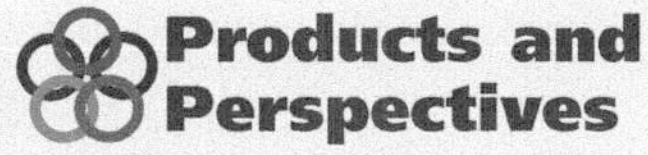

Products and Perspectives

Le Clézio's life has been marked by a series of travels. The experience that most affected him was the time that he spent among the Embera Indians in Panama. One theme that appears in his works is that of a search for cultural identity. He has said that he has been influenced by the works of James Joyce and Robert Louis Stevenson. How do the lives of these three authors compare? 2.2

Postreading

Make a list of nouns, adjectives, and adverbs derived from verbs that students know. Have students try to come up with the verb and guess the meaning of the derived word. Have students look for any typical prefixes or suffixes that were used in creating the new words. (**pêcher/pêcheur: -eur** suffix)

Differentiated Instruction

ADVANCED LEARNERS

If students are familiar with Ernest Hemingway's novel *The Old Man and the Sea,* you might ask them to compare it to this reading selection. Do they see any similarities in the characters, the setting, the ideas expressed by the characters, or the style of writing? 3.1

SPECIAL LEARNING NEEDS

Students with Auditory Impairments
Students with significant auditory impairment will have trouble following along as others are reading aloud in class. Such an activity will be of no benefit to them and may make them feel excluded. Supply them with the audio recording and let them listen to the text on their own with a headset during this time.

Language Examination

Through the practice of listening and reading comprehension, **Variations littéraires** helps students prepare for the **Interpretive Reading and Listening** and the **Presentational Writing** sections of the AP Language and Culture Exam.

Références

La France

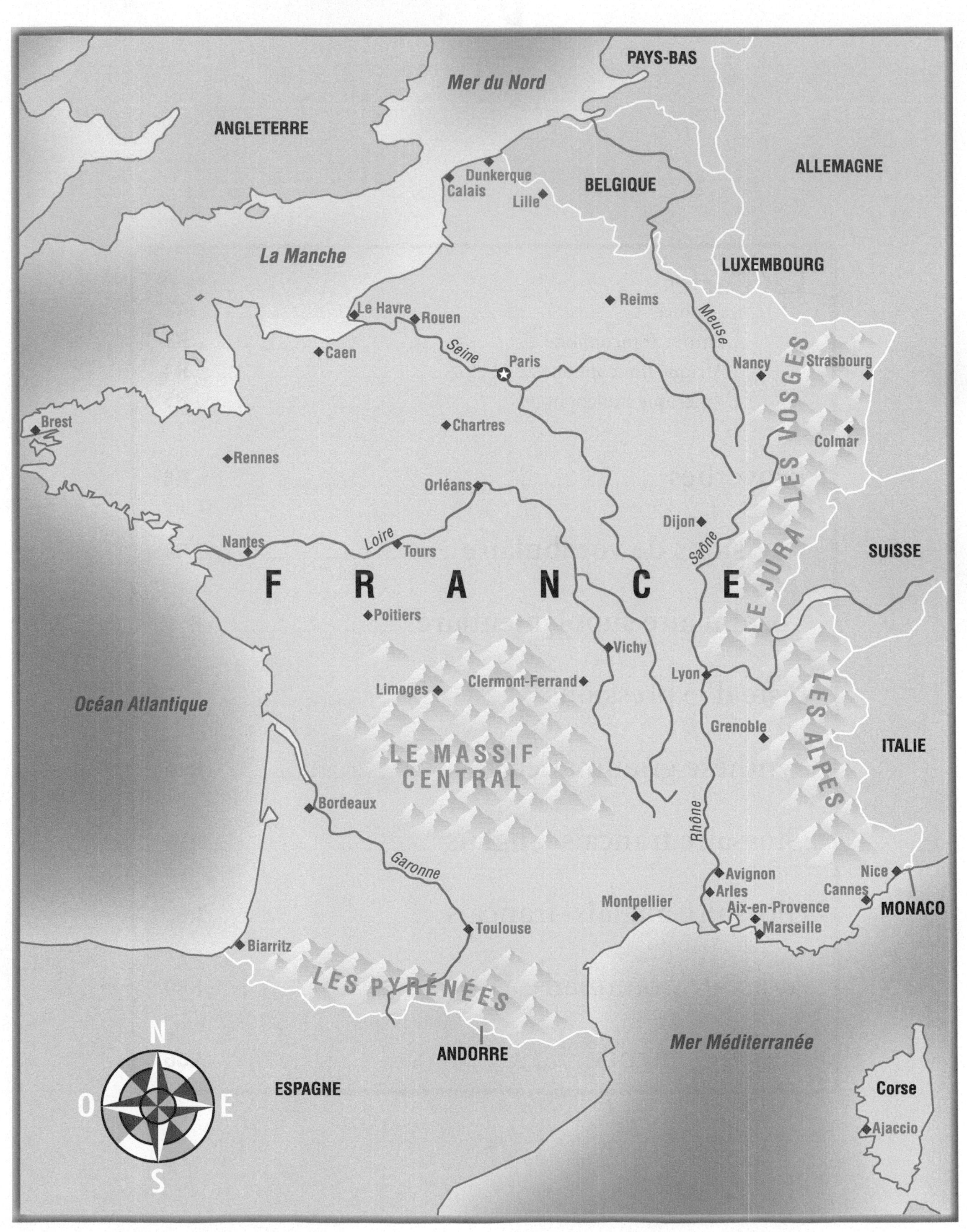

PAYS-BAS
Mer du Nord
ANGLETERRE
ALLEMAGNE
Dunkerque
Calais
BELGIQUE
Lille
La Manche
LUXEMBOURG
Reims
Meuse
Le Havre
Rouen
Caen
Seine
Paris
Nancy
Strasbourg
LES VOSGES
Brest
Chartres
Colmar
Rennes
Orléans
Dijon
Nantes
Loire
Tours
Saône
SUISSE
LE JURA
F R A N C E
Poitiers
Vichy
Lyon
Limoges
Clermont-Ferrand
Océan Atlantique
LES ALPES
Grenoble
ITALIE
LE MASSIF CENTRAL
Bordeaux
Rhône
Garonne
Avignon
Nice
Arles
Cannes
Montpellier
Aix-en-Provence
MONACO
Toulouse
Marseille
Biarritz
LES PYRÉNÉES
ANDORRE
Mer Méditerranée
N
O
E
S
ESPAGNE
Corse
Ajaccio

L'Europe francophone

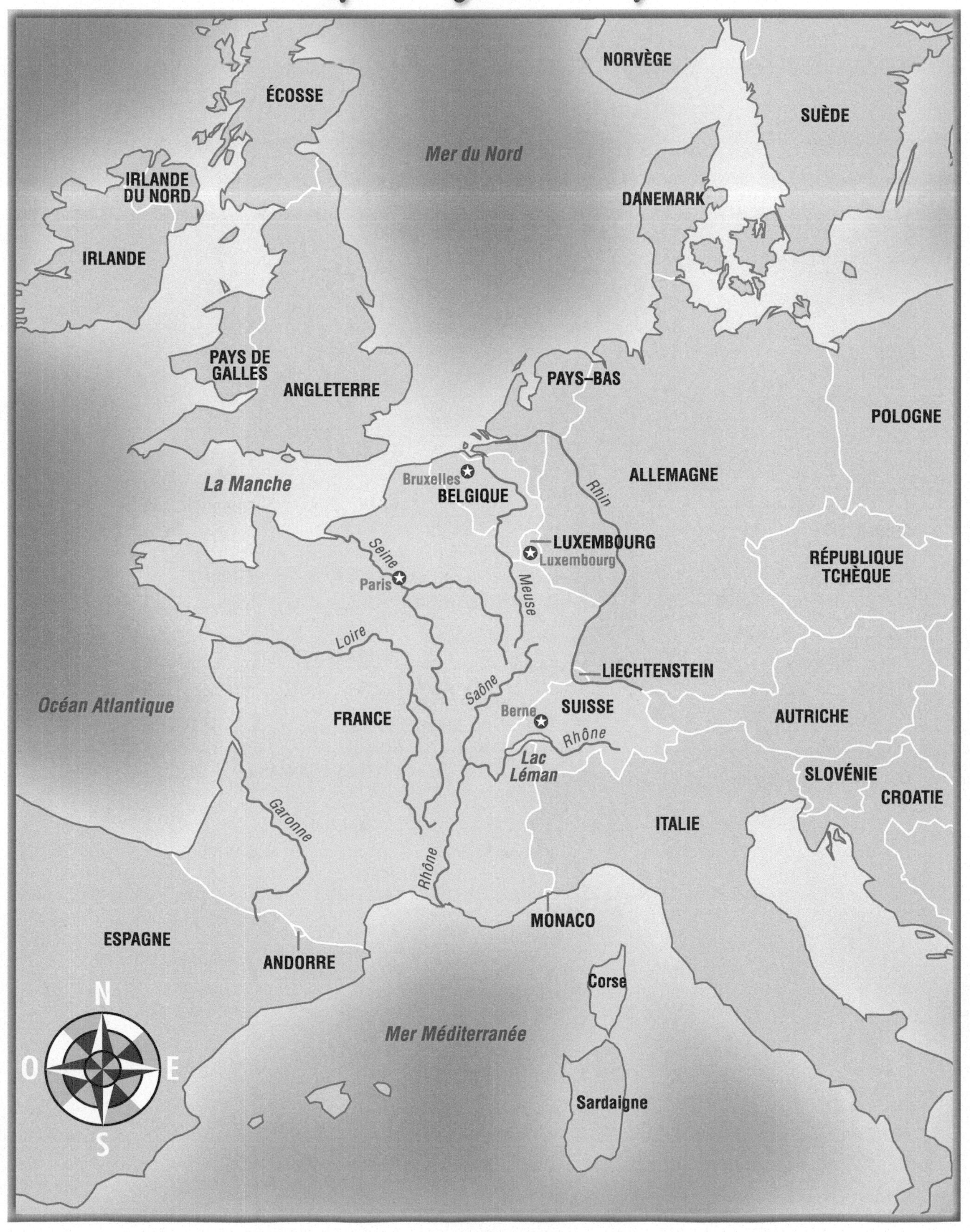

L'Europe francophone

L'Afrique francophone

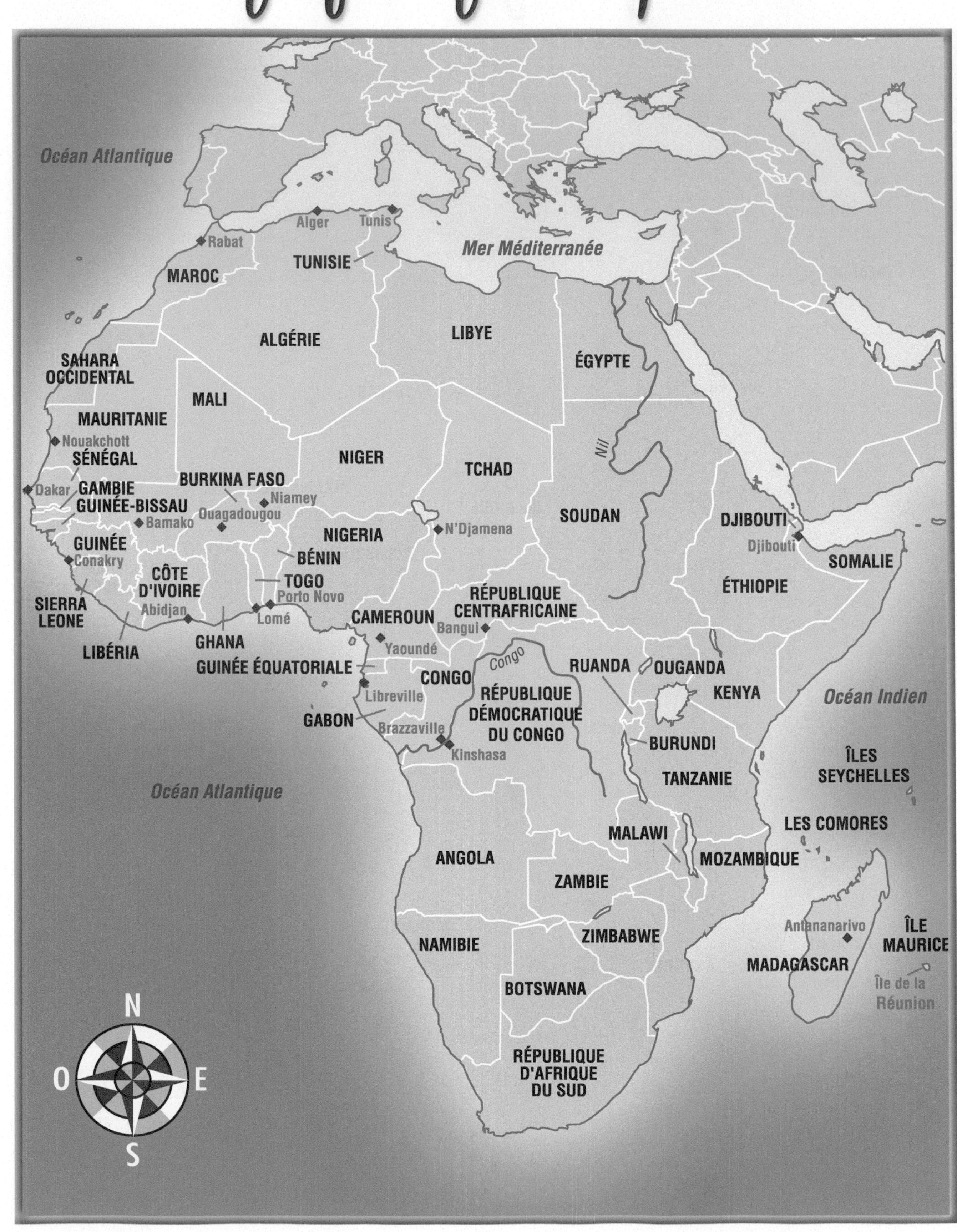

L'Afrique francophone

L'Amérique francophone

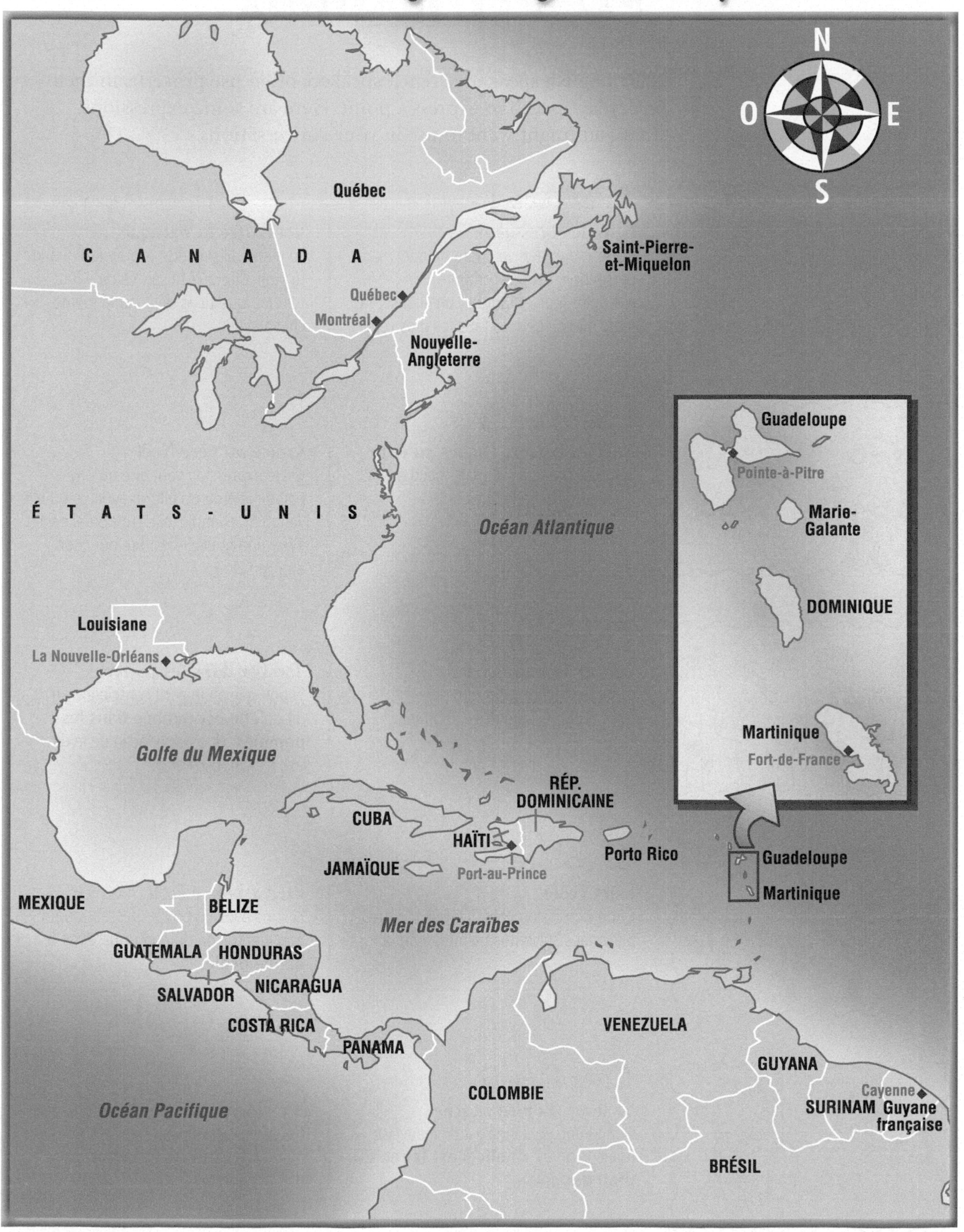

N
O
E
S
Québec
CANADA
Saint-Pierre-et-Miquelon
Québec
Montréal
Nouvelle-Angleterre
ÉTATS-UNIS
Océan Atlantique
Guadeloupe
Pointe-à-Pitre
Marie-Galante
DOMINIQUE
Martinique
Fort-de-France
Louisiane
La Nouvelle-Orléans
Golfe du Mexique
RÉP. DOMINICAINE
CUBA
HAÏTI
Porto Rico
JAMAÏQUE
Port-au-Prince
Guadeloupe
Martinique
MEXIQUE
BELIZE
Mer des Caraïbes
GUATEMALA
HONDURAS
SALVADOR
NICARAGUA
COSTA RICA
PANAMA
VENEZUELA
GUYANA
COLOMBIE
Cayenne
SURINAM
Guyane française
Océan Pacifique
BRÉSIL

Proverbes et expressions

Like English speakers, French speakers often use proverbs in their everyday speech to express a point. Here are some expressions that you might want to use in your conversations.

Chapitre 1

Faire les gros yeux
Cette expression veut dire qu'une personne n'est pas contente. Par exemple, si un enfant fait une bêtise, sa mère ou son père va faire les gros yeux.

Connaître la musique
Tu peux utiliser cette expression quand tu veux dire que tu sais ce qu'il faut faire ou que tu as déjà fait la même chose avant.

Chapitre 2

Noël au balcon, Pâques au tison
Selon ce proverbe, s'il fait chaud à Noël, il va faire froid à Pâques.

Croire au père Noël
Cette expression veut dire qu'une personne croit qu'elle va avoir ce qu'elle veut. Par exemple, elle croit qu'elle va avoir une nouvelle voiture pour son anniversaire.

Chapitre 3

Couper la poire en deux
Cette expression veut dire être diplomatique, faire des compromis.

Tomber dans les pommes
Si une personne perd conscience on dit qu'**elle est tombée dans les pommes.** Une autre façon de le dire est: s'évanouir *(faint)*.

Chapitre 4

Faire école
Cette expression veut dire que d'autres personnes suivent le même exemple.

Être à bonne école
Si vous avez un bon professeur ou un bon mentor, on dit que **vous êtes à bonne école.**

Chapitre 5

Se lever du pied gauche
Quand une personne est de mauvaise humeur, on dit qu'**elle s'est levée du pied gauche.**

S'endormir sur ses lauriers
Cette expression veut dire se contenter d'un premier succès et ne plus faire d'effort après.

Chapitre 6

Retomber en enfance
Quand un adulte agit comme un enfant, on peut dire qu'**il** ou **elle est retombé(e) en enfance.**

C'est un jeu d'enfant
Cette expression veut dire que quelque chose est facile à faire.

Chapitre 7

Rusé comme un renard
Cette expression veut dire que quelqu'un est rusé *(sly)*.

Les petits ruisseaux font les grandes rivières
Cette expression veut dire qu'une petite chose plus une autre petite chose finit par produire une chose importante.

Chapitre 8

Avoir un chat dans la gorge
Si vous avez mal à la gorge, vous pouvez dire que **vous avez un chat dans la gorge.**

Aux grands maux, les grands remèdes
Quand le mal est grave, il faut un traitement énergique. Il faut une solution proportionnée au mal ou aux problèmes.

Chapitre 9

Une histoire à dormir debout
Cette expression s'utilise pour qualifier une histoire tellement extraordinaire qu'elle est difficile à croire.

C'est toujours la même histoire.
Cette expression exprime souvent l'impatience face à un incident qui se reproduit. Par exemple, un(e) ami(e) est toujours en retard quand vous êtes pressé(e).

Chapitre 10

Faire une montagne de quelque chose
Cette expression veut dire voir des difficultés où il n'y en a pas.

Mener quelqu'un en bateau
Si une personne ne dit pas la vérité à une autre personne, on peut dire qu'**elle le/la mène en bateau.**

APRÈS la lecture

1. Can you think of English equivalents for some of these proverbs and expressions?
2. Pick a proverb that is not illustrated and work in groups of three to create an illustration to explain it.
3. On the Internet or at the library, find additional proverbs that use vocabulary and themes you've learned.
4. Work in small groups to create a mini-skit in which you use one or more of these proverbs in context.

Révisions de vocabulaire

This list includes words introduced in *Bien dit!* Level 1. If you can't find the words you need here, try the French-English and English-French vocabulary sections beginning on page R51.

Le calendrier *(Calendar)*

le jour	*day*
la semaine	*week*
le week-end	*weekend*
aujourd'hui	*today*
demain	*tomorrow*
hier	*yesterday*
lundi	*Monday*
mardi	*Tuesday*
mercredi	*Wednesday*
jeudi	*Thursday*
vendredi	*Friday*
samedi	*Saturday*
dimanche	*Sunday*
janvier	*January*
février	*February*
mars	*March*
avril	*April*
mai	*May*
juin	*June*
juillet	*July*
août	*August*
septembre	*September*
octobre	*October*
novembre	*November*
décembre	*December*
l'hiver	*Winter*
le printemps	*Spring*
l'été	*Summer*
l'automne	*Fall*

Les chiffres *(Numbers)*

zéro	*zero*
un/une	*one*
deux	*two*
trois	*three*
quatre	*four*
cinq	*five*
six	*six*
sept	*seven*
huit	*eight*
neuf	*nine*
dix	*ten*
onze	*eleven*
douze	*twelve*
treize	*thirteen*
quatorze	*fourteen*
quinze	*fifteen*
seize	*sixteen*
dix-sept	*seventeen*
dix-huit	*eighteen*
dix-neuf	*nineteen*
vingt	*twenty*
vingt et un/vingt et une	*twenty-one*
vingt-deux	*twenty-two*
vingt-trois	*twenty-three*
vingt-quatre	*twenty-four*
vingt-cinq	*twenty-five*
vingt-six	*twenty-six*
vingt-sept	*twenty-seven*
vingt-huit	*twenty-eight*
vingt-neuf	*twenty-nine*
trente	*thirty*
quarante	*forty*
cinquante	*fifty*
soixante	*sixty*
soixante-dix	*seventy*
soixante et onze	*seventy-one*

soixante-douze	*seventy-two*
quatre-vingts	*eighty*
quatre-vingt-un	*eighty-one*
quatre-vingt-dix	*ninety*
quatre-vingt-onze	*ninety-one*
cent	*one hundred*
cent un	*one hundred one*
deux cents	*two hundred*
mille	*one thousand*
million (m.)	*million*

Le corps *(Body)*

la bouche	*mouth*
les cheveux (m.)	*hair*
le nez	*nose*
les oreilles (f.)	*ears*
la tête	*head*
les yeux (m.)	*eyes*

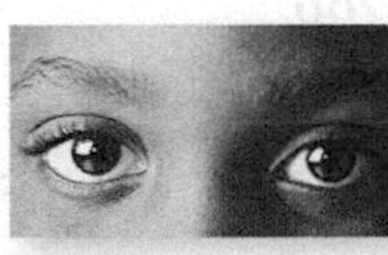

Les corvées *(Chores)*

arroser les plantes (f.)	*to water the plants*
balayer	*to sweep*
débarrasser la table	*to clear the table*
faire la cuisine	*to cook*
faire la lessive	*to do the laundry*
faire la vaisselle	*to do the dishes*
faire son lit	*to make one's bed*
laver la voiture	*to wash the car*
mettre la table	*to set the table*
nettoyer	*to clean*
passer l'aspirateur (m.)	*to vacuum*
promener le chien	*to walk the dog*
ranger sa chambre	*to pick up one's bedroom*
sortir la poubelle	*to take out the trash*
tondre la pelouse	*to mow the lawn*
vider le lave-vaisselle	*to empty the dish-washer*

Les couleurs *(Colors)*

blanc(he)	*white*
bleu (foncé)	*(dark) blue*
bleu (clair)	*(light) blue*
gris(e)	*grey*
jaune	*yellow*
marron	*brown*
noir(e)	*black*
orange	*orange*
rose	*pink*
rouge	*red*
vert(e)	*green*
violet(te)	*purple*

Les descriptions *(Descriptions)*

beau (belle)	*handsome, beautiful*
blond(e)	*blond*
bon (bonne)	*good*
brun(e)	*dark-haired*
châtain	*chestnut, light brown*
court(e)	*short*
créatif (créative)	*creative*
fort(e)	*strong*
généreux (généreuse)	*generous*
génial(e)	*fantastic, awesome*
gentil(le)	*kind*
grand(e)	*tall*
gros(se)	*big, fat*
intelligent(e)	*smart*
jeune	*young*
long (longue)	*long*
marrant(e)	*funny*
méchant(e)	*mean*
mince	*thin*
nouveau (nouvelle)	*new*
paresseux (paresseuse)	*lazy*
pénible	*tiresome, difficult*
petit(e)	*short*
roux (rousse)	*red-headed*
sérieux (sérieuse)	*serious*
sportif (sportive)	*athletic*
sympathique	*nice*
timide	*shy*
vieux (vieille)	*old*

En ville *(In town)*

à pied	*by foot*
à vélo	*by bicycle*
l'arrêt (m.) de bus	*bus stop*
la banque	*bank*
la bibliothèque	*library*
la boutique	*shop*
la cabine téléphonique	*phone booth*
le café	*café*
la campagne	*country*
le carrefour	*intersection*
le centre commercial	*mall*
le centre-ville	*downtown*
le club	*sport club*
le coiffeur	*hairdresser*
le cybercafé	*cybercafé*
le distributeur d'argent	*automatic cash machine*
l'école	*school*
l'église (f.)	*church*
en bus	*by bus*
en métro	*by subway*
en taxi	*by taxi*
en voiture	*by car*
le feu	*traffic light*
le fleuriste	*flower shop*
la grande surface	*hypermarket*
l'hôpital (m.)	*hospital*
le lac	*lake*
la librairie-papeterie	*books and stationery store*
le lycée	*high school*
la Maison des jeunes et de la Culture (MJC)	*recreation center*
le marché	*open air market*
la mer	*sea*
la montagne	*mountain*
le musée	*museum*
l'opéra (m.)	*opera house*
la patinoire	*skating rink*
le parc	*park*
la pharmacie	*pharmacy*
la plage	*beach*
le plan	*map*
le pont	*bridge*
la poste	*post office*
le rayon bijouterie	*jewelry section*
le rayon maroquinerie	*leathergood section*
le rayon sport et plein air	*sport section*
la rue	*street*
le stade	*stadium*
la station de métro	*subway station*
le théâtre	*theater*
le ticket	*ticket*
le zoo	*zoo*

La famille *(Family)*

le beau-père	*stepfather*
la belle-mère	*stepmother*
le chat	*cat*
le chien	*dog*
le/la cousin(e)	*cousin*
le demi-frère	*half-brother*
la demi-sœur	*half-sister*
divorcé(e)	*divorced*
un/une enfant (m./f.)	*child*
la famille	*family*
la femme	*wife*
la fille	*daughter*
le fils	*son*
le frère	*brother*
la grand-mère	*grandmother*
le grand-père	*grandfather*
les grands-parents (m.)	*grandparents*
le mari	*husband*
la mère	*mother*
le neveu	*nephew*
la nièce	*niece*
l'oncle	*uncle*
les parents (m.)	*parents*

le père — *father*
la petite-fille — *granddaughter*
le petit-fils — *grandson*
les petits-enfants (m.) — *grandchildren*
la sœur — *sister*
la tante — *aunt*

Les fournitures scolaires *(School supplies)*

le cahier — *notebook*
la calculatrice — *calculator*
le classeur — *binder*
le crayon (de couleur) — *pencil (colored)*
le dictionnaire — *dictionnary*
la feuille de papier — *sheet of paper*
la gomme — *eraser*
le livre — *book*
la règle — *ruler*
le sac (à dos) — *backpack*
le stylo — *pen*
le taille-crayon — *pencil sharpener*
la trousse — *pencil case*

L'heure *(Time)*

Quelle heure est-il? — *What time is it?*
Il est... heure(s) — *It is . . . o'clock.*
À quelle heure tu as... ? — *At what time do you have . . . ?*
de l'après-midi — *in the afternoon*
du matin — *in the morning*
du soir — *in the evening*
maintenant — *now*
midi — *noon*
minuit — *midnight*
moins le quart — *a quarter to*
moins vingt — *twenty minutes to*
et demie — *half past*
et quart — *a quarter past*

Les loisirs *(Leisure activities)*

le baladeur (MP3) — *MP3 player*
la bande dessinée (une BD) — *comic strip/comic book*
chanter — *to sing*
le dessin/dessiner — *drawing/to draw*
dormir — *to sleep*
écouter de la musique — *to listen to music*
les écouteurs (m.) — *headphones*
envoyer des e-mails (m.) — *to send e-mail*
étudier — *to study*
le journal — *newspaper*
lire — *to read*
le magazine — *magazine*
la musique classique — *classical music*
la musique moderne — *modern music*
parler anglais/français — *to speak English/French*
le portable/le mobile — *cell phone and laptop/cell phone*
la radio — *radio*
regarder la télé — *to watch T.V.*
le roman — *novel*
le SMS (un texto) — *instant message*
surfer sur Internet — *to surf the Internet*
téléphoner (à des amis) — *to telephone friends*
travailler — *to work*
les vacances (f.) — *vacation*
la voiture de sport (f.) — *sport car*

La maison *(House/Home)*

l'appartement (m.) — *apartment*
l'armoire (f.) — *wardrobe*
le balcon — *balcony*
la chaîne stéréo — *stereo*
la chambre — *bedroom*
la commode — *chest of drawers*
la cuisine — *kitchen*
l'escalier — *staircase*
l'étagère (f.) — *shelf*
le fauteuil — *armchair*
le garage — *garage*
l'immeuble (m.) — *appartment building*
le jardin — *yard, garden*
les jumelles (f.) — *binoculars*
la lampe — *lamp*
le lit — *bed*
la pièce — *room*
le placard — *closet, cabinet*
le premier étage — *second floor*
le rez-de-chaussée — *first floor*
la salle à manger — *dining room*

la salle de bain	*bathroom*
le salon	*living room*
le sofa	*couch*
la table basse	*coffee table*
la table de nuit	*night stand*
le tableau	*painting (hanging on a wall)*
le tapis	*rug*
les toilettes (f.)	*restroom*

La nourriture *(food)*

l'assiette (f.)	*plate*
le bacon	*bacon*
la baguette	*long loaf of bread*
la banane	*banana*
le beurre	*butter*
le bol	*bowl*
boire	*to drink*
le café (au lait)	*coffee with milk*
les céréales (f.)	*cereal*
le chocolat (chaud)	*(hot) chocolate*
le coca	*cola*
la confiture	*jelly*
le couteau	*knife*
le croissant	*croissant*
le croque-monsieur	*ham and cheese sandwich*
la cuillère	*spoon*
le déjeuner	*lunch*
le dîner	*dinner*
l'eau minérale (f.)	*mineral water*
la fourchette	*fork*
les frites (f.)	*french fries*
la glace	*ice cream*
la grenadine	*water with pomegranate syrup*
le jus d'orange/de pomme	*orange/apple juice*
le lait	*milk*
les légumes (m.)	*vegetables*
la limonade	*lemon soda*
manger	*to eat*
la nappe	*tablecloth*
les œufs (m.)	*eggs*
l'omelette (f.)	*omelet*
le pain	*bread*
le pamplemousse	*grapefruit*
les pâtes (f.)	*pasta*
le petit-déjeuner	*breakfast*
la pizza	*pizza*
le poisson	*fish*
le poivre	*pepper*
le porc	*pork*
le poulet	*chicken*
la quiche	*quiche*
le repas	*meal*
le riz	*rice*
saignant(e)/à point/ bien cuit(e)	*rare/medium/ well-done*
la salade	*salad*
le sandwich au fromage/ au jambon/au saucisson	*cheese/ham/ salami sandwich (with baguette)*
le sel	*salt*
la serviette	*napkin*
le sirop de menthe	*water with mint syrup*
le steak	*steak*
la tarte	*fruit pie*
la tartine	*slice of French bread*
le toast	*toast*
la tasse	*cup*
le verre	*glass*

Les présentations *(Introductions)*

C'est un ami/une amie.	*He/She's a friend.*
Ça, c'est...	*This is . . .*
Enchanté(e)!	*Delighted!*
Je te/vous présente...	*I'd like to introduce you to . . .*
Voici... /Voilà...	*Here is . . ./There is . . .*
Ça, c'est/ce sont...	*This is/These are . . .*
Qui c'est, ça?	*Who is that?*
Il/Elle s'appelle comment?	*What is his/her name?*
Tu t'appelles comment?	*What is your name?*
Il/Elle s'appelle...	*His/Her name is . . .*
Je m'appelle...	*My name is . . .*

La salle de classe *(Classroom)*

le bureau	*desk*
la carte	*map*
le CD	*CD*
la chaise	*chair*
le DVD	*DVD*

- **l'élève** — *student*
- **la fenêtre** — *window*
- **la fille** — *girl*
- **le garçon** — *boy*
- **le lecteur de CD/DVD** — *CD/DVD player*
- **l'ordinateur (m.)** — *computer*
- **la porte** — *door*
- **le poster** — *poster*
- **le/la prof(esseur)** — *teacher*
- **la table** — *table*
- **le tableau** — *blackboard*
- **la télé(vision)** — *television*

Au lycée *(In high school)*

- **l'allemand (m.)** — *German*
- **l'anglais (m.)** — *English*
- **les arts (m.) plastiques** — *art class*
- **la biologie** — *biology*
- **la chimie** — *chemistry*
- **les devoirs (m.)** — *homework*
- **l'école (f.)** — *school*
- **l'éducation musicale (f.)** — *music*
- **l'EPS (éducation physique et sportive) (f.)** — *physical education*
- **l'espagnol (m.)** — *Spanish*
- **l'examen (m.)** — *test*
- **le français** — *French*
- **la géographie** — *geography*
- **l'histoire (f.)** — *history*
- **l'informatique (f.)** — *computer science*
- **les mathémathiques (maths) (f.)** — *mathematics (math)*
- **les matières (f.)** — *school subjects*
- **la physique** — *physics*
- **la récréation** — *break*
- **la sortie** — *dismissal*

Les salutations *(Greetings)*

- **À bientôt.** — *See you soon.*
- **À demain.** — *See you tomorrow.*
- **À plus tard./ À tout à l'heure.** — *See you later.*
- **Au revoir.** — *Goodbye.*
- **Bonjour.** — *Good morning.*
- **Bonsoir.** — *Good evening.*
- **Salut!** — *Hi!*
- **Ça va?/Comment ça va?** — *Are you doing OK?/ How's it going?*
- **Comment allez-vous?** — *How are you doing?*
- **Et toi/vous?** — *And you?*
- **Bien.** — *Fine.*
- **Non, pas très bien.** — *No, not too good.*
- **Oui, ça va. Merci.** — *Yes, fine. Thank you.*
- **Pas mal.** — *Not bad.*
- **Plus ou moins.** — *So-so.*
- **Très bien.** — *Very well.*

Les sports et les passe-temps *(Sports and hobbies)*

- **aller à la piscine** — *to go to the pool*
- **aller au café** — *to go to a café*
- **aller au cinéma** — *to go to the movie theater*
- **l'appareil photo numérique** — *digital camera*
- **la balle/le ballon** — *ball*
- **la batte** — *bat*
- **le caméscope** — *camcorder*
- **la canne à pêche** — *fishing rod*
- **le casque** — *helmet*
- **le cerf-volant** — *kite*
- **danser** — *to dance*
- **discuter (avec des amis)** — *to chat (with friends)*
- **faire...**
  - **de l'aérobic (f.)** — *aerobics*
  - **de l'athlétisme (m.)** — *track and field*
  - **de la photo** — *take pictures*
  - **de la vidéo amateur** — *make videos*
  - **du jogging** — *jogging*
  - **du patin à glace** — *skating*
  - **du skate(-board)** — *skateboarding*
  - **du ski** — *skiing*
  - **du sport** — *sports*
  - **du surf** — *surfing*
  - **du théâtre** — *drama*
  - **du vélo** — *biking*
- **faire la fête** — *to party*
- **faire les magasins (m.)** — *to go shopping*

faire un pique-nique — *to have a picnic*
jouer...
à des jeux vidéo — *video games*
au base-ball — *baseball*
au basket(-ball) — *basketball*
au football — *soccer*
au hockey — *hockey*
au tennis — *tennis*
au volley — *volleyball*
aux cartes — *cards*
aux échecs — *chess*
de la batterie — *drums*
de la guitare — *guitar*
du piano — *piano*
le masque de plongée — *diving mask*
nager — *to swim*
les palmes (f.) — *fins*
la planche de surf — *surf board*
la raquette — *racket*
les skis — *skis*
le skate (board) — *skateboard*
sortir — *to go out*
le tuba — *snorkeling mask and tube*
le vélo tout terrain (VTT) — *mountain bike*
voir un film — *to see a movie*

Le temps *(Weather)*

Quel temps fait-il? — *What is the weather like?*
Il fait beau. — *It's nice weather.*
Il fait chaud. — *It's hot.*
Il fait froid. — *It's cold.*
Il fait mauvais. — *It's bad weather.*
Il neige. — *It's snowing.*
Il y a des nuages. — *It's cloudy.*
Il pleut. — *It's raining.*
Il y a du vent. — *It's windy.*
Il y a du soleil. — *It is sunny.*

Les vacances *(Vacation)*

à l'heure — *on time*
l'aéroport (m.) — *airport*
l'accès handicapé (m.) — *handicap access*
annuler — *to cancel*
l'arrivée (f.) — *arrival*
l'ascenseur (m.) — *elevator*
l'avion (m.) — *plane*
le bagage (à main) — *(carry-on) luggage*
le billet d'avion/de train — *plane/train ticket*
le bureau de change — *currency exchange office*
la carte d'embarquement — *boarding pass*
la chambre avec vue/non-fumeur — *room with a view/non-smoking*
les chèques de voyage (m.) — *traveler's checks*
la climatisation — *air conditioning*
le compartiment — *compartment*
composter — *to punch (a ticket)*
la consigne — *baggage locker*
le contrôleur — *ticket collector*
la correspondance — *connecting flight/connection*
la couchette — *sleeping car*
le départ — *departure*
demi-pension — *half-board*
disponible (pour) — *available (for)*
le distributeur de billets — *ticket machine*
emporter — *to take something (with)*
en avance — *early*
en retard — *late*
la gare — *train station*
la glacière — *ice chest*
le hall — *lobby*
l'hôtel — *hotel*
l'hôtesse — *stewardess*

le lit simple/double	*single/double bed*
manquer/rater	*to miss*
le parking	*parking*
le passager	*passenger*
le passeport	*passport*
le pilote	*pilot*
la place assise	*seat*
le porte-bagages	*luggage carrier/rack*
la porte d'embarquement	*boarding gate*
la première/ deuxième classe	*first/second class*
le quai/la voie	*platform/track*
la réception	*reception*
le/la réceptionniste	*receptionist*
le sac de voyage	*traveling bag*
le tableau d'affichage	*information board*
la tente	*tent*
le terminal	*terminal*
le train	*train*
la trousse de toilette	*vanity case*
la valise	*suitcase*
le visa	*visa*
le vol	*flight*
le wagon	*car (in a train)*
le wagon-restaurant	*dining car*

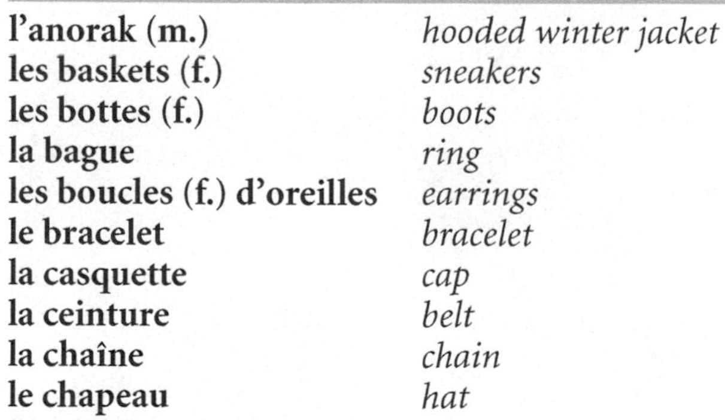

Les vêtements et les accessoires
(Clothes and accessories)

l'anorak (m.)	*hooded winter jacket*
les baskets (f.)	*sneakers*
les bottes (f.)	*boots*
la bague	*ring*
les boucles (f.) d'oreilles	*earrings*
le bracelet	*bracelet*
la casquette	*cap*
la ceinture	*belt*
la chaîne	*chain*
le chapeau	*hat*
les chaussures (f.) de randonnée	*hiking shoes*
les chaussettes (f.)	*socks*
les chaussures (f.)	*men's dress shoes*
la chemise	*shirt*
le chemisier	*blouse*
cher/chère	*expensive*
le collier	*necklace*
le costume/	*man's suit/*
le coupe-vent	*wind-breaker*
la cravate	*tie*
l'écharpe (f.)	*scarf (long, wool scarf)*
en argent	*in silver*
en coton	*made of cotton*
en cuir	*made of leather*
en jean	*made of denim*
en laine	*made of wool*
en lin	*made of linen*
en or	*in gold*
en soie	*made of silk*
étroit(e)/ serré(e)/	*tight*
le foulard	*scarf (as in a dressy silk scarf)*
les gants (m.)	*gloves*
l'imperméable (m.)	*raincoat*
le jean	*jeans*
la jupe	*skirt*
large	*loose*
les lunettes (f.) de soleil	*sunglasses*
le maillot de bain	*bathing suit*
le manteau	*coat*
la montre	*watch*
le pantalon	*pants*
le parapluie	*umbrella*
le portefeuille	*wallet*
le porte-monnaie	*coin purse*
le pull	*pullover*
la robe	*dress*
le sac (à main)	*handbag*
les sandales (f.)	*sandals*
le sweat-shirt/le tee-shirt	*sweat-shirt/ tee-shirt*
le tailleur	*woman's suit*
la veste	*jacket*

Vocabulaire supplémentaire

This list includes additional vocabulary that you may want to use to personalize activities. If you can't find the words you need here, try the French-English and English-French glossary sections beginning on page R51.

La famille *(Family)*

l'aîné(e)	*oldest child*
les ancêtres (m. pl.)	*ancestors*
le benjamin/ la benjamine	*youngest child in a family of more than 2 children*
le cadet/la cadette	*youngest child of 2*
le ménage	*household*
les parents (m. pl.)	*relatives*

Les adjectifs descriptifs *(Descriptive adjectives)*

actif/active	*active*
bavard(e)	*talkative*
bien élevé(e)	*well-mannered*
branché(e)	*in, with 'it'*
compréhensif/ compréhensive	*understanding*
débrouillard(e)	*resourceful*
égoïste	*selfish*
enthousiaste	*enthusiastic*
gâté(e)	*spoiled*
mal élevé(e)	*ill-mannered*
optimiste	*optimistic*
pessimiste	*pessimistic*
réservé(e)	*quiet, reserved*
sage	*quiet, well-behaved*
sévère	*strict*
têtu(e)	*stubborn*
travailleur/ travailleuse	*hard-working*

Les animaux domestiques *(Pets)*

le berger allemand	*German shepherd*
le cacatoès	*cockatoo*
le canary	*canary*
le caniche	*poodle*
le chat persan	*Persian cat*
le chat siamois	*Siamese cat*
le cochon d'Inde	*guinea pig*
le furet	*ferret*
le golden retriever	*golden retriever*
le hamster (m.)	*hamster*
l'iguane (m.)	*iguana*
le labrador	*labrador retriever*
le perroquet	*parrot*
le poisson rouge	*goldfish*

Au café/La nourriture *(At the café/ Food)*

le café-crème	*coffee with cream*
le café liégeois	*coffee ice-cream with coffee sauce and whipped cream*
le chocolat liégeois	*chocolate ice-cream with chocolate sauce and whipped cream*
la coupe Melba	*vanilla ice-cream with peach, red currant jelly, whipped cream, and almonds*

le croque-madame	*grilled ham, cheese, and egg sandwich*
l'eau (f.) gazeuse	*sparkling water*
les glaçons	*ice cubes*
le jus d'abricot	*apricot juice*
le jus d'ananas	*pineapple juice*
le jus de mangue	*mango juice*
le jus de pamplemousse	*grapefruit juice*
le jus de raisin	*grape juice*
le pan bagnat	*tuna and vegetable sandwich*
la salade niçoise	*salad with mixed vegetables and tuna*
le sandwich au saumon fumé	*smoked salmon sandwich*
le sandwich aux merguez	*spicy lamb sausage sandwich*
le sandwich grec	*gyro*
le sirop de cassis à l'eau	*black currant syrup with water*
le sirop de citron à l'eau	*lemon syrup with water*
le sirop de fraise à l'eau	*strawberry syrup with water*
le sirop de framboise à l'eau	*raspberry syrup with water*
le sirop de menthe à l'eau	*mint syrup with water*
la soupe à l'oignon	*onion soup*
le thé glacé	*iced tea*

Les fêtes *(Parties)*

le buffet (chaud, froid)	*(cold, warm) buffet*
commander	*to order*
le déguisement	*costume*
grignoter	*to snack*
les hors-d'œuvres	*hors d'oeuvres, appetizers*
livrer	*to deliver*
le masque	*mask*

les plats préparés	*prepared dishes*
les plats surgelés	*frozen dishes*
servir	*to serve*
se servir	*to help oneself*
la soirée à thème	*theme party*
le traiteur	*caterer*

Dans la cuisine *(In the kitchen)*

la casserole	*sauce pan*
le couvercle	*lid*
couvrir	*to cover*
la cuillère en bois	*wooden spoon*
cuire à feu doux	*to cook on low heat*
cuisiner	*to cook*
égoutter	*to strain*
l'égouttoir (m.)	*colander*
éplucher	*to peel*
le fouet	*whisk*
le/la gourmand(e)	*someone who likes to eat a lot*
le gourmet	*someone who appreciates good food*
la marmitte	*stock pot*
mesurer	*to measure*
mijoter	*to simmer*
le moule à gâteau	*cake dish*
le moule à tarte	*pie dish*
le plat à gratin	*ovenproof dish*
la poêle	*frying pan*

la râpe — *grater*
la recette — *recipe*
remuer — *to stir*
le saladier — *salad bowl, mixing bowl*
la spatule — *spatula*
le tablier — *apron*
végétarien(ne) — *vegetarian*
le verre à mesurer — *measuring glass*
verser — *to pour*

À la boucherie-charcuterie *(At the butcher's)*

l'agneau (m.) — *lamb*
le bifteck — *steak*
la caille — *quail*
la côtelette — *loin chop*
les cubes de bœuf — *beef cubes*
le filet de bœuf — *beef tenderloin*
le foie — *liver*
le jambon fumé — *smoked ham*
l'oie (f.) — *goose*
le rôti — *roast*
le veau — *veal*

À la poissonnerie *(At the fish monger's)*

le calmar — *squid*
la coquille Saint-Jacques — *scallop*
le crabe — *crab*
la crevette — *shrimp*
l'espadon (m.) — *swordfish*
le flétan — *halibut*
le homard (m.) — *lobster*
la langouste — *spiny lobster*
la moule — *mussel*

la palourde — *clam*
le saumon — *salmon*
la sole — *sole*
le thon — *tuna*
la truite — *trout*

Le basket-ball *(Basketball)*

l'anneau (m.) — *rim*
l'arrière (m.) — *guard*
l'entraîneur (m.) — *coach*
le filet — *net*
le panier — *basket*
le pivot — *center*
le terrain — *court*

Le base-ball *(Baseball)*

l'abri des joueurs — *dugout*
l'arbitre (m.) — *referee*
l'avant-champ — *infield*
la batte — *bat*
la base — *base*
le casque — *helmet*
centre — *center*
le champ — *field*
droit(e) — *right*
le frappeur — *batter*
le gant — *glove*
le lanceur — *pitcher*
le maillot — *team shirt*
le marbre — *home plate*
le masque — *mask*
le plastron — *chest protector*
la plaque du lanceur — *pitcher's plate*
le receveur — *catcher*

L'athlétisme *(Track and field)*

le bloc de départ — *starting block*
le couloir — *lane*
les haies (f. pl.) — *hurdles*
le lancer du disque — *discus throw*
le lancer du javelot — *javelin throw*
le lancer du poids — *shot put*
la ligne d'arrivée — *finish line*
le relais — *relay*
le saut à la perche — *pole vault*
le saut en hauteur — *high jump*
le saut en longueur — *long jump*
le tableau indicateur — *score board*
le témoin — *baton*

Au gymnase *(At the gym)*

les anneaux (m. pl.) — *rings*
les barres asymétriques (f. pl.) — *uneven parallel bars*
les barres parallèles (f. pl.) — *parallel bars*
le cheval d'arçons — *pommel horse*
le/la gymnaste — *gymnast*
le juge — *judge*
la note — *score*
la poutre — *balance beam*
le tapis — *floor mat*
le travail au sol — *floor exercise*
le tremplin — *springboard*
le vestiaire — *locker room*

Le matériel de bureau *(Office equipment)*

la ligne téléphonique — *telephone line*
la messagerie vocale — *voicemail*
le répondeur téléphonique — *answering machine*
le photocopieur — *photocopier*
la souris mécanique — *mechanical mouse*
la souris optique — *optical mouse*
le télécopieur — *fax machine*

Les professions *(Professions)*

l'assistant(e) social(e) — *social worker*
l'avocat(e) — *lawyer*
le/la chef d'entreprise — *business owner*
le/la comptable — *accountant*
l'électricien(ne) — *electrician*
l'employé(e) de bureau — *office worker*
l'infirmier/infirmière — *nurse*
l'ingénieur — *engineer*
le/la mécanicien (ne) — *mechanic*
le plombier — *plumber*
le policier — *police officer*
le pompier — *firefighter*
le prêtre — *priest*
le/la secrétaire — *secretary*

Les produits de soins et de beauté *(Body care and beauty products)*

l'après-rasage — *aftershave*
l'après-shampooing (m.) — *conditioner*
la crème de soin — *face cream*
la crème pour le corps — *lotion*
le démaquillant — *make-up remover*
l'eau de toilette — *cologne*
le fard à joues — *blush*
le fond de teint — *foundation*
le gel — *hair gel*
l'ombre à paupières (f.) — *eye shadow*
le parfum — *perfume*
la poudre — *powder*

À la campagne *(In the country)*

l'abreuvoir (m.)	*drinking trough*
l'agriculteur/ agricultrice	*farmer*
l'agriculture (f.)	*agriculture*
l'auge (f.)	*feeding trough*
le coq	*rooster*
cultiver	*to grow (crops)*
les cultures (f. pl.)	*crops*
l'élevage	*cattle raising*

l'étable (f.)	*barn*
le fermier/la fermière	*farmer*
le foin	*hay*
la moisson	*harvest*
planter	*to sow*

Le camping *(Camping)*

l'auvent (m.)	*canopy*
le couteau suisse	*Swiss Army knife*
la glacière	*cooler*
le gonfleur	*air pump*
le lit de camp pliant	*folding cot*
le matelas mousse	*foam pad*
le matelas pneumatique	*air mattress*
la pelle-pioche pliante	*folding shovel*
le piquet	*stake*
la tente igloo	*pop-up tent*

La nature *(Nature)*

l'aigle (m.)	*eagle*
aller observer les oiseaux	*to go bird watching*
le castor	*beaver*
le cerf	*deer*
la chasse	*hunting*
le corbeau	*raven*
la couleuvre	*garter snake*

faire du canoë	*to go canoeing*
faire du rafting	*to go rafting*
la grotte	*cave*
l'hirondelle (f.)	*swallow*
le lièvre	*hare*
la moufette (au Canada)	*skunk*
l'ornithologie (f.)	*bird watching*
le porc-épic	*porcupine*
le raton-laveur	*raccoon*
le renard	*fox*
le serpent à sonnette	*rattlesnake*
le tir à l'arc	*archery*
le vautour	*vulture*

Le corps humain *(The human body)*

l'avant-bras	*forearm*
le coude	*elbow*
le crâne	*skull*
la cuisse	*thigh*
la hanche	*hip*
le mollet	*calf*
la nuque	*nape*
l'omoplate (f.)	*shoulderblade*
le talon	*heel*
la tempe	*temple*
le ventre	*abdomen, stomach*

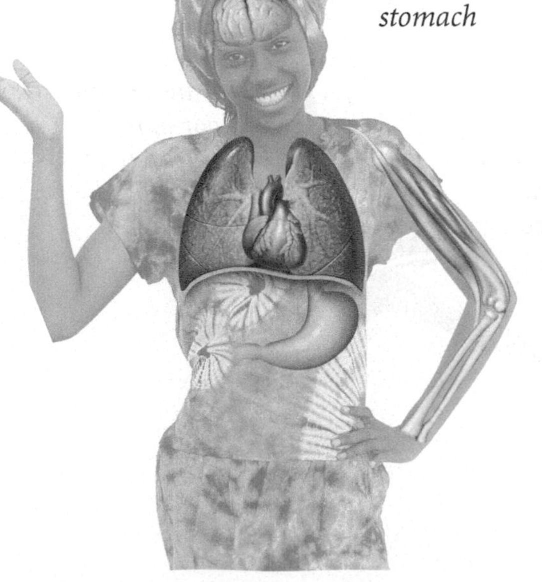

Les problèmes de santé *(Health issues)*

les allergies (f.)	*allergies*
l'angine (f.)	*tonsillitis*
avoir la nausée	*to be nauseous*

avoir mal à l'estomac	*to have a stomach ache*
le bandage	*bandage*
les béquilles (f.)	*crutches*
la bronchite	*bronchitis*
s'évanouir	*to faint*
la grippe	*flu*
le plâtre	*cast*
la radiographie	*x-ray*
le rhume	*cold*
la salle d'attente	*waiting room*
le sirop	*syrup*

Le cinéma *(Movies)*

la bande annonce	*movie trailer*
les cascades (f.)	*stunts*
le cascadeur	*stuntman*
le décor	*set*
les effets spéciaux (m. pl.)	*special effects*
le film doublé	*dubbed movie*

le film en noir et blanc	*black and white movie*
le générique	*credits*
l'intrigue (f.)	*plot*
la maquilleuse	*make-up artist*
le metteur en scène	*director*
le producteur	*producer*
le réalisateur	*director*

Quelques pays *(A few countries)*

l'Afrique (f.) du Sud	*South Africa*
l'Autriche (f.)	*Austria*
l'Australie (f.)	*Australia*
le Brésil	*Brazil*
le Cameroun	*Cameroon*
la Chine	*China*

l'Égypte (f.)	*Egypt*
la Grèce	*Greece*
l'Inde (f.)	*India*
l'Irlande (f.)	*Ireland*
le Japon	*Japan*
le Mexique	*Mexico*
la Nouvelle-Zélande	*New Zealand*
les Pays-Bas (m. pl.)	*Netherlands*
le Royaume-Uni	*United Kingdom*
la Russie	*Russia*
la Turquie	*Turkey*

Liste d'expressions

Functions are the ways in which you use a language for particular purposes. In specific situations, such as in a restaurant , in a grocery store, or at school, you will want to communicate with those around you. In order to do that you have to "function" in French: you buy food, tell what you like to do for fun, or talk about your daily routine.

Here is a list of the functions presented in this book along with the French expressions you'll need to communicate in a wide range of situations. Following each function is the chapter and page number from the book where it is introduced.

Socializing

Describing yourself and asking about others
Ch. 1, p. 7

Comment tu t'appelles?
Je m'appelle...
Tu as quel âge?
J'ai... ans.
De quelle couleur sont... ?
Il/Elle est comment, ton ami(e)?
Il/Elle est...

Wishing someone a good time
Ch. 2, p. 43

J'espère que tu vas passer...
Amuse-toi bien...
Bonne soirée!
Profite bien...
Je te/vous souhaite...

Exchanging information

Telling when you do something
Ch. 1, p. 21

Le lundi,... souvent... ... fois par semaine.
... tous les mercredis. ... au printemps... en été.
...rarement.

Checking if things have been done
Ch. 2, p. 57

Tu as déjà... ?
... pas encore.
Est-ce qu'il y a encore... ?
... c'est bon.
Tu as bien... ?
Mais oui!
Tu as pensé à... ?
J'ai complètement oublié!

Asking about food preparation
Ch. 3, p. 83

Comment est-ce qu'on fait... ?
Coupe... Ajoute... Mélange...
C'est facile de faire... ?
... c'est très simple.
... c'est compliqué.
Qu'est-ce qu'il y a dans... ?
Il y a...

Shopping for groceries
Ch. 3, p. 95

Qu'est-ce qu'il vous faut?
Il me faut...
Combien vous en faut-il?
À peu près...
... environ.
Vous les voulez comment,... ?
Bien mûrs / mûres,...
C'est... le kilo.
... je vais en prendre...
Ce sera tout?
... c'est tout pour aujourd'hui,...

Asking where things are
Ch. 3, p. 97

Madame,... s'il vous plaît?
Alors,... tout près...
Où est-ce que je pourrais trouver... ?
Si vous allez... , au bout du/de la/de l'...
... ça se trouve où,... ?
Au milieu du/de la/de l'...

Asking how something turned out
Ch. 4, p. 119

Au fait,...
Évidemment!
Comment s'est passée... ?
Je l'ai gagné(e).
Alors,...
Je n'en sais rien.
Dis-moi,... ?
... complètement...

Asking for information
Ch. 4, p. 131

Savez-vous comment... ?
Comment est-ce qu'on fait pour... ?
Qu'est-ce que tu utilises comme... ?
Quelle sorte de/d'... ?

Talking about your routine
Ch. 5, p. 159

... en premier... ensuite,...
Chaque...
... avant de...
... tous les deux...
... en même temps que...
... pendant que...

Saying when you do things
Ch. 5, p. 171

... tôt... | ... de bonne heure.
... tard. | Une fois que...
Après ça,... | ... au plus tard.

Talking about when you were a child
Ch. 6, p. 195

Quand j'étais (plus) jeune,...
Quand j'étais petit(e),...
Quand j'avais... ans,

Telling about an event in the past
Ch. 6, p. 197

Alors que... | À ce moment-là,...
Heureusement,... | Finalement,...
Pendant que...

Describing life in the country
Ch. 6, p. 208

... tellement...
Il y avait...
Ce qui était... , c'était...
Ce qui me manque, c'est...

Saying what happened
Ch. 7, p. 235

Figure-toi que... | Alors,...
À ce moment-là,... | Heureusement,...
Bref,...

Describing circumstances
Ch. 7, p. 237

J'étais en train de/d'... | Je venais de/d'...
Au moment où... | ... sur le point de/d'...

Telling what you will do
Ch. 7, p. 247

Tout à l'heure,... | Après-demain,...
... bientôt... | ... prochain...
La prochaine fois,...

Asking and telling how you feel
Ch. 8, p. 271

Qu'est-ce que tu as?
Je ne me sens pas très bien.
Je me sens mal.
Ça n'a pas l'air d'aller.
Tu n'as pas bonne mine...
Tu as mauvaise mine.
... je ne suis pas en forme.
... malade.
Tu as l'air...
... j'ai mal dormi.

Asking for information
Ch. 9, p. 313

Qu'est-ce qu'on joue... ?
Il y a...
C'est avec qui?
C'est avec...
Ça passe où?
Ça passe au...
Ça commence à quelle heure?
La séance est à...
Qu'est-ce que tu as lu d'intéressant... ?
... le dernier...
De quoi ça parle?
Ça parle de/C'est basé sur...
Qu'est-ce que ça raconte?
C'est l'histoire de/d'...

Liste d'expressions

Asking about TV habits/preferences
Ch. 9, p. 323
Qu'est-ce que tu aimes regarder à la télé?
Ce que je préfère, c'est...
Lequel de... est-ce que vous préférez?
Celui avec...
Tu as suivi... ?
... je déteste...
Tu as vu... ?
Je ne rate jamais...

Asking someone about a vacation
Ch. 10, p. 347
... pendant les vacances ?
Ça dépend,...
Qu'est-ce que tu fais de beau... ?
Je reste chez moi.
Tu fais de la voile... ?
J'en fais...
Ça t'arrive de/d'... ?
... j'y vais...

Asking about what has been done
Ch. 10, p. 361
Tu as bien pensé à... ?
Tu as bien fait de me le rappeler.
... déjà... ?
Évidemment que...
Tu n'as pas oublié de/d'... ?
Ah, mais si!

Expressing attitudes and opinions

Talking about likes and dislikes
Ch. 1, p. 9
J'adore.../ J'aime bien...
Moi aussi./Pas moi.
Moi, je n'aime pas...
Moi non plus.
Je n'aime pas beaucoup...
Moi si.
Qu'est-ce que/qu'... aime faire?
Il/Elle aime...

Inquiring about abilities and preferences
Ch. 1, p. 19
Il est bon,... ?
Excellent!/Pas mauvais.
Est-ce que tu joues bien... ?
Assez bien.
Ça te dit de/d'... ?
Tu as envie de/d'... ?
Pourquoi pas?
Tu veux... ?
... je n'ai pas le temps. Je dois...
Qu'est-ce que tu penses de... ?
Il est génial!

Asking for and giving advice
Ch. 2, p. 45
Tu as une idée de cadeau... ?
Tu pourrais lui offrir...
Bonne idée!
Qu'est-ce que je pourrais offrir... ?
Offre-lui...
Tu n'as pas une autre idée?
Il/Elle en a déjà plein.

Wondering what happened
Ch. 4, p. 121
Je me demande si...
... pour une fois.
Je parie que...
Oui, sans doute.
Tu crois?
Tu crois qu'il est arrivé quelque chose à... ?
C'est possible.
Tu as peut-être raison.
... quelqu'un... ?
... personne.

Making recommendations
Ch. 5, p. 173
Tu devrais...
Il est temps de/d'...
Va te coucher.
C'est l'heure de/d'...

Comparing life in the country and life in the city
Ch. 6, p. 207
... plus... que/qu'...
... c'est moins... que/qu'...
Il y a plus de... que/qu'...
... différent(e) de...
...autant... que/qu'...

Wondering what will happen
Ch. 7, p. 248
Je me demande si...
Tu crois que/qu'... ?
Est-ce qu'il va y avoir... ?
Est-ce que tu sais si... ?

Describing symptoms and giving advice
Ch. 8, p. 273

J'ai mal au/à la/à l'/aux	Je te conseille de...
Je me suis coupé...	Il est important que...
J'ai le nez qui coule.	Il faut que...
J'ai mal au coeur.	Tu dois...

Complaining and giving advice
Ch. 8, p. 283
Je suis fatigué(e).
Tu n'as qu'à...
Je suis au régime.
Tu devrais...
J'ai mal partout.
Pourquoi tu ne/n'... pas... ?
J'ai grossi.
Tu ferais bien de...
Je suis stressé(e).
Il faudrait que...

Describing a movie or a book
Ch. 9, p. 311
C'est drôle/amusant.
C'est trop long/ennuyeux/déprimant.
Il y a plein de rebondissements.
Il n'y a pas d'histoire.
Il y a beaucoup de...
C'est pas mal, sans plus.
C'est une histoire passionnante.
Ce n'est pas génial.
C'est une bonne adaptation... du...
Ça n'a rien à voir avec...

Recommending or advising against something
Ch. 9, p. 325
Je te recommande...
... ne vaut vraiment pas le coup.
... à ne pas manquer.
... ne m'a pas emballé(e).
Qu'est-ce qu'elle est bien,... !
... ennuyeux à mourir.
C'est le meilleur... que...
Je ne te conseille pas...

Saying what you would do if you could
Ch. 10, p. 348
... je partirais en vacances...
... faire le tour du monde.
Mon rêve, ce serait de...

Expressing necessity
Ch. 10, p. 359

Il faut que...	J'ai besoin de/d'...
Il ne faut surtout pas...	Je dois absolument...

Expressing feelings and emotions

Expressing frustration
Ch. 4, p. 133
Ça m'énerve!
Tout va de travers depuis...
... Rien ne marche... !
Je ne sais pas quoi faire!

Expressing impatience
Ch. 5, p. 161
Dépêche-toi!
Vous allez être en retard.
Tu es prêt(e)? Alors, on y va?
Arrête de traîner!

Sympathizing with someone
Ch. 8, p. 285

Ce n'est pas grave.	Ne t'en fais pas!
Ça va aller mieux.	Mon/Ma pauvre!
Je te plains.	

Persuading

Asking for help
Ch. 2, p. 55
Tu peux m'aider à... ?
D'accord... /Pas de problème.
Désolé(e), je n'ai pas le temps.
Ça t'ennuie de... ?
Bien sûr que non.
Pas maintenant. Je dois d'abord...

Making requests
Ch. 3, p. 85
Tu veux bien... ?
Tu me rapportes... ?
Oui, j'y vais tout de suite.
Non, je regrette mais...
... je suis trop occupé(e).
N'oublie pas...
... Tu n'as besoin de rien d'autre?

Synthèse de grammaire

ADJECTIVES

Adjective Agreement

Adjectives are words that describe or modify a noun. Adjectives agree in gender and in number with the nouns they modify. To make an adjective feminine, add an **-e** to the masculine singular form. To make an adjective plural, add an **-s** to the singular form.

	SINGULAR	PLURAL
MASCULINE	intelligent	intelligents
FEMININE	intelligente	intelligentes

Adjectives ending in *-eux*

If the masculine singular form of the adjective ends in **-eux**, change the **-x** to **-se** to make it feminine.

	SINGULAR	PLURAL
MASCULINE	heureux	heureux
FEMININE	heureuse	heureuses

Adjectives ending in *-if*

If the masculine singular form of the adjective ends in **-if**, change the **-f** to **-ve** to create the feminine form.

	SINGULAR	PLURAL
MASCULINE	sportif	sportifs
FEMININE	sportive	sportives

Adjectives with Irregular Feminine Forms

The following adjectives have irregular feminine forms.

SINGULAR		PLURAL	
MASCULINE	FEMININE	MASCULINE	FEMININE
long	longue	longs	longues
blanc	blanche	blancs	blanches
bon	bonne	bons	bonnes
gros	grosse	gros	grosses

Synthèse de grammaire

The Irregular Adjectives *beau, nouveau,* and *vieux*

Masculine Singular (before a consonant)	Masculine Singular (before a vowel)	Masculine Plural	Feminine Singular	Feminine Plural
beau nouveau vieux	bel nouvel vieil	beaux nouveaux vieux	belle nouvelle vieille	belles nouvelles vieilles

Adjective Placement

Most French adjectives come **after** the nouns they describe. Adjectives of **beauty, age, number, goodness,** or **size** usually come before the nouns they modify. The following adjectives fall into this group.

Category	Adjectives
*B*eauty *A*ge *N*umber *G*oodness *S*ize	beau, joli vieux, jeune un, deux, trois... bon, mauvais grand, petit

Mme Pasquier est une **belle** dame et elle a des enfants **intelligents.**

If the adjective comes before a plural noun, the word **des** becomes **de**.

Il y a **de** bons films au cinéma ce week-end.

Possessive Adjectives

Possessive adjectives agree in gender and in number with the nouns they modify. Possessive adjectives agree with the items (people, things, animals, etc.) possessed.

	Masculine Singular	Feminine Singular	Plural
my	mon	ma	mes
your	ton	ta	tes
his/her/its	son	sa	ses
our	notre	notre	nos
your	votre	votre	vos
their	leur	leur	leurs

In English, possession can be shown by using **'s**. In French, the preposition **de/d'** is used to show possession.

Le livre **de** Jacqueline est sur la table.

Demonstrative Adjectives

Words like *this, that, these,* and *those* are called demonstrative adjectives. There are four demonstrative adjectives in French: **ce, cet, cette,** and **ces.**

MASCULINE SINGULAR	MASCULINE SINGULAR (vowel sound)	MASCULINE PLURAL	FEMININE SINGULAR	FEMININE PLURAL
ce livre	**cet** ordinateur	**ces** livres	**cette** chaise	**ces** chaises

To distinguish between *this* and *that* and *these* and *those,* add **–ci** or **–là** to the end of any noun.

J'achète **cette robe-ci** parce que je n'aime pas **cette robe-là**!

Interrogative Adjectives

Certain adjectives in French can be used to form questions. The interrogative adjective **quel** means *what* and it has four forms.

	SINGULAR	PLURAL
MASCULINE	**Quel** restaurant?	**Quels** restaurants?
FEMININE	**Quelle** classe?	**Quelles** classes?

When a form of **quel** is followed by **est** or **sont**, it agrees in gender and number with the noun following the verb.

Quelle est ta couleur préférée?

Quel can also be used as an exclamation. Use a form of **quel** plus a noun to express the idea *"What a…"*

Quelle belle robe! *What a beautiful dress!*

Adjectives used as Nouns

When used as a noun, the adjective has a definite article in front of it. Both the adjective and the article will agree in gender and in number with the noun to which they refer.

—Tu préfères la grande maison ou **la petite?**
—Je préfère **la petite**.

The Adjectives *tout, tous, toute, toutes*

Tout and its forms are used in French to say *all* or *whole.* **Tout** has four forms and agrees in gender and in number with the noun it modifies.

	SINGULAR	PLURAL
MASCULINE	tout	tous
FEMININE	toute	toutes

Toutes les chemises sont chères!

Synthèse de grammaire

ADVERBS

Formation of Adverbs

Adverbs modify verbs, adjectives, or other adverbs and tell when, where, why, and to what extent an action is performed. In French, adverbs usually end in **-ment**. To form most adverbs in French, take the feminine form of the adjective and add **-ment**. Common French adverbs are **bien, souvent, de temps en temps, rarement,** and **régulièrement**.

Adjective (Masculine Singular Form)	Adjective (Feminine Singular Form)	Adverb (Feminine Singular Adjective + -ment ending)
sérieux	sérieuse	sérieusement

Paul et Luc étudient **sérieusement** pour leur examen final.

Placement of Adverbs

While adverbs are generally placed near their verbs, they can take other positions in the sentence. Here is a general overview that might help when deciding where to place French adverbs.

Type of adverb	Examples	Placement in the sentence
how much, how often, or how well something is done	**rarement, souvent, bien, mal**	after the verb
adverbs of time	**hier, maintenant, demain**	the beginning or the end of the sentence
some adverbs ending in **-ment**	**normalement, généralement**	the beginning or the end of the sentence

Nous allons **rarement** chez nos cousins.

Patricia a fait du vélo **hier.**

Normalement, je sors avec mes copains après les cours.

Some adverbs are exceptions to these rules and require a special place in the sentence or clause.

Adverb	Placement
comme ci comme ça	end of the clause
quelquefois	beginning or end of the clause or after the verb

Paul parle italien **comme ci comme ça**. Il voyage souvent en Italie et **quelquefois** il réussit à communiquer.

Synthèse de grammaire

The Adverbs *bien* and *mal*

The adjectives **bon** and **mauvais** have irregular adverbs.

ADJECTIVE	ADVERB
bon	bien
mauvais	mal

Ma mère chante **bien,** mais moi, je chante **mal.**

Adverbs with the *passé composé*

The following adverbs are helpful when talking about the past. They can be placed at either the beginning or at the end of a sentence.

hier (matin, après-midi, soir)
yesterday (morning, afternoon, evening)

la semaine dernière/le mois dernier/l'année dernière
last week/last month/last year

soudain *(suddenly)*

Hier, je suis allé au cinéma avec des amis.

Depuis, il y a, ça fait

To say what someone ***has been doing*** or ***for how long*** a person has been doing an activity, use **depuis + a time expression.** This expression can also be used to mean **since.**

Nous habitons à Paris **depuis** cinq ans. — *We've been living in Paris* ***for*** *5 years.*

Je travaille **depuis** six heures du matin. — *I've been working* ***since*** *6 a.m.*

You can also use the expressions **il y a** and **ça fait + a time expression** to say ***how long something has been going on.*** When you use these expressions, they must be followed by the word **que** and usually come at the beginning of the sentence.

Ça fait une semaine **que** nous attendons. — *We've been waiting for a week.*

Il y a trois mois **que** Marie est malade. — *Marie's been sick for three months.*

Synthèse de grammaire

ARTICLES

Definite Articles

There are four definite articles in French.

	MASCULINE (beginning with a consonant)	**FEMININE (beginning with a consonant)**	**MASCULINE OR FEMININE (beginning with a vowel or vowel sound)**
SINGULAR	le	la	l'
PLURAL	les	les	les

The definite article contracts with the preposition **à** to express *at the* or *to the.* It contracts with the preposition **de** to express *of the* or *from the.*

DEFINITE ARTICLE	**CONTRACTED FORM WITH *À***	**CONTRACTED FORM WITH *DE***
le	au	du
les	aux	des
l'	à l'	de l'
la	à la	de la

Je vais **au** café. — Je sors **du** café.

Paul répond **aux** questions. — Le père **des** garçons travaille beaucoup.

Vous retournez **à la** gare. — Le train part **de la** gare.

Chantal et Paul vont **à l'**école. — La porte **de l'**école est grande.

Indefinite Articles

The indefinite articles in French are **un, une,** and **des. Un** and **une** mean *a* or *an* and **des** means *some.* They agree in gender (masculine or feminine) and number (singular or plural) with the nouns they modify.

	SINGULAR	**PLURAL**
MASCULINE	**un** livre	**des** livres
FEMININE	**une** carte	**des** cartes

Un, **une**, and **des** become **de** after a negative.

Chantal a **un** cours de français. — Chantal n'a pas **de** cours de français.

Ils mangent **des** sandwichs. — Ils ne mangent pas **de** sandwichs.

If **de** comes before a noun beginning with a vowel or vowel sound, it changes to **d'**.

Synthèse de grammaire

The Partitive Articles

The partitive is used in French to express *a part* or *some* of an item.

Masculine Singular	Feminine Singular	Before a Noun Beginning With a Vowel	Plural
du café	de la salade	de l'eau	des petits pois

Je vais prendre **de l'**eau. Pierre va prendre **du** café.

The partitive will change to **de** after a negative.

Aurélie ne mange pas **de** tarte parce qu'elle ne veut pas grossir.

When speaking about a whole item, use the indefinite articles **un, une,** and **des**.

Tu veux **un** croissant ou **une** orange?

COMPARATIVES AND SUPERLATIVES

Comparing Adjectives

To compare adjectives, use the following expressions. Remember to make your adjectives agree in gender and in number with their noun.

To say	Use
more...than	**plus** + adjective + **que**
as...as	**aussi** + adjective + **que**
less...than	**moins** + adjective + **que**

Marie est **plus** généreuse **que** son frère.

Nous sommes **aussi** fatigués **que** vous.

Les amis de Xavier sont **moins** sportifs **que** les amis de David.

Comparing Nouns

To compare things, persons, places, or ideas, use the following expressions. Use **de** before the noun.

To say	Use
more...than	**plus** + **de** + noun + **que**
as...as	**autant** + **de** + noun + **que**
less...than	**moins** + **de** + noun + **que**

Marie a **plus de** livres **que** son frère.

Nous achetons **autant de** CD **que** vous.

Les amis de Xavier font **moins de** voyages **que** les amis de David.

The Superlative of Adjectives

The superlative is used to convey *the best, the most, the least,* or *the worst.* Make your adjective agree in gender and in number with the noun it modifies. Depending on the adjective, the superlative can come either before or after its noun.

C'est + definite article + plus/moins + adjective + noun + de + noun

C'est la plus jolie fille de la classe.

le (l')
C'est + definite article + noun + la (l') + plus/moins + adjective + de + noun
les

C'est la fille la plus intelligente de la classe.

Irregular Comparatives and Superlatives

The adjectives **bon** and **mauvais** have irregular forms in both the comparative and the superlative.

ADJECTIVE	COMPARATIVE	SUPERLATIVE
bon(s)/bonne(s)	meilleur(s)/meilleure(s) aussi bon(s)/bonne(s) moins bon(s)/bonne(s)	le meilleur/la meilleure les meilleurs/les meilleures
mauvais/mauvaise(s)	pire(s) aussi mauvais/mauvaise(s)	le pire/la pire/les pires

INTERROGATIVES

Inversion

One way of asking questions is by using inversion. The subject and verb switch positions and are connected by a hyphen.

Tu aimes le chocolat? → **Aimes-tu** le chocolat?

Vous parlez français? → **Parlez-vous** français?

If your subject is **il, elle,** or **on** and if your verb ends with a vowel, insert **-t-** between the verb and the subject.

Elle va au cinéma ce soir? → **Va-t-elle** au cinéma ce soir?

When you have a noun as the subject, such as a person's name, use the subject and then invert with the corresponding pronoun.

Est-ce que **Paul** préfère le vert? → **Paul préfère-t-il** le vert?

NEGATIVE EXPRESSIONS

Negative Expressions

The most common negative expression is **ne… pas**. To make a sentence negative, put **ne… pas** around the conjugated verb.

Vous travaillez bien! → Vous **ne** travaillez **pas** bien!

In the **passé composé**, the negative comes around the helping verb.

Ils **ont mangé** ensemble. → Ils **n'**ont **pas mangé** ensemble.

Here are more negative expressions in French.

Negative Expression		Example
ne… pas encore	*not yet*	Ils **n'**ont **pas encore** mangé.
ne… plus	*no longer*	Elle **ne** mange **plus** de croissants.
ne… ni… ni	*neither nor*	Je **n'**aime **ni** les bananes **ni** les pommes.
ne… jamais	*never*	Tu **ne** viens **jamais** au parc avec nous.
ne… personne	*no one*	Danièle **n'**entend **personne** au téléphone.
ne… rien	*nothing*	Nous **ne** faisons **rien** ce soir.
ne… que	*only*	Je **n'**aime **que** le chocolat suisse.

When used as subjects, both **rien** and **personne** come before **ne**.

Rien n'est impossible! **Personne n'**écoute Charles!

In the past tense **ne… personne** works differently. Put the **ne** before the helping verb, but position the word **personne** after the past participle.

—Hier soir, vous avez vu **Marie** au théâtre ?

—Non je **n'**ai vu **personne** au théâtre.

The negative expressions **ne… rien, ne… personne,** and **ne… que** are often used with the expressions **quelque chose** *(something)* and **quelqu'un** *(someone).*

Expression	Corresponding Negatives
quelque chose	ne… rien; ne… que
quelqu'un	ne… personne, ne… que

Tu veux **quelque chose?**	*Do you want something?*
Je **ne** veux manger **que** la salade.	*I only want the salad.*
Vous attendez **quelqu'un**?	*Are you waiting for someone?*
Non, nous **n'**attendons **personne**.	*No, we aren't waiting for anyone.*
Je **n'**attends **que** mes parents.	*I'm **only** waiting for my parents.*

Synthèse de grammaire

PRONOUNS

Subject Pronouns

Here are the subject pronouns in French.

PERSON	SINGULAR PRONOUNS		PLURAL PRONOUNS	
1ST	je (j')	*I*	nous	*we*
2ND	tu	*you*	vous	*you*
3RD	il/elle/on	*he/she/one, we*	ils/elles	*they*

Tu and **vous** both mean *you*. Here are the rules for using them.

TU	VOUS
• someone your own age	• someone older than you
• someone younger than you	• someone you've just met
• family members	• someone in authority
• friends	• groups
• someone called by his/her first name	

When referring to a group with both masculine and feminine nouns (people or things), use **ils**.

Direct Object Pronouns

A **direct object** is the person or thing that receives the action of a verb. A direct object can be either a noun or a pronoun. Direct objects can be replaced by **direct object pronouns**.

DIRECT OBJECT PRONOUNS	
me (m') *me*	**nous** *us*
te (t') *you (fam)*	**vous** *you (formal, plural)*
le/la (l') *him/her, it*	**les** *them*

Direct object pronouns come before the conjugated verb or infinitive.

Paul et Sophie **nous** invitent au restaurant.

Tu veux regarder **la télévision**? → Oui, je veux **la** regarder.

When using a direct object pronoun with a negative, place the negative expression around the direct object pronoun and its verb.

Pierre **n'**entend **pas ses amis.** → Pierre **ne les** entend **pas.**

In the **passé composé,** the direct object pronoun will come before the helping verbs **avoir** or **être**.

Tu **as** regardé **le film français** hier? → Tu **l'as** regardé hier?

In the **passé composé** with **avoir,** the past participle doesn't agree with the subject. It will agree with a preceding direct object.

Michel a écouté **la radio.** → Michel **l'**a écouté**e**.

Nicole n'a pas aimé **les croissants.** → Nicole ne **les** a pas aimé**s.**

Indirect Object Pronouns

An **indirect object** is the person who benefits from the action of the verb. Indirect objects indicate *to whom* or *for whom* something is done. In French, the indirect object is usually preceded by the preposition **à** and is often used with verbs of giving (**donner, offrir, envoyer**) and of communication (**parler, écrire, dire, téléphoner**).

Nous allons écrire une carte postale **à nos parents**.

Indirect Object Pronouns	
me (m') *to me*	**nous** *to us*
te (t') *to you*	**vous** *to you (formal, plural)*
lui *to him, to her*	**leur** *to them*

Indirect object pronouns come before the verb. In the present tense, place the object before the conjugated verb.

Paul et Sophie **nous** envoient une lettre.

If there is an infinitive in the sentence, place the indirect object pronoun in front of the infinitive.

Tu veux parler **à ta mère**? → Oui, je veux **lui** parler.

When using an indirect object pronoun with a negative, place the negative expression around the indirect object pronoun and its verb.

Pierre **ne** téléphone **pas à ses amis**. → Pierre **ne leur** téléphone **pas**.

In the **passé composé,** the indirect object pronoun will come before the helping verbs **avoir** or **être**.

J'ai dit **à ma cousine** de venir ce soir. → Je **lui** ai dit de venir ce soir.

The Pronoun *en*

The pronoun **en** replaces **de** + **noun**. **En** is best understood to mean *some, any, of it,* or *of them.*

Tu prends **du café?** *Do you want some coffee?*

Oui, **j'en** veux bien. *Yes, I'd really like some.*

You can use the pronoun **en** to replace nouns that follow numbers or expressions of quantity.

D'habitude, j'achète **beaucoup de pain.** D'habitude, j'**en** achète **beaucoup.**

Tu as combien **de sœurs?** J'**en** ai **une.**

If there is an infinitive in the sentence, the pronoun **en** comes before the infinitive.

Je peux **en** manger.

In the **passé composé,** the pronoun **en** comes before the helping verb **avoir** or **être**.

Nous avons fait **des gâteaux.** Nous **en** avons fait.

A negative expression comes around the pronoun **en** and its verb.

Paul ne veut pas **de glace?** Non, il **n'en** veut **pas.**

Synthèse de grammaire

The Pronoun *y*

The pronoun **y** replaces the names of places that start with prepositions like **à, dans, en, chez, sur,** and **sous.**

Monique travaille **au musée?** → Oui, elle **y** travaille.

If there is an infinitive in the sentence, the pronoun **y** comes before the infinitive.

Vous voulez voyager **en Italie** l'année prochaine?

Oui, je veux **y** voyager l'année prochaine.

In the **passé composé,** the pronoun **y** comes before the helping verb **avoir** or **être.**

Nous avons dîné **au restaurant.** → Nous **y** avons dîné.

Elles sont allées **à la bibliothèque.** → Elles **y** sont allées.

Double Object Pronouns

It is possible to have both a **direct object** and an **indirect object** in the same sentence. When this occurs, place the pronouns before the verb in the following order.

me										
te		le (l')								
se	→	la (l')	→	lui	→	y	→	en	→	verb
nous		les		leur						
vous										

J'envoie **la lettre à mes parents.** — *I am sending my parents the letter.*

Je **l'**envoie à mes parents. — *I am sending* ***it*** *to my parents.*

Je **leur** envoie la lettre. — *I am sending* ***them*** *the letter.*

Je **la leur** envoie. — *I am sending* ***it to them.***

The Relative Pronouns *qui, que, dont*

To refer to something or someone already mentioned in conversation, use the relative pronouns **qui** and **que** *(that, which, who,* or *whom).*

Qui, meaning *that, which,* or *who,* is used as the subject of the second clause and is always followed by a verb.

C'est un étudiant **qui est** très sérieux.

Que, meaning *that, which, whom,* is the object of the second clause and is followed by a subject and a verb.

Paul est un ami **que nous aimons** beaucoup.

If the **passé composé** follows **que**, the past participle agrees in gender and number with the noun to which **que** refers.

La maison que vous avez achetée est très grande!

Use the relative pronoun **dont** (*that, whom, whose*) to replace a prepositional phrase beginning with **de.**

Tu parles **de Céline?** Elle travaille à la boulangerie.

La fille **dont** tu parles travaille à la boulangerie.

Interrogative Pronouns

To ask *which one* or *which ones,* use the appropriate form of the interrogative adjective **lequel**. It refers back to someone or to something already mentioned and agrees in gender and in number with its noun.

	MASCULINE	FEMININE
SINGULAR	lequel	laquelle
PLURAL	lesquels	lesquelles

Voici un sandwich au jambon et un sandwich au poulet. **Lequel** veux-tu?

Les chaussures noires ou les chaussures blanches? **Lesquelles** achètes-tu?

Demonstrative Pronouns

The **demonstrative pronoun** is used to refer back to the person(s) or thing(s) already mentioned. Demonstrative pronouns agree in gender and in number with the nouns they replace.

	MASCULINE	FEMININE
SINGULAR	celui	celle
PLURAL	ceux	celles

Cette affiche est jolie.

Laquelle? **Celle** qui est sur la table.

To make a distinction between *this one* and *that one,* and to separate *these* from *those,* use **-ci** and **-là**.

Je veux des bananes. **Celles-ci** sont bonnes mais **celles-là** sont mauvaises.
I want some bananas. These are good but those are bad.

VERBS

Present Tense of regular *-er* verbs

Regular verbs ending in **-er** are formed by dropping the **-er** from the verb and adding the appropriate endings.

aimer	
j'	aime
tu	aim**es**
il/elle/on	aime
nous	aim**ons**
vous	aim**ez**
ils/elles	aim**ent**

Tu **aimes** chanter avec la radio, n'est-ce pas?

Verbs ending in *-ger* and *-cer*

Verbs ending in **-ger** or **-cer** have a slightly different conjugation pattern. Verbs ending in **-ger**, like **manger**, follow the regular pattern except for the **nous** form. Verbs ending in **-cer**, like **commencer**, also change in the **nous** form.

	manger *(to eat)*	**commencer** *(to begin)*
je	mange	commence
tu	manges	commences
il/elle/on	mange	commence
nous	mang**e**ons	commen**ç**ons
vous	mangez	commencez
ils/elles	mangent	commencent

Regular *-re* verbs

Regular verbs ending in **-re** are formed by dropping the **-re** ending and adding the appropriate endings.

attendre *(to wait for)*	
j'	attend**s**
tu	attend**s**
il/elle/on	attend
nous	attend**ons**
vous	attend**ez**
ils/elles	attend**ent**

Regular *-ir* verbs

Regular verbs ending in **-ir** are formed by dropping the **-ir** ending from the verb and adding the appropriate endings.

finir *(to finish)*	
je	fini**s**
tu	fini**s**
il/elle/on	fini**t**
nous	fini**ssons**
vous	fini**ssez**
ils/elles	fini**ssent**

Stem-changing verbs

Some **-er** verbs, like **préférer** and **acheter**, change their stems in the **je**, **tu**, **il/elle/on**, and **ils/elles** forms of the verb.

préférer *(to prefer)*		**acheter** *(to buy)*	
je **préfère**	nous préférons	j'**achète**	nous achetons
tu **préfères**	vous préférez	tu **achètes**	vous achetez
il/elle/on **préfère**	ils/elle **préfèrent**	il/elle/on **achète**	ils/elles **achètent**
Verbs like préférer: espérer, répéter		Verbs like acheter: amener, emmener, lever, promener	

Tu **préfères** le café.

Elles **achètent** de belles bananes au marché.

Other verbs like **appeler** *(to call)* change their stems by doubling a consonant. Verbs ending in **-yer,** like **nettoyer** *(to clean)*, change the **-y** to **-i.**

appeler *(to call)*		**nettoyer** *(to clean)*	
j'**appelle**	nous appelons	je **nettoie**	nous nettoyons
tu **appelles**	vous appelez	tu **nettoies**	vous nettoyez
il/elle/on **appelle**	ils/elles **appellent**	il/elle/on **nettoie**	ils/elles **nettoient**
Verbs like appeler: jeter, épeler, rappeler		Verbs like nettoyer: balayer, envoyer, essayer (de), payer	

J'**appelle** souvent mon frère.

Laurence ne **nettoie** jamais sa chambre!

The Irregular Verbs *avoir, être, aller,* and *faire*

The verbs **avoir**, **être**, **aller**, and **faire** are all irregular.

	avoir *(to have)*	**être** *(to be)*	**aller** *(to go)*	**faire** *(to make, to do)*
je/j'	ai	suis	vais	fais
tu	as	es	vas	fais
il/elle/on	a	est	va	fait
nous	avons	sommes	allons	faisons
vous	avez	êtes	allez	faites
ils/elles	ont	sont	vont	font
Past Participle	eu	été	allé	fait

The Irregular Verbs *vouloir, pouvoir,* and *devoir*

The verbs **vouloir**, **pouvoir**, and **devoir** are all irregular. They do not follow the normal conjugation pattern like regular **-ir** verbs.

	vouloir *(to want)*	**pouvoir** *(to be able to)*	**devoir** *(must, to have to)*
je	veux	peux	dois
tu	veux	peux	dois
il/elle/on	veut	peut	doit
nous	voulons	pouvons	devons
vous	voulez	pouvez	devez
ils/elles	veulent	peuvent	doivent

The Irregular Verb *prendre*

prendre *(to take, to have food or drink)*	
je prends	nous prenons
tu prends	vous prenez
il/elle/on prend	ils/elles prennent

Other verbs that follow the conjugation of **prendre** are: **apprendre, comprendre,** and **reprendre**.

The Verbs *dormir, sortir,* and *partir*

The verbs **dormir, sortir,** and **partir** follow a different conjugation pattern than regular **-ir** verbs.

	dormir *(to sleep)*	**partir** *(to leave)*	**sortir** *(to go out)*
je	dors	pars	sors
tu	dors	pars	sors
il/elle/on	dort	part	sort
nous	dormons	partons	sortons
vous	dormez	partez	sortez
ils/elles	dorment	partent	sortent

The Irregular Verbs *boire* and *voir*

The verbs **boire** and **voir** are both irregular.

	boire *(to drink)*	**voir** *(to see)*
je	bois	vois
tu	bois	vois
il/elle/on	boit	voit
nous	buvons	voyons
vous	buvez	voyez
ils/elles	boivent	voient

The Verbs *savoir* and *connaître*

Both **savoir** and **connaître** mean *to know* and they are irregular verbs.

savoir *(to know)*		**connaître** *(to know; to be acquainted with)*	
je sais	nous savons	je connais	nous connaissons
tu sais	vous savez	tu connais	vous connaissez
il/elle/on sait	ils/elles savent	il/elle/on connaît	ils/elles connaissent
Past participle: su		**Past participle:** connu	

Savoir means *to know about something.* It is used to express general knowledge, facts, and also means to know how to do something.

Nous **savons** l'heure. Il est trois heures et demie.

Connaître means *to know* as in the sense of being *acquainted with.* It is used with people, places, works of art, and literature.

Je **connais** bien cet hôtel.   Vous **connaissez** Martin?

The Irregular Verb *mettre*

The verb **mettre** is an irregular verb. Its past participle is **mis.**

mettre *(to put, to put on clothes)*	
je mets	nous mettons
tu mets	vous mettez
il/elle/on met	ils/elles mettent

Tu **mets** un pull bleu?   Chantal **met** le CD dans son sac.

The Irregular Verb *courir*

The verb **courir** is irregular. Its past participle is **couru.**

courir *(to run)*	
je cours	nous courons
tu cours	vous courez
il/elle/on court	ils/elles courent

The Verbs *ouvrir* and *offrir*

The verbs **offrir** and **ouvrir** end in **-ir,** but are conjugated like **-er** verbs.

offrir *(to offer)*	**ouvrir** *(to open)*
j'offre	j'ouvre
tu offres	tu ouvres
il/elle/on offre	il/elle/on ouvre
nous offrons	nous ouvrons
vous offrez	vous ouvrez
ils/elles offrent	ils/elles ouvrent

The Verb *recevoir*

The verb **recevoir** is irregular. Its past participle is **reçu**.

recevoir *(to receive, to get)*	
je reçois	nous recevons
tu reçois	vous recevez
il/elle/on reçoit	ils/elles reçoivent

The Irregular Verb *suivre*

The verb **suivre** is irregular. You can use this verb to say which courses you are taking this year.

suivre *(to follow)*	
je suis	nous suivons
tu suis	vous suivez
il/elle/on suit	ils/elles suivent

The *passé composé* with *avoir*

The **passé composé** tells what happened in the past. The **passé composé** has two main parts, a helping verb (usually the verb **avoir**) and a past participle.

To form the past participle of an **-er** verb, take off the **-er** and add **-é.** To form the past participle of an **-ir** verb, take off the **-r.** For **-re** verbs, drop the **-re** and add a **-u** to form its past participle.

Infinitive	Past Participle
écouter	**écouté**
choisir	**choisi**
perdre	**perdu**

	écouter *(to listen to)*	**choisir** *(to choose)*	**perdre** *(to lose)*
j'	ai écouté	ai choisi	ai perdu
tu	as écouté	as choisi	as perdu
il/elle/on	a écouté	a choisi	a perdu
nous	avons écouté	avons choisi	avons perdu
vous	avez écouté	avez choisi	avez perdu
ils/elles	ont écouté	ont choisi	ont perdu

To make the **passé composé** negative, put **ne** and **pas** around the helping verb.

Vous **n'**avez **pas** écouté le professeur.

Synthèse de grammaire

Past Participles of Irregular Verbs

Here is a list of some irregular verbs and their past participles.

INFINITIVE	PAST PARTICIPLE	INFINITIVE	PAST PARTICIPLE
être	**été**	faire	**fait**
avoir	**eu**	pleuvoir	**plu**
vouloir	**voulu**	connaître	**connu**
boire	**bu**	devoir	**dû**
lire	**lu**	dire	**dit**
voir	**vu**	écrire	**écrit**
mettre	**mis**	pouvoir	**pu**
prendre	**pris**	savoir	**su**

The *passé composé* with *être*

Some verbs, mainly verbs of motion like **aller,** use **être** instead of **avoir** as a helping verb in the **passé composé.** For these verbs, the past participle agrees with the subject.

aller *(to go)*	
je suis **allé(e)**	nous sommes **allé(e)s**
tu es **allé(e)**	vous êtes **allé(e)s**
il est **allé**	ils sont **allés**
elle est **allée**	elles sont **allées**
on est **allé(e)(s)**	

Les professeurs **sont arrivés** en retard pour leurs cours.

Here is a list of verbs that take **être** in the **passé composé.**

VERB	PAST PARTICIPLE	VERB	PAST PARTICIPLE
arriver	**arrivé**	partir	**parti**
descendre	**descendu**	rester	**resté**
entrer	**entré**	tomber	**tombé**
sortir	**sorti**	mourir	**mort**
retourner	**retourné**	naître	**né**
monter	**monté**	venir	**venu**

Verbs with *être* or *avoir* in the *passé composé*

Some verbs can take either **être** or **avoir** to form the **passé composé.** When these verbs have a direct object, the past participle agrees with the direct object if it comes before the past participle.

Anne **est sortie** hier soir avec ses amies.
Anne went out last night with her friends.

Anne **a sorti la poubelle** après le dîner.
Anne took out the trash after dinner.

Anne **l'a sortie** après le dîner.
Anne took it out (the trash) after dinner.

C'est versus *il/elle est*

Use C'est With	Use Il/Elle est With
• someone's name • an article/possessive adjective + a noun • an article + a noun + an adjective	• an adjective by itself • a profession

C'est **Pierre**. Il est **dentiste**. C'est **un restaurant italien**.

Venir and the *passé récent*

The verb **venir** means *to come* and is an irregular verb.

venir *(to come)*	
je viens	nous venons
tu viens	vous venez
il/elle/on vient	ils/elles viennent

A form of **venir** plus the preposition **de** plus an infinitive can be used to express an action that has just occurred.

Nous **venons de finir** nos devoirs. *We have just finished our homework.*

The Imperative

To give a command in French, use the imperative. The imperative form comes from the **tu, nous,** and **vous** forms. In **-er** verbs, the **-s** is dropped from the **tu** form.

	tu	nous	vous
écouter	écoute	écoutons	écoutez
finir	finis	finissons	finissez
attendre	attends	attendons	attendez

To make a command negative, put **ne** and **pas** around the verb.

Donne le livre à Monique! → **Ne donne pas** le livre à Monique!

Reflexive Verbs

Reflexive verbs are used when the same person does and receives the action of the verb. These verbs use reflexive pronouns.

se laver *(to wash oneself)*	
je me lave	nous nous lavons
tu te laves	vous vous lavez
il/elle/on se lave	ils/elles se lavent

Marie **se lave** les cheveux chaque soir et elle **se brosse** les dents.

Reflexive Pronouns with Infinitives

When you use the reflexive verb in the infinitive form, the reflexive pronoun will agree with the subject.

Nous n'allons pas **nous** ennuyer à la plage!

Synthèse de grammaire

Reflexive Verbs in the *passé composé*

All reflexive verbs use **être** to form the **passé composé.**

Paul **s'est déshabillé** et puis il **s'est couché.**

In the **passé composé** of reflexive verbs, the past participle usually agrees in gender and number with the reflexive pronoun.

se coucher *(to go to bed)*	
je me suis **couché(e)**	nous nous sommes **couché(e)s**
tu t'es **couché(e)**	vous vous êtes **couché(e)(s)**
il/elle s'est **couché/couchée**	il/elles se sont **couché(e)s**
on s'est **couché(e)(s)**	

The past participle agrees with the reflexive pronoun only if the pronoun is a direct object. The reflexive pronoun, however, is not always a direct object.

Monique **s'est lavée.** Monique **s'est lavé les mains.**

Commands with Reflexive Verbs

When you make an affirmative command with a reflexive verb, connect the reflexive pronoun to the verb with a hyphen.

Couche-toi! *Go to bed!*

If the command is negative, however, the reflexive pronoun comes before the verb and **ne… pas** comes around the whole structure.

Ne te couche **pas!** *Don't go to bed!*

The *imparfait*

The **imparfait** is used to describe events in the past or to emphasize that certain actions were done habitually. To form the imperfect, drop the **-ons** from the **nous** form of the verb and add the endings. The **only** verb that has an irregular stem is **être: ét-**.

	parler	**finir**	**vendre**
je	parlais	finissais	vendais
tu	parlais	finissais	vendais
il/elle/on	parlait	finissait	vendait
nous	parlions	finissions	vendions
vous	parliez	finissiez	vendiez
ils/elles	parlaient	finissaient	vendaient

Remember that **-ger** verbs, like **manger** and **-cer** verbs, like **commencer,** have a different stem in the **nous** and **vous** forms than in the other forms of the verb.

	manger	**commencer**
je	mangeais	commençais
tu	mangeais	commençais
il/elle/on	mangeait	commençait
nous	**mangions**	**commencions**
vous	**mangiez**	**commenciez**
ils/elles	mangeaient	commençaient

Synthèse de grammaire

The Future

The future tense in French is used to tell what will happen. To form the future tense, use the infinitive as the stem and add the future endings. Drop the **-e** from **-re** verbs before you add the future endings.

	parler	**finir**	**vendre**
je	parlerai	finirai	vendrai
tu	parleras	finiras	vendras
il/elle/on	parlera	finira	vendra
nous	parlerons	finirons	vendrons
vous	parlerez	finirez	vendrez
ils/elles	parleront	finiront	vendront

While the endings for the future are the same for all verbs, several verbs have irregular future stems.

aller	**ir-**	**j'irai, tu iras,**
avoir	**aur-**	**j'aurai, tu auras,**
devoir	**devr-**	**je devrai, tu devras**
être	**ser-**	**je serai, tu seras,**
faire	**fer-**	**je ferai, tu feras,**
pouvoir	**pourr-**	**je pourrai, tu pourras**
vouloir	**voudr-**	**je voudrai, tu voudras**
venir	**viendr-**	**je viendrai, tu viendras**
voir	**verr-**	**je verrai, tu verras**
envoyer	**enverr-**	**j'enverrai, tu enverras**
courir	**courr-**	**je courrai, tu courras**
mourir	**mourr-**	**je mourrai, tu mourras**

Verbs like **appeler, acheter, lever,** and **préférer** that have spelling changes in the present tense also have spelling changes in the future.

The Conditional

The conditional (**le conditionnel**) is used to tell what would happen. To form the conditional, use the infinitive as the stem (same as the future stem) and add the endings from the **imparfait**.

	parler	**finir**	**vendre**
je	parlerais	finirais	vendrais
tu	parlerais	finirais	vendrais
il/elle/on	parlerait	finirait	vendrait
nous	parlerions	finirions	vendrions
vous	parleriez	finiriez	vendriez
ils/elles	parleraient	finiraient	vendraient

The conditional can also be used to make polite requests.

Est-ce que **tu pourrais** m'aider? *Could you help me?*

Si clauses

To express what happens, will happen, or would happen in different circumstances, use two different types of clauses, an "if" clause and a "result" clause. The if clause will be in either the present or the **imparfait** and the result clause will be in either the present, the future, or the conditional.

Si tu étudies beaucoup, **tu réussis.**	*If you study a lot, you succeed.*
Si tu étudies beaucoup, **tu réussiras.**	*If you study a lot, you will succeed.*
Nous viendrions si nous avions le temps.	*We would come if we had the time.*

You can also use a **si** clause to make an invitation. To do this, you will use ***si*** + ***on*** + ***imparfait***.

Si on allait à la plage ce week-end?
How about going to the beach this weekend?

The *passé composé* versus the *imparfait*

Both the **imparfait** and the **passé composé** can be used to talk about the past.

The **imparfait** is generally used to talk about things that happened over and over again in the past or how things used to be.

Quand Nicole **était** petite, sa famille **rendait** visite à ses grands-parents en été.
When Nicole was little, her family used to visit her grandparents every summer.

The **imparfait** can also be used to give descriptions of the weather, people, or places.

Il **pleuvait** quand on est arrivés.
Yesterday, the weather was bad. It was raining!

The **passé composé** is used to tell what happened at a specific moment in the past.

Ce matin, **j'ai téléphoné** deux fois à Max mais il **n'a pas répondu**!
This morning I called Max two times but he didn't answer!

Use the Imparfait To:	Use the Passé Composé To:
give background information	tell what happened on a particular occasion
set the scene and explain the circumstances in a story	tell the sequence of events in a story **(d'abord, ensuite, puis, après)**
explain what used to happen repeatedly	indicate a sudden change or the reaction to something
Key words: **souvent, tous les jours, d'habitude, le lundi (mardi, jeudi…etc.)**	Key words: **soudain, à ce moment-là, au moment où, une fois, deux fois...**

Synthèse de grammaire

The Subjunctive of Regular Verbs

The present tense, the **passé composé,** and the future tense are in the indicative mood. There is another mood in French called the **subjunctive** mood that is used after certain expressions like **il faut que.** The subjunctive is used to express emotion, desire, and doubt.

Il faut que nous nous **dépêchions.**
We have to hurry!

Ma mère **est heureuse que** je **finisse** mes devoirs.
My mother is happy that I am finishing my homework.

Use the **subjunctive** with the following expressions:

Il faut que...
Il est important que...
Il est nécessaire que...
Il est bon que....
Je veux que...
Je suis content(e) que...
Je suis triste que...

To form the subjunctive, drop the **-ent** from the **ils/elles** present tense form of the verb and add the following endings: **-e, -es, -e, -ions, -iez, -ent**

	parler **ils** par**lent**	**finir** **ils** finiss**ent**	**vendre** vend**ent**
que je	parle	finisse	vende
que tu	parles	finisses	vendes
qu'il/elle/on	parle	finisse	vende
que nous	parlions	finissions	vendions
que vous	parliez	finissiez	vendiez
qu'ils/elles	parlent	finissent	vendent

The Subjunctive of Irregular Verbs

Some verbs in the subjunctive are irregular because they have different stems for the **nous** and **vous** forms of the verb.

boire	que je boive	que nous buvions
devoir	que je doive	que nous devions
prendre	que je prenne	que nous prenions
venir	que je vienne	que nous venions
voir	que je voie	que nous voyions

	aller	**être**	**avoir**	**faire**
que je (j')	aille	sois	aie	fasse
que tu	ailles	sois	aies	fasses
qu'il/elle/on	aille	soit	ait	fasse
que nous	allions	soyons	ayons	fassions
que vous	alliez	soyez	ayez	fassiez
qu'ils/elles	aillent	soient	aient	fassent

Present Participles

Form the **present participle** of French verbs by taking off the **-ons** from the **nous** form and adding the ending **-ant.**

verb	**nous** form	**present participle**
sortir	sortons	sortant
aller	allons	allant
attendre	attendons	attendant
finir	finissons	finissant
prendre	prenons	prenant
vouloir	voulons	voulant
dormir	dormons	dormant
faire	faisons	faisant

The present participles for **avoir, être,** and **savoir** are irregular.

Verb	**Present Participle**
être	étant
avoir	ayant
savoir	sachant

Use **en** or **tout en** + **present participle** to indicate that someone is doing one thing while another is going on. It can also show two activities that occur at the same time.

J'ai répondu au téléphone **en mangeant** un croissant.
I answered the phone while eating a croissant.

The present participle can also be used as an adjective. Remember to make it agree in gender and in number with its noun.

C'est une maison **charmante**!

Glossaire français-anglais

This vocabulary includes almost all of the words presented in the textbook, both active (for production) and passive (for recognition only). An entry in boldface type indicates that the word or phrase is active. Active words and phrases are practiced in the chapter and are listed in the **Résumé** pages at the end of each chapter. You are expected to know and be able to use active vocabulary.

All other words are for recognition only. These words are found in activities, in optional and visual material, in the **Géoculture, Comparaisons, Lecture et écriture,** the **Télé-roman,** and **Variations littéraires.** Many words have more than one definition; the definitions given here correspond to the way the words are used in *Bien dit!*

The number after each entry refers to the chapter where the word or phrase first appears or where it is presented as an active vocabulary word. Active words and phrases from Level 1 are indicated by the Roman numeral I.

(auto)biographie *(auto)biography,* 9
à *at/to,* 3; **À bientôt.** *See you soon.* I; **à ce moment-là** *at that moment,* 6; **à côté de** *next to,* I; **À demain.** *See you tomorrow.,* I; **à destination de** *heading for,* I; **à droite de** *to the right of,* I; **à gauche de** *to the left of,* I; à haute voix *aloud,* 5; **à l'** at/to, 3; à l'époque *at the time,* 3; **à l'étranger** *abroad,* 10; **à l'heure** *on time,* I; à l'inverse *conversely,* 10; **à la** *at/to,* 3; à la fois *at the same time,* 396; **à la télé** *on TV,* 9; **à mon avis** *in my opinion,* I; à partir de *from,* 1; à pas de loup *on tip toes,* 5; **à peine** *barely,* 7; **à peu près** *about,* 3; **à pied** *on foot,* I; **À plus tard.** *See you later.,* I; **à point** *medium,* I; **À quel nom?** *Under what name?,* I; **à quelle heure** *at what time,* I; **À quelle heure tu as... ?** *At what time do you have . . . ?,* I; **à tour de rôle** *taking turns,* 10; **À tout à l'heure.** *See you later.,* I; à travers *through,* 5; **à vélo** *by bicycle,* I; **À votre service.** *You're welcome.,* I
abasourdi(e) *astounded,* 7
les abdominaux (m. pl.) *abdominal muscles,* 8
l' abeille (f.) *bee,* 10
abîmer *to damage,* 10
l' abricot (m.) *apricot,* 3
absolument *absolutely,* 10
l' accès (handicapé) (m.) *handicap access,* I
les accessoires (m. pl.) *accessories,* I
accorder *to give,* 1; *to award,* 9
accorte *cheerful,* 1
s' accouder *to lean (one's elbows) on,* 1
accro *addicted (slang),* 9
accrocher *to hang; to attach,* 2
l' accueil (m.) *home page,* 4
accueillir *to welcome,* 7
l' achat (m.) *purchase,* 396
acheter *to buy,* 1
l' acteur (m.) *actor,* 1
l' activité (f.) *activity,* I
l' actrice (f.) *actress,* 1
actualiser *to refresh,* 4
l' addition (f.) *bill,* I
adorer *to adore,* 1
l' adresse (f.) *address,* 4; **adresse e-mail** *e-mail address,* I
s' adresser *to address,* I
Adressez-vous... *Ask . . . ,* I
aérien(ne) *air/air-related,* 10
l' aérobic (m.) *aerobics,* I
l' aéroport (m.) *airport,* I
l' affichage (m.) *view,* 4
l' affiche (f.) *poster,* 9
s' afficher *to show off,* 10
s' affronter *to confront each other,* 4
l' âge (m.) *age,* I
âgé(e) *elderly,* 1
l' agence (f.) de voyages *travel agency,* 10
agricole *agricultural,* 6
agroalimentaire *agro-food,* 5
l' aide (f.) *help,* 4
aider *to help,* I
l' ail (m.) *garlic,* 3
l' aile (f.) *wing,* 401
ailleurs *somewhere else,* 3
aimer *to like/to love,* 1; **aimer bien** *to like,* I; **aimer mieux** *to like better/to prefer,* I
ainsi *so, thus,* 4
aisé(e) *well-to-do,* 386
ajouta *added,* 385
ajouter *to add,* 3
alentour *around,* 6
alimentaire *food (adj.),* 3
l' alimentation (f.) *eating,* 8
l' Allemagne (f.) *Germany,* 10
l' allemand (m.) *German (language),* I
allemand(e) *German,* 10
aller *to go,* 2; **s'en aller** *to run along, to leave* 5; **aller de travers** *to go wrong,* 4
l' aller simple (m.) *one way,* I
l' aller-retour (m.) *round-trip,* I
l' allume-gaz (m.) *gas lighter,* 7
allumer (les bougies) *to light (the candles),* 2; *to turn on,* 9
les allumettes (f. pl.) *matches,* 7
alors *well/then,* 3; *so,* 4; **alors que** *while,* 6
l' alouette (f.) *lark,* 388

Glossaire français-anglais

l' amateur (m.) (de) *lover (of),* 9
l' âme (f.) *soul,* 6
amener *to bring someone along,* I
américain *American,* I
amputasse *amputate,* 399
l' ami(e) *friend,* I
amusant(e) *funny/amusing,* 9
les amuse-gueules (m.pl.) *snacks,* 2
s' amuser *to have fun,* 2
Amuse-toi bien... *Have fun...,* 2
l' anchois (m.) *anchovy,* 9
l' âne (m.) *donkey,* 6
l' ange (m.) *angel,* 9
l' anglais (m.) *English,* I
anglais(e) *English/British,* 10
l' Angleterre (f.) *England,* 10
l' animal(-aux) (m.) *animal(s),* I
l' animateur (animatrice) *disc jockey,* 9
animer *to animate,* 5
l' anneau (m.) *ring,* 4
l' anniversaire (m.) *birthday,* 2
annuler *to cancel, stop,* 4
l' anorak (m.) *winter jacket,* I
août *August,* I
l' appareil photo (numérique) *(digital) camera,* 1
l' apparition (f.) *appearance,* 385
l' appartement (m.) *apartment,* I
apparu(e) *appeared*
l' appel (m.) *call*
appeler *to call,* I; **s'appeler** *to be named,* I
apporter *to bring,* 388
apprécier *to appreciate,* 9
apprendre *to learn,* I
l' apprentissage (m.) *learning,* 1
après *after,* I; **après ça** *afterwards,* 5;
après-demain *day after tomorrow,* 7
l' après-midi (m.) afternoon, I
apprêter *to prepare,* 396
l' aquarelle (f.) *watercolor,* 382
l' arachide (f.) *peanut,* 396
l' araignée (f.) *spider,* 7
l' arbre (m.) *tree,* 7
les arènes (f. pl.) *amphitheater,* 9
l' argent (m.) *silver,* I; money, I
argenté(e) *silver,* 2
l' armoire (f.) *wardrobe,* I
l' arrêt (de bus) (m.) *(bus) stop,* I
arrêter *to stop,* 4
l' arrivée (f.) *arrival,* I
arriver *to arrive,* 2; *to happen (to someone),* 4
l' arrondissement (m.) *neighborhood or district in Paris,* 1
arroser *to water,* I
les arts plastiques (m. pl.) *visual arts,* I

l' ascenseur (m.) *elevator,* I
l' aspirateur (m.) *vacuum cleaner,* I
s' asseoir *to sit down,* 3
Asseyez-vous! *Sit down!,* I
assez *quite,* I; *pretty/rather,* 1; assez bien *pretty well,* 1
l' assiette (f.) *plate,* I
assis(e) *seated,* 4
l' assurance maladie (f.) *health insurance,* 8
l' atelier (m.) *workshop,* 3
l' athlétisme (m.) *track and field,* I
attendre *to wait,* 1; *to expect,* 10
attira *brought,* 389
attraper *to catch,* 7
au *to/at/at the,* 3; **au bord de la mer** *seashore,* 10; **au bout de** *at/ to the end of,* 3; au cours de *during,* 389; **au début de** *at the beginning of,* 384; au-dessus *above,* 10; **Au fait,...** *By the way,...,* 4; **au fond de** *at the end of,* I; *at the bottom of,* 10; **au milieu de** *in the middle of,* 3; **au moment où** *at the time (when)/ as,* 7; **au plus tard** *at the latest,* 5; au premier abord *at first glance,* 8; **Au revoir.** *Goodbye.,* I
l' aubergine (f.) *eggplant,* 3
aucun(e) *no other,* 1; *no, not any,* 4
aujourd'hui *today,* I
aurait dû *should have,* 3
aussi bien pour ... que pour ... *for ... as well as for ...,* 383
aussitôt que *as soon as,* 385
autant de *as many as,* 6
autant que *as much as,* 6
l' automne (m.) *fall,* I
autour de *around,* 3
autrefois *in the past,* 5
aux *at/to,* 3; at the, I; aux aguets *on guard,* 7
avancer *to go forward,* I
avant (de) *before,* 5
avec *with,* I; **avec qui** *with whom,* I; **Avec qui... ?** With whom ...?, I; **avec vue** *with a view,* I
l' aversion (f.) *dislike,* 5
l' avion (m.) *plane,* 10
l' avocat(e) *lawyer,* 384
avoir *to have,* 1; **avoir... ans** *to be ... years old,* 1; **avoir besoin de** *to need,* 3; **avoir bonne mine** *to look good (healthy),* 8; **avoir chaud** *to be hot,* I; avoir confiance *to trust,* 396; **avoir de la fièvre** *to have a fever,* 8; **avoir entraînement** *to have practice/ training,* 4; **avoir envie de** *to feel like,* I; **avoir faim** *to be hungry,* I; **avoir froid** *to be cold,* I; avoir honte *to be ashamed,* 7; **avoir intérêt à** *to be in one's best interest,* I; **avoir l'air** *to seem,* 8; **avoir le temps** *to have time,* 2; **avoir les yeux...** *to have... eyes,* I; avoir lieu *to take place,* 1; **avoir mal (à)** *to hurt/ache,* 8; **avoir mauvaise mine** *to look bad (unhealthy),* 8; **avoir raison** *to be right,* 4; **avoir soif** *to be thirsty,* I
avoisinant(e) *neighboring,* 389
avouer *to confess,* 4
avril *April,* I
l' awalé (m.) *African game like Backgammon,* 8

le bacon *bacon,* I
les bagages (à main) (m. pl.) *(carry-on) luggage,* I
la bague *ring,* I
la baguette *loaf of French bread,* I
la baie *bay,* 9
se baigner *to swim,* 7
la baignoire *bathtub,* 5
le bal populaire *village dance,* 2
le baladeur *walkman,* I
la balançoire *swing,* 6
balayer *to sweep,* I
le balcon *balcony,* I
la balle *ball,* 1
le ballon *(inflatable) ball,* I; *balloon,* 2
la banane *banana,* 3
la bande dessinée (BD) *comic strip,* 9
la banque *bank,* I
la barre de défilement *scroll bar,* 4
bas (basse) *low,* I
le bas-relief *raised surface sculpture,* 9
basé(e) sur *based on,* 9
le base-ball baseball, I
le basket(ball) *basketball,* 1
les baskets (f.) tennis shoes, I
la basse-cour barnyard, 6
le bassin de baignade *swimming area,* 383
le bateau: *boat,* 10; bateau-mouche *river boat (on the Seine),* 382
bateau à voiles *sailboat,* 10
le bâtiment *building,* 1
le bâton *stick,* 4

la batte *bat,* I
la batterie *drums,* 1
se battre *to fight,* 3
bavarder *to talk,* 4
beau *handsome,* 1
beaucoup *a lot,* 3
le beau-père *stepfather,* 1
la Belgique *Belgium,* 10
belle *beautiful,* 1
la belle-mère *stepmother,* 1
les bénéfices (m. pl.) *profit,* 397
bercer *to rock (cradle),* 394
la berge *bank (of a river),* 382
bête *fool,* 385
le beurre *butter,* I
la bibliothèque *library,* I
bien *well,* I; **bien cuit** *well-done,* I; bien des *many,* 399; **bien entendu** *of course,* I; **bien mûr(e)** *ripened,* 3
bien sûr *of course,* I; **Bien sûr que non.** *Of course not.,* 2
bientôt *soon,* 7
la bijouterie *jewelry,* I
le/la bijoutier (-ière) *jeweler,* 1
les billes (f.) *marbles,* 6
le billet *bill,* I; *ticket,* 10; **billet d'avion** *plane ticket,* I; **billet de train** *train ticket,* 10
les biscuits (m.) *cookies,* 2
blanc(he) *white,* I
se blesser *to injure oneself,* 8
bleu(e) *blue,* 1
blond(e) *blond(e),* 1
le blues *blues music,* 9
le bœuf *beef,* 3; *ox,* 4
boire *to drink,* 2
le bois *woods,* 7; wood, 5
boisé(e) *panelled,* 390
la boisson *drink,* I
la boîte *box,* 3; **boîte de conserve** *canned food,* 3
le bol *bowl,* I
bon *good,* I; *fine,* 2; **Bon anniversaire!** *Happy birthday!,* 2; **bon appétit** *enjoy your meal,* I; **bon marché** *inexpensive,* I; bon sang! *blast!, darn!,* 5
les bonbons (m. pl.) *sweets/candy,* 2
le bonheur *happiness,* 388
le bonhomme *sonny,* 3
Bonjour. *Hello.,* I; *Good morning.,* I
bonne *good,* I; **bonne année** *Happy New Year,* 2; **Bonne idée!** *Good idea!,* 2; **Bonne soirée!** *Have a good evening!,* 2
Bonsoir. *Hello./Good evening.,* I

la bonté *kindness,* 394
le bord *edge,* 10; *side,* 6
bosser *to work (slang),* 9
le bossu (la bossue) *hunchback,* 398
les bottes (f. pl.) *boots,* I
la bouche *mouth,* I
le boucher (la bouchère) *butcher,* 3
la boucherie *butcher shop,* 3
les boucles d'oreilles (f. pl.) *earrings,* I
bouger *to move,* 6
la bougie *candle,* 2
bouillir *to boil,* 3
le boulanger(-ère) *baker,* 3
la boulangerie *bakery,* 3
la boule *ball,* 3
le boulodrome *area to play pétanque,* 383
le bouquet de fleurs *bouquet of flowers,* 2
la boussole *compass,* 7
la bouteille d'eau *bottle of water,* 3
la bouteille isotherme *thermos,* 7
la boutique *shop,* I
le bovarysme *refers to the novel Madame Bovary,* 5
le bracelet *bracelet,* I
la branche *branch,* 7
branché(e) *tuned in; plugged in,* 9
le bras *arm,* 8
bref *in short,* 7
briller *to shine,* 389
la brindille *twig,* 401
le briquet *lighter,* 7
la brochure *brochure,* 10
le brocoli *broccoli,* 3
la bronche *bronchial tube*
la brosse *brush,* 5; **brosse à dents** *toothbrush,* 5
se brosser (les cheveux/les dents) *to brush (one's hair/one's teeth),* 5
la brousse *African bush (wilderness),* 7
le bruit *noise,* 6; bruit de fond, *background noise,* 9; bruits, *gossip,* 4
se brûler *to burn oneself,* 8
le brumatiseur *spray,* 383
brun(e) *brown(-haired),* I
bruyant(e) *noisy,* 6
la bûche de Noël *Yule log,* 2
le buisson *bush,* 7
le bulletin météo(rologique) *weather report,* 9
le bureau *desk,* I; **bureau de change** *currency exchange office, I*
le bus *bus,* 9
le but *goal,* 4
le butin *bounty,* 392

C

C'est l'heure de... *It's time to...,* 5
C'est pas mal, sans plus. *It's just O.K.,* 9
C'est... le kilo. *It's... per kilo.,* 3
ça *this/that,* I; **ça fait** *since/ago/for,* I; **Ça fait...** *It's... (euros).,* I; **Ça fait combien (en tout)?** *How much is it (total)?,* I; **Ça m'énerve!** *How annoying!,* 4; **Ça me plaît beaucoup.** *I really like it.,* 3; **Ça n'a rien à voir avec le roman.** *It has nothing to do with the novel,* 9; **Ça parle d'un petit garçon qui...** *It's about a little boy who...,* 9; **Ça s'écrit...** *It is spelled...,* I; **Ça t'ennuie de...?** *Would you mind...?,* ; **Ça te/vous dit de...?** *Do you feel like...?,* 1; **Ça te plaît,...?** *Do you like...?,* I; **Ça va?** *How are you? (informal),* I; **Ça va aller mieux.** *It's going to get better.,* 8; **Ça, c'est...** *This is...* I; **Ça, ce sont...** *These are...* I
la cabine de bains *beach hut,* 383
la cabine téléphonique *telephone booth,* I
le cabinet *study,* 390
les cacahuètes (f. pl.) *peanuts,* 2
cacher *to hide,* 396
le cadeau *present,* 2
le café *coffeehouse,* I; *coffee,* 1; **café au lait** *coffee with milk,* I; café du coin *neighborhood café,* 4
le cahier *notebook,* I
la caisse *checkout/cash register,* 3
le caissier (la caissière) *cashier,* 3
la calculatrice *calculator,* I
calme *calm,* 6
le caméscope *video camera,* 1
la campagne *countryside,* 6
camper *to camp out,* 7
le camping *camping,* 7; camping sauvage *primitive camping,* 7
le cap *cape (land),* 399
capter *to capture,* 9
le canard *duck,* 6
la canne à pêche *fishing pole,* I
la cantine *cafeteria,* 4
le car *bus,* 2
car *because,* 388
le caractère d'imprimerie *block letter,* 1
le carnet *notebook,* 396

la carotte *carrot,* 3
le carrefour *intersection,* I
le carreau *(window)pane,* 3
la carte *card,* I; *map,* I; *menu,* I; *playing card,* I; **carte bancaire** *bank card,* I; **carte d'anniversaire** *birthday card,* 2; **carte de vœux** *greeting card,* 2; **carte d'embarquement** *boarding pass,* I; **carte postale** *post card,* I; **carte téléphonique** *calling card,* I
le cas *case,* 5
la cascade *waterfall,* 7
le casque *helmet,* I
la casquette *cap,* I
se casser la jambe *to break one's leg,* 8
le caoutchouc *rubber,* 4
le CD *CD,* I
le CDI (centre de documentation et d'information) *library,* 4
ce *this,* I; Ce n'était pas la peine de... *It wasn't worth . . .,* 3; ce que *What (before subject),* 9; **ce qui** *what (before verb),* 6; **Ce sera tout?** *Will that be all?,* 3
la ceinture *belt,* I
cela *that,* 400
celles *those,* 5
la cellule *cell,* 391
celui *the one,* 9
cent *one hundred,* I
cent un *one hundred and one,* I
les centaines (f. pl.) *hundreds,* 9
le centre *center,* I; centre aéré *outdoor center,* I; **centre commercial** *mall,* I;
le centre-ville *downtown,* I
les céréales (f. pl.) *cereal,* I
le cerf-volant *kite,* I
la cerise *cherry,* 3
le cerveau *brain,* 8
ces *these,* I
C'est... *It's . . .,* I; **C'est combien (pour)...?** *How much is (it)... ?,* I; **C'est tout à fait toi.** *It's totally you.,* I; **C'est une bonne affaire!** *It's a good deal!,* I; **C'est... arobase... point...** *It's... @... dot...,* I
c'était une honte *it was a scandal,* 3
le certificat *diploma,* 4
cesser *to stop,* 388
cet *this,* I
cette *this,* I
ceux *those,* 388
la chaîne *chain,* I; *station,* 9; **chaîne stéréo** *stereo system,* I
la chaise *chair,* I
la chambre *bedroom,* I; **chambre avec vue** *room with a view,* I
le champ *field,* 6
le champignon *mushroom,* 3
le championnat *championship,* 1
changer (en) *to change (into),* I; **changer de l'argent** *to exchange money,* I
la chanson *song,* 6
le chant *song,* 6
chanter *to sing,* I
le chantier *construction site,* 393
le chapeau *hat,* I
chaque *each/every,* 5
la charcuterie *delicatessen,* 3
le charcutier *delicatessen dealer, butcher,* 3
le chariot *shopping cart,* 3
la chasse *hunting,* 391
le chasseur (la chasseuse) *hunter,* 7
le chat *cat,* 1
châtain(s) *light brown(-haired),* I
le château *castle,* 10; **château de sable** *sand castle,* 6
chaud *hot,* I
chauffer *to boil,* 3
les chaussettes (f. pl.) *socks,* I
les chaussures (f. pl.) *shoes,* I; **chaussures de randonnée** *hiking shoes,* I
le chef d'œuvre *masterpiece,* 1
le chemin de fer *train track,* 10
la chemise *man's shirt,* I; **chemise de nuit** *night gown,* 5
le chemisier *woman's blouse,* I
la chenille *caterpillar,* 4
le chèque *check,* I; **chèques de voyage** *travelers' checks,* 10; **chèque-cadeau** *gift card,* 2
cher (chère) *expensive,* I
chercher *to look for,* I
le cheval *horse,* 6
les cheveux (m. pl.) *hair,* 1
la cheville *ankle,* 8
la chèvre *goat,* 6
chez *at the house of,* 3; **chez moi** *at (my) home,* 8
le chien *dog,* 1
la chimie *chemistry,* I
les chips (m. pl.) *chips,* 2
le chocolat *chocolate,* 2; **chocolat chaud** *hot chocolate,* 1
le chœur *chorus,* 385
choisir *to choose,* 1
le choix *choice,* 2
la chose *thing,* I
la chouette *owl,* 391
le chroniqueur judiciaire *legal affairs correspondant,* 384
le chuchotement *whisper,* 4
la chute *(water)fall,* 3
le ciel (cieux, pl.) *heaven,* 1; *sky,* 6
le cimetière *cemetery,* I
le cinéaste *film maker,* 9
le cinéma *movie theatre/movies,* I
cinq *five,* I
cinquante *fifty,* I
le cirque *circus,* 6
citer *to cite, mention,* 394
clair *light,* I
la classe *class/classroom,* I
le classement *ranking,* 7
le classeur *binder,* I
classique *classical,* I
le clavier *keyboard,* 4
la clé *key,* I
cligner *to blink,* 4
la climatisation *air conditioning,* I
cliquer *to click,* 4
la cloche *bell,* 391
clouer *to nail,* 401
le club (de tennis, de foot) *(sports) club,* I
le coca *soda,* 1
le cochon *pig,* 6
le code postal *zip code,* I
le cœur *heart,* 8
se coiffer *to do one's hair,* 5
le coiffeur (la coiffeuse) *hairdresser,* I
le colis *package,* I
collectionner *to collect,* 6
le collège *middle school,* 5
le collégien (la collégienne) *middle school student,* 396
le collier *necklace,* I
colmater *to fill in,* 401
le colon *colonist*
la colonie de vacances *summer camp,* 10
le colorant alimentaire *food coloring,* 2
combien de (d') *how many/how much,* 3; **Combien vous en faut-il?** *How many do you need?,* 3
comblé(e) de *filled with,* 1
la comédie *comedy,* 9
comme *like,* 5
comme ci comme ça *so so,* 6
comme tout *as can be,* 3
commencer *to begin,* 1
comment *how,* 3; **Comment allez-vous?** *How are you? (formal),* I; **Comment ça s'écrit?** *How do you write that?,* I; **Comment ça va?** *How are you? (informal),* I; **Comment c'est,... ?** *How is...?,* I; **Comment dit-on... en français ?** *How do you say . . . in French?,* I; **Comment tu épelles... ?** *How do you spell . . . ?,* I; **Comment tu t'appelles?** *What is your name ?,* 1; **Comment tu trouves... ?** *What do you think of. . .?,* I

le commerce *business,* 10; *trade,* 393
la commode *chest of drawers,* I
la compagnie *company,* 10
le compartiment *compartment,* I
la compétition *contest/competition,* 4
complet *booked/full,* I
complètement *completely,* 4
le complexe sportif *sports complex,* 4
compliqué(e) *complicated,* 3
composter *to punch (a ticket),* I
comprendre *to understand,* I; *to include,* 393
le comprimé tablet, I
compter *to count,* 8; *to have,* 400
la comptine *nursery rhyme or song,* 6
la conciergerie *attendant's station,* 383
le concombre *cucumber,* 9
le concours *competition,* 3
conduire *to lead,* 400
les confettis (m. pl.) *confetti,* 2
la confiture *jam,* I
le confluent *merging,* 5
le congé *vacation,* 10
congeler *to freeze,* 2
connaître *to know,* 2
se consacrer *to dedicate (oneself),* 1
les conseils (m. pl.) *advice,* 8
conseiller *to advise,* I
le conseiller (la conseillère) d'éducation *school counselor,* 4
la consigne *baggage locker,* I
consigner *to record,* 396
consommer *to consume/eat,* 8
construire *to build,* 1
le conte *story,* 400
contemporain(e) *contemporary,* 7
content(e) *happy,* 6
continuer *to continue,* I
contre *against,* 395
la contre-valeur *exchange value,* 397
le contrôleur *ticket collector,* 10; *inspector,* 4
convenu(e) *agreed,* 397
le copain (la copine) *friend,* 1
le coq *rooster,* 6
la coque *hull (of a ship),* 401
le coquillage *shell,* 10
le cornet *cone,* 396
la corde *jump rope,* 6
le corps *body,* 8
la correspondance *connecting flight/connection,* I
corriger *to correct,* 4
le corsaire *privateer,* 392
la corvée *chore,* 8
le costume *suit,* 7
la côte *coast,* 401
le côté *side,* 390
le coton *cotton,* 7
le cou *neck,* 8
se coucher *to go to bed,* 5
la couchette *built-in bunk (train)* I
le coude *elbow,* 395
couler *to run/drip,* 8
la couleur *color,* I
les coulisses *backstage,* 384
la country *country music,* 9
couper *to cut,* 3; **se couper** *to cut oneself,* 8
le coupe-vent *windbreaker,* 7
la cour *courtyard,* 390; **cour de récré(ation)** *playground,* 4
le courant *current,* 386
la courgette *zucchini,* 3
courir *to run,* 7
couvrir *to spread,* 4
le courrier *mail,* I
le(s) cours *class(es),* I
la course du rhum *yacht race following the old rum route to Guadeloupe,* 393
le court métrage *short film,* 5
court(e) *short (length),* 1
le cousin (la cousine) *cousin,* 1
le coussin *cushion,* 3
le couteau *knife,* I
coûter *to cost,* I
le couturier *fashion designer,* 1
le couvert *table setting,* I
couvrir *to cover,* 7
la cravate *tie,* I
le crayon (de couleur) *(colored) pencil,* I
créatif(-ive) *creative,* I
créer *to create,* 1
la crème *cream,* 5; **crème à raser** *shaving cream,* 5; crème fraîche *sour cream,* 6; **crème solaire** *sunscreen,* 7
la crémerie *dairy market,* 3
la crevette *shrimp,* 3
le crime de lèse-majesté *crime against the king (terrible crime),* 5
croire *to think/believe,* 4; **croire que** *to think that,* 7
le croisement *intersection,* 1
la croisière *cruise ship,* 393
le croissant *croissant,* I
le croque-monsieur *toasted ham and cheese sandwich,* 1
les crudités (f. pl.) *vegetable salad,* 8
la cuillère *spoon,* I; **cuillerée à café** *teaspoon,* 3; **cuillerée à soupe** *tablespoon,* 3
le cuir *leather,* I
la cuisine *cooking,* I; **cuisine** *kitchen,* I,
la cuisinière *stove, 3*
cuit *cooked,* 8
le cuivre *copper,* 391
cultivé(e) *cultured,* 386
le cybercafé *Internet café,* I

d'abord *first,* I
D'accord. *Okay.,* 2
D'autre part... *On the other hand...,* 9
le Danemark *Denmark,* 10
dangereux(-euse) *dangerous,* 6
danois(e) *Danish,* 10
dans *in/inside,* 3
danser *to dance,* I
le danseur (la danseuse) *dancer,* 384
d'ailleurs *besides,* 397
d'après moi *in my opinion,* I
de *of/from,* I; **de bonne heure** *bright and early,* 5; **de l'** *of the,* I; *some,* 3; *from,* 3; **de la** *of the,* I; *some,* 3; *from,* 3; de la même façon *the same way;* de luxe *luxury,* 1; de nouveau *again,* 3; **De quelle couleur sont... ?** *What color are... ?,* 1; **De quelle couleur?** *In what color?,* 4; **De quoi ça parle?** *What's it about?,* 9; **De quoi tu as besoin?** *What do you need?,* I; **de temps en temps** *from time to time,* I
débarrasser *to clear (something),* I
le début *beginning,* 3
le débutant(e) *beginner,* 383
décembre *December,* I
décevoir *to disappoint,* 390
déchiffrer *to decode*
le décodeur *decoder (allows people who pay a monthly fee to watch the movies the channel shows),* 9
les décorations (f. pl.) *decorations,* 2
décorer *to decorate,* 2
la découverte *discovery,* 6
découvrir *to discover,* 1; *to find out,* 2
le défilé *parade,* 2
dégoûté(e) *disgusted,* 7
déjà *already,* 10
le déjeuner *lunch,* I
délicieux (délicieuse) *delicious,* I
demain *tomorrow,* I
se demander *to wonder,* 4
le démarrage *home (Internet),* 4
démarrer *to start up,* 4
demi(e) *half,* I
le demi-frère *half-brother,* I
la demi-pension *half-board,* I

le demi-pensionnaire *half-boarder,* 4
la demi-sœur *half-sister,* I
démonter la tente *to take down the tent,* 7
la dentelure *jagged outline,* 6
le dentifrice *toothpaste,* 5
le dentiste *dentist,* 8
les dents (f. pl.) *teeth,* 5
le déodorant *deodorant,* 5
le départ *departure,* I
le département *district,* 5
se dépêcher *to hurry,* 5
Dépêche-toi! *Hurry up!,* 5
dépendre *to depend,* 10
déposer *to deposit,* I
déprimant *depressing,* 9
depuis *since/ago,* 4
le député *representative (government),* 394
déranger *to disturb,* I
dernier(ière) *last/latest,* 9
se dérouler *to happen,* 4
derrière *behind,* I
des *of the,* I; *some,* 3; *from,* 3
dès lors *from then on,* 388; dès que *as soon as,* 396
se désaltérer *to quench one's thirst,* 383
descendre *to come down,* I; *to go down/to get out,* 1
le désespoir *despair,* 395
se déshabiller *to get undressed,* 5
le désinfectant *disinfectant,* 7
désirer *to want,* I
désolé(e) *sorry,* I
le dessin *drawing,* I; **dessin animé** *cartoon/movie cartoon,* I
le dessinateur *cartoonist,* 3
dessiner *to draw,* I
la destination *destination,* I
se détendre to relax, 382
détester *to hate,* 9
détruit(e) *destroyed,* 5
deux *two,* I
deux cent un *two hundred and one,* I
deux cents *two hundred,* I
deuxième *second,* I; **la deuxième classe** *second class,* I; la Deuxième Guerre mondiale *Second World War,* 388
devant *in front (of),* I
devenir *to become,* 1
deviner *to guess,* 5
la devise *motto,* 392
devoir *to have to/must,* 2
le devoir *homework,* I
d'habitude *usually,* I
le dictionnaire *dictionary,* I
Dieu *God,* 1
différent(e) de *different from,* 6
difficile *difficult,* I
diffuser *to broadcast,* 9
dimanche *Sunday,* I
dîner *to have dinner,* I
dire *to say,* 2; *to tell,* I
direct *live,* 9
discuter (avec des amis) *to talk (with friends),* I
Dis-moi,... *Tell me,...* 4
disponible (pour) *available (for),* I
disposer *to place,* 2
se distraire *to have fun,* 382
le distributeur: le distributeur d'argent *cash machine,* I; **distributeur de billets** *ticket machine,* I; distributeur automatique *vending machine,* 4
dites-moi *tell me,* I
le divertissement *entertainment,* 391
divorcer *to divorce,* I
dix *ten,* I
dix-huit *eighteen,* I
dix-neuf *nineteen,* I
dix-sept *seventeen,* I
le docteur *doctor,* 8
le document *document,* 4
le documentaire *documentary,* 9
le/la documentaliste *librarian,* 4
le doigt *finger,* 8; **doigt de pied** *toe,* 8
le domicile *home,* 7
donc *thus,* 5
donner *to give,* I
Donnez-moi... *Give me...,* I
doré(e) *gold,* 2; *golden,* 10
dormir *to sleep,* 1
le dos *back,* 8
doté(e) de *endowed with,* 388
la douche *shower,* 5
doux (douce) *sweet,* 1
la douzaine d'œufs *dozen eggs,* 3
douze *twelve,* I
le drame *drama,* 9
se dresser *to stand up,* 385
le droit *(legal) right,* 5
la droite *right,* I
drôle *funny,* 9
drôlement *strangely,* 3
du *of the,* I; *some,* 3; *from,* 3; **du... au** *from the... to the...,* I; du haut en bas *from top to bottom,* 385
durer *to last,* 5
le DVD *DVD,* I

l' eau (f.) *water,* I; eau d'érable *maple sap,* 3; **eau gazeuse** *sparkling water,* 8; **eau minérale** *mineral water,* I; eau pétillante *sparkling water,* 2
l' échange (m.) *exchange,* 1
échapper *to escape,* 5
l' écharpe (f.) *winter scarf,* I
les échecs (m. pl.) *chess,* I
échoué(e) *washed up,* 401
l' éclat (m.) *flash (of light),* 386
l' éclosion (f.) *birth,* 6
l' école (f.) *school,* I; école (f.) maternelle *kindergarten,* 1
les économies (f. pl.) *savings,* 396
écouter *to listen,* I
les écouteurs (m.pl.) headphones, I
l' écran (m.) *screen,* 4
écraser *to crush,* 10
écrire *to write,* 2
l' écritoire (m.) *writing case,* 399
l' écrivain *writer,* 384
l' édition (f.) *edition,* 4
l' éducation musicale music education, I
également *also,* 383
l' église (f.) church, I
s' élancer *to rush out,* 7
élégant (e) *elegant,* I
l' élève (m./f.) *student,* I
elle *she,* I; **Elle est comment,...?** *How is...?,* I
elles *they (fem),* I
s' éloigner *to move away,* 7
élu(e) *chosen,* 7; *elected,* 394
l' e-mail (m.) *e-mail,* I
emballer *to wrap,* 2; *to thrill (slang),* 9
embelli(e) *embellished (decorated),* 391
l' émission (f.) *program,* 9; **émission de variétés** *variety show,* 9; **émissions télé** *television programs,* 9
emmener *to take,* 10
l' employé(e) *employee,* I
emporter *to take (with),* 7
emprunter (un livre) *to borrow (a book),* 4
en *in/to,* 3; **en argent** *(of) silver,* I; **en avance** *early,* I; **en bas** *downstairs,* I; **en bus** *by bus,* I; en chemin *on the way,* 5; en clair *in other words,* 9; **en diamant** *made of diamonds,* I; **en face de** *across from,* I; en fait *in fact,* 9; en habit *dressed in,* 385; **en forme** *in shape,* 8; **en haut** *upstairs,* I; **en jean** *(of) denim,* I; **en laine** *(of) wool,* I; **en lin** *(of) linen,* I; **en même temps (que)** *at the same time (as),* 5; **en métro** *by subway,* I; en moyenne *on an average,* 9; **en or** *(of) gold,* I; **en premier** *first,* 5; **en provenance de** *from,* I; en plein *in the middle*

of, 398; **en retard** *late,* I; **en solde** *on sale,* I; en somme *in short,* 398; **en taxi** *by taxi,* I; **en train de** *in the middle of,* 7; en vente libre (médicaments) *over the counter (medecine),* 8; **en voiture** *by car,* I
en *some of it (them)/any of it(them),* 3
encadré(e) *supervised,* 383
Enchanté(e)! *Delighted!,* I
encore *more,* I; *yet/again,* I; *still,* 2
encourager *to encourage,* I
l’ encre (f.) *ink,* 385
s’ endormir *to fall asleep,* 5
l’ endroit (m.) *place,* 3
énerver *to annoy,* 4
l’ enfant *child,* I
s’ enfermer *to lock oneself in,* 384
s’ enorgueillir *to boast,* 388
s’ engouffrer *to dive,* 7
enlever ses vêtements *to take off one’s clothes,* 5
ennuyeux (-euse) *boring,* 1
enregistrer *to check in,* I
enrichissant(e) *enriching,* 6
l’ enseignement (m.) *education,* 5
enseigner *to teach,* 394
ensemble *together,* 385
ensuite *then/next,* 5
entasser *to pile up,* 7
entendre *to hear,* I
entier (entière) *whole,* 1
entouré *surrounded,* 6
entourer *to surround,* 386
entraîner *to drag along,* 388
entre *between,* I
l’ entrée (f.) *entrance,* 5; *first course,* 8
l’ entreprise (f.) *business,* 7
entrer *to enter,* 2
l’ entretien (m.) *interview,* 10
l’ enveloppe (m.) *envelope,* I
environ *approximately,* 3
envisager *to consider,* 4
s’ envoler *to fly away,* 5
envoyer *to send,* 2
épais (-se) *thick,* 394
l’ épaule (f.) *shoulder,* 8
épeler *to spell,* I
l’ épicerie (f.) *grocery store,* 3
les épices (f. pl.) *spices,* 3
l’ épicier(-ière) *grocer,* 3
l’ épine (f.) *thorn,* 7
épineux (-euse) *thorny,* 7
éplucher *to core (an apple),* 3
épouser *to wed,* 7
éprouver *to feel,* 1
l’ EPS (éducation physique et sportive) (f.) *Physical education (P.E.),* I

l’ équilibre (m.) *balance,* 8
équilibré *balanced,* 8
équilibrer *to balance,* 8
l’ équipe (f.) *team,* 1
l’ escalade (f.) *mountain climbing,* 10; *rock climbing,* 383
escalader *to climb,* 3
l’ escale (f.) *stopover,* I; *layover,* I
l’ escalier (m.) *staircase,* I
l’ escalope de dinde (f.) *turkey breast,* 8
l’ espace (m.) *space,* 6
l’ Espagne (f.) *Spain,* 10
l’ espagnol (m.) *Spanish,* I
espagnol(e) *Spanish,* 10
l’ espèce (f.) *species,* 393
espérer *to hope,* 2
l’ esprit (m.) *mind,* 399
essayer *to try (on),* I
essentiellement *primarily,* 9
l’ est (m.) east, 390
est-ce que *is it that / does,* 3
estival(e) *summer,* 382
l’ estomac (m.) *stomach,* 8
et *and;* **Et toi?** *(informal)* **Et vous?** *(formal) How about you?,* I
établir *to establish,* 394
l’ étage (m.) *floor,* I
l’ étagère (f.) *bookshelf,* I
l’ état (m.) *state,* 7
l’ été (m.) *summer,* 1
s’ éteindre *to turn off (a light),* 386
éternuer *to sneeze,* 8
l’ étoile (f.) *star,* 1
étonnamment *surprisingly,* 388
étonner *to surprise,* 400
étrange *strange,* 384
étranger (-ère) *foreign,* 10
être *to be,* 1; être censé(e) *to be supposed to,* 390; **être en forme** *to be in shape/healthy,* 8; **être en retard** *to be late,* 5; **être en retenue** *to be in detention,* 4; **être fatigué(e)** *to be tired,* 8; être issu(e) de *to stem from,* 10; être pris(e) au piège *to be trapped,* 387
étroit(e) *tight,* I
les études (f. pl.) *studies,* 4
étudier *to study,* I
eus *had,* 388
eût commencé *started,* 396
eût pu *could,* 385
évanouir (s’) *to faint,* 385
éveiller *to wake,* 390
l’ événement (m.) *event,* 7
évidemment *obviously,* 4
éviter *to avoid,* 2
évoluer *to evolve,* 2
excellent(e) *excellent,* 1
excusez-moi... *excuse-me...,* I
l’ exercice (m.) *activity,* I; *exercise,* 8

l’ exploitation (f.) agricole *farming,* 6
l’ exposition (f.) *exhibition,* 9
s’ extasieraient *would go into ecstasies,* 4
l’ extrait (m.) *excerpt,* 384

fabriquer *to create,* 384
fâcheux *upsetting,* 4
facile *easy,* I
le facteur *mail carrier,* I
la faïence *earthenware,* 5
la faim *hunger,* 397
faire *to do/to make,* 2; **faire** + *place to visit (France),* I; faire chauffer *to heat,* 401; **faire cuire** *to cook/ to bake,* 3; **faire de l’escalade** *to mountain climb,* 10; **faire de l’exercice** *to exercise,* 8; **faire de la balançoire** *to swing,* 6; **faire de la musculation** *to lift weights,* 8; **faire de la photo** *to do photography,* 1; **faire de la planche à voile** *to windsurf,* 10; **faire de la vidéo amateur** *to make amateur videos,* 1; **faire de la voile** *to go sailing,* 10; **faire des châteaux de sable** *to make sandcastles,* 6; faire des économies *to save money,* 3; **faire des farces** *to play practical jokes,* 6; **faire des pompes** *to do push-ups,* 8; **faire du camping** *to go camping,* 10; **faire du manège** *to go on a carousel,* 6; **faire du sport** *to play sports,* I; **faire du théâtre** *to do theater/drama,* 1; **faire du yoga** *to do yoga,* 8; **faire escale** *to make a stopover/ layover,* I; faire la connaissance *to meet,* 396; **faire la cuisine** *to cook,* I; **faire la fête** *to party,* I; **faire la lessive** *to do laundry,* I; faire la moue *to pout,* 388; **faire la poussière** *to dust,* 2; **faire la queue** *to stand in line,* I; **faire la sieste** *to take a nap,* 5; **faire la vaisselle** *to do the dishes,* I; faire le bonheur *to make happy,* 9; **faire le ménage** *to clean house,* 2; **faire le tour du monde** *to take a world tour,* 10; **faire les courses** *to go grocery shopping,* 2; **faire les magasins** *to go shopping,* I; **faire les valises** *to pack the bags,* I; **faire partie de** *to be part of,* 3; **faire sa toilette** *to clean (oneself) up,* 5; **faire sa valise** *to pack one’s*

suitcase, 10; **faire ses devoirs** *to do one's homework,* 5; **faire son lit** *to make one's bed,* I; **se faire très tard** *to be getting very late,* 3; **faire un pique-nique** *to go on a picnic,* I; **faire un régime** *to go on a diet,* 8; **faire un séjour** *to stay/to sojourn,* 10; **faire un voyage (organisé)** *to take a (an organized) trip,* 10; **faire une demande de visa** *to apply for a visa,* 10; **faire une expérience** *to do an experiment,* 4; **faire une randonnée** *to go hiking,* 10; faire une recherche *to do a web search,* 4; faire une réservation *to make a reservation,* 10; faire une visite guidée *to take a guided tour,* 10; se faire vacciner *to get vaccinated,* 10

falloir *to have to/to be necessary,* 10

la famille *family,* 1; famille d'accueil *host family,* 6

le fantôme *phantom, ghost,* 384

farci(e) *stuffed,* 9

la farine *flour,* 3

fascinant *fascinating,* I

la faute *mistake, error,* 4

le fauteuil *armchair,* I; **fauteuil pliant** *folding chair,* 7

le fauve *wild animal,* 7; *musky,* 394

le faux ami *false cognate,* 2

les favoris (m. pl) *favorites (Internet),* 4

la femme *wife,* I

la fenêtre *window,* 4

la ferme *farm,* 6; ferme d'accueil *host/bed and breakfast farm,* 7

fermer *to close,* I

la fête *party,* I; *holiday,* 2; **fête des mères** *Mother's Day,* 2; fête des rois *Epiphany,* 2; **fête nationale** *national holiday,* 2

le feu *traffic light,* I; **feu de camp** *campfire,* 7

la feuille *sheet,* I; *leaf,* 7; **feuille de papier** *piece of paper,* I

le feuilleton *television series,* 9

le feu d'artifice (m.) *fireworks,* 2

février *February,* I

le fichier *file,* 4

Figure-toi que *Imagine that,* 7

le filet *net,* 401; filet à provisions *string bag,* 3

la fille *girl,* I; *daughter,* I; **fille unique** *only daughter,* I

le film *film/movie,* 9; **film classique** *classic movie,* 9; **film comique** *comedy (movie),* 9; **film d'action** *action movie,* 9; **film d'aventures** *adventure movie,* 9; **film d'espionnage** *spy movie,* 9; **film d'horreur** *horror movie,* 9; **film de guerre** *war movie,* 9; **film de science-fiction** *science-fiction movie,* 9; **film étranger** *foreign film,* 9

le fils *son,* I; **fils unique** *only son,* I

la fin *end,* 397

fin(e) *fine,* 382

finalement *finally,* 6

finir *to finish,* 1

fis *made,* 388

la fissure *crack,* 401

fit *said,* 385

le flamant rose *flamingo,* 7

la fleur *flower,* 7

le fleuriste *flower shop,* I

le fleuve *river,* 7

florissant(e) *flourishing,* 396

la flotte *fleet,* 392.

la fois *time,* I; **fois par semaine** *times a week,* 1; **fois par...** *times per...,* I

foncé(e) *dark,* I

le fondement *foundation,* 394

fondu(e) *melted,* 387

le football *soccer,* I

la force *strength,* 4

la forêt *forest,* 7

le forfait *flat rate,* 4

la formation *training,* 4

former *to train,* 4

la formule *system,* 7

fort(e) *strong,* I

fortifié(e) *fortified, walled,* 3

le foulard *scarf,* I

la foule *crowd,* 2

se fouler la cheville/le poignet *to twist one's ankle/wrist,* 8

fonder *to found,* 3

le four *oven,* 3

la fourchette *fork,* I

la fourniture *supply,* I; **fournitures scolaires** *school supplies,* I

le fou rire *giggles,* 4

les frais (m. pl.) *expenses,* 8

frais (fraîche) *fresh,* 3

la fraise *strawberry,* 3

la framboise *raspberry,* 3

le français *French (language),* I

français(e) *French,* I

la France *France,* 10

franchement *honestly,* I;

la frayeur fright, 7

frémissant(e) *quivering,* 388

le frère *brother,* 1

frire *to fry,* 9

frissonna *shivered,* 385

les frites (f. pl.) *fries,* I

froid *cold,* I

le fromage *cheese,* I

la fromagerie *cheese market,* 3

le front *forehead,* 8

la frontière *border,* 6

le fruit *fruit,* 3; **fruits de mer** *seafood,* 3; **fruits secs** *dried fruit,* 2

fuire *to flee,* 10

fumer *to smoke,* 8

furent construits *were built,* 392

le fusil *rifle,* 391

fut *was,* 389

gagner *to win,* 4

la galette des rois *King's cake (eaten on Epiphany)*

gallois(e) *Welsh,* 392

les gants (m. pl.) *gloves,* I

le garage *garage,* I

le garçon *boy,* I

le garde barrière *crossing gate,* 10

le gardien (la gardienne) de but *goalie,* 4

la gare *train station,* I

le gâteau *cake,* 2

gauche *left,* I

le gel douche *shower gel,* 5

geler (gèle) *to freeze,* 3

gémissant *moaning,* 385

généreux(-euse) *generous,* I

génial(e) *great,* 3

le genou *knee,* 8

le genre *genre/type,* 9

les gens (m. pl.) *people,* 1

gentil(le) *sweet,* 1

la gentillesse *kindness,* 4

la géographie *geography,* I

le gibier *(wild) game,* 3

le gilet de sauvetage *life vest,* 10

la glace *ice cream,* 1; *ice,* 4

la glacière *ice cooler,* I

glauque *dull blue-green,* 386

glisser *to glide,* 400

la gomme *eraser,* I

la gorge *throat,* 8

la gourde *canteen,* 7

le goût *taste,* 2

le goûter *snack,* 8

grâce à *thanks to,* 382

grand(e) *big/tall,* 1

la grande surface *superstore,* I

les grandes vacances (f. pl.) *summer vacation (occurs in July and August),* 10

grandir *to grow (up),* I

la grand-mère *grandmother,* 1

le grand-parent *grandparent,* I

le **grand-père** *grandfather,* 1
la **grange** *burn,* 6
grapiller *to nibble,* 5
gratuit(e) *free (of charge),* 9
gratuitement *free (of charge),* 382
graver *to burn (a CD),* 4
le **graveur de CD/DVD** *CD/DVD burner,* 4
grec (grecque) *Greek,* 10
la **Grèce** *Greece,* 10
le gréement *rigging,* 393
le grelot *bell,* 2
la **grenadine** *pomegranate drink,* I; *pomegranate syrup,* 1
la **grenouille** *frog,* 7
grimper aux arbres *to climb trees,* 6
grignoter *to snack on,* 2
la **grippe** *flu,* 8
gris(e) *gray,* I
gros(se) *fat/big,* 1
grossir *to gain weight,* 1
guérir *to cure,* 7
guetter *to watch,* 389
le **guichet** *window/counter/ticket office,* I
le **guide** *guidebook,* 10
guidé(e) *guided,* 10
la guirlande *garland,* 2
la **guitare** *guitar,* 1
le **gymnase** *gymnasium,* 4

s' **habiller** *to get dressed,* 5
habiter *to live,* I
habituer (s') *to get used to,* 6
le **hall** *lobby,* I
le hanap *goblet,* 399
les **haricots verts** (m. pl.) *green beans,* 3
hâter le pas *to quicken one's step,* 397
haut(e) *high,* I
la haute couture *high fashion,* 1
la haute technologie *high-tech industry,* 9
l' hectare (m.) *unit of land measurement,* 5
hennir *to neigh,* 6
l' herbe (f.) *grass,* 382
l' **héroïne** (f.) *heroine,* 9
le **héros** *hero,* 9
l' **heure** (f.) *hour,* I
heureuse *happy,* I
heureusement *fortunately,* 6
heureux *happy,* I
hier *yesterday,* 1
le **hip-hop** *hip-hop,* 9
l' **histoire** (f.) *history,* I; *story,* 9
l' **hiver** (m.) *winter,* I
le **hockey** *hockey,* I
l' homme *man,* 6
l' **hôpital** (m.) *hospital,* 1
l' **horaire** (m.) *schedule,* I
horrible *horrible,* I
hors *out,* 7
l' **hôtel** (m.) *hotel,* 10
l' hôtesse (f.) *stewardess,* I
l' huile (d'olive) (f.) *(olive) oil,* 3
huit *eight,* I
l' **huître (f.)** *oyster,* 3
le hussard *horseman,* 398
l' **hymne national** (m.) *national anthem,* 2

il *he,* I; **Il/Elle me va,… ?** *How does… fit me?,* I; **Il/Elle n'est ni… ni…** *He/She is neither… nor…,* I; **Il/Elle ne te va pas du tout.** *It doesn't suit you at all,* I; **Il/Elle te plaît,…?** *Do you like… ?,* I; **Il en a déjà plein.** *He already has plenty of them.,* 2; Il est courant *It's common,* 3; **Il est génial!** *It's great!,* 1; **Il est important que tu le désinfectes.** *It is important that you disinfect it.,* 8; **Il est temps de…** *It's time to…,* 5; Il était une fois… *Once upon a time,* 7; **Il fait beau.** *It's nice outside.,* I; **Il fait chaud.** *It's hot.,* I; **Il fait froid.** *It's cold.,* I; **Il fait mauvais.** *It's bad weather.,* I; Il faudra *We'll have to,* 387; **Il faudrait que tu fasses du yoga.** *You should do yoga.,* 8; **il faut** *it is necessary,* 8; **Il me faut…** *I need…,* 3; Il suffit! *That's enough!,* 4; **Il te faut autre chose?** *Do you need something else?,* 3; Il vaut mieux *It's best,* 2
il y a *since/ago/for,* 4; *There is/are…,* 3; **Il y a des nuages.** *It's cloudy.,* I; **Il y a du soleil.** *It's sunny.,* I; **Il y a du vent.** *It's windy.,* I
Il y avait… *There were…,* 6
Il y en a… *There are… of them.,* I
l' île (f.) *island,* 7
ils *they (m.),* I; **Ils/elles sont soldé(e)s à…** *They are on sale for…* I
s' illuminer *to turn on (a light),* 386
immensément *immensely,* 5
l' **immeuble** (m.) *apartment building,* 8; building, 5
l' immigré(e) *immigrant,* 10
l' impératrice (f.) *empress,* 9
l' **imperméable** (m.) *raincoat,* I
imprescriptible *inalienable,* 5
l' **imprimante** (f.) *printer,* 4
imprimer *to print,* 4
l' incendie (m.) *fire,* 5
incroyable *unbelievable,* 3
l' **infirmerie** (f.) *nurse's office,* 4
l' **infirmier(-ière)** *nurse,* 4
les **informations** (f. pl.) *news,* 9
l' **informatique** (f.) *computer science,* 4
s' **informer** *to find out,* 10; **s'informer sur Internet** *to find out/to inquire on the Internet,* 10
initier *to begin,* 9
l' initié(e) *initiated,* 383
l' **insecte** (m.) *insect,* 7
l' inspecteur d'éducation (m.) *school superintendent,* 4
s' installer *to settle,* 396
l' instituteur (l'institutrice) *primary school teacher,* 1
intellectuel(-le) *intellectual,* 1
intelligent(e) *intelligent/smart,* 1
interdire *to forbid,* 5
intéressant (e) *interesting,* I
l' **intérêt** (m.) *interest,* I
l' **interface** (f.) *interface,* 4
Internet (m.) *Internet,* I
l' interprète (m., f.) *interpreter,* 9
l' **interro(gation)** (f.) *quiz,* 4
interroger *to ask,* 385
l' intervention (f.) médicale *medical attention,* 8
l' **invité(e)** *guest,* 2
l' **Italie** (f.) *Italy,* 10
italien(ne) *Italian,* 10
l' **itinéraire** (m.) *itinerary/route,* 10

J'ai le nez qui coule. *I have a runny nose.,* 8
J'ai mal au cœur. *I'm nauseated.,* 8
J'ai sommeil. *I'm sleepy.,* 8
J'aimerais… *I would like…* I
jamais *never,* 2
la **jambe** *leg,* 8
le **jambon** *ham,* 6
janvier *January,* I
le **jardin** *yard/garden,* I
jaune *yellow,* I
le **jazz** *jazz,* 9
je *I,* I
Je fais du… *I wear a size…,* I
Je me sens mal. *I feel ill.,* 8

Je n'arrive pas à me décider. *I can't decide,* I
Je ne me sens pas très bien. *I don't feel very well.,* 8
Je suis fatigué(e). *I'm tired.,* 8
Je suis stressé(e). *I'm stressed.,* 8
je suis trop occupé(e). *I'm too busy,* 3
Je te/vous présente... *I'd like you to meet...,* I
Je te plains. *I feel sorry for you.,* 8
Je voudrais... *I would like...,* I
le jean *jeans,* I
jeter *to throw,* I
le jeu *game,* 9; **jeu télévisé** *gameshow,* 9; **jeu vidéo** *video game,* I
jeudi *Thursday,* I
jeune *young,* 1
le jogging *jogging,* I
la joue *cheek,* 8
jouer (à) *to play,* 1; **jouer à chat perché** *[similar to tag],* 6; **jouer à des jeux vidéo** *to play video games,* I; **jouer à la marelle** *to play hopscotch,* 6; **jouer à la poupée** *to play dolls,* 6; **jouer au ballon** *to play ball,* 6; **jouer au base-ball** *to play baseball,* I; **jouer au basket-ball** *to play basketball,* I; **jouer au football** *to play soccer,* I; **jouer au tennis** *to play tennis,* I; **jouer au train électrique** *to play with electric trains,* 6; **jouer aux billes** *to play marbles,* 6; **jouer aux cartes** *to play cards,* I; **jouer aux dames** *to play checkers,* 6; **jouer aux échecs** *to play chess,* I; **jouer aux petites voitures** *to play with toy cars,* 6; jouer faux *to be out of tune,* 1
le jour *day,* I; **jour de l'an** *New Year's Day,* 2; jours gras *last two days before Lent,* 2
le journal *newspaper,* I
la journée *day,* 8
les joutes (f. pl.) *jousting (Medieval tournament),* 5
Joyeux Noël *Merry Christmas,* 2
juillet *July,* I
juin *June,* I
les jumelles (f. pl.) *binoculars,* I
la jupe *skirt,* I
le jus *juice,* I; **jus de fruit** *fruit juice,* 1; **jus de pomme** *apple juice,* I; **jus d'orange** *orange juice,* I
jusqu'à *until,* I
jusque-là *up until then,* 389
juste *fair,* 3; *true,* 388

le khalam *type of African guitar,* 394
le kilo(gramme) *a kilogram,* 3

la *(direct object) her/it,* 2
là *here/there,* I; **Là, c'est...** *Here is...,* I
la (l') *the,* I
le laboratoire *laboratory,* 4
le lac *lake,* 7
lâcher *to let go of,* 3
laid(e) *ugly,* 385
la laine *wool,* I
laisser *to allow,* 5; *to leave,* 396; se laisser moins rouler *to not be easily conned,* 3
le lait *milk,* I
la laitue *lettuce,* 3
la lamelle *slice,* 3
la lampe *lamp,* I; **lampe de poche** *flashlight,* 7
lancer *to throw,* I
la langouste *lobster,* 3
la lanterne *lantern,* 7
le lapin *rabbit,* 6
laquelle *which,* 9
large *loose,* I
les lattes de bois *wooden deck,* 382
le lavabo *sink,* 5
laver *to wash,* I; **se laver la figure** *to wash one's face,* 5; **laver la voiture** *to wash the car,* I; **se laver les cheveux** *to wash one's hair,* 5
le lave-vaisselle *dishwasher,* I
le *(direct object) him/it,* 2
le (l') *the,* I; le long de *along,* 383; **Le lundi,...** *On Mondays,...,* 1
le lecteur de CD/DVD *CD/DVD player,* I
léger *light,* 8
le légume *vegetable,* I; **légumes** *vegetables,* 3
lequel *which,* 9
les *the,* I
les *(direct object) them,* 2
lesquels *which,* 9
la lessive *laundry,* I
la lettre *letter,* I; lettre de marque *a license to cruise at sea and take an enemy's ship and merchandise,* 392; Lettres (f. pl.) *Literature and Linguistics,* 396
leur *their,* I
leur *(indirect object) (to) them,* 2
leurs *their,* I
lever *to raise,* I
se lever *to get up/stand up,* 5
la lèvre *lip,* 8
le lézard *lizard,* 7
la liberté *freedom,* 392
la librairie *bookstore,* I
libre *free,* I
le lien *link (Internet),* 4
se lier d'amitié *to become friends,* 7
le lieu *place,* 3
la limonade *lemon-lime soda,* 1
le lin *linen,* I
le liquide (argent) *cash,* I
lire *to read,* I
le lit *bed,* I; **lit double** *double bed,* I; **lit simple** *single bed,* I
le litre *liter,* 3; **litre de jus d'orange** *liter of orange juice,* 3
littéraire *literary,* 9
le livre *book,* I;
la livre *pound of,* 3; **livre de cerises** *pound of cherries,* 3
la loge *theater box,* 384
le logiciel *software,* 4
loin de *far from,* I
les loisirs (m.) *leisure-time activities,* I
long *long,* 9
long(-ue) *long,* 1
lors de *at the time of,* 2
lorsque *when,* 1
la lotion anti-moustiques *mosquito repellent,* 7
lui *(indirect object) (to) him/her,* 2
la lumière *light,* 10
lundi *Monday,* I
la lune *moon,* 10
les lunettes de protection (f. pl.) *safety glasses,* 4; **lunettes de soleil** *sunglasses,* 10
le lycée *high school,* 4

ma *my,* I; **Ma pauvre.** *Poor thing.,* 8
madame *Mrs.,* I; **Madame, s'il vous plaît?** *Ma'am,, please?,* 3
mademoiselle *Miss,* I
le magasin *shop/store,* I
le magazine *magazine,* I
maghrébin(e) *North African,* 7
se magner *to hurry (slang),* 5
mai *May,* I
maigrir *to lose weight,* 1
le maillot de bain *swimsuit,* I
la main *hand,* 8
maintenant *now,* I

le maire *mayor,* 4
mais *but,* I
la maison *house,* 2; **Maison des jeunes et de la culture (MJC)** *recreation center,* I
le maître *master,* 391
la maîtresse de maison *hostess,* 2
la maîtrise de Lettres *master's degree in literature,* 5
mal *badly,* I
malade *sick,* 8
malgré soi *despite oneself,* 1
le malheur *bad luck,* 2
malouin(e) *from Saint Malo,* 393
mamie *grandma,* 2
le mandat *money order,* I
manger *to eat,* 1
se manifester *to show itself,* 386
la manivelle *crank,* 10
manquer *to miss,* 10
le manteau *coat,* I
le maquillage *make-up,* 5
se maquiller *to put on make-up,* 5
le marchand *salesman,* 3
le marché *open air market,* I
marcher *to work/run,* 4; *to walk,* 7
mardi *Tuesday,* I
le mari *husband,* I
le marin *sailor,* 392
la maroquinerie *leather goods,* I
marrant(e) *funny,* 1
marron *brown(-eyed),* 1
mars *March,* I
le mascara *mascara,* 5
le masque de plongée *diving mask,* I
les matériaux (m. pl.) de récupération *recycled materials,* 7
les mathématiques (maths) (f. pl.) *mathematics (math),* I
la matière *school subject,* I
les matières grasses (f. pl.) *fatty substances,* 8
le matin *morning,* I
la matinée *morning,* 5
mauvais(e) *bad,* I
me (m') *(direct object) me,* 2; *(indirect object) (to) me,* 2
méchant(e) *mean,* I
le médecin *doctor,* 8
le (la) mendiant(e) *begger,* 396
le médicament *medicine,* I
la mendicité *begging,* 397
meilleur(e)(s) *best,* 1
mélanger *to mix,* 3
la mélasse *molasses,* 3
le melon *melon,* 3
le mensonge *lie,* 4
la menthe *mint,* I
la mer *sea,* 10
merci *thank you,* I
mercredi *Wednesday,* I; mercredi des Cendres *Ash Wednesday,* 9

la mère *mother,* 1
le merle *blackbird,* 4
mes *my,* I
le métro *subway,* I
le metteur en scène *(movie) director,* 9
mettre *to set,* I; to put, 2; to wear, I; **se mettre** *to put on,* 5; se mettre à + inf. *to begin to,* 3; mettre feu *to light a fire,* 7; **mettre la table** *to set the table,* I; **mettre le couvert** *to set the table,* I
les meubles (m. pl.) *permanent fixtures,* 9; *furniture,* 394
midi *noon,* I
mignon(-ne) *cute,* I
migrateur (-trice) *migratory,* 7
les milliers (m. pl.) *thousands,* 8
mince *thin,* 1
la mine *appearance,* 8
minuit *midnight,* I
le miroir *mirror,* 5
la mise en scène *set up,* 2
la misère *poverty,* 390
le mobile *cell phone,* I
la mode *fashion,* 7
moderne *modern,* I
moi *me,* I; **Moi aussi.** *Me too.,* 1; **Moi non plus.** *Me neither.,* 1; **Moi si.** *I do.,* I; **Moi, j'aime... Et toi?** *I like... And you?,* I; **Moi, je n'aime pas...** *I don't like...,* 1
le moine *monk,* 392
moins *minus,* I; **moins... que** *less... than,* 6
le mois *month,* I; **le mois dernier** *last month,* I
la moitié *half,* 4
le moment *moment,* I
mon *my,* I; **Mon pauvre.** *Poor thing.,* 8
le monde *world,* 10
la monnaie *change (coins),* I
monsieur *Mr.,* I
la montagne *mountains,* I; *mountain,* 10
le montant *sum, amount,* 397
monter *to go up,* 2; **monter à cheval** *to go horseback riding,* 10; **monter la tente** *to pitch a tent,* 7
la montre *watch,* I
moquer (se) de *to make fun of,* 398
le morceau *piece,* 3; **morceau de fromage** *piece of cheese,* 3
le mort *dead person,* 2
le mot apparenté *cognate,* 2
le moteur de recherche *search engine,* 4
le motif *reason,* 4
la mouche *fly,* 7
mourir *to die,* 2
la moustiquaire *mosquito net,* 7
le moustique *mosquito,* 7

le mouton *sheep,* 6
le moyen *way*
le Moyen Âge *Middle Ages,* 5
le MP3 *MP3,* I
muet(te) *silent,* 386
le mur *wall,* 394
mûr(e) *ripe,* 3
la muraille *wall,* 385
le muscle *muscle,* 8
le musée *museum,* I
la musique *music,* 1
musulman(ne) *Muslim*

n'importe où *wherever,* 5
n'importe quoi *whatever,* 5
nager *to swim,* I
le nageur (la nageuse) *swimmer,* 6
naître *to be born,* 2
la nappe *table cloth,* I
le naseau *nostril,* 6
la natte *mat,* 394
la nature *nature,* 7
le naufrage *shipwreck,* 10
le navigateur *browser,* 4
naviguer *to navigate,* 4
le navire *ship,* 392
navré(e) *sorry,* 397
ne: ne pas avoir le temps *to not have the time,* 1; **Ne t'en fais pas!** *Don't worry!,* 8; ne... guère *hardly,* 389; **ne... jamais** *never,* I; *not ever,* 2; **ne... pas** *not,* 2; **ne... pas encore** *not yet,* 2; **ne... personne** *no one,* I; *nobody,* 4; **ne... plus** *no longer,* I; *no more, not anymore,* 2; **ne... que** *only,* 4; **ne... rien** *nothing,* I; *not anything,* 2
néant *no result,* 5
la neige *snow,* I
neiger *to snow,* I
nerveux (-euse) *nervous,* 3
nettoyer *to clean,* I
neuf *nine,* I
le neveu *nephew,* I
le nez *nose,* I
la nièce *niece,* I
le Noël *Christmas,* 2
noir(e) *black,* I
le nom *name,* I
nombreux (-euse) *numerous,* 3
non *no,* I; **Non, ça ne me dit rien.** *No, I don't feel like it.,* I
non-fumeur *non-smoking,* I
normalement *normally,* 6
nos *our,* I

la **note** *grade,* 4
notre *our,* I
N'oublie pas... *Don't forget...,* 3
nourrir (se) *to feed oneself,* 8
nous *we,* I
nous *us,* 2
nous *(to) us,* 2
nouveau *new,* 1
nouvelle *new,* 1
la nouvelle *short story,* 4
novembre *November,* I
le nuage *cloud,* I
la nuit *night,* I
nul (le) *worthless,* 9
nulle part *nowhere,* 5
le numéro *number,* I; **numéro de téléphone** *phone number,* I

ô *oh,* 399
obéissant(e) *obedient,* 6
obtenir *to obtain,* 5
occupé(e) *busy,* I
s' occuper (de) *to take care (of),* 5
octobre *October,* I
l' œil (m.) *eye,* 8
l' œuf (m.) *egg,* I; **œuf dur** *hard-boiled egg,* 9
l' œuvre (f.) *work,* 386
l' office de tourisme (m.) *tourist center,* 10
offre-lui... *give him/her...,* 2
offrir *to offer,* 2; *to give,* 7
l' oignon (m.) *onion,* 3
l' oiseau (m.) *bird,* 7
l' olive (f.) *olive,* 3
l' olivier (m.) *olive tree,* 9
l' ombre (f.) *shadow,* 7
l' omelette (f.) *omelet,* I
on *one/we,* I
l' oncle (m.) *uncle,* 1
l' ongle (m.) *(finger)nail,* 387
onze *eleven,* I
l' opéra (m.) *opera,* I
l' or (m.) *gold,* I
l' orage (m.) *storm,* 7
l' orange (f.) *orange,* I
l' oranger (m.) *orange tree,* 3
l' ordinateur (portable) (m.) *(laptop) computer,* 4
l' ordonnance (f.) *prescription,* 8
ordonner *to order,* I
l' oreille (f.) *ear,* I
organisé(e) *organized,* 10
organiser *to plan/to organize,* 2; **organiser une soirée/fête** *to plan a party,* 2
orner *to adorn,* 5
l' os (m.) *bone,* 8
oser *to dare,* 385
les ossements (m.pl.) *bones,* 1
ou *or,* I
où *where,* 3; **Où ça?** *Where?,* I; **Où est-ce que je pourrais trouver...?** *Where could I find...?,* 3; **Où se trouve...?** *Where is...?,* I
oublier *to forget,* 2
l' ouest (m.) *west,* 388
oui *yes,* I; **Oui, je veux bien.** *Yes, I would indeed.,* I
l' ouïe (f.) *hearing,* 6
l' oursin (m.) *sea urchin,* 10
les outils (m. pl.) *tools,* 4
outre *besides,* 388
l' ouvre-boîte (m.) *can opener,* 7
ouvrir *to open,* I; **ouvrir une session** *to open a session,* 4

la page *page,* I
le pagne *loincloth,* 394
la paille *straw,* 7
le pain *bread,* I
le pain au chocolat *chocolate croissant,* 8
la paix *peace,* 394
le palais *palace,* 7; palais de justice *courthouse,* 5
les palmes (f. pl.) *flippers,* I
le palmier *palm tree,* 6
le pamplemousse *grapefruit,* I
le panneau *sign,* 5
le pansement *bandage,* I
le pantalon *pair of pants,* I
la papeterie *stationery store,* I
papi *grandpa,* 2
le papier *paper,* I
le paquet *package,* 3; **paquet de pâtes** *package of pasta,* 3
par: par habitude *out of habit,* 9; par rapport à *with regard to,* 9; par terre *on the ground,* 3
paraître *to appear,* 1
le parapluie umbrella, I
parce que *because,* I
pareil(le) *similar,* 6
parfois *sometimes,* 6
la parfumerie *perfume shop,* 1
parmi *among,* 9
la parole *word,* 6
le parasol *beach umbrella,* 382
le parc *park,* I
parcours des yeux *skim,* 2
pardon *excuse me,* I
le parent *parent,* I
paresseux(-euse) *lazy,* I
parier *to bet,* 4
le parking *parking,* I
parler *to speak,* 1
partager *to share,* 1
la partie *game, match,* 8
partir *to leave,* 1; partir à la remorque *to lag behind,* 388; **partir en voyage** *to go on vacation,* 10
partout *everywhere,* 8
le pas *step,* 7; **Pas bon du tout!** *Not good at all!,* I; **pas de** *not any,* 3; **pas de problème** *no problem,* 2; **pas du tout** *not at all,* I; **pas encore** *not yet,* I; **pas encore** *not yet,* 2; **Pas grand-chose.** *Not much.,* I; **Pas mal.** *Not bad.,* I; **Pas mauvais.** *Not bad.,* I; **Pas moi.** *Not me./I don't.,* I; **Pas moi.** *Not me./I don't.,* 1; **Pas question!** *Out of the question!,* I
le passeport *passport,* 10
passer (à un endroit) *to stop by,* I; **se passer** *to happen,* 4; *to play,* 9; *to spend,* 1; **passer l'aspirateur** *to vacuum,* I
se passeraient *would be spent,* 2
le passereau *sparrow,* 388
passionnant(e) *exciting,* 9
la pataugeoire *wading pool,* 383
la pastèque *watermelon,* 3
la pâte à beignet *frying batter,* 9
les pâtes (f. pl.) *pasta,* I
le patin à glace *ice-skating,* I
la patinoire *ice-skating rink,* I
la pâtisserie *pastry shop,* 3; *pastry,* 3
la patte *claw,* 3; *paw,* 3
patronner *to sponsor,* 7
la pauvreté *poverty,* 7
payer *to pay,* I; **payer avec une carte** *to pay with a credit card,* I; **payer en liquide** *to pay cash,* I; **payer par chèque** *to pay by check,* I
le pays *country,* 10
le paysage *landscape,* 6
le (la) paysan(-ne) *peasant,* 396
la pêche *peach,* 3; *fishing,* 7
le peigne *comb,* 5
se peigner (les cheveux) *to comb (one's hair),* 5
le peignoir *house coat,* 5
peint(e) *painted,* 5
le peintre *painter,* 5
la peinture *painting,* 3

Glossaire français–anglais

le pélican *pelican,* 7
la pelouse *lawn,* I
pendant *during,* 10; **pendant les vacances** *during vacation,* 10; **pendant que** *while/during,* 5
pendu(e) *hung,* 392
le pendule *pendulum,* 1
pénible *tiresome/difficult, annoying* I
penser *to think,* 1
la pension complète *full-board,* I
le perchoir *perch,* 399
perdre *to lose,* 1
le père *père,* 1
permettre *to allow,* 7
permis de conduire *driver's license,* 10
la perpétuité *perpetuity (time without end),* 386
le perron *steps,* 391
le personnage *figure,* 5; **personnage principal** *main character,* 9
la personne *person;* **ne... personne** *no one,* I; *nobody,* 4
se peser *to weigh oneself,* 8
la pétanque *type of lawn bowling,* 383
petit(e) *small,* I; *little,* 1
le petit-déjeuner *breakfast,* I
la petite-fille *granddaughter,* I
le petit-enfant *grandchild,* I
le petit-fils *grandson,* I
les petits pois (m. pl.) *peas,* 3
la peur *fear,* 7; peur bleue *scared stiff,* 7
peut-être *maybe,* 4
le phare *lighthouse,* 386
la pharmacie *pharmacy,* I
le (la) pharmacien(-ne) *pharmacist,* I
la photo *photo,* I
la physique *physics,* I
le piano *piano,* 1
le pic *peak,* 399
la pièce *room,* I; *coin,* 10; **pièce de théâtre** *play,* 9
le pied *foot,* 8
la pierre *stone,* 5
le pilote *pilot,* I
le pinceau *paintbrush*
le pique-nique *picnic,* I
pire(s) *worse/worst,* 6
la piscine *swimming pool,* I
la piste (d'athlétisme) *track,* 4
la pizza *pizza,* I
le placard *closet/cabinet,* I
la place *seat,* I; **place assise** *seat,* I
placer *to place,* I
le plafond *ceiling,* 4
la plage *beach,* 10
plaire *to please,* 5
le plaisir *pleasure,* 5
le plan *map,* 10
la planche planche à voile *windsurfing,* 10; **planche de surf** *surfboard,* I
la plante *plant,* I
planter *to crash (a computer),* 4
la plate-bande *flower bed*
plein(e) *full/plenty,* 9; **plein air** *open air/outdoors,* 7
pleurer *to cry,* 3
pleuvoir *to rain,* 2
la plongée sous-marine *scuba diving,* 393
plonger *to dive,* 10
la plupart *most*
plus *no longer,* I; **plus de ... que** *more of...than,* 6; **Plus ou moins.** *More or less.,* I; **plus... que** *more... than,* 6
plutôt *rather,* 388
le poignet *wrist,* 8
la pointure *shoe size,* I
la poire *pear,* 3
le pois chiche *chickpea,* 9
le poisson *fish,* I
la poissonnerie *fish market,* 3
le poissonnier (la poissonnière) *fish monger,* 3
le poivre *pepper,* I
le poivron *bell pepper,* 3
la poix *pitch (tar),* 401
poli(e) *polished,* 387
pollué(e) *polluted,* 6
la pomme *apple,* 3; **pomme de terre** *potato,* 3
les pompes (f. pl.) *push-ups,* 8
le pont *bridge,* I
la pop *pop music,* 9
le porc *pork,* I
le portable *cell phone/laptop,* I
la porte *door,* I; **porte d'embarquement** *boarding gate,* I
le porte-bagages *luggage carrier/ rack,* I
le portefeuille *wallet,* I
le porte-monnaie *change purse,* I
porter *to wear,* 7; *to bring,* 2
portugais(e) *Portuguese,* 10
le Portugal *Portugal,* 10
poser *to put down,* 3
posséder *to possess,* 388
la poste *post office,* I
le poste de télévision *television set,* 5
le poster poster, I
le pot *jar,* 3; **pot de confiture** *jar of jam,* 3
potager *vegetable garden,* 391
le pote *friend (slang),* 9
le poteau télégraphique *telegraph pole,* 395
la poubelle *trash,* I
la poule *hen,* 6
le poulet *chicken (meat),* I
le poumon *lung,* 8
la poupée *doll,* 6
pour *for,* I; **pour une fois** *for once,* 4
pourquoi *why,* 3; **Pourquoi pas ?** *Why not?,* I; **Pourquoi tu n'irais pas chez le docteur?** *Why don't you go to the doctor?,* 8
poursuivre *to continue,* 7
poussant *letting out,* 7
pousser à tort et à travers *to grow wildly,* 10
la poutine *french fries with cheese and gravy,* 3
pouvoir *to be able to/can,* 2
la prairie *meadow,* 6
précédente *back (Internet),* 4
préféré(e) *favorite,* I
préférer *to prefer,* 1
premier *first,* I
le premier étage *second floor,* I
la première classe *first class,* I
prendre *to take,* 2; **prendre du poids** *to gain weight,* 8; prendre fin *to end,* 393; **prendre la température** *to take someone's temperature,* 8; **prendre le bus** *to take the bus,* 5; **prendre le petit-déjeuner** *to have breakfast,* 5; **prendre un bain/une douche** *to take a bath/shower,* 5
préparer *to prepare,* 2; **se préparer** *to get ready,* 5; **préparer les amuse-gueules** *to prepare the snacks.* 2; **préparer son sac** *to get one's backpack ready,* 5
près de *next to,* I
le présentateur (la présentatrice) *newscaster,* 9
présenter *to introduce,* 1
presque *almost,* 4
prêt(e) *ready,* 5
prêt-à-porter *ready-to-wear,* 7
prétendre *to claim,* 4
prêter *to lend,* I
la preuve *proof,* 4
prévenir *to warn,* 3
prévoir à l'avance *to plan ahead,* 2
prier *to ask,* 388
la prière *prayer,* 7
primordial(e) *essential,* 394
principal *main,* 383
le printemps *spring,* 1
le prisonnier (la prisonnière) *prisoner,* 392
le prix *prize, award,* 7
priver (se) *to deprive oneself,* 8
le pro *professional (abbrev.),* 9
prochain(e) *next,* I; **prochaine fois** *next time,* 7
proche *near,* 6

Glossaire français–anglais

produire *to produce,* 3
le produit: produit d'artisanat *handicraft,* 7; **produits bio(logiques)** *organic products,* 8
le prof(esseur) *teacher,* I
profiter *to make the most of/to enjoy,* 2
le programme télé *t.v. program,* 9
projeter *to show,* 2
la promenade *walk,* 8
promener *to take for a walk,* I; *to walk (a dog),* I; **se promener** *to take a stroll,* 7
prononcer *to pronounce,* I
propre *clean,* 6; *own,* 1
le propriétaire *owner,* 7
provençal(e) *from Provence,* 10
provenir *to come from,* 400
pruneaux *the color of prunes,* 385
la publicité *advertising,* 9
puis *then,* I
puisque *since,* 389
le pull *pull-over sweater,* I; *sweater,* 10
punir *to punish,* 4
pur(e) *clear,* 6
pût *was able, could,* 385

Q

qu'est-ce que *what,* I; **Qu'est-ce qu'elle est bien, cette pub!** *What a good commercial!,* 9; **Qu'est-ce que ça veut dire... ?** *What does that mean?,* I; **Qu'est-ce que je pourrais offrir à... ?** *What could I get for... ?,* 2; **Qu'est-ce que tu as?** *What's wrong?,* 8; **Qu'est-ce que tu fais comme sport ?** *What sports do you play?,* I; **Qu'est-ce que tu fais de beau pendant tes vacances?** *What interesting things do you do during your vacation?,* 10; **Qu'est-ce que vous avez comme... ?** *What type of... do you have?,* I; **Qu'est-ce qu'il te faut pour...?** *What do you need for...?,* I
le quai *platform,* I
quand *when,* 3; **Quand j'avais... ans,...** *When I was... years old,...,* 6; **Quand j'étais petit(e),...** *When I was little,...,* 6; **Quand j'étais plus jeune,...** *When I was younger,...,* 6
quant à *as far as... is concerned,* 3
quarante *forty,* I
quart *quarter,* I
le quartier *neighborhood,* 3
quatorze *fourteen,* I
quatre *four,* I
quatre-vingt-dix *ninety,* I
quatre-vingt-onze *ninety one,* I
quatre-vingts *eighty,* I
quatre-vingt-un *eighty one,* I
que (qu') *what,* 3
quel(le)(s) *which,* I; **Quel jour sommes-nous ?** *What day is today?,* I; **Quel temps fait-il?** *What is the weather like?,* I; **Quelle est ton adresse email/mail?** *What is your e-mail address?,* I; **Quelle heure est-il ?** *What time is it?,* I; **Quelle pointure faites-vous?** *What shoe size do you wear?,* I; **Quelle sorte de /d'... ?** *What type of... ?,* 4; **Quelle taille faites-vous?** *What size do you wear?,* I
quelque chose *something,* I
quelquefois *sometimes,* 6
quelques *a few,* 5
quelqu'un *someone,* 4
la queue *line,* I
qui *who,* 3; **Qui c'est, ça?** *Who is that?,* I
la quiche *quiche,* I
quinze *fifteen,* 1
quitter *to leave,* 384
quoi *what,* 4
quotidien(ne) *daily,* 9

raconter *to tell,* 9
la radio *radio,* I
radiophonique *for the radio,* 386
la raffinerie de pétrole *oil refinery,* 386
le ramassage scolaire *school bus service,* 5
ramasser *to pick up,* 5
le rameur (-euse) *rower,* 6
la randonnée *hike,* 10
ranger *to put away/to tidy up,* 2; **ranger la maison** *to tidy up the house,* 2; **ranger sa chambre** *to pick up one's bedroom,* I; **ranger ses affaires** *to put one's things away,* 2
le rap *rap,* 9
râpé(e) *grated,* 6
rappeler *to call back,* I; *to remind,* 10
Rapporte-moi... *Bring me back...,* 3
rapporter *to bring back,* 3
la raquette *racket,* 1
rarement *rarely,* 1
se raser *to shave,* 5
le rasoir (électrique) *(electric) razor,* 5
rassurer *to reassure,* 5
rater *to miss,* I; *to fail (an exam, a class),* 4
rattacher à *to unite with,* 392
ravissant(e) *very beautiful,* 388
le rayon *department,* I; *ray,* 391; **rayon bijouterie** *jewelery department,* I; **rayon maroquinerie** *leather department,* I; **rayon plein air** *outdoor goods department,* I
le réalisateur *film maker,* 5
le rebondissement *twist,* 9
récemment *recently,* 9
la réception *reception,* I
la réceptionniste *receptionist,* I
recevoir *to receive,* 2; *to get,* 4
le réchaud *camping stove,* 7
la recherche *research,* 5
rechercher *to search,* 4
rechigner *to balk,* 2
la récolte *harvest, collection,* 3
récolter *to collect,* 3
recommander *to recommend,* I
reconstruit(e) *reconstructed,* 5
recouvert(e) de *covered in,* 2
la récréation *break,* I
recroquevillé(e) *curled up,* 395
le recueil de poésie *poetry collection,* 9
réfléchir *to think about,* 401
le reflet *reflection,* 6
la reflexion *thinking,* 8
se régaler *to have a wonderful time,* 7
regagner *to go back to,* 391
regarder *to look at,* I; *to watch,* I; **regarder des dessins animés** *to watch cartoons,* 6; **regarder la télé** *to watch TV,* I
le reggae *reggae,* 9
le régime *diet,* 8; **le régime équilibré** *balanced diet,* 8
la règle *ruler,* I; *rule,* 392
réglementé(e) *regulated,* 7
le règne *reign,* 390
regretter *to be sorry,* I; *to regret,* 3
régulièrement *regularly,* I
se rejoindre *to join (together),* 5; *to get back to,* 5
se relaxer *to relax,* 8
relier *to join,* 3
remarier *to remarry,* I
remarquer *to notice,* 398
rembourser *to reimburse,* 8
se remémorer *to recall,* 9
remercier *to thank,* 2
les remparts (m. pl.) *outer walls,* 392
remplacer *to replace,* I
remplir *to complete,* 4

remuer *to move,* 3
rencontrer *to encounter,* 10
le rendez-vous *date, appointment,* 1; *meeting,* 3
rendre *to give back,* I; *to make,* 5; **rendre (un livre)** *to return (a book),* 4; se rendre compte (de) *to realize,* 9; **rendre visite à (une personne)** *to visit (a person),* 10
renoncer *to abandon,* 7
renouveler *to renew,* 397
se renseigner *to become informed,* 10; **se renseigner dans une agence de voyages** *to get information in a travel agency,* 10
rentrer (à la maison) *to return (to the house),* 2
se répandre *to spread,* 4
réparti(e) *spread out,* 383
le repas *meal,* I
répéter *to repeat,* I
Répétez, s'il vous plaît? *Could you please repeat that?,* I
répliqua *replied,* 385
répondre (à) *to answer,* I
le reportage *report,* 9; **reportage sportif** *sports report,* 9
reposer (se) *to rest,* 8
reprendre *to take more,* I; *to have more,* I
reprit *responded,* 397
réputé(e) *renowned (famous),* I
requis(e) *required,* 7
rescapé(e) *saved,* 397
la réservation *reservation,* 10
réserver *to reserve,* I
ressembler *to look like,* 3
ressortir *to stand out,* 4
restant(e) *remaining,* 397
rester *to stay,* 2; *to remain,* 391; **rester chez soi** *to stay at home,* 10; rester dans le coup *to be in,* 9; rester dans le vent *to be left out,* 9
retirer *to withdraw,* I
rétorquer *to answer back,* 397
le retour *return,* 4
retourner *to return,* 2
Retournez à vos places! *Go back to your seats!,* I
retrouver (se) *to get together,* 1
réunir *to gather,* 7
réussir (à) *to pass/to succeed,* I; *to pass (an exam, a class),* 4
le rêve *dream,* 10
le réveil *alarm,* 5
se réveiller *to wake up,* 5
le réveillon *midnight feast,* 2
revendiquer *to claim,* 392
revendre *to resell,* 396
revenir *to return,* 10
rêver *to dream,* 5
le rez-de-chaussée *first floor,* I
le rhume *cold,* I
rien *nothing,* 2; **rien de mieux** *nothing better,* 9; **Rien de spécial.** *Nothing special.,* I; **rien ne marche** *nothing is working,* 4
rigoler *to laugh,* 3
les rillettes (f) *type of meat spread,* 2
la ringuette *game like ice hockey played by women in Canada,* 4
rire *to laugh,* 4
le rire *laughter,* 4
le rivage *shore,* 6
la rivière *river,* 7
le riz *rice,* I
la robe *dress,* I
le robinet *faucet,* 5
le rock *rock,* 9
le roi *king,* 2
le roller *rollerblading,* 9
le roman *novel,* 9; **roman classique** *classic novel,* 9; **roman d'amour** *romance novel,* 9; **roman fantastique** *fantasy novel,* 9; **roman historique** *historical novel,* 9; **roman policier** *mystery novel,* 9
le romancier (la romancière) *novelist,* 5
rose *pink,* I
la roseraie *rose garden,* 5
rouge *red,* I
le rouge à lèvres *lipstick,* 5
rouler *to roll,* 10
rousse *red-head(ed) (f.),* 1
la route *road,* 395
roux *red-head(ed) (m.),* 1
le royaume *kingdom,* 392
le ruban *ribbon,* 2
la rue *street,* I
le rugissement *roar,* 9
le ruisseau *stream,* 7
russe *Russian,* 9

sa *his/her,* I
le sable *sand,* 382
le sac (à dos) *bag, backpack,* I; **sac (à main)** *purse,* I; **sac de couchage** *sleeping bag,* 7; **sac de voyage** *traveling bag,* I; **sac en plastique** *plastic bag,* 3
sagement *quietly,* 5
saignant(e) *rare (meat),* I
la Saint-Sylvestre *New Year's Eve,* 2
la saison *season,* I
la salade *salad,* I; *lettuce,* 3
sale *dirty,* 6
la salle *room,* I; **salle à manger** *dining room,* I; **salle de bain** *bathroom,* I; **salle d'informatique** *computer room,* 4
le salon *living room,* I
la salopette *overalls,* 2
saluer *to greet,* 10
Salut. *Hi./Goodbye.,* I
samedi *Saturday,* I
le sanctuaire d'oiseaux *bird sanctuary,* 7
les sandales (f. pl.) *sandals,* I
le sandwich *sandwich,* I; **sandwich au jambon** *ham sandwich,* 1
le sang-froid *cool, calm,* 385
le sanglot *sob,* 4
sans *without,* I; sans avoir appris *without having learned,* 1; **sans doute** *without a doubt,* 4
la santé *health,* 8
le sapin de Noël *Christmas tree,* 2
le saucisson *salami,* I
le saumon fumé *smoked salmon,* 10
sauf *except,* 9
sauter *to skip,* 5
sauter: sauter à la corde *to jump rope,* 6; **sauter des repas** *to skip meals,* 8
sauvegarder *to save (a document),* 4
la saveur *flavor,* 1
savoir *to know (facts),* 2
le savon *soap,* 5
le scénario *screenplay,* 386
le scénariste (la scénariste) screenwriter, 3
la scène *stage,* 384
scolaire *scholastic,* I; *school (adj.),* 5
la scolarité *schooling,* 1
le sculpteur *sculptor,* 7
la séance *showing,* 9
sec (sèche) *dry,* 7
le sèche-cheveux *blow-dryer,* 5
se sécher les cheveux *to dry one's hair,* 5
le secours *help,* 7
seize *sixteen,* I
le séjour *stay (vacation),* 10
le sel *salt,* I
selon *according to,* 5
la semaine *week,* I; **semaine dernière (la)** *last week,* I
la semoule *type of flour made out of hard wheat,* 3
le sentier *path,* 7
sept *seven,* I
septembre *September,* I
serein(e) *serene, calm,* 394
la série *series,* 9
sérieux (-euse) *serious,* 1
le serpent *snake,* 7
serrer *to squeeze,* 395
serré(e) *tight,* I

la serviette *napkin, towel* I
ses *his/her,* I
le seuil *threshold,* 1
seul(e) *only,* 3
le shampooing *shampoo,* 5
le short *a pair of shorts,* 1
si *if,* 3; *yes (to negative question),* 10
le siècle century, 3
la sieste *nap,* 5
la signification *meaning,* 2
s'il te plaît *please,* I
s'il vous plaît *please,* 3
silence *quiet,* I
simple *simple,* 3
le sirop *syrup,* I; sirop d'érable *maple syrup,* 3; **sirop de menthe** *mint syrup,* 1
le sitcom *sitcom,* 9
le site *website,* 10; **site d'une compagnie aérienne** *airline website,* 10
se situer *to be located,* 1; *to take place,* 384
six *six,* I
le skate(board) *skateboarding,* I
le ski(s) *skiing/skis,* I
le SMS *instant message,* I
le soap *soap opera,* 9
la sœur *sister,* 1
le sofa *couch,* I
la soie *silk,* I
soigneusement *carefully,* 397
le soir *evening,* I
la soirée *party/mixer,* 2; soirée costumée *costume party,* 2; soirée habillée *formal dress party,* 2
soit *either,* 5
soixante *sixty,* I
soixante et onze *seventy one,* I
soixante-dix *seventy,* I
soixante-douze *seventy two,* I
le sol *ground,* 394
le soldat *soldier,* 392
les soldes (m.) *sale,* I
le soleil *sun,* I
sombre *dark,* 394
sombrer *to sink,* 386
le sommeil *sleep,* 8
le sommet *peak,* 10
son *his/her,* I
le son *sound,* 9
songer *to think,* 7
sonner *to ring,* 5; *to sound,* 7
la sono *sound system,* 2
la sorte *type,* 4
la sortie *dismissal,* I
sortir *to go out,* 1; *to take out,* I; **sortir la poubelle** *to take out the trash,* I
sot (sotte) *foolish, silly,* 1
se soucier de *to worry about,* 2
soudain *suddenly,* 10
le Soudan *Sudan (African country),* 394
souhaiter *to wish,* 2; **souhaiter une bonne nuit** *to say good night,* 5
soulager *to relieve,* 3
souper *to have supper,* 390
le souper *supper,* 391
le sourcil *eyebrow,* 8
sourd(e) *deaf,* 386; sourd(e) comme un pot *deaf as a post,* 1
sourire *to smile,* 1
le sourire *smile,* 4
la souris *mouse,* 4
sous *under,* I; sous les espèces *as a,* 385
le sous-marin *submarine,* 10
sous-marin(e) *underwater,* 386
le sous-sol *basement,* 1
les sous-titres (m. pl.) *subtitles,* 9
soutenir *to support,* 4
le souvenir *memory (of something),* 2
se souvenir *to remember,* 389
souvent *often,* 1
le spectacle *show,* 10; **spectacle son et lumière** *sound and light show,* 10
le sport *sports,* I
sportif(-ive) *athletic,* 1
le spot publicitaire *commercial,* 9
le stade *stadium,* 1
la station balnéaire *beach resort,* 393
la station de métro *subway station,* I
le steak *steak,* I
stressant(e) *stressful,* 6
stressé(e) *stressed,* 8
la strophe *stanza,* 1
stupéfié(e) *stunned,* 389
le styliste *fashion designer,* 7
le stylo *pen,* I; stylo plume *fountain pen,* 1
subite *sudden,* 385
subsister *to remain,* 4
la sucette *lollipop,* 3
le sucre *sugar,* 3
le sud *south,* 7
la Suède *Sweden,* 10
suffire *to be enough,* 396
suffisant(e) *enough,* 8
la Suisse *Switzerland,* 10
suivant(e) *next,* 2
suivante *forward (Internet),* 4
suivre *to follow,* 4; **suivre un cours** *to take a class,* 4
le supermarché *supermarket,* 3
supporter *to stand (tolerate),* 5
sur *on,* I; **sur le point de** *about to,* 7
le surf *snowboarding, surfing,* I
surfer *to surf,* I; **surfer sur Internet** *to surf the Net,* I
surgir *to appear,* 7
le surnom *nickname,* 392
surnommé(e) *nicknamed,* 392
surtout *especially,* 10
sus *knew,* 388
susciter *to incite,* 5
suspendu(e) *suspended,* 390
le suspense *suspense,* 9
le sweat-shirt *sweat-shirt,* I
sympathique *nice,* I

ta *your (informal),* I
la table *table,* I; **table basse** *coffee table,* I; **table de nuit** *night stand,* I
le tableau *board,* I; *painting,* I; **tableau d'affichage** *information board,* 10
la tablette *tablet,* 4
le tabouret *stool,* 394
la taille *clothing size,* I
le taille-crayon *pencil sharpener,* I
le tailleur *woman's suit,* I
Tant pis pour elle! *Too bad for her!,* 4
la tante *aunt,* 1
tape-à-l'œil *flashy,* I
taper *to bang (on),* 1
le tapis *rug,* I
le tarama *fish dip,* 2
tard *late,* 5
le tarif *fee,* I; **tarif réduit** *reduced fee/discount,* I
la tarte *pie,* I; **tarte aux pommes** *apple pie,* 1
la tartine *bread with butter or jam,* I
le tas de *loads of,* 3
la tasse *cup,* 3
le taxi *taxi,* I
te (t') *(to) you,* 2
la techno *techno,* 9
le tee-shirt *t-shirt,* I
le teint de bistre *dark complexion or coloring,* 385
tel(le) *such,* 5; tel(le)(s) que *such as,* 7
la télé(vision) *television,* I; télévision numérique terrestre (TNT) *digital TV,* 9
télécharger *to download,* 4
la télécommande *remote control,* 9
le téléphone *telephone,* I
téléphoner (à des amis) *to call (friends),* I
tellement *so/so much,* 6; *really,* 10
le temps *time,* I; *weather,* I; **temps libre** *free time,* I
tenailler *to gnaw,* 7

Glossaire français–anglais

se tenir *to stand,* 396
le tennis *tennis,* I
la tente *tent,* I
la tenue *outfit,* 2
le terminal *terminal,* I
terne *lifeless,* 388
le terrain de camping *campground,* 7
le terrain de sport *sports field,* 4
la terre *earth,* 1; *mud,* 5; *clay,* 7; terre battue *clay,* 1; terre cuite *pottery,* 3
tes *your (informal),* I
la tête *head,* I
le texto *instant message,* I
le théâtre *drama,* I; *theater,* I
le thiaf *grilled groundnuts (slang),* 397
le thon *tuna,* 9
le ticket *ticket,* 9
tiède *lukewarm,* 3
Tiens. *Here.,* I
le timbre *stamp,* I
timide *shy,* I
tiré(e) de *taken from,* 9
tirer *to shoot,* 391
le toast *toast,* I
toi *you,* I
la toile *cloth,* 2; **toile d'araignée** *spider web,* 7
les toilettes (f. pl.) *restroom,* I
le toit *roof,* 1; toit mansardé *sloping roof,* 3
la tomate *tomato,* 3
tomber *to fall,* I; tomber court *to be short of something,* 2
le ton *pitch,* 388
ton *your (informal),* I
tondre la pelouse *to mow the lawn,* I
le tonneau *barrel,* 3
la tortue *turtle,* 7
tôt *early,* 5
la touche *key,* 4
toujours *always,* I
la tour *tower,* 10
la tourelle *turret,* 390
le tourisme *tourism,* 10
tourner *to turn,* I
Tournez au/à la prochain(e)... *Turn at the next...,* I
le tournoi *tournament,* 1
tous: tous du pareil au même *all the same,* 3; **tous les deux (jours)** *every other (day),* 5; **tous les jours** *every day,* I; **tous les mercredis** *every Wednesday,* 1
la Toussaint *All Saint's Day,* 2
tousser *to cough,* 8
tout: tout à coup *suddenly,* 5; **tout à fait** *totally/absolutely,* I; **tout à l'heure** *very soon,* 7; tout de suite *right away/immediately,* I; tout droit *straight ahead,* I; **tout le monde** *everyone,* 5; tout près *right next to,* 3; Tout va de travers depuis... *Everything is going wrong since...,* 4
toute la nuit *all night,* I;
la toux *cough,* I
tracer *to draw,* 6
le tracteur *tractor,* 6
le traducteur (la traductrice) *translator,* 9
traduire *to translate,* 9
le trafic portuaire *port traffic,* 3
le train *train,* 10; **train éléctrique** *electric train,* 6
traîner *to trail behind/dawdle,* 5
traiter *to deal with,* 7
le trajet *distance,* 5
la tranche *slice,* 3; **tranche de jambon** *slice of ham,* 3
tranquille *peaceful,* 6
le transat *deck chair,* 382; *transatlantic crossing,* 393
le travail *work,* 5
travailler *to work,* I
traverser *to cross,* I
Traversez... *Cross...,* I
treize *thirteen,* I
tremper *to dip,* 399
trente *thirty,* I
trente et un *tthirty-one,* I
très *very,* 1; **très bien** *very well,* I; **très mal** *very badly,* I
triste *sad,* 6
trois *three,* I
trop (de) *too/too much,* 3
la trousse *pencil case,* I; **trousse de premiers soins** *first-aid kit,* 7; **trousse de toilette** *vanity case,* 10
trouver *to find/to think,* I; **trouver (se)** *to be located,* 3
tu *you,* I; **Tu as bien... ?** *Are you sure you ...?,* 2; **Tu as déjà... ?** *Did you already ...?,* 2; **Tu devrais...** *You should ...,* 5; **Tu es d'accord si... ?** *Is it all right with you if...?,* I; **Tu ferais bien...** *You would do well ...,* 8; **Tu pourrais lui offrir...** *You could give him/her...,* 2; **Tu pourrais me prêter... ?** *Could you lend me ...?,* I; **Tu veux bien... ?** *Would you mind ...?,* 3
le tuba *snorkel,* I
tuer *to kill,* 390

un/une *one,* I; **un peu trop...** *a little bit too ...,* I; **une fois que...** *once ...,* 5
unique *only,* I
l' unité centrale (f.) *CPU,* 4
l' urgence (f.) *emergency,* 8
utiliser *to use,* 4

les vacances (f. pl.) *vacation,* I
la vache *cow,* 6
la vague *wave,* 6
la vaisselle *dishes,* 8
le valet de chambre *manservant,* 390
valider *OK (Internet),* 4
la valise *suitcase,* 1
la vallée *valley,* 10
la vedette *movie star,* 9
la veille *the night before,* 2
le vélo *biking/bike,* I; **vélo tout terrain** *mountain bike,* I
vendre *to sell,* 1
vendredi *Friday,* I
venir *to come,* 2; **venir de** *to have just done something,* 7
le vent *wind,* I
la vente *sale,* 396
le ventre *stomach,* 396
la verdure *greenery,* 382
verni(e) *varnished, glazed,* 5
le verre *glass,* I
le vers *verse,* I
vers *around, about,* 3
versé(e) *paid,* 397
la version originale (VO) *original version,* 9
vert(e) *green,* 1
la veste *jacket,* I
les vêtements (m. pl.) *clothes,* I
la vidéo amateur *amateur film-making,* I
le vidéoclip *music video,* 9
vider *to empty,* I; se vider la tête *to clear one's head,* 9; **vider le lave-vaisselle** *to empty the dishwasher,* I
la vie *life,* 6
vieille *old (f.),* 1
vieux *old (m.),* 1
vif (vive) (couleur) *bright,* 9
le village *village,* 6

la ville *city,* 10
vingt *twenty,* I
vingt et un(e) *twenty-one,* I
vingt-cinq *twenty-five,* I
vingt-deux *twenty-two,* I
vingt-huit *twenty-eight,* I
vingt-neuf *twenty-nine,* I
vingt-quatre *twenty-four,* I
vingt-sept *twenty-seven,* I
vingt-six *twenty-six,* I
vingt-trois *twenty-three,* I
violet(te) *purple,* I
le visa *visa,* I
le visage *face,* 8
la visite *visit/tour,* 10; visite à domicile *house call,* 8
visiter (un endroit) *to visit (a place),* 10
les vitamines (f. pl.) *vitamins,* 8
vivant(e) *vibrant,* 6
vivre *to live,* 390
la voie *track,* I
voilà *here is . . . ,* 1
la voile *sail,* 10
voir *to see,* 2
le voisin (la voisine) *neighbor,* 1
le voisinage *neighborhood,* 6
la voiture *car,* I; **voiture de sport** *sports car,* I
la voix *voice,* 10
le vol *flight,* 10; vol d'aile *flap of a wing,* 387
le volley *volleyball,* I
vos *your (formal),* I
votre *your (formal),* I
vouloir *to want,* 2
voulut *wanted,* 385
vous *(to) you,* 2; **Vous devriez...** *You should . . . ,* I; **Vous êtes combien dans votre famille?** *How many are you in your family?,* I
le voyage *trip,* 10
voyager *to travel,* 1
vrai(e) *true,* 9
le VTT (vélo tout terrain) *mountain bike,* I
la vue *view,* I

le wagon *car (in a train),* I
le wagon-restaurant *buffet car,* I
le week-end *weekend,* 7

y *there,* 3
le yaourt *yogurt,* 3
les yeux (m. pl.) *eyes,* 1
le yoga *yoga,* 8

le zapping *surfing,* 9
zéro *zero,* I
le zoo *zoo,* I

Glossaire anglais–français

This vocabulary includes all of the words presented in the **Vocabulaire** sections of the chapters. These words are considered active–you are expected to know them and be able to use them. French nouns are listed with the definite article. Expressions are listed under the English word you would most likely reference. The number after each entry refers to the chapter in which the word or phrase is introduced. Words and phrases from Level 1 are indicated by the Roman numeral I.

To be sure you are using French words and phrases in their correct context, refer to the chapters listed. You may also want to look up French phrases in the **Liste d'expressions,** pages R22–R25.

abdominal muscles *les abdominaux,* 8
about *à peu près,* 3
about to *sur le point de,* 7
abroad *à l'étranger,* 10
absolutely *absolument,* 10
access *l'accès (m.),* I
accessories *les accessoires,* I
according to me *d'après moi,* I
across from *en face de,* I
action movie *le film d'action,* 9
activity *l'activité, l'exercice (m.),* I
to add *ajouter,* 3
address *l'adresse (f.),* 4
to address *s'adresser,* I
to adore *adorer,* 1
adventure movie *le film d'aventures,* 9
to advise *conseiller,* I
aerobics *l'aérobic,* I
after *après,* I
afternoon *l' après-midi (m.),* I
afterwards *après ça,* 5
again *encore,* I
age *l'âge (m.),* I
ago *il y a,* 4
air conditioning *la climatisation,* I
airline *la compagnie aérienne,* 10
airport *l'aéroport (m.),* I
alarm *le réveil,* 5
all *tout(e)(s), tous,* 5
already *déjà,* 10
always *toujours,* I
amateur film-making *la vidéo amateur,* I
American *américain(e),* I
and *et,* I
animal *l'animal(-aux) (m.),* I
ankle *la cheville,* 8
to annoy *énerver,* 4
annoying *pénible,* 1
to answer *répondre (à),* I
apartment *l'appartement (m.),* I
appearance *la mine,* 8
apple *la pomme,* I
apple juice *le jus de pomme,* I
apple pie *la tarte aux pommes,* 1
to apply for a visa *faire une demande de visa,* 10
approximately *environ,* 3
apricot *l'abricot (m.),* 3
April *avril,* I
arm *le bras,* 8
armchair *le fauteuil,* I
arrival *l'arrivée (f.),* I
to arrive *arriver,* 2
as much as *autant que,* 6
at (my) home *chez (moi),* I
at/to *à, au, à la, à l', aux,* 3
at that moment *à ce moment-là,* 6
at the end of *au fond de,* I; *au bout de,* 3
at the home of *chez,* 3
at the latest *au plus tard,* 3
at the same time (as) *en même temps (que),* 5
at the time (when) / as *au moment où,* 7
at what time *à quelle heure,* I
athletic *sportif(-ive),* I
August *août,* I
aunt *la tante,* I
available (for) *disponible (pour),* I

back (Internet) *la précédente,* 4
backpack *le sac (à dos),* I
bacon *le bacon,* I
bad *mauvais(e),* I
badly *mal,* I
baggage locker *la consigne,* I
baker *le/la boulanger(-ère),* 3
bakery *la boulangerie,* 3
balanced *équilibré(e),* 8
balcony *le balcon,* I
ball *le ballon (inflatable), la balle,* I
balloon *le ballon,* 2
banana *la banane,* I
bandage *le pansement,* I
bank *la banque,* I
bank card *la carte bancaire,* I
barely *à peine,* 7
barn *la grange,* 6
baseball *le base-ball,* I
basketball *le basket(-ball),* I
bat *la batte,* I
bathroom *la salle de bain,* I
bathtub *la baignoire,* 5
to be *être,* I
to be able to *pouvoir,* I
to be born *naître,* I
to be cold *avoir froid,* I
to be healthy *être en forme,* 8
to be hot *avoir chaud,* I
to be hungry *avoir faim,* I
to be in detention *être en retenue,* 4
to be in one's best interest *avoir intérêt à,* I
to be late *être en retard,* 5
to be located *se trouver,* I
to be named *s'appeler,* I
to be right *avoir raison,* 4
to be sorry *regretter,* I
to be thirsty *avoir soif,* I
to be tired *être fatigué(e),* 8
beach *la plage,* I
beautiful *beau, belle,* 1
to become informed *se renseigner,* 10

Glossaire anglais–français

bed *le lit,* I
bedroom *la chambre,* I
beef *le bœuf,* 3
before *avant (de),* 5
to **begin** *commencer,* I
behind *derrière,* I
Belgium *la Belgique,* 10
to **believe** *croire,* 4
bell pepper *le poivron,* 3
belt *la ceinture,* I
better *meilleur(e)(s),* 6
best *le/la/les meilleur(e)(s),* 6
to **bet** *parier,* 4
between *entre,* I
bicycle *le vélo,* I
big *grand(e), gros(-se),* I
biking *le vélo,* I
bill *l'addition (f.), le billet,* I
binder *le classeur,* I
binoculars *les jumelles,* I
biography *la biographie,* 9
bird *l'oiseau (m.),* 7
birthday *l'anniversaire (m.),* 2
birthday card *la carte d'anniversaire,* 2
black *noir(e),* I
blond *blond(e),* I
blouse *le chemisier,* I
blow-dryer *le sèche-cheveux,* 5
blue *bleu(e),* I
blues *le blues,* 9
board *le tableau,* I
boarding gate *la porte d'embarquement,* I
boarding pass *la carte d'embarquement,* I
boat *le bateau,* 10
body *le corps, (m.)* 8
boil *bouillir,* 3
bone *l'os (m.),* 8
book *le livre,* I
booked (full) *complet (-ète),* I
bookshelf *l'étagère (f.),* I
bookstore *la librairie,* I
boots *les bottes (f.pl.),* I
boring *ennuyeux(-euse),* I
to **borrow** *emprunter,* 4
bottle *la bouteille,* 3
bouquet of flowers *le bouquet de fleurs,* 2
bowl *le bol,* I
box *la boîte,* 3
box of chocolates *la boîte de chocolats,* 2
box of matches *la boîte d'allumettes,* 7
boy *le garçon,* I
bracelet *le bracelet,* I
brain *le cerveau,* 8
branch *la branche,* 7
bread *le pain,* I
bread with butter or jam *la tartine,* I
break *la récréation,* I
to **break one's leg** *se casser la jambe,* 8
breakfast *le petit-déjeuner,* I
bridge *le pont,* I
to **bring back** *rapporter,* 3
to **bring someone along** *amener,* I
broccoli *le brocoli (m.),* 3
brochure *la brochure,* 10
brother *le frère,* I
brown *marron (inv.),* 1
brown(-eyed) *avoir les yeux marron,* I
brown(-haired) *brun(e),* I
browser (Internet) *le navigateur,* 4
brush *la brosse,* 5
to **brush one's hair** *se brosser les cheveux,* 5
to **brush one's teeth** *se brosser les dents,* 5
buffet car *le wagon-restaurant,* I
built-in bunk *la couchette,* I
to **burn (a CD)** *graver,* 4
to **burn oneself** *se brûler,* 8
bus *le bus,* I
bus stop *l'arrêt de bus (m.),* I
busy *occupé(e),* 3
but *mais,* I
butcher *le/la boucher(-ère),* 3
butcher shop *la boucherie,* 3
butter *le beurre,* I
to **buy** *acheter,* I
to **buy a guidebook** *acheter un guide,* 10
by bicycle *à vélo,* I
by bus *en bus,* I
by car *en voiture,* I
by foot *à pied,* I
by subway *en métro,* I
by taxi *en taxi,* I
by the way *au fait,* 4

cafeteria *la cantine,* 4
cake *le gâteau,* 2
calculator *la calculatrice,* I
to **call** *appeler,* I
to **call** *téléphoner,* I
calling card *la carte téléphonique,* I
calm *calme,* 6
camera *l'appareil photo (m.),* I
to **camp out** *camper, faire du camping,* 7
camping *le camping,* 7
camping stove *le réchaud,* 7
can opener *l'ouvre-boîte (m.),* 7
to **cancel** *annuler,* I
candle *la bougie,* 2
candy *les bonbons (m.),* 2
canned food *la boîte de conserve,* 3
canteen *la gourde,* 7
cap *la casquette,* I
car *la voiture,* I
car (train) *le wagon,* I
card(s) *la/les carte(s),* I
carousel *le manège,* 6
carrot *la carotte,* 3
cartoon *le dessin animé,* 9
cash *le liquide (argent),* I
cash machine *le distributeur d'argent,* I
cash register *la caisse,* 3
cashier *le/la caissier(-ière),* 3
castle *le château,* 10
cat *le chat,* I
to **catch a fish** *attraper un poisson,* 7
CD *le CD,* I
CD burner *le graveur de CD,* 4
CD player *le lecteur de CD,* I
cell phone *le mobile, le portable,* I
cereal *les céréales (f.pl.),* I
chain (neck) *la chaîne,* I
chair *la chaise,* I
to **change** *changer,* I
change (coins) *la monnaie,* I
to **change** *changer,* I
to **change money** *changer de l'argent,* 10
change purse *la porte-monnaie,* I
check *le chèque,* I
to **check in** *enregistrer,* I
checkers *le jeu de dames,* 6
checkout (register) *la caisse,* 3
cheek *la joue,* 8
cheese *le fromage,* I
cheese market *la fromagerie,* 3
chemistry *la chimie,* I
cherry *la cerise,* 3
chess *les échecs (m.pl.),* I
chest of drawers *la commode,* I
chicken *le poulet,* I
chicken (animal/meat) *la poule/le poulet,* 6
child *l'enfant (m./f.),* I
chips *les chips,* 2
chocolate *le chocolat,* I
to **choose** *choisir,* I
chore *la corvée,* I
Christmas *le Noël,* 2
Christmas tree *le sapin de Noël,* 2
church *l'église (f.),* I
city *la ville,* I
class *la classe, le/les cours* I
classic movie *le film classique,* I
classical *classique,* I
clean *propre,* 6
to **clean** *nettoyer,* I
to **clean (oneself) up** *faire sa toilette,* 5
to **clean the house** *faire le ménage,* 2
clear *pur(e),* 6
to **clear (something)** *débarrasser,* I

to clear the table *débarrasser la table,* I
to click *cliquer,* 4
to climb trees *grimper aux arbres,* 6
to close *fermer,* I
closet *le placard,* I
clothes *les vêtements (m.pl.),* I
clothing size *la taille,* I
cloud *le nuage,* I
club *le club (de tennis, de foot),* I
coat *le manteau,* I
coffee *le café,* I
coffee (with milk) *le café au lait,* I
coffee house *le café,* I
coffee table *la table basse,* I
coin *la pièce,* I
cold (temperature) *froid(e),* I
cold (illness) *la rhume,* I
to collect *collectionner,* 6
color *la couleur,* I
colored pencil *le crayon de couleur,* I
comb *le peigne,* 5
to comb (one's hair) *se peigner (les cheveux),* 5
to come *venir,* I
to come down *descendre,* I
comedy *la comédie,* 9
comic strip *la bande dessinée (BD),* I
commercial *le spot publicitaire,* 9
company *la compagnie,* 10
compartment *le compartiment,* I
compass *la boussole,* 7
competition *la compétition,* 4
completely *complètement,* 4
complicated *compliqué(e),* 3
computer *l'ordinateur,* I
computer lab/room *la salle d'informatique,* 4
computer science *l'informatique,* I
confetti *les confettis,* 2
connecting flight *la correspondance,* I
to consume *consommer,* 8
to continue *continuer,* I
to cook *faire la cuisine,* I
to cook/bake *faire cuire,* 3
cookies *les biscuits,* 2
cooking *la cuisine,* I
to correct *corriger,* I
to cost *coûter,* I
costume party *la soirée costumée,* I
cotton *le coton,* I
couch *le sofa,* I
cough *la toux,* I
to cough *tousser,* 8
country *le pays,* 10
country music *la country,* 9
countryside *la campagne,* I
cousin *le/la cousin(e),* I
cow *la vache,* 6
CPU (computer) *l'unité centrale (f.),* 4
to crash (a computer) *planter,* 4
creative *créatif(-ive),* I
croissant *le croissant,* I
to cross *traverser,* I
crowd *la foule,* 2
cup *la tasse,* I
currency exchange office *le bureau de change,* I
to cut *couper,* 3
to cut oneself *se couper,* 8
cute *mignon(ne),* I

dairy market *la crémerie,* 3
to dance *danser,* I
dangerous *dangereux(-euse),* 6
Danish *danois(e),* 10
dark *foncé(e),* I
daughter *la fille,* I
to dawdle *traîner,* 5
day *le jour,* I
day after tomorrow *après-demain,* 7
December *décembre,* I
to decorate *décorer,* 2
decorations *les décorations (f.pl.),* 2
delicatessen *la charcuterie,* 3
delicious *délicieux(-euse),* I
denim (made of) *(en) jean,* I
Denmark *le Danemark,* 10
dentist *le/la dentiste,* 8
deodorant *le déodorant,* 5
department *le rayon,* I
departure *le départ,* I
to depend *dépendre,* 10
to deposit *déposer,* I
depressing *déprimant(e),* 9
to deprive onself *se priver,* 8
desk *le bureau,* I
destination *la destination,* I
dictionary *le dictionnaire,* I
to die *mourir,* I
diet *le régime,* 8
different *différent(e),* 6
difficult *difficile,* I
difficult (personality) *pénible,* I
digital camera *l'appareil photo numérique (m.),* I
dining room *la salle à manger,* I
director (movie) *le metteur en scène,* 9
dirty *sale,* 6
disc jockey *l'animateur (animatrice),* 9
discount *le tarif réduit,* I
dishes *la vaisselle,* I
dishwasher *le lave-vaisselle,* I
disinfectant *le désinfectant,* 7
dismissal *la sortie,* I
to disturb *déranger,* I
diving mask *le masque de plongée,* I
to divorce *divorcer,* I
to do *faire,* I
to do a web search *faire une recherche,* 4
to do an experiment *faire une expérience,* 4
to do drama *faire du théâtre,* 1
to do one's hair *se coiffer,* 5
to do one's homework *faire ses devoirs,* 5
to do photography *faire de la photo,* 1
to do the dishes *faire la vaisselle,* I
to do the laundry *faire la lessive,* I
to do theater *faire du théâtre,* 1
doctor *le médecin* 8
document *le document,* 4
documentary *le documentaire,* 9
dog *le chien,* I
doll *la poupée,* 6
donkey *l'âne, (m.),* I
door *la porte,* I
double bed *le lit double,* I
to download *télécharger,* 4
downstairs *en bas,* I
downtown *le centre-ville,* I
dozen *une douzaine de (d'),* 2
drama *le théâtre,* I
drama *le drame,* 9
to draw *dessiner,* I
drawing *le dessin,* I
dream *le rêve,* 10
dress *la robe,* I
dried fruit *les fruits secs,* 2
drink *la boisson,* I
to drink *boire,* I
driver's license *le permis de conduire,* 10
drums *la batterie,* I
to dry one's hair *se sécher les cheveux,* 5
duck *le canard,* 6
during *pendant,* 10
to dust *faire la poussière,* 2
DVD *le DVD,* I
DVD burner *le graveur de DVD,* 4
DVD player *le lecteur de DVD,* I

each *chaque,* 5
ear *l'oreille,* I
early *en avance,* I
early *tôt, de bonne heure,* 5
earrings *les boucles (f.) d'oreilles,* I
easy *facile,* I

Glossaire anglais–français

to eat *manger,* I
edge *le bord,* 10
edit *l'édition, (f.),* 4
egg *l'œuf (m.),* I
eggplant *l'aubergine (f.),* 3
eight *huit,* I
eighteen *dix-huit,* I
eighty *quatre-vingts,* I
eighty one *quatre-vingt-un,* I
elderly *âgé(e),* 1
electric train *le train électrique,* 6
elegant *élégant(e),* I
elevator *l'ascenseur (m.),* I
eleven *onze,* I
e-mail *l'e-mail (m.),* I
e-mail address *l'adresse e-mail, (f.),* I
employee *l'employé(e),* I
to empty *vider,* I
to empty the dishwasher *vider le lave-vaisselle,* I
to encourage *encourager,* I
England *l'Angleterre,* 10
English *l'anglais,* I
English (nationality) *anglais(e),* 10
to enjoy *profiter,* 2
enjoy your meal *bon appétit,* I
to enter *entrer,* 2
envelope *l'enveloppe (f.),* I
eraser *la gomme,* I
especially *surtout,* 10
evening *le soir,* I
every *chaque,* 5
every day *tous les jours,* I
every other (day) *tous les deux (jours),* 5
every Wednesday *tous les mercredis,* 1
everywhere *partout,* 8
every one *tout le monde,* 5
excellent *excellent(e),* I
exciting *passionnant(e),* 9
excuse-me *pardon,* I
exercise *l'exercice (m.),* 8
expensive *cher (chère),* I
eye *l'œil (m.),* 8
eyebrow *le sourcil,* 8
eyes *les yeux (m.pl.),* I

face *le visage,* 8
to fail (an exam, a class) *rater,* 4
fall *l'automne (m.),* I
to fall *tomber,* I
to fall asleep *s'endormir,* 5
family *la famille,* I
fantasy novel *le roman fantastique,* 9
far *loin (de),* I
farm *la ferme,* 6
fascinating *fascinant(e),* I
fat *gros(se),* I
father *le père,* I
fatty foods *les matières grasses,* 8
faucet *le robinet,* 5
favorite *préféré(e),* I
favorites (Internet) *les favoris,* 4
February *février,* I
fee *le tarif,* I
to feed oneself *se nourrir,* 5
to feel like *avoir envie de,* I
field *le champ,* 6
fifteen *quinze,* I
fifty *cinquante,* I
file *le fichier,* 4
film *le film,* I
finally *finalement,* I
to find *trouver,* I
to find out *s'informer,* 10
finger *le doigt,* 8
to finish *finir,* I
fireworks *les feux (m.) d'artifice,* 2
first *d'abord,* I
first *premier(ière),* I
first *en premier,* 5
first class *la première classe,* I
first floor *le rez-de-chaussée,* I
first-aid kit *la trousse de premiers soins,* 7
fish *le poisson,* I
fish market *la poissonnerie,* 3
fish monger *le/la poissonnier (-ière),* 3
fishing pole *la canne à pêche,* I
five *cinq,* I
flamingo *le flamant rose,* 7
flashlight *la lampe de poche,* 7
flashy *tape-à-l'œil,* I
flight *le vol,* I
flippers *les palmes (f.pl.),* I
floor (of a building) *l'étage (m.),* I
flour *la farine,* 3
flower *la fleur,* 7
flower shop *le fleuriste,* I
flu *la grippe,* 8
fly *la mouche,* 7
folding chair *le fauteuil pliant,* 7
to follow *suivre,* 4
foot *le pied,* I
for once *pour une fois,* 4
forehead *le front,* 8
foreign *étranger (-ère),* 10
foreign film *le film étranger,* 9
forest *la forêt,* 7
to forget *oublier,* I
fork *la fourchette,* I
fortunately *heureusement,* I
forty *quarante,* I
forward (Internet) *suivante,* 4
four *quatre,* I
fourteen *quatorze,* I
France *la France,* 10
free *libre,* I
free time *le temps libre,* I
French *le français,* I
Friday *vendredi,* I
friend *l'ami(e), le copain/la copine,* I
fries *les frites,* I
frog *la grenouille,* 7
from *en provenance de,* I
from *de, du/de la/de l'/ des,* 3
from time to time *de temps en temps,* I
fruit juice *le jus de fruit,* 1
fruit *les fruits (m.),* 3
full *plein(e),* 9
full (booked) *complet(-ète),* I
full-board *la pension complète,* I
funny *marrant(e),* I
funny *drôle, amusant(e),* 9

to gain weight *grossir,* I
game *le jeu,* I
garage *le garage,* I
garden *le jardin,* I
garlic *l'ail (m.),* 3
gas lighter *l'allume-gaz (m.),* 7
generous *généreux(-euse),* I
genre *le genre,* 9
geography *la géographie,* I
German *l'allemand,* I
German (nationality) *allemand (e),* 10
Germany *l'Allemagne,* 10
to get dressed *s'habiller,* 5
to get information in a travel agency *se renseigner dans une agence de voyages,* 10
to get one's backpack ready *préparer son sac,* 5
to get ready *se préparer,* 5
to get undressed *se déshabiller,* 5
to get up *se lever,* 5
to get vaccinated *se faire vacciner,* 10
gift card *le chèque-cadeau,* 2
girl *la fille,* I
to give *donner,* I
to give back *rendre,* I
glass *le verre,* I
glasses *les lunettes (f.pl.),* I
gloves *les gants (m.),* I
to go *aller,* I
to go down *descendre,* 1
to go fishing *aller à la pêche,* 7
to go forward *avancer,* I
to go grocery shopping *faire les courses,* 2
to go hiking *faire une randonnée,* 10
to go on a carousel *faire du manège,* 6
to go on a picnic *faire un pique-nique,* I
to go on vacation *partir en voyage,* 10

to **go out** *sortir,* I
to **go sailing** *faire de la voile,* 10
to **go shopping** *faire les magasins,* I
to **go to bed** *se coucher,* 5
to **go to summer camp** *aller en colonie de vacances,* 10
to **go to the circus** *aller au cirque,* 6
to **go to work** *aller au travail,* 5
to **go up** *monter,* I
to **go the wrong way** *aller de travers,* 4
goat *la chèvre,* 6
gold *l'or (m.),* I
gold (made of) *en or,* I
good *bon(ne),* I
Good evening *Bonsoir,* I
Goodbye *Au revoir,* I
grade *la note,* 4
grandchild *le petit-enfant,* I
granddaughter *la petite-fille,* I
grandfather *le grand-père,* I
grandmother *la grand-mère,* I
grandparent *le grand-parent,* I
grandson *le petit-fils,* I
grapefruit *le pamplemousse,* I
gray *gris(e),* I
great *génial(e),* I
Greece *la Grèce,* 10
Greek *grec (grecque),* 10
green *vert(e),* I
green beans *les haricots (m.pl.) verts,* 3
greeting card *la carte de vœux,* 2
grocer *l'épicier(-ière),* 3
grocery store *l'épicerie,* 3
to **grow (up)** *grandir,* I
guest *l'invité(e),* 3
guidebook *le guide,* 10
guided *guidé(e),* 10
guitar *la guitare,* I
gymnasium *le gymnase,* 4

hair *les cheveux (m.),* I
hairdresser *le coiffeur,* I
half *demi(e),* I
half-board *demi-pension,* I
half-brother *le demi-frère,* I
half-sister *la demi-sœur,* I
ham *le jambon,* I
ham sandwich *le sandwich au jambon,* 1
hand *la main,* 8
handicap access *l'accès handicapé,* I
handsome *beau (belle),* I
to **happen** *se passer,* 4
to **happen (to someone)** *arriver (à quelqu'un),* 4
happy *heureux(-euse),* I
happy *content(e),* 6
Happy Birthday! *Bon anniversaire!,* 2
Happy New Year! *Bonne année!,* 2
hat *le chapeau,* I
to **hate** *détester,* I
to **have** *avoir,* I
to **have a fever** *avoir de la fièvre,* 8
to **have breakfast** *prendre le petit-déjeuner,* 5
to **have dinner** *dîner,* I
to **have fun** *s'amuser,* I
to **have just done something** *venir de,* I
to **have more** *reprendre,* I
to **have practice** *avoir entraînement,* 4
to **have time** *avoir le temps de,* I
to **have to** *devoir,* I; *falloir (Il faut),* 8
to **have training** *avoir entraînement,* 4
he *il,* I
head *la tête,* I
heading for *à destination de,* I
headphones *les écouteurs (m.pl.),* I
health *la santé,* 8
to **hear** *entendre,* I
heart *le cœur,* 8
hello *Bonjour, Bonsoir,* I
helmet *la casque,* I
help (computer) *l'aide (m.),* 4
to **help** *aider,* I
here *là,* I
here is... *voilà,* I
Here. *Tiens, Voilà,* I
hero *le héros,* 9
heroine *l'héroïne (f.),* 9
hi *salut,* I
high *haut,* I
high school *le lycée,* I
hike *la randonnée,* I
hiking shoes *les chaussures (f.pl.), de randonnée,* I
hip-hop *le hip-hop,* 9
historical novel *le roman historique,* 9
history *l'histoire (f.),* I
hockey *le hockey,* I
home (Internet) *le démarrage,* 4
home page *l'accueil (m.),* 4
homework *le devoir,* I
honestly *franchement,* I
to **hope** *espérer,* I
hopscotch *la marelle,* 6
horrible *horrible,* I
horror movie *le film d'horreur,* 9
horse *le cheval,* 6
hospital *l'hôpital (m.),* I
hot *chaud(e),* I
hot chocolate *le chocolat chaud,* I
hotel *l'hôtel (m.),* I
hour *l'heure (f.),* I
house *la maison,* I
how *comment,* I
to **hurry** *se dépêcher,* 5
to **hurt** *avoir mal à,* I
husband *le mari,* I

I *je,* I
ice cooler *la glacière,* I
ice cream *la glace,* I
ice-skating *le patin à glace,* I
ice-skating rink *la patinoire,* I
if *si,* 3
in *dans,* I; en, 3
in front (of) *devant,* I
in my opinion *à mon avis,* I
in short *bref,* 7
in the middle of *au milieu de,* 3
in the process of *en train de,* 7
inexpensive *bon marché,* I
information board *le tableau d'affichage,* I
to **injure oneself** *se blesser,* 8
insect *l'insecte (m.),* 7
inside *dans,* 3
instant message *le SMS, le texto,* I
intellectual *intellectuel(le),* 1
intelligent *intelligent(e),* I
interest *l'intérêt (m.),* I
interesting *intéressant(e),* I
interface *l'interface (f.),* 4
Internet *Internet,* I
Internet café *le cybercafé,* I
intersection *le carrefour,* I
to **introduce** *présenter,* I
Italian *italien(ne),* 10
Italy *l'Italie,* 10
itinerary *l'itinéraire,* 10

jacket *la veste,* I
jam *la confiture,* I
January *janvier,* I
jar *le pot,* 3
jazz *le jazz,* 9
jeans *le jean,* I
jewelry *la bijouterie,* I
jewelry department *le rayon bijouterie,* I
jogging *le jogging,* I
juice *le jus,* I
July *juillet,* I
to **jump rope** *sauter à la corde,* 6
June *juin,* I

key *la clé,* I
key (computer) *la touche,* 4
keyboard *le clavier,* 4
kilogram *un kilo(gramme),* 3
kitchen *la cuisine,* I
kite *le cerf-volant,* I
knee *le genou,* 8
knife *le couteau,* I
to **know (facts)** *savoir,* I
to **know (to be familiar with)** *connaître,* I

laboratory *le laboratoire,* 4
lake *le lac,* I
lamp *la lampe,* I
landscape *le paysage,* 6
lantern *la lanterne,* 7
laptop *l'ordinateur (m.) portable,* 4
laptop *le portable,* I
last *dernier(-ière),* I
last month *le mois dernier,* I
last week *la semaine dernière,* I
late *en retard,* I; *tard,* 5
latest *dernier(-ière),* 9
to **launch a session** *ouvrir une session,* 4
laundry *la lessive,* I
lawn *la pelouse,* I
layover *l'escale (f.),* I
lazy *paresseux(-euse),* I
leaf *la/les feuille(s),* 7
to **learn** *apprendre,* I
leather *le cuir,* I
leather department *le rayon maroquinerie,* I
leather goods *la maroquinerie,* I
to **leave** *partir,* I
left *gauche,* I
leg *la jambe,* 8
lemon-lime soda *la limonade,* I
to **lend** *prêter,* I
less . . . than *moins... que,* 6
letter *la lettre,* I
lettuce *la laitue,* 3
librarian *le documentaliste,* 4
library *la bibliothèque, le CDI (centre de documentation et d'information),* I
life *la vie,* 6
life vest *le gilet de sauvetage,* 10
to **lift weights** *faire de la musculation,* 8
to **light** *allumer,* 7
light (color) *clair(e),* I
light *la lumière,* 10
to **light** *allumer,* 2
light (weight) *léger(-ère),* 8
light brown(-haired) *châtain(s),* I
lighter *le briquet,* 7
to **like** *aimer, aimer bien,* I
to **like better** *aimer mieux, préférer,* I
line *la queue,* I
linen *le lin,* I
linen (made of) *en lin,* I
link (Internet) *le lien,* 4
lip *la lèvre,* 8
lipstick *le rouge à lèvres,* 5
to **listen** *écouter,* I
liter *le litre,* 3
liter of orange juice *le litre de jus d'orange,* 3
literary *littéraire,* 9
little *petit(e),* 1
live *direct(e),* 9
to **live** *habiter,* I
living room *le salon,* I
lizard *le lézard,* 7
loaf of French bread *la baguette,* I
lobby *le hall,* I
long *long(ue),* I
to **look at** *regarder,* I
to **look for** *chercher,* I
loose *large,* I
to **lose** *perdre,* I
to **lose weight** *maigrir,* I
lot *beaucoup,* I
to **love** *aimer, adorer,* I
low *bas(se),* I
luggage (carry on) *les bagages (à main),* I
luggage rack *le porte-bagages,* I
lunch *le déjeuner,* I
lung *le poumon,* 8

magazine *le magazine,* I
mail *le courrier,* 4
mail carrier *le facteur,* I
main character *le personnage principal,* 9
to **make** *faire,* I
to **make a campfire** *faire un feu de camp,* 7
to **make a reservation** *faire une réservation,* 10
to **make a stopover** *faire escale,* I
to **make one's bed** *faire son lit,* I
to **make sandcastles** *faire des châteaux de sable,* 6
to **make videos** *faire de la vidéo amateur,* 1
make-up *le maquillage,* 5
mall *le centre commercial,* I
man's shirt *la chemise,* I
map *la carte, le plan,* I
marbles *les billes (f.),* 6
March *mars,* I
mascara *le mascara,* 5
mathematics *les mathématiques,* I
May *mai,* I
meadow *la prairie,* 6
meal *le repas,* I
mean *méchant(e),* I
medicine *le médicament,* I
medium *à point,* I
melon *le melon,* 3
menu *la carte,* I
Merry Christmas *Joyeux Noël,* 2
midnight *minuit,* I
midnight feast *le réveillon,* 2
milk *le lait,* I
mineral water *l'eau minérale,* I
mint *la menthe,* I
mint syrup *le sirop de menthe,* I
minus *moins,* I
mirror *le miroir,* 5
Miss *mademoiselle,* I
to **miss (someone)** *manquer,* I
to **miss (an event)** *rater,* I
to **mix** *mélanger,* 3
modern *moderne,* I
moment *le moment,* I
Monday *lundi,* I
money *l'argent (m.),* I
money order *le mandat,* I
month *le mois,* I
more *encore,* I
more of...than *plus de... que,* 6
more... than *plus... que,* 6
morning *le matin,* I; *la matinée,* 5
mosquito *le moustique,* 7
mosquito net *la moustiquaire,* 7
mosquito repellent *la lotion anti-moustiques,* 7
mother *la mère,* I
Mother's Day *la fête des mères,* 2
mountain *la montagne,* I
mountain bike *le vélo tout terrain/le VTT,* I
to **mountain climb** *faire de l'escalade,* 10
mountain climbing *l'escalade,* 10
mouse *la souris,* 4
mouth *la bouche,* I
movie *le film,* I
movie star *la vedette,* 9
movie theatre *le cinéma,* I
to **mow** *tondre,* I
to **mow the lawn** *tondre la pelouse,* I
MP3 *le MP3,* I

Mr. *monsieur,* I
Mrs. *madame,* I
muscle *le muscle,* 8
museum *le musée,* I
mushroom *le champignon,* 3
music *la musique,* I
music education *l'éducation (f.) musicale,* I
music video *le vidéoclip,* 9
my *mon/ma/mes,* I
mystery novel *le roman policier,* 9

name *le nom,* I
nap *la sieste,* 5
napkin *la serviette,* I
national anthem *l'hymne (m.) national,* 2
national holiday *la fête nationale,* 2
nature *la nature,* 7
to **navigate** *naviguer,* 4
neck *le cou,* 8
necklace *le collier,* I
to **need** *avoir besoin de,* I
nephew *le neveu,* I
never *jamais, ne... jamais* I
new *nouveau(-elle),* I
New Year's Day *le jour de l'an,* 2
New Year's Eve *la Saint-Sylvestre,* 2
news *les informations (f.),* 9
newscaster *le présentateur (la presentatrice),* 9
newspaper *le journal,* I
next *prochain(e),* I
next time *la prochaine fois,* 7
next to *à côté de, près de,* I
nice *sympa(thique),* I
niece *la nièce,* I
night *la nuit,* I
nightgown *la chemise de nuit,* 5
night stand *la table de nuit,* I
nine *neuf,* I
nineteen *dix-neuf,* I
ninety *quatre-vingt-dix,* I
ninety-one *quatre-vingt-onze,* I
no *non,* I
no longer *ne... plus,* I
no more *ne...plus,* 2
no one *ne... personne,* I
no problem *pas de problème,* 2
nobody *ne...personne,* 4
noise *le bruit,* 6
noisy *bruyant(e),* 6
non-smoking *non-fumeur,* I
noon *midi,* I
nose *le nez,* I
not *ne... pas,* I
not any *pas de,* 3
not anymore *ne... plus,* I
not at all *pas du tout,* I
not bad *pas mal, pas mauvais,* I
not much *pas grand-chose,* I
not yet *ne... pas encore,* I
notebook *le cahier,* I
nothing *ne... rien,* I
nothing special *rien de spécial,* I
novel *le roman,* I
November *novembre,* I
now *maintenant,* I
number *le numéro,* I
nurse *l'infirmier(-ière),* 8
nurse's office *l'infirmerie,* 4

obedient *obéissant(e),* 6
obviously *évidemment,* 4
October *octobre,* I
of *de,* I
of course *bien entendu, bien sûr,* I
to **offer** *offrir,* 2
often *souvent,* I
okay *d'accord,* I
old *âgé(e), vieux (vieille),* I
olive *l'olive (f.),* 3
olive oil *l'huile (f.) d'olive,* 3
omelet *l'omelette (f.),* I
on *sur,* I
on sale *en solde,* I
on time *à l'heure,* I
once *une fois que,* 5
one (number) *un(e),* I
one hundred *cent,* I
one hundred and one *cent un,* I
one way *aller simple,* I
onion *l'oignon (m.),* 3
only *ne... que,* 4
only daughter *la fille unique,* I
only son *le fils unique,* I
to **open** *ouvrir,* I
open-air market *le marché,* I
opera *l'opéra (m.),* I
or *ou,* I
orange *orange,* I
orange (n.) *l'orange (f.),* I
orange juice *le jus d'orange,* I
organic products *les produits (m.pl.) bio(logiques),* 8
to **organize** *organiser,* 2
organized *organisé(e),* 10
our *notre, nos* I
outdoor center *le centre aéré,* I
outdoor goods department *le rayon plein air,* I
outdoors *plein air,* I
oven *le four,* 3
oyster *les huître(s) (m.),* 3

to **pack one's suitcase** *faire sa valise,* 10
to **pack the bags** *faire les valises,* I
package *le colis, I; le paquet,* 3
page *la page,* I
painting *le tableau,* I
pants *le pantalon,* I
paper *le papier,* I
parade *le défilé,* 2
parent *le parent,* I
park *le parc,* I
parking *le parking,* I
party *la fête,* I
to **party** *faire la fête,* I
party *la soirée,* 2
to **pass** *réussir (à),* I
passenger *le passager,* I
passport *le passeport,* I
pasta *les pâtes (f.pl.),* I
pastry shop *la pâtisserie,* 3
path *le sentier,* 7
to **pay** *payer,* I
to **pay by check** *payer par chèque,* I
to **pay cash** *payer en liquide,* I
to **pay with a credit card** *payer avec une carte,* I
peaceful *tranquille,* 6
peach *la pêche,* 3
peak *le sommet,* 10
peanuts *les cacahuètes (f.pl.),* 2
pear *la poire,* 3
peas *les petits pois (m.pl.),* 3
pelican *le pélican,* 7
pen *le stylo,* I
pencil *le crayon,* I
pencil case *la trousse,* I
pencil sharpener *le taille-crayon,* I
pepper *le poivre,* I
pharmacist *le/la pharmacien(ne),* I
pharmacy *la pharmacie,* I
phone number *le numéro de téléphone,* I
photo *la photo,* I
physical education (P.E.) *l'EPS (éducation physique et sportive),* I
physics *la physique,* I
piano *le piano,* I
to **pick up one's bedroom** *ranger sa chambre,* I
picnic *le pique-nique,* I
pie *la tarte,* I
piece *le morceau,* 3
piece of paper *la feuille de papier,* I
pig *le cochon,* 6
pilot *le pilote,* I
pink *rose,* I
to **pitch a tent** *monter la tente,* 7
pizza *la pizza,* I

to place *placer,* I
to plan *organiser,* 2
to plan a party *organiser une soirée/ fête,* 2
plane *l'avion (m.),* I
plane ticket *le billet d'avion,* I
plant *la plante,* I
plastic bag *le sac en plastique,* 3
plate *l'assiette,* I
platform *le quai,* I
play *la pièce de théâtre,* 9
to play *jouer,* I
to play ball *jouer au ballon,* 6
to play baseball *jouer au base-ball,* I
to play cards *jouer aux cartes,* I
to play checkers *jouer aux dames,* 6
to play chess *jouer aux échecs,* I
to play dolls *jouer à la poupée,* 6
to play hopscotch *jouer à la marelle,* 6
to play marbles *jouer aux billes,* 6
to play practical jokes *faire des farces,* 6
to play soccer *jouer au football,* I
to play sports *faire du sport,* I
to play tennis *jouer au tennis,* 1
to play video games *jouer à des jeux vidéo,* I
to play with electric trains *jouer au train électrique,* 6
to play with matchbox cars *jouer aux petites voitures,* 6
playground *la cour de récré(ation),* 4
please *s'il te/vous plaît,* I
poetry collection *le recueil de poésie,* 9
polluted *pollué(e),* 6
pomegranate drink *la grenadine,* I
pool *la piscine,* I
poor *pauvre,* 8
pop music *la pop,* 9
pork *le porc,* I
portable stereo *le baladeur,* I
Portugal *le Portugal,* 10
Portuguese *portugais(e),* 10
post card *la carte postale,* I
post office *la poste,* I
poster *le poster,* I
potato *la pomme de terre,* 3
pound *la livre,* 3
to prefer *préférer,* I
to prepare *préparer,* 2
to prepare the snacks *préparer les amuse-gueules,* 2
present *le cadeau,* 2
pretty (rather) *assez,* 1
pretty well *assez bien,* I
to print *imprimer,* 4
printer *l'imprimante (f.),* 4
to pronounce *prononcer,* I
pull-over sweater *le pull,* I
to punch (a ticket) *composter,* I
purple *violet(te),* I
purse *le sac (à main),* I
push ups *les pompes,* 8
to put *mettre,* I
to put away *ranger,* I
to put on *se mettre,* 5
to put on a nightgown *se mettre en chemise de nuit,* 5
to put on makeup *se maquiller,* 5
to put on pajamas *se mettre en pyjama,* 5
to put one's things away *ranger ses affaires,* 5

quarter *le quart,* I
quiche *la quiche,* I
quiet *silence,* I
quite *assez,* I
quiz *l'interro(gation) (f.)* 4

rabbit *le lapin,* 6
racket *la raquette,* I
radio *la radio,* I
to rain *pleuvoir,* I
raincoat *l'imperméable (m.),* I
to raise *lever,* I
rap *le rap,* 9
rare (cooking) *saignant,* I
rarely *rarement ,* I
raspberry *la framboise,* 3
razor (electric) *le rasoir (électrique),* 5
to read *lire,* I
ready *prêt(e),* 5
to receive *recevoir,* 2
recently *recémment,* 9
reception *la réception,* I
receptionist *la réceptioniste,* I
to recommend *recommander,* I
recreation center *la Maison des jeunes et de la culture (MJC),* I
red *rouge,* I
red-head(ed) *roux (rousse),* 1
to refresh *actualiser,* 4
reggae *le reggae,* 9
register *la caisse,* 3
regularly *régulièrement,* I
to relax *se relaxer,* 8
to remarry *se remarier,* I
to remember *se rappeler,* I
to remind *rappeler,* 10
remote control *la télécommande,* 9
to repeat *répéter,* I
to replace *remplacer,* I
report *le reportage,* 9
reservation *la réservation,* I
to reserve *réserver,* I
to rest *se reposer,* 8
restroom *les toilettes (f.),* I
return *le retour,* 4
to return *retourner,* I
to return (a book) *rendre (un livre),* 4
to return (to the house) *rentrer,* 2
rice *le riz,* I
to ride a horse *monter à cheval,* 10
right *droite,* I
right away *tout de suite,* I
right next to *tout près,* 3
ring *la bague,* I
to ring *sonner,* 5
ripe *mûr(e),* 3
river *le fleuve, la rivière,* 7
rock *le rock,* 9
romance novel *le roman d'amour,* 9
room *la pièce, la salle,* I
room with a view *la chambre avec vue,* I
round-trip *l'aller-retour (m.),* I
rug *le tapis,* I
ruler *la règle,* I
to run *courir,* 7
to run (drip) *couler,* 8
to run along *s'en aller,* 5

sad *triste,* 6
safety glasses *les lunettes (f.) de protection,* 4
sail *la voile,* 10
salad *la salade,* I
salami *le saucisson,* I
sale *les soldes (f.pl.),* I
salt *le sel,* I
sand castle *le château de sable,* 6
sandals *les sandales (f.),* I
sandwich *le sandwich,* I
Saturday *samedi,* I
to save (a document) *sauvegarder,* 4
to say *dire,* I
to say good night *souhaiter une bonne nuit,* 5
scarf *le foulard,* I
schedule *l'horaire (m.),* I
scholastic *scolaire,* I
school *l'école (f.),* I
school counselor *le/la conseiller(-ère) d'éducation,* 4
school subject *la matière,* I

school supplies *les fournitures (f.pl.), scolaires,* I
science-fiction movie *le film de science-fiction,* 9
screen *l'écran (m.),* 4
scroll bar *la barre de défilement,* 4
sea *la mer,* I
seafood *les fruits de mer (m.pl.),* 3
to **search** *rechercher,* 4
search engine *le moteur de recherche,* 4
seashore *au bord de la mer,* 10
season *la saison,* I
seat *la place,* I
second *deuxième,* I
second class *la deuxième classe,* I
second floor *le premier étage,* I
to **see** *voir,* I
to **seem** *avoir l'air,* 8
to **seesaw** *faire de la bascule,* 6
to **sell** *vendre,* I
to **send** *envoyer,* I
to **send e-mails** *envoyer des e-mails,* I
to **send invitations** *envoyer les invitations,* 2
September *septembre,* I
series *la série,* 9
serious *sérieux(-euse),* I
to **set** *mettre,* I
to **set the table** *mettre la table, mettre le couvert,* I
seven *sept,* I
seventeen *dix-sept,* I
seventy *soixante-dix,* I
seventy-one *soixante et onze,* I
seventy-two *soixante-douze,* I
shampoo *le shampooing,* 5
to **shave** *se raser,* 5
shaving cream *la crème à raser,* 5
she *elle,* I
sheep *le mouton,* 6
sheet *la feuille,* I
shoe size *la pointure,* I
shoes *les chaussures (f.),* I
shop *la boutique,* I
shop *le magasin,* I
shopping cart *le chariot,* 3
short (length) *court(e),* I
shorts *un short,* I
shoulder *l'épaule (f.),* 8
show *le spectacle,* 10
shower *la douche,* 5
shower gel *le gel douche,* 5
showing *la séance,* 9
shrimp *les crevettes (f.),* 3
shy *timide,* I
sick *malade,* 8
silk *la soie,* I
silver *l'argent (m.),* I
silver (made of) *en argent,* I
simple *simple,* 3
since *depuis, ça fait,* 4
to **sing** *chanter,* I
single bed *le lit simple,* I
sink *le lavabo,* 5
sister *la sœur,* I
sit down *asseyez-vous,* I
sitcom *le sitcom,* 9
size (clothing) *la taille,* I
size (shoe) *la pointure,* I
six *six,* I
sixteen *seize,* I
sixty *soixante,* I
skateboarding *le skate(board),* I
skiing *le ski,* I
to **skip meals** *sauter des repas,* 8
skirt *la jupe,* I
skis *les skis (m.pl.),* I
sleep *le sommeil,* 8
to **sleep** *dormir,* I
sleeping bag *le sac de couchage,* 7
slice *la tranche,* 3
small *petit(e),* I
smart *intelligent(e),* I
to **smoke** *fumer,* 8
snacks *les amuse-gueules,* 2
snake *le serpent,* 7
to **sneeze** *éternuer,* 8
snorkel *le tuba,* I
snow *la neige,* I
to **snow** *neiger,* I
snowboarding *le surf,* I
so *alors,* I
so (so much) *tellement,* 6
soap *le savon,* 5
soap opera *le feuilleton,* 9
soccer *le football,* I
socks *les chaussettes (f.),* I
soda *le coca,* I
software *le logiciel,* 4
some *du/de la/de l'/des,* 3
some (of it/them) *en,* 3
someone *quelqu'un,* 4
son *le fils,* I
soon *bientôt, tout à l'heure,* 7
sorry *désolé(e),* I
sound *le son,* 9
sound and light show *le spectacle son et lumière,* 10
Spain *l'Espagne (f.),* 10
Spanish *l'espagnol,* I
Spanish (nationality) *espagnol(e),* 10
to **speak** *parler,* 1
to **spell** *épeler,* I
spices *les épices (f.pl.),* 3
spider *l'araignée (f.),* 7
spider web *la toile d'araignée,* 7
spoon *la cuillère,* I
sports *le sport,* I
sports car *la voiture de sport,* I
sports complex *le complexe sportif,* 4
sports field *le terrain de sport,* 4
sports report *le reportage sportif,* 9
spring *le printemps,* I
spy movie *le film d'espionnage,* 9
stadium *le stade,* I
staircase *l'escalier,* I
stamp *le timbre,* I
to **stand in line** *faire la queue,* I
to **stand up** *se lever,* 5
to **start up** *démarrer,* 4
station *la chaîne,* 9
stationary store *la papeterie,* I
to **stay** *rester,* I
stay (sojourn) *le séjour,* 10
to **stay (sojourn)** *faire un séjour,* 10
to **stay at home** *rester chez soi,* 10
steak *le steak,* I
stepfather *le beau-père,* I
stepmother *la belle-mère,* I
stereo system *la chaîne stéréo,* I
stewardess *l'hôtesse,* I
stomach *l'estomac (m.),* 8
stop *l'arrêt (m.),* I
stop (Internet) *arrêter, annuler,* 4
to **stop by** *passer (à un endroit),* I
stopover *l'escale,* I
story *l'histoire (f.),* 9
stove *la cuisinière,* 3
straight ahead *tout droit,* I
strawberry *la fraise,* 3
street *la rue,* I
stressed *stressé(e),* 8
stressful *stressant(e),* 6
strong *fort(e),* I
student *l'élève (m./f.),* I
to **study** *étudier,* I
subtitles *les sous-titres (m.pl.),* 9
subway *le métro,* I
subway station *la station de métro,* I
to **succeed** *réussir (à),* I
sugar *le sucre,* 3
suit *le costume, le tailleur* I
suitcase *la valise,* I
summer *l'été (m.),* I
summer camp *la colonie de vacances,* 10
suddenly *soudain,* 7
sun *le soleil,* I
Sunday *dimanche,* I
sunglasses *les lunettes (f.) de soleil,* I
sunscreen *la crème solaire,* 7
supermarket *le supermarché,* 3
superstore *la grande surface,* I
to **surf** *surfer,* I
to **surf the Net** *surfer sur Internet,* I
surfboard *la planche de surf,* I
suspense *le suspense,* 9
sweater *le pull,* 10
sweat-shirt *le sweat-shirt,* I
Sweden *la Suède,* 10
to **sweep** *balayer,* I
sweet *gentil(le),* I

to **swim** *nager,* I; se *baigner,* 7
swimming pool *la piscine,* I
swimsuit *le maillot de bain,* I
to **swing** *faire de la balançoire,* 6
Switzerland *la Suisse,* 10
syrup *le sirop,* I

t.v. program *le programme télé,* 9
table *la table,* I
table setting *le couvert,* I
tablecloth *la nappe,* I
tablespoon *la cuillerée à soupe,* 3
tablet *le comprimé,* I; *la tablette* 4
tag *jouer à chat perché,* 2
to **take** *prendre, emporter,* I
to **take a bath** *prendre un bain,* 5
to **take a class** *suivre un cours,* 4
to **take a guided tour** *faire une visite guidée,* 10
to **take a nap** *faire la sieste,* 5
to **take a shower** *prendre une douche,* 5
to **take a stroll** *se promener,* 7
to **take a test** *passer un examen,* 4
to **take a trip** *faire un voyage,* I
to **take a walk** *se promener,* I
to **take a world tour** *faire le tour du monde,* 10
to **take an organized trip** *faire un voyage organisé,* 10
to **take care (of)** *s'occuper (de),* 5
to **take down a tent** *démonter la tente,* 7
to **take more** *reprendre,* I
to **take off one's clothes** *enlever ses vêtements,* 5
to **take out** *sortir,* I
to **take out the trash** *sortir la poubelle,* I
to **take someone's temperature** *prendre la température,* 8
to **take the bus** *prendre le bus,* 5
to **talk** *parler, discuter,* I
taxi *le taxi,* I
teacher *le prof(esseur),* I
teaspoon *la cuillerée à café,* 3
techno (music) *la techno,* 9
telephone *le téléphone,* I
telephone booth *la cabine téléphonique,* I
television *la télé(vision),* I
television programs *les émissions télé,* 9
to **tell** *dire,* I; *raconter,* 9
ten *dix,* I
tennis *le tennis,* I
tennis shoes *les baskets,* I
tent *la tente,* I
terminal *le terminal,* I
to **thank** *remercier,* 2
thank you *merci,* I
that *ça,* I
the *le/la/les,* I
theater *le théâtre,* I
their *leur(s),* I
then *ensuite, puis,* I
there is/are . . . *il y a...,* 3
there were . . . *il y avait...,* 6
thermos *la bouteille isotherme,* 7
these *ces,* I
they *ils/elles,* I
thin *mince,* I
thing *la chose,* I
to **think** *penser,* I; *croire,* 4
thirteen *treize,* I
thirty *trente,* I
thirty-one *trente et un,* I
this *ce/cet/cette,* I
three *trois,* I
throat *la gorge,* I
to **throw** *jeter, lancer,* I
Thursday *jeudi,* I
ticket *le ticket, I; le billet,* 10
ticket collector *le contrôleur,* I
ticket machine *le distributeur de billets,* I
to **tidy up the house** *ranger la maison,* 2
tie *la cravate,* I
tight *étroit(e)/serré(e),* I
time *la fois,* I
time *le temps,* I
times a week *fois par semaine,* 1
times per... *fois par...,* I
to the left of *à gauche de,* I
to the right of *à droite de,* I
toast *le toast,* I
toasted ham and cheese sandwich *le croque-monsieur,* I
today *aujourd'hui,* I
toe *le doigt de pied,* 8
tomato *la tomate,* 3
tomorrow *demain,* I
too much *trop,* I
tools *les outils,* 4
toothbrush *la brosse à dents,* 5
toothpaste *le dentifrice,* 5
totally *tout à fait,* I
tour *la tour,* 10
tourism *le tourisme,* 10
tourist center *l'office de tourisme,* 10
towel *la serviette,* 5
track *la piste (d'athlétisme),* 4
track and field *l'athlétisme,* I
track (train) *la voie,* I
tractor *le tracteur,* 6
traffic light *le feu,* I
train *le train,* I
train station *la gare,* I
train ticket *le billet de train,* I
trash *la poubelle,* I
to **travel** *voyager,* I
travel agency *l'agence de voyages,* 10
travelers' check *le chèque de voyage,* I
traveling bag *le sac de voyage,* I
tree *l'arbre (m.),* 7
trip *le voyage,* I
to **try** *essayer,* I
t-shirt *le tee-shirt,* I
Tuesday *mardi,* I
to **turn** *tourner,* I
turtle *la tortue,* 7
twelve *douze,* I
twenty *vingt,* I
twenty-eight *vingt-huit,* I
twenty-five *vingt-cinq,* I
twenty-four *vingt-quatre,* I
twenty-nine *vingt-neuf,* I
twenty-one *vingt et un(e),* I
twenty-seven *vingt-sept,* I
twenty-six *vingt-six,* I
twenty-three *vingt-trois,* I
twenty-two *vingt-deux,* I
twist *le rebondissement,* 9
to **twist one's ankle/wrist** *se fouler la cheville/le poignet,* 8
two *deux,* I
two hundred *deux cents,* I
two hundred and one *deux cent un,* I
type *la sorte,* 4

umbrella *le parapluie,* I
uncle *l'oncle (m.),* I
under *sous,* I
to **understand** *comprendre,* I
upstairs *en haut,* I
to **use** *utiliser,* 4
usually *d'habitude,* I

vacation *les vacances (f.pl.),* I
to **vacuum** *passer l'aspirateur,* I
vacuum cleaner *l'aspirateur (m.),* I
valley *la vallée,* 10
vanity case *la trousse de toilette,* I
variety show *l'émission (f.) de variétés,* I
vegetable *le légume,* I
very *très,* I
vibrant *vivant(e),* 6
video camera *le caméscope,* I
video game *le jeu vidéo,* I

view *la vue,* I
view (computer) *l'affichage (m.),* 4
village *le village,* 6
village dance *le bal populaire,* 2
visa *le visa,* I
to visit (a person) *rendre visite à (une personne),* 10
to visit (a place) *visiter (un endroit),* 10
visit *la visite,* 10
visual arts *les arts plastiques,* I
vitamins *les vitamines (f.),* 8
volleyball *le volley,* I

to wait *attendre,* I
to wake up *se réveiller,* 5
to walk *se promener,* I
to walk the dog *promener le chien,* I
wallet *le portefeuille,* I
to want *désirer,* I
to want *vouloir,* I
war movie *le film de guerre,* 9
wardrobe *l'armoire (f.),* I
to wash *laver,* I
to wash one's face *se laver la figure,* 5
to wash one's hair *se laver les cheveux,* 5
to wash the car *laver la voiture,* I
watch *la montre,* I
to watch *regarder,* I
to watch cartoons *regarder des dessins animés,* 6
to watch TV *regarder la télé,* I
water *l'eau (f.),* I
to water *arroser,* I
to water the plants *arroser les plantes,* I
waterfall *la cascade,* 7
watermelon *la pastèque,* 3
we *nous,* I
to wear *mettre, porter,* I
weather *le temps,* I
weather report *le bulletin météo(rologique),* 9
web site *le site,* 10
Wednesday *mercredi,* I
week *la semaine,* I
weekend *le week-end,* I
to weigh oneself *se peser,* 8
well *bien,* I
well-done *bien cuit,* I
what *que (qu'),* I
when *quand,* I
where *où,* I
which *quel, quelle, quels, quelles,* I
which one *lequel, laquelle, lesquels, lesquelles,* 9
while *alors que,* 6
while *pendant que,* 5
white *blanc(he),* I
who *qui,* I
why *pourquoi,* I
wife *la femme,* I
to win *gagner,* 4
wind *le vent,* I
windbreaker *le coupe-vent,* I
window *la fenêtre,* I
window (counter) *le guichet,* I
to windsurf *faire de la planche à voile,* 10
windsurfing *la planche à voile,* 10
winter *l'hiver,* I
winter jacket *l'anorak,* I
winter scarf *l'écharpe (f.),* I
to wish *souhaiter,* 2
with *avec,* I
to withdraw *retirer,* I
without *sans,* I
without a doubt *sans doute,* 4
woman's blouse *le chemisier,* I
woman's suit *le tailleur,* I
to wonder *se demander,* 4
woods *le bois,* 7
wool *la laine,* I
wool (made of) *en laine,* I
to work *travailler,* I
to work (run) *marcher,* 4
world *le monde,* 10
worst *le/la/les pire(s),* 6
to wrap *emballer,* 2
to wrap the presents *emballer les cadeaux,* 2
wrist *le poignet,* 8
to write *écrire,* I

yard *le jardin,* I
yellow *jaune,* I
yes *oui,* I
yes (to negative question) *si,* 10
yesterday *hier,* I
yoga *le yoga,* 8
yogurt *le yaourt,* 3
you *tu/vous,* I
young *jeune,* I
your (formal) *votre/vos,* I
your (informal) *ton/ta/tes,* I
Yule log *la bûche de Noël,* 2

zero *zéro,* I
zip code *le code postal,* I
zoo *le zoo,* I
zucchini *la courgette,* 3

Index de grammaire

Page numbers in boldface type refer to the first presentation of the topic. Other page numbers refer to the grammar topic in subsequent presentations or in the *Bien dit!* features. The Roman numeral I preceding page numbers indicates Level 1; the Roman numeral II indicates Level 2. For more grammar references, see the **Synthèse grammaticale** on pages R26–R50.

Index de grammaire

Y

Remerciements

ACKNOWLEDGMENTS

Grateful acknowledgment is made to the following sources for permission to reproduce copyrighted material:

"Nos mains au jardin" from *Œuvre poétique 1950–1990* by Anne Hébert. Copyright © 1960 by Les Éditions du Boréal. Reproduced by permission of the publisher.

"Nuit" from *Œuvre poétique 1950–1990* by Anne Hébert. Copyright © 1960 by Les Éditions du Boréal. Reproduced by permission of the publisher.

"On a fait le marché avec papa" from *Le petit Nicolas a des ennuis* by Jean-Jacques Sempé and René Goscinny. Copyright © 1964, 2004 by Éditions Denoël. Reproduced by permission of the publisher.

"Le vieux piano" from "La lanterne magique" from *Les Plus Beaux Poèmes de Maurice Carême* by Maurice Carême. Copyright © 1985 by Fondation Maurice Carême. All rights reserved. Reproduced by permission of the copyright holder.

"L'Enfant à l 'harmonica" from "Au clair de la lune" from *Les Plus Beaux Poèmes de Maurice Carême* by Maurice Carême. Coyright © 1985 by Fondation Maurice Carême. All rights reserved. Reproduced by permission of the copyright holder.

"Le matin du monde" from *Gravitations* by Jules Superveille. Copyright © 1947 by Librairie Gallimard. Reproduced by permission of Éditions Gallimard.

"En sortant de l'école" from *Paroles* by Jacques Prévert. Copyright © 1980 by Éditions Gallimard. Reproduced by permission of Éditions Gallimard and electronic format by permission of Fatras.

"Les droits imprescriptibles du lecteur" from *Comme un roman* by Daniel Pennac. Copyright © 1992 by Éditions Gallimard. Reproduced by permission of the publisher.

"Naissance de l'alchimiste" from *Comme un roman* by Daniel Pennac. Copyright © 1992 by Éditions Gallimard. Reproduced by permission of the publisher.

From *Mondo et autres histoires* by J. M. G. Le Clézio. Copyright ©1978 by Éditions Gallimard. Reproduced by permission of the publisher.

Acte I, Scène 6 from *Intermezzo* by Jean Giraudoux. Copyright © 1933 by Éditions Bernard Grasset. Reproduced by permission of Société des Éditions Grasset et Fasquelle.

"Comment guérir la peur" by Amsata Dieye from *Contes wolof du Baol,* edited by Jean Copans and Philippe Couty. Copyright © 1988 by Karthala; copyright © by Union Générale d'Editions. Reproduced by permission of Editions Karthala.

"Est-ce le fantôme?" from *Le fantôme de l'Opéra* by Gaston Leroux. Copyright © 1959 by Librairie Générale Française. Reproduced by permission of the publisher.

"La mendiante et l' écolière" from *La préférence nationale et autres nouvelles* by Fatou Diome. Copyright © 2001 by Éditions Présence Africaine. Reproduced by permission of the publisher.

"Je suis seul" from "Poèmes divers" from *Œuvre poétique* by Léopold Sèdar Senghor. Copyright © 1964, 1972, 1979, 1984 and 1990 by Éditions du Seuil. Reproduced by permission of the publisher.

"Et nous baignerons mon amie" from "Nocturnes" from *Œuvre poétique* by Léopold Sèdar Senghor. Copyright © 1964, 1972, 1979, 1984 and 1990 by Éditions du Seuil. Reproduced by permission of the publisher.

From *Ces enfants de ma vie* by Gabrielle Roy. Copyright © 1977 by Éditions Internationales Alain Stanké Ltée. Reproduced by permission of the publisher.

"National Standards Report" from *Standards for Foreign Language Learning: Preparing for the 21st Century.* Copyright © 1996 by National Standards in Foreign Language Education Project. Reproduced by permission of the copyright holder.

PHOTOGRAPHY CREDITS

Abbreviations used: c-center, b-bottom, t-top, l-left, r-right, bkgd-background

FRONT COVER: (tl) Renault Philippe/Monde/Hémisphères; (tr) PhotoDisc/Getty Images; (bl) Gavriel Jecan/Corbis; (br) Hervé Gyssels/Photononstop.

AUTHORS: Page iii (DeMado) courtesy John DeMado; (Champeny) Victoria Smith/HRW; (M.Ponterio) courtesy Marie Ponterio; (R. Ponterio) courtesy Robert Ponterio.

TABLE OF CONTENTS: Page vi (l) Goodshoot; (r) Victoria Smith/HRW; vii (l) Victoria Smith/HRW; (r) Royalty-Free/CORBIS; viii Sam Dudgeon/HRW; ix Sam Dudgeon/HRW; x Victoria Smith/HRW; xi Victoria Smith/HRW; xii Sam Dudgeon/HRW; xiii Sam Dudgeon/HRW; xiv Victoria Smith/HRW; xv Victoria Smith/HRW.

WHY STUDY FRENCH: Page xvi (bl) Sam Dudgeon/HRW; (br) Royalty-Free/Corbis; (tl) courtesy of Margot Steinhart; (tr) Victoria Smith/HRW; xvii (bc, br) Sam Dudgeon/HRW; (bl, tr) Victoria Smith/HRW.

INSTRUCTIONS: Page xx Sam Dudgeon/HRW; xxi Victoria Smith; xxi Sam Dudgeon/HRW.

CHAPITRE 1 All photos by Victoria Smith except: Page xviii (c) Pix06/Getty Images; (t) Pixtal; 1 (tl) Stephen Simpson/Getty Images; (tr) ART on FILE/Corbis; (c) Steve Vidler/eStock Photo; (bl) Robert Holmes/Corbis; 2 (tl) Tim De Waele/Corbis; (tc) Reuters/Corbis; (tr) Christian Liewig/Corbis; (cl) Underwood & Underwood/Corbis; (b) Ruggero Vanni/Corbis; 3 (tl) Sam Dudgeon/HRW; (cr) Patrick Robert/Corbis Sygma; (bc) James Worrell/Photonica; (br) Stéphanie Cardinale/People Avenue/Corbis; 8 (t) PhotoDisc/Getty Images; (b) Réunion des Musées Nationaux/Art Resource, NY; 13 (tr) Robert Harding Picture Library/Alamy; (cl) John Langford/HRW; (c) Don Couch/HRW; (cr) Corel; (bl) Purestock/PunchStock; (br) BananaStock/PunchStock; 15 John Langford/HRW; 16 (t) Mermet/Photononstop; (b) Jean-Marc Romain/Photononstop; 17 (t) TREAL Cecile/Ruiz Jean-Michel/Hoa-Qui/Hachette; (b) John Henley/Corbis; 18 (tr) Jeff Greenberg/Alamy; (cl) Jim Sugar/Corbis; (bl) Gary Burchell/Getty Images; (br) Brand X Pictures; 19 (tl) Bill Wymar/Alamy; (tr) Laura Dwight/Corbis; 20 (1) Creatas; (2) Artville/Getty Images; (4) Sam Dudgeon/HRW; (5) Brand X Pictures; 23 (tr) Andy Christiansen/HRW; (cl) Franck Seguin/Corbis; (c) Steve Chenn/Corbis; (cr) Pitchal Frederic/Corbis Sygma; (bl, br) Sam Dudgeon/HRW; (bc) Royalty-Free/Corbis; 30 Jeannine Burny; 38 (a) PhotoDisc/Getty Images; (b)

Remerciements

HRW; (c) Artville/Getty Images; (d) Peter Van Steen/HRW; 39 The Bridgeman Art Library/Getty Images.

CHAPITRE 2 All photos by Victoria Smith except: Page 40–41 Owen Franken/Corbis; 42 (tl) Gyori Antoine/Corbis Sygma; (tr) Owen Franken/Corbis; (cr) Reuters/Corbis; (bl) Goodshoot; (bc) Sam Dudgeon/HRW; 44 (a) Wetzel & Company; (b) Sam Dudgeon/HRW; (c) PhotoDisc/Getty Images; (d) Brand X Pictures; (bl) Pascal Bouclier/Photononstop; 45 (tl) Stephanie Friedman/HRW; (tr) PhotoDisc/Getty Images; 47 (tr) Sam Dudgeon/HRW; (1) Peter Tumley/Corbis; (2) Stockdisc Premium/Getty Images; (4) Don Couch/HRW; 48 Corbis; 52 (tl) François Le Diascorn/Rapho/Hachette; (cl, cr, bl, bc, br) Sam Dudgeon/HRW; 53 (t) Image Source Limited; (b) Guy Bouchet/Photononstop; 56 (tl, tc, tr, bl, br) Sam Dudgeon/HRW; (bc) HBJ Photo/Mark Antman; 59 (tr) Stephanie Friedman/HRW; (c) John Langford/HRW; (bl) Kate Mitchell/Corbis; (bc, br) Sam Dudgeon/HRW; 66 (l) M Llorden/Getty Images; (r) Brand X Pictures; 67 (l) G. Schuster/Corbis; (r) Brand X Pictures; 68 (l) G. Schuster/Corbis; (b) Brand X Pictures; 70 (tl) Sam Dudgeon/HRW; (tr) Ingram Publishing; (br) PhotoDisc/Getty Images; 74 (b) Design Pics Inc./Alamy; (c) Marshall Gordon/Getty; (d) Don Couch/HRW; 75 Réunion des Musées Nationaux/Art Resource, NY.

CHAPITRE 3 All photos by Sam Dudgeon except: Page 76 (t) Dave G. Houser/Corbis; 77 (tl) Nik Wheeler/Corbis; (tr) Ludovic Maisant/Corbis; (bl) Bill Brooks/Alamy; (br) J.A. Kraulis/Masterfile; 78 (tr) Pierre Soulard/Musée de la civilisation; (cl) Louise Leblanc; (bl) Phillipe Renault/Monde/Hemisphère Images; (br) Jean-François Brière/Alt-6/Alamy; 79 (t, cr) Andy Christiansen/HRW; (cl) Stephanie Friedman/HRW; (bl) Ron Watts/Corbis; (br) Richard Cummins/Lonely Planet Images; 83 (b) Victoria Smith/HRW; 87 Victoria Smith/HRW; 92 (t) Bill Brooks/Alamy; (br) Victoria Smith/HRW; 93 (t) Rougemont Maurice/Gamma; (b) Bill Bachmann/Alamy; 96 (a, b, c, e) Victoria Smith/HRW; (d) Shout/Alamy; 98 Victoria Smith/HRW; 101 (tr, 1, 2, 4) Victoria Smith/HRW; (3) Royalty-Free/Corbis; 106 (tl) Courtesy Editions Denoel; (tc) AP/Wide World Photo; 106 (c, bl), 107, 108 Illustrations from Les adventures du petit Nicolas by Sempé and Goscinny ©1964; 109 Robert Fried; 115 Erich Lessing/Art Resource, NY.

CHAPITRE 4 All photos by Sam Dudgeon except: Page 119 (t) Stephanie Friedman/HRW; 120 (tr, 1, 4) Andy Christiansen/HRW; (2) Victoria Smith/HRW; (3) Stephanie Friedman/HRW; 123 (tr, 1, 2, 3, 4) Victoria Smith/HRW; 128 (t) Darryl Dyck/IPhotoInc./NewsCom; (c, bl, bc, br) Victoria Smith/HRW; 129 (t) Victoria Smith/HRW; (b) Janine Wiedel Photolibrary/Alamy; 130 (l) Comstock; (r) Royalty-Free/Corbis; 131 (l, r) PhotoDisc/Getty Images; 132 Victoria Smith/HRW; 133 (a) Photo on cover PhotoDisc/Getty Images/Sam Dudgeon/HRW; (c, e) PhotoDisc/Getty Images; (d) Victoria Smith/HRW; 135 (tr) Royalty-Free/Corbis; (cl, cr, bl, bc, br) PhotoDisc/Getty Images; (c) Digital Vision/Getty Images; 137 (tr, 1, 2, 3, 4) Victoria Smith/HRW; 142 (t) Roger Viollet/Getty Images; (br) Comstock; 143, 144 Andy Christiansen/HRW; 145 Victoria Smith/HRW; 146 (l) Alvaro Ortiz/HRW; (cl) Victoria Smith/HRW; (cr) Andy Christiansen/HRW; (r) Don Couch/HRW; 150 (c) Andy Christiansen/HRW; (d) Image Source Limited; 151 Clément & Mongeau.

CHAPITRE 5 All photos by Victoria Smith except: Page 152 (c) Gamma Presse; 153 (tl) François Le Divenah/Photononstop; 154 (tc) Charle Abad/Photononstop (br) Goupy Didier/Corbis; (bl) Grégoire Maisonneuve/AFP/Getty Images; 155 (tl) Eric Doll; (cl) Gelalande Raymond/JDD/Gamma; (cr) Comstock; (bl) Urbain Huchet, Selling Lobsters in Brittany, Watercolor; 160 (all) Sam Dudgeon/HRW; 163 (4) PhotoDisc/Getty Images; 168 (t) David Martyn Hughes/images-of-france/Alamy; (cr, bl, bc, br) Sam Dudgeon/HRW; (cl) Hughes Hérvé/Hemisphères Images; 169 (b) Blend Images/Alamy; 170 (tc) Sam Dudgeon/HRW; (bl, bc) Andy Christiansen/HRW; 171 (tl, tr, bc, br) Andy Christiansen/HRW; 172 (c, cl, bl, bc, br) Andy Christiansen/HRW; 175 (t) ImageState; (1) Punchstock; (3) William Koechling/HRW; (4) Peter Van Steen/HRW; 182 Souloy Frédéric/Gamma; 186 (1) Sam Dudgeon/HRW; (3, 4) Andy Christiansen/HRW; 190 (b) Digital Vision/Getty Images; (t) SuperStock/Alamy; 191 Edouard Manet/The Bridgeman Library/Getty Images.

CHAPITRE 6 All photos by Victoria Smith except: Page 194 (br) Myrleen Ferguson Cate/Photo Edit; (cr) David Young-Wolff/Photo Edit; (tc) Vincent Leblic/Photononstop; 195 (tr, bl, br) Sam Dudgeon/HRW; (tc) Spencer Grant/Photo Edit; (bc) Mel Curtis/Getty Images; 196 (tr) Getty Images/RubberBall Productions; (1) Ollvier Martel/Corbis; (4) PhotoDisc/Getty Images; (tl) Sam Dudgeon/HRW; 198 Book Cover: Les Aventures de Tintin On a marché sur la lune by Herge reprinted with permission of ©Casterman, 1982; 199 (tr) Royalty-Free/Corbis; (1) Don Couch/HRW; (2) Gary Moss/Jupiter; (3) Rolf Bruderer/Corbis; (4) Getty Images/PhotoDisc; 203 (tl, cl) Corbis; (tr) PhotoDisc/Getty Images; (bl) Comstock; (br) Sam Dudgeon/HRW; 204 (t) Daniel Thierry/Photononstop; (b) Govin-Sorel/Photononstop; 205 (t) Alain Le Bot/Photononstop; (b) Bubbles Photolibrary/Alamy; 208 (a, d, e) PhotoDisc/Getty Images; (b) ImageState; (c) Royalty-Free/Corbis; 209 (1, 3) Getty Images/PhotoDisc; (2) Ingram Publishing; (4) plainpicture GmbH & Co. KG/Alamy; 211 (tr) David Martyn Hughes/images-of-france/Alamy; (1) Peter Adams Photography/Alamy; (2) Owen Franken/Corbis; (3) Joel Demase/Photononstop; 218 Martinie/Roger-Viollet/The Image Works; 222 (tl) Alvaro Ortiz/HRW; (1r, 1l, 2r, 3r) Corbis; (2l) Spencer Grant/Photo Edit; (3l) Getty Images/Digital Vision; (4r) Don Couch/HRW; (4l) Getty Images/Brand X Pictures; 226 (c) Getty Images/PhotoDisc; (l) Brand X Pictures; (r) ImageState; 227 Erich Lessing/Art Resource, NY.

CHAPITRE 7 All images by Sam Dudgeon except: Page 228 (c) Andrew Burke/Lonely Planet Images; (br) Brian Atkinson/Alamy; 229 (cl) M. ou Mme. Desjeux, Bernard/Corbis; (cr) Phillippe Crochet/Photononstop; 230 (t) Nic Bothma/epa/Corbis; (l) Pierre Verdy/Agence France Presse/NewsCom; (r) Benali Remi/Gamma; (b) Quidu Noel/Gamma; 231 (tl) Stephanie Friedman/HRW; (tr) Pierre Holtz/epa/Corbis; (c) AFP/Getty Images; (bl) rtrphotos/Newscom; (br) Ahmed Ouoba/Panapress/Maxppp/NewsCom; 235 (bl) PhotoDisc/Getty Images; (cl) Ingram Publishing; (br) Stephanie Friedman/HRW; 241 (tr) Caroline Woodham/Getty Images; (1) Patrick Molnar/Getty Images; (2) PhotoDisc/Getty Images; (3) Stephen Frink/Corbis; (4) Michael DeYoung/Corbis; 243 (tr, 2) Victoria Smith/HRW; (1) HRW; (3) Shalom Ormsby/Getty Images; (4) David Phillips; 244 (t) Ariadne Van Zandbergen/Lonely Planet Images; (c, bl) PhotoDisc/Getty Images; (br) imagebroker/Alamy; 245 (t) M. Alexis BRU; (b) Jason Lindsey/Alamy; 246 (tl, tr) Royalty-Free/Corbis; (bl) Buddy Mays/Corbis; (bcl) Joe McDonald/Corbis; (bcr) Paul A. Souders/Corbis; (br) Anthony Bannister/Photo Researchers; 247 (cr) The Garden Picture Library/Alamy; (c) Inga Spence/Getty Images; (tl) Andrew Darrington/Alamy; (bl) PhotoDisc/Getty Images; (cl) Joseph T. Collins/Photo Researchers; (bc) Royalty-Free/Corbis; 253 (tr) Comstock; (1) Victoria Smith/HRW; (2) Don Couch/HRW; (3) Getty Images/PhotoDisc; 261 Frank Herholdt/Getty Images; 266 (tl) Andrew Burke/Lonely Planet Images; (br) Theo Allots/Corbis; 267 Giraudon/Art Resource, NY.

CHAPITRE 8 All photos by Sam Dudgeon except: Page 270 (bl) Custom Medical Stock Photos; (br) Larry Dale Gordon/Getty Images; (tl) Artville/Getty Images; (tr) BananaStock/PunchStock; 273 (tr) Phototake/Alamy; (1) MedioImages Fresca Collection/Alamy; (2) Pierre Bourrier/Getty Images; (3) StockDisc/PunchStock; (4) Mary Kate Denny/Photo Edit; 275 (tr) Image Source/Getty Images; (1) Jochen Tack/Alamy; (2) Punchstock; (3) Victoria Smith/HRW; 279 Royalty-Free/CORBIS; 281 (t) Victoria Smith/HRW; (b) Corbis Sygma; 282 (inset) PhotoDisc/Getty Images; 284 (tl) Fotosearch; (tr) Digital Archives Japan/Alamy; (bl) Victoria Smith/HRW; (br) Peter Van Steen/HRW; 285 (tr) Richard Radstone/Getty Images; (1) Custom Medical Stock Photos; (2) Royalty-Free/Corbis; (3) Medio Images/PunchStock; (4) Visual&Written SL; 287 (1) Victoria Smith/HRW; (2) SuperStock/Alamy; (3) Image Ideas/Jupiter Images; 294 (l) Alan Bailey/Rubberball/Alamy; (tr) Brand X Pictures; (br) Stockbyte; 295 D. Hurst/Alamy; 296 (l) HRW/Corbis; (br) John Langford/HRW; 302 (a) ThinkStock/FotoSearch; (b) Ron Chapple/Getty Images; (c) Larry Dale Gordon/Getty Images; (d) Victoria Smith/HRW.

CHAPITRE 9 All photos by Victoria Smith except: Page 304 (t) Courtesy of Marion Burmondy; (c) Steve Vidler/eStock Photo; 305 (tl) Barry Mason/Alamy; (tr, br) Gail Mooney/Corbis;

(bl) Dan Herrick/Lonely Planet Images; 306 (tl) 2012 Artist's RIght's Society (ARS), NY/CNAC/MNAM Dist. Reuinion des Musees Natonaux/Art Resource; (tc) Musee National d'Art Moderne,© 2012 Artist's RIght's Society (ARS), NY/ADAGP, Paris. Centre Georges Pompidou, Paris, France/Art Resource, NY; (tr) Matisse, Henri (1868-1954), "Madame Matisse: Madras Rouge", summer, 1907. oil on canvas, 99.4 x 80 cm. The Barnes Foundation. © 2012 Succession H. Matisse/Artists Rights Society (ARS); (bl) Ruth Tomlinson/Robert Harding World Imagery/ Getty Images; (c, br) (c) Paul Shawcross/Alamy; (br) Valery Hache/AFP/Getty Images; 307 (t) NICOLAS José/hemis.fr/ Getty Images; (cl) Ludovic Maisant/Corbis; (bl, bc, br) Sam Dudgeon/HRW; 310 (tl) Everett Collection; (tc) Paramount/ courtesy Everett Collection; (tr) AF archive/Alamy; (cl) Everett Collection; (c) Mary Evans/PARAMOUNT PICTURES/Ronald Grant/Everett Collection(10396797); (cr)Photos 12/Alamy; (bl) Pictorial Press Ltd/Alamy; (bc) MGM/courtesy Everett Collection; (br)Mary Evans/MGM/Ronald Grant/Everett Collection; 311 (tl) Book Cover: Le Mystère de la chambre jaune by Gaston Leroux reprinted with permission of ©Gaston Leroux, 1960; (tcl) Book Cover: Madame Bovary by Gustave Flaubert reprinted with permission of ©1986, Flammarion, Paris; (tcr) Book Cover: De La Terre à La Lune by Jules Verne reprinted with permission of ©Librairie Hachette, 1944; (tr) Book Cover: Le Rouge et Le Noir by Stendhal reprinted with permission of ©1964, Garnier-Flammarion, Paris; (bl) Book Cover: 50 Poèmes by Claude Revil reprinted with permission of ©Hachette 1986; (bc) Book Cover: La cantatrice chauve suivi de La leçon by Eugene Ionesco reprinted with permission of ©Éditions Gallimard, 1954; (br) Book Cover: L'enfant noir by Camara Laye reprinted with permission of ©Librairie Plon, 8, rue Garancière, Paris, 1953; 315 (tr) Courtesy Théâtre du Temple/Action Gitanes, All rights reserved; (bl) Courtesy Turner Entertainment Company, All rights reserved; (bc) Courtesy of LucasFilms Ltd, All rights reserved; (br) Courtesy of TM & ©2001 DreamWorks LLC, All rights reserved; 317 (tr, 2) Sam Dudgeon/HRW; (1) Yasuhide Fumoto/Digital Vision/Getty Images/Houghton Mifflin Harcourt; (3) Hugh Threlfall/Alamy/Houghton Mifflin Harcourt; (4) Brand X Pictures; 319 (t) Photos 12/Alamy; (b) Mary Evans/Ronald Grant/Everett Collection; 320 (tl) Niviere/ Niko/Loreenvu/SIPA; (cl) All rights reserved Leblanc; (cr) Alerte Orange; 321 (t) Fuse/Getty Images; (b) David Leahy/ Getty Images; 322 (tl) Patrick Hertzog/Getty Images; (tc) 2004 Getty Images; (tr, c) TFI/Sipa; Ron P. Jaffe/©CBS/Courtesy Everett Collection; (cr) Gallo Images/Corbis; (bl) Erik Dreyer/ Getty Images; (bc) Photos 12/Alamy; (br) Pascucci/TFI/SIPA; 327 (tr) Ryan McVay/PhotoDisc/Getty Images; (tr inset) Fabrice Vallon/Cub Sept/Corbis; (1) PhotoDisc/Getty Images; (2, 3) Sam Dudgeon/HRW; (4) Punchstock; 329 (t) © Eric Fougere/ VIP Images/Corbis; (b) Steve Bloom Images/Alamy; 342 (l) Tony Barson/WireImage/Getty Images; (r) Christian Liewig/Corbis; 343 Erich Lessing/Art Resource, NY.

CHAPITRE 10 All photos by Victoria Smith except: Page 346 (tl) Dorset Media Service/Alamy; (tl inset) Photononstop/ SuperStock; (tr) nagelstock.com/Alamy; (tr inset) blickwinkel/ Alamy; (bl) GP Bowater/Alamy; 347 (tl) Janine Wiedel Photolibrary/Alamy; (tr) david sanger photography/Alamy; (cl) Dougal Waters/Getty Images; (bl) Hemis/Alamy; (br) Don Couch/HRW; 351 (tr) Corbis; (1) goodshoot.com; (3) Marty Granger/HRW; (4) Russell Mountford/Lonely Planet Images; 352 Eric Gaillard/Reuters/Corbis; 353 (tr) The Flat Earth Collection www.picture-gallery.com; (1) Rob Boudreau/Getty Images; (2) Mark Lewis/Alamy; (3) Keith Levit/Alamy; (4) Tony Wheeler/ Lonely Planet Images; 355 (l) Royalty-Free/Corbis; (r) Steve Dunwell/Getty Images; 357 (t) Medioimages; (b) Richard T. Nowitz/Corbis; 358 Web page: Corel; 359 (tl) Sam Dudgeon/ HRW; (tr) Royalty-Free/Corbis; (bl) PhotoDisc/Getty Images; (br) Don Couch/HRW; 360 (a, d) Sam Dudgeon/HRW; (b, c) Andy Christiansen/HRW; 363 (tr) Book Cover: Quebec: Guides Bleus Évasion, Courtesy of ©Hachette Livre, 2000, All rights reserved; (1) PhotoDisc/Getty Images; (4) Brand X Pictures; 364 Ray Juno/Corbis; 366 (1a) Getty Images/PhotoDisc; (1b) Ingram Publishing; (2a, 2b, 4b) PhotoDisc/Getty Images; (3b) ImageState; (4a) Book Cover: Paris, by Knopf Guides, Courtesy of Knopf Guides, All rights reserved; 370 (cl) Mali/Gamma/ getty Images; 373 (cl) Philip Coblentz, Brand X Pictures; 374 (3) Royalty-Free/Corbis Images; (4) Don Couch/HRW; 378 (t) Corbis; (c) Don Couch/HRW; (b) Getty Images/PhotoDisc; 379 Matisse, Henri (1869-1954), Woman on the Terrace, 1906. Oil on canvas, 65 X 80.5 cm, Hermitage, St. Petersburg, Russia. © 2012 Succession H. Matisse/ARS, NY. Photo: Archives H. Matisse.

VARIATIONS LITTÉRAIRES: Page 382 (tl, bl) Victoria Smith/ HRW; (r) PhotoDisc/Getty Images; 383 (tl) Dave King/Getty Images; (cl) Victoria Smith/HRW; (cr) Sebastien Baussais/Alamy; (bl) Steve Gorton/Getty Images; (br) PhotoDisc/Getty Images; 384 (tr) Victoria Smith/HRW; (cl) Image Farm, (inset) Mary Evans Picture Library/Alamy; (cr) Stephanie Friedman/HRW; (b) The Everett Collection; 385 (bkgd) Kaz Chiba/Getty Images; (tl) PhotoDisc/Getty Images, (inset) Warner Bros./ZUMA/ Corbis; (br) AF archive/Alamy, (inset) Really useful films/Joel Schumacher Prods./The Kobal Collection/Bailey, Alex; 386 (tl) Andersen Ulf/Gamma/getty Images; (bl) Stuart Westmorland/ Getty Images; (tr) Yves Marcoux/Getty Images; 387 (bkgd) Royalty-Free/Corbis; 388 (tl) Everett Collection Inc/Alamy; (bl) Arco Images/Alamy; (bc) PunchStock; 389 (tc) ClassicStock/ Alamy; (tr) jonathan & angela/Getty Images; (branch composite) PhotoDisc/Getty Images, Brand X Pictures; 390 (tl) Réunion des Musées Nationaux/Art Resource, NY; 392 (tl) Philippe Renault/ Hemisphères Images; (br) Russell Mountford/Lonely Planet Images; 393 (t) JB Autissier/Panoramic/ZUMA; (c) Patrick Frilit/ Hemis/Alamy; (b) Rocco Fasano/Lonely Planet Images; 394 (tl) Pelletier Micheline/Gamma/Getty Images; (c, cr, bl, br) Sam Dudgeon/HRW; 396 (tl) Eric Robert/VIP Production/Corbis; (tr, bl) Sam Dudgeon/HRW; 397 Sam Dudgeon/HRW; 398 (all cds) PhotoDisc/Getty Images; (tl book) Photo: Victoria Smith/ HRW, Book Cover Les Trois Mousquetaires by Alexandre Dumas Reprinted with permission of Éditions Gallimard; (tl dvd) Photo: Victoria Smith/HRW, DVD Cover: Les Trois Mousquetaires Reprinted with permission of Buena Vista Home Entertainment (France)/Disney Enterprises; (tc) PhotoDisc/Getty Images; (tr) Everett Collection; (cl book) Photo: Victoria Smith/HRW, Book Cover: Le hussard sur le toit by Jean Giono reprinted with permission of © Éditions Gullimard, 1951, cover Illustration by Patrick Siméon; (cl dvd) Photo: Victoria Smith/HRW, DVD Cover: Hussard reprinted with permission of Hachette Première et Cie/France 2 Cinéma/Centre Européen Cinematographique Rhone-Alps/Pathe Video; (bl book) Photo: Victoria Smith/ HRW, Book Cover: Cyrano de Bergerac by Edmond Rostand reprinted with permission of © Éditions Gallimard 1983, Coquelin dans Cyrano de Bergerac, Théâtre de la Porte Saint-Martin 1897, d'après une photographie de Nadar, Bibl.nat., Paris. ©S.P.A.D.E.M., 1983, All Rights Reserved; (bl dvd) Photo: Victoria Smith/HRW, DVD Cover: Cyrano de Bergerac reprinted with permission of ©1990 President Films/©2004 MGM Home Entertainment; (br) Sam Dudgeon/HRW; 399 (tcr, tr) Everett Collection; (tl, tcl) Hachette/ZUMA; (film strip) Siede Preis/ Getty Images; 400 Andersen Ulf/Gamma/getty Images.

REVISIONS DE VOCABULAIRE: Page R8 (t) Victoria Smith/ HRW; (b) Sam Dudgeon/HRW; R9 (tl) RubberBall/Alamy; (tr) Stephanie Friedman/HRW; (bl) Sam Dudgeon/HRW; (br) Victoria Smith/HRW; R10 (tl) Victoria Smith/HRW; (tr) PhotoDisc/Getty Images; (br) Sam Dudgeon/HRW; R11 (tl, r) Sam Dudgeon/HRW; (bl) Stephanie Friedman/HRW; R12 (tl, bl) Victoria Smith/HRW; (tr) Sam Dudgeon/HRW; (br) Comstock Images; R13 (tl) Stephanie Friedman/HRW; (cl, tr, br) PhotoDisc/Getty Images; (bl) Victoria Smith/HRW; R14 (tl) Stephanie Friedman/HRW; (tr) Victoria Smith/HRW; (bl) PhotoDisc/Getty Images; R15 (tl, bl) PhotoDisc/Getty Images; (tr) Victoria Smith/HRW; (br) Sam Dudgeon/HRW.

VOCABULAIRE SUPPLÉMENTAIRE: Page R16 (tl) Royalty-Free/ Corbis; (tr, bl) PhotoDisc/Getty Images; (cr) Victoria Smith/ HRW; (br) Brand X Pictures; R17 (t, b) Sam Dudgeon/HRW; (c) PhotoDisc/Getty Images; R18 (tl) Brand X Pictures; (tr, br) PhotoDisc/Getty Images; (bl) Victoria Smith/HRW; R19 (tl) Sam Dudgeon/HRW; R19 (tr) Ronnie McMillan/Alamy, (cr, bl) PhotoDisc/Getty Images; (br) Stockbyte; R20 (tl) Royalty-Free/ Corbis; (tr) Corel; (bl) HRW; R21 (tl, bl) Victoria Smith/HRW; (tr) Mountain High Maps® Copyright©1997 Digital Wisdom, Inc.; (cl) Sam Dudgeon/HRW; (br) PhotoDisc/Getty Images.

TÉLÉ-ROMAN STILL PHOTOS: All taken by Edge Media

ICONS: All Icon photos taken by Edge Media/HRW except: Page xviii PhotoDisc/Getty Images; 76 Sam Dudgeon/HRW; 152 Victoria Smith/HRW; 220 Sam Dudgeon/HRW; 304 Victoria Smith.

TEACHER EDITION PHOTO CREDITS:

All photos by Sam Dudgeon except: T3 (DeMado) courtesy John DeMado; T3 (Champney) Victoria Smith/HRW; T3 (Marie) courtesy Marie Ponterio; T3 (Robert) courtesy Robert Ponterio; T5 Comstock; T6 Victoria Smith/HRW; T8 Goodshoot; T8 Victoria Smith/HRW; T9 Victoria Smith/HRW; T9 Royalty-Free/Corbis; T12, T13, T16, T17 Victoria Smith/HRW; T22 (tl) Royalty-Free/Corbis; T22 (bl) PhotoDisc/Getty Images; T23 (bl) Medioimages; T23 (tl) Brand X Pictures; T23 (cl) Royalty-Free/Corbis; T24 (cl) Victoria Smith/HRW; T24 (bl) Brian Atkinson/Alamy; T24 (tl) Goodshoot; T25 (cl, bl) Victoria Smith/HRW; T26 (tl) Royalty-Free/Corbis; T26 (bl) Victoria Smith/HRW; T27, T28, T29 Victoria Smith/HRW; T30 (tl) Victoria Smith/HRW; T30 (bl) Edge Productions/HRW; T31 (tl) Glen Allison/PhotoDisc/Getty Images; T32 (bl) Mark Antonan/HRW; T33 (cl) Marty Granger/HRW; T33 (bl) Marty Granger/HRW; T33 (tl) Cindy Verheyden/HRW; T44 (tl) image100; T46 (tl) Comstock; T48 (l) Royalty-Free/Corbis; T48 (c) Victoria Smith/HRW; T51 (l, c) Victoria Smith/HRW; T52 courtesy Margot Steinhart; T52 (b) Victoria Smith/HRW; T53 (b) BananaStock; T54 courtesy Paul Sandrock; T56 courtesy Kylene Beers; T57 (Tomlinson) courtesy Carol Ann Tomlinson; T57 (Strickland) courtesy Cindy Strickland; T58 (Ponterio) courtesy Robert Ponterio; T58 (LeLoup) courtesy Jean LeLoup; T59 courtesy Nancy Humbach; T60 Victoria Smith/HRW; T61 (t) Sam Dudgeon/HRW/SCRABBLE® is a trademark of Hasbro in the United States and Canada. © 2002 Hasbro, Inc. All Rights Reserved.; T62 Victoria Smith/HRW; T63 PhotoDisc/Getty Images; T64 Royalty-Free/Corbis; T65 Victoria Smith/HRW; 3D (t) Victoria Smith/HRW; 3D (b) PhotoDisc/Getty Images; 13 courtesy of Genevieve Delfosse; 28 Edge Media; 37 courtesy of Sue Mistric; 38 Image Source Limited; 39C Getty Images/PhotoDisc; 39D (t) Goodshoot; 39D (b) PhotoDisc/Getty Images; 59 courtesy of Elaine Bind; 64 Edge Media; 74 (l) courtesy of Jodi Mahlmann; 74 (r) Victoria Smith/HRW; 79D (t) HRW; 79D (b) Corel; 104 Edge Media; 113 courtesy of Cindy McDaniel; 114 courtesy of Todd Bowen; 115D Brian Hagiwara/Getty Images; 133 courtesy of Rachel Norwood; 140 Edge Media; 148 courtesy of Sandra Behensky; 151A Victoria Smith/HRW; 151B Victoria Smith/HRW; 155C HRW 155D Victoria Smith/HRW; 181 Edge Media; 190 (l) courtesy of Bill Heller; 190 (r) Victoria Smith/HRW; 191C PhotoDisc/Getty Images; 191D Victoria Smith/HRW; 211 courtesy of Barbara Tentinger; 216 Edge Media; 225 courtesy of Nancy Rodman; 226 Victoria Smith/HRW; 231D Victoria Smith/HRW; 237 courtesy of Pam Seccombe; 257 Edge Media; 264 courtesy of Todd Losie; 267C Marty Granger/Edge Productions/HRW; 267D (t) Owen Franken/Corbis; 267D (b) Food Features/Alamy; 277 courtesy of Dena Hooley; 281 courtesy of Lynn Payne; 292 Edge Media; 303A Victoria Smith/HRW; 303B PhotoDisc/Getty Images; 307C Victoria Smith/HRW; 307D (t) Victoria Smith/HRW; 307D (b) PhotoDisc/Getty Images; 333 Edge Media; 340 courtesy of Jon Baker; 342 Victoria Smith/HRW; 343C Image Source Limited; 343D (t) Victoria Smith/HRW; 343D (b) Getty Images/PhotoDisc; 347 courtesy of Laura Grable; 368 Edge Media; 378 Victoria Smith/HRW.